Rehabilitation and Health Assessment

Elias Mpofu, PhD, CRC, is Associate Professor and Head of Discipline of Rehabilitation Counseling at the University of Sydney, Australia. Formerly professor of rehabilitation services at the Pennsylvania State University, he is the recipient of three national research awards in rehabilitation: the Mary Switzer Distinguished Research Award, the National Council on Rehabilitation Education Researcher of the Year Award, and the American Rehabilitation Counseling Association Research Award (2007). Dr. Mpofu has more than 12 years of research and test development experience and in the practice of assessment for intervention in educational and rehabilitation settings. He was a keynote speaker on equitable assessment practices at the annual conference of the International Test Commission in October 2004.

Thomas Oakland, PhD, ABPP, ABPN, is a University of Florida Research Foundation Professor. He is president of the International Foundation for Children's Education, president-elect of the International Association of Applied Psychology's Division of Psychological Assessment and Evaluation, and past-president of the International School Psychology Association and of the International Test Commission. He has worked in more than 40 countries. Dr. Oakland has authored or edited 7 books, more than 140 chapters and articles, and 6 psychological tests. He was a coauthor of *Standards for Educational and Psychological Testing* and the 2002 APA code of ethics. He is a licensed psychologist, board certified in school psychology and neuropsychology, and has an active clinical and forensic practice. His interests center on the psychological and educational characteristics of children and youth, cultural diversity, international issues, and professionalism. He is the recipient of Distinguished Service Awards from APA's Division of School Psychology and the International School Psychology Association, and he received the 2002 National Association of School Psychology's Legend Award.

Rehabilitation and Health Assessment

Applying ICF Guidelines

Elias Mpofu, PhD
Thomas Oakland, PhD

SPRINGER PUBLISHING COMPANY
New York

Springer Publishing Company, LLC
11 West 42nd Street
New York, NY 10036
www.springerpub.com

Acquisitions Editor: Philip Laughlin
Production Manager: Mark Frazier
Cover design: Steve Pisano
Composition: Apex CoVantage, LLC

EBook ISBN: 978-0-8261-5735-5

09 10 11 12/5 4 3 2 1

Library of Congress Cataloging-in-Publication Data

Rehabilitation and health assessment : applying ICF guidelines / [edited by] Elias Mpofu and Thomas Oakland.
p. ; cm.
Includes bibliographical references and index.
ISBN 978-0-8261-5734-8 (alk. paper)
1. People with disabilities—Functional assessment. 2. Disability evaluation. I. Mpofu, Elias. II. Oakland, Thomas. III. International classification of functioning, disability and health.
[DNLM: 1. Rehabilitation. 2. Disability Evaluation. 3. Disabled Persons—classification. 4. Needs Assessment. WB 320 R34413 2009]
RM930.8.R44 2009
616.07'5—dc22 2009014947

Printed in the United States of America by the Hamilton Printing Company

To the thousands of professionals who develop tests and use them daily in ways that serve others and our professions. They are to be commended for their involvement in this important technology. We trust that they share our commitment to continuing efforts to ensure that the laudatory goals of the ICF are achieved.

Contents

Contributors

Jerome E. Bickenbach, PhD, Professor of the Department of Philosophy, School of Medicine, Queen's University, Kingston, Ontario, Canada

Malachy L. Bishop, PhD, CRC, Associate Professor, Coordinator, Rehabilitation Counseling Program, Special Education and Rehabilitation Counseling Department, University of Kentucky, Lexington

Eva M. Björck-Åkesson, PhD, Dean, Professor of Education/Special Education, Jönköping University, Sweden

David R. Brown, PhD, Assistant Professor of Counseling, Cincinnati Christian University, Cincinnati, Ohio

Mary G. Brownsberger, PsyD, Mt Sinai Hospital, New York City

Carrie Bruce, MA, CCC-SLP, ATP, Center for Assistive Technology and Environmental Access, Georgia Institute of Technology, Atlanta

Lawrence R. Burns, PhD, Assistant Professor, Department of Psychology, Grand Valley State University, Allendale, Michigan

Marsha Carlin, MS, Center for Functional Assessment Research, Department of Rehabilitation Medicine, School of Medicine and Biomedical Sciences, University at Buffalo, The State University of New York

Marcia J. Carter, ReD, CPRP, CTRS, Associate Professor, Western Illinois University—Quad Cities, Moline

Fabienne Cazalis, PhD, Brain Injury Research Center, University of California, Los Angeles

Luke B. Connelly, PhD, Professor, Health Economics and Director of the Australian Centre for Economic Research on Health, The University of Queensland; Faculty of Health Sciences (School of Medicine); Faculty of Business, Economics and Law (School of Economics), Brisbane, Australia

Robert A. Cummins, PhD, Professor, Personal Chair in Psychology, School of Psychology, Deakin University, Melbourne, Australia

Patrick Devlieger, PhD, Professor, Department of Social and Cultural Anthropology, University of Leuven, Belgium

Chandra M. Donnell, PhD, CRC, LLPC, Assistant Professor, Department of Counseling, Educational Psychology, & Special Education, Michigan State University, East Lansing

Robert D. Enright, PhD, Professor of Educational Psychology, Department of Educational Psychology Human Development and Family Studies, University of Wisconsin—Madison

Amy N. Evans, BS, Department of Psychology, Grand Valley State University, Allendale, Michigan

Ellen S. Fabian, PhD, Associate Professor, University of Maryland, College Park

Michael Gilewski, PhD, Department of Physical Medicine and Rehabilitation, Loma Linda University Health Care, California

Mats Granlund, PhD, Professor of Psychology, School of Education and Communication, Jönköping University and Mälardalen University, Sweden

Carl V. Granger, MD, Chairman Emeritus, Professor, Department of Rehabilitation Medicine, School of Medicine and Biomedical Sciences, University at Buffalo, The State University of New York

Jennifer L. Harman, PhD, Psychology Fellow, Yale Child Study Center and the University of Florida, Gainesville

Jill Harris, PhD, Coordinator of Autism Center of Excellence Locations, Children's Specialized Hospital, Hamilton, New Jersey

Jolie Haun, PhD, LMT, College of Medicine, University of Arizona, Tucson

Trevor Hawkins, Grad Dip RC, MSc, Lecturer and Program Coordinator for Rehabilitation Counseling, Discipline of Rehabilitation Counseling, The University of Sydney, Lidcombe, Australia

Alicia A. Heapy, PhD, Research Psychologist, VA Connecticut Healthcare System, West Haven; Department of Psychiatry, Yale University School of Medicine, New Haven, Connecticut

Nancy L. Heath, PhD, Faculty of Education, McGill University, Montreal, Quebec, Canada

Mary Hibbard, PhD, NYU Langone Medical Center, New York City

Andreas Hirschi, PhD, Department of Counselor Education, Counseling Psychology and Rehabilitation Services, College of Education, Pennsylvania State University, University Park

Anthony C. Holter, PhD, Faculty, The Mary Ann Remick Leadership Program in The Alliance for Catholic Education, Concurrent Assistant Professor of Psychology Institute for Educational Initiatives, University of Notre Dame, Indiana

Karen Hwang, EdD, Department of Physical Medicine and Rehabilitation, University of Medicine and Dentistry of New Jersey, Department of Outcomes Research, Kessler Research Foundation, West Orange, New Jersey

Elise P. Johnson, PhD, LPC, Counselor and Therapist, Walton Career Academy, Monroe, Georgia

Robert D. Kerns, PhD, Professor of Psychiatry, Neurology, and Psychology, VA Connecticut Healthcare System, West Haven; Department of Psychiatry, Yale University School of Medicine, New Haven, Connecticut

Anna L. D. Lau, PhD, Assistant Professor, Department of Rehabilitation Sciences, Hong Kong Polytechnic University, China

Marisa Macy, PhD, Assistant Professor of Special Education, Department of Educational and School Psychology and Special Education, The Pennsylvania State University College of Education, University Park

Chad M. Magnuson, PhD, Department of Educational Psychology, Human Development and Family Studies, University of Wisconsin—Madison

David Mellor, PhD, Associate Professor, School of Psychology, Deakin University, Melbourne, Australia

Elias Mpofu, PhD, Associate Professor and Head of Discipline of Rehabilitation Counselling, Faculty of Health Sciences, University of Sydney, Lidcombe, Australia

Thomas Oakland, PhD, Research Foundation Professor, University of Florida, College of Education, Gainesville

Steven J. Osterlind, PhD, Professor of Measurement and Statistics and Director of Educational Psychology program, University of Missouri—Columbia

Mark S. Parrish, PhD, Assistant Professor, Department of Counseling and Educational Psychology, University of West Georgia, Carrollton

David B. Peterson, PhD, CRC, NCC, Associate Professor, Licensed Clinical Psychologist, California State University, Los Angeles

Russell A. Poldrack, PhD, Associate Professor, Department of Psychology, University of California, Los Angeles

Michael J. Prince, PhD, Lansdowne Professor of Social Policy, University of Victoria, British Columbia, Canada

Stacia L. Robertson, PhD, CRC, Assistant Professor, Rehabilitation Institute, Southern Illinois University—Carbondale

Patricia H. Rosenberger, PhD, Research Psychologist, VA Connecticut Healthcare System, West Haven; Department of Psychiatry, Yale University School of Medicine, New Haven, Connecticut

Robert Ruchinskas, PsyD, ABPP, Neuropsychologist, New Jersey Institute for Successful Aging, School of Medicine, University of Medicine and Dentistry of New Jersey (UMDNJ), Stratford

Frank R. Rusch, PhD, Professor of Education, Department of Educational and School Psychology and Special Education, The Pennsylvania State University College of Education, University Park

Jon A. Sanford, MArch, Director, and Adjunct Associate Professor of Architecture, Center for Assistive Technology and Environmental Access, Georgia Institute of Technology, Atlanta

Andrea Sauer-Lee, PhD Cand., University of North Carolina at Chapel Hill

Caren L. Sax, EdD, CRC, Professor and Chair, San Diego State University Interwork Institute, California

Marcia J. Scherer, PhD, MPH, FACRM, President, Institute for Matching Person & Technology, Webster, New York; Professor of Physical Medicine and Rehabilitation, University of Rochester Medical Center, New York

Maria T. Schultheis, PhD, Research Associate Professor, Department of Psychology, Drexel University, Philadelphia, Pennsylvania

Rune J. Simeonsson, PhD, MSPH, Professor of Education, Research Professor of Psychology, School of Psychology Program, University of North Carolina, Chapel Hill

Tina M. Smith-Bonahue, PhD, Associate Professor, Educational Psychology, College of Education, University of Florida, Gainesville

Mark Stokes, PhD, Associate Professor, School of Psychology, Deakin University, Melbourne, Australia

Norma J. Stumbo, PhD, CTRS, Director, Midwest Alliance, University of Illinois at Urbana—Champaign

Timothy N. Tansey, PhD, CRC, CVE, Assistant Professor, Department of Counseling, Educational Psychology, & Special Education, Michigan State University, East Lansing

Jessica R. Toste, PhD, Faculty of Education, McGill University, Montreal, Quebec, Canada

Michael Ungar, PhD, Associate Professor, School of Social Work, Dalhousie University, Halifax, Nova Scotia, Canada

Gitendra Uswatte, PhD, Associate Professor, Department of Psychology, University of Alabama at Birmingham

Floyd Webster Rudmin, PhD, Professor of Social and Community Psychology, Psychology Department, University of Tromsø, Norway

Foreword

Throughout my 40 years in rehabilitation counseling/rehabilitation psychology, including the last 33 at the University of Wisconsin-Madison, assessment has been a primary focus of my work, and I have taught graduate courses in assessment at both the master's and Ph.D. levels. As a result, I have become familiar with a number of the myriad of textbooks available on the topic of assessment, and I have found that they often look very similar to one another in content, organization, and format, particularly those focusing on psychological assessment. In contrast, this text, *Rehabilitation and Health Assessment: Applying ICF Guidelines*, is quite different from others.

Particularly unique is the application of assessment to the *International Classification of Functioning, Disability and Health* (*ICF*). The *ICF* represents a landmark development, with official endorsement in 2001 by all 193 Member States of the World Health Organization (WHO) as an internationally accepted standard for describing health and disability. The *ICF* provides a comprehensive specification of health-related human functioning in the domains of body functions and structures, including both physical and psychological functions of body systems (e.g., mental, sensory, neuromuskuloskeletal, and movement-related functions, in addition to pain); activities and participation, ranging from basic (e.g., dressing and eating) to complex (e.g., working and living independently); and environmental factors that provide a context for understanding functioning, disability, and health.

The *ICF* holds great promise in facilitating understanding and the formulation of responses to the disability and health-related needs of both individuals and groups. For individuals, the *ICF* provides a framework for identifying and understanding rehabilitation needs and developing comprehensive service and treatment plans to address those needs. Beyond the individual level, the *ICF* can facilitate the understanding of the needs of entire communities, regions, nations, and the world as a whole, leading to the development of policies and strategies to address rehabilitation and health-related needs at broad societal levels. However, the *ICF* provides only a framework for understanding and does not identify methods or technology to conduct assessments in the domains specified, and it is this need that Mpofu and Oakland have addressed through their text, reviewing the state of the art and issues in assessment as applied to the *ICF* domains.

A reading of the table of contents of the text will clearly indicate the unique content covered. Beginning with an introductory "Part 1: Professional Issues in the ICF Context," and concluding with a trends and future perspectives chapter in "Part 5: Looking Ahead," the other three sections focus on assessment procedures and measures that look very different from other texts on assessment. To highlight some examples, "Part 2: Measures and Procedures" includes chapters on real and virtual world tools for assessment of functioning, in addition to assessment of healthcare quality and costs, environmental context, predisposition and use of assistive technology, universal design, and life care planning. "Part 3: Measures of Adaptation and Adjustment" includes chapters on measures of acculturation, values, subjective well-being, pain, self-efficacy and resilience, and spirituality and religiosity. "Part 4: Measures of Participation" includes chapters on measures of physical and functional performance, community integration, sexual function, and recreation and leisure. Further, all content, to the extent possible, applies the *ICF* in reviewing the current state of the art in the various domains of assessment.

The authors of the individual chapters in the text represent a diversity of backgrounds and expertise, another unique feature of the book. Among the disciplines represented are rehabilitation, medical, educational, counseling, and clinical psychology; cognitive science and neuroscience; medicine; occupational therapy; social work; therapeutic recreation; disability policy; economics; public administration; measurement and statistics; and design and architecture. The authors comprise a distinguished group of authorities in their respective disciplines, and they also bring international perspectives, coming from the U.S., Canada, Australia, and Norway, with many international involvements that are directly related to the topics of their respective chapters. The broad array of disciplines represented is important in adequately addressing assessment in the various domains represented in the *ICF*, and international perspectives are also important.

Finally, Elias Mpofu and Tom Oakland bring particular expertise to their role as co-editors of the text. Both have long and distinguished professional and academic careers and I have had the honor and privilege to work with both of them. I have a particularly long association with Elias Mpofu, knowing him since 1995 when he came to the University of Wisconsin—Madison as a Fulbright Scholar to pursue a Ph.D. degree in our rehabilitation psychology program. I had opportunities to work with him in all aspects of his doctoral study, including serving on his dissertation committee, and he was enrolled in my core Ph.D. seminar, Assessment in Rehabilitation Psychology. Both co-editors have extensive backgrounds in assessment with both children and adults and are particularly respected researchers and scholars, with extensive international involvements, and I have the highest regard for their work, including their work in compiling and editing this text.

I see the text as an important and unique contribution to the literature on assessment in rehabilitation, disability, and health. The text reviews the state of the art in assessment, with a focus on the domains of the *ICF*, and it should facilitate assessment practice, while also identifying research and development needs to improve assessment procedures, measures, and practices in the various *ICF* domains. It should become a widely used textbook in assessment courses in a variety of rehabilitation and health-related disciplines, including those represented by the chapter authors, either as a primary or supplementary text. In addition, it should be included in the professional libraries of practitioners, academicians, and researchers in rehabilitation, disability, and health-related disciplines.

Norman L. Berven
Professor and Chair
Rehabilitation Psychology Program
University of Wisconsin—Madison

Preface

Rehabilitation and health assessment constitutes a rapidly evolving resource, with continuous advances derived through research and other forms of scholarship, including technology, leading to a larger number of quality tests, increased awareness of the value of test data, improved professional preparation on test use, and years of dedicated service from committed professionals who artfully utilize test and other data. Advances in assessment lead to advances in personally tailored health and wellness interventions, resulting in a more rapid return to wellness and increased longevity—conditions seen more clearly in the developed countries. Changes in our clientele base and our resources for responding to their needs also are apparent.

This is an exciting time as we examine new models for describing behaviors, treating them, and linking assessment and intervention methods. For example, more infants who otherwise would have died now survive, some with chronic and others with acute rehabilitation and health needs. One the one hand, our population is aging, resulting in a significant increase in physical, mental, social, and other disorders—ones that were observed less frequently 50 years ago due to higher death rates at earlier ages. On the other hand, the aging generation is seeking health outcomes to support preferred lifestyles, making it ever more important to provide rehabilitation services that enhance the quality of life in the twilight years. The accurate assessment of the rehabilitation and health needs in an increasingly diverse and complex clientele constituency is important for accountable and evidence-based quality of care.

Global health initiatives exert a growing influence on rehabilitation and health assessment as exemplified by the wide adoption of the World Health Organization's (2001) International Classification of Functioning, Disability, and Health (ICF), a model that promotes an understanding of the complexity of health and well-being practices. The receptivity of the ICF by those engaged in rehabilitation and other health services reflects their desire to move more fully to a multidiscipline/multiprofessional service model. The ICF provides a professionally agreed upon framework for viewing behaviors from three broad and different perspectives: physiologic, physical–environmental, and psychosocial functions. The ICF's focus centers directly on the work of rehabilitation specialists who partner with clients to promote functional life activities and participation in social and other settings. The ICF's de-emphasis on the exact cause of pathology or the need to diagnose also helps to reframe our work that now increasingly centers on current and future functional performance outcomes.

This is a great time to be engaged in rehabilitation science and services. Consumers prefer rehabilitation and health services that result in personally meaningful outcomes that support their preferred lifestyle and promote full community inclusion. Moreover, the importance of subjective aspects of health to functioning is receiving increasing recognition at all levels of rehabilitation and health practices. Thus, we are engaged in the provision of rehabilitation services to a wide range of persons who display a common need and desire: to be active partners in acquiring or reacquiring and maintaining needed functional behaviors and skills, preventing loss of function, or maximizing quality of life. This book is significant in its comprehensive survey of assessment tools and procedures important to personalizing and individualizing rehabilitation and health care interventions.

This is a great time to rely on reliable and valid tests and other assessment methods to assist us in our work. The availability of an estimated 5,000 or more tests in English alone constitutes a resource that few of us developed yet most of us are able to use and rely on. Professions engaged in rehabilitation services may be the envy of other professions that lack these resources and thus must continue to rely on less reliable and valid methods when making professional decisions. *Rehabilitation and Health Assessment: Applying ICF Guidelines* reflects these themes.

The contributing authors were selected due to their renowned expertise in rehabilitation and health assessment. Most have a solid scientist–practitioner understanding of using assessment to promote health and well-being rather than engaging merely in ameliorating symptoms of the disease, illness, or disability. The contributing authors were selected carefully to reflect the diversity of backgrounds of professionals in rehabilitation and health, including research and practice in rehabilitation services, rehabilitation counseling, communication and speech disorders, engineering, health economics, ethics and law, occupational therapy, physiotherapy, physical medicine and rehabilitation, psychology, neuropsychology, leisure and recreation, policy studies, and public health. Our science and services increasingly reflect multidiscipline/multiprofessional efforts. It is imperative for both pre-service and in-service rehabilitation and health professionals to keep abreast of assessments to support effective services.

Rehabilitation and Health Assessment: Applying ICF Guidelines is designed to meet the needs of students in upper division and graduate courses that provide foundation knowledge and skills in measurement and assessment. It also is intended to serve as a resource for professional researchers and practitioners who want to refresh or advance their knowledge and practice. Additionally, consumers of rehabilitation services who seek to understand the evidentiary basis of the assessment procedures that influence specific services are likely to find this book is an excellent resource.

Chapter content addresses issues important to young children through the elderly. Aspects of rehabilitation science and practice addressed in this book focus more on adults with chronic health care needs than on children. Although the content of this book necessarily reflects this somewhat skewed emphasis, the inclusion of chapters on the ICF for children and youth reflect our interest in them. The contents of other chapters also are relevant to this younger age group.

The book's title, *Rehabilitation and Health Assessment: Applying ICF Guidelines,* was selected deliberately to provide focus to the use of test data in light of the ICF. Chapter authors were asked to discuss their topic, when possible, in ways that promote an understanding of test use within an ICF framework. This is a tall request. Very few tests were designed, standardized, and normed to be consistent with this model. Thus, at this time, scholars and practitioners mainly can examine how existing resources may align and be used within the ICF model.

This book does not provide a list of tests that can be used in ways consistent with the ICF. In fact, the development of tests that fully implement the ICF is an evolving professional activity. Tests are tools to be used skillfully and respectfully by experienced professionals. When they are reliable and valid, tests can assist professionals in decision making. Thus, given the complex nature of the ICF, professionals will continue to be the decision makers who rely on assessment, a process much broader and complex than test use. Rehabilitation and health professionals must avoid becoming psychometricians—those who focus exclusively on test data and not on the individual client and his or her environment.

We believe most chapters advance an understanding of test use in the context of rehabilitation science and practice and within an ICF model. The first four chapters discuss professional issues in the ICF context. Chapter 1, "Concepts and Models in Disability, Functioning, and Health," provides a foundation for the other 30 chapters. The discussion of the International Classification of Functioning, Disability, and Health: Children & Youth Version (ICF-CY; WHO, 2007) by one of the ICF-CY authors provides information rarely found elsewhere in summary form. An understanding of important ethical, cultural, and diversity issues promotes an understanding of the broader context of our work.

Chapters included in Part 2: Measures and Procedures reflect recent advances that add to the diverse ways in which tests and other assessment methods impact services. For example, item response theory may bring new perspectives to assessment for some readers. Topics such as virtual world tools, functional magnetic resonance imaging, and universal design were not widely known 20 years ago. Information on assessment of capacity, life cares planning, and program evaluation lies at the heart of many rehabilitation services.

The concepts of adaptation/adjustment as well as participation are a centerpiece in rehabilitation services, are important in the ICF, and are addressed in this book. Part 3 focuses on measures of adaptation and adjustment. Services commonly strive to assist clients in acquiring, restoring, or maintaining functional adaptive skills and behaviors. The process of examining the concepts of adaptation and adjustment may be similar to the process of examining light through a prism. These concepts are multifoci in nature and better understood by knowing about assessment of adaptive behaviors in young children, values, subjective well-being, pain, forgiveness, self-efficacy and resilience, spirituality and religiosity, and perfectionism—that is, the topics addressed in Part 3.

Part 4, Measures of Participation, focuses on the actual display of desired behaviors in the contexts within which society expects them to occur. Topics include physical performance, community integration, society safety, sexual functioning, and health literacy. These issues impact a person's ability to participate in meaningful ways at home, in the neighborhood, and in the community.

The editors and chapter authors were committed to producing a book that would be of value to those entering the profession as well as to the more seasoned professionals. Various instructional features aid in the acquisition, retention, and application of chapter information.

Chapters open with a brief overview followed by a delineation of key learning objectives that highlight key concepts, terms, and information found in the chapter. Discussion and research boxes are used to promote an understanding and application of information. Many chapters include case studies or vignettes as well learning exercises and field-based experiential assignments to further illustrate key information.

Elias Mpofu
Thomas Oakland
February 2009

References

World Health Organization. (2001). *ICF: International Classification of Functioning, Disability and Health.* Geneva: Author.

World Health Organization. (2007). *ICF: International Classification of Functioning, Disability and Health: Children & Youth Version.* Geneva: Author.

We want to thank the more than 40 authors who contributed to this book. Their instrumental knowledge of both the science and practices that make up rehabilitation services is clearly evident. We also want to thank Philip Laughlin, Senior Editor at Springer Publishing Company, and others associated with Springer Publishing Company for marshalling this book from its contract, through the manuscript phase, to its successful completion.

Part 1

Professional Issues in the ICF Context

Concepts and Models in Disability, Functioning, and Health

David B. Peterson
Elias Mpofu
Thomas Oakland

1

Overview

This chapter reviews the historical and contemporary concepts, terms, and scholarship associated with disability, health, and functioning in rehabilitation and health-related services. We believe that an understanding of key concepts in disability, health, and functioning will encourage an appreciation of assessment procedures used in rehabilitation and health by providing a common language that bridges disciplinary perspectives (see Peterson & Kosciulek, 2005; Peterson & Rosenthal, 2005a; World Health Organization [WHO], 2001). For example, common concepts and language among a multidisciplinary rehabilitation team and customers alike facilitate shared understanding of intervention goals, procedures, and outcomes, thus improving the potential of quality care when different disciplines share a common taxonomy and related knowledge base.

Learning Objectives

By the end of the chapter, the reader should be able to:

1. Outline historical conceptions of health, functioning, and disability;
2. Explain how disability, health, and functioning are conceptualized from the perspective of WHO's ICF, and ICD;
3. Apply the conceptual framework of the ICF to the classification of functioning, health, and disability; and
4. Evaluate the potential of multidisciplinary applications of the ICF to classification of health and functioning.

Introduction

The International Classification of Functioning, Disability, and Health (ICF; WHO, 2001) provides core concepts in disability, health, and functioning that are increasingly embraced in the rehabilitation and health community. In this chapter, we present the ICF as the international standard for classification of disability, health, and functioning.

The ICF is not an assessment system. It is "a classification of human functioning and disability" (WHO, 2001, p. 21). Classification systems used in health care map the domains of functioning that become the target for detailed investigation using clinical assessment tools. The goals of assessment in rehabilitation and health are to describe the health status–related qualities within domains of functioning. Rehabilitation interventions are intended to maintain functioning, prevent the loss of functioning, and enhance recovery and independence (Stucki, Üstün, & Melvin, 2005). Accurate classification of functioning will inform assessment within domains of functioning and related rehabilitation interventions. Üstün, Chaterji, Bickenbach, Kastanjsek, and Schnieder (2003) wrote that "[t]he ICF is shown to be an essential tool for identifying and measuring efficacy and effectiveness of rehabilitation services, both through functional profiling and intervention targeting" (p. 565). The primary goal of this chapter is to consider the assessment implications of the ICF, broadly construed.

We present a brief historical overview of models of health care as a context for assessment of health, functioning, and disability, and we review the ICF within the context of its applications in health care. We conclude the chapter with a discussion regarding current and future implications for practice and research, including future multidisciplinary applications of the ICF to classifying disability, health, and functioning.

Historical Conceptualizations of Disability, Health, and Functioning

Several models of health care have influenced professional thinking over the years: the medical model, social model, and biopsychosocial model (Peterson & Elliot, 2008). We consider each of these models in this section, as they relate to contemporary definitions of disability, health, and functioning according to the ICF.

Models of Disability, Functioning, and Health

According to the medical model, disability, health, and functioning are to be explained primarily by objective physical qualities of a person. Therefore, *disability* is from impairment of anatomical structures from disease or physical trauma, *health* is the absence of disease, and *functioning* is explained by residual physical capacity and performance following impairment. The medical model of disability suggests that disability is a personal aspect that could be evaluated and defined or diagnosed and is the focus of a health care intervention that seeks to ameliorate or eliminate the condition. It focuses on the diagnosis and treatment of disease, disorder, or injury (WHO, 2001).

The medical model influenced the development of the International Classification of Impairments, Disabilities, and Handicaps (ICIDH; WHO, 1980; see also Brandsma, Lakerveld-Heyl, & Van Ravensberg, 1995; De Kleijn-De Vrankrijker, 2003), the forerunner of the ICF. For instance, the ICIDH defined *impairment* as a *problem* in body function and structure due to a significant deviation or loss. *Handicap* was defined as a barrier in the environment, and *disability* was the manifestation of impairment within the environment. These definitions were strongly influence by the medical model, having a "problem" orientation, without much reference to healthy functioning. The 1990 Americans with Disabilities Act (ADA) was developed using two key terms that paralleled their use with the ICIDH: *impairments* and *disability* (Nieuwenhuijsen, 1995). The International Statistical Classification of Diseases and Related Health Problems, 10th revision (ICD-10) is also a good example of the medical model's influence on the classification of health (WHO, 1992). In existence since 1893, the ICD-10 provides an etiological (pertaining to causes) classification of health conditions (e.g., diseases, disorders, injuries) related to mortality and morbidity.

A growing body of research suggests that diagnostic information alone may not adequately reflect an individual's health condition (Basset, Chase, Folstein, & Regier, 1998; Burns, 1991; Gatchel, Polatin, Mayer, & Garcy, 1994; Massel, Liberman, Mintz, & Jacobs, 1990; McCrone & Phelan, 1994; National Advisory Mental Health Council, 1993; Ormel, Oldehinkel, Brilman, & vanden Brink, 1993; Rabinowitz, Modai, & Inbar-Saban, 1994; Segal & Choi, 1991). Further, medically diagnosed diseases or impairments may manifest differently across individuals, and similar functioning does not imply similar diagnoses (WHO, 2001).

Leonardi, Bickenbach, Üstün, Kostanjsek, and Chatterji (2006) stated that it is important to distinguish between objective descriptions of the "disability experience" and an individual's satisfaction with that experience (p. 1220). They assert that these distinctions are of equal importance in health and related policy considerations, but "data about disability are objective descriptions that differ from subjective appraisals." They go on to argue, "Data about quality of life, wellbeing, and personal satisfaction with life are useful for health and policy planning; but these data are not necessarily predicted by the presence or extent of disability" (p. 1220).

Although the medical model continues to be influential, its limitations and disability activism gave rise to a competing social model of health care and

Discussion Box 1.1

DEPRESSION AS A CO-OCCURRING DIAGNOSIS

Consider someone with a disabling condition secondary to a traumatic accident, one of the sequelae of which is a co-occurring diagnosis of depression. According to the *Diagnostic and Statistical Manual of Mental Disorders* (4th ed., text rev.; *DSM-IV-TR*), the person who is depressed may experience any of nine characteristic symptoms. These symptoms can range from an inability to concentrate to weight gain or loss. The functional implications of either of these symptoms may be quite different, and of course, the person may show neither symptom. The possible combinations of the seven diagnostic criteria remaining highlight the fact that diagnostic information alone is limited without clear descriptions of function (Peterson & Rosenthal, 2005a, pp. 82–83).

Consult the *DSM-IV-TR* criteria for depression and related differential diagnosis. Based on your study of the *DSM-IV-TR* criteria for depression and the discussion box description, discuss how functioning would be different with combinations of symptoms within the depressive disorders syndrome.

disability. The social model considers the role of environmental facilitators and barriers in health and functioning. The social model of disability, health, and functioning considers the environment the "major determinant of individual functioning" (Pledger, 2003, p. 281). It proposes that disability is a social construct, impairment as it manifests in a given context in society, and suggests that disability in and of itself is not problematic, but societal attitudes and barriers can be so. Health status is not limited to being a personal attribute; it also includes the interaction between the individual's functioning and the environment (Hurst, 2003; Smart, 2005; WHO, 2001), which is influenced by societal attitudes and barriers in the environment.

The social model is most preferred by advocates for the civil rights of persons with disability (Olkin, 1999). From a social model, it is critically important that inequalities from the experience of disability are identified, measured, and ultimately remedied. According to Leornadi et al. (2006), "inequality can only be identified by comparison of people who benefit from the way society is organized with those who do not benefit" (p. 1220). However, a classical social model perspective would underemphasize assessment and focus on social constructions of disability, health, and functioning disability and the consequences of those constructions on individuals and society. The underemphasis on assessment by proponents of the social model may result from regard of psychological methods as part and parcel to the medical model, which overlooks important personal and contextual factors (see Hansen, 2004; Peterson & Elliott, in press; see also Olkin & Pledger, 2003).

A model of health care and disability that incorporates useful aspects of both the medical and social models is the biopsychosocial model (Peterson &

Elliott, 2008; Peterson & Rosenthal, 2005b; Simeonsson et al., 2003; Ueda & Okawa, 2003), which integrates diagnostic information (medical and psychological) with psychosocial aspects of life (e.g., personality traits, coping abilities, stress, and social support; see Elliott, Kurylo, & Rivera, 2002), giving equal consideration to all factors impacting health and functioning. The biopsychosocial perspective is consistent with contemporary rehabilitation processes and practice (Frank & Elliott, 2000; Parker, Szymanski, & Patterson, 2005; Peterson & Elliott, 2008; Rubin & Roessler, 2000). The biopsychosocial model does not discount either perspective but integrates them into contemporary conceptualizations of disability, health, and functioning.

The biopsychosocial model affected the evolution of the ICIDH to its current iteration, the ICF. The ICF's conceptual framework illustrates how facilitators and barriers in the environment interact with and influence health and functioning. Consistent with values proposed by the social model, ethical use of the ICF requires that the individual's appraisals of environmental assets and liabilities, personal body functions, and his or her ability to participate in desired personal and social activities are considered along with professional classification of functioning, disability, and health (see Peterson & Threats, 2005; WHO, 2001; see also Figure 1.1). The change in title from ICIDH to ICF is consistent with the shift away from a focus on the "consequence of disease" to "functioning as a component of health" (Üstün et al., 2003, p. 566).

1.1

Interactions between the components of ICF.

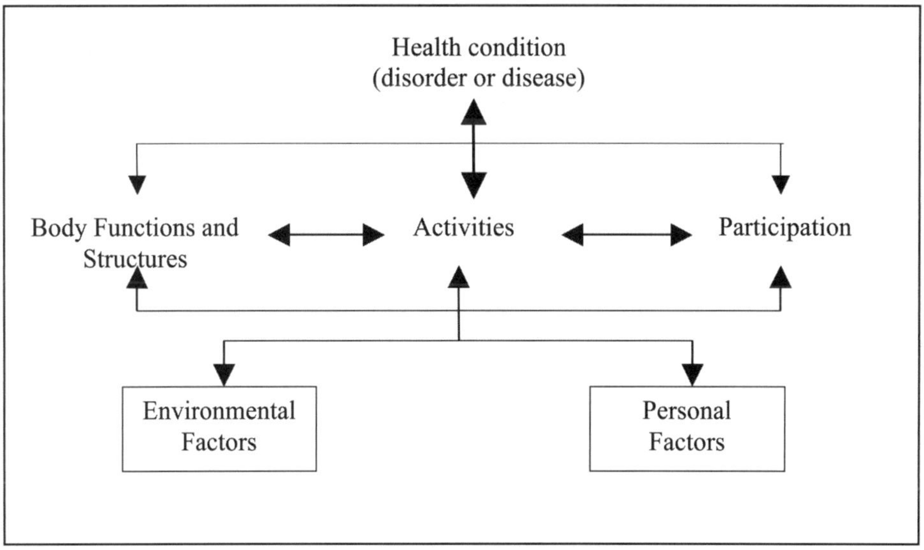

From *The International Classification of Functioning, Disability and Health* (p. 18), by the World Health Organization, 2001, Geneva: Author. Copyright ©2001 by the World Health Organization. Reprinted with permission.

Contemporary Conceptualization of Disability, Health, and Functioning

The ICF defines *disability* as "an umbrella term for impairments, activity limitations and participation restrictions. Functional limitations occur as a result of the interaction between an individual (with a health condition) and that individual's contextual factors (environmental and personal factors)" (WHO, 2001, p. 17). *Impairments,* according to the ICF, are the manifestations of dysfunction in the body structures or functions. Etiology of dysfunction is not the focus of the ICF, but it is the focus of its sister classification, the ICD-10; the ICF does not focus on the underlying pathology itself. Impairments do not necessarily imply the presence of a disorder or disease but "represent a deviation from certain generally accepted population standards" of functioning (WHO, 2001, p. 12). Determination of impairment is made by "those qualified to judge physical and mental functioning according to these standards" (p. 12). *Disability,* then, refers to "the outcome or result of a complex relationship between an individual's health condition and personal factors, and of the external factors that represent the circumstances in which the individual lives" (WHO, 2001, p. 17). *Disability* is meant to focus on the individual, societal, and body-related aspects of impairments, activity limitations, and participation restrictions in the environment.

According to the ICF, the term *health* refers to components of health that are typically a focus of health care professionals, for example, seeing, hearing, speaking, remembering, learning, and walking. Further, the ICF delineates health-related components of well-being that are not typically a focus of health care systems, such as labor, education, employment, social interactions, and transportation. The ICF was not designed to classify disability exclusively; it classifies health and health-related states that make up a universe of well-being. The ICF encourages flexibility to accommodate different conceptualizations of health and health-related states (WHO, 2001). Its focus is on human functioning, and the components of health make it universally applicable regardless of health condition (Bickenbach, Chatterji, Badley, & Üstün, 1999).

Within the ICF, the term *impairment* (a problem with a body function or structure) was redefined as an *activity limitation,* and the term *handicap* was replaced with the term *participation restriction,* meaning a problem an individual may experience in life situations due to environmental influence. *Impairment* here refers to a significant variation from established statistical norms (i.e., as a deviation from a population mean; WHO, 2001, p. 213). According to Leonardi et al. (2006), "Impairments are interactions affecting the body; activity limitations are interactions affecting individual's actions of behavior; participation restrictions are interactions affecting person's experience of life" (p. 1220). *Disability,* then, can be conceptualized in terms of *activity limitations* and *participation restrictions.*

The ICF Conceptual Framework

The ICF describes the situation of the person being evaluated within an array of health or health-related *domains,* which are practical and meaningful sets of related physiological functions, anatomical structures, actions, tasks, or areas of life within a given context. The ICF classifies both limitations in functioning and positive experiences with respect to bodily functions, activities, and participation in the environment (e.g., communicating, tending to personal hygiene, working, and studying; WHO, 2001).

The model of functioning proposed in the ICF suggests dynamic and reciprocal relationships between the various health-related conditions within the context of environmental and personal factors. Both functioning and disability are conceptualized within the dynamic interaction between health conditions and contextual factors. Figure 1.1 provides an illustration of the components and interactions that can be used to describe the relationship between disability and functioning (WHO, 2001, p. 18).

ICF Structure

There are two versions of the ICF: the full version, which provides four levels of classification detail, and the short version, which provides two levels of classification. The units of classification are qualified with numeric codes that specify the magnitude or extent of disability or function in a given category, or, within the case of environment, the extent to which a factor in the environment is a facilitator or a barrier. Once someone becomes familiar with the basic structure of the ICF, the user can search purposefully for information related to health and functioning in different domains (Peterson, 2005). In addition to an alphabetical index available in the hardcopy version of the ICF, WHO created an electronic version of the ICF that is searchable through the ICF browser or CD-ROM (WHO, 2001).

The ICF is made up of two parts, each with two components. The first part of the ICF describes the individual via Functioning and Disability, and the second part addresses Contextual Factors. Respective components are further divided into chapters that contain categories of function within a given domain of health and health-related states.

Part 1: The Individual

Part 1 addresses the individual with respect to functioning and disability and comprises two components. The *Body* component consists of two parallel classifications: *Body Functions* and *Body Structures*. The second component, *Activities and Participation,* covers domains of functioning from both an individual and societal perspective.

The two components of functioning within the first part of the ICF can be expressed either as nonproblematic functioning or as disabilities (i.e., impairment, activity limitation, or participation restriction) and are operationalized through four separate but related qualifiers. Body functions and structures are interpreted through changes in physiological systems or anatomical structures, and activities and participation are interpreted though capacity and performance. These qualifiers are elaborated upon further in their respective sections.

Part 2: The Context

The second part of the ICF classification describes *Contextual Factors* through two components: *Environmental Factors* and *Personal Factors.* Environmental Factors are factors in the physical, social, or attitudinal world ranging from the

1.1 ICF Core Structure

Part 1: The Individual: Function and Disability		Part 2: Contextual Factors	
Body Functions and Structures	Activities and Participation	Environmental Factors	Personal Factors

Note: The ICF is comprised of two parts, each with two components (WHO, 2001).
From ICF: International Classification of Functioning, Disability and Health, by the World Health Organization, 2001. Geneva: Author.

immediate to more general environment. These factors are qualified as either facilitating or hindering functioning. The second component, Personal Factors, is not currently classified in the ICF due to the complex nature of social and cultural variation (WHO, 2001). A summary of the ICF core structure is illustrated in Table 1.1.

Levels of Classification

Each ICF code is designed to be mutually exclusive. The classes and subclasses reflect the various levels that make up the hierarchical order of the ICF, with more basic levels comprising all aspects of more detailed levels (WHO, 2001). Domains within the ICF are practical and meaningful sets of related physiological functions (including psychological functions) and anatomical structures, as well as actions, tasks, and areas of life described from bodily, individual, and societal perspectives that make up the different chapters within each component of the ICF. Essential attributes of the domains (e.g., qualities, properties, and relationships) are defined by both inclusions and exclusions.

The one-level classification of the ICF expands on the core structure: (1) the Body Functions component contains eight chapters that address "physiological functions of body systems (including psychological functions)" (WHO, 2001, p. 12); (2) the Body Structures component contains eight chapters that parallel the Body Functions component and deal with "anatomical parts of the body such as organs, limbs, and their components" (p. 12); (3) the Activities and Participation component contains nine chapters, with *Activities* addressing "the execution of a task or action by an individual" and *Participation* addressing "involvement in a life situation" (p. 14); and (4) the Environmental Factors component contains five chapters focusing on "the physical, social, and attitudinal environment in which people live and conduct their lives" (p. 171), organized from the immediate to more general environment. The categories of function for a given domain begin at a general level of detail and expand to levels of greater detail. The one-level classification is further illustrated in Table 1.2.

The two-level classification, the first branching level of the ICF, has specific chapter headings. Alphanumeric codes begin with a letter (*b* for Body Functions, *s* for Body Structures, *d* for Activities and Participation, and *e* for Environmental

1.2 ICF: One-Level Classification

Components:	Body Functions	Body Structures	Activities and Participation	Environmental Factors
Code letter:	b	s	d	e
	8 parallel chapters		9 chapters	5 chapters
Chapter 1	Mental functions	Structures of the nervous system	Learning and applying knowledge	Products and technology
Chapter 2	Sensory functions and pain	The eye, ear, and related structures	General tasks and demands	Natural environment and human-made changes to environment
Chapter 3	Voice and speech functions	Structures involved in voice and speech	Communication	Support and relationships
Chapter 4	Functions of the cardiovascular, hematological, immunological, and respiratory systems	Structures of the cardiovascular, immunological, and respiratory systems	Mobility	Attitudes
Chapter 5	Functions of the digestive, metabolic, and endocrine systems	Structures related to the digestive, metabolic, and endocrine systems	Self-care	Services, systems, and policies
Chapter 6	Genitourinary and reproductive functions	Structures related to the genitourinary and reproductive systems	Domestic life	
Chapter 7	Neuromusculoskeletal and movement-related functions	Structures related to movement	Interpersonal interactions and relationships	
Chapter 8	Functions of the skin and related structures	Skin and related structures	Major life areas	
Chapter 9			Community, social, and civic life	

From ICF: International Classification of Functioning, Disability and Health, by the World Health Organization, 2001. Geneva: Author.

Factors) and a three-digit numeric classification indicating chapter and specific categories within each chapter. For example, the classification associated with the psychological function of emotion is found in the first chapter of Body Functions (its code begins with "b") under the *Specific mental function* section, called *Emotional functions,* or alphanumeric code b152 (WHO, 2001).

The more *Detailed Classification with Definitions* lists all categories within the ICF along with their definitions, inclusions, and exclusions, providing specificity using four- and five-digit numeric codes. Examples of level of detail within emotional functions could include *Appropriateness of emotion* (b1520), *Regulation of emotion* (b1521), and *Range of emotion* (b1522). Code groups also offer *Other specified* (e.g., b1528) and *Unspecified* (e.g., b1529) codes for functions not detailed in the current classification (WHO, 2001). As units of classification become more detailed, they share the attributes of the broader units above them. For example, *Range of emotion,* b1522, shares the attributes of the higher level of classification *Emotional functions,* b152.

Body Functions and Structures

The Body Functions and Structures component of the ICF comprises two classifications: physiological functions of body systems, or body functions (including psychological functions); and anatomical parts of the body, or body structures (e.g., organs, limbs, and their components). They are separate but parallel chapters (see Table 1.2). Within Body Functions, "hearing functions" has a parallel structure within Body Structures of "ear and related structures." Both classifications are arranged according to the same body system taxonomy. The criteria for impairment are the same for body functions and structures and are classified according to (a) loss or lack, (b) reduction, (c) addition or excess, and (d) deviation.

Impairments are further qualified in terms of severity. Codes have no meaning without the use of qualifiers, which are one or more numbers indicated after a multilevel code, separated by a decimal point (or separator), indicating a magnitude or level of health for a given code. The Body Function component uses a generic qualifier that addresses severity through values ranging from 0 through 4 indicating, respectively, "NO," "MILD," "MODERATE," "SEVERE," and "COMPLETE" impairment (WHO, 2001, p. 47). Relevant to all components of the ICF, qualifiers describe the extent of problems for a given code using this same generic scale with slight modifications depending upon the component qualified (i.e., substituting the term *problem* with "impairment" or "barrier" or "facilitator" depending upon the context). See Table 1.3 for an example of the ICF generic qualifiers.

The Body Structure component uses the generic qualifier as a first qualifier, and a second qualifier to indicate the nature of the change in a body structure as follows: 0 = no change in structure; 1 = total absence; 2 = partial absence; 3 = additional part; 4 = aberrant dimensions; 5 = discontinuity; 6 = deviating position; and 7 = qualitative changes in structure, including accumulation of fluid (WHO, 2001, p. 105). A third qualifier indicates the location of impairment as follows: 0 = more than one region; 1 = right; 2 = left; 3 = both sides; 4 = front; 5 = back; 6 = proximal; and 7 = distal. All three qualifiers have a "not specified" (8) and a "not applicable" (9) qualifier as appropriate.

1.3 Generic Qualifiers

Code	Extent	Qualitative Descriptors: impairment, limitation, restriction, barrier	Percentages*
xxxx.0	NO problem	none, absent, negligible…	0–4%
xxxx.1	MILD problem	slight, low…	5–24%
xxxx.2	MODERATE problem	medium, fair…	25–49%
xxxx.3	SEVERE problem	high, extreme…	50–95%
xxxx.4	COMPLETE problem	total…	96–100%
xxxx.8	not specified		
xxxx.9	not applicable		

* Percentages are to be calibrated in different domains with reference to relevant population standards as percentiles. "Having a "problem" may mean an impairment, limitation, restriction, or barrier, depending on the construct." (WHO, 2001, p. 222) "xxxx" is an exemplar that stands for a given second-level domain number within the ICF classification code, which precedes the qualifier (Adapted from WHO, 2001, p. 22).

Activities and Participation, and Capacity and Performance

The second component under Functioning and Disability, which is Activities and Participation, classifies nine domains of different aspects of functioning from both individual and societal perspectives (see Table 1.2). In all instances, the Body Functions and Structures component is intended to be used with the Activities and Participation component.

Activity is defined as the execution of a task or action by an individual, such as sitting, copying, calculating, or driving. *Participation* is involvement in a life situation. As with the term *impairment, Activity limitations* and *Participation restrictions* "are assessed against a generally accepted population standard" for someone without a similar health condition (WHO, 2001, p. 15).

The ICF proposes four possible conceptualizations of the relationship between activities and participation. First, the user can code each category as either an activity or participation issue, resulting in two mutually exclusive lists, which is how Australia conceptualizes it in its clinical implementation manual (see http://www.aihw.gov.au/disability/icf). Alternatively, one can use the domains for both activity and participation simultaneously or as an overlapping list, which is how the U.S. version of a clinical implementation manual in progress is proceeding (Reed et al., 2005; Threats & Worrall, 2004). Two other variations between separate and overlapping lists will not be discussed here, but are referred to in Annex 3 of the ICF.

The domains of the Activities and Participation component are operationalized through the use of the qualifiers *capacity* and *performance*. The capacity qualifier "describes an individual's ability to execute a task or an action," or more specifically, "the highest probable level of functioning that a person may reach in a given domain at a given moment" (WHO, 2001, p. 15). One must apply the capacity qualifier in the context of a "'uniform' or 'standard' environment that thus reflects the environmentally adjusted ability of the individual" (p. 15). In order to make international comparisons, such environments have to be defined similarly across countries. A heuristic for capacity could be *what a person can do.*

The performance qualifier describes "what a person does in his or her current environment" (p. 15). Another way to describe this qualifier is as "involvement in a life situation" or "the lived experience" of a person in the environment (p. 15). A heuristic for performance could be *what a person does do.*

Differences between capacity and performance can be used to target discrepancies in functioning and to formulate what could be done to an individual's environment in order to maximize his or her ability and function and to increase opportunity for full participation in society. The performance and capacity qualifiers are rated on the same 0 to 4 scale as the generic qualifier, substituting the term *difficulty* for *impairment.* Performance and capacity can be considered both with and without assistive devices or personal assistance, forming four possible scenarios (performance with and without assistance, and capacity with and without assistance).

Contextual Factors

Environmental factors (the physical, social, and attitudinal worlds) are classified within the ICF in terms of whether they facilitate or hinder functioning. Environmental Factors are organized into three levels: the individual level (e.g., support network), the services level (e.g., vocational rehabilitation), and the cultural/legal systems level (e.g., world views, laws). Table 1.2 lists the five chapters of Environmental Factors.

Environmental factors are qualified on a scale not unlike the generic scale, ranging from 0 to 4—NO to COMPLETE—substituting *barrier* or *facilitator* for the *impairment* or *problem* in previously reviewed qualifiers. Positive environmental support or facilitators are noted with a plus sign; barriers follow the decimal point unaltered. One can use the Environmental Factors coding to describe an individual's mobility within the community, whether they are able to access public transit effectively to travel where needed (facilitator), or whether the individual is reliant on others for transportation (barrier). Societal forces can be captured through classification of the impact of prevailing attitudes toward disability, which can either create barriers or facilitate inclusion of people with disabilities.

The Personal Factors component of the ICF is currently defined by personal characteristics such as gender, race, age, fitness, religion, lifestyle, habits, upbringing, coping styles, social background, education, profession, past and current experience, overall behavior pattern and character, individual psychological assets, and other health conditions (WHO, 2001). It is clear that all of these descriptors can impact health and functioning, and users are encouraged to consider these issues qualitatively while classifying other areas of health and functioning. Thus, while the ICF classifies aspects of human health and some health-related components of well-being, it does not classify personal circumstances such as socioeconomic status, race, gender, religion, or culture that may restrict full participation in society for reasons not related to health. The Personal Factors component within the conceptual framework of the ICF, while not currently classified, highlights the need to consider complex social circumstances that may influence the information that is classified. Table 1.4 provides an overview of the many ICF concepts presented. Inspection of the table highlights the positive aspects of health and functioning, including concepts that are consistent with the medical model, reflecting the biopsychosocial model that informs the ICF conceptual framework.

1.4 Overview of the ICF

Two Parts: (A dynamic interaction)	Part 1: Functioning and Disability		Part 2: Contextual Factors	
Each part has two components:	Body Functions and Structures	Activities and Participation	Environmental Factors	Personal Factors
Domains (Contain the categories or units of classification of the ICF)	1. Body Functions (including psychological functioning) 2. Body Structures	Life areas (tasks, actions)	External influences on functioning and disability	Internal influences on functioning and disability
Constructs (Defined through use of qualifiers that modify the extent or magnitude of function or disability)	Change in body function (physiological) Change in body structure (anatomical)	Capacity: Executing tasks in a standard environment ("can do") Performance: Executing tasks in the current environment ("does do")	Facilitating or hindering impact of features of the physical, social, and attitudinal world	Impact of attributes of the person
Positive Aspect	Functioning Functional and structural integrity Activities Participation		Facilitators	*Not classified in the ICF*
Negative Aspect	Disability Impairment Activity limitation Participation restriction		Barriers/ hindrances	

Note: Units of classification are situations, not people (Adapted from WHO, 2001, p. 11).
From ICF: International Classification of Functioning, Disability and Health (p. 11), by the World Health Organization, 2001, Geneva: Author. Adapted with permission.

Great interest has been expressed by a variety of stakeholders to further develop this component of the ICF (e.g. Hurst, 2003; Institute of Medicine, 2007). In its current iteration, these issues must be considered because they may affect the outcome of a given health care intervention when classifying health and functioning using the ICF. Much work remains to be done with respect to incorporating the subjective and ipsative nature of an individual's health, functioning, and disability being classified through the ICF taxonomy.

Discussion Box 1.2

BRIEF EXAMPLE OF THE GENERATION OF AN ICF CODE

A health care recipient has survived a motor vehicle accident in which she lost her left arm at the elbow. An orthopedic surgeon or physiatrist could begin to classify the patient's health status with respect to body structure using an ICF "s" code "Structures related to movement," specifically, s73018, "Structure of the forearm, other specified." With the structural focus established, the surgeon would further describe her health status with the qualifier "COMPLETE impairment," indicated by adding the first qualifier code after a decimal point, ".4." Because the forearm is missing, the first qualifier would be followed by the second qualifier "1" to indicate "total absence" of the forearm. A third qualifier would be added to the ICF code to indicate the location of the absence as "left" forearm, or the number 2. The complete code would be written as s73018.412.

Related ICF codes would be generated to establish resultant functioning (via the "b" codes of body functioning, which parallel the "s" code, see Table 1.3), the person's ability to be active and participate in the environment ("d" codes of activities and participation, used in tandem with the "s" and "b" codes), and the degree to which the environment presents as a facilitator or a barrier (via the "e" codes). As described previously, each unique code generated is followed with a qualifier to indicate level of severity if impairment exists. Finally, the Personal Factors component of the ICF's Contextual Factors, while not currently classified but part of the ICF conceptual framework, reminds us to consider unique individual circumstances and their impact on overall health and functioning.

This brief example may suggest that coding with the ICF is quite complex at first and requires appropriate guidance and training. See the clinical implementation discussion later in this chapter for details on appropriate training for effective use of the ICF.

What kinds of issues would you imagine as a focus of clinical attention for this woman who is missing her left forearm? What other body structures might become involved? How might her impairment limit her capacity to perform within her social environment? What environmental facilitators or barriers might be present?

Impact of and Benefits of Using the ICF

The ICF has influenced many health care entities internationally. It is now in use in several countries including the United States, Australia, Canada, and the Netherlands (Bickenbach, 2003; Holloway, 2004, Peterson & Rosenthal, 2005b). Canada adopted the ICF through the Canadian Institute for Health Information, and the Australian Institute of Health and Welfare has applied the ICF to its national data dictionaries (Madden, Choi, & Sykes, 2003). Work on the World Health Survey, built upon the ICF conceptual framework, has been implemented in 74 countries (Üstün et al., 2003). In the United States, the ICF framework had a direct impact on the scope of practice statement for the speech language pathology profession (American Speech-Language-Hearing Association, 2004; Threats, 2003) and has influenced activities related to data collection, framing assessment interventions, measuring clinical research outcomes (Threats, 2002), and investigating the role of communication in the quality of life (Threats & Worrall, 2004).

Contemporary literature reviews addressing the ICF suggest that there is a growing body of scholarship supporting the potential utility of the ICF (see Bruyère, Van Looy, & Peterson, 2005; Peterson, 2005). Posited applications of the ICF include:

1. The ICF can improve communication between different users, such as health care workers, researchers, policy makers, and the public, including people with disabilities" (WHO, 2001, p. 5).
2. The ICF provides the basis for a systematic coding scheme for global health information systems.
3. Data from ICF-based systems can be used to identify facilitators and barriers that affect the full participation of people with disabilities in society.
4. Research using ICF structure may permit comparison of data across countries, health care disciplines, services, and time.
5. Data from the ICF can contribute to an international database of scientific knowledge of health and health-related states, thus stimulating research on the consequences of health conditions.
6. The ICF can be used to create informative profiles of an individual's functioning, disability, and health, and such data can enhance health care service provision. (Reed et al., 2005)

Üstün and associates (2003) predicted that "(t)he ICF will become the generally accepted framework to describe functioning in rehabilitation" (p. 567).

Future Directions in ICF Research and Practice

To date, the ICF has been used as a statistical tool for population studies and in systems of information management; as a research tool to measure outcomes, environmental factors, and quality of life; as a clinical tool in treatment planning, vocational assessment, and rehabilitation outcome evaluation; as a social policy tool for social security planning, compensation systems development,

Research Box 1.1

MAPPING PARTICIPATION

Seekins, T., Ipsen, C., & Arnold, N. L. (2007). Using Ecological Momentary Assessment to measure participation: A preliminary study. *Rehabilitation Psychology, 52,* 319–330.

Objective: Participation is a key outcome of rehabilitation and health interventions, yet, there are fewer measures to assess it in community settings than should be the case. The study developed a participation measure (the Ecological Momentary Assessment: EMA) based on the ICF and useful for assessing functioning in everyday settings.

Method: Five adults with mental health and neuromuscular conditions receiving vocational rehabilitation services were participants. They were all residents of a rural community. Participants used personal data assistants (PDAs) with memory cards to record their activity at the prompt of the PDA, which was programmed to allow for comprehensive time sampling of participant activities over the day. Data were collected over 7 weeks.

Results: The EMA was useful for mapping the level and quality of participation in a variety of everyday settings. Participants reported greater community engagement and personal fulfillment based on their self-observations.

Conclusion: Participation in everyday settings can be reliably measured using tools that are time and context sensitive.

Questions:

1. How may self-observation influence data on participation by rehabilitation customers? Consider ways in which the reliability of data from self-observations using PDAs can be enhanced.
2. What alternative methods to measure participation are possible? How would they compare with the use of PDAs?

and policy design and implementation; as an educational tool in curriculum design; and to raise awareness and take social action (Peterson & Kosciulek, 2005; WHO, 2001, p. 5).

The greatest contribution of the ICF to health care is the opportunity for health care stakeholders, consumers, and providers, alike, to participate fully in ongoing interdisciplinary cooperation to improve health care intervention targeting, helping people with disabilities to maximize their personal achievement and full participation in society. However, it is important to note that as a major classification system, the ICF is in its nascent stages of development.

Future research and implementation efforts with the ICF promise to: (1) revolutionize the way stakeholders in health care delivery systems think about and classify health, (2) improve the quality of health care for individuals across the world, (3) generate innovative outcome-based research, and (4) influence culturally sensitive global health policy (Peterson & Rosenthal, 2005b; Stucki, Ewert, & Cieza, 2003).

Linking ICF to Functional Outcome Measures

As advancement in medical technology has resulted in improved treatment of acute medical conditions and longer life expectancy, the cost of medical care over the average person's lifetime has increased significantly (Jaet & McMahon, 1999; Peterson & Aguiar, 2004; Peterson & Elliott, in press; Tarvydas, Peterson, & Michaelson, 2005). The managed care industry has forced health professionals to be more outcomes-focused in their reports to third-party payers rather than reporting only traditional diagnostic information. The ICF provides a system to document functional outcomes that complement diagnostic information in health classification efforts.

A variety of health care disciplines have focused on research that links the ICF to commonly used clinical tests and health outcome measures. Research has also focused on identifying ICF core sets for use by physicians, nurses, and others in acute care to help maintain functioning early in the treatment process (Stucki et al., 2005). ICF core sets are priority categories selected for their appropriateness to address need in specific patient populations, and these core sets have been developed for patients with cardiopulmonary, musculoskeletal,

Discussion Box 1.3

ICF CORE SETS

The ICF comprises about 1,500 categories and is somewhat cumbersome to use in everyday rehabilitation settings. To enhance the utility of the ICF categories, ICF core sets have been developed for several health conditions. ICF core sets have fewer categories that are also clinically most relevant to the rehabilitation needs of patients or customers with particular health conditions. However, physicians, nurses, and other acute care rehabilitation service providers were significantly less reliable and confident in scoring the items that measured functioning in everyday settings (Korner-Bitensky, Mayo, & Poznanski, 1990; Gurka et al., 1999; Turner-Stokes, Nyein, Turner-Stokes, & Gatehouse, 1999), which compromised their ability to plan for discharge or to evaluate changes in patients or people with disabilities that predicted readiness for community reintegration. ICF core sets would make the ICF more user-friendly, but measurement problems with service providers require attention.

How would you enhance the reliable use of ICF core sets by a multidisciplinary rehabilitation team?

and neurological conditions. The ICF core sets for these patient populations are undergoing trials in Austria, Germany, and Switzerland. Similarly, ICF categories most relevant for evaluating the outcome of health resort programs have been identified and are currently in use in several European countries and Japan (Morita, Weigl, Schuh, & Stucki, 2006). Health resort programs are holiday or respite destinations typically consisting of residential health spa and fitness programming, often with both physical and spiritual components.

Theory Development

The ICF and its conceptual framework can be used to define concepts, build constructs, hypothesize relationships, and propose new theories that will further research and practice well into the 21st century (Bruyère & Peterson, 2005; Bruyère, Van Looy, & Peterson, 2005; Peterson, 2005; WHO, 2001). However, the conceptual framework of the ICF requires further study to establish construct-related evidence for validity (e.g., can relationships between the proposed constructs be hypothesized and tested?) and criterion-related evidence for validity (e.g., can these variables be used to predict health and health-related states?). As data are collected relating various concepts within the model, researchers can explore relationships and research causal links to inform future theory development. For example, do differences between Activity (what a person can do) and Participation (what a person does do) predict future health and functioning?

Mapping the ICF to Seminal Assessment Tools

Ongoing and future research efforts include mapping the ICF onto items within ubiquitous and contemporary assessment and classification instruments in health care (Stucki et al, 2003). The 2005 meeting of the North American Collaborating Center (NACC) focused on efforts to map the ICF to other clinical assessment, evaluation, and classification tools. Attendees represented seven different countries working with the ICF. As these data are agglomerated, various health care disciplines can create bridging texts and documents to facilitate the ICF's dissemination into their respective classification protocols. Within the area of mental health, the *Diagnostic and Statistical Manual of Mental Disorders* (4th ed., text rev.; *DSM-IV-TR*) is currently linked with the ICD-10 codes. Linking its sister-classification, the ICF, would provide classification of functioning within a mental health context that moves beyond multiaxial diagnoses alone to descriptions of health and health-related states (see previous example using depression).

Developing Instruments Based Upon the ICF

Item response theory holds great promise to convert the ICF into measurement systems that individualize the assessment process, reduce respondent burden, and increase measurement precision (Velozo, 2005). Professionals from the disciplines of rehabilitation psychology (DiCowden, 2005), nursing (Coenen, 2005; Harris, 2005), occupational therapy (Velozo, 2005), and physical therapy (Brandt, 2005; Mayo & McGill, 2005) have developed instruments and protocols based upon the ICF model. For example, Velozo (2005) was awarded a National Institute on Disability and Rehabilitation Research (NIDRR) field-initiated grant to develop a computerized adaptive measurement system for the Activity dimension of the ICF.

Medical Ontology Research

Olivier Bodenreider (2005), of the Lister Hill National Center for Biomedical Communications, applied the ICF to the National Library of Medicine's (NLM) Unified Medical Language System (UMLS). The UMLS facilitates the development of computer systems that work with the meaning of the language of biomedicine and health. The NLM produces and distributes the UMLS Knowledge Sources (databases) and associated software tools (programs) for use by system developers in building or enhancing electronic information systems that create, process, retrieve, integrate, and aggregate biomedical and health data and information, as well as in informatics research (U.S. National Library of Medicine, n.d., ¶1). Preliminary efforts have focused on mapping the ICF into the UMLS. ICF concepts were associated with related terms within the UMLS so that in the future the ICF could be cross-referenced with other information systems that are already mapped to the UMLS. Previous UMLS initiatives were primarily influenced by the medical model. The biopsychosocial approach embraced by the ICF has challenged the UMLS to develop new categories to better reflect functional information rather than diagnostic information alone.

Bioinformatics and Medical Informatics

The ICF can provide direction, consistency, and assurance to managing the ever-increasing amount of medical information (Rock, 2005). Chute (2005) suggested that the evolving knowledge base of medical information has outgrown our ability to consume it effectively and that systems like the ICF can help us to develop shared semantics, vocabularies, and terminologies in a way that helps us to use medical knowledge effectively when treating people in health care settings. For example, common taxonomies used between psychiatry, neuropsychology, neurology, physiatry, speech language pathology, occupational therapy, and physical therapy may facilitate better coordination of subacute rehabilitation services provided for people with traumatic brain injury. Chute suggested that while informatics is a very complex area of research, measures and classifications of functioning are the overall metric of organic well-being and, thus, important to include in this evolving research area.

Savova, Harris, Pakhomov, and Chute (2005) presented a method of semantic processing of a portion of the ICF (Self-Care), using Natural Language Processing (NLP) techniques, or computational methods of processing information to autocode text descriptions of health care scenarios. NLP is a subfield of artificial intelligence and linguistics that studies the problems of automated generation and understanding of natural human languages. While their study suggested that some ambiguities existed within the ICF itself, overall, they were able to use the Berkely FrameNet (FN), a computational lexicography resource, to provide relevant and complete coverage for the ICF Self-Care domain.

ICF and Youth

During the ICIDH revision processes of the '90s, a task force was created to specifically address using the ICIDH with children. Simeonsson et al. (2003) attempted to incorporate the sensibilities needed when classifying youth who are in constant developmental transition, resulting in the ICF-Youth (ICF-Y).

Recent research suggests that the ICF and the ICD-10 can be used together as a common language to document disability characteristics of children in early interventions and in child service systems more generally (Simeonsson, Scarborough, & Hebbeler, 2006). There is need for more research on use of the ICF with children.

Legal and Professional Issues of Clinical Implementation of the ICF

According to Leonardi and associates (2006), in many countries the 2010 census efforts, based upon the recommendation of the UN Population division, will include queries regarding disability status. As national health and disability surveys are established, they predict an increased attention on nonfatal health care outcomes (such as disability associated with aging), necessitating common agreement on the meaning of disability, health, and functioning, which can be facilitated by the ICF's "consistent and complete conceptualization of disability" (p. 1220).

Research from the ICIDH field trials suggests that training and structured guidance would be useful to future users of the classification system (Reed et al., 2005). To date, most of the 191 member states who are encouraged to use the ICF have lacked such guidance in its clinical implementation. In order to facilitate implementation of the ICF in clinical settings in the United States and allied member states, the American Psychological Association (APA) and WHO formed a series of interdisciplinary team expert groups to develop *The Procedural Manual and Guide for the Standardized Application of the ICF: A Manual for Health Professionals.* While many have speculated on its date of completion (Daw, 2002; Holloway, 2004; Peterson, 2005; Threats & Worrall, 2004), unanticipated coding issues have delayed its production.

A prototype manual for several ICF chapters was disseminated for field testing (Holloway, 2004), and the results were used on subsequent iterations of the manual. Most recently, the Environmental Factors, the newest addition to the ICF, received increased attention as the APA-coordinated effort progressed. The size of the volume to date (over 800 pages) argues for exploring the utility of using computerized and automated matching systems in employing the ICF (Peterson & Rosenthal, 2005b; Reed et al., 2005). Once the *Procedural Manual* is published, the guide can be used for training that promotes consistent coding. Further, studies will need to be conducted that evaluate the clarity of the manual, the utility of the manual in clinical practice, and ultimately, the application of the ICF given the new implementation guidelines (Peterson & Rosenthal, 2005b; Reed et al., 2005).

Summary and Conclusion

Assessment is more usable and accurate within clearly specified domains of disability, health, and functioning. The ICF provides a classification system for disability, health, and functioning that would be common basis for locating assessment needs and relating assessment findings from diverse sources to a common framework. The ICF also provides a common language on disability, health, and functioning that would enhance the quality of treatment by multidisciplinary rehabilitation teams.

The ICF uses a universal, culturally sensitive, integrative, and interactive model of health and functioning that is sensitive to psychosocial and environmental aspects of health and disability and covers the entire lifespan of human development (Bruyère & Peterson, 2005; Peterson & Kosciulek, 2005; Üstün et al., 2003; WHO, 2001). Its conceptual framework presents disability as an interaction between impairment, functioning, and environment and can be used to describe both how environmental factors are key to understanding disability and how advocacy occurs through social change (Hurst, 2003; Peterson & Rosenthal, 2005a). The ICF can be used to identify, mitigate, or remove societal hindrances to the full participation of people with disabilities in mainstream society (Peterson, 2005; Peterson & Rosenthal, 2005a; Scherer et al., 2004). As the ICF is revised based on user evidence, the scope and precision of health care's conceptions of health, functioning, and disability based on that classification system will be enhanced.

References

American Speech-Language-Hearing Association (ASHA). (2004). Scope of practice in audiology. *ASHA Supplement 24*. Rockville, MD: Author.

Bassett, S. S., Chase, G. A., Folstein, M. F., & Regier, D. A. (1998). Disability and psychiatric disorders in an urban community: Measurement, prevalence and outcomes. *Psychological Medicine, 28,* 509–517.

Bickenbach, J. E. (2003). Functional status and health information in Canada: Proposals and prospects. *Health Care Financing Review, 24*(3), 89–102.

Bickenbach, J. E., Chatterji, S., Badley, E. M., & Üstün, T. B. (1999). Models of disablement, universalism and the International Classification of Impairments, Disabilities and Handicaps. *Social Science and Medicine, 48,* 1173–1187.

Bodenreider, O. (2005, June). *Mapping new vocabularies to the UMLS: Experience with ICF.* Symposium conducted at the meeting of the World Health Organization's North American Collaborating Center, Mayo Clinic, Rochester, MN.

Brandsma, J. W., Lakerveld-Heyl, K., & Van Ravensberg, C. D. (1995). Reflection on the definition of impairment and disability as defined by the World Health Organization. *Disability & Rehabilitation: An International Multidisciplinary Journal, 17*(3–4), 119–127.

Brandt, D. (2005, June). *Physical therapy and the ICF: Functional stepping stones to the future.* Symposium conducted at the meeting of the World Health Organization's North American Collaborating Center, Mayo Clinic, Rochester, MN.

Bruyère, S. M., & Peterson, D. B. (2005). Introduction to the special section on the International Classification of Functioning, Disability and Health (ICF): Implications for rehabilitation psychology. *Rehabilitation Psychology, 50,* 103–104.

Bruyère, S. M., Van Looy, S. A., & Peterson, D. B. (2005). The International Classification of Functioning, Disability and Health (ICF): Contemporary literature review. *Rehabilitation Psychology, 50,* 113–121.

Burns, C. (1991). Parallels between research and diagnosis: The reliability and validity issues of clinical practice. *The Nurse Practitioner, 16*(10), 42–45, 49–50.

Chute, C. G. (2005, June). *The spectrum of clinical data representation: A context for functional status.* Symposium conducted at the meeting of the World Health Organization's North American Collaborating Center, Mayo Clinic, Rochester, MN.

Coenen, A. (2005, June). *Mapping ICF to the International Classification for Nursing Practice (ICNP).* Symposium conducted at the meeting of the World Health Organization's North American Collaborating Center, Mayo Clinic, Rochester, MN.

Daw, J. (2002). Reconceptualizing health care: APA's work will guide health-care professionals in using a new system for classifying human functioning. *Monitor on Psychology, 33*(1), 70.

De Kleijn-De Vrankrijker, M. W. (2003). The long way from the International Classification of Impairments, Disabilities, and Handicaps (ICIDH) to the International Classification of Functioning, Disability and Health (ICF). *Disability and Rehabilitation, 25,* 561–564.

DiCowden, M. A. (2005, June). *The impact of ICF coding in practice.* Symposium conducted at the meeting of the World Health Organization's North American Collaborating Center, Mayo Clinic, Rochester, MN.

Elliott, T., Kurylo, M., & Rivera, P. (2002). Positive growth following an acquired physical disability. In C. R. Snyder & S. Lopez (Eds.), *Handbook of positive psychology* (pp. 687–699). New York: Oxford University Press.

Frank, R. G., & Elliott, T. R. (2000). Rehabilitation psychology: Hope for a psychology of chronic conditions. In R. G. Frank & T. R. Elliott (Eds.), *Handbook of rehabilitation psychology* (pp. 3–8). Washington, DC: American Psychological Association.

Gatchel, R. J., Polatin, P. B., Mayer, T. G., & Garcy, P. D. (1994). Psychopathology and the rehabilitation of patients with chronic low back pain disability. *Archives of Physical Medicine and Rehabilitation, 75,* 666–670.

Gurka, J. A., Felmingham, K. L., Baguley, I. J., Schotte, D. E., Crooks, J., & Marosszeky, J. E., (1999). Utility of the Functional Assessment Measure after discharge from inpatient rehabilitation. *Journal of Head Trauma and Rehabilitation, 14,* 247–256.

Hansen, J. T. (2004). Thoughts on knowing: Epistemic implications of counseling practice. *Journal of Counseling and Development, 82,* 131–138.

Harris, M. R. (2005, June). *Clinical and administrative mappings to the ICF.* Symposium conducted at the meeting of the World Health Organization's North American Collaborating Center, Mayo Clinic, Rochester, MN.

Holloway, J. D. (2004, January). A new way of looking at health status. *Monitor on Psychology, 35,* 32.

Hurst, R. (2003). The international disability rights movement and the ICF. *Disability and Rehabilitation, 25,* 572–576.

Institute of Medicine. (2007). *The future of disability in America.* Washington, DC: Author.

Jaet, D. N., & McMahon, B. T. (1999). Implications of disability legislation for case managers. In F. Chan & M. J. Leahy (Eds.), *Health care & disability case management* (pp. 213–238). Lake Zurich, IL: Vocational Consultants Press.

Korner-Bitensky, N., Mayo, N. E., & Poznanski, S. G. (1990). Occupational therapists' accuracy in predicting sensory, perceptual-cognitive, and functional recovery post-stroke. *The Occupational Therapy Journal of Research, 10,* 237–248.

Leonardi, M., Bickenbach, J., Üstün, T. B., Kostanjsek, N., & Chatterji, S. (2006). Comment: The definition of disability: What is in a name? *The Lancet, 368*(9543), 1219–1221.

Madden, R., Choi, C., & Sykes, C. (2003). The ICF as a framework for national data: The introduction of the ICF into Australian data dictionaries. *Disability and Rehabilitation, 25,* 676–682.

Massel, H. K., Liberman, R. P., Mintz, J., & Jacobs, H. E. (1990). Evaluating the capacity to work of the mentally ill. *Psychiatry: Journal for the Study of Interpersonal Processes, 53,* 31–43.

Mayo, N. E., & McGill, J. (2005, June). *Standardizing clinical assessments to the ICF.* Symposium conducted at the meeting of the World Health Organization's North American Collaborating Center, Mayo Clinic, Rochester, MN.

McCrone, P., & Phelan, M. (1994). Diagnosis and length of psychiatric in-patient stay. *Psychological Medicine, 24,* 1025–1030.

Morita, E., Weigl, M., Schuh, A., & Stucki, G. (2006). Identification of relevant ICF categories for indication, intervention planning and evaluation of health resort programs: A Delphi exercise. *International Journal of Biometeorol, 50,* 183–191.

National Advisory Mental Health Council. (1993). Health care reform for Americans with severe mental illness: Report of the National Advisory Mental Health Council. *American Journal of Psychiatry, 150,* 1447–1465.

Nieuwenhuijsen, E. R. (1995). The ICIDH in the USA: Applications and relevance to ADA goals. *Disability and Rehabilitation, 17*(3–4), 154–158.

Olkin, R. (1999). *What psychotherapists should know about disability.* New York: Guilford Press.

Olkin, R., & Pledger, C. (2003). Can disability studies and psychology join hands? *American Psychologist, 58,* 296–304.

Ormel, J., Oldehinkel, T., Brilman, E., & vanden Brink, W. (1993). Outcome of depression and anxiety in primary care: A three wave 3 1/2 year study of psychopathology and disability. *Archives of General Psychiatry, 50,* 759–766.

Parker, R. M., Szymanski, E. M., & Patterson, J. B. (Eds.). (2005). *Rehabilitation counseling: Basics and beyond* (4th ed.). Austin, TX: PRO-ED.

Peterson, D. B. (2005). International Classification of Functioning, Disability and Health (ICF): An introduction for rehabilitation psychologists. *Rehabilitation Psychology, 50,* 105–112.

Peterson, D. B., & Aguiar, L. (2004). History & systems: United States. In T. F. Riggar & D. R. Maki (Eds.), *The handbook of rehabilitation counseling* (pp. 50–75). New York: Springer Publishing Company.

Peterson, D. B., & Elliott, T. R. (2008). Advances in conceptualizing and studying disability. In S. Brown & R. Lent (Eds.), *Handbook of counseling psychology* (4th ed., pp. 212–230). Hoboken, NJ: Wiley.

Peterson, D. B., & Kosciulek, J. F. (2005). Introduction to the special issue of *Rehabilitation Education:* The International Classification of Functioning, Disability & Health (ICF). *Rehabilitation Education, 19,* 75–80.

Peterson, D. B., & Rosenthal, D. R. (2005a). The International Classification of Functioning, Disability and Health (ICF): A primer for rehabilitation educators. *Rehabilitation Education, 19,* 81–94.

Peterson, D. B., & Rosenthal, D. R. (2005b). The International Classification of Functioning, Disability and Health (ICF) as an allegory for history and systems in rehabilitation education. *Rehabilitation Education, 19,* 75–80.

Peterson, D. B., & Threats, T. T. (2005). Ethical and clinical implications of the International Classification of Functioning, Disability and Health (ICF) in rehabilitation education. *Rehabilitation Education, 19,* 129–138.

Pledger, C. (2003). Discourse on disability and rehabilitation issues: Opportunities for psychology. *American Psychologist, 58,* 279–284.

Rabinowitz, J., Modai, I., & Inbar-Saban, N. (1994). Understanding who improves after psychiatric hospitalization. *Acta Psychiatrica Scandidavica, 89,* 152–158.

Reed, G. M., Lux, J. B., Bufka, L. F., Trask, C., Peterson, D. B., Stark, S., et al. (2005). Operationalizing the International Classification of Functioning, Disability and Health (ICF) in clinical settings. *Rehabilitation Psychology, 50,* 122–131.

Rock, M. (2005, June). *Welcome WHO/ICF NACC to Mayo Clinic.* Symposium conducted at the meeting of the World Health Organization's North American Collaborating Center, Mayo Clinic, Rochester, MN.

Rubin, S. E., & Roessler, R. T. (2000). *Foundations of the vocational rehabilitation process* (5th ed.). Austin, TX: PRO-ED.

Savova, G., Harris, M., Pakhomov, S., & Chute, C. G. (2005, June). *Frame representation of ICF.* Symposium conducted at the meeting of the World Health Organization's North American Collaborating Center, Mayo Clinic, Rochester, MN.

Scherer, M. J., Blair, K. L., Banks, M. E., Brucker, B., Corrigan, J., & Wegener, J. H. (2004). Rehabilitation psychology. In W. E. Craighead & C. B. Nemeroff (Eds.), *The concise Corsini encyclopedia of psychology and behavioral science* (3rd ed., pp. 801–802). Hoboken, NJ: Wiley.

Seekins, T., Ipsen, C., & Arnold, N. L. (2007). Using Ecological Momentary Assessment to measure participation: A preliminary study. *Rehabilitation Psychology, 52,* 319–330.

Segal, S. P., & Choi, N. G. (1991). Factors affecting SSI support for sheltered care residents with serious mental illness. *Hospital and Community Psychiatry, 42,* 1132–1137.

Simeonsson, R. J., Leonardi, M., Lollar, D., Björck-Åkesson, E., Hollenweger, J., & Martinuzzi, A. (2003). Applying the International Classification of Functioning, Disability and Health (ICF) to measure childhood disability. *Disability and Rehabilitation, 25,* 602–610.

Simeonsson, R. J., Scarborough, A. A., & Hebbeler, K. M. (2006). The ICF and ICD codes provide a standard language of disability in young children. *Journal of Clinical Epidemiology, 59,* 365–373.

Smart, J. (2005). The promise of the International Classification of Functioning, Disability & Health (ICF). *Rehabilitation Education, 19,* 191–199.

Stucki, G., Ewert, T., & Cieza, A. (2003). Value and application of the ICF in rehabilitation medicine. *Disability and Rehabilitation, 25,* 628–634.

Stucki, G., Ustun, T. B., & Melvin, J. (2005). Applying the ICF for the acute hospital and early post-acute rehabilitation facilities. *Disability Rehabilitation, 27*(7–8), 349–352.

Tarvydas, V. M., Peterson, D. B., & Michaelson, S. D. (2005). Ethical issues in case management. In F. Chan, M. Leahy, & J. Saunders (Eds.), *Case management for rehabilitation health professionals* (2nd ed., pp. 144–175). Osage Beach, MO: Aspen Professional Services.

Threats, T. (2002). Evidence based practice research using the WHO framework. *Journal of Medical Speech-Language Pathology, 10,* xvii–xxiv.

Threats, T. (2003). The framework for ASHA's revised scope of practice in speech-language pathology. *Speech Pathology Online.* Retrieved June 6, 2003, from: http://www.speechpathology.com.

Threats, T. T., & Worrall, L. (2004). Classifying communication disability using the ICF. *Advances in Speech Language Pathology, 6*(1), 53–62.

Turner-Stokes, L., Nyein, K., Turner-Stokes, T., & Gatehouse, C. (1999). The UK FIM+FAM: Development and evaluation. *Clinical Rehabilitation, 13,* 277–287.

Ueda, S., & Okawa, Y. (2003). The subjective dimension of functioning and disability: What is it and what is it for? *Disability and Rehabilitation, 25,* 596–601.

U.S. National Library of Medicine. (n.d.). *Fact sheet: Unified Medical Language System.* Retrieved May 26, 2007, from: http://www.nlm.nih.gov/pubs/factsheets/umls.html.

Üstün, T. B., Chaterji, S., Bickenbach, J., Kastanjsek, N., & Schnieder, M. (2003). The International Classification of Functioning, Disability and Health: A new tool for understanding disability and health. *Disability and Rehabilitation, 25,* 565–571.

Velozo, C. A. (2005, June). *Tutorial: Developing measures based on the ICF.* Symposium conducted at the meeting of the World Health Organization's North American Collaborating Center, Mayo Clinic, Rochester, MN.

World Health Organization. (1980). *ICIDH: International Classification of Impairments, Disabilities, and Handicaps. A manual of classification relating to the consequences of disease.* Geneva: Author.

World Health Organization. (1992). *ICD-10: International Statistical Classification of Diseases and Related Health Problems* (10th rev.). Geneva: Author.

World Health Organization. (2001). *ICF: International Classification of Functioning, Disability and Health.* Geneva: Author.

Developmental and Health Assessment in Rehabilitation with the ICF for Children and Youth

Rune J. Simeonsson
Andrea Sauer-Lee
Mats Granlund
Eva Björck-Åkesson

2

Overview

Prior to 2001, there was no standard universal classification of dimensions of health and human functioning for the field of rehabilitation. The World Health Organization's (WHO) 2001 International Classification of Functioning, Disability, and Health (ICF) provided the first standard taxonomic approach applicable to health and rehabilitation services for adults. A comparable universal taxonomy for the corresponding fields of child habilitation, special education, and early childhood intervention became available in 2007 with the publication of the ICF version for Children and Youth (ICF-CY; WHO, 2007). It offers a new way to conceptualize, implement, and document characteristics of children and youth with disabilities and their environments. This chapter provides a brief overview of the ICF-CY, describes its use as a resource in assessment of child health and development, and identifies specific issues in its application in assessment practice.

Learning Objectives

By the end of the chapter, the reader should be able to:

1. Describe the main features of the ICF-CY and evaluate its contributions to assessment practice;
2. Identify and describe sources of evidence for assigning ICF-CY codes to assessment results; and
3. Apply scale values to the ICF-CY universal qualifier.

Introduction

The ICF was developed to provide a universal method and common language for documenting dimensions of human health, functioning, and disability. However, the 2001 ICF was not sufficiently comprehensive to include coverage of health and functioning characteristics in children, particularly those displayed during the very early years of childhood (Simeonsson, Leonardi, Björck-Åkesson, Hollenweger, & Lollar, 2003). In addition, the ICF did not meet the need for a classification inclusive of children and youth (Simeonsson, Lollar, Hollowell, & Adams, 2000). In contrast to the task of documenting functioning in adults, documenting child characteristics can be more challenging in that the developing child is a "moving target," manifesting rapid changes in physical, social, and psychological functioning during the first 2 decades of life (Simeonsson, 2005). The development of the ICF-CY required expansion of the scope and content of the ICF to encompass the developmental characteristics of children and youth from birth through age 17. This age range parallels the age range for defining childhood covered by another universal document, the United Nations (UN) Convention on the Rights of the Child (UN, 1989).

Overview of Defining Features of the ICF-CY

The ICF-CY provides a classification system derived from the ICF. Thus, the ICF-CY and the ICF's organizational and structural features are consistent. Its division of domains and hierarchical structure of chapters, blocks, and codes are identical to that of the ICF. The ICF-CY's new features are found in the expansion of content and increased specificity of detail. The ecological model described by Bronfenbrenner and Ceci (1994), in which the child's adaptation during the developmental years is the product of the child's ongoing interactions with the environment over time, guided the addition of content. This developmental perspective was emphasized in the ICF-CY in two ways: through the addition of content and through the expansion of the definition of the universal qualifier. The universal qualifier is a scale value assigned to ICF-CY codes to quantify the extent of problems characterizing the body function or structure and activity or participation of an individual. Further, the universal qualifier also can be used to quantify the extent to which an environment constitutes a barrier or facilitator for an individual's functioning.

In keeping with the ICF's taxonomical structure, new content was added to the four ICF-CY domains using neutral terms such as *adaptability* (b1250) in Body Functions and *acquiring language* (d133) in Activities and Participation. These additions to the ICF-CY codes reflect developmental aspects of body functions and structures and activities and participation displayed by infants, toddlers, children, or adolescents. The nature of children's functioning and their ongoing interactions with the environment are reflected in the ICF-CY codes through the use of the 4, 5, and 6 character levels across the four domains (i.e., Body Functions, Body Structure, Activities and Participation, and Environmental Factors). For example, the code for *basic interpersonal relationships* (d710) is documented by the letter *d* to indicate the domain of Activity and Participation, *7* as the chapter for interpersonal, and *10* to designate the *basic nature of the relationship.* The expansion of content in the ICF-CY in many cases reflected the addition of codes defining developmentally earlier forms of more mature levels of functioning manifested later in the individual's life. For example, the addition of the code *learning to read* (d140) is a precursor of the ICF code *reading* (d166). As shown in Table 2.1, most new codes were added in the domain of Activities and Participation and were made at the fifth character level, that is, a domain code plus four digits. Although not constituting the addition of new codes, substantial modifications were made for codes in Body Functions and Structures at the fifth character level to encompass characteristics of children. For example, these additions and modifications resulted in a total of 1,658 classes in the ICF-CY compared to 1,454 classes in the ICF.

The use of codes within the four ICF-CY domains provides the common language for documenting limitations that may characterize a child in activities

2.1 Additions and Modifications to Content Defined by the ICF-CY

	Changes to inclusion/ exclusion criteria	New class at 4th character	New class at 5th character	New class at 6th character	Total new classes
Body Function	24	4	28	6	38
Body Structure	0	0	8	11	19
Activities & Participation	75	14	128	17	159
Environmental Factors	12	0	6	9	15
Total	111	18	170	43	231

such as learning, moving, or interacting with others. The use of the code also provides the basis for documenting the role of the environment in facilitating or restricting the child's functioning and development.

A developmental perspective also was emphasized by an expansion of the definition of the universal qualifier to include the concept of developmental delay. Use of the universal qualifier is required to record the presence and extent of impairments, limitations, restrictions, and environmental barriers experienced by an individual child. In the ICF-CY, the qualifier is defined by five levels (0–4) with the first (0) indicating no impairment or difficulty and the last (4) indicating complete impairment or difficulty.

The qualifier is universal in that it is applied to all codes across all domains with the same meaning of severity. Expanding the definition of the universal qualifier to include the concept of developmental delay was done to provide the option of recording problems or difficulties as possible lags in maturation or development rather than fixed impairments. Thus, a difficulty or problem displayed by a child can be noted as a developmental concern without the necessary implication that the difficulty or problem is permanent. The concept of developmental delay is well established and widely used to define infants and young children in need of early intervention and support in lieu of, or in conjunction with, a formal diagnosis—for example, when defining eligibility under the Individuals with Disabilities Education Improvement Act (U.S. Department of Education, 2004).

The ICF-CY universal qualifier is applied by specifying the extent of a problem or difficulty (i.e., to designate its severity) by using numerals from 0 to 4 following the decimal point for the code. When referencing the environmental domain, the qualifier can be used to document environmental factors that may be hindering functioning, health, and activities and participation. In this situation, the decimal is followed by a minus (–) sign and the numeric value of the qualifier, thus signifying the relative strength of the barrier from no barrier (0) to a complete barrier (4). The universal qualifier also can be used in a positive manner to indicate the extent to which an environment may serve to facilitate a child's body function or activity or participation. Environmental factors that have a facilitating role are coded by adding a plus (+) sign and the numeric value of the qualifier. The application of the universal qualifier in coding assessment data is described more fully later in this chapter.

Using the ICF-CY in Developmental and Health Assessment

The domain framework and common language provided by the ICF-CY may be used in various ways and for different purposes. The ICF-CY offers a wide range of applications, including documenting clinical, administrative, and surveillance data; health informatics; and policy and research information. Importantly, the ICF-CY can serve as a companion resource to the UN Convention on the Rights of the Child (1989) to provide needed documentation of deprivation of children's rights in terms of access to services and support (Lansdown, 2000; Simeonsson, Björck-Åkesson, & Bairrao, 2006). With reference to assessment of child health, functioning, and development, the ICF-CY offers a conceptual framework and a common terminology for recording problems displayed by children and adolescents. The ICF-CY defines child health and health-related components of well-being and contributing environmental factors. With reference to assessment in clinical practice and research, the ICF-CY can (a) offer a framework for interdisciplinary assessment practice, (b) provide a systematic approach to assessment, and (c) yield data to profile child functioning and clarify clinical diagnoses.

Framework for Interdisciplinary Assessment Practice

At a global level, the domain structure of the ICF-CY provides a useful framework for interdisciplinary practice as suggested in the adapted ICF-CY model shown in Figure 2.1. The common language of the ICF-CY addresses an important problem in current interdisciplinary practice, namely, the use of discipline-specific languages may restrict a holistic and integrated view of the child. The comprehensive framework of ICF-CY domains changes the focus from classifying children on the basis of discipline-specific diagnoses to a dimensional classification of functional characteristics. This distinction is important and is consistent with a holistic and nonstigmatizing approach to disability. Thus, the ICF-CY provides a framework for integrating interdisciplinary efforts on behalf

2.1

The ICF-CY: A unifying framework for interdisciplinary assessment practice.

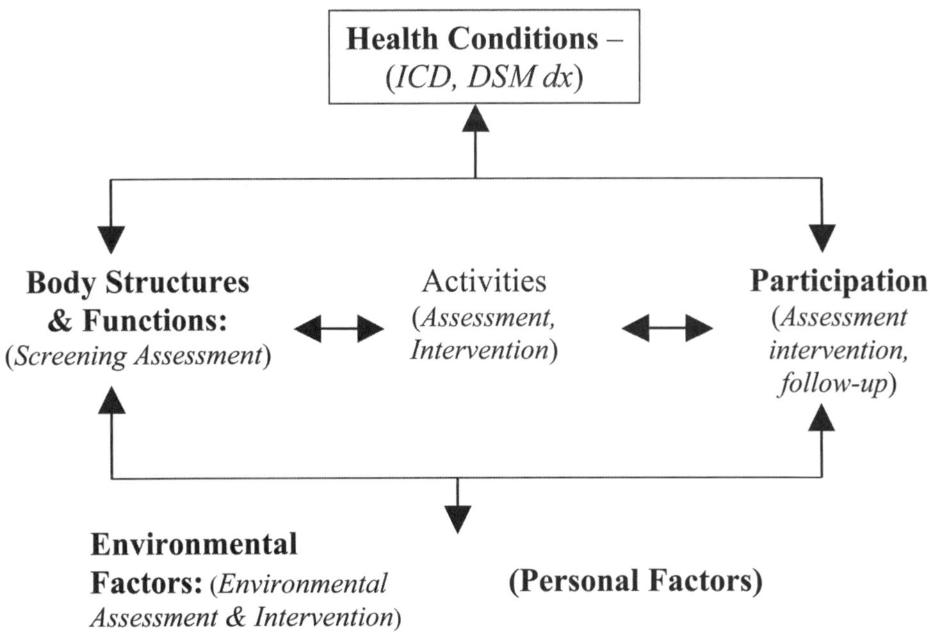

of children with disabilities. Although the disciplinary activities of medicine, allied health, nursing, psychology, and special education are likely to focus on different components of the ICF-CY model, all disciplines can share the common language of the ICF in describing characteristics of the child and identifying interventions and environmental supports.

In Sweden, the ICF-CY has been tested as a framework for habilitation services for children and youth with disability provided by habilitation teams. Habilitation teams are interdisciplinary and involve occupational therapists, physiotherapists, physicians, psychologists, social workers, and special educators, among others. Results from these field trials show that professionals perceive the use of the ICF-CY facilitates interdisciplinary communication and collaborative goal setting (Ibragimova, Granlund, & Björck-Åkesson, 2009; Pless, Ibragimova, Adolfsson, Björck-Åkesson, & Granlund, 2009).

ICF-CY and Systematic Approach to Assessment

The use of the underlying framework of domains of health and functioning in the ICF-CY is important when conceptualizing policy and service applications. However, the primary utility of the ICF-CY may rest on the description and subsequent coding of information about the child's functioning in the environmental contexts within which that child functions. To this end, coding applications of clinical, research, and statistical data require matching characteristics of children and their environments to ICF-CY codes closest to those characteristics.

With reference to assessment, the ICF-CY may be used to document impairments, limitations, restrictions, and environmental barriers experienced by a child. Implementation of the ICF-CY requires the application of the qualifier to codes that indicate the severity of problems. The ICF-CY is a classification tool, not a measurement tool. Thus, in reference to assessment, the ICF-CY may be helpful by (a) defining the focus of assessment, (b) guiding the selection of assessment evidence, and (c) coding the nature and extent of a disability. At the most basic level, the practitioner must consider the purpose of conducting an assessment prior to choosing measures, administering these tools, and then attempting to interpret the results in a way that is meaningful for both the child and for persons in their proximal environment in order to develop interventions that meet the child's needs.

Traditional assessment practices typically focus on assessment of defined constructs (e.g., perception, memory, cognition, and self concept) that describe a child's daily functioning indirectly. In contrast, the ICF-CY provides the basis for an assessment that focuses on universally displayed functions, activities, and participation. Thus, the ICF-CY encourages practitioners to describe a child's daily functioning more directly and functionally. Its multidimensional framework can be used to design assessments that encompass a broad domain of interests (e.g., body function, structures, activities/participation, and environmental factors). The ICF-CY also can be used as a model to help guide and organize the practitioner's thoughts about what information is needed and why. This information then can be used to identify appropriate assessment tools that yield data important in collaborative problem-solving methods.

The correspondence of assessment instruments with elements of the ICF-CY can be in terms of a domain (e.g., Activities and Participation) or at the chapter level (e.g., General Tasks and Demands). Assessment results from specific subscales or variables are likely to correspond to particular ICF-CY codes in order to document a particular function, activity, or form of participation. Assessment may be more general when used for screening and more specific when used for intervention and treatment planning and evaluation.

The match of assessment data to ICF-CY components will vary depending on the assessment purpose or goals. In the context of clinical, child habilitation, or special education settings, assessment data representing codes from the Activity and Participation and Environmental Factors domains are likely to be acquired in that they help document the reality of the child's limitations of everyday functioning in context. Assessment data related to the domains of Body Functions and Body Structures also are likely to be acquired for children who display acquired problems (e.g., traumatic brain injury), chronic health conditions (e.g., Prader-Willy Syndrome), or neuromuscular disorders (e.g., spina bifida; Simeonsson, McMillen, & Huntington, 2002). The nature and extent of a child's presenting difficulties will define and reflect the comprehensiveness of the developmental assessment and the scope of ICF-CY codes. To this end, assessment planning is likely to prioritize those aspects of the child's functioning important for intervention planning and outcome documentation.

This priority is consistent with a focus on the steps of the intervention cycle in intervention planning (Simeonsson et al., 1996). Following the first step of defining intervention expectations, the goal of assessment is described and the child's problems are explained. This leads to the steps of goal setting in an individualized intervention and implementation of services. The last step is an evaluation of outcomes following a prescribed period of intervention. A cycle designed to address the child's next developmental goals then is initiated. Using this framework, problems and goals often can be described in terms of Activities and Participation, while problem explanations may encompass information from all ICF-CY components. The following vignette illustrates a preschool child's problems of social interaction and participation in class activities. Within the framework of the ICF-CY, these problems reflect the influence of impairments of body functions, limitations in performing activities, and experience of environmental barriers on participation. Intervention methods occur externally to the child and therefore need to be phrased in terms of the environmental factors (Björck-Åkesson & Granlund, 2004; Raghavendra, Bornman, Granlund, & Björck-Åkesson, 2007).

Vignette: Defining Intervention Expectations

Anna, a 5-year-old girl, attends a preschool. Its staff reports Anna spends almost all her time alone or with staff. Anna plays functional games (e.g., pretend feeding a doll) and with toys, yet she seldom is involved with other children in her play. Anna's speech is difficult to understand because of articulation problems and restricted vocabulary. Her parents confirm these difficulties. Anna is referred to habilitation services by the preschool psychologist to define intervention priorities.

As can be seen in the table, Anna's problems are primarily identified within the Activities and Participation component in terms of using spoken language; engaging in conversation with peers in preschool; starting, sustaining, and ending conversations; and lack of peer relations. Barriers in the environment include peers' lack of attention and communication invitations to Anna as well as the preschool staff's lack of knowledge about how to set up communicative temptations involving peers. Parents and preschool staff agree on having Anna's informal relationship with peers as their long-term goal with objectives focusing on speaking, starting conversations, and conversing with one person (peer). Intervention methods are defined in terms of environmental factors and include using iconic symbols and preschool walls (e 125) to augment spoken messages and providing training material regarding communication to staff and parents (e 1300) to change communicative responsiveness of communication partners. These training materials are to be used to train staff (e 330) in setting up communicative temptations involving peers and to train peers (e 325) in adjusting their conversation to Anna. In addition, Anna is provided with a personal assistant (e 340) at preschool.

TABLE: Assessment and intervention planning for Anna

Steps in intervention cycle	Body function/ Body structure	Activity and participation	Environment
Assessment: problem description & explanation	b 16710 Mental functions of language, expression of language b 1400 Sustaining attention b 1402 Dividing attention, b 1403 Sharing attention b 16710 Mental functions of language b 7356 Muscle tone of all body	d 330 speaking d 3500–3504 conversation d 7504 Informal relationships with peers d 330 speaking d 3500–3504 Conversation	e 325 Peers e 330 People in positions of authority, e.g. teachers
Identification of intervention plan & goals		d 330 Speaking d 3500 Starting conversation, d 3503 Conversing with one person d 7504 Informal relationships with peers	
Implementing intervention			e 125 Products and technology for communication e 1300 Products and technology for education e 325 Peers e 330 Teachers e 340 Personal assistant
Evaluating intervention outcomes		Above codes on communication and social relationships	

Questions

1. What specific interventions could staff be trained in to support Anna in her school adjustment? How would those interventions map onto the ICF framework?
2. What other evidence would be needed for a maximally responsive intervention with Anna? Explain your answer.

Table 2.2 summarizes an approach that may be useful when using the ICF-CY to guide assessments of children's functioning in their primary environments (e.g., home, school, and community). First, the practitioner identifies the purpose of assessment. In the context of this chapter, the purpose is likely to focus on an assessment of key dimensions of functioning with the goal to (a) document the nature and extent of limitations or disability, (b) confirm a diagnosis, (c) identify priorities for intervention, and/or (d) provide evidence of intervention outcome. A second step is to identify assessment methods that can provide evidence of the specific aspect of functioning. A related third step is to match, as closely as possible, the best available scale of quantification to the universal qualifier.

To this end, successive steps can be followed to address six broad assessment questions: (a) How does the child's mind and body function? (b) How does the child learn? (c) How does the child respond/adapt to situational demands? (d) What is the nature of the child's independence? (e) What is the nature and level of the child's participation? (f) What barriers or facilitators impact functioning in the child's primary environments? Codes from the domains of Body Function and Body Structures are likely to be central to the first two questions, whereas codes from the Activities and Participation and Environmental Factors domains relate to the remaining questions focused on the child's functioning and participation.

Identifying Sources of Evidence

Applications of the ICF-CY to document child functioning and disability require assessment data to determine the values of the universal qualifier. In addition, an assessment of how the environment impacts the child's functioning is important. Compared to more limited assessments, comprehensive assessments are likely to yield information that can be used for developing interventions that will meet the child's needs. The ICF-CY provides a useful framework for organizing information typically provided by a comprehensive assessment (e.g., by matching assessment goals related to a child's mobility to the Activities and Participation component of Mobility [chapter 4] to the block level of walking and moving [d-450–469] and to the specific code of moving around using equipment [d465]).

The ICF-CY framework can serve the following three important purposes: to encourage practitioners to consider the relevance of the desired information, to encourage practitioners to consider if the desired information is relevant to the development of subsequent interventions, and to help practitioners

2.2 Identifying Sources of Evidence for Documenting ICF-CY Codes

Step 1: Defining the purpose of assessment with reference to key ICF-CY content	Step 2: Representative forms of assessment for obtaining evidence	Step 3: Quantification and coding with the universal qualifier
a) How does the child's mind and body function? BF Chapters 1–8 BS Chapters 1–8	- Standardized and criterion-referenced measures of cognition, perception, attention, sensation - Tests of vision and audition - Physical measurement - Laboratory measures	- Standard scores - Percentile scores and ranks - Descriptive terms - Ratings based on clinical judgment
b) How does the child learn? -BF Chapter 1: Mental Functions -A/P Chapters 1, 3: Learning and Applying Knowledge; Communication	- Standardized and criterion-referenced measures of learning, communication, academic achievement - Problem-solving tasks - Observations of learning context - Self-, teacher-, parent-report of functioning	- Standard scores - Percentile scores and ranks - Description - Ratings based on clinical judgment
c) How does the child respond/adapt to situational demands? -A/P Chapter 2: General Tasks and Demands	- Problem-solving tasks - Observations within everyday situations - Self-, teacher-, parent-report of functioning - Artifacts	- Standard scores - Percentile scores and ranks - Description - Ratings based on clinical judgment
d) What characterizes the child's independence? -A/P Chapters 4, 5, 6: Mobility, Self-Care, Domestic Life	- Normative and criterion-referenced measures of mobility, adaptive and independent behavior Self-, teacher-, parent-report of independent functioning - Observation of daily tasks and activities	- Standard scores - Percentile scores and ranks - Description - Ratings based on clinical judgment
e) What is the nature and level of the child's participation? -A/P Chapters 7, 8, 9: Interpersonal Interactions and Relationships, Major Life Areas; Community, Social and Civic Life	- Normative and criterion-referenced measures of social relationships and behavior - Self-, teacher-, parent-report of participation - Official records from schools, etc. - Observation	-Standard scores -Percentile scores and ranks -Description -Ratings based on clinical judgment

2.2 Identifying Sources of Evidence for Documenting ICF-CY Codes — *Continued*

Step 1: Defining the purpose of assessment with reference to key ICF-CY content	Step 2: Representative forms of assessment for obtaining evidence	Step 3: Quantification and coding with the universal qualifier
f) What barriers/facilitators impact functioning in the child's primary environments? -EF Chapters 1–5: Products & Technology; Natural Environment/Human-Made Changes; Support and Relationships; Attitudes; Services, Systems, Policies	- Normative and criterion-referenced measures of physical, social, and attitudinal environments - Self-, teacher-, parent-report of environment - Observation of person/environment interaction - Photographic, audio, & video documentation	- Standard scores - Percentile scores and ranks - Description - Ratings based on clinical judgment

Note: BF = Body Functions, BS= Body Structures, A/P = Activity and Participation, EF = Environmental Factors

organize and execute collaboratively based interventions that include the child, those responsible for the child's welfare, professionals, and other key informants in the child's proximal environment.

Practitioners must identify the form of assessment that will provide evidence to match ICF-CY elements at the level of chapters or codes. Assessment instruments and methods should yield data that correspond to the information needed and should not be selected simply due to convenience or their availability. To this end, evidence can take a number of forms, including observation; artifacts; criterion referenced tools; data-based measures; and judgments from clinicians, caregivers, and the person herself/himself. Table 2.2 identifies forms of evidence relative to the kind of data needed to document ICF-CY codes. The instruments and methods that can be matched to these forms of evidence vary widely. The choice of specific assessment tools or methods will depend on the nature and level of evidence needed. The match between data and the ICF-CY codes may be more difficult and inconsistent in that existing measures were not developed within an ICF-CY framework.

Information obtained from observations, interviews, and behavioral measures completed by children, those responsible for their welfare and care (e.g., parents, teachers), or peers may be aligned closely with the ICF-CY codes. Artifacts (e.g., drawings, completed school assignments or reports, and school records of academic performance) may provide data needed in a number of chapters in the Activities and Participation domain, including those on learning, general tasks and demands, and communication. Other useful sources for ICF-CY–related data include clinical judgment of professionals as well as indices commonly obtained in health and developmental assessments (e.g., measures of auditory and visual acuity, height and weight, and body mass index [BMI])—the latter to document representative ICF-CY body functions. Criterion-referenced instruments can yield evidence with face validity, and norm-referenced measures offer evidence with known reliability and validity. However, as noted previously, the match between data and the ICF-CY codes may be difficult and inconsistent because existing measures were not developed within an ICF-CY framework. Thus, the development of measures that correspond closer to the ICF-CY codes is an important priority.

Coding Functional Limitations and Disability

ICF-CY universal qualifiers are used to specify the severity of the delays, impairments, limitations, or restrictions displayed by the child. The terms defining the universal qualifier and associated percentage values proposed to quantify the extent of the problem or difficulty are presented in the first few rows of Table 2.3. The universal qualifier can be used to document the extent to which the environment is a facilitator or barrier to the child's functioning. Assignment of values 0 to 4 of the universal qualifier requires evidence based on subjective or objective assessment. The ICF-CY definition for levels of severity reported in terms of incremental amounts of a problem or disorder from 0% to 100% does not readily correspond to the conceptualization of severity in many informal and standardized measures. Instead, levels of severity based on clinical judgment and assessment measures often are conceptualized in terms of decreasing levels of typical functioning—from no problem (0) to successively higher levels of reduced functioning (e.g., 1, 2, 3, and 4). In this context, assignment of values for the universal qualifier may differ depending on how severity is operationalized in particular assessment methods or tools.

Table 2.3 summarizes some ways in which levels of severity are defined and could be used to match the levels defined by the ICF-CY universal qualifier. Although the correspondence between levels of the universal qualifier and assessed levels of severity may be less than exact, the different forms of quantification illustrated in the table may serve as a useful reference. The need to clarify the universal qualifier may be related to different applications as described by Okawa, Ueda, Shuto, and Mizoguchi (2008) with reference to data from population surveys.

Thus, when evidence for coding ICF-CY content is obtained following data collection, assignment of universal qualifiers is likely to occur through clinical judgment. As referenced in Table 2.3, clinical judgment is likely to be based on an ordinal scale that corresponds to mild, moderate, severe, or profound deviations from a typical or normal state of functioning. Clinical judgment of severity may be relatively straightforward for some characteristics (e.g., walking, speech, or aspects of self-care) and may be more difficult for many characteristics in the domains of Body Functions and Activities and Participation. Attempts to define and measure participation are ongoing issues of discussion. The use of criterion-referenced instruments as the source of evidence for coding ICF-CY content may provide summary data from which a relative level of severity may be derived for the child's behavior. Criterion-referenced instruments also may yield qualitative data that can be matched to corresponding values of the universal qualifier.

Norm-referenced measures generally report quantified data in terms of severity levels through percentiles and standard scores. As noted in Table 2.2,

2.3 Operationalizing Levels of Severity for Assessment Data in the Application of the ICF-CY Universal Qualifier

Universal qualifier (ICF-CY, p. 21)	0 No problem	1 Mild problem	2 Moderate problem	3 Severe problem	4 Complete problem
Percentage of problem (ICF-CY, p. 21)	0–4%	5–24%	25–49%	50–95%	96–100%
Quantifying words (ICF-CY, p. 21)	(none, absent, negligible)	(slight, low)	(medium, fair)	(high)	(total)
Descriptive terms for use in self-report, by key respondents, or in quantification of artifacts or common indices	average and above	slightly below average	moderately low	very low	extremely low
Clinical judgment	No difference or limitation for age, gender, or context	Slight difference or limitation	Moderate difference or limitation	Serious difference or limitation	Extreme difference or limitation
Standard Score example, where Mean = 100, SD = 15 SS points	86+	71–85	56–70	41–55	<40
Scaled Score example, where Mean = 10, SD = 3 scaled points	> 7	5–7	2–4	1	<1
T-Scores (mean = 50, SD = 10)	> 41	31–40	21–30	11–20	0–10
Percentile Ranks (may vary from test to test)	> 23	11–23	4–11	1–4	<1
Standard deviation units below the mean	0, +SDs	−1 to −2	−2 to −3	−3 to −4	>4

these data can be matched to levels of the ICF-CY universal qualifier. Information on the relative frequency of an observed or assessed characteristic can be used to assign a qualifier value for severity. For example, height or weight charts or their combination, such as BMI, for defined ages provide information about an individual's relative place in the distribution. Percentile values below specified levels (e.g., <5%, <1%) can be set to correspond to severity levels of the universal qualifier. For example, when BMI values are used as reference for Growth Maintenance (b560) in the domain of Body Functions, the percentile

Discussion Box 2.1

One means for providing evidence suggested in this chapter is to use existing assessment instruments (norm-referenced, criterion-referenced, or standardized instruments). Their use in an ICF-CY model requires ICF-CY codes to be informed by data at the item level. Several research studies have used such an approach to investigate the utility of existing instruments in describing child functioning in light of the ICF model (e.g., Østensjo, Bjorbaekmo, Carlberg, & Vøllestad, 2006).

This research has identified difficulties in linking data from existing instruments to ICF or ICF-CY codes. Research has identified the need to link item data, not subtest or total score data, to ICF-CY chapters. Almost all instruments contain items that can be linked with several different ICF-CY codes. Some can be linked with different ICF-CY chapters. Additionally, an in-depth understanding of the aim of specific items in the original instrument is needed to be able to assign the best fitting ICF-CY codes. Cieza et al. (2005) have developed rules for how items from existing instruments can be linked to ICF codes.

Questions:

1. What does "linking" refer to in the context of the ICF-related instrument development?
2. What are the relative advantages of linking at the item, rather than subtest or total score level, when developing instruments to map the ICF framework?
3. Explain why items from existing measures could be linked to several ICF-CY codes?
4. Why is in-depth understanding of the original instrument important to assigning items to ICY-CY codes?

value of > 96 could be set to correspond to the severe level (3) of the universal qualifier resulting in the code of b560.3.

Standardized tests represent a hallmark of assessment in rehabilitation and habilitation. Various standardized measures are available to assess the child's physical, psychological, social, and educational status and can provide a range of subtest and composite scores that are useful when defining level of severity of functioning. Scores from standardized tests provide important data to use when assigning values to the universal qualifier. Thus, data from standardized measures can serve a useful purpose when utilized properly and their limitations are recognized. In any application of the ICF-CY, the manner in which data relate to the universal qualifier needs to be specified. This is necessary because the percentage values for the universal qualifier in the ICF-CY are conceptualized in terms of increasing levels of a problem, ranging from a state of no problem to a complete problem. This formulation of the universal qualifier contrasts with the conceptualization of problem severity in most population-based measures, in which severity levels are defined by decreasing levels from a state of full functioning to progressively lesser levels of typical functioning.

Within this conceptualization of problem severity, standard scores may be assigned to levels of severity of the universal qualifier (Table 2.3). The prototype application of standard scores to the severity levels of mild, moderate, severe, and profound is found in the concept of mental retardation based on results obtained from tests of intelligence and adaptive behavior. For example, the *Diagnostic and Statistical Manual of Mental Disorders,* fourth edition (*DSM-IV;* American Psychiatric Association [APA], 1994) defines mild mental retardation, in part, by IQs falling in the range between 70 to 50–55 (i.e., 2 to 3 standard deviations below the mean). Ranges of IQs at moderate, severe, and profound levels of mental retardation would correspond to successively lower standard deviation units below the mean. However, when documenting cognitive limitations in the ICF-CY, a detailed approach that defines limitations in terms of one or more specific cognitive functions should be followed rather than reliance on a single summary index score (e.g., an IQ; Simeonsson, Granlund & Björck-Åkesson, 2006).

Although an official formulation for assigning standardized scores for the universal qualifier has not been established, methods that define levels of severity in terms of standard deviation units from the mean would seem to provide a useful approach to convey the relative levels of severity when evidence is drawn from standardized measures. Given the levels of the universal qualifier as defined in the ICF-CY, one method could be to set mild, moderate, severe, and extreme (i.e., profound) levels to corresponding standard deviation units below the mean for values between 1 to 2, 2 to 3, 3 to 4, and > 4 for applicable standardized measures. However, any use of this and other methods to assign levels for the universal qualifier described in Table 2.3 should be accompanied by documentation of how the values are set to correspond to respective universal qualifier levels. This is essential to ensure proper interpretation of the meaning of ICF-CY codes in terms of the extent of limitation or disability.

ICF-CY Applications

Indicators and Profiles of Child Functioning

The ICF-CY model can contribute to clinical practice by providing a profile of ICF-CY codes to portray the child's functional limitations. The purpose of the ICF is not to classify individuals on the basis of a diagnosis, but rather to classify their health status and acknowledge the impairments of body function or structure and activity limitations or participation restrictions they may experience. This distinction between classifying individuals on the basis of diagnoses and classifying them based on their health and functioning is in keeping with a holistic and nonstigmatizing approach to disability determination, intervention, and evaluation. ICF-CY codes can be used to document a single problem or a profile of limitations that help define a child's health and functioning difficulties. In addition, environmental factors that represent barriers to functioning and performance of activities can be identified. Codes for the four domains of the ICF-CY (i.e., Body Function, Body Structure, Activities and Participation, and Environmental Factors) emphasize that disability is not one-dimensional and instead is manifested in different ways and across different domains among children.

Assessment framed within the ICF-CY encourages direct involvement of children and youth as well as their parents and caregivers in defining personal functioning. The functional language of the ICF-CY lends itself to assessment approaches for engaging children in describing their thoughts and feelings of their health and development. Children as young as age 5 may be able to describe well-being using words that reflect activity and participation (Almqvist, Hällnäs, Stefansson, & Granlund, 2006). However, when describing illness, they may use words that refer to body functions.

Classifying different manifestations of disability with applicable codes from the four domains can generate profiles of codes and accompanying qualifiers that document the nature and extent of a child's impairments, activity limitations, and participation restrictions. Such profiles reflect intraindividual characteristics that can help define needs unique to each child as well as environmental factors that may facilitate or hinder the child's functioning.

Clarification of Clinical Diagnoses and Comorbidity

The derivation of diagnoses in clinical practice (e.g., for autism or attention deficit hyperactivity disorder) typically is based on evidence of the presence of a defined number of symptoms within a broader set of symptoms. For example, the *DSM-IV* (APA, 1994) diagnosis of autistic disorder (299.0) specifies criteria of: (1) a combination of impairments in the three domains of social function, communication, and atypical behavior; (2) delayed or abnormal functioning evident before age three; and (3) the exclusion of other disorders. Although these criteria are used to establish the diagnosis of autism in clinical practice and research, the idiosyncratic expression and/or possible combinations of symptoms that provide evidence for impairment in the three domains contribute to variability in children with this diagnosis because the diagnosis of autism can be based on different combinations involving two or more impairments of social function—one or more in communication and one or more in atypical/repetitive behavior. Different combinations of impairments will be associated with children presenting with different expressions and severity of problems. To this end, ICF-CY codes can be used to describe functional characteristics that illustrate the individuality of the child. In this way, the use of ICF-CY codes can clarify clinical diagnoses by differentiating the presenting characteristics of children who share the same diagnosis.

Table 2.4 presents information on two children who share the clinical diagnosis of autism yet present with different functional limitations and thus with implications for different intervention priorities. The profiling of functional characteristics has the advantage of reflecting problems of current functioning that have direct significance for intervention. Profiles of functional characteristics may change following subsequent assessments, whereas clinical diagnoses often remain permanent and fail to convey information with implications for immediate intervention.

The ICF-CY also may be used to address the problem of comorbidity in the assignment of multiple diagnoses to document presenting symptoms. In this

2.4 Profiles of ICF-CY Codes to Clarify the Diagnosis of Autism in Two Children

Child A	Child B
• b1142.3 orientation to person • b120.2 general cognitive functions • d310.3 communicating • d510.2 self care • d710.3 interpersonal interactions • Stereotyped movements • Severe mental retardation	• b1142.3 orientation to person • b144.2 memory functions • d1600.2 attending to touch, face, and voice • d130.3 copying • d310.3 communicating • d330.3 speaking • Moderate Mental Retardation • Fragile X-syndrome

regard, the use of ICF-CY codes may clarify both "successive" and "concurrent" comorbidity by displaying profiles of children's functional limitations without making assumptions about the existence of separate and unique diagnosable conditions (Knapp & Jensen, 2006). This application is illustrated in Table 2.4 for child B, who presents with the diagnoses of autism, mental retardation, and Fragile-X syndrome, yet for whom an integrated profile of ICF-CY codes describes the individuality of this child.

Continuing Issues in the Implementation of the ICF-CY

The dissemination of the ICF has contributed to a rapid growth of applications in fields such as nursing, physical medicine, rehabilitation, and psychology (Institute of Medicine, 2007; Mueller, Boldt, Grill, Strobl, & Stucki, 2008; Reed et al., 2005; Stucki & Grimby, 2004; Walsh, 2004). The availability of the ICF-CY is likely to result in similar expanded applications in policy, practice, and research involving children and youth (Lollar & Simeonsson, 2005; Simeonsson et al., 2003). The development of "core sets" in physical medicine has promoted ways to document chronic health conditions such as osteoarthritis, diabetes mellitus, depression, or stroke (Cieza et al., 2006). Core sets have been defined as "a list of ICF categories that includes as few categories as possible to be practical, but as many as necessary to be sufficiently comprehensive to describe in a comprehensive assessment, the typical spectrum of problems in functioning of patients with a specific condition" (Cieza et al., 2004, pp. 9–11).

Initially, practitioners typically describe the ICF-CY as too comprehensive and complex for practical use. Nevertheless, the approach of deriving a limited set of ICF codes to define key functional characteristics of specific health conditions has relevance for ICF-CY–guided assessment. For example, "developmental" core sets could be derived for specified age groups, or "service" core sets could define child characteristics related to service settings (e.g., early intervention, special education, mental health, vocational rehabilitation). Such core sets could be used to define eligibility as well as to match child needs to services and supports. Core sets also are important for facilitating the inclusion of ICF-CY in clinical practices and may provide a way to facilitate adoption and use of this model (Pless et al., submitted).

The view of children's disabilities as variations of human functioning rather than diagnosed disorders is consistent with parallel efforts of viewing children with chronic health conditions in a noncategorical framework (Stein & Silver, 1999, 2002). The focus on classification of functioning and the dimensional approach of the ICF-CY are consistent with emerging trends in child health, habilitation, and special education (Florian et al., 2006; Simeonsson, Simeonsson, & Hollenweger, 2008).

The ICF-CY's emphasis on documenting the impact of environment factors has important implications for children with disabilities. For example, continued advances in assistive technology hold promise for enhancing children's responses to assessment as well as facilitating their engagement in activities and participation in everyday life. Assessment approaches that match functional problems in thinking, remembering, and learning with assistive technology is an important dimension of rehabilitation (Scherer, 2005). The development of measures sensitive to environmental factors in the ICF-CY should be compatible with the universal classification system defined by the International Organization for Standardization (ISO) 9999:2007 (ISO, 2007). Furthermore, attempts to engineer the physical and social environments in the form of universal design are likely to result in expanded opportunities for children to become more independent and to attain higher levels of achievement. Measures that identify environmental factors that influence children's functioning and performance in daily life settings, as well as those that engage the child directly as a respondent, are developmental priorities (Lollar, Simeonsson, & Nanda, 2000). The development of measures that assess personal support and relationships, as well as attitudes of people in the environment that impact interventions focused on the social environment, may be especially important (Zakirova-Engstrand, & Granlund, submitted).

Summary

The ICF-CY is a new taxonomy that offers a universal language of functioning, disability, and health for children and youth. It provides a structure for interdisciplinary collaboration in assessment and is compatible with existing practices and approaches to assessment. This chapter has presented an approach for understanding how to use the ICF-CY in the assessment of children's health, development, and well-being. This approach incorporates various assessment methods and data sources as well as a way to conceptualize how the information from an assessment reflects a profile of a child or youth's functioning within a child-environment interaction perspective. The common language of the ICF-CY can facilitate the match between children's needs and environmentally-based resources, thereby enhancing their experiences and contributing to a fuller realization of their potential.

References

Almqvist, L., Hällnäs, P., Stefansson, M., & Granlund, M. (2006). I can play—Young children's perceptions of health. *Pediatric Rehabilitation, 9*(3), 275–284.

American Psychiatric Association. (1994). *Diagnostic and statistical manual of mental disorders* (4th ed.). Washington, DC: Author.

Björck-Åkesson, E., & Granlund, M. (2004) Early intervention in Sweden—A developmental systems perspective. In M. Guralnick (Ed.), *A developmental systems approach to early intervention* (pp. 571–591). Baltimore, MD: Brookes Publishing.

Bronfenbrenner, U., & Ceci, S. J. (1994). Nature-nurture reconceptualized in developmental perspective: A bioecological model. *Psychol. Rev., 101*(4), 568–586.

Cieza, A., Ewert, T., Üstün, T. B., Chatterji, S., Kostanjsek, N., & Stucki, G. (2004). Development of ICF core sets for patients with chronic conditions. *Journal of Rehabilitation Medicine 44*(suppl.), 9–11.

Cieza, A., Geyh, S., Chatterji, S., Kostanjsek, N., Üstün, B., & Stucki, G. (2005). ICF linking rules: An update based on lessons learned. *Journal of Rehabilitation Medicine, 37,* 212–218.

Cieza, A., Geyh, S., Chatterji, S., Kostanjsek, N., Üstün, B. T., & Stucki, G. (2006). Identification of candidate categories of the International Classification of Functioning Disability and Health (ICF) for a Generic Core Set based on regression modeling. *BMC Medical Research Methodology, 6,* 36–52.

Florian, L., Hollenweger, J., Simeonsson, R. J., Wedell, K., Ridell, S., Terzi, L., et al. (2006). Cross-cultural perspectives on the classification of children with disabilities: Issues in the classification of children with disabilities. Part I. *Journal of Special Education, 40*(1), 36–45.

Ibragimova, N., Granlund, M., & Björck-Åkesson, E. (2009). Field trial of ICF version for children and youth (ICF-CY) in habilitation services for children and youth in Sweden: developmental issues and clinical use. *Developmental Neurorehabilitation, 12*(1), 3–11.

Institute of Medicine—Committee on Disability in America. (2007). *The future of disability in America.* Washington, DC: National Academies Press.

International Organization for Standardization. (2007). *ISO 9999: 2007-Assistive technology for persons with disability-classification.* Geneva: Author.

Knapp, P., & Jensen, P. S. (2006). Recommendations for *DSM-V.* In P. S. Jensen, P. Knapp, & D. A. Mrazek (Eds.), *Toward a new diagnostic system for child psychopathology* (pp. 162–181). New York: Guilford Press.

Lansdown, G. (2000). Implementing children's rights and health. *Archives of Disease in Childhood, 83*(4), 286–288.

Lollar, D. J., & Simeonsson, R. J. (2005). Diagnosis to function: Classification of children and youth. *Journal of Developmental and Behavioral Pediatrics, 26*(4), 323–330.

Lollar, D. J., Simeonsson, R. J., & Nanda, U. (2000). Measures of outcomes for children and youth. *Arch. Phys. Med. Rehabil., 81*(2, Supp.), S46–S52.

Mueller, M., Boldt, C., Grill, E., Strobl, R., & Stucki, G. (2008). Identification of ICF categories relevant for nursing in the situation of acute and early post-acute rehabilitation. *BMC Nursing, 7,* 3–11.

Okawa, Y., Ueda, S., Shuto, K., & Mizoguchi, T. (2008). Development of criteria for The qualifiers of activity and participation in the "International Classification of Functioning, Disability and Health" based on the accumulated data of population surveys. *International Journal of Rehabilitation Medicine, 31,* 97–103.

Østensjo, S, Bjorbaekmo, W., Carlberg, E. B., & Vøllestad, N. K. (2006). Assessment of everyday functioning in young children with disabilities: An ICF-based analysis of concepts and content of the Pediatric Evaluation of Disability Inventory (PEDI). *Disability & Rehabilitation, 28,* 489–504.

Pless, M., Ibragimova, N., Adolfsson, M., Björck-Åkesson, E., & Granlund, M. (2009). Evaluation of inservice training in using the ICF and ICF version for children and youth. *Journal of Rehabilitation Medicine, 41*(6) 451–458.

Raghavendra, P., Bornman, J., Granlund, M., & Björck-Åkesson, E. (2007). The World health Organization's International Classification of Functioning, Disability and Health: Implications for clinical and research practice in the field of augmentative and alternative communication. *Augmentative and Alternative Communication, 23*(4), 349–361.

Reed, G. M., Lux, J. B., Bufka, L. F., Trask, C., Peterson, D. B., Stark, S., et al. (2005). Operationalizing the International Classification of Functioning Disability and Health (ICF) in clinical settings. *Rehab. Psychology, 50,* 122–131.

Schere, M. J. (2005). Assessing the benefits of using assistive technologies and other supports for thinking, remember and learning. *Disability Rehabilitation, 27*(13), 731–739.

Simeonsson, R. J. (2005). Defining and classifying childhood disability. In Institute on Medicine (Ed.), *Disability in America*. Washington, DC: National Academy Press.

Simeonsson, R. J., Björck-Åkesson, E., & Bairrao, J. (2006). Rights of children with disabilities. In G. Albrecht (Ed.), *Encyclopedia of disability* (pp. 257–259). Thousand Oaks, CA: Sage.

Simeonsson, R. J., Granlund, M., & Björck-Åkesson, E. (2006). Classifying mental retardation: Impairment, disability, handicap, limitations or restrictions? In S. Greenspan & H. Switzky (Eds.), *What is mental retardation? Ideas for the new century* (pp. 245–266). Washington, DC: American Association on Mental Retardation.

Simeonsson, R. J., Huntington, G. S., McMillen, J. S., Haugh-Dodds, A. E., Halperin, D., Zipper, I. N., et al. (1996). Services for young children and families: Evaluating intervention cycles. *Infants and Young Children, 9*(2), 31–42.

Simeonsson, R.J., Leonardi, M., Björck-Åkesson, E., Hollenweger, J., & Lollar, D. (2003). Applying the International Classification of Functioning Disability and Health to measure childhood disability. *Disability & Rehabilitation, 25*(11–12), 602–610.

Simeonsson, R. J., Lollar, D., Hollowell, J., & Adams, M. (2000). Revision of the International Classification of Impairments, Disabilities & Handicaps: Developmental issues. *Journal of Clinical Epidemiology, 53,* 113–124.

Simeonsson, R. J., McMillen, J., & Huntington, G. S. (2002). Secondary conditions in children with disabilities: Spina bifida as a case example. *Mental Retardation and Developmental Disabilities Research Reviews, 8*(3), 198–205.

Simeonsson, R. J., Simeonsson, N. E., & Hollenweger, J. (2008). International Classification of Functioning, Disability and Health: A common language for special education. In L. Florian & M. McLaughlin (Eds.), *Disability classification in education* (pp. 207–226). New York: Corwin Publishers.

Stein, R.E.K., & Silver, E. J. (1999). Operationalizing a conceptually based noncategorical definition. *Archives of Pediatric and Adolescent Medicine. 153,* 68–74.

Stein, R. E., & Silver, E. J. (2002). Comparing different definitions of chronic conditions in a national data set. *Ambulatory Pediatrics, 2*(1), 63–70.

Stucki, G., & Grimby, G. (2004). Applying the ICF in medicine. *Journal of Rehabilitation Medicine 44*(suppl.), 5–6.

United Nations. (1989). *U.N. Convention on the Rights of the Child.* New York: Author.

U.S. Department of Education. (2004). *Individuals with Disabilities Education Act.* Retrieved May 19, 2009, from http://IDEA.ed.gov

Walsh, N. E. (2004). The Walter J. Zeiter lecture: Global initiatives in rehabilitation medicine. *Arch. Phys. Med. Reh., 85*(9), 1395–1402.

World Health Organization. (2001). *International Classification of Functioning, Disability and Health.* Geneva: Author.

World Health Organization. (2007). *International Classification of Functioning, Disability and Health-Children and Youth.* Geneva: Author.

Zakirova-Engstrand, R., & Granlund, M. (2009, June). The International classification of functioning, disability and health–children and youth (ICF-CY): testing its utility in classifying information from eco-cultural family interviews with ethnically diverse families with children with disabilities in… *Disability & Rehabilitation, 31*(12), 1018–1030.

Ethical Considerations in Applying the ICF

Jerome E. Bickenbach

3

Overview

This chapter discusses some of the ethical issues that may arise as the ICF is applied in clinical, health information, and research contexts. Because the World Health Organization (WHO) intends the ICF to have a multitude of uses across countries around the world, the potential risks from misuse are considerable. The discussion begins with a review of the underlying principles that govern the model of disability in the ICF and the approach it takes to the description and classification of disability phenomena, including, in particular, the importance of the inclusion of environmental factors in that description. Next, a distinction is made between ethical concerns raised by the ICF itself and ethical concerns raised by the application of the ICF in various contexts. Ethical objections that are intrinsic to the ICF are briefly reviewed. The discussion then moves to discussion of the ethical guidelines found in the ICF (Annex 6) that are designed to apply to the use of the ICF. The significance and application of these guidelines is explained in terms of the underlying ICF principles. Finally, a brief discussion of the future development of the ethical use of the ICF closes the chapter.

Learning Objectives

By the end of the chapter, the reader should be able to:

1. Describe and understand the underlying principles governing the ICF conception of functioning and disability: multidimensionality, interactivity, the essential role of the environment, universality, and etiological neutrality;
2. Explain the significance and power of the ICF conception of disability, in light of these principles governing the ICF conception of functioning and disability;
3. Outline the basic structure of the ICF Ethical Guidelines and show how these Guidelines deal with distinct ethical problem areas (respect and confidentiality, the clinical use of ICF, and the social use of ICF information);
4. Differentiate between an ethical objection to the ICF itself and ethical concerns about ICF in use;
5. Provide the rationale for each of the ICF Ethical Guidelines and demonstrate how they may be applied, alone or together in context; and
6. Project possible future amendments or additions to the ethical dimension of ICF application.

Introduction

The International Classification of Functioning, Disability and Health (ICF; WHO, 2001) is many things: a taxonomy, a multipart classification of human functioning, a coding structure for data collection and collation, a model of disability for health systems organization and research, among others (see chapter 1; Peterson, 2005). The ICF is a multidimensional tool intended to reflect the multidimensionality of disability phenomena, as well as the multidisciplinary character of disability science, scholarship, and clinical practice. Finally, the ICF is an *international* classification, which means it purports to be valid and useable across cultures and languages (Trotter et al., 2001).

An international, collaborative effect, spanning nearly a decade and involving preliminary item-pool development, drafting, field trialing, and iterative redrafting, produced a classification that is unique in the world. The ICF was motivated by WHO's constitutional mandate to produce health classification instruments with the widest possible range of uses. In addition, WHO insisted that the ICF would be a complex character of the lived experience of disability (Üstün, Chatterji, & Bickenbach, 2003; Üstün, Chatterji, Kostansjek, & Bickenbach, 2003; Stucki, Ewert, & Cieza, 2003). The various dimensions, uses, and applications of the ICF in rehabilitation are reflected throughout this volume, particularly in the domain of assessment. In this chapter, however, the focus is entirely on the ethical considerations that are raised by the application of the ICF.

WHO's own agenda for the ICF follows from its obligation to its member states to collect valid and reliable information about the health of populations. This is critical input into international public health policy. Mortality statistics have long been collected on the basis of WHO's *International Statistical Classification of Diseases and Related Health Problems* (ICD-10; 1992). Though useful for measuring life expectancy as a proxy for population health, mortality data alone does not capture the overall health status of living populations. This data is missing information about levels of functioning and disability across all areas of life—what might be called the *lived* experience of health. Without information about functioning and disability, policy makers are left with profound information gaps in both the health sector (e.g., service needs, intervention effectiveness, service utilization, and cost effectiveness) and the social sector (e.g., lost productivity from disability, social needs assessment, and social outcomes of antidiscrimination and other human rights laws).

WHO decided it could not rely on the disability data that were reported to it by member states. There were vast differences in prevalence estimates of "severe disability" in different countries. Either one could conclude that, unlikely though it seems, there was a 60-fold difference in disability prevalence between Syria and Norway, or else, more plausibly, these two countries were using very different and incomparable definitions of *disability*. WHO concluded that the second option was more likely and discovered as well that, within national legislation, what counted as *disability* is not uniform. Surveys of U.S. federal legislation, for example, reveal nearly 100 different definitions in use. If some consistency and regularity could be brought to the definition of disability it would be very beneficial to many stakeholders.

It bears remarking that this lack of a common understanding of disability has unfortunately been repeated in the recently approved *UN Convention on the Rights of Persons with Disabilities* (2007). After several years of debating the issue, in the end, the Convention drafters failed to reach consensus on the definition, with the result that this UN Convention offers no binding characterization of the people to whom its guarantees of rights and freedoms apply. This flaw may well undercut the value of this important document as countries around the globe attempt to implement its provisions, especially because Article 31 of the Convention requires states to "undertake to collect appropriate information, including statistical and research data, to enable them to formulate and implement policies to give effect to the present Convention."

Whatever WHO's motivations for producing the ICF and the history of its creation and testing, the ICF now must stand or fall on its own. Much has been written about the ICF and its uses, but one aspect of the ICF has received relatively little attention so far, and that is the focus of this chapter: the ethical dimension of the application of the ICF.

Ethical considerations raised by the ICF can best be put into context by reviewing the guiding principles and underlying theoretical premises of the ICF, and a review of these will start off this chapter. The ICF is explicit in the conception of human functioning and disability it relies on, and one of its primary functions is to set out a transparent, understandable, and useful model of disability. This model, and the underlying philosophy of the ICF, is governed by a set of principles that need to be clearly enunciated because they have direct ethical significance.

The chapter then moves on to a closer look at ethical issues that arise from the model of disability itself, before turning to the main focus of this chapter: the ethics of the ICF in application. These issues will be considered in light of the Ethical Guidelines that are included in the ICF in Annex 6. Along the way it will be necessary to make some general remarks about the nature of ethics as it applies to epidemiology in general and classificatory instruments like the ICF, in particular, as well as more global issues of disability advocacy and human rights.

The ICF's Guiding Principles and Their Ethical Significance

Disability, as everyone knows, is a contentious concept, both scientifically and politically. There is a long history to the notion, one that reflects a developing understanding of the disability experience. Disability has been understood as individual fault or misfortune, as a purely medical phenomena, and, more recently, as a complex notion that incorporates the role of the person's physical and social environment in the production of disability. We now know that *disability* is a notion that forces us to acknowledge the complexity of the *disabling process* and also to address the role of social arrangements in the creation of the disadvantages associated with disability. The key to understanding the ICF is that it was intentionally designed to embody a specific conceptual understanding of disability—and an appreciation of the lived experience of disability. That understanding, or *model of disability,* embodies the collective wisdom of many decades of research and clinical practice both within and outside of the rehabilitation disciplines The so-called biopsychosocial model of disability that forms the core of the ICF is structured in terms of the following principles.

Disability Is a Multidimensional Notion

The term *disability* in ordinary use, both lay and professional, is ambiguous because it refers to three separate dimensions: a biomedical dimension (which in the ICF is represented by impairments of body function or structure), a person dimension (activities and activity limitations), and a fully contextualized social dimension (participation and participation restrictions). *Disability* is an amalgamation of all three dimensions, and no single dimension is prior or more fundamental than any other. Most of the confusion found in disability literature, not to mention disability law and social policy, can be traced to a failure to properly identify which dimension of the complex notion of disability one is talking about (Bickenbach, 1999; Bickenbach, Chatterji, Badley, & Üstün, 1999). Health and rehabilitation practice and research is no exception. The perfectly justifiable need to focus clearly on one dimension—whether impairment, capacity level, or actual performance—does not relieve the user of the ICF from the responsibility to take note of the effects, on research or on clinical practice, of the other dimensions. It is as much an error to say that "disability is just an impairment" as it is to say that "disability is just the product of an inaccessible social environment."

Most often, the temptation is to reduce disability to a matter of impairment alone and leave others to worry about how the impairment interacts with the person's environment. But this is a distortion of the experience. This is not merely a matter of bad descriptive science; it is also a question of ethical distortion. As the disability rights community has insisted for decades, it is insulting, demeaning, and ethically objectionable to reduce all that a person is to a single dimension of functional limitation.

Disability Is Interactive

In the ICF, *disability phenomena* are outcomes of complex interactions between intrinsic features of the physiological or functional states of individuals and the physical, human-built, attitudinal and social environmental context in which they live. It is a complex matter to determine the degree to which the difficulties that a person with disabilities experiences can be traced to health-related functional limitations rather than features of the person's environment. In some cases—muscular pain, for example—the difficulty is entirely a problem with the body; but in others—access to employment opportunities, for example—the difficulty may be entirely a matter of social attitudes, stigma, and false perceptions about disability. However, the fact that disability is a result of both intrinsic and extrinsic factors is fundamental to the ICF conception of disability.

This means that a person's physical and social environment is always relevant to the description of the nature and extent of the person's disability. Ethically speaking, this requires both practitioner and researcher to take the person's environment into account and, in particular, not to make assumptions about the degree to which a person's functional status needs to be altered in order to be "normal" and fit into the environment in which he or she lives. Why is this a matter of ethics as well as scientific accuracy? Because misdescriptions of the causes of disability can stand in the way of essential social reform (e.g., the removal of environmental barriers or the provision of accessibility). When the environment is responsible for the difficulties that a person experiences, it is ethically objectionable to credit the problems to the functional alone. Once again, as the disability rights community has long argued, the disadvantages associated with disability are often created by the environment, not the impairment, and a failure to appreciate this is a further disadvantage that the person with the disability has to face.

Disability Is a Universal Human Experience

Instead of viewing disability as abnormality—a deviation from the normal functional parameters of a human being—the ICF adopts the view that disability is a universal human experience, both epidemiologically and normatively. The case for epidemiological normality is almost trivial because everyone, at some point in their lives, will experience functional limitation in some domain to some extent, and, as one ages, the severity of that limitation is bound to increase. In short, everyone experiences impairments of one degree or another, and many people experience participation restrictions that are directly caused by features

Discussion Box 3.1

DISABILITY AND CULTURE

Is the ICF "culturally insensitive"? A common objection to the ICF is that it is insensitive to cultural differences (see Ingstad & Reynolds, 1995). If this were true, then the ICF, which calls itself "an international language of functioning and disability," would be a fraud. But it is not clear what "insensitive to cultural differences" means. Does it mean that a person who has severe visual acuity difficulty in one culture will not have visual acuity difficulty in another culture? How could this be possible? Or does it mean that a person who has difficulties dressing herself in one culture may not have those difficulties in another (because the culturally appropriate clothing requires different muscles and a different level of coordination)? Is the ICF "insensitive" to a cultural difference such as this? Is the "culturally insensitive" criticism of ICF fair or misconceived?

of the physical or social environmental (from inaccessible buildings and other failures to accommodate functional limitations, to benign neglect, to outright discrimination). This is what is meant by the *universality* of disability.

Ethically speaking, the universality of disability stands directly opposed to the view that people with disabilities are the "other," a discrete and insular minority of people different from normal people. Instead, the ICF stands for the proposition that we are all people with disabilities, and as such, we have the moral obligation to make our built environment and our social environment appropriate to the full range and variety of functional circumstances that characterize the human condition.

Continuity and Etiological Neutrality

The ICF presumes that functioning and disability are not categorical but continuous phenomena. Disability is not a matter of "yes or no" but "more or less." In the case of body functions, for example, there is a potentially infinite gradation of functional capacity that individuals can exhibit in whatever physiological domain we choose (sensory, speech, cardiovascular, digestive, neuromusculoskeletal, and so on). There is no *a priori* or scientific threshold of functionality that separates the normal from the impaired, and certainly, the ICF as a scientific classification does not impose threshold or standards of normality or dysfunctioning. Admittedly, resource allocation and other practical considerations require that such lines be drawn, but inasmuch as the functionality lies on a continuum, the decision where to drawn these lines is, morally speaking, a matter of political negotiation between and among service providers, funders, and consumers. This is ethically significant because it implies that decisions about when levels of functioning warrant intervention are not medical decisions, but, in the end, political decisions that require us to listen to the voices of everyone, not merely experts or professionals.

For similar reasons, the ICF does not identify or describe impairments, or other aspects of disability, in terms of their etiology. Indeed, and more generally, the ICF's model does not presume any causal linkage between the three dimensions of disability. In part, this is to ensure that the model remains neutral about how disabilities arise. Hypotheses about how specific kinds of disabilities arise should be confirmed or rejected on the basis of evidence, not on the basis of presumptions that are built into a classification.

Etiological neutrality also reinforces the core tenet of the ICF model of disability, which is that the day-to-day lived experiences of people, and the social restrictions they face, are not caused by their health condition or impairment but rather are outcomes of an interaction with physical, social, and attitudinal factors in their world. Astigmatism, as an impairment, is associated with a person's limited capacity to read print, but neither the functional state nor the limited capacity *cause* restricted employment opportunities; these are results of employer attitudes, the availability of assistive devices or other accommodations, as well as other features of the environment in which the person lives.

The ICF, in other words, mainstreams the experience of disability by shifting the focus of attention from health *causes* of disability to a fuller understanding of the nature of the lived experience of disability—an experience that is normal to the human condition, not a mark of a special class or group of people ("the disabled"). Rather than emphasizing people's disabilities and labeling them as *disabled,* the ICF allows us to focus on the level of health and functional capacity of all people, their strengths and their weaknesses. Mainstreaming has ethical

Discussion Box 3.2

ETIOLOGICAL NEUTRALITY

What is the impact of the ICF principle of "etiological neutrality" on ethical clinical practice? Etiological neutrality is the name given to a guiding principle of the ICF that each category of disability (whether impairment, activity limitation, or participation restriction) must be considered causally independent of any other, so that no assumptions are built into the ICF classifications to the effect that, if a patient exhibits this impairment, then they are bound to have this capacity limitation or that participation restriction. The ethical rationale of etiological neutrality is that these assumptions are what form the basis of stereotypes about people with disabilities. For example, if we assume that a person who is blind cannot hold down a job as a lawyer, we are making an unfair judgment about a person's capacities that may not be warranted by the evidence. The ICF is a descriptive tool, not an evaluative tool. Still, as every rehabilitation practitioner knows full well, if a client has a set of impairments associated with, for example, arthritis in the knees, then the chances are that they won't have the capacity to walk 10 miles. What is the difference between that assumption and the earlier assumption about blind lawyers? Why is one a sensible, professional judgment and the other a discriminatory stereotype?

Discussion Box 3.3

MENTAL AND PHYSICAL DISABILITY

Why doesn't the ICF distinguish between "physical disability" and "mental disability"? If you read through the entire ICF you will never find the phrase "mental disability" (you won't find the phrase "physical disability" either). The reason for this is that the ICF does not categorically distinguish at the Activity and Participation levels between those difficulties that can be traced to physical or mental functioning. Chapter 1 of Body Functions is filled with functions that most of us would say are "mental." So, the ICF could make the distinction if it wanted to, but is there an ethical reason why the ICF does not follow this tradition? Does it have to do with the fact that the social dynamics of "physical disabilities" are different from those of "mental disabilities" (e.g. there tends to be far more stigma associated with the latter)?

importance because it opens the door to law, policy, and social practices that are inclusive and that emphasize the rights of all to participate fully in all areas of human life. The ICF is fully in line with the human rights approach to disability.

The Ethical Dimension of the ICF

As a branch of philosophy, ethics is traditionally divided into systematic theories of ethics, on the one hand, and applications of these theories in practical human contexts on the other. One of the prominent areas of so-called practical ethics is *bioethics,* the ethics of health care, understood broadly. Bioethics, in turn, is divided into the clinical ethics and public health ethics. Within clinical bioethics, one would expect to see discussions of patient autonomy, informed consent to treatment, and confidentiality (as well as ethical concerns about medical practices involving the beginning and end of life). Public health bioethics, by contrast, looks at more systematic issues, such as the right to health care and fair access to health resources, the rights of research subjects, confidentiality of records, and the ethics of epidemiology, as well as ethical concerns about specific public health interventions such as health promotion, vaccination, and guaranteeing. The domain of human rights intersects both clinical and public health ethics, but the application of these rights differs. Clinical ethics is primarily concerned—to use the standard ethical framework of Beauchamp and Childress (1994; cf. Kitchener, 2000)—with the ethical principles of autonomy, nonmaleficence ("do no harm"), and beneficence ("strive to benefit"), whereas public health ethics is concerned with systematic and political issues of justice and fairness, especially in the distribution of and access to resources and opportunities.

What kinds of ethical issues and concerns does the ICF create? Roughly, there are two sets of issues: those that arise from the intrinsic characteristics of the ICF and, in particular, its characterization of disability; and those that arise from the application of the ICF in various contexts and sectors. Our concern in this chapter is primarily with the latter, but it might be helpful to spend a moment with the first set of issues, if for no other reason than to review the common ethical objections to the ICF that are found in the literature.

During the revision process that led up to the ICF, voices were heard objecting to WHO's project of creating an international classification of disability. Most often heard were two related objections: one, that WHO was creating a classification that would *medicalize* disability, and two, that it would therefore *enforce normality* to the detriment of people with disabilities. Together, these objections offer a global ethical critique of the ICF (indeed, a critique of any scientific classification or assessment tool). At bottom, the critique claims that the ICF distorts the nature of disability in a manner that is fundamentally unfair and demeans people with disabilities.

David Pfeiffer, in particular, has argued that the ICF medicalizes disability, thereby allowing "medical personnel to make decisions having nothing to do with medicine such as measuring the quality of life of a person with a disability." This, he argues, puts WHO on a path that can only lead to wholesale social abuses such as eugenics and involuntary euthanasia: "People with poor quality of life first are denied resources (not just health services) and then become the prime candidates for euthanasia" (Pfeiffer, 1994, p. 486; and cf. 1992, 1998, 2000, 2001). The claim that the ICF opens the door to the very extinction of persons with disabilities has been raised directly or in passing by others (e.g., Barile, 2003; Metts, 2001).

The ICF is a health classification, not a medical one. Medicine is a health discipline, but it is not the only one, and WHO's mandate covers the complete realm of health. Moreover, unless one takes the bizarre view that "disability has nothing to do with the body but everything to do with society" (Oliver, 1996, p. 22)—an early version of the so-called social model, which has been abandoned by many disability advocates (see Shakespeare, 2006)—it can hardly be an ethical objection that the ICF is designed to be used in the health sector (see Üstün, Bickenbach, Badley, & Chatterji, 1998). Arguably, to deny the central importance of the health sector to people with disabilities can only serve to further disadvantage people with disabilities (Bury, 2000; Shakespeare, 2006), so this part of the critique is ill-conceived.

What gives ethical power to Pfeiffer's critique, however, is the supposed link between ICF and eugenics and related practices. As Pfeiffer notes, this link is made only if one assumes that to *describe* functional states—which is indeed what the ICF does—is at the same time to *evaluate* those states and, in particular, to identify people with functional limitations as biologically inferior. But this is certainly not what the ICF purports to do, nor does Pfeiffer give us any reason to think this assumption is even plausible (cf. Hays, Hahn, & Marshall, 2002). History is certainly filled with horrors and abuses that have been directed against people with disabilities and other "deviants," but it is an unhelpful exaggeration to suggest that a multipurpose health classification could be responsible for these abuses happening again. (If society degenerated to such an extent that people with disabilities are killed off as a matter of public policy, surely it would take more than the ICF to bring this about.)

Closely linked to the objection to medicalization is that the ICF is a dehumanizing scientific tool that represents people as a series of numbers (Duchan, 2004), or as utterly vulnerable and open to manipulation and abuse (Reeve, 2002). But does the ICF devalue people with disabilities by judging them inferior against a standard of "normality"? Some critics believe so. Tom Koch has recently seen this danger in all quality of life instruments, insisting that "contemporary medicine and mainline bioethics hold the view that any divergence resulting in negative cognitive, physical, or sensory abilities when compared to those of a mundane population norm results in a person who will be necessarily disadvantaged." He goes on to say that "deviations from the norm are...a harm resulting in suffering to be avoided where possible. In the extreme, severe deviations from the norm result in a life unworthy of continuance" (Koch, 2002, p. 421).

These are powerful objections to the ICF, but it is important to notice that they apply across the board to all forms of scientific assessment. The ICF is not an assessment tool, merely a classification, but it is probably easy enough to group it together with the myriad other assessment and measurement instruments used in clinical and research practice across health disciplines. Far from "enforcing normality," however, the ICF makes a point of universalizing disability and, by virtue of its continuous and etiological approach, utterly destroying the plausibility of a dichotomy between the "disabled: and the "normal."

But, we should not be naïve. The ICF may, as a matter of its theory, be immune from these objections, but practice is something else again. We cannot assume that an ethically positive theoretical underpinning can prevent the ICF from being used in precisely the kinds of ways these critiques suggest are implicit in the very structure of the ICF. To deal with these ethical concerns, therefore, we must turn to the arena of actual practice.

Ethical Issues Arising From Application and Use of the ICF

The ICF is a multiuse classification. As mentioned, WHO's own use of the ICF is in line with its constitutional duties in international public health data collection, collation, and analysis. The ICF also has myriad clinical uses across the spectrum of health care disciplines; it provides a common language for the collection and management of health and health systems information that can be used for needs assessment, intervention studies, and quality assessment. The research applications of the ICF—both as a model of disability and as a data tool—are unlimited. Finally, the ICF has a great potential, as yet untapped, in social policy analysis, not merely in the health sector, but also in all areas of policy in which the needs of individuals with disabilities are relevant—education, employment, income security, transportation, communications, housing, and human rights.

With so many potential uses, there are many opportunities for potential misuse. The ICF itself provides its own set of ethical guidelines in Annex 6: "Ethical Guidelines For the Use of ICF." Although some of these guidelines are specific to the ICF, its governing principles and its applications, others are either standard bioethical principles, or similar to those found in ethical statements of professional organizations such as the American Occupational Therapy Association, the American Physical Therapy Association, and the American College of Epidemiology (ACE). Because of the ICF's public health focus, ACE's code of ethics (2000) is the most similar to the ICF Guidelines. (The ICF Guidelines that deal with ICF-generated information are similar to the principles enunciated in Article 31, "Statistics and Data Collection," in the *UN Convention on the Rights of Persons with Disabilities,* 2007.)

The ICF Guidelines are organized into three sections: Respect and Confidentiality, Clinical Use of the ICF, and Social Use of ICF Information. Although schematic, the Guidelines attempt to encompass the full range of ethical issues that might arise when applying the ICF in clinical, epidemiological, and public health; health informatics; and research contexts. A brief review of each section will help to survey the kinds of ethical issues that were thought by WHO to be likely in the application of the ICF. This review will also set the stage for suggestions about revision or expansion of the ethical framework for the ICF (see McAnaney, 2005; Peterson & Threats, 2005). We return to these suggestions in the final section of this chapter.

Respect and Confidentiality

The four guidelines in this section are common statements of ethical behavior governing the patient–health professional relationship. They rely on the standard bioethical value of autonomy (Beauchamp & Childress, 1994; Dworkin, 1988; Rothman, 2001) and entail as practical correlates the rules requiring informed consent and confidentiality. In bioethics, autonomy is often thought to be the central value, inasmuch as abuse of the professional relationship can nearly always be characterized as paternalism or some other form of disrespect of the decision-making authority of the individual. Autonomy is most clearly expressed in Guidelines 1 and 3, and especially in the requirement that all interventions require the "full knowledge, cooperation, and consent" of the patient, or of the substitute decision maker if the person is not competent to consent. In most jurisdictions, a detailed legal framework is in place that formalizes all aspects of informed consent, competency to consent, substitute decision making, advanced directives, and a number of related issues, all of which rest on the importance of securing autonomous decision making. It should be noted that the value of autonomy has also been a central value of the disability rights movement, and arguably, it is on this value that the bioethical tradition and the disability rights movement converge (Asch 2001; Shakespeare, 2006).

Exhibit 3.1

RESPECT AND CONFIDENTIALITY

1. ICF should always be used so as to respect the inherent value and autonomy of individual persons.
2. ICF should never be used to label people or otherwise identify them solely in terms of one or more disability categories.

3. In clinical settings, ICF should always be used with the full knowledge, cooperation, and consent of the persons whose levels of functioning are being classified. If limitations of an individual's cognitive capacity preclude this involvement, the individual's advocate should be an active participant.
4. The information coded using ICF should be viewed as personal information and subject to recognized rules of confidentiality_appropriate for the manner in which the data will be used.

Because the ICF is a scientific classification rather than a health intervention, as such, the ethical parameters of its use extend somewhat beyond the traditional scope of autonomy. Guideline 2, for example, prohibits labeling or identifying people solely in terms of a disability category, an issue of considerable concern to the disability community. Perhaps ironically, the ICF is open to misuse in this manner in part because of an attempt by the ICF drafters to avoid exactly this misuse: The ICF identifies the unit of classification as a category of functioning, not the individual person (WHO, 2001, p. 8). Nonetheless, a clinical practitioner—unintentionally, as a shorthand mechanism—may take the extra step and identify a person with the functional category that the ICF reveals during an assessment.

Guideline 4 suggests a second area in which the ICF Guidelines extend beyond traditional autonomy protection. The ICF is a potentially powerful tool for collecting, organizing, and analyzing health information, derived either from clinical encounters or administrative records. The greater the scope of the use of the ICF, the greater the usefulness of the data that it creates. In general, this is a good thing, but it does raise the concern that ICF-generated data—which remains personal information—can be abused if confidentiality is not strictly enforced. We will return to this issue more completely later in this chapter.

Clinical Use of the ICF

The guidelines in this section are designed to be "fit for purpose" for anticipated clinical uses of the ICF, uses that may raise ethical concerns that are less frequently covered by the standard bioethical framework. Standardly, clinical and research issues involving persons with disabilities are covered under the rubric of "vulnerable populations" (see, e.g., Beauchamp et al., 1991; Coughlin & Beauchamp, 1996), furthering the stereotypes of child-like, frail creatures needing professional help. Although it might seem harmless, even beneficial, to identify a group of people as "vulnerable" so that efforts can be made to protect them from harm, there is also a considerable cost in dignity and respect. In recent years, led by the disability rights advocates, this picture of vulnerability has been challenged as discriminatory and insulting. In its place is a *participatory* paradigm, in which persons with disabilities are viewed as contributors, collaborators, and coparticipants in therapy or research, rather than patients or subjects.

Exhibit 3.2

CLINICAL USE OF THE ICF

1. Wherever possible, the clinician should explain to the individual or the individual's advocate the purpose of the use of the ICF and invite questions about the appropriateness of using it to classify the person's levels of functioning.
2. Wherever possible, the person whose level of functioning is being classified (or the person's advocate) should have the opportunity to participate and, in particular, to challenge or affirm the appropriateness of the category being used and the assessment assigned.
3. Because the deficit being classified is a result of both a person's health condition and the physical and social context in which the person lives, the ICF should be used holistically.

This participatory approach follows directly from the ICF's universalism and, in particularly, is reflected in Guidelines 5 and 6. The user of the ICF is directed to facilitate a coequal participation by the person with disabilities in clinical assessment. Ensuring collaboration and participation, it must be emphasized, is a stronger ethical requirement than respecting autonomy; one can respect a person's decision-making authority without directly involving them in the determination of the options that are available. Guidelines 5 and 6 ethically require the ICF user not merely to provide information and ask for consent, but to actively invite the person whose functional status is being described to "challenge or affirm the appropriateness of the category being used and the assessment assigned." This invitation obviously goes far beyond consenting or withholding consent—which the value of autonomy mandates—into a realm in which the person with disabilities is a contributor, indeed an expert, in assessment. The slogan of Disabled Persons International is, "Nothing about us, without us." Arguably, these two guidelines put this important slogan into effect in areas of intervention and research where professionals are usually thought to be in complete charge.

Guideline 7 in conjunction with Guidelines 8 and 11 are the ethical rules most clearly designed to respond to, and complement, the underlying philosophy of the ICF. As noted previously, in the ICF, disability is multidimensional and interactive; disability is the outcome of an interaction between intrinsic health features of the individual and extrinsic features of the individual's physical, human-built, interpersonal, attitudinal, and social environment. On this conception of disability, it is scientifically inaccurate to generalize the overall disability situation from a description or assessment of any single dimension. Not only can we not infer disability from diagnosis (the principle of etiological neutrality), we cannot infer activity or participation levels from the presence or severity of impairments. The environment—which is an essential component of the ICF model of disability and the classification of which is an essential part of the ICF classification—is always a relevant feature of the description of disability.

But acknowledging and assessing all dimensions of disability, including the role of the person's environment as a barrier or facilitator, are not merely scientific *desiderata;* they are also requirements of the ethical use of the ICF. As Guideline 7 states, "ICF should be used holistically." A partial or selective application of the ICF is not merely a scientific misdescription of phenomena; it is also a *moral* misdescription. A person with a disability is not simply a person with an impairment, nor is a disability the same thing as an impairment (or worse yet, as a disease or other health state). An understanding of the holistic notion of disability, in ICF terms, requires a complete description of the lived experience, which includes the role of the person environment. A complete description is one true to the reality of disability; a partial description distorts this reality, with, experience tells us, unfair social consequences for persons with disabilities.

Social Use of ICF Information

Bioethics has only recently broadened its agenda from issues arising out of clinical practice—where the governing ethical values are respect for autonomy, beneficence, and nonmaleficence—to those that arise in population or public health arenas (Brock, 2000; Gostin, 2002, pp. xxiii–xxv; Illingworth & Parmet, 2006, pp. 12–14). Interestingly, bioethics became aware of the disability rights movement at more or less the same time as it saw the need to go beyond clinical to social issues (see Asch, 2000; Parens & Asch, 2000). Both shifts in agenda forced traditional bioethicists to look more closely at human rights and the demands of social justice. The ICF was drafted to be in accordance with the *UN Standard Rules on the Equalization of Opportunities for Persons with Disabilities* (1994), a predecessor of and model for the UN *Convention on the Rights of Persons with Disabilities.* Both documents are in a long tradition of UN declarations, covenants, and conventions that affirm the human rights of persons with mental and physical disabilities. The ICF Ethical Guidelines reflect this affirmation.

Exhibit 3.3

SOCIAL USE OF ICF INFORMATION

8. ICF information should be used, to the greatest extent feasible, with the collaboration of individuals to enhance their choices and their control over their lives.
9. ICF information should be used toward the development of social policy and political change that seeks to enhance and support the participation of individuals.
10. ICF, and all information derived from its use, should not be employed to deny established rights or otherwise restrict legitimate entitlements to benefits for individuals or groups.
11. Individuals classed together under the ICF may still differ in many ways. Laws and regulations that refer to ICF classifications should not assume more homogeneity than intended and should ensure that those whose levels of functioning are being classified are considered as individuals.

One word here about the notion of human rights. It is common these days for disability advocates to say that "disability is a human rights issue," rather than a medical or social policy issue. As a bit of rhetoric, this phrase has power and has done a lot of good. Unfortunately, to say that something is a human rights issue does not really say much of substance, at least ethically speaking, until we answer the question "rights to what?" In the UN documents just mentioned, there are lists of specific legal entitlements that member states are requested to put into effect for the benefit of persons with disabilities (e.g., the UN Convention mentioned previously includes right to life; security of the person; protection against violence; independent living; rights to education, health, and employment; and many others). But rights are mere expressions of aspiration (or inspiration) without enforcement remedies; unless the state is prepared to act and expend resources to remedy a situation where rights are violated, the "human rights approach" to disability will remain in the realm of rhetoric.

Still, it is here in the ICF Guidelines that the issue of human rights is raised. One might think of these Guidelines as the beginnings of a social justice agenda for the ICF. As Peterson and Threats note, all health care professionals are obliged, by the ethical codes of their professions, to be advocates for those they serve. So, in this sense, health care professionals (like all social professionals, from social workers, to lawyers, the police, and government officials) are professionally obliged to be advocates and concerned about social justice. Although the ICF is merely a scientific tool, open to use by all, it is true that it carries an implicit ethical responsibility to use it in order to facilitate "the empowerment and inclusion of persons with disabilities in society" (Peterson & Threats, 2005, p. 134). This is an important declaration of the ethical content of the ICF, although, admittedly, it is not always easy to see how, in one's day-to-day practice, this obligation can be fulfilled.

Guidelines 8, 9, and 10 set out the social justice agenda in a manner that is directly relevant to the primary purpose of the ICF. This agenda extends the traditional concern about the confidentiality as personal information beyond the uses made of this information by clinicians and researchers directly involved in collecting the data. These Guidelines demand that the "upstream" uses of ICF-generated data also be protected against unauthorized use. It was often argued during the drafting of the ICF that data collection is not an ethically or politically neutral activity, but one that can have profound effects on the lives of persons with disabilities (see Gross & Hahn, 2004; Hurst, 2000, 2003). The ICF recognizes this. Data can be used to disenfranchise people, to support efforts to deny them needed resources and services, and in general, to devalue their lives. Although technically the ICF is neither an assessment tool nor a quality of life measure, nothing prevents the ICF from being used in these ways. People with disabilities are justifiably concerned about the ethics of quality of life determinations and are frequently the victims of judgments that their lives are not sufficiently valuable to have access to scarce medical resources on par with people without disabilities.

Increasingly, concern has been expressed about the justice of medical allocation procedures that rely on implicit or explicit judgments about the quality of the lives of certain groups of people, including people with disabilities (Asch, 2001; Rhodes, Battin, & Silvers, 2002). Guidelines 9 and 10 require the user of ICF-generated data to ensure that these data "enhance and support" the

Discussion Box 3.4

DISABILITY ADJUSTED BY LIFE YEARS

Health economists have developed various versions of summary measures of health, such as quality-adjusted life years, disability-adjusted life years, health-adjusted life expectancy, and others. At the heart of these notions is the idea that disability should be taken into account when evaluating the health status of a person. This is typically done by discounting or adjusting a year of life lived with a disability so that its value is less than 1 (the value of a normal life year). For example, a year of life lived as a quadriplegic might be set at .25 years. (Usually these values are set by health care experts and researchers.) One use of these measures is in resource allocation: If we have only one kidney to transplant and two people who require it to live, we can compare the expected outcomes of each in years left to live. If one of these people is a quadriplegic, then that disability would make his remaining years worth less than the other person, and we could say the expected outcome for the disabled individual is worse. Allocating scarce resources in terms of a cost/benefit calculation, we would give the kidney to the normal person. In terms of ICF principles, how would you argue against using summary measures of health in this way?

participation of persons with disabilities in all areas of human life and draw the user's attention to potential misuses of these data that would threaten rights or legitimate entitlements to benefits. Guideline 8 provides guidance into how this might be accomplished: by ensuring that data collection and use is done in collaboration with the people this information is about.

Guideline 11, finally, highlights an implicit ethical dimension of the ICF, related to the value of human dignity. If autonomy demands that, wherever possible, we should respect the decision-making capacity of the individual, the value of human dignity demands that when we engage in public health and focus on the common good, we not overlook the distinctness of each individual person.

By its nature, public health merges individuals into a composite or aggregate. "The public" becomes a kind of homogenous entity that has health needs of its own that need to be served by the best medical science we have. Population-based policies look at prevention and health promotion strategies whose outcomes are measured in terms of the health of the population as a whole. The ICF can serve a vital role in these strategies, and in public health as a whole, by organizing the information we require to develop, implement, monitor, and test the effectiveness of our strategies. But as every epidemiologist knows, the causes of the incidence of ill-health need not be the same as the causes of the prevalence of ill-health, and, as a result, population-based prevention strategies (which seek to reduce prevalence) may be useless at the level of the individual (Rose, 1992). Guideline 11 reminds us that, despite the enormous advantages of aggregation of data, we must not lose sight of the individual and his or her individual differences. In particular, we must not assume that people who share impairments share more than that, or that, for example, "the blind" are a distinct and homogenous group of people who think and act alike and share the same aspirations and goals in life. The ICF makes data aggregation possible, but it must not be used to merge all differences and undermine the intrinsic dignity of the individual.

The Future of Ethics and the ICF

It is inevitable that our understanding of the ethical dimension of the ICF will develop over time as we get more experience with the application of the ICF in clinical, health systems, and research contexts. The Ethical Guidelines presented in the ICF are a first attempt at creating a suitable ethical response to what will inevitably be myriad applications of the ICF, across professions and disciplines, and across sectors and around the globe.

Donal McAnaney (2005) has recently argued that more thought should be given to the ethical dimension of the ICF and that it is "legitimate to question whether or not these brief guidelines are sufficient to support the ethical global deployment and dissemination of what is a very powerful classification" (p. 3). The ICF is "powerful," McAnaney claims, not only because of its potential to document and explain disability phenomena across linguistic and cultural boundaries, but also because as it becomes incorporated into professional, academic, institutional, and administrative structures, the ICF will become authoritative and exert a strong influence. In the first instance, this influence will be felt in the area of data collection procedures, but soon enough it will be felt on health and social policy that dramatically affects the lives of people with disabilities.

It is the ICF's potential power that makes ethical scrutiny necessary because, McAnaney argues, "the main ethical concerns with regard to the use of the ICF arise from inequalities of power" (2005, p. 3). This inequality creates a number of potential risks inherent in the use of the ICF: the risk of denying a person eligibility for supports and services, of imposing interventions against the will of the individual, and, in the worst case, of characterizing lives as having so little value as to justify denying them scarce health resources. With more and more sophisticated information retrieval processes and the call for personal identification numbers and other universal identifying mechanisms, ICF-information will fill the data universe, providing health providers and health planners with information that may undermine the rights of people with disabilities.

These are substantial risks, and the more the ICF is used and relied on, the more serious these risks become. Arguably, the current Ethical Guidelines in the ICF, in particular Guidelines 6 and 8–11, anticipate these risks by insisting on the full participation of persons with disabilities in their assessment and the use of information derived from the ICF. But guidelines are not enough, and McAnaney (2005) recommends the development of a more comprehensive Code of Practice governing all applications of the ICF, a Code that professional associations could incorporate into their own ethical guidelines and that people with disabilities and their families and carers would be made aware of. In addition to a Code, McAnaney recommends national and international ethical monitoring of ICF applications. Moreover, to assist in the equalization of power between professionals and persons with disabilities, McAnaney recommends legal requirements that the ICF and the consequences of its use be explained to those to whom the ICF is applied and that there be an avenue of administrative investigation and redress, perhaps assisted by an ombudsperson, to deal with grievances and allegations of misuse.

These are all good suggestions, fully within the spirit of the underlying philosophy of the ICF. One must always recognize, of course, that however powerful the legal and administrative apparatus that is put into place, misuse will slip by undetected and unremedied. In the end, the best safeguard against the ethical misuse of the ICF, as with all facets of professional care and research, is the education of professionals in the inherent dangers in their tools and procedures and the development, through practice, of a sense of professionalism that recognizes the possibilities of unethical behavior and guards against them.

References

American College of Epidemiology. (2000). *Ethics Guidelines.* Retrieved May 10, 2009, from: http://acepidemiology2.org/policystmts/EthicsGuide.asp

Asch, A. (2001). Disability, bioethics and human rights. In G. L. Albrecht, K. Seelman, & M. Bury (Eds.), *Handbook of disability studies* (pp. 297–326). Thousand Oaks, CA: Sage.

Barile, M. (2003). Globalization and ICF eugenics: Historical coincidence or connection? The more things change the more they stay the same. *Disability Studies Quarterly, 23*(2), 203–223.

Beauchamp, T. L., & Childress, J. F. (1994). *Principles of biomedical ethics* (4th ed.). Oxford: Oxford University Press.

Beauchamp, T. L., Cook, R. R., Fayerweather, W. E., et al. (1991). Ethical guidelines for Epidemiologists. *Journal of Clinical Epidemiology, 44* (Suppl. I), 151S–169S.

Bickenbach, J. E. (1999). Minority rights or universal participation: The politics of disablement. In M. Jones & L. A. Marks (Eds.), *Disability, diversability and legal change* (pp. 101–115). Dordrecht: Martinus Nijhoff.

Bickenbach, J. E., Chatterji, S., Badley, E. M., & Üstün, T. B. (1999). Models of disablement, universalism and the ICIDH. *Social Science and Medicine, 48*(9), 1173–1187.

Brock, D. (2000). Broadening the bioethics agenda. *Kennedy Institute of Ethics Journal, 10*(1), 21–38.

Bury, M. (2000). A comment on the ICIDH2. *Disability & Society, 15*(7), 1073–1077.

Coughlin, S. S., & Beauchamp, T. L. (Eds.). (1996). *Ethics and epidemiology.* New York: Oxford University Press.

Duchan, J. F. (2004). Where is the person in the ICF? *Advances in Speech-Language Pathology, 6*(1), 63–65.

Dworkin, G. (1988). *The theory and practice of autonomy.* New York: Cambridge University Press.

Gostin, L. O. (Ed.). (2002). *Public health law and ethics.* Berkeley: University of California Press.

Gross, B. H., & Hahn, H. (2004). Developing issues in the classification of mental and physical disabilities. *Journal of Disability Policy Studies, 15,* 130–134.

Hays, R. D., Hahn, H., & Marshall, G. (2002). Use of the SF-36 and other health-related quality of life measures to assess persons with disabilities. *Archives of Physical Medicine and Rehabilitation, 83*(12), S4–S9.

Hurst, R. (2000). To revise or not to revise? *Disability & Society, 15*(7), 1083–1087.

Hurst, R. (2003). The international disability rights movement and the ICF. *Disability and Rehabilitation, 25,* 572–576.

Illingworth, P., & Parmet, W. E. (Eds.). (2006). *Ethical health care.* Upper Saddle River, NJ: Pearson Education, Inc.

Ingstad, B., & Reynolds Whyte, S. (1995). *Disability and culture.* Berkeley: University of California Press.

Kitchener, K. S. (2000). *Foundations of ethical practice, research, and teaching in psychology.* Mahwah, NJ: Lawrence Erlbaum Associates.

Koch, T. (2000). Life quality vs the "quality of life": Assumptions underlying prospective quality of life instruments in health care planning. *Social Science & Medicine, 5,* 419–427.

McAnaney, D. (2005). Is the current Ethical Framework for the ICF sufficient? *RIVM Newsletter on the WHO-FIC, 3*(2), 3–4.
Metts, R. L. (2001). The fatal flaw in the disability adjusted life year. *Disability and Society, 16*(2), 449–452.
Oliver, M. (1996). *Understanding disability: From theory to practice.* Basingstoke: Macmillan.
Parens, E., & Asch, A. (Eds.). (2000). *Prenatal testing and disability rights.* Washington, DC: Georgetown University Press.
Peterson, D. B. (2005). International Classification of Functioning, Disability and Health: An introduction for rehabilitation psychologists. *Rehabilitation Psychology, 50,* 105–112.
Peterson, D. B., & Threats, T. M. (2005). Ethical and clinical implications of the International Classification of Functioning, Disability and Health (ICF) in rehabilitation education. *Rehabilitation Education, 19*(2 & 3), 129–138.
Pfeiffer, D. (1992). Disabling definitions: Is the World Health Organization normal? *New England Journal of Human Services, 11,* 4–9.
Pfeiffer, D. (1994). Eugenics and disability discrimination. *Disability & Society, 9,* 481–99.
Pfeiffer, D. (1998). The ICIDH and the need for its revision. *Disability & Society, 13,* 503–23.
Pfeiffer, D. (2000a). The devils are in the details: The ICIDH2 and the disability movement. *Disability & Society, 15*(7), 1079–1082.
Pfeiffer, D. (2000b). The disability paradigm. Disability policy: Issues and implications for the new millennium—A report on the 21st Mary E. Switzer Memorial Seminar, held September 1999.
Pfeiffer, D. (2001). The conceptualization of disability. Exploring theories and expanding methodologies: Where we are and where we need to go. In S. N. Barnartt & B. M. Altman (Eds.), *Research in social science and disability* (Vol. 2, pp. 29_52). New York: Elsevier Science.
Reeve, D. (2002). Negotiating psycho-emotional dimensions of disability and their influence on identity constructions. *Disability and Society, 17*(5), 493–508.
Rhodes, R., Battin, M., & Silvers, A. (Eds.). (2002). *Medicine and social justice: Essays on the distribution of health care.* New York: Oxford University Press.
Rose, G. (1992). The population strategy of prevention. In G. Rose (Ed.), *The strategy of prevention medicine* (pp. 95–129). New York: Oxford University Press.
Rothman, D. (2001). The Origins and consequences of patient autonomy: A 25 year retrospective. *Health Care Analysis, 9,* 255–264.
Shakespeare, T. (2006). *Disability rights and wrongs.* London: Routledge.
The Standard Rules on the Equalization of Opportunities for Persons with Disabilities. Adopted by the United Nations General Assembly at its 48th session on 20 December 1993 (resolution 48/96). New York, United Nations Department of Public Information, 1994.
Stucki, G., Ewert, T., & Cieza, A. (2003). Value and application of the ICF in rehabilitation medicine. *Disability & Rehabilitation, 25*(11–12), 528–634.
Trotter, R. T. II, et al. (2001). Cross-cultural applicability research on disablement: Models and methods for the revision of an international classification. *Human Organization, 60*(1), 3–27.
Üstün, T. B., Bickenbach, J. E., Badley, E., & Chatterji, S. (1998). A reply to David Pfeiffer "The ICIDH and the need for its revision." *Disability & Society, 13*(5), 829–831.
Üstün, T. B., Chatterji, S., & Bickenbach, J. (2003). The International Classification of Functioning, Disability and Health: A new tool for understanding disability and health. *Disability & Rehabilitation, 25*(11–12), 565–571.
Üstün, T. B., Chatterji, S., Kostansjek, N., & Bickenbach, J. E. (2003). The World Health Organization's International Classification of Functioning, Disability and Health (ICF) and functional status information in health records. *Health Care Financing Review, 24*(3), 77–88.
UN Convention on the Rights of Persons with Disabilities. (2007). Retrieved May 10, 2009, from: http://www.un.org/disabilities/convention/conventionfull.shtml
World Health Organization. (1992). *International statistical classification of diseases and related health problems, tenth revision (ICD-10).* Geneva: Author.
World Health Organization. (2001). *International classification of functioning, disability and health (ICF).* Geneva: Author.

Measures of Culture and Diversity in Rehabilitation and Health Assessment

Chandra M. Donnell
Stacia L. Robertson
Timothy N. Tansey

4

Overview

There exists consistent evidence in published research that indicates health care disparities for persons from racial and ethnic groups in access and quality of treatment (Smedley, Stith, & Nelson, 2002). Similarly, discussion regarding disparities in vocational rehabilitation has increased in the literature. This literature highlights inequity in access, levels of rejection (Wilson, 2000; Wilson, Harley, & Alston, 2001), successful case closures, training, and case-expenditures (Atkins, 1980; Dodd, Nelson, Ostwald, & Fischer, 1991; Dziekan & Okocha, 1993; Faubion, Calico, & Roessler, 1998; Smart & Smart; 1994). Given the nature of these outcomes, it is thus imperative that rehabilitation professionals and health care providers carefully examine the potential precursors to inequitable services. This requires a much closer look at what is generally the first point of interaction with persons of color seeking services: assessment. As set forth in Niemeier, Burnett, and Whitaker (2003), we also utilize the definition and guidelines for the terms *ethnicity* and *people of color* for our purposes:

> *established by the US government classification system and used by the National Institutes of Health (NIH). This system specifies that categories of race are American Indian/Alaska Native, African American, Asian and other Pacific Islander, and white. The 2 categories for ethnicity are Hispanic or Latino or not Hispanic or Latino. Of the categories listed above, all are referred to as* 'underrepresented' *in biomedical and behavioral science careers, based on each minority group's representation in the total population, except whites and Asians. (p. 1240)*

In this chapter, we present the most critical factors relevant to the provision of culturally appropriate assessment in rehabilitation.

Learning Objectives

By the end of the chapter, the reader should be able to:

1. Identify and describe provider and client characteristics that affect the health assessment process in culturally diverse contexts;
2. Explain why culturally appropriate health assessments are necessary for successful rehabilitation and health outcomes;
3. Examine various approaches to conducting culturally appropriate assessment in terms of their potential in rehabilitation and health settings; and
4. Evaluate the evidence for the use of culturally appropriate assessment tools in rehabilitation and health settings.

Introduction

Culturally appropriate assessment must be the cornerstone of any culturally relevant and successful intervention. It has been suggested that "successful service provision starts with an accurate assessment of the consumer's needs and wishes" (Stone, 2005, p. 229). The yield then becomes successful outcomes for the people we work with. In the process of assessment, a relationship between the clinician and the person being served must exist. This relationship is an essential piece of the assessment formula. The complexity involved in developing this relationship with culturally and ethnically diverse clients calls for the clinician to develop culturally competent knowledge, attitudes, and skills (Lu, Russell, & Mezzich, 1995). Concerted effort toward developing these attributes enhances the strength of the clinician/client/consumer relationship.

The client or consumer (or patient), after all, is the best source of the client's story. Within their story is access to the day-to-day subjective information that provides insight into the client's perspective of their health experience. Whatever the nature or duration of the assessment, there are key features that should be included:

Intentional Questioning → Intentional and Active Listening → Developing Relationship

Addressing these areas can occur in structured, testing environments; clinical environments; or in brief assessment-based settings. While they are depicted in a linear and sequential manner, they often occur simultaneously, thus a better illustration is featured in Figure 4.1.

The challenge for most practitioners is to incorporate these skills simultaneously. Examination of clinician culture and client culture are equally essential to the process of assessment. This chapter briefly reviews the history of assessment, presents definitions of relevant terminology, and illustrates various techniques and assessment tools that can be useful to service providers in

4.1

Key features of assessment.

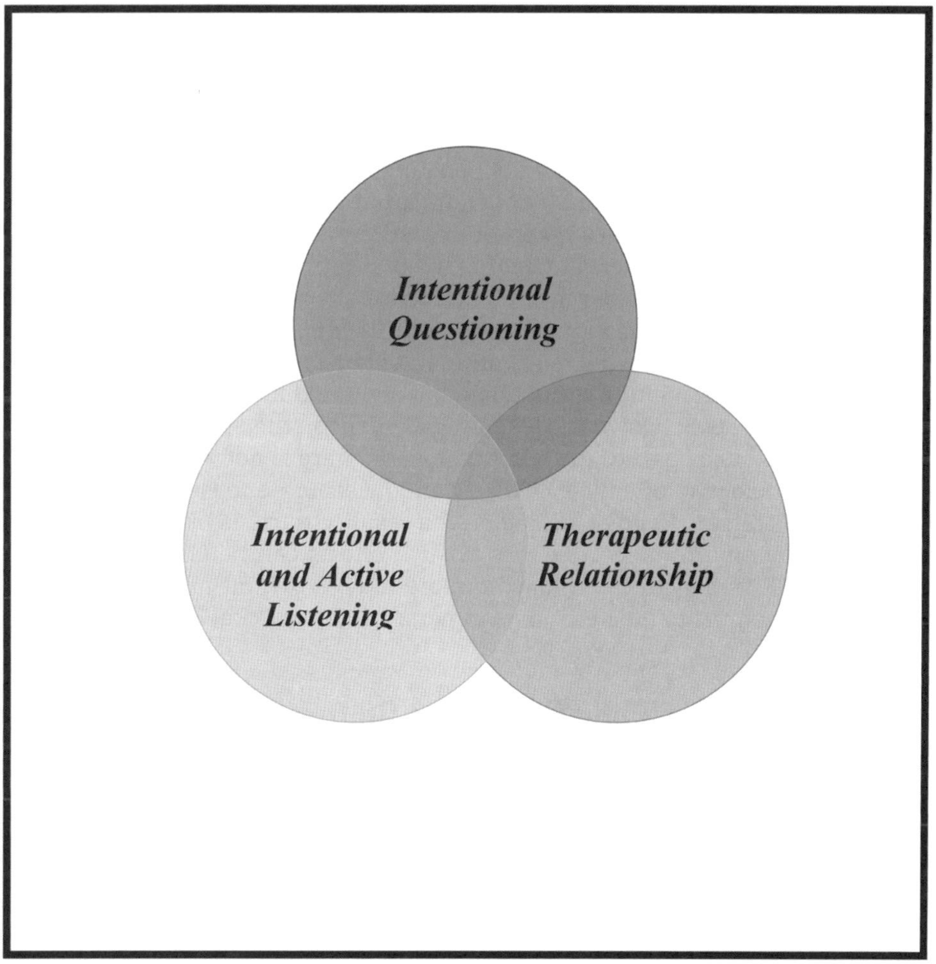

conducting culturally appropriate assessments that will generate the most useful information for accurate assessment.

Assessment of Culture and Diversity in the Context of the ICF

Assessment in rehabilitation and other health professions generally involves: *a systematic process of collection, review, and integration of information from varied sources for treatment and intervention decisions*. Client/consumer/patient information, psychological tests, medical records, and clinical interviews are often the main sources of information utilized in the assessment process. Accurate assessment facilitates health, vocational, educational, and mental health interventions. Assessment should involve a partnership between the service provider and the person being assessed.

Culture and diversity can be considered as contextual factors within the International Classification of Functioning, Disability, and Health (ICF). The ICF framework delineates contextual factors as being made up of environmental and personal factors. Environmental factors, those factors external to individuals, are intended to capture those variables that impact the ability of individuals to live within a society (Peterson, 2005). Variables such as the physical surroundings (i.e., accessibility), opportunities for socialization, and the attitudes held by those in society can facilitate or restrict the opportunities of individuals to fully participate in society as well as moderate the behaviors exhibited by individuals (Reed et al., 2005). As such, environmental factors are the only factors within the ICF that can be classified as either assets or limitations (Homa & Peterson, 2005).

Personal factors, or internal factors affecting functioning and disability, are intended to capture the wide range of characters specific to individuals such as race, religion, gender, education, and age, but they also incorporate additional factors associated with the diversity within individuals, such as coping styles, social background, behavior patterns, character style, and individual psychological assets (Peterson, 2005). However, despite agreement on the existence and impact of personal factors as part of the ICF framework, there is not yet any agreement on the methodology to effectively classify and incorporate these factors into the framework (Peterson; Reed et al., 2005). As a result, clinicians may want to focus on influencing environmental factors as such efforts can be clearly expressed within the ICF framework and may be more likely to result in successful outcomes than attempts to create change in personal factors (Reed et al., 2005).

History of Research and Practice in Culture and Diversity Assessment

Assessment as a practice for deciding psychological, educational, and vocational interventions has been in place for over 100 years (Tyack, 1974), with widespread use during the Industrial Revolution. Issues with standardized testing specifically for children whose native language was not English gained increased attention in the 1940s (McLean, 1995). Researchers found that test results for children who spoke their native language versus those children whose native language was English highlighted the cultural bias that negatively affected intelligence test scores. Since that time, psychological and physical health disciplines have also examined the intersection of culture and assessment.

Service providers generally have limited access to culturally appropriate assessments for diverse populations (Niemeier et al., 2003). This is due in part to the standardization of norm-referenced tests, which were historically based on majority, White American, English-speaking perspectives and values. Oakland (2004) informs us that there are currently over 5,000 standardized instruments that are generally constructed in the United States and Western Europe and are mostly in English. Population estimates in the United States, hugely affected by immigration patterns, indicate an increasingly diverse society. This is particularly true in urban area hospitals and rehabilitation facilities (Niemeier et al., 2003). Still, consumer diversity and professional preparedness to understand cultural variances are not the sole contributors to issues and bias in assessment. van de Vijver and Tanzer (2004) posed an example of bias inherent in the construction of some instruments that is mainly the result of the worldview and perspective of test constructers. van de Vijver and Tanzer illustrate the following example in Exhibit 4.1 (p. 119–120).

This is a common problem illustrating the bias that can occur in assessment. Bias in assessment then reflects systematic advantage or disadvantage to members of certain groups when the differentiation occurs on a basis other

Exhibit 4.1

Suppose that a geography test contains the item "What is the capital of Poland?"

This test is administered to pupils in a large international educational achievement survey. The proportion of correct answers to the item will depend on, among other things, the pupils' level of intellectual abilities, the quality of their geography education, and the distance of their country to Poland.

Assuming that samples have been carefully composed, the question will enable an adequate comparison of the differences in knowledge of this particular item across all countries.

However, suppose that the domain of the test is broader and that this item is used to assess geographical knowledge. Pupils from central Europe are put at an advantage in comparison with pupils from, say, Australia and USA.

than the characteristic being assessed. In the example by van de Vijver and Tanzer (2004), the score differences on the construct (i.e., knowing that Warsaw is the capital of Poland) do not correspond to the differences of the underlying trait (e.g., geography knowledge; p. 120). The former illustration highlights one of three deficiencies in assessment that might lead to culturally inappropriate assessment: *test construction, test administration,* and *test interpretation.*

Test Construction

Test construction and development is a critical first step in which bias can be addressed and corrected. Bias occurs quite easily in this area when a particular measured construct is not consistent across cultural groups. Consider the following example:

Discussion Box 4.1

You are administering the WAIS-IV to Anthony, a second generation Cuban American from Hialeah, Florida, where he was raised and lived until 1 year ago. Anthony is bilingual, very proficient in English, and has recently relocated to Tennessee. During administration, you notice Anthony having particular difficulty with the Verbal Comprehension subtest, which assesses his ability to understand abstract social conventions, rules, and expressions.

Question: Given Anthony's cultural background and hometown; what might limit his familiarity with common U.S. social conventions and norms?

Although Anthony is second generation, here are some facts about his hometown of Hialeah, Florida, that might disadvantage him on this particular section of the WAIS and might not typically present as an issue for second-generation immigrants:

- Hialeah has the second largest population of Cubans and Cuban Americans in the United States, and it is a very close-knit community.
- As of 2000, Spanish as a first language accounted for 92% of the population.
- *Telemundo,* the second largest Spanish network television channel, is headquartered in Hialeah.

As a second-generation immigrant, one might assume that Anthony would speak English proficiently. However, the culture of his environment called for Anthony to remain immersed in his native culture, and thus, he might not be familiar with U.S. social conventions and expressions or mainstream English. Instead of assessing Anthony's verbal comprehension, this particular section might more accurately measure his level of immersion into U.S. social customs (see also chapter 17). This representation of construct bias should be acknowledged and accounted for in test selection in addition to any linguistic issues that might also affect assessment bias.

In order to counter bias in test construction, test adaptation may be necessary. Adaptation involves modification of an assessment instrument to allow for evaluation of individuals or groups with qualities other than those for which the test was originally constructed for. Oftentimes, translation and accommodations for chronic illness or disability are the most common types of adaptations made to test construction. Oakland (2004) indicates that adaptations are needed generally for three reasons:

1. When tests are used in countries other than those in which they were developed,
2. When tests are designed for use in two or more countries in which cross-national practices occur, and
3. For use with persons who differ in linguistic, cultural, or functional qualities. (p. 168)

Pena (2007) identifies translation methods specifically as a means to introduce bias to the validity of an instrument. Various methods of gaining equivalence in translation can greatly diminish the potential for bias. Subsequently, as providers seek alternative measures to address linguistic differences, they should carefully evaluate the psychometric properties of the instrument, including methods for translation (Mpofu & Ortiz, in press). Pena discussed four translation methods.

- *Linguistic equivalence* is the translation of instructions and instruments, and then using back-translation (translation from the first language to the second, and then back to the first by a second person) as a means of verification.
- *Functional equivalence* is a translation method that allows for elicitation of the same construct as the original instrument.
- *Cultural equivalence* is a method that considers the underlying meaning of an item for various cultural and linguistic groups.
- *Metric equivalence* is a method that implements congruence between item and question difficulty across the assessment instruments.

Gonzalez-Calvo, Gonzalez, and Lorig (1997) and Pena (2007) submit that a combination of translation methods should be taken into account. A combination of methods greatly reduces the potential for bias. Gonzalez-Calvo et al. suggest that when selecting appropriate instruments, service providers should refer to those that employed a qualitative technique to assess universality prior to item construction. This process typically identifies instruments that took specific steps to *ensure* universality versus ones constructed on the *assumption* of universality.

Test Administration

Test administration is yet another area where bias can occur. Issues with administration tend to surround test selection and translation challenges for persons who do not speak English as their first language or those whose daily lives are not typical to the Western/U.S. models of medical care and intervention. General levels of difference in communication styles and patterns can affect administration. van de Vijver and Tanzer (2004) support this notion, that lack of understanding of testing language by the interviewee, or the interviewers' violation of cultural norms, can hinder the collection of information during administration. Translation and other linguistic issues can pose particular challenges for persons with chronic illness and disability because health status is often described differently among various cultural groups.

Cultural attitudes and beliefs about disability and illness are central to the administration of assessments and can be particularly relevant during intake assessments. These attitudes can vary widely from culture to culture and can affect responses to treatment (Niemeier et al., 2003). Consider the example of a spiritually committed African American woman who resides in the rural south and consistently complains about her "nerves." Assessment instruments regarding anxiety or depression might seem like foreign concepts as well as diagnostic and negative. Language that suggests that this woman is unable to "heal" herself through faith and prayer may be in conflict with her spiritual beliefs. These are beliefs that might also prevent her from implementing a medicinal intervention. Niemeier et al. further illustrates this assertion in the anecdotal reference regarding some American Indians, who for example, still believe that disability is contagious and may, as a result, discourage their children from touching assistive technology devices (p. 1242).

In addition to the diverse cultures of the persons we will serve, there is also a culture that exists for the service provider. Yes, our identity as rehabilitation and health professionals also represents a cultural identity. As a result of training on the philosophies that guide our disciplines and other training experiences, it is likely that the rehabilitation professional has also been indoctrinated with *provider culture* (Spector, 2002). This provider culture also consists of norms, beliefs, and practices that partially shape providers' attitudes toward disability and health. During the assessment, these provider beliefs might conflict with the beliefs of the person being assessed. For example, a major tenet of the rehabilitation philosophy is person-centered planning. While the heart of this concept posits that professionals should view individuals comprehensively, persons from a collectivistic orientation may not readily understand a concept titled *person-centered*. The very terminology itself might be antithetical to an individual who is oriented as being "part of a whole," as you will find in some indigenous peoples and East Indian cultures. A later section discusses current practices on how to effectively examine and address the various dimensions of identity for the rehabilitation profession and preempt a biased assessment.

Test Interpretation

Test interpretation can thus be affected by both test construction and administration. Interpretation is a critical component of the assessment process. Following interpretation, treatment plans and interventions are designated. Inaccurate interpretation can derail a successful rehabilitation, health, or therapeutic outcome, therefore, test interpretation is worthy of further discussion.

Previous research indicates that there are several components that might impact accurate interpretation of assessment data. The first major issue is to recognize that the assessment data collected is not the final step. As proposed by Mitroff and Sagasti, "another way to put this is to note that data are *not* information; information is that which results from the *interpretation* of data" (as cited in Messick, 1980, p. 1014). Practitioners must not only be proficient in the selection and delivery of the assessment but also in the accurate interpretation of the data results. Accurate interpretation will again call upon the rehabilitation or health professionals' ability to consider the impact of cultural differences on the assessment results. This, however, should not diminish the relevance of scores, but it should temper the interpretation, which might be affected by disability status and cultural or linguistic differences. A second key issue surrounds factors external to the instrument. Test interpretation requires a service provider to consider the cultural factors at play during administration so that they are able to accurately interpret the findings. Consequently, professional preparation in psychometrics and evaluation plays a significant role as an external factor affecting interpretation. Oakland (2004) emphasizes the dearth of graduate training programs that focus on psychometrics and test development. As previously asserted, rehabilitation and health professionals who are "under-trained," in regard to assessing psychometric properties and test adaptations that allow for culture-fair assessments, will lack the ability to provide accurate diagnoses and treatment planning needed to facilitate successful outcomes.

Current Practices in Culture and Diversity Assessments in Rehabilitation and Health Settings

In any discussion of current practices in culture and diversity, it is imperative that the contextual implications of *cultural competency* are discussed. While there are several variations in the literature of what contributes to cultural competence, the most widely used definition was developed by Cross (1989), who defined cultural competence as: "a set of congruent behaviors, attitudes, and policies that come together in a system, agency, or among professionals that enables effective work in cross-cultural situations."

Developing Cultural Competence

A central piece to the definition of cultural competence includes employing four pertinent strategies on an on-going basis (reflected in Figure 4.2): (a) the

Discussion Box 4.2

How we perceive our cultural identity is key to our interpretation of cultural issues that impact the persons we serve. Culture is a multidimensional construct that is highly dynamic and often contextual. Given that, it is essential to examine the dimensions of our cultural selves frequently to enhance our own cultural awareness as rehabilitation and health professionals. This awareness assists greatly in enhancing our cultural responsiveness during testing and assessment. Consider the key features of your cultural self (ethnicity, spirituality, gender, nationality, family system, etc.).

Questions:
Name two characteristics that have strong cultural relevance to your daily interactions as a professional. How might these cultural features impact your interpretation of test data collected from a client with characteristics dissimilar from the two you named?

4.2

Strategies toward cultural competency.

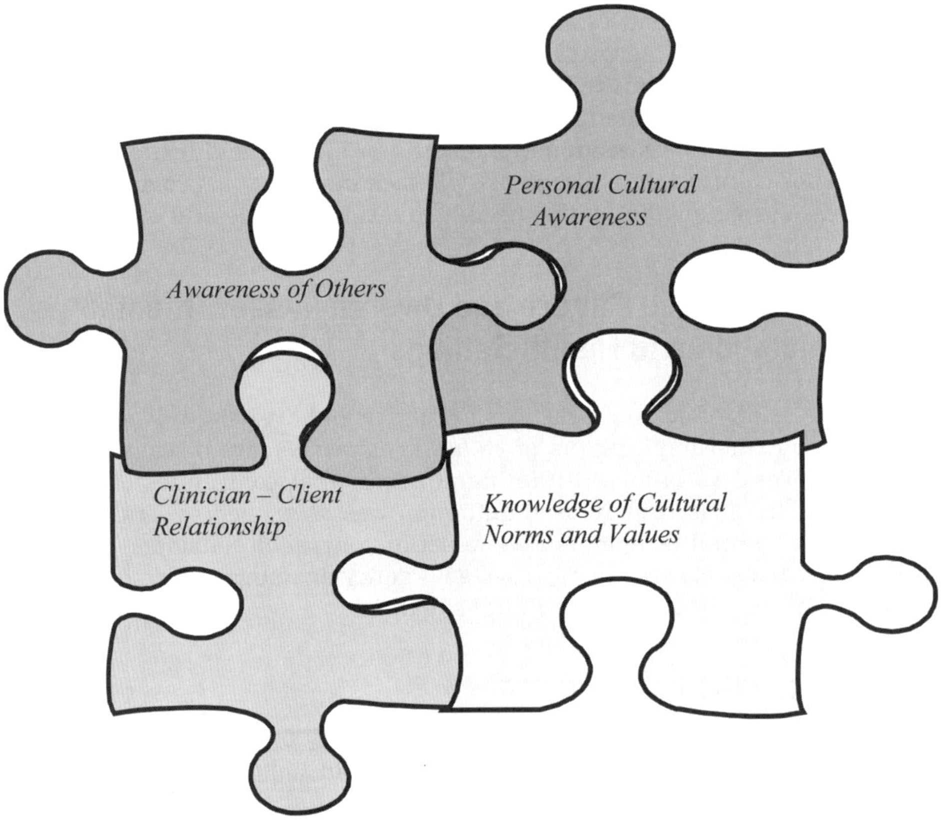

From "Psychometric Evaluation of the Cultural Competence Assessment Instrument Among Healthcare Providers," by A. Z. Doorenbos, S. Myers-Schim, R. Benkert, & N. N. Borse, 2005, *Nursing Research, 54*, pp. 324–331. Adapted with permission.

clinician's insight into their own culture and awareness of values, (b) the clinician's awareness of the individual client's cultural viewpoint and values as they relate to the client's group identity, (c) the clinician's knowledge of various cultural norms and values, and (d) the clinician's ability to build a relationship with the client given their awareness and knowledge.

Also inherent in attaining cultural competence is an understanding of culture. We see culture as consisting of multiple identities that are multidimensional, dynamic, and evolving as well as contextual. To further understand the various dimensions of culture, it might be useful to refer to Arredondo and Glauner's (1992) *Dimensions of Identity*.

They define identity across three areas: Dimension A, which defines those qualities such as ethnicity and gender that are at the person level and are to some degree predetermined; Dimension B, which defines those levels of identity that, although also at the person level, are those that can be impacted by the individual (e.g., work experiences and spirituality); lastly, Dimension C, which

4.3

Dimensions of personal identity.

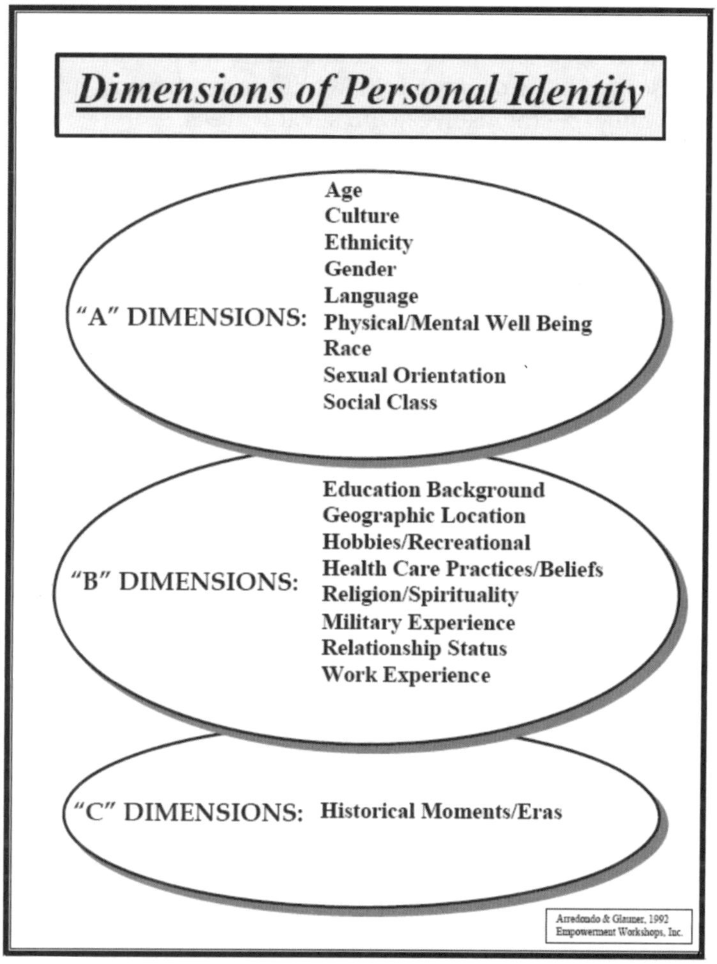

From *Personal Dimensions of Identity Model*, by P. Arredondo and T. Glauner, 1992, Boston: Empowerment Workshops. Copyright ©1992 by Empowerment Workshops, Inc. Reprinted with permission.

includes those events that exist outside the individual but have the ability to shape other aspects of the individual's identity (e.g., being raised during the Civil Rights Era or personally defining historical events). This broad definition of culture allows for all levels of identity to be considered as they intersect and impact the individual's identity and perceptions of health and disability (e.g., a person of Eastern European nationality living in poverty will likely conceptualize health vastly different from a wealthy person from Eastern Europe).

These pieces fit together and should be interlocking. This model is perhaps an extension of the Doorenbos, Myers-Schim, Benkert, and Borse (2005) model of provider level cultural competency. The current model highlights the additional relevance of the clinician and client relationship/communication—a relationship enhanced by the other features of the interlocking pieces. In regard to health status and assessment, communication between the provider and the client/patient/consumer is critical. The relationship and resultant patterns of communication are integral to the framework of cultural competence (Betancourt, Green, Carrillo, & Ananeh-Firempong, 2003). However, perhaps the most central piece is the clinician's own personal cultural awareness. We firmly believe that seeking self-understanding is pivotal in working toward cultural competency and must occur prior to implementation of culturally responsive practices in assessment. In order to initiate this understanding, the service provider should familiarize themselves with several areas:

1. How they define their own central group identities (this would include any defining identities such as race/ethnicity, nationality, gender, disability status, socioeconomic status, etc.).
2. What are their individually unique characteristics that distinguish them from their group identities? For example, perhaps they were raised in a very homogenous, rural, farming community, yet they have an affinity for exotic East Asian foods.
3. Lastly, the clinician should reflect on personal life experiences and challenges that have shaped their perspective on life. This will help maintain understanding of universal human elements of experiencing various emotions (e.g., joy, disappointment, frustration, honor, pride). At this universal level, there can always be a connection between the clinician and the person being assessed.

These efforts by the service provider, when coupled with standardized tests and appropriate test batteries, can yield a culturally responsive and comprehensive assessment environment for all clients and could significantly impact rehabilitation, counseling, and health outcomes (Roysircar, 2005).

Acculturation

Acculturation is one other key feature of cultural competency that should be a focal point when discussing culturally responsive assessments. By definition,

Case Study 4.1

A 28-year-old man, originally from Sudan, immigrated to the United States 4 years before sustaining a severe brain injury. He was assaulted one evening as he returned home from his pizza delivery job.

The oldest of six children and the only son of a merchant in Khartoum, the patient hoped to help the rest of his family relocate to America. Initially, following the injury, the patient could not speak English, and his native Arabic was garbled and halting. He declined to eat, even though he had been cleared for swallowing by the speech and language pathologists. He also refused to be bathed or to dress in front of female staff.

Ultimately, staff familiar with the religious, social, and dietary practices of his country addressed relevant cultural issues, and his behaviors began to be seen as being understandable within the context of his worldview and the customs of Sudan. When family from Indiana arrived, bringing food native to the patient's culture, he began to participate in more rehabilitation therapies. His speech, specifically his second language, English, improved, and he revealed himself to be a very personable, bright, and hard-working man (Niemeier et al., 2003).

QUESTIONS

1. Identify and explain the social attitudinal variables that would explain the patient's preferences in the rehabilitation setting.
2. How might assessments with culturally diverse individuals best be responsive to their values or worldviews? (See also chapter 18.)

acculturation is a psychological and sociological adaptive process through which the values, customs, and norms of a culture are incorporated in the cultural behavior of someone from a different culture (Marin, 1992). Sodowsky and Lai (1996) purport that acculturation as a process is a response to the dominant culture, such that a person integrates the cultural behaviors of the dominant culture into their existing framework. Recall our earlier example of Anthony, the second-generation Cuban American who now lives in Tennessee. A second-generation resident of the United States, Anthony's adaptation of some cultural behaviors of the majority culture are likely to be greater than what might have been seen with his parents—first-generation residents of the United States. While his parents still speak mostly Spanish and have a limited mastery of the English language, Anthony has gained proficiency of the English language. Language acquisition of the dominant culture can be seen as instrumental in the acculturation process. As addressed earlier, linguistic differences can impact the assessment process. Acculturation is a viable factor that could mediate responses and interactions with rehabilitation and health care professionals during assessment and treatment (Niemeier et al., 2003). Thus, various degrees of such must also be examined and considered during the assessment process.

What this discussion of cultural competence naturally guides us to is reflection on the construct of "universality." Pena (2007) asserts that a "cross-cultural approach can help to identify universals in test development and to discover variation attributable to linguistic and cultural differences" (p. 1261). Specific to issues related to disability, Zola (1989) also presented a view on the need for universalism. As a universalist, Zola's strategy calls for a respect for difference through policy that recognizes difference, yet simultaneously broadens the definition of what is deemed, in this case, "normal" (Bickenback, Chatterji, Badley, & Üstün, 1999). In the case of measures of culture and assessment, universalism would be represented as assessment instruments that were culturally appropriate across various dimensions of culture and accurately adapted for linguistic differences. Furthermore, a universal approach would contend that health constructs vary greatly among various cultural groups and that dimensions of health should be investigated *within* cultural groups (Maramaldi, Berkman, & Barusch, 2005).

While not all assessment instruments have reached the aforementioned level of universalism, there are quite a few that have been adapted to address cultural distinctions among test populations. It would be too cumbersome to identify each of those instruments here, so we have chosen to focus on several culturally responsive administration strategies and several culturally appropriate instruments that focus on general mental health characteristics and one physical health survey with widespread use.

Culturally Appropriate Assessment Considerations

Prior to Administration (Test Selection)

- Rehabilitation and health professionals should receive and participate in on-going multicultural training and field-related experiences to enhance cultural competence for working with culturally diverse populations (Betancourt et al., 2003; Donnell, 2008; Niemeier et al., 2003; Spector, 2002).
- It is imperative that rehabilitation and health professionals administering assessments receive adequate training in assessment and illustrate understanding of terminology such as construct validity (Maramaldi et al., 2005).
- Rehabilitation and health professionals should gain familiarity and proficiency in examining various methods of instrument translation, adaptation, and accommodations utilized to achieve psychometric equivalence (Pena, 2007).

During Administration

- Professionals may need to implement various forms of assessment to counter any potential bias evident to the administrator in the instruments selected (Downing, 2003).
- Qualitative measures of assessment across varying settings may also need modifications to prevent provider-defined concepts of illness, health, and disability from being transferred onto the client. An example of this might be a modified intake process with questions that allow for the individual to define their perception of health.

Following Administration (Interpretation)

- Rehabilitation and health professionals must understand the importance of interpretation and regard it as similar to the "scientific method of theory development or hypothesis generation" (Downing, 2003, p. 837).
- As previously mentioned and aptly framed by Mitroff and Sagasti (as seen in Messick, 1980), the data retrieved is not the final step. Interpretation and cultural consideration of linguistic and other cultural factors are as critical at this point as they are at any other point during assessment.

These represent a minimal level of consideration for rehabilitation and health care providers when assessing health status of culturally diverse persons. Integrating these directives will enhance a culturally appropriate and unbiased assessment that may yield more positive rehabilitation and health outcomes. While there are various methods of adapting and accommodating instruments, clinicians should implement these considerations at each critical juncture during assessment. The following is an example of several widely used instruments that illustrate fusing cultural considerations with rigorous test construction and development.

Culturally Responsive Assessment Instruments

Modified Intake Assessment

During most assessments, clients tend to expect a professional with a notepad or keyboard. This tends to place an immediate, typically impenetrable boundary between the clinician and the client. Instead, a more relaxed approach of "let's get to know each other" can be more effective, while still maintaining appropriate professional boundaries (see Exhibit 4.2).

The General Acculturation Index

The General Acculturation Index (GAI; Balcazar, Castro, & Krull, 1995) is a more recently developed instrument that is a five-question measure of acculturation. Although the GAI was initially developed to study cancer risk in Mexican American women, this instrument was useful in assessing levels of acculturation for the person being evaluated. The GAI reports a Cronbach's alpha of .82. It should be noted that this measure was found to correlate with education level. This, however, would be congruent with the purpose of the instrument, which seeks to assess acculturation using factors that typically influence the adaptation of migrant populations to foreign lifestyles (Jaber, Brown, Hammad, Zhu, & Herman, 2003). This index inquires about language typically written and spoken, geographic location of childhood, ethnicity of friends, and degree of pride in one's background. Answers are chosen based on a five-point Likert scale. This is a useful introductory scale to administer to gain insight into the level of adherence to other cultural trends and, potentially, definitions of health and wellness that might impact client involvement in treatment.

The Beck Depression Inventory–II

The Beck Depression Inventory–II (BDI-II; Beck, Steer, & Brown, 1996) is the most widely used self-report instrument for assessment of depression. The BDI-II has received substantial revisions since the 1961 version to maintain consistency with the American Psychiatric Association's (APA) *Diagnostic and Statistical Manual of Mental Disorders* (4th edition, text revision; *DSM-IV TR*). The BDI-II is available in approximately 16 language translations, including Xhosa, Dutch, French, German, and Persian. The BDI-II is not a standardized measure and thus does not include any normative data in the manual. This could potentially allow for cultural interpretations of the results. Despite

Exhibit 4.2

CULTURALLY APPROPRIATE TRADITIONAL ASSESSMENT QUESTIONS

Tell me a little about your background.	Current residence Place of origin Family network Previous careers/education Past health issues
Tell me what your interests are.	Hobbies Career interests/goals Educational goals
When in trouble, where do you find strength or help?	Social networks Family relationships Health resources Community resources Past experiences seeking assistance
How do you deal with difficult times?	Behavioral cues Cognitive resilience Psychological functioning Community resources Familial resources
How would you describe your health?	Health status/perception Description of health-related issues/problems Understanding of health-related issues
What have you been told is affecting you?	Understanding of health-related issues Health status/perception

several shortcomings of the BDI-II, it boasts high internal consistency (yielding a Cronbach's alpha of .92), high content validity, and strong international propagation.

General Health Questionnaire

The General Health Questionnaire (GHQ; Goldberg, 1978) is a measure of the mental health issues related to depression, anxiety, and social withdrawal. The GHQ has been translated into over 38 different languages (including Arabic, Hindi, Japanese, and Yoruba) and is available in 4 versions, using 12, 28, 30, or 60 items. The 28-item version, GHQ 28, is used most widely and most often is used within "working populations." Although the GHQ seeks to assess the presence of more common mental health issues, it was not developed for predictive uses. Its scores are used to indicate "psychiatric caseness." This "is a probabilistic term—whereby, if such respondents presented in general practice, they would be likely to receive further attention" (Jackson, 2007, p. 79). Reliability coefficients have ranged from 0.78 to 0.95 in various studies.

State-Trait Anxiety Inventory

The State-Trait Anxiety Inventory (STAI; Spielberger, Gorsuch, Lushene, Vagg, & Jacobs, 1970) was designed to measure anxiety in adults. A later version was developed for children (STAIC; Spielberger, Edwards, Montuori, & Lushene, 1973). A key feature of the STAI is that it distinguishes feelings of anxiety from depression. The STAI is appropriate for those with a sixth-grade reading level, which increases it's applicability across various levels of literacy. The inventory includes two subscales, one that assesses "state" anxiety (a temporal condition of anxiety), and one that assesses "trait" anxiety (a more long-standing behavioral condition of anxiousness). The inventory illustrates high concurrent validity with other scales utilized to assess anxiety. The STAI also has high relevance for culturally responsive assessment. The STAI has been adapted into 48 languages, including Arabic, Hindi, Korean, and Portuguese, and can be effectively used to measure a particular population in study regardless of their racial, spiritual, or gender background (De Jong, Merckelbach, & Nijman, 1990).

The SF-36® Health Survey

The SF-36 (Coons, Rao, Keiner, & Hays, 2002) is an example of a health-related quality of life instrument with consistently strong validity that was intended for use in the general population. The SF-36 consists of eight cluster scales: physical functioning, role functioning, bodily pain, general health, vitality, social functioning, role-emotional, and mental health. These eight clusters then form two general measures of health: physical health and mental health. In addition to English, the SF-36 has been translated, adapted, and published in 13 other forms through the International Quality of Life Assessment (IQOLA) Project and is used in over 50 countries. A key feature in the development of the SF-36 perhaps is represented not only in the array of adapted versions available but more so in the diligence taken to not operationally define health constructs for diverse populations. The Physical Functioning domain presents a Cronbach's alpha of 0.90, and test-retest reliabilities for the eight domains ranged from 0.73 to 0.96. There exist four English language versions (United States, Canada, Australia/New Zealand, and the United Kingdom), which is indicative of the complexity and potential danger with straight language translations as well as the necessity to consider cultural distinctions when investigating issues of health and disability across diverse cultural groups. The SF-36 is an excellent illustration of a culturally responsive assessment instrument that not only considers the language of the population but also various regional cultural trends and norms toward health and illness.

Discussion Box 4.3

WHAT EXACTLY IS THE "NORM"?

The term *race* in the United States has lost the original anthropology-based definition. Individuals and society as a whole tend to classify individuals based more on outward appearances than on genetics or biology. To this end, some researchers believe that race is a social construct, or something that has been giving meaning based on the thoughts and beliefs of the society in which you live. Similarly, when we talk about disability in the field of rehabilitation, often we believe we are all talking about the same construct. But what if my definition of disability is different than your definition of disability? Does *disability* mean the same thing in Japan as it does in England? Does this also make the term *disability* a social construct? Often we take things that we know for granted. What does it mean to be disabled? What does it mean to be Latino? The answers to these questions are based more on our thoughts and beliefs about these constructs than on outward appearances. What other terms do we assume mean the same to everyone? In July 2008, in the United States, the headlines read "Pregnant man, gives birth to daughter." The "pregnant man" had been born, biologically, a woman. After extensive surgery and living as a male, "she" became "he" by legally changing his gender. So what is "normal"?

Questions:
Is "normal" static? Does it stay the same over time? Is there anything that was "normal" in the 1940s that isn't "normal" now? Are there things that are considered every day, routine, or "normal" now that were not "normal" 5, 10, 15, or 20 years ago? Who decides what is or is not considered "normal"? How does this shift in "normal" affect how we view disability, health, and/or rehabilitation? How does it affect what is or isn't considered a physical or psychological disorder? What do you think will shift our beliefs about disability over the next 10 years? How do you suspect these shifts will affect how we conduct assessments?

Legal and Professional Issues in Culture and Diversity Assessments

In 1994, the APA recognized the effect of culture and ethnicity on assessment, diagnosis, and treatment and actively acknowledged this impact in the revised *DSM-IV* (Lu et al., 1995). Additionally, the Commission on Rehabilitation Counselor Certification also addressed assessment bias in the revised Code of Ethics. According to the Code of Ethics, consideration of culture should occur: (a) during diagnosis of mental disorders; (b) during test selection; and (c) during scoring and interpretation of test results. These efforts illustrate awareness of the potential for cultural bias in assessment.

More recent efforts by the APA (2000), the American Psychological Association (2002), and the American Counseling Association (2005) have introduced guidelines for the ethical practice of conducting quantitative assessments. These guidelines highlight the culturally responsive practice of identifying the norm group of the client so that assessments are interpreted in context of the client. Effective assessments also require that the "person(s) doing the assessment has accumulated significant knowledge about the history, customs, and modes of interaction of the groups in question" (Lonner & Ibrahim, 2008, p. 40).

An often cited source is the International Test Commission (ITC; 2001). The ITC is an "association of national psychological associations, test commissions, publishers and other organizations committed to promoting effective testing and assessment policies and to the proper development, evaluation and uses of educational and psychological instruments." The ITC developed guidelines on test use that compiled common practices from multiple codes of ethical practice, standards, and practices of organizations that develop and administer educational and psychological tests. The guidelines for test use are available at http://www.intestcom.org.

Issues Critical to Culture Diversity Assessments in Rehabilitation and Health Settings

As discussed in this chapter, there are three major areas in which the counselor must be cognizant of cultural bias within the assessment process. These areas include: possible bias as introduced by the instrument and the development of the instrument; the bias that can be introduced during the test administration; and the cultural competency of the counselor conducting the assessment process, where bias can be introduced throughout the process from interview to interpretation.

Critical to approaching the assessment process, counselors must start with the basic questions of: "what treatment, by whom, is most effective for this individual, with that specific problem, and under which set of life circumstances" (Paul, 1967, p. 111). Although not specific to multicultural counseling, these questions can be used in determining the specific assessment for the individual in a specific cultural environment. In multicultural training, although counselors are guarded against making generalizations, training materials often refer to individuals based on ethnic or demographic categories. In assessment, this "ecological fallacy" leads one to draw conclusions about an individual based on an analysis of group data (Hofsteded, 1980, 2001; Pedersen, Draguns, Lonner, & Trimble, 2002). An example of this would be to assume that an assessment is appropriate for a person from the Philippines because the assessment was conducted on Asian Americans. Similar to other cultural/racial groups, Asian Americans represent many different cultures, languages, and worldviews (Bryan, 1999). Likewise, the assessment concerns for a racially Black Latino individual may be drastically different than the assessments concerns for a racially White Latino because of their different life experiences.

Examining within-group differences is especially important in rehabilitation and health settings. As mentioned previously in this chapter, cultural attitudes and beliefs about disability, along with definitions of health and ill health, vary across cultural groups (Ibrahim & Ohnishi, 2001; Niemeier et al., 2003). These cultural differences in attitudes, beliefs, and definition of disability or health affect two areas of the assessment process. The first is the individual and his or her responses to the outcomes of the assessment. The second area is cultural context and definition of the "problem."

How the individual is treated and their life experiences and worldviews may be affected by the cultural beliefs regarding disability or ill health. For example, Tsao (2000) pointed out that in her family, her disability and the family's cultural beliefs regarding disability "overshadowed many traditional Asian values" (p. 27). There are many areas in the assessment process this may affect. One such area would be in the interpretation of the data received. In interpreting the assessment information, it could be the case that scores cannot be compared to other individuals with disabilities because of the Asian cultural background, but also, they cannot be compared to other Asian populations because of the disability.

As the definition of disability, health, and ill health vary across cultural groups (Niemeier et al., 2003; Ibrahim & Ohnishi, 2001), so do the definitions of terms such as *intelligence, abilities, personality,* and *pathology* (Pedersen et al., 2002). It can be argued that these terms, often assessed to determine disability or illness, hold different meanings for different cultural groups. For example, Cheung and Leung (1998) noted, "prior to the importation of Western psychology into China, personality was studied in terms of the ideal moral character in Chinese philosophy" (p. 233). Using the cultural norms of China, standardized personality measures such as the Minnesota Multiphasic Personality Inventory (MMPI) can be translated into the Chinese language, however, the items do not translate into a Chinese cultural context. Researchers have found that individuals who are Chinese score high on depression scales on the MMPI (and the revisions) because the items endorsed do not "reflect depression in the Chinese cultural context" (Cheung & Leung, p. 235).

Therefore, in returning to the original questions of "what treatment, by whom, is most effective for this individual, with what specific problem, and under which set of life circumstances" (Paul, 1967, p. 111), there are several complexities. Critical to assessment in rehabilitation and health care settings it is necessary to identify if the "problem" is actually a problem within the individual's cultural group and if cultural group norms, as defined for other members of the group, are the same for the individual with a disability. Recognizing the complexities of the assessment process not only includes examining general multicultural competencies but also an ability to examine within-group differences and how these differences may affect the assessment process.

Aspects of Culture and Diversity Assessment for Research and Other Forms of Scholarship

Since *Griggs v. Duke Power* (401 U.S. 424 [1971]), health service providers have had to be aware of the potential of systematic errors in assessment instruments. Of particular concern have been those systematic errors that result in differential impact for individuals as a function of their race, ethnicity, or culture. At the heart of this case were concerns regarding the design of the assessments and, more importantly, the valid use of test results. Efforts to understand and implement assessment programs for specific purposes must incorporate the relative strengths or limitations of the instruments and interpreting results in light of individual factors and contextual demands (Dana, 2008). As such, developers of assessment instruments and researchers attempting to understand the implications of scores from assessments must consider much more than content, construct, or criterion validity of instruments. Meeting the demands of equitable testing and research on instrumentation requires the development of cultural competencies and rethinking approaches to evaluating the psychometric properties and utility of different assessment instruments.

Cultural Competence

Conceptualizations of the term *cultural competence* vary according to professional orientation and specific discipline (Dana, 2008). Broadly, cultural competence can be considered the possession or development of congruent behaviors, attitudes, and policies that enable individuals to work effectively with individuals from different ethnic or cultural backgrounds (Isaacs & Benjamin, 1991). Individuals are considered to be increasing their cultural competence as they begin the process of seeking and integrating knowledge regarding groups of people into specific attitudes, practices, standards, and policies to increase the quality of services and outcomes (Davis, 1997). However, it is unclear to what extent that the researchers conducting experiments to evaluate psychometric instruments have developed a level of cultural competence prior to engaging in their explorations. There are some indications that individuals who consider themselves to possess high levels of cultural competence on surveys are more confident in providing services to clients from different cultural backgrounds (Nagai, 2008). However, self-report of cultural competency may fall prey to concerns regarding respondents supplying socially desirable responses (Ponterotto, Gretchen, & Chauhan, 2006). As such, a need persists to develop measures, such as indirect assessments, that reduce the likelihood of socially desirable response patterns (Antonak & Livneh, 1995). Alternative methods to measure cultural competency will increase the likelihood that individuals conducting research will consider the broad array of experiences and values of persons from diverse cultural and ethnic backgrounds.

In addition to developing better tools to measure the cultural competency of researchers, further research is also needed regarding the health impact of the provision of services by persons with varying levels of cultural competence. As previously stated, existing research may lack sufficient credibility among policy makers to create progressive changes in existing preservice and in-service training programs, community initiatives, and future guidelines or laws. With the promotion of research on evidence-based practices to guide clinicians and administrators (Chan, Rosenthal, & Pruett, 2005), further investigation that incorporates empirically sound instrumentation is necessary to guide policy and training toward creating services that are consistent with the diversity of the clientele requesting services.

Summary

The essential argument of this chapter is that the providers of health care, counseling, and rehabilitation services must consider the implications of culture on the assessment process. Both the provider culture and the culture of persons receiving assessment services must be considered. This is by no means a simple task, but one that requires adequate assessment training that infuses exposure to: culturally diverse field experiences, training on selecting and utilizing culturally relevant and appropriate assessment instruments, and structured examination of personal cultural awareness. It was best articulated by Doorenbos et al. (2005): "the cultural competence of healthcare providers is central to the healthcare system's ability to provide access to and delivery of high-quality, high-value healthcare and is instrumental in reducing health disparities" (p. 324).

It is imperative to note again that persons with disabilities and persons from diverse cultural groups—although there are some shared variables—are not homogenous. Hence, rehabilitation and health providers need to examine the cultural beliefs and perceptions of the individual they are working with. Cultural group information should serve one dimension of identity, but the individual layer adds yet another dimension of characteristics to be considered during assessment. Culturally competent service providers will know to utilize the client/consumer as a key source of information that will provide some direction toward the culturally appropriate assessment and treatment interventions (Stone, 2005). Proficient service provision requires culturally competent and sensitive providers who are able to understand the impact of culture on health and disability status, utilization, and treatment outcomes (Gonzalez-Calvo, Gonzalez, & Lorig, 1997). Consequently, the success of rehabilitation and health outcomes depends on our cultural competence and ability to effectively and appropriately assess the needs and abilities of the persons we serve.

Research Box 4.1

Warner, T. D., Dede, D. E., Garvan, W. G., & Conway, W. (2002). One size does not fit all in specific learning disability assessment across ethnic groups. *Journal of Learning Disabilities, 35,* 500–508.

Objectives: The purpose of this study was to examine whether the use of minimum IQ scores and simple difference methods is appropriate in diagnosing specific learning disabilities (SLD) in African American college students. Noting that, on average, African American IQ scores differ by 1 *SD* from those of European American scores, the simple difference method uses a minimum IQ score cut-off point, and SLD diagnosis is determined based on the discrepancy between the IQ and Achievement test scores. The researchers, replicating previous research, postulate that more sound statistical analysis can be used to provide a more balanced interpretation of severe discrepancy, thus more accurately diagnosing SLD.

Method: Participants were full-time college students referred for SLD evaluation over the course of 3 years. A total of 117 individuals participated in the study: 50 were African American and 67 were European Americans. Participants were between the ages of 18 and 25 (African American $M = 19.7$, $SD = 1.4$; European American $M = 20.6$, $SD = 1.8$) with the majority being male (African American M = 88%, European American M = 55.2%). IQ and achievement test scores were obtained and converted to standard scores. Severe discrepancies between IQ scores and Achievement scores were determined through both a simple difference method and a regression-based method.

Results: As the researchers expected, significant differences were found for the WAIS-R Full Scale IQ scores, favoring European American students. Similar to findings in other research, African American students were, on average, 1 *SD* lower than those of the European American students. Using the minimum IQ score of 85 to differentiate SLD from low functioning would have excluded 3% of the European American participants and 33% of the African American participants from further evaluation for a SLD diagnosis. In examining the differences between the simple differences and regression-based methods for determining a severe discrepancy between IQ and Achievement, one-third more African Americans (54%) were identified as having SLD using the regression-based method. Equally important, when determining SLD in European American students, there was no significant difference found between the two methods.

Conclusion: The findings of the study call for researchers, educators, and psychologist to examine the methods used to determine SLD diagnosis. Warner et al. call for the establishment of a uniform guideline in determining SLD. The differences in average IQ scores found when comparing minority students to nonminority students have been a concern for a number of years. Thus, the use of minimum IQ score cut offs and the use of discrepancy criteria provides inaccurate information, when used with minority students, and limits the number of students eligible for services.

The study indicates that the assessment process can also be biased in the manner in which the results are interpreted. In this particular study, the authors presuppose that the statistical methods psychologists use to interpret the results of the scores and a lack of standardized methods of interpretation build bias into the diagnosing process for minorities.

Questions:
What are the ways in which biases can be built into both IQ and achievement tests? How would you determine if these instruments are appropriate for your consumers? Aside from the bias that may be included in the assessment construction, what are other ways that the assessment process can be biased? How can you adapt the assessment and diagnosing process so as to avoid introducing additional bias into your assessment process? As a supplement to standardized assessments (such as IQ tests), what are other ways to assess for learning disabilities?

References

American Psychiatric Association. (2000). *Diagnostic and statistical manual of mental disorders* (4th ed., text revision). Washington, DC: Author.

Antonak, R. F., & Livneh, H. (1995). Direct and Indirect Methods to Measure Attitudes Toward Persons With Disabilities, With an Exegesis of the Error-Choice Test Method. *Rehabilitation Psychology, 40,* 3–24.

Armour-Thomas, E. (1992). Intellectual assessment of children from culturally diverse backgrounds. *School Psychology Review, 21*(4), 552–565.

Arredondo, P., & Glauner, T. (1992). *Personal Dimensions of Identity Model.* Boston: Empowerment Workshops.

Balcazar, H., Castro, F., & Krull, J. (1995). Cancer risk reduction in Mexican-American women: The role of acculturation, education, and health risk factors. *Health Education Quarterly, 22,* 61–84.

Beck, A. T., Steer, R. A., & Brown, G. K. (1996). *Manual for the Beck Depression Inventory-2,* San Antonio, TX: Psychological Corporation.

Betancourt, J. R., Green, A. R., Carrillo, J. E., & Ananeh-Firempong, O. (2003). Defining cultural competence: A practical framework for addressing racial/ethnic disparities in health and healthcare. *Public Health Reports, 118,* 293—302.

Bickenbach, J. E., Chatterji, S., Badley, E. M., & Üstün, T. B. (1999). Models of disablement, universalism and the international classification of impairments, disabilities and handicaps. *Social Science and Medicine, 48,* 1173–1187.

Bryan, W. V. (1999). *Multicultural aspects of disabilities: A guide to understanding and assisting minorities in the rehabilitation process.* Springfield, IL: Charles C. Thomas Publisher, LTD.

Chan, F., Rosenthal, D. A., & Pruett, S. R. (2008). Evidence-based practice in the provision of rehabilitation services. *Journal of Rehabilitation,72,* 3–5.

Cheung, F. M., & Leung, K. (1998). Indigenous personality measures: Chinese examples. *Journal of Cross-Cultural Psychology, 29,* 233—248.

Coons, S. J., Rao, S., Keiner, D. L., & Hays, R. D. (2000). A comparative review of generic quality of life instruments. *Pharmocoeconomics, 17*(1), 13—35.

Dana, R. H. (2008). Multicultural issues in assessment. In B. Bolton & R. Parker (Eds.), *Handbook of measurement and evaluation in rehabilitation* (pp. 569–690). Austin, TX: Pro Ed.

Davis, K. (1997). *Exploring the intersection between cultural competency and managed behavioral health care policy: Implications for state and county mental health agencies.* Alexandria, VA: National Technical Assistance Center for State Mental Health Planning.

De Jong, P. J., Merckelbach, H., and Nijman, H. (1990). Conjugate lateral eye movements, cerebral dominance, and anxiety. In R. I. Takens (Ed.), *European perspectives in psychology* (Vol. 2., pp. 369–379). New York: Wiley.

Dodd, J. M., Nelson, J. R., Ostwald, S. W., & Fischer, J. (1991). Rehabilitation counselor education programs' response to cultural pluralism. *Journal of Applied Rehabilitation Counseling, 22*(1), 46–48.

Donnell, C. M. (2008). Examining the multicultural counseling competencies of rehabilitation counseling graduate students. *Rehabilitation Education, 22,* 13–17.

Doorenbos, A. Z., Myers-Schim, S., Benkert, R., & Borse, N. N. (2005). Psychometric evaluation of the Cultural Competence Assessment Instrument among healthcare providers. *Nursing Research, 54,* 324–331.

Downing, S. M. (2003). Validity: On the meaningful interpretation of assessment data. *Medical Education, 37,* 830–837.

Dziekan, K. I., & Okocha, A. G. (1993). Accessibility of rehabilitation services: Comparison by racial-ethnic status. *Rehabilitation Counseling Bulletin, 36,* 84–95.

Faubion, C. W., Calico, J., & Roessler, R. T. (1998). Meeting the needs of underserved populations: Vocational rehabilitation and the Cherokee Nation 130 Project. *Rehabilitation Counseling Bulletin, 41,* 173–189.

Goldberg, D. (1978). *General Health Questionnaire (12-item).* Windsor: NFER-Nelson.

Gonzalez-Calvo, J., Gonzalez, V. M., & Lorig, K. (1997). Cultural diversity issues in the development of valid and reliable measures of health status. *Arthritis Care and Research, 10,* 448–456.

Griggs v. Duke Power, Inc. 401 U.S. 424 (1971).

Hofstede, G. (1980). Beyond the Rorschach. *Journal of Personality Assessment, 52,* 578–609.
Hofstede, G. (2001). *Culture's consequences: Comparing values, behaviors, institutions, and organizations across nations* (2nd ed.). Thousand Oaks, CA: Sage.
Homa, D. B., & Peterson, D. B. (2005). Using the International Classification of Functioning, Disability and Health (ICF) in teaching rehabilitation client assessment. *Rehabilitation Education, 19,* 119–128.
Ibrahim, F. A., & Ohnishi, H. (2001). Posttraumatic stress disorder and the minority experience. In D. B. Pope-Davis & H.L.K. Coleman (Eds.), *The intersection of race, class, and gender in multicultural counseling* (pp. 89–126). Thousand Oaks, CA: Sage.
International Test Commission. (2001.) *ITC guidelines on test use.* Retrieved January 4, 2009, from: http://www.intestcom.org/guidelines/index.php
Isaacs, M., & Benjamin, M. (1991). *Towards a culturally competent system of care, volume II, programs which utilize culturally competent principles.* Washington, DC: Georgetown University Child Development Center, CASSP Technical Assistance Center.
Jaber, L. A., Brown, M. B., Hammad, A., Zhu, Q., & Herman, W. H. (2003). Lack of acculturation is a risk factor for diabetes in Arab immigrants in the US. *Diabetes Care, 26,* 2010–2014.
Jackson, C. (2007). The General Health Questionnaire. *Occupational Medicine, 57,* 79.
Lonner, W. J., & Ibrahim, F. A. (2008). Appraisal and assessment in cross-cultural counseling. In P. B. Pedersen, J. G. Draguns, W. J. Lonner, & J. E. Trimble (Eds.), *Counseling across cultures* (pp. 37–55). Thousand Oaks, CA: Sage.
Maramaldi, P., Berkman, B., & Barusch, A. (2005). Assessment and the ubiquity of culture: Threats to validity in measures of health-related quality of life. *Health and Social Work, 30*(1), 27–38.
McLean, Z. Y. (1995). History of bilingual assessment and its impact on best practices used today. *New York State Association for Bilingual Education Journal, 10,* 6–10.
Mead, H., Cartwright-Smith, L., Jones, K., Ramos, C., Woods, K., & Siegel, B. (2008). *Racial and ethnic disparities in U.S. health care: A chartbook.* New York: The Commonwealth Fund.
Messick, S. (1980). Test validity and ethics of assessment. *American Psychologist, 35,* 1012—1027.
Mpofu. E., & Ortiz, S. (in press). Equitable assessment in diverse settings. In E. Grigorenko (Ed.)., *Multicultural psychoeducational assessment.* New York: Springer.
Niemeier, J. P., Burnett, D. M., & Whitaker, D. A. (2003). Cultural competence in the multidisciplinary rehabilitation setting: Are we falling short of meeting needs? *Archive of Physical Medicine and Rehabilitation, 84,* 1240–1245.
Oakland, T. (2004). Use of educational and psychological tests internationally. *Applied Psychology: An International Review, 53,* 152—172.
Olmedo, E. L. (1979). Acculturation: A psychometric perspective. *American Psychologist, 34,* 1061–1070.
Paul, G. L. (1967). Strategy outcome research in psychotherapy. *Journal of Consulting Psychology, 31,* 109–119.
Pedersen, P. B., Draguns, J. G., Lonner, W. J., & Trimble, J. E. (Eds.). (2002). *Counseling across cultures* (5th ed.). Thousand Oaks, CA: Sage.
Pena, E. D. (2007). Lost in translation: Methodological considerations in cross-cultural research. *Child Development, 78,* 1255–1264.
Peterson, D. B. (2005). International Classification of Functioning, Disability and Health: An introduction for rehabilitation psychologists. *Rehabilitation Psychology, 50,* 105–112.
Ponterotto, J. G., Gretchen, D., & Chauhan, R. V. (2006). Quantitative and qualitative tools for the clinician. In A. Suzuki, J. Ponterotto, & P. Miller (Eds.), *Handbook of multicultural assessment* (pp. 67–100). San Francisco, CA: Jossey-Bass.
Reed, G. M., Lux, J. B., Bufka, L. F., Trask, C. Peterson, D. B., Stark, S., et al. (2005). Operationalizing the International Classification of Functioning, Disability and Health in clinical settings. *Rehabilitation Psychology, 50,* 122–131.
Smart, J. F., & Smart, D. W. (1994). Rehabilitation of Hispanics: Implications for training and educating service providers. *Rehabilitation Education, 8*(4), 360–368.
Smedley, B. D., Stith, A. Y., & Nelson, A. R. (2002). *Unequal treatment: Confronting racial and ethnic disparities in health care.* Washington, DC: Institute of Medicine.
Sodowsky, G. R., & Lai, E.W.M. (1996). Acculturation instrumentation. In G. R. Sodowsky & J. C. Impara (Eds.), *Multicultural assessment in counseling and clinical psychology* (pp. 347–354). Lincoln, NE: Buros Institute of Mental Measurements.

Spector, R. E. (2002). Cultural diversity in health and illness. *Journal of Transcultural Nursing, 13,* 197–199.

Spielberger, C. D., Edwards, C. D., Montuori, J., & Lushene, R. (1973). *Manual for the State-Trait Anxiety Inventory for Children.* Palo Alto, CA: Consulting Psychologists Press.

Spielberger, C. D., Gorsuch, R. L., & Lushene, R. E. (1970). *Manual for the State-Trait Anxiety Inventory.* Palo Alto, CA: Consulting Psychologists Press.

Stone, J. H. (2005). Understanding immigrants with disabilities. In J. H. Stone (Ed.), *Culture and disability: Providing culturally competent services* (pp. 225–230). Thousand Oaks, CA: Sage.

Tyack, D. B. (1974). *The one best system: A history of American urban education.* Cambridge, MA: Harvard University Press.

Vijver, F. J. R. van de, & Tanzer, N. K. (2004). Bias and equivalence in cross-cultural assessment: An overview. *European Review of Applied Psychology, 54*(2), 119–135.

Warner, T. D., Dede, D. E., Garvan, W. G., & Conway, W. (2002). One size does not fit all in specific learning disability assessment across ethnic groups. *Journal of Learning Disabilities, 35,* 500–508.

Wilson, K. B. (2000). Predicting vocational rehabilitation eligibility based on race, education, work status, and source of support at application. *Rehabilitation Counseling Bulletin, 43,* 97–105.

Wilson, K. B., Harley, D. A., & Alston, R. J. (2001). Race as a correlate of vocational rehabilitation acceptance: Revisited. *Journal of Rehabilitation, 67*(3), 35–41.

World Health Organization. (2001). *International classification of functioning, disability and health (ICF).* Geneva: Author.

Zola, I. K. (1989). Toward the necessary universalizing of a disability policy. *The Milbank Quarterly, 67,* 401.

Part 2

Measures and Procedures

Item Response Theory and Computer Adaptive Testing

Steven J. Osterlind
Elias Mpofu
Thomas Oakland

5

Overview

Measures constructed using item response theory (IRT) are gaining increased attention in rehabilitation and health settings. Most computer-administered measures are IRT-based, thus adding to the efficiency, accuracy, and amount of patient-oriented data collected. This chapter describes IRT, including some of its basic tenants. The chapter also discusses differences between IRT and classical test theory (CCT), common IRT models for assessment (i.e., 1-, 2-, and 3-parameter models), and item information characteristics (difficulty, discrimination), as well as IRT's basic mathematical features. The chapter reviews research and practice issues in the construction of IRT methods for use in rehabilitation and health measures. Practical features of IRT modeling (e.g., its focus on estimating measurement characteristics of test questions in light of a person's abilities) make it ideal for use in rehabilitation and health settings wherein test information at the item level has clinical significance.

Learning Objectives

By the end of the chapter, the reader should be able to:

1. Contrast item response to classical test theories of assessment;
2. Explain the conceptual basis of IRT and computer adaptive testing (CAT);
3. Describe item characteristic and person ability measures with IRT-based measures;
4. Describe how IRT and CAT are applied in assessment in rehabilitation and health;
5. Discuss how IRT and its application in CAT can be used to aid research and practice in assessment in rehabilitation and health; and
6. Evaluate the merits of IRT in constructing measures for use in rehabilitation and health settings.

Introduction

Item response theory (IRT) is a cognitively-based theory of assessment. It posits a latent trait (e.g., neurological functioning, health-related quality of life) that can be estimated within an individual. It uses sophisticated statistics to calculate a test score that reflects the individual's status on that health-related quality (e.g., physical and functional performance, neurological functioning, subjective well-being). Thus, IRT is both a theory of assessment and a set of powerful statistics that puts the theory into practice.

IRT often is contrasted with classical test theory (CTT), an approach to testing that is more familiar to many laypersons. In CTT, assessment focuses on estimating an individual's "true score" by presenting a set of test items that sample a domain of content. (A sample of items is used because an attempt to devise and administer all questions in a given content domain is impracticable.) Then, the number of questions answered correct by the examinee is summed to produce an estimate of the true score. CTT is presumed to be on an *additive* model of assessment. The degree to which one test score is consistent with test scores from other samples of items is an indication of reliability in the measurement.

In contrast, the statistics undergirding IRT are based on probability theory wherein the "likelihood" of an examinee's response being either correct or incorrect on a set of test items with known statistical characteristics is calculated as the final score. For example, if an examinee answers correctly a set of questions that are increasingly difficult, there is a high likelihood of obtaining yet another correct response on the next, more difficult item and so forth until the examinee begins to miss items—then the likelihood of passing more difficult items decreases. However, if another examinee responded inconsistently to the same set of items (getting some correct and some incorrect), there is a lower likelihood that he or she would respond correctly to the next, and more difficult, item. A test score based on IRT methods is thought to more accurately reflect the examinee's real, and underlying, ability or proficiency.

As a cognitive theory–based model for individual appraisal, IRT is determinedly focused on the underlying psychological dimensions of a trait or construct. As discussed later, this feature of IRT is of great interest to patient-oriented rehabilitation practitioners wherein health status is perceived to be on an objective continuum from lower to superior health. IRT brings a theory of measurement closer to rehabilitation assessment models in which health statuses are defined as constructs useful for case conceptualization as well as rehabilitation treatment design and evaluation (Cella & Chang, 2000; Mpofu et al., 2006; Vickers, 2003). IRT produces more accurate and psychologically-based appraisals and can be implemented in computer adaptive frameworks (Hays, Morales, & Reise, 2000; Ware, Bjorner, & Kosinski, 2000). This makes IRT appropriate for testing persons in individual settings—common circumstance in rehabilitation practice.

The purpose of this chapter is to introduce IRT along with one of its important advantages: implementing IRT via computers through *computer adaptive testing* (CAT). Although an attempt is made to discuss IRT in layman's terms, the internal process of implementing IRT-based tests involves statistics. Thus, its description requires knowledge and use of some statistics that are explained later in the chapter.

History of Research and Practice in IRT and CAT

IRT may be traced to L. L. Thurstone's work on test scaling in the 1920s (Thurstone, 1925) in which he statistically linked responses to test questions to a theory of learning and achievement. Major advances have occurred in the theory of measurement as well as in the statistics employed to represent it since that early work (e.g., Lord, 1952). Following are descriptions of some seminal stops along this evolutionary road.

One early point along this road concerned the procedures used to determine the difficulty level of a given test item. Prior to IRT developments, individual test items were statistically treated as being equally difficult in most CTT scoring schemes. Attempts to determine whether an item was easy or difficult depended entirely upon the group of examinees to whom the test was administered. An item that most people responded to correctly is considered to be easy *because* most members of the group got it right. The reverse also is true: Items that most examinees answer incorrectly are considered difficult *because* they typically are missed. This aspect for items is termed "group-dependence," and it is a shaping feature of CTT.

In 1942, Ferguson (1942) began to move away from this idea and investigated methods by which a test item could be calibrated as easy, medium, or difficult regardless of who took it. However, the early scholarship on IRT by Ferguson and others (e.g., Carroll, 1950; Lawly, 1943) did not attract much attention, probably due to their highly technical descriptions with formulae requiring lengthy hand calculations in pre-calculator days. Still, mental-appraisal work associated with World War II personnel created considerable interest in various types of tests, including those used for achievement testing, health and rehabilitation, and clinical appraisal. In 1952, Fredrick Lord, a brilliant graduate student working on his dissertation, developed IRT as a full-fledged test theory as well as models for its use. Further advances in the mathematics of IRT suddenly came fast and furious, especially from the Danish mathematician Georg Rasch (1960).

The importance and use of IRT grew during the 1970s and through the 1990s due, in large part, to the availability of powerful computers to do the complex statistical analyses. The progress also brought out strong advocates of IRT such as Benjamin Wright at the University of Chicago (Wright & Stone, 1979). Since then, developments have been profound and profuse. Now IRT's role is considered mainstream in the testing industry. IRT's role in representing various social and psychological phenomena, including in rehabilitation research and practice, is becoming increasingly important.

Understanding the Theory Behind IRT

An understanding of the cognitive base for IRT and its elegant statistics requires knowledge of CTT. IRT does not refute CTT; rather, it extends it in assorted and significant ways. CTT rests its foundation on the notion of a *true score*. A true score is thought to represent the actual amount of a trait or proficiency possessed by an individual in a given content domain. The goal of CTT is to determine this true score as accurately as possible.

Estimating an examinee's true score requires several steps. It begins during the initial development of a test when the content to be appraised is accurately and completely described or defined. In CTT, the content is conceived as a domain of knowledge with limits that prescribe its parameters. The domain may be any type of mental attribute, such as an academic achievement, a belief, an attitude, a personality, a proficiency (e.g., relearning), or any other important personal quality in rehabilitation.

Next, test questions (technically called *items* because not all are in a question format) covering varying aspects of the domain are developed according to criteria. One criterion is that a set of items must represent the entire domain fairly and accurately. For example, when developing a test of elementary mathematics, items would be developed that assess all four functions (i.e., addition, subtraction, multiplication, and division) rather than just one or two of them.

This approach to test construction is called *domain sampling*. A domain sampling model for test development is much like taking a poll to sample opinions held by the entire population. Just as a polltaker asks questions of many people to gauge the population's opinion, in domain-sampling testing, test items are developed to cover the breadth and depth of the targeted domain. Achieving the proper scope and sequence for items is difficult. Additionally, the domains may change over time, such as when new knowledge is uncovered. The process of constructing suitable test items requires considerable skill and care. Persons new to item development often are surprised at the difficulty involved and the amount of time needed.

CTT recognizes these challenges in test construction and acknowledges them as *error* in the measurement process. In fact, CTT acknowledges error as a component of the measurement process. Without error, measurement would be a true and accurate reflection of an examinee's ability or proficiency. In fact, the *true and accurate* reflection is the examinee's *true score*. Putting these notions together yields the basic true score formula: $T = X - e$ where T is true score, X is observed score, and e is the error.

Looked at another way, a person's true score equals the person's observed score (i.e., the one reported after scoring a test) minus the error. A test's reliability is used to indicate the amount of error. A perfectly reliable test has no error. Under this condition, the observed score equals the true score. Although the development of a test without error is a laudatory goal, this never is achieved in sophisticated mental appraisals.

IRT, like CCT, also has an observed score and one that includes measurement error. However, IRT takes a fundamentally different approach to assessment, one that is more psychologically based. IRT focuses on cognitive processes rather than on content domains. Such cognitive processes may include mental areas such as achievement, acuity, perception, personality, temperament, and various other qualities considered commonly by specialists in rehabilitation and other health professions. These personal qualities are veiled and not directly apparent. Thus, they are labeled as *latent,* or as *latent traits.* Being complex humans, we have countless numbers of latent traits, including our ability to read, do math, have opinions, and exhibit personality characteristics such as extroversion and introversion. The extent to which we express these traits is one's *ability* or *proficiency.* In testing, the latent traits often are operationalized as constructs.

In the IRT model, a trait is expressed along a continuum that ranges from none to infinite, technically shown as range $[-\infty, +\infty]$. A test is administered to determine the amount of proficiency an examinee displays. Because a test is composed of separate and individual test questions, obtaining information on the items' characteristics is important, including each item's difficulty level, its discriminating value, and so forth. Information on an item's difficulty is useful to building tests that are appropriate to a particular examinee and that reflect the wide range within the latent trait.

Item Formats

The format for the test's questions is an important component. Some tests use multiple-choice questions, while others use other formats (e.g., open-ended questions). Although the use of multiple-choice questions may be an efficient means to apprise a large body of knowledge, they often are not the best means to an effective appraisal. Other methods (e.g., open-ended questions, observations, demonstrations) may provide a more targeted appraisal when assessing a particular proficiency. Test questions often are termed *stimuli,* a term that embraces many format types, including multiple-choice, demonstrations, and other activities (e.g., relearning to walk after a severe stroke). A stimulus is anything reasonable that the test maker deliberately uses to evoke and thus test proficiency.

Given this background information, one can identify two ingredients that need to be quantified in the appraisal process: the characteristics of the test's stimuli (e.g., its difficulty) and the examinee's ability or proficiency. The IRT formulae determine both ingredients. For the items, the formulae allow one to gauge where a test's stimuli lay along a continuum from easy to difficult (called "item fit" in IRT parlance). Knowing this, a test can be composed of items representing a range of difficulty as well as other characteristics. Additionally, the IRT formulae gauge an examinee's ability or proficiency in the construct being

5.1

Line representing a trait continuum, with people and test stimuli scaled along it.

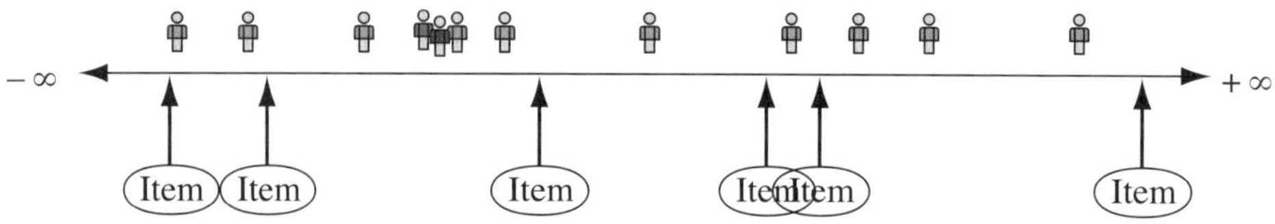

appraised. Thus, the formulae also determine where the examinee lies on the continuum. *Scaling* refers to the process of determining a test item's difficulty and an individual's proficiency. Both the test items and an individual's proficiency are *scaled.* Figure 5.1 displays this theoretical notion of the test stimuli and the examinee's proficiency being scaled.

Scaling of the Test Items

The test's stimuli and the examinee's proficiency are mapped to the same scale. Hence, much of IRT involves a search process to determine where the test stimuli (i.e., the questions) map onto the scale and where the test taker also maps onto the same scale. In other words, a central goal of an IRT-validated assessment is to determine where the items should lie on the scale as well as where each examinee's proficiency lies on that scale.

Using a simple example to understand this point, realize that testing is more informative when the difficulty of the items is appropriate to the proficiency of an examinee. Thus, not all persons need to take the identical set of items because persons with higher proficiency can be given more difficult items, and those with less proficiency can be given easier items. A good test exists when a test's items and the examinee's characteristics overlap so that appropriately difficult stimuli are presented (e.g., when the test is neither too easy nor too difficult) to each examinee.

Of course, the test stimuli (i.e., items) that are an appropriate level of difficulty are different for each examinee because their abilities and other personal qualities differ. Attempting to assess an examinee with test items that are too difficult or too easy is not a good fit and provides little useful information. Thus, the essence of an IRT process is found in its statistical methods that determine where along the scale (i.e., the trait's continuum) the items and the examinees fit best.

The Item Dependence/Examinee Dependence Problem in Testing

All test development methods provide information about the test's items and examinees' scores. When using CCT, this information is known through the information about examinees. Additionally, information about examinees' true score is known through the item information. Thus, we have a tautology (i.e., a proposition that, because of itself, is logically true). Each kind of test-related information is known only through each other, including the characteristics for a test's stimuli (e.g., the difficultly of the test's items) and the level of an examinee's proficiency. Although this concept, central to IRT, takes a bit of mental wrestling to get used to, it does make sense. The following example illustrates the principle.

Imagine that a test of functional performance is administered to two groups of patients, one with complete spinal cord injury (SCI) and another with incomplete SCI. As expected, the two groups will differ in their ambulatory functional performance. Those with complete SCI will earn functional performance scores well below those with incomplete of SCI for the same level of injury. Does this information indicate the test's items are necessarily too difficult for patients with complete SCI and too easy for those with incomplete SCI?

Using a CCT model, we cannot answer these questions with certainty. An examination of the difficulty of single test items, when considered only from the perspective of the patients with complete SCI (i.e., those who score low on most items of functional performance), is likely to conclude the items generally are too difficult. However, an examination of the same items, when considered only from the perspective of the patient with incomplete SCI (i.e., those who pass most functional performance items), is likely to conclude the items generally are too easy. Thus, opposite conclusions are reached for the same items depending on the group from whom the evidence is obtained and viewed. Therefore, in CCT, item information is *group dependent.*

The corollary for examinee information also occurs. Two patients with objectively different types of SCI received average functional performance scores for their respective types of SCI. The patient with complete SCI failed most of the functional performance test's items, while the patient with incomplete SCI passed most of the items. We may conclude the patient with complete SCI has low functional ability and that the patient with incomplete SCI is quite agile. Thus, an interpretation of these patients' abilities depends upon the items administered. This is termed *item dependence.*

When using CCT, we have no way to learn the absolute difficulty level of the items. Without this information, we cannot estimate the proficiency level of any examinee. We know only he or she passed more or fewer questions than did their peers. In contrast, when using an IRT model, information about items and examinees is separate and can be known independently. Returning to the two groups of patients with SCI, the difficulty level of the functional performance items can be determined regardless of who took them. Additionally, patients' abilities are estimated (i.e., they receive scores) regardless of the particular functional performance items they took. Thus, in IRT, *item information is group independent, and an examinee's estimated ability is item independent.* This group-and-item independence feature is a major advantage of using IRT.

IRT item statistics from different ability samples may be used interchangeably. This is a distinct advantage for rehabilitation outcome measurement in that the same items may be used with people with a variety of disabling conditions (as discussed later in this chapter). A person who passes a particular item at a specified level of difficulty can be reliably said to possess a certain

Discussion Box 5.1

EFFICIENT MEASURES WITH IRT

In real-world rehabilitation intervention settings, service providers or rehabilitation customers may not be able to (self) report on all behaviors or dispositions likely to influence a rehabilitation outcome. Moreover, there are constraints on the time available for rehabilitation service, necessitating use of short and efficient measures. Often, the same measure may be used with a diversity in rehabilitation customers (e.g., by disability, severity, demographics, environments). Efficient measures save effort and time in that they are typically briefer and allow for more focused or precise evaluation. A person's status of a health-related variable can be reliably established from the person's responses to any set of questions that are equivalent in measuring the construct of interest. Ideally, service providers and their customers wish to reliably establish status on a health construct of interest even though the customer took different test items on different occasions or skipped some questions.

Which of CCT- or IRT-based measures would be optimal to use the rehabilitation context as described, and why? What are efficient measures? In what ways and under what conditions are shorter measures (a) more efficient measures? (b) less efficient measures?

level of competence on the underlying trait that the test item measures. In terms of rehabilitation outcomes measurement, the result of that individual's test performance may be used for treatment planning based on knowledge of the individual's standing on the latent health variable (Heinemann & Hamilton, 2000).

Some Common IRT Models and Measures

IRT item information usually is discussed in reference to two main characteristics: an item's discrimination and its difficulty. On occasion, a third characteristic, guessing or pseudo-chance, also may be discussed. Each of these features for a test item (stimuli) is described here.

Item Discrimination

The purpose of a test is to discriminate, that is to determine the extent people differ from others (i.e., interindividual differences) and whether their personal qualities differ (i.e., intraindividual differences). Thus, to be successful, a test should discriminate.

An item's *discrimination index* indicates the rate at which each item differentiates examinees for a whole test. An item passed or failed by every examinee does not distinguish otherwise low- and high-scoring examinees. Thus, its discrimination index is zero, the item has little informative value, and it may be discarded. When using a CCT model, bi-serial or point bi-serial correlation methods (i.e., correlation relationship between a correct response to a given item and the examinee's total test score) commonly are used to determine the discrimination index. Using an IRT model, and for persons familiar with regression, the discrimination is expressed as the slope of a regressed score on the ability scale. This is explained later in more detail.

Item Difficulty

Item difficulty refers to the degree an item is easy or difficult. Using a CCT model, an item's difficulty is expressed using a *p-value* that indicates the percent (or proportion of 100) of examinees who responded correctly to an item. Using an IRT model, an item's difficulty is expressed using an item's calibration value to the proficiency scale. The less often mentioned estimate of pseudo-chance or guessing refers to the probability of a low-ability examinee passing difficult items. This construct is of little value in health assessments as people generally do not guess their well-being. Thus, this issue is not featured in this chapter.

When only the item's difficulty is considered, the IRT model is called a one-parameter (1PL) model because only one item characteristic is estimated. When both item discrimination and item difficulty are estimated, the IRT model is called a two-parameter (2PL) model. A three-parameter model (3PL) also would include the guessing parameter, giving further information about the probability of guessing correctly on an item.

Discussion Box 5.2

IRT MEASUREMENT MODELS

The 2-parameter IRT model is an extension of the 1-parameter (or Rasch) model. It estimates both an item difficulty parameter and an item discrimination parameter. Higher discriminating items have a steeper slope and are more effective in partitioning ability on adjacent points on the latent trait continuum. The probability of endorsement of a highly discriminating item increases as the distance between person ability and item difficulty narrows. Items with low discrimination are less affected by the discrepancy between ability and item difficulty. The choice of the appropriate measurement model to use in test development depends on the purposes of the research and how closely the data approximates the assumptions for the specific model.

Questions:

1. In developing measures, which of item difficulty and item discrimination would your prefer to use and why?
2. Explain why highly discriminating items have a narrower gap between person ability and item difficulty.

Person and Item Location

IRT statistical methods are used to determine the two essential maps: (1) where the item (stimuli) fits on the scale, and (2) where an examinee's proficiency lies on the same scale. To understand the first mapping issue, consider this proposition.

A patient has a particular probability of passing a health and well-being item. A number expresses this probability. This probability is dependent upon the interaction of the item's characteristics and the patient's proficiency in the assessed health construct. For example, individuals with higher well-being have a high probability of passing items that have low functional performance difficulty. Conversely, individuals with lower well-being have low probability of passing items that have high functional performance difficulty. In Figure 5.1, a very difficult item would fall to the right end of the scale. This also means that all but the healthiest individuals on the construct of interest have a low probability of "passing" the item.

IRT is a method to determine the utility of a test item (or group of items) by the information that the item (or group of items) contributes toward estimating a person's ability (i.e., likelihood of endorsing or "passing" an item) on

Discussion Box 5.3

ESTIMATING ABILITY AND ITEMS

IRT allows co-joint analysis of item difficulties and person abilities in that both items and persons have objective locations on the scale of the construct (see Figure 5.1). Items toward the lower end of an item difficulty hierarchy (easier items) can be considered as measuring lower abilities on the target health construct more than they do higher level abilities. Items toward the upper end of the item difficulty hierarchy could be regarded as measuring higher abilities. Thus, endorsing a higher placed transition ability item presumes that the individual is capable (probabilistically) of the lower placed abilities on the item hierarchy. Similarly, persons placed lower on a person-item hierarchy will have objectively lower ability. Person-item maps routinely available with IRT software are useful for charting health statuses in the absence of intervention. Changes in person-item maps over time or across cohorts (e.g., by disability, rehabilitation interventions received, age) are a reliable method for assessing a measure's sensitivity to change at the group level.

Questions:

1. What is the advantage to rehabilitation and health assessments of stable items difficulty and person ability locations on a health construct of interest?
2. How would you interpret changes in person locations with intervention?

an underlying construct (or latent trait; Andrich, 2003; Rasch, 1960). A person's ability is an estimate of the person's endorsement of a set of items that measure a latent trait (e.g., patient-centered care). For example, a health service provider who "passes" a particular item at a specified level of difficulty (e.g., endorses educating clients on treatment procedure) can be reliably said to possess a certain level of competence on the underlying trait that the item measures (i.e., patient-oriented care). In the context of IRT modeling, item difficulty is a measure of the ability (or trait) level needed to endorse an item at a given level. IRT modeling enables the joint prediction of the likelihood that a patient with a certain health care quality status will answer a particular item in a given direction. For example, a health care provider who endorses an item on patient education also is likely to endorse an item on supporting patients in their health care management decisions. The joint probability estimation with IRT modeling enables the prediction of service qualities for patients across a broad range of indicators.

Fit Statistics

IRT item statistics are commonly presented on an ordered hierarchy of a parameter (e.g., item difficulty, item discrimination). *Fit statistics* are used in IRT-based models to determine the extent to which each item and person ability are consistent with each other or the hierarchy of item difficulties or abilities. *Infit* statistics are used to identify unexpected answers close to the person's ability, whereas *outfit* statistics describe unexpected responses far from the person's ability. In measure development, infit and outfit statistics are helpful in identifying poorly written items because they reveal atypical responses relative to a person's ability or hierarchy of item difficulties. For example, unusually low infit and outfit statistics may suggest redundancy in the item pool (Hawley, Taylor, Hellawell, & Pentland, 1999), or items with double negatives (Hays et al., 2000).

Infit and outfit diagnostics are relevant to rehabilitation outcome measurement in that unexpected deviations from an individual's ability may be clinically significant. For example, if the deviation is unexpected but close to a person's ability (infit statistics), that may indicate potential for change with rehabilitation intervention. If the deviation is unexpected and far from the person's ability, the result may suggest that the person has specialized ability in that domain of functioning, which may be a resource for supporting rehabilitation intervention in related areas or an area on which fewer rehabilitation resources need to be expended.

Pivot Anchoring

Pivot anchoring as a method of item development is possible with application of IRT methodology. *Pivot anchoring* is variously defined (Cella & Chang, 2000; Hays et al., 2000). Clinically, it is the critical or transition point on the continuum of a latent trait that marks the difference between well-being and being unhealthy. The pivot score may be a minimum total score on a unidimensional scale or a choice point on a polytomous rating scale. IRT is useful for determining whether response categories on a polytomous rating scale are distinct and understandable.

Anchor-based applications of IRT are particularly important in health outcomes measurement in that people who score at a certain level on the trait continuum may evidence a unique health pattern and responsive to an identifiable rehabilitation intervention. For example, an individual with an acceptance of disability status at or above a certain point of the continuum of the latent trait adjustment to disability may be ready to participate in his or her own rehabilitation planning and management as compared to someone at a lower level of acceptance. Anchor-based approaches also enable the prediction of health status on the basis of a current proxy health status variable. For example, a measure of personal valuing (e.g., self-perception as a worthy being) at admission following acquired disability may prospectively predict time to achieve functional independence, discharge, and community reintegration. Personal valuing below a critical level for successful community participation at discharge may suggest a lower preparedness for employment and independent living. Anchor-based approaches to health outcome measurement have been infrequently applied to rehabilitation outcome measurement (Samsa et al., 1999; Testa, 2000).

Best Measurement Qualities

A test performs best and proficiency is assessed most accurately when the examinee has a 50% chance of getting an item correct. In such a case, the item is well suited to the examinee. The item is neither too easy nor too difficult, and as a consequence, the item is likely to reveal the examinee's proficiency in the trait.

The chance of an examinee passing an item is termed a *probability* because there is no certainty this will occur. Many personal and test conditions impact test performance, resulting in some very able examinees missing easy items and less able examinees passing difficult items. The mathematics used in IRT account for this occurrence.

The Probability Function of IRT

This section describes the probability function of IRT and is useful to understanding how the IRT formulae operate. The probability is described with only minimal reference to statistics to enable persons with elementary statistical training to follow. Remember, do not lose the flow of our overall point: to learn about IRT and its applications in CAT.

The Concept of Probability

Probability, expressed as *P*, ranges from 0 (no known probability) to 1 (perfect or 100% probability). Syntactically, the IRT-based relationship between probability and an examinee's proficiency is written as $P(U_i \mid \theta)$, where U is a response to a randomly selected item (i), and θ (theta) represents proficiency. The previous term reads as follows: For a randomly selected patient, the probability of a response to a randomly selected functional performance item is dependent upon—that is, is a *function of* or is *conditioned upon*—his or her ability.

By convention, an IRT proficiency estimate is represented by theta (θ), and the term $P(U_i \mid \theta)$ implies a correct response. The probability of not getting an item correct is expressed as Q. Accordingly $= 1 - P(U_i \mid \theta)$. These statements present the complete set of probabilities for a dichotomous item by including the probabilities of both a correct and incorrect response.

Remember, the probability of passing an item is determined in reference to an examinee's ability or proficiency in the trait (or belief, condition, personality characteristic, or other measured quality) and is not an absolute property of an item or an examinee. Thus, two separate examinees, when presented with the same item, are unlikely to have the same probability of correctly responding to the item. The examinee with the higher ability will have a higher probability of responding correctly than the one with the lower ability. Additionally, when completing to two different items, one examinee will not respond correctly to them with the same probability.

The Item Characteristic Curve (ICC)

The relationship between the probability of a correct response and an examinee's ability is displayed graphically for one hypothetical item in Figure 5.2. Study this figure carefully because it reveals how IRT works. The probability is displayed on the vertical axis (ordinate, Y axis). A proficiency scale in standardized units is displayed on the horizontal axis (abscissa, x axis). As is shown, as proficiency increases from left (low) to right (high), the probability also increases on the Y axis (from low to high). Note, too, that the relationship is not strictly linear, as would be shown if the line were straight. Instead, the relationship is

5.2

Curve for one item representing the relationship between examinees' ability and probability of a correct response.

displayed as a curve, called an *ogive*. This curvilinear relationship reflects the real-world practicality that test items are not equally discriminating along the entire range of abilities. The curve begins relatively flat, thus revealing that examinees of several abilities (e.g., from about −3 to −2 standard deviations) have roughly the same probability of passing the item. Thus, the item does not strongly discriminate among examinees who have varying low abilities. In fact, for motivational purposes, the initial items on many tests are intentionally easy to allow most examinees to pass.

The item in Figure 5.2 begins to discriminate when an examinee is about −1 standard deviation to about +2 standard deviations. At that level, its discrimination trails off (i.e., asymptotes) for examinees of higher ability who generally can be anticipated to pass the item. There also is little discrimination among examinees whose score is at the high end. Here, the item does not differentiate between highly able and very highly able persons: Both tend to get this item correct. This item performs best for examinees that are in the middle ranges of ability.

Realize, too, that Figure 5.2 displays only one test item. A figure for an entire test would have such a curve for every test item. When an examinee completes a set of test items, the probability of a correct response for *each* item ranges from zero to one (i.e., no chance to 100% chance). However, the probability of success on the entire test score is not the sum of the probabilities for individual items. Consistent with probability theory, success is based on a *joint probability*. A joint probability is the product of two (or more) individual probabilities; that is, the individual probabilities are multiplied.

For example, let us assume an examinee completes two items. The chances of responding correctly are 80% on the first item and only 50% on the second. The joint probability of being correct on *both* items is thus 40%, the product of the individual probabilities ($.8 \times .5 = .4$). If the examinee is presented with a third item for which there is, say, a 60% chance of being passed by an examinee with his ability, the joint probability of passing all three is 24% ($.8 \times .5 \times .6 = .24$).

Note from the example that the joint probability decreased as the number of items increased. As can be imagined, the joint probability of obtaining a perfect score on a test with many items diminishes to a very small figure. For a long test, when all the probabilities (one for each item, and remember that each of them is less than 1) are multiplied together, the joint probability for the entire test (getting every item correct) will be a very small number. As an illustration, each year only a few persons among the more than 1 million examinees obtain a perfect score on the college-entrance exam SAT, thus reflecting that the joint probability of getting all items correct is very small indeed, even for the most talented.

While determining the joint probability is a simple calculation, realize that responding (whether correctly or incorrectly) to a set of items is a function of the examinee's ability or proficiency. Therefore, in testing, the two ideas are linked. The function between them expressed mathematically is called a *likelihood*. A likelihood that is dependent on an examinee's ability is written as $L \mid \theta$ which reads, *likelihood is a function of ability* (theta). We saw above that there are two probabilities: a probability of getting the item correct (P) and another probability of getting the item wrong (Q). Hence, there are two probabilities, each of which is expressed as a likelihood. A ratio is constructed, called a *likelihood ratio,* to view them together.

The primary goal of the IRT mapping procedure is to locate the maximum likelihood ratio of achieving a particular response—either P or Q—to the set of items on a test for a given theta value (i.e., the examinee's ability or proficiency). This value is expressed as the *maximum likelihood estimate.* Maximum likelihood estimates differ for all thetas within the range measured by a test. An ability/proficiency estimate is determined by identifying the maximum likelihood estimate for each examinee who takes the test. This is their IRT score, usually termed their *theta value.* Understanding this process is critical to comprehending IRT.

IRT Test Scores

How theta values are expressed as a test score is another important IRT issue. As previously noted, each probability is limited to the range between 0 and 1. The joint probabilities become smaller as the test length increases and may approach zero. These probabilities are expressed on a log scale in order to ameliorate this situation (as well as to simplify some mathematics discussed later). That is, instead of saying a .5 probability, it is expressed as the log of .5, or –.03. When these log values are multiplied time and time again, they do not approach zero. Hence, the joint probability is more interpretable when expressed in log units (e.g., something like, a value of, say, a 1.2 in log metric) versus a near-zero value of, say, .00000001 in normal or non-log metric.

Finally, the log values are standardized onto a z scale on which, by definition, the mean is 0 and the standard deviation is 1. At last, we have arrived at a number than can be readily interpreted. A score (or theta value) of 0 is the median score, just as a score of ±1 is one standard deviation above or below the median. The scale on the bottom (X) axis in Figure 5.2 is expressed in these standardized units. Of course, as you likely know, standardized values also can be expressed as percentiles, making interpretation even more accessible. A theta of ±1 is at the 16th or 84th percentile, respectively.

Depicting these characteristics graphically is common in IRT. Figure 5.3 presents such information for two items.

Two items are shown simultaneously in Figure 5.3, each with its own curve. The curves differ, reflecting differing characteristics of the two items. As is evident, they are not equally difficult, nor do they discriminate among abilities to the same degree. The curve for Item 2 is much flatter (less slope) than for Item 1. This means that Item 2 is less discriminating than Item 1 because the probability of getting it correct (as shown along the Y axis) is about the same for everyone regardless of their proficiency (the X axis). Item 1 is more discriminating because it reveals a higher probability of a correct response by highly proficient examinees than less proficient examinees. Other item features also are revealed. For example, Item 2 begins higher at the left than does Item 1, showing that the item is more difficult for low ability examinees than is Item 1. On the opposite end of the curve for Item 2 (the right side), the item is less difficult than Item 1 for highly able examinees. However, at the point noted in the figure, both items are equally discriminating.

5.3

Two-item characteristic curves.

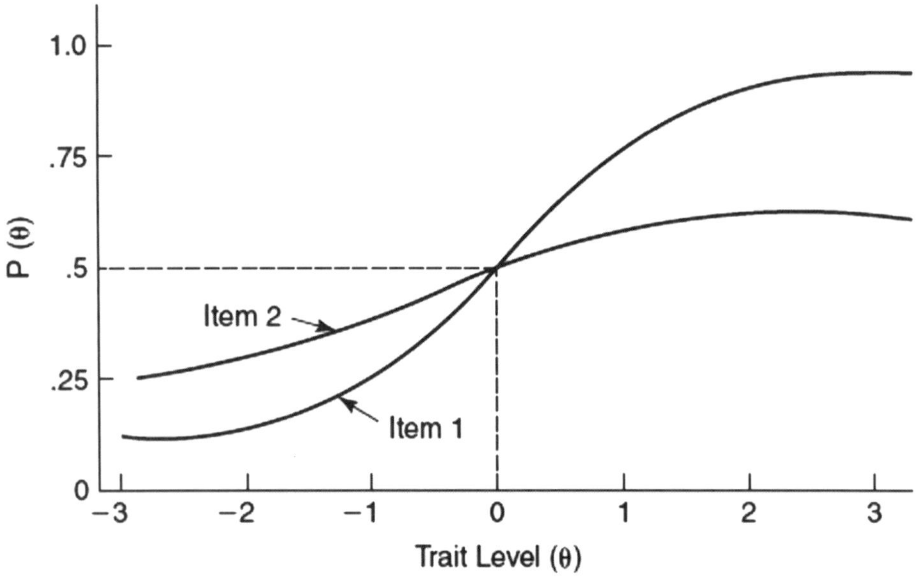

Computer Adaptive Testing

The usual approach to rehabilitation outcome measurement is for a health care professional to complete every question on a form and submit it for scoring. This is inherently inefficient. On most scales, responses to some items are subsumed in the responses to others.

For example, on the Functional Assessment Inventory (Crewe & Athelstan, 1981), if we know that a patient "Has little ability to control and coordinate movements," then very little information is gained by completing items that assess ambulation or upper extremity functioning. The information for each of these categories already is subsumed by the coordination rating. Rather than administer "fixed-item" measures, where all questions on an outcome measure are rated, it is possible to sequentially select items to maximize information, update the estimated score, and then evaluate whether there is enough information to terminate testing. In measurement this is called *adaptive* or *tailored testing*. In statistics, this is called *sequential testing.* Tailored item selection can result in reduced standard errors and greater precision with only a handful of properly selected items. The use of computers to deliver tests is becoming increasingly popular given its greater precision and efficiency of assessment.

Computer adaptive testing is an approach to testing that utilizes a computer to implement an IRT-developed test. In CAT, both the test item and the examinee proficiency are mapped to the line we described in Figure 5.1. However, in CAT, each examinee takes a different set of items via the computer. The items presented to each examinee depend upon his or her unique proficiency and are successively selected based on their responses to prior items. The less able examinees are presented only the simpler items (given the assumption they would likely miss difficult items: lower probabilities). The more able examinees are presented only the difficult items. This selection process means less wasting of valuable testing time by asking an individual to complete only items that are appropriately suited to their ability or proficiency. Because the set of items presented is appropriate to just the given examinees likelihood, CAT sometimes is termed *tailor testing* or *personal testing.* This individual approach to testing is a boon to rehabilitation professionals who are less interested in group proficiencies.

Procedure

The IRT-CAT process works in the following way. First, a large number of test items is prepared—many more than would be developed for a typical paper-and-pencil–administered test. Next, the items are administered via computer to a pilot group of examinees (sometimes called a *calibration* sample) in order to acquire pretest data. These data will not be used to evaluate the performance of individuals within this pilot group. Instead, the values are used to determine the items' characteristics (e.g., their difficulty and their discrimination values) onto the IRT scale, as we saw in Figure 5.1. Importantly, this calibration group must be similar in all important ways to other examinees who later will take the test (e.g., by type of disability, gender, training, etc.). Thus, they must come from the same population as the future examinees.

A test is ready to use with the intended examinees after a large number of items have been field-tested and their properties are known. To begin their computer adaptive test, the examinees take an initial small set of *locator items* selected from the item pool, usually from 6 to 20 items. By design, these locator items represent a wide range of item characteristics; some are easy, others are difficult. Then, based on an individual's responses to these few locator items, the IRT CAT algorithm selects a next item for each examinee.

The responses by each examinee to the locator set of items determine the selection and presentation of the next item. Of course, the "next" items for each examinee differ. The CAT algorithm selects a "next" item that is targeted at .5 probability of a correct response (the optimal point for IRT assessment) for each examinee. For example, if an examinee responded correctly to all or nearly all of the locator items, the next item presented to that examinee would have item characteristics (e.g., difficulty) much higher than the characteristics of the locator items. However, if an examinee responded incorrectly to all or nearly all of the locator items, the next item presented would have item characteristics much lower than those of the locator items.

For example, suppose a test has a set of 16 locator items. All examinees take these 16 items to get an initial starting point. Each examinee's responses to the locator items are used to preliminarily estimate the examinee's ability, thus leading to the selection of the next item. After taking this next item, the IRT search routines now have data on 17 items with which to prepare a more refined yet still somewhat tentative proficiency estimate. The computer adaptive testing algorithm again selects a "next" item, this time it is the 18th item. After the examinee responds to that item, proficiency estimates now are recalculated

Research Box 5.1

ADVANTAGES OF CAT IN REHABILITATION MEASUREMENT

Ware, J., Gandek, B., Sinclair, S., & Bjorner, J. B. (2005). Item response theory and computerized adaptive testing: Implications for outcomes measurement in rehabilitation. *Rehabilitation Psychology, 50*(1), 71–78.

Objective: To evaluate measures of rehabilitation outcomes that had been administered by IRT-based computer adaptive tests, with CAT software.

Method: A pilot study composed of 169 selected items from the Activity Measure for Post-Acute Care (AM-PAC) was administered to 485 patients who were receiving rehabilitation services to evaluate CAT software for its potential to be used in real situations. Items were calibrated with only one-parameter (difficulty) considered, making this Rasch analysis. Results were contrasted with scores garnered by structured interviews.

Results: By examinee responses, only 77 items were selected more than once during the first trial, with 10 more items selected on subsequent trials. Analysis showed virtual elimination of "floor" and "ceiling" effects; no examinee reached all the items. Reliability estimates ranged from .88 to .90. Also, examinees tended to prefer the CAT administered items to an interview format.

Conclusion: Improved scores can be IRT based. Reduced testing time is an advantage for examinees. However, the breadth of the content domain may not be fully appraised via CAT in the study.

Questions:
1. What are several advantages and disadvantages of CAT on the basis of this study?
2. What are instrument floor and ceiling effects, and how may these be influenced by patient characteristics? Discuss with reference to disability types of your choice.
3. This study used only a single IRT parameter (difficulty). Would there be some additional advantages if item discrimination was also used? Explain your answer.

based on his or her responses to all 18 items, only now the proficiency estimate is a little bit more accurate because more items are involved in the calculation of ability.

Thus, each iteration of the CAT process yields more information, resulting in the ever-more accurate estimates of the examinee's proficiency. The process of presenting ever-more-suited items continues, and ability estimate becomes increasingly stable. Finally, after the test developer's criterion for proficiency stability is met, the test ends for that examinee and the last and final ability estimate is calculated. A standard error of measurement typically is designated as the criterion for ending an assessment. The final proficiency estimate is the examinee's test score.

Remember that because each examinee responds to a different set of items and order of administration, the number of next items needed to obtain stable ability estimates also differs. When test items are calibrated by their characteristics, and if an examinee's responses are consistent (i.e., he or she passes easy items and fails difficult ones), the ability estimate may stabilize very quickly. However, if an individual responds inconsistently (i.e., he or she fails some easy items and passes difficult items), more items are needed to identify the optimal probability for him or her, thus making the test longer. The on-going process of revising item and ability estimates is not trivial mathematically. This introduction provides the basic ideas for this process.

Online CAT

Online CAT measures increasingly are being used in rehabilitation and health assessment. They offer several advantages. First, they allow the practitioner to easily and quickly enter data. This typically results in better data for a larger number of patients. Second, online CAT measures that require little to no training facilitate patient self-assessment. Their use also opens a wide range of research opportunities into cognitive as well as physical changes. Online CAT use allows one to systematically collect data that traditionally have been difficult to obtain, including changes over time, item sensitivity to improvement, and corresponding affective data.

Research on the Use of IRT-Based Rehabilitation and Health Assessments

There is abundant literature from patient-oriented rehabilitation outcomes research in which IRT-based measures were used (e.g., Bode, Lai, Cella, & Heinemann, 2003; Fisher, Harvey, Taylor, Kilgore, & Kelly, 1995; Hawley et al., 1999; Kilgore, Fisher, Silverstein, Harley, & Harvey, 1993; Linn, Blair, Harper, O'Hara, & Macuira, 1999). Studies on patient oriented outcomes assessments have investigated the structure of the dimensionality (or factor structure) of the measures (e.g., Hawley et al., 1999; Silverstein, Fisher, Kilgore, Harley, & Harvey, 1992). For example, Fisher, Eubanks, and Marier (1997) demonstrated that various measures of physical and functional performance could be placed on a common metric using IRT procedures. Studies have also examined how measures of the same health status compare in terms of item difficulties as ability hierarchies (Fisher et al., 1997; Fisher et al., 1999; McHorney & Cohen, 2000) as well as incremental value of measures constructed using IRT methodology to predicting patient oriented outcomes (e.g., Harvey et al., 1992; Hawley et al., 1999; Linn et al., 1999; Kilgore et al., 1993; Tesio & Cantagallo, 1998). Others studies have focused on rehabilitation measure equating to create more robust instruments or those with greater range and sensitivity across

Research Box 5.2

IRT IN INSTRUMENT DEVELOPMENT

Orlando, M., Wenzel, S. L., Ebener, P., Edwards, M. C., Mandell, W., & Becker, K. (2006). The dimensions of change in therapeutic community treatment instrument. *Psychological Assessment, 18*(1), 118–122.

Objective: To refine and preliminarily evaluate an IRT-based measure of treatment process, *Dimensions of Change in Therapeutic Community Treatment Instrument (DCI),* for youth and adults in community detention programs.

Method: A preliminary 99-item version of the DCI was administered to a sample of 990 substance-abuse clients. IRT-based statistics were used to develop scores for the clients and relevant characteristics (e.g., difficulty, discrimination) for the instrument's items. Item invariance was conducted by comparing the IRT scores across several subgroups of clients (e.g. males versus females, prison adults versus residential adults). Each group's performance on each test item as well as within the test's dimensions was contrasted.

Results: The authors reduced the DCI to 54 items by combing the IRT invariance test results with data from a companion factor analytic study, resulting in a more sharply focused instrument. All of the test's 17 dimensions (9 reflecting aspects of the community environment and 8 reflecting aspects of personal development) were retained.

Conclusion: The DCI has evidence for construct invariance and can be reliably employed for assessing specific dimension. Both study objectives are met, although continued validity-related research is needed.

Questions:

1. What is the unique measurement advantage of using a heterogeneous sample of respondents to develop an instrument, as in this study?
2. What is the meaning of "sharply focused instrument" in this case? How is that an advantage to measurement using an IRT approach?
3. Given the focus of IRT on latent traits for individuals, how is the use of IRT more useful that other approaches to examining construct invariance in behavioral health assessments?

the ability continuum (Fisher et al., 1995; Fisher et al., 1997); use of IRT-based measures in rehabilitation treatment planning and programming with various inpatient care facilities (Harvey et al., 1992); and construct equivalence across instruments and samples (Bode et al., 2003; Fisher, 1997; Stineman et al., 1996). Research on the use of IRT-constructed measures also has evaluated the reliability of rehabilitation outcome measure training systems (Granger, Deutsch, & Linn, 1998; Turner et al., 1999).

Studies by Fisher et al. (1995) and Bode et al. (2003) demonstrated that IRT-based measures could be used across disability types due to their group independence (as discussed previously). The research by Bode et al. exemplifies this line of research. Bode et al. investigated the utility of the Medical Outcomes Study 36-Item Short Form Health Survey (SF-36) for measuring physical functioning in four groups of patients who differed by illness: cancer (399), HIV/AIDS (328), stroke (328), and multiple sclerosis (433). They concluded that the SF-36 could be reliably used to assess health and well-being with people with diverse chronic illness or disability.

Issues for Research and Other Forms of Scholarship

The *Standards for Educational and Psychological Testing* (American Educational Research Association, American Psychological Association, National Council for Measurement in Education, 1999) cites a number of relevant general concerns with testing as well as some that more specifically involve computers and IRT (cf. Standard 13.18). Many such issues center on *construct-irrelevant variance.* This term means that the test measures variables other than those it is designed and intended to assess. These variables are irrelevant to the interpreted construct and thus contribute to error.

For example, if an examinee is unfamiliar with computers or especially nervous about taking a test via computer, then the process of navigating through a test while using a screen, a mouse, and a keyboard introduces qualities irrelevant to what is being assessed, thus interferes with the accuracy of the assessment, and thus contributes to construct-irrelevant variance. The examinee's score will differ from what it would be without this added irrelevant variance. Therefore, should this occur, the examinee's score cannot be interpreted properly. This is an important consideration for those engaged in rehabilitation work (e.g., identifying compensatory skill).

CAT can be an enormously valuable administrative tool if these and related concerns can be addressed properly. The ability estimates it provides are more accurate because each test is uniquely suited to that examinee, and item parameter estimates are refined constantly.

Professionals involved in rehabilitation and other heath care systems increasingly will use IRT-based tests as technology advances and practical issues associated with their use are resolved. However, fewer studies have considered rehabilitation outcome measurement from the perspective of the patient or person with a disability (Heinemann, Bode, Cichowski, & Kan, 1998; Ozer & Kroll, 2002), even though provider and patient views about what constitutes significant functional change often differ (Djikers, 2003; Kane, Rockwood, Finch, & Philip, 1997). Furthermore, the transition points that herald clinically significant changes in health and well-being in acute care settings and that also predict successful psychosocial functioning are unknown for many measures used in rehabilitation and health settings (Bajo, Hazan, Fleminger, & Taylor, 1999; Samsa et al., 1999). These transition markers (also called *pivot points*) are important for monitoring client rehabilitation progress or response to rehabilitation therapies (Gurka et al., 1999).

In reference to quality improvement care, interest by health service providers to collect and use data on patient experiences for quality care improvement is increasing (Asch et al., 2006; Davies & Cleary, 2005; Davis, Schoenbaum, & Audet, 2005; Institute of Health Improvement, 2006; Swenson et al., 2004). However, patient-centered care surveys currently are limited in that they mistakenly treat the concrete counts of indicators of quality of care (e.g., response choices on patient experience items) as abstract measures of amount. They were developed based on CCT models of measurement. Thus, the use of these measures assumes that the respondents use every scale point and that there is a ratio (e.g., that a score of "4" is twice the value of a score of "2" on a 4-point Likert scale) or an equal interval across the scale points. In real terms, response options are used inconsistently for specific items in a scale so that the scale in fact is made up of items that essentially function on a different scale. This situation arises from the fact that response categories and item scores are not necessarily the same thing. The analysis of data from most CCT-developed tests makes little or no use of this information so that little is known about the distribution of patient health care experiences.

Achieving metric equivalence of health care measures using IRT modeling would enable comparative analysis of health care qualities by patient characteristics, add to our understanding of patient-centered care as a quality improvement construct, and enhance the quality of evaluations of interventions aimed at quality care improvement (see also chapter 7).

IRT measures have the potential to help identify sources of disparities in patient experiences of care influenced by the patient's service environment and patient personal and group membership attributes (e.g., social class, gender, race/ethnicity). Measures developed using IRT are objective in the sense of measuring the same attribute with precision regardless of group membership (Embretson & Reise, 2000). Items could be identified to enable quality of care comparisons by patient and service environment attributes known to influence health status.

Summary and Conclusion

IRT is a method of scoring tests that does not rely solely upon number-correct scoring. Instead, characteristics of the test stimuli (e.g., the questions, whether multiple-choice, performance such as relearning to speak or walk, or some other form) are considered. These item characteristics are matched to an examinee using a search routine to locate an accurate estimate of the examinee's proficiency. Imaginably, the mathematics of this process is complex and requires persons with training in psychometrics to accommodate it. Further, computers are used in the IRT algorithms. Computers, too, can be employed in administering the assessment, using an IRT CAT process. The primary advantages of IRT CAT are that the assessment is tailored to an individual (rather than all examinees receiving the same test) and that the proficiency estimates (the final score) are more accurate. Both advantages are important for those engaged in rehabilitation counseling.

As CAT grows in popularity and availability, one may anticipate that persons in rehabilitation work also will find increasing contact with IRT CAT. The trend of increased use of IRT methodology will continue.

Finally, as professionals engaged in rehabilitation seek ever-more sophisticated means to gather information about their clients, IRT and IRT-based CAT are likely to be used more commonly.

References

American Educational Research Association, American Psychological Association, National Council for Measurement in Education. (1999). *Standards for educational and psychological testing.* Washington, DC: American Educational Research Association.

Andrich, D. (2003). On the distribution of measurements in units that are not arbitrary. *Social Science Information, 42,* 557–589.

Asch, S. M., Kerr, E. A., Keesey, J., Adams, J. L., Setodji, C. M., Malik, S., et al. (2006). Who is at greatest risk of receiving poor-quality health care? *New England Journal of Medicine, 354*(11), 1147–1156.

Bajo, A., Hazan, J., Fleminger, S., & Taylor, R. (1999). Rehabilitation on a cognitive behavioral unit is associated with changes in FAM, not FIM. *Neuropsychological Rehabilitation, 3/4,* 413–419.

Bode, R. K., Lai, J., Cella, D., & Heinemann, A. W. (2003). Issues in the development of an item bank. *Archives of Physical Medicine and Rehabilitation, 84,* 52–60.

Carroll, J. B. (1950). Problems in the factor analysis of tests with varying difficulty. *American Psychologist, 5,* 369–375.

Cella, D., & Chang, C. (2000). A discussion of item response theory and its applications in health status assessment. *Medical Care, 38,* 11–72.

Crewe, N. M., & Athelstan, G. T. (1981). Functional assessment in vocational rehabilitation: A systematic approach to diagnosis and goal setting. *Archives of Physical Medicine and Rehabilitation, 62,* 299–305.

Davies, E., & Cleary, P. D. (2005). Hearing the patient's voice? Factors affecting the use of patient survey data in quality improvement. *Quality and Safety in Health Care, 14*(6), 428–432.

Davis, K., Schoenbaum, G., & Audet, A. J. (2005). A 2020 vision of patient-centered primary care. *Journal of General Internal Medicine, 20*(10), 953–957.

Djikers, M. P. (2003). Individualization in quality of life measurement: Instruments and approaches. *Archives of Physical Medicine and Rehabilitation, 84,* 3–14.

Embretson, S. E., & Reise, S. P. (2000). *Item response theory for psychologists.* Mahwah, NJ: Lawrence Erlbaum Associates.

Ferguson, G. A. (1942). Item selection by constant process. *Psychometrika, 7,* 19–29.

Fisher, W. P. (1997). Physical disability construct convergence across instruments: Towards a universal metric. *Journal of Outcomes Measurement, 1,* 87–113.

Fisher, W. P. (1999). Foundations for health status metrology: The stability of MOS, SF-36, PF-10 calibrations across samples. *Journal of the Louisiana State Medical Society, 151,* 566–578.

Fisher, W. P., Harvey, R. F., Taylor, P., Kilgore, K. M., & Kelly, C. K. (1995). Rehabits: A common language of functional assessment. *Archives of Physical Medicine & Rehabilitation, 76,* 113–122.

Fisher, W. P., Eubanks, R. L., & Marier, R. L. (1997). Equating the MOS, SF-36 and the LSU HIS physical functioning scales. *Journal of Outcomes Measurement, 1,* 329–362.

Granger, C. V., Deutsch, A., & Linn, R. T. (1998). Rasch analysis of the Functional Independence Measure (FIM) Mastery Test. *Archives of Physical Medicine and Rehabilitation, 79,* 52–57.

Gurka, J. A., Felmingham, K. L., Baguley, I. J., Schotte, D. E., Crooks, J., & Marosszeky, J. E. (1999). Utility of the Functional Assessment Measure after discharge from inpatient rehabilitation. *Journal of Head Trauma and Rehabilitation, 14,* 247–256.

Harvey, R. F., Silverstein, B., Venzon, M. A., Kilgore, K. M., Fisher, W. P., Steiner, M., et al. (1992). Applying psychometric criteria to functional assessment in medical rehabilitation: III. Construct validity and predicting level of care. *Archives of Physical Medicine and Rehabilitation, 73,* 887–892.

Hawley, C. A., Taylor, R., Hellawell, D. J., & Pentland, B. (1999). Use of the functional assessment measure (FIM + FAM) in head injury rehabilitation: A psychometric analysis. *Journal of Neural Psychiatry, 67,* 749–754.

Hays, R. D., Morales, L. S., & Reise, S. (2000). Item response theory and health outcomes measurement in the 21-st century. *Medical Care, 38,* 28–42.

Heinemann, A. W., Bode, R., Cichowski, K. C., & Kan, E. (1998). Measuring patient satisfaction with medical rehabilitation. In E. A. Dobrzykowski (Ed.), *Essential readings in rehabilitation outcomes measurement: Application, methodology, and technology* (pp. 92–103). Gaithersburg, MD: Aspen.

Heinemann, A. W., & Hamilton, B. B. (2000). Relation of rehabilitation intervention to functional outcome. *Journal of Rehabilitation Outcome Measures, 4,* 18–21.

Institute of Health Improvement. (2006). Patient-centered care: General. Retrieved April 19, 2006, from: http://www.ihi.org/IHI/Topics/PatientCenteredCare/PatientCenteredCare General/

Kane, R., Rockwood, T., Finch, M., & Philip, I. (1997). Consumer and professional ratings of the importance of functional status components. *Health Care Financing Review, 19,* 11–22.

Kilgore, K. M., Fisher, W. P., Silverstein, B., Harley, J. P., & Harvey, R. F. (1993). Application of Rasch analysis to the Patient Evaluation Conference System. *Physical Medicine and Rehabilitation Clinics of North America, 4,* 493–515.

Lawley, D. N. (1943). On problems connected with item selection and test construction. *Recordings of the Royal Society of Edinburgh, 61,* 273–287.

Linn, R. T., Blair, R. S. Granger, C. V., Harper, D. W., O'Hara, D. W., & Maciura, E. (1999). Does the Functional Assessment Measure (FAM) extend the Functional Independence Measure (FIM) instrument? A Rasch analysis of stroke inpatients. *Journal of Outcome Measurement, 3,* 339–359.

Lord, F. M. (1952). *A theory of test scores. Psychometric Monograph No. 7.* Psychometric Society.

McHorney, C. A., & Cohen, A. S. (2000). Equating health status measures with item response theory: Illustrations with functional status items. *Medical Care, 38,* S43–59.

Mpofu, E., Caldwell, L., Smith, E., Flisher, A. J., Mathews, C., Wegner, L., et al. (2006). Rasch modeling of the structure of health risk behavior in South African adolescents. *Journal of Applied Measurement, 7,* 323–334.

Orlando, M., Wenzel, S. L., Ebener, P., Edwards, M. C., Mandell, W., & Becker, K. (2006). The dimensions of change in therapeutic community treatment instrument. *Psychological Assessment, 18*(1), 118–122.

Ozer, M. N., & Kroll, T. (2002). Patient centered rehabilitation: Problems and opportunities. *Critical Review in Physical and Rehabilitation Medicine, 14,* 273–289.

Rasch, G. (1960). *Probabilistic models for some intelligence and attainment tests.* Copenhagen: Denmark Pedogogiske Institute. (Reprinted in 1980, Chicago: University of Chicago Press.)

Samsa, G., Edelman, D., Rothman, M. I., Williams, G. R., Lipscomb, J., & Matchar, D. (1999). Determining clinically important differences in health status measurement: A general approach with illustrations to the Health Utilities Index mark II. *Pharmacoeconomics, 15,* 141–155.

Silverstein, B., Fisher, W. P., Kilgore, K. M., Harley, J. P., & Harvey, R. F. (1992). Applying psychometric criteria to functional assessment in medical rehabilitation: II. Defining interval measures. *Archives of Physical Medicine and Rehabilitation, 73,* 507–518.

Stineman, M. G., Shea, J. A., Jette, A., Tassoni, C. J., Ottenbacher, K. J., Fiedler, R., et al. (1996). The Functional Independence Measure: Tests of scaling assumptions, structure and reliability across 20 diverse impairment categories. *Archives of Physical Medicine and Rehabilitation, 77,* 1101–1108.

Swenson, S. L., Buell, S., Zettler, P., White, M., Ruston, D. C., & Lo, B. (2004). Patient-centered communication: Do patients really prefer it? *Journal of General Internal Medicine, 19*(11), 1069–1079.

Tesio, L., & Cantagallo, A. (1998). The functional Assessment measure (FAM) in closed traumatic brain injury outpatients: A Rasch based psychometric study. *Journal of Outcome Measurement, 2*(2), 79–96.

Testa, M. A. (2000). Interpretation of quality of life outcomes: Issues that affect magnitude and meaning. *Medical Care, 38,* 166–174.

Thurstone, L. L. (1925). A method of scaling psychological and educational tests. *Journal of Educational Psychology, 16,* 412–433.

Turner-Stokes, L., Nyein, K., Turner-Stokes, T., & Gatehouse, C. (1999). The UK FIM+FAM: Development and evaluation. *Clinical Rehabilitation, 13,* 277–287.

Vickers, A. J. (2003). Statistical considerations for use of composite health-related quality-of-life scores in randomized trails. *Quality of Life Research, 13,* 717–723.

Ware, J. E., Bjorner, J. B., & Kosinski, M. (2000). Practical implications of item response theory and computerized testing. *Medical Care, 14,* 73–82.

Ware, J., Gandek, B., Sinclair, S., & Bjorner, J. B. (2005). Item response theory and computerized adaptive testing: Implications for outcomes measurement in rehabilitation. *Rehabilitation Psychology, 50*(1), 71–78.

Wright, B. D., & Stone, M. H. (1979). *Best test design.* Chicago: Mesa.

Real and Virtual Tools for Objectively Measuring Function During Everyday Activities

Gitendra Uswatte
Maria T. Schultheis

6

Overview

The World Health Organization's (WHO) International Classification of Functioning, Disability, and Health (ICF) characterizes human health into two super domains: (a) Body Functions and Structures and (b) Activities and Participation. Rehabilitation consumers, health care professionals, and payors generally believe improvements in activities and participation constitute the most important outcome (Keith, 1995; Uswatte & Taub, 2005). Behaviors in this domain traditionally have been assessed using performance tests administered in laboratory or clinic settings. However, behaviors observed and tested in these settings may be considerably different from those displayed in daily life settings (Uswatte & Taub, 2005). Thus, there is a need to directly assess activities outside of the treatment setting, especially with respect to use of impaired body parts and structures. This chapter outlines research and practice in the use of real and virtual world tools for measuring function during everyday activities.

Learning Objectives

By the end of the chapter, the reader should be able to:

1. Explain the importance of assessing function directly in daily life;
2. Describe the shortcomings of self-report instruments;
3. Discuss the use of accelerometers to measure upper-extremity function outside the laboratory after stroke;
4. Outline the advantages and challenges of using virtual reality–based driving simulation systems to assess driving in health care consumers with acquired brain injury; and
5. Evaluate real and virtual world tools for use in the design of rehabilitation interventions for everyday functioning.

Introduction

Although functional independence (i.e., how much assistance a rehabilitation consumer needs from others or devices to accomplish important activities of daily living [ADL]) is a valuable outcome, measures of functional independence (see chapter 23 for a discussion of functional independence measures) are relatively insensitive to differences in the actual function of a body structure in daily life (Uswatte & Taub, 2005). Knowledge of the actual function of a body structure in daily life is becoming increasingly salient given recent breakthroughs in rehabilitation and neuroscience that suggest forthcoming treatments for restoring function of a body structure, thus supplanting current efforts to teach consumers how to compensate for an impairment by using other intact body structures (Taub, Uswatte, & Elbert, 2002). Most measures of function in daily life rely on self-report, which may be limiting (Uswatte & Taub, 2005).

This chapter presents two models for objectively measuring the actual function of body structures in daily life. The first employs accelerometers—sensors that monitor movement to assess how much consumers after stroke use their affected arm outside of the treatment setting. The second employs driving simulators to assess how well consumers drive after brain injury. The use of virtual reality technology permits health care professionals to safely approximate real-world circumstances. Accurate measurement of real-world function of body structures permits clinicians and researchers to identify treatments that make the largest differences in the daily lives of consumers.

A Theory of Excess Motor Deficit

Research with monkeys from whose forelimbs somatic sensation had been surgically abolished has shown that, following injury to the nervous system, chronic disuse of a body part or function frequently exceeds what is warranted by damage to the physiological structures (Taub, 1977). Excess motor deficits are more likely when (a) organic damage results in an initial inability to use a body part, resulting in an animal being punished (by failure) when attempting to use that part of the body and rewarded for use of other parts of the body, and b) slow recovery of the organic damage permits the animal to recover the physical ability to use that body part, while leaving the conditioned suppression of use that developed during the acute phase in place. This type of motor deficit, termed *learned nonuse* (Taub, 1977), may be overcome by repetitive practice of use of the impaired body part or function. Such repetitive practice counter-conditions the behavior learned during the acute phase. These findings have important implications for the treatment and measurement of motor impairment in humans after central nervous system (CNS) damage and other injuries (Taub, 1980; Taub & Uswatte, 2000).

Some portion of a motor disability may be associated with a learning process that may be reversed many months or even years after the initial injury by the application of an appropriate technique, leading to a substantial improvement in the use of an extremity. Moreover, the adult CNS has the capacity for substantial plasticity (Taub et al., 2002). The University of Alabama at Birmingham's (UAB) Constraint-Induced Therapy Research Group has developed and tested a new family of rehabilitation techniques, known as constraint-induced (CI) movement therapy, or CI therapy, based on knowledge of this plasticity and counter-conditioning learned nonuse (Taub & Uswatte, 2006; Taub et al., 1993). The treatment to rehabilitate affected-arm use in stroke survivors with mild-to-moderate hemiparesis may be the most well-known intervention in this family. The three main components of this treatment are: intensive training of affected-arm use on functional tasks for several hours per day for 10 consecutive weekdays, physically restricting use of the unaffected arm by placing the unaffected hand and wrist in a protective safety mitt, and the use of behavioral techniques (e.g., behavioral contracting, self-monitoring, problem-solving) designed to transfer gains from the treatment to real-world settings (Taub et al., 2006).

Estimates of rehabilitation outcome should consider that the spontaneous use of a body structure in natural settings may differ considerably from their impairment and use when assessed in laboratory or clinical settings. Large discrepancies may exist between *ability* and *actual behavior* due to the presence of learned nonuse as well as other factors (Uswatte & Taub, 1999). Reliance on information impacted by learned nonuse may underestimate deficits in behavior (Uswatte & Taub, 1999; Uswatte et al., 2000), resulting in grossly under-treating deficits displayed in more natural environments (i.e., activities and participation in the ICF model). Evidence for learned nonuse is discussed in the following section.

Limb Nonuse After Somatosensory Deafferentation in Monkeys

When a single forelimb is deafferented in a monkey, the animal does not make use of it in the free situation (Knapp, Taub, & Berman, 1963; Mott & Sherrington, 1895). Several converging lines of evidence (Taub, 1977, 1980), suggest that nonuse of a single deafferented limb is a learned response that involves a conditioned suppression of movement.

As a background for this explanation, substantial neurological injury usually leads to a depression in motor and/or perceptual function. Recovery processes then come into operation so that, after a period of time, functional movements may be accomplished successfully. In monkeys, the initial period of depressed function lasts from 2–6 months following forelimb deafferentation (Taub, 1977; Taub & Berman, 1968). Thus, immediately after an operation, monkeys cannot use a deafferented limb, resulting in a long period of recovery from the initial depression of physical function. An animal with one deafferented limb typically tries unsuccessfully to use that extremity in the immediate postoperative situation. The animal generally can function somewhat well in a laboratory environment on three limbs and therefore is positively reinforced for this pattern of behavior, resulting in its being strengthened. Moreover, continued attempts to use the deafferented limb often lead to painful and otherwise aversive consequences, including incoordination and falling, loss of food objects, and failure of other activities attempted with the deafferented limb. These aversive consequences condition the animal to avoid using their deafferented limb, resulting in the failure by the monkey to learn that the limb has become potentially useful several months after the operation. In addition, following stroke and presumably after extremity deafferentation, the size of the cortical representation of the affected limb is markedly contracted (Liepert, Bauder, Miltner, Taub, & Weiller, 2000). This may help explain why persons, following stroke, often report movement of the hemiparetic arm is effortful. The three processes of punishment of use of the deafferented limb, reinforcement of use of the intact limb only, and plastic brain reorganization (see Figure 6.1) interact to produce a vicious spiral downward that results in a normally permanent "learned nonuse" of the affected extremity (Taub et al., 2002).

6.1

Schematic model of development of learned nonuse.

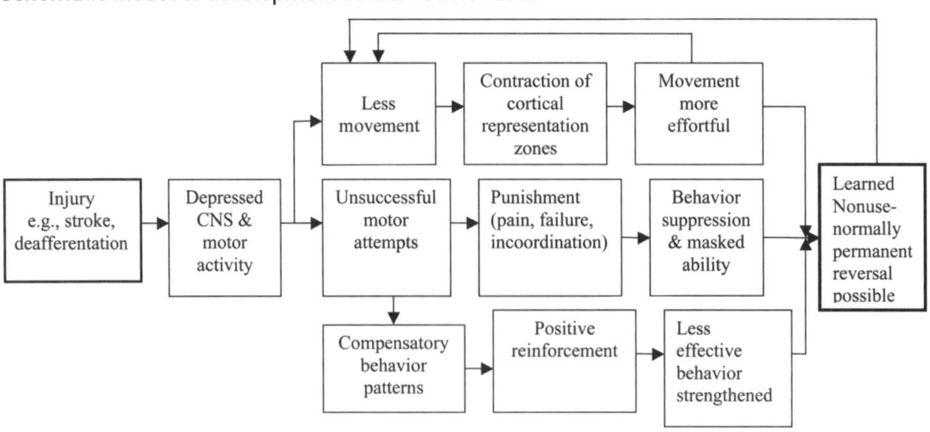

Note: CNS = central nervous system.

Learned nonuse of a deafferented limb can be overcome by either intensive training of the deafferented extremity, particularly by the operant conditioning technique termed *shaping*, or by continuous restraint of the intact limb over a period of a week or more (Taub, 1977). Both procedures have the effect of changing the contingencies of reinforcement for the use of the affected extremity (see Figure 6.2). For example, when the movements of the intact limb are restricted several months after unilateral deafferentation, the animal either uses the deafferented limb or it cannot with any degree of efficiency feed itself, walk, or carry out a large portion of its normal activities of daily life. This dramatic change in motivation overcomes the learned nonuse of the deafferented limb. If the movement restriction device remains on for several days or longer, use of the deafferented limb acquires strength and then is able to compete successfully with the very well-learned habit of learned nonuse of that limb in the free situation. As noted, other effective means of rehabilitating use of the deafferented limb are conditioned response and shaping techniques (summarized in Taub, 1977). The conditioned response and shaping techniques, similar to the restriction of the intact limb, also involve major alterations in the contingencies of reinforcement; the animal must use its deafferented limb or forego food or other reinforcements. Although the monkeys show some improvement in dexterity of movement with the deafferented limb subsequent to application of these techniques, the most striking gain in motor function is how much animals spontaneously use their deafferented limb in their everyday normal environments.

Evidence for Nonuse after Stroke and Other Injuries in Humans

The poor transfer of rehabilitation gains made in the clinical setting to daily life is a source of frustration for many rehabilitation professionals. However,

6.2

Schematic model of mechanism for overcoming learned nonuse.

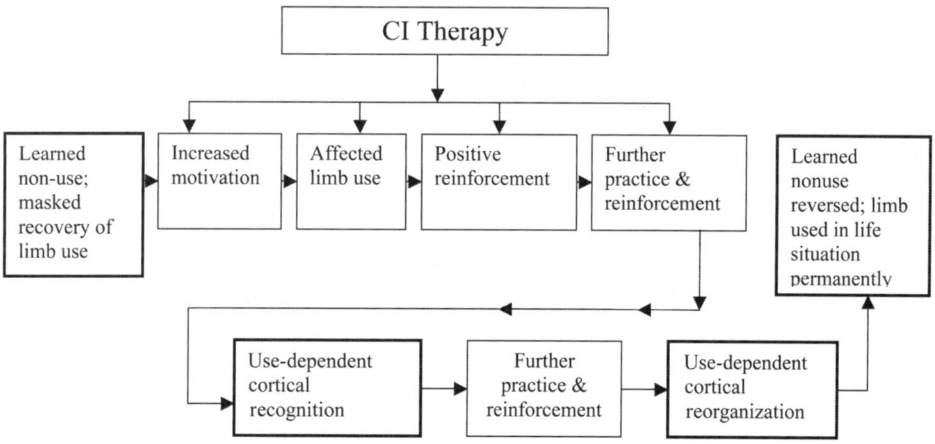

Note: CI = constraint-induced movement.

research rarely examines discrepancies between potential and actual motor ability of an extremity as seen in clinical and normal life situations. A notable exception is a study of 29 consecutive admissions to a day hospital program in a department of geriatric medicine (Andrews & Stewart, 1979). Among the patients, 25% to 45% performed ADL less well in the home than in the hospital.

Data from a study of 11 chronic stroke patients with mild to moderate motor impairment of their more-affected arm enrolled in a clinical trial of CI therapy support these findings (Taub, Uswatte, & Pidikiti, 1999). Prior to treatment, there was no association between motor ability tested in the laboratory and real-world arm function (Uswatte et al., 2000). A separate study of 10 chronic stroke patients with a similar degree of motor impairment found they did not spontaneously use their more impaired arm to help perform 25% of the bilateral upper-extremity tasks tested, even though they performed the tasks in a similar length of time when *asked* to perform them using both arms (Uswatte & Taub, 2005).

As noted previously, the theory of learned nonuse is based on the observation that, after neurological injury, the amount of use of the more affected extremity displayed in daily life activities is often less than that warranted by the level of motor impairment. This theory also is consistent with the effect of CI therapy on motor ability and daily life motor functions. For example, an effect size (d') of 3.3 was found for gains in use of the more-impaired arm in daily life, as measured by a structured interview, across several CI therapy studies in persons with chronic stroke with mild to moderate motor deficits (Taub et al., 1999). The magnitude of the improvement in more-impaired arm motor ability assessed by a motor test carried out in the laboratory setting was .9. A d' of .57 is considered to reflect a large effect size (Cohen, 1988). Thus, although the effect size based on data acquired in the laboratory showed a large improvement, it was less than one-third of the effect size found in actual daily use (Taub et al., 1999). Similar differential effects of CI therapy on actual daily use of arm and motor ability have been observed in other studies with persons having similar motor deficits (Kunkel et al., 1999; Miltner, Bauder, Sommer, Dettmers, & Taub, 1999; Sterr et al., 2002), as well as those with more severe motor deficits (Taub et al., 1999). Furthermore, an index of learned nonuse before treatment, based on the difference between scores on an interview measure of real-world arm use and motor performance test of arm motor ability, predicts CI therapy outcome, $r\ (63) = .47, p < .001$ (Mark, Taub, Perkins, Gauthier, & Uswatte, 2008), while the individual components of this composite variable (i.e., actual use and motor ability considered separately) do not predict treatment outcome. These findings are consistent with CI therapy producing a greater treatment change in the learned reduction in spontaneous use of the more-impaired extremity as opposed to a deficit in motor ability per se.

Differences between functional activities that older community residents can do and actually perform has been described using data from the MacArthur Studies of Successful Aging (Glass, 1998). Among 78 low-functioning interviewees (mean age = 75) who reported that they could do heavy housework, 23% said that they did not do any heavy housework. Among 928 low- and high-functioning interviewees who reported no functional limitations, 30% reported levels of productive activity in the lowest third relative to all 1,354 interviewees. In cognitive rehabilitation, differences between performance on laboratory tests and actual behavior in daily life have been discussed in terms of ecological validity (e.g., Sbordone, 1996).

The learned nonuse model does not claim that, in general, there is no relationship between the amount of neural damage following stroke and the amount of motor function that is recovered on the more-affected side. However, the fact that some patients with a given lesion size and location recover more movement than other patients with stroke having similar lesions suggests that additional factors may impact recovery and motor use. The learned nonuse model also does not claim to provide a complete account of excess motor deficit (Uswatte & Taub, 2005). The term does not incorporate some modifiers (e.g., comorbidities or psychosocial support) that could potentially influence the extent of excess motor deficit. For example, the quality of social support (e.g., overprotective caregiving) may affect the functional independence of persons with stroke (Garraway, Akhtar, Hockey, & Prescott, 1980).

Case Study 6.1

BREAKING ONE ARM TO FIND ANOTHER ONE

A 55-year-old woman had severe paresis of her right (dominant) arm immediately after a stroke. She was unable to lift her right arm to a table top while sitting or open her right hand in the first week after stroke. However, by the third month after her stroke, she was able to lift her right arm above her head and was able to coordinate movements of her fingers, albeit in a clumsy fashion. Nevertheless, she continued to avoid using her right arm while engaged in daily life activities. In the fourth month, she fell and broke her left arm, which was placed in a cast for 6 weeks. She began to use her right arm again to accomplish daily tasks and continued to do so after the cast was removed from her left arm. She even noticed that the fingers on her right hand moved more dexterously.

Discussion Questions. How can you explain this seemingly miraculous recovery in real-world stroke affected-arm function? What may account for the increase in the dexterity of right-hand finger movement?

Real-World Measures of Arm Activity After Stroke

History of Arm Activity Assessment

A structured interview, the Motor Activity Log (MAL), was developed to provide a direct assessment of arm activity in daily life after stroke (Taub et al., 1993). During interviews, stroke survivors are asked to rate how much and how well they have used their affected-arm to accomplish 30 common ADL over a specified period (e.g., for the week prior to starting to rehabilitation). Examples of ADL tasks include opening a drawer, wiping off a kitchen countertop or other surface, and using a key to open a door (Uswatte, Taub, Morris, Light, &

Thompson, 2006). Rating scale values range from 0 (no use of the affected arm) to 5 (normal use, i.e., use of the affected arm that is as good as pre-stroke). The MAL Arm Use scale has adequate test–retest reliability, r (115) = .82 (Uswatte, Taub, et al., 2006), and its convergent validity has been demonstrated against other self-report measures of real-world arm function, correspondent MAL reports (Uswatte, Taub, Morris, Vignolo, & McCulloch, 2005; Uswatte, Taub, et al., 2006) and an objective measure of real-world arm movement (discussed later). Other instruments that assess arm function in daily life after stroke are the ABILHAND (Massimo Penta, Tesio, Arnould, Zancan, & Thonnard, 2001) and Stroke Impact Scale (Duncan et al., 1999).

On the ABILHAND, participants are asked to rate their difficulty in performing 23 bimanual ADL without assistance, irrespective of which arm they use, whether compensatory strategies are employed, and whether they actually display the ADL in their daily lives. However, there are several circumstances with respect to measuring rehabilitation outcome where affected-arm use and general manual ability may diverge, making the ABILHAND less valuable than the MAL as a measure of arm activity in daily life. For example, stroke survivors may make substantial gains in affected-arm motor ability and increase use of their affected-arm in daily life as a result of an upper-extremity intervention. However, unless these improvements pass a certain threshold, patients may not register gains on the ABILHAND (i.e., the improvements in affected-arm function, although substantial, may not be sufficient to surpass the efficiency of compensatory strategies for performing bimanual tasks that the patients employed prior to treatment). Conversely, stroke survivors may be taught compensatory strategies that substantially increase their ABILHAND scores (i.e., ability to perform bimanual tasks) but do not result in gains in affected-arm use. Additionally, stroke patients may make gains in their ability to perform bimanual tasks and not make full use of those gains in general manual ability in their daily lives.

The Hand Function scale of the Stroke Impact Scale (SIS; Duncan et al., 1999) requires participants to rate their difficulty in using their affected-arm to carry out five ADL. However, this approach shares one of the limitations of the ABILHAND. Stroke survivors may make gains in their ability to use their affected-arm and not make full use of those gains in their daily lives.

Although the MAL has good psychometric properties, confidence in this instrument is limited by the fact that it is susceptible to the types of bias and error common to self-report measures (e.g., inaccurate recall, demand characteristics, and experimenter bias). For example, participants may not be able to recall their arm use accurately or may modify their responses to please interviewers (an example of demand characteristics). Interviewers may subtly cue participants to give desirable responses (e.g., an example of experimenter bias). Given these limitations, the use of objective measures of arm activity in daily life is desirable.

History of Objective Measures of Physical Activity

Accelerometers are sensors that measure acceleration movement. Prior to work by Uswatte et al. (2000), accelerometers had been used in health research to measure overall levels of physical activity and, with these data, to estimate caloric expenditure. Four accelerometers were used to measure time spent ambulating, transferring, standing, sitting, and lying down in individuals with a transtibial amputation (Bussman, Reuvekamp, Veltink, Martens, & Stam, 1998). Three accelerometers were used to estimate energy expenditure in college students without any motor impairment (Melanson & Freedson, 1995). Other technologies (e.g., step counters and tilt counters) also have been used to measure overall physical activity (Tryon, 1991).

Objective, Accelerometer-Based Measures of Arm Activity

Accelerometry technology has been applied to measure arm activity in daily life after stroke (Uswatte et al., 2000). In this application, Actigraphs (Manufacturing Technologies Incorporated, 2001), which are plastic units about the size and weight of a large wristwatch, are worn proximal to the wrist on modified wristbands. Actigraphs contain a single piezoelectric crystal sensor (Uswatte et al., 2000) that deforms and produces a charge when it is subjected to acceleration. This charge is digitized at a 10 Hz sampling rate, summed over a user-specific time epoch, and reported as an activity count for each epoch (Tryon & Williams, 1996). For example, approximately 20 activity counts are recorded in response to a human arm movement (e.g., lifting a book from a stool 78 cm off the floor to a shelf 80 cm away in 1 second; Uswatte & Taub, 2005). The acceleration recordings are stored in the unit's RAM and can be downloaded to a PC using a computer interface reader unit. When a 2 second recording epoch is specified, the units can record continuously for approximately 72 hours (Uswatte & Taub, 2005). A more modern Actigraph has a higher sampling rate and longer recording period.

A series of studies showed these accelerometers provide an accurate, reliable, and stable measure of the duration of arm movement and that this parameter is a valid measure of arm use in daily life. A short recording epoch (2 sec) and a simple data transformation of the raw accelerometer recordings were used to obtain an accurate measure of the duration of extremity movement (Uswatte et al., 2000). The data transformation involves setting raw acceleration values above a low threshold to 1 and values below the threshold to 0. The number of 2-second epochs with a transformed value of 1, multiplied by two, represents the duration of movement in seconds. Using this "threshold-filter" approach, the accelerometer recordings gave a virtually perfect reflection of the duration of movement for each patient tested in two experiments, involving simple standardized movements performed repetitively along fixed tracks as well as complex ADL-like movements by normal subjects in the laboratory. The measurement error across ADL tasks using threshold-filtering accelerometer recordings from 12 persons was small; the average standard deviation across subjects was 3% of the mean (Uswatte et al., 2000).

Threshold-filtered accelerometer data from spontaneous behavior of healthy subjects and stroke patients have been compared to coded data of their movement from videotape using a reliable behavioral observation system (mean agreement between independent observers for duration of arm movement was 95%). Ten subjects wore a set of four accelerometers (one on each arm, the chest, and leg) and were videotaped while carrying out their usual activities at home (n = 5) or in an occupational therapy clinic (n = 5). Correlations between the threshold-transformed accelerometer values and observer coding of the duration of body part movements were significant: impaired arm, r (9) = 0.93; torso, r (9) = 0.93; ambulation, r (9) = 0.99 (Uswatte et al., 2000). Accelerometer recordings for 3 consecutive days were obtained from 9 upper-extremity CI therapy patients before and after 2 weeks of treatment and 9 stroke survivors in the community before and after a 2-week no-treatment period (Uswatte, Foo, et al., 2005). The CI therapy patients showed an increase in movement that was specific to the affected arm, while the no-treatment control group showed an increase in movement in all monitored body parts. One may expect changes in overall levels of physical activity would affect recordings from the affected- and unaffected-arm roughly equally. Thus, the ratio of affected- to unaffected-arm accelerometer recordings was examined as a measure of treatment outcome. The CI therapy patients showed a significant increase in this ratio, $d' = .9$, while the no-treatment controls did not, $d' = .3$. Thus, this ratio measure provides a responsive and stable measure of upper-extremity rehabilitation outcome. Test–retest reliability was supported by the finding that, for this ratio, the correlation between values from the two recording occasions in the no-treatment control group was high, $r = .88$. Data from a multisite trial of CI therapy (Wolf et al., 2006) confirm the reliability of the ratio measure, $r = .9$ (Uswatte, Giuliani, et al., 2006), and provide further support for its validity as an index of more-impaired arm activity in daily life. Using data from this large trial ($n = 169$), the ratio measure correlated with other measures of arm activity strongly (e.g., MAL, r [168] = .52, $p < .001$) and with a measure of mobility weakly (SIS Mobility scale, r [168] = .16, $p < .05$). However, affected-arm recordings alone were influenced by differences in levels of physical activity. Affected-arm recordings alone correlated moderately with both the MAL, r (168) = .41, $p < .001$, and SIS Mobility scale, r (168) = .32, $p < .001$.

An alternate system of uniaxial accelerometers (ULAM) for measuring upper-extremity movement has been developed by Schasfoort, Bussman, Zandbergen, and Stam (2003). It permits a breakdown of arm movement by type of overall physical activity (e.g., duration of arm movement during walking, sitting, or lying down). Although such information is desirable, it comes at the cost of a reduced recording period (24 hr) and more cumbersome (7 sensors connected by wires to a central recording unit), complex, and expensive equipment. In contrast, two accelerometers have been found to be adequate for the purpose of assessing whether rehabilitation has an effect on arm function outside the laboratory (Uswatte, Giuliani, et al., 2006). Complementary self-report measures such as the MAL, when used simultaneously with accelerometry, can provide rich information about the specific types of upper-extremity activities in which changes have occurred.

Virtual-World Measures of Driving Behaviors After Brain Injury

Importance of Virtual Reality Technology for Driving Rehabilitation

The application of virtual reality (VR) for driver rehabilitation can offer numerous unique and innovative advantages to the assessment and rehabilitation of

Discussion Box 6.1

CULTURE AND ACCELEROMETRY

A multisite trial of CI therapy (Wolf et al., 2006) revealed that African Americans had a significantly higher percentage of missing accelerometer data than European Americans (37% vs. 22%), $\chi^2 = 6, p < .05$ (Uswatte, Giuliani et al., 2006). All participants were asked to wear an accelerometer on each arm for 3 days outside the treatment setting both before and after CI therapy. Possible reasons for missing data were (a) errors in programming the accelerometers to record data, downloading data, or storing data; (b) participants wearing accelerometers for an insufficient time; (c) participants putting on only one unit or putting units on after the programmed recording period; (d) participants switching limb placement of units for part of the recording period; (e) recordings that did not appear veridical; and (f) recordings that clearly indicated accelerometer malfunction. The breakdown of reasons data were missing was similar for African American and European American participants, except that 10% of African Americans versus 1% of European Americans wore only one unit or made a similar mistake.

Discussion Questions:
What factors may have been responsible for the differential missing data rates in African American and European American participants? How may this disparity in data collection rates be remedied?

driving skills for persons with neurological compromise. Continuing advances in VR technology, along with concomitant system cost reductions, have supported the development of more usable, useful, and accessible VR systems. VR simulation, which typically involves hardware (e.g., head-mounted display, computer) and software elements, allows the presentation of 3-D interactive computer-generated environments that allow the user to "enter" and become immersed in these simulated environments. VR offers the potential to deliver systematic human testing and training environments that allow for the precise control of complex dynamic 3-D stimulus presentations, where sophisticated behavioral recording is possible. As such, VR offers the unique opportunity to obtain objective measurements of complex human behavior within relevant and functional environments. Furthermore, VR allows the presentation of varying levels and types of stimuli that can allow for the evaluation of challenging and potentially risky behaviors and situations, while maintaining user safety.

History of Virtual Reality Technology in Rehabilitation and Health Care

Although VR remains a developing technology, it is not a new method of assessment and treatment in health care. Various studies serve to document the successful integration of VR to myriad aspects of health care, including surgical training (Haluck, Marshall, Krummel, & Melkonian, 2001; Satava, 2001), education of patients and medical students (McCloy & Stone, 2001), and treatment of sensory mobility deficits (Burdea, Popescu, Hentz, & Colbert, 2000). VR treatment of psychological dysfunction, including anxiety disorders and phobia, also has been successful, including fear of flying and fear of heights (Emmelkamp, Bruynzeel, Drost, & van der Mast, 2001; Rothbaum, Hodges, Smith, Lee, & Price, 2000). VR treatment also has been applied to post-traumatic stress disorder (Rothbaum et al., 1999), eating disorders (Riva, 1997; Riva, Bacchetta, Baruffi, Rinaldi, & Molinari, 1999), and pain management (Hoffman, Patterson, & Carrougher, 2000; Sander Wint, Eshelman, Steele, & Guzzetta, 2002).

In rehabilitation medicine, VR has been integrated into physical (Burdea et al., 2000) and cognitive (Matheis et al., 2006; Rose, Brooks, & Rizzo, 2005) rehabilitation and for the evaluation and retraining of ADL (Christiansen et al., 1998; Zhang et al., 2003) and community ambulation (McComas, MacKay, & Pivik, 2002). VR applications to rehabilitation medicine also have been reviewed extensively (Gourlay, Lun, Lee, & Tay, 2000; Rizzo, Schultheis, Kerns, & Mateer, 2004; Rizzo, Schultheis, & Rothbaum, 2002; Schultheis & Rizzo, 2001). One specific rehabilitation application of VR, its use in driving assessment and retraining among clinical populations, has received a lot of attention from researchers and clinicians in the last decade (Liu, Miyazaki, & Watson, 1999; Schultheis & Mourant, 2001; Wald & Liu, 2001).

Virtual Reality and Driving Assessment

Driving is important for individuals with neurological compromise, their families, and health care professionals and constitutes a public safety issue. A need to ensure driver competence prior to returning to the roads is obvious. Unfortunately, current methods for driving assessment are fraught with limitations (Schultheis & Mourant, 2001). Specifically, current driver rehabilitation assessment protocols are limited to paper and pencil cognitive test, computerized tasks, driving simulators, or behind-the-wheel driving evaluations. To date, there is a lack of standardization as to what and how these measures are used to determine driving capacity after neurological compromise. VR driving simulation offers a variety of unique assets that could address many of the limitations of these measures. For example, computerized tasks typically are designed to target individual or component demands of driving and do not allow the simultaneous evaluation of interactions of various driving behaviors. Similarly, while driving simulators may offer more complex driving scenarios and more user interaction, they typically are unavailable to clinicians due to their high cost (for a complete review see Schultheis & Rizzo, 2001).

Research from Schultheis and coworkers (2005) has focused on the development and use of the VR-based driving simulation system (VRDS). The VRDS uses a head-mounted simulator that allows the user to "drive through" a specified route with a variety of driving zones (e.g., highway, residential, commercial, school). The virtual route takes approximately 30 minutes to traverse and offers the option to present a variety of challenging driving situations (e.g., a pedestrian suddenly crossing the street or speeding vehicles entering the highway). The VRDS automatically records four primary measures of driving behavior while the individual is driving through the route: the vehicle's speed, lane position, head turning position, and distance from target object (i.e., stop signs, traffic lights). These preliminary driving behaviors were selected based on prior VR programming experience (Mourant & Ge, 1999; Mourant, Tsai, Al-Shihabi, & Jaeger, 2001) and clinical experience. Additional driving performance measures can be calculated by combining the four primary output measures. Research with the VRDS has included both healthy normal drivers and individuals with neurological compromise (i.e., stroke, brain injury). Findings from these studies have provided insight into both the benefits and challenges of using this technology for driver assessment and rehabilitation.

The Benefits of VR Driving

VR's unique capacity to objectively measure driving performance in simulated challenging environments constitutes its most obvious benefit to driving

Research Box 6.1

MATCHING USERS AND TECHNOLOGY

The impact of the user-technology match commonly is overlooked when using innovative technologies to assess human performance. The following case is presented to highlight the importance of this consideration, in particular in the development of future clinical assessment tools.

Driver performance was examined using a new virtual reality driving simulator that relied on a head-mounted display (HMD). Specifically, the researchers believed the HMD allowed participants to better engage in the simulation by minimizing outside distractions. All participants were required to drive through a virtual driving route using the HMD unit. The researchers were examining behaviors at a stop sign, specifically whether individuals were scanning appropriately and the length of time they remained stopped at the signed intersection. Participants with a diagnosis of brain injury generally scanned less than participants without brain injury. The researchers preliminary conclusion was that drivers with brain injury were more likely to have scanning problems at stop sign intersections than those drivers without brain injury. Further analysis revealed greater subjective discomfort with the HMD in individuals with brain injury.

Discussion Questions:
How may the findings of subjective HMD comfort potentially influence the findings on group differences in scanning behavior? What other participant characteristics related to technology use may influence performance on the driving simulator? What are the potential ethical considerations in the development of new technologies without the inclusion of usability analysis (e.g., user-technology match, user-comfort)?

assessment. The benefits are twofold: It allows clinicians to observe objective and detailed responses made by the individual, and VR methods can collect these measures in both simple, nonchallenging conditions or during difficult, cognitively demanding, and potentially hazardous situations.

Most measures of driving capacity following neurological compromise remain limited to gross performance measures. The VRDS was used to demonstrate the use of VR driving simulators to measure more specific behaviors of driving (e.g., driving behaviors for managing a stop sign intersection). Stop sign management is at high risk among normal drivers and is likely to be higher among those with medically challenging conditions. Thus, specific measures of driving performance related to stop sign intersections were assessed using 15 drivers with acquired brain injury and 9 healthy controls (Schultheis et al., 2006). Both groups were matched on driving experience; the acquired brain injury group included only drivers who had regained driving privileges.

New driving performance measures included: full stop, distance from the stop sign, time at stop sign, approaching speed, and departing speed from the stop sign. Comparison of these measures found a pattern of improved performance with repeated exposure. Specifically, this was seen in two variables: a decreased frequency of no stops at the stop sign and the distance participants stopped from the stop sign as they progressed through the environment. As expected, both groups demonstrated atypical performance at initiation (Stop Sign 1). This was due to unfamiliarity with the VRDS and the virtual environment and a lack of depth and perceptual accommodation. Interestingly, while both groups showed learning patterns across the three stop sign intersections, the observed patterns differed for the two groups, with the acquired brain injury group showing greater difficulties.

A second auxiliary benefit of using a VRDS is its face validity. Specifically, because VR driving so closely resembles real-life driving, it often is well-received by patients, family members, and clinicians. In fact, a recent study attempted to quantify the overall user ratings regarding comfort and reception of the VRDS among individuals with stroke, brain injury, and healthy controls (Schultheis, Rebimbas, Mourant, & Millis, 2007). Results indicated that all three groups generally rated the use of the VRDS favorably, with healthy control providing the highest ratings, followed by brain injury users and stroke users.

Negative Aspects of Using VR Driving

One of the predominant negative side effects identified in VR exposure is simulation sickness. By definition, simulation sickness can include symptoms similar to those seen in motion sickness, including vertigo, dizziness, and headaches, but within a lesser degree of severity. For example, although an individual may experience nausea in simulator sickness, this rarely results in vomiting, a condition often seen in motion sickness. The occurrence of simulator sickness occurs at approximately the same frequency in clinical populations as in healthy control subjects, at a less then 20% occurrence rate (Nichols & Patel, 2002).

Preliminary analysis of the incidence of simulation sickness among a sample of 21 adults with brain injury, 15 adults with stroke, and 21 healthy controls indicated an unexpected high incidence in all three groups (Schultheis, Rebimbas, Mourant, & Millis, 2005). Specifically, there was a 32% incidence of simulation sickness in the entire sample, with a 24% incidence among the healthy control group, 30% among the traumatic brain injury group, and 46% among the stroke group. Thus, the use of VR driving simulation must occur cautiously. That is, VR driving simulation is not suitable for everyone, whether a clinical or nonclinical application. Although not severe in nature, simulation sickness is an adverse event that can leave an individual feeling uncomfortable for several hours. This fact underscores the need to ensure that the use of VR exposure is clinically validated and that the measures obtained from using this approach are safe, relevant, and useful for clinical decision making.

Limited attention has been paid to human–computer interactions, more specifically to the potential confounding factors of driving performance in a virtual environment. For example, the use of virtual environments with head-mounted displays is common practice and offers unique assets to the evaluation and therapy of clinical populations. However, research examining the effects of this technology on clinical populations is sparse. Understanding how wearers interact with the head-mounted displays is vital. Discomfort that leads to altered use of the head-mounted display could confound performance measures that may eventually be used as a tool for clinical decision making. A post-hoc analysis of the relationship between head-mounted display use and discomfort was conducted to examine potential contributing factors for a high incidence of simulator sickness in a head-mounted display–based driving simulator (Simone, Schultheis, Rebimbas, & Millis, 2006). Pearson correlation analysis was used to evaluate objective and subjective measures of head-mounted display performance and self-reported user comfort ratings. Correlations between these variables were weak, thus indicating the complexity of quantifying user discomfort and head-mounted display performance.

Some Outstanding Questions

While researchers and clinicians are recognizing the potential advantages offered to the area of driving rehabilitation, much work remains to be done before VR driving simulation can be viewed as a valid and viable method for determining driving capacity. In fact, VR technology has the potential to allow us to evaluate and treat various functional daily activities. Although the utility of the concept has been demonstrated, further validation work that addresses issues of user–computer interaction and identifies systems that minimize negative side effects (e.g., simulation sickness) is warranted. Results of current studies have identified both some of the positive and negative aspects of applying VR technology and directions for improving this technology.

Summary

Theory and data suggest that a substantial gap between what a person can do when tested in the clinical or laboratory setting and what they actually do at home can develop after neurological and other injuries. The conditions that support the development of such learned nonuse include an injury that results in an initial severe deficit in function that gradually resolves along with punishment of attempts to use the impaired function during the initial recovery period.

Relatively little attention has been paid to this aspect of recovery in rehabilitation and health care. Thus, this type of deficit largely has gone undiagnosed and untreated. This limitation can start to be remedied by developing methods for assessing actual function of an impaired body structure or function in daily life. A few self-report measures of this area of function have been developed. However, like other self-reports, they are subject to inaccurate recall, demand characteristics, and experimenter bias.

This chapter presented two models for objectively measuring actual function in daily life. The first was mounting accelerometers on stroke survivors' arms for 3 days outside the clinical setting to index arm use in daily life after stroke. The second was using a virtual reality driving simulator to evaluate driving behaviors in a clinical setting. The use of virtual reality here permits approximation of actual driving behaviors in a safe setting along with objective and highly quantitative metrics of driving behavior. These approaches may be extended to other areas, such as cognitive rehabilitation in which the ability of clients to report activity outside the laboratory accurately is likely to be even more severely compromised.

Author Note

Portions of this chapter, including the figures, are adapted from Uswatte, and Taub (2004). Implications of the learned nonuse formulation for measuring rehabilitation outcomes: Lessons from constraint-induced movement therapy. *Rehabilitation Psychology, 50,* 34–42. Copyright 2005 by the American Psychological Association. Adapted with permission.

Work on this chapter was supported by the American Heart Association Southeast Affiliate Grant 0365163B, James S. McDonnell Foundation Grant HD34273, National Institute of Disability and Rehabilitation Research Grant H133G050222, and National Institutes of Health Grants HD34273.

References

Andrews, K., & Stewart, J. (1979). Stroke recovery: He can but does he? *Rheumatology and Rehabilitation, 18,* 43–48.

Burdea, G., Popescu, V., Hentz, V., & Colbert, K. (2000). Virtual reality-based orthopedic telerehabilitation. *IEEE Transactions on Rehabilitation Engineering, 8,* 430–432.

Bussman, H., Reuvekamp, P., Veltink, P., Martens, W.L.J., & Stam, H. J. (1998). Validity and reliability of measurements obtained with an "Activity Monitor" in people with and without a transtibial amputation. *Physical Therapy, 78,* 989–998.

Christiansen, C., Abreu, B., Ottenbacher, K., Huffman, K., Masel, B., & Culpepper, R. (1998). Task performance in virtual environments used for cognitive rehabilitation after traumatic brain injury. *Archives of Physical Medicine and Rehabilitation, 79,* 888–892.

Cohen, J. (1988). *Statistical power analysis for the behavioral sciences* (2nd ed.). Hillsdale, NJ: Lawrence Erlbaum Associates.

Duncan, P. W., Wallace, D., Lai, S. M., Johnson, D., Embretson, S., & Laster, L. J. (1999). The stroke impact scale version 2.0. Evaluation of reliability, validity, and sensitivity to change. *Stroke, 30,* 2131–2140.

Emmelkamp, P. M., Bruynzeel, M., Drost, L., & van der Mast, C. A. (2001). Virtual reality treatment in acrophobia: A comparison with exposure in vivo. *Cyberpsychology & Behavior, 4,* 335–339.

Garraway, W. M., Akhtar, A. J., Hockey, L., & Prescott, R. J. (1980). Management of acute stroke in the elderly: Follow-up of a controlled trial. *British Medical Journal, 281,* 827–829.

Glass, T. A. (1998). Conjugating the "tenses" of function: Discordance among hypothetical, experimental, and enacted function in older adults. *The Gerontologist, 38,* 101–112.

Gourlay, D., Lun, K. C., Lee, Y. N., & Tay, J. (2000). Virtual reality for relearning daily living skills. *International Journal of Medicine and Information, 60,* 255–261.

Haluck, R. S., Marshall, R. L., Krummel, T. M., & Melkonian, M. G. (2001). Are surgery training programs ready for virtual reality? A survey of program directors in general surgery. *Journal of American College of Surgeons, 193,* 660–665.

Hoffman, H. G., Patterson, D. R., & Carrougher, G. J. (2000). Use of virtual reality for adjunctive treatment of adult burn pain during physical therapy: A controlled study. *Clinical Journal of Pain, 16,* 244–250.

Keith, R. A. (1995). Conceptual basis of outcome measures. *American Journal of Physical Medicine and Rehabilitation, 74,* 73–80.

Knapp, H. D., Taub, E., & Berman, A. J. (1963). Movements in monkeys with deafferented limbs. *Experimental Neurology, 7,* 305–315.

Kunkel, A., Kopp, B., Muller, G., Villringer, K., Villringer, A., Taub, E., et al. (1999). Constraint-Induced Movement therapy: A powerful new technique to induce motor recovery in chronic stroke patients. *Archives of Physical Medicine and Rehabilitation, 80,* 624–628.

Liepert, J., Bauder, H., Miltner, W.H.R., Taub, E., & Weiller, C. (2000). Treatment-induced cortical reorganization after stroke in humans. *Stroke, 31,* 1210–1216.

Liu, L., Miyazaki, M., & Watson, B. (1999). Norms and validity of the DriVR: A virtual reality driving assessment for persons with head injuries. *Cyberpsychology & Behavior, 2,* 53–67.

Manufacturing Technologies Incorporated. (2001). *Activity Monitor Model 7164 [Manual].* Shalimar, FL: Author.

Mark, V. W., Taub, E., Perkins, C., Gauthier, L., & Uswatte, G. (2008). MRI infarction load and CI therapy outcomes for chronic post-stroke hemiparesis. *Restorative Neurology and Neuroscience, 26,* 13–33.

Massimo Penta, I., Tesio, L., Arnould, C., Zancan, A., & Thonnard, J. (2001). The ABILHAND questionnaire as a measure of manual ability in chronic stroke patients. *Stroke, 32,* 1627–1634.

Matheis, R., Schultheis, M. T., Tierksy, L., DeLuca, J., Millis, S. R., & Rizzo, A. (2006). Is learning and memory in a virtual environment different? *The Clinical Neuropsychologist, 21,* 146–157.

McCloy, R., & Stone, R. (2001). Science, medicine, and the future. Virtual reality in surgery *British Medical Journal, 323,* 912–915.

McComas, J., MacKay, M., & Pivik, J. (2002). Effectiveness of virtual reality for teaching pedestrian safety. *Cyberpsychology & Behavior, 5,* 185–190.

Melanson, E. L., Jr., & Freedson, P. S. (1995). Validity of the Computer Science Applications, Inc. (CSA) activity monitor. *Medicine and Science in Sports and Exercise, 27,* 934–940.

Miltner, W.H.R., Bauder, H., Sommer, M., Dettmers, C., & Taub, E. (1999). Effects of Constraint-Induced Movement therapy on chronic stroke patients: A replication. *Stroke, 30,* 586–592.

Mott, F. W., & Sherrington, C. S. (1895). Experiments upon the influence of sensory nerves upon movement and nutrition of the limbs. *Proceedings of the Royal Society of London, 57,* 481–488.

Mourant, R. R., & Ge, Z. (1999). *Measuring attentional demand in a virtual environment driving simulator.* Paper presented at the 41st Annual Meeting of the Human Factors and Ergonomics Society, Albuquerque, New Mexico.

Mourant, R. R., Tsai, F., Al-Shihabi, T., & Jaeger, B. K. (2001). Measuring divided attention capability of young and older drivers. *Transportation Research Record, 1779,* 40–45.

Nichols, S., & Patel, H. (2002). Health and safety implications for virtual reality: A review of empirical evidence. *Applied Ergonomics, 33,* 251–271.

Riva, G. (1997). Virtual reality and the body experience: A new approach for the treatment of eating disorders. *Presence: Teleoperators and Virtual Environments, 6,* 106–117.

Riva, G., Bacchetta, M., Baruffi, M., Rinaldi, S., & Molinari, E. (1999). Virtual reality based experiential cognitive treatment of anorexia nervosa. *Journal of Behavioral Therapy and Experimental Psychiatry, 30,* 221–230.

Rizzo, A. A., Schultheis, M. T., Kerns, K., & Mateer, C. (2004). Analysis of assets for virtual reality applications in neuropsychology. *Neuropsychological Rehabilitation, 14,* 207–239.

Rizzo, A. A., Schultheis, M. T., & Rothbaum, B. O. (2002). Ethical issues for the use of virtual reality in the psychological sciences. In S. Bush & M. Drexler (Eds.), *Ethical issues in clinical neuropsychology* (pp. 243–279). Lisse, Netherlands: Swets & Zeitlinger Publishers.

Rose, F., Brooks, B., & Rizzo, A. (2005). Virtual reality in brain damage rehabilitation: A review. *Cyberpsychology and Behavior, 8,* 241–262.

Rothbaum, B. O., Hodges, L. F., Alarcon, R., Ready, D., Shahar, F., Graap, K., et al. (1999). Virtual reality exposure therapy for PTSD Vietnam Veterans: A case study. *Journal of Traumatic Stress, 12,* 263–272.

Rothbaum, B. O., Hodges, L., Smith, S., Lee, J. H., & Price, L. (2000). A controlled study of virtual reality exposure therapy for the fear of flying. *Journal of Consulting and Clinical Psychology, 68,* 1020–1026.

Sander Wint, S., Eshelman, D., Steele, J., & Guzzetta, C. E. (2002). Effects of distraction using virtual reality glasses during lumbar punctures in adolescents with cancer. *Oncology Nursing Forum, 29,* E8–E15.

Satava, R. M. (2001). Surgical education and surgical simulation. *World Journal of Surgery, 25,* 1484–1489.

Sbordone, R. J. (1996). Ecological validity: Some critical issues for the neuropsychologist. In R. J. Sbordone (Ed.), *Ecological validity of neuropsychological testing* (pp. 15–42). Delray Beach, FL: GR Press/St. Lucie Press.

Schasfoort, F. C., Bussman, J.B.J., Zandbergen, A.M.A.J., & Stam, H. J. (2003). Impact of upper limb complex regional pain syndrome type 1 on everyday life measured with a novel upper limb-activity monitor. *Pain, 101,* 79–88.

Schultheis, M. T., & Mourant, R. R. (2001). Virtual reality and driving: The road to better assessment of cognitively impaired populations. *Presence: Teleoperators and Virtual Environments, 10,* 436–444.

Schultheis, M. T., Rebimbas, J., Mourant, R., & Millis, S. R. (2005). Examining the usability of a virtual reality driving simulator. *Archives of Physical Medicine and Rehabilitation, 86,* e12.

Schultheis, M. T., Rebimbas, J., Mourant, R., & Millis, S. R. (2007). Examining the usability of a virtual reality driving simulator. *Assistive Technologies, 19,* 1–8.

Schultheis, M. T., & Rizzo, A. A. (2001). The application of virtual reality technology for rehabilitation. *Rehabilitation Psychology, 46,* 296–311.

Schultheis, M. T., Simone, L. K., Roseman, E., Nead, R., Rebimbas, J., & Mourant, R. (2006). Stopping behavior in a VR driving simulator: A new clinical measure for the assessment of driving? *IEEE Engineering in Medicine & Biological Science, 1,* 4921–4924.

Simone, L., Schultheis, M. T., Rebimbas, J., & Millis, S. R. (2006). Head mounted displays for clinical virtual reality applications: Pitfalls in understanding user behavior while using technology. *CyberPsychology & Behavior, 9,* 591–602.

Sterr, A., Elbert, T., Berthold, I., Kölbel, S., Rockstroh, B., & Taub, E. (2002). Longer versus shorter daily Constraint-Induced Movement therapy of chronic hemiparesis: An exploratory study. *Archives of Physical Medicine and Rehabilitation, 83,* 1374–1377.

Taub, E. (1977). Movement in nonhuman primates deprived of somatosensory feedback. In *Exercise and sports science reviews* (Vol. 4, pp. 335–374). Santa Barbara, CA: Journal Publishing Affiliates.

Taub, E. (1980). Somatosensory deafferentation research with monkeys: Implications for rehabilitation medicine. In L. P. Ince (Ed.), *Behavioral psychology in rehabilitation medicine: Clinical applications* (pp. 371–401). New York: Williams & Wilkins.

Taub, E., & Berman, A. J. (1968). Movement and learning in the absence of sensory feedback. In S. J. Freedman (Ed.), *The neuropsychology of spatially oriented behavior* (pp. 173–192). Homewood, IL: Dorsey Press.

Taub, E., Miller, N. E., Novack, T. A., Cook, E. W., III, Fleming, W. C., Nepomuceno, C. S., et al. (1993). Technique to improve chronic motor deficit after stroke. *Archives of Physical Medicine and Rehabilitation, 74,* 347–354.

Taub, E., & Uswatte, G. (2000). Constraint-Induced Movement therapy: Rehabilitation based on behavioral neuroscience. In R. G. Frank & T. R. Elliott (Eds.), *Handbook of rehabilitation psychology* (pp. 475–496). Washington, DC: American Psychological Association.

Taub, E., & Uswatte, G. (2006). Constraint-Induced Movement therapy: Answers and questions after two decades of research. *NeuroRehabilitation, 21,* 93–95.

Taub, E., Uswatte, G., & Elbert, T. (2002). New treatments in neurorehabilitation founded on basic research. *Nature Reviews Neuroscience, 3,* 228–236.

Taub, E., Uswatte, G., King, D. K., Morris, D., Crago, J., & Chatterjee, A. (2006). A placebo controlled trial of Constraint-Induced Movement therapy for upper extremity after stroke. *Stroke, 37,* 1045–1049.

Taub, E., Uswatte, G., & Pidikiti, R. (1999). Constraint-Induced Movement therapy: A new family of techniques with broad application to physical rehabilitation—A clinical review. *Journal of Rehabilitation Research and Development, 36,* 237–251.

Tryon, W. W. (1991). *Activity measurement in psychology and medicine.* New York: Plenum Press.

Tryon, W. W., & Williams, R. (1996). Fully proportional actigraphy: A new instrument. *Behavior Research Methods, Instruments, & Computers, 28,* 392–403.

Uswatte, G., Foo, W. L., Olmstead, H., Lopez, K., Holand, A., & Simms, M. L. (2005). Ambulatory monitoring of arm movement using accelerometry: An objective measure of upper-extremity rehabilitation in persons with chronic stroke. *Archives of Physical Medicine and Rehabilitation, 86,* 1498–1501.

Uswatte, G., Giuliani, C., Winstein, C., Zeringue, A., Hobbs, L., & Wolf, S. L. (2006). Validity of accelerometry for monitoring real-world arm activity in patients with subacute stroke: Evidence from the Extremity Constraint-Induced Therapy Evaluation trial. *Archives of Physical Medicine and Rehabilitation, 87,* 1340–1345.

Uswatte, G., Miltner, W. H. R., Foo, B., Varma, M., Moran, S., & Taub, E. (2000). Objective measurement of functional upper extremity movement using accelerometer recordings transformed with a threshold filter. *Stroke, 31,* 662–667.

Uswatte, G., & Taub, E. (1999). Constraint-Induced Movement therapy: New approaches to outcome measurement in rehabilitation. In D. T. Stuss, G. Winocur & I. H. Robertson (Eds.), *Cognitive neurorehabilitation* (pp. 215–229). Cambridge: Cambridge University Press.

Uswatte, G., & Taub, E. (2005). Implications of the learned nonuse formulation for measuring rehabilitation outcomes: Lessons from Constraint-Induced Movement therapy. *Rehabilitation Psychology, 50,* 34–42.

Uswatte, G., Taub, E., Morris, D., Light, K., & Thompson, P. (2006). The Motor Activity Log-28: Assessing daily use of the hemiparetic arm after stroke. *Neurology, 67,* 1189–1194.

Uswatte, G., Taub, E., Morris, D., Vignolo, M., & McCulloch, K. (2005). Reliability and validity of the upper-extremity Motor Activity Log-14 for measuring real-world arm use. *Stroke, 36,* 2493–2496.

Wald, J., & Liu, L. (2001). Psychometric properties of the driVR: A virtual reality driving assessment. *Student Health and Technology Information, 81,* 564–566.

Wolf, S. L., Winstein, C., Miller, J. P., Taub, E., Uswatte, G., Morris, D., et al. (2006). Effect of Constraint-Induced Movement therapy on upper extremity function 3–9 months after stroke: The EXCITE randomized clinical trial. *Journal of the American Medical Association, 296,* 2095–2104.

Zhang, L., Abreu, B. C., Seale, G. S., Masel, B., Christiansen, C. H., & Ottenbacher, K. J. (2003). A virtual reality environment for evaluation of a daily living skill in brain injury rehabilitation: Reliability and validity. *Archives of Physical Medicine and Rehabilitation, 84,* 1118–1124.

Health Care Quality Assessments

Karen Hwang
Elias Mpofu

7

Overview

Persons who display complex medical conditions require an interdisciplinary approach to health care, one that involves strategic communication between providers, payers, and consumers to deliver care in a reliable, timely, effective, and efficient manner. People with disabilities are more likely to report dissatisfaction in key areas of access and care than typically developing others. Inefficient allocation of resources leads to health risks and poorer health-related quality of life as well as additional financial costs that society can ill afford, given already overburdened health care systems. Little is known about disability-specific care experiences from the perspective of those receiving those services. This is unfortunate in that quality health care requires one to take into account the choices and values of the person receiving health care as well as recognition of a need to make critical choices correctly. This chapter describes commonly used current measurement tools for assessing health care quality. It also discusses critical issues for the development of health care quality measures that are responsive to consumer needs in their diversity and that would add value to the use of health care quality information by health service providers.

Learning Objectives

By the end of the chapter, the reader should be able to:

1. Outline the actual or prospective role of the federal and state governments in monitoring quality health care standards;
2. Explain the importance of tracking health care quality for different consumer populations;
3. Describe and evaluate some currently available health care quality assessment measures;
4. Identify and describe criteria for selecting appropriate health care quality measures; and
5. Discuss critical issues in the development of health care quality assessment instruments.

Introduction

Most traditional models of health care have been fragmented, acute-based, and expensive. By contrast, emerging health care models emphasize increased attention to preventive efforts for chronic concerns, including increasing patient education and empowerment in communicating with health care providers and making relevant health care decisions (Kaplan & Greenfield, 2004). The benefits of preventive health care include greater consumer satisfaction with the services, improved health outcomes, and cost savings. In short, the patient-centered approach is a cost-effective way to promote health-related quality of life for people who display complex chronic medical conditions. Assessing health care quality performance indicators is pivotal in health care systems that seek to be responsive to their clients—ensuring that services are appropriate for a population's genuine needs (Swenson et al., 2004). Feedback from consumers using these and other assessment measures can inform providers about their patients' needs and concerns.

People with complex chronic conditions use up to three to five times as many health care services relative to the general population (Bodenheimer, Chen, & Bennett, 2009), and they are at particular risk for breakdowns in communication among multiple services (Coulter, 1997; Schmittdiel, Shortell, Rundall, Bodenheimer, & Selby, 2006). Quality of health care for people with chronic illness or disability requires integrated global planning and an interdisciplinary approach to organizing health care providers, payers, and consumers to deliver care in a reliable, timely, and efficient manner (Kroll & Neri, 2004). Consumer-oriented data are critical to evidence-informed health care services with this population.

Definition of Key Concepts and Terms

The Institute of Medicine (1994) considers quality health care to be respectful of and responsive to the preferences of patients, including their needs and values, and to prioritize patient values in the provision of health care services. Audet, Davis, and Schoenbaum (2006) identified seven areas of patient-centered care: (1) access to care, (2) patient engagement in care, (3) information systems, (4) care coordination, (5) care integration, (6) consumer feedback, and (7) public dissemination about quality. Health care quality is characterized by a collaborative relationship between consumers and providers. Patients as partners in health care are presumed interested in participating in decisions affecting their treatment, to comprehend the information about the potential risks and benefits of treatment options with appropriate explanation, and to request necessary health care services for their well-being. There is evidence to suggest that patients want to be informed of treatment alternatives and want to be involved in treatment (Brody, Miller, Lerman, Smith, & Caputo, 1998; Guadagnoli & Ward, 1998; Kaplan & Greenfield, 2004).

The terms *care coordination* and *access barriers* are commonly associated with the research and practice in health care quality improvement. *Care coordination* refers to "the activities performed to ensure that multiple parties to delivery of health and disability care—including physicians, nurses, therapists, equipment providers, payers, attendants, and others—work together to deliver needed services, drugs, and equipment" (Hwang et al., 2008, p. 3). Health care coordination is particularly relevant to people with disabling conditions because they tend to have multiple health issues. However, population surveys have indicated that people with disabilities face multiple barriers to receiving quality health care services (Kroll, Jones, Kehn, & Neri, 2006). Barriers may be structural or procedural (i.e., process).

Structural–environmental barriers refer to the physical and social environment in which health care services are delivered. These include lack of ramps or parking spaces at buildings where services are provided, inaccessible examination rooms, fixed-height examination tables, scales that do not accommodate wheelchairs, and inaccessible washrooms. Transportation barriers include unavailability of needed transportation services to medical appointments or inaccessible transportation services. People with chronic illness or disability may also lack reliable personal attendant care necessary for accessing adequate management of their health conditions.

Process barriers are difficulties that individuals experience in the course of actual service delivery. The most commonly cited difficulties involve convenience of care, receipt of preventive teaching, and aspects of communication between providers and consumers. Examples of process barriers include inordinately long wait times and difficulty in scheduling appointments, disrespectful treatment from service providers, and denials and restrictions in insurance coverage. Both structural–environmental and procedural barriers can result in patients foregoing nonemergency or even emergency care because of the perceived burden involved. Without adequate health care, people with chronic illness or disabilities are constrained in their community participation or citizenship (see also chapters 13 and 26).

Research Box 7.1

DISABILITY AND PREVENTIVE HEALTH SERVICES

Diab, M. E., & Johnston, M. V. (2004). Relationships between level of disability and receipt of preventive health services. *Archives of Physical Medicine and Rehabilitation, 85,* 749–757.

Objective: The objective of this study was to examine relationships between level of disability and receipt of preventive health services along with any potential demographic confounders.

Design: States reporting disability rates (13 in 1998, 18 in 2000) supplied data from the *Behavioral Risk Factor Surveillance System,* a nationwide telephone survey. People with and without disabilities living in the community submitted information on how often they received recommended preventive health services, including colorectal, cervical, and breast cancer screening and influenza and pneumococcal vaccination. An ordinal index of disability severity was constructed from questions on activity limitations.

Results: People with severe disabilities were less likely to receive flu shots or pneumonia vaccines than people without disabilities or those with mild and moderate disabilities. Women with disabilities received fewer Pap tests and clinical breast examinations, but rates of mammograms did not differ significantly. Access to routine checkups affected all preventive services independent of disability level.

Conclusion: Severity of disability is related to receipt of certain preventive services in ways that were not necessarily simple or linear. Regardless of disability, access to services was an important determinant of receipt of preventive health services. Rates of preventive care remained suboptimal for almost all services and groups studied.

Questions:

1. Why may people with more severe disabilities receive the fewest preventive services? What barriers may impede people with severe disabilities from receiving preventive checkups?
2. How may differences in health insurance (e.g. Medicaid/Medicare vs. HMO vs. PPO) affect rates of primary care for people with disabilities? What interventions may be enacted to encourage more people with disabilities to receive preventive care services?

Applicable ICF Concepts

The World Health Organization (WHO; 2004) described a conceptual model of disablement that encompasses *impairment* (including medical diagnosis), *disability* (describing functional status), and *participation* (encompassing the roles one plays in the world and society). The use of an additional scale, *environment,* helps acknowledge ways environmental access can impact on both functional disability and social role fulfillment, including its possible impact on one's decisions that influence access, coordination, and quality of health care services. Health care quality assessments address important personal and environmental aspects of health care access. Such assessments provide input on consumers' satisfaction with the health care services they receive as well as on the specific areas of health care that are most in need of change for improvement. Firsthand consumer-level data are essential to providing information on ways environmental factors (e.g., access to health care) can affect both social role participation and functional disability (e.g., through general health outcomes).

Data from health care quality assessments can be interpreted with respect to experiences of health care in light of personality or group characteristics. For example, national health care quality norms could be used to track possible group disparities in the provision of health care. Group specific norms may be more appropriate for capturing cultural nuances that influence perceptions of health care services (see also chapter 18). For example, Sinclair, Fleming, Radwinsky, Clupper, and Clupper (2002) reported that health care service aspects valued by patients with heart disease influenced their perception of service qualities by patients. Consumers of health care services from groups that historically relied on alternative, complementary health care systems or mistrusted formal health care services due to a history of exclusion from social services would perceive salient health care qualities differently (Cooper et al., 2003; Hunt, Gaba, & Lavizzo-Mourey, 2005). For instance, Hunt et al. (2005) observed that regardless of health care plan, racial minority patients in the United

Discussion Box 7.1

ASSESSING CULTURALLY DIVERSE POPULATIONS

A public health research student wants to administer the *Consumer Assessment of Healthcare Providers and Systems* (CAHPS) and the Health Related Self-Efficacy Scales to elderly residents of San Francisco's Chinatown. Because of potential language difficulties, she first translates all the measures into Chinese. Results showed that the elderly Chinese subjects use fewer health care services and have lower levels of satisfaction and health-related self-efficacy, relative to national norms. Based on these findings, she concludes that elderly Chinese in San Francisco use fewer primary health care services because they lack the self-confidence to manage their own health care. Is this a valid conclusion? Support your answer with reasons. What other possible ways could one interpret the data?

States were less satisfied with physicians and also trusted them less compared to White patients.

History of Pertinent Research and Practice

Originally hatched in New York State around the mid-1980s, the health care quality initiatives have since been implemented by many other countries as part of their health care systems. This development is driven both by the need for quality improvement by health care organizations, as well as a mission to stimulate active consumer participation by enabling consumers to make informed choices about their health care providers (Faber, Bosch, Wollersheim, Leatherman, & Grol, 2009). Between 1992 and 1996, the Agency for Health Care Policy and Research (now the Agency for Health care Research and Quality; AHRQ) sponsored the development of a series of 19 health care quality clinical practice guidelines. Users can access the clinical practice guidelines through an electronic full-text retrieval system, *Health Services Technology Assessment Text* (HSTAT), at the National Library of Medicine. Each guideline has several versions designed for use by both clinicians and practitioners. The *Consumer Assessment of Healthcare Providers and Systems* (CAHPS; Hargraves, Hays, & Cleary, 2003) is the main project funded and administered by the AHRQ. The CAHPS project seeks to develop reliable surveys of patients' experiences with ambulatory and facility-level care (AHRQ, 2008). It also provides informational chart books and data sets to the public.

There continues to be increasing interest by health service providers in the United States to collect and use data on patient experiences for quality care improvement (Davis, Schoenbaum, & Audet, 2005; Davies & Cleary, 2005; Institute of Health Improvement, 2006; Swenson et al., 2004). International interest in health care quality is also growing (Davis, 1999). International versions of the CAHPS have been applied to patient samples in South Korea (Kang et al., 2006), the Netherlands (Arah et al., 2006; Delnoij et al., 2006) and the United Kingdom (Davies et al, 2008). In addition, the Healthcare Effectiveness Data and Information Set (HEDIS) has been used with Canadian hospital inpatients to assess quality of inpatient hospital care (Naylor, 1999).

Other research has focused on the influence of patient-provider relationships on health care outcomes, as well as the use of consumer report cards in health care decision making. In particular, studies have shown that better physicians were perceived to be patient-oriented—that is, having a respectful attitude toward their patients, expressing positive affect during visits, and providing more health care information (Beach, Roter, Wang, Duggan, & Cooper, 2006). Similarity of values between patient and therapist also had a positive influence on patient progress in the treatment (Kelly & Strupp, 1992; Street, O'Malley, Cooper, & Haidet, 2008). Qualities of care such as instrumental care, expressive care, and communication effectiveness appeared to explain satisfaction and wellness in patients with heart disease (Sinclair et al., 2002). Doeschler, Saver, Franks, and Fiscella (2000) explored racial/ethnicity differences in patients in the United States with regard to physician style and trust in physician. The satisfaction with physician indicators included perceived listening skills, explanations, and thoroughness. The trust in physicians scale included the extent to which physicians

Discussion Box 7.2

CHALLENGES IN THE DELIVERY OF PATIENT-ORIENTED HEALTH CARE

Challenges to the collection and use of patient experience of care data for enhancing the quality of health care service include heavy case loads, staff lacking experience in patient-oriented care, health care plans that may not prioritize patient perspectives, and competing priorities for service providers. The barriers to patient-oriented care mean that health care quality information may not be valued even by well-meaning service providers.

Questions:

1. Name and describe other barriers to the collection and/or use of health care quality data that you envisage.
2. What strategies would be helpful to increasing the collection and use of health care quality data by service providers?

were perceived to place patient's needs above other considerations, appropriate referral, performance of needed procedures, and being influenced more by insurance rules rather than by patient health care needs. Racial minority patients reported less satisfaction with and trust of physicians, after controlling for socioeconomic class and continuity of care with physician. Studies on sources of racial disparities in patient experience of health care are ongoing, and findings will be helpful to quality of care improvement efforts by service providers.

Concepts are still evolving on the specific uses to which consumer health care quality evaluations can be put. For example, Schauffler and Mordavsky (2001) observed that consumer health care report cards appeared not to make a difference in health care decision making, improvement of health care quality, or the competitiveness of health care services. They proposed a rethink of the use of consumer health care reports, observing that what consumers seemed to value most was provider specific information and particularly information on rates of errors and adverse outcomes. Thus, health care quality assessments may be used prospectively by consumers to compare different health services or health plans on salient qualities such as free provider choice or cost of services (Faber et al., 2009). Patients also valued health care services that were responsive to their requests for specific needs for care (Kravitz et al., 2002).

Professional Regulators in Rehabilitation and Health

Three leading organizations in the regulation of health care quality in the United States are: the AHRQ; National Committee for Quality Assurance (NCQA), and Institute for Clinical Research and Health Policy Studies (ICRHPS). The AHRQ is a prototypical example of an organization focused on improving the quality, safety, efficiency, and effectiveness of health care for all consumers. It is 1 of 12 agencies within the U.S. Department of Health and Human Services that support health services research. Its mission is to improve the quality of health care and promote evidence-informed decision making. The AHRQ provides information to both clinicians and consumers on:

- *Safety and quality:* reducing the risk of harm by promoting delivery of the best possible health care.
- *Effectiveness:* improving health care outcomes by encouraging the use of evidence to make informed health care decisions.
- *Efficiency:* transforming research into practice to facilitate wider access to effective health care services and reduce unnecessary costs.
- *Organizational excellence:* using efficient and responsive business processes to maximize the Agency's resources and the effectiveness of its programs.

The AHRQ's typical annual budget exceeds $300 million and mainly is used to support grants and contracts focused on improving health care. Its Web site also maintains a comprehensive list of measures and projects related to health care quality and patient safety (see http://www.qualitymeasures.ahrq.gov).

The NCQA is a private, not-for-profit organization dedicated to improving health care quality. Since its founding in 1990, NCQA has been a central player in motivating care improvements throughout the U.S. health care system, helping to elevate health care quality issues to the top of the national agenda. The NCQA provides statistics that track the quality of care delivered by the nation's health plans. Every year for the past 5 years, these numbers have improved

Discussion Box 7.3

YOUR OWN FACILITY

The AHRQ's latest research program (2008) is the development of a new survey to identify the strengths and weaknesses of disaster response plans in hospitals and nursing facilities. Under this program, hospitals conduct real-time simulations of community-wide disasters. Observers complete a set of standardized checklists, covering such areas as decontamination, triage, and treatment, as well as a post-treatment debriefing exercise to solicit feedback from all the participants. Summary data about these drills then are submitted periodically to the AHRQ. Using the results of the assessments, hospitals can identify areas for improvement, make appropriate changes, and set benchmarks to track those changes over time, ensuring that hospitals are adequately prepared for the sudden demand for service and provide high-quality care during a disaster event.

Question:
Thinking about your own facility or other facility with which you are familiar, how would you rate the facility's disaster response program?

in scope and accuracy: health care protocols have been refined, doctors have learned new ways to practice, and patients have become more engaged in their care. Those improvements in quality care translate into lives saved, illnesses avoided, and costs reduced. The NCQA also issues accreditations and certifications to help professionals and consumers identify and select high-caliber health plans and health care providers. Lists of the most highly rated plans are available at their Web site: http://www.ncqa.org/tabid/60/Default.aspx.

The ICRHPS at Tufts Medical Center maintains a database of public domain assessment measures of health care quality. The ICRHPS offers both research and training programs dedicated to the study of clinical, functional, and social outcomes of health care interventions. Their specific research programs cover biostatistics, cardiovascular health, and genetic testing, among others. Further details are available at their Web site: http://160.109.101.132/icrhps/default.asp.

Assessment Methods That Are Useful to Health-Related Practices

More than 400 patient-oriented health care quality indicators have been identified (Asch et al., 2006), and many of these are shared or duplicated in some way among several health care quality instruments. In the United States, the AHRQ maintains several resources for researchers, clinicians, and consumers interested in information regarding quality of care. For instance, the CAHPS surveys are among the more comprehensive available to researchers and service providers for assessing direct health care qualities.

Direct Health Care Quality Instruments

These surveys fall into two categories: the *CAHPS Ambulatory Care Services* (which assesses consumers' experiences with outpatient health care services) and the *CAHPS Facility Services* (which asses consumers' experiences with hospitals and nursing homes).

The CAHPS Health Plan Survey

Originally developed in 1997, the CAHPS Health Plan Survey is regarded as the national standard for measuring and reporting on the experiences of consumers with their health plans and providers (AHRQ, 1997). This survey contains different but related modules for adults (ages 18 and over) and children (ages 17 and under) and for different types of health coverage plans (Medicaid and Medicare vs. private commercial insurance). The CAHPS Health Plan Survey contains a core set of 39 multiple-choice, self-report items covering individuals' overall assessments of primary care, specialist care, and health insurance plans. The questionnaires are also available in English and Spanish language versions.

The CAHPS Clinician and Group Survey

The CAHPS Clinician & Group Survey is designed to assess the experiences of patients with physicians and medical groups. Using a format similar to the

CAHPS Health Plan Survey, the CAHPS Clinician & Group Survey also contains four different but related modules addressing children and adults and covers primary and specialty care. Each module consists of 23 items that address an individual's specific experiences with primary and specialist care providers, including wait times, cost, and provider–patient communication dynamics.

The ECHO® Survey

The Experience of Care and Health Outcomes (ECHO) Survey includes questionnaires that survey consumers who receive behavioral health care services from either managed care organizations or managed behavioral health care organizations. The ECHO survey contains 63 self-report items covering 17 dimensions of mental health treatment, including scheduling treatment, client–clinician rapport, and perceived effectiveness of treatment. These instruments are available for adults in English or Spanish as well as an English-only version for children. The CAHPS ambulatory care kit also contains supplemental item sets that address dental care and home care, as well as screening measures for children with chronic conditions and persons with mobility impairments, among others currently in development.

CAHPS Hospital and Other In-Residence Surveys

This survey, sometimes known as H-CAHPS or Hospital CAHPS, is a standardized survey of adult inpatient experiences with hospital care and services. This survey was developed in conjunction with the Centers for Medicare and Medicaid Services that collect data regularly on hospital quality care. The H-CAHPS contains 23 items covering patients' perceptions of such areas as nursing care, cleanliness of the room, and discharge planning. It is available in English, Spanish, and Chinese language versions.

CAHPS Nursing Home Surveys

These surveys are supported jointly by the AHRQ and the Centers for Medicare & Medicaid Services. These surveys provide information on the experiences of nursing home residents and their family members. The CAHPS Nursing Home Surveys include two separate modules, one for residents currently living in nursing home facilities for longer than 30 days and one for those recently discharged after short stays. The *Long-Stay Residents* version contains 45 items that cover such areas as cleanliness of the facility, quality of the food, and treatment by staff. The *Discharged Resident Instrument* is similar and covers outpatient services. The CAHPS *Long-Stay Residents* survey includes an additional survey assessing the experiences of family members of people currently residing in nursing homes. The *CAHPS Family Member Instrument* contains 50 items and asks respondents to report on their own experiences (not the resident's) with the nursing home and their perceptions of the quality of care provided by the facility to their family, including how well the staff meets a resident's basic needs such as eating, bathing, and toileting; the cleanliness of the facility; and the level of engagement of residents in therapeutic and recreational activities.

The CAHPS In-Center Hemodialysis Survey

This survey assesses the experiences of patients receiving services from dialysis facilities. The survey contains 58 core items covering such areas as quality of the kidney doctors, helpfulness of the staff, and length of time spent in the waiting room. The questionnaire also includes 20 supplemental items dealing with structural accessibility of the facility, availability of interpreter services, and transportation care. The instrument is available in English and Spanish versions. (All CAHPS survey measures are designed to be standardized and applicable across different health plans and providers and can be downloaded as PDF files at http://www.cahps.ahrq.gov/cahpskit.)

The Patient Assessment of Chronic Illness Care

The Patient Assessment of Chronic Illness Care (PACIC; Glasgow et al., 2005) measures the quality of care consumers experienced in the health care delivery system. The survey includes 20 items that cover such areas as provision of information, shared decision making, and appropriate referrals. The PACIC is designed to be a complementary measure to the Assessment of Chronic Illness Care (ACIC) and thus to provide complementary consumer and provider assessments of important aspects of care for chronically ill patients. The PACIC is a public domain instrument available at: http://www.improvingchroniccare.org/index.php?p=PACIC_Survey&s=36.

The Primary Care Assessment Survey

The Primary Care Assessment Survey (PCAS; Safran, Rogers, Talra, Ueberman, & Ware, 1998), available from the ICRHPS, includes 51 items that measure 7 domains of care through 11 summary scales, including accessibility, continuity, comprehensiveness clinical interaction, interpersonal treatment, and trust. The PCAS can be downloaded at http://160.109.101.132/icrhps/resprog/thi/pcas.asp. The ICRHPS has also published Child Health Ratings Inventories (CHRIs) useful for health care evaluations with pediatric populations.

Cost-Tracking Instruments

In addition to CAHPS, the AHRQ has also developed health care quality instruments to track cost of services and outcomes of care materials at the institutional level. These include the Healthcare Cost and Utilization Project (HCUP), the Medical Expenditure Panel Survey (MEPS), and the Community Tracking Survey (CTS; see also chapter 8).

The Healthcare Cost and Utilization Project

The HCUP is sponsored jointly through a partnership between industry, state governments, and the AHRQ. The HCUP provides data on hospitalization, ambulatory surgery, and emergency care through its public domain search engine, HCUPnet. The HCUP databases have tracked hospital care data in the United States since 1988, combining information from federal, state, and industry sources, and are available to researchers studying longitudinal trends in medical expenses and continuity of care.

The Medical Expenditure Panel Survey

The MEPS provides large-scale statistics that track the cost of health care services for families and individuals, their medical providers, and employers nationwide. The MEPS is sponsored by AHRQ and contains data on different age groups, racial minorities, and types of insurance coverage as well as the uninsured. The MEPS survey contains two major components: the *Household Component* and the *Insurance Component.* The *Household Component* provides data from individual households and their members, which is supplemented by data from their medical providers, on such topics as health care costs, racial disparities in health care, and quality of care. The *Insurance Component* surveys employers and provides data on employer-based health insurance, including the number and types of private health insurance plans offered, benefits, premiums, eligibility requirements, and employer characteristics. Details of the MEPS can be found at: http://www.meps.ahrq.gov/.

The Community Tracking Survey

The CTS data are from a national study designed to track changes in the U.S. health care system and their effects. The fourth round was administered to households in the 60 CTS sites: 51 metropolitan areas and 9 nonmetropolitan areas that were randomly selected to form the core of the CTS and to be representative of the nation as a whole. The first round of the CTS was conducted in 1996–1997, the second round in 1998–1999, and the third in 2000–2001. Respondents to the fourth round (2003–2004) provided information about health insurance coverage, use of health services, unmet needs for health care, children's special health care needs, out-of-pocket medical costs, patient trust in physicians, sources of health information, attitudes about medical care, and satisfaction with health care and health plans. Health status, chronic conditions, risk attitudes, and smoking behavior were additional topics covered by the fourth-round questionnaire. The data include variables on height and weight, employment, income, ethnicity, race, U.S. citizenship, household composition, and demographic characteristics. The instrument is available in both English and Spanish.

The Healthcare Effectiveness Data and Information Set

HEDIS (NCQA, 2009) measures the performance of health plans across multiple providers. Thus, it is somewhat analogous to the CAHPS. Health plans use HEDIS results to determine where improvement efforts are most needed. HEDIS consists of 71 self-report items covering 8 domains of care, including preventive care, health care for selected chronic conditions, actual use of services, and perceptions of care. The HEDIS questionnaires can be found at the National Center for Quality Assurance Web site (http://web.ncqa.org).

The Assessment of Chronic Illness Care

The ACIC (Bonomi, Wagner, Glasgow, & VonKorff, 2002) is used by health service providers to rate the quality of services they provide to their patients with chronic conditions. The ACIC contains three multipart sections covering organization of health care delivery programs, community linkages, and patient–provider interactions. Results of the survey are used by practitioners and policy holders to improve quality. The ACIC can be downloaded at: http://www.improvingchroniccare.org/index.php?p=ACIC_Survey&s=35.

Community Participation–Oriented Measures

These are not specifically designed to address issues around health care quality. However, they may contain items of relevance to investigators interested in understanding the effects of health care disparities among people with disabilities (see also chapter 24).

Chronic Disease Self-Management Scales

The Chronic Disease Self-Management Scales (CDSS) were developed by the Stanford Patient Education Research Center at Stanford University's School of Medicine. This measure is part of a multiyear project to develop and evaluate self-management programs for persons with chronic health conditions. It is designed to help people gain a sense of control over how their health problems affect their lives. These scales contain separate modules for assessing an individual's self-confidence in managing their health conditions, communicating with providers, and pursuing occupational and social activities of daily living. They have been translated into Chinese, Vietnamese, Norwegian, Somali, Bengali, Dutch, German, Hindi, Korean, Welsh, and Italian languages. The scales can be downloaded free at http://patienteducation.stanford.edu/research/.

Craig Handicap Assessment and Reporting Technique

The Craig Handicap Assessment and Reporting Technique (CHART; Whiteneck, Charlifue, Gerhart, Overhosler, & Richardson, 1992) was developed in conjunction with WHO-ICF guidelines and measures the degree to which impairments and disabilities result in handicaps. First developed in 1992 and revised in 1995, the CHART's 32 questions cover 5 of the original WHO dimensions of handicap: physical independence, mobility, occupation, social integration, and economic self-sufficiency. A scale measuring cognitive independence also is included. High subscale scores indicate lesser degrees of a disability (i.e., higher social and community participation). The CHART also is available in a 19-item short form, the CHART-SF. Detailed information about the CHART, including a downloadable rating form, can be accessed from the Web site: http://www.tbims.org/combi/chart/index.html.

Craig Hospital Inventory of Environmental Factors

The goal underpinning the development of the Craig Hospital Inventory of Environmental Factors (CHIEF) was to provide insight into the degree to which environmental participation affects the lives of people with disabilities. The CHIEF's 25-items ask respondents to rate the frequency in which they encounter environmental barriers within the political, structural, occupational, attitudinal, and assistive dimensions. Further details about the CHIEF can be found online at: http://www.tbims.org/combi/chief/index.html.

Generic and Disability Specific Measures

These instruments are health care–related in focus and address issues that impact perceptions of care by consumers with a variety of health conditions.

Assessment of Health Plans and Providers by People With Activity Limitations

The Assessment of Health Plans and Providers by People with Activity Limitations (AHPPPAL) Survey was developed under the joint sponsorship of the National Institute for Disability Rehabilitation and Research and the California Health Care Foundation (Palsbo, Mastal, & O'Donnell, 2006). Originally developed from the Medicaid CAHPS and HEDIS instruments, the AHPPPAL has revised wording and included additional content areas of interest for people with disabilities. This project is part of a larger study to develop organizational performance measures of the care provided to people with activity limitations arising from chronic illness or long-term disability. The AHPPPAL contains 168 self-report items taken from the CAHPS, the Persons with Mobility Impairments (PWMI) screener, and HEDIS, plus additional items derived from focus groups of consumers with disabilities. In addition to mobility impairments, the AHPPAL contains items relating to cognitive, sensory, and psychiatric disabilities. The AHPPPAL is being adapted for use with those with spinal cord injury and traumatic brain injury. The AHPPPAL is publicly available at: http://obslap.com/AHPPPAL.html.

The SF-36 and the SF-12

The SF-36 Health Survey is a 36-item short-form survey of general health status on 8 domains, including physical functioning, pain, and general health perceptions, among others. It has been widely used to assess patient-reported outcomes both domestically and in more than 30 foreign countries. The SF-12 Health Survey is a 12-item subset of the SF-36 that measures the same 8 domains of health. The SF-36 and the SF-12 are not public domain and can be purchased online at: http://www.qualitymetric.com/products/sf36v2.aspx.

Practices in the International Community

A number of consumer health care assessment instruments have been utilized in the United Kingdom, most notably the Improving Practice Questionnaire (IPQ; Greco, Powell, & Sweeney, 2003) and the General Practice Assessment Questionnaire (GPAQ; Mead, Bower, & Roland, 2008; Ramsay, Campbell, Schroter, Green, & Roland, 2000). Both instruments have been widely used throughout the United Kingdom but have not been applied to U.S. participants due to differences between U.S. and U.K. health service systems. The GPAQ has been applied to populations in Thailand (Jaturapatporn, Manataweewat, & Hathirat, 2006). An earlier version, the General Practice Assessment Survey (GPAS), was applied to populations in Chile (Pantoja, Beltrán, & Moreno, 2009).

A review of 18 articles on consumer assessment questionnaires for primary care out-of-hours services found four questionnaires (Garratt, Danielsen, &

Hunskaar, 2007): two from the United Kingdom, the Patient Satisfaction with Out-of-Hours Care (PSOC) and Short Questionnaire for Out-of-Hours Care (SQOC); and two from the Netherlands, the van Uden and Moll van Charante questionnaires. Other consumer assessments of health care services developed and tested in European countries include the OutPatient Experiences Questionnaire (OPEQ) in Norway (Garratt, Bjaertnes, Krogstad, & Gulbrandsen, 2005), the Health Care Communication Questionnaire (HCCQ) in Italy (Gremigni, Sommaruga, & Peltenburg, 2008), and a measure of outpatients' consultation departments in France (Gasquet et al., 2004). The Picker Patient Experience Questionnaire (Jenkinson, Coulter, & Bruster, 2002) is a measure of inpatient hospital quality and has been field tested in the United Kingdom, Germany, Sweden, Switzerland, and the United States.

The General Practice Clinical Linkages Interview (GP-CLI) was developed in Australia and is a nine-item tool with three underlying factors: referral and advice coordination, shared care and care planning linkages, and community access and awareness linkages. It measures the comprehensiveness and quality of a general practice's coordination with external health care providers. In particular, it is used to assess the communication, support, and referral arrangements between services as experienced by persons with chronic health conditions (Amoroso et al., 2007). The Health Management Information system (HMIS) is a measure developed in Pakistan that is used to assess and improve patient satisfaction with health services (Shaikh & Rabbani, 2005). Other health care assessments developed independently in East Asian countries and targeted especially toward individuals with disabilities could not be located in PUBMED and MEDLINE.

Issues for Research and Other Forms of Scholarship

We previously noted ongoing debate about the perceived relevance by service providers and consumers of consumer health care report cards (Fitzpatrick et al., 1992; Schauffler & Mordavsky, 2001). As evidence accumulates to support their use to inform health care interventions or plans, consumer health care report cards are likely to be used to a greater extent as part of any comprehensive heath care service system. Researchers and service providers interested in applying any of these health care quality measures need to be alert to the following cautions: relevance to the client population and service setting, influence of health management care plans, and the evidentiary basis of the measures.

Are the Measures Applicable to the Population Under Study?

Health researchers need to be certain that the selected assessment surveys are appropriate to the disability population under investigation before using them. Important considerations include whether the surveys were appropriately normed for use with persons with disabilities. For example, the CAHPS and the PCAS are generic measures of health care quality and may not accurately capture the access-related experiences of persons with chronic illnesses and disabilities. The PWMI and the AHPPPAL are designed to be inclusive and cross-disability. Therefore, researchers interested in specific populations should consider complementing these health care assessments with population-specific outcome measures.

Health care service qualities may also differ in their salience by demographic characteristics of patients or consumers. Patients or consumers of heath care services would mostly likely consider quality of care in part from their subjective evaluation of the extent to which the indicators of quality care are consistent with their individual preferences, expectations, or abilities. Little is known about the distribution of patient health care experiences within and across race/ethnicity. Patient self-reported experiences of health care are useful for determining whether there are race/ethnicity disparities in patient-oriented care (Asch et al., 2006) and if the data support: (1) what service qualities are associated with those disparities, and (2) what quality of

Research Box 7.2.

PATIENT INVOLVEMENT IN MEDICAL CARE

Brody, D. S., Miller, S. M., Lerman, C. E., Smith, D. G., & Caputo, G. C. (1998). Patient perceptions of involvement in medical care: Relationships to illness attitudes and outcomes. *Journal of General Internal Medicine, 4,* 506–511.

Objective: The study explored patients' perceptions about self-reported wellness following physician visits in which they perceived themselves to have been active or passive participants.

Method: Adult patients completed a self-report measure on their experience of care 1 day after and also 1 week after their medical visits. They also self-reported on their role perception (47% = active vs 62% = passive) during the medical consultation. The data were analyzed adjusting for age, sex, baseline illness ratings, and physician ratings of potential to achieve better health.

Results: Active patients reported greater symptom relief and general wellness compared to passive patients. They also reported higher satisfaction with their physicians and a greater sense of control over their illness than passive patients.

Conclusion: Patients' perceptions of their involvement in treatment consultation appeared to influence their attitudes toward illness and also recovery.

Questions:
1. To what extent can this study suggest that patients want to be involved in their treatment? Explain your answer.
2. Comment on the use of patient self-report of experience of care measures.
3. What limits the interpretation of the findings of this study?

care improvements are possible. In addition, research is needed to assess the validity of proxy data submitted by caregivers of individuals with severe disabilities (Sneeuw et al., 1997).

Influence of Health Management Plans

Systematic outcomes research on the specific ways in which consumer experiences with health care plans and providers affect actual health behaviors is needed (Ngui & Flores, 2006). Does poor coordination of services lead individuals to forgo nonemergency or even emergency car because of perceived burden? How do restrictions imposed by health plans affect care-seeking behaviors. As previously observed, this is particularly important for people with complex medical conditions who typically use about three to five times as many medical services as typically developing others. Findings from such research would be important for quality of care improvement efforts. Patient education on making the most of their visit to the health center would tremendously add to the value of patient health care quality information (Kaplan & Greenfield, 2004). It would also add to patient self-efficacy in their health management, leading to better preventive health (Marks, Allegrante, & Lorig, 2005; Orbell, Johnston, Rowley, Davey, & Espley, 2001).

Are the Measures Constructed Using an Efficient Measurement Model?

Indicators of patient experience on most patient surveys of quality care improvement are interpreted in a piecemeal fashion (e.g., percentage endorsement) without mapping them against other measures that are equivalent in mapping the overarching of construct of health care quality or constructing them to be transportable across patient or health consumer populations. To reliably identify robust indicators of health care or those important to patients and service providers and across settings, measures of health care quality constructed using item response theory (IRT) are needed. IRT measures are constructed to be objective in their assessment of a construct regardless of participants or context (see also chapter 5).

Many health care quality measures are quite lengthy, and they may compromise their utility in high patient enrollment health care settings and also with patients or clients with significant disability. Shorter versions of health care quality surveys with evidence for validity in their use with client populations would enhance the likelihood that patient or health care consumer data will be collected and used in treatment settings. Shorter and efficient measures of health care quality are possible with the use of IRT measurement models and use of computer adaptive testing (see also chapter 5).

Summary and Conclusion

Public reporting of patient or consumer experience of health care is important for accountability and transparency in health care service provision. Measures need to be developed to be responsive to patient or consumer characteristics and also health care service qualities. The AHRQ oversees the quality, cost, and efficiency of health care services for the U.S. Department of Health and Human Services. It maintains several databases dealing with different aspects of health care across all U.S. populations. The CAHPS is widely considered as the gold standard of consumer-rated health care quality. However, the CAHPS contains only generic items that may limit its applicability to persons with disabilities and chronic illnesses. Numerous research-based assessments can complement the CAHPS in order to provide a more comprehensive understanding of health care access, coordination, and quality. The PWMI and the AHPPPAL represent the newest generation of health care quality assessments designed to capture the experiences of persons with physical, cognitive, sensory, and psychiatric disabilities. However, more research leading to the development of versions of existing instruments that target the unique factors associated with specific disability diagnoses and of interventions to promote health-related self-efficacy is needed. Reliability and validity data are being gathered for many of the measures. Survey measures also need to be calibrated using IRT measurement models for wider application across patient populations and service provider settings.

Author Note

This book chapter contribution was supported, in part, by an ARRT research training fellowship from the University of Medicine and Dentistry of New Jersey, Department of Physical Medicine and Rehabilitation, sponsored by grant H 133P970011 from the National Institute on Disability and Rehabilitation, and a Mary Switzer Research Training Fellowship. Grateful appreciation to Mark Johnston, PhD, David Tulsky, PhD, and Trevor Dyson-Hudson, MD, for their support and mentorship on this project.

References

Agency for Healthcare Research and Quality. (1997). *The CAHPS Program.* Retrieved May 9, 2009, from https://www.cahps.ahrq.gov/content/cahpsOverview/OVER_Program.asp?p=101&s=12

Amoroso, C., Proudfoot, J., Bubner, T., Jayasinghe, U. W., Holton, C., Winstanley, J., et al. (2007). Validation of an instrument to measure inter-organisational linkages in general practice. *International Journal of Integrated Care, 3,* e46.

Arah, O. A., ten Asbroek, A. H., Delnoi, J.D.M., de Koning, J. S., Stam, P. J., Poll, A. H., et al. (2006). Psychometric properties of the Dutch version of the Hospital-level Consumer Assessment of Health Plans Survey instrument. *Health Services Research, 4,* 284–301.

Asch, S. M., Kerr, E. A., Keesey, J., Adams, J. L., Setodji, C. M., Malik, S., et al. (2006). Who is at greatest risk of receiving poor-quality health care? *New England Journal of Medicine, 354*(11), 1147–1156.

Audet, A. M., Davis, K., & Schoenbaum, S. C. (2006). Adoption of patient-centered care practice by physicians: Results from a national survey. *Archives of Internal Medicine, 166,* 754–759.

Beach, M. C., Roter, D. L., Wang, N. Y., Duggan, P. S., & Cooper, L. A. (2006). Are physicians' attitudes of respect accurately perceived by patients and associated with more positive communication behaviors? *Patient Education and Counseling, 62,* 347–354.

Bodenheimer, T., Chen, E., & Bennett H. D. (2009). Confronting the growing burden of chronic disease: Can the U.S. health care workforce do the job? *Health Affairs, 28,* 64–74.

Bonomi, A. E., Wagner, E. H., Glasgow, R. E., & VonKorff, M. (2002). Assessment of chronic illness car (ACIC): A practical tool to measure quality improvement. *Health Services Research, 37,* 791–820.

Brody, D. S., Miller, S. M., Lerman, C. E., Smith, D. G., & Caputo, G. C. (1998). Patient perceptions of involvement in medical care: Relationships to illness attitudes and outcomes. *Journal of General Internal Medicine, 4,* 506–511.

Cooper, L. A., Roter, D. L., Johnson, R. L., Ford, D. E., Steinwachs, M. D., & Powe, N. R. (2003). Patient-centered communication ratings of care and concordance of patient and physician race. *Annals of Internal Medicine, 139*(11), 907–915.

Coulter, A. (1997). Partnerships with patients: The pros and cons of shared clinical decision-making. *Journal of Health Services Research and Policy, 2,* 112–121.

Davies, E., & Cleary, P. D. (2005). Hearing the patient's voice? Factors affecting the use of patient survey data in quality improvement. *Quality and Safety in Health Care, 14*(6), 428–432.

Davies, E., Shaller, D., Edgman-Levitan, S., Safran, D. G., Oftedahl, Sakowski, J., et al. (2008). Evaluating the use of a modified CAHPS survey to support improvements in patient-centred care: Lessons from a quality improvement collaborative. *Health Expectations, 11,* 160–176.

Davis, K. (1999). International health policy: Common problems, alternative strategies. *Health Affairs, 3,* 135.

Davis, K., Schoenbaum, G., & Audet, A. J. (2005). A 2020 vision of patient-centered primary care. *Journal of General Internal Medicine, 20*(10), 953–957.

Delnoij, D. M., ten Asbroek, G., Arah, O. A., de Koning, J. S., Stam, P., Poll, A., et al. (2006). Made in the USA: The import of American Consumer Assessment of Health Plan Surveys (CAHPS) into the Dutch social insurance system. *European Journal of Public Health, 16,* 652–659.

Diab, M. E., & Johnston, M. V. (2004). Relationships between level of disability and receipt of preventive health services. *Archives of Physical Medicine and Rehabilitation, 85,* 749–757.

Doeschler, M. P., Saver, B. G., Franks, P., & Fiscella, K. (2000). Racial and ethnic disparities in perceptions of physician style and trust. *Archives of Family Medicine, 9,* 1156–1163.

Faber, M., Bosch, M., Wollersheim, H., Leatherman, S., & Grol, H. (2009). Public reporting in health care: How do consumers use quality-of-care information?: A systematic review. *Medical Care, 47,* 1–8.

Fitzpatrick, R., Fletcher, A., Gore, S., Jones, D., Spiegelhalter, D., & Cox, D. (1992). Quality of life measures in health care. I: Applications and issues in assessment. *British Medical Journal, 305*(6861), 1074–1077.

Garratt, A. M., Bjaertnes, Ø. A., Krogstad, U., & Gulbrandsen, P. (2005). The Outpatient Experiences Questionnaire (OPEQ): Data quality, reliability, and validity in patients attending 52 Norwegian hospitals. *Quality & Safety in Health Care, 14,* 433–437.

Garratt, A. M., Danielsen, K., & Hunskaar, S. (2007). Patient satisfaction questionnaires for primary care out-of-hours services: A systematic review. *British Journal of General Practice, 57,* 741–747.

Gasquet, I., Villeminot, S., Estaquio, C., Durieux, P., Ravaud, P., & Falissard, B. (2004). Construction of a questionnaire measuring outpatients' opinion of quality of hospital consultation departments. *Health Quality of Life Outcomes, 4,* 2–43.

Glasgow, R. E., Wagner, E. H., Schaefer, J., Mahoney, L. D., Reid, R. J., & Greene, S. M. (2005). Development and validation of the Patient Assessment of Chronic Illness Care (PACIC). *Medical Care, 43,* 436–444.

Greco, M., Powell, R., & Sweeney, K. (2003). The Improving Practice Questionnaire (IPQ): A practical tool for general practices seeking patient views. *Education for Primary Care, 14,* 440–448.

Gremigni, P., Sommaruga, M., & Peltenburg, M. (2008). Validation of the Health Care Communication Questionnaire (HCCQ) to measure outpatients' experience of communication with hospital staff. *Patient Education and Counseling, 71,* 57–64.

Guadagnoli, E., & Ward, P. (1998). Patient participation in decision-making. *Social Science and Medicine, 47,* 329–339.

Hargraves, J. L., Hays, R. D., & Cleary, P. D. (2003). Psychometric properties of the Consumer Assessment of Health Plans Study (CAHPS) 2.0 adult core survey. *Health Services Research, 38,* 1509–1527.

Hunt, K. A., Gaba, A., & Lavizzo-Mourey, R. (2005). Racial and ethnic disparities and perceptions of health care: Does health plan type matter? *Health Services Research, 40,* 551–576.

Hwang, K., Johnston, M. V., Tulsky, D., Wood, K. D., Dyson-Hudson, T., & Komaroff, E. (2008). Access and coordination of health care service for people with disabilities. *Journal of Disability Policy Studies 20,* 1–7.

Institute of Health Improvement. (2006). Patient-centered care: General. Retrieved April 19, 2006, from: http://www.ihi.org/IHI/Topics/PatientCenteredCare/PatientCenteredCareGeneral/

Institute of Medicine. (1994). Retrieved May 9, 2009, from http://www.iom.edu/CMS/3809/27708.aspx

Jaturapatporn, D., Manataweewat, B., & Hathirat, S. (2006). Reliability and validity of a Thai version of the General Practice Assessment Questionnaire (GPAQ). *Journal of the Medical Association of Thailand, 89,* 1491–1496.

Jenkinson, C., Coulter, A., & Bruster, S. (2002). The Picker Patient Experience Questionnaire: Development and validation using data from in-patient surveys in five countries. *International Journal for Quality in Health Care, 14,* 353–358.

Kang, N. M., Kim, S., Hong, S., Ryu, S., Chang, H. J., & Kim, J. (2006). The evaluation criteria of internet health information. *Studies in Health Technology Information, 122,* 886.

Kaplan, S. H., & Greenfield, S. (2004). The patient's role in reducing disparities. *Annals of Internal Medicine, 141,* 222–223.

Kelly, T. A., & Strupp, H. H. (1992). Patient and therapist values in psychotherapy: Perceived changes, assimilation, similarity, and outcome. *Journal of Consulting and Clinical psychology, 60,* 34–40.

Kravitz, R. L., Bell, R. A., Azari, R., Krupat, E., Kelly-Reif, S., & Thom, D. (2002). Request fulfillment in the office practice: Antecedents and relationships to outcomes. *Medical Care, 40,* 38–51.

Kroll, T., Jones, G. C., Kehn, M., & Neri, M. T. (2006). Barriers and strategies affecting the utilization of primary preventive services for people with physical disabilities: A qualitative inquiry. *Health and Social Care in the Community, 14,* 284–293.

Marks, R., Allegrante, J. P., & Lorig, K. (2005a). A review and synthesis of research evidence for self-efficacy-enhancing interventions for reducing chronic disability: Implications for health education practice (Part I). *Health Promotion Practice, 6,* 7–43.

Mead, N., Bower, P., & Roland, M. (2008). The General Practice Assessment Questionnaire (GPAQ)—development and psychometric characteristics. *BMC Family Practice, 20,* 9–13.

National Committee for Quality Assurance. (2009). *HEDIS & quality measurement.* Retrieved May 9, 2009, from http://www.ncqa.org/tabid/62/Default.aspx

Naylor, C. (1999, May/June). Health care in Canada: Incrementalism under duress. *Health Affairs, 18,* 9–26.

Ngui, E. M., & Flores, G. (2006). Satisfaction with care and ease of using health care services among parents of children with special health care needs: The roles of race/ethnicity, insurance, language and adequacy of family centered care. *Pediatrics, 117,* 1184–1196.

Orbell, S., Johnson, M., Rowley, D., Davey, P., & Espley, A. (2001). Self-efficacy and goal importance in the prediction of physical disability in people following hospitalization: A prospective study. *British Journal of Health Psychology, 6,* 25–40.

Palsbo, S. E., Mastal, M. F., & O'Donnell, L. T. (2006). Disability care coordination organizations: Improving health and function in people with disabilities. *Lippincott's Case Management, 11,* 255–264.

Pantoja, T., Beltrán, M., & Moreno, G. (2009). Patients' perspective in Chilean primary care: A questionnaire validation study. *International Journal of Quality in Health Care, 21*(1), 51–57.

Ramsay, J., Campbell, J., Schroter, S., Green, J., & Roland, M. (2000). The General Practice Assessment Survey (GPAS): Tests of data quality and measurement properties. *Family Practice, 17,* 372–379.

Safran, D. G., Kosinski, M., Tarlov, A. R., Rogers, W. H., Taira, D. H., Lieberman, N., & Ware, J. E. (1998). The Primary Care Assessment Survey: Test of data quality and measurement performance. *Medical Care, 36,* 711–723.

Schauffler, H. H., & Mordavsky, J. K. (2001). Consumer reports in health care: Do they make a difference? *Annual Review of Public health, 22,* 69–89.

Schmittdiel, J. A., Shortell, S. M., Rundall, T. G., Bodenheimer, T., & Selby, J. V. (2006). Effect of primary health care orientation on chronic care management. *Annals of Family Medicine, 4,* 117–123.

Shaikh, B. T., & Rabbani, F. (2005). Health management information system: A tool to gauge patient satisfaction and quality of care. *East Mediterranean Health Journal, 11,* 192–198.

Sinclair, R. R., Fleming, W. D., Radwinsky, R., Clupper, D. R., & Clupper, J. H. (2002). Understanding patients' reactions to services: The role of personal service values in heart patient satisfaction and wellness. *Journal of Applied Social Psychology, 32,* 424–442.

Sneeuw, K. C., Aaronson, N. K., Sprangers, M. A., Detmar, S. B., Wever, L. D., & Schornagel, J. H. (1997). Value of caregiver ratings in evaluating the quality of life of patients with cancer. *Journal of Clinical Oncology, 15,* 1206–1217.

Street, R. L., Jr., O'Malley, K. J., Cooper, L. A., & Haidet, P. (2008). Understanding concordance in patient physician relationships: Personal and ethnic dimension of shared identify. *Annals of Family Medicine, 6,* 198–205.

Swenson, S. L., Buell, S., Zettler, P., White, M., Ruston, D. C., & Lo, B. (2004). Patient-centered communication: Do patients really prefer it? *Journal of General Internal Medicine, 19*(11), 1069–1079.

Whiteneck, G. G., Charlifue, S. W., Gerhart, K. A., Overhosler, J. D., & Richardson, G. N. (1992). Quantifying handicap: A new measure of long-term rehabilitation outcomes. *Archives of Physical Medicine and Rehabilitation, 73,* 519–526.

World Health Organization. (2004). *International classification of functioning, disability, and health (ICF).* Retrieved May 7, 2009, from http://www.who.int/classifications/icf/en/

8 Economic Evaluations with Prescored Health Status Instruments

Luke B. Connelly

Overview

An economic evaluation is a systematic way of quantifying the additional costs and benefits that are expected to arise when a product or process is adopted. These evaluations typically seek to measure the costs of interventions in dollars and to quantify their health effects using measures of whatever improvements in the quality and/or quantity of life can be expected to result, based on the available clinical evidence. This chapter provides a brief overview of economic evaluation, generally, and cost-utility analysis (CUA), in particular. It provides a conceptual account of how economists think about costs and the way that economic analyses focus on incremental (or marginal) changes. It also introduces some of the ways that health-related quality of life (HRQoL) may be measured, focusing on prescored instruments in particular. The latter focus is pragmatic: prescored instruments are popular because they are simple and quick to administer and provide a useful way of measuring HRQoL for the purpose of CUA.

Learning Objectives

By the end of the chapter, the reader should be able to:

1. Explain the economic concept of opportunity cost and the technique of marginal analysis;
2. Distinguish between the different types of economic evaluation technique and the questions they may be used to answer;
3. Describe the way that primary health state preference data are collected for use in a CUA;
4. Describe and evaluate the use of prescored measures for HRQoL assessments;
5. Discuss some of the difficulties that are associated with health state measurement and health preferences; and
6. Demonstrate a basic appreciation of discounting and sensitivity analysis.

Introduction

Human beings routinely have to make choices between alternatives. Some choices are made without much thought or consequence, while others are made very carefully and systematically. Economic evaluation techniques provide a systematic way to examine the costs and benefits of alternative patterns of resource allocation. There has been a growth in the application of these techniques in the health sector. As the capacity of health technologies to extend and improve the quality and quantity of life has advanced, individuals and societies have often been willing to invest a greater share of their incomes in pursuit of better health and longer lives. At the same time, more spending on health means less spending on other things, and there has been pressure on governments and other third-party payers (such as insurers) to limit the growth of health expenditure. Economic evaluations have become a routine part of decision making in the health sector because they provide decision makers with a methodical way of comparing the costs and consequences of health sector interventions. Although these techniques may also be usefully applied in private sector applications, the emphasis in this chapter is on applications of these techniques for public sector resource allocation.

In this chapter, you will learn about some of the concepts that underpin an economic evaluation, including the framework that economists typically use to evaluate costs, benefits, and the effects of different patterns of resource allocation on social welfare.

That discussion is followed by an introduction to the basic economic evaluation approach, an overview of two methods that may be used to generate primary data on individuals' preferences over different health states, a discussion of prescored health state instruments (which elicit health state values and are quick and convenient to administer), and a brief discussion of discounting and sensitivity analysis. At the end of this chapter, you should have a good understanding of the ideas that drive an economic evaluation and a grasp of how prescored health state measures may be used to collect data on health states that may be useful for the conduct of an economic evaluation.

To get started, consider two of the primary concepts that underpin the economic way of thinking: opportunity cost and marginal analysis.

Opportunity Cost and Marginal Analysis

Economics is concerned with making the best use of scarce resources. The notion of opportunity cost and the technique of marginal analysis are useful in this regard irrespective of whose perspective or preferences are considered relevant to determining the purpose to which resources are to be put. Applying these two concepts from the viewpoint of individual consumer, a provider (or firm), or society as a whole is a productive way to consider the costs and benefits of different patterns of resource allocation.[1]

The use of resources for one purpose typically entails forgoing some alternatives that would also have produced benefits. When resources are being allocated between competing alternatives, the relevant notion of the cost of each alternative is the benefit that the next-best alternative could produce. This is the notion of opportunity cost. It is an encompassing concept that includes all of the benefits foregone, irrespective of whether they have a monetized value (e.g., where a benefit is not a traded good). Moreover, opportunity costs do not always bear a close resemblance to market prices.

For an illustration of the concept, consider the challenge of providing physiotherapy services in a busy rehabilitation unit in a tertiary care hospital. Suppose that the budget has been determined, along with the number of staff, and that the physiotherapy staff must use the resources available to treat the admitted patients, the case-mix for whom is beyond their control. The staff of the hospital must make decisions (probably after some consultation with other treating clinicians) about how to distribute their finite supply of physiotherapy labor and capital (by which economists usually mean equipment) across the patients who have been admitted for rehabilitation. That is, the staff will need to make decisions about how much physiotherapy each patient will get. If the department is focused on making the best use of its resources for the patients they treat, that decision, in turn, could be guided by the capacity of each patient to benefit from physiotherapy, in particular, because each hour of physiotherapy received by Patient A implies that an hour less time is available for the physiotherapy staff to spend with other patients. In this example, the opportunity cost of treating Patient A for an extra hour is the benefit that would have been generated by spending that extra time on the patient or patients who would have received the greatest benefit from that hour of treatment.

Note that in an example like this one, the trade-offs of whom to treat and for how long are likely to become more acute with a lower staff-to-patient ratio. In

1. The question of whose preferences determine the question of what is "best" is addressed later in this chapter.

Discussion Box 8.1

OPPORTUNITY COST

How is the concept of opportunity cost affected by the particular circumstances of a person, or a group of people (including an entire country)? Can technological and economic advancement affect the opportunity cost of one activity (say, an increase in the proportion of the nation's resources devoted to health care and rehabilitation) vis-à-vis another?

principle, of course, one could determine the number of hours of physiotherapy that would maximize the benefit each patient received and increase the budget to that level. Doing so would mean that each individual had as much therapy as would produce any benefit, and the question of rationing within the unit would no longer be a problem. Does this mean that the opportunity cost would fall to zero if we increased the physiotherapy staff? The answer is "no." It doesn't cause the opportunity cost to fall to zero, provided there are other activities that the same labor and capital could be used with elsewhere in the economy. This shows how the "perspective" that is adopted—whether we take the perspective of the economy as a whole, a particular firm, or a unit within a firm—matters. (This is an issue that is explored in further detail in the next section.)

This physiotherapy example also introduced the concept of marginal analysis along the way. *Marginal* or *incremental analysis* involves analyzing what happens if or when small changes—or changes "at the margin"—occur. More precisely, economists are typically interested in the marginal benefits and the marginal (opportunity) costs of resource allocation decisions. In the previous example, the increment that was considered was 1 hour of treatment by a physiotherapist. The benefit and cost calculus involved a comparison of the extra benefits that Patient A would receive from 1 hour of physiotherapy with those that other patients could derive from that treatment.

Maximizing Net Benefits: The Kaldor-Hicks Criterion

What type of decision rule could be used to allocate physiotherapist time (at the margin) in the foregoing example?[2]

One approach would be to try to maximize the benefits that the physiotherapy team produces for people who use the rehabilitation service, that is, the customers. That approach requires that each hour of physiotherapy be used so that the benefits it produces outweigh the benefits of the opportunities foregone. In turn, this means that the marginal recipient of an extra hour of physiotherapy is the individual who stands to gain the greatest benefit from that treatment.

This suggestion is underpinned by several value judgments. First, measuring the benefits produced by the service as the sum of the benefits received by all of the users of it implies that we place equal importance on the benefits

2. For simplicity, assume that the allocation of physiotherapy staff to this unit is, itself, optimal.

received by each of the patients. This value judgment follows the utilitarian conception of social welfare: Society's happiness is conceived as the sum of the happiness of all the individuals within it. In addition, in valuing each patient's benefits in this way, we actually apply a rule that means that those rehabilitation recipients who have the greatest capacity to benefit from physiotherapy receive more services than those with less capacity to benefit (at the margin). This follows another value judgment, called the Kaldor-Hicks criterion, which is commonly applied in welfare economics.

According to the Kaldor-Hicks criterion, a change in resource allocation increases social welfare if the individuals who are made better off by that change could compensate the individuals who are made worse off by it, and still be better off. In the physiotherapy example, suppose Patient B could receive greater benefit than Patient A from the last hour of physiotherapy available. The Kaldor-Hicks principle suggests that changing the pattern of resource allocation so that Patient B receives an extra hour of physiotherapy and Patient A receives an hour less results in a net improvement in social welfare.[3]

The importance of the preceding value judgments is that they are, by nature, not verifiable or falsifiable.[4] One may disagree with the Kaldor-Hicks criterion and/or with a utilitarian notion of social welfare.

These techniques are decision aids, not substitutes for decision making, so it is important to be aware of their inherent assumptions and the concerns that a conventional application may not capture. A common example is a concern about the distributional consequences of alternative courses of action: taken together, the Kaldor-Hicks criterion and utilitarianism suggest an indifference between precisely which individuals receive the benefits and bear the costs of different patterns of resource allocation—what matters according to these criteria is what happens to the sum of individuals' utilities. In practice, though, policy makers may not be indifferent as to who benefits and who loses as a result of a resource allocation decision.

For example, suppose we were evaluating two mutually exclusive, publicly funded, rehabilitation programs for people who have suffered a stroke. Both programs cost the same amount, but suppose that the lion's share of benefits from rehabilitation program A are conferred on wealthy people, while benefits of program B are conferred on people from across the wealth spectrum, including poor people. If the net benefit of Program A were equal to that of Program B, the normal cost-benefit rules (applying the Kaldor-Hicks principle) would suggest that we ought to be indifferent between the programs. However, this judgment may not be acceptable to decision makers or the electorate: The benefits conferred by Program B may be more highly valued due to their distributional consequences (i.e., the help that they provide to poorer households). For this reason, presenting the estimated costs and benefit data in a disaggregated form can increase their value as decision aids. Doing so may enable decision makers

3. Implicitly, we also assume that there are no changes within this margin (e.g., 40 minutes more for Patient B and 20 minutes more for Patient A) that would pass the Kaldor-Hicks test.

4. Economists and others (e.g., moral philosophers) also refer to such statements as "normative" statements. Normative statements are not verifiable or falsifiable, whereas "positive" statements are. An example of a normative statement is "any person with a disability should receive social security payments." An example of a positive statement is "all people with disabilities receive social security payments." The first statement is neither verifiable or falsifiable. The second statement can be verified/falsified (and, of course, it is false).

to explore considerations, such as distributional issues, using the data that have been systematically considered for the economic evaluation itself, along with any additional information the decision makers may bring to bear.[5]

Cost-Benefit Analysis, Cost-Minimization Analysis, Cost-Effectiveness Analysis, and Cost-Utility Analysis: What Are the Differences?

There are four basic approaches to economic evaluation, and each of them has a distinct purpose. These four techniques are cost-benefit analysis (CBA), cost-minimization analysis (CMA), cost-effectiveness analysis (CEA), and cost-utility analysis (CUA). This chapter is mostly concerned with CUA, which is the most commonly used economic evaluation technique for health sector interventions. So it is sufficient for our purposes here to provide only a brief overview of the other techniques and highlight how they differ from CUA. A basic description of those differences will suffice, and we will set aside issues that are common to all forms of economic evaluation (e.g., discounting, sensitivity analysis) for a moment and return to them toward the end of the chapter.

Cost-Benefit Analysis

The most general form of economic evaluation is CBA, which involves the monetization of both costs and benefits. In other words, in a CBA costs and benefits are all valued in dollars (pounds, etc.).

The advantage of this approach is that it enables a direct comparison of the costs and benefits. Specifically, one is able to subtract the costs of the investment from the benefits that it creates. The general decision rule in CBA is to invest in any and all projects for which the benefits exceed the costs. The decision rule involves the value judgments that were discussed in the last section: A project or program of work is considered worthwhile (for society) if the people who gain as a result of that change could compensate the losers for their losses and still remain better off than they were prior to the change.

Although CBA is a very powerful form of economic evaluation, and even though ingenious ways of valuing benefits of all kinds (including health benefits) do exist, it is not a popular economic evaluation technique for health sector applications.

CBA is unpopular in the health sector because many people do not feel comfortable about monetizing improvements in quality of life or life-years gained. Although it is easy to understand that disposition, avoiding CBA for this reason usually just leads one to substitute an implicit valuation of life rather than an

---

5. The foregoing example seems fairly straightforward, but it involves some measurement issues that can, in principle, be captured in the evaluation itself. For example, if individuals value services provided to poor households, the notion of a "caring externality" may be applied and valued. We could measure the amount that individuals would be willing to pay to support poorer households. Doing so would serve to include (at least some of) the distributional adjustment that we have in mind if we prefer Program B over Program A. Therefore, one may argue that the example implies that the benefits of Program B were not fully captured. If they were, its net benefits would exceed those of Program A, and Program B would have been preferred.

explicit one. It is worth emphasizing that none of the remaining techniques that we will consider enables one to answer, explicitly, the question "is this intervention worthwhile?" That question can only be answered explicitly via CBA; each of the other forms of economic evaluation involves an assessment of some intervention relative to the other interventions that are available.

Cost-Minimization Analysis

CMA can be used when a specified health outcome can be produced by more than one technique or approach. A CMA might be appropriate if, for example, one were considering the provision of manipulative physiotherapy for low-back pain either at a clinic or in the home. If a decision has been made to supply the service, and the health outcomes are known not to be contingent upon where the treatment takes place, one need only measure the costs of the two alternatives and choose the least-cost option.

In reality, there are not very many examples that fit this bill. For example, people who receive the treatment may not be indifferent between where they receive it, meaning that they do not consider the two alternatives to be equally beneficial (or costly). Admittedly, it is possible to deal with some of these issues within the CMA framework (e.g., by ensuring that the costs of each alternative are captured properly for all parties), and CMA is sometimes an acceptable way to compare two programs/interventions with outcomes that are virtually identical in quantity and quality.

Furthermore, sometimes when there are qualitative differences in the outcomes, but it is known that consumers prefer the presumably lower-cost alternative, it may be superfluous to quantify the outcome directly. For example, Coast et al. (1998) conducted a CMA that compared inpatient and hospital-in-the-home (HITH) care for hospitalized but medically stable patients in Bristol, England. They found that HITH was cheaper than inpatient hospital treatment for this group. If it were known in advance that patients generally prefer HITH to in-hospital treatment, one's conclusion about the best approach to treatment would not change. On the other hand, if patients preferred to be treated in the hospital rather than via HITH, the question would not have been amenable to CMA. Some of these issues are not obvious in advance, so setting out to do a CMA is unwise unless you are sure that the two interventions you wish to compare have outcomes that are identical in quantity and quality.

Cost-Effectiveness Analysis

CEA requires the measurement of both the costs and the outputs (or outcomes, if you prefer) produced by the alternatives under consideration. The way that CEA differs from CBA, however, is that it does not require monetization of the health outcomes data. The outcome of a CEA is called an incremental cost-effectiveness ratio (ICER), which is a ratio of costs—which are monetized—to benefits, which are not monetized but expressed in physical units (such as life-years).

As with a CMA, a CEA becomes relevant once it has already been decided to achieve a particular outcome and the remaining question is only how to do so at the least cost. The difference between CEA and CMA is that the quantity of the output produced by each intervention need not be equal. Suppose, for example, that a government decides to prevent dental cavities by adding fluoride to drinking water. A range of alternatives might exist (e.g., fluoridate the general water supply, fluoridate bottled drinking water only, distribute fluoride tablets to parents of young children, etc.), and those alternatives might be quite disparate in terms of both their costs and their effectiveness (i.e., the number of teeth they prevent from decay). These alternatives could be compared by estimating their costs and their consequences and expressing these for each alternative as a ratio (e.g., the "cost per decayed tooth prevented"). The decision rule in CEA is usually to choose the intervention that has the lowest ICER. This will not always be considered an acceptable decision rule, however, if the alternatives available affect different numbers and/or types of individuals. For example, a program that fluoridates the water supply only of major cities is likely to be more cost-effective than one that fluoridates both urban and rural supplies, but it may not be acceptable on political or other normative grounds (e.g., considerations of equity). Although CEA applies more generally than CMA, it does require that the measured outputs be homogenous. This is an important limitation in the health sector, where interventions may not only affect the quantity, but the quality of life. Conventional CEA generally cannot deal with qualitative differences that arise in the outputs or outcomes of different investments.

Cost-Utility Analysis

The limitation of CEA is obviously important in the health sector because many health sector interventions affect the quality of life.

CUA is similar to CEA—technically it is a type of CEA—in the sense that it also involves monetizing costs but measuring benefits in physical units. The point of difference is that CUA involves an adjustment for qualitative differences in outcomes. The most commonly used measure for outcomes in this kind of analysis is the quality-adjusted life-year (QALY). The output from a CUA itself is also an ICER, such as the incremental cost per QALY saved.

The historical basis of CUA was a study by Klarman, Francis, and Rosenthal (1968) of different interventions that keep people with end-stage renal (i.e., kidney) disease alive. The interventions they were interested in were dialysis and transplantation. Their argument was that although both dialysis and transplantation can be equally effective at prolonging life, the quality of life for transplant recipients is generally much better than it is for people who are dialyzed. Although a CBA wasn't necessary in their study—it had already been determined that people with end-stage renal disease could not just be allowed to die—a standard CEA could not cope with this difference in the quality of life due to dialysis and transplantation. Therefore, in order to make some adjustment to their CEA, the authors weighted each year of life gained due to transplantation as 1.25 and each year of life gained by dialysis equal to 1. These weights were somewhat arbitrary, but they nevertheless represented an attempt to adjust the quantities of life for its quality.

Since that study, much work has been undertaken to derive measures of HRQoL from individuals' preferences over health states. A variety of approaches has been used, and we mention them briefly here (the sources at the end of this chapter will be useful to readers who want to learn more about these approaches). For practical reasons, though, the discussion in this chapter mostly focuses on prescored HRQoL measures. Several prescored measures have been tested and used in the health economics and clinical literatures, and they are popular because they are generally quite easy to administer and score. Of course, these methods also have their limitations, and we address some of those issues as we progress; but the general approach that we take is to introduce the methods first and then discuss their conceptual basis.

QALYs

The concept of the QALY was developed as a summary measure of both the longevity and morbidity-reducing effects of interventions that are designed to improve health. Thus, the QALY measure is useful when the purpose of a study is to compare the cost-effectiveness of health-improving products or processes that (a) extend life, but do not create a state of "perfect health" or (b) do not extend life, but improve quality of life. This section presents an overview of how QALYs can be generated and how the resulting data may be interpreted.

QALYs are generated using preference-based data on health states. These can be elicited via a number of different methods, the two most common of which are the standard gamble (SG) technique and the time trade-off (TTO) technique.

The Standard Gamble

The basic SG approach involves asking an individual to choose between a state of imperfect health and a state that involves an intervention that results in perfect health but also carries a risk of death. For example, suppose the health state of interest is paraplegia. Respondents would be given a description of the functional limitations that may be associated with paraplegia and asked to imagine being in this health state. They would then be asked to consider a choice between the state of imperfect health (in this case, paraplegia) and a state of perfect health, which may only be achieved by risking one's life. For example, consider the two scenarios in Exhibit 8.1.

Exhibit 8.1

THE STANDARD GAMBLE

Health State 1: Paraplegia for 10 years, followed immediately by death.

Health State 2: An intervention that results in EITHER (a) perfect health immediately, sustained for 10 years and followed by death [with a chance of ρ], or (b) immediate death [with a chance of $(1 - \rho)$].

Note that Health State 1 (HS1) is certain, while Health State 2 (HS2) carries the chance, ρ, that the person will be restored to full health and the chance $(1 - \rho)$ that s/he will not survive the intervention. The interviewer would give a hypothetical value for ρ (the chance of success) and $1 - \rho$ (the chance of failure) and would ask the respondent, "Which HS would you choose?" Then, based on the response, the interviewer would change the value of ρ with the objective of finding the point at which the individual becomes indifferent between Health State 1 (HS1) and (the risky) Health State 2 (HS2). For example, suppose that the interviewer started with a value of $\rho = 0.90$ (implying that 90% of people survive the intervention and are returned to full health, while 10% die from the intervention), and the respondent chose HS1. In this case, the interviewer would increase the value of ρ and continue to do so until the preference between the health states was reversed, and the respondent chose HS2. Conversely, if the respondent chose HS2 when the risk of death in HS2 was 0.10, the interviewer would lower ρ until the individual chose HS1. Of course, some individuals may not change their choice, irrespective of the proposed value of ρ.[6]

Generally, though, individuals *are* willing to make such trade-offs. The strength of their preference for one health state over the other is indicated by the level of risk that is necessary to make the individual indifferent between the two choices. So, how is this information used to generate a QALY?

Suppose that, in the preceding example, the individual chose HS2 for all values of ρ above 0.60, but changed his/her preference to HS1 when ρ was less than 0.60. We might estimate the point of indifference as the midpoint between the ρ that led to a choice of HS2 and the ρ that led to a choice of HS1. Suppose that the respective bids were $\rho = 0.59$ and $\rho = 0.61$: We could take the midpoint ($\rho = 0.60$) as an estimate of the point of indifference. The interpretation of this outcome is, "the respondent preferred the risky option that would return her to perfect health when the risk of death was less than 0.40 (or 40%), but preferred the certain option in the nominated health state [paraplegia] when the risk of death for the uncertain state exceeded 0.40." The utility weight for this health state, for this individual, is 0.60 on the zero-to-one QALY scale, where zero is death and one is perfect health. This essentially implies that this hypothetical individual would be indifferent between living for 6 years in perfect health or 10 years with paraplegia. Another implication is that if there were, indeed, an intervention that could repair the spinal cord and reverse paraplegia, it would be highly valued by this individual: Restoring her from paraplegia to full health adds 0.40 QALYs per year. Over 5 years, such an intervention—which (by assumption) improves quality of life but does not extend it—would produce two QALYs. In other words, the benefits it produces are comparable to the benefits that are produced by an intervention that prolongs a healthy life for 2 years. The SG method can also be adapted for use with conditions that are not chronic in nature by modifying the end-point in HS2 to a health state that is worse than full health but better than death.

The advantage of the SG approach is that it is consistent with von Neumann-Morgenstern consumer theory, which describes individuals' choices under risk and uncertainty. In this regard, the SG approach yields values that some economists are comfortable to describe as "utilities." There are some obvious drawbacks of the SG technique, too. One of these is that the concept of risk, which is so central to this technique, is not particularly easy to convey or for respondents

6. Such preferences are described as *lexicographic* preferences. For example, the preferences of an individual who was not willing to take any chance of loss of life, no matter how small, for restoration of "perfect health" would be described as lexicographic.

to understand. This problem is usually addressed by invoking visual aids, such as a probability wheel, where a disc is divided into two colors, one of which represents the chance of perfect health and the other of which represents the risk of death in HS2. The interviewer adjusts the disc in a manner that corresponds with the risk that s/he wants the subject to consider. In any event, the SG approach is also quite time-consuming for both the interviewer and the respondent, and data collection is best done via face-to-face interviews. The latter may be problematic for studies that would otherwise rely on a computer-assisted telephone interview (CATI) approach or Web-based completion of survey instruments. Admittedly, some of these limitations could be overcome with clever applications of Web-based technologies.

The Time Trade-Off

The TTO approach is easier to administer than the SG approach because the task is generally more intuitive. The basic approach involves asking respondents to choose between a health state that is worse than perfect health for T years and a perfect health state for $t < T$ years. Once again, the objective is to identify the respondent's point of indifference between these states, but with this technique the variable is time in the healthy state. To apply the TTO to the paraplegia health state described previously, the choices in Exhibit 8.2 could be constructed.

Exhibit 8.2

THE TIME TRADE-OFF

Health State 1: Paraplegia for *T years,* followed immediately by death.

Health State 2: Perfect health for *t < T years,* followed immediately by death.

For example, suppose T is 10 years and applies to HS1; a period of less than 10 years (say, 5 years) would be used for HS2. The objective is to find the value of t at which the respondent is indifferent between HS1 and HS2. Suppose that the interviewer started with $t = 4$ and that the respondent chose HS1 (for 10 years) over HS2 (for 4 years). The interviewer would then increase t and ask the respondent to choose again. The interviewer would continue to do so until the indifference point was located. For example, if the respondent preferred HS1 to HS2 when $t = 5$ but preferred HS2 to HS1 when $t = 6$, one may conclude that the point of indifference is between these two points. One could then either continue to modify the value of t (e.g., take t down by 0.5 to 5.5) in order to get closer to the point of indifference, or accept the midpoint of the existing bids (i.e., 5.5) as an approximation. The utility weight is then found by dividing t by T, which, in this case, yields 0.55. In other words, 1 year in HS2 is considered to be of equivalent value, by this respondent, to 0.55 years of perfect health.

The TTO's advantage—its simplicity due to the omission of risk in the choice set—is also its shortcoming. Choices are not generally made under conditions of certainty, but the TTO approach involves a choice between certain alternatives. For that reason, it does not accord as closely as the SG technique does with conventional economic consumer theory, and the values it generates are not generally regarded as "utilities" but rather as health state values. The TTO is, nevertheless, a fairly popular approach in practice because of its relative simplicity in application.

Prescored Measures

An alternative to collecting health state preferences directly using the TTO or SG (for example) is to use prescored HRQoL instruments. There are numerous instruments, including the EQ5D Dolan et al. (1995), the Quality of Well-Being (QWB) index (Kaplan, Bush, & Berry, 1979), the Health Utilities Index (Mark 2 and Mark 3; HUI2, HUI3; Feeny et al., 2002; Torrance et al., 1996), the SF-6D (Brazier, Roberts, & Deverill, 2002), and the AQoL (Hawthorne, Richardson, & Day, 2001). The creators of these instruments have derived a set of scoring weights that can be used to convert individuals' responses to these questionnaires into QALY-type measures of HRQoL.

For instance, the SF-6D—which is based on the popular SF-36 health status measure—is an instrument that has six health status–related attributes and a scoring table that is used to convert respondents' self-reported health attributes into utility weights (which fall on the zero to one scale). Thus, the idea is that researchers can administer the SF-6D, which contains statements that are easy for subjects to understand, and use their responses to generate corresponding utility weights.

The scoring algorithm for the SF-6D was derived by taking a random sample of the UK population and administering the SG technique with health scenarios that comprise various levels of the dimensions of the SF-6D (six dimensions, with four to six levels each). In total, 249 health states were valued using this approach, and the authors then used regression analysis to estimate the relationship between each health state's characteristics and the corresponding utility scores that were obtained via the SG technique. The scoring algorithm they derived is composed of the coefficients of the estimated regression. The HUI3 and related instruments were derived in a similar way, using the SG technique on a Canadian sample taken from Hamilton, Ontario.

The EuroQol EQ-5D is another very popular instrument made up of two parts. The first part is a prescored measure that has five health "dimensions" (mobility, self-care, usual activity, pain/discomfort, and anxiety/depression), each of which has three levels (no problems, some problems, substantial problems), thus yielding 243 combinations (i.e., health states). The items on the EQ-5D appear in Table 8.1. The second part of the EQ-5D is the visual analogue scale (VAS) that is presented as Figure 8.1. The endpoints of the EQ-5D VAS are zero ("Worst imaginable health state") and 100 ("Best imaginable health state") and appear on a scale that looks like a thermometer (see Figure 8.1). Respondents are asked to indicate their current health state on the VAS scale by drawing a line from the "Your health state today" box to a point on the scale. The VAS

8.1

The EuroQol EQ-5D Visual Analogue Scale (VAS).

To help people say how good or bad a health state is, we have drawn a scale (rather like a thermometer) on which the best state you can imagine is marked 100 and the worst state you can imagine is marked 0.

We would like you to indicate on this scale how good or bad your own health is today, in your opinion. Please do this by drawing a line from the box below to whichever point on the scale indicates how good or bad your health state is today.

Your own health state today

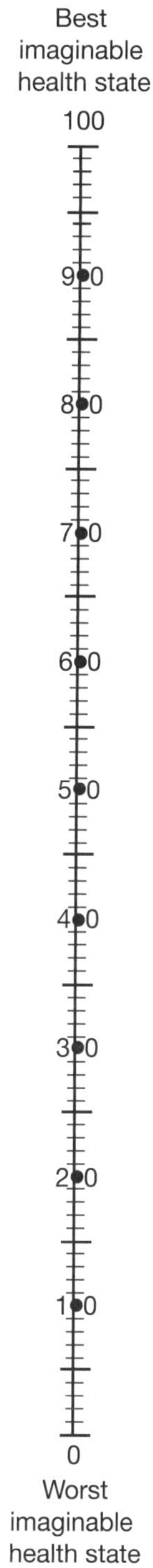

8.1 The EuroQol EQ-5D

EQ-5D (UK English version)

By placing a tick in one box in each group below, please indicate which statements best describe your own health state today.

Mobility

I have no problems in walking about ☐
I have some problems in walking about ☐
I am confined to bed ☐

Self-Care

I have no problem with self-care ☐
I have some problems washing or dressing myself ☐
I am unable to wash or dress myself ☐

Usual Activities (*e.g., work, study housework, family or leisure activities*)

I have no problems with performing my usual activities ☐
I have some problems with performing my usual activities ☐
I am unable to perform my usual activities ☐

Pain/Discomfort

I have no pain or discomfort ☐
I have moderate pain or discomfort ☐
I have extreme pain or discomfort ☐

Anxiety/Depression

I am not anxious or depressed ☐
I am moderately anxious or depressed ☐
I am extremely anxious or depressed ☐

From EQ-5D User Guide, Version 1.0, by M. Oppe, R. Rabin, and F. de Charro, 2008, Rotterdam, the Netherlands: The EuroQol Group.

score is a number between 0 and 100 corresponding to the point at which the respondent marks the line.

Responses to the EQ-5D (Table 8.1) may be used to generate an index of HRQoL by applying scoring weights. This index does not require a response to the EQ-VAS (Figure 8.1), just the EQ-5D questions that appear in Table 8.1. A set of scoring weights for the UK (Dolan, Gudex, Kind, & Williams, 1995) is presented in Table 8.2.

Applying the scoring weights is fairly simple:

1. First, summarize each EQ-5D response by creating a five-digit code, where each digit in the code indicates the level that the respondent has checked for the five dimensions, in order.
   - For example, we would write "22311" if a respondent ticked the second boxes in both the mobility and self-care dimensions, the third box for the

usual activities dimension, and the first box for the pain/discomfort and anxiety/depression dimensions of the EQ-5D.

2. Second, add the scoring weights in Table 8.2 that correspond to these levels, plus the "Constant" term if there is any dysfunction (i.e., the respondent answered level 2 or 3 for any dimension) and the N3 term if any of the EQ-5D dimensions was rated at level 3.
   - Thus, for the response "22311," we compute: 0.069 + 0.104 + 0.094 + 0 + 0 + 0.081 + 0.269 = 0.617
3. Third, subtract this total from 1.00.
   - For the response "22311" we get 1– 0.617 = 0.383.

In other words, simply subtract the relevant scores from 1.00 to derive a QALY estimate for the respondent's health state.

The values in Table 8.2 were derived by taking a random sample of the noninstitutionalized adult population of England, Scotland, and Wales. The researchers interviewed 3,395 respondents, face-to-face in their homes, and the interviewees responded to a TTO exercise based on health state descriptions from the EQ-5D. The researchers constructed 45 health states from across the range of (245) states for the EQ-5D and administered various subsets of these

8.2 The EuroQol EQ-5D Scoring Algorithm for England, Scotland, and Wales

Dimensions		Coefficient
Constant		0.081
	Mobility	
level 2		0.069
level 3		0.314
	Self-Care	
level 2		0.104
level 3		0.214
	Usual activity	
level 2		0.036
level 3		0.094
	Pain/discomfort	
level 2		0.123
level 3		0.386
	Anxiety/depression	
level 2		0.071
level 3		0.236
N3		0.269

From Dolan et al. (1995).

to the respondents, along with the states of perfect health (11111), immediate death (33333), and unconsciousness. The scores, in fact, are the regression coefficients that were obtained by estimating the TTO values they obtained as a function of the corresponding health state dimensions and levels that were described in the survey.

Deriving QALYs from the EQ-VAS is not as straightforward for several reasons. First, QALYs are usually expressed on the zero (death) to one (perfect health) scale, so EQ-VAS scores have to be re-scaled if there are health states that the respondent considers worse than death. Second, note that there is a difference between administering the EQ-5D and EQ-VAS to respondents in whose own health state you are interested. Specifically, the value that is elicited by the EQ-VAS is the respondent's own rating of his/her health state compared to the nominated endpoints. By contrast, when we create the EQ-5D index, we do so by applying population-based health state preference information to the individual's responses. The next section provides a brief discussion of why this distinction is potentially important.

Finally, it is worth pointing out that at least 17 EQ-5D "value sets" now exist for a range of European countries, the United Kingdom, the United States, New Zealand, and Zimbabwe. These population-based value sets allow the construction of the EQ-5D index for each of those countries. A list of the available value sets, by country and derivation method, may be found in Oppe, Rabin, and de Charro (2008), and a collection of value sets may be found in Szende, Oppe, and Devlin (2007).

Whose Health State Preferences?

The Washington Panel on Cost-effectiveness in Health and Medicine (Russell et al., 1996) recommended that economic evaluations use population-based health state values. This recommendation is widely followed in the health economics literature and has been adopted by a number of countries in their guidelines on the conduct of cost-utility analyses in the health sector (Mann, Brazier, & Tsuchiya, 2008). There are several arguments for asking the general population about their health state preferences, including the fact that the general population is typically the "society" in whose welfare we are interested and of whose resources the allocation decision will affect.

This is an interesting problem, partly because it doesn't usually affect health state valuations in the direction that one might imagine. People who have less-than-perfect health or have a disability are liable to rate their HRQoL as better than people who have not experienced that health state. This is believed to be due, in part, to the capacity of people to adjust to many health states and also the tendency of individuals who are asked to react to a health state to, essentially, overreact based on their fear of it, for example. More generally, as Dolan and Kahneman (2008, p. 217) have argued:

> *decision utilities will always reflect the focus of the respondent's attention at the time of the assessment, rather than what they will attend to while experiencing a particular health state. Patients' decision utilities may be free of some of the biases associated with public values but they do not take due account*

> *of any losses associated with adaptation that may have already taken place. Whilst the public may overestimate the losses associated with a given state of health, patients may underestimate such losses and, importantly in a policy context, the relative ranking of different health states may well vary from one another.*

Indeed, there is substantial evidence that—with some notable exceptions, including pain and progressive diseases (e.g., muscular dystrophy)—individuals generally do adapt or adjust (Dolan & Kahneman, 2008). The result is that health status measures collected from "patients" or from people with disabilities tend to be lower than one might expect.

There are several interesting studies of this kind that pertain to people with a spinal cord injury (SCI). For example, Shulz and Decker (1985) found that the happiness of a group of middle-aged and elderly people with paraplegia was only marginally lower than the average population values for people of the same age; Wortman and Sliver (1987, cited in Dolan & Kahneman, 2008) found that people with quadriplegia did not have any greater frequency of negative feelings than the nonparaplegic population. An earlier study by Brickman, Coates, and Janoff-Bulman (1978) also showed that the mean happiness scores of people who had an accident within the last year and sustained either paraplegia or quadriplegia were, although lower than the general population, still fairly high (the group with disabilities recorded an average score of 2.96, compared to an average score of 3.82 on a 0-to-5 scale for the comparison group, which did not have SCIs). Interestingly, in the latter study, the group with SCIs also rated their pre-injury happiness considerably higher than the non-SCI group (the former recorded a mean score of 4.41, and the latter recorded a mean score of 3.32). This possibly is evidence of a "response shift" (see, e.g., Joore, Potjewijd, Timmerman, & Anteunis, 2002, Dolan & Kahneman, 2008), wherein the quality of life prior to an intervention is reassessed in the light of the intervention itself.

Another example of the disparate nature of assessments of health characteristics comes from the literature on hearing loss. There is some evidence that many people who are prelingually deaf and learn to communicate in sign language simply do not regard their hearing deficit as a disability. Some authors (e.g., Access Economics, 2006, p. 21) have embraced this notion, arguing that prelingual deafness is not, in fact, a disability but a "cultural-linguistic experience." Certainly, there is evidence that this view is shared by some people with prelingual deafness: An example is that of a U.S. couple who evidently sought a profoundly deaf IVF donor who had five generations of deafness in his family to maximize the chance that their child would be born profoundly deaf (Savulescu, 2002).

However, there is also evidence to the contrary: In a recent U.S. study (Smith-Olinde, Grosse, Olinde, Martin, & Tilford, 2008), caregivers of children with hearing losses that ranged from mild to profound provided HRQoL ratings for their children that suggested a very substantial loss of HRQoL was generally attributed to the children's' hearing deficit. Of course, in the latter study, the reported health state information is not "self-reported" by the person with a disability.

In another study, however, that does depend on self-reported data, Fellinger, Holzinger, Gerich, and Goldberg (2007) compared the HRQoL of German adults with acquired (and partial) hearing loss (AHL) with both a German sample of people who sign and the general (hearing) population. They collected measures of social functioning and of physical and mental health. Two particular aspects of their results are especially interesting. First, for their measures of social functioning, the authors found that the group with AHL had statistically significantly worse mean outcomes not only than the general population but also than the signing deaf population. Thus, the extent of the loss of functioning did not correlate well with the extent of a hearing deficit, at least between these two groups. Second, the authors also found that the signing deaf population had worse mean physical health than both the AHL and hearing population groups (between the latter two of which there was no statistically significant difference). This study is interesting because even if individuals in the prelingually deaf group did not view themselves as having a disability, their physical health status was generally rated as worse than that of their hearing counterparts and people with AHL. Furthermore, the magnitude of the loss of social function was not correlated with an audiological measure of hearing loss. Indeed, the latter finding—that there is a poor correlation between reported levels of disability or HRQoL and audiological measures of hearing loss—is a consistent theme in the hearing loss literature, even between people with mild, moderate, and severe AHLs (see, e.g., Helvik, Jacobsen, and Hallberg, 2006, and the references contained therein).

More generally, there is fairly strong evidence (Dolan & Kahneman, 2008) that values for HRQoL that are elicited from "patients" are often greater than those elicited from the general population. A review of 38 separate studies by de Wit, Busschbach, and de Charro (2000) found that patient-rated HRQoL was generally, but not always, greater than HRQoL values elicited from the general public. They found that 27 of the 38 studies concluded that patient values were different or sometimes different from other groups' health state values, while in the remaining 11 studies there was no difference between the rater groups. In the 27 studies that had divergent results for rater groups, the patient ratings were higher than the other groups' ratings in 22 studies, while 2 produced lower patient values, and the remaining 3 reported contradictory results. They concluded that the current evidence would be most supportive of the conclusion that patients' values are higher than values of other rater groups.

Discussion Box 8.2

HEALTH STATES—WHOSE PREFERENCES?

Interestingly, the general population often places lower health state values on states of less-than-perfect health than do individuals who, themselves, are in that health state. For example, people with paraplegia and quadriplegia are liable to rate their HRQoL more highly than a member of the general population would assume it to be. This has the implication that if "patient" (or "first-person") preferences are used to generate QALY measures, interventions that benefit people with disabilities will have a higher cost per QALY than they would if population values were used. What are the potential equity implications, then, of using first-person ("patient"), rather than third-party ("population") values?

Ubel, Lowenstein, and Jepson(2003, p. 599) caution that the differences in values that arise between patients and the public could arise for a variety of reasons:

> *Discrepancies might occur because patients and the public interpret health state descriptions differently—for example, making different assumptions about the recency of onset of the health state, or about the presence of co-morbidities. Discrepancies might also arise if patients adapt to illness and the public does not predict this adaptation; because of response shift in how people use quality of life scales; because of a focusing illusion whereby people forget to consider obvious aspects of unfamiliar health states; because of contrast effects, whereby negative life events make people less bothered by less severe negative life events; and because of different vantage points, with patients viewing their illness in terms of the benefits that would result from regaining health, while the public views the illness in terms of the costs associated with losing good health.*

A novel piece of work on this topic by Mann et al. (2008) seeks to compare health state values from both the EQ-VAS and EQ-5D components for non-patient and patient groups across eight patient groups (via eight studies): varicose veins, chest pain, chronic obstructive pulmonary disease, irritable bowel syndrome, osteoarthritis, low back pain, elderly women, and patients admitted to intensive care. The patient data comprise 4,137 EQ-5D profiles and 3,376 EQ-VAS profiles, while the general population data were taken from the UK EQ-5D valuation set. The authors (a) compare the patient-rated EQ-VAS with the population EQ-VAS results for the same health states and (b) estimate a model that relates patient VAS values to the EQ-5D dimensions and levels, in order to compare the resulting coefficients with the population-based EQ-5D coefficients (recall Table 8.1). In (a), they found that patient VAS scores were slightly lower than those for the general population, but via (b), they found mixed evidence about the direction of influence of patient ratings (compared with population ratings), by condition. For example, for osteoarthritis and low back pain, patient VAS values were statistically significantly lower than those elicited from the general population, while they were significantly higher for patient groups than the general population for chest pain, irritable bowel syndrome, and intensive care.[7] The only patient group for which there was no statistically significant difference was elderly women. Thus, the most recent evidence on differences between patient and population values is still fairly mixed and perhaps more complicated than was previously thought.

If patient ratings of HRQoL do exceed those of the general public, what are the ramifications of patient HRQoL values? An important one is that the QALY denominator will tend to be deflated by the use of patient values with a concomitant increase in the related cost-utility ratio (i.e., the cost per QALY). Thus, perhaps ironically, an implication of using patient values is that the interventions that would assist those patients, if funded, may appear less cost-effective than they would be if general population values were used.

7. It is worthwhile to note, in this context, that an instrument that was specifically developed for use with people who have osteoarthritis—the WOMAC (Bellamy, 1989, 2002)—also exists and that an algorithm has also been developed to map WOMAC responses to the HUI3 (Grootendorst et al., 2007).

Research Box 8.1

MENTAL DISTRESS AND QUALITY OF LIFE IN THE HARD OF HEARING

Fellinger, J., Holzinger, D., Gerich, J., & Goldberg, D. (2007). Mental distress and quality of life in the hard of hearing. *Acta Psychiatrica Scandinavica, 115*(3), 243–245.

Objectives: These authors sought to take measures of the psychological HRQoL and functions of people with (generally) prelingual deafness ("signing deaf"), people who had AHL (i.e., who were "hard of hearing"), and the general population.

Method: A total of 373 members with AHL completed the brief WHO's Quality of Life (WHO-QoL), 12-item General Health Questionnaire, and Brief Symptom Inventory and provided details about their initial and current level of hearing loss.

Results: People with AHL had worse social relationships than people who were prelingually deaf, and they were disadvantaged relative to the general population on all areas that were measured. For the AHL group, HRQoL was related to the level of satisfaction with the hearing achieved by hearing aids. See the following table.

TABLE: Means and (Standard Deviations) for the WHO Quality of Life (WHO-QoL) BREF Domain Scores for the General Population, People with Acquired Hearing Loss, and People Who Are Prelingually Deaf ("Signing Deaf")

WHO-QOL Scale	A: Hearing (general population) (n= 2048–2055)	B: acquired hearing loss (n=369–371)	C: signing deaf (n=228–232)
Physical	76.92 (17.68)	71.68α (18.49)	68.13 α (14.38)
Psychological	74.02 (15.68)	63.83α (18.60)	64.16 α (17.17)
Social	71.83 (18.52)	62.15α (23.47)	70.19 (18.06)
Environment	70.38 (14.17)	68.09α (16.29)	67.68 α (14.51)

Notes: The scores reported in this table are the unweighted means of quality of life subscales from the *WHO-QoL* that range from 0 to 100, upon which higher scores correspond with a higher quality of life rating; (unweighted) standard deviations are reported in parentheses; NS = not significant; $^{\alpha}$ indicates that the value is statistically different from the general population value (group A) at the 5% level or less, based on a two-tailed *t*-test; blue text indicates that the values for the AHL respondents (group B) is statistically different from that for the signing deaf sample (group C) at the 5% level or less, based on a test of the hypothesis that the standardized partial regression coefficient for the AHL is equal to zero.

From "Mental Distress and Quality of Life in the Hard of Hearing," by J. Fellinger, D. Holzinger, J. Gerich, and D. Goldberg, 2007, *Acta Psychiatrica Scandinavica,* 115(3), p. 244.

Conclusion: The findings of this study suggest that individuals who have an AHL may be socially isolated by comparison with both the general population and people who are prelingually deaf and sign. Nevertheless, the physical health status of the latter group may not be as good as that of the general population. This result is consistent with much of the literature on the effects of hearing loss, which suggests that "physical" (or audiological) measures of the severity of hearing disability do not correlate well with reductions in HRQoL.

Questions:
What are the implications of this study for the measurement of HRQoL and, in particular, the question of whose preferences should be used to create health scale values? For example, if the deaf community comprises individuals who do not regard themselves as having a disability, is the appropriate QALY weight for prelingual deafness 1.00 (i.e., perfect health)?

What are the implications of adopting the latter for interventions that may benefit members of the deaf community?

Discounting

In an economic evaluation, individual's preferences over the timing of costs and benefits are also considered important. Costs and benefits that are incurred or received in future time periods are usually discounted to reflect the fact that—on a dollar-for-dollar basis—benefits and costs that will arise at some time in the future typically do not have the same importance to people as benefits and costs that are more imminent.

Suppose that you have won a lottery where the prize can be taken as either:

Option 1: $2 million today; OR
Option 2: $500,000 today, and $500,000 per year for the next 3 years, payable on the anniversary of the first payment.

These two streams have the same nominal monetary value ($2 million), but most people would not be indifferent between them. An obvious reason to favor Option 1 is that inflation will erode the real value of the $500,000 to be received at anniversaries 1 through 3: If prices rise over time (as they usually do), Option 2 results in a lower total payment than Option 1.

Now suppose that the lottery company recognizes the preceding problem and offers you the same choice but promises to index the $500,000 payments at the applicable rate of inflation for anniversaries 1 through 3. In other words, Option 2 now involves payments that are equal to $2 million of today's money. (Also assume that you face zero risk of default on payments, irrespective of the option you choose.) Would you be indifferent between these two options? Once again, most people wouldn't be. Most people would still prefer Option 1 because money received today and deposited would earn a real rate of interest (i.e., the rent that is paid by the bank on your principal, over and above the rate of inflation). For example, if the real rate of interest were 2%, your \$2 million deposit, compounding annually, would earn \$40,000 interest in the first year. If you left the \$2 million principal, plus the first year's interest in the bank, the following year you would earn \$41,800in interest (i.e., 2.04m x 1.02). Indeed, by the final anniversary, your bank balance would have grown to \$2,122,416 if you had left it untouched.

The simple way to work out the future value of a sum of money earning a given rate of interest is to use the compounding formula:

$$FV = P(1 + r)^t \tag{1}$$

where *FV* is the future value, *P* is the principal (in this case, \$2 million), *r* is the rate of interest (0.02), and *t* is the number of time periods (in this case, 3 years) the principal is left in the bank. Taking Option 1 would leave you \$61,612 better off than Option 2, if you banked your payments. Of course, putting your money in the bank may not be the best option available to you: You may derive greater marginal benefit by investing it elsewhere, or using it for consumption purposes. The most important point to make here, however, is that inflation plays no role in this example.

Now suppose that we wanted to estimate the present value of \$500,000 of today's money received 3 years from now. The present value formula is the inverse of the *FV* formula, namely:

$$PV = P\left(\frac{1}{(1+r)^t}\right) \tag{2}$$

Thus, we multiply \$500,000 by 0.94232 ($\approx 1/(1.02)^3$), which gives us \$471,161. Once again, inflation takes no part in this computation. We discounted the future flow of \$500,000 to get a measure of the present value of that money to us, based on the 2% rate of interest we assumed was available.

To complicate matters slightly more, imagine that the lottery company modified Option 2: Now the offer is that you can take \$2 million now, or \$2,122,416 in 4 years from now, indexed for inflation. That's a much better deal than the previous two iterations, but is it good enough? The answer to that question depends upon your preferences and the opportunities that are open to you. If you expect to generate a better return by taking the \$2 million today and using it for investment or consumption, you may still (rationally) prefer Option 1 over Option 2. The question is, at what future offer or stream of future offers would you become indifferent between taking a payment of \$2 million now and accepting a payment of x at some future time point? Suppose the answer to this question is that you would be indifferent between a payment of \$2 million now, or \$2.662 million 3 years from now. If that were the case, your rate of time preference (which corresponds to the value of *r* in our present value formula) is 10%. This is another way of saying that \$2.662 million received 3 years from now is, to you, worth \$2 million received right now.

Economic evaluations usually involve discounting both the costs and benefits of the interventions. The rate of discount (RoD) that is used corresponds to

r in Equation (2), and the expression in parentheses is known as the discount factor. The higher the rate of discount (r), the smaller the weight that is attached to costs and benefits that are received in future years and the farther into the future (t) a payment is made, or received, the less its value.

It is beyond the scope of this chapter to discuss the theoretical arguments around the selection of a rate of discount. It is sufficient to note that, although a range of discount rates is used in practice, most analysts typically use rates of between 3% and 8%. This brings us to the next and final installment on economic evaluations: sensitivity analysis.

Sensitivity Analysis

Most economic evaluations are performed under conditions of uncertainty, and it is usually necessary to make some assumptions (e.g., about the correct value of the RoD) to proceed with the analysis. Some assumptions may have an important impact on the results of the analysis. Sensitivity analysis is the name that is given to analyses where the modeler changes some key assumptions and evaluates their effect on the outcome of interest (e.g., the CUA ratio).

Good economic evaluations contain a sensitivity analysis wherein the key assumptions are varied and the effect on the CUA ICER is examined. A common example is the use of a range of discount rates, which enables one to accommodate a range of assumptions about the appropriate RoD and to examine whether the cost-per-QALY of the competing alternatives is affected by those assumptions. More sophisticated analyses include "*n*-way" sensitivity analyses, wherein a number (n) of key assumptions are allowed to vary simultaneously, producing a set of CUA ICER estimates. This practice is useful because it serves to highlight the range of estimates that may be produced by adopting relatively conservative or radical assumptions over parameters about which the analyst cannot be certain.

CUA Decision Rules

A common question economists are faced with is: "What is the cost per QALY cut-off?" Meaning, at what cost per QALY should we draw the line to distinguish those interventions that should be subsidized and those that should not? Obviously, this question is inherently normative. Actually, it requires that the QALY, itself, be valued. In other words, in order to answer this question directly, we should go back to the Kaldor-Hicks principle and conduct an appropriate economic evaluation—in the form of a CBA—that measures, directly, the benefits associated with life-years.

Nevertheless, for argument's sake, suppose that the government of your country has announced a universal health care system under which all interventions that have an incremental cost per QALY of less than or equal to $50,000 will be provided to the population. What does this decision imply? It implies that:

- Sufficient resources will be allocated to the health budget to cover all interventions that fall below the threshold;

- The opportunity cost of the last QALY saved via the health budget is equal to $50,000;
- Saving further QALYs, with interventions that fall above the threshold, does not maximize social welfare; and
- The opportunity cost of saving QALYs beyond this point exceeds $50,000.

Will this decision rule lead to "too much", "not enough" or the right amount of health sector spending? That depends very much on the opportunities that are available in the health sector and elsewhere and the preferences of your country's population over those alternatives. We must apply the concepts of opportunity cost and marginal analysis again to answer the question: At the margin, would allocating, for example, an extra $1 million to the health sector produce greater social benefit than the next best alternative?

While the use of cost-per-QALY ICER thresholds is problematic and controversial, there is evidence that thresholds are applied in practice. The National Institute for Health and Clinical Excellence (NICE), which provides guidance on the use (and nonuse) of existing and new medical technologies in the United Kingdom, has stated a "range of acceptable cost-effectiveness" of £20,000 to £30,000 per QALY (Devlin & Parkin, 2004). However, Culyer et al. (2007) have responded to criticisms of this threshold (see, e.g., Birch & Gafni, 2007) by arguing that NICE is not entitled to set ICER thresholds but rather has sought to identify the thresholds above/below that which new medical technologies would likely be approved/not approved for funding under the National Health Service (NHS). In Australia, George, Harris, and Mitchell (2001) conducted an empirical study with a similar intent. They studied the recommendations of the Pharmaceutical Benefits Advisory Committee (PBAC) during the period 1992–1996. They found that the PBAC was unlikely to recommend a new drug for subsidization under the Pharmaceutical Benefits Scheme (PBS) if its cost per QALY ICER was greater than AU$76,000 and unlikely to recommend rejection of a drug if its ICER was less than AU$42,000.

Summary

This chapter has provided a brief overview of some of the central components of economic evaluation. In so doing, we skipped a lot of the details that you would need to come to terms with to conduct an economic evaluation yourself. For example, we really said little about measuring costs, concentrating mostly on the concept of opportunity cost. That was necessary in order for us to explore the question of health status measurement within CUA, which is, by far, the most popular economic evaluation technique in health sector applications. The learning materials that accompany this chapter provide some suggestions for readers who are interested to learn more about economic evaluation or health economics in general.

References

Access Economics. (2006). *Listen hear! The economic impact and cost of hearing loss in Australia.* Technical Report. Canberra: Author.

Bellamy, N. (1989, May). Pain assessment in osteoarthritis: Experience with the WOMAC osteoarthritis index. *Seminars in Arthritis and Rheumatism, 18*(4 Suppl 2), 14–17.
Bellamy, N. (2002). WOMAC: A 20-year experiential review of a patient-centered self-reported health status questionnaire. *Journal of Rheumatology, 29*(12), 2473–2476.
Birch, S., & Gafni, A. (2007). Economists' dream or nightmare? Maximizing health gains from available resources using the NICE guidelines. *Health Economics, Policy and Law, 2(2)*, 193–202.
Brazier, J., Roberts, J., & Deverill, M. (2002). The estimation of a preference-based measure of health from the SF-36. *Journal of Health Economics, 21*(2), 271–292.
Brickman, P., Coates, D., & Janoff-Bulman, R. (1978). Lottery winners and accident victims: Is happiness relative? *Journal of Personality and Social Psychology, 36*(8), 917–927.
Coast, J., Richards, S. H., Peters, T. J., Gunnell, D. J., Darlow, M. A., & Pounsford J. (1998). Hospital at home or acute hospital care? A cost minimisation analysis. *British Medical Journal, 316*(7147), 1802–1806.
Culyer, A. J., McCabe, C., Briggs, A., Claxton, C., Buxton, M., Akehurst, R., et al. (2007). Searching for a threshold, not setting one: The role of the national institute for health and clinical excellence. *Journal of Health Services Research and Policy, 12*(1), 56–58.
Devlin, N., Szende, A., & Oppe, M. (2006). *EQ-5D value sets: Inventory, comparative review and user guide* (EuroQoL Group Monographs, vol. 2). Berlin: Springer-Verlag.
Devlin, N., & Parkin, D. (2004). Does NICE have a cost-effectiveness threshold and what other factors influence its decisions? A binary choice analysis. *Health Economics, 13*(5), 437–452.
de Wit, G. A., Busschbach, J. J., & de Charro, F. T (2000). Sensitivity and perspective in the valuation of health status: Whose values count? *Health Economics, 9*(2), 109–126.
Dolan, P., Gudex, C., Kind, P., & Williams, A. (1995). *A social tariff for EuroQol: Results from a UK general population survey* (Centre for Health Economics Discussion Paper No. 138). York: University of York, Centre for Health Economics.
Dolan, P., & Kahneman, D. (2008). Interpretations of utility and their implications for the valuation of health. *Economic Journal, 118,* 215–234.
Feeny, D., Furlong, W., Torrance, G. W., Goldsmith, C. H., Zhu, Z., DePauw, S., et al. (2002). Multiattribute and single-attribute utility functions for the Health Utilities Index Mark 3 system. *Medical Care, 40*(2), 113–128.
Fellinger, J., Holzinger, D., Dobner, U., Gerich, J., Lehner, R., Lenz, G., et al. (2005). Mental distress and quality of life in a deaf population. *Social Psychiatry and Psychiatric Epidemiology, 40*(9), 737–742.
Fellinger, J., Holzinger, D., Gerich, J., & Goldberg, D. (2007). Mental distress and quality of life in the hard of hearing. *Acta Psychiatrica Scandinavica, 115*(3), 243–245.
George, B., Harris, A., & Mitchell, A. (2001). Cost-effectiveness analysis and the consistency of decision making: Evidence from pharmaceutical reimbursement in Australia (1991 to 1996). *Pharmacoeconomics, 19*(11), 1103–1109.
Grootendorst, P., Marshall, D., Pericak, D., Bellamy, N., Feeny, D., & Torrance, G. W. (2007). A model to estimate health utilities index mark 3 utility scores from WOMAC index scores in patients with osteoarthritis of the knee. *Journal of Rheumatology, 34*(3), 534–542.
Hawthorne, G., Richardson, J., & Day, N. A. (2001). A comparison of the assessment of Quality of Life (AQoL) with four other generic utility instruments. *Annals of Medicine, 33*(5), 358–370.
Helvik, A-S., Jacobsen, G., & Hallberg, L. R-M. (2006). Psychological well-being of adults with acquired hearing impairment. *Disability and Rehabilitation, 28*(9), 535–545.
Joore, M. A., Potjewijd, J., Timmerman, A. A., & Anteunis, L.J.C. (2002). Response shift in the measurement of quality of life in hearing impaired adults after hearing aid fitting. *Quality of Life Research, 11*(4), 299–307.
Kaplan, R. M., Bush, J. W., & Berry, C. C. (1979). Health status index: Category rating versus magnitude estimation for measuring levels of well-being. *Medical Care, 17*(5), 501–525.
Klarman, H. E., Francis, J. O., & Rosenthal, G. D. (1968). Cost-effectiveness analysis applied to the treatment of chronic renal disease. *Medical Care, 6,* 48–54.
Mann, R., Brazier, J., & Tsuchiya, A. (2008). A comparison of patient and general population weightings of EQ-5D dimensions. *Health Economics, 18*(3), 363–372.
Oppe, M., Rabin, R., & de Charro, F. (2008). *EQ-5D user guide, Version 1.0.* Rotterdam, the Netherlands: The EuroQoL Group.
Russell L. B., Wienstein, M. C., Gold, M. E., & Siegel, J. E. (1996). Panel on cost-effectiveness in health and medicine. *Medical Care, 34*(12 Suppl), DS197–DS199.

Savulescu, J. (2002). Education and debate: Deaf lesbians, "designer disability," and the future of medicine. *British Medical Journal, 325*(7367), 771–773.

Schulz, R., & Decker, S. (1985). Long-term adjustment to physical disability: the role of social support, perceived control, and self-blame. *Journal of Personality and Social Psychology, 48,* 1162–1172.

Smith-Olinde, L., Grosse, S. D., Olinde, F., Martin, P. F., and Tilford, J. M. (2008). Health state preference scores for children with permanent childhood hearing loss: a comparative analysis of the QWB and HUI3. *Quality of Life Research, 17*(6), 943–953.

Szende, A., Oppe, M., & Devlin, N. (Eds.) (2007). *EQ-5D value sets: Inventory, comparative review and user guide.* Dordrecht: Springer.

Torrance, G. W., Feeny, D. H., Furlong, W. J., Barr, R. D., Zhang, Y., & Wang, Q. (1996). Multi-attribute utility function for a comprehensive health status classification system. Health Utilities Index Mark 2. *Medical Care, 34*(7), 702–722.

Ubel, P. A., Loewenstein, G., & Jepson, C. (2003). Whose quality of life? A commentary exploring discrepancies between health state evaluations of patients and the general public. *Quality of Life Research: An International Journal of Quality of Life Aspects of Treatment, Care and Rehabilitation, 12*(6), 599–607.

fMRI: Functional Magnetic Resonance Imaging

Fabienne Cazalis
Russell A. Poldrack

9

Overview

This chapter provides information on functional magnetic resonance imaging (fMRI), a brain imaging technique that allows researchers to visualize variation of blood flow in the brain in relation to a specific task, from simple sensorimotor tasks to complex cognitive tasks, such as learning, problem solving, reading, or language production.

This chapter describes important technical characteristics, limits, and constraints related to fMRI. Its main focus, however, is a description of the present and future use of fMRI for assessment, diagnosis, treatment planning, and treatment evaluation. The role of brain plasticity on treatment and prognosis, as demonstrated by fMRI exams, is discussed.

Learning Objectives

By the end of the chapter, the reader should be able to:

1. Outline the basic fMRI principles, including some technical aspects and typical paradigms;
2. Describe current and potential uses of fMRI for assessment, including clinical as well as experimental uses, with a detailed review of current research on the topic; and
3. Evaluate the requirements and constraints related to fMRI.

Introduction

fMRI is an imaging method that is used to measure functional activity in the brain. fMRI has been a major tool for research on brain functions during the last decade, especially in the field of cognitive neuroscience and neuropsychology. As such, it has progressively gained importance as a clinical tool for diagnosis, prognosis, treatment planning, and assessment for individuals with brain injury or disease. This chapter first reviews standard methods for fMRI; then it reviews the fields of clinical application and outlines the constraints, issues, and limits related to the use of fMRI as an assessment tool.

Definition of fMRI

In order to determine the context in which fMRI is used, one should have a basic understanding of its functioning. Understanding of the various parameters of fMRI paradigm is also necessary to be able to interpret fMRI results.

Basis of fMRI Functioning

Magnetic resonance imaging (MRI) is an imaging method that detects the characteristics of tissues using the principles of magnetic resonance. MRI is based on the fact that, depending on their composition and density, tissues differ in the way that they respond to radio frequency excitation. The MRI scanner measures those variations and reconstructs a map that provides an accurate in vivo image of tissue features. MRI is a noninvasive and spatially precise technique, which makes it a tool of choice for routine brain imaging in the clinical setting (see Figure 9.1). fMRI is a specialized MRI method that, to date, has been used primarily in research settings. fMRI allows indirect measurement of neuronal activity in the brain, due to the fact that local changes of neuronal activity induce local changes of blood concentration in oxygen; oxygenated and deoxygenated hemoglobin differ in their magnetic characteristics, which can be detected using special MRI methods. This effect is called the BOLD (Blood Oxygen Level dependent) effect and is the foundation for most current fMRI methods. Statistical postprocessing is used to reconstruct a map that represents local levels of neural activity, hence described as functional activation maps.

9.1

MR image of a brain is used to detect neuronal tissue loss after brain injury.

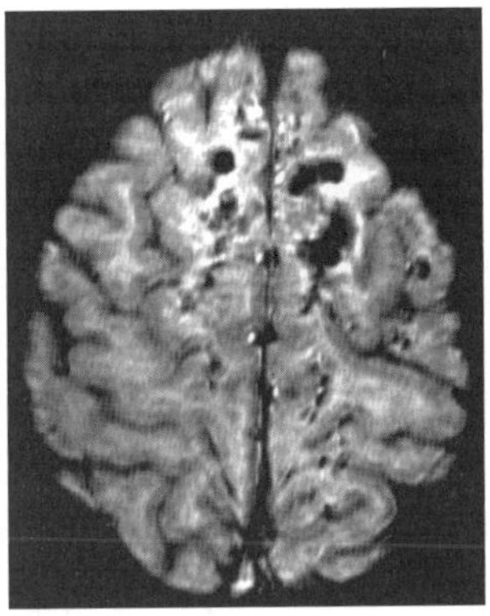

Overview of fMRI Paradigm

Understanding the experimental paradigm used in fMRI is of major importance when it comes to interpreting the results.

The standard fMRI protocol includes anatomical MRI scanning and functional MRI, that is, scanning while the individual is accomplishing a task (sensory, motor, or cognitive). Individuals lie in a reclined position within the scanner. Various devices may be used to setup the task: screen goggles, keyboard, headphones, and so forth. Low signal-to-noise ratio requires postprocessing in order to extract significant information. It's the most time-consuming part of the protocol. Processing is a statistical analysis that produces functional maps that indicate brain activation related to the functional task that is studied (see Figure 9.2).

In the standard fMRI paradigm, the subject performs a set of tasks; for example, the subject might alternate every 20–30 seconds between tapping the fingers on their right hand and resting. FMRI activation maps are always relative, meaning that each map reflects a comparison between different sets of scans. The results are read as the difference of activation between the different states engaged during those different sets of scans; for example, the comparison of right handed finger tapping and rest would isolate regions that are activated in response to finger tapping.

There are a number of different paradigms that can be used for fMRI acquisition. In the most common approach, a task of interest is compared to a "control" or "baseline" condition that is meant to "subtract" out all mental processes except for those of interest. Alternatively, it is possible to compare performance across multiple levels of task intensity or difficulty; for example, a subject might be asked to tap their fingers at several different rates. In this case, the analysis would identify regions where activity increases or decreases systematically as task intensity changes. This approach can allow activation to be related to task performance across conditions, which may be of interest in individuals with cognitive or physical impairments. Another innovation in fMRI methods is the ability to use paradigms where conditions are not presented in separate blocks but instead are interspersed throughout the scan. This "event-related" approach allows analysis based on the subject's performance (e.g., comparison of trials on which the subject succeeded versus failed on the task) and also reduces the predictability of the task.

9.2

fMRI activation maps.

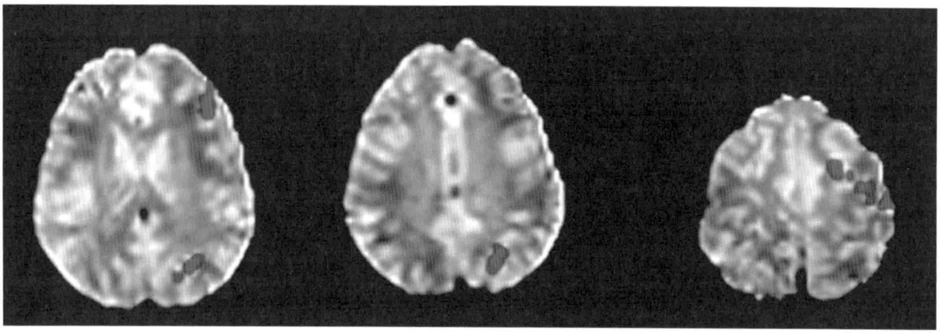

A major issue in the use of fMRI in assessment is that clinical evaluation is generally conducted on single subjects. However, there may be substantial variability across individuals, and in group studies, it is generally thought that a minimum of 15 to 20 subjects is necessary to obtain results that are generalizable to the wider population. For this reason, case studies and individual analysis must be very carefully interpreted and compared to very well-demonstrated results whenever possible. It should also be remembered that the absence of activation on a map does not imply that this part of the brain is not activated, but merely indicates that if there is activation in the region, it is not consistent enough to obtain statistical significance.

Current Assessment Methods for fMRI

The use of fMRI as a clinical assessment tool is still early in its development. Larger scale research is needed for standardization of the results and also for a better evaluation of normal versus abnormal variability between subjects. However, because of its safety and noninvasiveness, fMRI holds great promise for future clinical practice. This section reviews the current uses of fMRI for diagnosis, treatment planning, neuropsychological assessment, and treatment evaluation.

Diagnostic

The use of fMRI in diagnosis is currently limited to a small range of disorders. It is generally combined with other imaging methods, including other types of MRI that are sensitive to different aspects of brain function (e.g., MR spectroscopy, diffusion weighted imaging) or other imaging modalities, such as electroencephalography (EEG) or magnetoencephalography (MEG). Because anatomy can be difficult to discern from fMRI images, fMRI is always coupled with high-resolution structural MRI to allow precise localization.

Discussion Box 9.1

CAN fMRI DETECT CONSCIOUS AWARENESS?

Recent research using fMRI has shown what may be the only evidence of conscious awareness in some patients. For example, a group of British scientists has studied patients with severe brain damage who met criteria for being in a vegetative state, a condition in which coma has progressed to a state of wakefulness without detectable awareness. In this study, they asked a patient to imagine actions, such as playing tennis, while the patient's brain was being scanned using fMRI. This patient showed activation patterns that were similar to the patterns seen in healthy individuals (Owen et al., 2006).

Does this mean that the patient has more chance of recovery? Should such results influence the treatment of the patient?

Cochlear Implantation

fMRI is used in candidates for cochlear implantation when the diagnosis obtained through standard testing (e.g., tympanometry, otoacoustic emission, subjective residual hearing) remains inconclusive regarding the potential usefulness of such an implant. Prior to surgery, it is necessary to assess the integrity of the neuronal auditory pathway posttympanic from the cochlear nerve to the primary cortex of audition. A protocol using noninvasive electrostimulation of the nerve associated with fMRI can demonstrate the responsiveness of the primary auditory cortex, which is suggestive of approval for cochlear implantation (Bartsch, Homola, Biller, Solymosi, & Bendszus, 2006).

Unconscious Brain

fMRI of minimally conscious patients has helped investigate functions of their brains and led to the understanding of various degrees of responsiveness, opening the way to the use of fMRI as a tool for prognostic and health care planning. The research for signs, even modest, of responsiveness for patients in an unconscious state, varying from comatose to vegetative to minimally conscious, is a major step in the decision for treatment planning (cf. Schiff, 2006, for a review). For example, Owen et al. (2006) used fMRI to assess awareness in a patient in a vegetative state and found results suggesting that the patient was able to discriminate between fully meaningful sentences, sentences with semantically ambiguous meaning, and simple noise. Furthermore, an additional study was conducted during which a patient was instructed to perform mental imagery task, and the activation maps were similar to the one obtained in healthy controls. These preliminary results suggest that such fMRI protocols could be used to assess levels of awareness in patients in an unconscious, vegetative, or minimally conscious state; however, it is important to point out that a lack of activation cannot be taken as strong evidence against awareness, as outlined previously.

Research Box 9.1

EVALUATION OF CEREBRAL IMPLANTATION SUCCESS

Seghier, M., Boex, C., Lazeyras, F., Sigrist, A., & Pelizzone, M. (2005). fMRI evidence for activation of multiple cortical regions in the primary auditory cortex of deaf subjects users of multichannel cochlear implants. *Cerebral Cortex, 15,* 40–48.

Objective: The aim of this study is the exploration and understanding of auditory cortex activation in deaf subjects using a cochlear implant.

Method: Three deaf subjects, users of the Ineraid cochlear implant, underwent fMRI exam after the safety limits of the scanner in regard to interference with implanted electrodes were addressed. Once safe experimental conditions were obtained, electrical stimuli were applied on each implanted electrode. This was received as auditory sensations of various pitches, as reported by patients themselves. Such methods provided auditory sensory input without the noise of the scanner interfering with the measures.

Results: The stimulus produced activation in the primary auditory cortex, predominantly in the left hemisphere. Stimulation of each different intracochlear electrode produced distinct activation, but no clear tonotopic organization was identified.

Conclusion: The results suggest that there is a functional organization in the auditory cortex of persons with a cochlear implant.

Questions:

1. What type of knowledge on brain plasticity is demonstrated by this research study? How can such knowledge on brain plasticity following cochlear implant be useful regarding patient assessment and management?
2. Why did the authors pay so much attention to safety in the case of implanted electrodes?

Early Detection of Neurodegenerative Diseases

fMRI holds substantial promise in the early detection of neurodegenerative disorders. In a prospective fMRI study of persons genetically at risk for Alzheimer's disease, Bookheimer et al. (2000) showed an increase of activation in the network associated to a memory task related to genetic risk. Further memory testing, 2 years later, confirmed that fMRI signal was predictive of subsequent memory loss. More recently, Rombouts, Goekoop, Stam, Barkhof, and Scheltensb (2005) have shown that elderly persons with mild cognitive impairment

Research Box 9.2

EVALUATION OF LEVEL OF CONSCIOUSNESS

Moritz, C. H., Haughton, V. M., Rowley, H. A., Badie, B., Jones, J., & Meyerand, M. E. (2002). Assessment of comatose brain injured patients with functional MR imaging. *Proceeding of the International Society of Magnetic Resonance in Medicine 10,* 729.

Objective: Prognostic evaluation for neurological recovery can have a significant impact on severe traumatic brain injury treatment and outcome. This study aims at evaluating the use of fMRI as a prognosis tool for outcome in patients with severe traumatic brain injury. The authors argue that the use of conventional electrophysiological assessment techniques, such as evoked potentials, can be misleading. They report results of fMRI exams on comatose patients with brain injury.

Method: fMRI exams were performed on two patients with severe traumatic brain injury, in a comatose state, using a 1.5T scanner. Three types of stimulation were studied: blinking light, listening to a narrated text, and bilateral palm scratch.

Results: In patient #1, all three stimulations produced activation in the expected brain areas, consistent with literature on functional brain imaging. Such results were followed by aggressive medical management until the patient was fully conscious and able to recover fluent speech, visual ability, and motor functions 3 months later.

In patient #2, stimulations produced only partial response. General condition further declined, life support was withdrawn, and the patient died after 3 days.

Conclusion: These results suggest that cortical functions can be, at least partially, preserved in comatose patients.

Questions:
What does this study suggest regarding the use of fMRI in evaluation of brain functions in nonresponsive brain trauma patients? Do you think that this study brought determining results, provided that patient #1 had a living will directing the use of no extraordinary measures in the event of unlikely neurological recovery? What would be the limits of the use of fMRI as an assessment tool for comatose patients?

exhibited a BOLD signal that is slightly temporally delayed when compared to healthy matched controls but not as much delayed as patients with diagnosed Alzheimer's disease. Mild cognitive impairment in elderly persons is thought to be indicative of an early stage of neurodegenerative disease, and those results therefore suggest that fMRI could be used in complement to other testing in early detection of dementia.

Presurgical Mapping

When brain surgery is needed, either to respect a tumor or arteriovenous malformation or remove a central focus of epilepsy, it is of major importance that the neurosurgeon knows which regions are responsible for eloquent functions. All the efforts tend toward minimization of damage during surgical intervention in order to limit postsurgery impairments, such as paralysis or aphasia. The standard tool to identify regions of interest for language and motoricity prior to surgery is the Wada test, which involves injection of an anesthetic that temporarily suppresses functions of one hemisphere. The side of injection that suppresses language is the side of hemispheric dominance for that function. fMRI has been shown to have good concordance with Wada test results (Desmond et al., 1995). Further, fMRI is not only much safer, but also allows a finer-grained localization of specific functions, such as motor or language function. fMRI has been shown to be more cost-effective than the Wada test (Medina, Aguirre, Bernal, & Altman, 2004).

Identification of Motor Areas

Primary motor areas can be identified with fMRI through the use of simple tasks, such as finger tapping, toe flexion, or lip contraction. Thanks to its somatotopical organization, area M1 is identified. This paradigm is considered to be reliable enough to be used in clinical routine (Krainik et al., 2006). For instance, real time fMRI, that is fMRI with fast real-time postprocessing, has been successfully used to identify primary sensory motor areas prior to neurosurgery (Möller et al., 2005).

Identification of Hemispheric Dominance for Language

Language functions involve several cortical areas: inferior prefrontal cortex (Broca's area), superior temporal cortex (Wernicke's area), the supramarginal gyrus, and the angular gyrus. In most individuals, those language areas are localized in the left hemisphere. However, factors such as handedness and gender influence language laterality in favor of more bilaterally localized eloquence areas. Recent studies suggest that even in the case of a marked lateralization of language, the right hemisphere may contribute significantly to some aspects of language production and understanding (cf. Lindell, 2006, for a review). In any case, individual variation is large, and for this reason, it is important to determine the hemispheric dominance of a patient prior to surgery in order to leave the dominant hemisphere intact when possible. Various tasks are used in order to assess different levels of language: story listening, verbal fluency, rhymes detection, and so forth. If hemispheric dominance is not obviously exhibited via those tasks, a laterality index is computed. It can be a simple count of activated voxels—[(left−right)/(left+right)]—or it can be a more recent method of direct statistical comparison by flipping the right hemisphere to the left hemisphere (Jansen et al., 2006).

Other Uses of Presurgical fMRI

fMRI proves useful when a lesion's mass effect renders anatomical localization impossible. In the case of patients with seizures, a combination of EEG and fMRI can be realized in order to determine foci of pathological EEG activity. Other studies report that fMRI was useful in combination with perfusion MRI in a case of frontal tumor resection, or in combination with fiber tractography technique (processed from diffusion weighted imaging) to identify pyramidal motor tracts in order to improve presurgical planning and intraoperative navigation (cf. Bartsch et al., 2006, for a review).

Limitations

Presurgical use of fMRI has to be preceded by a detailed study of the individual's anatomy. It must be stressed that interpretation of single-subject fMRI data requires caution; in particular, the lack of activation must not be taken as a strong indication that a region is not necessary for the function of interest, as there are many potential reasons for null results in fMRI. However, this technique can complement other diagnostic tools to facilitate presurgical planning and improve patient outcome.

Assessment of Neuroplasticity in Healthy Subjects

In order to understand the basis of neuroplasticity assessment in brain-injured patients, it is necessary to review the effect of practice on healthy subjects. Contrary to what was long believed, there are experience-induced modifications of human brain during all its life. Practice and learning of new skills modifies durably the pattern of brain activation, as observed with fMRI. As described in reviews by Poldrack (2000) and Kelly, Foxe, and Garavan (2006), the nature and dynamics of these changes depend on the type of task that is practiced and on other parameters. Four types of neuroplasticity are observed with fMRI in healthy subjects who undergo training for a task: increase of activity, decrease of activity, redistribution of functional activations, and functional reorganization of activations. It must be noted that in most cases, the terms *increase* or *decrease* refer to a spatial change (i.e., the extent of activation), however some studies refer to *increase* as an increase of signal intensity for a given location. However, this is not a robust distinction because preprocessing of fMRI smoothes the data so that the higher signal is also the more extensive.

Reliability of fMRI Signals

Study of long-term changes in neural function using fMRI requires that the signal be reliable across time. This means that the experimenter needs to make sure that there is no signal drift across time that would render longitudinal comparison impossible. Recent work has shown that fMRI signal is reliable across very long time scales (more than a year; Aron, Gluck, & Poldrack, 2006). This suggests that changes in signal should be robustly detectable with fMRI.

Increase of Activity and Sensorimotor Functions

A long-term increase of activation in primary motor areas has been observed after extensive task practice (Kami et al., 1995). It is the case with simple motor tasks such as finger-to-thumb opposition as well as with complex motor tasks such as practice of musical instruments. A similar increase with practice is observed in primary somatosensory areas, for example, finger sensitivity for Braille readers as compared to nonreaders, and also primary auditory cortex for tones in musicians (Kelly et al., 2006). This increase is interpreted as a marker of efficiency of neural response to this task, as well as a cortical specialization that may be associated with better performance (accuracy and/or response time) to this task. However, it is important to note that differences in behavior (e.g., faster rate of movement) can result in increased fMRI signals, so it is important to control for the details of behavior.

Decrease of Activity and Cognitive Functions

Contrary to sensorimotor tasks, practice of cognitive tasks involving executive functions is generally associated with a decrease of activity as measured by fMRI. This is understood as an increase of neural efficiency, fewer neurons being needed as the neural representation becomes more precise with practice, whereas the initial novelty of the tasks elicited a greater cognitive control. Improvement of performance is often observed in conjunction of activity decrease for cognitive tasks.

Redistribution of Functional Activations

Most tasks cannot be simply categorized as executive functions or motor functions because they involve a combination of those processes. In that case, brain activation related to task-execution is exhibited as a complex pattern of several cortical and subcortical areas. Practice of the task modifies the intensity of the fMRI signal or the extent of activation, but not uniformly: Some areas decrease, while others increase. This combination of increases and decreases within the same network reflects the changes associated with training, that is, a modification of respective contributions of those areas, while the cognitive process itself is unchanged. More precisely, this dynamic balance of activity is interpreted as a decrease of the cognitive demand, while there is an increase on storage capacity (Cazalis et al., 2003).

Functional Reorganization of Activations

In some cases, practice on a task induces more than a greater efficiency of the processes involved. Training can help reach a level where processes are replaced by new processes, which in turn allow a higher level of performance. This shift of problem-solving strategy, called *functional reorganization of activations,* is seen as a pattern of both increases and decreases in activation. In order to interpret a change of brain activation pattern after training, it must be hypothesized whether the underlying cognitive processes involved in the early stages of the practice are still in use at the end of the training time (persistence), or whether new processes have been involved, leading to recruitment of new cortical areas (process-switching).

Commercial Use of fMRI for Assessment

Two areas of commercial use for fMRI are currently emerging: neuromarketing and lie detection. Neuromarketing involves the use of neural measures such as fMRI to measure the response to advertisements. For example, a recent study by McClure et al. (2004) found that subjects presented with soda during fMRI scanning exhibited stronger brain activity when they received information about particular soda brands as compared to the blind tasting condition, showing that brand knowledge impacts neural activity. Use of fMRI for marketing purposes has raised controversy ("Brain Scam?," 2004), both for ethical reasons (as medical research is being used to advance commercial interests) and because there is no current evidence that imaging data are any more effective than standard methods such as focus groups. The use of neuroimaging methods for lie detection or guilty knowledge detection has also been promoted by private companies. Recent work has shown that it is possible to detect differential patterns of brain activity between lying and truth-telling (Davatzikos et al., 2005), but it is not clear how well this extends beyond laboratory situations.

Assessment of Spontaneous Neuroplasticity in Patients With Brain Disorders

fMRI is used to investigate the evolution of brain function following an injury or during a neurological disease. Cross-sectional group studies of patients at various levels of severity and longitudinal studies have provided understanding of the mechanisms of neuronal plasticity associated with recovery of cognitive functions. Two major causes of disability induced by a brain lesion are reviewed here: stroke and traumatic brain injury.

Stroke

Stroke is a condition that has been extensively studied using fMRI. Many important longitudinal studies of recovery of motor functions after stroke have been published, producing a wealth of information on neuroplasticity of motor functions in the brain. When a stroke destroys a cerebral area involved in motor function, patients experience impaired movement, ranging from loss of fine motor control or muscle weakness to paralysis. Recovery may be observed and is associated with recruitment of alternative cortical areas that become activated when the impaired motor function is induced. It is considered that recruitment of alternative cortical areas is a process of compensation. Initial studies led to the belief that efficient recovery was associated with recruitment of the equivalent motor areas contralateral to the areas affected, using interhemispheric pathways. However, further studies have shown that a good outcome is more associated with ipsilateral compensatory processes, that is, recruitment of cortical areas adjacent or close to the lesion (Levin, 2006). For instance, Calautti et al. (2007) show that the recruitment of contralesional hemisphere for primary motor area is associated with poor recovery in patients who have suffered from stroke-induced hemiparesis, whereas recruitment of the ipsilesional areas is associated with a better recovery level.

Traumatic Brain Injury

Traumatic brain injury (TBI) is the major cause of disability in young adults in the United States. Contrary to stroke, most fMRI studies of TBI involve a cognitive task rather than a sensorimotor task. Therefore, resulting activation maps should be interpreted as described in the previous section concerning healthy groups: Local decrease is expected for recovery in the case of simple cognitive tasks, redistribution is expected in the case of improvement of complex cognitive tasks, and functional reorganization is expected when new cognitive processes participate to the enhanced performance. The presence of a TBI does not necessarily involve a focal lesion of the brain cortex; most TBI are characterized by transitory or persistent diffuse subcortical microlesions named diffuse axonal lesions (DAL). The presence of DAL is sufficient to disorganize the patterns of brain activation, as shown in fMRI studies of patients with severe TBI (Cazalis et al., 2006). On the other hand, the absence of cortical lesions potentially allows a functional reorganization that is similar to healthy subjects' in patients who exhibit a good level of recovery. For this reason, fMRI assessment of recovery in patients with TBI is very promising because it may help distinguish between rehabilitation that induces compensatory alternative processes versus rehabilitation that induces recovery of the initial processes.

So far, quite a few fMRI studies have been published on patients with TBI (cf. Strangman et al., 2005, for a review). One convergent result of these studies is that patients with TBI exhibit a disruption of activation patterns in the prefrontal cortex as compared to control groups, all of them showing an increase of activation or a functional reorganization in the frontal lobes, sometimes associated with changes in parietal or temporal lobes. Also, an experimental issue arises regarding the most appropriate behavioral task to be used with patients suffering from brain injury because comparison can be made with control subjects only on the basis of equivalent performance (succeeded trials). However, tasks that challenge cognitive abilities are more instructive for the understanding of the evolution of the patients. One response to this problem is to use parametric tasks in event-related paradigm, which potentially allows the comparison of trials of comparable success, while getting information on failed attempts.

Assessment of Therapy-Induced Neuroplasticity in Patients With Injured Brain

Extensive research on healthy subjects has shown that practice can induce neuroplasticity of the brain along with the improvement of performance in simple tasks as well as in complex cognitive tasks. In individuals with injured brain or cognitive impairment, research is more limited. However, many studies' results indicate that efficient rehabilitation resulting in improved performance or reduced impairment for the patients can be demonstrated using fMRI, as these behavioral changes are exhibited on the activation maps. Therefore, fMRI can be used as an assessment tool to evaluate the efficiency of a rehabilitation program. How brain activation changes depends on several factors: initial level of impairment, presence of lesions, and extent of practice (see previous sections). Changes of activation might either reflect improvement of existing skills, creation of compensatory processes recruiting areas distinct from the injured area, or even involvement of compensatory functions recruiting new areas.

Use of fMRI to Assess Intervention-Effect in Patients With Stroke

Stroke is the leading cause of adult disability in the United States. Although most patients exhibit spontaneous recovery at some level within 3 months postinjury, rehabilitation is often suggested as a way to improve outcome. fMRI is used to assess the effects of intervention and to understand the underlying mechanisms of enhanced recovery. It should be noted that patients with severe disability are usually excluded from such studies because they would require sedation in order to stay still in the scanner or because they would not be able to perform the tasks. As reviewed by Hodics, Cohen, and Cramer (2006), several rehabilitation methods have been evaluated with fMRI: medication, brain stimulation, robotic or device-based therapy, and several types of physical therapies such as constraint-induced movements therapy. All studies reported positive effects of the intervention, with improved motor behavior, even when the timeframe of spontaneous poststroke recovery had passed months or years ago. All studies reported cortical changes associated with behavioral improvement, most of those being an increase of activation in motor areas located ipsilaterally to the lesion. Change of laterality index is also reported, as well as a few contralateral increases, the later being associated to more severe cases, consistently with the notion that contralateral compensatory activation indicates a lesser level of recovery. Hopefully, further research will be able to identify fMRI indicators of what methods of restorative therapies are more adapted to what types of stroke-caused impairments.

Use of fMRI to Assess Mental Practice With Motor Imagery in Poststroke Rehabilitation

Along with the various existing methods of motor rehabilitation for stroke-induced paralysis, as mentioned previously, mental practice has recently emerged as a promising technique to be used along with classical physical therapy. During a mental practice exercise, individuals simply imagine a movement instead of executing it or trying to execute it. It is considered a mental simulation of the movement without overt execution. There is strong evidence that this practice recruits part of the same cerebral network as the actual movement, and furthermore, research suggests that mental practice is sufficient to modify motor performance and that it can adequately be used as a rehabilitation method (cf. Butler & Page, 2006, for a review). fMRI studies of mental practice with motor imagery show that a change of cortical activation is observed along with behavioral improvement (Szameitat, Shen, & Sterr, 2007).

Pharmacological fMRI

As reviewed by Honey and Bullmore (2004), pharmacological fMRI (or phMRI) involves the use of fMRI to assess the effects of a substance on brain function. Pharmacological agents are evaluated for their ability to modify neural activity in specific brain systems. phMRI can also be used to understand the pharmacodynamics of a drug. The properties of a substance can also be used to test a scientific hypothesis about the role of a neurotransmitter in a cognitive process. For instance, Mattay et al. (2000) used dextroamphetamine, a stimulant of dopamine release, to evaluate performance in a working memory task using fMRI in healthy subjects. They found that the drug improved performance of individuals with a low working memory span, whereas individuals with a high working memory capacity were impaired and exhibited significantly higher activation change in their frontal cortex. phMRI results demonstrate the importance of interindividual variability and may help targeting medication. For example, in the phMRI study of an antidepressant, Davidson, Irwin, Anderle, and Kalin (2003) showed that patients with the greater activation pattern exhibited the most robust treatment response.

Cultural, Legislative, and Professional Issues That Impact the Specific Counseling Aspects or Procedures

Clinical use of fMRI presents several constraints that must be considered before planning for its use. A major limit of fMRI is its safety requirements that are described in the following section. In addition, one must consider the costs of scanning as well as the availability of an MRI scanner before planning for fMRI use. Also, one must meet the criteria required by the local committee for legal protection of human research subjects in biomedical research.

Discussion Box 9.2

ETHICAL AND SCIENTIFIC IMPLICATIONS OF CONSCIOUSNESS ASSESSMENT USING fMRI

Vegetative state can be a transient, reversible condition with examples of spontaneous recovery, but in some cases it is a chronic and irreversible condition. What are the ethical implications of these findings? Should fMRI be offered to every individual diagnosed as vegetative, and how should we respond if they are found to have evidence of awareness?

Our knowledge of the mechanisms involved in coma and vegetative state is still limited. What would be the implications of this research for our understanding of coma?

Safety Limits of fMRI

MRI is considered noninvasive and safe as long as the scanned individuals and operators are screened for any metallic object that could become a deadly hazard when entering the strong magnetic field of the scanner room. External objects such as watches, coins, and glasses must be removed, while internal objects such as bone plates must be approved for MRI-compatibility. A metal-screening form is filled by the person or by his/her legal representative prior to every exam in order to ensure safety for the patient and the personnel.

Another safety limit concerns fetuses because the effects of a strong magnetic field have not been fully examined regarding their interaction with pregnancy. For this reason, pregnant women are generally not allowed in the scanner room. However, specific protocols now include pregnant women when the benefits of the experiment have been evaluated by the local ethical committee as able to encompass potential risk.

Persons suffering from claustrophobia are usually not considered as good fMRI candidates because the tightness of the MRI scanner bore may trigger a claustrophobia attack. However, in that case, pre-exposure in an MRI scanner simulator may help the subject accommodate to the environment and reduce the risk of attack. Unfortunately, open MRI systems generally are not sufficient to perform fMRI scanning.

Other Constraints of fMRI

The main constraint associated with fMRI is that it is very sensitive to motion. Motion, such as head movements of an amplitude superior to a few millimeters, produces very blurry pictures that can't be processed. Therefore, if an individual moves too much during the scan, results will most likely be unusable. For this reason, the person has to stay still during the scan, and this can prove difficult for individuals with behavioral conditions.

Another constraint of fMRI is the cost of the scanner, which limits the number and duration of scans and can be related to the limited availability of scanners. Another main constraint to consider is the delay necessary for processing data.

Legal and Ethical Constraints Related to the Experimental Nature of fMRI

Routine clinical fMRI is thought to be feasible but has not yet spread (Detre, 2006), with the notable exception of presurgical evaluation fMRI that has been recently approved for clinical routine and is used in an increasing number of centers.

All other fMRI protocols are still considered research protocols and therefore require an approval from the local Institutional Review Board (IRB) in order to ensure the protection of human research subjects.

National/State and Federal or International Practices in fMRI

The American College of Radiology has addressed the safety issues related to the practice of magnetic resonance imaging. The guidelines, referred to as the

ACR white paper on radiology, have been published in 2002 and revised in 2004 (http://www.acr.org/.../quality_safety/guidelines/WhitePaperonMRSafetyCombinedPapersof2002and2004Doc11.aspx). They include safety issues such as biostimulation device interference, movement of ferromagnetic bodies, and incidental localized heating.

Multidisciplinary or Interdisciplinary Approaches

fMRI is by essence a multidisciplinary technique. It involves knowledge from various scientific fields. Psychology is necessary to construct experimental paradigm; statistics are essential to data processing; and neuroanatomy is indispensable, as well as some skills in computer programming. Basic understanding of physics and neurophysiology are also helpful.

Summary

fMRI is a brain imaging technique that can be used for clinical diagnosis, treatment planning, and assessment of recovery. Brain activity is observed in relation to a sensorimotor or cognitive task in order to determine which brain regions are engaged by the task. However, due to a broad interindividual variability, case studies must be compared to well-established group results.

fMRI is experimentally used as a complementary diagnosis tool for a small range of disorders, such as candidate screening for cochlear implantation, research of brain responsiveness in patients with altered consciousness, and early detection of neurodegenerative diseases. The use of fMRI in treatment planning is routinely used as an alternative or a complement to Wada testing in order to identify regions of eloquent cortex prior to surgery. fMRI is experimentally used to assess neural plasticity associated with recovery in patients with brain disorder. It has been shown that spontaneous poststroke neuroplasticity involves recruitment of new regions in lieu of the destroyed tissue. fMRI is also used to evaluate the efficiency of rehabilitation programs, such as mental imagery, for instance. After brain injury, disturbance of neural networks is commonly observed, and functional reorganization may be related to the degree of recovery.

fMRI is considered to be noninvasive as long as safety constraints are respected: metallic objects, including internal objects such as pace-makers, must not enter the scanner room, and pregnant women and persons suffering from claustrophobia are excluded from experimental protocols. The use of fMRI is limited by its financial cost, its limited availability, and legal protection of human research subjects in biomedical research.

References

Aron, A. R., Gluck, M. A., & Poldrack, R. A. (2006). Long-term test-retest reliability of functional MRI in a classification learning task. *NeuroImage, 29*(3), 1000–1006.

Bartsch, A. J., Homola, G., Biller, A., Solymosi, L., & Bendszus, M. (2006). Diagnostic Functional MRI: Illustrated clinical applications and decision-making. *Journal of Magnetic Resonance Imaging, 23,* 921–932.

Bookheimer, S., Trojwas, M., Cohen, M., Saunders, A., Pericak-Vance, M., Mazziotta, J., et al. (2000). Patterns of brain activation in people at risk for Alzheimer's disease. *The New England Journal of Medicine, 343*(7), 450–456.

Butler, A. J., & Page, S. J. (2006). Mental practice with motor imagery: Evidence for motor recovery and cortical reorganization after stroke. *Archives of Physical Medicine and Rehabilitation, 87*(12), 2–11.

Calautti, C., Naccarato, M., Jones, P. S., Sharma, N., Day, D. D., Carpente, A. T., et al. (2007). The relationship between motor deficit and hemisphere activation balance after stroke: A 3T fMRI study. *NeuroImage, 34*(1), 322–331.

Cazalis, F., Feydy, A., Valabregue, R., Pelegrini-Issac, M., Pierot, L., & Azouvi, P. (2006). fMRI study of problem-solving after severe traumatic brain injury. *Brain Injury, 20*(10), 1019–1028.

Cazalis, F., Valabregue, R., Pelegrini-Issac, M., Asloun, S., Robbins, T. W., & Granon, S. (2003). Individual differences in prefrontal cortical activation on the Tower of London planning task: Implication for effortful processing. *European Journal of Neuroscience, 17,* 2219–2225.

Davatzikos, C., Ruparel, K., Fan, Y., Shen, D. G., Acharyya, M., Loughead, J. W., et al. (2005). Classifying spatial patterns of brain activity with machine learning methods: Application to lie detection. *Neuroimage, 28*(3), 663–668.

Davidson, R. J., Irwin, W., Anderle, M. J., & Kalin, N. H. (2003). The neural substrates of affective processing in depressed patients treated with venlafaxine. *American Journal of Psychiatry, 60*(1), 64–75.

Desmond, J. E., Sum, J. M., Wagner, A. D., Demb, J. B., Shear, P. K., Glover, G. H., et al. (1995). Functional MRI measurement of language lateralization in Wada-tested patients. *Brain, 118*(6), 1411–1419.

Detre, J. A. (2006). Clinical applicability of Functional MRI. *Journal of Magnetic Resonance Imaging, 23,* 808–815.

Brain scam? (2004). *Nature Neuroscience 7,* 683.

Hodics, T., Cohen, L., & Cramer, S. (2006). Functional imaging of intervention effects in stroke motor rehabilitation. *Archives of Physical Medicine and Rehabilitation, 87*(12), S1, 36–42.

Honey, G., & Bullmore, E. (2004). Human pharmacological MRI. *Trends in Pharmacological Sciences, 25*(7), 366–374

Jansen, A., Menke, R., Sommer, J., Förster, A., Bruchmann, S., Hempleman, J., et al. (2006). The assessment of hemispheric lateralization in functional MRI—Robustness and reproducibility. *NeuroImage, 33*(1), 204–217.

Kami, A., Meyer, G., Jezzard, P., Adams, M. M., Turner, R., & Ungerleider, L. G. (1995). Functional MRI evidence for adult motor cortex plasticity during motor skill learning. *Nature, 377*(6545), 155–158.

Kelly, C., Foxe, J. J., & Garavan, H. (2006). Patterns of normal human brain plasticity after practice and their implications for neurorehabilitation. *Archives of Physical Medicine and Rehabilitation, 87*(12), S20–S29.

Krainik, A., Rubin, C., Grand, S., David, O., Baciu, M., Jaillard, A., et al. (2006). Functional magnetic resonance imaging in clinical practice. *Journal de Radiologie, 87*(6), 607–617.

Levin, H. (2006). Neuroplasticity and brain imaging research: Implications for rehabilitation. *Archives of Physical Medicine and Rehabilitation, 87*(12), S1.

Lindell, A. K. (2006). In your right mind: Right hemisphere contributions to language processing and production. *Neuropsychology Review, 16* (3), 131–148.

Mattay, V., Callicott, J., Bertolino, A., Heaton, I, Frank, J., Coppola, R., et al. (2000). Effects of dextroamphetamine on cognitive performance and cortical activation. *NeuroImage, 12*(3), 268–275.

McClure, S. M., Li, J., Tomlin, D., Cypert, K. S., Montague, L. M., & Montague, P. R. (2004). Neural correlates of behavioral preference for culturally familiar drinks. *Neuron, 44*(2), 379–387.

Medina, L. S., Aguirre, E., Bernal, B., & Altman, N. R. (2004). Functional MR imaging versus Wada test for evaluation of language lateralization: Cost analysis. *Radiology, 230*(1), 49–54.

Möller, M., Freund, M., Greiner, C., Schwindt, W., Gaus, C., & Heindel, W. (2005). Real time fMRI: A tool for the routine presurgical localisation of the motor cortex. *European Radiology, 15*(2), 292–295.

Moritz, C. H., Haughton, V. M., Rowley, H. A., Badie, B., Jones, J., & Meyerand, M. E. (2002). Assessment of comatose brain injured patients with functional MR imaging. *Proceeding of the International Society of Magnetic Resonance in Medicine 10,* 729

Owen, A. M., Coleman, M. R., Boly, M., Davis, M. H., Laureys, S., & Pickard, J. D. (2006). Detecting awareness in the vegetative state. *Science, 313,* 1402.

Poldrack, R. A. (2000). Imaging brain plasticity: Conceptual and methodological issues—A theoretical review. *NeuroImage, 12*(1), 1–13.

Rombouts, S., Goekoop, R., Stam, C. J., Barkhof, F., & Scheltensb, P. (2005). Delayed rather than decreased BOLD response as a marker for early Alzheimer's disease. *NeuroImage, 26* (4), 1078–1085.

Schiff, N. D. (2006). Measurements and models of cerebral function in the severely injured brain. *Journal of Neurotrauma, 23*(10), 1436–1449.

Seghier, M., Boex, C., Lazeyras, F., Sigrist, A., & Pelizzone, M. (2005). fMRI evidence for activation of multiple cortical regions in the primary auditory cortex of deaf subjects users of multichannel cochlear implants. *Cerebral Cortex, 15,* 40–48.

Strangman, G., O'Neil-Pirozzi, T., Burke, D., Cristina, D., Goldstein, R., Rauch, S., et al. (2005). Functional neuroimaging and cognitive rehabilitation for people with traumatic brain injury. *American Journal of Physical Medicine and Rehabilitation 84*(1), 62–75.

Szameitat, A. J., Shen, S., & Sterr, A. (2007). Motor imagery of complex everyday movements. An fMRI study. *NeuroImage, 34*(2), 702–713.

Jon A. Sanford
Carrie Bruce

Measuring the Physical Environment

10

Overview

This chapter focuses on measuring the demands of the physical environment to develop effective environmental rehabilitation interventions. Three important models of person-environment fit are presented. Although the models do not provide guidance on the measurement of environmental demands, they do suggest that demands are inherent in environmental attributes, rather than environmental features. When attributes interact with human activity, potential demands are converted to kinetic demands, the strength of which is primarily dependent on the design of the environment and an individual's ability. However, demand strength is also situational; varying as situations change from one moment to the next as well as across environments. As a result, it is important to recognize the conditions and circumstances under which environmental demands and performance outcomes are measured such that the limitations of environmental rehabilitation interventions can be understood.

Learning Objectives

By the end of the chapter, the reader will be able to:

1. Discuss the strengths and limitations of major ecological models, including Environmental Press, Enabling–Disabling Process, and International Classification of Functioning, Disability, and Health (ICF), as they relate to measuring the impact of the physical environment on performance and participation;
2. State the difference between environmental features and attributes;
3. Describe differences between actual and potential environmental demands; and
4. Identify three reasons why contextual variability is an important factor in determining the impact of the physical environment on performance outcomes.

Introduction

The environment is that part of our context in which activity occurs. It encompasses all things in the physical world of buildings, objects, technologies, landscapes, and geography, as well as the social world of friends, families, services, organizations, and culture. Because we live all of our lives within physical and social environments, it stands to reason that environmental factors play an important role in human activity.

While important, the environment, in and of itself, neither determines nor dictates human performance. Rather, the environment creates opportunities for positive or negative performance outcomes through the strength of the demands that it exerts on an individual. As such, the environment acts as an independent variable that has contributions that can only be assessed in relation to an individual's performance outcomes. Whereas both the physical and social environments are equally important in providing opportunities for individuals to engage in activities and to participate in society, this chapter focuses specifically on measuring the demands of the physical environment.

Importance of the Physical Environment in Rehabilitation and Health

Traditional medical models attribute performance outcomes primarily on an individual's functional abilities. More specifically, these models predict that impairment causes functional limitations, which, in turn, result in negative performance outcomes. More recently, social construction models have begun to suggest that performance outcomes are situational—the result of the interaction between an individual's abilities (as opposed to limitations) and the demands of the environment. As a result, social construction models view performance as an expression of the fit or *mis*fit between an individual and his/her environment. An environment that fits an individual will facilitate positive performance outcomes that are manifest in his/her ability to participate in activities when, where, and with whom he/she desires. In contrast, an environment that does not fit an individual will result in negative performance outcomes or performance deficits that may prevent an individual from participating in an activity altogether.

Differences between medical and social construction models have important implications in rehabilitation. Medical models suggest that rehabilitation involves changing the person (i.e., eliminating or minimizing impairment) or compensating for a functional limitation (i.e., providing assistive technology). In contrast, social models suggest that rehabilitation can also involve eliminating or minimizing the demands of the individual's circumstances (e.g., physical environment).

Among the various social construction models that have been suggested over the past 3 decades, three models of person–environment (P–E) interaction—Environmental Press, Enabling–Disabling Process Model, and the International Classification of Functioning, Disability, and Health (ICF)—have been particularly important in rehabilitation and health. Although each model presents a different perspective on the role of the environment in promoting activity and participation, each has contributed to our fundamental understanding of the importance of the physical environment as a rehabilitation strategy.

Environmental Press Model

Based on Lawton and Nahemow's (1973) work in psychology and aging, the Environmental Press Model provides a broad conceptualization of P–E fit that describes an individual's behavior as the outcome of a transactional relationship (first described by Lewin, 1951) between an individual's competence (i.e., abilities) and environmental demands. Illustrated in Figure 10.1, the level of an individual's competencies (e.g., functional, cognitive, social, and behavioral skills and abilities) is represented on the Y-axis, and the strength of environmental demands is represented on the X-axis. The outcome of a transaction is depicted on the graph at the intersection of an individual's skill level and demand strength.

Optimal P–E fit (zone of maximum comfort to maximum performance) occurs when an individual's abilities and the environmental demands are compatible. Conversely, P–E misfit occurs when the environment is either too challenging (i.e., demands exceed abilities) or not challenging enough (i.e., abilities exceed demands). Therefore, as an individual moves farther to the right or the left of his/her baseline adaptation level, behavioral outcomes, defined by negative affect (i.e., emotion) and maladaptive (i.e., maladjusted or inappropriate) behavior, are negatively impacted. Although the psychological derivation of the model expresses outcomes as negative behaviors, they can be equally applied to poor functional performance. In either case, negative outcomes adversely impact activity and participation.

Two general principles derived from the Environmental Press Model are important in understanding the impact of the environment on people with

10.1

Environmental Press Model.

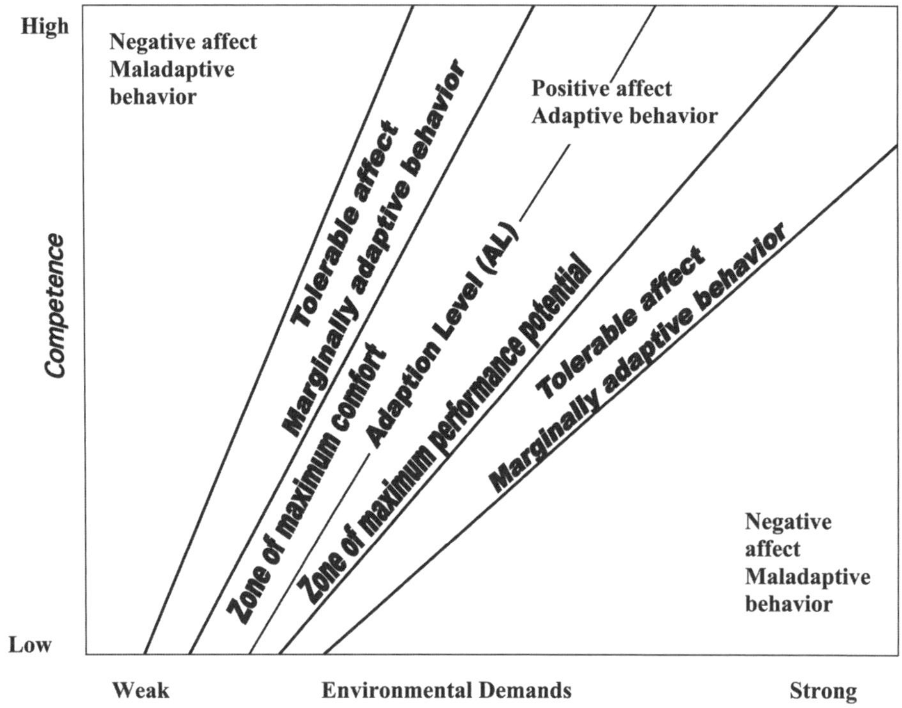

From "Ecology and the Aging Process," by M. P. Lawton and L. Nahemow, in *Psychology of Adult Development and Aging*, by C. L. Eisdorfer & M. P. Lawton (Eds.), 619–674, 1973, Washington, DC: American Psychological Association.

reduced capacities. First, the Environmental Docility Hypothesis (Lawton & Simon, 1968; Lawton, 1990) suggests that the impact of demands is a function of an individual's ability. In other words, individuals with less ability will be more challenged by the same environmental demands than individuals with greater levels of ability. Second, Excess Disability (Lawton & Nahemow, 1973) suggests that when demands exceed abilities, an individual's level of dependency will be greater than expected given the level of impairment alone.

Clearly, Lawton and Nahemow's (1973) conceptualization of the transactional relationship between a person's competence and the demands of the environment has played a major role in defining environmental contributions to activity and participation. However, the real impact of the model in rehabilitation is its contention that an environment that is commensurate with an individual's level of competence will promote engagement in meaningful activities and participation. As such, the Environmental Press Model establishes the theoretical basis for using environmental intervention as an effective rehabilitation strategy. However, this is as far as the Environmental Press Model takes us. Because it does not provide a basis for measuring either an individual's competence level or the demands of the environment, the model does not provide a mechanism that can be used to specifically inform rehabilitation intervention.

Enabling–Disabling Process Model

The Institute of Medicine's (IOM) Enabling–Disabling Process Model (Brandt & Pope, 1997) specifically identifies the environment as a pathway for rehabilitation intervention. The model suggests that the *disabling process* is the dislocation of an individual from his/her prior integration in an environment due to increasing needs relative to the environment. In contrast, the *enabling process* is either the restoration of the individual's function or environmental modification to remove barriers that limit performance.

Clearly, the model identifies linkages between the environment and disability and explicitly articulates the two potential pathways to rehabilitation. However, the model is predicated on the misfit between an existing, unchanged environment and an individual's altered needs due to impairment and functional limitation. Because the model presumes that the environment is constant, it does not account for environmental changes that might promote further disability. Furthermore, while the model identifies needs, quantifies disability, and suggests that rehabilitation interventions are possible, it offers little insight into identifying and measuring the environmental factors that account for the misfit. As a result, the model does not provide explicit guidance for environmental modification as a rehabilitation pathway.

International Classification of Functioning, Disability, and Health

In contrast to the previous models, the World Health Organization's (WHO) ICF (2001) is a health model, rather than a rehabilitation model. As a result, it assumes a continuum of degrees of ability in all people, rather than a specific set of limitations in an individual. The ICF (see Figure 10.2) also associates specific environmental factors with performance outcomes by attributing the difference between what an individual can do (capacity to engage in activities and participation based on body function and structure) and what he or she actually does (performance of activities) to the influence of personal and environmental factors.

The ICF not only provides a model that describes performance as the impact of the physical environment on all components of an individual's functional ability, it also provides an extensive taxonomy of environmental features, organized in sequence from the individual's most immediate environment to the general environment, that may either facilitate or create barriers to activity and participation (see Figure 10.3). Accompanying the taxonomy is a rating scale that denotes the strength of a particular feature as a facilitator (from 0 to positive 4) or barrier (from 0 to negative 4). The taxonomy and rating scale provide a mechanism by which the ICF can be used as a research and clinical tool to measure needs, rehabilitation outcomes, and environmental factors (WHO, 2001).

Interestingly, as illustrated in Figure 10.4, the environment is the only ICF construct, including body structure/function and personal contextual factors, that is defined by features rather than by demand-producing attributes. Thus,

10.2

Interactions between ICF components.

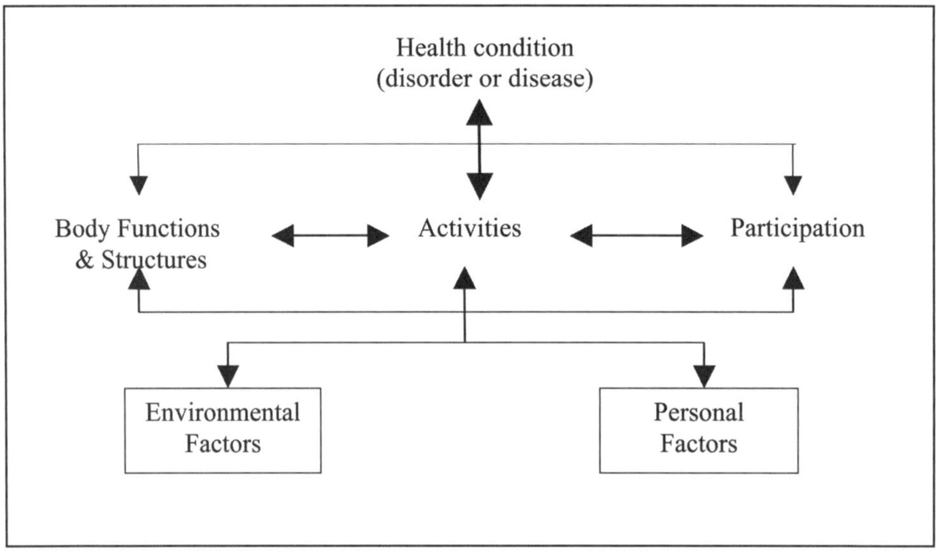

From *International Classification of Functioning, Disability and Health*, by World Health Organization, 2001, Geneva: Author.

10.3

Example of ICF taxonomy of the environment features.

ENVIRONMENTAL FACTORS

CHAPTER 1 PRODUCTS AND TECHNOLOGY

e160 Products and technology of land development

e1602 Products and technology of urban land development

Products and technology in urban land areas as they affect an individual's outdoor environment through the implementation of urban land use policies, design, planning and development of space, such as kerb cuts, ramps, signposting and street lighting.

From *International Classification of Functioning, Disability and Health*, by World Health Organization, 2001, Geneva: Author.

the focus on environmental features in the taxonomy limits measurement of environmental factors to that of categorical descriptions of what exists (i.e., a ramp that is provided or not provided), rather than quantifiable, demand-producing attributes (i.e., a ramp has a 1:12 slope). For example, personal factors are characterized by a variety of individual attributes, such as age, gender, education, coping style, and social background. In contrast, physical environmental factors are defined by products, built environment, and nature.

The differences between the ICF's characterization of environmental factors and the other constructs is important because, as we describe later in this chapter, the demands exerted by a particular feature (such as a ramp) are not inherent properties of that feature (i.e., common to all features of the same type) but rather vary with the attributes (e.g., slope and length) of that feature. As a result, the degree to which environmental modification will be an effective rehabilitation strategy is dependent on documenting and measuring the specific demand-producing attributes that must be changed. Without a framework

10.4

An overview of the ICF.

	Part 1: Functioning and Disability		**Part 2: Contextual Factors**	
Components	Body Functions and Structures	Activities and Participation	Environmental Factors	Personal Factors
Domains	Body functions Body structures	Life areas (task, actions)	External influences on functioning and disability	Internal Influences on functioning and disability
Constructs	Change in body functions (physiological) Change in body structures (anatomical)	Capacity Executing tasks in a standard environment Performance Executing tasks in the current environment	Facilitating or hindering impact of features of the physical, social, and attitudinal world	Impact of attributes of the person
Positive aspect	Functional and structural integrity	Activities Participation	Facilitators	Not applicable
	Functioning			
Negative aspect	Impairment	Activity limitation Participation restriction	Barriers/ hindrance	not applicable
	Disability			

Quantifiable Attributes **Categorical Descriptions**

From *International Classification of Functioning, Disability and Health*, by World Health Organization, 2001, Geneva: Author.

for quantifying environmental demands, the ICF, as the other models, lacks a mechanism to use environmental intervention as a rehabilitation strategy.

Comparison of the Models

This section provided background on three important models that help us understand environmental contributions to activity and participation. Lawton and Nahemow's Environmental Press Model establishes the basis for measuring the impact of the environment on activity and participation and suggests that environmental intervention can be an effective rehabilitation strategy. It also identifies basic qualities of both the person (i.e., competence) and the environment (i.e., demands) that contribute to P–E fit. However, while the interaction of these qualities provides a conceptual basis for environmental interventions, the model does not link specific environmental attributes or personal competence to performance outcomes. As a result, it does not provide explicit guidance for rehabilitation interventions. The Enabling–Disabling Process Model also suggests that disability is the result of a misfit between the person and his/her environment. In addition, it goes a step further than the Environmental Press Model by explicitly identifying the person and the environment as potential pathways to rehabilitation. However, unlike the Environmental Press Model, which suggests that P–E misfit is the result of the interaction between measurable competencies and potentially measurable demands, only the person side (i.e., impairment) of the P–E misfit equation is measurable in the Enabling–Disabling Process model. The environment, in contrast, is literally a black box, with no recognition that there are specific measurable factors that contribute to the misfit. Finally, the ICF's taxonomy and rating scale are the first attempt to identify and measure salient environmental factors that contribute to P–E misfit. However, the focus on environmental features in the taxonomy (even

Discussion Box 10.1

RETHINKING THE ICF'S UNDERSTANDING OF ENVIRONMENT

As described in the text, there is an inconsistency in the classification of the physical environment in the ICF compared to the other constructs of structure and function; capacity and performance; and personal contextual factors. This is a rather challenging issue because it makes it difficult to clearly identify the specific attributes of an environmental feature that lead to person–environment interaction problems. In conducting an environmental assessment, what do you need to know about the physical environment in order to suggest specifications for an intervention or a new design? What is the result of only recognizing features as barriers or facilitators? Why do you think the ICF was designed in this way? How would you propose making changes to the ICF based on this issue? What challenges might be encountered if changes were to be made to the physical environment construct?

though other constructs clearly focus on specific attributes) limits measurement of environmental factors to that of categorical descriptions of what exists, rather than measurable demand-producing attributes. As a result, the ICF, as the other models, lacks a mechanism to guide measurement and prescription of specific environmental interventions as a rehabilitation strategy.

History of Research and Practice in Reducing the Demands of the Physical Environment

As suggested by the environmental models described previously, the outcomes of the fit between an individual and his/her environment can be far reaching, impacting not only an individual's behavior and functional performance but also the activities in which the person engages and his/her participation in the community. As a result, providing manageable demands through environmental modification has become an increasingly important rehabilitation strategy to compensate for functional limitations; maintain or improve performance outcomes; increase independence; ensure safety, ease of use, security, self-esteem, and self confidence; reduce caregiver upset; and reduce the costs of health care and personal care services. These positive impacts have been demonstrated by a growing body of evidence, particularly in relation to environmental interventions in the home (e.g., Administration on Aging, 2000; Connell & Sanford, 1997, 2001; Gitlin, Corcoran, Winter, Boyce, & Hauck, 2001; Gitlin, Miller, & Boyce, 1999; Gitlin et al., 2002; Mann, Ottenbacher, Fraas, Tomita, & Granger, 1999; Sanford et al., 2006; Sanford & Hammel, 2007).

While these and other studies have demonstrated the rehabilitative impact of reducing environmental demands, rehabilitation practice has made little attempt to quantitatively measure demands themselves. Rather, the strength of demands has been associated with the type of abilities an environment (characterized by *typical design, accessible design,* or *universal design,* as described in Chapter 12) is expected to support. Similarly, research has not attempted to quantify demands but instead has focused on demonstrating that typical environments are not usable and on describing accessible and universally designed environments that are usable.

Issues That Impact Environmental Measures: Differentiating Features and Attributes

We have described the major limitation of existing ecological models as their failure to provide a framework for environmental intervention. Whereas all of the models link the environment to performance outcomes, they all also fail to provide a mechanism to quantify environmental demands that impact performance. Even the ICF, which quantifies the overall strength of demands exerted by environmental features, does not specifically quantify the demands themselves. As a result, it, too, fails to provide guidance for environmental intervention. In this section, we further elaborate on the differences between features and attributes and propose a framework for identifying and measuring demand-producing attributes of the physical environment.

Environmental Features and Attributes

- *Environmental Feature* (n). Any identifiable (i.e., has a name) artifact, either natural or man-made, including products, devices, pieces of equipment, technologies, rooms, buildings, and spaces (e.g., door, window, toilet, ramp, walkway, park, lake). Features are either present in the environment or not. As a result, features are categorical variables that are only measurable by their presence or absence (e.g., yes/no). Features of a particular type have the same inherent properties (e.g., a ramp is inclined, a sidewalk is hard, and a lake has water). Because properties are identifiable characteristics of all features in a particular category, basic assumptions can be made about the contributions of those features to human performance (i.e., facilitator or barrier) irrespective of personal capacity (i.e., a wheelchair will roll across a sidewalk, but not a lake).
- *Attribute of an Environmental Feature* (adj.). A measurable (i.e., quantifiable or describable) characteristic of a feature, such as height, length, width, color, texture, and condition (see Figure 10.5). Because attributes vary widely, even among features of a particular type, these characteristics will act as either facilitators or barriers only when they interact with personal capacity.

Taxonomy of Features and Attributes

A *taxonomy* is an organizational scheme in which related constructs are presented in a hierarchical progression. For our purposes we have presented a framework (see Table 10.1) of a taxonomy of environmental features and

10.5

Example of ramp attributes.

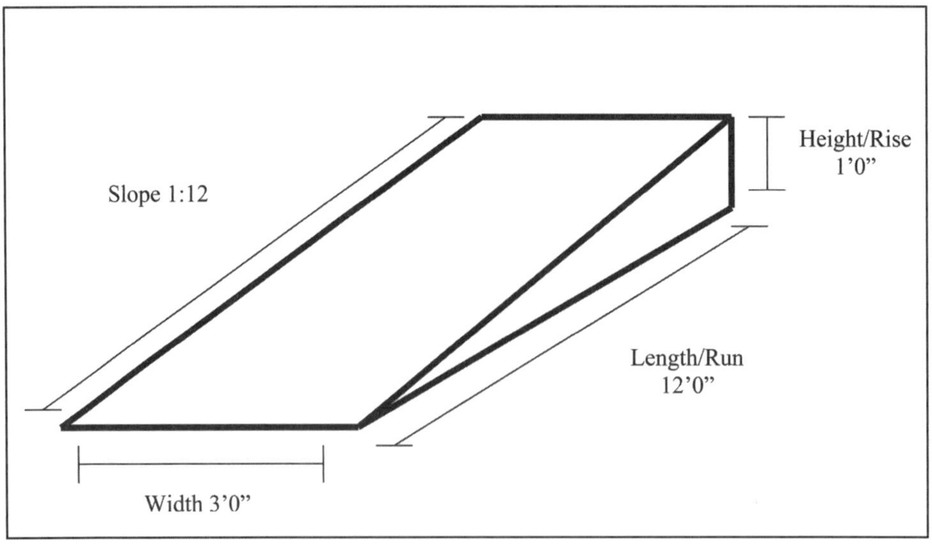

10.1 Common Attributes of Physical Environment Features

Spaces	Products, Devices, and Technologies	User Interfaces
• Configuration/layout • Entry • Circulation/level changes • Orientation cues • Location of products, devices, and technologies • Location of environmental controls • Ground/floor and wall materials/finishes • Ambient conditions	• Product type • Dimensions • Weight • Location of user interfaces • Materials/finishes	• Type of interface • Minimum approach distance and angle • Dimensions • Activation force required • Operational attributes • Materials/finishes • Feedback mechanisms • Layout of user interfaces

demand creating attributes that can potentially impact performance outcomes. The framework is strictly conceptual and uses common attributes to illustrate the concept. It is not meant to be comprehensive. To propose a taxonomy of specific features would essentially undertake the task of rewriting the ICF. Thus, the table presents a possible taxonomy of environmental features and attributes organized by decreasing scales of the environment from spaces to products, devices, and technologies to user interfaces.

Spaces

The physical attributes of elements, such as buildings, walls, landscapes, rooms, and other spaces, place demands on people that can affect successful performance. Common attributes of spaces that can create demands include:

- Space configuration/layout (e.g., size of space/subspaces, orientation of structures, arrangement of key elements);
- Entry (e.g., location, width, entryway height, threshold height);
- Circulation routes/level changes (e.g., location of routine and emergency egress/ingress, visibility, width, length, slope);
- Orientation cues (e.g., location of signage, landmarks);
- Location of products, devices, and technologies (e.g., clear floor space for approach and use, mounting height);
- Location of environmental controls (e.g., mounting height and clear floor space at switches and outlets);
- Ground/floor and wall materials/finishes (e.g., color, type, texture, reflectivity, slip resistance); and
- Ambient conditions (e.g., light levels, temperature, shade, acoustic properties, and noise levels).

Products, Devices, and Technologies

The design of products themselves, such as fixtures, appliances, switches, and furniture, can also create demands that impact performance outcomes. Product attributes of interest include:

- Product type;
- Dimensions (e.g., height, shape, width);
- Weight;
- Location of user interfaces (mounting height and location, space between controls); and
- Materials/finishes (type, texture, and color contrast).

User Interfaces

User interfaces include a variety of controls and hardware. They can be either operable (such as a doorknob) or fixed (such as a drawer pull or grab bar). Generally their function is to operate products, although occasionally inoperable hardware, such as grab bars, function independent of a product or device. In addition, although many operable interfaces are located on products or devices, environmental controls, whether wired or remote, including light switches, elevator call buttons, thermostats, and alarm systems, are typically located in the surrounding spatial environment rather than attached directly to the product.

Interfaces often require use of upper extremities (arms) and fine motor control (fingers) for grasping, twisting, rotating, pushing, or pulling. In fact, many interfaces require multiple manipulations, such as a doorknob that requires pushing and twisting to lock, or a computer mouse that requires fingering, holding, and pushing/pulling to highlight, drop, and drag text. However, interfaces can also be operated by voice recognition and may require visual and cognitive abilities to discriminate between the control and the environment in which it is located. Specific attributes of user interfaces that affect performance include:

- Type of interface (dispenser, toilet handle, lock, assist, receptacle, control);
- Minimum approach distance and angle (space needed to use the device);
- Size (diameter, length, width);
- Activation method (voice, grip required);
- Operational characteristics (direction and distance interfaces need to be moved, calibration, type of sensory feedback, force required, voice sensitivity);
- Materials/finish (type, texture, and color contrast);
- Configuration of interface; and
- Feedback mechanisms (level of auditory or visual feedback, if provided).

Measuring the Physical Environment: A Framework for Linking Environmental Attributes, Activity, and Performance Outcomes

As noted earlier in this chapter, environmental features, in and of themselves, do not exert demands on individuals. Rather, the attributes of those features, such as the number and height of steps, the height of a toilet, the width of a walkway, the size of text on a sign, or the amount of force required to open a door, create demands that impact performance outcomes. However, there are no existing ecological models that provide a framework to enable us to specify which environmental attributes create demands during the performance of specific activities. For example, spatial attributes, such as the layout of the tub and toilet in a bathroom, will influence whether a person in a wheelchair can get close enough to transfer; the height of a thermostat will affect whether a person can reach it to adjust the temperature; and light levels can determine if an individual with low vision can see enough to read the label on a medicine bottle. Similarly, product level attributes, such as the location of controls at the rear of a stove, may be too far for an individual in a wheelchair to reach to operate the appliance, or the weight of a pot may be too much for an individual with limited strength to pick up. Finally, user interface attributes, such as a black knob on a black appliance, might not have sufficient contrast for someone with a vision impairment to locate or the sound of an oven control clicking when it reaches a specified heat setting may not be loud enough for an individual with a hearing impairment.

To identify the environmental attributes that create demands during the performance of specific activities, we need a framework that links attributes to both activity and ability. The conceptual framework proposed in this chapter is based on research conducted by the authors over the past 20 years. It was originally constructed to identify environmental attributes associated with performance deficits among people with hand and upper extremity impairments for the purpose of proposing recommendations for technical specifications in the Minimum Guidelines and Requirements for Accessible Design (MGRAD) (Feurstein, Steinfeld, Sanford, & Shiro, 1987). Over the years, it was expanded to guide the identification and measurement of demand-producing attributes in a variety of environmental features in many different settings, including toilets and bathing fixtures in homes and public facilities (Sanford, Echt, & Malassigné, 1999; Sanford & Megrew, 1995; Sanford, 2002); various features of the home associated with basic activities of daily living (Connell & Sanford, 1997, 2001); and accessible seating in theaters and stadiums (Sanford & Connell, 1998). More recently, the framework has been used to identify applicable attributes to be measured in the home environment for the provision of remote rehabilitation services (Hoenig et al., 2006; Sanford & Butterfield, 2005; Sanford et al., 2007; Sanford, Jones, Daviou, Grogg, & Butterfield, 2004).

Identifying Activity-Relevant Environmental Demands: Linking Attributes to Activity

Surely, everyone is familiar with the popular philosophical riddle: *If a tree falls in a forest and no one is around to hear it, does it make a sound?* We might also ask: If a tree falls in a forest and no one is around to hear it, does it exert auditory demands? We probably would all agree that the sound can occur in the absence of human perception. But would we agree that demands do not occur in the absence of human activity?

For example, if an individual does not cook on a stove, then the stove controls will not exert any demands. In this case, we would not need to measure the activation force required or how far the individual will need to reach to operate a stove control. Conversely, if he/she does cook on a stove, the controls will exert demands, and thus, we would need to measure the attributes of the stove controls. As the example illustrates, activity defines the relevant demand-producing environmental attributes. Therefore, for any activity, activity-relevant environmental attributes must be identified.

One application of this framework was the identification of attributes of home environments associated with routine household activities for the purpose of making appropriate environmental modifications (Connell & Sanford, 1997; Jones & Sanford, 2002; Stark & Sanford, 2005). The framework includes a comprehensive list of activities (e.g., bathing, toileting, preparing meals, cleaning) and their associated tasks (undress, grasp faucet, turn water on, transfer into fixture, etc.). Specific environmental features and their demand-producing attributes are then associated with each task (see Table 10.2). This framework provides us with a mechanism to measure the relevant environmental attributes for any activity, which, when linked to performance outcomes (as described later), will enable us to determine appropriate environmental interventions.

10.2 The Framework with Examples of Attributes Linked to Household Activities

Activities and Tasks		Activity-Relevant Features & Attributes		
Activity	Task	Space	Product	User Interface
Bathe/Shower	Dress/undress Grasp faucet Turn water on/off Regulate water temperature	Bathroom	Tub/shower, seat, grab bars, towel rack	drain, faucet, hand-held shower, soap dish, storage
	Transfer to/from fixture Reach/grab soap, shampoo Wash self Reach/grab towel	• location • layout • door width • floor finish • lighting	• location • height • finish • color	• location • height • type of handle • force required
Wash face/hands	Use mirror Turn water on/off Regulate water temperature	Bathroom	Mirror, sink, soap dish, towel rack	faucet, soap
	Reach/grab soap Wash face/hands Reach/grab towel Put soap/towel away	• location • layout • door width • floor finish • lighting	• location • height • finish • color	• location • height • type of handle • force required

Measuring Demand Strength: Linking Attributes to Ability

While the specific attributes associated with an activity will define the types of demands that will be exerted, the impact of demands (i.e., the amount of influence that the environment has on performance), as you might recall from our discussions of the Environmental Docility Hypothesis and the ICF earlier in the chapter, is a function of the interaction between the strength of environmental demands and human ability.

Like energy, the environment possesses both potential and kinetic (actual) demand. Whereas a body possessing stored potential energy requires a force to release kinetic energy (e.g., a pitcher winding up for a fastball, or the giant New Years Eve ball in Times Square at 11:59 P.M. before it descends), environmental characteristics have stored-up, demand-producing potential that is only exerted (thus becoming an actual demand) when it is released by an action or, in this case, human activity. Therefore, while both potential and actual demand strength can be measured, it is important to differentiate between the two.

Potential Demand

The concept of demand potential is illustrated by the Enabler (see Figure 10.6), which has been applied to measuring the potential demands of the physical environment in order to assess accessibility in a variety of environments, including public facilities (Steinfeld et al., 1979) and personal residences (Iwarsson, 1997). The Enabler identifies a set of typical impairments and functional limitations as a surrogate for ability or, in this case, disability. Characteristics of features are then systematically rated in relation to these disabilities to measure the strength of potential demands that would be encountered during routine activities.

The Enabler model assesses the relationship between expected levels of (dis)ability and a specific set of environmental characteristics to predict potential demands. However, measuring potential demands has its limitations. As you recall from our discussion of the ICF model, contextual factors (including environmental demands and personal factors) account for the difference between individual capacity (i.e., what people can do) and performance (i.e., what they actually do). If we don't know what people can do, how can we be sure that the potential demand strength accurately reflects what individuals actually do?

Clearly, the measurement of demand potential is helpful when there is no single client whose abilities can be determined (such as accessibility of public buildings) or when actual performance for specific activities cannot be determined, such as assessing the home environment for a patient prior to his/her discharge from a clinic or a work environment prior to employment. However, when performance outcomes can be determined, as is the case when an individual is living at home or working at a job, then measurement of actual (i.e., kinetic) demand strength will provide a more accurate picture of environmental demands than prediction of demand potential will.

Actual Demand

Actual demand, in contrast to potential demand, is based on real interactions between individuals and their environments in the course of conducting

10.6

Excerpt from *The Enabler.*

The Enabler

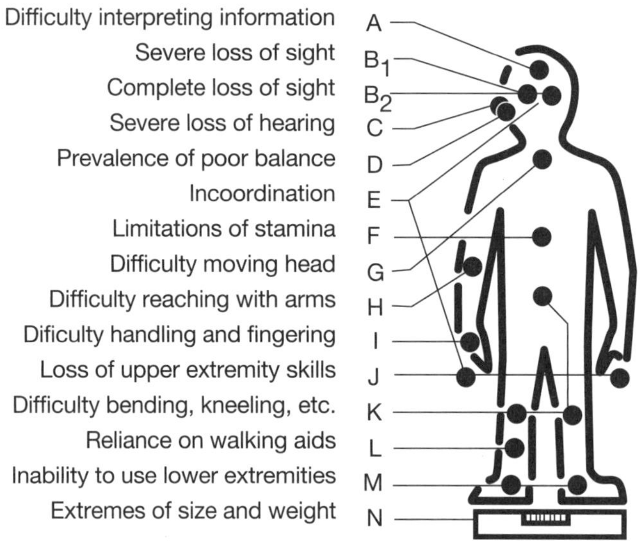

A. Outdoor environment	A	B1	B2	C	D	E	F	G	H	I	J	K	L	M	N
General (pp. 37–42, 183–96)															
1. Narrow paths (less than 1.3 m).					3	3							3	3	1
2. Irregular walking surface (includes irregular joins, sloping sections, etc.).		2	3		1	1		3					3	3	
3. Unstable walking surface (loose gravel, sand, clay, etc.).		2	3		3	3	2						3	4	
4. Path surfaces not level (cracks, holes deeper than 5 mm).		2	3		3	3	2						3	3	
5. Steep gradients (more than 1:12; does not include ramp at entrance–rate under B23).		2	3		2	2	3						3	3	1

From T*he Enabler: A Method for Analysing Accessibility Problems for Housing,* by S. Iwarsson, 1997, Lund, Sweden: Lund University, Department of Community Health Services

activities, such as bathing or using the computer. Such interactions can be assessed through a variety of methods, including direct observation of task performance, physical traces from prior activities (e.g., room temperature is too high because the thermostat cannot be reached or a light is left on because the light switch cannot be reached), or reported problems with performance from individuals, caregivers, or others, such as family members, friends, coworkers, supervisors, or teachers, who are knowledgeable about the situation.

Although most assessments (e.g., for home modification or workplace accommodation) include some level of information about an individual's abilities and preferences, performance problems, and the environmental attributes that impact performance, the specific information typically varies according to discipline bias, individual preference, and level of expertise. Because a large number of environmental assessments are conducted by rehabilitation professionals with limited experience in the identification and measurement of activity-related environmental attributes, environmental demands are often overlooked in the assessment process. As a result, environmental modifications are often underrepresented as a rehabilitation strategy.

Moreover, other than assessments for home modifications, there are few assessment instruments for environmental modifications that are intended to assist rehabilitation professionals in identifying and measuring activity-related attributes. Among the home modification assessments, the Comprehensive Assessment and Solutions Process for Aging Residents (CASPAR) is perhaps the most comprehensive in terms of measuring demand-producing attributes (Sanford & Butterfield, 2005; Sanford, Pynoos, Gregory & Browne, 2002). CASPAR is a client-directed assessment that enables an older adult, family member, or caregiver to identify high-priority problem areas in the home that are in need of modification. CASPAR enables someone without professional expertise in environmental assessment to collect the same critical information about activity-relevant home environment attributes that would be collected by a specialist. CASPAR documentation includes self-reported information on functional abilities under typical conditions (e.g., turn on a light switch, open a drawer, and turn a doorknob) and types of performance problems with P–E transactions (e.g., going up steps to the entry door, locking and unlocking the door, and stepping over the doorway threshold). It also includes detailed measures of activity-relevant environmental attributes of the home, such as the narrowest width of steps, door threshold height, height and location of toilet, and location of bathroom (see Figure 10.7).

10.7

Examples of CASPAR attribute measures.

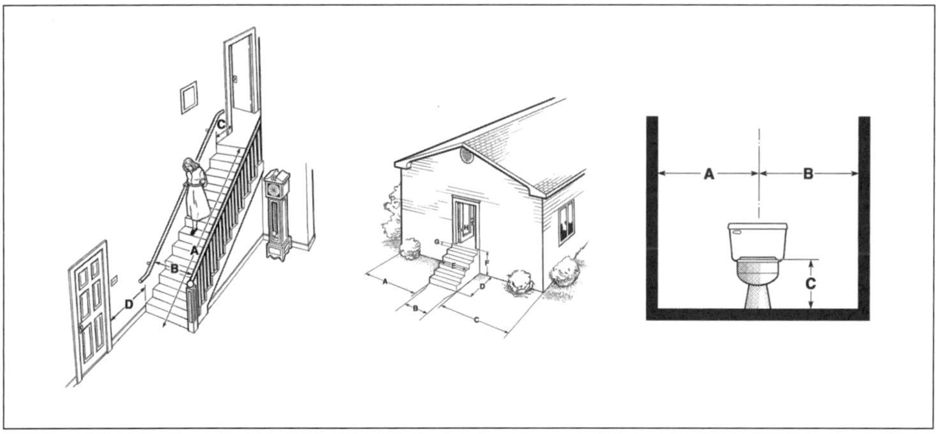

Major Issues That Need Attention in Measuring Environmental Demands

The biggest issue impacting the measurement of environmental demands is *contextual variability* that limits generalizability. Because activities vary across settings, no two setting types (e.g., home, office, school, places of worship, restaurant) have the same features and attributes. As a result, identification and measurement of demands, even across the range of human abilities, in one setting may not carry over to other settings. Unfortunately, there is also a high degree of intrasetting variability, despite having many attributes that are the same. For example, the strength of demands in residential bathrooms and kitchens can vary from low to high due to layout, size, and location of fixtures, cabinets, and appliances, even though there is very little variability in the products and user interfaces that are commonly found in these areas themselves. Such variability suggests that a comprehensive taxonomy of environmental attributes is a task that will need to be undertaken one setting at a time and is most likely unattainable.

A second issue that further complicates contextual variability is the effect of *transient attributes* of the individual (e.g., fatigue and pain) and environment (e.g., lighting, temperature, noise) that may or may not be present or may change from one moment to the next. Specifically, environmental factors that are transient include ambient conditions (e.g., lighting, sound), weather conditions (e.g., ice, rain, humidity, temperature), vehicular traffic (e.g., number and speed of cars), the presence of other individuals (e.g., too many or too few), and other situational conditions (e.g., water spills or objects in the path of travel). Transient conditions can create distractions, such as a loud noise, or alter the physical conditions, such as a liquid spill or the sun's glare on a tile floor, that may compound the demands of the existing attributes. Similarly, transient conditions can compensate for environmental attributes, such as using additional lighting on stairs, to minimize demands of existing attributes. In either case, because transient attributes are variable, frequently unpredictable, and often not replicable, it is not only difficult to precisely measure the strength of their demands but also the strength of fixed environmental attributes with which they interact. As a result, transient conditions create a reliability and validity dilemma in which knowing when, and under what conditions, attributes and performance outcomes are representative of predictable and usual events and are repeatable is not a trivial task.

Despite the impact of variability, validity and reliability issues are even more basic, being strongly influenced by the ways in which demand strength is measured. Clearly, the measurement of demand potential, which is the way in which environmental demands are commonly measured in settings where modifications are generalized (i.e., public settings) rather than individualized (i.e., home, work, and school), is more susceptible than actual demand strength to validity and reliability problems. First, because actual performance is not being measured, we don't really know whether the attributes being measured are the right ones to measure (content validity), and even if they are, they may not predict actual performance in the way that we think they will (criterion validity). Second, because many instruments, such as the Enabler, do not precisely quantify attributes but use qualitative judgments about the attributes, such as wide, narrow, poor condition or insufficient light to describe their condition, measurements are more susceptible to failing to accurately assess the features that they set out to measure (construct validity) and to inconsistencies in measurement among raters (interrater reliability).

Research Box 10.1

REMOTE ASSESSMENT

Sanford, J. A., & Butterfield, T. (2005). Using remote assessment to provide home modification services to underserved elders. *The Gerontologist, 45*(3), 389–398.

In many areas of the rural United States, it is often difficult for individuals to get services related to health care or functional limitations. This is due in part to the limited number of professionals available to provide services, as well as transportation issues that might be experienced by either the individual traveling to get the service or the professional traveling to see the person. As a result, remote methods for collecting information and providing services are becoming more popular. However, a lack of research exists that demonstrates how useful remote protocols are in measuring the environment and a person's performance of activities to determine what environmental modifications are needed. Sanford and Butterfield (2005) investigated the use of remote protocols to gather information about home environments in order to understand how the environment can be measured and modifications identified.

Method: The investigators compared a paper-and-pencil remote protocol, CASPAR, and a televideo remote protocol for determining home modifications. Traditional in-home assessments were performed in addition to either a paper-and-pencil or televideo assessment in 73 homes. Paper-and-pencil assessment data was collected by an individual inexperienced in home modifications and then sent to a home modifications expert for complete analysis. In the televideo protocol, an individual inexperienced in home modifications was directed by an expert to collect information about the environment using teletechnology, which included a videophone that connected to a standard residential landline telephone service, wireless video camera, and wireless earphone and microphone.

Results: Both paper-and-pencil and televideo remote protocols had significant results for problem identification and agreement in proposed environmental modifications. Thus, remote protocols have potential in collecting appropriate measures of the environment for determining modifications and interventions.

Questions:

1. What does this research indicate regarding using remote protocols for collecting information about the environment?
2. What are some specific considerations that should be acknowledged in a remote assessment?
3. What are some environmental measures that might be difficult to gather using a remote protocol?
4. What are some anticipated issues with using televideo equipment to collect data? What might be different if Internet or cell transmission was used instead of landline phone connection?

Summary

This chapter focused specifically on measuring the demands of the physical environment. Three important models that assume differing perspectives on the disparity between an individual's ability to function and the demands of the environment were presented. The first is the Environmental Press Model, a psychological model that describes the behavioral outcomes associated with fit or misfit between a person's competence and level of environmental demands. Second, the Enabling–Disabling Model is a rehabilitation model that describes the misfit that results from functional limitation and an existing (disabling) environment as well as the fit that results from environmental modifications (enabling) to accommodate those limitations. Finally, the ICF, which is a public health model, attributes the difference between what individuals can and actually do to environmental demands and personal factors. Although, these models provide the basis for considering environmental modifications as a rehabilitation strategy, none specifically define, describe, or differentiate the environmental demands that would enable us to develop specific environmental interventions. Clearly, the development of effective environmental interventions is dependent on identifying and measuring the demands associated with specific performance outcomes.

Despite the lack of guidance in the identification of specific demands, it is important to understand that design attributes, rather than design features, account for those demands. Environmental features were defined as any identifiable artifact, including products, devices, equipment, technologies, rooms, buildings, and spaces. Attributes were defined as characteristics of a feature, such as height, length, width, color, texture, and condition. Features are categorical (exist or not). As a result, they can be associated with the level of overall environmental demands and their impact on performance and activity. In contrast, attributes are measurable. Therefore, the strength of the demands can be associated with specific measures of any particular attribute. Importantly, attributes can be modified to reduce demands.

A general taxonomy of environmental features and attributes organized by scales of the environment (space, product, and user interface) was suggested. However, attributes only create demands during the performance of activities.

To identify the demand-producing attributes as well as the strength of the demands associated with specific activities, we proposed a framework that links attributes to activity. The framework provides us with a mechanism to measure the relevant environmental attributes for any activity, which, when linked to performance outcomes, will enable us to determine appropriate environmental modifications.

Finally, while the specific attributes associated with an activity will define the types of demands that will be exerted, demand impact is a function of the interaction between demand strength and human ability. Demand strength is analogous to potential and kinetic energy. Environmental characteristics have stored-up, demand-producing potential that is only exerted when it is released through human activity. Measuring actual demand of environmental attributes, in contrast, is based on real interactions between individuals and their environments in the course of conducting activities, such as bathing or using the computer.

Despite the typology and framework proposed in this chapter, because demands are situational, measuring the physical environment is neither a simple nor straightforward task. While attributes of environmental features may be static, transient characteristics ensure that the overall setting is dynamic. To further complicate matters, no two settings are identical. In other words, the impact of demands varies as situations change from one moment to the next as well as across environments. As a result, it is important to recognize the conditions and circumstances under which environmental demands and performance outcomes are measured such that the limitations of environmental rehabilitation interventions can be understood.

References

Administration on Aging. (2000). Retrieved July 14, 2008, from: http://www.aoa.dhhs.gov/eldrachn/homemodf.html.

Brandt, E. N., & Pope, A. M. (1997). *Enabling America: Assessing the role of rehabilitation science and engineering.* Washington, DC: National Academies Press.

Connell, B. R., & Sanford, J. A. (1997). Individualizing home modification recommendations to facilitate performance of routine activities. In J Hyde & S. Lanspery (Eds.), *Staying put, changing the place not the people* (pp. 113–147). Amityville, NY: Baywood Publishing Co., Inc.

Connell, B. R., & Sanford, J. A. (2001). Difficulty, dependence, and housing accessibility for people aging with a disability. *Journal of Architecture and Planning Research, 18*(3), 234–242.

Feurstein, M., Steinfeld, E., Sanford, J. A., & Shiro, G. (1987). *Hands on architecture.* Proceedings of the Eighteenth Annual Conference Environmental Design Research Association, Ottawa, Canada, May 29–June 2.

Gitlin, L. N., Corcoran, M. A., Winter, L., Boyce, A., & Hauck, W. W. (2001). A randomized, controlled trial of a home environmental intervention to enhance self-efficacy and reduce upset in family caregivers of persons with dementia. *The Gerontologist, 41,* 15–30.

Gitlin, L. N., Miller, K. S., & Boyce, A. (1999). Bathroom modifications for frail elderly renters: outcomes of a community-based program. *Technology and Disability, 10,* 141–149.

Gitlin, L. N., Winter, L., Dennis, M., Corcoran, M., Schinfield, S., & Hauck, W. (2002). Strategies used by families to simplify tasks for individuals with Alzheimer's disease and related disorders: Psychometric analysis of the Task Management Strategy Index (TSMI). *The Gerontologist, 42,* 61–69.

Hoenig, H., Sanford, J. A., Butterfield, T., Richardson, P., Hargraves, K., & Griffiths, P. M., et al. (2006). Development of a tele-technology protocol for in-home rehabilitation. *Journal of Rehabilitation R&D, 43*(2), 287–298.

Iwarsson, S. (1997). *The enabler: A method for analysing accessibility problems for housing.* Lund, Sweden: Individual Health Society, Department of Community Health Sciences.

Jones, M. L., & Sanford, J. A. (2002). Home modifications and environmental controls. In D. A. Olson & F. DeRuyter (Eds.), *Clinician's guide to assistive technology,* (pp. 405–423). Chicago: Mosby Inc.

Lawton, M. P. (1990). Residential environment and self-directness among older people. *American Psychologist, 45*(5), 638–640.

Lawton, M. P., & Nahemow, L. (1973). Ecology and the aging process. In C. L. Eisdorfer & M. P. Lawton (Eds.), *Psychology of adult development and aging* (pp. 619–674). Washington, DC: American Psychological Association.

Lawton, M. P., & Simon, B. (1968). The ecology of social relationships in housing for the elderly. *Gerontologist, 8,* 108–115.

Lewin, K. (1951). *Field theory in social science.* New York: Harper.

Mann, W. C., Ottenbacher, K. J., Fraas, L., Tomita, M., & Granger, C. V. (1999). Effectiveness of assistive technology and environmental interventions in maintaining independence and reducing home care costs for the frail elderly. *Archives of Family Medicine, 8,* 210–217.

Sanford, J. A. (2002). Time to get rid of those old gray grab bars and get yourself a shiny new pair. *Alzheimer's Care Quarterly, 3*(1), 26–31.

Sanford, J. A., & Butterfield, T. (2005). Using remote assessment to provide home modification services to underserved elders. *The Gerontologist, 45*(3), 389–398.

Sanford, J. A., & Connell, B. R. (1998). Accessible seating in stadiums and arenas. *The Journal of Urban Technology, 5*(1), 65–86.

Sanford, J. A., Echt, K., & Malassigné, P. (1999). An E for ADAAG: The case for "ADA Accessibility Guidelines for the Elderly" based on three studies of toilet transfer. *Journal of Physical and Occupational Therapy in Geriatrics, 16*(3/4), 39–58.

Sanford, J. A., Griffiths, P. M., Richardson, P., Hargraves, K., Butterfield, T., & Hoenig, H. (2006, November). The effects of in-home rehabilitation on task self efficacy in mobility impaired adults: A randomized clinical trial. *Journal of American Geriatrics Society, 54,* 1641–1648.

Sanford, J. A., & Hammel, J. (2006). *Impact of accessibility modifications to the home environment on community living and activity.* Symposium presentation at Gerontological Society of America Annual Conference, Dallas, TX, November 17.

Sanford, J. A., Hoenig, H., Griffiths, P. M., Butterfield, T., Richards, P., & Hargraves, K. (2007). A comparison of televideo and traditional in-home rehabilitation in mobility impaired older adults. *Physical and Occupational Therapy in Geriatrics, 25*(3), 1–18.

Sanford, J. A., Jones, M. L., Daviou, P., Grogg, K., & Butterfield, T. (2004). Using telerehabilition to identify home modification needs. *Assistive Technology, 16*(1), 43–53.

Sanford, J. A., & Megrew, M. B. (1995, Fall). An evaluation of grab bars to meet the needs of elderly people. *Assistive Technology, 7*(1). 36–47.

Sanford, J. A, Pynoos, J., Gregory, A., & Browne, A. (2002). Development of a comprehensive assessment to enhance delivery of home modifications. *Journal of PT and OT in Geriatrics, 20*(2), 43–56.

Stark, S. L., & Sanford, J. A. (2005). Environmental enablers and their impact on occupational performance. In C. H. Christiansen & C. M. Baum (Eds.), *Occupational therapy: Performance, participation, and well-being* (pp. 299–327). Thorofare, NJ: Slack, Inc.

Steinfeld, E., Schroeder, S., Duncan, J., Faste, R., Chollet, D., Bishop, M., et al. (1979). *Access to the built environment: A review of literature.* Washington, DC: U.S. Government Printing Office.

World Health Organization. (2001). *International classification of functioning, disability and health.* Geneva: Author.

Measures of Assistive Technology Predisposition and Use

Marcia J. Scherer
Caren L. Sax

11

Overview

It is crucial to apply a consumer-centered assessment approach when matching an individual with relevant assistive technology. Research on assistive technology use increasingly highlights the fact that consumers are less likely to use recommended devices when their needs are neither fully addressed nor understood during the technology selection process. Rehabilitation professionals who partner with consumers in the technology assessment and selection process preserve the highly valued *personal touch* and achieve the outcome of a good match of person and selected technology. The importance of integrating the various elements known to impact technology use and assessing their relevance for each consumer is emphasized.

Learning Objectives

By the end of the chapter, the reader should be able to:

1. Describe the value of assessing a person's predisposition to the use of technology prior to recommending equipment;
2. Describe the theoretical background and underlying constructs for measures of predisposition to technology use;
3. Describe the reliability and validity of the Assistive Technology Device Predisposition Assessment;
4. Provide examples of how the Match Person and Technology assessment surveys are relevant for assessing ICF domains impacted by technology use; and
5. Explain the importance of using person-centered assessment measures in the identification of appropriate assistive technology and how it impacts service delivery and outcomes measurement.

Introduction

Every year hundreds of new assistive technologies appear in the marketplace. More than 30,000 different devices currently are available (Abledata, 2009). Assistive technology use is dynamic. As the features and options of devices have continued to evolve, they have been more widely considered and recommended. In turn, assistive technology use resulting in positive outcomes tends to lead to more demand for assistive technology products.

The definition of assistive technology most frequently used originated in the U.S. *Technology-Related Assistance of Individuals with Disabilities Act of 1988* (P.L. 100–407):

> *[A]ny item, piece of equipment, or product system, whether acquired commercially off the shelf, modified, or customized, that is used to increase, maintain, or improve functional capabilities of individuals with disabilities.*

This generally accepted definition internationally covers a broad of range of products, including wheelchairs, splints, lifts, modified vans, voice input computers, environmental control systems/electronic aids to daily living, augmentative and alternative communication devices, and devices for those with limited or no eyesight or hearing.

In spite of the increased variety and availability of assistive technologies, approximately 30% of those obtained continue to be abandoned or discarded within a year (e.g., Scherer & Craddock, 2002). While there are many positive, as well as undesirable, reasons for this rate of discard, a major reason remains inadequate assessment of consumer needs and preferences.

The availability of skilled assistive technology professionals who understand the importance of a consumer-driven process and are able to provide appropriate and adequate services is key to an individual obtaining a quality assessment of needs and the most personally appropriate devices (e.g., Scherer, 2002, 2005). The importance of assistive technology services is underscored in various federal statutes, including the Americans with Disabilities Act, together with state policies. Nevertheless, many professionals who provide services to persons with disabilities are unaware of assistive technologies, do not know how to obtain and fund them, and do not have an effective process for matching a person with the most suitable devices. Moreover, although many professionals realize they need to be more consumer-responsive, they lack the training needed to accomplish this.

Professionals increasingly are better able to respond to consumers' different needs and preferences because the variety of assistive technology options continues to expand. However, the increased availability of assistive technology options has made the process of matching a person with the most appropriate device more complex because people's predisposition to, expectations for, and reactions to technologies and their features are highly individualized and personal. These predispositions, expectations, and reactions emerge from varying needs, abilities, preferences, and past experiences with and exposures to technologies (e.g., Elliott & Umlauf, 1995; Scherer, Jutai, Fuhrer, Demers, & DeRuyter, 2007). Predispositions to technology use also depend on adjustment to disability, subjective quality of life or sense of well-being, a person's outlook and goals for future functioning, expectations held by one's self and others, and financial and environmental support for technology use. The Matching Person and Technology model accounts for all of these influences.

Discussion Box 11.1

TRAINING CONSIDERATIONS

Rehabilitation counselors constitute one group of professionals who play key roles in facilitating the match between individuals with disabilities and assistive technology. Few graduate programs that offer master's degrees in rehabilitation counseling include required courses in assistive technology. Programs increasingly are offering elective courses or introducing the topic through guest speakers or specialized modules within related courses. Rehabilitation counselors employed in state or community agencies often have little familiarity and even less of a comfort level in exploring, recommending, and purchasing assistive technology. Orientation training for new counselors may provide an introduction to specific technologies (e.g., alternative computer access, vehicle modifications, ergonomic keyboards). Unless a counselor has a specialized caseload (i.e., blind/low vision, deaf/hard of hearing) where he/she becomes familiar with commonly used devices, counselors are unlikely to know the right questions to ask and the appropriate resources to access. With training budgets stretched to the limit, how can counselors effectively work with their consumers in assessing individual needs and finding the right assistive technology match? With time at a premium and administrative accountability at an all-time high, how can holistic assessment approaches, such as the Matching Person and Technology (MPT) model, be integrated into the rehabilitation process in a way that ensures a client-centered perspective?

The Matching Person and Technology (MPT) Model

The MPT model emerged from research on the use and nonuse of recommended assistive technology by consumers with a variety of disabilities (Scherer, 1986). The model has three crucial areas of foci that represent the primary components that most influence use of assistive technologies: (a) the *m*ilieu/ environment(s) in which the user will interact with the technology; (b) the needs and preferences, and predisposition to use, of the unique *p*erson; and (c) the functions and features of the most desirable and appropriate technology (see Vignette 11.1).

Vignette 11.1: Applying Theory to Practice

Hundreds of practicing rehabilitation counselors have used the MPT model in an interactive 12-week online course, Applications of Rehabilitation Technology, in order to complete the major class assignment. Rehabilitation counselors identify a focus individual who might benefit from the use of assistive technology to improve access to employment, education, recreation, or the community. The rehabilitation counselors and the individual organize an interdisciplinary tech team in order to assess the three primary components of the MPT. Rehabilitation counselors who complete the tech team projects report increased knowledge and comfort levels with completing the MPT assessment. They are able to more effectively utilize expertise from related professionals, (e.g., occupational therapists, physical therapists, rehabilitation engineers) and, as a result, play a more active role in this process.

One student, who identified herself at the beginning of a course as having very limited experience with assistive technology, described the MPT process in her final paper. She identified a 48-year-old man with cerebral palsy who had moved from an institution into an apartment. He moved from an environment in which assistive technology, if used at all, was selected to meet the priorities of the caregivers rather than those of the assistive technology user, to an environment where he would depend on assistive technology for increasing his independence in mobility and communication. An interdisciplinary team was formed and, through the use of the MPT survey forms, that team identified potential devices and training techniques to enable the assistive technology user to more easily integrate these devices into his new lifestyle. The student found the whole process to be enlightening, commenting that without a guide, some written prompt, or assessment tool, it is difficult to identify all possible technology needs for someone with a disability. A guide who can identify the needs alone is not a holistic guide. Unless the individual's temperament and desires are considered, such a device may go unused. The MPT is a holistic guide/assessment to navigate the way through the technology needs and selection process, going beyond the identification of functional needs to the assessment of the person's strengths, limitations, support needs, and propensity for using technology.

Each component contributes either a positive or a negative influence on technology use and degree of satisfaction with its use. Satisfaction with technology use is greatly reduced when there are more negative influences. Although a technology may appear perfect for a given need, it may be used inappropriately or even go unused when critical person/social characteristics or needed environmental support are not considered, thus leading to personal frustration and wasted resources. On average, one-third of assistive technologies are abandoned by their users (e.g., Scherer, 2002).

The use and nonuse of assistive technology as conceptualized in the MPT model has been confirmed by several other assistive technology researchers and authors (e.g., Cook & Hussey, 2002; Lasker & Bedrosian, 2001; Wielandt, Mckenna, Tooth, & Strong, 2006). The MPT model was operationalized by developing an assessment process consisting of a series of measures that provide a person-centered and individualized approach to matching individuals with the most appropriate technologies for their use. It includes an assessment process consisting of a collaborative approach in which a consumer and professional engage in a range of assessments that may include a quick screen, to specialized evaluations (completed in about 15 minutes), to a comprehensive evaluation (completed in about 45 minutes) by someone trained and experienced in their use. The MPT process is applicable across a variety of users and settings and is depicted in Figure 11.1.

The specific steps with accompanying measures are as follows:

Step 1: Determine initial goals that the professional and the consumer have established. Potential interventions supportive of these goals and technologies needed to support the attainment of the goals are recorded (Initial Worksheet for the MPT model).

Step 2: Further identify need for assistive technology by reviewing supports used in the past, satisfaction with those supports, and those that are desired and needed but not yet available to the consumer (History of Support Use).

11.1

Assessment process.

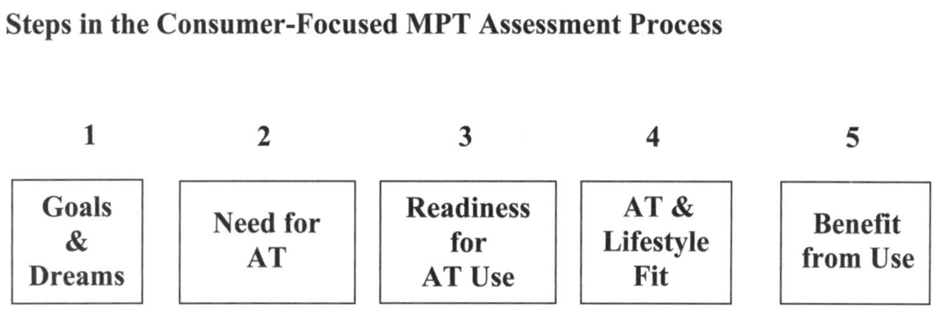

Steps 3–5: Specific technology matching for readiness for use, fit with lifestyle, and comfort in use. The consumer is asked to complete the appropriate form depending on the type of technology under consideration:

- General: Survey of Technology Use (SOTU)
- Assistive: Assistive Technology Device Predisposition Assessment (ATDPA)
- Educational: Educational Technology Device Predisposition Assessment (ETPA)
- Workplace: Workplace Technology Device Predisposition Assessment (WTPA)
- Health care: Health Care Technology Device Predisposition Assessment (HCTPA)
- Hearing: Hearing Technology Predisposition Assessment (HT PA)
- Cognitive disability: Cognitive Support Technology Predisposition Assessment (CST PA)
- Childhood and adolescence: Matching Assistive Technology & CHild (MATCH) for Early Intervention and ages 0–8; Matching Student and Technology (MST) for children and adolescents in inclusive education.

Subsequent steps to the assessment ideally include trial use of the selected device(s) and then periodic follow-up with users after they acquire their technologies in order to determine the success of the match and whether adjustments need to be made in the device, milieu, or person and the desirability of considering upgraded or additional supports.

Samples of the actual user forms can be found at: http://matchingpersonandtechnology.com, and they are described more fully in the following paragraphs. While the forms were created to provide a sequence of measures to inform professional practice, it is also appropriate to use just any one of the measures alone. Additionally, each measure is composed of separate scales, and in some cases, one scale may be used alone. This is most often appropriate when a battery of measures is used and there is a need to document that particular factors were taken into consideration.

Profiles derived from the results of the forms and process can be used to help provide a rationale for funding and training, demonstrate improvement in skills, organize information about the needs of a particular consumer, and provide information as to those factors that contribute to or detract from the use of the desired technology. With such information, the professionals can identify potential or existing problem areas and intervene to better ensure that the use of the technology will enhance quality of life and the consumer's community, workplace, and educational experiences. A written summary of this information can specify what needs to be done, for whom, by whom, by when, and with what resources, thus equipping professionals with appropriate questions to ask technology providers and vendors (see Vignette 11.2).

Form 1. Initial Worksheet for the MPT Process

The Initial Worksheet is organized by areas in which persons may experience loss of function (e.g., speech/communication, mobility, hearing, and eyesight) or have important strengths. It is designed to be used collaboratively, with professionals working together with individuals with disabilities to identify areas to

Vignette 11.2: Results of the MPT Process

Rehabilitation counselors who have used the MPT forms in an online course, Applications of Rehabilitation Technology, were asked to report the results of using the assessment model. They submitted information via an online survey including which forms were used, who was involved in completing the forms, what the major incentives and disincentives were for the individual to access and integrate assistive technology into their lives, and which forms were most/least useful for their particular tech team. The following responses demonstrate the ease of using this assessment approach as well as the value of employing a user-centered strategy. One counselor commented that she found all forms were helpful. They were a springboard for discussion and led to other questions or points that needed to be addressed. The areas dealing with quality of life gave me so much information and really helped her see more clearly what was most important to my focus individual. Another rehabilitation counselor reported that the forms helped him understand more about the individual's prior technology experiences and her view of her own abilities and disabilities. Yet another commented that the forms helped her ask the right questions, which helped her team narrow down which assistive technology device the client was interested in obtaining. This process put the client in control in deciding on a device that best fit her needs. The forms helped determine if the client had experience working with technology and how comfortable she felt using it. These are important issues and concerns to consider.

strengthen through the use of a technology (or other support/strategy) or environmental accommodation.

Assessment should identify both existing strengths as well as difficulties/limitations together with goals and beginning strategies for goal attainment. The strategies may involve a technology, or a change in the environment, or both. When introducing a new technology, one works from an area of strength. Each area or category on the Initial Worksheet should be addressed, regardless of beliefs of its relevance for an individual. Connection may be triggered or observations made that may impact later decision making. When working with young children, this form is typically completed in collaboration with the parent. The Matching Assistive Technology & Child, a different MPT form, is available for them.

Form 2. History of Support Use

The History of Support Use form is used to understand technologies that have been attempted, their success, and why a new technology may be better. The organization of this form is consistent with areas of functioning found in the Initial Worksheet for the MPT Process. It includes space for listing three technologies (or supports/strategies) that have been tried for each area.

Forms 1 and 2 focus on a person's separate areas of functioning, given the belief that key obstacles to optimal technology use are identified only when each area is considered. For example, if a focus on communication leads to a recommendation for a device that requires good vision, problems may be encountered when using the recommended device if vision has not yet been assessed. A goal that emphasizes the need to focus on the whole person is achieved by considering the many parts that make up the whole and their relationship to one another.

Form 3. Survey of Technology Use

After a technology is determined to be viable, the individual is asked to complete the Survey of Technology Use (SOTU), a 29-item checklist that inquires into the respondent's present experiences and feelings toward technologies. This information is gathered and evaluated in an attempt to identify and introduce new technology that builds and capitalizes on existing skills and comfort in their use. Respondents also provide information about their general mood, personal characteristics and preferences, and social involvement. These areas have been identified through research to impact a favorable predisposition toward technology use.

The SOTU provides two identical forms, one for use by professionals and one by consumers. Both forms are meant to be used as a set, thus possibly providing different perspectives from the professional and consumer that may need to be addressed.

Form 4. Assistive Technology Device Predisposition Assessment

The Assistive Technology Device Predisposition Assessment (ATD PA; Person and Device Forms) has supporting materials: (a) computerized scoring and interpretations and (b) an interactive CD training program for professionals. The Person Form has 54 items divided into 3 sections. Section A (9 items) asks for consumer ratings of functional capabilities; Section B (12 items) provides information on quality of life or subjective well-being in the context of the World Health Organization's (WHO) International Classification of Functioning, Disability and Health (ICF; 2001) domains of Activity and Participation; and Section C (33 items) produces data on personal and psychosocial characteristics through 8 subscales that assess mood, self-esteem, self-determination, autonomy, family support, friend support, therapist and program reliance, and motivation to use support.

The Device Form's 12 items ask respondents to rate their predisposition to using the specific assistive technology under consideration. A follow-up version of this form exists to assess satisfaction with use of the selected device.

The professional forms of the ATD PA allow them to determine and evaluate incentives and disincentives to the use of the device by a particular consumer and to compare perspectives held by the consumer and the professional.

Form 5. Educational Technology Device Predisposition Assessment

The Educational Technology Device Predisposition Assessment (ET PA) is a 43-item self-report checklist developed to assist professionals and teachers in compiling comprehensive pre- and post-learning profiles of a student provided with educational technology to determine whether its use enhances the student's educational experience. These profiles can be used to help demonstrate improvement in skills for individual students and organize information about the needs of a particular student population.

A companion teacher/educator version of this form allows for an assessment of the view of both a student and his or her teacher in four key areas: characteristics of the educational goal and need that a teacher is attempting to address through the use of a specific technology, characteristics of the particular educational technology being reviewed, characteristics of the psychosocial environments in which the technology will be used (e.g., the presence of supportive family, peers, and/or teachers), and the student's characteristics that may influence technology use (e.g., learning styles and preferences).

Several MPT measures are suitable for use with WHO's ICF and thus are relevant for use in assessing ICF domains impacted by technology use. Table 11.1 lists the principle ICF domains, examples of assistive technologies and other supports, and the MPT measures most appropriate for the assessment of each ICF domain.

History of Research and Practice

Development and validation of the MPT assessments followed the recommended steps of professionally approved standards as found in *Standards for Educational and Psychological Testing:* (a) concept definition and clarification, (b) draft of items and response scales, (c) pilot testing, and (d) determination of measure quality and usefulness (Scherer, 1995).

A consumer's perspective of their needs and preferences may be obtained by having them identify and prioritize their desired outcomes and then rate progress in achieving them. This approach was used in developing the MPT measures and has also been used in developing other tools such as Goal Attainment Scaling (e.g., Donnelly & Carswell, 2002) and the Individually Prioritised Problem Assessment (IPPA); Wessels et al., 2002). Such a person-centered approach allows outcomes to be measured in reference to changes in a person's *satisfaction* to achieve desired goals, not merely their functional ability to achieve them. An idiographic evaluation is used (i.e., the person is the unit of analysis and serves as his or her own control), not a normative one (i.e., the person is compared to his or her peers). An idiographic evaluation best captures a consumer-directed and social model perspective of outcomes assessment (Punch, 1996).

The results of studies that examine psychometric qualities and test usefulness of the MPT measures are summarized in the following section.

Interrater Reliability

Thirty rehabilitation professionals or graduate students rated videotaped interviews, supplemented with written information, of individuals using assistive or educational technologies. Item modes (the most common response identified) were calculated, and the differences between the mode and individual rater responses were computed. Items on the measure that were related to technology

11.1 ICF Domains

ICF Activities and Participation	Examples of AT and other Supports	MPT Measure
LEARNING AND APPLYING KNOWLEDGE: learning, applying the knowledge that is learned, thinking, solving problems, and making decisions.	Note taking, real-time captioning services, personal digital assistant (PDA) and laptop computers, audio recording devices, computer software, electronic calculators	SOTU, ET PA, CST PA, MST
GENERAL TASKS AND DEMANDS: carrying out single or multiple tasks, organizing routines, and handling stress.	Personal assistance, service animals, timers, memory aids	ATD PA Sections B and C
COMMUNICATION: communicating by language, signs and symbols, including receiving and producing messages, carrying on conversations, and using communication devices and techniques.	Sign language interpreters, electronic and manual communication devices, computer input and output devices, modified telephones and text messaging devices, radio and television adaptations, signaling and alerting devices	Initial Worksheet, History of Support Use, ATD PA Section B, HT PA
MOBILITY: changing body position or location or transferring from one place to another, by carrying, moving or manipulating objects; by walking, running, or climbing; and by using various forms of transportation.	Manual and power wheelchairs, canes and walkers, transfer boards, vehicle modifications, lifts, relief maps, global positioning system (GPS)	ATD PA Sections A and B
SELF-CARE: caring for oneself, washing and drying oneself, caring for one's body and body parts, dressing, eating and drinking, and looking after one's health.	Modified eating utensils, nonslip mats, robotic devices, buttonhooks, liquid soap dispensers, electric toothbrushes	ATD PA Sections A and B
DOMESTIC LIFE: acquiring a place to live, food, clothing and other necessities; household cleaning and repairing; caring for personal and other household objects; and assisting others.	Bottle and can openers, tilt tables, modified lighting, support bars and rails, remote- or voice-activated environmental controls	ATD PA Sections A and B
INTERPERSONAL INTERACTIONS AND RELATIONSHIPS: basic and complex interactions with people (strangers, friends, relatives, family members, and lovers) in a contextually and socially appropriate manner.	Manual and electronic communication devices, life skills coach, sexual aids	ATD PA Sections B and C

11.1 ICF Domains — *Continued*

ICF Activities and Participation	Examples of AT and other Supports	MPT Measure
MAJOR LIFE AREAS: tasks and actions required to engage in education, work, and employment and to conduct economic transactions.	Remote control devices, customized workstations, structural modifications, alternative computer access	ATD PA Sections A and B, other MPT measures
COMMUNITY, SOCIAL AND CIVIC LIFE: actions and tasks required to engage in organized social life outside the family, in community, social, and civic areas of life.	Signaling and alerting devices, noise reduction devices, adapted recreational and leisure devices, transportation accommodations	ATD PA Sections A and B, other MPT measures

From: Scherer, M. J., & Glueckauf, R. (2005). Assessing the benefits of assistive technologies for activities and participation. *Rehabilitation Psychology, 50*(2), 138–139.

itself and its use within the family or workplace displayed high interrater reliability. Items concerned with user characteristics and whether each was an incentive or disincentive to technology use displayed lower interrater reliability (Scherer & McKee, 1992).

Validity

The concurrent validity of the quality of life (QoL) subscale of the ATD PA was estimated by correlating it with the Diener's Satisfaction with Life Scale (Diener, Emmons, Larsen, & Griffin, 1985) and the depression subscale of the Brief Symptom Inventory (BSI; Heinrich, Tate, & Buckelew, 1994). Twenty persons with a newly acquired spinal cord injury (50% males) completed items from the QoL subscale of the ATD PA, the Satisfaction with Life Scale (SWLS), and the BSI while in acute rehabilitation (Scherer & Cushman, 2001). One month post-discharge, they rated their satisfaction with their assistive technology.

Negative correlations with the BSI depression subscale were found with all items on the Satisfaction with Life Scale (–.64) and the QoL subscale of the ATD PA (–.71). The correlation between the total scores from the QoL subscale of the ATD PA and the Satisfaction with Life Scale was .89 ($p < 01$). Fourteen consumers subsequently provided data on their satisfaction with their assistive technology at 1 month post–acute rehabilitation. Nine (64%) indicated they were satisfied with their assistive technology, and 5 (36%) reported being not satisfied. An independent-samples t test was used to evaluate the hypothesis that the QoL scale of the ATD PA would better discriminate *(predictive validity)* between the two groups than Diener's Satisfaction with Life scale. The depression subscale of the BSI was not tested because of its low correlation with assistive technology satisfaction (–.04). Persons not satisfied with their assistive technology (mean = 23, SD = 7.6) generally scored lower on the QoL subscale of the ATD PA than those who were satisfied (mean = 34.6, *SD* = 9.3). The effect size was estimated with the eta square index (.34) indicating a large effect size.

Item analyses on the QoL subscale of the ATD PA examined its internal consistency by correlating each item with the total score after removing that item from the analysis. Coefficient alpha was .80.

In another study, a researcher in Ireland found that the QoL subscale of the ATD PA had high internal consistency with a coefficient alpha above .80 (Craddock, 2003, 2006). This study also examined technology needs and preferences of students with disabilities, including many with hearing or vision loss, who were transitioning from secondary education to employment or university.

Research on the validity of using the MPT in a consumer-peer provider (services delivered by nonprofessionals) partnership in reference to technology selection, training, and outcomes is on-going in Ireland (Craddock & McCormack, 2002). A similar model in a New York State Tech Act-fund project used peer mentors and the MPT assessments to help consumers identify the best technologies for their use (Heerkens, Briggs, & Weider, 1997).

Criterion-Related Validity

Older adults (mean age 65) with normal hearing and comparably aged users of assistive listening devices completed the following measures: (a) Hearing Handicap Inventory for the Elderly, (b) the Communication Profile for the Hearing Impaired, and (c) the ATD PA. The results between assistive listening device users and nonusers suggested the value of assessing personality and psychosocial factors involved in technology use. Compared to device nonusers, device users generally attributed more value to assistive listening devices, had a higher psychological readiness for adopting technical assistance, and perceived fewer difficulties with technology use around family, friends, at work, or at school.

Behavioral and audiological data were obtained from 40 persons, ages 61–81. Group A included 20 persons with normal audiological thresholds. Group B included 20 persons with mild-to-moderate degrees of high-frequency hearing loss. Each person completed a hearing loss screening survey, the ATD PA, and the Profile of Hearing Aid Performance. The Profile of Hearing Aid Performance and hearing loss screen were adequate assessments of self-reported hearing loss, as was the subjective rating of hearing section of the ATD PA. People with high-frequency marginal hearing loss reported less satisfaction with their personal independence (doing things on their own), reduced emotional well-being, and more limitation from their hearing loss than those with normal hearing. Discriminant analyses showed that the ATD PA was the best predictor of membership in Group A or Group B, correctly classifying 85% of the participants and providing psychosocial markers associated with awareness of and adaptation to hearing loss (Scherer & Frisina, 1994, 1998).

Using a conceptual framework developed from the MPT model (Scherer, 1998) and a career construct of environmental strategies use, a qualitative research study investigated the experiences of using environmental strategies for mobility and independence among people aging with multiple sclerosis (Bruner-Canhoto, 2004). Forty-five people with multiple sclerosis ages 50 and older were interviewed using a semistructured interview guide. Personal, milieu, and environmental strategies factors influenced the environmental strategies experience. Disability, age, psychological characteristics, religion, and productive activity were determined to be important personal factors associated with the use of environmental strategies. Conditions associated with other people in their lives, time of year and day, location, therapeutic opportunities, and policies/programs facilitated or hindered milieu factors. Aesthetics, reliability, usability, cost-effectiveness, and likeability were environmental strategies–specific factors that impacted their experience.

Respondents were classified into one of three groups based on their environmental strategies career: optimal users, who maximized their use of environmental strategies and expressed positive reactions to use; partial users, who used some environmental strategies and expressed ambivalent reactions; and avoidant users, who did not use much, if any, environmental strategies and expressed negative reactions. Personal factors were most important to optimal users. Milieu and environmental strategies factors often contributed to environmental strategies careers among partial and avoidant users.

Predictive Validity

The usefulness of the ATD PA in determining reasons for device nonuse or abandonment was investigated in 47 persons with mixed diagnoses discharged from an acute inpatient rehabilitation unit. They completed the ATD PA at the time of discharge and at 3 months postdischarge. Their occupational and physical therapists completed the ATD PA professional form. Among all participants, 128 devices were prescribed; of these, 86 were in use at the 3-month follow-up. Nonuse of the prescribed devices most commonly was attributed to their no longer being needed. Yet, functional improvement (as measured by the Functional Independence Measure) corresponded with device nonuse for just half the devices. A comparison of data from consumer- and therapist-completed forms showed consumers viewed some assistive devices more positively than others, with the least positive being walkers. The views of consumers and therapists differed regarding the benefits of an assistive device, with the adaptations required for use of an assistive device not well recognized by consumers. Consumers were found to have positive expectations toward using the devices. If later performance fell short of their expectations, they discarded use of the device—an action that may be prevented by longer trial periods with devices in a variety of situations (Cushman & Scherer, 1996).

Over 150 vocational rehabilitation counselors in 25 states within the United States, each having at least one consumer receiving a new assistive device, were provided training in the MPT model (Scherer, Sax, Vanbiervliet, Cushman, & Scherer, 2005). Each counselor asked a working-age adult consumer who was thought to possibly benefit from the use of an assistive device to complete the ATD PA. The results showed that the ATD PA items differentiated consumer predispositions to assistive technology use as well as assistive device and user match at follow-up. Differences due to gender, physical locality, or age were not significant. Thus, the ATD PA appears to be a valid measure of predisposition to use an assistive device as well as the subsequent match of assistive device and user. Rehabilitation practitioners who used the ATD PA achieved enhanced assistive technology service delivery outcomes while using an evidence-based measure.

Case Study 11.1

THE ENDS JUSTIFY THE MEANS

J. T., the rehabilitation counselor, began working with Mr. C. to explore possible assistive technology solutions to reach his employment goal of becoming a writer. Mr. C. graduated with a journalism degree and uses assistive technology for mobility and activities of daily living. Due to cerebral palsy that resulted in spastic quadriplegia, Mr. C.'s speech is severely affected. However, his personal attendant often acts as an interpreter when others are not available. Mr. C. gestures, makes facial expressions, responds to yes/no questions, and uses multiple repetitions in order to be understood. He used a speech board at one point and found it cumbersome and time-consuming. Through the use of the MPT process, J. T. learned about Mr. C. and his apparent incentives and disincentives regarding assistive technology use. While the process of interviewing Mr. C. was slow, the results helped J. T. understand Mr. C.'s underlying anxiety about the next stage of his life. J. T. saw inconsistencies in Mr. C.'s responses in the initial interview as compared with the responses on the forms, prompting a conversation about Mr. C.'s perception of his life and the ways in which he copes. Had it not been for Mr. C.'s responses on the forms, J. T. would not have understood his level of depression. The survey results highlighted autonomy and self-determination and a high level of support from his family, all of which would strengthen his ability to adopt assistive technology. A communication device was recommended for purchase through the Department of Rehabilitation.

J. T.'s reflections of the process revealed the added value of the MPT model. She compared it to the traditional process rehabilitation counselors use in procuring assistive technology services and equipment—to authorize an evaluation, receive a report, request three bids, and authorize the equipment. J. T. described that process as relinquishing all knowledge about the individual and expecting the outside evaluator to figure everything out. She felt that administering the MPT assessment enabled her to play an essential role in gathering information from Mr. C. and in sharing that information with the evaluator who could incorporate the MPT results in his recommendations.

Data on outcomes after using assistive devices provide important indicators of a quality service delivery process (e.g., Ripat & Booth, 2005). Recent developments in assessment research confirm the importance of therapeutic assessment and an appropriate early assessment of consumer needs for assistive technology.

The influence of consumer expectations and preferences, as well as their personal characteristics, on their predisposition to use and their subjective need for an assistive device (as well as their subjective subsequent match with the assistive device at 6 months follow-up) was examined in a study of 139 individuals who had one or more mobility ATDs and were followed over time in order to gain a better understanding of the factors influencing the continued or discontinued use of mobility devices, which include canes, walkers, wheelchairs, and crutches. Participants were enrolled in a rehabilitation outcomes study and were recruited at discharge from a large acute care hospital or on admission to one of two rehabilitation hospitals in the greater Boston, MA, region (Haley et al., 2004; Jette, Keysor, Coster, Ni, & Haley, 2005). Participants had diagnoses of hip fracture, stroke, or complex medical conditions and all completed the ATD PA at baseline and 6 months follow-up.

Respondents varied in their predispositions to using a device according to their ATD PA Device form total scores (weak, moderate, strong predisposition at baseline and match at 6-month follow-up). Discriminant function analyses were used to determine which predictor variables discriminate among the three predisposition groups. The predictors were the 45 Section B and Section C items on the ATD PA Person form. For both baseline and 6-months follow-up, the overall Wilks' Lambda was significant at the $p = .01$ level or better, indicating that the 45 predictors (45 Section B and Section C items) strongly differentiated the three groups. The findings gained further strength when prediction of group membership was calculated. Predictions that participants could be placed into one of the three groups (weak, moderate, strong assistive device predisposition) at 6 months follow-up were accurate for 98.7%. Thus, those who reported their quality of life, outlook, and personal characteristics to be more positive were more favorably predisposed to assistive device use and were better matched with the selected assistive device at 6 months follow up.

At 6 months, the 139 individuals had either continued, discontinued, or substituted use of the initial ATD, and again, the ATD PA baseline data strongly discriminated the three groups. General Linear Model (GLM) multivariate analyses showed a significant difference between the three groups (continued use of the primary device, discontinued use, or substituted use at 6 months) in the subscale scores (F = 2.07, df = 16 and 194, p = .01; Graves, Scherer, & Sax, 2006; Scherer, Jutai, Fuhrer, Demers, & DeRuyter, 2006). Univariate tests showed that, for this population, the subscale scores differentiated the groups as follows:

A. Cognitive/sensory (F = 4.20, df = 2 and 104, p = .01); Mobility (F = 6.50, df = 2 and 104, p = .002); Upper extremity (F = 4.78, df = 2 and 104, p = .01).
B. Subjective well-being (F = 9.07, df = 2 and 104, p = .001);
C. Social support (F = 3.06, df = 2 and 104, p = .05); engagement in therapy (F = 4.76, df = 2 and 104, p = .01); resistance to change (F = 6.45, df = 2 and 104, p = .002).

The results also showed that these three factors account for 96% of the variance found in the Section A items. The reliability of the quality of life/subjective well-being scale (Section B) items were analyzed to determine if they form a unidimensional scale (Graves et al., 2006). The reliability of the test was .90, thus demonstrating good discrimination and coverage of a wide range along the well-being continuum. The 33-item Section C of the ATD PA accounted for 58%

of the variance with reliability statistics ranging from .39 to .62., thus showing that the underlying dimensions of the ATD PA Person form are well-defined with acceptable measurement properties (Graves et al., 2006).

A person's perceived quality of life/subjective well-being is important because it influences his or her performance in activities and participation in various social settings (e.g., school, work, community life). Relationships between one's level of education, current employment status, and perceived quality of life may not be as strong among older adults as for those of working age. Thus, it is important to keep in mind that individual items can have more or less importance depending on the needs, preferences, and priorities of the population under study.

In another study (Fuhrmann, 2007), 43 adults with spinal cord injury (SCI) receiving care at University of Rochester Medical Center completed the ATD PA and were categorized into three groups according to time since injury: 60.5% (n = 26) were injured within the past year, 14% (n = 6) had been injured for 1–3 years, and 14% (n = 6) had been injured for more than 3 years. Depending on the time since injury, discriminant analyses showed that the three groups had statistically significant different perceptions of well-being and activity level (p = .00) and could be grouped accurately 100% of the time. Those injured 1–3 years ago rated themselves as having the highest well-being and activity levels. Patients injured less than 1 year ago rated themselves having the lowest well-being. In addition, depending on time since injury, the three groups showed different SCI educational needs (p = .00; 100% accurate classification). Patients injured 1–3 years ago reported the most need for further education on SCI issues. Patients injured for more than 3 years reported the least need.

In conclusion, a series of studies provide evidence for addressing several constructs when evaluating a person's predisposition to use a technology and for determining the outcome of a successful match. The studies simultaneously provided data regarding the psychometric properties of measures in the MPT model.

Cross-Disciplinary and Cross-National Relevance and Applications

In addition to the studies discussed previously, a study conducted in Montreal, Quebec, Canada, by occupational therapists showed that items from the ATD PA focus well on the pertinent factors related to individuals' decisions to use or not use an assistive technology (Vincent & Morin, 1999). Another study focused on adolescents who used functional electrical stimulation (FES) to stand and who were administered the ATD PA and several other measures. The results supported the use of the ATD PA and highlighted the need to consider psychosocial aspects of MPT (Brown, 1996; Brown & Merbitz, 1995).

A study in Australia investigated the ability of client, assistive technology, and intervention-related factors to predict the postdischarge use of rails and bathing, toileting, and dressing assistive technologies, which had been recommended by an occupational therapist during hospitalization (Wielandt et al., 2006). Variables found to predict assistive technology use included participants' perceptions of the characteristics of the device, the presence or absence of anxiety, and their ability to recall assistive technology training. Additionally, four other variables (intended postdischarge use of assistive technology, negative perceptions about disability/illness, perceived benefit of the assistive technology, and having a choice during the device selection process) were strongly related to assistive technology use. Although these four variables were not included in the best final model, they are nevertheless important and need to be considered when recommending assistive technology. The authors concluded that occupational therapists need to ensure that assistive technology is recommended using a client-centered approach, where clients' perceptions and opinions are considered along with their needs and goals. They recommend use of the MPT model to guide the process of recommending assistive technologies.

In Ireland, Craddock (2003, 2006) has used all of the MPT measures (except the Workplace and Health Care Predisposition Assessments) in providing assistive technology assessments nationally. His work includes using the assessments to determine differences between successful and unsuccessful technology users as they transitioned from secondary to postsecondary education.

To assess the effectiveness of a college course on adapted computer use in the United States, 14 college students with disabilities (more than half having complete or partial eyesight loss) identified factors that influenced them to adopt or reject a device for computer access. The results provide evidence of the usefulness of the MPT model and the ATD PA items as applied to computer access technology for college students (Goodman, Tiene, & Luft, 2002). For students in secondary or elementary school, educational researchers have found the ET PA to have utility when preselecting person characteristics relevant to the use of educational technologies (Albaugh & Fayne, 1996; Albaugh, Piazza, & Scholsser, 1997).

Other authors have used the MPT model as the theoretical foundation for concept papers or the development of companion assessments (e.g., Beigel, 2000; Demers, Weiss-Lambrau, & Ska, 1996; Zapf & Rough, 2002). Table 11.2 summarizes the evaluation of the psychometric properties of the MPT assessments.

Assessment Methods Useful to Health-Related Practices

Based on the results of research studies conducted to date, the MPT measures have been shown to have good reliability and validity. Thus, the measures are useful both practically and in outcomes research. The testing of the MPT model has determined that the model adequately represents the relevant influences on technology use and nonuse or abandonment/discard. Even so, MPT users have said that they require more training in how to maximize benefit from the process and measures, and they would like the forms to be scored and interpreted, with a particular focus on next steps and strategies to pursue with consumers. Therefore, computerized scoring with interpretations of ATD PA results and a CD interactive program that trains users in the comprehensive MPT process were developed (Scherer & Cushman, 2002). Updated information about these resources, general developments with the MPT assessments, and sample portions of each of the assessment forms can be obtained from the homepage of the Institute for Matching Person & Technology: http://matchingpersonandtechnology.com.

11.2 References for the Psychometric Properties of the Matching Person and Technology Assessments

Reference	Study Population	MPT form	Interrater Reliability	Internal Consistency	Criterion-Related Validity	Concurrent And construct Validity	Predictive Validity
Albaugh & Fayne, 1996; Albaugh, Piazza & Scholsser,1997	Adolescents; variety of disabilities	ET PA		√	√	√	√
Brown, 1996; Brown & Merbitz, 1995	Adolescents with spinal cord injury	ATD PA			√	√	
Bruner-Canhoto, 2004	Adults with Multiple sclerosis	MPT				√	
Craddock, 2003	Adolescents and adults with a variety of disabilities	MPT process; SOTU, ETPA, ATD PA		√	√		√
Cushman & Scherer, 1996	Adults with spinal cord injury	ATD PA				√	√
Fuhrmann, 2007	Adults with spinal cord injury	ATD PA					√
Goodman, Tiene, & Luft 2002; Scherer & Cushman, 2001; Vincent & Morin, 1999	Adolescents and adults with a variety of disabilities	ATD PA		√	√	√	√

Graves, Scherer, & Sax, 2006	Older adults with hip replacement, complex medical conditions, or stroke	ATD PA		√		√	
Scherer & Craddock, 2002	Adolescents with a variety of disabilities	ATD PA, ET PA, SOTU		√	√	√	√
Scherer & Frisina, 1994, 1998	Adults with hearing loss	ATD PA		√	√		
Scherer, Jutai, Fuhrer, Demers, & DeRuyter, 2006	Older adults with hip replacement, complex medical conditions, or stroke	ATD PA		√			√
Scherer & McKee, 1992	Adults with a spinal cord injury or cerebral palsy	ATD PA, ET PA	√	√	√	√	
Scherer, Sax, Vanbiervliet, Cushman, & Scherer, 2006	Adults with a variety of mobility disabilities	ATD PA		√			√
Wielandt, 2003		MPT				√	

Discussion Box 11.2

SOME RESEARCH ISSUES IN ASSESSMENT

1 Measures undergo years of development and validation. Individual items have been assessed for the quality and strength of information they contribute, and if scales exist in the measure, they, too, have undergone a great deal of examination. Describe why it is inappropriate to develop a new measure based on combining items or scales from a number of existing measures.

2 In order to obtain the must useful and helpful information for research or for guiding a technology or other intervention and achieving positive outcomes, an investment of time needs to be devoted to gathering that information. Each MPT measure requires approximately a half hour to complete, and this is not unusual for comprehensive assessments. Yet, such time may not be available, reimbursed, or otherwise devoted to assessment. Why is this being "penny wise and pound foolish?" In other words, why is saving a little time or money initially apt to result in the loss of a great deal of time and money later on?

Questions:

Service Domain

1. What makes predispositions to technology use important when working with people with disabilities? How may predispositions to technology use influence the outcomes of assistive technology service delivery?
2. Three major factors directly influence use and nonuse of assistive technology: characteristics of the milieu of use, the person, and the technology itself. Why should the consumer be consulted about these?
3. What is the importance of subjective quality of life and well-being on consumers' decisions about using assistive technology?
4. What is the value of completing a comprehensive assessment before providing an individual with an assistive technology? What circumstances may affect the decision to complete a more or less comprehensive assessment?

Research Domain

5. What are some key differences among individuals that are likely to affect their predisposition to the use of one or more technologies?

Policy Domain

How do the factors that influence the use of assistive technology coincide with the ICF? What are the implications for using the ICF in policy development for rehabilitation?

Critical Research Issues

The typology developed by WHO in the ICF (2001) provides an overview of important life domains to be considered when assessing the need for and evaluating the effectiveness of assistive technology. The ICF is divided into the following four domains: Body Functions, Body Structures, Activities (e.g., Activities of Daily Living and Instrumental Activities of Daily Living), and Participation (i.e., the capability to perform activities enables participation in social, educational, vocational, civic, and other broader pursuits).

The Context consists of Environmental and Personal Factors that either can facilitate or hinder participation. Environmental factors can include access to health care and rehabilitation, access to assistive technology and personal assistance, and access to information. Assistive technology is a Contextual Factor of the Physical Environment. Contextual factors are dynamic and subject to influence. For example, considering Personal Contextual factors, an individual's attitudes toward assistive technology may be negative initially. However, following later experiences using well-matched assistive technology to carry out desired activities, an individual's attitudes may change, resulting in the consideration of additional needed assistive technology.

The ICF applies the term *Facilitators* to all contextual factors that promote health and functioning. The terms *Barriers/Hindrances* applies to all contextual factors that have a negative impact. A barrier exists if resources to purchase assistive technology are not available as well as when policies set a low priority on resource allocation for assistive technology. Barriers within the social environment exist when trained personnel to assist in selecting and obtaining assistive devices are not available and when a service provider fails to require a needed comprehensive assessment of consumer needs, priorities, and assistive technology preferences at the beginning of the assistive technology and support selection process.

The use of assessment methods that are evidence-based and allow easy comparisons with other disability statistics are needed. A common tool, such as that provided by the ICF, can greatly facilitate this occurring.

Issues Impacting the Use of the Assessments

To avoid technology nonuse, inappropriate use, or abandonment/discard, all but the simplest technology require an evaluation early in the process of selecting interventions and devices for a given consumer. Professionals may not engage in these critical evaluations due to limited time and support for them, primarily because funding sources and their own managers may view these evaluations to be a low priority. Managers have limited resources and thus often emphasize cost-effectiveness and cost-efficiency; therefore, they may be somewhat inclined to adopt a minimum data set as being sufficient. A balance is needed among three qualities: consumer needs and preferences, quality service delivery, and cost-effectiveness and cost-efficiency. When these three are seen as stool legs, if one were eliminated, the stool becomes unstable. Therefore, methods to balance and satisfy critical issues for consumers, professionals, and administrators/funding sources are needed.

Discussion Box 11.3

GLOBALIZATION OF REHABILITATION

Given the attention to globalization of rehabilitation, consider the interface of assistive technology assessment and the ICF. The ICF describes how people live with their health conditions and emphasizes functional status over diagnoses. The classification system is not just about people with traditionally acknowledged disabilities diagnostically categorized. Instead it is about all people. For the first time, the ICF also calls for the elimination of distinctions, explicitly or implicitly, between health conditions that are mental or physical. Significant issues remain as to how to reconcile the competing interests of individuals and practitioners with those of administrators and policy makers. Individual will (e.g., coping and adaptation, motivation), goals and preferences, opportunities, and appropriate support selection constitute key considerations for individuals and practitioners. However, administrators and policy makers may have a different frame of reference, namely the largest number of people who can be served with the limited resources available (i.e., people, fiscal, time). In other words, group statistics rather than individual needs may drive their considerations. What impact do these competing interests have on current service delivery systems for assistive technology services and equipment? How may these interests differ when considering services in the United States as compared with other countries using the ICF?

Assistive technology service delivery models have been scrutinized. According to Ripat and Booth (2005, p. 1462):

> *The literature describes some models of service provision that result in the end-user receiving a product or device... No preferred method has emerged as the method of choice in the field of AT service delivery; each method needs to consider the unique social, financial and political environments in which it exists. Despite the lack of uniformity of service delivery models, certain characteristics may be essential for enabling the best possible solution for the end-user of the technology.*

The authors go on to advocate the need to match assistive technology to the individual in context and recommend use of the MPT process.

The system of assistive technology service delivery in Italy was modified and the interdisciplinary Assistive Device Evaluation and Prescription Protocol was implemented (Verza, Lopes Carvalho, Battaglia, & Messmer Uccelli, 2006). A study of its outcomes revealed that the system reduced inappropriate assistive technology recommendations and nonuse of assistive technology devices. The authors further state, "The MPT utilized as a precursor to the Assistive Device Evaluation and Prescription Protocol would provide the team with valuable insight on possible effective interventions, the user's way of thinking and incentives and disincentives to acceptance and use" (Ripat & Booth, 2005, p. 93).

Thus, the MPT process and measures have been found to be of use in matching the most appropriate technology to any given individual user. Its value as an important component of improved assistive technology service delivery is being recognized.

Future Trends

Consumer-centered methods to select and evaluate technologies have been described. Although considerable progress has been achieved during the last decade, additional progress is needed to provide technologies to those who can benefit from their use. These efforts require attention to information dissemination, training assistive technology providers together with primary and secondary users, and funding.

Success in closing service gaps requires changes in the rehabilitation service delivery process. This includes ensuring that consumers receive a comprehensive and individualized evaluation by a qualified professional. Professionals, administrators, and funding sources acknowledge that consumers have a right to select the technologies and other resources they will be using, and therefore, they should be involved in the processes of needs evaluation, selection, and outcomes evaluation. Professionals realize that they can no longer impress their view of what is best on the consumer. Relevant features across the ICF domains help monitor service delivery and determine rehabilitation success. Follow-up evaluations of how well consumer needs are met need to become a regular part of the rehabilitation service delivery process.

Summary

A good match between a person and needed technologies and other supports requires attention to aspects of the environments in which the technology will be used, the needs and preferences of the user, and the functions and features of the technology/support. Improvements in person-centered assistive technology services and outcomes assessment are needed, given reports of a high level of dissatisfaction and nonuse of technology by consumers.

As this chapter has discussed, it is important to ensure an evidence-based, client-centered assessment for determining the match of individuals with the most appropriate technologies for their use. Achieving a desired outcome begins at the point of technology consideration and then progresses to product selection (Scherer et al., 2007). Research increasingly highlights the fact that consumers are less likely to use recommended devices when their needs are neither fully addressed nor understood during the technology selection process (e.g., Scherer et al., 2007). Both practitioners and researchers who partner with consumers and apply the principles of evidence-based practice will more likely make decisions that result in better outcomes.

Acknowledgments

Information in this chapter about the MPT measures and accompanying materials was supported in part by funding from:

- National Center for Medical Rehabilitation Research at the National Institutes of Health (Grants HD038220 and HD052310)
- Centers for Disease Control and Prevention (Grant DD000219)
- National Institute on Disability and Rehabilitation Research (Grant H133A010401)

References

Abledata. (2009). Retrieved May 2, 2009, from: http://www.abledata.com

Albaugh, P. R., & Fayne, H. (1996). The ET PA for predicting technology success with learning disabled students: Lessons from a multimedia study. *Technology & Disability, 5*(4), 313–318.

Albaugh, P. R., Piazza, L., & Scholsser, K. (1997). Using a CD-ROM encyclopedia: Interaction of teachers, middle school students, library media specialists, and the technology. *Research in Middle Level Education Quarterly, 20*(3), 43–55.

Beigel, A. R. (2000). More than the device. *Intervention in School and Clinic, 35*(4), 237–243.

Brown, D. (1996). Personal implications of functional electrical stimulation standing for older adolescents with spinal cord injuries. *Technology and Disability, 5*(4), 295–311.

Brown, D. L., & Merbitz, C. (1995). Comparison of technology match between two types of functional electrical stimulation hand grasp systems. *Proceedings of the RESNA '95 Annual Conference* (pp. 381–383). Arlington, VA: RESNA Press.

Bruner-Canhoto, L. A. (2004). *Environmental strategies among people growing older with Multiple Sclerosis.* Unpublished doctoral dissertation, University of Massachusetts, Boston.

Cook, A. M., & Hussey, S. M. (2002). *Assistive technology: Principles and practices* (2nd ed.). St. Louis, MO: Mosby.

Craddock, G. M. (2003). *The impact of assistive technology on the quality of life and participation, self-esteem and autonomy of students with disabilities transitioning from second level to post second level education.* Unpublished doctoral dissertation, University College Dublin, Ireland.

Craddock, G. M. (2006). The AT continuum in education: Novice to power user. *Disability and Rehabilitation: Assistive Technology, 1*(1/2), 17–27.

Craddock, G. M., & McCormack, L. (2002). Delivering an AT service: A client-focused, social and participatory service delivery model in assistive technology in Ireland. *Disability and Rehabilitation, 24*(1/2/3), 160–170.

Cushman, L. A., & Scherer, M. J. (1996). Measuring the relationship of assistive technology use, functional status over time, and consumer-therapist perceptions of ATs. *Assistive Technology, 8*(2), 103–109.

Demers, L., Weiss-Lambrou, R., & Ska, B. (1996). Development of the Quebec User Evaluation of Satisfaction with assistive Technology (QUEST). *Assistive Technology, 8*(1), 3–13.

Diener, E., Emmons, R., Larsen, R., & Griffin, S. (1985) The Satisfaction With Life Scale. *Journal of Personality, 49,* 71–75.

Donnelly, C., & Carswell, A. (2002). Individualized outcome measures: A review of the literature. *Canadian Journal of Occupational Therapy, 69,* 84–94.

Elliott, T. R., & Umlauf, R. L. (1995). Measurement of personality and psychopathology following acquired physical disability. In L. A. Cushman & M. Scherer (Eds.), *Psychological assessment in medical rehabilitation* (pp. 325–359). Washington, DC: APA Books.

Fischer, C. T. (2000). Collaborative, individualized assessment. *Journal of Personality Assessment, 74*(1), 2–14.

Fuhrmann T. (Preceptors N. Namassivaya & M. Scherer). (2007). *Assessing the concerns of SCI patients in order to improve treatment.* Basic Science and Clinical Research, 2007 Student Research Poster Session, University of Rochester Medical Center, New York.

Goodman, G., Tiene, D., & Luft, P. (2002). Adoption of assistive technology for computer access among college students with disabilities. *Disability and Rehabilitation, 24*(1–3), 80–92.

Graves, D., Scherer, M., & Sax, C. (2006). Dimensional structure of the Assistive Technology Device Predisposition Assessment. *Archives of Physical Medicine and Rehabilitation, 87*(10), E23; *Neurorehabilitation and Neural Repair,* 20(4).

Haley, S. M., Coster, W. J., Andres, P. L., Ludlow, L. H., Ni, P., Bond, T. L., et al. (2004). Activity outcome measurement for postacute care. *Medical Care, 42*(1 Suppl), I49–I61.

Heerkens, W. D., Briggs, J., & Weider, T. G. (1997). Using peer mentors to facilitate the match of person & technology. In S. Sprigle (Ed.), *Proceedings of the 1997 RESNA Annual Conference* (pp. 484–486). Arlington, VA: RESNA Press.

Heinrich, R. K., Tate, D., & Buckelew, S. P. (1994). Brief Symptom Inventory norms for SCI. *Rehabilitation Psychology, 39,* 49–56.

Jette, A. M., Keysor, J., Coster, W., Ni, P., & Haley, S. (2005). Beyond function: Predicting participation in a rehabilitation cohort. *Archives of Physical Medicine and Rehabilitation, 86*(11), 2087–2094.

Lasker, J. P., & Bedrosian, J. L. (2001). Promoting acceptance of augmentative and alternative communication by adults with acquired communication disorders. *Augmentative & Alternative Communication, 17*(3), 141–153.

Punch, K. F. (1996). *Introduction to social research: Quantitative & qualitative approaches.* Thousand Oaks, CA: Sage.

Ripat, J., & Booth, A. (2005). Characteristics of assistive technology service delivery models: stakeholder perspectives and preferences. *Disability and Rehabilitation, 27*(24), 1461–1470.

Scherer, M. J. (1986). Values in the creation, prescription, and use of technological aids and assistive devices for people with physical disabilities (Doctoral dissertation, University of Rochester, and final report to the National Science Foundation). *Dissertation Abstracts International, 48*(1), 49.

Scherer, M. J. (1995). A model of rehabilitation assessment. In L. C. Cushman & M. J. Scherer (Eds.), *Psychological assessment in medical rehabilitation* (pp. 3–23). Washington, DC: APA Books.

Scherer, M. J. (1998). *The Matching Person & Technology (MPT) model manual.* Webster, NY: The Institute for Matching Person & Technology, Inc.

Scherer, M. J. (Ed.). (2002). *Assistive technology: Matching device and consumer for successful rehabilitation.* Washington, DC: APA Books.

Scherer, M. J. (2005). *Living in the state of stuck: How assistive technology impacts the lives of people with disabilities* (4th ed.). Cambridge, MA: Brookline Books.

Scherer, M. J., & Craddock, G. (2002). Matching Person & Technology (MPT) assessment process (reliability and validity). *Technology & Disability, Special Issue: The assessment of assistive technology outcomes, effects and costs, 14*(3), 125–131.

Scherer, M. J., & Cushman, L. A. (2000). Predicting satisfaction with assistive technology for a sample of adults with new spinal cord injuries. *Psychological Reports, 87,* 981–987.

Scherer, M. J., & Cushman, L. A. (2001). Measuring subjective quality of life following spinal cord injury: A validation study of the Assistive Technology Device Predisposition Assessment. *Disability & Rehabilitation, 23*(9), 387–393.

Scherer, M. J., & Cushman, L. A. (2002). Determining the content for an interactive training programme and interpretive guidelines for the Assistive Technology Device Predisposition Assessment. *Disability and Rehabilitation, 24*(1/2/3), 126–130.

Scherer, M. J., & Frisina, D. R. (1994). Applying the Matching People with Technologies Model to individuals with hearing loss: What people say they want—and need—from assistive technologies. In M. J. Scherer (Ed.), *Technology & Disability: Deafness and Hearing Impairments, 3*(1), 62–68.

Scherer, M. J., & Frisina, D. R. (1998). Characteristics associated with marginal hearing loss and subjective well-being among a sample of older adults. *Journal of Rehabilitation Research and Development, 35*(4), 420–426.

Scherer, M. J., Jutai, J., Fuhrer, M., Demers, L., & DeRuyter, F. (2006, June). Factors impacting consumers' assistive technology device (ATD) selection. *Proceedings of the 29th Annual RESNA Conference, Atlanta.* Retrieved from: http://www.resna.org/ProfResources/Publications/Proceedings/2006/Research/Outcomes/Scherer.php

Scherer, M., Jutai, J., Fuhrer, M., Demers, L., & DeRuyter, F. (2007). A framework for modelling the selection of assistive technology devices (ATDs). *Disability and Rehabilitation: Assistive Technology, 2*(1), 1–8.

Scherer, M., & McKee, B. (1992, April). *Early validity and reliability data for two instruments assessing the predispositions people have toward technology use: Continue integration of quantitative and qualitative methods.* Paper presented at the Annual Meeting of the American Educational Research Association, San Francisco. (ERIC Document Reproduction Service #ED 346 124.)

Scherer, M. J., Sax, C., Vanbiervliet, A., Cushman, L. A., & Scherer, J. V. (2005). Predictors of assistive technology use: The importance of personal and psychosocial factors. *Disability and Rehabilitation, 27*(21), 1321–1331.

Technology-Related Assistance for Individuals with Disabilities Act of 1988, Pub. L. 100–407, 29 U.S.C. 2201 et seq.

Verza, R., Lopes Carvalho, M. L., Battaglia, M. A., & Messmer Uccelli, M. (2006). An interdisciplinary approach to evaluating the need for assistive technology reduces equipment abandonment. *Multiple Sclerosis, 12,* 88–93.

Vincent, C., & Morin, G. (1999). L'Utilisation ou non des aides techniques: Comparaison d'un modeleamericain aux besoins de la realite quebecoise. *Canadian Journal of Occupational Therapy 66*(2), 92–101.

Wielandt, T., Mckenna, K., Tooth, L., & Strong, J. (2006). Factors that predict the post-discharge use of recommended assistive technology (AT). *Disability and Rehabilitation: Assistive Technology, 1*(1–2), 29–40.

Wessels, R., Persson, J., Lorentsen, O., Andrich, R., Ferrario, M., Oortwijn, W., et al. (2002). IPPA: Individually Prioritised Problem Assessment. *Technology and Disability, 14*(3), 141–145.

World Health Organization. (2001). *International Classification of Functioning, Disability and Health.* Geneva: Author.

Zapf, S. A., & Rough, R. B. (2002). The development of an instrument to match individuals with disabilities and service animals. *Disability and Rehabilitation, 24*(1–3), 47–58.

Assessing Universal Design in the Physical Environment

Jon A. Sanford

12

Overview

This chapter focuses on assessing the environmental demands of universal design to understand its effect on activity and participation of all individuals. Universal design is defined by the Principles of Universal Design and is contrasted to typical and accessible design as well as to ergonomic and human factors design. Universal design is generally assessed either by standards of accessibility or by broader performance guidelines. Further, the strength of demands attributed to either prescriptive standards or performance guidelines can be measured either by their expected (i.e., potential) or actual (i.e., kinetic) effects on activity performance and participation. Therefore, the extent to which any design is universal is a function of the degree to which the attributes of design features minimize demands on the widest range of users. Several tools are presented to illustrate strengths and weaknesses of assessing prescriptive standards. In addition, two tools for assessing universal design are introduced: *the Universal Design Performance Measures* and *the Universal Design Assessment Protocol.*

Learning Objectives

By the end of the chapter, the reader will be able to

1. Describe differences between typical design, accessible design, and universal design approaches in supporting functional abilities;
2. Discuss the similarities and differences between universal design and human factors and ergonomic design as they relate to measuring the impact of the physical environment on activity performance and participation;
3. State the relationship between the Principles of Universal Design and the ICF constructs of activity and participation;
4. Describe different types of universal design assessments and how assessing actual and potential environmental demands informs our understanding of universal design in the physical environment; and
5. Identify three reasons why assessing the impact of universal design on activity and participation is difficult.

Introduction

Universal design is the design of all products and environments to be usable by all people to the greatest extent possible without the need for adaptation or specialized design (Mace, Hardie, & Place, 1991). Although originally intended to describe design of physical artifacts, such as manufactured objects, controls, hardware and other user interfaces, buildings, and public spaces, it has subsequently been extended to encompass the design of systems (e.g., telecommunications) and programs (e.g., educational). At its core, universal design is predicated on design to meet the needs of the wide array of users. In essence, universal design seeks to minimize demands (see chapter 10 for a discussion of the Environmental Press Model) for everyone by infusing accessibility for all types and levels of abilities into the design of objects, spaces, and technologies for the general public.

Approaches to Environmental Design in Rehabilitation and Health

In contrast to accessible design, which is disability-focused, universal design is compatible with the ICF concept that disability is not a single point requiring specialized intervention but a continuum of ability that would benefit from less demanding design. Also unlike accessible design, which only minimizes demands on people with specific types and levels of disability, universal design minimizes demands on all types and levels of ability. Simply put, *universal design is typical design that minimizes demands for everyone.* To understand the role of universal design, we must first understand the implications of different environmental design approaches in rehabilitation and health.

Typical Design

Typical design is the way in which buildings, objects, and spaces are usually designed and produced. To the extent that such designs are based on human functioning at all, they are based on body structure, body function, and capacities of a male in the 95th percentile. That is, typical design is based on someone who has fairly high levels of ability across all abilities, including motor, vision, hearing, touch, communication, and cognition. Because very few individuals actually have high levels of ability in all of their abilities, the demands exerted by typical design invariably result in a misfit between design and some abilities for almost everyone (a VCR, for example).

Accessible Design

Accessible design is a disability-specific approach that is compatible with the Institute of Medicine's (see chapter 10) concept that enabling environments will restore function (Brandt & Pope, 1997). Accessible design includes specialized and assistive products, devices, and technologies that are intended to minimize demands for people with specific types and levels of ability (i.e., disabilities). For example, a ramp and curbless shower minimize demands on one's lower body motor abilities (i.e., eliminate need to lift one's leg onto or over a step); high contrast signage or tactile warnings minimize demands on visual abilities; and an augmentative and alternative communication device minimizes demands on communication abilities.

Accessible design that minimizes demands should not be confused with an assistive technology device, which is *any item, piece of equipment, or product system, whether acquired commercially, modified, or customized, that is used to increase, maintain, or improve functional capabilities of individuals with disabilities* (U.S. Congress, 1988, 1998). Although both assistive technologies and accessible design are aimed at improving task performance of individuals who have specific limitations in ability, the two clearly have different approaches to achieve this end. Whereas accessible design focuses on changing characteristics of the environment (e.g., lowering shelves) to enable performance of a given individual's specific level of ability (e.g., limited reach), assistive technology focuses on changing the functional capabilities of a person (e.g., a reacher stick to reach objects on high shelves).

Accessible design is usually mandated through codes and standards (e.g., Americans with Disabilities Act Accessibility Guidelines [ADAAG], Uniform Federal Accessibility Standards [UFAS], and American National Standards Institute [ANSI] A117.1) that prescribe or stipulate technical requirements for design that are expected to minimize environmental demands on individuals with limitations in specific types of abilities. For example, to minimize demands on individuals who cannot ambulate, a ramp is specified to have a maximum slope of 1 inch of rise for every 12 inches of run and a maximum length of 30 feet between level landings. Whereas these requirements are intended to minimize demands on a wheelchair user, the specifications may or may not actually achieve that end, depending on the interaction between the ramp and the actual motor abilities of the individual while using the wheelchair.

Universal Design

Accessible design, as defined previously, prescribes the requirements that are necessary (i.e., tells you what you must do) to minimize demands on a group of individuals with a specific type of disability (e.g., a ramp shall have a maximum slope of 1:12 to permit a wheelchair user to access the door). Universal design, in contrast, is more descriptive than prescriptive. In other words, universal design describes how a design can minimize demands on all users (e.g., a *level* entrance will enable all people to access the door). As a result, universal design opens up the world of possibilities of what you can do.

Examples of accessible and universal design features are shown in Table 12.1. It is important to note that while many of the design features that exemplify these design strategies are the same, the characteristics of the design features differ between the two approaches. Whereas many characteristics of accessible design are specific prescriptions for accessibility, universal design is typically less prescriptive and more descriptive of the type of characteristics that will promote usability.

The differences between accessible and universal design are shown in Table 12.2. While accessible design purports to ameliorate disability by reducing environmental demands on people with specific ability limitations, universal design promotes usable environments by reducing demands on all individuals with all levels of abilities. As a result, accessible design is a reactive band-aid approach intended to compensate for deficiencies in typical design that impeded task performance for individuals with limitations in some abilities, whereas universal design is a proactive, problem-solving approach that is intended to prevent design deficiencies regardless of one's level of ability. Clearly, the differences are akin to the glass being half empty versus the glass being half full.

12.1 Examples of Accessible and Universal Design Features

Accessible Design	Universal Design
• Ramp with 1:12 slope (max) • Fixed grab bars in specified location • Toilet safety frame or 17–19" high toilet • Lever door handle • 32" clear door • Shower w/ seat in a specified location • Amplified phone • 36" width walkway, 60" every 200'	• Sloping walkway (a slope of 1:20 or less is defined as a walkway) • Swing-up grab bars where needed • Toilet at an appropriate height • Lever door handle • Door width as needed • Curbless (i.e., roll-in) shower, with seat as desired • Large button, amplified phone, auto dial • Walkway width as needed

12.2 Comparison of Accessible and Universal Design

	Design Objective	Approach	Design Strategy	Result
Accessible Design	Reduce environmental demands on individuals with specific types and levels of disability through specialized design	Reactive, band-aid approach in response to a problem	Prescriptive: For example, what is the maximum ramp slope I can use to get wheelchair users into the building?	Specialized technology and designs where usability is added in after or late in the design process
Universal Design	Reduce environmental demands on individuals with all types and levels of ability through better design overall	Proactive, problem-solving approach that tries to prevent problems from occurring	Performance: For example, what is the best way to get everyone into the building?	Usability is the design goal

Some authors (e.g., Johnson, 2006) have equated universal design with human-factors design and ergonomics, although universal design encompasses and transcends them both. Like universal design, both human factors and ergonomic designs are user-centered, that is, designed for the user rather than forcing the user to accommodate the design. The two disciplines, however, differ in their approaches to user-centered design. Human factors, which is modeled after the design process used by the U.S. military, seeks to achieve comfort, safety, performance, and privacy based on rigorous measures of human physical, sensory, and cognitive abilities. Ergonomics, on the other hand, which has well-established applications in the work environment and product design, is more closely linked to goals of comfort and ease of use based on the physical, psychological, and social needs of individuals. Universal design, by its very nature as design for all, not only incorporates all of the design goals but is also based on the entire set of needs and abilities included in both human factors and ergonomic design.

In 1997, a group a group of architects; industrial, landscape, and graphics designers; and engineers at the Center for Universal Design, North Carolina State University, established the Principles of Universal Design (Center for Universal Design, 1997), which define the general performance goals for universal design. They include: equitable use, flexibility in use, simple and intuitive use, perceptible information, tolerance for error, low physical effort, and size and space for approach and use (see Table 12.3).

Clearly, the human factors and ergonomics goals of performance, ease of use, comfort, security, and privacy are evident in the seven principles. However, social and contextual integration, the two goals that differentiate universal design from other user-centered approaches, are not evident. Both goals are included in equitable use, but the intent is unclear. Social integration (i.e., inclusion) is defined by use (the same means of use for all users and avoiding

12.3 Principles of Universal Design

Principle One. Equitable Use:

The design is useful and marketable to people with diverse abilities.

1a. Provide the same means of use for all users: identical whenever possible; equivalent when not.
1b. Avoid segregating or stigmatizing any users.
1c. Provisions for privacy, security, and safety should be equally available to all users.
1d. Make the design appealing to all users.

Principle Two. Flexibility in Use:

The design accommodates a wide range of individual preferences and abilities.

2a. Provide choice in methods of use.
2b. Accommodate right- or left-handed access and use.
2c. Facilitate the user's accuracy and precision.
2d. Provide adaptability to the user's pace.

Principle Three. Simple and Intuitive Use:

Use of the design is easy to understand, regardless of the user's experience, knowledge, language skills, or current concentration level.

3a. Eliminate unnecessary complexity.
3b. Be consistent with user expectations and intuition.
3c. Accommodate a wide range of literacy and language skills.
3d. Arrange information consistent with its importance.
3e. Provide effective prompting and feedback during and after task completion.

Principle Four. Perceptible Information:

The design communicates necessary information effectively to the user, regardless of ambient conditions or the user's sensory abilities.

4a. Use different modes (pictorial, verbal, tactile) for redundant presentation of essential information.
4b. Provide adequate contrast between essential information and its surroundings.
4c. Maximize "legibility" of essential information.
4d. Differentiate elements in ways that can be described (i.e., make it easy to give instructions or directions).
4e. Provide compatibility with a variety of techniques or devices used by people with sensory limitations.

Principle Five. Tolerance for Error:

The design minimizes hazards and the adverse consequences of accidental or unintended actions.

5a. Arrange elements to minimize hazards and errors: most used elements, most accessible; hazardous elements eliminated, isolated, or shielded.
5b. Provide warnings of hazards and errors.
5c. Provide fail-safe features.
5d. Discourage unconscious action in tasks that require vigilance.

Principle Six. Low Physical Effort:

The design can be used efficiently and comfortably and with a minimum of fatigue.

6a. Allow user to maintain a neutral body position.
6b. Use reasonable operating forces.
6c. Minimize repetitive actions.
6d. Minimize sustained physical effort.

12.3 Principles of Universal Design — *Continued*

Principle Seven. Size and Space for Approach and Use:
Appropriate size and space is provided for approach, reach, manipulation, and use regardless of user's body size, posture, or mobility.

7a. Provide a clear line of sight to important elements for any seated or standing user.
7b. Make reach to all components comfortable for any seated or standing user.
7c. Accommodate variations in hand and grip size.
7d. Provide adequate space for the use of assistive devices or personal assistance.

From *Principles of Universal Design*, by the Center for Universal Design, 1997, Raleigh: North Carolina State University, School of Design.

segregating users) rather than by outcome. The idea that social integration is an outcome of use fails to recognize that use (i.e., activity) and integration (i.e., participation), despite being linked, are separate constructs that must be independently considered in design (WHO, 2001). Contextual integration (i.e., fits with the context) is similarly vague, being captured by the guideline to avoid stigmatizing users. Moreover, the clarity of the two goals is further confounded by their being lumped together in the same guideline to avoid segregating or stigmatizing users.

To address these deficiencies, this writer, who was one of the authors of the Principles of Universal Design, has previously suggested revising our understanding of equitable use and the addition of two new principles that specifically address the goals of social and contextual integration (Sanford, 2004; see Table 12.4). Whereas these changes clearly distinguish between seven "usability" principles and two "integration" principles, the goals of universal design, unlike those of human factors (i.e., performance, comfort, security and privacy) and ergonomics (i.e., ease of use and comfort), remain unstated.

Ed Steinfeld, Director of the Rehabilitation Engineering Research Center on Universal Design in the Built Environment and one of the author's of the principles, has suggested that a set of key goals for universal design can be generated from the principles (see Table 12.5). The first four—body fit, comfort, awareness, and understanding—are derived from human factors and ergonomic goals and provide support for activities. The second three—social integration, personalization, and appropriateness—are related to support for social participation (Steinfeld & Danford, 2007).

History of Research and Practice in Assessing Design for Rehabilitation Intervention

Accessibility Standards and Guidelines 1961–1991

Despite differences between universal and accessible design, universal design owes its origins to the latter about 3 decades earlier with the sponsorship of the American National Standards Institute (ANSI) *A117.1 Making Buildings and*

12.4 Suggested Revisions to the Principles of Universal Design

Principle One. Equitable Use and Appeal:
The design is useful and marketable to people with diverse abilities.

- 1a. Provide the same outcome(s) for all users.
- 1b. Provide opportunity for concurrent use by all users.
- 1c. Provide the same opportunities for privacy for all users.
- 1d. Provide the same opportunities for safety/security for all users.
- 1e. Is equally suitable for use by all users.
- 1f. Would be in demand by any individual.

Principle Eight. Social Integration:
The design provides opportunities for individuals to participate in activities with others.

- 8a. Enables engagement in activities **when** wanted or needed.
- 8b. Enables engagement in activities **where** wanted or needed.
- 8c. Enables engagement in activities **with whom** is desired or needed.

Principle Nine. Contextual Integration:
The design is compatible with the context.

- 9a. Design is not stigmatizing.
- 9b. Looks, feels, smells, and sounds like it is an integral part of the overall design.

From *Development and Testing of a Universal Design Assessment Protocol*, by J. A. Sanford, 2004. Presentation at EDRA 35, the Thirty-fifth Annual Conference of the Environmental Design Research Association.

Facilities Accessible to and Usable by People with Disabilities by the President's Committee on Employment of the Physically Handicapped and the National Society for Crippled Children in 1959. In 1961, ANSI made A117.1 the first published national standard for accessibility for the design and construction of new buildings and facilities as well as the alterations to existing facilities (U.S. Department of Transportation, 2009). The new standard provided a minimal set of recommendations for basic accessibility for specific parts and features of buildings (e.g., an entrance, a bathroom, a water fountain, and a route from the entrance to the accessible features), based primarily on consensus opinion and what little human factors and ergonomic data that was available at the time. As its name suggests, ANSI was a standard, not a required code. As such, it served as a model with recommendations that could be voluntarily adopted into the various building codes adhered to by federal, state, and local agencies.

In 1965, the Vocational Rehabilitation Amendment Act (P.L. 89-333) was passed to encourage public facilities to voluntarily comply with ANSI A117.1, thus establishing the importance of the accessibility standard. Recognizing the ineffectiveness of voluntary compliance, Congress passed the Architectural Barriers Act (ABA) in 1968, which required for the first time that buildings or facilities owned, funded, or leased by the federal government be accessible. The four agencies responsible for federal construction (the U.S. Department of Defense, the U.S. Department of Housing and Urban Development, the U.S. General Services Administration, and the U.S. Postal Service) were required to develop accessibility standards based on ANSI A117.1.

12.5 Goals of Universal Design

- Body fit—accommodating a wide range of body sizes and abilities
- Comfort—keeping demands within desirable limits of body function and perception
- Awareness—ensuring that critical information for use is easily perceived
- Understanding—making methods of operation and use intuitive, clear, and unambiguous
- Social integration—treating all groups with dignity and respect
- Personalization—incorporating opportunities for choice and the expression of individual preferences
- Appropriateness—respecting and reinforcing cultural values and the social and environmental context of any design project

From *Universal Design and the ICF,* by E. Steinfeld & G. S. Danford, June 6, 2007. Presentation at 12th Annual North American Collaborating Center Conference on ICF, Vancouver, Canada.

The technical provisions of ANSI A117.1 were reaffirmed without changes in 1971. However, the drive to achieve access for people with disabilities gained momentum with the passage of the Rehabilitation Act in 1973. Section 502 of the Rehabilitation Act established the U.S. Architectural and Transportation Barriers Compliance Board (later changed to U.S. Access Board) as an independent regulatory agency with authority to enforce the ABA. To support this role, the Access Board published the Minimum Guidelines and Requirements for Accessible Design (MGRAD) in 1982. The technical specifications of MGRAD were largely based on ANSI A117–1980, which completely overhauled and expanded the original ANSI standards, in a large part based on the seminal work of Ed Steinfeld and his colleagues at Syracuse University (Steinfeld et al., 1979). In addition, MGRAD added with scoping specifications derived from its own research, state accessibility codes, public comment, and existing federal agency standards. Based on MGRAD, the four agencies responsible for federal construction published the Uniform Federal Accessibility Standards (UFAS) in 1984 to replace ANSI A117.1 as the basis for accessibility in federal facilities.

In 1990, Congress passed the American Disabilities Act (ADA), which guaranteed for people with disabilities equal opportunity in accommodations, commercial facilities, employment, transportation, state and local government services, and telecommunications. Title V of the ADA requires the U.S. Access Board to issue minimum guidelines for accessible design to ensure that buildings, facilities, rail passenger cars, and vehicles are accessible in terms of architecture and design, transportation, and communication to individuals with disabilities (ADA, 1990, Section 504). To comply with this mandate, the Access Board published the Americans with Disabilities Act Accessibility Guidelines (ADAAG) in 1991. ADAAG is based on specifications established in MGRAD. ADAAG, in turn, were adopted by the U.S. Department of Justice (U.S. DOJ) and the U.S. Department of Transportation (U.S. DOT) as the basis for enforceable accessibility standards for public facilities and transportation facilities, respectively.

From Accessibility to Universal Design 1991–Present

Clearly, the initial development of ANSI A117.1 in 1961 and its continued revision has had a profound influence on guidelines and legislation pertaining to accessible design in the United States, culminating with the ADAAG in 1991. However, accessible design intended to meet the requirements of federal legislation was historically identified with the use of assistive technology devices, durable medical equipment, and expensive, out-of-place, clinical-looking features such as ramps and stainless steel grab bars. As a result, builders, owners, and the public resisted including accessibility features as they increased cost, had undesirable aesthetics, and decreased marketability.

On the other side of the coin, the aesthetics of accessible design were often stigmatizing to people with disabilities because they clearly called attention to those individuals as different from the general population. At the same time, accessible design features were repeatedly located in isolated parts of buildings that were hard to get to, if one could find them at all. Such strategies effectively segregated people with disabilities and frequently denied them the right to full inclusion and participation in activities.

To overcome the stigma, segregation, and other shortcomings of accessible design, architect Ron Mace, himself an individual with a disability and a staunch advocate of accessibility legislation, developed the concept of universal design. Although, he first developed the concept in the late 1980s, his ideas were fittingly first published in 1991, the same year as the ADAAG. Until his untimely death in 1998, Ron Mace not only advocated for good aesthetics and finding accessibility solutions that were invisible, but also for designs that were good for everyone, regardless of ability. From a market standpoint, such ideas also make good sense as design for everyone creates economies of scale that are considerably more cost effective than specialized products and features required by accessible design.

Research in Accessible and Universal Design

Research related to the interaction between the physical environment and disability dates back to the mid-1960s following the publication of the initial ANSI A117.1 in 1961. However, research focusing on developing technical specifications (i.e., identifying the attributes) of accessible design really began to flourish in the 1970s (e.g., Johnson, 1981; Steinfeld et al., 1979; Templer, 1977, 1979; Woods, 1980) after the passage of the Architectural Barriers Act (ABA) in 1968 and the Rehabilitation Act in 1973, which established the U.S. Architectural and Transportation Barriers Compliance Board (later changed to the U.S. Access Board). Additionally, ANSI developed a completely new and more comprehensive version of A117.1 in 1980, which extended the standard into residential environments.

ANSI A117.1–1980 became the model standard that was the basis for most accessibility provisions in local U.S. building codes prior to the passage of the ADA in 1990. During this time, the federal government, under the auspices of the Access Board, began supporting research to provide technical specifications for accessible design in federal construction. These specifications were published as the MGRAD, which were used to establish UFAS in 1984. Importantly, the Access Board supported a range of studies to develop design specifications for MGRAD on a number of specific issues, including detectability of tactile warning surfaces by individuals with visual impairments (Sanford, 1985; Steinfeld, Richmond, & Sanford, 1986); operability of interfaces by people with hand and upper extremity impairments (Feurstein, Steinfeld, Sanford, & Shiro, 1987); ramp slope and length for people with ambulatory impairments (Sanford, Story, & Jones, 1997); and children's environments (Connell, Sanford, Moore, Bostrom, & Ostroff, 1994).

By the mid to late 1990s, the nature of environment and disability research changed dramatically. The Access Board changed its focus from applied research to broader use of consensus panels to develop design specifications for the ADAAG. With this change, accessibility studies were driven by researchers' desire for new knowledge and the development of effective interventions rather than by standards development and the specific interests of the Access Board. As a result, studies in the United States, funded to a large extent by the Department of Veterans Affairs Rehabilitation Research and Development Service (VARRD) and the National Institute on Disability and Rehabilitation Research (NIDRR), became more innovative and began to incorporate aging issues (e.g., Connell & Sanford, 2001; Sanford, 2002; Sanford, Echt, & Malassigné, 1999; Sanford & Megrew, 1995).

In the mid-1990s, at about the same time as the Access Board scaled back on accessibility research, widespread interest in universal design moved it from concept to practice. Although much of the initial effort in universal design focused on practice, NIDRR was among the first to recognize that this paradigm shift had research implications, beginning with the change in name and focus of the Center on Accessible Housing at NC State University, which became known as the Center on Accessible and Universal Design in Housing in the mid-1990s

Discussion Box 12.1

DESIGNING FOR ALL

While standards such as the Americans with Disabilities Act Accessibility Guidelines (ADAAG) provide guidelines to promote accessibility of the physical environment, there is no guarantee that accessibility will be achieved. There are several reasons for this, including variance in the abilities and needs of all potential users of a space and the contextual variability of spaces. Is it possible to truly design the physical environment to accommodate the needs of every person? Universal design has emerged as an area of research and practice that attempts to make this possible. Discuss whether universal design can accomplish what accessible design has had difficulty doing. Does the type of space make a difference? For example, is it easier or more difficult to employ universal design in a residential space versus a public space? What influence do specific activities to be performed or features of the space have on design? What would be an advantage to applying accessible design standards when building a new space?

and eventually the Center for Universal Design in the Built Environment at the turn of the 21st century.

Nonetheless, significant gaps in the knowledge base of universal design still exist. While research on assessment of accessible design has appropriately addressed questions of "fit" between both typical and accessible environments and people with disabilities, universal design has been less successful in addressing its specific (cl)aims of improving usability for all individuals and enhancing the social integration and participation of people with disabilities. The primary motivation in asking questions about the effects of universal design has been an understanding of how much and what kind of difference universal design makes in the lives of people with and without disabilities (Connell & Sanford, 1999). Unfortunately, research in universal design assessment has continued to focus on activity performance and the usability of the physical environment for people with specific functional limitations rather than participation in life roles and the community of all individuals regardless of ability. As a result, to date, much of what has been labeled research in assessing universal design has failed to be much more than assessment of accessible design in a different wrapper.

Methods of Assessing Universal Design

The extent to which any design is universal is a function of the degree to which the attributes of design features minimize demands on the widest range of users. Therefore, to assess universal design, it is necessary to identify the magnitude of demands as well as the type (i.e., sensory, motor, cognitive, communicative) and level (i.e., continuum from none to full) of ability (i.e., capacity) of any particular user.

Universal design in the physical environment can be assessed either by standards of accessibility or by broader performance guidelines. The former are based on either empirical evidence or expert consensus that comprises the accepted knowledgebase of prescriptive accessibility standards. The latter is typically based on the Principles of Universal Design (Center for Universal Design, 1997), a set of ideal performance guidelines developed by expert consensus. These assessments represent specific applications of environmental assessments described previously in chapter 10, "Measuring the Physical Environment." As suggested by the chapter's discussion of environmental demands, the strength of demands attributed to prescriptive standards and performance guidelines can be measured either by their expected (i.e., potential) or actual (i.e., kinetic) effects on activity performance and participation. Expected demands are based on predefined assumptions of activity and participation by individuals with specific functional limitations given an environment with specific attributes. In contrast, actual demands are based on tangible interactions between individuals and their environment.

Whichever approach is used, assessment methods should provide objective identification of mismatches between the demands of the environment and the capacities of the user. There are many objective methods for measuring the usability of products, including naturalistic observations, focus groups, interviews and surveys of users, checklists of environmental attributes, and simulation studies (Keates & Clarkson, 2004). However, such methods are not only limited to usability, but such studies are relevant to usability studies, in general, and have been described elsewhere (e.g., Nielsen, 1993). As a result, this chapter will focus on assessment tools that are unique to assessment of universal design.

Assessment of Prescriptive Accessibility Guidelines and Standards

Assessment of Potential Demands

The underlying assumption of this assessment method is that prescriptive requirements (typically embodied in codified accessibility standards) are effective at facilitating independent activity performance for a specific target population (see Table 12.6). As a result, they represent the gold standard of usable design that promotes independent activity performance. The assessment of potential demands of these design attributes, therefore, entails the verification that they actually meet the prescriptive requirements for accessibility.

Assessments of potential demand are generally manifest as checklists. Perhaps the two most well-known are the ADA Checklist (Adaptive Environments Center and Barrier Free Environments, 1995) and the UFAS Checklist (Barrier Free Environments, 1990), which assess precise technical specifications (e.g., # provided and physical dimensions) in their respective guidelines and standards for public accommodations. A third, well-known assessment of potential demand is *The Enabler* (Steinfeld et al., 1979), which is described in chapter 10 and has been applied to both public and residential environments. Unlike the other two checklists, the Housing Enabler (Iwarsson, 1997), for example, was not developed to assess mandatory code compliance. Rather, it is intended to inform decisions about modifying residential environments to reduce demands. As a result, it includes both technical specifications (e.g., 1:12 ramp slope) as well as less precise subjective evaluation (e.g., wide, narrow, poor condition) of environmental attributes that are believed to reduce demands and promote usability.

Although potential demands are assessed based on the anticipated performance of specific user groups, the ADA and UFAS checklists do not explicitly identify those groups. For example, a ramp with a slope of 1:12 or less is intended to facilitate performance of manual wheelchair users. Yet, whether we know that or not is not important. Because the technical requirements represent a gold standard, those user groups do not need to be identified. The design simply either meets or does not meet the standard. In contrast, the unique aspect of the Enabler is that it differentiates the expected impact of design by user group. Specifically, it assigns a measure of potential demand based on expected interaction between design attributes and users' functional limitations. As a result, identification of the user group is essential for assessing potential demands. For example, ramp slope might differentially impact performance of manual wheelchair users as well as people with shuffling gait and people who use walkers.

There are four major limitations in assessing the potential demands of accessibility requirements. First, expected demands are often based on technical specifications that are only concerned with independent functioning in performance of activities. Second, technical requirements were developed through consensus opinion and lack validation through empirical evidence. Third, the requirements presume demands based on interactions between person and environment that may or may not occur. Fourth, they are population-specific. That is, potential demands can only be generalized to populations for which consensus standards or research data exist. For example, a ramp slope of 1:12 slope is assumed to facilitate performance of manual wheelchair users, but the extent to which the same slope might impact performance of people with other types of impairments, such as shuffling gait or vision loss, is empirically unknown. As a result, the more we are able to demonstrate that specific accessibility requirements reduce demands on a broader population of users, the more generalizable (and therefore universal, although only in terms of independent performance of activity) those requirements will be.

Assessment of Actual Demands

One way of increasing the generalizability of prescriptive requirements is to measure real demands of technical specifications under conditions of actual use. Typically, this implies conducting research with a range of user groups to generate actual usability data. Under these circumstances, characteristics of accessible features can be applied to populations for whom they were not intended, thus providing a better assessment of their generalizability to these populations.

Unfortunately, not many assessments of actual demands have been developed, and those that have, have been primarily for research purposes. As a result, they are either difficult to locate or obtain. Assessments of potential demands, such as those described previously, could be adapted to assess actual demands on new populations. However, this would require expanding their focus from verification that specific conditions exist (e.g., a ramp has 1:12 slope) to include an assessment of the effects of that condition on actual task performance of specific user groups (e.g., can people who use walkers ascend a ramp with a slope of 1:12). In addition, outcomes used to measure usability would have to be expanded beyond independent functioning to include activity-appropriate measures, such as task difficulty, task performance time, exertion, and pain.

Despite these changes, modified assessments of potential demands would still be constrained by the technical specifications for environmental attributes upon which they are based. For example, even though objective measures can be used to determine difficulty of ascending a ramp by people who use walkers, it is still based on a ramp with a slope of 1:12. These assessments would have to be fundamentally changed to determine if other slopes (e.g., slopes of 1:10, 1:14, 1:16, etc.) might be more or less usable (e.g., less difficult than 1:12) by other user groups.

There are some assessments of actual demands in which the measures of environmental attributes are open-ended rather than specified, as in the accessibility guidelines. Typically, these assessments, such as Comprehensive Assessment and Solutions Process for Aging Residents (CASPAR), also described in chapter 10, are designed to determine usability of environmental attributes by an individual rather than user groups. However, they have been shown to be readily adaptable to assessing actual demands on different user groups. For example, CASPAR is an individualized housing assessment (Sanford & Butterfield, 2005; Sanford, Pynoos, Gregory, & Browne, 2002) that has been adapted to collect performance data on difficulty and dependence of various user groups across a number of housing features with a range of attributes (Hammel, Fogg, Walens, Garcia, & Sanford, 2005; Sanford & Hammel, 2006).

Assessment of Universal Design

Assessments of prescriptive accessibility guidelines are one-dimensional, focusing only on functional aspects of design. In contrast, assessments of performance guidelines based on the Principles of Universal Design are multidimensional, including functional, social, and contextual aspects of design (see Table 12.6). In addition, the universal design principles provide a more robust understanding of function as a defined set of usability outcomes (i.e., flexibility, simple and intuitive, perceptibility, ease, limiting error, and sufficient space) than the focus on either dependence or difficulty that is associated with accessibility requirements.

Many universal design assessments have been reported in the literature. However, few actual assessments have been published, and those that have,

12.6 Generalizability of Assessment by Type of Design and Demand

Design Type	Potential Demands	Actual Demands
Prescriptive Requirements for Accessibility	Assumptions of independent activity performance of specific user groups based on expected demands of prescriptive standards (e.g., ADAAG, UFAS) Generalizable to target populations	Observed activity performance of any user group to determine demands of prescriptive standards on that group Generalizable to populations observed (the more generalizable, the more universally usable)
Performance Requirements for Universal Design	Assumption of activity performance and participation of any user group based on expected demands of performance standards (i.e., Principles of Universal Design) Generalizable to all populations	Observed activity performance and participation of all user groups to determine demands of performance standards on all users Generalizable to all populations

have largely been based on the Principles of Universal Design. On the positive side, the principles have received widespread acceptance and consensus acknowledgement throughout the world. On the negative side, they are based on consensus opinion, not empirical data; they lack measurable outcomes and are therefore open to interpretation; and they have not been validated to any large extent.

Nonetheless, two assessments developed at the Center for Universal Design at NC State have undergone some validation and therefore warrant discussion. Both assessments use the Principles of Universal Design and their guidelines as assessment items. The first assessment, the *Universal Design Performance Measures* (Story, 1998; Story, Mueller & Montoya-Weiss, 2001), focuses on product assessment. The second assessment, the *Universal Design Assessment Protocol* (Sanford, 2004), focuses on the scale of spaces, buildings, and building elements.

Two versions of the Universal Design Performance Measures assessment were developed to identify potential areas for improvement for a product, comparing relative strengths of similar products and identifying potential strengths of a product such as for marketing purposes. Both versions of the assessment comprise 29 performance measures (i.e., environmental demands) that correspond to the 29 guidelines associated with the 7 Principles of Universal Design. In addition, both versions use rating scales from *strongly agree* to *strongly disagree* to assess the strength of each specific demand.

One version, *Evaluating the Universal Design Performance of Products* (Center for Universal Design, 2000), was intended to be used by product designers to assess potential demands in order to guide the development of more universally usable products (see Figure 12.1). Specifically, it was designed to help product developers with some knowledge of aging and disability to evaluate product usability for all users throughout its life cycle, including packaging, instructions, set-up, use, maintenance, and disposal, and to develop product testing and focus group methodologies for product evaluation (Center for Universal Design, 2000).

12.1

Example of designer's rating scale.

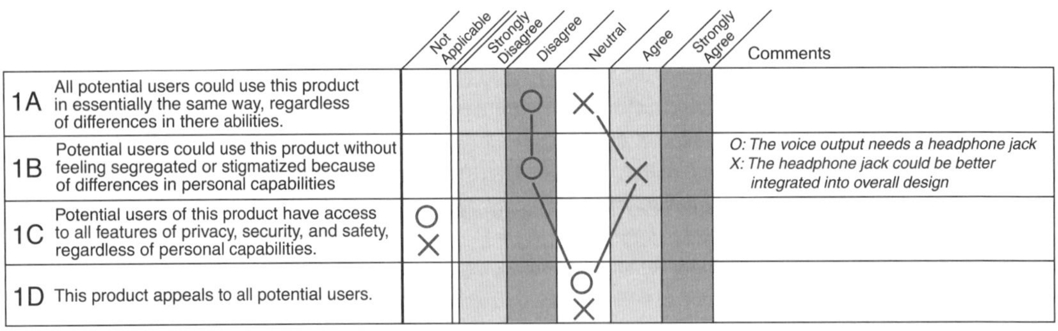

From *Universal Design Performance Measures for Products: Evaluating the Universal Design Performance of Products*, by the Center for Universal Design, 2000, Raleigh: North Carolina State University, School of Design. Copyright © 2000 by the Center for Universal Design. Reprinted with permission.

The second version, *Product Evaluation Countdown* (Center for Universal Design, 2002), is intended to be used by consumers to assess actual demands of products given their own types and levels of functional ability. This enables consumers to consider their own needs when purchasing products and to compare products already on the market.

The purpose of the Universal Design Assessment Protocol was to provide an understanding of the universal nature of buildings, spaces, and building elements based on functional, social, and contextual criteria. Performance guidelines in the existing principles were the source for the functional assessment criteria. To address social and contextual integration, two new principles, as described previously, were added to further clarify issues of segregation and stigmatization included in Principle 1. In total, the 9 principles included 34 performance guidelines, each representing a different environmental demand.

In addition, the instrument was intended to assess any design from the perspective of the full range of users. As a result, the assessment allowed each of the 34 guidelines to be assessed by the demands (either potential or actual) placed on individuals with any type and level of ability. A total of 18 types of abilities were identified (see Figure 12.2), including 5 types of motor function (e.g., changing position, moving around, manipulating objects), 5 types of mental function (e.g., perceiving space, remembering), 4 types of perception and sensation (e.g., seeing, hearing); and 4 types of communication (e.g., producing and receiving communication).

Demand strength was rated for each guideline by the level of ability (on a scale from severe [4] to no limitations [1]) that was supported by a specific design feature. The higher the overall score (i.e., the greater the severity of functional limitations supported by a particular feature), the more universal a particular environmental feature is.

The instrument was designed to be implemented at all stages of the design process by people who are likely to make or influence decisions about the design of a building or space. This includes architects, landscape architects, interior designers, and access consultants. As a result, it can be used to assess both potential and actual demands. Like the *Product Evaluation Countdown* assessment, the Universal Design Assessment Protocolcan be used during the design process to measure potential demands on expected users. Similarly, it can be used after construction to measure real kinetic demands under conditions of actual use.

Although the assessment was designed to embrace activity and participation of people with all types of abilities, the 612 cell matrix (34 guidelines x 18 abilities) proved, in the end to be overly complex, unwieldy, and impractical for the intended audiences to use. As a result, it represents a model for what a universal design assessment is, rather than what a universal design assessment should be.

Major Issues That Need Attention in Measuring Environmental Demands

The hallmark of universal design is the notion of design for all. Not surprisingly, therefore, the biggest issue impacting the general assessment of universal design is its generalizability across user groups. Unless design can be shown, at a

12.2

Example of motor function and scoring from Universal Design Assessment Protocol.

COMPETENCE	Person-Environment Fit (Demands / Abilities)	MOTOR FUNCTION						
	Demands	**Maintain Posture** Initiating & sustaining body positions to perform tasks	**Change Position** Transitioning from lying, standing or sitting positions to other positions	**Move Around** Moving oneself across space	**Manipulate Objects** Reaching, lifting, handling and transporting objects	**Coordinate Movements** Performing movements in a purposeful, orderly combination	**Types of ABILITIES**	Sketch of motor abilities
	Abilities	✓ Balance ✓ Stand ✓ Sit	✓ Whole Body Position ✓ Lie Down ✓ Sit to Stand ✓ Whole Body Transfer	✓ Ambulate ✓ Ambulate or Propel with the aid of a device- ✓ Climb ✓ Crawl	✓ Reach ✓ Grasp ✓ Lift/Lower ✓ Push/Pull ✓ Carry Objects ✓ Release ✓ Turn/Twist	✓ Coordinate Hand ✓ Coordinate Eye-Hand-Foot ✓ Coordinate Lower Body ✓ Coordinate Upper Body ✓ Coordinate Foot-Hand	Examples of ABILITIES	
	ABILITY LEVEL 1.0 Full Ability — 3.0 Some Ability — 5.0 No Ability	The **ENVIRONMENTAL FEATURE** (FILL IN) **UD GUIDELINE** (FILL IN) people with **ABILITY LEVEL** (CHOOSE LOWEST LEVEL FROM 1-5) to **TYPE OF ABILITY** (FILL IN) **0 = Guideline is applicable, but not present in environmental feature** **9 = Guideline is not applicable to environmental feature** **X = Guideline is not applicable to the ability**					**TOT APP DEMANDS**	**IDENTIFY BARRIERS (notes)**

Research Box 12.1

UNIVERSAL DESIGN FOR RAMPS

Sanford, J. A., Story, M. F., & Jones, M. L. (1997). An analysis of the effects of ramp slope on people with mobility impairments. *Assistive Technology, 9*(1), 22–33.

According to technical accessibility specifications, ramps should have a maximum slope of 1:12. However, this requirement is based on young adult manual wheelchair users. There is general lack of research that demonstrates how useful this slope is for older adults, many of whom lack the strength and stamina to propel a wheelchair up a slope or control it on the way down. Sanford, Story, and Jones (1997) investigated performance of individuals with a wide range of abilities on slopes ranging from 1:8 to 1:18.

Method: The investigators compared people with a range of abilities going up and down slopes from 1:8 to 1:18. Subjects were scored on time, veering, collisions with ramp, and self-reported difficulty. The order of the slopes was randomized to counterbalance the effects of fatigue.

Results: The investigators found that many younger people could negotiate 1:10 slopes, although older adults had difficulty negotiating slopes steeper than 1:16. However, there were not enough participants in this category to warrant recommending changes to the accessibility codes.

Questions:

1. What does this research indicate regarding the specification of a universally usable ramp?
2. What are some of the difficulties in conducting research to develop technical specifications for universal design?
3. What are some additional measures that might be used to assess universal ramp usability?
4. Even if a universal ramp slope were developed, would all ramps designed to this specification be universally designed? Why or why not?

minimum, to be usable by users with a range of abilities, then it cannot claim to be universal. As a result, many assessments, even if they are based on the Principles of Universal Design, are not truly measuring universal design because they fail to look across users' abilities. Unfortunately, assessment has, for the most part, tended to be more ability *specific* than it has been ability *generic*.

A second issue that is tied to the generalizability across user groups is the complexity that results from trying to account for a range of abilities. This problem was painfully illustrated by the Universal Design Assessment Protocol, which, despite its best intentions to include all users, ultimately required ratings of 612 cells for a single doorknob.

Finally, the most prominent issue that needs attention as it concerns this chapter is the relationship of the Principles of Universal Design to the ICF. Whereas, Steinfeld and Danford (2007) have suggested a crosswalk between the two, issues go deeper than that. Despite their near universal acceptance, the principles are subjective performance standards that have never have been validated. As a result, both validity and reliability of the principles are suspect. We have no idea if they are being interpreted and applied in the same manner. Similarly, the extent to which the one inclusion/integration principle (or the two, if the author's additional principles are considered) and the six usability principles are the appropriate outcomes to assess the ICF's constructs of social participation and activity performance is unknown. Such validation against accepted measures of activity and performance is imperative.

Ultimately, the best assessment of universal design would be the measurement of functionality/usability and inclusiveness/contextual appropriateness of a particular design feature for all users under conditions of actual use. Clearly, the inclusion of all users representing the widest range of abilities is not practical, given the resources it would require. However, conceptually, such an undertaking is the only way to establish the links between the goals of universal design with those of the ICF. Even then, it isn't clear what goals of universal design are appropriate. Certainly, the principles are widely acknowledged, and this author has suggested revisions and additions to more closely align them with the ICF. On the other hand, Steinfeld and Danford (2007) have articulated an alternative, although not incompatible, set of goals that supports activity (i.e., body fit, comfort, awareness, and understanding) and participation (i.e., social integration, personalization, and contextual appropriateness). Thus, even if assessment of design for all users is not practical, such issues need to be resolved to fully assess and quantify universal design as a facilitator of activity and participation.

Summary

This chapter focused specifically on assessing environmental demands of universal design to understand its effect on activity and participation of all individuals. The discussion of the three design approaches provides insight into the strength of demands. Clearly, typical design creates the strongest demands on all individuals, but particularly on those with functional limitations. Accessible design uses specialized interventions to reduce the demands of typical design on people with impairments. Universal design is merely typical design that reduces demands on all individuals.

The extent to which any design is universal is a function of the degree to which the attributes of design features minimize demands on the widest range of users. Universal design can be assessed either by standards of accessibility or by broader performance guidelines such as the Principles of Universal Design.

Both approaches to universal design assessment have their strengths and weaknesses. Prescriptive guidelines need little interpretation and are easy to objectively verify in the field (e.g., 1:12 ramp slope over 30 feet). However, prescriptive accessibility guidelines are unidimensional, focusing entirely on usability as defined by reducing demands on independent activity performance as the main outcome measure. In addition, the knowledgebase used to develop prescriptive guidelines is generally limited to performance of specific users (e.g., young wheelchair users or people with low vision). This effectively limits generalizability across user groups (e.g., older users with mobility impairments or blind cane users) and creates questions as to the extent that such designs are actually universal. The wider the range of user groups that are accommodated by the design, the more universal (at least in terms of usability and activity performance) the design will be.

In contrast to function-oriented accessibility guidelines, assessment of universal design based on the Principles of Universal Design is multidimensional, incorporating both ICF constructs of activity and participation. Activity is manifest in six dimensions of usability (i.e., flexibility, simple and intuitive, perceptibility, ease, limiting error, and sufficient space); participation is measured by social and contextual integration. Nonetheless, each principle is subject to interpretation by both the individuals who implement the designs as well as those that assess them, making objective measurement difficult. As a result, universal design may be solely in the eye of the beholder. You should keep the limitations of each approach in mind as we examine specific applications of each.

It is important to remember that the hallmark of universal design is its generalizability across user groups. Designs intended for specific users (e.g., accessible design) are not likely to be universal. Nonetheless, while all accessible design is not universal, all universal design is accessible.

References

Adaptive Environments Center and Barrier Free Environments. (1995). *ADA checklist for readily achievable barrier removal.* Boston, MA: Adaptive Environments Center.

Barrier Free Environments. (1990). *UFAS accessibility checklist.* Washington DC: US Access Board.

Brandt, E. N., & Pope, A. M. (1997). *Enabling America: Assessing the role of rehabilitation science and engineering.* Washington, DC: National Academies Press.

Center for Universal Design. (1997). *Principles of universal design.* Raleigh: North Carolina State University, School of Design, Author.

Center for Universal Design. (2000). *Universal design performance measures for products: Evaluating the universal design performance of products.* Raleigh: North Carolina State University, School of Design, Author.

Center for Universal Design. (2002). *Product evaluation countdown.* Raleigh: North Carolina State University, School of Design, Author.

Connell, B. R., & Sanford, J. A. (1999). Research implications of universal design. In E. Steinfeld & S. Danford (Eds.), *Measuring enabling environments* (pp. 35–37). New York: Springer-Verlag.

Connell, B. R., & Sanford, J. A. (2001). Difficulty, dependence, and housing accessibility for people aging with a disability. *Journal of Architecture and Planning Research, 18*(3), 234–242.

Connell, B. R., Sanford, J. A., Moore, R., Bostrom, J. A., & Ostroff, E. (1994). Accessibility standards for children's environments. *Proceedings of the RESNA '94 Annual Conference* (pp. 48–50). Arlington, VA: RESNA Press.

Feurstein, M., Steinfeld, E., Sanford, J. A., & Shiro, G. (1987, May 29–June 2). Hands on architecture. *Proceedings of the Eighteenth Annual Conference Environmental Design Research Association,* Ottawa, Canada.

Hammel, J., Fogg, L., Walens, D., Garcia, J., & Sanford, J. (2005, October). Examining the impact of home modifications on community living and participation with people aging with disability. *The Gerontologist, 45*(Special Issue II), 429.

Iwarsson, S. (1997). *The enabler: A method for analysing accessibility problems for housing.* Lund, Sweden: Lund University, Department of Community Health Services.

Johnson, B. (1981). *Door-use study.* Ottawa, Canada: National Research Council, Division of Building Research.

Johnson, M. (2006). Universal design: Integrating innovative products and spatial design. *Architectural Record.* Retrieved September 5, 2008, from: http://continuingeducation.construction.com/article.php?L=39&C=191&P=1

Keates, S., & Clarkson, J. (2004). *Countering design exclusion: An introduction to inclusive design.* New York: Springer.

Mace, R., Hardie, G., & Place, J. (1991). *Accessible environments: Toward universal design.* In E. T. White, (Ed.), *Innovation by design* (pp. 155–175). New York: Van Nostrand Reinhold-Publishers.

Nielsen, J. (1993). *Usability engineering.* Boston, MA: AP Professional.

Sanford, J. A. (1985, March). Designing for orientation and safety. *Proceedings of the First Annual Conference on Building Use and Safety Technology,* National Institute of Building Sciences.

Sanford, J. A. (2002). Time to get rid of those old gray grab bars and get yourself a shiny new pair. *Alzheimer's Care Quarterly, 3*(1), 26–31.

Sanford, J. A. (2004, June.). *Development and testing of a universal design assessment protocol.* Presentation at edra 35, the Thirty-fifth Annual Conference of the Environmental Design Research Association.

Sanford, J. A., & Butterfield, T. (2005). Using remote assessment to provide home modification services to underserved elders. *The Gerontologist, 45*(3), 389–398.

Sanford, J. A., Echt, K., & Malassigné, P. (1999). An E for ADAAG: The case for accessibility guidelines for the elderly based on three studies of toilet transfer. *Journal of Physical and Occupational Therapy in Geriatrics, 16*(3/4), 39–58.

Sanford, J., & Hammel, J. (2006, October). Impact of accessibility modifications to the home environment on community living and activity. *The Gerontologist, 46*(Special Issue I), 129–130.

Sanford, J. A., & Megrew, M. B. (1995, Fall). An evaluation of grab bars to meet the needs of elderly people. *Assistive Technology, 7*(1), 36–47.

Sanford, J. A., Pynoos, J., Gregory, A., & Browne, A. (2002). Development of a comprehensive assessment to enhance delivery of home modifications. *Journal of PT and OT in Geriatrics, 20*(2), 43–56.

Sanford, J. A., Story, M. F., & Jones, M. L. (1997, Winter). An analysis of the effects of ramp slope on people with mobility impairments. *Assistive Technology, 9*(1), 22–33.

Steinfeld, E., & Danford, G. S. (2007, June 6). *Universal design and the ICF.* Presentation at 12th Annual North American Collaborating Center Conference on ICF, Vancouver, Canada.

Steinfeld, E., Richmond, G., & Sanford, J. A. (1986, April 9–13). Detectable tactile surface treatments. *Proceedings of the Seventeenth Annual Environmental Design Research Association Conference, Atlanta, GA.*

Steinfeld, E., Schroeder, S., Duncan, J., Faste, R., Chollet, D., Bishop, M., et al. (1979). *Access to the built environment: A review of literature.* Washington, DC: U.S. Government Printing Office.

Story, M. F. (1998). Assessing usability: The principles of universal design. *Assistive technology, 10*(1), 4–12.

Story, M., Mueller, J. L., & Montoya-Weiss, M. (2001). Completion of universal design performance measures. *Proceedings of 2001 Conference of the Rehabilitation Engineering Society of North America* (pp. 109–111). Washington, DC: RESNA Press.

Templer, J. (1977). *Priority Accessible Network: A manual for making the city accessible to the elderly and handicapped pedestrian.* Manual prepared for the U.S. Dept. of Transportation, Federal Highway Administration.

Templer, J. (1979). *Provisions for elderly and handicapped pedestrians.* Final report prepared for the U.S. Dept. of Transportation, Federal Highway Administration.

Uniform Federal Accessibility Standards. *Federal Register,* August 7, 1984 (49 FR 31528).

U.S. Congress. (1988, *1998). Technology Assistance Act (P.L. 105–394).*

U.S. Congress. (1990). Americans with Disabilities Act (P.L. 101–336).

U.S. Department of Transportation. (2009). *Disability rights legislation and accessibility guidelines and standards in the United States.* Retrieved May 5, 2009, from http://www.fhwa.dot.gov/environment/sidewalks/chap1.htm

World Health Organization. (2001). *International classification of functioning, disability and health.* Geneva: Author.

Woods, W. (1980). *Disability and building codes: A quantitative study.* Tucson: Southwest Arthritis Center, University of Arizona.

Robert
Ruchinskas

13 Assessment of Capacity

Overview

This chapter explores issues related to the assessment of decision-making capacity (DMC), or deciding "who gets to decide." We first review the basic ethical principals and assessment methods related to decisional capacity and relate these to the International Classification of Functioning, Disability, and Health (ICF; World Health Organization, 2001). The second half of the chapter focuses on cultural and situational differences in capacity assessment, along with the challenges of a multidisciplinary approach to DMC.

Learning Objectives

By the end of the chapter, the reader should be able to:

1. Differentiate between DMC and competency;
2. Outline the history of capacity models and examine how they have changed over time;
3. Identify and examine the core components of DMC;
4. Discuss various capacity assessment instruments and their limitations;
5. Determine the extent that medical, personal, and situational variables affect capacity; and
6. Demonstrate an understanding of how to ethically and scientifically balance the competing interests in capacity evaluations.

Introduction

Rehabilitation professionals deal with a wide variety of individuals facing a diverse set of challenges. Often, such challenges involve conditions that may affect the structure or integrity of the brain and therefore cause changes in thinking, memory, reasoning, and other cognitive skills. In addition, changes to the brain and the body can increase the likelihood of emotional reactions such as depression. An individual who has a new or chronic illness that needs rehabilitation experiences significant changes in their life and must adapt to their circumstances. This means that the rehabilitation professional will have to assist individuals as they make significant, and often life-changing, decisions. However, because some individuals in the rehabilitation setting may have difficulties with thinking and reasoning or may be suffering from depression or other mental health disorders, questions often arise regarding whether the individual is making the "best" decision for themselves or if their ability to make the "best" decision is compromised. Ultimately, this is a question that may need to be answered not by the person, but by the rehabilitation professional through an assessment process, which will be further examined in this chapter.

Importance of Capacity Assessment to Rehabilitation and Health

A person makes literally hundreds of decisions each day. These decisions usually are automatic and not questioned. However, their ability to make decisions may be doubted by others if they experienced a change in their functioning (e.g., suffered a stroke) or had a chronic disease that affected their decision making (e.g., dementia or schizophrenia). The judgment by others as to whether an individual can make rational and informed choices that are health sustaining and consistent with his or her long-held values may seem relatively simple. In reality, this process is extremely difficult yet one that embodies the ideals of the ICF. The ICF model provides tools that enable professionals to determine the fit between a person's abilities and environmental needs. Challenges exist when attempting to determine the goodness of such a fit because no simple and reliable method exists for determining DMC. It is for this and other reasons to be reviewed in this chapter that evaluations of DMC should be considered the last resort and should be made only when all viable remediation and accommodation strategies have failed. This cautiousness must occur in response to important legal, ethical, and practical considerations when deciding to limit a person's decision making. As we shall see, the process of assessing capacity involves evaluating the person's values, environment, and capabilities, as well as, to some degree, societal wishes.

History of Research and Practice in the Assessment of Capacity

Our understanding of capacity has been enhanced through recent research. During the last few decades, the pendulum has swung from the opinion that the "doctor knows best" to the current environment that emphasizes patient rights and patient–physician collaboration. The passage of the 1990 Patient Self-Determination Act underscored the federal government's commitment to ensure a patient's right to participate in and direct his or her own health care decisions, to accept or refuse medical or surgical treatment, and to prepare an advance directive (i.e., a treatment guide if one becomes incapacitated). An emphasis on these rights led to increased scrutiny of the process of decision making, as occasionally the treatment team and/or society disagreed with an individual's

Discussion Box 13.1

THE VAGUENESS OF DECISION-MAKING CAPACITY

The following list identifies a few areas where decision-making capacity may need to be addressed:

- Consent for research
- Consent for medical or psychological treatment
- Medical decision making
- Handling finances
- Estate planning
- Living alone
- Sexual relationships between individuals with possibly impaired capacity
- Driving
- Parenting

Think of a familiar clinical situation, be it something you've experienced or seen in the movies or on TV, where there has been an ethical dilemma. Try to imagine at least two sides to the issue and come up with three good reasons that a person in that situation may or may not have decision-making capacity. Upon completing this exercise, discuss the ethical dilemmas associated with your decisions.

choices. The term *DMC* and the more generic term *capacity* are interchangeable throughout this chapter. The term *competency* often is used mistakenly to mean capacity. However, in this chapter, *competency* is used to refer to decisions made by a judge—often after weighing a professional's testimony about DMC.

Autonomy

Capacity typically is conceptualized under the biomedical ethical construct of *autonomy,* a personal quality that requires at least three separate abilities. In order to act autonomously, an individual must act *intentionally* to display the will and/or desire to perform such an act; display *understanding* to know and be able to explain one's self; and be *generally free of outside influences that could affect how he or she decides*. The first criteria essentially is a yes–no dichotomy. The next two criteria rarely are dichotomous. Based on the nature of the decision, some degree of understanding is required—understanding that can range from minimal to substantial, depending on the amount of risk present with the decision—together with a minimal degree of outside influence. Autonomy does have inherent limits. For example, each state has minimum age requirements for a variety of decision-making situations (e.g., marriage, voting, medical decision making, etc.; Beauchamp & Childress, 2001).

Capacity

Being autonomous does not automatically mean that you have the abilities to make decisions. Autonomy is a necessary but not sufficient condition, as other behaviors must be present for adequate DMC. Besides the capacity to understand the information *(understanding),* an individual must also be able to apply the information to one's situation *(appreciation),* to make a judgment about the presented information in light of values that generally are long-held and consistent over time *(reasoning),* and to freely communicate one's wishes *(communication)*.

The Sliding Scale

A *sliding scale* is typically used when deciding a person's DMC. Standards governing the previously discussed four criteria are raised when the nature and extent of risk inherent in a decision increase. Two popular views guide the height of the standards to be employed when utilizing a sliding scale. The first viewpoint suggests that as risk grows the need for higher levels of DMC also increases (e.g., sharper logic and reasoning are needed when making immediate life or death decisions than when decisions involve lower levels of risk). The difficulty with this standard is that it may automatically declare a substantial proportion of the population who lack such high-level thinking, abstraction, or vocabulary skills to be incapable. In addition, such a standard tends to exclude rationally based decisions that are not considered normal (i.e., a decision that may be adequately contemplated by the patient yet seen by others as idiosyncratic or wrong).

Another viewpoint suggests the level of evidence for determining DMC rises with increased risk. Thus, as risk increases, the standard for judgment rises from minimal to significant evidence that the person has basic abilities for understanding, appreciation, reasoning, and communication (Beauchamp & Childress, 2001). This standard shifts the burden from the need for higher cognitive skills as risk increases to higher confidence in the evaluator that these basic skills are present. The use of this standard decreases the chance for restraint of autonomous behavior and increases the chance for informed yet odd or wrong decisions, ones that may lead to feelings of distress amongst the rehabilitation team.

Case Study 13.1

Four principles of medical ethics generally include the following:

- Autonomy—an individual's right to act without coercion to make a decision in one's best interests
- Beneficence—the promotion of good outcomes and the reduction of bad outcomes
- Nonmaleficence—above all, do no harm
- Justice—a fair and equal distribution of often-scarce resources among individuals as well as a society's right to ensure the safety of its citizens

Think of a situation that is common in medical practice, and try to think of the root principles at stake. For example, end-of-life care issues often revolve around obeying a person's wishes (autonomy) to the point of not doing any harm or promoting a good outcome (beneficence and nonmaleficence). However, when the rehabilitation team members believe that further treatments are futile (e.g., the further use of aggressive treatment is unlikely to produce significant recovery), the concept of justice becomes active. For example, let us assume a patient whose future treatments will be futile occupies a bed in an intensive care unit (which is scarce in many hospitals) and will likely not recover or survive. Should they be occupying this limited resource when it may lower the chance for survival of another patient who cannot be admitted to intensive care because no beds are available? In this situation, which ethic principal should prevail? Do we prioritize an individual's autonomy in that all heroic medical measures should be undertaken despite the limited chance of success? Should the medical teams' belief that such treatment will not work and may open the door to potentially harmful events (e.g., pain, infections, trouble breathing) take precedence? Does a hospital have the right to distribute beds in its intensive care unit to those who will most benefit from such care? How would you go about (1) identifying the core ethical principles at odds in this scenario? and (2) balancing these competing rights?

Simply put, capacity evaluations attempt to balance competing interests and provide the best outcomes for difficult situations.

Historically, DMC evaluations utilized a model in which a person was assessed once, and the data from the evaluation was used to answer the dichotomous question: Is DMC present or absent? Current evaluations of DMC are guided by serial assessments that should consider the individual's mental status and wishes (noting that both can change), the likelihood of risk inherent in the decision, and the degree of certainty the evaluator has in predicting risk.

Most evaluations for legal competency ask for opinions regarding the potential for the individual to regain DMC, the likelihood that treatments will restore DMC, and an estimated time frame for the person to regain DMC (Melton, Petrila, Poythress, & Slobogin, 1997). This legal framework also is helpful in clinical settings because it facilitates the move away from the historic model of using one evaluation to make dichotomous decisions toward other models that consider treatments and accommodations.

Current Assessment Methods in Capacity

An assessment specialist may use various tests and other assessment methods when conducting a capacity evaluation. The evaluator may use two methods for assessing aspects of capacity: indirect and direct. Indirect methods involve the assessment of processes presumed to be involved in capacity decisions. Many cognitive processes are assumed to be necessary in order to properly understand, apply information, reason, and communicate. Thus, brief instruments such as the Mini-Mental State Examination (Folstein, Folstein, & McHugh, 1975) often are utilized to gain a broad and general understanding of an individual's cognitive status. Scores below a certain cutoff are often misapplied to indicate a lack of cognitive abilities necessary to make most any decision. In reality, most everyone maintains some level of DMC. For example, one study reported that 36% of individuals in a long-term care facility who had significant cognitive compromise (Mini-Mental State Exam < 15) displayed the capacity to consistently designate a health care proxy or state a decision to not name one (Sansone, Schmitt, & Nichols, 1998).

Neuropsychological Tests

Given limitations inherent in the use of the Mini-Mental State Examination, lengthier and more thorough neuropsychological batteries often are used to examine cognitive capabilities. In general, the qualities assessed by many neuropsychological tests are associated with various activities of daily living (Baird, Podell, Lovell, & McGinty, 2001; Patrick, Perugini, & Leclerc, 2002). Additionally, as cognitive skills deteriorate, one's ability to exhibit needed components of DMC also tends to decline (Marson, Hawkins, McInturff, & Harrell, 1997).

Any attempt to directly relate data from neuropsychological tests to a person's actual behavior is difficult. The relationship between abilities tested with cognitive measures and a criterion of real-life skills is far from exact. For example, there is a belief that *executive functioning* (i.e., one's ability to plan, reason, monitor, and change behavior) is the key to successful functioning in one's environment. However, some evidence suggests executive functioning accounts for only 18%–20% of the variance associated with a patient's successful independent functioning (Chaytor & Schmitter-Edgecombe, 2003), meaning that there are many other factors that explain functioning. This and other research that examines the ecological validity of data from neuropsychological tests underscores the difficulty when attempting to account for the multiple variables that impact complex human behaviors.

Research Box 13.1

HOW DECREASED COGNITION AFFECTS DECISION-MAKING CAPACITY

Earnst, K., Marson, D., & Harrell, L. (2000). Cognitive models of physicians' legal standard and personal judgments of competency in patients with Alzheimer's Disease. *Journal of the American Geriatrics Society, 48,* 919–927.

Objective: To investigate how cognitive variables predict physicians' judgments of capacity to consent to medical treatments.

Method: Twenty-one patients with either mild or moderate Alzheimer's disease and 10 controls were videotaped as they completed a specific instrument to measure capacity to make medical decisions. They were also administered a battery of neuropsychological tests. Five physicians experienced in capacity evaluation watched the videotapes and rated the subjects as either having or not having capacity based on five specific legal standards that ranged from evidence of a treatment choice to fully understanding the treatment situation and choices. The use of legal standards in such decisions has been shown to improve judgmental accuracy amongst raters.

Results: As the legal standards became more stringent, more cognitive variables predicted the physician's decisions. For more lenient standards, receptive language skills (understanding) and measures of semantic knowledge (being able to name pictures) predicted capacity determinations. As standards became more stringent, measures of short-term memory and reasoning also predicted capacity determinations.

Conclusion: Semantic knowledge, short-term memory, and reasoning should be assessed when faced with capacity decisions in those with Alzheimer's disease.

Question:
The research supports the idea that people with more severe cognitive deficits are more likely to be unable to make decisions that carry significant associated risk. How does this research impact the evaluation and standards to be utilized with those with milder forms of cognitive deficits?

Additionally, research on the contributions of most cognitive skills (memory, reasoning, attention, etc.) to capacity decisions is in its infancy. In general, measures that are sensitive to cognitive decline (e.g., memory, visual-spatial functioning, language, reasoning, cognitive set shifting) predict broad functional skills such as driving or independent living (Ruchinskas & Blair, 2008). When examining more specific behaviors (e.g., one's ability to manage money or one's capacity to consent for treatment based on legal standards), data from measures of specific cognitive domains have significant predictive power (e.g., measures of language when asked to communicate choice, measures of abstraction and reasoning when asked to provide the rationale for a decision).

Thus, data from neuropsychological batteries may provide valuable yet incomplete information when evaluating a patient's DMC. Therefore, some direct assessment of capacity also is warranted (Sullivan, 2004).

Direct assessment involves the use of tests specifically designed to assess the components of DMC (understanding, reasoning, appreciation, and communication). Such instruments are similar in many aspects, yet each has unique properties. For example, most tests that are marketed as being able to evaluate capacity utilize a structured or semistructured interview that employs standardized questions or vignettes (which are often hypothetical in nature). Also, most instruments have some studies that suggest adequate reliability (usually interrater and test–retest) and validity (usually comparison of the test results with experts' clinical judgments). The majority of these instruments assess understanding. However, their definitions of understanding often differ (Dunn, Nowrangi, Palmer, Jeste, & Saks, 2006). Not all instruments assess reasoning, the appreciation of consequences, or other core components of capacity. (For a review of these instruments see Dunn et al., 2006; Vellinga, Smit, Leeuwen, Tilburg, & Jonker, 2004.)

Tests That Assess DMC

The increasing incidence of capacity evaluations has lead to an explosion of tests designed to assess capacity. Some instruments with a stronger research base are reviewed here.

Competence Assessment Tool-Treatment

The Competence Assessment Tool-Treatment was designed to assess a patient's capacity to make treatment decisions (Grisso, Appelbaum, & Hill-Fotouhi, 1997). The administration time for the Competence Assessment Tool-Treatment is approximately 15–20 minutes and aims to tap a broad spectrum of abilities as part of the DMC evaluation. While this tool is rooted in research, it is intended for use in clinical practice in both psychiatric and general medical settings. The instrument utilizes a semistructured interview process that integrates information specific to a patient's situation while assessing the four primary components of capacity (i.e., reasoning, understanding, appreciation, and expression). The information is scored using standardized procedures. The domains assessed include the patient's ability to understand information relevant to his/her clinical situation, to demonstrate adequate reasoning processes about the benefits and risks of treatment options in his/her situation, to appreciate how the treatment information and options impact his/her situation and the consequences of various treatment choices, and to express a choice among treatment options. Essentially, if a patient can paraphrase the information he/she has received regarding the disease/disorder, the treatment that has been recommended, and the risks and benefits of the treatment, then they will be considered to have a necessary level of understanding in order to make a decision. Reasoning is displayed when a patient is able to explain his/her treatment decisions. An ability to compare and contrast alternate approaches is displayed when a patient uses logical and rational cognitive processes when acknowledging treatment alternatives as well as their benefits and risks. Appreciation is displayed when a patient acknowledges the information being discussed applies to him/her and has potential treatment benefits and limitations. The ability to express a choice is displayed when a patient states a preference for a treatment option.

Patient responses are rated as inadequate or adequate. Summary ratings are obtained for each of the assessed capacities. The authors note that other contextual and clinical information must be considered in light of the ratings when making judgments regarding capacity. The test authors suggest the use of this instrument enables a clinician to document the standardized evaluation process and create a record that allows a clinician to explain to others how the capacity decision was made. Although this decision-making process has subjective elements, training is available (via manual, book, and videotape) on administration and scoring methods to achieve suitable interrater reliability.

Aid to Capacity Evaluation

As previously stated, direct measures of capacity generally display similar, although not uniform, formats. For example, the Aid to Capacity Evaluation is a brief question-and-answer–based consent to treatment assessment tool that takes approximately 10 minutes to administer and score (Tunzi, 2001). It assesses a patient's understanding of his or her medical condition and treatment options and ability to foresee consequences of accepting and/or rejecting the proposed treatment. The possibility that mood and/or other psychiatric issues are affecting the decision also is considered. While this interview offers a structured set of questions and scoring options for responses, the results of this evaluation must be utilized in the context of a broader evaluation. Thus, as with other instruments designed to measure specific decision-making capabilities, additional information besides the test is needed to fully understand a patient's DMC. This tool is available from the University of Toronto Joint Centre for Bioethics and can be obtained through their Web site at http://www.utoronto.ca/jcb/home/main.htm.

The Hopkins Capacity Assessment Test

The Hopkins Capacity Assessment Test (Janofsky, McCarthy, & Folstein, 1992) assesses a patient's ability to provide informed consent to treatment or provide *advance directives* (i.e., instructions the treatment team should follow if the individual becomes incapacitated). When taking this test, a patient simultaneously hears and reads a short essay regarding issues of durable power of attorney and informed consent. The information is available on three different reading levels (6th-, 8th-, and 13th-grade levels). After receiving the information, a patient is asked related questions, and the responses are scored. The suggested cutoff score of 4 (within a range of a low of 0 to a high of 10) displays both sensitivity (define) and specificity (define) of 100% in accurately predicting clinical capacity as determined independently by a psychiatrist. Adequate interrater reliability was established in a subsequent study by Barton, Mallik, Orr, and Janofsky (1996). Since its publication, the measure has gained acceptance in both clinical and research communities as a potential means for assessing capacity to give advance directives, although comfort in using this instrument in clinical settings will increase as more reliability and validity studies are published.

Summary

While many more tests are available, the review of three commonly used measures highlights the fact that tests aimed at determining a patient's DMC should be used as tools, not decision makers or solutions, as they all have inherent limitations.

Discussion Box 13.2

LIMITATIONS OF TESTS FOR CAPACITY

Below are some of the limitations of test designed to assess specific areas of decisional capacity:

- Difficulty developing a consensus on definitions of domains such as understanding, appreciation, reasoning, and communicating.
- Inability to account for individual differences and situational variables.
- Need to validate data using criteria other than professional judgment or the presence or absence of capacity.
- Limited in scope, for example, only addresses decision-making capacity for one type of situation.
- Responses of patients to hypothetical vignettes versus real-life decisions may different.
- Professionals may require extensive training on administration and scoring to use them.
- Need for further reliability and validity studies for most instruments.

After reading the overview of these instruments, discuss how these instruments may be useful when assessing decision-making capacity. Consider other limitations of these tests when conducting complex capacity evaluations.

How would you change these tests to design a measure of decision-making capacity for use with individuals from minority cultures?

In addition to concerns cited in the discussion box, the amount of research on issues, such as how cultural differences or variations in information processing across age groups affect these instruments, is limited (Moye, 2000). Thus, although several standardized measures are available to assist in the assessment of specific functional components involved in DMC, their use with patients receiving rehabilitation services is limited. Thus, knowledge of their strengths and limitations requires further research.

Risk Assessment and Integrating Such Into DMC Assessment Instruments

Methods to validly measure and quantify *risk* are needed in capacity evaluations yet are substantially ignored in the research literature. Recall that a sliding scale often is used to gauge the degree of a patient's *understanding, appreciation, reasoning, and communication* when determining whether a patient is *capable* to make the decision in question. Such a scale is determined by the nature of risk involved in the decision, with increased risk raising the need for more components of capacity.

The process of evaluating a patient's core components of capacity has been extensively researched. Conversely, the accuracy of an evaluator's judgment of the inherent level of risk for the decision in question, by which the "sliding scale" for necessary components of DMC is established, has been essentially ignored in the research literature. Thus, risk assessment, which is a crucial aspect of the DMC process, often relies on imperfect research or the inherently limited process called *clinical judgment.* Examples of such difficulties include trying to utilize instruments created through research on groups for decisions regarding individuals seen in clinical practice. Frequently used research designs can also limit the utility of an instrument when it aims to predict a worrisome, yet infrequent, event (e.g., automobile crashes, falling after discharge from the hospital, bankruptcy). For example, when developing a new test for use in a clinical population, validity studies often select samples in which half has a particular condition and half do not have the condition (i.e., 50% are incapacitated, and 50% have DMC). When clinically utilizing such a measure in a population in which the incidence of incapacity may be much lower (e.g., < 10%), then claims that an instruments has 100% sensitivity and specificity (or the ability to detect those with and without capacity) are overly generous, meaning that the instrument adds less predictive or diagnostic value (Macciocchi & Stringer, 2001).

Difficulties in Assessing Risk

Risk is difficult to quantify, in part, because clinicians often do not predict the occurrence of risk accurately when working with patients who may display infrequent or low base rate (e.g., the rate an incident occurs per person in a population) behaviors. One study (Ruchinskas, 2003) found predictions by physical and occupational therapists, considered to be experts in gait dysfunction, of a patient falling during the first month postdischarge from acute rehabilitation to be accurate 34% of the time when predicting falling and 82% of the time when predicting not falling. Thus, the use of clinical judgment did not improve the specialist's predictive accuracy beyond that of simply knowing that those with a prior history of falling or the presence of a neurological disorder were at increased risk for falls. In addition, the clinician was incorrect more often than correct when trying to predict an infrequent event. As is human nature, we usually make such predictions with great confidence because we rarely get feedback about our decisional accuracy, and we often utilize variables that have poor predictive power when we are trying to predict unfortunate events such as falls (Ruchinskas, Macciocchi, Howe, & Newton, 2001).

This research reinforces the fact that behavior is driven by numerous complex factors, and the ability to predict most any behavior by utilizing only one or two predictors (which is our natural tendency) is unacceptably low. The only exception may be with patients who are obviously incapacitated, and such individual's capacity for many decisions is rarely called into question due to their inherent lack of DMC abilities. For example, a person who is completely bed bound is unlikely to fall, and a person diagnosed with severe mental retardation is unlikely to have a high-income profession (Fisher, 1959). The challenge is that the majority of capacity and risk evaluations are conducted for patients who are in the "grey area," where either capacity or incapacity is not grossly obvious.

Base rate issues also affect the identification of individuals of questionable capacity. Most nonpsychiatric professionals are not proficient at detecting cognitive dysfunction or diagnosable psychiatric illness (e.g., Guilmette, Snow, Grace, & Giuliano, 1992). For example, despite having worked with patients for 6 to 10 days on average, members of a multidisciplinary team correctly identified only about 37% of those with cognitive impairment and between 0% and 14% of those with significant depressive symptoms (Ruchinskas, 2002). Professionals who cannot adequately identify those at risk for decisional incapacity also are likely to inaccurately identify individuals who need and do not need these evaluations.

Research Critical to Issues in Capacity Assessment

Research on DMC is rapidly increasing. The attainment of clarity on issues impacting DMC requires significant effort due to their nature and complexity. Each capacity decision is unique due to individual differences together with differences in environmental and situational variables. Thus, when attempting to assess capacity, applications of research findings conducted on groups to an individual, who is likely to differ in important ways from mean group characteristics, poses major obstacles. Additionally, research on DMC is limited by the lack of consensus on many basic concepts and terms that are being examined (e.g., understanding, appreciation, etc.). Furthermore, each DMC evaluation is unique based on the nature of the circumstances, person, and decision being made, which challenges the replication of most research.

Research on DMC often focuses on specific aspects of the person's cognitive processes. Issues associated with how well professionals evaluate risk have not received wide attention. Moreover, professionals lack best practice standards or guidelines on conducting risk assessment. Without such guidelines, professionals rely on clinical judgment—a process that often is unreliable (Meehl & Rosen, 1955). Despite longstanding knowledge of the limitations of clinical judgment, many tests that assess DMC skills still rely on expert clinical judgment when validating their tests.

Cultural, Legislative, and Professional Issues That Impact the Specific Counseling Aspects or Procedures

Although some readers may not anticipate their careers to include DMC evaluations, trends suggest that such work will be standard in many rehabilitation and other professional services settings. For example, institutional review boards that review research protocols have noticed changes in ethics codes regarding informed consent (e.g., the American Psychological Association, 2002) and are increasingly requesting documentation that research participants understand (i.e., comprehend) what they are volunteering for in terms of risks, benefits, and options. Thus, consistent with DMC evaluations, statements that describe the definition, assessment, and documentation of the research participant's understanding are becoming more common for research protocols.

Practitioners must take note of recent legislative changes, which are often in reaction to tragic, high-profile legal cases, regarding the prediction of negative events. During the last 20 years, both legislation and case law have established the duty of mental health professionals, in many states, to protect an individual from doing harm to him/her and to others. This protective duty is being expanded to other areas of society. For example, professionals increasingly are being asked to report individuals who they consider to be potentially unsafe drivers (Snyder & Bloom, 2004). Some states are broadening the requirements to include anyone of adequate training, not only physicians, as being able to judge a person's capacity to drive and subsequently report unsafe drivers to state agencies.

A duty to warn may cause a dilemma. First, the prediction of an infrequent event (e.g., car crashes) is inherently difficult. Additionally, technology (e.g., cognitive tests, driving simulators) has limited benefit in predicting events (Edwards, Hahn, & Fleishman, 1977). Although states may offer immunity to those who report potentially unsafe drivers, few states shield practitioners from lawsuits if an unreported driver causes an accident. Thus, professionals may face the following dilemma: Do they report a potentially unsafe driver based on indirect evidence and therefore possibly deprive the person of a well-valued privilege, or do they not report and risk a potential lawsuit?

Case Study 13.2

Many states require professionals to report potentially unsafe drivers. However, the professionals may not be offered protection from suits if they do not report individuals who subsequently get into a car accident. Imagine that you are a practitioner in a rural area where public transportation does not exist. Your patient had a stroke about 6 months ago, the effects of which have mildly slowed his reflexes and left him with a small blind spot in his vision. Gross deficits in cognition are not apparent. He has been driving for the past 3 months and has not had an accident. The patient reports that he lives alone and has no friends or family. He would be unable to attend his doctors' appointments and his rehabilitation therapies if he couldn't drive. He also describes needing to drive daily in order to get food, prescriptions, and other necessities of life. Your options are to (1) do nothing and hope for the best; (2) report him to a department of motor vehicles, which will result in his loosing his license until he can be evaluated in 6 to 8 weeks; or (3) encourage him to attend a driving school which is 100 miles away and costs money that he doesn't have. Which option would you choose? What other options exist?

Capacity is imbued with cultural and social issues, including differences in values, morals, and norms. Individualism, individual rights, and individual autonomy are strongly held values in the United States. Nevertheless, society does impose limitations on an individual's actions. These limits vary from country to country. For example, in contrast to large expenditures of money to maintain life of the elderly in this country, other countries view the end of life differently and thus may ration health care toward the end of life. In addition, the multicultural fabric of the United States is becoming more obvious. Many immigrants come from counties that emphasize social cohesion as opposed to individualism. The interaction—some may say clash—between the concepts of autonomy and capacity and the values of social cohesion and individualism has not been explored through research yet is seen daily in clinical practice.

Multidisciplinary or Interdisciplinary Approaches

DMC evaluations encompass many different aspects of a person's functioning. Thus, information provided by various professions that describes a patient's performance in reference to multiple relevant life domains can be valuable. Capacity can change over time, be displayed differently across settings, and be viewed differently by individual professionals. A team-based assessment helps address some of these conditions by offering observational and evaluative information of behaviors displayed in many settings and at different intervals. This method helps to avoid the historic practice of conducting one evaluation from which various life-transforming decisions may be made (Moye, Karel, Gurrera, & Azar, 2006).

Rehabilitation team evaluations may allow each professional specialty to describe an individual's capabilities. This information then is synthesized during team meetings. While team evaluations have intuitive appeal, standardized team evaluation methods to assess DMC do not exist.

Team Approaches to DMC

Still, it is not difficult to imagine the issues that would be faced if such a model were being created. For example, standardized methods for screening and later identifying those at risk for impaired decisional capacity must be established. This screening should rely on objective measures of the concepts being evaluated (i.e., cognitive compromise, depression, balance) because professional judgments regarding a patient's mental status, mood, and fall risk are unreliable (Ruchinskas, 2002, 2003). After identifying impairments in areas that could potentially limit capacity, the team should clearly define what specific decisions may be problematic for the individual. Oftentimes such questions are phrased too generally (e.g., "Can she go home safely?") instead of addressing specific potential skill deficits (e.g., "What is the likelihood that he will fall?" or "What is the likelihood that he will mismanage his medications?") The team also should avoid recommending an overly restrictive regimen for the patient once potential skill deficits are found and instead acknowledge that capacity should be assumed to be present until proven otherwise.

After recognizing potential incapacities, then a standardized evaluation can be measured objectively by at least one team member (e.g., assess balance, cognition, money management, and awareness of deficits). These functional evaluations are conducted with the recognition that in some sense they are artificial. For example, making a meal in the kitchen of an occupational therapist and at one's home differ significantly. Differences between performing an activity in clinical and more common settings must be recognized and appreciated.

The need for a standard protocol that guides the evaluation of risk also is needed. For example, a professional's ability to predict worrisome events (e.g., falls, dangerousness to others, unsafe driving, etc.) based on information acquired in a clinic setting tends to be unreliable (Ruchinskas, 2003) because such events have many potential causes, both patient-centered (e.g., poor balance, decreased vision, trouble solving problems, weakness, etc., in the case of falls) and environmental (e.g., presence of throw rugs, cords, pets, unsteady flooring). Once the level of risk is established, the most prudent course is to not immediately start a DMC evaluation but instead to determine if the conditions that contribute to risk may be remedied (improve balance, raise the level of awareness into deficits, etc.) or modified (have team members secure loose rugs, remove potential obstacles, recommend installation of grab bars in the patient's home, etc.).

Basically, the team needs to improve a person's abilities in order to meet the demands of their environment, decrease the demands of the environment in order to meet a person's current abilities, or do both. In essence, this approach is consistent with the spirit of the ICF guidelines, in that a formal evaluation of a person's decisional abilities is viewed as a last resort. Instead, beginning on the first day of admission, the evaluation process should focus on an assessment of the underlying components of decision making and quantifying risk, with the goal to improve outcomes through modifying or accommodating potential barriers to a person's autonomy.

Each practice setting varies tremendously and creates differences that affect the functioning of any multidisciplinary team engaged in capacity evaluation.

For example, the protocols for team functions as well as the range and immediacy of questions of capacity experienced when working in an emergency room and in a long-term care facility differ significantly. Although the issues encountered in the various settings in which they work are not more or less important, differences in settings must be considered when designing interdisciplinary evaluation strategies.

Major Issues That Need Attention in Capacity Assessment

The assessment of DMC is complex and requires more than obtaining a number from a neuropsychological test or an instrument designed to assess capacity. Additional research leading to the development of reliable and valid tools and other methods that enable clinicians to make informed determinations of DMC is needed. Research needs to focus on ways to improve the assessment of individual decisional skills, clinician's reliability in making DMC determinations, risk assessment, applications of legal and ethical standards, and methods that help apply professional knowledge and skills across cultures.

These goals can be accomplished by continuing research that helps identify the exact cognitive and affective components to each hypothesized capacity construct. This effort first requires more uniform definitions of constructs such as *understanding, appreciation, reasoning,* and *expression.* A better understanding of cognitive qualities that provide a foundation for DMC would provide important insight and guidance during the capacity evaluation process. Cultural qualities of the patient, professionals, and the assessment process that impact decision making are not well understood. In addition to culture, generational influences need further study because they have an important impact on decision making. Given the importance of DMC on important life outcomes, we need to establish some form of *continuous quality improvement* based on research and other forms of scholarship that helps us to understand individual decision making; we need to develop more accurate methods to quantify capacity and risk; and we need to improve professional judgments during DMC evaluations.

Summary

The assessment of DMC frequently occurs in rehabilitation settings. Although rehabilitation specialists traditionally have displayed paternalistic forms of care toward patients, recent legal and social changes currently emphasize a need to respect an individual's desires when they are arrived at autonomously. DMC is evaluated to determine if a patient's desires are arrived at autonomously and guided by adequate consideration.

DMC evaluations can take many forms. Clinical judgment typically is used despite its flaws. Various tests assess a patient's neuropsychological qualities, including cognitive qualities thought to underlie the four components of capacity: understanding, appreciation, reasoning, and communication. Practices that rely solely on data from these instruments should be avoided, given difficulties using these tests to predict a patient's behaviors displayed at home, work/school, and in the community. In contrast to these indirect measures of DMC, other direct measures are available. Such tests typically use structured or semi-structured interviews to present hypothetical vignettes or actual material about a person's current situation in order to evaluate how well they comprehend and reason in these circumstances. Again, these data do not provide complete evidence of DMC and need to be integrated with other collateral information and, ultimately, clinical judgment.

Additional research is needed to inform and improve DMC practices. While considerable research focuses on individual decision making, little has been done on methods to improve risks associated with DMC. Thus, professional decisions as to a patient's DMC must be somewhat tentative, knowing that standards that differentiate those who are and are not likely to display risky behaviors are not well established—and thus rely heavily on clinical judgment. Furthermore, the impact of individual differences in culture, social class, and race/ethnicity on DMC and risk largely is unknown.

Thus, when professionals need to consider a patient's DMC and associated risk, the most prudent course is to: (1) initially assume that capacity is present, (2) clarify exactly what specific areas of capacity may be an issue (as rarely is a person incapable of making all decisions), and (3) systematically assess the domains that underlie capacity. After completing the assessments, the most prudent step would be to implement a practical program aimed at remedying areas that could limit decisional capacity or modifying the environment to decrease risk. Pragmatically, it is more efficacious to improve DMC or reduce risk, when possible, than to engage in an ethically and scientifically challenging process of determining DMC. If ultimately faced with a DMC evaluation, caution must be utilized so as to not unduly restrain autonomy based on potentially flawed evaluations of an individual's capacity and/or the risk inherent in the situation.

References

American Psychological Association. (2002). Ethics principles of psychologists and code of conduct. *American Psychologist, 57,* 1060–1073.

Baird, A., Podell, K., Lovell, M. R., & McGinty, S. B. (2001). Complex real world functioning and neuropsychological test performance in older adults. *The Clinical Neuropsychologist, 15,* 369–379.

Barton, C., Mallik, H., Orr, W., & Janofsky, J. (1996). Clinicians' judgment of capacity of nursing home patients to give informed consent, *Psychiatric Services, 47,* 956–960.

Beauchamp, T., & Childress, J. (2001). *Principles of biomedical ethics* (5th ed.). New York: Oxford University Press.

Chaytor, N., & Schmitter-Edgecombe, M. (2003). The ecological validity of neuropsychological tests: A review of the literature on everyday cognitive skills. *Neuropsychology Review, 13,* 181–197.

Dunn, L., Nowrangi, M., Palmer, B., Jeste, D., & Saks, E. (2006). Assessing decisional capacity for clinical research or treatment: A review of instruments. *American Journal of Psychiatry, 163,* 1323–1334.

Earnst, K. S., Marson, D. C., & Harrell, L. E. (2000). Cognitive models of physician's legal standard and personal judgments of competency in patients with Alzheimer's disease. *Journal of the American Geriatric Society, 48,* 919–927.

Edwards, D., Hahn, C., & Fleishman, E. (1977). Evaluation of laboratory methods for the study of driver behavior: Relations between simulator and street performance. *Journal of Applied Psychology, 62,* 559–566.

Fisher, J. (1959). The twisted pear and the prediction of behavior. *Journal of Consulting Psychology, 23,* 400–405.

Folstein, M. F., Folstein, S. E., & McHugh, P. R. (1975). Mini-mental state: A practical method for grading the cognitive state of patients for the clinician. *Journal of Psychiatric Research, 12,* 189–198.

Grisso, T., Appelbaum, P. S., & Hill-Fotouhi, C. H. (1997). The MacCAT-T: A clinical tool to assess patients' capacities to make treatment decisions. *Psychiatric Services, 48,* 1415–1419.

Guilmette, J., Snow, M., Grace, J., & Giuliano A. (1992). Emotional dysfunction in a geriatric population: staff observations and patients' reports. *Archives of Physical Medicine and Rehabilitation, 73,* 587–593.

Janofsky, J. S., McCarthy, R. J., & Folstein, M. F. (1992). The Hopkins Competence Assessment Test. *Hospital and Community Psychiatry, 43,* 132–136.

Macciocchi, S., & Stringer, A. (2001). Assessing risk and harm: The convergence of ethical and empirical considerations. *Archives of Physical Medicine and Rehabilitation, 82*(Suppl. 2), S15–S19.

Marson, D. C., Hawkins, L., McInturff, B., & Harrell, L. E. (1997). Cognitive models that predict physician's judgments of capacity to consent in mild Alzheimer's disease. *Journal of the American Geriatrics Society, 45,* 458–464.

Meehl, P., & Rosen, A. (1955). Antecedent probability and the efficiency of psychometric signs, patterns, or cutting scores. *Psychological Bulletin, 52,* 194–216.

Melton, G., Petrila, J., Poythress, N., & Slobogin, C. (1997). *Psychological evaluations for the courts: A handbook for mental health professionals and lawyers* (2nd ed.). New York: Guilford Press.

Moye, J. (2000). Mr. Franks refuses surgery: Cognition and values in competency determination in complex cases. *Journal of Aging Studies, 14,* 385–401.

Moye, J., Karel, M. J., Gurrera, R. J. & Azar, A. R. (2006). Neuropsychological predictors of decision-making capacity over 9 months in mild-to-moderate dementia. *Journal of General Internal Medicine, 21,* 78–83.

Patrick, L., Perugini, M., & Leclerc, C. (2002). Neuropsychological assessment and competency for independent living among geriatric patients. *Topics in Geriatric Rehabilitation, 17,* 65–77.

Ruchinskas, R. (2002). Rehabilitation therapists' recognition of cognitive and mood disorders in geriatric patients. *Archives of Physical Medicine and Rehabilitation, 83,* 609–612.

Ruchinskas, R. (2003). Clinical prediction of falls in the elderly. *American Journal of Physical Medicine and Rehabilitation, 82,* 273–278.

Ruchinskas, R., & Blair, K. (2008). Assessment of capacity and competency in the rehabilitation setting. In S. Gontkovsky & C. Golden (Eds.), *Neuropsychology within the inpatient rehabilitation environment* (pp. 221–236). New York: Nova Science Publishers.

Ruchinskas, R., Macciocchi, S., Howe, G., & Newton, R. (2001) Clinical decision-making in the prediction of falls. *Rehabilitation Psychology, 46,* 262–270.

Sansone, P., Schmitt, L., & Nichols, J. (1998). Determining the capacity of demented nursing home residents to name a health care proxy. *Clinical Gerontologist, 19,* 35–50.

Snyder, K., & Bloom, J. (2004). Physician reporting of impaired drivers: A new trend in state law? *Journal of the American Academy of Psychiatry and the Law, 32,* 76–79.

Sullivan, K. (2004). Neuropsychological assessment of mental capacity. *Neuropsychology Review, 14,* 131–142.

Tunzi, M. (2001). Can the patient decide? Evaluating patient capacity in practice. *American Family Physician, 64,* 299–306.

Vellinga, A., Smit, J. H., Leeuwen, E., Tilburg, W., & Jonker, C. (2004). Instruments to assess decision-making capacity: An overview. *International Psychogeriatrics, 16,* 397–419.

World Health Organization. (2001). *ICF: International Classification of Functioning, Disability and Health.* Geneva: Author.

Marisa Macy
Frank R. Rusch

Life Care Planning Evaluation

14

Overview

The following chapter explores issues related to the evaluation of life care plans (LCPs). First, we define life care planning, as well as content related to life care plans. Second, we outline the brief history of life care planning. Third, a framework for the evaluation of life care plans is presented. The final sections of the chapter relate to research and an interdisciplinary perspective of life care plans.

Learning Objectives

By the end of the chapter, the reader should be able to:

1. Define life care planning and its importance to rehabilitation and health;
2. Establish organizing principles of a life care plan;

3. Identify a systems model to evaluate life care plans;
4. Utilize a systems approach to outcome-based evaluation; and
5. Compare and contrast critical issues with an interdisciplinary perspective.

Introduction

Michael, a student at a university, was walking across a street in his college town with his two friends when a car hit him. He was severely injured. Six months later, the local newspaper reported that Michael was not making sufficient progress for his insurance company to continue paying up to $2,000 daily for rehabilitation. A life care plan is a vital tool for Michael as we consider his rehabilitation and health throughout this chapter. The *evaluation* of a life care plan is of paramount importance. This chapter describes life care planning, discusses the brief history of life care planning, offers a model for evaluating life care plans, applies the evaluation model to Michael's life care plan, reviews research related to life care plans, and then reviews interdisciplinary approaches to life care planning.

Importance of Life Care Planning to Rehabilitation and Health

Life care planning is an activity that can facilitate aspects of daily living for a person with a catastrophic injury, chronic health condition, or disability. A life care plan (LCP) is an individualized, working document that describes information for the provision of appropriate services and support, and it is updated regularly to capture any changes. It should be easy to use, culturally appropriate (Munoz & Hemmila, 2004), and legally sound (Brown & Smith, 2004; Deutsch, 2004; Vierling, 2004).

LCP leadership teams and organizations (e.g., American Academy of Nurse Life Care Planners) interested in life care planning came to an official agreement in 1998 on a shared definition that states, "A *Life Care Plan* is a dynamic document based upon published standards of practice, comprehensive assessment, data analysis and research, which provides an organized concise plan for current and future needs with associated costs, for individuals who have experienced catastrophic injury or have chronic health care needs" (Weed, 2004, p. 3).

Life care plans can address the needs of people of all ages, including infants and toddlers (Accardo & Accardo, 2004; Riddick-Grisham, 2004), children, adults, and the elderly (McCollom, 2000b, 2004). They are created for a variety of cases, such as spinal cord injury in Michael's case. Prior to writing a LCP, a multidisciplinary team will have conducted a comprehensive assessment. The information gathered during the assessment process will be used to develop the LCP as shown in Figure 14.1a.

Assembling appropriate information is the beginning of the LCP process. Referral, case intake, data gathering, research, interviewing, and needs assessment are activities that will take place to develop a LCP. Eliff (1995) notes that preparing a LCP takes approximately 20 to 40 hours. Sources of information

14.1a

A linked system framework for LCP.

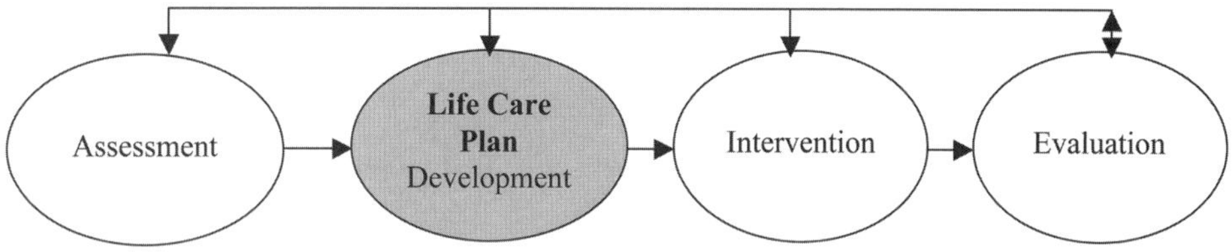

are medical records and documentation, the individual and his/her family and friends, and others who are knowledgeable about the person and his/her needs.

A life care plan contains the following features: (a) area of need; (b) types of care, services, and equipment; (c) goals and projected outcomes with timelines; and (d) associated costs. The LCP will describe the individual's current and long-term needs. A statement about the individual's present levels of functioning will provide information about strengths and areas of need. Information about the injury, condition, or disability will also be useful. Projected evaluations, by providers, will be accounted for on the LCP. Potential future needs will be forecasted.

The types of care, services, and equipment will vary by individuals. The LCP describes the care, services, and equipment followed by an explanation of the purpose of each (Barker, 1999). For example, Michael will need a physiatrist (care/service) to monitor his physical condition and rehabilitation (purpose). The age of the individual and the year will be recorded, as well as when the care, service, or equipment is to begin and end. When appropriate, the LCP will have information about vendors and equipment. Care, services, and equipment that must be considered are:

- Aids for independent function (e.g., assistive technology, adaptive clothing)
- Architectural renovations (e.g., tub and toilet safety grab bars in the bathroom)
- Attendant or supervisory care
- Case management
- Counseling
- Diagnostic testing
- Educational services/plans
- Facility care/services
- Home care/services
- Medical equipment and/or replacements
- Medical care and/or interventions (both routine and nonroutine)
- Medication
- Nursing
- Options for alternative situations (e.g., returning to work)
- Orthotic or prosthetic devices

- Possible complications
- Supplies (e.g., catheter)
- Surgical intervention/treatment
- Therapeutic modalities (e.g., alternative medical therapies like acupuncture, occupational, physical, recreational, rehabilitation, and speech therapies)
- Transportation (e.g., adaptive van)
- Vocational services/plans
- Wheelchair needs (Mayo, 1994; McCollom & Crane, 2001; Reid, Deutsch, Kitchen, & Aznavoorian, 1999; Weed, 1995, 2004)

The LCP should help the individual address meaningful outcomes (Kuntz, 2005). In order to achieve projected outcomes, goals will be identified with target dates and timelines. Goals are observable and measurable statements that the individual can realistically achieve in a certain amount of time. Measurability refers to behaviors that can be directly counted (e.g., duration, frequency, distance measures, etc.). Goals can provide a basis for determining: (a) whether anticipated outcomes are being met and (b) whether care, services, and equipment are appropriate.

A three-step process can be used to develop goals. The first step is to decide the purpose of the goal. Goals can be considered to refine, reinforce, or develop a skill or behavior. *Refinement* involves a skill or behavior that is emerging but has *not yet* been mastered. *Reinforcement* includes a skill or behavior that *has* been mastered but not beyond an initial trial; more proof is needed to show robust evidence. *Growth/development* is a behavior that may be missing or underdeveloped and needs to be added to an individual's repertoire.

The second step is to consider the antecedent, behavior, and criteria for each goal. The *antecedent* describes the context for the goal. *Behavior* is the observable skill or performance. *Criteria* are needed to measure the goal. For example, "During meals (antecedent), Michael will drink from a cup with a lid with some spilling (behavior), observed two times a day, each day, for 2 weeks (criteria)." Prioritize goals in order of importance. Once the goals are written, developing a measurement system will follow.

The third step involves choosing a method for collecting data related to the goal. Decide how often to measure progress toward reaching the goal. Identify what the goal will look like once it is accomplished. It will be necessary to decide what materials, resources, information, people, time, and financial support are needed to achieve the goal. These three steps can be taken for developing goals during the process of writing and implementing a LCP.

Associated costs are identified for each item described in the LCP. For example, Michael will need a physiatrist (care/service) to monitor his physical condition and rehabilitation (purpose) twice a month (frequency) at $100 each session (cost) from 2007 to life (years) for $2400 (annual cost) by Dr. Galliano (provider). The total annual costs will be reported. A LCP may need to predict the life expectancy of the individual in order to estimate costs (Katz, 2003; Katz, Haig, Clark, & DiPaola, 1992; Kessler, 2004; Plioplys, 2004). Funding sources will also need to be researched for the LCP (Ehlert & Rubin, 2004). An overall financial plan may be needed to help the individual, family, and/or insurers budget associated costs and anticipate future needs.

History of Life Care Planning

The history of life care planning can be traced to the 1980s (Weed, 2004). LCPs were originally used by professionals in the legal field (e.g., attorneys) to help determine damages involving personal injury and product liability lawsuits (Toran, 1999; Weed, 2004). Next, the allied health fields adopted life care plans and started to develop a professional literature base, professional organizations, certification guidelines, and LCP training programs (Riddick-Grisham, 2004; Weed, 2004).

Since 1996, leaders in the field of rehabilitation have established practice and certification guidelines for life care planners (May & Lubinskas, 2004; McCollom, 2000; Toran, 1999). The Commission on Health Care Certification (CHCC) provides credentials in life care planning service delivery and organizes practice principles around: (1) moral and legal standards, (2) disability examiners and life care planners–patient relationship, (3) patient advocacy, (4) professional relationships, (5) public statements/fees, (6) confidentiality, (7) assessment, (8) research activities, (9) competence, and (10) credentials, which include Certified Disabilities Examiners (CDE), Certified Post Offer Evaluators (CPOE), and Certified Life Care Planners (CLCP; CHCC, 2007; Weed, 2004). Today, there are several training programs across the United States and Canada to become a life care planner. The need for life care planners is growing. About 300 professional certified life care planners are working in the field, while it is projected that 1,500 are needed to meet demand (Rice, Hicks, & Wiehe, 2000).

One aspect of life care planning that remains critical to recommended practice is evaluation. Once a comprehensive assessment has been used to create the LCP, intervention will take place to address meaningful LCP goals. Evaluation involves collecting ongoing data that is necessary to monitor progress and program efficacy. In a linked system, the evaluation component is designed to connect to all of the other components (i.e., diagnostic assessment, LCP goal development, intervention, and an initial evaluation or re-evaluation). Figure 14.1b highlights the role of evaluation in the linked system framework.

Because life care planning focuses on individuals, interdisciplinary providers, and programs that organize services and providers, the evaluation model we propose recognizes at least three levels of *outcome-based evaluation:* (a) participant, (b) family/provider, and (c) program. Figure 14.2 displays each of these three levels as well as recognition that the larger "community" is important to the quality of those services provided at each of these three levels.

14.1b

A linked system framework for LCP.

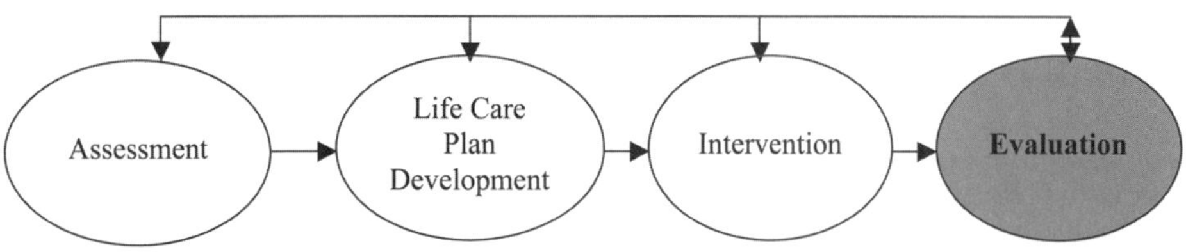

14.2

Systems approach to outcome-based evaluation.

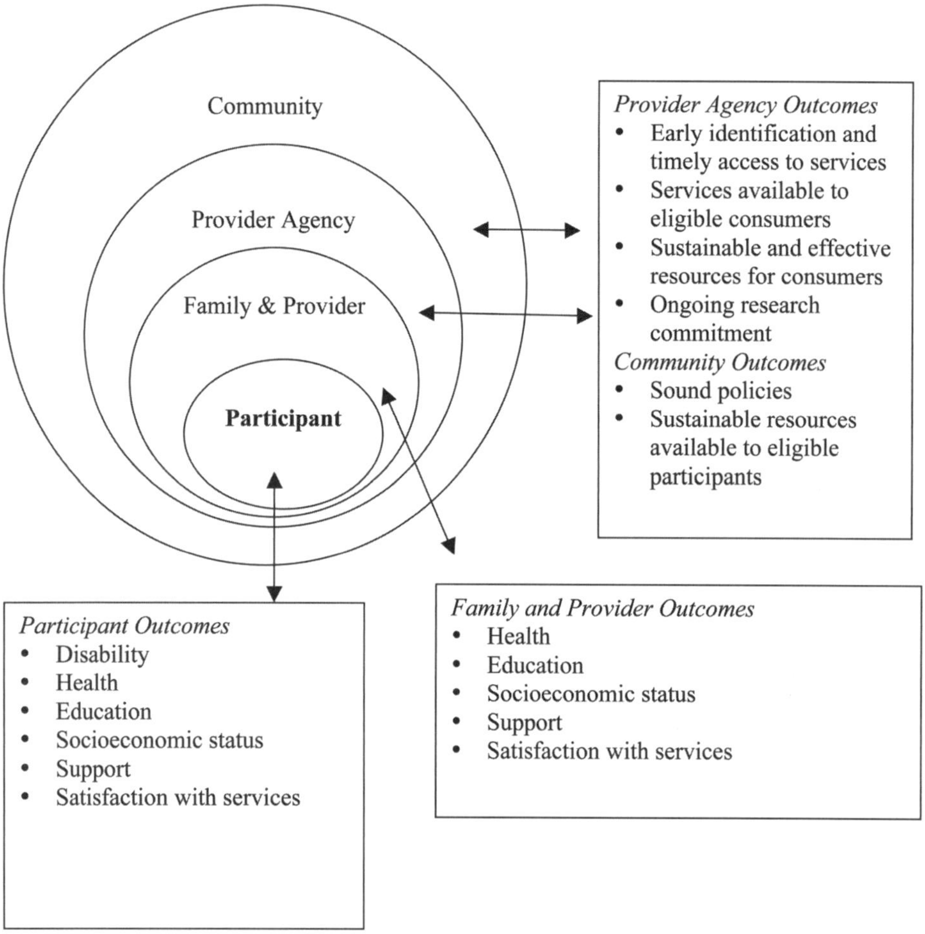

Outcome-based evaluation addresses desired and expected participant outcomes and family/provider and program outcomes as promised. Essentially, outcome-based evaluation asks questions that focus upon the extent to which programs meet stated goals and objectives and whether the life care program made a difference in a participant's life.

Systems Approach to Outcome-Based Evaluation

The systems approach recognizes that there are multiple, interrelated service levels that define impact and effectiveness. Typically, *impact* is assigned to outcomes evaluation at the participant level and *effectiveness* at the family/provider and the program levels. Families/providers and programs provide services, and the questions that are asked are directed toward their effectiveness; participants receive services, and most often concern is focused on the impact of these services in improving their quality of life. Table 14.1 displays five steps that broadly define the structure of outcome-based evaluations, including: (step 1) identifying the focus of the evaluation (participant, family/provider, program), (step 2) identifying stakeholders who are central to providing life care planning, (step 3) identifying questions, (step 4) identifying the evaluation procedures, and (step 5) evaluating the outcomes as promised and/or expected. The following three sections provide overviews for evaluating impact and effectiveness at each of three levels (i.e., participant, family/provider, and program).

Participant Outcome-Based Evaluation (Impact Evaluation)

Participant outcomes are primarily directed toward physical and material well-being, emotional well-being, self-determination, and interpersonal relations. Consequently, the purpose of evaluation at this level is fairly conscribed.

14.1 Outcome-Based Evaluation Model

Steps	Questions to Ask
1	Identify the Purpose of the Evaluation • Is the focus of the evaluation participant outcomes? • Is the focus of the evaluation family or provider impact? • Is the focus of the evaluation program evaluation?
2	Identify Stakeholders • Who are the stakeholders (participants, family/providers, or program)?
3	Identify Questions for the Outcome-Based Evaluation • What questions do the stakeholders (including the participant) want answered?
4	Develop an Outcome-Based Evaluation Design • What information is needed to answer the questions? • What are appropriate measures? • How will information be collected? • What procedures need to be in place to ensure data quality? • How frequently will data need to be collected? • How will the data be analyzed?
5	Evaluate Outcomes • Are the outcomes those that were expected? • Do the goals need to be revised? • Do the methods need to be revised? • How will results of the evaluation be communicated with stakeholders? • What are/were constraints, if any, of the evaluation (e.g., time, financial resources, personal biases, available methodologies)?

Discussion Box 14.1

> Why is it important to consider multiple participants when evaluating life care plans (LCPs)? Typically, LCPs involve numerous participants and multiple perspectives. Consequently, we propose utilizing the systems approach to evaluation in an effort to capture these multiple perspectives. The value of this approach is found in the equal weighting of diverse but complementary opinions.

Physical and material well-being includes objectives and goals that are principally performance-oriented (e.g., health status and wellness indicators). This is the same for material well-being, with employment, residential, and educational status serving as the primary performance areas. Emotional well-being, self-determination, and interpersonal relations are primarily addressed through questions that are directed at a participant's opinion about how well he or she is doing.

As depicted in Table 14.1, step 1 of outcome-based evaluations identifies the level of evaluation by asking what is the intent of the evaluation. If the intent of the evaluation is to determine whether participant health and wellness has improved, for example, then identifying the stakeholders (step 2) and questions (step 3) is straightforward. For example, if a participant were to identify medication utilization and nutritional status as important outcomes associated with weight loss, then members of the medical community and family members would be likely stakeholders, and the types of questions would also be fairly transparent. These questions might be framed around monitoring medication trials, monitoring weight gain/loss and blood pressure, and monitoring caloric intake and nutritional values. Identifying stakeholders includes identifying anyone with information related to whether the life care planning and service provision impacted the life of the participant as expected by that participant.

Table 14.2 displays a model for evaluating life care planning goals, the procedures for attaining those goals, and whether the results were attained as expected. The upper row asks whether individuals who are similar to the participant set similar goals (e.g., young women just out of high school, retired men of color, children attending elementary school), utilize similar procedures to attain their goals (e.g., exercise in local health centers, attend yoga classes at holistic health centers, and participate in summer youth sports programs), and attain results that are viewed as important by the participant as well as their peers (e.g., increase their strength in order to operate a wheel chair, increase their range of motion in order to climb stairs leading to an apartment, and regaining soccer skills in order to rejoin friends who participate in soccer during recess). Each of these three areas (i.e., goals, procedures used to attain goals, and the results as expected/promised) is evaluated by obtaining information through social comparison, which requires that the evaluation process include obtaining actual data on goals, procedures, and results on persons who are members of similar social networks (i.e., young women, retired men, children).

The lower row of Table 14.2 highlights the importance of asking the participant's opinion about whether she believes: (1) she met her goals; (2) she

14.2 Life Care Planning Social Validation at the Participant Level

	Social Validation		
	Goals	Procedures	Results
Social Comparison	Collect performance indicators on individuals who have similar goals	Collect information on procedures used to attain desired goals	Collect performance information on similar individuals
Subjective Evaluation	Ask participant if he/she believes the goals are important	Ask participant if he/she agrees to the use of certain procedures to meet stated goals/objectives	Ask participant if he/she believes that the goals have been attained as promised

was provided an opportunity to engage in activities that are valued by her; and (3) whether the results achieved were the ones that were promised and consequently valued by her. These measures are collected by administering surveys that ask stakeholders to rate goals as important, procedures as appropriate, and results as expected. Table 14.3 provides an example of how a participant (Michael) met two of his self-determined leisure goals (spending time with his friends and bowling). Michael decided that he wanted to spend time with his friends by participating in a bowling league with them on a weekly basis. Because Michael has had to learn how to use a wheel chair as a result of a spinal cord injury, he has been able to bowl on a fairly regular basis.

Developing an outcome-based design (step 4) and evaluating the outcomes (step 5) are the final two steps depicted in the outcome-based evaluation model (refer to Table 14.1). Developing an outcome-based design requires stakeholders to align design methodology with the questions that are posed. At the participant level, these questions typically address whether the participant set relevant goals, identified acceptable procedures to meet those goals, and viewed the results as effective. Consequently, the primary focus of participant outcome-based evaluation is impact evaluation; that is, was there a valued change in the participant's life as judged objectively (social comparison) and subjectively (subjective evaluation)? As displayed in Table 14.1, there are several questions that drive the formation of outcome-based design, including: (a) What information is needed to answer the questions? (b) What are appropriate measures? (c) How will information be collected? (d) What procedures need to be in place to ensure data quality? (e) How frequently will data need to be collected? and (f) How will the data be analyzed?

The final step in participant outcome-based evaluation is evaluating outcomes (step 5). The questions that are posed here include: (a) Are the outcomes those that were expected? (b) Do the goals need to be revised? (c) Do the methods need to be revised? (d) How will results of the evaluation be communicated with stakeholders? and (e) What are/were constraints, if any, of the evaluation (e.g., time, financial resources, personal biases, available methodologies)?

14.3 Sample Social Comparison and Subjective Evaluation

Evaluation Procedure	Social Validation Targets		
	Goals	Procedures	Results
Social Comparison (Collecting Objective Data)	Michael's friends like to get together and bowl.	Michael's team of bowlers participate in a league.	Michael's team members all routinely attend bowling once per week.
Michael	Michael bowls with his friends.	Michael participates in a bowling league.	Since his spinal cord injury, Michael has bowled on a regular basis using his Quickie™ wheelchair. During the past 6 months, Michael attended 80% of the weekly sessions. Reasons for missing some sessions included: 10% of the time he missed the bus, and 10% of the time he was not feeling well.
Subjective Evaluation (Collecting Subjective Data)	Michael's friends have elected to continue bowling as a means to get together.	Michael's friends like to compete in a league.	Michael's friends are improving their bowling scores as well as enjoying more time together.
Michael	Michael has elected to continue bowling to meet with his friends.	Michael enjoys bowling as a way to get together regularly.	Michael has posted his bowling score each week and likes the fact that he is getting better.

Family/Provider Outcome-Based Evaluation (Effectiveness Evaluation)

Family/provider outcome-based evaluation is directed toward whether the goals of the treatment and the procedures utilized to attain the goals were adhered to as prescribed in the life care plan. The principle concern at this level is fidelity—was the life-care treatment protocol adhered to? After reidentification of the purpose of the evaluation (step 1), stakeholders (step 2), and questions (step 3), the treatment protocol is addressed in an effort to ensure that appropriate measures are being collected and how these measures are collected, including addressing the quality and quantity of the measures (step 4). For example, Michael indicated that he wanted to return to his "normal" life as soon as possible after his car accident. He identified socializing with his friends and continuing to be physically active as two outcomes that were important to him. His life care planning team followed the five steps outlined in the outcome-based evaluation model and decided, with Michael's input, that participating in a bowling league was an appropriate activity, one that met both of his goals (i.e., socializing and participating).

Developing the outcome-based evaluation design was fairly straightforward once the stakeholders and questions were identified (steps 2 and 3). The team, which included Michael, his wife, and a long-time friend, identified Michael's attendance and bowling scores and his friends' attendance and bowling scores (social comparison). They agreed that Michael's and his friends' opinions (subjective evaluation) were appropriate measures and that the social comparison measures (attendance and scores) would be collected every week. The subjective evaluation measures (whether they enjoyed bowling and whether they had appropriate opportunities to socialize) would be collected on a biweekly basis. To ensure data quality, a decision was made to collect bowling score cards marked by Michael's bowling team and to obtain printouts of the bowling alley's electronic scores; also, in addition to asking Michael and a team member how they liked bowling and whether they were enjoying one another's company, Michael's wife, who regularly watched the team bowl, and his long-time friend were asked to occasionally collect satisfaction measures.

Addressing fidelity is critical to step 4. To evaluate the overall effectiveness of the goals that are outlined in a life care plan, the team must follow the prescribed procedures that are expected to effect change from where a participant is before treatment compared to where they are as a result of receiving treatment. The final step is supported by evaluating treatment measures and the veracity of those measures. Step 5 includes five questions, including revising the goals and methods as a result of inspecting the social comparison and subjective evaluation outcomes. Meeting or exceeding the goals, for example, may result in identifying new and more frequent opportunities for Michael to participate in athletically focused sports (e.g., wheel chair tennis, golfing, Para Olympics).

Program Outcome-Based Evaluation (Effectiveness Evaluation)

Program outcome-based evaluation is focused on the overall effectiveness of multiple teams' efforts. The primary question being addressed is whether the life care program's rehabilitation and medical teams, as a group, are capable

Discussion Box 14.2

Private and public funding agencies require the use of outcome data in order to make decisions regarding life care plans (LCPs). Policy makers support an accountability model. Advocates are concerned that such a movement may prove detrimental to individuals with disabilities, their families, and their programs. Accountability methods must be equitable, meet professional standards, and reflect the individuality and diversity of the progress made on a LCP. How could you advocate for equitable and quality individualized practices? Policies?

of achieving participant-directed goals and objectives. These evaluations are usually completed on an annual or semiannual basis because of the overall effort that is expended to collect these measures. It is not uncommon for external teams of evaluators to be hired by a program to evaluate the results of several teams' effectiveness at impacting participant's lives. As a result of this broader focus, multiple evaluation methods are used to address participant outcomes, family/provider impact, and program effectiveness; the stakeholders also include multiple audiences, such as participants attempting to select effective programs and communities attempting to spend scarce resources on effective programs.

Program evaluations usually address whether a program has improved (is more effective) or whether a program is more effective than the alternative. The key outcome variables might well include costs, fidelity to the program's treatment model, participant satisfaction, and indicators of the programs effects on participants' physical, social and emotional well-being. Additional indicators may include how well services are coordinated, financial stability, staff turn over, and access to services. Utilizing the social validation model discussed previously, these questions would also address whether the program measures compare to standards (goals), procedures, and results attained by alternative programs.

Research Critical to Issues in Evaluation of Life Care Plans

Life care planning is a relatively new field. There are few studies on the evaluation of life care plans. In 2001, McCollom and Crane conducted a study with 10 people with spinal cord injury. They found that the LCPs were consistent across time in terms of the projected and actual needs of the participants. In a similar study by Sutton and colleagues (2002), 65 LCPs were compared at two points in time (ranging between 1 and 5 years). Their results suggest that the LCPs were reliable over time in the areas of "Home and Facility Care" and "Routine Medical Care" (Sutton, Deutsch, Weed, & Berens, 2004). A study on vocational outcomes for participants who had traumatic brain injury examined 44 LCPs (Deutsch, Kendall, Daninhirsch, Cimino-Ferguson, & McCollom, 2006). The retrospective study by Deutsch and colleagues found that over half of the participants returned to supported work environments, and all participants were involved in litigation during both the initial and updated evaluations. More research is needed in the area of life care planning. Future research efforts could focus on investigating the reliability, validity, and utility of LCPs, as well as program evaluation research.

Interdisciplinary Approach to LCP

The creation, implementation, and evaluation of a life care plan is a team effort. The LCP involves people across a variety of disciplines that have diverse backgrounds, training, and experiences. LCP teams comprise members who should

Research Box 14.1

Kendall, S. L., & Casuto, D. (2005). A quantitative reappraisal of a qualitative survey to assess reliability and validity of life care planning process. *Journal of Life Care Planning,* 4(2–3), 75-84.

Background: Life care plans (LCP) need to be valid and reliable for clients and their families. A dependable LCP is one that produces similar and consistent results for clients with similar characteristics and disability. Kendall and Casuto (2005) examined the reliability and validity of LCPs related to a pediatric case load.

Method: A survey was developed and administered over the phone to 22 pediatric client families. This survey was used in a previous study to determine the reliability of recommendations made by a life care planner. The purpose of the current retrospective case review study was to examine intra-planner reliability and validity.

Results: Clients were receiving the predicted level of physical, occupational, and speech therapies. Occupational, counseling, and speech therapies were not implemented as proscribed in the LCP. Attendant care services on the LCP were consistently provided at the level suggested.

Conclusions: Services are not always implemented at the level recommended on LCPs.

Questions:
1. What are drawbacks of LCPs that are not implemented as proscribed by a life care planner?
2. How could practitioners ensure that the LCPs they create are valid and reliable?
3. Why do you think treatment validity is an important component of LCPs?

be prepared for their roles. In addition to an individual and his/her family, the following service providers may be involved in a LCP: audiologists (Higdon, Higdon, & Gladstone, 2004), legal professionals (Kessler, 2004), case managers (Demoratz, 2004), economists (Dillman, 2004), home care providers (Gunter & Matteson, 2004), life care planners, medical professionals, neurologists, neuropsychologists (Evans, 2004), nurses, nutritionists, occupational therapists, pediatric physicians, physiatrists (Bonfiglio, 2004), physical therapists, psychologists, rehabilitation counselors (Shahnasarian, 2002), social workers (Rice et al., 2000), speech-language pathologists (Higdon, 2004), special education teachers (Hill, 2004), and vocational counselors.

Interdisciplinary LCP team members practice within their own areas of expertise. Members of LCP teams should be involved in every aspect of the LCP process so that information is communicated accurately. Decision making should be a shared process with everyone working toward a common vision that is generated by the individual and/or the individual's family. LCPs are dependent upon effective partnerships (Klinger, Baptiste, & Adams, 2004; Kuntz, 2005).

One innovative practice occurred in 2001 when the World Health Organization (WHO) approved the use of the International Classification of Functioning, Disability, and Health (ICF; Peterson, 2005; WHO, 2001). The ICF facilitates interdisciplinary collaboration in at least three ways. First, a "common language" is used to make communication more efficient. Second, the "comparison of data" allows users a standard format for collaboration. Third, a "systematic coding scheme" can be used to further support the partnerships and interdisciplinary work that often occurs when creating a life care plan.

Summary

This chapter covered life care planning content, history, evaluation, research related to life care plans, and an interdisciplinary perspective. A well-developed life care plan is essential for the participant, his/her family, service providers, an agency, and the overall community. Utilizing a systems approach is central to all aspects of a life care plan because this approach addresses varying levels of influence of the plan in relation to the impact of planned services on the participant's life and the overall effectiveness of the plan.

References

Accardo, P. J., & Accardo, J. (2004). The role of the developmental pediatrician in life care planning. In S. Riddick-Grisham (Ed.), *Pediatric life care planning and case management* (pp. 139–148). Boca Raton: CRC Press.

Barker, E. (1999). Life care planning. *RN, 62*(3), 58–61.

Bonfiglio, R. P. (2004). The role of the physiatrist in life care planning In R. O. Weed (Ed.), *Life care planning and case management handbook* (pp. 17–23). Boca Raton: CRC Press.

Brown, G. W., & Smith, A. W. (2004). Evaluating life care plans from a legal defense perspective. In S. Riddick-Grisham (Ed.), *Pediatric life care planning and case management handbook* (pp. 733–749). Boca Raton: CRC Press.

Demoratz, M. J. (2004). Incorporating life care planning concepts in case management. *Case Manager, 15*(3), 48–50.

Deutsch, P. M. (2004). Daubert v. Merril Dow: Implications for the life care planner. In S. Riddick-Grisham (Ed.), *Pediatric life care planning and case management handbook* (pp. 759–780). Boca Raton: CRC Press.

Deutsch, P. M., Kendall, S. L., Daninhirsch, C., Cimino-Ferguson, S., & McCollom, P. (2006). Vocational outcomes after brain injury in a patient population evaluated for Life Care Plan reliability. *NeuroRehabilitation, 21*(4), 305–314.

Dillman, E. G. (2004). The role of the economist in life care planning. In R. O. Weed (Ed.), *Life care planning and case management handbook* (pp. 265–278). Boca Raton: CRC Press.

Ehlert, M. A., & Rubin, B. (2004). Understanding Medicaid and other funding sources. In S. Riddick-Grisham (Ed.), *Pediatric life care planning and case management handbook* (pp. 865–872). Boca Raton: CRC Press.

Eliff, B. (1995). Preparing and using life care plans. *National Medical-Legal Journal, 6*(1), 6–7.

Evans, R. W. (2004). The role of the neuropsychologist in life care planning. In R. O. Weed (Ed.), *Life care planning and case management handbook* (pp. 77–87). Boca Raton: CRC Press.

Gunter, K., & Matteson, S. (2004). Role of the home care provider in life care planning. In S. Riddick-Grisham (Ed.), *Pediatric life care planning and case management* (pp. 351–363). Boca Raton: CRC Press.

Higdon, C. W. (2004). The role of speech-language pathologists and audiologists in life care planning. In S. Riddick-Grisham (Ed.), *Pediatric life care planning and case management* (pp. 177–275). Boca Raton: CRC Press.

Higdon, C. W., Higdon, L., & Gladstone, V. S. (2004). The role of the audiologist in life care planning. In R. O. Weed (Ed.), *Life care planning and case management handbook* (pp. 217–263). Boca Raton: CRC Press.

Katz, R. T. (2003). Life expectancy for children with cerebral palsy and mental retardation: implications for life care planning. *NeuroRehabilitation, 18*(3), 261–270.

Katz, R. T., Haig, A. J., Clark, B. B., & DiPaola, R. J. (1992). Long-term survival, prognosis, and life-care planning for 29 patients with chronic locked-in syndrome. *Archives of Physical Medicine and Rehabilitation, 73*(5), 403–408.

Kendall, S. L., & Casuto, D. (2005). A quantitative reappraisal of a qualitative survey to assess reliability and validity of life care planning process. *Journal of Life Care Planning, 4*(2–3), 75–84.

Kessler, M. W. (2004). Critical analysis of the life expectancy research from an attorney's perspective. In S. Riddick-Grisham (Ed.), *Pediatric life care planning and case management handbook* (pp. 797–816). Boca Raton: CRC Press.

Kuntz, K. R. (2005). Life care plans provide a pathway to improved outcomes. *Journal for Specialists in Pediatric Nursing, 10*(3), 143–146.

May, R. V., & Lubinskas, P. (2004). The commission on health care certification (CHCC): Credentialing in life care planning service delivery. In R. O. Weed (Ed.), *Life care planning and case management handbook* (pp. 761–789). Boca Raton: CRC Press.

Mayo, C. (Ed.). (1994). *Life care planning: An overview for professionals.* Washington, DC: National Head Injury Foundation.

McCollom, P. (2000a). Life care planning: A tool for elder care management. *Case Manager, 11*(1), 37–40.

McCollom, P. (2000b). Proposed practice guidelines for excellence in life care planning. *Case Manager, 11*(2), 67–71.

McCollom, P. (2004). Application of life care planning principles in elder care management. In R. O. Weed (Ed.), *Life care planning and case management handbook* (pp. 591–611). Boca Raton: CRC Press.

McCollom, P., & Crane, R. (2001). Life care plans: Accuracy over time. *Case Manager, 12*(3), 85–87.

Munoz, C. C., & Hemmila, L. (2004). Cultural considerations in life care planning for pediatric patients. In S. Riddick-Grisham (Ed.), *Pediatric life care planning and case management handbook* (pp. 855–864). Boca Raton: CRC Press.

Pearl, P. L. (2004). The role of the pediatric neurologist in life care planning. In S. Riddick-Grisham (Ed.), *Pediatric life care planning and case management* (pp. 117–124). Boca Raton: CRC Press.

Peterson, D. B. (2005). International classification of functioning, disability, and health: An introduction for rehabilitation psychologists. *Rehabilitation Psychology, 50*(2), 105–112.

Plioplys, A. V. (2004). Life expectancy of severely disabled children: A brief review. In S. Riddick-Grisham (Ed.), *Pediatric life care planning and case management handbook* (pp. 781–795). Boca Raton: CRC Press.

Reid, C., Deutsch, P. M., Kitchen, J., & Aznavoorian, K. (1999). Life care planning. In F. Chang & M. J. Leahy (Eds.), *Health care and disability case management* (pp. 415–453). Lake Zurick: Vocational Consultants Press.

Rice, J., Hicks, P. B., & Wiehe, V. (2000). Life care planning: A role for social workers. *Social Work in Health Care, 31*(1), 85–94.

Riddick-Grisham, S. (Ed.). (2004). *Pediatric life care planning and case management.* Boca Raton: CRC Press.

Shahnasarian, M. (2002). The rehabilitation counselor as forensic expert, life care planner, and case manager in catastrophic disability: A case illustration. *Journal of Applied Rehabilitation Counseling, 33*(4), 5–9.

Sutton, A. M., Deutsch, P.M., Weed, R. O., & Berens, D. E. (2004). Reliability of life care plans: A comparison of original and updated plans. In R. O. Weed (Ed.), *Life care planning and case management handbook* (pp. 685–692). Boca Raton: CRC Press.

Toran, M. R. (1999). Maps to the future. Life care planning. *Case Manager, 10*(1), 35–37.

Vierling, L. E. (2004). Americans with disabilities act (ADA): From case law to case management and life care planning practice. In R. O. Weed (Ed.), *Life care planning and case management handbook* (pp. 693–705). Boca Raton: CRC Press.

Weed, R. O. (1995). Life care plans as a managed care tool. *Medical Interface, 8*(2), 111–114.

Weed, R. O. (2004a). Life care planning: past, present, and future. In R. O. Weed (Ed.), *Life care planning and case management handbook* (2nd ed., pp. 1–13). Boca Raton: CRC Press.

Weed, R. O. (Ed.). (2004b). *Life care planning and case management handbook.* Boca Raton: CRC Press.

World Health Organization. (2001). *International classification of functioning, disability and health (ICF)*. Geneva: Author.

Rehabilitation Outcome Assessment in Program Evaluation

Ellen S. Fabian

15

Overview

Rehabilitation and health-related services are intended to improve the lives of the people with disabilities who use or participate in them. The evaluation of their effectiveness is critical to efforts to improve service quality and thus improve the quality of life of the individuals they serve. The use of outcome assessments constitutes one approach to program evaluation. It may focus broadly (e.g., on comprehensive community services) or more narrowly (e.g., on individual treatment). Single or multiple assessment methods may be used depending on many conditions (e.g., the purpose of the assessment, available resources, the type of service or program, and the consumers and/or other stakeholders involved). The key issue that distinguishes outcome assessment from individual appraisal or assessment is its purpose: to measure the objective and subjective results of rehabilitation processes (Heinemann, 2005). Rehabilitation outcome assessment is one way of evaluating the effectiveness of rehabilitation programs. This chapter examines how client outcome assessment tools and techniques can be applied to evaluating and improving rehabilitation programs and interventions. The chapter briefly reviews the history and practice in outcome assessment.

Learning Objectives

By the end of this chapter, the reader should be able to:

1. Define the context of rehabilitation outcome assessment;
2. Differentiate among rehabilitation outcome assessment approaches and techniques;
3. Explain the underlying assumptions and values regarding rehabilitation outcome assessment as a tool in program evaluation;
4. Demonstrate an awareness of core considerations, including ethical and cultural issues, in rehabilitation outcomes assessment; and
5. Discuss the significance of rehabilitation outcomes assessment within comprehensive rehabilitation evaluation programs.

Introduction

Outcome assessment generally is conducted in order to evaluate the effectiveness of a specific rehabilitation or health-related treatment intervention, the degree to which programs or services benefited participants, clients' satisfaction with services, and the impact of program services on one's quality of life. Outcome assessment is one of many methods used in program evaluation. Program evaluations may use various methods in addition to outcome assessments, including process assessment, cost-benefit analysis, utilization analysis, and accessibility analysis. Process evaluation monitors service implementation; cost-benefit analysis focuses on monetary indicators of service efficiency; and utilization and accessibility analyses explore patterns of service use and people's access to services.

Outcome assessment has attracted more attention during the last 2 decades due to increased accountability demands from the public, the focus on evidence-based practices, and the availability of more sophisticated evaluation methodologies (Heinemann, 2005).

All health-related fields, including rehabilitation, recognize the importance of assessing whether, and the extent to which, specific interventions benefit recipients. For example, the Council on the Accreditation of Rehabilitation Facilities (CARF) requires programs to evaluate outcomes, not just processes (Heinemann, 2005). Insurance-based managed care organizations emphasize the importance of identifying specific outcome criteria in their reimbursement of empirically supported treatments. Consumer groups encourage rehabilitation and health providers to incorporate outcome assessments that clearly demonstrate the benefits of services (Busch & Sederer, 2000).

Discussion Box 15.1

PROCESS AND OUTCOME METHOD IN EVALUATION

In program evaluation, there is generally a minimal requirement to measure processes and outcomes. Processes are the implementation standards that characterize a program (such as the number of treatment days or whether a particular behavioral intervention occurred), and outcome evaluation is concerned with the effects of the intervention implemented. For a treatment program designed to improve memory functions of individuals with traumatic brain injury, what types of implementation standards or indicators might be used? How would they be measured? What methods, such as reports and observations, could be used?

The importance of outcome assessment also is implied in the philosophy and policies reflected in consumer choice and self-determination. Consumers are requesting information from outcome assessments that document anticipated benefits and disadvantages associated with participating in a specific program. Information from outcome assessments also is important to professionals who either recommend or provide an intervention service as evidenced by client changes resulting from such an intervention. Additionally, federal policy and practices also underscore the importance of evaluating rehabilitation services. For example, the National institute on Disability and Rehabilitation Research's (NIDRR) Long Range Plan calls for improved outcome measures in order to more fully capture the subjective and objective consequences of diverse types of rehabilitation services (NIDRR, 2000).

The first part of this chapter is a brief discussion of the context of outcome assessment in rehabilitation, including its relevance to the International Classification of Functioning (the ICF) developed by the World Health Organization, and described in other chapters in this book. The ICF is used in this chapter as the framework for organizing the different types of rehabilitation outcome assessment, with particular focus on three of its components: activities, participation, and the environment. The chapter also discusses some of the challenges involved in rehabilitation outcome assessments, particularly as these challenges relate to purposes, people, and assessment products. The chapter ends with a discussion of some of the significant ethical issues involved in outcome assessment, as well as recommendations related to cultural diversity.

History of Research and Practice in Outcome Assessment

Earlier efforts to measure rehabilitation outcomes focused almost exclusively on measures of individual change, consistent with a prevailing medical model of disability that emphasized remediating problems or deficits within the individual, rather than within the broader social and physical environments

(Nagi, 1970; Pope & Tarlov, 1991). As the philosophy regarding disability shifted toward seeing disability as the interaction between a person and his or her environment, appreciation for the ways that environments impacted functioning increased (Whiteneck et al., 2004). For example, in its 1993–2003 Long Range Plan, NIDRR wrote that, "disability is a product of an interaction between the characteristics of the individual (e.g., conditions, or impairments, functional status, or personal and social qualities) and the characteristics of the natural, built, cultural, and social environments" (p. 8–9). The World Health Organization's (WHO) International Classification of Functioning, Disability, and Health (ICF; 2001) is providing a universally endorsed framework for developing outcome assessments in rehabilitation. As noted in the first chapter of this book, the ICF's general intent is to improve health care and services in order to enhance the lives of people with disabilities (Reed et al., 2005). This mission is dependent on efforts to evaluate existing programs and services in order to maintain costs, improve access, and increase program effectiveness.

Those engaged in working with the ICF are making important strides toward developing a classification of functional impairments as well as a classification of the environmental domains that either facilitate or impede functioning. Environmental domains include products and technology, natural environment and human-made changes, support and relationships, attitudes, and service systems and policies. The ICF is applicable across the range of disabilities. Although the ICF is not an evaluation system, it shows potential as a framework for rehabilitation outcome assessment in that it depicts the relationship between individual impairments and activities and participation, and it highlights the importance of environmental factors. As indicated in chapter 1 in this text, the ICF provides a dynamic approach to assessing the reciprocal interaction between person and environment and, as such, is an overarching model for outcome assessment in rehabilitation.

Current Assessment Methods in Outcomes Assessment

The ICF framework may be valuable to outcome evaluation efforts by providing a model for conceptualizing the manner in which impairments in body systems may affect an individual's capacity to perform and participate in society. Thus, the model focuses on the functional outcomes or consequences of impairments within an environmental context. It has stimulated rehabilitation outcome assessment by focusing on developing and/or refining functional assessment batteries to be consistent with the ICF framework (e.g., Reed et al., 2005). Although not all rehabilitation outcome assessments have been designed within the ICF framework, the next section of this chapter illustrates several examples of outcome assessments that have been derived from it.

Outcome Assessment Instruments

Functional Activity Assessment

Rehabilitation outcome assessment generally has emphasized measuring individual capacity or skills acquisition for different populations of individuals with disabilities. According to the ICF framework, measuring individual capacity would constitute an "activity," defined as the execution of a task or action by an individual across the domains of learning and applying knowledge, communication, movement, self-care, domestic life, interpersonal relationships, and performing the simple to complex tasks involved in major life activities (Gray & Hendershot, 2000). Functional assessments of individual capacity have focused on most of these domains (Mermis, 2005).

Assessment typically considers an individual's capacity to perform instrumental activities of daily living (e.g., hygiene, food preparation, money management, shopping, and use of community resources). These activities require the use of complex physiological structures such as cognition, communication, and mobility. The goal of most rehabilitation programs is to impact multiple personal qualities or skills. Consequently, the interest in rehabilitation outcome assessment has been on instruments that assess change across multiple domains that are viewed as fundamental to acquiring the skills to live, learn, and work successfully in the community.

Hundreds of instruments that measure individual performance domains are available. However, only a few assess performance or activity across multiple domains (Cohen & Marino, 2000; Neath, Bellini, & Bolton, 1997). Most multiple functional capacity instruments are from physical medicine and rehabilitation due, in part, to the pervasive influence of the medical model in physical rehabilitation and the demand to develop functional inventories that assessed change following clinical treatment.

Evaluations of psychiatric rehabilitation efforts also are aided by hundreds of measures of individual functional capacities (e.g., occupational skills, independent living, social skills, and cognition). However, relatively few psychometrically sound instruments have achieved widespread use. An exception is the Global Assessment of Functioning (GAF) scale, which is included in the *Diagnostic and Statistical Manual of Mental Disorders-IV-TR* (American Psychiatric Association, 2000). Although the GAF is not a test, it is widely used in psychiatric rehabilitation to describe activity (capacity) and participation (utilization and involvement) and to use as a baseline when assessing progress. The use of the GAF may be limited for individuals with significant mental illness (Iyer, Rothmann, Vogler, & Spaulding, 2005).

Some of the more widely known and used functional assessment instruments are reviewed in the following paragraphs. Most have suitable psychometric properties (i.e., suitable reliability and validity) to possibly warrant their use in outcome assessments.

The Barthel Index and the Functional Independence Measure are two of the most widely used instruments in physical rehabilitation outcome assessment . The primary domains measured by the Barthel Index (Mahoney & Barthel, 1965) include basic activities of daily living (e.g., self-care, hygiene, and mobility). This measure is most appropriate for individuals with significant physical impairments. The Barthel Index has adequate empirical validity and strong reliability (Cohen & Marino, 2000). A trained caregiver observes and records the desired behaviors for a few minutes up to an hour. Its long history and associated research warrants its frequent use as a benchmark for validating newer functional assessment batteries.

The Functional Independence Measure (FIM) was developed in the 1980s by a national taskforce from the World Rehabilitation Congress and the American Academy of Physical Medicine and Rehabilitation (Granger, 1998). It is designed to assess the extent to which individuals with disabilities can perform basic life activities, or a measure of capacity. The FIM measures multiple life domains (i.e., self-care, mobility, locomotion, communication, and social-cognition). The cognitive domain seemingly is insufficient for individuals with spinal cord injury (SCI; Cohen & Marino, 2000). The FIM is used primarily in in-patient settings and typically is administered by a trained clinician. However, it can be used as a self-report inventory. Its psychometric properties generally are considered to be adequate (Heinemann, Linacre, Wright, Hamilton, & Granger, 1994).

The Level of Rehabilitation Scale (LORS; Carey & Posavac, 1978) is used in physical rehabilitation to measure four functional domains: activities of daily living, mobility, communication, and cognition. The Patient Evaluation and Conference System (PECS; Harvey & Jellinek, 1981) is used in outpatient rehabilitation programs to measure self-care, mobility, communication, and cognition. According to Cohen and Marino (2000), there have been a number of studies supporting the construct validity of the PECS, but few studies exploring its reliability. The PECS has primarily been used for individuals with acquired brain injury, such as stroke (e.g., Chaudhuri, Harey, Sulton, & Lambert, 1988; Korner-Bitensky, Mayo, Cabot, Becker, & Coopersmith, 1989), and traumatic brain injury, where Rao and Kilgore (1992) found that the PECS was the most robust predictor of return to work for 57 hospitalized individuals with traumatic brain injury.

Measures of Participation

Participation is defined as "an individual's involvement in life situations in relation to health conditions, body functions and structures, activities and contextual factors" (WHO, 2001). While "activities" assess the degree to which people with disabilities can perform tasks associated with daily activities—such as hygiene, eating, mobility—participation assesses the degree to which individuals are "socially integrated, productive and involved in the community" (Heinemann, 2005, p. 9). As Heinemann notes, the key word in this definition is *involvement* because most rehabilitation interventions have integration or involvement of the individual in the community as their desired outcome.

Measures of participation, distinct from activity, represent a more recent assessment emphasis in rehabilitation, due in part to the influence of the ICF and

Discussion Box 15.2

OUTCOME ASSESSMENTS AND PSYCHIATRIC DISABILITIES

There are fewer valid outcome assessment for individuals with psychiatric disabilities than for those with physical disabilities. Why is this? What types of functional assessments used in rehabilitation outcome assessment could be used with people with psychiatric disabilities? What specific functional domains would be important to include? To what extent do you think psychiatric diagnosis would be important in designing functional inventories?

the movement away from a medical model of disability to one that considers the interaction of the individual within his or her environment. Similar to the array of instruments available to measure activity, many instruments designed to measure participation reflect a physical medicine perspective. However, broad measures of participation (i.e., those that measure quality of life) have achieved some influence in measuring rehabilitation outcomes for individuals with psychiatric disabilities. Some of the well-known measures of participation are reviewed in the following paragraphs.

The Craig Handicap Assessment and Reporting Technique (CHART; Whiteneck, Charlifue, Gerhart, Overholser, & Richardson, 1992) may be the most widely used rehabilitation outcome assessment of multiple domains. It measures the social integration of people with disabilities across six scales: physical independence, mobility, occupation, social integration, economic independence, and orientation. The CHART consists of 32 items that can be administered by a clinician or completed by the patient (a short form of the CHART has also been developed, see http://www.tbims.org/combi/chartsf/index.html). The CHART displays good reliability and validity estimates (Cusick, Gerhart, & Mellick, 2000), including adequate validity when used with diverse populations (e.g., people with spinal cord injury, acquired brain injury, amputation, and multiple sclerosis).

The Community Integration Questionnaire (CIQ; Willer, Rosenthal, Kreutzer, Gordon, &, Rempel, 1993) also is widely used, particularly with individuals who display acquired brain injury and other physical disabilities. It measures home integration, social integration, and productivity. This brief scale (15 items) generally has adequate reliability and validity estimates (Dijkers, Whiteneck, & El-Jaroudi, 2000).

Multiple functional scales for use with individuals with psychiatric disabilities are less widely reported, probably as a result of the comprehensive nature of psychiatric rehabilitation programs and the unique characteristics of individuals with significant mental illness (Blankertz & Cook, 1998). As a result, functional assessment in psychiatric rehabilitation often targets specific and somewhat narrow domains, such as work (the Endicott Work Productivity Scale; Endicott & Nee, 1997) or social adjustment (Weissman, Sholomskas, & John, 1981), although there are multiple assessment batteries described in the literature (Slaton & Westphal, 1999).

Interest in assessing quality of life across multiple domains for individuals with psychiatric disabilities has increased, resulting in several well-known instruments to assess it. Lehman's Quality of Life Scale (Lehman, 1983) combines objective and subjective ratings of multiple life domains from the perspective of the individual. Similarly, the Quality of Life Inventory (Frisch, Cornell, Villanuerva, & Retzlaff, 1992) provides a measure of general life satisfaction. The lack of quality rehabilitation outcome assessments in psychiatric rehabilitation generally has been recognized and identified as a specific need for development (Anthony, Buell, Sharratt, & Althoff, 1972; Slaton & Westphal, 1999).

Environmental Assessment

In the ICF, *environment* is defined as those "physical, social and attitudinal environments in which people live and conduct their lives" (WHO, 2001). Within the ICF framework the individual interacts with the environment in ways that either facilitate or impede functioning. For example, an individual who is hearing impaired may function well in an environment that is relatively quiet and well lit, enabling the person to focus on spoken communication. However, if that individual's work environment is dark and noisy, his or her capacity to communicate through speech is compromised (Schneidert, Hurst, Miller, & Üstün, 2003). Although the environmental context is an important aspect of the ICF framework, few instruments assess it (Whiteneck et al., 2004). Available instruments tend to focus on one aspect of the environment. An example is The ADA Checklist for Readily Achievable Barrier Removal, which monitors compliance with physical accessibility standards under the Americans with Disabilities Act (Adaptive Environmental Center, 1995). Although these types of assessments are central to assessing compliance with building codes and architectural design, they rely on generic standards (e.g., curb cuts) rather than focusing on an individual's needs. The need to move away from generic measures to those needed by individuals is underscored by the belief that some generic items (e.g., curb cuts) vital to some individuals (e.g., those using wheelchairs) may pose barriers to others (e.g., those with visual impairments) (Whiteneck et al., 2004).

Scales measuring attitudes toward individuals with disabilities also are available. A review identified 14 direct and 10 indirect methods for assessing attitudes, including those that rank various types of disability, such as the Handicapped Ranking Scale (Barsch, 1964), to those that ask respondents to associate certain characteristics with disability (Antonak & Livneh, 2000). Although self-report measures on which people rate or identify barriers to participation in various environments (e.g., Quebec Environmental Scale; Fougeyrollas, 1995) have been developed, their psychometric properties generally are marginal.

The Craig Hospital Inventory of Environmental Factors (CHIEF; Whiteneck et al., 2004) measures the frequency and magnitude of physical, attitudinal, service productivity, and policy barriers that individuals with physical and sensory disabilities encounter in school, at home, and work. The CHIEF consists of 25 items and can be completed in about 15 minutes. Measures that assess the extent to which communities create livable environments for people with disabilities (e.g., transportation, housing, and access to community resources) represent a recent trend in environmental assessment (Jensen, Iwarsson, & Stahl, 2002).

Discussion Box 15.3

IDENTIFYING EVALUATION INSTRUMENTS

Assume you are responsible for designing a program evaluation of an in-patient hospital unit serving adults with acquired brain injury. The unit provides multiple services (e.g., physical therapy, adjustment to disability counseling, and identification of potential needs for accommodation). Describe the type of program evaluation you would conduct, including the types of outcome assessments you would use. Identify at least three instruments you would use. Identify and discuss some of the most important qualities you may need to consider when establishing a program evaluation.

Challenges in Outcome Assessments

Methods used in outcome assessment in rehabilitation and other health-related fields vary considerably in the number of behaviors and traits they assess (e.g., from somewhat simple tasks such as bathing to complex tasks such as driving), the environments in which the data are collected (e.g., clinic setting, work, home), the sources of data (e.g., from the client or others, from observations), and the number of times the data are obtained. Thus, the instruments range from single-method, one-dimensional scales to multidimensional instruments that may use multiple assessment methods. Rehabilitation outcome assessment increasingly is moving toward the use of multidimensional scales, given the belief they more fully capture the broad purpose of rehabilitation intervention—namely to increase an individual's participation in society, leading ultimately to improvements in his or her quality of life (Jette, Keysor, Coster, Pengsheng, & Haley, 2005). However, multidimensional assessments typically have focused on individuals rather than attempting to assess environments or the fit between individual functioning and environmental resources.

The increased attention given to broad outcome assessment also has highlighted some of the challenges involved. The inclusion of heterogeneous groups of people with disabilities and the diversity of rehabilitation and health-related programs developed to assist them pose complex challenges. Many rehabilitation and health-related programs encompass multiple treatment domains (e.g., medical, social, and vocational). Locating suitable outcome measures that adequately measure possible change across all of multiple treatment domains is almost impossible. The finding that improvement in one area or domain does not necessarily predict improvement in another limits the generalizability of the results (Iyer et al., 2005). For example, individuals with psychiatric disabilities may be able to perform a job with appropriate supports, yet still be managing the active symptoms of their illnesses, such as hallucinations (Mueser, Meyer, Penn, Clancy, & Clancy, 2006).

Although the ICF framework itself provides a classification of functions, the nine domains it describes (learning and applying knowledge; general tasks and demands; communication; mobility; self-care; domestic life; interpersonal interactions and relationships; major life areas; and community, social, and civic life) are not conceptually linked to each other to assist in the development of outcome measures. For example, a discrete skill, such as toileting, represents a physical function, while coping with the psychological consequences of needing assistance in toileting represents a psychosocial function. Teaching clients how to make maximal use of their functional capacities in toileting may be the desirable outcome of a physical therapy program. Helping clients to adjust to the psychosocial aspects of needing this assistance may be the desirable outcome of rehabilitation counseling or therapy. When all of the professionals involved in the rehabilitation process are aware of and can map the physical and psychosocial processes to each other, it can certainly assist in more effectively and efficiently achieving rehabilitation goals (Mermis, 2005). Such a classification or taxonomy of rehabilitation outcome measures does not currently exist.

The identification of methods that assess individual skill changes is challenging. For example, the evaluation of programs designed to improve bathing skills in the elderly following a stroke may appear to be simple. However, contextual factors (i.e., the generalization of skills acquired in an acute care rehabilitation facility to the home) and person factors (e.g., motivation, prior physical or mental impairments, whether there is a desire to bathe) illustrate how assessment of the acquisition of one discrete function may be complicated by environmental and person qualities.

Outcome assessments of more complex or multidimensional capacities (e.g., complex cognition or social skills—purchasing food or opening a bank account) present other challenges, including specifying anticipated outcomes of the intervention and then designing or locating psychometrically sound instruments to operationalize these outcomes. Outcome assessment in rehabilitation ultimately focuses on client or consumer acquisition of behaviors or skills intended to improve participation in specific environments. Thus, the need to assess more complex skills in diverse environmental contexts is critical. For example, the ICF framework indicates that individual functioning should be understood in the context of how it affects individual participation in important domains of life, with or without environmental supports.

Another challenge in outcome assessment is the various stakeholders who are involved in the implementation, funding, and monitoring of programs and practices, each of whom has specific needs and demands that may be in conflict. These issues pose another challenge to outcome assessments. For example, services of more than eight stakeholders may be involved in psychiatric rehabilitation outcome: physicians, insurance companies, consumers, families, communities, employers, educators, counselors, and other practitioners (Iyer et al., 2005). Another potential conflict can be seen in the externally imposed financial constraints by federal, state, or insurance policies that may result in vocational counselors establishing goals that can be achieved somewhat immediately and thus differ from those preferred or needed by a client. Thus, the choice of outcomes as well as understanding the potential for conflict need to be considered in designing evaluation protocols for rehabilitation outcome assessment.

Ensuring construct validity is critical to evaluation efforts and often poses a major challenge. Construct validity refers to the degree test scores accurately indicate a person's standing on the construct measured by the test. Assurance of construct validity requires an evaluator to clearly define the constructs to be assessed and then develop or select tests that operationalize them. Definitional issues may include the location in which the behavior occurs, its frequency, quality, degree of allowable assistance as well as the source of the data (reports by self or others, naturalistic observation, or demonstration).

Issues regarding cultural assumptions and cultural values may need to be considered in rehabilitation outcome assessment. Standards for what is considered to be normal in our increasingly multicultural society may be changing (Dijkers et al., 2000). For example, independence has been one of the benchmarks of rehabilitation outcomes. This standard reflects an individualist approach (in which an individual is expected to assume control of his or her life) rather than a collectivist approach to life (in which control lies in the hands of groups with whom an individual is affiliated). Thus, the goal of independence may not be relevant across all cultures. Moreover, research investigating test validity, including construct validity, should evaluate their utility and validity using participants from diverse racial and ethnic backgrounds.

Professional Issues Central to Rehabilitation Outcome Assessment: The Three P's

Stakeholders engaged in health care services have an abiding interest in questions that pertain to treatment effectiveness: Was the patient cured? Did behavior improve? Was the patient able to return to work? Did the patient return to work? Answers to these and other questions help determine the effectiveness of treatment outcomes. Accreditation and regulatory agencies, such as the Commission on Rehabilitation Facilities (CARF) and the Joint Commission on the Accreditation of Health Care Organizations, require evidence of treatment outcomes achieved. Thus, the goals and methods of rehabilitation outcome assessment have become more visible and salient. Although rehabilitation outcome assessment is not new, it is receiving considerably more attention in the literature. Central issues to consider in rehabilitation outcome assessment relate to three main areas: purpose, people, and products.

Purpose of the Evaluation

Rehabilitation outcome assessments are initiated for various purposes, including those associated with accreditation, after developing a new treatment intervention, for quality assurance purposes, or for research or other internal programmatic issues. Although each of these shares in common a need to examine program effectiveness, each requires different evaluation designs and data collection methods. For example, consider the following two purposes: to determine whether an intervention worked or to determine why an intervention worked. Attempts to answer these questions will require different evaluation methods and thus different measurement instruments (Busch & Sederer, 2000). An answer to the first question may rely more on quantitative methods while answers to the second may rely more on qualitative methods.

People Who May Benefit From Evaluation Efforts

Multiple users and stakeholders may benefit from rehabilitation outcome assessments. These include clients and consumers, accreditation and regulatory agencies, those who provide rehabilitation services, as well as community, state, and federal agencies. Their needs and desires for information will guide program evaluation methods.

Clients and their families are the primary recipients of services and thus constitute one of the most important consumers of this information. The degree to which programs are effective will affect the quality of their lives directly. Programs often ask clients to complete measures of satisfaction upon the termination of services as a part of their program outcome assessments (e.g., Attkisson & Greenfield, 1996). Accreditation and other regulator agencies (e.g., CARF) may require programs to provide data as to the effectiveness of their programs or their fidelity to evidence-based practice (Heinemann, 2005). Community, state, and federal agencies also may be important stakeholders and thus require outcome reports to forecast funding and shape policy.

Products: The Inputs and Outcomes of Evaluation

Products of an outcome evaluation refer to both the measures and strategies that are used for data gathering, such as the functional instruments described earlier, as well as the outcome that is produced as a result of the process, such as an evaluation report or a research study. Prior to initiating an outcome assessment, evaluators first determine the issues to be investigated, the qualities to be measured, at what level (e.g., functional capacities or activities, or participation), in what environment (e.g., home, community, hospital, rehabilitation center), and when the assessment will occur (e.g., whether data will be acquired when consumers are receiving treatment, immediately after, or perhaps when they have been reintegrated into the community). The selection of instruments must consider these issues. The end-users or audience for the results of the outcome assessment should also be considered in determining what behaviors are to be measured and how (Busch & Sederer, 2000).

The type of desired product or report of the assessment results also should be considered. For example, some outcome assessments may analyze and report administrative data (e.g., presenting symptoms, duration and frequency of rehabilitation services, and demographic and disability information) in order to compare program outcomes across time periods and among different service users. This type of outcome report can be internally useful for personnel and resource allocation decisions. On the other hand, outcome assessment results may be designed to analyze or document treatment or program effectiveness. Thus, data collected and analyzed may include functional improvement after using one of the instruments described earlier in this chapter. This type of outcome report requires multiple data collection efforts as well as more substantial investment of time and money. The end result of the outcome assessment process is important issues to consider, including the type of required product and the intended audience.

Cultural and Ethical Issues That Impact Rehabilitation Outcome Assessment

Most professional codes of ethics are built around five basic principles: autonomy, nonmaleficence, beneficence, fidelity, and justice (Kitchener, 2000). Autonomy refers to a patient's self-determination and choice. Nonmaleficence refers to avoiding harm to others. Beneficence refers to facilitating a client's well-being. Fidelity refers to loyalty and honesty in practice. Justice refers to fairness and equitable distribution of resources.

In rehabilitation counseling, these principles are operationalized through the Code of Ethics for Rehabilitation Counselors (Commission on Rehabilitation Counselor Certification, 2007) and are intended to protect consumers of rehabilitation services. For example, the rehabilitation counseling code of ethics addresses issues such as client confidentiality and informed consent. These are important considerations in rehabilitation outcome assessment. Informed consent requires that clients be fully informed of the purpose, nature, and ultimate use of testing or evaluation activities. Some rehabilitation consumers, particularly those with significant cognitive or neurological disabilities, may require assistance from family members or other advocates when deciding to give their consent to participate in various assessment activities (Aman & Handen, 2006). Informed consent applies when assessments are being used for individual clinical purposes as well as when rehabilitation outcome assessment is being conducted for program evaluation or research purposes. In the latter case, organizations (e.g., hospitals or agencies) whose programs are being evaluated establish ethical review boards to ensure the protection of consumers who participate in these programs and their role in the evaluation of them.

Client confidentiality, particularly the confidentiality of medical records, is another example of consumers' rights and evaluator responsibilities regarding the administration and sharing of assessment data. Client confidentiality generally is consistent with the ethical principles of autonomy and nonmaleficence, values intended to protect individuals from potential harm should the private assessment information or data gathered by health care professionals be revealed to others (e.g., government entities, public officials, private individuals, and family members). Client confidentiality places limits on the release of program evaluation data where individual identity may be revealed.

Rehabilitation outcome assessment also requires sensitivity to cultural issues and values. For example, the state and federal vocational rehabilitation program is predicated on the value of productivity, particularly productive employment as the prime indicator of successful outcome. As a result, consumers are served and the program is evaluated on the basis of whether clients achieved paid employment. However, in some cultures, return to work after injury is not uniformly viewed as the primary desirable outcome—in fact, it may have no value. People from cultures that have a more holistic or traditional view of healing and health (e.g., traditional Asian cultures) may find little value in American-style vocational rehabilitation with its emphasis on productivity.

Given this example, values and life assumptions that differ among cultures are unavoidably linked to rehabilitation outcome assessment decisions. What one cultural group values (e.g., human interaction or intrapersonal "wholeness") may be vastly different than what most funding agencies require as evidence (i.e., health improvement and symptom alleviation; Banja, 1998). In psychiatric rehabilitation, consumers have identified "recovery" as the desired outcome of treatment interventions, with recovery viewed as a dynamic and changing intentional process of attaining desirable life goals, not a static end state (Anthony, 1993). As a result, the development of instruments that measure the construct of recovery requires a collaborative process among consumers, families, and researchers together with the use of qualitative evaluation methods (e.g., action research) that stimulate self-awareness and self-control in goal identification and achievement.

Implicit assumptions regarding values also are bound up in decisions regarding what behavior is important to measure and how it should be measured. These issues become particularly complex when dealing with individuals with significant mental health disorders whose symptoms present in patterns of remission and exacerbation, or those with multiple sclerosis. Is the desirable outcome alleviation of symptoms, alleviation of pain, improvement in self-control or self-management, overall quality of life, or other desired conditions? Although there are no universally correct answers to these questions, an understanding of how these and similar questions are bound up with cultural values

Discussion Box 15.4

ETHICS AND OUTCOME ASSESSMENTS

Ethical issues in assessment and program evaluation can sometimes be overlooked. For example, if the program evaluation is being conducted in order to publish or disseminate the results, are consumers adequately informed, even if individuals cannot be identified in the subsequent publication? What would you recommend in situations where consumers refuse to participate in research studies of program effectiveness even when they are participants in the treatment intervention? How important is their refusal? To what extent should program evaluation design and methods involve clients and consumers in design, methods, data collection, analysis, and dissemination of results?

and ethical considerations demonstrates the complexity underlying decisions in this area, particularly when the treatment beneficiary may be unable to articulate his or her own consent, desires, or goals.

Summary

Rehabilitation outcome assessment is an important aspect of overall program evaluation. Although instruments used in individual appraisal also may be relevant to outcome assessment, their purposes differ. The purpose of individual assessment is to accurately describe personal qualities. The purpose of test use in rehabilitation outcome assessment is to provide data that assists in evaluating the effects of rehabilitation and other health-related program interventions. As such, their focus is broader than when used in individual assessments.

Rehabilitation outcome assessment methods and measures reflect various trends. For example, the focus in outcome assessment has shifted from emphasizing individual skills or capacity attainment to examining the extent to which attainment of new skills or capacity improve community integration. In this regard, rehabilitation outcome assessment reflects the person–environment interaction perspective on disability and functioning as described in the ICF. Measures that help assess key components of the ICF model, including activities, participation, and environment, are targeted for development and use.

Although interest in designing such functional outcome measures to use in rehabilitation is apparent, rehabilitation specialists currently lack comprehensive tools that can be used across multiple domains with diverse populations. The biopsychosocial approach to rehabilitation can be seen in the way that many rehabilitation and health-related programs offer holistic and multidisciplinary treatment across major life domains of living, learning, and working. However, our capacity to measure the extent to which such programs have benefited participants remains constrained by the limited instruments available to assess it. Interest in developing such instruments among practitioners, accreditation agencies, and the federal government is intense.

Rehabilitation and other health-related outcome assessment methods and measures need to be sensitive to potential bias issues for people with disabilities. For example, Hartley and MacLean (2006) identified response bias among people with significant intellectual disabilities responding to tests that use Likert-type rating scales. Abedi (2006) urged caution in the use of standardized tests used to make referrals to special education for students whose primary language is not English. Ysseldyke et al. (2004) reviewed empirical studies of high stakes testing for students with disabilities, concluding that more studies on the consequences of these types of tests need to be conducted, particularly regarding the consequences of testing.

The challenges of rehabilitation outcome assessment will need to be addressed in order to respond to the increased demands for quality services from the public (Busch & Sederer, 2000). Many future issues in this area need to be resolved, including the availability of reliable and valid measures, developing useable and affordable methods of evaluation, and disseminating research instruments in order to enable broader evaluation of their applicability and merits to diverse populations. The availability of a universal framework for assessment, in part through the ICF, holds promise for addressing these challenges in the future.

References

Abedi, J. (2006). Psychometric issues in the ELL assessment and special education eligibility. *Teacher's College Record, 108,* 2282–2303.

Adaptive Environmental Center. (August, 1995). *The Americans with Disabilities Act. Checklist for readily achieving barrier removal. Checklist for existing facilities. Version 2.1.* Boston: Barrier Free Environments.

Aman, M. G., & Handen, B. (2006). Reactions to "ethical challenges and complexities of including people with intellectual disabilities as participants in Research" by Teresa Iacono. *Journal of Intellectual Disability, 31,* 180–182.

American Psychiatric Association. (2000). *Diagnostic and statistical manual of mental disorders* (4th ed., text rev.). Washington, DC: Author.

Anthony, W. A. (1993). Recovery from mental illness: The guiding vision of the mental health service system in the 1990's. *Psychosocial Rehabilitation Journal, 16*(4), 11–23.

Anthony, W. A., Buell, G. J., Sharratt, S., & Althoff, M. E. (1972). Efficacy of psychiatric rehabilitation. *Psychological Bulletin, 78,* 447–456.

Antonak, R. F., & Livneh, H. (2000). Measurement of attitudes towards persons with disabilities. *Disability and Rehabilitation, 22,* 211–224.

Atkisson, C. C., & Greenfield, T. K. (1996). The Client Satisfaction Questionnaire (CSQ) Scales and the Service Satisfaction Scale-30 (SSS-30). In L. I. Sederer & B. Dickey (Eds.), *Outcome assessment in clinical practice* (pp. 120–127). Baltimore, MD: Wiley.

Banja, J. D. (1998). Values and outcomes: The ethical implications of multiple meanings. In E. A. Dobrzkowski (Ed.), *Essential readings in rehabilitation outcomes measurement* (pp. 52–59). Gaithersburg, MD: Aspen Publications.

Barsch, R. H. (1964). The handicapped ranking scale among parents of handicapped children. *American Journal of Public Health, 54,* 1560–1567.

Blankertz, L., & Cook, J. A. (1998). Choosing and using outcome measures. *Psychiatric Rehabilitation Journal, 22,* 167–174.

Busch, A. B., & Sederer, L. I. (2000). Assessing outcomes in psychiatric practice: Guidelines, challenges and solutions. *Harvard Rev. Psychiatry, 8,* 323–327.

Carey, R. G., & Posavac, E. J. (1978). Program of a physical medicine and rehabilitation unit: A new approach. *Archives of Physical Medicine and Rehabilitation, 59,* 330–337.

Chaudhuri, G., Harvey, R. F., Sulton, C. D., & Lambert, R. W. (1988). Computerized tomography head scans as predictors of functional outcome of stroke patients. *Archives of Physical Medicine and Rehabilitation, 69,* 496–498.

Cohen, M. E., & Marino, R. J. (2000). The tools of disability outcomes research functional status measures. *Archives of Physical Medicine and Rehabilitation, 81* (Supp. 2), S21–S29.

Commission on Rehabilitation Counselor Certification. (2007). *Code of Professional Ethics for Rehabilitation Counselors.* Retrieved July 20, 2007, from: http://www.crccertification.com/pages/30code.html

Cusick, C. P., Gerhart, K. A., & Mellick, D. C. (2000). Participant-proxy reliability in traumatic brain injury outcome research. *Journal of Head Trauma Rehabilitation, 15,* 739–749.

Dijkers, M., Whiteneck, G., & El-Jaroudi, R. (2000). Measures of social outcomes in disability research. *Archives of Physical Medicine and Rehabilitation, 81* (Supp. 2), S63–S80.

Endicott, J., & Nee, J. (1997). Endicott Work Productivity Scale (EWPS): A new measure to assess treatment effects. *Psychopharmacology Bulletin, 33,* 13–16.

Fougeyrollas, P. (1995). Documenting environmental factors for preventing the handicap creation process. Quebec contributions relating to the ICIDH and social participation of people with functional differences. *Disability and Rehabilitation, 17,* 145–153.

Frisch, M. B., Cornell, J., Villanuerva, M., & Retzlaff, P. J. (1992). Clinical validation of the Quality of Life Inventory: A measure of life satisfaction for use in treatment planning and outcome assessment. *Psychological Assessment, 4,* 92–101.

Granger, C. V. (1998). The emerging science of functional assessment: Our tool for outcomes analysis. *Archives of Physical Medicine and Rehabilitation, 78,* 235–240.

Gray, D. B., & Hendershot, G. E. (2000). The ICIDH-2: Developments for a new era of outcomes research. *Archives of Physical Medicine and Rehabilitation, 81* (Supp. 2), S10–S14.

Hartley, S. L., & MacLean, W. E. (2006). A review of the reliability and validity of Likert-type scales for people with intellectual disability. *Journal of Intellectual Disability, 50,* 813–827.

Harvey, R. F., & Jellinek, H. H. (1981). Functional performance assessment: A program approach. *Archives of Physical Medicine & Rehabilitation, 62,* 456–461.

Heinemann, A. W. (2005). Putting outcome measurement in context: A rehabilitation psychology perspective. *Rehabilitation Psychology, 50,* 6–14.

Heinemann, A. W., Linacre, J. M., Wright, B. D., Hamilton, B. B., & Granger, C. V. (1994). Measurement characteristics of the Functional Independent Measure. *Topics in Stroke Rehabilitation, 1*(3), 1–15.

Iyer, S. N., Rothmann, T. L., Vogler, J. E., & Spaulding, W. D. (2005). Evaluating outcomes of rehabilitation for severe mental illness. *Rehabilitation Psychology, 50,* 43–55.

Jensen, G., Iwarsson, S., & Stahl, A. (2002). Theoretical understanding and methodological challenges in accessibility assessments, focusing the environmental component: An example from travel chains in urban public bus transport. *Disability and Rehabilitation, 24,* 231–242.

Jette, A. M., Keysor, J., Coster, W., Pengsheng, N., & Haley, S. (2005). Beyond function; Predicting participation in a rehabilitation cohort. *Archives of Physical Medicine and Rehabilitation, 86,* 2087–2094.

Kitchener, K. S. (2000). *Foundations of ethical practice, research, and teaching in psychology.* Mahwah, NJ: Lawrence Erlbaum Associates.

Korner-Bitensky, N., Mayo, N., Cabot, R., Becker, R., & Coopersmith, H. (1989). Motor and functional recovery after stroke: Accuracy of physical therapists' predictions. *Archives of Physical Medicine and Rehabilitation, 70,* 95–99.

Lehman, A. F. (1983). The well-being of chronic mental patients: Assessing their quality of life. *Archives of General Psychiatry, 40,* 369–373.

Mahoney, F. I., & Barthel, D. W. (1965). Functional evaluation: The Barthel Index. *Maryland State Medical Journal, 14,* 61–65.

Mermis, B. J. (2005). Developing a taxonomy for rehabilitation outcome measurement. *Rehabilitation Psychology, 50,* 15–23.

Mueser, K. T., Meyer, P. S., Penn, D. L., Clancy, R., & Clancy, D. M. (2006). The illness management and recovery program: Rationale, development, and preliminary findings. *Schizophrenia Bulletin, 32,* S32–S43.

Nagi, S. Z. (1970). *Disability and rehabilitation: Legal, clinical and self concepts and measurements.* Columbus: Ohio State University Press.

National Institute on Disability and Rehabilitation Research. (1993—2003). *Long Range Plan.* Retrieved May 5, 2009, from http://www.ed.gov/rschstate/research/pubs/nidrr-irp-99-03.pdf

Neath, J., Bellini, J., & Bolton, B. (1997). Dimensions of the Functional Assessment Inventory for five different disability groups. *Rehabilitation Psychology, 42,* 183–207.

Pope, A. M. & Tarlov, A. R. (1991). *Disability in America: Toward a national agenda for prevention.* Washington, DC: National Academy Press.

Rao, N., & Kilgore, K. M. (1992). Predicting return to work in traumatic brain injury using assessment scales. *Archives of Physical Medicine and Rehabilitation, 73,* 911–916.

Reed, G. M., Lux, J. B., Burka, L. F., Peterson, D. B., Threats, T. T., Trask, C., et al. (2005). Operationalizing the International Classification of Functioning, Disability and Health in clinical settings. *Rehabilitation Psychology, 50,* 122–131.

Schneidert, M., Hurst, R., Miller, J., & Üstün, B. (2003). The role of environment in the International Classification of Functioning, Disability and Health (ICF). *Disability and Rehabilitation, 25,* 588–595.

Slaton, K. D., & Westphal, J. R. (1999). The Slaton-Westphal Functional Assessment Inventory for adults with psychiatric disabilities: Development of an instrument to measure functional status and psychiatric rehabilitation outcome. *Psychiatric Rehabilitation Journal, 23,* 119–126.

Weissman, M. M., Sholomskas, D., & John, K. (1981). The assessment of social adjustment: An update. *Archives of General Psychiatry, 38,* 1250–1258.

Whiteneck, G., Charlifue, S. W., Gerhart, K., Overholser, D., & Richardson, G. N. (1992). Quantifying handicap: A new measure of long-term rehabilitation outcomes. *Archive of Physical Medicine and Rehabilitation, 73,* 519–526.

Whiteneck, G. G., Harrison-Felix, C. L., Mellick, D. C., Brooks, C. A., Charlifue, S. B., & Gerhart, K. A. (2004). Quantifying environmental factors: A measure of physical, attitudinal, service, productivity, and policy barriers. *Archives of Physical Medicine and Rehabilitation, 85,* 1324–1335.

Willer, B., Rosenthal, M., Kruetzer, J. S., Gordon, W. A., & Rempel, R. (1993). Assessment of community integration following rehabilitation for traumatic brain injury. *Journal of Head Trauma Rehabilitation, 8,* 75–87.

World Health Organization. (2001). *International classification of functioning, disability and health (ICF).* Geneva: Author.

Ysseldyke, J., Nelson, J., Christen, S., Johnson, D. R., Dennison, A., Triezenberg, H., et al. (2004). What we know and need to know about the consequences of high-stakes testing for students with disabilities. *Exceptional Children, 71,* 75–94.

Part 3

Measures of Adaptation and Adjustment

Assessment of Adaptive Behavior Development in Young Children

Jennifer L. Harman
Tina M. Smith-Bonahue
Thomas Oakland

16

Overview

This chapter provides an overview of adaptive behavior during early childhood and discusses professional and legal issues regarding the assessment of adaptive behavior. Theory and the history of research related to adaptive skills of young children are presented. Next, the assessment of adaptive behavior in young children is discussed. Finally, the utility of assessing young children's adaptive behavior among various discipline and specialty areas is discussed through the use of two case study presentations.

Learning Objectives

By the end of the chapter, the reader should be able to:

1. Outline the legal definition of adaptive behavior;
2. Explain the concept of adaptive behavior in young children;
3. Outline the reasons for assessing adaptive behavior in young children;
4. Name and describe two forms of legislation that address the area of adaptive behavior with regard to education;
5. Describe common ways of assessing adaptive behavior in young children; and
6. Examine how various discipline and specialty areas could utilize the assessment of adaptive behavior skills and deficits in providing interventions for young children.

Introduction

Federal legislation, specifically the 1986 amendment to the Education of the Handicapped Act (PL 99–457), requires the assessment of infants and young children at-risk for disabilities to be comprehensive, multidisciplinary, and to focus on functional abilities. In many ways, adaptive skills are the quintessential functional abilities in that they encompass key functional developmental tasks that typically are acquired first shortly after birth and continue throughout adulthood. For infants, these tasks comprise behaviors necessary for their survival.

Initially, infants are unable to display all needed functional skills themselves and thus rely on care providers to meet most of their needs. Immediately after birth, instinctive reflexes pave the way for the acquisition of adaptive skills needed for life outside the womb, including the ability to communicate basic needs. As infants grow into toddlers, their ability to accomplish tasks independently escalates as seen in various discreet areas, including their learning to feed themselves, self-soothing, and mobility. Infants' adaptive behaviors are inextricably associated with and evidence of their cognitive, language, and motor competence. As such, adaptive skills can be conceptualized as the visible manifestation both of infants' functional adaptation to their environment and their ongoing development.

This chapter provides an overview of adaptive behavior during early childhood. Discussions center on professional and legal definitions of adaptive behavior, two theories related to adaptive behavior in young children, and the assessment of adaptive behavior in young children through the use of three measures. The utility of assessing young children's adaptive behavior is illustrated through the use of two case studies.

Professional and Legal Definition of Adaptive Behavior

Adaptive behavior refers to the ways in which individuals meet their daily personal needs and cope with the natural and social demands in their environment.

Thus, adaptive behavior includes qualities that have a functional and pervasive impact on the quality of one's life, including the ability to function effectively and independently at home, school, work, and the community.

The American Association on Intellectual and Developmental Disabilities (AAIDD)[1] has provided leadership in reference to defining adaptive behavior, in part, due to the inclusion of adaptive behavior in its definition of mental retardation as well as its efforts to promote the development of functional skills in the lives of those with mental retardation.[2] AAIDD emphasizes the importance of describing strengths and limitations in adaptive skills that lead to the development of a profile of needed support and services. It also emphasizes the view that life functioning generally improves with appropriate personalized educational efforts provided over a sustained period (AAIDD, 2002).

AAIDD's emphasis on improving adaptive behavior, not merely assessing it, led to their placing greater emphasis on adaptive qualities that can be improved. Evidence that the more general construct of adaptive behavior can be improved is meager. Evidence is more robust that specific features of the construct of adaptive behavior, seen at the skill level and especially at the item level, can be improved. This knowledge led to highlighting the belief that specific skills that have a functional impact on the quality of one's life can be improved through education and suitable reinforcement methods.

This belief led to an emphasis on the importance of adaptive skills, not merely adaptive behavior, as found in AAIDD's 1992 definition of mental retardation: "Mental retardation refers to substantial limitations in present functioning. It is characterized by significantly subaverage intellectual functioning, existing concurrently with related limitations in two or more of the following applicable adaptive skill areas: communication, self-care, home living, social skills, community use, self-direction, health and safety, functional academics, leisure, and work. Mental retardation manifests before age 18" (p. 5). AAIDD's 2002 definition emphasized three broad adaptive skills by defining adaptive behavior as "the collection of conceptual, social, and practical skills that have been learned by people in order to function in their everyday lives" (p. 73).

Important features of the 1992 and 2002 definitions can be combined to show the relationship between the earlier emphasis on the 10 adaptive skills and the latter emphasis on the 3 broader adaptive domains: the conceptual domain includes communication, functional academics, and self-direction skills; the social domain includes social and leisure skills; and the practical domain includes self-care, home or school living, community use, health and safety, and work skills. These qualities, with motor skills substituted for work skills, form the foundation for the assessment of adaptive behavior and skills as measured by the *Adaptive Behavior Assessment System-II* (Harrison & Oakland, 2003) for children from birth through age 5 and the *Bayley Scales of Infant and Toddler Development: Third Edition* (Bayley, 2006).

History and Legal Standards Governing the Use of Measures of Adaptive Behavior for Young Children

Rehabilitation counselors, psychologists, occupational therapists, speech language pathologists, and other professionals who use tests are familiar with and rely heavily on various standards intended to impact practices. These include ethics codes, best practice guidelines, and authoritative scholarship. However, none of these sources may be more important than legal standards. Legal standards typically are defined first through legislation and later given clarity through administrative policy and case law. Two forms of legislation pertinent to work with young children in the context of schooling are summarized here.

No Child Left Behind Act of 2001

The No Child Left Behind Act of 2001 (NCLB) provides the most sweeping reform of the Elementary and Secondary Education Act since its enactment in 1965. NCLB redefines the federal role in K-12 education, with the goal to help close the achievement gap between disadvantaged and minority students and their middle-class and higher performing peers. The Act is based on four reform principles: accountability for results, flexibility and increased local control, research-based reforms, and expanded parental options (http://www.nochildleft behind.gov/). Issues pertaining to assessment often focus on state-mandated achievement tests typically given to students starting in grade 3 and extending through high school. Thus, this Act generally does not impact the education of young children directly. Nevertheless, the implementation of this Act and the Individuals with Disabilities Education Act seemingly is modifying the role of professionals providing indirect (e.g., assessments) and direct (e.g., academic, behavioral, language, and motor interventions) services.

Individuals With Disabilities Education Improvement Act

Approximately 6.5 million children and youth with special education needs receive special education and related services in the United States (U.S. Department of Education, 2006).The Individuals with Disabilities Education Improvement Act (IDEIA) governs the provision of early intervention, special education, and related services by state and local educational agencies for children ages 2 through 21 (U.S. Code Service, 2007).

Part C of IDEIA addresses assistance for infants and toddlers with disabilities by authorizing states to develop and maintain early intervention programs for them (Apling & Jones, 2005). Thus, Part C is pertinent to the use of measures that assess adaptive behavior in young children. Eligibility is based on a diagnosis of developmental delay that requires early intervention services. The assessment of adaptive behavior provides data that can be helpful in establishing impairment and eligibility for these services and pinpointing interventions.

Part B of IDEIA addresses assistance for students with disabilities ages 3 through 21 (Apling & Jones, 2005). Eligibility for services is based on meeting criteria for one or more 13 disability categories (U.S. Department of Education, 2006). Data on adaptive behavior are needed to determine eligibility for students with developmental and intellectual disabilities, may be helpful for determining the strengths and weaknesses in daily living skills of all students suspected of having a disability, and may inform educational programming efforts, help determine progress, and provide information for reevaluations (Ditterline, Banner, Oakland, & Becton, 2008).

Local educational agencies are required to use multiple assessment methods and sources of information to document disabilities. These data have three purposes: to assist in determining whether a child has a disability, to inform the content of an educational plan, and to provide baseline data useful for determining later changes (Council for Exceptional Children, 2004). Local education agencies are encouraged to emphasize the assessment of functional skills, thereby informing interventions that can have a direct and functional impact on important practical life skills.

For example, the results of a measure of adaptive behavior may show a weakness in practical daily life skills, such as those associated with communication, functional academics, and self-direction skills—the three components of the conceptual domain. An examination of item data may help identify specific skill deficits that warrant interventions. The ABAS-II Interpretative Report assists this process by suggesting empirically validated interventions that promote skill development (Harrison & Oakland, 2008). Instructional support strategies may include group and individual instruction, guided practice, modeling, consultation, and independent monitoring. Subsequent evaluations of adaptive behavior may show improvement toward meeting performance goals.

Theories Related to Adaptive Behavior in Young Children

Adaptive behavior, as discussed previously, includes the ability to meet daily needs and handle the demands of the environment. Two prominent theories of early development contribute to our understanding of adaptive skill development during the early childhood years: attachment theory and the synactive theory of development.

Attachment Theory

Attachment refers to the natural inclination for a child to form a bond with caregivers or a few special adults (Bowlby, 1958; Grossman & Grossman, 2005). Grossman and Grossman state "attachments are the natural pre-requisite for becoming emotionally and socially acculturated" (p. 10). Attachment theory promotes the preeminent importance of social acculturation, first for survival and ultimately for successful adaptation to later life. Social acculturation incorporates adaptive skills of being able first to socially interact with others and later to be responsive to the needs of others—critical components of adaptive skills development.

The instinctive inclination to form an attachment with one's caregiver serves other adaptive functions as well. For example, from an evolutionary perspective, the formation of attachments helps infants ensure access to emotional and social resources and other resources they need to survive. As such, the skills required to form attachments are among the most important early adaptive skills infants must acquire. The formation and maintenance of secure attachments help children acquire these resources and thus foster their mental and physical health (Grossman & Grossman, 2005).

Clinicians focus on the abilities and behaviors displayed by an infant or toddler when assessing adaptive skills. The framework of attachment theory may trigger the following two questions: What roles do infants play in forming this attachment? How successful are they at establishing and maintaining the attachment? Typically, developing children begin life with several instinctual drives that assist in this task. For example, normal healthy newborns are able to suck, cling, cry, and smile. Attachment is developed through the expression of these drives (Bowlby, 1958). Thus, secure attachments are critically important adaptive skill for infants. For example, an infant may cry for its mother, then soothe when in her arms. Likewise, infants smile when approached by special adults in their lives, again helping to foster a secure attachment with those individuals important to an infant's survival (Bowlby, 1958). To measure these critical abilities, the adaptive behavior scale of the Bayley-III asks parents to rate how often their infant or toddler displays a special closeness or relationship to a parent, runs to greet special family members and friends, and responds differently to familiar and unfamiliar people.

The importance of assessing such adaptive skills as sucking, crying, and the ability to be soothed is highlighted by the fact that not all newborns are equipped to employ these instinctive drives successfully. For various reasons, some infants lack the ability or stamina to demonstrate these instinctive behaviors, thus placing them at-risk for less than optimal development. For example, infants with craniofacial anomalies may lack the physical capacity to employ these skills; premature infants may not have all skills in place at time of birth, or they may lack the stamina to use them. Scenarios such as these illustrate the need to examine adaptive behavior when assessing the development of infants and toddlers.

Synactive Theory of Development

Similar to attachment theory, the *synactive theory of development* assumes that early adaptive functioning relies heavily on instinctive abilities being present at birth. However, this theory focuses on infants' reactions to the world around them rather than their reactions solely to their social partners. The synactive theory of development recognizes that a neonate's primary job is to adapt to life outside the womb and develop neurobehavioral competence. For example, the newborn first needs to gain control over his or her physiological system, including breathing, heart rate, and temperature control. Next, the newborn needs to organize and differentiate his or her motor system, including learning to gain control of the range, smoothness, and complexity of his/her movements (Brazleton, 2000; Robertson, Bacher, & Huntington, 2001). Newborns also organize their states of consciousness, including deep sleep, light sleep, indeterminate drowsy, wide awake alert, fussy alert, and crying. Infants achieve control over the transitions between states of consciousness as they develop their adaptive skills.

The synactive theory of development provides a framework for understanding infants' neurobehavioral competencies and organization (e.g., sleep–wake cycles, crying, attention, self-regulation) by highlighting five subsystems that guide an infant's interaction with his/her environment. These subsystems include the autonomic system, the motor system, the state-organizational system, the attention and interaction system, and a self-regulatory balancing system that integrates and organizes the other subsystems. According to this theory,

Discussion Box 16.1

From the first moments after birth, neonates begin communicating with their caregivers. Crying initially is utilized to communicate needs. As the infant grows, gestures, differential use of facial expressions, and utterances become more common. Language assessment almost always includes assessment of the components of language in isolation (e.g., expressive and receptive abilities). However, in order for the evaluation to provide optimal information for diagnostic and planning purposes, more functional pragmatic communication skills and abilities must be evaluated. When examining the pragmatics of language, the observer also should consider the child's ability to use and manipulate verbal as well as nonverbal communicative strategies in a social context. As mentioned previously, and with the development of many adaptive skills, the environment can enhance or interfere with the promotion of functional communication skills. For example, parenting behaviors (e.g., trips to the library and reading to infants and toddlers), have been related to adaptive communication among preschoolers (Arterberry & Bornstein, 2007).

The intersection of pragmatic function and ability can be addressed through adaptive skills assessment and thus can be critical to understanding developmental disabilities. For example, functional assessment of skills may be one of the most useful methods to distinguish children with autism spectrum disorders from those with general developmental delay. Observation of home movies enabled blind observers to distinguish infants who later would be diagnosed with autism from those who were typically developing as well as those who later would be diagnosed with mental retardation. In particular, early functional communications skills (e.g., orienting to name, eye gaze) differed among the samples with and without autism (Osterling, Dawson, & Munson, 2002).

Consider issues in the assessment of functional communication of neonates. What issues should be considered, and how should they be assessed?

these subsystems interact with one another during each stage of development. The purpose of the self-regulatory subsystem is to balance and synthesize the actions of the other four subsystems.

Autonomic System

The autonomic system includes the regulation of bodily functions. For example, this subsystem addresses the infant's immediate need to regulate cardiopulmonary activity, bowel movements, hiccoughing, gagging, and blood flow (Als, 1982). The newborn is learning to utilize information from the environment while mastering the demands of the autonomic nervous system. The world around newborns helps them to learn about themselves (Brazleton, 1990a). Various senses are employed while they are exploring their world. Specifically, newborns often rely upon their olfactory senses. For example, Schaal (2005) hypothesizes that amniotic fluid, which commonly contacts the nasal receptors in utero, carries odors similar to the odors present in new mother's breast milk. Similarity, its smell likely serves an adaptive function by increasing the likelihood that babies are enticed to nurse. Some newborns and mothers must learn to nurse. A neonate's ability to rely on his/her olfaction senses to aid in the process of nursing may constitute an adaptive skill. The adaptive behaviors related to the autonomic system predominately are assessed formally by pediatric specialists.

Motor System

The motor system includes posture, movement abilities, and muscle tone (Als, 1988). Items on the ABAS-II, Bayley-III, and Vineland-II assess infants' motor abilities, progressing from the ability to follow a moving object by moving his/her head, lifting one's head to look around, and rolling over, through the ability to manipulate materials such as shaking toys, reaching for objects, and ultimately using objects as tools. Infants' gross motor skills progress from gaining basic trunk and head control, moving to and maintaining a sitting position, standing with and without support, and progressing through a series of complex gross motor activities required to accomplish other functional tasks (e.g., squatting to lift a desired object, balancing then hopping on one foot, running, and skipping). The synactive theory underscores the importance of motor abilities in their enabling an infant to accomplish other important functional and social tasks.

State-Organizational System

The state-organizational system addresses the infant's ability to cycle between quiet sleep, active sleep, active–quiet transitional sleep, sleep–wake transition, and wakefulness—including crying. A study of respiration and body movements of sleeping newborns found that, consistent with the synactive theory of development, neonates commonly cycle among quiet sleep, active sleep, active–quiet transitional sleep, sleep–wake transition, and wakefulness (Thoman & McDowell, 1989). One of the most important jobs of the neonate is "learning to control alert states and maintain habituated states in sleep" (Brazleton, 1990a, p. 1662). The infants' caretakers play a primary role in helping them acquire the skills needed to adapt to sleep schedules that meet both the infants' and the families' needs (Brazleton, 1990b, 2000). Therefore, a primary goal in the assessment of the neonate is estimating the state control and effective sleep states of the newborn (Brazleton, 1990a, 2000; Thoman & McDowell, 1989). Accordingly, the ABAS-II and the adaptive scale of the Bayley-III ask caregivers how often infants and toddlers sleep through most of the night.

Attention and Interaction System

The attention and interaction system addresses an infant's ability to attain and maintain an alert and attentive state. The primary developmental task of neonates is the *differentiation,* or shifting and internal organizing, of the attentional–interactive system. Importantly, the newborn has the help of primary caregivers when working toward this adaptive skill, again highlighting the importance of attachment in acquiring adaptive skills (Als, 1988; Als, Butler, Kosta, & McAnulty, 2005). Moreover, the attentional–interactive system addresses the adaptive functions of crying. The adaptive purposes of cries often are apparent shortly after birth. For example, infants commonly cry in response to physiological needs such as hunger and discomfort. These cries serve the purpose of letting the infant's primary caretaker know the infant is in need of something (Brazleton, 1990b). The presence of crying to communicate physiological needs is an adaptive skill. The ABAS-II, the Vineland-II, and the adaptive scale of the Bayley-III ask caregivers if infants are able to raise and lower voices to express different feelings and to cry to communicate.

Assessment of Adaptive Behavior

Measurement of Adaptive Behavior in Young Children

The assessment of adaptive behavior often is considered essential when evaluating young children, especially when assessing children suspected of developmental delays. When assessing adaptive behavior, the examiner needs to know what a child typically does, not what a child is capable of doing. Therefore,

Discussion Box 16.2

SELF-HELP SKILLS

As the young child develops, so does his/her adaptive self-help skills. For example, an infant may go from being able to swallow only liquids, to then swallow strained and mashed food, and then to feed him/herself solid foods. Positive feeding experiences are related both to an infant's health status and a mother's evaluation of caregiving experiences (Pridham, Chin-Yu, & Brown, 2001).

The intersection of physical and motor development, cultural expectations, and environmental opportunities can result in different behavior patterns exhibited by children of similar ages. For example, a study of Caucasian, Puerto Rican, and Filipino infants found differences in such daily living skills associated with eating. For example, the eating of solid foods, on average, occurred at 6.2 months for Filipino children and at 10.1 months for Puerto Rican children. The independent use of a training cup typically was acquired at 12.0 months for Caucasian children, 17.1 months for Puerto Rican children, and 21.9 months for Filipino children (Carlson & Harwood, cited in Center on the Social and Emotional Foundations for Early Learning, 2001).

In small groups discuss how you think your culture might have impacted your adaptive development. What needs to be considered with regard to diversity when assessing adaptive behavior development?

Discussion Box 16.3

FUNCTIONAL ADAPTIVE SKILLS

Functional adaptive skills (i.e., communication, community use, health and safety, leisure, self-care, self-direction, home living, social and motor skills) are influenced by the unfolding of biological qualities, parental expectations, home environments, and early care techniques. Both the home environment and early care techniques employed (e.g., Kangaroo Care, which includes skin-to-skin contact between mothers and infants and exclusive breastfeeding) impact the motor and functional communication development among high-risk, premature infants (Feldman, Eidelman, Sirota, & Weller, 2002). Likewise, children with special needs who received higher quality of care displayed higher adaptive behaviors (Booth & Kelly, 2002).

Maternal reports of adaptive behavior for 20-month-olds in rural and urban settings in Italy and the United States suggest differences in adaptive skills by gender, setting, and country. Compared to U.S. children, those in Italy displayed higher adaptive communication and motor skills. Compared to boys, girls displayed higher general adaptive behavior and communication skills and lower motor skills. Compared to children in rural settings, those in urban settings demonstrated higher motor skills and lower daily living skills (Bornstein, Giusti, Leach, & Venuti, 2005).

In small groups, discuss what you think might have contributed to the differences found based on gender, setting, and country. What clinical implications might this study have?

assessments of adaptive behavior commonly are conducted through the use of third-party informants. Individuals who spend many hours a day with children are the best informants to utilize when assessing adaptive skills. These individuals often are the ones who best know the child's typical behaviors in various settings. Informants such as parents, grandparents, and childcare providers often are asked to participate in the assessment of adaptive behavior in young children. Three measures frequently utilized in the assessment of adaptive behavior in young children include the *Adaptive Behavior Assessment Scale—Second Edition* (ABAS-II; Harrison & Oakland, 2003), the Adaptive Behavior Scale of the *Bayley Scales of Infant and Toddler Development, Third Edition* (Bayley-III; Bayley, 2006), and the *Vineland Adaptive Behavior Scales, Second Edition* (Vineland-II; Sparrow, Cicchetti, & Balla, 2005). Each of these measures is described here.

Adaptive Behavior Assessment Scale—Second Edition

The ABAS-II (Harrison & Oakland, 2003) is designed to measure the adaptive behavior and skills of persons from birth through age 89. Five forms are provided: Parent/Primary Caregiver Form (for ages 0–5), Teacher/Day Care Provider Form (for ages 2–5), Parent Form (for ages 5–21), Teacher Form (for ages 5–21), and an Adult Form (for ages 16–89). Its standardization sample is representative of 1999–2000 U.S. census data in reference to gender, race/ethnicity, parental education, and proportion of individuals with disabilities. Parent forms are available in Spanish, and all five forms are available in French-Canadian.

The ABAS-II is consistent with models advocated by the AAIDD (1992, 2002). Ten skill area scores combine to produce standard scores in their respective domains: conceptual (communication, functional academics, and self-direction skills), social (social and leisure skills), and practical (self-care, home or school living, community use, health and safety). Work is assessed for adults and motor skills for young children; they do not contribute to one of the three domains. A general adaptive composite is derived from the skill scores.

The ABAS-II demonstrates strong psychometric qualities. Internal consistency is high, with reliability coefficients of .85 to .99 for the general adaptive composite, three adaptive behavior domains, and skill areas. Test–retest reliability coefficients are in the .80s and .90s for the general adaptive composite, three adaptive behavior domains, and skill areas. Interrater reliability coefficients (e.g., between teachers, daycare providers, and parents) range from the .60s to the .80s for the skill areas and are in the .90s for the general adaptive composite.

Its construct validity is strong as displayed through factor analyses. Its concurrent validity with the Vineland Adaptive Behavior Scales-Classroom Edition's Adaptive Behavior Composite is .82. Clinical validity is extensive and highly evident.

Critical reviews of the ABAS-II noted several advantages over other measures of adaptive behavior (Meikamp & Suppa, 2005). The ABAS-II behavior domains align well with the newest AAIDD recommendations. The scale allows for multiple respondents from multiple settings. The ABAS-II allows one to guess about behaviors. The scale provides respondents the opportunity to answer each question without a trained interview present.

In a separate review, Burns (2005) noted that the ABAS-II is based on sound theory and empirical methodology, the norm group is sufficiently representative and large, scores from the general adaptive composite are adequate for eligibility and entitlement decisions, and domain scores are useful for clinical and intervention utility.

Reviewers Rust and Wallace (2004) note that the items, manual, and record forms are easy to use. The ABAS-II conforms to revised AAIDD domain guidelines and, as such, provides an important addition to the assessment of adaptive behavior. The ABAS-II strengthens the comprehensive assessment of adaptive behavior for mental retardation and is technically superior to its competitors. Thus, the ABAS-II is viewed as being technically sound and valuable when assessing an individual's adaptive functioning pursuant to diagnosis, planning for effective services, and use in subsequent evaluations.

Bayley Scale of Infant and Toddler Development—Third Edition

The Bayley-III, the newest revision of the *Bayley Scales of Infant Development,* is an individually administered instrument whose primary purposes are to identify children with developmental delay and provide information for intervention planning. The Bayley-III assesses infant and toddler development across five domains: cognitive, language (receptive and expressive), motor (gross and fine), social-emotional, and adaptive. Assessment of the first three scales is conducted using items administered to the child. Assessment of the last two scales is conducted using primary caregiver responses to a questionnaire.

The Adaptive Behavior Scale of the Bayley-III is derived from items for children, ages birth through 5, on the ABAS-II. These scales are based on (1) a concept of adaptive behavior promoted by AAIDD; (2) legal and professional standards applicable to disability classifications, special education classifications, the *Diagnostic and Statistical Manual of Mental Disorders- Fourth Edition, Text Revision (DSM-IV-TR),* and federal (i.e., the *Individuals with Disabilities Education Act)* and state special education regulations; and (3) diagnostic, classification, and intervention research conducted to investigate the skills of people with various disabilities (Bayley, 2006).

Purposes

The Adaptive Behavior Scale of the Bayley-III evaluates the functional skills necessary for infants and young children to become more independent. This scale focuses on a parent or caregiver's report of observable behaviors as to what a child is observed to be unable to do, able do with assistance, and able to do independently, as well as a caregiver's thoughts on what a child may be able to do if provided with the appropriate opportunity. Parents determine what their child is able to do, may be able to do, and is unable to do based on their previous interactions with their child (Bayley, 2006).

Definition of Adaptive Behavior

The AAIDD concluded that adaptive behavior comprises "the collection of conceptual, social, and practical skills that have been learned by people in order to function in their everyday lives" (2002, p. 41). Therefore, the ABAS-II, and thus the Adaptive Behavior Scale of the Bayley-III, defines the adaptive skills measured as practical, everyday skills required for children to function and meet environmental demands.

Adaptive Qualities Assessed

Ten specific skill areas are measured by the Adaptive Behavior Scale of the Bayley III: communication (e.g., speech, nonverbal communication, and listening), community use (e.g., infant or toddler's interest in activities outside the home and the infant or toddler's recognition of different facilities), health and safety skills (e.g., skills related to being cautious and keeping out of physical danger), leisure (e.g., an individual's skills related to playing, engaging in games at home, and following rules), self-care (e.g., eating, toileting, cleaning self, and bathing), self-direction (e.g., making independent choices, following directions, and utilizing self-control), functional pre-academics (e.g., letter recognition, counting, and drawing shapes), home living (e.g., helping adults with household tasks and taking care of personal possessions), social skills (e.g., getting along with others, using manners, assisting others, and recognizing emotions), and motor skills (e.g., locomotion and manipulation of the environment; Bayley, 2006). As noted later in this chapter, some skill areas develop later than others. Thus, not all 10 skill areas are assessed at every age.

The Adaptive Behavior Scale of the Bayley-III is identical to the Parent/Primary Caregiver Form of the ABAS-II for ages 0–5. Therefore, both the ABAS-II for ages 0 through 5 and the Adaptive Behavior Composite of the Bayley-III comprise 241 items. When assessing infants from birth through 11 months, the following skill areas are addressed: communication, health and safety, leisure, self-care, self-direction, social, and motor. For toddlers and preschoolers ages 12 through 42 months, these same skill areas are addressed as well as the following: community use, functional pre-academics, and home living. Data from all assessed skill areas are used to compute the Adaptive Behavior Scale Composite, which is the total score. The Adaptive Behavior Scale also provides scores on three domains (i.e., conceptual, practical, and social) and all assessed skills. The skill areas included in each of the three adaptive domains are outlined in Table 16.1.

Scoring the Adaptive Behavior Scale of the Bayley-III

The Adaptive Behavior Scale of the Bayley-III is congruent with the ABAS-II. Thus, both use the same scoring methods. After the Adaptive Behavior Scale of the Bayley- III has been completed by parents or other care providers, the examiner can derive scores either by entering the total scores for each skill area into a computer scoring program or by consulting tables found in the appendix

16.1 Skill Areas Comprising Adaptive Domains for the Parent/Primary Caregiver of the ABAS-II and the Adaptive Behavior Composite of the Bayley-III

Adaptive Domain	Birth–11 months (ABAS-II)	1–5 years (ABAS-II), and 1–3.5 years (Bayley-III)
Conceptual	Communication	Communication
	Self-Direction	Functional Pre-academics
		Self-Direction
Social	Leisure	Leisure
	Social	Social
Practical		Self-Care
		Home Living
		Health & Safety
		Community Use

From: *Adaptive Behavior Assessment System–Second Edition*, by P. Harrison & T. Oakland, 2003, San Antonio,TX: Harcourt Assessment.

of the Bayley-III manual. If the computer option is employed, an assessment summary provides norm-referenced scaled scores for each skill area (mean = 10, standard deviation = 3), the three domains, and the composite (mean = 100, standard deviation = 15), and then graphs the data. The computer scoring program compares a child's development between the skill areas within each adaptive domain and between domains to enable the examiner to identify the child's strengths and weaknesses.

Psychometric Properties of the Bayley-III Adaptive Behavior Scale

Internal Consistency

Data on the ABAS-II's internal consistency and test–retest reliability can be used to establish internal consistency for the Bayley-III Adaptive Behavior Scale (Bayley, 2006). The internal consistency of the Adaptive Behavior Scale was examined for children in 10 age groups: 0–3 months, 4–7 months, 8–11 months, 12–15 months, 16–19 months, 20–23 months, 24–29 months, 30–35 months, 36–41 months, and 42–47 months. Internal consistency estimates ranged from .86 to .98 for the composite score, from .90 to .92 for the three adaptive domains, and .79 to .92 for the skill areas (Bayley, 2006).

Test–Retest Reliability

Test–retest reliability was estimated by having 207 parents of infants, toddlers, or preschoolers to complete the ABAS-II on two different days, 2 days to 5 weeks apart. The test–retest reliability for the composite score ranged from .86 to .92 for the following three age groups: birth to 11 months, 12 to 23 months, and 24 to 35 months. The test–retest reliabilities generally were above .80 for the three adaptive domains and above .70 for each skill area.

Content Validity

The theory and constructs of the ABAS-II (and consequently those items used for the Bayley-III Adaptive Behavior Scale) are based on AAIDD's definition of adaptive behavior; legal and professional standards applicable to disability classifications, special education classifications, the *DSM-IV-TR,* and federal (i.e., the *Individuals with Disabilities Education Act)* and state special education regulations; and diagnostic, classification, and intervention research that investigated the skills of people with various disabilities. Therefore, evidence of content validity is considerable. Readers are encouraged to see Harrison & Oakland (2003) for a more complete discussion of the test's reliability and validity.

Vineland Adaptive Behavior Scales—Second Edition

The Vineland-II are designed to measure the adaptive behavior and skills of persons from birth through age 90. Each of the Vineland-II measures is administered through parent or teacher interview or through parent or teacher ratings. Moreover, scoring the Vineland-II scales is facilitated by the use of a computer scoring program (Sparrow, Cicchetti, & Balla, 2005).

The Vineland-II is used in the assessment of individuals with developmental delays, developmental disabilities, and intellectual deficits. The Vineland-II is recommended for use to support diagnoses, provide daily caregivers' perspectives on a child's behavior, determine eligibility for special education, plan interventions, and monitor progress (Sparrow et al., 2005).

Purposes

The Vineland II assesses the personal and social skills needed for young children's everyday living. This measure focuses on a parent, primary caregiver, or teacher's report of observable behaviors a child *usually* performs without physical help or reminders, *sometimes or partially* without help or reminders, or *never* without help or reminders. Parents, caregivers, and teachers decide what their child is able to perform, is sometimes or partially able to perform, or never is able to perform based on their daily interactions with the child (Sparrow et al., 2005).

Definition of Adaptive Behavior

The Vineland-II defines adaptive behaviors in young children as personal and social skills needed for daily living (Sparrow et al., 2005). For example, based on the Synactive Theory of Development and Attachment Theory, a baby's ability to respond to their caregiver's voice, an early skill assessed by the Vineland-II, is an adaptive behavior that promotes development. Likewise, a young child's ability to open his/her mouth when offered food, another adaptive skill addressed in the Vineland-II, is necessary for typical daily living.

Adaptive Qualities Assessed

The Vineland-II Survey Interview Form and the Parent/Caregiver Rating Form assess four skill areas: communication, daily living, socialization, and motor skills. The Vineland-II Teacher Rating Form also provides an assessment of those four skill areas. The communication domain assesses how a child lets his or her wants and needs be known (i.e., expressive communication); a child's ability to listen, attend, and understand (i.e., receptive communication); and how a child understands the function of letters and words (i.e., written communication). The daily living skills domain assesses a child's ability to care for oneself, whereas the socialization domain assesses a child's ability to get along with others and have appropriate interpersonal relationships. Additionally, the motor domain assesses a child's use of small muscle groups (e.g., fine motor skills) and large muscle groups (e.g., gross motor skills). Ratings of maladaptive behaviors (e.g., externalizing, or acting out behaviors, and internalizing behaviors) also may be obtained through the use of the Vineland-II (Sparrow et al., 2005).

Scoring the Vineland-II

After a parent, caregiver, or teacher has completed the scale, the examiner can obtain scores either by entering the total scores for each area assessed into a computer scoring system or by consulting the tables found in the appendix of the appropriate Vineland-II administration and scoring manual (e.g., parent or teacher rating, or interview form). If computer scoring is employed, as assessment summary provides norm-referenced V-scale scores for each subdomain and subscale (mean = 15, standard deviation = 3), a standard score (mean = 100, standard deviation = 15) for each of the four major domain areas, percentile ranks, age-equivalents, and a list of relative strengths and weaknesses (Sparrow et al., 2005).

Psychometric Properties of the Vineland-II

Reliability

The Vineland-II demonstrates strong psychometric qualities. Internal consistency is strong, with most reliability coefficients higher than .75. The majority of test–retest reliability coefficients are in the .80s and .90s for the general adaptive composite, the four adaptive behavior domains, and individual subscales (e.g., receptive communication, expressive communication, written communication, personal daily living skills, domestic daily living skills, community daily living skills, interpersonal relationships, play and leisure time, coping skills, gross motor skills, and fine motor skills). More than 50% of the 154 subdomain reliabilities reported in the Vineland-II manual are greater than .90, and only 6 had reported internal consistency reliabilities less than .80. Interrater reliability coefficients (e.g., between teachers, daycare providers, and parents) range from the .50s to the .80s for four adaptive behavior domains, the skill areas, and the general adaptive composite (Sparrow et al., 2005).

Validity

The Vineland-II manual describes a strong link between theoretical and empirical information, test content, and the behaviors and skills important in adaptive functioning at various ages. Its concurrent validity with the ABAS-II is .82. Clinical validity is provided in the test manual (Sparrow et al., 2005).

Adaptive Behavior Viewed Within the Context of the ICF, Children & Youth Version

The International Classification of Functioning, Disability and Health: Children & Youth Version (ICF-Y; World Health Organization [WHO], 2007) provides a downward extension of WHO's (2001) International Classification of Functioning, Disability and Health (ICF). As discussed in chapter 2 of this book, the ICF-Y provides a universal method and common language to describe a child's health, functioning, and disability.

The model's emphasis on activities and participation includes many behaviors common to the assessment of adaptive behavior. The term *activities* refer to tasks or actions a client is able to perform. Examples for younger children include naming 20 or more familiar objects or walking. The term *participation*

Research Box 16.1

TEACHER RATING OF ADAPTIVE BEHAVIOR

Voelker, S. L., Johnston, T. C., Agar, C., Gragg, M., & Menna, R. (2007). Vineland Survey: Self-administered checklist format for teachers of young children in rehabilitation. *Journal of Developmental Physical Disabilities, 19,* 177–186.

Objective: The objective of this study was to examine the feasibility of using the Vineland-II Checklist Teacher Form to assess the adaptive abilities of low functioning preschool children.

Method: Participants included 36 preschool children in a self-contained, highly structured day-treatment rehabilitation center in Canada. The measures utilized included the Vineland Classroom Edition, the Vineland Survey Edition, and the Diagnostic Inventory for Screening Children. Lead teachers, all whom held masters degrees in special education, concurrently completed the Vineland Classroom and Survey Editions for each participating child in a checklist format. The Vineland Survey Edition was also administered to each child's mother. Teacher and parent reports were administered within one week of each other.

Findings: The Classroom Edition of the Vineland yielded statistically significant higher ability levels than the Classroom Survey or Parent Survey form of the Vineland. Results from the two survey forms (parent and teacher) did not statistically differ from one another when the Teacher Survey Form was administered in a checklist format.

Conclusion: The authors concluded that there is support for the use of the Classroom Survey Edition of the Vineland in a checklist format.

Questions:

1. Do you think it was essential for the researchers to assess adaptive skills as reported by teachers and parents when conducting this study? Why or why not?
2. Why might the Classroom Edition yield spuriously high results with this population?

   a. Answer: floor effects

3. Would you consider using the Vineland Classroom Edition in a checklist format after considering these results? Why or why not?
4. In what ways could the methods of this study be improved upon in a follow-up study?

refers to activities that become integrated into one's life. Examples for young children include regularly describing their room through the use of correct terms or walking to the store with a parent. The use of the ICF-Y model allows clinicians to indicate whether a child has an activity or performance deficit.

This distinction between activities and participation was incorporated in the ABAS-II and Bayley-III. A child who displays an activity deficit never has demonstrated a particular skill (e.g., never has walked without help) and receives a score of 0 for that item. A child who displays a performance deficit has demonstrated a skill (e.g., has walked without help) yet never or almost never displays this skill when needed; thus, the child receives a score of 1 on that item. This distinction between an activity and performance deficit may be important when guiding developmental and rehabilitation efforts. For example, activity deficits require the initial development of a skill. In contract, participation deficits require the elicitation and use of a skill in ways that are rewarded and become self-sustaining.

Activities and participation include the following nine domains (with examples of corresponding adaptive skills in parentheses): learning and applying knowledge (e.g., functional academics), general tasks and demands (e.g., work), communication, mobility (e.g., fine and gross motor skills), self-care, domestic life (e.g., school and home living), interpersonal interactions and relationships (e.g., social skills), major life areas (e.g., health and safety, leisure skills), and community, social, and civic life (e.g., community use; Ditterline & Oakland, 2010). Thus, these nine domains are found on both the ABAS-II and the Bayley-III. Clinicians should rely on the Bayley-III for a more detailed assessment of a child's cognitive and communication skills.

Summary

In this chapter, adaptive behavior was defined as the ways in which individuals meet their daily personal needs and deal with the natural and social demands in their environment. Specifically, adaptive behavior development in young children was discussed, and two prominent theories of early development (attachment theory and the synactive theory of development) were explained to facilitate the understanding of adaptive skill development during the early childhood years. Additionally, professional and legal issues regarding the assessment of adaptive behavior also were discussed. Two specific forms of legislation pertinent to work with young children were discussed: the No Child Left Behind Act of 2001 and the Individuals with Disabilities Education Improvement Act (IDEIA). Next, the assessment of adaptive behavior in young children through the use of the ABAS-II, the Bayley-III, and the Vineland-II were discussed. Finally, the utility of assessing young children's adaptive behavior is illustrated through two case studies in the accompanying manual.

References

Als, H. (1982). Toward a synactive theory of development: Promise for the assessment and support of infant individuality. *Infant Mental Health Journal, 3*(4), 229–243.

Als, H., Butler, S., Kosta, S., & McAnulty, G. (2005). The assessment of preterm infants' behavior (APIB): Furthering the understanding and measurement of neurodevelopmental competence in preterm and full-term infants. *Mental Retardation and Developmental Disabilities, 11,* 94–102.
American Association on Intellectual and Developmental Disability. (1992). Definitions, classifications, and systems of supports (9th ed.). Washington, DC: Author.
American Association on Intellectual and Developmental Disability. (2002). Mental retardation: Definition, classification, and systems of support (10th ed.). Washington, DC: Author.
Apling, R. N., & Jones, N. L. (2005). *Congressional research service report for Congress, Individuals with Disabilities Education Act (IDEA): Analysis of changes made by P.L. 108–446.* Washington, DC: The Library of Congress.
Arterberry, M., & Bornstein, M. (2007). Early attention and literacy experiences predict adaptive communication. *First Language, 27*(2), 175–189.
Bayley, N. (2006). *Bayley Scales of Infant and Toddler Development, Third Edition: Technical manual.* San Antonio, TX: Harcourt Assessment Inc.
Booth, C. L., & Kelly, J. F. (2002). Child care effects on the development of toddlers with special needs. *Early Childhood Research Quarterly, 17(*2), 171–196.
Bowlby, J. (1958). The nature of the child's tie to his mother. *International Journal of Psychoanalysis, 39,* 350–373.
Brazleton, T. B. (1990a). Saving the bathwater. *Child Development, 61,* 1661–1671.
Brazleton, T. B. (1990b). Crying and colic. *Infant Mental Health Journal, 11*(4), 349–356.
Brazleton, T. B. (2000). In response to Louis Sander's challenging paper. *Infant Mental Health Journal, 21*(1–2), 52–62.
Burns, M. K. (2005). Review of the Adaptive Behavior Assessment System–Second Edition. In R. Spies & B. Plake (Eds.), *The sixteenth mental measurements yearbook* (pp. 1–3). Lincoln, NE: Buros Institute of Mental Measurements.
Council for Exceptional Children. (2004). *The New IDEA: CEC's summary of significant issues.* Arlington, VA: Council for Exceptional Children.
Ditterline, J., Banner, D., Oakland, T., & Becton, D. (2008). Adaptive behavior profiles of students with disabilities. *Journal of Applied School Psychology, 24,* 191–208.
Ditterline, J., & Oakland, T. (2010). Adaptive behavior. In E. Mpofu & T. Oakland (Eds.), *Assessment in rehabilitation and health.* Boston: Allyn & Bacon.
Feldman, R., Eidelman, A. I., Sirota, A., & Weller, A. (2002). Comparison of Skin-to-Skin (Kangaroo) and traditional care: Parenting outcomes and preterm infant development. *Pediatrics, 110,* 16–26.
Grossman, K. E., & Grossman, K. (2005). *Universality of human social attachment as an adaptive process.* Regensburg, Germany: Institut für Psychologie, Universität Regensburg.
Harrison, P., & Oakland, T. (2003). *Adaptive Behavior Assessment System–Second Edition.* San Antonio, TX: Harcourt Assessment.
Harrison, P., & Oakland, T. (2008). *ABAS-II Interpretative Report.* San Antonio, TX: Harcourt Assessment.
Meikamp, J., & Suppa, C. H. (2005). Review of the Adaptive Behavior Assessment System—Second Edition. In R. Spies & B. Plake (Eds.), *The sixteenth mental measurements yearbook* (pp. 1–3). Lincoln, NE: Buros Institute of Mental Measurements. Association of School Psychologists.
Osterling, J.A., Dawson, G., & Munson, J.A. (2002). Early recognition of 1-year-old infants with autism spectrum disorder versus mental retardation. *Development and Psychopathology, 14,* 239-251.
Pridham, K., Chin-Yu, L., & Brown, R. (2001). Mothers' evaluation of their caregiving for premature and full-term infants through the first year: Contributing factors. *Research in Nursing and Health, 24,* 157–169.
Robertson, S. S., Bacher, L. F., & Huntington, N. L. (2001). The integration of body movement and attention in young infants. *Physiological Science, 12*(6), 523–526.
Rust, J. O., & Wallace, M. A. (2004). Test review: Adaptive Behavior Assessment System—Second Edition. *Journal of Psychoeducational Assessment, 22,* 367–373.
Schaal, B. (2005). From Amnion to Colostrum to Milk: Odor bridging in early developmental transitions. In B. Hopkins & S. P. Johnson, (Eds.), *Prenatal development of postnatal functions* (pp. 51–102).Westport, CT: Praeger Publishers/Greenwood Publishing Group.
Sparrow, S. S., Cicchetti, D. V., & Balla, D. A. (2005). *Vineland Adaptive Behavior Scales, Second Edition.* Circle Pines, MN: AGS Publishing.

Thoman, E. B., & McDowell, K. (1989). Sleep cyclicity in infants during the earliest postnatal weeks. *Physiology and Behavior, 45*(3), 517–522.

U.S. Code Service. (2007). *20 USCS § 1400: Individuals with Disabilities Education Act.* Retrieved June 12, 2007, from: http://web.lexis-nexis.com/universe/document?_m=6af9d78cf01c007d8151e26c38f4192dand_doc num=1andwchp=dGLbVlz-zSkVband_md5=412bb646231d76b75426f221f 837233a

U.S. Department of Education. (2006). *The Individuals with Disabilities Education Improvement Act of 2004.* Retrieved June 13, 2007, from: http://www.ed.gov/about/offices/list/osers/osep/index.html

Voelker, S. L., Johnston, T. C., Agar, C., Gragg, M., & Menna, R. (2007). Vineland Survey: Self-administered checklist format for teachers of young children in rehabilitation. *Journal of Developmental Physical Disabilities, 19,* 177–186.

World Health Organization. (2001). *International classification of functioning, disability and health* (ICF). Geneva: Author.

World Health Organization, (2007). *International Classification of Functioning, Disability and Health: Children & Youth Version.* Geneva: Author.

Floyd Webster Rudmin

17 Acculturation Measures

Overview

All nations are multicultural to some degree, and this is increasing due to economic and demographic disparities. Cultures have tremendous resilience and may survive even in minority status facing coercive assimilation practices. Medical research and medical services have begun to gauge the social, psychological, and biological consequences of cultural minority status. This is important in an epidemiological frame, to predict illnesses for cultural groups and to predict a population's comprehension of, and cooperation with, preventative public health programs. But minorities are in complex relationships with dominant groups, often with historic racist overtones that may still leave some residue of beliefs that minority culture should be less healthful than mainstream culture. This chapter provides a comprehensive overview of the history, current practices, and research on the assessment of acculturation. It addresses the many problems and difficulties in the assessment of acculturation and in the use of acculturation research to understand health-related issues.

Learning Objectives

By the end of the chapter, the reader should be able to:

1. Outline the history of the concept of acculturation as an aspect of how cultural minorities react to continuous contact with a dominating majority and with the dynamic forces of modernization;
2. Relate the concept and theory of acculturation to three other concepts: (1) acculturative stress as both a motivator of acculturation and a consequence of acculturation, (2) acculturation attitudes and orientations, and (3) acculturative learning;
3. Evaluate the origins of acculturation measures (1) in the numerous permutations of pairing specific minority and dominant cultures, (2) in the different research traditions, and (3) in the competing psychometric approaches;
4. Explain the importance to health care research of valid and reliable measures of acculturation; and
5. Critically synthesize the evidence for recommendations on the health consequences of acculturation.

Introduction

When newspapers, TV, or medical journals report that Native Americans face a suicide epidemic, or that Hispanics have a greater risk of diabetes, or that immigrants are not using health services, then there is need to see if such health disparities are due in part to continued reliance on minority culture practices, or to the loss of minority culture through assimilation, or to the stresses of being bicultural. Such processes of culture contact and culture change are called *acculturation* (Redfield, Linton, & Herskovits, 1936).

There is a long history of concern that acculturation processes may adversely affect health (Rudmin, 2003a, 2003b, 2003c). Past stereotypes of immigrants and native peoples considered them to be unhygienic, ignorant, and disease-prone, qualities that assimilation was thought to correct (Escobar, Nervi, & Gara, 2000; Escobar & Vega, 2000; Hunt, Schneider, & Comer, 2004; Lara, Gamboa, Kahramanian, Morales, & Bautista, 2005; Thielman, 1985). However, the first empirical study of immigrants by Thomas and Znaniecki (1918) concluded that assimilation leads to personality problems because the old mental schema (habits of perception, cognition, and emotion), based on traditional culture in rural communities, become dissociated from new mental schema needed for modern, urban, industrialized life. Thomas and Znaniecki conceived that there are three general acculturation orientations for the immigrant: (1) assimilate and suffer personality disintegration; (2) refuse to assimilate and live a restricted, maladaptive life; or (3) maintain traditional schema but creatively adjust them so as "to widen the control of his [sic] environment, to adapt to his purposes a continually increasing sphere of social reality" (p. 1856). During the nine decades following this formulation of acculturation, more than 100 such taxonomies of acculturation orientations were proposed (Rudmin, 2003a, 2003b).

In the 1930s and 1940s, the adjustment of immigrants in learning to accept American culture began to be measured with psychometric self-report scales (e.g., Campisi, 1947; Chief, 1940; Hoffman, 1934). In the 1950s, the concept of "acculturative stress" came into use but without definition (e.g., Ausubel, 1960; Barnett, Broom, Siegel, Vogt, & Watson, 1954). In the 1980s, academics and medical professionals in the United States began to study the effects of acculturation on the health of Hispanics (also labeled as Chicanos, Latinos, or as national identities). The first reviews of this research appeared in the early 1990s (e.g., Moyerman & Forman, 1992; Negy & Woods, 1992b; Rogler, Cortes, & Malgady, 1991). A similar focus came onto Asian immigrants (e.g., Kurasaki, Okasaki, & Sue, 2002; Salant & Lauderdale, 2003; Tabora & Flaskerud, 1994). A search of MEDLINE and of PsychINFO reveals that approximately 33% of all acculturation research is about Hispanic-Americans, and 25% is about Asian-Americans. In contrast, only 4% is about Black Americans, and only 2% is about aboriginal peoples.

Unfortunately, the quality of acculturation research has not been high. Reviews have often lamented the many faults in acculturation research:

> *The conceptualization and methods are so variant that it is almost impossible to integrate them, whether intuitively or by some objective procedure such as formal meta-analysis. (Taft, 1986, p. 343)*
>
> *The research needs new directions, proceeding from but not constricted by the assumptions and procedures in the work already done. (Rogler et al., 1991, p. 585)*
>
> *The primary deficiency in ACC [acculturation] studies is the lack of agreement as to the definition of the construct. (Negy & Woods, 1992b, p. 224)*
>
> *[S]tudies have been mainly descriptive and have not been used to develop and evaluate strategies to improve health care. (Sheldon & Parker, 1992, p. 104)*
>
> *The experience of psychiatric epidemiology has shown that no explanatory power is gained by the inclusion of multidimensional acculturation scales. (Escobar & Vega, 2000, p. 739)*
>
> *Because of the lack of consistency in study designs and findings, we are unable to draw conclusions about the effects of dietary acculturation on overall diet quality, immigrant associated dietary patterns, and chronic disease risk. (Satia-Abouta, Patterson, Neuhouser, & Elder, 2002, p. 1116)*
>
> *[T]his literature is highly fragmented in both how acculturation is assessed and how it relates to health. (Salant & Lauderdale, 2003, p. 87)*
>
> *Literature reviews that have examined the relationship between acculturation and the mental health status of Hispanic groups . . . have found a plethora of inconsistent and inconclusive findings. (Cabassa, 2003, p. 139)*
>
> *Despite its prominence in current research on the unequal distribution of poor health among ethnic minorities in the US, acculturation as a variable in health research is riddled with serious conceptual and factual errors. (Hunt et al., 2004, p. 981)*

> *The literature on acculturation to date lacks sufficient breadth and methodological rigor to make comprehensive and definitive evidence-based recommendations. (Lara et al., 2005, p. 383)*

> *There are numerous scales available to measure acculturation, perhaps reflecting its diverse conceptualizations. (Abraído-Lanza, Armbrister, Flórez, & Aguirre, 2006, p. 1343)*

This chapter cannot completely review and find correctives for thousands of studies done in several different disciplines across three decades. The goals here are more modest. Acculturation constructs are defined and the history of their measurement is briefly reviewed. The variety of methods of measuring these constructs are presented. Some of the confounds that have plagued acculturation research are explained, and recommendations are made for best practice. The chapter closes with a review of a few tentative findings on acculturation and health.

Importance of Acculturation to Rehabilitation and Health Services

Acculturation is not indexed in World Health Organization's (WHO) International Classification of Functioning, Disability and Health (ICF). Acculturation as a risk factor for illness is not easy to establish and, if established, acculturation is not easy to change at individual or community levels. Nevertheless, valid acculturation measures would be useful in the planning, implementation, and evaluation of public health campaigns directed at minority or multicultural communities, for example, concerning smoking reduction, nutrition promotion, or utilization of health services.

As shown in Table 17.1, the appearance of acculturation research in the medical and psychological literature is accelerating. There are several relatively new health journals with a focus on acculturation and related issues, for example, Cultural Diversity and Ethnic Minority Psychology, Ethnicity and Disease

17.1 Number of Articles Per Year With the Search Word "Acculturation" in the Title, Abstract, or Index Keywords

	ARTICLES PER YEAR IN	
DECADE	MEDLINE	PsychINFO
1950s	0.9	9.9
1960s	11.2	11.7
1970s	21.6	32.4
1980s	52.8	89.3
1990s	115.6	215.9
2000s	172.1	366.7

Journal, Journal of Cross-Cultural Gerontology, Journal of Immigrant and Minority Health, and Journal of Immigrant and Refugee Services.

The reasons for this acceleration are several. First, there are ever more minorities in the economically developed nations: high standards of living and labor shortages encourage immigration. Wars, oppression, and environmental pressures create increasing numbers of refugees. Also, demographic shifts follow from the high birth rates of some minority populations relative to the low birth rates of affluent majority populations. A recent U.S. Census Bureau headline announced that "Minority Population Tops 100 Million": one-third of the U.S. population is now ethnic minorities (Bernstein, 2007). Finally, as more minority individuals enter the health professions, they take interest in the health of their own group, and they have the cultural and research skills to undertake studies of acculturation and health.

Concepts of Culture, Enculturation, and Acculturation

Acculturation is concerned with *culture,* which is notoriously difficult to define (Olmedo, 1979). Culture includes visible aspects, such as behaviors, language, clothing, foods, architecture, and so on, and invisible aspects, which must be inferred, such as values, beliefs, social roles, or concepts of cleanliness. A very common error is to define culture by reference to nations or to geographic regions. Thus, there are studies, for example, about people of Hispanic culture adapting to American culture, or about Asian people adapting to Western culture. The findings of such studies are doubtful regardless of the details. Nations, regions, continents, and civilizations *contain* cultures; they are not cultures (Hunt et al., 2004). It is safe to say that there are no pure unicultural nations in the world. By one estimation, there are about 600 living languages and about 5,000 identifiable ethnic groups, all contained within fewer than 200 nations (Krymlicka, 1995). Even within well-defined ethnic groups, there are subcultures differentiated by social classes, castes, genders, age cohorts, or vocations.

Cultures are transmitted from one generation to the next. The process of learning one's first culture during childhood is called enculturation, that is, socialization into one's maternal culture. This involves natural learning processes such as imitation, but it also involves schooling and other forms of overt socialization. Culturally based behaviors, ways of thinking, social roles, and lifestyles become habituated and unconscious to the degree that they are "normal," "natural," and nearly invisible to the people in the culture. Enculturation is a life-long process because we encounter and learn new aspects of our own culture as we age, as we take on new social or vocational roles, and as we enter new institutions or move to new geographic regions. Furthermore, cultures are dynamic; they are always changing. Hence, people are continually learning the new aspects of their own culture, a recent example being cell phone etiquette.

If enculturation is first-culture acquisition, then acculturation is second-culture acquisition. It, too, is a process of cultural learning across the life span, and it, too, can involve natural learning as well as formal schooling. When one considers acculturation in contrast to enculturation, it is difficult to differentiate within-culture learning from between-culture learning, especially considering (1) that individuals do not know many aspects of their own culture,

(2) that cultures are dynamic and changing, and (3) that this dynamism includes diffusion from other cultures. For example, is an American learning yoga acculturating to Indian culture or enculturating to a new aspect of U.S. culture? When Campisi (1947) made his acculturation scale, he noted that it is difficult to specify American culture, for example, specific games, gestures, holidays, or foods, because these invariably came from some other cultures. For example, the decorated Christmas tree came from German culture; peanut butter and jazz came from Black culture.

History of Research and Practice in Assessment of Acculturation

The assessment of acculturation has diverged into three related measurement issues:

1. How distressing is cultural contact, and how much does this distress change?
2. What is the orientation of the acculturating person or group to acculturative learning?
3. How far has acculturative learning progressed?

Early Acculturation Constructs and Measures

The word *acculturation* was coined in 1880 by William Powell, director of the American Bureau of Ethnography, referring to processes of "mental evolution" when so-called primitive or inferior peoples use modern technology or otherwise imitate the behavior of superior peoples (Rudmin, 2003c). However, in 1888, anthropologist Franz Boas (1940) argued that acculturation is a universal human process regardless of cultural dominance or supposed superiority; he gave the example of European and American whalers imitating the harpoon head developed by the Eskimos. In 1936, a committee of the U.S. Social Science Research Council made the authoritative definition: "Acculturation comprehends those phenomena which result when groups of individuals having different cultures come into continuous first-hand contact, with subsequent changes in the original culture patterns of either or both groups" (Redfield et al., 1936, p. 149). Redfield et al. noted that minorities have several possible different ways to react: (1) acceptance of the dominant culture's traits resulting in eventual assimilation; or (2) reaction against the new culture, especially if acceptance entails imposed inferiority; or (3) adaptation by fusing two cultures or (4) alternating between the two cultures. Redfield et al. also noted that "psychic conflict" can arise from incompatible cultural norms (p. 152).

The first psychometric measure of acculturation was probably Hoffman's (1934/1977) 24-item scale of language use with which he demonstrated that bilingualism did not cause low intelligence in immigrant children as contemporary research had claimed. An early comprehensive measure of acculturation was Campisi's 1947 scale based on the definition that "the complex totality of acculturation" was synonymous with "biculturalism" such that his measures were indices of "(1) the degree to which a person has internalized certain aspects of American culture and (2) the degree to which that same person has retained his

Exhibit 17.1

EARLY PSYCHOMETRIC ITEMS ABOUT ACCULTURATION

Example items from Campisi's (1947) 10 types of acculturation measures.

i) How many songs that are sung only by people of your nationality can you sing or hum?
ii) The gestures I use in talking are:
  a) Completely American
  b) Mostly American
  c) Both American and of my nationality,
  d) Mostly of my nationality
  e) Completely of my nationality.
iii) With which of the following persons do you feel most at ease?
  a) Americans of American descent
  b) Americans of your nationality
  c) immigrants of your nationality
iv) In what type of neighborhood do your best friends live?
  a) A mostly American neighborhood
  b) A mixed neighborhood
  c) A neighborhood mostly of your nationality
v) What language do you use to tease and joke?
  a) Almost always English
  b) Mostly English
  c) Occasionally either language
  d) Mostly the language of my nationality group
  e) Almost always the language of my nationality group.
vi) Do you eat catsup, mustard or mayonnaise
  a) As part of your regular diet
  b) About every two weeks
  c) About once a month
  d) About once in six months
  e) Almost never
vii) Do you feel that people of your nationality should stick together?
  a) Always
  b) Often
  c) Somewhat
  d) Rarely
  e) Never
viii) I am
  a) Completely Americanized
  b) Mostly Americanized
  c) About half Americanized
  d) Little Americanized
  e) Not at all Americanized
ix) I would wish myself to be
  a) Completely Americanized
  b) Mostly Americanized

c) About half Americanized
d) Little Americanized
e) Not at all Americanized

x) I would wish my food to be:
a) Completely American
b) Mostly American
c) Both American and of my nationality
d) Mostly of my nationality
e) Completely of my nationality

or her ancestor's non-American way of life" (pp. 14–15). The Campisi acculturation exhibit shown lists examples of each of the 10 types of questions devised by Campisi. Notable is his use of the bipolar, zero-sum format, with American behaviors at the low end and ethnic behaviors at the high end. Early Hispanic scales adopted this format (e.g., Szapocznik, Scopetta, Kurtines, & Aranalde, 1978: Szapocznik & Kurtines, 1980; Szapocznik, Kurtines, & Fernandez, 1980).

Campisi's (1947) scale was used in Weinstock's 1964 study of Hungarian immigrants in the United States and in Gold's 1967 study of Saskatchewan Indians in Canada. But most subsequent empirical studies involved the development of original psychometric measures, for example, Eisenstadt (1952), Zajonc (1952), Richardson (1957), Taft (1963), Jones and Lambert (1959). The problem of idiosyncratic measures was noted by Triandis in 1977 and a decade later by Taft in 1987 in their presidential addresses to the International Association for Cross-Cultural Psychology. The proliferation of acculturation scales has continued unabated (Escobar & Vega, 2000).

Early Acculturative Stress Constructs and Measures

Acculturative stress was measured by DeVos and Miner in 1959 using Rorschach methods to show that "attenuation of traditional beliefs in the urbanized Arab is related to increasing intro-psychic tensions" (p. 345), thus confirming that acculturative stress causes psychiatric disorders (Murphy, 1973). However, acculturative stress was also then conceived to be a motivator of acculturative change. For example, Levine (1963) described "innovative adaptations to acculturative stress" (p. 125). Levy and Kunitz (1971) explained American Indian alcoholism as "a retreatist reaction to acculturative stress" (p. 102). Fabrega (1971) wrote of a shaman's role "as an innovator of curing procedures under acculturative stress" (p. 184).

Ausubel (1960) operationalized acculturative stress as self-report of low self-esteem. Cawte (1968) and Inkeles (1969) operationalized acculturative stress as check lists of psychosomatic symptoms. Berry (1970, 1976) carried this into psychology, measuring it also as marginal personality (Mann, 1958). Such methods of measuring acculturative stress have continued in the social sciences and health sciences.

Acculturative stress has been defined in various ways, often vaguely, for example, as "difficulties and stressors arising as part of this adaptation process"

(Joiner & Walker, 2002, p. 462) or as "losses that occur when adjusting to or integrating a new system of beliefs, routines, and social roles" (Caplan, 2007, p. 94). For Kaplan and Nunes (2003), acculturative stress included low socioeconomic status (SES) and family separation. The definition by Berry, Kim, Minde, and Mok (1987) is probably most useful because it makes salient the idea that stress is an imbalance that motivates a coping reaction, and it makes salient some of the confounds:

> *Stress is considered to be a generalized physiological and psychological state of the organism, brought about by the experience of stressors in the environment, and which requires some reduction (for normal functioning to occur), through a process of coping until some satisfactory adaptation to the new situation is achieved . . . The concept of acculturative stress refers to one kind of stress, that in which the stressors are identified as having their source in the process of acculturation; in addition, there is often a particular set of stress behaviors which occurs during acculturation, such as lowered mental health status (specifically confusion, anxiety, depression), feelings of marginality and alienation, heightened psychosomatic symptom level, and identity confusion. (p. 492)*

Five-Stage Causal Chain of Acculturation

Acculturation might be best illustrated as a five-stage causal chain, drawing on the theory of Berry (1970, 1980), Born (1970), Tadmor and Tetlock (2006), and others:

1		2		3		4		5		SES
										⇓
Cultural Contact	⇒	Acculturative Stress at T1	⇒	Acculturation Orientations	⇒ ⇐	Acculturation Processes	⇒	Δ Acculturative Stress at T2	⇒	Δ Health
										⇑
										Discrimination

The strangeness of a new culture causes stress at time of contact (T1), which motivates the individuals or group to orient themselves to assimilate to the new culture, or to separate from it, or to integrate into both cultures, or to just endure the stress of marginalization. These orientations in turn affect the amount of acculturation and learning. This is a simplified sequence, of course. The research of Tartakovsky (2002) and Kim (as reviewed in Rudmin, 2003b, 2006b) shows that acculturation orientation may be determined prior to contact. It is also plausible that acculturation orientations are not only causes of acculturative learning but are also consequences (Rudmin & Ahmadzadeh, 2001). In any case, new behaviors and subsequent changes in stress at T2 will produce changes in health, for the better or the worse. Health is also affected by SES and discrimination, even for nonminority people (Wamala, Boström, & Nyqvist, 2007).

To illustrate this causal chain, imagine a Japanese man coming to the United States and encountering such strange things as driving on the right, wearing shoes in the house, using first names, and having a female boss. He knew about such aspects of America before coming and probably has a precontact acculturation attitude. However, cultural contact causes extra alertness, fear of faux pas, and feelings of discomfort or anxiety. This motivates him to do something to relieve the stress, for example, to assimilate (e.g., learn English well, take a driving course, imitate American colleagues), to separate (e.g., give up driving, withdraw into an enclave of Japanese friends), to integrate (e.g., have green tea and bagels for breakfast), or to marginalize (e.g., stop socializing, drink alone). The acculturation orientation will determine, in part, how much acculturative learning takes place, for example, in mastering English or enjoying American football. The success or difficulty of learning may make him change his orientation.

More cultural competence may result in lower acculturative stress and better health, for example, lower blood pressure, but this may be offset by new behaviors that are unhealthful, for example, eating fewer vegetables (Stimpson & Urrutia-Rojas, 2007). Changing one culture for another, or not changing, or alternating between them may make some aspects of health better and some aspects worse. That is an empirical issue, to be answered a posteriori, after the data, not a priori according to stereotypes or ideologies. It should not be considered a paradox if immigrants are not as unhealthy as expected or if cultural separation leads to better health (Franzini, Ribble, & Keddie, 2001; Markides & Coreil, 1986; Palloni & Arias, 2004; Sam, 2006; Sam, Vedder, Ward, & Hoarenczyk, 2006).

Current Assessment Methods

Empirical data depends on methods of measurement. Acculturative stress has been measured in many different ways, as have acculturation orientations and acculturative learning. In addition to psychometric measures, these constructs have also been approximated by proxy measures as used in large-sample epidemiological studies that draw on census type data.

Measures of Acculturative Stress

Acculturative stress, as stress, is fundamentally a physiological phenomenon and hence best measured physiologically, for example, as cortisol level or as blood pressure. To date, only one acculturation study has measured cortisol (Decker, 2001); however, many have measured blood pressure. Kaplan and Nunes (2003) reviewed 17 studies and concluded that longer duration of cultural contact and more cultural learning results in higher blood pressure. In dramatic contrast, Steffen, Smith, Larson, and Butler (2006) conducted a meta-analysis on 125 studies and concluded that blood pressure has greatest increase at the time of immigration, with rapid decrease during the first 5 years, but with detectable differences from control groups even 10 years later. Thus, physiological measures of acculturative stress are still inconclusive, but the weight of evidence is that time-since-arrival may prove to be a useful proxy measure for acculturative stress at T2.

The vast majority of studies, however, measure acculturative stress as the negative effects that stress is presumed to cause. These proxy measures are of two types. Most used are existing scales designed for psychiatric screening or other such purposes. A search of "acculturative stress" in PsychINFO,

MEDLINE, and Dissertation Abstracts identified 10 depression scales (e.g., Zung's Self-Rating Depression Scale: Zung, 1965), 5 stress scales (e.g., Perceived Stress Scale: Cohen, Kamarck, & Mermelstein, 1983), 2 satisfaction scales (e.g., Satisfaction With Life Scale: Diener, Emmons, Larsen, & Griffin, 1985), and 2 personality scales (e.g., Rosenberg's Self-Esteem Scale: Rosenberg, 1965). The second type are multidimensional scales created for the purpose of measuring acculturative stress. The literature search identified 17 such scales. However, neither type will be described in detail here because this review will, for five reasons, recommend that acculturative stress not be measured in cross-sectional survey research on acculturation.

First, a single measure of acculturative stress cannot differentiate T1 stress from T2 stress. Second, a single measure of stress cannot differentiate stress as a cause of poor health from stress as a consequence of poor health. Third, in studies of minority mental health, of which there are many, operationalizing acculturative stress as depression/anxiety confounds the predictor variable (stress) with what is predicted (mental illness), thereby producing positive correlations that spuriously support the belief that acculturation causes mental illness. Fourth, a single measure of stress cannot differentiate acculturative stress from other sources of stress. Joiner and Walker (2002) have noted that "people undergoing acculturation pressures may, like everyone else, experience general life stress" (p. 465). Their study found that acculturative stress and general stress were positively correlated ($r = +.46$), such that a strong positive correlation of acculturative stress and suicidality ($r = +.50$) collapsed ($r = +.04$) after controlling for general stress. Similarly, Spasojevic, Heffer, and Snyder (2000) found that acculturation no longer predicted marital discord after controlling for the stress underlying PTSD symptoms. In an early study, Ødegaard (1973) found that Norwegians migrating to Minnesota were more depressed than people born in Minnesota but were less depressed than Norwegians moving to Oslo, indicating that it was relocation per se, not acculturation, that was causing depression.

Finally, multidimensional scales of acculturative stress confound the constructs, as so many critics have noted. For example, the Cultural Adjustment Difficulties Checklist (CADC) has a subscale of cultural competence (Sodowsky & Lai, 1997), and the Adolescent Stress Measure for Asian Americans (ASMAA) has a subscale of linguistic competence (Kim-Bae, 1999). Cultural and linguistic competence are aspects of acculturative learning, which is predicted by acculturative stress and which predicts acculturative stress but is not acculturative stress. Falk's (1995) measure of acculturative hassles contains a subscale of financial stress, thus confounding measures of acculturative stress and SES. The acculturative stress scale used by Joiner and Walker (2002) contains a subscale of perceived discrimination, as do several other acculturative stress scales (e.g., Abouguendia & Noels, 2001; Kim-Bae, 1999; Lay & Nguyen, 1998; Sandhu & Asrabadi, 1994).

Perceived Discrimination and Acculturative Stress

Acculturative stress should be differentiated from perceived discrimination because numerous studies have shown that perceived discrimination is often more distressing than is acculturation (Beiser & Hou, 2006; Gee, Ryan, Laflamme,

& Holt, 2006; Lam, Tsoi, & Chan, 2005; McDonald, Vechi, Bowman, & Sanson-Fisher, 1996; Moghaddam, Taylor, Ditto, Jacobs, & Bianchi, 2002; Sam, 2001; Stevens, Vollebergh, Pels, & Crijnen, 2005a, 2005b; Virta, Sam, & Westin, 2004; Ying, Lee, & Tsai, 2000). In a Finnish study of six immigrant groups (Jasinskaja-Lahti, Liebkind, & Perhoniemi, 2006) and in a Spanish study of five immigrant groups (Zlobina, Basabe, Paez, & Furnham, 2006), perceived discrimination strongly predicted psychological stress. In a study of 42 samples of immigrant teenagers in 13 nations (N = 5366), perceived discrimination was the strongest predictor of poor psychological adaptation (measured as mental health, self-esteem, and satisfaction with life), much more influential than acculturation (Vedder, van de Vijver, & Liebkind, 2006). This was replicated in further analyses of Turks and Vietnamese (Vedder, Sam, van de Vijver, & Phinney, 2006). In a Swedish sample (N = 33,328) consisting mostly of nonminority Swedes, perceived discrimination, operationalized as experiences of humiliation, was a strong predictor of psychological distress, and 25% of this effect was related to low SES (Wamala et al., 2007).

This Swedish study measured perceived discrimination with a single item: "Have you during the past 3 months been treated in a way that made you feel humiliated?" with responses of "no" (none), "yes, once" (some) or "yes, several times" (frequent). However, several scales of perceived discrimination have been developed (e.g., Krieger, Smith, Naishadham, Hartman, & Barbeau, 2005; Paradies, 2006; Phinney, Madden, & Santos, 1998; Verkuyten, 1998).

SES and Acculturative Stress

Socioeconomic status is another source of stress distinct from acculturative stress, as first noted by Murphy back in 1973. Many studies have found that low SES is a major predictor of ill health among minorities, often more predictive than are acculturation variables (e.g., Buriel & Saenz, 1980; Canabal & Quiles, 1995; Cuéllar, Arnold, & Maldonado, 1995; Gallagher-Thompson, Tazeau, Basilio, et al., 1997; Griffith & Villavicencio, 1985; Pham & Harris, 2001; Schalk-Soekar, van de Vijver, & Hoogsteder, 2004; Simich, Hamilton, & Baya, 2006; Solis, Marks, Garcia, & Shelton, 1990). Based on a meta-analysis of 49 studies of acculturation, Moyerman and Forman (1992) wrote that "SES was the most influential study characteristic" and that "lower SES samples had sharper increases in symptomology and conflict as they acculturated" (p. 117). Negy and Woods (1992a) examined acculturation and several different indices of SES and reported significant positive correlations, leading to the conclusion that "acculturation and SES are intricately intertwined" (p. 250).

For more than a decade, critical reviews of acculturation research have warned of the danger of ignoring socioeconomic variables. For example, Sheldon and Parker (1992) warned that "Multiculturalist ethnic health explanations also tend to displace more material explanations of health outcomes" (p. 104). Recio-Adrados (1993) reviewed drug abuse literature and warned that "social class of stratum is not accounted or controlled for by the acculturation scales, which is a symptom of the 'disembodied' treatment of acculturation that prevails in the field" (p. 59). Hunt et al. reported that "the studies we reviewed routinely fail to seriously explore the role of socio-economic, educational, and related factors" (2004, p. 980). After reviewing studies of acculturation and health, Caetano and Clark (2003) argued that "analyses must control for the effects of

Research Box 17.1

SOCIAL CONFORMITY BIAS AND THE FUNDAMENTAL ERROR OF ATTRIBUTION

Kvernmo, S., & Heyerdahl, S. (2003). Acculturation strategies and ethnic identity as predictors of behavior problems in Arctic minority adolescents. *Journal of the American Academy of Child and Adolescent Psychiatry, 42*, 57–65.

Conformity bias causes people to adjust their perceptions, or their reported perceptions, to match those of others. The classic experiments by Asch have people at a table identifying lines of the same length, with the confederates all saying publicly that the two lines have different lengths, thus putting conformity pressure on the subject to give a similar answer. Acculturation research is not so very different. For example, Kvernmo and Heyerdahl (2003, p. 63) cited the conformity pressures that "integration has been regarded as the most healthy mode of acculturation" and then concluded that their own data showed integration to be "a protective factor for mental health problems" when in fact their data showed 7 of 8 independent correlations of integration and stress to be statistically nonsignificant.

The Fundamental Error of Attribution argues that people have a tendency to overestimate internal personal characteristics as a cause of behavior and to underestimate the external contexts. In acculturation research, this bias is evident in the near-universal paradigm of seeking to find the causes of acculturation and its problems in the attitudes of minority individuals, and not in the contexts in which the minority individuals find themselves. Said one refugee in Norway, "Do you think I am stupid? Of course I know it is better that I learn to speak Norwegian. But I have three small children, no relatives, no car, and the Norwegian lessons on the other side of city just at supper time. I cannot go." It was not attitudes that were blocking cultural learning, but lack of resources. That is why it is so important to consider the effects of socioeconomic status in studies of acculturation and health. What appears to be a cultural effect that arises from the individual's lifestyle may be merely a lack of money.

various sociodemographic factors to protect against reporting spurious associations" (p. 223). Similarly, Yamada, Valle, Barrio, and Jeste (2006) argued that "the effects of socioeconomic status should be considered separately from acculturation in accounting for psychological adjustment and well-being" (p. 553). Finally, Abraído-Lanza et al. (2006) warned that research "can inadvertently fuel week explanations of health disparities by focusing attention on culture rather than on structural constraints (e.g., lack of access to resources)" (p. 1344). In sum, acculturation studies should always measure SES, in addition to perceived discrimination, so that health theories, minority health policies, and specific interventions do not become overly focused on acculturation.

Constructs With Confounds

Confounded constructs, misoperationalizations, and unarticulated theory have led to the faulty acculturation research that reviewers complain about. As Escobar and Vega (2000) noted, "Through a convoluted logic, acculturation is equated with stressful life experiences encountered in the culture change process" (p. 738). For example, perceived discrimination has been conceived to be a component of acculturation (e.g., Malcarne, Chavira, Fernandez, & Liu, 2006; Richman, Gaviria, Flaherty, Birz, & Wintrob, 1987). If acculturation were mismeasured as stress, predicting acculturative stress mismeasured as depression, predicting mental illness, that would seem to show that acculturation causes mental illness. Rudmin (2003b, 2007) has traced an actual error like this. The orientation of marginalization (rejection of both cultures) was misoperationalized with items about acculturative stress, and this mismeasure loaded in a factor with other measures of acculturative stress, leading to dozens of prominent scholars in high-status journals for two decades citing that as evidence for the generalized claim that marginalization is the most stressful mode of acculturation.

Measures of Acculturation Orientation and Acculturative Learning

There are a plethora of psychometric measures of acculturation. Unlike the measurement of depression, for example, for which there are 12 or 15 scales each with robust psychometric properties and a record of use in numerous studies, there are hundreds of acculturation scales, often with weak psychometric properties and often used in only one or two studies. There are at least three reasons for this proliferation of scales.

Causes of the Proliferation of Acculturation Scales

First, schisms divide acculturation research communities. One major split is between scholars who study Hispanic acculturation in the United States and others who study other ethnic groups in the United States or who study acculturation outside the United States. For example, Rogler's et al. (1991) published a review of Hispanic acculturation literature in *American Psychologist,* including 53 articles from the 1980s. LaFromboise, Coleman, and Gerton (1993) published a review of acculturation literature in *Psychological Bulletin,* including 68 articles from the 1980s. The two reviews, published in high level journals, had only two references in common for the 1980s. There are other splits in the literature of the different academic disciplines that study acculturation. Rudmin's (2003a, 2003b) multidisciplinary tabulations of acculturation taxonomies show a century of poor citations of prior research and a continual reinvention of theory and terminology.

Second, acculturation scales should inquire about important aspects of culture, and these will be different for different societies. For example, Kim's (1984) scale for Koreans in Canada, recommended by Berry, Kim, Power, Young, and Bujaki (1989), has items about furniture preferences; Rudmin and Ahmadzadeh's (2001) scale for Iranians in Norway has an item about celebrating the spring equinox. Each acculturation study and its measures should inquire about the specific cultures in question. A scale created for Hispanics in the United States would not be suitable for Koreans in Japan, or Brits in Hong Kong. The large study of 42 minority samples in 13 nations (Berry, Phinney, Sam, & Vedder, 2006) asked about the same five topics in all contexts (language use, marriage expectations, friendships, social activity participants, and attachment to cultural traditions), but the resulting data were psychometrically defective, with poor validity, poor divergent validity, poor reliability, and excessive acquiescence bias (Rudmin, 2008).

Third, there are at least seven types of question formats, illustrated in Exhibit 17.1, with hypothetical attitude items about language use for Mexicans acculturating in the United States. Full psychometric scales would be made of questions in the same format about several different cultural topics. The response options shown are Likert 5-point measures of agreement, but responses could be yes–no check lists; true–false responses; 3-point, 4-point, 7-point Likert scales; and so forth.

1. Unipolar scales about minority culture are measures of how much minorities are unassimilated.
2. Unipolar scales about the dominant culture are measures of how much minorities are assimilated.
3. Bipolar scales impose zero-sum competition between cultures, such that as scores for one culture increase scores for the other decrease. The bicultural, midscale response indicates preference for both cultures or rejection of both, making it ambiguous.

Exhibit 17.2

BIAS EFFECTS IN ACCULTURATION RESEARCH

Seven types of acculturation question formats, illustrated with attitude items about language for Mexicans acculturating to the United States answered on a Likert scale.

1) One scale made of unipolar items about attachment to the minority culture:
   I like to speak Spanish. Disagree 1 2 3 4 5 Agree

2) One scale made of unipolar items about assimilation to the dominant culture:
   I like to speak English. Disagree 1 2 3 4 5 Agree

3) One scale made of bipolar items with minority culture at one end and dominant at the other:

I most like to speak Spanish.		*I like speaking both languages equally*		*I most like to speak English.*
1	2	3	4	5

4) Bilineal scales made of two independent unipolar scales, one for each culture:
 i) Minority culture: *I like to speak Spanish.* Disagree 1 2 3 4 5 Agree

 ii) Dominant culture: *I like to speak English.* Disagree 1 2 3 4 5 Agree

5) Four ipsative scales made of items questioning both cultures simultaneously:

i) Assimilation:	*I like English but dislike Spanish.*	Disagree 1 2 3 4 5 Agree
ii) Separation:	*I dislike Spanish but like English.*	Disagree 1 2 3 4 5 Agree
iii) Integration:	*I like both Spanish and English.*	Disagree 1 2 3 4 5 Agree
iv) Marginalization:	*I dislike both Spanish and English.*	Disagree 1 2 3 4 5 Agree

6) Four ipsative scales made of categorical forced-choice items:
 For language, I like: 1) *English* 2) *Spanish* 3) *Both* 4) *Neither*

7) Proxy measures from census-type sources, which by inference reflect acculturation:
 Primary home language? a) *English,* b) *Spanish,* c) *native Indian,* d) other:_________

4. Bilineal scales are composed of two independent unipolar scales, thus avoiding zero-sum presumptions but allowing that possibility if the two scales are negatively correlated. This format also allows several different ways to compute a measure of biculturalism (Arends-Tóth & van de Vijver, 2006; Rudmin, 2006b).
5. Four ipsative scales inquire about cultural predominance or preference patterns that define acculturation orientation of assimilation, separation, integration, and marginalization. *Ipsative* means nonindependent: as scores for one scale increase, the scores to the other scales should decrease. It is not plausible to give maximum agreement to all four scales as is possible with the two independent scales of the bilineal format.
6. Forced-choice ipsative scales also measure assimilation, separation, integration, and marginalization constructs but in a more efficient, constrained manner.
7. Proxy measures are made from information found in census data or similar sources that by inference indicate acculturation status. For example, census information that a person (a) is an immigrant from Mexico and (b) now has English as the primary language infers that the person has acculturated; whereas, being (a) from Mexico and (b) now speaking Spanish infers that the person has not acculturated.

Reviews of Acculturation Scales

To date, acculturation scales have been collected and compared in 16 summary reviews. (Reviews by Freeman, Lewis, and Colon, 2002, and by Kurasaki et al., 2002, were not available for this report.) The first was Olmedo's 1979 review of 7 psychometric measures, all of which he considered tentative and exploratory. Hoffmann (1983) examined 32 studies of Native Americans and identified 27 quantitative measures of acculturation, which asked about 23 different acculturation constructs or dimensions. Dana (1996) recommended 5 acculturation scales for Hispanics, which he considered to be well conceptualized and validated. Mariño, Stuart, Wright, Klimidis, and Minas (2001) reviewed 43 scales and argued that acculturation scales should not mix items about psychology (attitudes, values, preferences, loyalties) and items about behavior (language and cultural skills). The bipolar format was most common, but the authors recommended bidimensional methods that allow measurement of biculturalism. Kim and Abreu (2001) reviewed 33 scales for U.S. minorities, made between 1978 and 1999, finding 25 to be bipolar, 6 to be bilineal, and 2 to be unipolar. They argued that acculturation scales should demonstrate construct validity, should use bilineal measures, and should separately measure psychological and behavioral aspects of acculturation.

Skinner (2002) examined 24 acculturation measures and recommended that future research avoid unipolar scales and avoid items about personal history. Satia-Abouta et al. (2002) examined 11 acculturation measures used in diet research and faulted all of them for poor validation and poor sampling. Zane and Mak (2003) examined the content of 22 acculturation scales, 15 of which were bipolar and 7 unipolar. They found language to be the most common topic, followed by daily living habits, social affiliations, and cultural identity. Zea, Asner-Self, Birman, and Buki (2003) surveyed the literature on acculturation scales and focused on 6 scales, plus their own, that were bilineal and that separately measured psychological and behavioral dimensions, the latter defined as language proficiency. Collier (2004/2007) examined 9 acculturation scales and gave extended discussion of the 8-item Acculturation Quick Screen (AQS) because it was not specific to any minority group and was not based on self-report but on information in school files, for example, years in the United States or proficiency in English.

Yamada et al. (2006) reviewed 32 acculturation scales for Hispanics and described in detail 15 scales shown to be valid for middle-aged and older Latinos. Only 3 of these 15 scales used the bilineal format. This study also recommended against using demographic items in acculturation scales. Kang (2006) reviewed 14 bilineal measures in order to discover item characteristics that contribute to negative correlations between the two scales, indicating that they are zero-sum measures like the bipolar measures. Measures that used items asking about frequency, for example, "How much do you speak Chinese?" and "How much do you speak English?," result in negative correlations between scales because a higher response to an item asking about frequency requires a lower response to the corresponding item in the other scale. This study also found that language items were important for predicting different aspects of well-being in different contexts, for example, at home or with friends. Loue (2006) reviewed 7 self-report measures of ethnic identity, 11 self-report measures of acculturation, and 19 proxy measures of immigration status. Loue argued that immigration status is frequently overlooked but might be predictive of immigrants' use of medical services.

The largest review of acculturation measures to date is Matsudaira's (2006) descriptive tabulation of 51 scales, reporting number of items (ranging from 4 to 80), Cronbach alpha coefficients (ranging from .47 to .97), and the target minority group (usually Hispanics). The cultural domain most commonly questioned by these scales was language, and the domain most neglected was values. Matsudaira found the greatest failing to be lack of external validity criteria for acculturation scales and recommended that scales (a) avoid demographic questions, (b) use the bilineal format, and (c) use qualitative data to validate acculturation measures.

Several further critical evaluations of acculturation scales, but without reference to a declared sample of scales, should be considered. Cabassa (2003) argued that proxy measures and bipolar scales should be avoided, instead advocating bidimensional scales. More technical were his recommendations to avoid "how well" (in Spanish, que tan bien) because it encourages acquiescence and to include "no opinion" or "don't know" answer options, which would not be summated into the scale score. Abraído-Lanza et al. (2006) recommended that acculturation questions ask about the health issue being studied, for example, studies of body weight should ask questions about diet. More unique was his recommendation that acculturation studies should consider the possibilities that immigrants may be acculturating to other minority groups, for example, Chinese-Americans eating Mexican food, or that the dominant group may be acculturating to the immigrants, for example, Americans eating pizza. Arends-Tóth and van de Vijver (2006) recommended the bilineal format because the four scale ipsative format often uses double-barreled items, negations, or other complex formulations. Rudmin (2003b, 2006b, 2008) has criticized this format for the further reasons of lack of logic, lack of validity, lack of reliability, faulty factor structure, inducement of acquiescence bias, and inducement of ideological biases.

Recommendations for Acculturation Assessment

This review of the psychometric literature on acculturation comes to several recommendations for acculturation measures intended for health research.

1. Identify and culturally describe a specific minority group and a specific dominant group. Avoid categories such as Hispanic or Asian American.
2. Articulate stereotyped beliefs about the minority group so as to be consciously aware of potential biases.
3. Identify comparison control groups in addition to the dominant group, for example, other minorities, the same minority in a different nation, people of the minority nationality who migrated internally within their own nation, or applicant immigrants who have not yet arrived.
4. Identify a specific health issue, problem, or illness and describe its epidemiological parameters for the minority group, the dominant group, and the control group, if possible.
5. Do not measure acculturative stress. Measures of depression, blood pressure, self-esteem, poverty, and so forth should not be relabeled and called "acculturative stress."

6. Measure acculturation orientation using bilineal scales with attitude or preference items suitable for the two cultures in question.
7. Measure acculturation learning using bilineal scales with behavioral or knowledge items, for example, about language, driving, recreation, politeness, and so forth.
8. For both acculturation measures, use the bilineal format of two independent scales, one for each culture. Avoid bipolar and ipsative question formats.
9. For both acculturation measures, avoid demographic questions and frequency questions.
10. Examine the validity of the measures on a sample of subjects using qualitative data.
11. Compute measures of biculturalism for the orientation and learning scales, if needed.
12. Use education, income, and employment information to make a measure of SES.
13. Make an independent measure of perceived discrimination, using a standard scale that does not confound discrimination with other constructs.
14. Statistically remove the effects of SES, perceived discrimination, and other sources of nonacculturative stress, for example, war trauma or family separation.
15. In literature reviews, discount studies that have used undefined groups, undefined health issues, confounded measures, or no covariate controls for SES and perceived discrimination.
16. Do not use acculturation research scales for single case analysis because they lack established norms and lack covariate control of SES and discrimination. For single cases, Donohue et al. (2006) have developed an Ethnic Culture in Therapy Scale with validation by clinical interview. Rudmin (2006a) has proposed a measure modeled on the Apgar score used in obstetrics.

Clinical Applications

As shown in Table 17.2, the majority of clinical studies using measures of acculturation are focused on mental health and lifestyle illnesses. The results in Table 17.2 cannot be summated because the categories are not mutually exclusive. Nevertheless, it seems clear that mental health is frequently studied, especially stress, depression, and anxiety, the very constructs that are most confounded in the misoperationalizations of acculturation and acculturative stress.

The consensus of reviewers of this literature is that the research methods are too various and too faulty to allow confident conclusions about the effects of acculturation on health. For example, Satia-Abouta et al. (2002) reviewed 18 studies of dietary acculturation and concluded "we are unable to draw conclusions" because of inconsistent research designs and findings (p. 1116). Lindberg and Stevens (2007) examined studies of weight loss and found that faulty methods "precluded conducting a formal meta-analysis on the available data" (p. 397). The RAND Corporation group reviewed research on acculturation and Latino health and also concluded that definitive conclusions could not be drawn. However, they did find five studies showing acculturation to have a negative effect on diet, namely, more fat and less fruit and vegetables (Lara et al.,

17.2 Topics of Acculturation Research in MEDLINE and PsychINFO Cumulatively Through 2006

	MEDLINE	PsychINFO
Total studies on "acculturation"	3292	6299
STUDIES OF MENTAL HEALTH		
acculturation AND mental	587	974
acculturation AND stress	384	765
acculturation AND depression	274	473
acculturation AND anxiety	123	228
acculturation AND suicid*	76	76
acculturation AND (psychosis OR psychotic)	48	31
acculturation AND schizophren*	44	40
STUDIES OF LIFESTYLE ILLNESSES		
acculturation AND alcohol*	284	280
acculturation AND (obes* OR weight)	194	100
acculturation AND smok*	174	113
acculturation AND cancer	162	87
acculturation AND sexual	142	208
acculturation AND cardio*	76	23
acculturation AND "blood pressure"	63	20

Note: Asterisks indicate truncation search; for example, "suicid*" would locate titles and abstracts containing the words "suicide," "suicides," and "suicidal." Categories are not exclusive, that is, studies may be about depression, and anxiety, and alcoholism.

2005). This was confirmed by a large scale (N = 16,539) blood survey showing that Hispanics born in Mexico had the highest levels of carotenoids and those born in the United States and who speak English, had the lowest (Stimpson & Urrutia-Rojas, 2007).

However, there is other evidence that acculturation is not damaging to health. Inkeles (1969) administered a 9-item checklist of psychosomatic symptoms to approximately 6,000 young men in 6 developing nations and found 72 of the 74 acculturating samples not to be distressed compared to matched nonacculturating control groups. Murphy (1973) confirmed this finding by an intensive study of 138 Yoruba from Nigeria, using a 79-item questionnaire, administered by a psychiatrist, with additional behavioral information, concluding that "contact per se with the forces of cultural change is not inevitably noxious to psychological well-being" (p. 256). Escobar, Nervi, and Gara (2000) reviewed five large studies of Hispanics' mental health and found that "Mexican-born immigrants have better mental health profiles than do U.S.-born Mexican Americans," thus disproving "the old idea that immigrants are necessarily disadvantaged" (p. 64). In a large nationally representative American sample (N = 201,379), Read,

Amick, and Donato (2005) found that Arab Americans had health equal to that of nonimmigrant Whites and that recent immigrants had the best health.

For high school students, Harker (2001) found in a large national sample (N = 13,350) that first-generation immigrants were less depressed and had more positive well-being than their nonimmigrant classmates and that second-generation immigrants were not different on these measures from the nonimmigrants. Lam et al. (2005) found that mainland China students in Hong Kong had better well-being (measured as depression, life purpose, and life satisfaction) than their nonacculturating classmates. Sam et al. (2006) used a 15-item scale of depression, anxiety, and psychosomatic symptoms to examine almost 8,000 students in 13 developed nations and found that immigrant teenagers had better well-being than matched samples of nonimmigrant teenagers. This pattern was evident in the data of each of the 13 nations examined.

Conclusion

In retrospect, we took three decades to go from the diary study by Thomas and Znaniecki (1918) to the psychometric study by Campisi (1947). We took several more decades to make measures of acculturative stress (e.g., Inkeles, 1969) and one decade more to establish the bipolar and the ipsative formats (e.g., Berry, 1976; Szapocznik et al., 1978). Three decades later, we now know to stop using those formats and to stop using proxy measures of acculturative stress. Hopefully, in one more decade, by 2018, on the one-century anniversary of Thomas and Znaniecki, acculturation constructs and their operationalization will be robust, reliable, and unconfounded to the degree that useful information about acculturation and health can be confidently compiled.

Summary

Acculturation measures must be directed to specific minorities in specific dominant cultures. Generic acculturation measures have yet to be demonstrated. This fact has resulted in a myriad of measures. Adding further complications is the fact that there are several psychometric measurement formats. One consequence of this proliferation of scales is that few, if any, are well-documented for validity, reliability, or clinical utility. Another consequence is that comparisons between acculturation measures are difficult or impossible. Much theoretical and empirical psychometric research remains to be done before health research is able to confidently measure acculturation and its effects on health.

Acknowledgments

Helpful criticisms of early drafts were provided by Daniel Geschke, Andrew Ryder, and Ann Marie Yamada. Eugene Tartakovsky kindly critiqued early figures. Thomas Hoffmann and Rodrigo Jose Marino kindly provided copies of unpublished manuscripts. Elias Mpofu and Tom Oakland were patient and encouraging editors.

References

Abouguendia, M., & Noels, K. A. (2001). General and acculturation-related daily hassles and psychological adjustment in first- and second-generation South Asian immigrants in Canada. *International Journal of Psychology, 36,* 163–173.

Abraído-Lanza. A. F., Armbrister, A. N., Flórez, K. R., & Aguirre, A. N. (2006). Toward a theory-driven model of acculturation in public health research. *American Journal of Public Health, 96,* 1342–1346.

Arends-Tóth, J., & van de Vijver, F.J.R. (2006). Assessment of psychological acculturation. In D. L. Sam & J. W. Berry (Eds.), *Cambridge Handbook of Acculturation Psychology* (pp. 142–160). Cambridge: Cambridge University Press.

Ausubel, D. P. (1960). Acculturative stress in modern Maori adolescence. *Child Development, 31,* 617–631.

Barnett, H. G., Broom, L., Siegel, B. J., Vogt, E. Z., & Watson, J. B. (1954). Acculturation: An exploratory formulation: The Social Science Research Council Summer Seminar on Acculturation, 1953. *American Anthropologist, 56,* 973–1000.

Beiser, M. N., & Hou, F. (2006). Ethnic identity, resettlement stress and depressive affect among Southeast Asian refugees in Canada. *Social Science & Medicine, 63,* 137–150.

Bernstein, R. (2007). *Minority population tops 100 million.* U.S. Census Bureau. Retrieved September 24, 2007, from: http://www.census.gov/Press-Release/www/releases/archives/population/010048html

Berry, J. W. (1970). Marginality, stress, and ethnic identification in an acculturated Aboriginal community. *Journal of Cross-Cultural Psychology, 1,* 239–252.

Berry, J. W. (1976). *Human ecology and cognitive style.* New York: John Wiley & Sons.

Berry, J. W. (1980). Social and cultural change. In H. C. Triandis & R. W. Brislin (Eds.), *Handbook of cross-cultural psychology: Social psychology* (vol. 5, pp. 211–279). Boston: Allyn and Bacon.

Berry, J. W., Kim, U., Minde, T., & Mok, D. (1987). Comparative studies of acculturative stress. *International Migration Review, 21,* 491–511.

Berry, J. W., Kim, U., Power, S., Young, M., & Bujaki, M. (1989). Acculturation attitudes in plural societies. *Applied Psychology: An International Review, 38,* 185–206.

Berry, J. W., Phinney, J. S., Sam, D. L., & Vedder, P. (Eds.). (2006). *Immigrant youth in cultural transition: Acculturation identity and adaptation across national boundaries.* London: Lawrence Erlbaum Associates.

Boas, F. (1940). The aims of ethnology. Reprinted in F. Boas, *Race, language, and culture* (pp. 626–638). New York: Macmillan. (Originally published in 1888.)

Born, D. O. (1970). Psychological adaptation and development under acculturative stress. *Social Science and Medicine, 3,* 529–547.

Buriel, R., & Saenz, E. (1980). Psychocultural characteristics of college-bound and noncollege-bound Chicanas. *Journal of Social Psychology, 110,* 245–251.

Cabassa, L. J. (2003). Measuring acculturation: Where we are and where we need to go. *Hispanic Journal of Behavioral Sciences, 25,* 127–146.

Caetano, R., & Clark, C. L. (2003). Acculturation, alcohol consumption, smoking, and drug use among Hispanics. In K. M. Chun, P. Balls Organista, & G. Marín (Eds.), *Acculturation: Advances in theory, measurement and applied research* (pp. 223–239). Washington, DC: American Psychological Association.

Campisi, P. J. (1947). *A scale for the measurement of acculturation.* Unpublished doctoral dissertation, University of Chicago.

Canabal, M. E., & Quiles, J. A. (1995). Acculturation and socioeconomic factors as determinants of depression among Puerto Ricans in the United States. *Social Behavior and Personality, 23,* 235–248.

Caplan, S. (2007). Latinos, acculturation, and acculturative stress: A dimensional concept analysis. *Policy, Politics, & Nursing Practice, 8,* 93–106.

Cawte, J. (1968). *Arafura, Aboriginal town: The medico-sociological expedition to Arnheim Land in 1968.* Sydney: University of New South Wales.

Chief, E. H. (1940). An assimilation study of Indian girls. *Journal of Social Psychology, 11,* 19–30.

Cohen, S., Kamarck, T., & Mermelstein, R. (1983). A global measure of perceived stress. *Journal of Health and Social Behavior, 24,* 385–396.

Collier, C. (2007). The assessment of acculturation. In G. B. Esquivel, E. C. Lopez, & S. G. Nahari (Eds.), *Handbook of multicultural school psychology: An interdisciplinary perspective.* London: Lawrence Erlbaum Associates. (Pre-publication manuscript from 2004.)

Cuéllar, I., Arnold, B., & Maldonado, R. (1995). Acculturation Rating Scale for Mexican Americans-II: A revision of the original ARSMA Scale. *Hispanic Journal of Behavioral Sciences, 17,* 275–304.

Dana, R. H. (1996). Assessment of acculturation in Hispanic populations. *Hispanic Journal of Behavioral Sciences, 18,* 317–328.

Decker, S. A. (2001). *Modernity, affluence, and well-being: A comparison of stress and social life in a remote-rural and central-urban community in Botswana.* Unpublished doctoral thesis, Emory University, Georgia.

DeVos, G., & Miner, H. (1959). Oasis and Casbah: A study in acculturative stress. In M. K. Opler (Ed.), *Culture and mental health* (pp. 333–350). New York: Macmillan.

Diener, E., Emmons, R. A., Larsen, R. J., & Griffin, S. (1985). The Satisfaction with Life Scale. *Journal of Personality Assessment, 49,* 71–75.

Donohue, B., Strada, M. J., Rosales, R., Taylor-Caldwell, A., Hise, D., Ahman, S., et al. (2006). The semistructured interview for consideration of Ethnic Culture in Therapy Scale: Initial psychometric and outcome support. *Behavior Modification, 30,* 867–891.

Eisenstadt, S. N. (1952). The process of absorption of new immigrants in Israel. *Human Relations, 5,* 223–246.

Escobar, J. I., Nervi, C. H., & Gara, M. A. (2000). Immigration and mental health: Mexican-Americans in the United States. *Harvard Review of Psychiatry, 8,* 64–72.

Escobar, J. I., & Vega, W. A. (2000). Mental health immigration's AAAs: Where are we and where do we go from here? *Journal of Nervous and Mental Disease, 188,* 736–740.

Fabrega, H., Jr. (1971). Medical anthropology. *Biennial Review of Anthropology, 7,* 167–229.

Falk, S. A. (1995). *Validation of a stress scale for Asian American college students and variables related to their perceptions of stress.* Unpublished doctoral dissertation, Loyola University, Chicago.

Franzini, L., Ribble, J. C., & Keddie A. M. (2001). Understanding the Hispanic paradox. *Ethnicity and Disease, 11,* 496–518.

Freeman, R. C., Lewis, Y. P., & Colon, H. M. (2002). *Handbook for conducting drug abuse research with Hispanic populations.* Westport, CT: Praeger.

Gallagher-Thompson, D., Tazeau, Y., Basilio, L., Hansen, H., Polich, T., Menéndez, A., & Villa, M. L. (1997). The relationship of dimensions of acculturation to self-reported depression in older Mexican American women. *Journal of Clinical Geropsychology, 3,* 123–137.

Gee, G. C., Ryan, A., Laflamme, D. J., & Holt, J. (2006). Self-reported discrimination and mental health status among African descendants, Mexican Americans, and other Latinos in the New Hampshire REACH 2010 Initiative: The added dimension of immigration. *American Journal of Public Health, 96,* 1821–1828.

Gold, D. (1967). Psychological changes associated with acculturation of Saskatchewan Indians. *Journal of Social Psychology, 71,* 177–184.

Griffith, J., & Villavicencio, S. (1985). Relationships among acculturation, sociodemographic characteristics and social supports in Mexican-American adults. *Hispanic Journal of Behavioral Sciences, 7,* 75–92.

Harker, K. (2001). Immigrant generation, assimilation, and adolescent psychological well-being. *Social Forces, 79,* 969–1004.

Hoffman, M.N.H. (1934). *The measurement of bilingual background.* New York: Columbia University. (Republished 1977, New York: AMS Press.)

Hoffmann, T. A. (1983). *Measures of Native American acculturation.* Unpublished manuscript, Psychology Dept., University of Arkansas, Fayetteville.

Hunt, L. M., Schneider, S., & Comer, B. (2004). Should "acculturation" be a variable in health research? A critical review of research on US Hispanics. *Social Science & Medicine, 59* 973–986.

Inkeles, A. (1969). Making men modern: On the causes and consequences of individual change in six developing countries. *American Journal of Sociology, 75,* 208–225.

Jasinskaja-Lahti, I., Liebkind, K., & Perhoniemi, R. (2006). Perceived discrimination and well-being: A victim study of different immigrant groups. *Journal of Community and Applied Social Psychology, 26,* 267–284.

Joiner, T. E., Jr., & Walker, R. L. (2002). Construct validity of a measure of acculturative stress in African Americans. *Psychological Assessment, 14,* 462–466.

Jones, F. E., & Lambert, W. E. (1959). Attitudes toward immigrants in a Canadian community. *Public Opinion Quarterly, 23,* 537–546.

Kang, S.-M. (2006). Measurement of acculturation, scale formats, and language competence: Their implications for adjustment. *Journal of Cross-Cultural Psychology, 37,* 669–693.

Kaplan, M. S., & Nunes, A. (2003). The psychosocial determinants of hypertension. *Nutrition, Metabolism and Cardiovascular Diseases, 13,* 52–29.

Kim, B.S.K, & Abreu, J. M. (2001). Acculturation measurement: Theory, current instruments, and future directions. In J. G. Ponterotto, J. M. Casas, L. A. Suzuki, & C. M. Alexander (Eds.), *Handbook of multicultural counseling* (2nd ed., pp. 394–424). Thousand Oaks, CA: Sage.

Kim, U. (1984). *Psychological acculturation of Korean immigrants in Toronto: A study of modes of acculturation, identity, language, and acculturative stress.* Unpublished MA thesis, Queen's University, Kingston, Ontario.

Kim-Bae, L. S. (1999). *Cultural identity as a mediator of acculturative stress and psychological adjustment in Vietnamese-American adolescents.* Unpublished doctoral dissertation, Arizona State University.

Krieger, N., Smith, K., Naishadham, D., Hartman, C., & Barbeau, E. M. (2005). Experiences of discrimination: Validity and reliability of a self-report measure for population health research on racism and health. *Social Science and Medicine, 61,* 1576–1596.

Krymlicka, W. (1995). *Multicultural citizenship: A liberal theory of minority rights.* Oxford: Clarendon Press.

Kurasaki, K. S., Okasaki, S., & Sue, S.(Eds.). (2002). *Asian American mental health: Assessment theories and methods.* New York: Kluwer Academic.

LaFromboise, T., Coleman, H.L.K., & Gerton, J. (1993). Psychological impact of biculturalism: Evidence and theory. *Psychological Bulletin, 114,* 395–412.

Lam, A.M.C., Tsoi, K. W., & Chan, T. S. (2005). Adolescent Chinese immigrants in Hong Kong: A comparison with locally born students and factors associated with their psychological well-being. *International Journal of Adolescent Medicine and Health, 17,* 157–168.

Lara, M., Gamboa, C., Kahramanian, M. I., Morales, L. S., & Bautista, D.E.H. (2005). Acculturation and Latino health in the United States: A review of the literature and the sociopolitical context. *Annual Review of Public Health, 26,* 367–397.

Lay, C., & Nguyen, T. (1998). The role of acculturation-related and acculturation non-specific daily hassles: Vietnamese-Canadian students and psychological distress. *Canadian Journal of Behavioural Science, 30,* 172–181.

LeVine, R. A. (1963). Culture and personality. *Biennial Review of Anthropology, 3,* 107–145.

Levy, J. E., & Kunitz, S. J. (1971). Indian reservations, anomie, and social pathologies. *Southwestern Journal of Anthropology, 27*(2), 97–128.

Lindberg, N. M., & Stevens, V. J. (2007). Review: Weight-loss interventions with Hispanic populations. *Ethnicity and Disease, 17,* 397–402.

Loue, S. (2006). Measures of ethnicity, ethnic identification, acculturation, and immigration status. In S. Loue, *Assessing race, ethnicity and gender in health* (pp. 119–135). New York: Springer.

Malcarne, V. L., Chavira, D. A., Fernandez, S., & Liu, P.-J. (2006). The Scale of Ethnic Experience: Development and psychometric properties. *Journal of Personality Assessment, 86,* 150–161.

Mann, J. (1958). Group relations and the marginal personality. *Human Relations, 11,* 77–92.

Mariño, R., Stuart, G. W., Wright, F.A.C., Klimidis, S., & Minas, H. (2001). *Quantitative measures of acculturation: A review.* Unpublished manuscript, School of Health, University of New England, Australia.

Markides, K. S., & Coreil, J. (1986). The health of Hispanics in the southwestern United States: An epidemiologic paradox. *Public Health Reports, 101,* 243–265.

Matsudaira, T. (2006). Measures of psychological acculturation: A review. *Transcultural Psychiatry, 43,* 462–487.

McDonald, R., Vechi, C., Bowman, J., & Sanson-Fisher, R. (1996). Mental health status of a Latin American community in New South Wales. *Australian and New Zealand Journal of Psychiatry, 30,* 457–462.

Moghaddam, F. M., Taylor, D. M., Ditto, B., Jacobs, K., & Bianchi, E. (2002). Psychological distress and perceived discrimination: A study of women from India. *International Journal of Intercultural Relations, 26,* 381–390.

Moyerman, D. R., & Forman, B. D. (1992). Acculturation and adjustment: A meta-analytic study. *Hispanic Journal of Behavioral Sciences, 14,* 163–200.

Murphy, J. M. (1973). Sociocultural change and psychiatric disorder among rural Yorubas in Nigeria. *Ethos, 1,* 239–262.

Negy, C., & Woods, D. J. (1992a). A note on the relationship between acculturation and socioeconomic status. *Hispanic Journal of Behavioral Sciences, 14,* 248–251.

Negy, C., & Woods, D J. (1992b). The importance of acculturation in understanding research with Hispanic-Americans. *Hispanic Journal of Behavioral Sciences, 14,* 224–247.

Ødegaard, Ø. (1973). Norwegian emigration, re-emigration and internal migration. In C. Zwingmann & M. Pfister-Ammende (Eds.), *Uprooting and after* . . . (pp. 161–177). Berlin: Springer-Verlag. (Originally published in 1936.)

Olmedo, E. L. (1979). Acculturation: A psychometric perspective. *American Psychologist, 34,* 1061–1070.

Palloni, A., & Arias, E. (2004). Paradox lost: Explaining the Hispanic adult mortality advantage. *Demography, 41,* 385–415.

Paradies, Y. (2006). A systematic review of empirical research on self-reported racism and health. *International Journal of Epidemiology, 35,* 888–901.

Pham, T. B., & Harris, R. J. (2001). Acculturation strategies among Vietnamese-Americans. *International Journal of Intercultural Relations, 25,* 279–300.

Phinney, J., Madden, T., & Santos, L. J. (1998). Psychological variables as predictors of perceived ethnic discrimination among minority and immigrant adolescents. *Journal of Applied Social Psychology, 28,* 937–953.

Read, J. G., Amick, B., & Donato, K. M. (2005). Arab immigrants: A new case for ethnicity and health? *Social Science and Medicine, 6,* 77–82.

Recio-Adrados, J.-L. (1993). Acculturation: The broader view. Theoretical framework of the acculturation scales. *NIDA Research Monographs, 130,* 57–78.

Redfield, R., Linton, R., & Herskovits, M. (1936). Memorandum on the study of acculturation. *American Anthropologist, 38,* 149–152.

Richardson, A. (1957). The assimilation of British immigrants in Australia. *Human Relations, 10,* 157–166.

Richman, J. A., Gaviria, M., Flaherty, J. A., Birz, S., & Wintrob, R. M. (1987). The process of acculturation: Theoretical perspectives and an empirical investigation in Peru. *Social Science and Medicine, 25,* 839–847.

Rogler, L. H., Cortes, D. E., & Malgady, R. G. (1991). Acculturation and mental health status among Hispanics: Convergence and new directions for research. *American Psychologist, 46,* 585–597.

Rosenberg, M. (1965). *Society and the adolescent self-image.* Princeton: Princeton University Press.

Rudmin, F. W. (2003a). Catalogue of acculturation constructs: Descriptions of 126 taxonomies, 1918–2003. In W. J. Lonner, D. L. Dinnel, S. A. Hayes, & D. N. Sattler (Eds.), *Online readings in psychology and culture.* Bellingham, WA: Center for Cross-Cultural Research, Western Washington University. Retrieved January 30, 2006, from: http://www.ac.wwu.edu/~culture/rudmin.htm

Rudmin, F. W. (2003b). Critical history of the acculturation psychology of assimilation, separation, integration, and marginalization. *Review of General Psychology, 7,* 3–37.

Rudmin, F. W. (2003c). Field notes from the quest for the first use of "acculturation." *Cross-Cultural Psychology Bulletin, 37*(4), 24–31.

Rudmin, F. W. (2006a). *APGAR-type measure of acculturation for use in medical settings.* Presented at the 8th NTNU Conference on Social and Community Psychology, Trondheim, November 9–10.

Rudmin, F. W. (2006b). Debate in science: The case of acculturation. *AnthroGlobe Journal.* Retrieved January 30, 2007, from: http://anthroglobe.info/docs/rudminf_acculturation_061204.pdf

Rudmin, F. W. (2007). Acculturation alchemy: How miscitations make biculturalism appear beneficial. *Psykologisk Tidsskrift, 11*(2), 4–10.

Rudmin, F. W. (2008). Review of "Immigrant youth in cultural transition: Acculturation, identity, and adaptation across national contexts," edited by Berry et al. *Journal of Cross-Cultural Psychology, 39,* 230–233.

Rudmin, F. W., & Ahmadzadeh, V. (2001). Psychometric critique of acculturation psychology: The case of Iranian migrants in Norway. *Scandinavian Journal of Psychology, 42,* 41–56.

Salant, T., & Lauderdale, D. S. (2003). Measuring culture: A critical review of acculturation and health in Asian immigrant populations. *Social Science and Medicine, 57,* 71–90.

Sam, D. L. (2001). Satisfaction with life among international students: An exploratory study. *Social Indicators Research, 53,* 315–337.

Sam, D. L. (2006). Acculturation and health. In D. L. Sam & J. W. Berry (Eds.), *Cambridge Handbook of Acculturation Psychology* (pp. 452–468). Cambridge: Cambridge University Press.

Sam, D. L., Vedder, P., Ward, C., & Hoarenczyk, G. (2006). Psychological and sociocultural adaptation of immigrant youth. In J. W. Berry, J. S. Phinney, D. L. Sam, & P. Vedder. (Eds.), *Immigrant youth in cultural transition: Acculturation, identity and adaptation across national contexts* (pp. 117–141). London: Lawrence Erlbaum Associates.

Sandhu, D., & Asrabadi, B. (1994). Development of an acculturative stress scale for international students: Preliminary findings. *Psychological Reports, 75,* 435–448.

Satia-Abouta, J., Patterson, R. E., Neuhouser, M. L., & Elder, J. (2002). Dietary acculturation: Applications to nutrition research and dietetics. *Journal of the American Dietetic Association, 102,* 1105–1118.

Schalk-Soekar, S.R.G., van de Vijver, F.J.R., & Hoogsteder, M. (2004). Attitudes toward multiculturalism of immigrants and majority members in the Netherlands. *International Journal of Intercultural Relations, 28,* 533–550.

Sheldon, T. A., & Parker, H. (1992). Race and ethnicity in health research. *Journal of Public Health Medicine, 14,* 104–110.

Simich, L., Hamilton, H., & Baya, B. K. (2006). Mental distress, economic hardship and expectations of life in Canada among Sudanese newcomers. *Transcultural Psychiatry, 43,* 418–444.

Skinner, J. H. (2002). Acculturation: Measures of ethnic accommodation to the dominant American culture. In J. H. Skinner, J. A. Teresi, H. Douglas, S. M. Stahl, & A. L. Stewart (Eds.), *Multicultural measurement in older populations* (pp. 37–51). New York: Springer.

Sodowsky, G. R., & Lai, E.W.M. (1997). Asian immigrant variables and structural models of cross-cultural distress. In A. Booth, A. C. Crouter, & N. Landale (Eds.), *Immigration and the family: Research and policy on U.S. immigrants* (pp. 211–234). Mahwah, NJ: Lawrence Erlbaum Associates.

Solis, J. M., Marks, G., Garcia, M., & Shelton, D. (1990). II. Acculturation, access to care, and use of preventative services by Hispanics: Findings from HHANES 1982–1984. *American Journal of Public Health, 80*(Supplement), 11–19.

Spasojevic, J., Heffer, R. W., & Snyder, D. K. (2000). Effects of posttraumatic stress and acculturation on marital functioning in Bosnian refugee couples. *Journal of Traumatic Stress, 13,* 205–217.

Steffen, P. R., Smith, T. B., Larson, M., & Butler, L. (2006). Acculturation to western society as a risk factor for high blood pressure: A meta-analytic review. *Psychosomatic Medicine, 68,* 386–397.

Stevens, G.W.J.M., Vollebergh, W.A.M., Pels, T.V.M., & Crijnen, A.A.M. (2005a). Predicting externalizing problems in Moroccan immigrant adolescents in the Netherlands. *Social Psychiatry and Psychiatric Epidemiology, 40,* 571–579.

Stevens, G.W.J.M., Vollebergh, W.A.M., Pels, T.V.M., & Crijnen, A.A.M. (2005b). Predicting internalizing problems in Moroccan immigrant adolescents in the Netherlands. *Social Psychiatry and Psychiatric Epidemiology, 40,* 1003–1011.

Stimpson, J. P., & Urrutia-Rojas, X. (2007). Acculturation in the United States is associated with lower serum carotenoid levels: Third national health and nutrition examination survey. *Journal of the American Dietetic Association, 107,* 1218–1223.

Szapocznik, J., & Kurtines, W. (1980). Acculturation, biculturalism and adjustment among Cuban Americans. In A. M. Padilla (Ed.), *Acculturation: Theory, models, and some new findings* (pp. 139–159). Boulder, CO: Westview.

Szapocznik, J., Kurtines, W., & Fernandez, T. (1980). Bicultural involvement and adjustment in Hispanic-American youths. *International Journal of Intercultural Relations, 4,* 353–365.

Szapocznik, J., Scopetta, M., Kurtines, W., & Arnalde, M. A. (1978). Theory and measurement of acculturation. *Interamerican Journal of Psychology, 12,* 113–130.

Tabora, B., & Flaskerud, J. H. (1994). Depression among Chinese Americans: A review of the literature. *Issues in Mental Health Nursing, 15,* 569–584.
Tadmor, C. T., & Tetlock, P. E. (2006). Biculturalism: A model of the effects of second-culture exposure on acculturation and integrative complexity. *Journal of Cross-Cultural Psychology, 37,* 173–190.
Taft, R. (1963). The assimilation orientation of immigrants and Australians. *Human Relations, 16,* 279–293.
Taft, R. (1986). Methodological considerations in the study of immigrant adaptation in Australia. *Australian Journal of Psychology, 38,* 339–346.
Taft, R. (1987). Presidential address: Cross-cultural psychology as psychological science. In C. Kagitcibasi (Ed.), *Growth and progress in cross-cultural psychology* (pp. 3–9). Lisse, the Netherlands: Swets & Zeitlinger.
Tartakovsky, E. (2002). Acculturation attitudes of potential emigrants: Jewish youths in Russia. *Journal of Applied Social Psychology, 32,* 1845–1862.
Thielman, S. B. (1985). Psychiatry and social values: The American Psychiatric Association and immigration restriction, 1880–1930. *Psychiatry, 48*(4), 299–310.
Thomas, W. I., & Znaniecki, F. (1918). *The Polish peasant in Europe and America.* New York: Dover.
Triandis, H. C. (1977). Presidential address: Impediments to the progress of cross-cultural psychology. In Y. H. Poortinga (Ed.), *Problems in cross-cultural psychology* (pp. 3–11). Lisse, the Netherlands: Swets & Zeitlinger.
Vedder, P., Sam, D. L., van de Vijver, F., & Phinney, J. S. (2006). Vietnamese and Turkish immigrant youth: Acculturation and adaptation in two ethnocultural groups. In J. W. Berry, J. S. Phinney, D. L. Sam, & P. Vedder. (Eds.), *Immigrant youth in cultural transition: Acculturation, identity and adaptation across national contexts* (pp. 185–210). London: Lawrence Erlbaum Associates.
Vedder, P., van de Vijver, F., & Liebkind, K. (2006). Predicting immigrant youth's adaptation across countries and ethnocultural groups. In J. W. Berry, J. S. Phinney, D. L. Sam, & P. Vedder (Eds.), *Immigrant youth in cultural transition: Acculturation, identity and adaptation across national contexts* (pp. 143–165). London: Lawrence Erlbaum Associates.
Verkuyten, M. (1998). Perceived discrimination and self-esteem among ethnic minority adolescents. *Journal of Social Psychology, 138,* 479–493.
Virta, E., Sam, D. L., & Westin, C. (2004). Adolescents with Turkish background in Norway and Sweden: A comparative study of their psychological adaptation. *Scandinavian Journal of Psychology, 45,* 15–25.
Wamala, S., Boström, G., & Nyqvist, K. (2007). Perceived discrimination and psychological distress in Sweden. *British Journal of Psychiatry, 190,* 75–76.
Weinstock, S. A. (1964). Some factors that retard or accelerate the rate of acculturation with specific reference to Hungarian immigrants. *Human Relations, 17,* 321–340.
World Health Organization. (2001). *ICF: International classification of functioning, disability and health.* Geneva: Author.
Yamada, A. M., Valle, R., Barrio, C., & Jeste, D. (2006). Selecting an acculturation measure for use with Latino older adults. *Research on Aging, 28,* 519–561.
Ying, Y.-W., Lee, P. A., & Tsai, J. L. (2000). Cultural orientation and racial discrimination: Predictors of coherence in Chinese American young adults. *Journal of Community Psychology, 28,* 427–442.
Zajonc, R. B. (1952). Aggressive attitudes of the "stranger" as a function of conformity pressures. *Human Relations, 5,* 205–216.
Zane, N., & Mak, W. (2003). Major approaches to the measurement of acculturation among ethnic minority populations: A content analysis and al alternative empirical strategy. In K. M. Chun, P. Balls Organista, & G. Marín (Eds.), *Acculturation: Advances in theory, measurement and applied research* (pp. 39–60). Washington, DC: American Psychological Association.
Zea, M. C., Asner-Self, K. K., Birman, D., & Buki, L. P. (2003). The Abbreviated Multidimensional Acculturation Scale: Empirical validation with two Latino/Latina samples. *Cultural Diversity and Ethnic Minority Psychology, 9,* 107–126.
Zlobina, A., Basabe, N., Paez, D., & Furnham, A. (2006). Sociocultural adjustment of immigrants: Universal and group-specific predictors. *International Journal of Intercultural Relations, 30,* 195–211.
Zung, W.W.K. (1965). A self-rating depression scale. *Archives of General Psychiatry, 12,* 63–70.

Elias Mpofu
Malachy Bishop
Andreas Hirschi
Trevor Hawkins

18 Assessment of Values

Overview

The personal values held by rehabilitation and health care clients influence in important ways how they comprehend and respond to health challenges or treatment interventions. For instance, affirming important personal values is associated with a willingness to participant in challenging or potentially high reward activities (Crooker, Niiya, & Mischkowski, 2008). Accurate assessment is the basis of effective rehabilitation interventions. Values assessment in rehabilitation and health care is in its infancy (Mpofu & Oakland, 2006). This chapter considers the nature of values and their relevance to and assessment in rehabilitation and health care. It surveys values assessment instruments with potential for rehabilitation intervention and suggests some ways in which research and practice in values assessment in rehabilitation and health care settings can be enhanced.

Learning Objectives

By the end of this chapter, the reader should be able to:

1. Define values in the context of rehabilitation and health care;
2. Explain the relevance of personal values to rehabilitation interventions;
3. Describe the commonly used instruments and procedures for assessing values;
4. Evaluate the evidence for using specific values assessment instruments in rehabilitation and health settings; and
5. Discuss key considerations in developing and using client- or patient-oriented measures of values for rehabilitation and health interventions.

Introduction

Despite the spectacular advances in medical technology in the last half century, the costs of rehabilitation and health care continue to escalate phenomenally, and many health care providers and rehabilitation clients or patients experience difficulties with meeting the costs of health care. A large proportion of these health care costs are from treating preventable health conditions that patients have or develop from a primary health condition (Werthamer & Chatterji, 1998; World Health Organization [WHO], 1999, 2001b) or from use of treatment interventions in which patients are not committed (Mpofu, Crystal, & Feist-Price, 2000; Mpofu & Oakland, 2006). A way to de-escalate health costs is to develop efficacious treatments that meaningfully engage patients in their rehabilitation or health care. Patients or rehabilitation clients would be more willing partners in preventive health if the procedures and outcomes for preventive health were built more on patients' health-related values than is currently the case.

Personal values play a significant role in the ways patients or individuals with chronic illness or disability interpret the meaning of a chronic illness or disability (Danford & Steinfeld, 2003; Schwartz & Sprangers, 1999; Scofield, Pape, McCracken, & Maki, 1980; Wright, Rudicel, & Feinstein, 1994) and, indirectly, their rehabilitation progress through the affirmation of their self-worth or integrity (Mpofu & Bishop, 2006; Mpofu & Oakland, 2006; Orbell, Johnston, Rowley, Davey, & Espley, 2001; Sinclair, Fleming, Radwinsky, Clupper, & Clupper, 2002). For example, presurgery personal goals predicted activity and participation at 9 months after knee-joint replacement (Orbell et al., 2001). The prospective health predictions of more than 75% of people with chronic illness or disability were unreliable if based only on knowledge of their physical functioning (Kivioja & Franklin, 2003). The meanings that patients impute on their conditions influence their health outcomes beyond those explained by objective functional limitations. Patient health-related values motivate their recovery and sustenance of good health.

Surprisingly, there currently are no measures of health-related values for use in rehabilitation and health settings that could be used to plan, monitor, or evaluate rehabilitation interventions. For example, a search for client values associated with rehabilitation and health care from the major databases on health measures (e.g., Health and Psychosocial Instruments and the Citation Index of Allied Health Literature) using an array of search terms (e.g., value(s), measure(s)/ment, scales, and consumer, customer, disability, activity, participation, community living) was unproductive. Measures of values are more developed for career interventions with typically developing others in vocational or work settings rather than rehabilitation and health settings, despite the fact that work is a widely acknowledged rehabilitation and health intervention. This chapter considers prospective assessment for health-related values for use in rehabilitation and health settings.

Definitions and Theories of Values

The concept of *values* is one that is widely recognized across the various specialties of psychology and the health sciences (Kluckhohn, 1951; Kluckhohn & Strodtbeck, 1961; Rokeach & Ball-Rokeach, 1989; Wright, 1983). The conceptual richness of the construct of values has encouraged several definitions and associated theories. For example, Kluckhohn (1951) defined values as "a conception of the desirable which influences the selection from available modes, means, and ends of action" (p. 395). Similarly, Rokeach (1973) defined values as "an enduring belief that a specific mode of conduct or end-state of existence is personally or socially preferable to an opposite or converse mode of conduct or end-state of existence" (p. 3). The significance of value-directed goals is also acknowledged by Schwartz, who defined values as "desirable, transituational goals varying in importance, that serve as guiding principles in people's lives" (1996, p. 2), and by Nevill and Super (1986), who defined values as need-based models of behavior that are behind a person's goal setting and implementation activity. Mpofu and Bishop (2006) weighted process factors in value enactment at the individual level when they defined values as "preferences or personally derived decisions about the importance or meaning of some aspect or component of self that are manifested cognitively, socially, and behaviorally through prioritizing, emphasis, or the investment of resources, such as time or psychological attention" (p. 148). Values are inherently related to the self-concept. By representing the ideals and goals by which the self is evaluated in the present, and toward which the self is directed in the future, values create an integral aspect of the experience and evaluation of self (see Table 18.1).

Characteristics of Values

Although specific definitions of values vary somewhat in focus and content, researchers have consistently identified several common characteristics of values. First, values influence behavior (Hitlin & Pilliavin, 2004). Although it is certainly the case that other motivational forces also function to shape individual and group behavior, values represent the goals or ideals toward which

18.1 Types of Values and Their Functions

Rokeach, 1973		Nevill & Super, 1986a
Instrumental Values	*Terminal Values*	*Ability Utilization*
Ambitious	A comfortable life	Achievement
Broad-minded	An exciting life	Aesthetics
Capable	A sense of accomplishment	Altruism
Cheerful	A world at peace	Autonomy
Clean	A world of beauty	Creativity
Courageous	Equality	Economic rewards
Forgiving	Family security	Lifestyle
Helpful	Freedom	Physical activity
Honest	Happiness	Prestige
Imaginative	Inner harmony	Risk taking
Independent	Mature love	Social interaction
Intellectual	National security	Variety
Logical	Pleasure	Working conditions
Loving	Salvation	Cultural identity
Obedient	Self-respect	Physical prowess
Polite	Social recognition	Personal identity
Responsible	True friendship	Advancement
Self-controlled	Wisdom	Economic security

From "Assessment of Value Change in Adults with Acquired Disabilities," by E. Mpofu and T. Oakland, 2006, in M. Hersen (Ed.), *Clinician's Handbook of Adult Behavioral Assessment* (pp. 601–630). New York: Academic Press.

behavior is directed. As Sagiv, Roccas, and Hazan suggested (2004), values are social and cognitive representations of the goals that influence individuals' perceptions and direct their decisions, choices, and behaviors. Conversely, from an assessment perspective it may also be said that behavior reflects values, or that through observing one's actions, decisions, and behaviors, one's values may be inferred.

Second, although values are enduring in their influence of behavior (as reflected in the consistency and continuity of personality and culture), they are also learned and shaped by developmental, personal, and social experiences. The concept of value change, discussed later in this chapter, and the various theories that describe value change as a response to changing health, represent conceptions of the mechanisms by which this modification of the value structure may occur.

Third, values are socially learned and culturally dependent and exist within a complex and fluid system. Values develop and are modified, prioritized, and reprioritized as the result of social influence, cultural and societal movements, and personal experiences (Kluckhohn & Strodtbeck, 1961; Nicholson & Stepina, 1998; Rohan & Zanna, 1996; Rokeach, 1973; Seligman & Katz, 1996). For instance, goals that, due to changes at the personal, societal, and external environmental level, become ineffectual, counterproductive, or maladaptive may be modified or restructured. At the individual level, social and cultural influence, including the family's influence on the individual, are essential to both value development and value change throughout the lifespan.

Finally, researchers (Rokeach, 1973; Schwartz, 1996) agree that values occur in the context of a system but differ with respect to their salience in expressing the core identity of the system they represent. Values are also perceived to differ in number and organization within a system and also in the goals to which they are aligned (Montgomery, Persson, & Ryden, 1996; Rokeach, 1973). For example, Rokeach (1973), Schwartz (1996), and Nevill and Super (1986a, 1986b) have all offered differing conceptual frameworks. Montgomery et al. and Schwartz have both suggested models in which a larger set of values, 82 and 56 respectively, could be assimilated into a smaller group of 10 factors or types. Rokeach and Nevill and Super postulated that the number of values that are possessed by individuals is relatively small. Rokeach (1973) proposed a total of 36 values, divided into 2 primary groups: terminal and instrumental. In this approach, *terminal* values are defined as the idealized end states. *Instrumental* values are regarded as the desirable attitudes or behaviors for accomplishing these terminal values. Nevill and Super proposed a model consisting of 21 different values. These models are further described later in this chapter.

Applicable ICF Concepts

Within the International Classification of Functioning, Disability, and Health (ICF) structure (WHO, 2001a), values as a health construct fall under the personal domain, particularly to the extent that they are an aspect of the self-concept, which is impacted by health conditions. Values are also an aspect of the participation in the sense that individuals, in their efforts to engage in preferred activities, negotiate environments that are value-laden and influence their rehabilitation outcomes (Mpofu & Bishop, 2006).

Self and Values

The congruence in the relationship between one's values and one's behavior is an important element of well-being (Kasser, 2006; Kasser & Ryan, 2001; Sagiv et al., 2004). Research in this area concerns such questions as whether certain values are inherently healthy or health promoting. Other research has examined the negative impact of values on health and well-being (e.g., Deci & Ryan, 1985; Sagiv et al.) and also how values may be modified or made salient for the promotion of health (e.g., Carver & Baird, 1998; Chirkov, Ryan, Kim, & Kaplan, 2003; Harvey et al., 1992). For instance, competing personal values are linked to intrinsic and extrinsic goals that influence health and well-being (Carver & Baird, 1998; Chirkov et al., 2003; Sheldon & Elliot, 1999). Understanding personal values as goals or motivators that shape behavior leads to a number of important implications for health and well-being.

Value-change theories propose that an adaptive shift in the importance and/or awareness of values occurs in response to disability, illness, or other life stresses (e.g., Dembo, Leviton, & Wright, 1956; Linkowski, 1971; Mpofu & Houston, 1998; Sprangers & Schwartz, 1999; Wright, 1983). Such models include, for example, value change (Dembo et al., 1956; Wright, 1983), "preference drift" (Groot & Van Den Brink, 2000), "domain compensation" (Misajon, 2002), "disability centrality" (Bishop, 2005), "systemic" (Mpofu & Oakland, 2006), and "response shift" (Schwartz & Sprangers, 1999, 2000). For example, the response shift model suggests that adaptation involves a change in the individual's values (Schwartz & Sprangers, 1999, 2000).

Researchers have proposed the occurrence of an adaptive value-change process (Linkowski, 1971; Menzel, Dolan, Richardson, & Oslen, 2002; Schwartz & Sprangers, 2000; Sprangers & Schwartz, 1999; Wright, 1983). For example, in Wright's approach, specific forms of value restructuring are aimed at normalizing the disability experience or regarding the disability as non-devaluing. Schwartz and Sprangers (2000) have explained value change from the experience of disability as a response shift to accommodate the disability experience in the most adaptive way. Rehabilitation clients' or patients' responses to chronic illness or disability are influenced by their personal values, and these values are reflected in their attitudes and behaviors toward rehabilitation interventions (Livneh & Antonak, 1994).

Activity, Participation, and Values

Activity and participation have been explored in terms of their implications for health promotion, self-management, psychosocial adaptation to chronic illness and disability, psychological well-being, adherence to treatment, help-seeking,

Discussion Box 18.1.

DEVELOPMENTAL EFFECTS OF DISABILITY

Studies (e.g., Mpofu & Bishop, 2006; Mpofu & Houston, 1998) have documented potential differences in disability- and health-related values in people with acquired disabilities compared to those with developmental disabilities. For instance, individuals with developmental disabilities appear to construct a value system that accommodates their disability-related difference over the life span, whereas those with acquired disabilities seem to reconstruct or reprioritize their value system in response to the experience of disability.

Questions:
In what specific ways could the history of a disability influence adaptation or living with a disability? How may such differences be assessed?

Would the quality of adaptation to a developmental disability be superior to adaptation to an acquired disability? Explain your answer.

and other concerns (Cooper et al., 2003; Karel, 2000; Levine, Plume, & Nelson, 1997; Ozer & Kroll, 2002; Pellissier & Venta, 1996; Sinclair et al., 2002). For example, rehabilitation clients or patients are likely to be motivated in their rehabilitation goals if they perceive rehabilitation interventions to be relevant to enhancing their participation in preferred activities and environments (Ozer & Kroll, 2002). Overvaluing of service provider perspectives (which reflect provider rather than patient values) could hinder effective rehabilitation planning and intervention because service provider perspectives may be at variance with those of the rehabilitation client (Heinemann, Bode, Cichowski, & Kan, 1998; Sneeuw et al., 1997). Rehabilitation service providers may misperceive client motivation and commitment to rehabilitation outcomes, with the result being that clients are hampered in their participation of the rehabilitation process and outcomes (Davies & Cleary, 2005; Lynch & Thomas, 1994; Rosenthal & Berven, 1999). The experience of chronic illness or disability in a family member impacts the family's resource utilization (personal, time, and material) and involvement with the individual with a disability, which in turn influences the quality of family and community participation of the person with a disability (Mpofu & Wilson, 2004; Rees et al., 2002). Family values mediate the impact of disability on activity and community participation by the individual with a disability. Communities that in their attitudes are disability friendly (as reflected in enabling legislation, infrastructure, and service systems) project values that make it likely that the individual with a disability will attain a preferred lifestyle (Livneh, Martz, & Wilson, 2001).

Values are unlike traits in that they are malleable and allow for more cognitive control in their expression as compared to traits. Values change as a function of different demands in the environment and from interactions with other people (Rohan, 2000). Positive changes in values will, in part, enable the individual with disabilities to experience greater participation in preferred environments.

History of Research and Practice in the Assessment of Values

One of the earliest models of human values was by the German philosopher Eduart Spranger (1928). Spranger proposed that six basic attitudes or value types (theoretical, economic, aesthetic, political, social, and religious; Rohan & Zanna, 2001) are present in each person, with different proportions, and with one of them dominating. This work later became the basis for one of the earliest standardized value assessment instruments: the Study of Values (Allport, Vernon, & Lindzey, 1960). The Study of Values measure assessed the relative importance of the six values proposed by Spranger and became one of the most popular value measures for years (see Braithwaite & Scott, 1991, for a more detailed discussion of early value measures). The basic assumption of Spranger's model of values was that there is a universally valid set of human values and that individual differences in values are explained by how values are organized or how much importance is attributed to them by each person. Both these notions appear to have received empirical support (e.g., Schwartz, 1992).

Important historical milestones in the development of measures of values include the works by Rokeach (1973), Schwartz (1992), Super (1970), and Dawis and Lofquist (1984).

Rokeach's Value Theory

Rokeach's (1973) value theory is credited as a major force in the assessment of values. He distinguished between goals (terminal values) and modes of conduct (instrumental values). Terminal values refer to desired ends (e.g., a comfortable / prosperous life), while instrumental values refer to desired means (e.g., being broad-minded or being helpful). Based on this distinction, he created the Rokeach Value Survey (Rokeach, 1973), which remains one of the most popular values inventories.

The *Rokeach's Values Survey* (RVS; Rokeach, 1973) contains a list of 18 terminal values and 18 instrumental values and asks the client to rank the values according to their importance. Based on the rankings, the most and the least important terminal and instrumental values of a client can be identified. Ranking of values was the preferred assessment method because in real live situations values are often in competition with each other and a person is forced to choose among them. However, others have argued that scaling values is more desirable because of preferable statistical proprieties. For example, it allows for longer lists of values to be assessed, and it also allows test-takers to give equal weights to values of equal subjective importance (Schwartz, 1994). Finally, there is some empirical evidence to suggest that rating offers more predictive validity because people who are forced to rank values often do so based on trivial distinction (Maio, Roese, Seligman, & Katz, 1996).

Applications of the RVS to rehabilitation and health care settings appears rare to nonexistent (Braithwaite & Law, 1985; Mpofu & Houston, 1998; Mpofu & Oakland, 2006). Braithwaite and Law criticized the RVS for not including values important to physical fitness and well-being. Rokeach's model of values and the instrument upon which it is based has also been criticized for merely presenting a list of unrelated values without a supporting theory of an underlying value structure. The lack of supporting interpretive theory makes it impossible to understand the consequences of high priorities on some values rather than others (Rohan, 2000). Finally, the usefulness and empirical validity of the instrumental vs. terminal value dichotomy has been questioned because instrumental values and terminal values influence each other (Mpofu & Oakland, 2006; Schwartz, 1992).

Schwartz's Circumplex Model of Universal Values

Shalom Schwartz's (1992) work explicitly drew upon Rokeach's work. He proposed a set of universally human values that can be organized into two dimensions: Openness to Change versus Conservation, and Self-enhancement versus Self-Transcendence. Openness to Change versus Conservation is defined by the conflict between being motivated "to follow their own intellectual and emotional interests in unpredictable and uncertain directions" or "to preserve the status quo and the certainty it provides in relationships with close others, institutions, and traditions" (p. 43). Self-Enhancement versus Self-Transcendence relates to the conflict between concern for the consequences of one's own and others' actions for the self and concern for the consequences of one's own and others' actions in the social context.

Schwartz proposed 10 values that are arranged along the 2 dimensions defined previously so that some values are closely related, while others can be considered as opposites and in conflict to each other: (1) Power: Social status and prestige, control or dominance over people and resources; (2) Achievement: Personal success through demonstrating competence according to social standards; (3) Hedonism: Pleasure or sensuous gratification for oneself; (4) Stimulation: Excitement, novelty, and challenge in life; (5) Self-direction: Independent thought and action—choosing, creating, exploring; (6) Universalism: Understanding, appreciation, tolerance, and protection for the welfare of all people and for nature; (7) Benevolence: Preservation and enhancement of the welfare of people with whom one is in frequent personal contact; (8) Tradition: Respect, commitment, and acceptance of the customs and ideas that traditional culture or religion provide; (9). Conformity: Restraint of actions, inclinations, and impulses likely to upset or harm others and violate social expectations or norms; and (10) Security: Safety, harmony, and stability of society, of relationships, and of self. Schwartz and colleagues have currently the most active research project on human values, which provides support for the accuracy and cross-cultural validity of this value model (e.g., Schwartz & Boehnke, 2004; Schwartz & Sagie, 2000).

The *Schwartz Value Survey* (SVS; Schwartz et al., 2001) contains less-abstract items that are more accessible to a wider population than the SVS, which is broadly applied in value research but not conceived as a tool for assessment practice. Research could not be identified on the use of the SVS in rehabilitation and health settings.

Super's Theory of Values

Super (Nevill & Super, 1986a; Super & Sverko, 1995) distinguished among 5 basic value orientations (utilitarian, individualistic, self-actualization, social, and adventurous) and 18 specific values (e.g., advancement, autonomy, social interactions). Super's model is the basis for the Values Scale.

The Values Scale (VS; Nevill & Super, 1986b) is a frequently applied inventory in counseling practice. The Values Scale is a 105-item scale that measures extrinsic and intrinsic life and work values according to the importance attributed to 21 different values, such as ability utilization, achievement, autonomy, economic rewards, working conditions, or cultural identity. Each value is assessed with five items, and results can be interpreted as the relative score obtained for each value. For example, the values can be ranked according to their scores to create a values hierarchy for a client (Nevill & Kruse, 1996). No norms data are yet available to compare the scores of an individual test-taker to a representative sample. Ranking values based on the obtained scores can present interpretation problems if a client rates all of the values as "very important."

The *Salience Inventory* (SI; Nevill & Super, 1986a) is a 170-item measure designed to assess the importance of five life–career goals: home and family, community service, studying, working, and leisure activities. Items include 50 participation items, 50 commitment items, and 70 value expectation items.

Participation measures what an individual actually does or has recently done in each area; commitment rates the degree to which a person is committed to pursuing each life role; and value expectation is based on the degree to which an individual expects that major life satisfactions or values are found in each role (Nevill & Calvert, 1996, for a review of the applications of the SI). Based on a large-scale study of values in 10 countries, Super and Sverko (1995) developed the *Work Importance Study* (WIS), which measures both general and work specific values. The WIS does not account for how work values are influenced in their salience by different aspects of work itself (Zytowski, 1994).

The VS was low to moderately correlated with Minnesota Importance Questionnaire (MIQ; Gay, Weiss, Hendel, Dawis, & Lofquist, 1971) scores in students with hearing impairment. There is very limited evidence to support the use of the VS, SI, and the WIS with rehabilitation and health populations.

Dawis and Lofquist's Model of Values

Dawis and Lofquist (1984) proposed that work values and needs congruence to job characteristics were the most important aspects of job choice and satisfaction. They proposed that 20 vocational needs (e.g., ability utilization, variety, social-service, creativity) can be identified. Factorial analysis of these needs revealed six underlying values: achievement, comfort, status, altruism, safety, and autonomy.

The Dawis and Lofquist values model was the basis for the MIQ (Gay et al., 1971). The MIQ assesses the degree to which a person emphasizes 20 psychological needs, which can be summarized into six work values. The goal of the MIQ is to identify needs and values of a client and to match those to corresponding work environments. The rationale behind this approach is that a person's needs affect his or her career choices, and the degree to which a person's needs are met influences satisfaction with work. The MIQ allows the comparison of one's needs and values to the reinforcement patterns of different occupations in order to locate a good match for one's preferences.

There are two forms of the MIQ, and both are self-administered. In both versions, clients are presented with 20 different statements. In the first, test-takers are asked to rank these statements in groups of five according to their personal preference regarding an ideal job. The second version requires clients to decide which of two statements is more important to them when thinking about an ideal job, which results in 190 pairs of statements to be rated. The results can be compared to normative data for different age groups and by gender. An ipsative (intraindividual) approach to results interpretation is possible in which the observed preferences are only interpreted in the light of the personal meaning for the client instead of giving priority to the actual values of the obtained scores (Brooke & Ciechalski, 1994). Regardless of whether norm data are applied or not, a possible approach to interpretation is to use the obtained scores to create an individual's hierarchy of needs and use this as a starting point to explore suitable career options.

The MIQ was developed, in part, to assess changes in vocational needs in clients from the impact of acquired disability and also their use of leisure time (Gay et al., 1971). There is limited evidence for the use of the MIQ with rehabilitation and health clients (Mpofu & Oakland, 2006). The factorial structure has, among

Discussion Box 18.2

VALUE CATEGORIES

The Schwartz Value Survey and similar measures of personal values have isolated broad categories of values, such as Power/Status/Prestige, Achievement, Hedonism, Self-Direction/Autonomy, Benevolence/Altruism, Conformity and Security, Achievement/Advancement, and Creativity. A more extensive list of values is included in Table 18.1 in this chapter.

Questions:

1. Using these personal values as a starting point, to what extent do you think they are relevant in a general rehabilitation setting in terms of their impact on the smooth progression of the rehabilitation process?
2. Take two values and outline how one may hinder and how the other may assist in the client's smooth transition through the rehabilitation process.
3. Using two different personal values, discuss how each of these may impact upon the vocational outcome for a client where the aim of their rehabilitation process is to go back to alternate appropriate work to enter the workforce for the first time.
4. What value does the assessment of personal values bring to the task of career decision making in a general sense?

others, been replicated among vocational rehabilitation clients (Lofquist & Dawis, 1978). MIQ measures correlated significantly with measures of work satisfaction in workers with mental retardation. The comparative judgment format may present difficulties to clients with significant cognitive impairment or other severe disability.

Current Practices in Values Assessment

Values are dynamic constructs best assessed with measures that combine both qualitative and quantitative approaches (Mpofu & Houston, 1998). Important considerations are the ability of the rehabilitation client or patient to identify values that are important to him or her (rather than being constrained by a predetermined set of values) and the ability then to express his or her experience with these values in a personally meaningful way. A related issue is the limited use of qualitative assessment techniques in values assessment.

Qualitative Approaches

Qualitative assessments typically involve examining forms of construction such as narrative, autobiography, life story, and the subjective career (Savickas, 1992;

Young & Collin, 2004). Instead of objectively assessing an individual's values in order to match a client to the most suitable occupation, the aim of assessment from a constructivist stance is to "open up avenues of movement, promote empowerment, support transitions, and assist the client gain eligibility for more participation [in their future]" (Peavy, 1998, p. 180). Qualitative assessments can be used in combination with more formal assessment measures (such as the ones discussed previously; see also McMahon & Patton, 2002; Whiston & Rahardja, 2005). Counselors could also use a qualitative follow-up session to a standardized value assessment where the subjective meaning of the retrieved results and their integration in the client's life story are the focus. Cart Sorts and Genograms are two commonly used qualitative approaches to the assessment of values.

Cart Sort Procedures

The *Personal Values Cart Sort* (PVCS; Miller, C'de Baca, Matthews, & Wilbourne, 2001) is a card-sorting tool that is available for free from the authors' Web site (http://casaa.umd.edu). It includes 50 different values that can be sorted into five categories ranging from "least important" to "most important." The top values are then sorted according to their subjective importance, which can be used as the basis for further discussion.

The *Career Values Cart Sort* (CVCS) planning kit (Knowdell, 2002) uses 54 different values that are to be stored in one of five categories: "Always Valued," "Often Valued," "Sometimes Valued," "Seldom Valued," and "Never Valued." Clients are then asked to sort the cards in each category according to their relative importance and copy the results to a summary sheet. With the help of a worksheet, clients are then encouraged to name their eight most important values and think about how they relate to their current career decision and possible conflicts that might arise in trying to satisfy these values. Evidence for the use of the PVCS and CVCS with rehabilitation and health clients could not be found.

The Values Genogram

Research shows that the family has a strong influence on value development. For example, parents' social class, vocation, education, and specific family characteristics, such as childrearing practices, all shape values of the children (Hitlin & Piliavin, 2004). The family is also among the strongest influences of career development beginning in childhood and continuing into adulthood (Whiston & Keller, 2004).

A genogram is a qualitative assessment method to gather information about a client's history, background, and life experience. The process can enrich a client's understanding of his or her present situation and facilitate planning for the future. Gysbers (2006) described how a career genogram can be conducted and integrated into the counseling process. The first step is to share the purpose of the genogram activity, such as gaining a better understanding of the client's values and how they were influenced by his family, community, and life experiences. The second step is for the client to draw a genogram with names of all the family members over three generations. A value-specific genogram can then be created if the counselor asks the client to identify which values were most important to each person represented on the genogram. This can be done in writing with a follow-up discussion and more in-depth questions from the counselor, such as "What was most important for this person in his/her life?" "What did this person aspire to be or to achieve in his/her life?" "How would you describe this person's life-motto?" The information gained about the client's family values can then be related to his or her present situation to get a better understanding of the client's own values and how they influence the individual's life and career decisions. Research on the use of value genograms in rehabilitation settings could not be identified.

Research Box 18.1

EFFECTS OF WRITING ABOUT VALUES

Crooker, J., Niiya, Y., & Mischkowski, D (2008). Why does writing about important values reduce defensiveness? Self-affirmation and the role of positive other-directed feelings. *Psychological Science: Research, Theory and Application in Psychology and Related Sciences, 19*(7), 740–747.

Objective: The study investigated the influence of affirming personal values in explaining acceptance of potentially threatening messages to the self. The authors hypothesized that writing about values important to self would enhance positive self-perceptions as a loving and caring person, which would extend to openness to messages that ordinarily would trigger defensiveness.

Method: A culturally diverse sample of 102 psychology undergraduate students participated in the study (70% White, 12% Asian, 18% other; 27% smokers). They were in two conditions: experimental and control. In the experimental condition, participants wrote about a value important to them, and in the control condition, they wrote about a value unimportant to them. They then took a scale to assess the extent to which they experienced love and other positive feelings (e.g., joyful, proud, connected). After, they were given a task to assess the scientific merit of a fake research article on the effects of smoking (a presumed threatening message to smokers) to evaluate the scientific merits of the study findings.

Findings: Participants who wrote about values important to them reported higher feelings of love and connectedness compared to those who wrote about values unimportant to them. Smokers who wrote about values important to them were more positive in their assessment of the threatening message about smoking from the research article than were nonsmokers.

Conclusion: Writing about values important to the self enhanced the sense of love and being involved with others beyond self-serving interests. It also reduced defensiveness to potentially threatening information from an external source. Priming values important to self has positive effects on well-being.

Questions:

Explain the openness to a potentially threatening message by smokers compared to nonsmokers.

To what extent does this study support the significance of values to health behavior?

Would asking people to write about a value important to the self be an acceptable measure of personal values in rehabilitation and health settings? Explain your answer.

Based on your reading of this chapter, what type of assessment procedure would writing about values important to self be? How could the scientific credibility of this procedure be enhanced?

Quantitative Approaches

The development of health values assessment tools has focused primarily on check lists or rating scales. The RVS and MIQ (previously considered) exemplify quantitative approaches to the assessment of values. In this section, we consider the Acceptance of Disability Scale (Livneh & Antonak, 1994) and O*NET-based value measures.

The *Acceptance of Disability Scale* (ADS; Linkowski, 1971) is a 50-item, Likert type, self-report measure of changes in values following disability. Items were written consistent with the value-change theory proposed by Beatrice Wright and colleagues (i.e., Dembo et al., 1956). Dembo et al. considered that adjustment to disability involved up to four value shifts: containment of disability effects (e.g., A physical disability may limit a person in some ways, but this does not mean he/she should give up and do nothing with his/her life in full), enlargement of scope of values (e.g., Though I am disabled, my life is full), subordination of physique (e.g., There are many things a person with a disability is able to do), and transformation from comparative to assertive values (e.g., Personal characteristics such as honesty and willingness to work hard are much more important than physical appearance and ability). Construct validity studies supported a one-factor structure that accounted for about 45% of the variance (Livneh & Antonak, 1994; Mpofu & Herbert, 2006). The measure has been used in research rather than as a clinical instrument.

The O*Net Measures

These comprise two measures based on the MIQ with updated and extended information (e.g., McCloy et al., 1999). The application and interpretation of the results is otherwise the same as for the MIQ. As is the case with the MIQ, the goal of the O*NET measures is to locate suitable occupations based on one's values and needs. O*NET draws upon an extensive database of occupations that is more up-to-date and extensive than the one available from the MIQ. This database is also continuatively updated based on actual job analyses. The measures can be downloaded and used for free from the U.S. Department of Labor's O*NET Web site (http://www.onenetcenter.org).

Super's *Work Values Inventory—Revised* (Zytowski, 2006) has been published as an online inventory on http://www.kuder.com and is an updated version of Super's (1970) original inventory focusing explicitly on work values. The inventory measures the importance of 12 work values (e.g., achievement, lifestyle, or variety) with 6 items each. The reading level is approximately sixth grade and the inventory takes 10–20 minutes to complete. Results are retrieved online as a two-page narrative and graph showing the assessed individual rank order of the values. A major advantage of the online inventory to the older paper-and-pencil version is that it provides a link to the O*NET database to locate potentially matching occupations with the test-takers values for further consideration and exploration.

The *Work Importance Profiler* (WIP; O*NET Resource Center, 2008) is a computerized version that uses the multiple-rank order format of the MIQ. The program then presents a list of occupations that match the test-taker's profile, sorted into categories that reflect different levels of educational requirements. The *Work Importance Locator* (WIL; O*NET Resource Center, 2008) is a shorter paper-and-pencil measure that uses a card-sorting task to determine the relative importance of the MIQ needs. This version might be useful if there is limited access to computers or for group administration.

Mixed Method Approaches

Some notable examples from the field of health-related quality of life (HRQoL) offer examples of potentially useful models of a combined qualitative and quantitative approach. For example, rather than presenting a patient with a set of predetermined HRQoL domains and asking the patient to rate his or her experience with them, the *Schedule for the Evaluation of Individual* QOL (SEIQOL; O'Boyle, McGee, Hickey, O'Malley, & Joyce, 1992; McGee, O'Boyle, Hickey, O'Malley, & Joyce, 1991) and the *Patient Generated Index of Quality of Life* (PGI; Ruta, Garratt, Leng, Russell, & Macdonald, 1994) have been designed to allow the individual's selection of personally important domains, and then to allow for the individual weighting of domain importance. The increased use of such approaches, combined with open-ended interviews and decision analytic approaches, would be an important development.

Particularly relevant for rehabilitation and health assessment is the notion that personal values change due to a change in health status when people adapt their values to cope with the new situation (Sprangers & Schwartz, 1999). The *Thentest* (Schwartz & Sprangers, 1999) is a measure of the extent that rehabilitation and health clients change their values to accommodate or adapt to disability experience. The basic procedure is to collect rehabilitation status data from a client using a preferred measure at a point in time (e.g., pretreatment) and then at another point in time (e.g., posttreatment or present time). The posttreatment perceptions of health are then retrospectively compared with previous perceptions (hence the *then* aspect of the test). For example, Schwartz, Sprangers, Carey, and Reed (2004) used the *Thentest* to assess value change in patients with multiple sclerosis at 5 years postillness. The patients showed a recalibration of personal values in valuing psychological functioning more than they did physical functioning earlier in the progression of the illness.

Research Critical to Values Assessment in Rehabilitation and Health

Research on values in rehabilitation and health settings is still in its early stages (Mpofu & Oakland, 2006). In the main, the focus has been on identifying the correlates of value change in specific rehabilitation settings and interventions (Livneh & Antonak, 1994; Mpofu & Herbert, 2006; Schwartz et al, 2004); the salience of rehabilitation values in specific disability populations and their differentiation by gender, severity of disability, and independent and community living status (Mpofu, 2008); the mechanisms of change or recalibration of values over the rehabilitation period (Schwartz et al., 2004); and defining priority issues in patient-oriented care (Cooper et al., 2003; Swenson et al., 2004). With increased use of values assessment in health and rehabilitation, several important research questions remain to be explored.

Correlates of Value Change in Specific Disability Populations

Rehabilitation client characteristics (e.g., by type of disability) and service context (community setting) influenced observed changes in client values toward health and well-being. For example, clients with community and independent living reported higher adaptive value changes (Mpofu & Herbert, 2006). Patients with progressive physical/neurological disabilities recalibrated their values to emphasize physical rather than mental health functioning (Schwartz et al., 2004). Measures are still to be constructed to assess changes in specific value domains influenced by disability experience. The empirical evidence for the specific progression in value change with acquired or chronic illness or disability is still to be documented.

Research on gender differences in values has produced inconsistent results. Some studies report statistical differences in general values between men and women. The studies that found significant differences generally report that men value materialistic and extrinsic values more than women, who, in turn, endorse more social and intrinsic values (e.g., Beutel & Marini, 1995). Analyzing gender differences in 10 basic values across 70 countries, Schwartz and Rubel (2005) came to the conclusion that men generally score higher on power, stimulation, hedonism, achievement, and self-direction values, whereas the reverse is true for benevolence and universalism values. However, Schwartz and Rubel also noted that gender differences are rather small and typically explain less variance than age and much less than culture. The literature is, however, quite clear on the notion that gender plays a major role in work values, where men were found to be more likely to espouse extrinsic values and women more likely to espouse social values (e.g., Duffy & Sedlacek, 2007a; Hitlin & Piliavin, 2004). It is unclear how gender effects influence disability-related values in rehabilitation clients.

Studies show that values change over time for different age cohorts. For example, over the period 1952–1970, a change of students' values toward a focus on personal gratification and personal freedom and a weakened sense of social responsibility was observed—but also some return to older values in the early 1980s (Hoge, Hoge, & Wittenberg, 1987). Students' values also appear to have shifted toward private materialism and away from personal self-fulfillment from the early 1970s to the mid-1980s (Easterlin & Crimmins, 1991). Studies concerning the last two decades report that adolescents and college students attributed increasing value to intrinsic and self/actualizing values, while extrinsic and prestige values declined (Duffy & Sedlacek, 2007b; Sinisalo, 2004). The manner in which these age-cohort value changes intersect disability-related values is in need of investigation.

Research confirms the theoretical notion that values and personality traits are two related yet distinct concepts (Olver & Mooradian, 2003). Studies showed that agreeableness correlates most positively with benevolence and tradition values, openness with self-direction and universalism values, extroversion with achievement and stimulation values, and conscientiousness with achievement and conformity values (Roccas, Sagiv, Schwartz, & Knafo, 2002). Values were also shown to predict vocational interests better than basic personality traits (Berings, Fruyt, & Bouwen, 2004). Studies to chart the evolution of adaptive disability-related values within personality types could be helpful to targeted interventions that address personality variables as mediators.

The Mechanisms of Value Change Over the Rehabilitation Period

Several theoretical constructs have been proposed to explain value change over the rehabilitation period. For example, Schwartz and Sprangers (1999) proposed a response-shift characterized by a change of the meaning of one's self-evaluation of a target construct as a result of: (a) a change in the consumer's internal standards (i.e., scale recalibration), (b) a change in the consumer's values (i.e., relative importance of the domains constituting the target construct),

Discussion Box 18.3

GENDER DIFFERENCES IN VALUES

The work of Schwartz and Rubel (2005) across 70 countries isolated some interesting and apparent differences in the predominant personal values of men and women. The basic difference is that men place more emphasis on extrinsic values and women place more emphasis on social values. There is also evidence to suggest that values can change as is evidence by changes in the personal values of Generation X and Generation Y.

Questions:
Given the reported difference in values orientations between males and females, how do you think that these differences will impact upon the nature of the adjustment to disability process for men and women?

and (c) redefining the target construct or value (i.e., reconceptualization). The specific triggers for such changes in disability-related values and their reliable measurement in rehabilitation and health settings are still a matter for study. The *Thentest* (as previously described) and other self-report approaches are susceptible to memory decay or selective forgetting effects and also social desirability. There is a possibility that patients in their self-evaluation of coping or living with a disability are influenced by self-comparisons, particularly in reference to others with more severe disabilities (e.g., a downward social comparison). These self comparisons may be associated with changes in one's internal standards (e.g., "Although I have a disability, others have more severe disabilities"; Mpofu & Bishop, 2006). The effects of self-comparisons in the construction of personal disability-related values and their reprioritization are unknown.

Measurement Issues

Among the issues that need attention are the identification of appropriate values for assessment in the health and rehabilitation context, instrument and measurement issues including the use of qualitative approaches, and increased attention to the perspective of the health care consumer in instrument development.

Indicators of disability-related values on current surveys (e.g., ADS: Linkowski, 1971; MIQ: Gay et al., 1971) are interpreted without regard of their equivalence in mapping the latent construct of adaptation to disability. However, in reality, clients experiencing negative personal self-worth on one indicator disability value domain (e.g., subordination of physique) may also experience self-efficacy problems in containing the effects of disability to areas in which activity and participation may be objectively constrained. If these indicators of disability-related value statuses are not considered conjointly, using a mathematical measurement model, valuable information for understanding sources of disparities in health care is lost. Item response measurement models (see chapter 5) are useful for constructing measures with conjoint properties, and instruments that enable meaningful aggregation of data from multiple settings are useful for identifying the status and development of adaptive disability-related values (Mpofu & Oakland, 2006).

It is also clear from the discussion in this chapter that values may be either general or more narrowly associated with specific life domains (e.g., work values). In the broad context of health, discussions of values and values systems may include both broad values systems and more specific health-related values (e.g., health care values concerning the meanings of pain management, the importance of choice and control, and risk taking in medical decision making; values about the meaning and components of physical and psychological health; or values about body image). Increased attention to the development of health-specific values and value systems and their assessment in rehabilitation and health is necessary. Increased attention to the specificity and sensitivity to changes of values and value assessment instruments in the context of health and rehabilitation is also required.

Theoretical Issues

Researchers who have explored values change using more general or universal values systems (such as Rokeach's values system; e.g., Keany & Glueckauf, 1993;

Research Box 18.2

VALUE INFLUENCES ON MEDICAL CONSULTATION

Source: O'Connor, A. M., Wells, G. A., Tugwell, P., Laupacis, A., Elmslie, T., & Drake, E. (1999). The effects of an "explicit" values clarification exercise in a woman's decision aid regarding postmenopausal hormone therapy. *Health Expectations, 2,* 21–32.

Objective: To evaluate the incremental effect of a graphic weigh-scale values clarification exercise to explicitly consider the personal importance of the benefits versus the risks in a woman's decision aid regarding postmenopausal hormone therapy.

Method: Among a sample of 201 women aged 50–69 years from Ottawa, Canada, who had never used hormone therapy, a decision aid including information on the options, benefits, and risks and their probabilities was either followed by: (1) a graphic weigh-scale values clarification exercise to explicitly consider the personal importance of each benefit and risk; or (2) a summary of the main benefits and risks to implicitly consider benefits versus the risks.

Outcome: Perceived clarity of values, a subscale of the decisional conflict scale; congruence between personal values of benefits and risks (measured on 0–10 importance rating scale) and choices (accept, decline, unsure regarding preventive hormone therapy) using discriminant function analysis.

Results: There were no statistically significant differences between interventions in perceived clarity of values and overall congruence between values and choices. Among those choosing HRT, there was a trend in those exposed to the graphic weigh-scale exercise to have better congruence between values and choices compared to implicit values clarification.

Conclusion: The use of the graphic weigh-scale exercise in a decision aid conveys no overall short-term benefit. Further study is needed to specifically determine effects in those changing the status quo and on the quality of patient–practitioner communication and persistence with decisions.

Questions:

Decision aids are increasingly being used by medical and rehabilitation professionals as a means of assisting patients in making decisions about their treatment. Personal values are consistently identified as a critical element in decision aids. What is not clear is what values are important to include. How should personal values be used to assist patients in evaluating their treatment options?

Aside from the sort of values clarification used in this study, how should "personal values" be defined for this purpose, and how should these values be measured?

What sort of health-related and other values would you consider in making a decision about whether to begin using a potentially effective treatment that also might have risks associated with it?

Persson, Engstrom, Ryden, Larsson, & Sullivan, 2005), have claimed that frequently, value changes failed to occur. This raises the question whether in fact the experience of changing health conditions would cause an individual to change the degree of importance that he or she places on such general values as harmony, knowledge, or comfort (generally no theory-based rationale is suggested for such changes). The sensitivity of measures based on such universal goals to assess changes in health-related values makes such efforts unlikely to produce significant results, particularly in the course of the relatively short amount of time such efforts involve. This example highlights the importance of delineating theoretical postulates in values research, operationalizing values appropriately, and selecting sufficiently sensitive and reliable instruments for values assessment.

Major Issues Requiring Attention in Values Assessment

Many theoretical and practical issues associated with the assessment of values and translating values constructs into health and rehabilitation interventions remain to be resolved. It will be important, as values assessment methods and instruments are continually developed, to explore the appropriateness of different assessment methods and techniques in different clinical and research settings. Issues involved in the accurate, valid, and reliable assessment of values include both methodological and theoretical issues.

The Consumer Perspective in Values Assessment

The ability of rehabilitation and health care professionals to reliably and accurately determine the experience and importance of the consumer's values is inherently limited (Heinemann et al., 1998; Mpofu & Oakland, 2006). Thus, the direct involvement of consumers in the development of values assessment instruments is critical. This approach is consistent with the principles of participatory action research (Walker, 1993) and authentic testing practices (Darling-Hammond, 1994). Some notable examples from the field of HRQoL offer examples of potentially useful models of patient-oriented approaches to values assessment (see previous discussion). The increased use of such approaches, combined with open-ended interviews and decision analytic approaches, would be an important development.

Researchers need to evaluate the benefits and disadvantages of constructing measures of consumer values using items developed by persons with chronic health concerns, illnesses, or disabilities and their families and caregivers, as compared to those items developed and typically used by health professionals. The fact that professionals design measures based on specific theories of values or the need to cover specific health status or service questions makes it unlikely that the resulting measures will be adequate for assessing and comprehensively understanding the experiences of consumers (Mpofu & Oakland, 2006).

Subjective Nature of Values

Values are dynamic constructs best assessed with measures that combine both qualitative and quantitative approaches (Mpofu & Houston, 1998). Assessment in rehabilitation and health often includes the use of proxies or caregivers (Heinemann et al., 1998). In using proxies and caregivers, it will be important to use a patient feedback procedure to estimate the extent to which proxy or caregiver information accurately reflects the rehabilitation client's values.

Type of Measures

Values assessment has primarily been conducted through ranking or rating scales, open-ended interviews, check lists, decision analysis, and card-sort methods (Karel, 2000; Karel, Moye, Bank, & Azar, 2007). Most values scales have employed a ranking approach, in which respondents are asked to rank the relative importance of values from a list. Arguments concerning this issue have focused on the relative merits and drawbacks of ranking procedures (Maio et al., 1996). It has been suggested that rankings provide more informative data because they force people to differentiate between similarly regarded values (Maio et al. 1996; Rokeach & Ball-Rokeach, 1989). Using a ratings approach, people may score several values identically, thus, value rankings may have greater predictive validity than value ratings (Maio et al., 1996). Alternately, however, as rankings do not allow people to assign equal importance to different values, the use of rankings may force distinctions that are "arbitrary and unimportant to the person ranking the values, and these arbitrary distinctions might lower the predictive validity of rankings." (Maio et al., p. 172).

To Weight or Not to Weight?

The utility and validity of weighting approaches are related methodological concerns and of significant importance as values about health care are increasingly assessed in the context of health care decision making. Weighting involves the application of an importance scale to values assessment, such that the rater identifies the relative importance of a value by assigning a scaled number to it. Quality of life (QoL) researchers have reported that the practice of importance weighting, typically achieved by multiplying QoL domain ratings by importance ratings, may add little if any sensitivity to a ranking (Cummins, McCabe, Gullone, & Romeo, 1994; Russell, Hubley, Palepu, & Zumbo, 2006; Trauer & Mackinnon, 2001). A number of methodological and theoretical concerns with this approach have also been identified and may, to some extent, account for these findings.

Methodological limitations of the importance-weighting approach include relatively low reliability, or internal consistency of importance scores, and their low temporal stability—features that have been noted across several studies (Russell et al., 2006). Conceptually, importance itself may be defined by an individual rater in a variety of ways, making its use in this context potentially unreliable unless a specific context for defining importance is provided in the importance scale. It is important from both a theoretical and a practical perspective to further explore these methodological questions.

Summary and Conclusion

Personal values held by the rehabilitation customer influence adaptation to disability and also the perceived efficacy of rehabilitation interventions. The accurate assessment of rehabilitation client values is important for successful rehabilitation of the client. Yet, there is a paucity of values assessment instruments with evidence for valid use in rehabilitation and health settings.

A majority of extant instruments to assess values have been developed in research settings with typically developing others or nonpatient populations or settings. There is scarce evidence for their use in rehabilitation and health settings. Prospectively, several of these instruments could be studied in rehabilitation and health settings to provide evidence for their potential utility in those settings. Extant value assessment instruments are based on value models that are developed in occupational or education settings rather than in rehabilitation and health settings. Consequently, they are short of health-related values, and efforts to use instruments developed in nonhealth settings will need to address the limitations in their conceptual frameworks to extend these to address pertinent values with chronic illness or disease.

The topic of value change also relates to the question of whether values can be changed intentionally through systematic interventions. Unfortunately, not many evaluation studies exist to prove such effects. However, the existing literature shows that because values are often simply truisms (Maio & Olson, 1998), values can indeed be changed if they are directly confronted and questioned about their reasons and their adaptability (Bernard, Maio, & Olson, 2003). Instruments that can reliably measure value change over the rehabilitation or health care period are an important priority in values assessment. Where qualitative approaches are used to assess values in rehabilitation and health care, the reliability and psychometric adequacy of qualitative measures will need to be established with the same rigor that is used in the development and use of quantitative measures (Mpofu & Oakland, 2006). Due care in the construction and design of qualitative and combined approaches to values assessment for use in rehabilitation and health care settings is critical.

References

Allport, G. W., Vernon, P. E., & Lindzey, G. (1960). *Study of Values. Manual and test booklet* (3rd ed.). Boston: Houghton Mifflin.

Berings, D., Fruyt, F. D., & Bouwen, R. (2004). Work values and personality traits as predictors of enterprising and social vocational interests. *Personality and Individual Differences, 36,* 349–364.

Bernard, M. M., Maio, G. R., & Olson, J. M. (2003). The vulnerability of values to attack: Innoculation of values and value-relevant attitudes. *Personality and Social Psychology Bulletin, 29,* 63–75.

Beutel, A. M., & Marini, M. M. (1995). Gender and values. *American Sociological Review, 60,* 436–448.

Bishop, M. (2005). Quality of life and psychosocial adaptation to chronic illness and acquired disability: Preliminary analysis of a conceptual and theoretical synthesis. *Rehabilitation Counseling Bulletin, 48,* 219–232.

Braithwaite, V. A., & Law, H. G. (1985). Structure of human values: Testing the adequacy of the Rokeach Value Survey. *Journal of Personality and Social Psychology, 49,* 250–263.

Braithwaite, V. A., & Scott, W. A. (1991). Values. In P. Robinson, P. Shaver, & L. Wrightsman (Eds.), *Measures of personality and social psychological attitudes* (pp. 661–753). New York: Academic.

Brooke, S. L., & Ciechalski, J. C. (1994). Review of the Minnesota Importance Questionnaire. In J. T. Kapes, M. M. Mastie, & E. A. Whitfield (Eds.), *A counselors guide to career assessment instruments* (pp. 222–225). Alexandria, VA: National Career Development Association.

Carver, C. S., & Baird, E. (1998). The American dream revisited: Is it what you want or why you want it that matters? *Psychological Science, 9*(4), 289–293.

Chirkov, V., Ryan, R. M., Kim, Y., & Kaplan, U. (2003). Differentiating autonomy from individualism and independence: A self-determination perspective on internalization of cultural orientations and well-being. *Journal of Personality and Social Psychology, 84,* 97–109.

Cooper, L. A., Roter, D. L., Johnson, R. L., Ford, D. E., Steinwachs, M. D., & Powe, N. R. (2003). Patient-centered communication, ratings of care and concordance of patient and physician race. *Annals of Internal Medicine, 139*(11), 907–915.

Crooker, J., Niiya, Y., & Mischkowski, D. (2008). Why does writing about values reduce defensiveness? Self affirmation and the role of positive other directed feelings. *Psychological Science: Research, Theory and Application in Psychology and Related Sciences, 19*(7), 740–747.

Cummins, R. A., McCabe, M., Gullone, E., & Romeo, Y. (1994). The comprehensive quality of life scale (comqol): Instrument development and psychometric evaluation on college staff and students. *Educational and Psychological Measurement, 54,* 372–382.

Danford, S., & Steinfeld, E. (2003). Measuring the influences of physical environments on the behaviors of people with impairments. In E. Steinfeld & G. S. Danford (Ed.), *Enabling environments: Measuring the impact of environment on disability and rehabilitation* (pp. 111–136). New York: Kluwer.

Darling-Hammond, L. (1994). Performance-based assessment and educational equity. *Harvard Educational Review, 64,* 5–32.

Davies, E., & Cleary, P. D. (2005). Hearing the patient's voice? Factors affecting the use of patient survey data in quality improvement. *Quality and Safety in Health Care, 14*(6), 428–432.

Dawis, R. V., & Lofquist, L. H. (1984). *A psychological theory of work adjustment: An individual differences model and its applications.* Minneapolis: University of Minnesota Press.

Deci, E. L., & Ryan, R. M. (1985). *Intrinsic motivation and self-determination in human behavior.* New York: Plenum Publishing Co.

Dembo, T., Leviton, G. L., & Wright, B. A. (1956). Adjustment to misfortune: A problem of social-psychological rehabilitation. *Artificial Limbs, 3,* 4–62.

Duffy, R. D., & Sedlacek, W. E. (2007a). The work values of first-year college students: Exploring group differences. *Career Development Quarterly, 55,* 359–364.

Duffy, R. D., & Sedlacek, W. E. (2007b). What is most important to students' long-term career choices: Analyzing 10-year trends and group differences. *Journal of Career Development, 34,* 149–163.

Easterlin, R. A., & Crimmins, E. M. (1991). Private materialism, personal self-fulfillment, family life, and public interest: the nature, effects, and causes of recent changes in the values of American youth. *Public Opinion Quarterly, 55,* 499–533.

Gay, E. G., Weiss, D. J., Hendel, D. D., Dawis, R. V., & Lofquist, L. H. (1971). *Manual for the Minnesota Importance Questionnaire.* Minneapolis: University of Minnesota, Vocational Psychology Work Adjustment Project, Department of Psychology.

Groot, W., & Van Den Brink, H. M. (2000). Life satisfaction and preference drift. *Social Indicators Research, 50,* 315–328.

Gysbers, N. C. (2006). Using qualitative career assessment in career counseling with adults. *International Journal for Educational and Vocational Guidance, 6,* 95–108.

Harvey, R. E., Silverstein, B., Venzon, M. A., Kilggore, K. M., Fisher, W. P., Steiner, M., & Harley, J. P. (1992). Applying psychometric criteria to functional assessment in medical rehabilitation: III. Construct validity and predicting level of care. *Archives of Physical Medicine and Rehabilitation, 73,* 887–892.

Heinemann, A. W., Bode, R. K., Cichowski, K., Kan, E. Y. (1998). Measuring patient satisfaction with medical rehabilitation. *Journal of Rehabilitation Outcomes Measurement, 1*(4), 52–65,

Hoge, D. R., Hoge, J. L., & Wittenberg, J. (1987). The return of the fifties: Trends in college students' values between 1952 and 1984. *Sociological Forum, 2,* 500–519.

Karel, M. J. (2000). The assessment of values in medical decision making. *Journal of Aging Studies, 14*(4), 403–422.

Karel, M. J., Moye, J., Bank, A., & Azar, A. R. (2007). Three methods of assessing values for advanced care planning: comparing persons with and without dementia. *Journal of Aging & Health, 19*(1), 123–151.

Kasser, T. (2006). The good life or the goods life? Positive psychology and personal well-being in the culture of consumption. In P. A. Linley & S. Joseph (Eds.), *Positive psychology in practice* (pp. 55–67). Hoboken, NJ: John Wiley & Sons.

Kasser, T., & Ryan, R. M. (2001). Be careful what you wish for: Optimal functioning and the relative attainment of intrinsic and extrinsic goals. In P. Schmuck & K. M. Sheldon (Eds.), *Life goals and well-being: Towards a positive psychology of human striving* (pp. 116–131). Ashland, OH: Hogrefe & Huber Publishers.

Keany, K. C. M-H., & Glueckauf, R. L. (1993). Disability and value change: An overview and analysis of loss theory. *Rehabilitation Psychology, 38,* 198–211.

Kivioja, A., & Franklin, R. D. (2003). Recovery of function. In R. D. Franklin (Ed.), *Prediction in forensic and neuropsychology: Sound statistical practices* (pp. 209–258). Mahwah, NJ: Lawrence Erlbaum Associates.

Kluckhohn, C. K. (1951). Values and value orientations in the theory of action. In T. Parsons & E. A. Shils (Eds.), *Toward a general theory of action* (pp. 1–65). Cambridge, MA: Harvard University Press.

Kluckhohn, F. R., & Strodtbeck, F. L. (1961). *Variations in value orientations.* Evanston, IL: Row Petersen.

Knowdell, R. (2002). *Knowdell Career Values Card Sort.* San Jose, CA: Career Research and Testing.

Levine, A. S., Plume, S. K., & Nelson, E. C. (1997). Transforming patient feedback into strategic action plans. *Quality Management in Health Care, 5,* 28–40.

Linkowski, D. C. (1971). A scale to measure acceptance of disability. *Rehabilitation Counseling Bulletin, 14,* 235–244.

Livneh, H., & Antonak, R. F. (1994). Indirect methods to measure attitudes toward persons with disabilities. *Rehabilitation Education, 8,* 103–137.

Livneh, H., Martz, E., & Wilson, L. M. (2001). Denial and perceived visibility as predictors of adaptation to disability among college students. *Journal of Vocational Rehabilitation, 16,* 227–234.

Lofquist, L. H., & Dawis, R. V. (1978). Values as second-order needs in the Theory of Work Adjustment. *Journal of Vocational Behavior, 13,* 12–19.

Lynch, R. T., & Thomas, K. R. (1994). People with disabilities as victims: Changing an ill-advised paradigm. *Journal of Rehabilitation, 6*(1), 8–11.

Maio, G. R., & Olson, J. M. (1998). Values as truisms: Evidence and implications. *Journal of Personality and Social Psychology, 74,* 294–311.

Maio, G. R., Roese, N. J., & Seligman, C, & Katz, A. (1996). Rankings, ratings, and the measurement of values: Evidence for the superior validity of ratings. *Basic and Applied Social Psychology, 18*(2), 171–181.

McCloy, R., Waugh, G., Medsker, G., Wahl, J., Rivkin, D., & Lewis, P. (1999). *Development of the computerized Work Importance Profiler.* Raleigh, NC: National Center for O*NET development.

McGee, H., O'Boyle, C. A., Hickey, A., O'Malley, K., & Joyce, C.R.B. (1991). Assessing the quality of life of the individual: The SEIQoL in a healthy and gastroenterology unit population. *Psychological Medicine, 21,* 749–759.

McMahon, M., & Patton, W. (2002). Using qualitative assessment in career counselling. *International Journal for Educational and Vocational Guidance, 2,* 51–66.

Menzel, P., Dolan, P., Richardson, J., & Oslen, J. A. (2002). The role of adaptation to disability and disease in health state valuation: A preliminary normative analysis. *Social Science and Medicine, 55,* 2149–2158.

Miller, W. R., C'de Baca, J., Matthews, D. B., & Wilbourne, P. R. (2001). *Personal values card sort.* Albuquerque: University of New Mexico.

Misajon, R. A. (2002). *The homeostatic mechanism: Subjective quality of life and chronic pain.* Unpublished doctoral dissertation, Deakin University, Australia.

Montgomery, H., Persson, L. O., & Ryden, A. (1996). Importance and attainment of life values among disabled and non-disabled people. *Scandinavian Journal of Rehabilitation Medicine, 28,* 233–240.

Mpofu, E. (2008). *Constructing consumer values for independent and community living.* Unpublished manuscript, Pennsylvania State University, University Park.

Mpofu, E., & Bishop, M. (2006). Value change theory and adjustment to disability: Implications for rehabilitation education and practice. *Rehabilitation Education, 20,* 147–161.

Mpofu, E., Crystal, R., & Feist-Price, S. (2000). Tokenism among rehabilitation clients: Implications for rehabilitation education. *Rehabilitation Education, 14,* 243–256.

Mpofu, E., & Herbert, J. (2006). *Rasch modeling of the Acceptance of Disability Scale.* Paper Presented at the 6th Annual conference of the National Council on Rehabilitation Education, San Diego, CA, February.
Mpofu, E., & Houston, E. (1998). Assessment of value change in persons with acquired physical disabilities: Current and prospective applications. *Canadian Journal of Rehabilitation, 12,* 53–61.
Mpofu, E., & Oakland, T. (2006). Assessment of value change in adults with acquired disabilities. In. In M. Hersen (Ed.), *Clinician's handbook of adult behavioral assessment* (pp. 601–630). New York: Academic Press.
Mpofu, E., & Wilson, K. B. (2004). Opportunity structure and transition practices with students with disabilities: The role family, culture, and community. *Journal of Applied Rehabilitation Counseling, 35*(2), 9–16.
Nevill, D. D., & Calvert, P. (1996). Career assessment and the Salience Inventory. *Journal of Career Assessment, 4,* 399–412.
Nevill, D. D., & Kruse, S. J. (1996). Career assessment and the values scale. *Journal of Career Assessment, 4,* 383–397.
Nevill, D., & Super, D. E. (1986a). *The Salience Inventory: Theory, application, and research.* Palo Alto, CA: Consulting Psychologists.
Nevill, D. D., & Super, D. E. (1986b). *The Values Scale.* Palo Alto, CA: Consulting Psychologists Press.
Nicholson, J. D., & Stepina, L. P. (1998). Cultural values: A cross-national study. *Cross Cultural Management—An International Journal, 5*(1), 34–49.
O'Boyle, C., McGee, H., Hickey, A., O'Malley, K., & Joyce, C.R.B. (1992). Individual quality of life in patients undergoing hip-replacement. *Lancet, 339,* 1088–1091.
O'Connor, A. M., Wells, G. A., Tugwell, P., Laupacis, A., Elmslie, T., & Drake, E. (1999). The effects of an "explicit" values clarification exercise in a woman's decision aid regarding postmenopausal hormone therapy. *Health Expectations, 2,* 21–32.
Orbell, S., Johnston, M., Rowley, D., Davey, P., & Espley, A. (2001). Self-efficacy and goal importance in the prediction of physical disability in people following hospitalization: A prospective study. *British Journal of Health Psychology, 6,* 25–40.
Olver, J. M., & Mooradian, T. A. (2003). Personality traits and personal values: A conceptual and empirical integration. *Personality and Individual Differences, 35,* 109–125.
Ozer, M. N., & Kroll, T. (2002). Patient centered rehabilitation: Problems and opportunities. *Critical Review in Physical and Rehabilitation Medicine, 14,* 273–289.
O*NET Resource Center. (2008). *Work Importance Profiler.* Retrieved May 28, 2009, from http://www.onetcenter.org/WIP.html
Peavy, R. V. (1998). *Sociodynamic counselling: A constructivist perspective.* Victoria, BC: Trafford.
Pellissier, J. M., & Venta, E. R. (1996). Introducing patient values into the decision making for breast cancer screening. *Women & Health, 24,* 47–67.
Persson, L. O., Engstrom, C. P., Ryden, A., Larsson, S., & Sullivan, M. (2005). Life values in patients with COPD: Relations with pulmonary functioning and health related quality of life. *Quality of Life Research, 14,* 349–359.
Rees, J. E., Waldron, D., O'Boyle, C. A., & MacDonagh, R. P. (2002). Response shift in individualized quality of life in patients with advanced prostate cancer. *Clinical Therapeutics, 24*(Supplement B), 33–34.
Roccas, S., Sagiv, L., Schwartz, S. H., & Knafo, A. (2002). The big five personality factors and personal values. *Personality and Social Psychology Bulletin, 28,* 789–801.
Rohan, M. J. (2000). A rose by any name? The values construct. *Personality and Social Psychology Review, 4,* 255–277.
Rohan, M. J., & Zanna, M. P. (2001). Values and ideologies. In A. Tesser & N. Schwarz (Eds.), *Blackwell handbook of social psychology: Intraindividual processes.* Oxford: Blackwell Publishing Ltd.
Rohan, J. J., & Zanna, M. P. (1996). Value transmission in families. In J. Olson, C. Seligman, & M. Zanna (Eds.), *The psychology of values: The Ontario symposium* (Vol. 8). Hillsdale, NJ: Lawrence Erlbaum Associates.
Rokeach, M. (1973). *The nature of values.* New York: Free Press.

Rokeach, M., & Ball-Rokeach, S. J. (1989). Stability and change in America value priorities: 1968–1981. *American Psychologist, 44,* 775–784.

Rosenthal, D. A., & Berven, N. L. (1999). Effects of client race on clinical judgement. *Rehabilitation Counseling Bulletin, 42,* 243–265.

Russell, L. B., Hubley, A. M., Palepu, A., & Zumbo, B. D. (2006). Does weighting capture what's important? Revisiting subjective importance weighting with a quality of life measure. *Social Indicators Research, 75,* 141–167.

Ruta, D. A., Garratt, A. M., Leng, M., Russell, I. T., & Macdonald, L. M. (1994). A new approach to the measurement of quality of life: The patient-generated index. *Medical Care, 32,* 1109–1126.

Sagiv, L., Roccas, S., & Hazan, O. (2004). Value pathways to well-being: Healthy values, valued goal attainment, and environmental congruence. In P. A. Linley & S. Joseph (Eds.), *Positive psychology in practice* (pp. 68–85). Hoboken, NJ: Wiley.

Savickas, M. L. (1992). New directions in career assessment. In D. H. Montross & C. J. Shinkman (Eds.), *Career development: Theory and practice* (pp. 336–355). Springfield, IL: Charles C. Thomas.

Schwartz, C. E., & Sprangers, M. A. G. (1999). The challenge of response shift for quality of life based clinical oncology research. *Annals of Oncology, 10,* 747–749.

Schwartz, C. E., & Sprangers, M. A. G. (2000). *Adaptation to changing health: Response shift in quality of life research.* Washington, DC: American Psychological Association.

Schwartz, C. E., Sprangers, M. A. G., Carey, A., & Reed, G. (2004). Exploring response shift in longitudinal data. *Psychology and Health, 19,* 51–69.

Schwartz, S. H. (1992). Universals in the content and structure of values: Theory and empirical tests in 20 countries. In M. Zanna (Ed.), *Advances in experimental social psychology* (Vol. 25, pp. 1–65). New York: Academic Press.

Schwartz, S. H. (1994). Are there universal aspects in the structure and content of human values? *Journal of Social Issues, 50,* 19–45.

Schwartz, S. H. (1996). Value priorities and behavior: Applying a theory of integrated value systems. In C. Seligman, J. M. Olson, & M. P. Zanna (Eds.), *The psychology of values: The Ontario symposium* (Vol. 8, pp. 1–24). Hillsdale, NJ: Lawrence Erlbaum Associates.

Schwartz, S. H., & Boehnke, K. (2004). Evaluating the structure of human values with confirmatory factor analysis. *Journal of Research in Personality, 38,* 230–255.

Schwartz, S. H., Melech, G., Lehmann, A., Burgess, S., Harris, M., & Owens, V. (2001). Extending the cross-cultural validity of the theory of basic human values with a different method of measurement. *Journal of Cross-Cultural Psychology, 32,* 519–542.

Schwartz, S. H., & Rubel, T. (2005). Sex differences in value priorities: Cross-cultural and multimethod studies. *Journal of Personality and Social Psychology, 89,* 1010–1028.

Schwartz, S. H., & Sagie, G. (2000). Value consensus and importance: a cross-national study. *Journal of Cross-Cultural Psychology, 31,* 465–497.

Schwartz, C. E., & Sprangers, M. A. G. (1999). The challenge of response shift for quality of life based clinical oncology research. *Annals of Oncology, 10,* 747–749.

Schwartz, C. E., & Sprangers, M. A. G. (2000). *Adaptation to changing health: Response shift in quality of life research.* Washington DC: American Psychological Association.

Scofield, M. E., Pape, D. A., McCracken, N., & Maki, D. R. (1980). An ecological model for promoting acceptance of disability. *Journal of Applied Rehabilitation Counseling, 11*(4), 183–187.

Seligman, C., & Katz, A. (1996). Rankings, ratings, and the measurement of values: Evidence for the superior validity of ratings. *Basic & Applied Social Psychology, 18*(2), 171–182.

Sheldon, K. M., & Elliot, A. J. (1999). Goal striving, need satisfaction, and longitudinal well-being: The self-concordance model. *Journal of Personality & Social Psychology, 76*(3), 482–497.

Sinclair, R. R., Fleming, W. D., Radwinsky, R., Clupper, D. R., & Clupper, J. H. (2002). Understanding patients reactions to services: The role of personal service values in heart patient satisfaction and wellness. *Journal of Applied Social Psychology, 32,* 424–442.

Sinisalo, P. (2004). Changing work values and expressed educational plans of adolescents: A cross-sectional follow-up of three cohorts in Finland. *European Journal of Psychology of Education, 19,* 227–236.

Sneeuw, K. C., Aaronson, N. K., Sprangers, M. A., Detmar, S. B., Wever, L. D., & Schornagel, J. H. (1997). Value of caregiver ratings in evaluating the quality of life of patients with cancer. *Journal of Clinical Oncology, 15,* 1206–1217.

Spranger, E. (1928). *Types of men: The psychology and ethics of personality.* Halle, Germany: Max Niemeyer Verlag.

Sprangers, M. A. G., & Schwartz, C. E. (1999). Integrating response shift into health-related quality of life research: A theoretical model. *Social Science & Medicine, 48,* 1507–1515.

Super, D. E. (1970). *Work Values Inventory.* Chicago: Riverside.

Super, D. E., & Sverko, B. (Eds.). (1995). *Life roles, values, and careers: International findings of the work importance study.* San Francisco, CA: Jossey-Bass.

Swenson, S. L., Buell, S., Zettler, P., White, M., Ruston, D. C., & Lo, B. (2004). Patient-centered communication: Do patients really prefer it? *Journal of General Internal Medicine, 19*(11), 1069–1079.

Trauer, T., & Mackinnon, A. (2001). Why are we weighting? The role of importance ratings in quality of life measurement. *Quality of Life Research, 10,* 579–85.

Walker, M. L. (1993). Participatory action research. *Rehabilitation Counseling Bulletin, 37*(1), 2–5.

Werthamer, L., & Chatterji, P. (1998). Prevention intervention cost effectiveness and cost benefit. Retrieved February 22, 2006, from: http://www.drugabuse.gov/about/organization/despr/hsr/da-pre/werthamerpreventive.htm

Whiston, S. C., & Keller, B. K. (2004). The influences of the family of origin on career development: A review and analysis. *The Counseling Psychologist, 32,* 493–568.

Whiston, S. C., & Rahardja, D. (2005). Qualitative career assessment: An overview and analysis. *Journal of Career Assessment, 13,* 371–380.

World Health Organization. (1999). *ICIDH-2: International classification of impairments, disabilities and handicaps: A manual of classification relating to the consequences of disease.* Geneva: Author.

World Health Organization. (2001a). *ICF: International Classification of Functioning, Disability and Health.* Geneva: Author.

World Health Organization. (2001b). *Literature review on the role of environmental factors in functioning and disability.* Geneva: Author. Available at http://www.who.int/icidh/env_fact/index.html

Wright, B. A. (1983). *Physical disability: A psychosocial approach* (2nd ed.). New York: Harper & Row.

Wright, J. G., Rudicel, S., & Feinstein, A. R. (1994). Ask patients what they want. *The Journal of Bone and Joint Surgery, 76,* 229–234.

Young, R. A., & Collin, A. (2004). Introduction: Constructivism and social constructivism in the career field. *Journal of Vocational Behavior, 64,* 373–388.

Zytowski, D. G. (1994). A super contribution to vocational theory: Work values. *The Career Development Quarterly, 43,* 25–31.

Zytowski, D. (2006). *Super Work Values Inventory–Revised: Technical manual (Version 1.0).* Retrieved from http://www.Kuder.com/PublicWeb/swv_manual.aspx

Robert A. Cummins
David Mellor
Mark Stokes
Anna L. D. Lau

19 Measures of Subjective Well-Being

Overview

This chapter describes the contemporary methodology used to measure subjective well-being (SWB). This account is embedded within a theoretical explanation of SWB so that the measurement technology can be understood within this context. The importance of subjective well-being measurement is its ability to identify a life worth living.

Learning Objectives

By the end of the chapter, the reader should be able to:

1. Define subjective well-being;
2. Explain the concept of SWB homeostasis;

3. Identify and select appropriate instruments to measure SWB;
4. Differentiate between medical health and SWB;
5. Discuss the importance and limitations to using SWB as an outcome measure; and
6. Explain how SWB can be used as an index of public health.

Introduction

Over the past few decades, quality of life (QoL) has emerged as an important and controversial topic in the field of rehabilitation and health (Schalock et al., 2002). It has become generally accepted that, beyond the maintenance of human life through increasingly sophisticated interventions, maintained lives must be worth living. Such assessment of life quality can be made through either objective or subjective measurement. The global subjective dimension is called subjective well-being.

SWB can be defined as a normally positive state of mind that involves the whole life experience. This implies that it is normal to feel positive about oneself and that such feelings of positivity are not directed to any specific aspect of one's life, but to the experience of life as a whole.

It is interesting to note that in terms of the International Classification of Functioning, Disability, and Health (ICF; World Health Organization [WHO], 2001a), SWB is an important omission. This is quite curious because Brundtland (2002), the then–Director-General of WHO, stated "While traditional health indicators are based on the mortality (i.e. death) rates of populations, the ICF shifts focus to 'life,' i.e., how people live with their health conditions and how these can be improved to achieve a productive, fulfilling life" (p. 1). Despite these fine words, the ICF fails to include the necessary subjective indicators to measure a "fulfilling life."

History of Research and Practice in the Assessment of SWB

The systematic study of SWB is now over 30 years old. While there had been some prior research, two extraordinary publications (see Andrews & Withey, 1976; Campbell, Converse, & Rodgers, 1976) launched the idea that SWB could be reliably measured. They also found such measures to be remarkably stable, and it is this stability and reliability of measurement that has made SWB such an attractive area for study. However, there are also some special difficulties in studying this area, and one of the most vexing is terminology (see Diener, 2006, for a review), particularly in relation to the word *happiness*. In common English usage, this term generally refers to a state of mind that has been caused by a specific experience, such as licking an ice cream cone on a hot day. In the context of SWB research, however, the term refers to a disposition, determined by the person's overall genetic make-up. This trait or dispositional happiness is what we refer to as SWB in order to avoid terminological confusion.

Despite three decades of research, SWB still has limited acceptance among policy makers as a valid measure of life quality. Much preferred are the traditional measures of life quality with their focus on the objective circumstances of living. These variables are more tangible. They can be simultaneously observed by a number of people, usually as estimates of frequencies or quantities. These may be the number of friends a person has or the degree of their physical disability. Certainly such measures involve degrees of subjective judgment, but when they are carefully performed, such measures can yield a high degree of interrater agreement.

Subjective variables are quite different. They can only be directly experienced by each individual person, such as their degree of felt happiness or satisfaction. Consequently, they can only be measured by asking the individual concerned how they feel about their life. It is not valid to infer SWB either from ratings made by other people (i.e., proxy responses—see later) or from objective measures.

Interestingly, these two forms of objective and subjective measurement generally show little relationship to one another. For example, people who are disabled usually have quite normal levels of SWB. The reason for this is a psychological/neurological system, SWB homeostasis, which operates to maintain normal levels of well-being in adverse conditions (see Cummins, 2000a, for a review). This is why there is generally a low correlation between, for example, objectively measured physical health and SWB (Cummins, Woerner, Tomyn, Gibson, & Knapp, 2006).

Homeostasis involves various mechanisms. Some of these are dispositional and include processes of adaptation, selective attention, and social comparison. Others are the external resources, such as money and relationships, which can be used to defend the self against adverse circumstances (see later). These act in concert to maintain the average level of SWB at around 75% of the measurement scale maximum (Cummins, Eckersley, Pallant, Van Vugt & Misajon, 2003). That is, people on average feel 75% satisfied with their lives.

So, how should life quality be measured? The answer is that both objective and subjective dimensions are important. Some authors, such as Schalock (1997), consider it is how people *feel* about their life quality that is the ultimate test of a life worth living. And certainly in circumstances where basic material needs are met, as is most common with Western society, authors generally agree that life quality can be most meaningfully assessed by subjective variables (e.g., Cummins, 2000a; Headey, 1981; Spilker, 1990). The influence of objective circumstances on SWB is most keenly felt when they challenge homeostasis. This may be either directly, such as having an abusive partner, or indirectly through a lack of a resource, such as money. However, such challenges do not necessarily defeat the homeostatic system, and it is a shock for many people to discover that physically able and rich people are not necessarily more satisfied with their lives than people who are disabled with a modest income. Due to the homeostatic system, disability is only a risk factor for SWB, not an insurmountable barrier to high life quality. The whole notion of a "healthy mind in a healthy body" (Juvenal, 55–127 A.D.) is a nonsense that has been damaging general perceptions of people who are disabled for two millennia, at least.

Current Assessment Methods in SWB

Qualitative Approaches

Researchers collect qualitative data for various reasons—sometimes the wrong ones. Some do not know the QOL literature and use qualitative methods because they think they are trail-blazing, when they are actually investigating a well-worn track. For example, if "qualitative" is entered as a search-word into the Bibliography of the Australian Centre on Quality of Life (ACQOL; 2007a), the search produces a list of over 50 publications. This is far from the complete set of studies that contain qualitative data relating to life quality, but it is indicative of the many, many studies reporting such data. Moreover, qualitative studies in this area tend to report much the same findings.

Qualitative researchers are usually looking for themes that they can shape into domains for subsequent investigation. The following two themes, at least, are almost guaranteed to be found: relationships, such as with partner, family, and friends; and money. in terms of earned income, purchases, or the worry attached to income uncertainty.

Other themes that are discovered from the use of focus groups or in-depth interviews are likely to be influenced by the biases of the interviewer. No one can conduct a value-free session of qualitative data gathering. Focus groups are a major hazard in this regard. The initial exploration of ideas will inevitably take the thoughts of the group in some general direction, and then the group will start to operate within that conceptual framework to search for further ideas and experiences. Even one-on-one interviews are not immune from bias because the interviewer is almost certain to provide cues for the direction of the conversation, even by showing differential positive feedback in relation to some topics rather than others. Largely because of such biases, interviews with people who have an intellectual disability will come up with "rights" and "community integration" as big issues; interviews with mothers will come up with the future security of their children, and so forth. These kinds of data have little general utility. There is no basis for ranking them in terms of their relative importance to life quality, and there can be no assurance that major domains have not been missed, most particularly in relation to taboo topics. Most importantly, there is no way to check the reliability of the findings.

Despite these problems, there is a place for a qualitative approach under certain conditions. This is especially true when the group under investigation is so different from the mainstream Western culture that there is a distinct possibility that some new domain may be discovered in addition to those that are known. However, even in this situation, it is vital that the interviewer is expert in the extant QOL literature concerning life domains. Only with this information can they avoid areas already known and seek new possibilities. This is the precise opposite of the Grounded Theory approach (Glaser & Strauss, 1967), which is an upside-down alternative to the conventional scientific method. Instead of testing hypotheses, researchers using Grounded Theory collect qualitative data and then deduce themes, which they then use as the basis for theory building. In relation to QOL research, this technique is most unlikely to yield new theoretical understanding.

Quantitative Approaches

It is an unfortunate fact that few quantitative researchers are aware of the array of potential scales available. Worse, they tend to apply scales on the rationale that some previous researcher has done so instead of making a selection based on the application of theory and strong psychometric criteria. As a sad consequence, many of the data that have been reported have been generated by such poor scales that the results cannot be simply interpreted. Therefore, a starting point for the quantitative researcher is to appreciate the vastness of the contemporary scale-bank for QOL measurement.

The Directory of Instruments that is available through ACQOL (2007b) lists over 700 scales that purport to measure some aspect of life quality. Most claim to measure well-being in some form. How can a researcher make a choice from such a daunting list? The answer is to know what to look for, and this means having an appreciation of the instruments at a deeper level than their psychometric surface-structure. If we are seeking an instrument to measure SWB, then we need to understand the SWB construct. With such understanding in place, we can apply selection criteria based on both the theoretical properties of the data generated by the instrument and its psychometric properties. One basis for such understanding comes from the perspective of SWB homeostasis.

SWB Homeostasis

The theory of subjective well-being homeostasis proposes that, in a manner analogous to the homeostatic maintenance of body temperature, SWB is actively controlled and maintained (see Cummins & Nistico, 2002, for an extended description). The operation of SWB homeostasis is most evident at the level of general, personal well-being. That is, homeostasis attempts to maintain a positive view of the self at a nonspecific, abstract level, exemplified by the classic question, "How satisfied are you with your life as a whole?" Given the extraordinary generality of this question, the response that people give does not represent a cognitive evaluation of their life. Rather, it reflects a deep and stable positive mood state that we call *core affect* (Davern, Cummins, & Stokes, 2007). It is this general and abstract state of SWB that the homeostatic system seeks to defend. As one consequence, the level of satisfaction people record to this question has the following characteristics:

1. It is remarkably stable. While unusually good or bad events will cause it to change in the short term, over a period of time homeostasis will normally return global satisfaction with life to its previous level (see Hanestad & Albrektsen, 1992; Headey & Wearing, 1989).
2. Each person has a level of core affect that is set genetically. This "set-point" for SWB lies in the "satisfied" sector of the dissatisfied–satisfied continuum. That is, on a scale where 0 represents complete dissatisfaction with life and 100 represents complete satisfaction, people's set-point normally lies within the positive sector of the scale (see Cummins, Gullone, & Lau, 2002).
3. At a population level within Western nations, the average set-point is 75. In other words, on average, people feel that their general satisfaction with life is about three-quarters of its maximum extent (Cummins, 1995, 1998).

While this generalized sense of well-being is held positive with remarkable tenacity, it is not immutable. A sufficiently adverse environment can defeat the homeostatic system, and when this occurs, the level of SWB falls below its homeostatic range. For example, people who experience strong, chronic pain from arthritis or the stress of caring for a severely disabled family member at home have low levels of SWB (e.g., Cummins, 2001a). However, for people who are maintaining a normally functioning homeostatic system, their levels of SWB will show little relationship to normal variations in their chronic circumstances of living.

Homeostatic Buffers

The homeostatic maintenance of the set-point is under constant pressure. Interaction with the environment constantly threatens to move well-being up or down in sympathy with momentary positive and negative experience. And to some extent, this does occur. However, most people are adept at avoiding strong challenges through the maintenance of established life routines that make their daily experiences predictable and manageable. Under such predictable conditions, the momentary mood-state varies by perhaps 10 points or so from one moment to the next, and this is the set-point range. Homeostasis works hardest at the edges of this range to prevent more drastic mood changes, which, of course, do occur from time to time. Strong and unexpected positive or negative experience will shift the sense of personal well-being to abnormally higher or lower values, usually for a brief period of time, until adaptation occurs. However, if the negative experience is sufficiently strong and sustained, homeostasis will fail to restore equilibrium and SWB will remain below its set-point range. Such homeostatic defeat is marked by a sustained loss of positive mood and a high risk of depression.

There are two kinds of defenses against homeostatic defeat. The first line of defense is to avoid, or at least rapidly attenuate, negative environmental interactions. This is the role of the external buffers.

External Buffers

The most important external buffer is a relationship with another human being that involves mutual sharing of intimacies and support. Almost universally, the research literature attests to the power of such relationships to moderate the influence of potential stressors on SWB (for reviews see Henderson, 1977; Sarason, Sarason, & Pierce, 1990).

The second important external buffer is money, but there are misconceptions as to what money can and cannot do in relation to personal well-being. For example, it cannot shift the set-point to create a perpetually happier person. Set-points for SWB are proposed to be under genetic control (Cummins et al., 2003), so in this sense, money cannot buy happiness. No matter how rich someone is, their average level of SWB cannot be sustained higher than their set-point range. People adapt readily to luxurious living standards, so genetics trumps wealth after a certain level of income has been achieved. The real power of wealth is to protect well-being through its capacity to be used as a highly flexible resource (Cummins, 2000b), which allows people to minimize the negative potential inherent within their environment. Wealthy people pay others to perform tasks they do not wish to do themselves. Poor people, who lack such resources, must fend for themselves to a much greater extent. Poor people, therefore, have a level of SWB that is far more at the mercy of their environment.

Internal Buffers

Our internal buffers comprise protective cognitive devices that are brought into action when SWB is threatened because we have failed to control our environment. They have the role of protecting the set-point setting for SWB against the conscious reality of life. While these buffers all act to minimize the impact of personal failure, the ways they do this are highly varied. For example, one can find meaning in the event ("God is testing me"), fail to take responsibility for the event ("it was not my fault"), or regard the event [dropping a vase] as unimportant ("I did not need that old vase anyway"). There are many such devices, collectively called secondary control techniques (Rothbaum, Weisz, & Snyder, 1982); detailed discussions of these systems in relation to SWB are provided in Cummins and Nistico (2002) and Cummins et al. (2002).

Diagnostic Ranges

Because individuals have set-points within the positive range, it is sometimes difficult to be precise concerning the diagnostic meaning of an individual SWB score. In making such interpretations, there are two forces to be considered. These are the set-point, which lies somewhere in the positive range between 50 and 100 points, and the chronic negative life experiences that are challenging homeostatic control. The additional information is that, on an average basis, some loss of homeostatic control occurs below 70 points (Cummins, 2003), and below 50 points all set-points have been defeated. Resulting from this, the following scheme is a guide to the interpretation of scores: 70+ points = normal; 51–69 points = either a low set-point or strong homeostatic challenge, even defeat; 50 or less = homeostatic defeat and depression.

In summary, SWB is a stable mood-state that normally operates within a narrow range of values for each individual. The level of this set-point-range is genetically determined, and a homeostatic system acts to maintain SWB within this range. However, if the level of challenge to SWB becomes too great, homeostasis fails, and SWB drops below the set-point range. This loss of positive mood is depression.

Recommended Scales

There are three scales that we recommend for use within the framework that has been outlined. The first is one of the oldest. It is the single question, "How satisfied are you with your life as a whole?" (Andrews and Withey, 1976). This question perfectly fulfills the criteria for an item measuring SWB to be personal and abstract. No one can compute the answer to the question in terms of cognition, so it is answered in reference to the ongoing mood state, which normally approximates the set-point core affect. The drawback to using this question, however, is that it is a single item. As such, it is not as reliable as a multi-item scale, so two alternative scales have been devised.

The first is the most widely used index of SWB, the Satisfaction with Life Scale (SWLS; Diener, Emmons, Larsen, & Griffin, 1985). This scale is designed to measure global life satisfaction through five items, each of which involves an overall judgment of life in general. The scores from these items are then summed as a measure of SWB. For a copy of the scale go to http://s.psych.uiuc.edu/~ediener/hottopic/hottopic.html. The psychometric properties of the scale can be accessed through the publications listed on this Web page.

The importance of the SWLS is that it represents an expanded version of "life as a whole." The items are not designed to give individual insights into the structure of SWB. This differs from the second scale to be recommended. The Personal Wellbeing Index (PWI; International Wellbeing Group [IWBG], 2006) has a quite different design. It is intended to represent the "first-level deconstruction" of satisfaction with life as a whole. That is, it contains the minimum number of items (domains) that, together, describe life as a whole. The PWI contains eight such domains, as satisfaction with Standard of Living, Health, Relationships, Achieving, Safety, Connection to Community, Future Security, and Spirituality/Religion. Each domain represents a broad, semi-abstract area of life. A more detailed description of the PWI is found in the manual, which is available from IWBG (2006).

The PWI is designed to be a "work in progress," with the scale evolving as new data show ways for it to be successfully modified. The IWBG oversights this evolution, and, the eighth domain, of spiritual/religious satisfaction, was added to the scale in 2006.

The disadvantage of the PWI over the SWLS is that, because the domains are slightly more specific in their focus, they are further away from the mood state of core affect. The advantage of the PWI is that each of the domains carries its own information concerning a broad aspect of life. Because of this, the scale can be analyzed at either the level of individual domains or by combining the domains to form a single SWB score. There are also parallel versions of the PWI for adults who have a cognitive or intellectual disability, school children, and preschool children (IWBG, 2006).

Scales That Are Not Recommended

If other scales are chosen to measure SWB, the researcher must be clear about what, exactly, the scale in question is measuring. For many scales this is problematic because there are many separate constructs that are used to represent "well-being" that share considerable variance with one another. These are perceived control, self-esteem, optimism, positive affect, extraversion, and others. It is important from a research perspective to keep such measures separate from one another so that data can be precisely interpreted. Unfortunately, many scales combine elements of these constructs to yield a composite score. This leads to very imprecise measurement and uncertain data interpretation. Some examples are given here.

Oxford Happiness Inventory

Despite its explicit title, the Oxford Happiness Inventory (Hills & Argyle, 2002) scale is a good example of a "rag-bag" scale that contains a little bit of everything. It contains items on control, self-esteem, optimism, positive affect, personality, and negative affect. As a consequence, it tends to correlate quite highly with almost any other well-being scale. However, how such correlations are to be interpreted is most uncertain. The composite score has no simple conceptual structure, and because of this, it cannot be recommended. For a detailed critique see Kashdan (2004).

Scales of Psychological Well-Being

Due to its title, many researchers assume that the popular Scales of Psychological Well-Being (Ryff, 1989) can be used as a measure of SWB. This is not correct. The instrument has six subscales: self-acceptance, positive relations with others, autonomy, environmental mastery, purpose of life, and personal growth. These subscale names are what it purports to measure, not SWB. For a detailed critique see Clarke, Marshall, Ryff, and Wheaton (2001) and Kafka and Kozma (2002).

Health Related QOL: The SF-36 Scale

Health Related QOL: The SF-36 scale (McHorney, Ware, & Raczek, 1993) exemplifies the schism that has developed between medicine and the social sciences. Within medicine, "subjective life quality" is operationalized as health-related quality of life (HRQoL). Here, "excellent" corresponds to the absence of patient-reported symptoms of pathology. This is quite different from the SWB measures, where "excellent" corresponds to a highly positive state of mind and satisfaction with life in general. The symptoms measured by HRQoL scales are important diagnostic and outcome measures in their own right, but they must not be confused with SWB. For a detailed critique of the HRQoL construct see Cummins, Lau, and Stokes (2004).

Summary

On the assumption that it is important to be as precise as possible about the interpretation of the measures we make, SWB should be measured using either the SWLS or the PWI.

Research Critical to Issues in SWB Assessment

There are three major issues when researching SWB assessments: scale weightings, proxy reports, and data cleaning.

Scale Weightings

It seems intuitive that the responses to questions of domain satisfaction should be weighted by their level of perceived importance. After all, if someone responds that they are very satisfied with their wealth and yet ascribes no importance to wealth, surely the level of wealth satisfaction should be discounted in the computation of their SWB? Surprisingly, the answer to this question is a nonintuitive—no. In fact, all such differential item-weighting schemes are logically and psychometrically flawed. Trauer and Mackinnon (2001) have empirically demonstrated the invalidity of using such multiplicative composites (importance x satisfaction), which are actually interaction terms, as dependant variables. In relation to importance as a weighting factor, there is an additional problem in that people can regard areas of their life as important for a wide variety of reasons. For example, they may see something as important because they do not have it and want it (e.g., an expensive car), or because they have it and do not want it (e.g., chronic pain), or because they have it and wish to retain it (e.g., political power). The logical link to satisfaction between these alternatives is very mixed. It is, therefore, not surprising that scales based on importance ratings form a fragile factorial structure (Lau & Cummins, 2007).

Proxy Responding

The technique of proxy responding, where one person responds for another, is commonly used to measure the SWB of people unable to provide self-reports. This may be because such people have a severe intellectual or cognitive disability. Unfortunately, however, proxy responses are neither valid nor reliable (Cummins, 2002a). The reasons include the lack of direct access to SWB by the proxy and the inherent biases caused by SWB homeostasis that make us assume lower well-being in others. This review also concludes that validity is not improved by the use of multiple proxies, nor is it likely that acceptable validity could be achieved through proxy training.

Research Box 19.1

ASSESSING LIFE QUALITY

Bach, J. R., Campagnolo, D. I., & Hoeman, S. (1991). Life satisfaction of individuals with Duchenne Muscular Dystrophy using long-term mechanical ventilatory support. *American Journal of Physical Medicine & Rehabilitation, 70,* 129–135.

Objective: Bach et al. (1991) wished to determine the validity of proxy responding for people with severe muscular dystrophy (MS) who had mechanically assisted breathing.

Method: They collected data from three groups: Health-care professionals rating their own SWB; these same professionals rating the SWB of the people with MS (proxy responses); the people with MS rating their own SWB.

Results: Professionals' self ratings = 72.7 points; Proxy ratings = 25.0 points; People with MS self-ratings = 65.7 points.

Conclusion: Proxy ratings are invalid and should be considered unethical in a professional context.

Data Cleaning

It is quite disturbing how few empirical papers report the systematic use of data cleaning techniques prior to data analysis. In the absence of such a procedure, data sets will inevitably contain random errors that will compromise the results. However, SWB data often contain a more sinister form of error that is systematic, most particularly in data derived from people who have limited understanding. Such data sets are almost certain to contain some consistently high scores representing an acquiescent response mode. Unless these data are removed from the data-set prior to analysis, they will form a subset of high scores that will systematically distort both difference and relationship statistics. The defense against this problem is a combination of pretesting to establish response competence and data-screening.

Cultural, Legislative, and Professional Issues That Impact the Assessment of SWB

It is common to find reports that produce comparative lists of SWB or happiness between countries and for the authors to assume that such differences represent valid international comparisons. This assumption is incorrect, and such simplistic comparisons are invalid. There are two reasons. The first is the simple problem of translation—that there is often no simple equivalence between the terms used to describe emotions in different languages. The second reason is more important and concerns cultural response bias. Such bias has been well-documented (e.g., Lee, Jones, Mineyama, & Zhang, 2002; Stening & Everett, 1984) and shows that when data are compared between equivalent demographic groups, people from Asian cultures show less tendency to rate themselves at the ends of the response scale when compared to Westerners. The reason for this, as documented by Lau, Cummins, and McPherson (2005), is a combination of modesty, concern at tempting the fates by rating oneself too high, and having a different view of what the maximum scale score represents. This tendency by indigenous Asians to avoid the ends of the scale results in lower overall scores and the appearance that, on average, the people from these countries have lower levels of SWB than do people from Western countries. This difference is, in fact, contaminated by response bias.

Interdisciplinary Approaches to Measuring Health

There are two quite different ways of measuring "health," and each has an uncertain relationship with SWB. Consider first the familiar medical-functioning measure of health, and consider the person who has undiagnosed high blood pressure. This medical condition will probably not impact on SWB because the pathology is not available to consciousness. Unless people are aware of their condition, it cannot influence feelings about the self. Moreover, even after diagnosis and awareness of the condition, the effect of high blood pressure on SWB is minimal (Cummins et al., 2006). This is because the on-going nature of the pathology is still not accessible to direct experience.

Consider, now, someone with paraplegia. Clearly, this condition is very available to consciousness through all of the functional limitations it imposes. Even here, however, the disability will not necessarily defeat homeostasis and cause SWB to fall below the normal range. There are two reasons. First, the person can usually adapt to their circumstances. Such a person will devalue the functions they have lost and value more other abilities that they possess, such as being productive in a job or family role. Such successful adaptation certainly requires the provision of external resources to diminish the negative pressure from obvious potential stressors. But if these support systems are in place and the person adapts successfully, the crucial feature is a separation of SWB from the measures of medical dysfunction. Health-related QoL scales do not measure SWB.

The second way of measuring health is by asking people to rate their own perceived health. This has a stronger link to SWB, but the relationship is not linear. For example, widows in Australia are generally elderly people who have not only lost their partner but also have lower than normal health satisfaction due to the medical conditions associated with old age. Surprisingly, however, they still maintain an age-appropriate level of SWB that lies above the normative population range (Cummins et al., 2006). One reason is due to the phenomenon of *domain compensation*—when one domain is adversely affected, satisfaction with other domains rises in order to maintain overall levels of SWB (Best, Cummins, & Lo, 2000). If, however, health satisfaction falls too low, and most particularly if it is associated with pain, then homeostasis fails and SWB falls.

The message from this section is that life quality is both objective and subjective. Because of this, QoL assessments for the purpose of judging service effectiveness and for determining resource allocation should employ both subjective and objective measurement.

National/State and Federal or International Practices in SWB Assessment

SWB measurement can inform national policy through the generation of normative data and an understanding of homeostasis. Normative tables for the Australian population (Cummins et al., 2006) indicate that group mean scores within Australia should lie within the range of 73.4 to 76.4 points when SWB is measured using the PWI (IWBG, 2006). That is, any group with a mean score of <73.4 points can be regarded as having insufficient resources to meet the needs of at least some of its members. Such normative data may be generated for each country.

Through a comparison with such normative ranges, population subgroups can be identified that have below-normal SWB and require additional resources in order to regain homeostatic control. Selective resource enrichment can be argued from the perspective that low SWB groups constitute an economic burden to society. Depression, which is the consequence of homeostatic failure, constitutes a terrible burden to individuals and a substantial economic burden to the State. When people are depressed, they lack the normal motivation for living. They are less likely to sustain gainful employment and meaningful personal relationships (e.g., Burg, Benedetto, & Soufer, 2003; Roberts, Roberts, &

Discussion Box 19.1

SUPPOSE THAT YOU ARE ASKED TO ASSESS THE QUALITY OF LIFE OF A PERSON WHO IS ELDERLY: HOW WOULD YOU GO ABOUT IT?

In making such an assessment, there are two major approaches: the medical/functional and the psychological. The medical approach seeks to document the various functional limitations that age and disease have imposed on the person. These are very important to discover, not only because they may be treatable or remediable through assistive technology, but also to determine whether the person is living under conditions acceptable to our society. For example, it may be discovered that the person cannot stand upright first thing in the morning and is in the habit of slowly dragging themselves on the floor to the toilet. If the person has developed this behavior over many years of gradually deteriorating mobility, they may well have adapted to their condition and consider this a normal part of their daily routine. An observer, however, would conclude that this is unacceptable in our society and that some form of human or mechanical assistance is required.

The second approach is psychological, where the person is asked to rate their satisfaction with life, to give a measure of subjective well-being. The importance of this is twofold. The first is as a diagnostic device to detect depression. If the person provides a score of <50 on the standardized 0–100 scale, they are at very high risk of depression. The second is to determine whether their SWB may benefit from the provision of additional resources as indicated by a score between 50 and 70. This is the grey area for SWB, where the person may either be under strong homeostatic challenge and therefore benefit from additional resources, or just have a low set-point. The only sure way of deciding which of these possibilities is most likely is to provide additional resources and measure the effect on SWB.

Note that both forms of measurement must be made to assess life quality and that one measure cannot be substituted for the other. If the person has fully adapted to dragging themselves to the toilet each morning, their SWB may well be unaffected. Thus, SWB cannot be used to infer normality of functional status, and neither can normal functional status be used to infer normal range SWB.

Chen, 2000). They also display increased morbidity (e.g., Davidson, Rieckmann, & Lesperance, 2004; Murphy, Monson, Olivier, Sobol, & Leighton, 1987). As one consequence, they are voracious consumers of medical and social resources. The WHO (2001b) report ranked depression as the fourth leading cause of burden among all diseases. Clearly, the maintenance of normative SWB for disadvantaged population subgroups may be one of the most effective public health initiatives.

Major Issues That Need Attention in SWB Assessment

There are two issues that require the attention of health practitioners, both relating to SWB stability. The first of these is the idea that because SWB is so stable, it is not worth measuring. Two earlier papers (Cummins, 2001b, 2002b), I provided a detailed argument that subjective QoL measurement is useful precisely *because* it is so stable. The analogy is made with the medical vital signs, which are crucial diagnostic indices for pathology precisely because they are normally so predictable. Because blood pressure and body temperature are held under tight homeostatic control, deviations from their normal ranges are highly diagnostic of pathology. So it is also for SWB. Deviations from the normal range, invariably downward, are indicative of homeostatic failure.

The second issue requiring attention is failure to understand the nonlinear relationship between SWB and whatever is causing it to change. Due to homeostasis, whenever SWB is used as an outcome measure, the influence of homeostasis must be considered. Whether SWB changes or not due to the intervention will depend not only on the efficacy of the intervention but also on the baseline values of the group in question. If an intervention is applied to a group that is already operating within the normal SWB range, it will fail to show change. Homeostasis will maintain normal-level SWB both before and after the intervention. Clearly, therefore, a crucial issue for researchers is to establish that the SWB of the treatment group lies below the normative range prior to the intervention.

Summary

- Subjective well-being can be defined as a normally positive state of mind that involves the whole life experience. This implies that it is normal to feel positive about oneself.
- SWB homeostasis is the psychological/neurological system for maintaining normal levels of well-being. Because of this system, there is generally a low correlation between medical health and subjective measures of life quality.
- While there are many scales that purport to measure well-being, very few measure SWB according to established theoretical and psychometric principles. The Satisfaction with Life Scale and the Personal Wellbeing Index fulfill these criteria.
- Scales of satisfaction should not be weighted by importance and proxy responding should not be employed.
- Due to cultural response bias, it is not usually valid to compare countries in terms of their measured SWB. QoL assessments for the purpose of judging service effectiveness and for determining resource allocation should employ both subjective and objective measurement. SWB measurement can inform national policy through the generation of normative data. The maintenance of normative SWB for disadvantaged population subgroups may be one of the most effective public health initiatives.
- A crucial issue for researchers or practitioners using SWB as an indicator variable is to establish that SWB lies below the normative range prior to the intervention.

References

Andrews, F. M., & Withey, S. B. (1976). *Social indicators of well-being: American's perceptions of life quality.* New York: Plenum Press.

Australian Centre on Quality of Life. (2007a). *Bibliography.* Retrieved December 27, 2006, from: http://www.deakin.edu.au/research/acqol/bibliography/biblio_list_by_letter.php

Australian Centre on Quality of Life. (2007b). *Directory of Instruments.* Retrieved December 27, 2006, from: http://www.deakin.edu.au/research/acqol/instruments/index.htm

Bach, J. R., Campagnolo, D. I., & Hoeman, S. (1991). Life satisfaction of individuals with Duchenne Muscular Dystrophy using long-term mechanical ventilatory support. *American Journal of Physical Medicine & Rehabilitation, 70,* 129–135.

Best, C. J., Cummins, R. A., & Lo, S. K. (2000). The quality of rural and metropolitan life. *Australian Journal of Psychology, 52,* 69–74.

Brundtland, G. H., (2002). *Director-General, WHO Opening Address.* WHO Conference on Health and Disability, Trieste, April 18. Retrieved December 28, 2006, from: http://www.who.int/directorgeneral/speeches/2002/english/20020418_disabilitytrieste.html

Burg, M. M., Benedetto, M. C., & Soufer, R. (2003) Depressive symptoms and mortality two years after coronary artery bypass graft surgery (CABG) in men. *Psychosomatic Medicine, 65*(4), 508–510.

Campbell, A., Converse, P. E., & Rodgers, W. L. (1976). *The quality of American life: Perceptions, evaluations, and satisfactions.* New York: Russell Sage Foundation.

Clarke, P. J., Marshall, V. W., Ryff, C. D., & Wheaton, B. (2001). Measuring psychological well-being in the Canadian Study of Health and Aging. *International Psychogeriatrics, 33,* 79–90.

Cummins, R. A. (1995). On the trail of the gold standard for life satisfaction. *Social Indicators Research, 35,* 179–200.

Cummins, R. A. (1998). The second approximation to an international standard of life satisfaction. *Social Indicators Research, 43,* 307–334.

Cummins, R. A. (2000a). Objective and subjective quality of life: An interactive model. *Social Indicators Research,* 52, 55–72.

Cummins, R. A. (2000b). Personal income and subjective well-being: A review. *Journal of Happiness Studies, 1,* 133–158.

Cummins, R. A. (2001a). The subjective well-being of people caring for a severely disabled family member at home: A review. *Journal of Intellectual and Developmental Disability, 26,* 83–100.

Cummins, R. A. (2001b). Self-rated quality of life scales for people with an intellectual disability: A reply to Ager and Hatton. *Journal of Applied Research in Intellectual Disabilities, 14,* 1–11.

Cummins, R. A. (2002a). Proxy responding for subjective well-being: A review. *International Review of Research in Mental Retardation, 25,* 183–207.

Cummins, R. A. (2002b). The validity and utility of subjective wellbeing: A reply to Hatton and Ager. *Journal of Applied Research in Intellectual Disabilities, 15,* 261–268.

Cummins, R. A. (2003). Normative life satisfaction: Measurement issues and a homeostatic model. *Social Indicators Research, 64,* 225–256.

Cummins, R. A., Eckersley, R., Pallant, J., Van Vugt, J., & Misajon, R. (2003). Developing a national index of subjective wellbeing: The Australian Unity Wellbeing Index. *Social Indicators Research, 64,* 159–190.

Cummins, R. A., Gullone, E., & Lau, A.L.D. (2002). A model of subjective wellbeing homeostasis: The role of personality. In E. Gullone & R. A. Cummins (Eds.), *The universality of subjective wellbeing indicators: Social Indicators Research Series* (pp. 7–46). Dordrecht: Kluwer.

Cummins, R. A., Lau, A.L.D., & Stokes, M. (2004). HRQOL and subjective wellbeing: non-complementary forms of outcome measurement. *Expert Reviews in Pharmacoeconomics Outcomes Research, 4,* 413–420.

Cummins, R. A., & Nistico, H. (2002). Maintaining life satisfaction: The role of positive cognitive bias. *Journal of Happiness Studies, 3,* 37–69.

Cummins, R. A., Woerner, J., Tomyn, A., Gibson, A., & Knapp, T. (2006). *Australian Unity Wellbeing Index: Report 16.0—"The Wellbeing of Australians—Mortgage payments and home ownership."* Melbourne: Australian Centre on Quality of Life, School of Psychology, Deakin University. Retrieved December 28, 2006, from: http://www.deakin.edu.au/research/acqol/index_wellbeing/index.htm

Davern, M., Cummins, R. A., & Stokes, M. (2007). Subjective wellbeing as an affective/cognitive construct. *Journal of Happiness Studies, 8*(4), 429–449.
Davidson, K. W., Rieckmann, N., & Lesperance, F. (2004). Psychological theories of depression: Potential application for the prevention of acute coronary syndrome recurrence. *Psychosomatic Medicine, 66,* 165–173.
Diener, E. (2006). Guidelines for national indicators of subjective well-being and ill-being. *Journal of Happiness Studies, 7,* 397—404.
Diener, E., Emmons, R. A., Larsen, R. J., & Griffin, S. (1985) The satisfaction with life scale. *Journal of Personality Assessment, 49,* 71–75.
Glaser, B. J., & Strauss, A. (1967). *The discovery of grounded theory: Strategies for qualitative research.* Chicago: Aldine Publishing.
Hanestad, B. R., & Albrektsen, G. (1992). The stability of quality of life experience in people with Type 1 diabetes over a period of a year. *Journal of Advanced Nursing, 17,* 777–784.
Headey, B. (1981). The quality of life in Australia. *Social Indicators Research, 9,* 155–181.
Headey, B., & Wearing, A. (1989). Personality, life events, and subjective well-being: Toward a dynamic equilibrium model. *Journal of Personality and Social Psychology, 57,* 731–739.
Henderson, S. (1977). The social network, support and neurosis. The function of attachment in adult life. *British Journal of Psychiatry, 131,* 185–191.
Hills, P., & Argyle, M. (2002). The Oxford Happiness Questionnaire: a compact scale for the measurement of psychological well-being. *Personality and Individual Differences, 33,* 1073–1082.
International Wellbeing Group. (2006). *Personal Wellbeing Index.* Retrieved December 28, 2006, from: http://www.deakin.edu.au/research/acqol/instruments/wellbeing_index.htm
Juvenal (55–127 A.D.). Roman poet & satirist. Retrieved December 28, 2006, from: http://www.quotationspage.com/quote/29034.html
Kafka, G. J., & Kozma, A. (2002). The construct validity of Ryff's Scales of Psychological Well-Being (SPWB) and their relationship to measures of subjective well-being. *Social Indicators Research, 57,* 171–190.
Kashdan, T. B. (2004). The assessment of subjective well-being (issues raised by the oxford Happiness Questionnaire). *Personality and Individual Differences, 36,* 1225.
Lau, A.L.D., & Cummins, R. A. (2007). *Why perceived importance is not worth measuring: Quality of life among stroke survivors in Hong Kong.* Unpublished manuscript.
Lau, A.L.D., Cummins, R. A., & McPherson, W. (2005). An Investigation into the cross-cultural equivalence of the Personal Wellbeing Index. *Social Indicators Research, 72,* 403–430.
Lee, J. W., Jones, P. S., Mineyama, Y., & Zhang, X. E. (2002). Cultural differences in responses to a Likert scale. *Research in Nursing and Health, 25,* 295–306.
McHorney, C. A., Ware, J. E., & Raczek, A. E. (1993). The MOS 36-item short-form health survey (SF-36): 11. Psychometric and clinical tests of validity in measuring physical and mental health constructs, *Medical Care, 31,* 247–263.
Murphy, J. M., Monson, R. R., Olivier, D. C., Sobol, A. M., & Leighton, A. H. (1987) Affective disorders and mortality: A general population study. *Archives of General Psychiatry, 44,* 473–480.
Roberts, R. E., Roberts, C. R., & Chen, I. G. (2000). Fatalism and risk of adolescent depression. *Psychiatry, 63,* 239–252.
Rothbaum, F., Weisz, J. R., & Snyder, S. S. (1982). Changing the world and changing the self: A two-process model of perceived control. *Journal of Personality and Social Psychology, 42,* 5–37.
Ryff, C. D. (1989). Happiness is everything, or is it? Explorations on the meaning of psychological well-being. *Journal of Personality and Social Psychology, 57,* 1069–1081.
Sarason, B. R., Sarason, I. G., & Pierce, G. R. (Eds.). (1990). *Social support: An interactional view.* New York: Wiley.
Schalock, R. L. (1997). The conceptualization and measurement of quality of life: Current status and future considerations. *Journal of Developmental Disabilities, 5,* 1–21.
Schalock, R. L., Brown, I., Brown, R., Cummins, R. A., Felce, D., Matikka, L., et al. (2002). The conceptualisation, measurement, and application of quality of life: Report of an international panel of experts. *Mental Retardation, 40,* 457–470.
Spilker, B. (1990). Introduction. In B. Spilker (Ed.), *Quality of life assessments in clinical trials* (pp. 3–9). New York: Raven Press.

Stening, B. W., & Everett, J. E. (1984). Response styles in a cross-cultural managerial study. *Journal of Social Psychology, 122,* 151–156.

Trauer, T., & Mackinnon, A. (2001). Why are we weighting? The role of importance ratings in quality of life measurement. *Quality of Life Research, 10,* 579–585.

World Health Organization. (2001a). *ICF: International Classification of Functioning, Disability and Health.* Geneva: Author.

World Health Organization. (2001b). *The world health report. Mental health: New understanding.* Geneva: New Hope.

Patricia H. Rosenberger
Alicia Heapy
Robert D. Kerns

20 Pain Assessment

Overview

This chapter provides a brief history of pain assessment methods and discusses theories guiding pain assessment research. The most commonly used methods of pain assessment are reviewed, and their strengths and limitations are discussed. Diagnosis of pain conditions using the International Classification of Functioning, Disability, and Health (ICF; World Health Organization [WHO], 2001) is reviewed. The chapter addresses important issues in the field of pain assessment and treatment, including the establishment of multidisciplinary pain clinics, the increasing recognition and demand for appropriate pain assessment and treatment, the challenges of assessing pain in special populations, and the practical considerations associated with choosing a pain assessment strategy.

The chapter ends with a discussion of current issues facing the area of pain assessment.

Learning Objectives

By the end of the chapter, the reader should be able to:

1. Describe the gate-control theory of pain and explain why it has provided a heuristic for pain research;
2. Describe the most commonly used pain assessment methods, including the psychosocial/behavioral interview, pain questionnaires and inventories, observational methods, and psychophysiological methods;
3. State the strengths and weaknesses of the various assessment methods, including cultural limitations, and the practical considerations involved in the choice of measures to include in a pain evaluation;
4. Examine two initiatives in the past decade mandating appropriate assessment and treatment of pain; and
5. Evaluate practices in pain assessment.

Introduction

There is probably no greater source of human suffering than pain. Complex in nature, pain has been traditionally difficult to classify and requires a broadband approach to assessment. This chapter reviews assessment methods for *chronic pain*. By definition, chronic pain persists over time, lasting at least 3 months and often lasting many years. Individuals with chronic pain frequently develop complications including functional disability and affective distress, particularly depression (Banks & Kerns, 1996). Proper assessment and treatment of chronic pain is critical to minimize both the pain experience and the physical and psychosocial complications arising from persistent, intractable pain.

Considerable evidence supports the role of psychosocial factors in the experience and the maintenance of chronic pain. Because chronic pain has both physiological and psychosocial components, and because it has far-reaching effects in terms of overall adjustment and quality of life, assessment strategies must necessarily emphasize the multidimensional aspects of the chronic pain experience. It is necessary to use multiple assessment strategies that include diverse measures of important variables to document the extent of the individual's pain, disability, and distress (Jensen & Karoly, 2001). A comprehensive and multidimensional assessment of pain may include the identification of possible contributors to the development and perpetuation of pain, potential problem areas, and potential targets for treatment. Thus, the assessment serves to generate hypotheses regarding the amount of influence of these contributors and their interaction with other contributors. In addition, baseline information obtained from a comprehensive assessment can be used as a basis for comparison following any intervention. Finally, the assessment process can serve to engage the individual in taking an active role in treatment planning and intervention efforts (Kerns, 1994).

History of Research and Practice in the Assessment of Pain

Many theories of chronic pain have been introduced, all with implications for research and practice in the assessment of pain. Traditional physiological theories emphasized the role of nociception at the site of structural pathology (Campbell et al., 1989). *Nociception* is a neurophysiological term denoting specific activity in nerve pathways and is considered the transmission mechanism for physiological pain. Traditional medical theories assumed a one-to-one correspondence between amount of physiological damage (e.g., structural damage resulting from injury) and the amount of pain experienced. Although this simplistic model of pain transmission spurred much research over the years, it was unable to account for clinical pain states rich in neurological and psychological complexity (Chapman & Okifugi, 2004). Research on the neurophysiology of pain has confirmed that pain is not a primitive sensory message somehow recognized by the cortex but the end product of complex processing within the brain and including the interdependent processes of emotion and cognition.

The first theory to acknowledge these interdependent processes, and the most influential theory of pain on the field of pain assessment, is the gate control theory of pain, introduced in 1965 by Canadian psychologist Ronald Melzack and British physiologist Patrick Wall. This theory expanded the conceptualization of pain from a purely sensory phenomenon to a multidimensional model incorporating both sensory-physiological components with motivational-affective and cognitive-evaluative components (Turk & Melzack, 2001). The theory offered a new heuristic for pain research and stimulated much work on the modulation of pain perception within the nervous system by psychosocial variables. That is, factors such as fatigue, depression, family support, and confidence in one's ability to successfully manage pain directly influenced pain perception and self-report of pain intensity. Central to the theory was the view that pain was multidimensional in nature and that a single measure of pain intensity would not adequately summarize its multidimensional aspects. Other integrative models of pain, such as the biopsychosocial model of chronic pain (Flor, Birbaumer, & Turk, 1990) and the diathesis-stress model of chronic pain (Kerns & Jacob, 1993), were introduced and continued to guide research in this area. In particular, these multidimensional models of chronic pain led to the development of comprehensive pain assessment, including multiple measures of pain for purposes of diagnosis, decisions about treatment, predictions of response to treatment, and evaluation of treatment effects (Turk & Okifuji, 2003). In addition, clinicians began to recognize that interdisciplinary collaboration was key to understanding and treating pain. The past 3 decades have seen tremendous growth in established multidisciplinary pain clinics. Many of these clinics offer a variety of therapeutic approaches to effective pain management, including physical therapy, acupuncture, transcutaneous electronic nerve stimulation (TENS), and psychological methods such as relaxation training, hypnosis and guided imagery, and cognitive-behavioral treatment.

The tasks of comprehensive pain assessment are considerable, and the specific goals of assessment will dictate choice of measures. Nevertheless, two primary components include assessment of the pain experience and the impact of pain on functioning, relationships, and quality of life. A range of assessment methods are available, including the psychosocial interview; questionnaires, inventories, and diaries; observational methods; and psychophysiological measures, and individual measures may be tailored to specific populations (e.g., children, individuals with specific medical disorders). The most common measures are reviewed here.

Pain Assessment Methods

Psychosocial/Behavioral Interview

The most frequently used method of pain assessment is the psychosocial/behavioral interview. Typically, the interview begins by collecting demographic information and obtaining background information about history of the injury, illness, and/or other sources of pain; location of pain sites; and intensity, frequency, and duration of the pain. In addition, information about the impact of pain on interpersonal and occupational functioning, mood, attitudes, and coping mechanisms is obtained. The presence of psychopathology and substance abuse may also be evaluated, as well as past treatment and outcome information. Pain behaviors during the interview are noted. Sometimes family members participate in the interview and offer their perspective on the impact of pain on the person's functioning and interpersonal relationships.

The advantages of the interview include ease of administration and the ability to obtain detailed and specific information about the person's pain history. Structured interviews offer the advantage of reliability and consistency of information obtained across pain assessment interviews. The validity of any interview, however, is dependent on the validity of the information provided by the person with pain.

Questionnaires and Inventories

Numerous questionnaires and inventories have been developed to assess various aspects of chronic pain, including pain intensity, assessment of psychosocial impact and interference with functioning, and pain beliefs and coping. While some questionnaires are narrow in focus, other questionnaires take a broadband approach and assess multidimensional aspects of pain. Some of the most widely used questionnaires and inventories are reviewed here.

Pain Intensity

A primary objective in assessing persons experiencing pain is to attempt to quantify the private experience of perceived pain by determining level of pain intensity. Decrease in pain intensity from baseline to posttreatment is often the primary outcome measure used in evaluating the efficacy of a given treatment. Three commonly used measures of pain intensity are Numeric Rating Scales (NRS), Verbal Rating Scales (VRS), and Visual Analog Scales (VAS). The McGill Pain Questionnaire (MPQ; Melzack, 1975) assesses both pain intensity and the quality of the pain experience.

Discussion Box 20.1

PAIN ASSESSMENT PSYCHOSOCIAL/BEHAVIORAL INTERVIEW TEMPLATE

A sample of topics covered in a pain assessment interview is outlined below. Review the outline and consider the strengths and limitations of this method of pain assessment. In what situations would an interview become less feasible or appropriate?

Demographics (e.g., age, marital status, ethnicity)

Referral Source/Purpose of Referral

Behavioral Observations:
Note pain behaviors observed during the interview (e.g., grimacing, wincing, frequent change of positions). In addition, note any behaviors indicative of psychiatric disturbance (e.g., symptoms of depression, anxiety, or psychotic state). Otherwise, state "no pain behaviors observed, affect and behavior within normal limits."

Pain Complaints and Treatment History:
Determine patient location of pain sites, then review questions below for each pain site.

- *Location of pain*

  [ ] Head/face [ ] neck [ ] shoulder [ ] arm [ ] hands [ ] stomach/abdomen [ ] upper back [ ] lower back [ ] hip [ ] leg [ ] knee [ ] foot [ ] anal [ ] genital [ ] whole body [ ] other sites (specify)

- *Intensity of pain*

  The patient rates their present level of pain as follows:

  0-----1-----2-----3-----4-----5-----6-----7-----8-----9-----10
  No Pain Worst Possible Pain

  Worst pain gets: Best pain gets: Average pain rating:

- *Quality of pain* (Don't prompt; use patient's own words when possible)

  [ ] dull [ ] stabbing [ ] hot-burning [ ] shooting [ ] aching [ ] piercing [ ] tingling [ ] numb [ ] squeezing [ ] throbbing [ ] pulling [ ] sharp [ ] cramping [ ] gnawing [ ] heavy [ ] tender [ ] radiating [ ] deep [ ] other (specify)

- *Onset and duration of pain problem*
- *Pain variations/patterns/rhythms*

  The pain is [ ] constant [ ] intermittent [ ] episodic/recurring [ ] other (specify)

- *What relieves the pain?*

  [ ] sitting [ ] lying down [ ] standing [ ] heat [ ] cold [ ] rest [ ] distraction [ ] exercises [ ] movement [ ] other (specify)

- *What causes or increases the pain?*

  [ ] sitting [ ] lying down [ ] standing [ ] heat [ ] cold [ ] rest [ ] exercises [ ] movement [ ] other (specify)

- *Consequences of pain*

  Other associated symptoms: [ ] nausea [ ] vomiting [ ] dyspnea [ ] confusion [ ] weakness [ ] numbness [ ] other (specify)

The pain affects the patient's

  [ ] sleep [ ] movement [ ] energy [ ] lifestyle [ ] personal relationships [ ] work [ ] emotions [ ] concentration [ ] appetite [ ] motivation [ ] Activities of daily living (ADLs) [ ] other (specify)

- *Patient's pain goals* (if appropriate, add brief descriptors of patient goals regarding reduced level of pain intensity, goals related to function, ADLs, quality of life, etc.):

  [ ] sleep comfortably [ ] comfort at rest [ ] comfort with movement [ ] stay alert [ ] perform activity (specify) [ ] other (specify)

  Pain severity goal: patient acceptable level of pain rating (0–10 scale)

- *Pain medications* (Current use, dosage, and general effectiveness of pain medications and patient perception of effectiveness)

- *History of nonpharmacological methods of pain relief and effectiveness* (For each method patient has used, note which pain sites are involved, past or present use, and effectiveness (yes/no))

  [ ] Physical Therapy [ ] Surgical Interventions [ ] Psychotherapy [ ] Relaxation [ ] Biofeedback [ ] Manual Treatments [ ] TENS [ ] Heat Application [ ] Cold Application [ ] Occupational Therapy [ ] Distraction [ ] Exercises [ ] Stretching [ ] Other (specify)

Relevant Medical History:
Significant recent medical history

Psychosocial History and Present Status:
Significant mental health and substance abuse historyCurrent employment status, current living arrangements

A *Numeric Rating Scale* (NRS) is a single-item rating scale of pain intensity that can be administered in an oral or written format. Patients are asked to specify their pain on a scale from 0 to 10, with 0 representing "no pain" and 10 representing "the worst pain imaginable" or extreme pain. Advantages of a NRS include ease of administration and scoring and high rates of completion by respondents (Jensen & Karoly, 2001). It has been widely used to rate pain intensity, and studies have supported its general validity (Jensen & Karoly, 2001; Jensen, Turner, Romano, & Fisher, 1999). Farrar Portenoy, Berlin, Kinman, and Strom (2000) have suggested that a two-point decrease on the NRS may be indicative of clinically important change in pain intensity.

Verbal Rating Scales (VRS) contain a list of pain descriptors that range in intensity. Patients are asked to select the descriptor that best characterizes their level of pain. The descriptors are then assigned a number value based on intensity level (e.g., "no pain" = 0, "mild pain" = 1, "considerable pain" = 2, and "severe pain" = 3). Depending on the number of descriptors included, scales range from 4 to 15 points. Strengths of this type of measure include ease of administration and score and high completion rate by respondents. However, in order to select the appropriate descriptor, respondents must read through all of the adjectives, which can be difficult for patients with reading difficulties. While VRS are significantly correlated with other measures of pain intensity (Jensen & Karoly, 2001), the scales may be psychometrically limited in that they are not true ratio scales.

Visual Analog Scales (VAS) consist of a line, typically 10 centimeters long, that features labeled endpoints denoting "no pain" at one end and "pain as bad as it could be" at the other. Respondents are asked to place a mark on the line that best characterized their pain intensity. The distance from the "no pain" endpoint to the respondent's mark is then measured to arrive at the pain intensity score. Studies support the validity of VAS and their sensitivity to treatment effects (Jensen & Karoly, 2001; Wallenstein, 1991). While VAS have the advantage of minimal vocabulary, however, some studies indicate that respondents may prefer VRS and NRS instruments (de C Williams, Oakley-Davies, & Chadury, 2000). In addition, VAS are more likely than NRS measures to result in missing or incomplete data, possibly due to cognitive or motor disabilities (Bruera, Kuehn, Miller, Selmser, & MacMillan, 1991).

In summary, several pain sensitivity measures are available. Studies comparing pain sensitivity measures indicate that none of the measures are clearly superior to the other (Jensen, Miller, & Fisher, 1998; Wallenstein, Heidrich, Kaiko, & Houde, 1980). Choice of measure should depend on the purposes of assessment and the respondent group involved.

The *McGill Pain Questionnaire* (MPQ; Melzack, 1975) is a more lengthy measure designed to assess the quality of the pain experience, not simply pain intensity. Respondents choose the descriptors that best characterize their pain from a list of 78 potential descriptors that fall into 20 pain categories. These descriptors assess four pain domains: sensory, affective, evaluative, and miscellaneous. Within each category the individual descriptors reflect varying degrees of intensity and are assigned corresponding numerical values that reflect this difference. Respondents also indicate the location of their pain on a figure drawing and provide information about the factors that increase and decrease their pain intensity. The MPQ generates four scores: (1) the Pain Rating Index-Mean

Scale Values, which is the sum of all words chosen in the available categories; (2) the Pain Rating Index-Rank Values, which is the sum of the value of each descriptor; (3) Number of Words Chosen, a score that reflects the number of words chosen from each of the four categories; and (4) the Present Pain Intensity, a rating of current pain on a scale from 1 (mild) to 5 (excruciating).

The MPQ and its individual subscales have been extensively used in a variety of pain studies, supporting its validity as a pain assessment measure, and it has been translated into several languages (Jensen & Karoly, 2001; Melzack & Wall, 1999). It is broader in scope than the pain intensity measures described previously and may be less sensitive as a "pure" measure of pain intensity A 15-item short-version of the MPQ (SF-MPQ) is also available (Melzack, 1987).

Assessment of Psychosocial Impact and Interference With Functioning

Several measures assessing the psychosocial impact of pain and interference with functioning are available. They vary widely in both breadth of focus and the types of functioning assessed. The most widely used are reviewed here.

The *West Haven-Yale Multidimensional Pain Inventory* (WHYMPI; Kerns, Turk, & Rudy, 1985) is a self-report instrument designed to measure psychosocial and behavioral aspects of chronic pain, and it is an extensively used and well-validated measure across a variety of pain complaints. The WHYMPI includes 52 items rated on 7-point Likert scales and takes approximately 10–15 minutes to complete. Its focus on pain is multidimensional and consists of three sections. Section one includes six scales measuring pain-related interference across several domains, including work, leisure activities, and interpersonal relationships, as well as perceived support from spouse or significant other, pain severity and suffering, perceived life control, and negative mood. Section two assesses the patient's perception of their significant other's responses to their overt expressions of pain, classifying responses as solicitous, distracting, or negative. Section three measures the frequency with which patients engage in four clusters of everyday activities, including household chores, social activities, outdoor work, and activities away from home.

The psychometric properties of the WHYMPI have been well-documented (Kerns et al., 1985; Riley, Zasacki, Robinson, & Geisser, 1999). Turk and Rudy have proposed an empirically derived taxonomy of the WHYMPI that includes three reliable profiles of persons with persistent pain, labeled as Dysfunctional, Interpersonally Distressed, and Adaptive Copers (Turk & Rudy, 1988); these findings have been replicated in numerous samples of persons with various pain conditions (Turk & Rudy, 1990).

The measure has been used in several empirical studies, including clinical trials of psychological and pharmacological interventions, studies of the psychosocial impact of pain, and studies examining the role of psychosocial factors as contributors to the development and maintenance of persistent pain. Recently, a consensus group of academic, industry, and government experts, termed IMMPACT (Initiative on Methods, Measurement and Pain Assessment in Clinical Trials), recommended the use of the Interference Scale of the WHYMPI as an outcome measure in pain clinical trials (Dworkin et al., 2005).

Case Study 20.1

WEST HAVEN-YALE MULTIDIMENSIONAL PAIN INVENTORY PROFILES

Turk and Rudy (1988) have proposed a model for the Multiaxial Assessment of Pain based on the identification of reliable subgroups of persons. The subgroups are based on profiles of scores on the West Haven-Yale Multidimensional Pain Inventory, one of the most commonly employed measures of the psychosocial dimensions and impact of chronic pain. Preliminary evidence suggests that this categorization may aid in the development of individually tailored approaches to pain treatment and rehabilitation.

Three subgroups have been identified and are labeled: *Adaptive Copers,* characterized by persons reporting relatively low levels of pain intensity, pain-related interference, and emotional distress, as well as strong perceptions of self-control; *Interpersonally Distressed,* including persons reporting moderate levels of pain interference and distress, the relative absence of perceived social support, and high rates of perceived negative responses from significant others; and *Dysfunctional,* characterized by particularly high levels of pain, interference, and distress; low levels of perceived control; and low overall activity.

Here are narratives from three elderly persons who were interviewed about their experience of pain and their interest in learning self-management strategies for coping with pain. See if you can match the description with their profile of scores on the Multidimensional Pain Inventory.

Mrs. S is a 91-year-old married Caucasian women living in an apartment in New York City who has a longstanding history of moderately severe osteoarthritis.

> *"It (the pain) is not that terrible ... At my age, if that's the only problem I have then I'm a lucky duck ... I've gone through a lot of that (therapy) in the past. I'd rather stay here and go out when I want and have people for dinner and that's it."*

Mrs. B is an 83-year-old widowed African American woman with persistent low back pain presumed to be associated with degenerative disk disease.

> *"It's horrible. I can't do the things I used to be able to do because of the pain. I am terribly depressed because I cannot take part in activities that bring meaning and joy to my life like going to museums and to shows. Now it takes everything I have to walk two blocks because of the pain."*

Mr. V is a 76-year-old married Hispanic male who reports diffuse pain throughout his body without identifiable cause.

> *"No one seems to understand my pain. Doctors can't find anything wrong with me, and my wife and children think I'm just a complainer. As hard as I try, I can't find any relief or anyone who can help me."*

Discussion Box 20.2

INITIATIVE ON METHODS, MEASUREMENT, AND PAIN ASSESSMENT IN CLINICAL TRIALS (IMPACT)

The mission of IMMPACT is to develop consensus recommendations for improving the design, execution, and interpretation of clinical trials of treatments for chronic pain. IMMPACT participants include representatives from academia, government agencies, and industry. Since 2002, seven meetings of the group have been held, including one on pediatric pain. The first meeting of the group resulted in recommendations for the core and supplemental outcome domains for pain clinical trials, especially trials conducted on new analgesic medications. The second meeting led to the recommendations of specific measures to assess each of these domains. It is hoped that these recommendations will foster better standardization of pain clinical trials that can promote comparison of effects from different studies and aggregation of findings across studies.

Core Outcome Domains	**Recommended Measures**
Pain severity	■ 11-point (0–10) numeric rating scale ■ Categorical rating of pain intensity when numeric ratings are problematic (e.g., none, mild, moderate, severe) ■ Use of rescue medications
Physical functioning	■ Multidimensional Pain Inventory Interference Scale ■ Brief Pain Inventory Interference items
Emotional functioning	■ Beck Depression Inventory ■ Profile of Mood States
Participant ratings of global improvement/satisfaction with treatment	■ Patient Global Impression of Change
Symptoms and adverse events	■ Documentation of spontaneously reported adverse events and symptoms (e.g., adverse medication side effects)
Participant disposition (Adherence to premature withdrawal from the trial)	■ Detailed information regarding participant *treatment regimen and* recruitment and progress through trial, including all information specified in CONSORT guidelines

The second section of the measure that focuses on significant other responses has been particularly valuable in evaluating the role of such responses as predictors of severity of pain and pain-related disability and distress (Kerns, Haythornthwaite, Southwick, & Giller, 1990). Modifications of the original version of the scale have enhanced its overall reliability, validity, and clinical utility (Bruehl, Lofland, Sherman, & Carlson, 1999; Okifuji, Turk, & Eveleigh, 1999; Rudy, 1989). A significant other version of the measure has also been published (Kerns & Rosenberg, 1995).

The *Pain Disability Index* (PDI; Pollard, 1984) is a brief measure of pain-related interference with role functioning. The PDI includes 7 items assessing perceived disability in the following seven areas of functioning: family/home responsibilities, recreation, social activity, occupation, sexual behavior, self-care, and life-support activity. Each item is rated on an 11-point Likert scale ranging from 0 (no disability) to 10 (total disability). Empirical data from several studies have supported its reliability and validity as a measure of pain interference (Gronblad et al., 1993; Gronblad, Jarvinen, Hurri, Hupli, & Karaharju, 1994; Tait, Pollard, Margolis, Duckro, & Krause, 1987).

The *Brief Pain Inventory* (BPI; Cleeland & Ryan, 1994) was originally developed to measure pain intensity and interference in patients with cancer pain, although it has been widely used to assess noncancer pain. Patients are asked to identify the pain location, and a list of descriptors is provided to describe pain quality. The 15-item BPI is short, easy to administer, reliable, and well-validated (Keller et al., 2004). Demonstrations of its responsivity to change as a function of treatment for chronic pain and its availability in multiple languages have contributed to it being recommended by IMMPACT for use as a measure of physical functioning in pain clinical trials (Dworkin et al., 2005).

The *Oswestry Disability Questionnaire* (ODQ; Fairbank, Couper, Davies, & O'Brien, 1980) was developed to measure functional status in persons with low back pain. Respondents are asked to indicate the degree of interference they experience in 10 functional categories (e.g., sleep, lifting, traveling) as a result of pain using a multiple choice format. This measure is widely used and is available for use in nine languages (Roland & Fairbank, 2000). The ODQ has been recommended for use in functional evaluations (Deyo et al., 1998) and spinal fusion outcomes assessment (Blount, Krompinger, Maljanian, & Browner, 2002). The major drawback of this measure is that it is specifically written for, and validated on, patients with low back pain and cannot be used with persons with other types of pain complaints.

The Roland and Morris Disability Survey (Roland & Morris, 1983) includes 24 items describing a variety of behaviors that could be affected by back pain. The scale score is determined by calculating the number of positively endorsed items. A strength of the survey is its brevity and ease of administration; however, like the ODQ, it is specific to back pain. The Roland and Morris Disability Survey has been used extensively and has demonstrated acceptable reliability and validity (Deyo et al., 1998).

Pain Beliefs and Coping

While assessment of the pain experience and impact on functioning represent the two primary components of pain experience, several additional measures have been developed to assess pain beliefs and coping because of their utility in predicting outcome. These measures are most important to include when predicting pain-related outcomes as a priority of the assessment.

The *Survey of Pain Attitudes* (SOPA; Jensen, Karoly, & Huger, 1987) was developed to measure beliefs about chronic pain. It was developed based on the principles of cognitive behavioral theory, which specifies that a person's beliefs about their pain influences important pain-related outcomes, including emotional and physical functioning. Originally, the measure included five domains: perceived ability to control pain (Control), perceived level of pain-related disability (Disability), belief in medical cures for pain (Medical Cures), belief that others should be solicitous toward them when they are in pain (Solicitude), and the importance of medication as a treatment for pain (Medication). In its current version, two new dimensions have been added: belief in the influence of emotions on pain (Emotions) and belief that pain indicates underlying physical damage that necessitates the limiting of physical activity (Harm; Blount et al., 2002; Jensen, Karoly, O'Riordan, Bland, & Burns, 1989; Jensen, Turner, Romano, & Lawler, 1994). The SOPA has 57 items rated on a 0 (this is very untrue for me) to 4 (this is very true for me) scale. A 30-item brief form of the SOPA, the SOPA-B (Tait & Chibnall, 1997), and a 35-item short version (Jensen, Turner, & Romano, 2000) are also available.

The various versions of the SOPA have been psychometrically supported (Jensen et al., 1994; Tait & Chibnall, 1997); analysis has demonstrated a seven-factor structure (Strong, Ashton, & Chant, 1992). A main strength of the SOPA subscales is their correlation with clinical treatment outcomes. The Disability scale of the SOPA (belief that one is disabled) is significantly correlated with physical and emotional functioning (Jensen & Karoly, 1991; Jensen et al., 1994; Strong, Ashton, & Chant, 1990); the Harm scale is significantly correlated with reported physical disability; and the Medication scale with treatment utilization (Jensen et al., 1994).

As evidence has mounted supporting the efficacy of psychological treatments for chronic pain (Hoffman, Papas, Chatkoff, & Kerns, 2007), attention has turned to identification of persons who could potentially benefit from such treatments but fail to be successfully engaged. An important step in this direction has been the development of the *Pain Stages of Change Questionnaire* (PSOCQ; Kerns, Rosenberg, Jamison, Caudill, & Haythornthwaite, 1997). The PSOCQ measures persons' beliefs about their degree of personal responsibility for pain control and their interest in making behavioral changes to cope with pain. The measure is a 30-item self-report measure composed of four distinct subscales. The *Precontemplation* subscale measures the degree to which a person endorses little personal responsibility for pain control and no interest in making behavioral changes. *Contemplation* represents an increasing recognition of personal responsibility for pain control and interest in behavioral changes that support pain management. The *Action* subscale measures the extent to which persons believe that they are actively learning pain management skills. The *Maintenance* subscale quantifies persons' degree of commitment to using self-management strategies in their daily life and a high degree of personal responsibility for pain management.

Empirical data has supported the reliability of the PSOCQ (Kerns & Habib, 2004). The utility of the PSOCQ, however, hinges on its ability to predict important

Research Box 20.1

READINESS TO CHANGE AS A PREDICTOR OF PAIN TREATMENT OUTCOME

Glenn, B., & Burns, J. (2003). Pain self-management in the process and outcome of multidisciplinary treatment of chronic pain: Evaluation of a stage of change model. *Journal of Behavioral Medicine, 26,* 417–433.

Psychological treatment approaches that emphasize acquisition and practice of self-management skills for coping and managing pain have emerged as commonly accepted alternatives to traditional medical and surgical interventions for persistent pain. Among persons with chronic pain, perceived *readiness to adopt a self-management approach* may influence participation and success in such treatments. Psychologists Beth Glenn and John Burns studied 65 chronic pain patients enrolled in a multidisciplinary pain treatment program emphasizing use of pain coping skills, such as mental relaxation, exercise, use of coping self-statements, assertive communication, activity pacing, and similar skills. Before beginning treatment, half-way through treatment, and at the end of treatment, participants completed the Pain Stages of Change Questionnaire (PSOCQ) designed to measure patients' readiness to adopt a self-management approach. Readiness was defined by endorsement of items on the PSOCQ consistent with beliefs about the potential usefulness of a self-management approach and a commitment to learning and practicing new pain coping skills. Participants also completed measures of important outcomes such as pain intensity, interference with daily functioning, and depressive symptom severity. Consistent with theory and prior research on the PSOCQ that suggested that readiness to change may *mediate* improved outcomes during pain treatment, Glenn and Burns hypothesized that increases in *readiness* during the first half of treatment would predict subsequent improvements in outcomes during the second half of treatment, but not vice versa.

The investigators employed a sophisticated series of statistical analyses to test the study hypothesis. As predicted, increases in PSOCQ scores consistent with increased readiness in the early phase of treatment were reliably (that is, statistically significantly) related to improvements in pain severity, interference, and depression during the second half of treatment. Importantly, improvements in outcomes during the first half of treatment were generally not significantly related to subsequent changes in readiness. Glenn and Burns concluded that their data provided the strongest evidence to date of the important role of a commitment to a self-management approach as a mediator of successful self-management treatment. The investigators suggested that the incorporation of explicit therapeutic efforts to promote a commitment to a self-management approach may lead to further enhancement of pain treatment outcomes.

treatment process variables. Mixed results have been reported in the literature. For example, PSOCQ subscales predicted completion of outpatient (Kerns & Rosenberg, 2000) and inpatient (Biller, Arnstein, Caudill, Federman, & Guberman, 2000) self-management treatment programs and improvements in pain coping during treatment (Strong, Westbury, Smith, McKenzie, & Ryan, 2002). Furthermore, changes in PSOCQ scores during treatment consistent with increased readiness to change or "forward stage movement" were associated with improvements in pain and physical and emotional functioning (Glenn & Burns, 2003; Kerns & Rosenberg, 2000). In another study (Strong et al., 2002), however, a measure of self-efficacy had greater predictive validity than the PSOCQ.

The *Chronic Pain Coping Inventory* (CPCI; Jensen, Turner, Romano, & Strom, 1995) is a 64-item questionnaire designed to assess an individual's use of pain coping strategies. Thus, unlike other measures in this category, the CPCI focuses on behavioral strategies as opposed to cognitive strategies. The questions contained in the scale fall into three broad categories and comprise eight subscales: wellness-focused coping strategies (exercise, relaxation, task persistence, coping self-statements), illness-focused coping strategies (guarding, asking for assistance, resting), and neutral coping strategies (seeking social support). Respondents are asked to report the number of days in the last week that they used each strategy.

The CPCI subscales have demonstrated good reliability and validity (Jensen et al., 1995), and the eight subscale structure has been supported empirically (Hadjistavropoulos, MacLeod, & Asmundson, 1999; Tan, Nguyen, Anderson, & Thornby, 2005). Illness-focused coping strategies are significantly associated with poorer patient adjustment and outcomes, and wellness-focused strategies are significantly associated with better patient adjustment and outcomes (Hadjistavropoulos et al., 1999; Jensen & Nielson, 2003; Tan et al., 2005). Further, CPCI subscales predict patient-reported pain-related interference, depressive symptoms severity, disability, and activity level (Tan et al., 2005; Truchon & Cote, 2005).

Observational Assessment

Although pain is a private, subjective experience, it is possible to observe signs that a person is experiencing pain by direct *behavioral observation*. Individuals can communicate that they are experiencing pain and the intensity of the pain through facial expressions, crying, moaning, limping, guarding, and rubbing affected areas. Behavioral observation of patients with chronic pain can provide valuable adjunct information beyond that gathered using a self-report format and is crucial to the evaluation of patients with cognitive or physical limitations that interfere with verbal communication. Behavioral observation methods have been developed for the assessment of persons with a range of painful medical conditions, including cancer pain (Ahles et al., 1990), rheumatoid arthritis (Anderson et al., 1987), osteoarthritis (Keefe et al., 1987), and low back pain (Keefe & Block, 1982). In order to obtain reliable and valid behavioral observation data, it is necessary to have a systematic plan for behavioral observation, coding, and interpretation of the data, and as such, the use of these methods requires considerable technological sophistication and expense (Keefe, Williams, & Smith, 2001). As a result, the use of behavioral observation methods is commonly limited to research settings and is not frequently employed in clinical settings.

Psychophysiological Assessment

Psychophysiological assessment methods are designed to determine the contribution of psychological factors to the initiation and maintenance of chronic pain symptoms (Flor, 2001). In the clinical setting, psychophysiological assessment may serve several useful purposes. For example, demonstration of the relationship between experiences of personal and mental stress and psychophysiological processes may be quite compelling in helping patients to understand the importance of these relationships and the potential value of engaging in psychological interventions targeting the experience of stress (Flor, Turk, & Birbaumer, 1985). Psychophysiological assessment data may be particularly valuable in monitoring response to pain treatment, such as biofeedback (Flor & Birbaumer, 1991). Examples of psychophysiological assessment measures are electromyography recordings, skin temperature and conductance readings, and heart rate and blood pressure values. Most recently, investigators have begun to employ neuroimaging and neurophysiological methods such as EEG, fMRI, and PET to more explicitly examine the role of specific brain structures in central processing of pain and in the development and maintenance of persistent pain (Flor et al., 1995). More work integrating laboratory-based methods assessing central functioning and peripheral psychophysiological methods needs to be done in the area of assessment of clinical pain conditions.

Diagnosis of Pain-Related Conditions: The ICF

The ICF represents an important alternative to traditional diagnostic systems as well as other conventional methods for the quantitative assessment of pain, pain-related disability, and other pain-relevant variables described in this chapter. The ICF provides a sophisticated nomenclature for the characterization of the "person with pain" that emphasizes the multidimensional experience of pain within the context of an ICF organization that attends to painful body functions and structures, pain-related interference with activities and participation, and environmental factors that moderate, mediate, and/or modify the effects of pain on functioning and health (Bruyere, van Looy, & Peterson, 2005; Peterson, 2005; Reed et al., 2005).

Classification of pain within the ICF is informed by the definition of pain from the International Association for the Study of Pain, which is that "pain is an unpleasant sensory and emotional experience associated with actual or potential tissue damage" (Merskey, 1979). This definition concurs with biopsychosocial perspectives of pain that account for the common phenomenology of pain as a subjective experience involving the interpretation by the brain of sensory information from the peripheral nervous system along with other cognitive and emotional inputs. Of central importance is the understanding that pain can occur in the absence of demonstrable structural pathology. Pain can even be experienced in a body part that no longer exists, which is known as *phantom pain*. Pain is experienced as physical discomfort and can be described qualitatively using various terms, including aching, pressure, burning, sharpness, among many others. Intensity can range from mild to severe. In contrast to other ICF codes, subcodes employed within the ICF for the *Sensation of pain b280* do not obviously represent "functions." Therefore, qualifier ratings for the *Sensation of pain b280* represent the severity of pain rather than severity of impairment. Another caveat to the use of the ICF coding system for pain is the recognition that reliable pain assessment hinges most often on the self-report of the person. Observational methods and vital signs do not reliably reflect the presence of pain or its severity. Of course, multiple factors influence the reliability of self-report, including language and cultural factors, cognitive impairment that interferes with verbal report, and a range of psychological and social factors. For these reasons, and despite apparent limitations of the physical exam and other medical diagnostic procedures, a comprehensive pain assessment that includes a detailed history and physical and that is commonly supplemented by diagnostic procedures is recommended.

Codes from the *Body Structures* section of the ICF can be used to identify the location of the pain experienced. Codes are available for sensations of generalized or localized pain, pain in a dermatome, stabbing pain, burning pain, dull pain, and aching pain, as well as myalgia, analgesia, and hyperalgesia. Specific codes are available for a broad array of body parts (e.g.,. head and neck, stomach and abdomen, lower limb). These codes are supplemented by a number of codes that accommodate to persons' experience of pain that is localized in more than one site and pain that extends across multiple sites. Reliable use of these codes requires knowledge of the structure and functioning of the peripheral nervous system and considerable experience in assessing persons' reports of pain. Concepts such as dermatomes (i.e., the distribution of peripheral nerve pathways) and radiating pain (i.e., a descriptive term that is useful in characterizing pain that radiates from one body site to other regions of the body) are used to differentiate among persons' descriptions of the sites and nature of their pain experiences. More broadly, appreciation of nervous system function and common sources and types of dysfunction may prove critical to reliable coding. In some cases, it may prove more informative to code certain painful conditions using other codes associated with specific body functions. For example, it may be useful to code dysuria under *Sensations associated with urinary functions b630,* or pain associated with spasm among persons with Multiple Sclerosis under *Sensations related to muscle and movement functions b780.*

Further development and evaluation of the ICF for use in characterizing and classifying painful experience is clearly required. Given the limited experience of providers in the application of the ICF for the clinical assessment of pain thus far and, in particular, the paucity of research that has evaluated the reliability of the codes, caution is encouraged in their use as the sole method for assessing pain and its impact and changes in pain and functioning as a result of intervention. On the other hand, the future availability of a reliable system for assessing pain and pain-related functioning, such as that conceived of by the developers of the ICF, may provide a ground-breaking opportunity for informing a paradigmatic shift toward a more thorough, and meaningful, assessment of the human experience of pain and its social and psychological context.

Research Critical to Pain Assessment

Assessment and treatment of complex pain syndromes, such as fibromyalgia, recurrent headache, temporomandibular disorders, complex regional pain syndrome, and cancer, are important current topics of pain research. The continued development of psychological and assessment methods designed for persons with specific painful conditions, as well as the evaluation of the psychometric properties of these measures, is an ongoing process. This includes specific examination of the psychometric properties among persons with similar disorders, given the diverse experiences of pain across individuals who have the same medical condition.

Another direction of pain assessment research is the development of patient-oriented outcome measures. One recent example is a study identifying types of pain coping strategies that are commonly employed among older persons living in the community. Using a more qualitative approach, Barry and colleagues collected information that may be useful in developing an age-appropriate quantitative measure of pain coping that may be more valid than existing coping measures for this population (Barry, Gill, Kerns, & Reid, 2005). Several other investigator groups are currently working on the development and validation of more comprehensive measures for assessing patient-oriented outcomes, and the future availability of these methods promises to provide alternatives to existing methods that may have increased sensitivity to important and meaningful changes in pain and its impact, at least from patients' perspectives.

Finally, research on measures of predictors of both treatment engagement and adherence is critical to advancing pain management intervention strategies. While psychological treatment methods have proven their effectiveness in chronic pain management, many patients continue to adhere to a unidimensional, biomedical, sensory model of pain and are reluctant to consider any treatment outside pharmaceutical or surgical approaches (Kerns, 1994). Difficulty in engaging the pain patient in psychological treatment limits the effectiveness of these interventions. In addition, some patients willing to participate in psychological interventions have difficulty adhering to treatment recommendations, such as practicing techniques that may be useful in managing chronic pain. Accurate assessment of engagement and adherence may facilitate both the identification of patients most likely to benefit from treatment and components of treatment strategies that promote engagement and adherence.

Cultural, Legislative, and Professional Issues That Impact Pain Assessment

Research investigating the influence of culture on pain report and treatment indicates that cultural background profoundly impacts pain behavior (Streltzer, 1997). Pain intensity ratings have been shown to differ across ethnic groups (Bates, 1996). Furthermore, infants as young as 2 months have shown different facial and behavioral pain responses depending on cultural background (Rosmus, Johnson, Chan-Yip, & Yang, 2000). Ethnicity and pain studies have similarly reported differences in the report of pain across ethnic groups, specifically levels of clinical pain, pain tolerance, pain threshold, and reports of unpleasantness (Edwards, Doleys, Fillingim, & Lowery, 2001; Edwards & Fillingim, 1999; Sheffield, Biles, Orom, Maxiner, & Sheps, 2000). An extensive discussion of cultural differences in pain behavior is beyond the scope of this chapter, however, research supports that the person's ethnic and/or cultural background must be taken into account when conducting pain assessment and interpreting pain measures.

Significant legislative and professional issues impacting pain assessment have occurred in the last decade. Adequate assessment and treatment of chronic pain has become a priority as individuals experiencing severe pain, families, and health care providers have worked together to make effective pain management a priority for research and treatment. An example of this effort is the Pain Patient's Bill of Rights (Health and Safety Code) and Intractable Pain Law (Business and Professionals Code), two laws dealing with the issue of treatment for chronic intractable pain passed by the State of California in 1997. These laws acknowledge that inadequate pain treatment is a significant health problem and that, for some individuals, pain management may be the single most important focus of their medical care. In addition, the laws provide guidelines regarding the use of prescription opiates to manage pain. Similar intractable pain laws have been passed in other states as well. These legislative initiatives mandate that patients suffering from chronic pain should have access to appropriate pain treatment in order to maintain quality of life.

Relevance to Health Care Professionals and Client Needs

Given the broad array of existing methods and measures for the psychological and behavioral assessment of persons with chronic pain, pragmatic issues related to their use in the clinical setting should be addressed. First, the goal of the pain assessment should dictate the particular methods and measures chosen. Different measures may be more or less appropriate, depending on purpose of the assessment. Diagnosis, treatment planning, treatment decision making, or pain outcome represent different assessment goals and require consideration of different measures. Treatment planning that considers maximum pain relief will likely dictate different measures than when considering overall quality of life. Similarly, if documenting change over time is a critical goal, measures that demonstrate sensitivity to change are most appropriate. Second, the costs of the assessment on the person (e.g., time, degree of complexity) is a critically important factor to consider when selecting measures for use in the clinical setting. Providers are encouraged to consider specific objectives of the assessment and the importance of reaching a balance between the desire for more thorough assessment and patient burden. Third, measurement precision, brevity, and financial costs of the assessment process are critical to consider in making decisions about the use of psychological assessment strategies. As already emphasized, the clinical interview and examination remain the core, or essential, methods for clinical assessment and should not be displaced by the use of questionnaires, diaries, and other methods. Finally, from a practical standpoint, managed care reimbursement methodologies must be considered in most clinical settings.

Agency Regulations in Pain Assessment and Treatment

The importance of reliable and valid pain assessment and adequate pain treatment has continued to gain recognition over the past 20 years. In 1998, the National Pain Management Strategy was initiated by the Veterans Health Administration (VHA), the largest health care provider in the United States, and established pain management as a national priority (Kerns et al., 2006). The objectives of the Pain Management Strategy were to provide a system-wide standard of care for pain management, including mandatory pain screening in all clinic settings to ensure consistent recognition of pain, inclusion of patients and families as active participants in pain management, continual monitoring of pain treatment and outcomes, and utilizing an interdisciplinary, multimodal approach to pain management.

Similarly, the Joint Commission on Accreditation of Healthcare Organizations (JCAHO), a U.S.-based nonprofit organization whose purpose is to evaluate and accredit health care organizations, initiated a collaborative pain assessment and management project in 1997, with pain management standards approved in 1999. The standards represented a strategy to improve pain management health care facilities throughout the country. All patient care organizations accredited by JCAHO-hospitals, ambulatory care, long-term care pharmacies, health care networks, and home and long-term care programs are required to implement these standards.

These initiatives by national health care organizations were in response to the growing awareness that pain was a major, yet treatable, public health problem. From recognition of the multidimensional nature of chronic pain, multidimensional pain assessment has become part of the standard of care for appropriate pain treatment provided by health care organizations in this country.

Major Issues or Additional Assessment Methods Needed to More Fully Address Pain

As comprehensive pain assessment and treatment methods continue to develop, pain assessment methods continue to be introduced to the field. As previously stated, given the proliferation of measures, ongoing research establishing the psychometric properties of these measures, as well as establishing their efficacy with specific populations of pain patients, their ability to detect change, and their validity depending on the particular assessment purpose, is critical. In addition, reliable and valid pain assessment with challenging populations is another important area of research. For example, one area of ongoing research is the development of reliable and valid strategies for the assessment of pain among persons who are significantly cognitively impaired or otherwise unable to communicate. In the absence of existing reliable methods, clinical scholars have encouraged the use of an array of methods, including reliance

Research Box 20.2

RESEARCH FOCUS: INTERACTIVE VOICE RESPONSE (IVR) TECHNOLOGY

Heapy, A. A., Sellinger, J. J., Higgins, D. M., Chatkoff, D. K., Bennett, T. C., & Kerns, R. D. (2007). Using interactive voice response to measure pain and quality of life. *Pain Medicine, 8,* S145–154.

Despite the popularity and ease of use of retrospective self-report to assess pain experience, this method may be biased by pain level and emotional state at the time of recall, as well as the influence of recent and extreme (positive or negative) events on memory. An alternative method of assessing pain and pain-related variables is the use of electronic methods such as Interactive Voice Response (IVR) technology. IVR allows respondents to provide their responses to prerecorded questions using the numeric keypad on their telephone. Respondents can be instructed to call daily, thereby reducing the effects of memory bias on recall. The call information is automatically stored in a computerized database and given a time and date stamp, verifying that respondents completed diary questions daily.

As an assessment tool, IVR technology has several advantages for both research and clinical applications. For example, daily reporting of pain-relevant variables (e.g., pain intensity, medication adherence, sleep, and pain-related interference) can result in important clinical information about how well a treatment is working. IVR technology also allows patients and research participants to report at times that are convenient to their schedules and independent of researchers' and clinicians' work schedules. Daily IVR diaries are especially useful when examining pain conditions that fluctuate significantly over time, such as headaches.

on systematic observation and reports from significant others. With a growing population of older persons with significant dementia, efforts designed to develop reliable and valid strategies for pain assessment among persons with cognitive impairment is a current priority for clinical investigation.

Finally, technological advances have provided new methodologies of pain assessment. Palmtop computers can be used to gather self-report data at specified timepoints, eliminating the need for retrospective reporting. Computerized assessment techniques can provide individualized feedback in the moment and can be incorporated into treatment strategies. New technology will continue to impact the field of pain assessment, providing innovative methods that reliably and accurately assess the multidimensional aspects of pain.

Summary

This chapter provides an overview of chronic pain assessment, emphasizing the multidimensional nature of pain and the impact of chronic pain on physical and psychological functioning over time. The most commonly employed pain assessment strategies are reviewed, including the psychosocial interview, questionnaires and inventories, observational methods, and psychophysiological methods. Various methods of assessment may be used in combination with one another, depending on the primary goal of assessment. In applied settings, practical issues such as patient burden, time, and cost of evaluation will necessarily influence choice of measures. Classification of pain conditions using the ICF, a comprehensive diagnostic system emphasizing the multidimensional experience of pain, allows for the coding of painful body functions or structures, pain-related interference with functioning, and environmental factors that modify the effects of pain on health.

Adequate pain assessment and treatment has become an important national issue, and the past decade has witnessed initiatives mandating appropriate assessment and care. State legislation has been passed such that individuals have the right to proper assessment and treatment in order to maintain quality of life. Health care organizations have developed and incorporated standards of care for patients with pain, including routine pain screening. This reflects the recognition that when pain is assessed and managed appropriately, it need not have such a devastating impact on quality of life.

Research has provided empirical evidence of reliable differences in the experience of pain among persons of differing racial/ethnic backgrounds, gender, and age. When possible, specific consideration of culturally specific norms for the measures is important, and caution is encouraged when employing reviewed assessment strategies with persons that differ in racial/ethnic backgrounds than the sample on which norms were developed.

The differences in pain sensitivity across individuals, and the profound impact of pain on diverse aspects of functioning, make pain an especially challenging but exciting area of assessment. Because adequate pain treatment starts with careful pain assessment, the importance of reliable and accurate assessment measures and techniques cannot be underestimated.

References

Ahles, T., Coombs, D., Jensen, L., Stukel, T., Maurer, L., & Keefe, F. (1990). Development of a behavioral observation technique for the assessment of pain behaviors in cancer patients. *Behavior Therapy, 21,* 449–460.

Anderson, K., Bradley, L., McDaniel, L., Young, L., Turner, R., Agudelo, C., et al. (1987). The assessment of pain in rheumatoid patients: Validity of a behavioral observation method. *Arthritis and Rheumatism, 30,* 36–43.

Banks, S., & Kerns, R. (1996). Explaining high rates of depression in chronic pain: A diathesis-stress framework. *Psychological Bulletin, 119,* 95–110.

Barry, L., Gill, T., Kerns, R., & Reid, M. (2005). Identification of pain-reduction strategies used by community-dwelling older persons. *Journal of Gerontology, 60,* 1569–1575.

Bates, M. (1996). *Biocultural dimensions of chronic pain: Implications for treatment of multiethnic populations.* New York: SUNY Press.

Biller, N., Arnstein, P., Caudill, M., Federman, C., & Guberman, C. (2000). Predicting completion of a cognitive-behavioral pain management program by initial measures of a chronic pain patient's readiness for change. *Clinical Journal of Pain, 16,* 352–259.

Blount, K., Krompinger, W., Maljanian, R., & Browner, B. (2002). Moving toward a standard for spinal fusion outcomes assessment. *Journal of Spinal Disorders and Techniques, 15,* 16–23.

Bruehl, S., Lofland, K., Sherman, J., & Carlson, C. (1999). The Variable Responding Scale for detecting random responding on the Multidimensional Pain Inventory. *Psychological Assessment, 10,* 3–9.

Bruera, E., Kuehn, N., Miller, M., Selmser, P., & MacMillan, K. (1991). The Edmonton Symptom Assessment System (ESAS): A simple method for the assessment of palliative care patients. *Journal of Palliative Care, 1,* 6–9.

Bruyere, S., van Looy, S., & Peterson, D. (2005). The International Classification of Functioning, Disability, and Health: Contemporary literature overview. *Rehabilitation Psychology, 50,* 113–121.

Business and Professions Code Intractable Pain Law, Code 2241.5, State of California (1997).

Campbell, J., Raja, S., Cohen, R., Manning, D., Khan, A., & Meyer, R. (1989). Peripheral neural mechanisms of nociception. In P. Wall & R. Melzack (Eds.), *Textbook of pain* (pp. 22–45). New York: Churchill Livingstone.

Chapman, C., & Okifugi, A. (2004). Pain: Basic mechanisms and conscious experience. In R. Dworkin & W. Breitbart (Eds.), *Psychosocial aspects of pain: A handbook for health care providers.* Seattle: IASP Press.

Cleeland, C., & Ryan, K. (1994). Pain assessment: Global use of the Brief Pain Inventory. *Annals of Academic Medicine, 23*(2), 129–138.

de C Williams, A., Oakley-Davies, H., & Chadury, Y. (2000). Simple pain ratings hide complex idiosyncratic meaning. *Pain, 85,* 457–463.

Deyo, R., Battie, M., Beurskens, A., Bombardier, C., Croft, P., Koes, B., et al. (1998). Outcome measures for low back research: A proposal for standardized use. *Spine, 23,* 2003–2013.

Dworkin, R., Turk, D., Farrar, J., Haythornthwaite, J., Jensen, M., Katz, N., et al. (2005). Core outcome measures for chronic pain clinical trials: IMMPACT recommendations. *Pain, 113*(1–2), 9–19.

Edwards, R., Doleys, D., Fillingim, R., & Lowery, D. (2001). Ethnic differences in pain tolerance: clinical implications in a chronic pain population. *Psychosomatic Medicine, 63,* 316–323.

Edwards, R., & Fillingim, R. (1999). Ethnic differences in thermal pain processes. *Psychosomatic Medicine, 61,* 346–354.

Fairbank, J., Couper, J., Davies, J., & O'Brien, J. (1980). The Oswestry Low Back Pain Questionnaire. *Physiotherapy, 66,* 271–273.

Farrar, J., Portenoy, R., Berlin, J., Kinman, J., & Strom, B. (2000). Defining the clinically important difference in pain outcome measures. *Pain Medicine, 88,* 287–294.

Flor, H. (2001). Psychophysiological assessment of the patient with chronic pain. In D. Turk & R. Melzack (Eds.), *Handbook of pain assessment* (pp. 76–96). New York: Guilford Press.

Flor, H., & Birbaumer, N. (1991). Comprehensive assessment and treatment of chronic back pain patients without physical disabilities. In M. Bond (Ed.), *Proceedings of the VIth world congress on pain.* Amsterdam: Elsevier.

Flor, H., Birbaumer, N., & Turk, D. (1990). The psychobiology of chronic pain. *Advances in Behavior Research and Therapy, 12,* 47–84.

Flor, H., Elbert, T., Knecht, S., Wienbruch, C., Pantev, C., Birbaumer, N., et al. (1995). Phantom limb pain as a perceptual correlate of cortical reorganization. *Nature, 357,* 482–484.

Flor, H., Turk, D., & Birbaumer, N. (1985). Assessment of stress-related psychophysiological reactions in chronic back pain patients. *Journal of Consulting and Clinical Psychology, 53,* 354–364.

Glenn, B., & Burns, J. (2003). Pain self-management in the process and outcome of multidisciplinary treatment of chronic pain: Evaluation of a stage of change model. *Journal of Behavioral Medicine, 26,* 417–433.

Gronblad, M., Hyupli, M., Wennerstrand, P., Jarvinen, E., Lukinmnaa, A., & Khouria, J. (1993). Intercorrelation and test-retest reliability of the Pain Disability Index (PDI) and the Owestry Disability Questionnaire (ODQ) and their correlation with pain intensity in low back pain patients. *Clinical Journal of Pain, 9,* 189–193.

Gronblad, M., Jarvinen, E., Hurri, H., Hupli, M., & Karaharju, E. (1994). Relationship of the Pain Disability Index (PDI) and the Oswestry Disability Questionnaire (ODQ) with three dynamic physical tests in a group of patients with chronic low-back and leg pain. *Clinical Journal of Pain, 10,* 197–203.

Hadjistavropoulos, H., MacLeod, F., & Asmundson, G. (1999). Validation of the Chronic Pain Coping Inventory. *Pain, 80,* 471–481.

Heapy, A. A., Sellinger, J. J., Higgins, D. M., Chatkoff, D. K., Bennett, T. C., & Kerns, R. D. (in press). Using interactive voice response to measure pain and quality of life. *Pain Medicine.*

Hoffman, B., Papas, R., Chatkoff, D., & Kerns, R. (2007). Meta-analysis of psychological interventions for chronic low back pain. *Health Psychology, 26,* 1–9.

Jensen, M., & Karoly, P. (1991). Control beliefs, coping efforts, and adjustment to chronic pain. *Journal of Consulting and Clinical Psychology, 59,* 431–438.

Jensen, M., & Karoly, P. (2001). Self-report scales and procedures for assessing pain in adults. In D. Turk & R. Melzack (Eds.), *Handbook of pain assessment* (pp. 15–34). New York: Guilford Press.

Jensen, M., Karoly, P., & Huger, R. (1987). The development and preliminary validation of an instrument to assess patients' attitudes toward pain. *Journal of Psychosomatic Research, 31,* 393–400.

Jensen, M., Karoly, P., O'Riordan, E., Bland, F., & Burns, R. (1989). The subjective experience of acute pain. An assessment of the utility of 10 indices. *Clinical Journal of Pain, 5,* 153–159.

Jensen, M., Miller, L., & Fisher, L. (1998). Assessment of pain during medical procedures: A comparison of three scales. *Clinical Journal of Pain, 14,* 343–349.

Jensen, M., & Nielson, W. K., RD. (2003). Toward the development of a motivational model of pain self-management. *Journal of Pain, 4,* 477–492.

Jensen, M., Turner, J., & Romano, J. (2000). Pain belief assessment: A comparison of short and long versions of the Survey of Pain Attitudes. *Journal of Pain, 1,* 138–150.

Jensen, M., Turner, J., Romano, J., & Fisher, L. (1999). Comparative reliability and validity of chronic pain intensity measures. *Pain Medicine, 83,* 157–162.

Jensen, M., Turner, J., Romano, J., & Lawler, B. (1994). Relationship of pain-specific beliefs to chronic pain adjustment. *Pain, 57,* 301–309.

Jensen, M., Turner, J., Romano, J., & Strom, S. (1995). The Chronic Pain Coping Inventory: Development and preliminary validation. *Pain, 60,* 203–216.

Keefe, F., & Block, A. (1982). Development of an observation method for assessing pain behavior in chronic low back pain patients. *Behavior Therapy, 13,* 363–375.

Keefe, F., Caldwell, D., Queen, R., Gil, R., Martinez, S., Crisson, S., et al. (1987). Osteoarthritic knee pain: A behavioral analysis. *Pain, 28,* 309–321.

Keefe, F., Williams, D., & Smith, S. (2001). Assessment of pain behaviors. In D. Turk & R. Melzack (Eds.), *Handbook of pain assessment* (pp. 170–190). New York: The Guilford Press.

Keller, S., Bann, C., Dodd, S., Schein, J., Mendoza, T., & Cleeland, C. (2004). Validity of the Brief Pain Inventory for use in documenting the outcomes of patients with noncancer pain. *Clinical Journal of Pain, 20,* 309–318.

Kerns, R. (1994). Pain management. In M. Hersen & R. Ammerman (Eds.), *Handbook of prescriptive treatments for adults* (pp. 443–461). New York: Plenum Press.

Kerns, R., Booss, J., Bryan, M., Clark, M., Drake, A., Gallagher, R., et al. (2006). Veterans Health Administration National Pain Management Strategy: Update and future directions. *American Pain Society Bulletin, 16,* 1–15.

Kerns, R., & Habib, S. (2004). A critical review of the Pain Readiness to Change Model. *Journal of Pain, 5,* 357–367.

Kerns, R., Haythornthwaite, J., Southwick, S., & Giller, E. (1990). The role of marital interaction in chronic pain and depressive symptom severity. *Journal of Psychosomatic Research, 34,* 401–408.

Kerns, R., & Jacob, M. (1993). Psychological aspects of back pain. In S. Newman & M. Shipley (Eds.), *Psychological aspects of rheumatic disease* (pp. 337–356). London: Bailliere Tindall.

Kerns, R., & Rosenberg, R. (1995). Pain relevant responses from significant others: Development of a significant other version of the WHYMPI scales. *Pain, 61,* 245–149.

Kerns, R., & Rosenberg, R. (2000). Predicting responses to self-management treatments for chronic pain: Application of the pain stages of change model. *Pain, 51,* 49–55.

Kerns, R., Rosenberg, R., Jamison, R., Caudill, M., & Haythornthwaite, J. (1997). Readiness to adopt a self-management approach to chronic pain: The Pain Stages of Change Questionnaire. *Pain, 72,* 227–234.

Kerns, R., Turk, D., & Rudy, T. (1985). The West Haven-Yale Multidimensional Pain Inventory (WHYMPI). *Pain, 23,* 345–356.

Melzack, R. (1975). The McGill Pain Questionnaire: Major properties and scoring methods. *Pain, 1,* 277–299.

Melzack, R. (1987). The Short-Form McGill Pain Questionnaire. *Pain, 30,* 191–197.

Merskey, J. (1979). Pain terms: A list with definitions and notes on usage recommended by the IASP Subcommittee on Taxonomy. *Pain, 6,* 249–252.

Okifuji, A., Turk, D., & Eveleigh, D. (1999). Improving the rate of classification of patients with the Multidimensional Pain Inventory (MPI): Clarifying the meaning of "significant other." *Clinical Journal of Pain, 15,* 290–296.

Pain Patient's Bill of Rights, Division of Health & Safety Code Part 4.5, 402, Code 124690, State of California (1997).

Peterson, D. (2005). The International Classification of Functioning, Disability, and Health: An introduction for rehabilitation psychologists. *Rehabilitation Psychology, 50,* 105–112.

Pollard, C. (1984). Preliminary validity study of the pain disability index. *Perceptual and Motor Skills, 59,* 974.

Reed, G., Lux, J., Bufka, L., Trask, C., Peterson, D., Stark, S., et al. (2005). Operationalizing the International Classification of Functioning, Disability, and Health in clinical settings. *Rehabilitation Psychology, 50,* 122–131.

Riley, J., Zasacki, T., Robinson, M., & Geisser, M. (1999). Empirical test of the factor structure of the West Haven—Yale Multidimensional Pain Inventory. *Pain, 15,* 24–30.

Roland, M., & Fairbank, J. (2000). The Roland-Morris Disability Questionnaire and the Oswestry Disability Questionnaire. *Spine, 25,* 3115–3124.

Roland, M., & Morris, R. (1983). A study of the natural history of back pain: Part I. Development of a reliable and sensitive measure of disability in low back pain. *Spine, 8,* 141–144.

Rosmus, C., Johnson, C., Chan-Yip, A., & Yang, F. (2000). Pain response in Chinese and non-Chinese Canadian infants: Is there a difference? *Social Science Medicine, 51,* 175–184.

Rudy, T. (1989). *Multiaxial assessment of pain: Multidimensional Pain Inventory. Computer program users' manual. Version 2.1.* Pittsburgh, PA: Pain Evaluation and Treatment Institute.

Sheffield, D., Biles, P., Orom, H., Maxiner, W., & Sheps, D. (2000). Race and sex differences in cutaneous pain perception. *Psychosomatic Medicine, 62,* 517–523.

Streltzer, J. (1997). Pain. In W. Tseng & J. Streltzer (Eds.), *Culture and psychopathology: A guide to clinical assessment* (pp. 87–100). New York: Brunner/Mazel.

Strong, J., Ashton, R., & Chant, D. (1990). Pain intensity measurement in chronic low back pain. *Clinical Journal of Pain, 7,* 209–218.

Strong, J., Ashton, R., & Chant, D. (1992). The measurement of attitudes towards and beliefs about pain. *Pain, 48,* 227–236.

Strong, J., Westbury, K., Smith, G., McKenzie, I., & Ryan, W. (2002). Treatment outcome in individuals with chronic pain: Is the Pain Stages of Change Questionnaire (PSOCQ) a useful tool? *Pain, 97,* 65–73.

Tait, R., & Chibnall, J. (1997). Development of a brief version of the Survey of Pain Attitudes. *Pain, 58,* 229–235.

Tait, R., Pollard, C., Margolis, R., Duckro, P., & Krause, S. (1987). The Pain Disability Index: Psychometric and validity data. *Archives of Physical and Medical Rehabilitation, 68,* 438–441.

Tan, G., Nguyen, Q., Anderson, K. O., Jensen, M., & Thornby, J. (2005). Further validation of the Chronic Pain Coping Inventory. *Journal of Pain, 6,* 29–40.

Truchon, M., & Cote, D. (2005). Predictive validity of the Chronic Pain Coping Inventory in subacute low back pain. *Pain, 116,* 205–212.

Turk, D., & Melzack, R. (2001). The measurement of pain and the assessment of people experiencing pain. In D. Turk & R. Melzack (Eds.), *Handbook of pain assessment* (2nd ed., pp. 3–11). New York: Guilford Press.

Turk, D., & Okifuji, A. (2003). Clinical assessment of the person with chronic pain. In T. Jensen & P. R. Wilson, ASC (Eds.), *Clinical pain management: Chronic pain* (pp. 89–100). London: Arnold.

Turk, D., & Rudy, T. (1988). Toward an empirically derived taxonomy of chronic pain patients: Integration of psychological assessment data. *Journal of Consulting and Clinical Psychology, 56,* 233–238.

Turk, D., & Rudy, T. (1990). The robustness of an empirically derived taxonomy of chronic pain patients. *Pain, 43,* 27–36.

Wallenstein, S. (1991). The VAS relief scale and other analgesic measures. *Advances in Pain Research and Therapy, 18,* 97–103.

Wallenstein, S., Heidrich, G., Kaiko, R., & Houde, R. (1980). Clinical evaluation of mild analgesics: The measurement of clinical pain. *British Journal of Clinical Pharmacology, 10,* 319S–327S.

World Health Organization. (2001). *ICF: International Classification of Functioning, Disability and Health.* Geneva: Author.

Anthony C. Holter
Chad M. Magnuson
Robert D. Enright

21 Application and Assessment of Interpersonal Forgiveness

Overview

Moral issues within psychology have been an object of study since the 1890s (see, for example, Hall, 1891). The majority of studies in the 20th century have centered on themes of justice, not mercy (see, for example, Killen & Smetana, 2006). In the 1980s, almost a century after the emergence of moral psychology, the construct of forgiveness began to emerge as a possible area of basic and applied research within psychology. From its humble beginnings, the psychology of forgiveness has now begun to emerge as a field worthy of researchers' time. For example, in 1985 a perusal of the American Psychological Association's database yielded no entries for the word "forgiveness." An examination of that site (PsychINFO) in October 2006 revealed a total of 218 entries for 2005–2006 alone. Those entries are as wide-ranging as social, developmental, clinical, and counseling psychology; family studies; and psychiatry. Forgiveness is even making inroads into the study of law (Sullivan & Tifft, 2006) and peace studies (Bole, Christiansen, & Henemeyer, 2004). This chapter discusses the research and practice in interpersonal forgiveness applied to the health professions.

Learning Objectives

By the end of the chapter, the reader should be able to:

1. Define the construct of interpersonal forgiveness;
2. Understand the history and current application of forgiveness research;
3. Identify the role of interpersonal forgiveness in rehabilitation and health; and
4. Examine current assessment measures of interpersonal forgiveness.

Introduction

The psychology of forgiveness is growing as a field, we think, because of its centrality to healthy relationships and healthy emotional functioning. To be able to forgive is an action that can benefit those forgiven and those doing the forgiving. If this is so, then it is important for our field to find effective ways to apply forgiveness when people are hurt by the injustices of others and to assess accurately a person's current level of forgiveness if effective applications are to ensue.

In this chapter, first, it is vital to understand the construct if we are to proceed well in the areas of application and assessment. Second, we review the intervention studies in this newly emerging area. All of the studies reviewed (with one exception in McCullough & Worthington, 1995) rely on the "gold standard" of intervention research: randomization to group, pretesting, posttesting, and follow-up testing with well-validated instruments. Third, we review assessment approaches so that the reader might select the best instrument for a given situation. Let us begin by examining the meaning of forgiveness.

History of Research and Practice in the Assessment of Forgiveness

The concept of *forgiveness* finds its roots in the ancient writings of the Hebrew and Christian scriptures. Accounts such as Joseph forgiving his brothers (Genesis 50) and the father forgiving his prodigal son (Luke 15) are just two narratives that portray forgiveness as a cessation of resentment and an offering of a beneficent response toward offenders, all in the context of unconditional love. Although other ancient religious or philosophical systems—such as Islam, Buddhism, and Confucianism—deal with notions of forgiveness in their treatment of such concepts as compassion and mercy, the most explicit and thorough ancient references come from Judaism and Christianity (Enright, Eastin, Golden, Sarinopoulos, & Freedman, 1992).

About 20 years ago, forgiveness remained largely outside the purview of social science, until Smedes (1984), Enright, Santos, and Al-Mabuk (1989), and Worthington and DiBlasio (1990) planted forgiveness on the scholarly landscape. Since then, the growing wave of forgiveness research has continued to shed light on the processes and outcomes of forgiveness interventions. Although not all scholars agree on the exact definition of forgiveness, most agree that forgiveness entails the giving up of anger and resentment, and many would suggest that those negative emotions be replaced by positive ones, such as benevolence and love. Enright (2001) provides a comprehensive definition of forgiveness:

> *When unjustly hurt by another, we forgive when we overcome the resentment toward the offender, not by denying our right to the resentment, but instead by trying to offer the wrongdoer compassion, benevolence, and love; as we give these, we as forgivers realize that the offender does not necessarily have a right to such gifts. (p. 25)*

Thus, forgiveness includes cognitive, affective, and behavioral components. Also important in describing forgiveness is defining what forgiveness is not. Forgiveness is not condoning, excusing, forgetting, justifying, calming down, or reconciling (Enright, 2001).

It is important to note here that there is healthy discourse across several disciplines—psychology, philosophy, and others—regarding what forgiveness is and is not. The definition we present here is not the only definition of forgiveness; rather, it represents one definition based on nearly 2 decades of academic inquiry and empirical research. (See Murphy (2000); McCullough, Pargament, & Thoresen (2000); and Rye et al. (2001) for an overview of alternative definitions of forgiveness.)

Regarding the implementation of forgiveness, two basic models exist in the literature: decision models and process models. Decision models emphasize a cognitive decision to let go of resentment, bitterness, and any need for vengeance (DiBlasio, 1998). In so doing, the forgiver separates reason from emotion and, as an act of the will, decides to forgive (DiBlasio, 2000; Worthington & Scherer, 2004). The process model of forgiveness, on the other hand, maintains that forgiveness is a complex process that takes time and hard work. One key feature of process models is a "roadmap" of forgiveness that identifies how people actually forgive one another. For example, in Enright's Process Model of Forgiveness (2001; see Exhibit 21.1), people journey through four phases of forgiveness: uncovering anger, deciding to forgive, working on forgiveness, and discovery and emotional release (see also Enright & Fitzgibbons, 2000). In making this journey, the forgiver moves at his or her own pace through different developmental guideposts, often revisiting some and sometimes skipping others.

Forgiveness interventions have proven effective with a variety of populations with myriad hurtful experiences. As a result of forgiveness interventions, elderly females showed higher forgiveness profiles and decreased in depression and anxiety (Hebl & Enright, 1993); college students increased in positive affect toward the offender and reported decreased vengeful feelings and increased conciliatory behavior (McCullough & Worthington, 1995); parentally love-deprived adolescents experienced significantly lower anxiety and higher self-esteem, hope, forgiveness, and positive attitudes toward their parents (Al-Mabuk, Enright, &

Exhibit 21.1

ENRIGHT PROCESS MODEL OF FORGIVENESS

The Enright Process Model of Forgiveness

The Phases and Units of Forgiving and the Issues Involved

UNCOVERING PHASE

1. Examination of psychological defenses and the issues involved
2. Confrontation of anger; the point is to release, not harbor, the anger
3. Admittance of shame, when this is appropriate
4. Awareness of depleted emotional energy
5. Awareness of cognitive rehearsal of the offense
6. Insight that the injured party may be comparing self with the injurer
7. Realization that oneself may be permanently and adversely changed by the injury
8. Insight into a possibly altered "just world" view

DECISION PHASE

9. A change in heart/conversion/new insights that old resolution strategies are not working
10. Willingness to consider forgiveness as an option
11. Commitment to forgive the offender

WORK PHASE

12. Reframing, though role-taking, who the wrongdoer is by viewing him or her in context
13. Empathy and compassion toward the offender
14. Bearing/accepting the pain
15. Giving a moral gift to the offender

DEEPENING PHASE

16. Finding meaning for self and others in the suffering and in the forgiveness process
17. Realization that self has needed others' forgiveness in the past
18. Insight that one is not alone (universality, support)
19. Realization that self may have new purpose in life because of the injury
20. Awareness of decreased negative affect and, perhaps, increased positive affect, if this begins to emerge, toward the injurer; awareness of internal, emotional release

From *Helping Clients Forgive: An Empirical Guide for Resolving Anger and Restoring Hope,* by R. D. Enright and R. P. Fitzgibbons, 2000, Washington, DC: American Psychological Association. Reproduced with permission.

Cardis, 1995); and female survivors of incest reported significant reductions in anxiety and depression and significant increases in hope, forgiveness, and self-esteem (Freedman & Enright, 1996). Furthermore, because of these interventions, college students showed more empathy and forgiveness (McCullough et al., 1997); men who were hurt by their partner's abortion decreased significantly in anxiety, anger, and grief and increased significantly in forgiveness (Coyle & Enright, 1997); residential drug rehab patients showed reduced depression, anger, and anxiety (Lin, Mack, Enright, Krahn, & Baskin, 2004); divorced individuals reported reduced depression (Rye et al., 2005); and emotionally abused women were able to improve in depression, trait anxiety, posttraumatic stress symptoms, self-esteem, forgiveness, environmental mastery, and finding meaning in suffering (Reed & Enright, 2006).

Importance of Forgiveness to Health and Rehabilitation

Until recently, psychological and social interventions and research have focused on the remediation or suppression of negative emotions associated with mental or physical illness. The current applications of interpersonal forgiveness are part of a growing trend in psychological research to focus on aspects of positive functioning that "lead to well-being, to positive individuals, and to thriving communities" (Seligman & Csikszentmihalyi, 2000, p. 5). This new focus is known as the Positive Psychology movement.

The empirical link between forgiveness and health has strengthened in the last several years. The link between mental health and forgiveness has been clearly established by various studies. Forgiveness has been shown both to decrease negative affect, such as depression, anger, anxiety, grief, and vengeful feelings, and to increase such positive traits as self-esteem, hope, positive attitudes, conciliatory behavior, positive affect, and empathy (Al-Mabuk et al., 1995; Coyle & Enright, 1997; Freedman & Enright, 1996; Hebl & Enright, 1993; Lin et al., 2004; McCullough & Worthington, 1995; McCullough et al., 1997; Reed & Enright, 2006; Rye et al., 2005). A recent meta-analytic study of forgiveness indicated that interventions based on the process model of forgiveness yielded an effect size for forgiveness between 0.53 and 2.16, which can be considered a large effect size (Baskin & Enright, 2004; Lipsley, 1990). Furthermore, participants who received individual treatment, rather than treatment within a large group, demonstrated significantly greater increases in forgiveness (Baskin & Enright, 2004).

The link between forgiveness and physical health, although somewhat less supported, is gaining strength as well. Huang and Enright (2000) discovered a relationship between forgiveness reasoning and blood pressure levels. Lawler et al. (2003) reported that state forgiveness was correlated with lower blood pressure levels and heart rate, and trait forgiveness was linked to lower blood pressure levels. Worthington and Scherer (2004) review literature demonstrating, through brain activity, hormonal patterns, the sympathetic nervous system, tension in facial muscles, and measures of blood chemistry, that the state of unforgiveness is stressful and that forgiveness can alleviate that stress. They also offer some initial support for propositions that forgiveness reduces hostility and affects both the immune and central nervous systems at various levels

(Worthington & Scherer, 2004). Forgiveness, then, is important to well-being, both mentally and physically.

Current Assessment Methods in Interpersonal Forgiveness

Since the social-scientific study of interpersonal forgiveness is a relatively new construct within the field of psychology and counseling (Enright, Gassin, & Wu, 1992; Enright & Human Development Study Group, 1991), there is some debate regarding what forgiveness is and is not and how it is most effectively measured (McCullough et al., 2000; Rye et al., 2001). These definitional considerations are paramount to issues of measurement and assessment. Perhaps more than any other variable, a researcher's or practitioner's conceptualization and definition of forgiveness will determine the types of outcomes they expect to find and the tools with which they assess those outcomes. Therefore, it is appropriate to

Discussion Box 21.1

WHAT IS FORGIVENESS?

The study of interpersonal forgiveness has burgeoned in the past 2 decades. Once absent from the social sciences, interpersonal forgiveness has inspired countless empirical articles and books that examine the theory, process, application, and measurement of the construct. And yet, despite the increasing academic interest in the study of interpersonal forgiveness, there is currently no academic consensus regarding the essential components or operational definition of interpersonal forgiveness. Therefore, before implementing or analyzing forgiveness programs or interventions, it is important to explore and articulate a working definition. Your response to these questions will likely impact your intervention model and assessment methods.

What is forgiveness?
Is forgiveness the absence of negative or the presence of positive thoughts, feelings, and actions? How is forgiveness different than excusing or condoning the unjust action? Can someone forgive without forgetting? Is there any act beyond the scope of forgiveness? Does authentic forgiveness necessarily involve reconciliation with the offender? Is forgiveness *a decision or a process of many decisions?*

Who is forgiving?
Is the person I am counseling or evaluating open to forgiveness? Does the intensity of the unjust and deep hurt prevent him/her from considering forgiveness as an option? Is she/he able to discuss their deep hurt rationally? Does he/she have preconceptions about forgiveness that are inaccurate or incomplete?

examine the components of forgiveness—definition, process, and participant—before choosing an assessment of the construct.

The definition of forgiveness discussed earlier in the chapter (Enright, 2001) and the Enright Process Model of Forgiveness describe forgiveness as a process of gradual changes in thoughts, feelings, and actions toward a wrongdoer. Subsequently, the measurement tool designed by Enright and Rique (1999) to assess interpersonal forgiveness is multidimensional in its construction and asks questions within affective, behavioral, and cognitive domains. Conditions such as construct-measurement match are essential to the accurate assessment of interpersonal forgiveness. Therefore, when choosing a forgiveness assessment, consider the following questions (adapted from Enright and Fitzgibbons, 2000):

Assessment Guidelines

1. Does it appropriately reflect the construct you are measuring?
2. Is it easy to complete, and is it developmentally appropriate?
3. Does it have strong psychometric properties of reliability and validity?

In the following section, we present three measures of interpersonal forgiveness that have been reported in published research: The Enright Forgiveness Inventory (EFI), The Enright Forgiveness Inventory for Children (EFI-C), and The Forgiveness Scale. These three measures were chosen as exemplary measures for three primary reasons. First, each measure assesses interpersonal forgiveness in a manner that is consistent with and reflective of the cognitive, affective, and behavioral assumptions represented in our earlier discussion of the construct of forgiveness, and each contains both positive and negative variables in assessing these categories. Second, each of the three measures assesses "transgression-specific" forgiveness—actual expressions of forgiveness based on a real experience of hurt—rather than an assessment of general forgiveness tendency or dispositional forgiveness. Finally, these three measures were chosen for their strength of construction (e.g., broad age range, general ease of use, and high internal reliability). Additionally, we will provide information on how to obtain copies of these measures for use in counseling, educational, or other research programs.

The Enright Forgiveness Inventory (EFI)

The Enright Forgiveness Inventory (EFI; see Exhibit 21.2) is based on the definition presented earlier in the chapter and the Enright Process Model of Forgiveness.

The EFI was developed over a 2-year period where graduate students and professors specializing in development and measurement met to explore what forgiveness is and how it could be measured. A total of 60 questions were constructed across 3 major domains—affect, behavior, and cognition—with a balance of 10 positive and 10 negative questions within each domain. For example, participants respond to questions such as "I feel warm toward him/her," "I would avoid him/her," and "I think he or she is worthy of respect," which were created to assess both positive and negative thoughts, feelings, and actions toward the

Exhibit 21.2

DESCRIPTION OF THE ENRIGHT FORGIVENESS INVENTORY (EFI)

ATTITUDE SCALE

We are sometimes unfairly hurt by people, whether in family, friendship, school, work, or other situations. We ask you now to think of the **most recent** experience of someone hurting you **unfairly** and **deeply**. For a few moments, visualize in your mind the events of that interaction. Try to see the person and try to experience what happened.

1. **How deeply were you hurt when the incident occurred?**
(circle one)

No hurt A little hurt Some hurt Much hurt A great deal of hurt

2. **Who hurt you?**

Child Spouse Relative Friend of the same gender Friend of the opposite gender Employer

3. **Is the person living?**

Yes No

4. **How long ago was the offense?**
(Please write in the number of days or weeks, etc.)

____ days ago ____ months ago
____ weeks ago ____ years ago

5. **Please briefly describe what happened when this person hurt you:**

Now, please answer a series of questions about your current attitude toward this person. We do **not** want your rating of past attitudes, but your ratings of attitudes **right now**. All responses are confidential so please answer honestly. Thank you.

SAMPLE AFFECT QUESTIONS

This set of items deals with your current **feelings** or **emotions** right now toward the person. Try to assess your actual **feeling** for the person on each item. For each item please check the appropriate number matching your level of agreement that **best** describes your current feeling. Please do not skip any item. Thank you.

I feel __________ toward him/her. (Place each word in the blank when answering each item.)

I feel...	Strongly Disagree	Disagree	Slightly Disagree	Slightly Agree	Agree	Strongly Agree
1 warm	1	2	3	4	5	6
2 negative	1	2	3	4	5	6

20 items total on the Affect subscale (10 positive and 10 negative affect items).

SAMPLE BEHAVIOR QUESTIONS

This set of items deals with your current **behavior** toward the person. Consider how you **do act** or **would act** toward the person in answering the questions. For each item please check the appropriate number matching your level of agreement that **best** describes your current behavior or probable behavior. Please do not skip any item. Thank you.

Regarding this person, I do or would _______. (Place each word in the blank when answering each item.)

I do or would...	**Strongly Disagree**	**Disagree**	**Slightly Disagree**	**Slightly Agree**	**Agree**	**Strongly Agree**
21 show friendship	1	2	3	4	5	6
22 avoid	1	2	3	4	5	6

20 items total on the behavior subscale (10 positive and 10 negative behavior items).

SAMPLE COGNITIVE QUESTIONS

This set of questions deals with how you currently **think** about the person. Think about the kinds of thoughts that occupy your **mind** right **now** regarding this particular person. For each item please check the appropriate number matching your level of agreement that **best** describes your current thinking. Please do not skip any items. Thank you.

I think he or she is __________. (Place each word in the blank when answering each item.)

I think he or she is...	**Strongly Disagree**	**Disagree**	**Slightly Disagree**	**Slightly Agree**	**Agree**	**Strongly Agree**
46 dreadful	1	2	3	4	5	6
47 loving	1	2	3	4	5	6

20 items total on the cognitive subscale (10 positive and 10 negative cognitive items).

SAMPLE PSEUDOFORGIVENESS AND VALIDATION QUESTIONS

In thinking through the person and event you just rated, please consider the following questions.

	Strongly Disagree	**Disagree**	**Slightly Disagree**	**Slightly Agree**	**Agree**	**Strongly Agree**
61 There really was no problem now that I think about it	1	2	3	4	5	6

We have one final question.

To what extent have you forgiven the person you rated on this *Attitude Scale*?

Not at all		In progress		Complete forgiveness
1	2	3	4	5

6 total items in the pseudoforgiveness and validation subscale

Note: Reprinted with permission from Dr. Robert Enright; available at http://www.mindgarden.com.

wrongdoer. Participants respond to these questions on a 6-point Likert scale ranging from (1) *strongly agree* to (6) *strongly disagree.*

The EFI evaluation begins by asking participants to describe a recent experience of unfair and deep hurt. They are also asked to visualize the person (wrongdoer) who is responsible for the hurt. Participants are then asked to focus only on the wrongdoer they identified in the focusing exercise as they complete the forgiveness assessment.

In addition to the three domains of assessment, the EFI provides an additional set of questions to evaluate *pseudoforgiveness.* As the term suggests, pseudoforgiveness is not genuine forgiveness but likely an expression of condoning or excusing the unjust hurt and wrongdoer. These pseudoforgiveness questions follow the same 6-point Likert format as the others but are scored independently. Enright and Fitzgibbons (2000) report that a score of 20 or more on this scale is indicative of pseudoforgiveness and recommend that the data be removed from analysis.

The final question on the EFI is designed to allow for the assessment of construct validity—to ensure that the EFI measures forgiveness and not some other construct. Participants are asked about forgiveness for the first time in this question, which reads: "To what extent have you forgiven the person you rated on the *Attitude Scale?*" Participants respond on a 5-point Likert scale that ranges from (1) *Not at all* to (5) *Complete forgiveness.*

The content and sequence of the EFI was originally validated through a study conducted by Subkoviak et al. (1992, 1995). Subkoviak and colleagues administered the EFI to 394 participants; half of the participants were college students, and the other half consisted of the same-sex parent of the student. Results from this study yielded a Cronbach's alpha for internal consistency of.98 and a correlation of.68 for the relationship between the construct validity question and the EFI. Both of these results are considered strong and have been replicated in numerous studies across diverse populations, as can be seen in Table 21.1.

The Enright Forgiveness Inventory for Children (EFI-C)

The Enright Forgiveness Inventory for Children (EFI-C; see example in Exhibit 21.3) is based on the adult version (EFI) and is representative of the definition and model of forgiveness presented earlier in the chapter. The EFI-C is designed to provide helping professionals and researchers an accurate and reliable assessment of children's expressions of interpersonal forgiveness.

The EFI-C begins by asking the children to describe a recent experience of deep hurt and to focus on the person responsible for that hurt. The children are

21.1 Reliability and Validity of the Enright Forgiveness Inventory (EFI)

Study	Sample Size	Cronbach's α	Correlation of EFI and 1-item forgiveness question
Subkoviak et al. (1995)	394	.98	.68
Gassin (1995)	19	.99	.74
Coyle & Enright (1997)	10	.95	Not given
Sarinopoulos (2000)	219	.99	.60
Konstam, Chernoff, & Deveney (2001)	138	.98	Not given
Rye et al. (2001)	328	.99	.71
Lin et al. (2004)	14	.96	Not given
Maltby, Day, & Barber (2005)	224	> .92	Not given
Reed & Enright (2006)	20	.94	Not given

then guided through 30 questions across the 3 major domains—affect, behavior, and cognition—with a balance of 5 positive and 5 negative questions within each domain. For example, the children respond to questions such as "Do you feel happy about him or/her?," "Would you get back at him/her?," and "Do you hope they are happy?" The children are asked to respond to such questions by indicating (1) *Yes,* (2) *A little bit yes,* (3) *A little bit no,* and (4) *No.* The EFI-C also includes questions that assess pseudoforgiveness and construct validity.

The language throughout the measure is crafted to be developmentally appropriate for children as young as age 7. Because the EFI-C is designed especially for young children, it is advised that a trained practitioner guide each child through the assessment in an informal interview format and record their responses. Practitioners can even use colorful response boards whereby the children indicate their responses by pointing to a word or picture.

The EFI-C is a relatively new measure of interpersonal forgiveness and has only recently been implemented in empirical research with elementary-age children (Enright, Knutson Enright, Holter, Baskin, & Knutson, 2006). University researchers have successfully used the EFI-C to assess forgiveness levels of first through fifth grade students in elementary schools throughout the United States and in Northern Ireland. Preliminary use of the measure with third grade children in the United States and Northern Ireland has indicated levels of reliability consistent with the EFI (Cronbach's $\alpha = .94$). However, further research is needed to properly validate the measure and establish expected norms.

Forgiveness Scale

Rye et al. (2001) developed a forgiveness scale that is "relatively brief and contains questions about both positive and negative responses toward offenders"

Exhibit 21.3

DESCRIPTION OF THE ENRIGHT FORGIVENESS INVENTORY FOR CHILDREN (EFI-C)

INTRODUCTION

Please remember a time when a person *hurt you very, very much*. Think back to what he/she did. Try to see in your mind what happened. How did this make you feel?

Circle the answer that is most appropriate:

Very Awful A Little Awful Not Awful Not at all Awful

Who was the one who made you feel this way?______________________

How long ago did this happen? ___________ months, weeks, days (circle one)

Please tell me about it (record what the child says):

SAMPLE AFFECT QUESTIONS

These questions deal with your current *feelings right now* about [state person's name]. Try to tell me your actual *feeling* for the person for each question.

Do you feel _______ about him/her?

1. happy	Yes	A little bit yes	A little bit no	No
2. had	Yes	A little bit yes	A little bit no	No

10 total items in the affect subscale (5 positive and 5 negative)

SAMPLE BEHAVIOR QUESTIONS

These questions deal with how you act right now toward the person. This about how you *do act* or *would act* toward the person in answering the questions.

Would you _______?

11. be a friend to him or her	Yes	A little bit yes	A little bit no	No
12. not talk to him/her	Yes	A little bit yes	A little bit no	No

10 total items in the behavior subscale (5 positive and 5 negative)

SAMPLE COGNITIVE QUESTIONS

These questions deal with how you *think* about the person. Think about the kinds of thoughts in your mind *right now* regarding [name].

Do you *think* [name] _______?

21. is mean	Yes	A little bit yes	A little bit no	No
22. is a good person	Yes	A little bit yes	A little bit no	No

10 total items in the affect subscale (5 positive and 5 negative)

SAMPLE PSEUDOFORGIVENESS AND VALIDATION QUESTIONS

34. Have you forgiven [name]	Yes	No
35. Do you know what forgiveness is?	Yes	No

Tell me what it is:

5 total items in the pseudoforgiveness and validation subscale

Note: Reprinted with permission from Dr. Robert Enright; available by request at director@forgivenessinstitute.org.

(p. 262). The *Forgiveness Scale* examined in this study is a reworked version of an earlier scale designed for romantic relationships. For the purposes of this study, Rye et al. conceptualize forgiveness as "a response toward an offender that involves letting go of negative affect (e.g., hostility), cognitions (e.g., thoughts of revenge), and behavior (e.g., verbal aggression), and may also involve positive responses toward the offender (e.g., compassion)" (p. 261). This conceptualization is similar in format to the Enright and Fitzgibbons (2000) definition but lacks a strong emphasis on positive affect, behavior, and cognition toward a wrongdoer.

The Forgiveness Scale begins by instructing the participant to think about how he/she has responded to a wrongdoer and then complete a series of questions. There are 15 questions in this scale, and participants respond to each question on a 5-point Likert scale ranging from (1) *strongly agree* to (5) *strongly disagree*. For example, participants are asked to respond to questions such as "I wish good things to happen to the person who wronged me," "I have compassion for the person who wronged me," and "I hope the person who wronged me is treated fairly by others in the future."

A sample of college students (N = 328) was solicited to validate the Forgiveness Scale. Analysis of the data revealed an overall Cronbach alpha of.87, which is an acceptable measure of internal consistency. The data also confirm that the Forgiveness Scale is significantly correlated with the subscales of the EFI. Copies of this scale are available by contacting Dr. Mark Rye at Mark.Rye@notes.udayton.edu.

Secondary Measures of Forgiveness

In addition to the primary measures of forgiveness (EFI, EFI-C, and Forgiveness Scale), practitioners and researchers may want to consider what we are calling secondary measures of forgiveness. As the review of research suggests, individuals who participate in forgiveness interventions often demonstrate decreases in negative emotional variables (anger, anxiety, depression, etc.) and increases in positive emotional variables (self-esteem and hope). The following is a list of exceptional instruments for measuring these secondary outcomes: Spielberger State-Trait Anxiety Scale (Spielberger, Gorsuch, Lushene, Vagg, &

Jacobs, 1983); Beck Anger Inventory, Beck Depression Inventory (Beck & Steer, 1987); and the Coopersmith Self-Esteem Inventory (Coopersmith, 1981).

Research Critical to Issues in Forgiveness Assessment

Although the term *forgiveness* is not specifically listed in the ICF, the practice of interpersonal forgiveness is directly related to several of the domains within the ICF (WHO, 2006). Research presented earlier in the chapter is relevant to all four of the categories identified by WHO—Body Function, Body Structure, Activities and Participation, and Environmental Factors. By targeting the psychological variables associated with experiences of deep hurt (i.e., anger, depression, self-esteem, etc.), forgiveness interventions have demonstrated positive effects with regard to personal mental health, physical well-being, and interpersonal relationships (see introduction for review). Each of these general benefits has the potential to promote successful functioning within general environmental and support structures such as the immediate family, work environment, and personal relationships.

Forgiveness interventions are clearly connected to the mission and objectives of the ICF (Reed et al., 2005; WHO, 2006), yet there is a dearth of forgiveness research situated in the specific language of the ICF categories—a paucity that is present across several psychological domains of study (Bruyere, Van Looy, & Peterson, 2005). Implementation of ICF standards in forgiveness research would allow researchers and practitioners from across the world—working with diverse populations and within diverse cultures—a common metric for the comparison of human functioning with regard to interpersonal forgiveness (Reed et al., 2005). Furthermore, the complexity of the ICF standards would allow for a concurrent assessment of positive and negative health factors from "biological, individual, and societal perspectives" all at the same time (Reed et al., 2005, p. 122).

Cultural and Professional Considerations

An important question for those in the helping professions to ask is how culture impacts interventions. For example, McLernon, Cairns, Herstone, and Smith (2004) warn that, in some societies, harboring anger and revenge is viewed as a way of memorializing or actively remembering the victim in order to minimize the tendency to trivialize or forget the offenses. Some, like Nietzsche (1887), might regard forgivers as morally weak and inferior. If by forgiveness one means excusing, condoning, or any form of pseudoforgiveness, then this assessment might be true. Genuine forgiveness, however, requires great courage and is one way to deal with injustices by preserving the inherent worth of the individual (even the one responsible for the hurt).

Still, cultural differences do impact the practice of forgiveness. For example, Rabbi Marc Gopin offers a five-point summary to helping professionals regarding cultural differences (Enright, 2000): (1) those from different religious backgrounds probably understand forgiveness differently; (2) some might look for acts of genuine repentance, while others proceed from the standpoint of unconditional love; (3) some might insist on evidence of responsibility and trust;

Discussion Box 21.2

PERSONAL AND CULTURAL CONSIDERATIONS

Interpersonal forgiveness is indeed a personal choice. However, the support or encouragement one receives for offering forgiveness may be impacted by religious beliefs, cultural expectations, family dynamics, and so on. Our recent research in Belfast, Northern Ireland, highlights the impact of family experiences and cultural expectations on interpersonal forgiveness. We encountered some initial reluctance and concern when meeting with several parents to discuss the implementation of a forgiveness education program at their children's school. Many of these families lived in interface areas and experienced significant intergroup violence. Parents from these areas were concerned that if their son or daughter practiced forgiveness, they would be targets for bullies at school and in the neighborhood. Anger was synonymous with strength. Forgiveness harkened weakness. We spent several hours meeting with these parents, listening to their concerns, and gaining an understanding of how their family dynamics and community experiences impacted their concept of forgiveness. In the end, parents and teachers alike were enthusiastic about forgiveness for their children. Consider the following when examining the impact of culture on the definition and application of interpersonal forgiveness. (1) How do you define forgiveness? (2) From where does this understanding come (cultural norms, etc.)? (3) Does repentance play an important role? (4) What role does trust play? (5) In each person's view, how deep is the injury? (Enright, 2000). What other questions might you add to this list?

(4) the depth of the injustice might be an important issue for some people; and (5) the forgiver's assessment of the offender's cultural history could impact the forgiveness process.

Although cultural differences do exist, Enright (2000) is quick to point out that many individuals and groups agree strongly in the words they use to describe forgiveness. Studies of forgiveness in the United States, Brazil, Australia, Israel, Korea, and Taiwan indicate general agreement that "to forgive is to cast off resentment, negative judgments, and revengeful behaviors toward the offender; they agree that to forgive is to substitute more positive emotions, thoughts, and behaviors toward the offender" (Enright, 2000, p. 14). Despite the universality of forgiveness terms, practitioners and others must recognize that the process of interpersonal forgiveness is highly individualized. The personal journey through forgiveness is therefore likely influenced by an individual's cultural identity, religious beliefs, personal history, and so on. These individual considerations are not prohibitive to forgiveness but may impact the process and assessment of the construct.

In dealing with painful offenses, many people are unaware that forgiveness is an option. Therefore, one of the responsibilities of those in the helping professions is to suggest effective options and alternatives to clients who desire wholeness. One such effective method for dealing with the anger and resentment stemming from personal injustice is forgiveness therapy. As professionals, it is important both to be aware of what forgiveness is and what it is not and to have a basic idea of how to help someone make the forgiveness journey. Texts such as *Helping Clients Forgive* (Enright & Fitzgibbons, 2000) and *Forgiveness is a Choice* (Enright, 2001) are helpful resources for helping professionals in that they provide a step-by-step forgiveness guide that can be easily followed. One should note that although the forgiveness process has a roadmap, the journey is not necessarily linear. Because forgiveness is a choice, it cannot be forced upon anyone. It is a choice, however, that should be presented as an option to those who harbor anger and resentment from deep and unjust hurt.

Multidisciplinary Approaches

Forgiveness intervention and assessment have taken place in multiple contexts. Forgiveness interventions have been successful in schools (Enright, Gassin, & Knutson, 2003; Gambaro, 2002; Gassin, Enright, & Knutson, 2005), marriages (DiBlasio, 2000), and inpatient drug rehab centers (Lin et al., 2004). Group interventions have helped elderly women (Hebl & Enright, 1993) and adolescents who felt deprived of love by their parents (Al-Mabuk et al., 1995). One-on-one interventions have helped women who survived incest (Freedman & Enright, 1996) and have experienced emotional abuse (Reed & Enright, 2006), men who were upset by their partners' decision to abort a baby (Coyle & Enright, 1997), and college students who experienced a variety of hurts (McCullough & Worthington, 1995; McCullough et al., 1997). The effectiveness of forgiveness interventions across multiple contexts and domains increases its credibility and viability as a treatment option. In the future, forgiveness interventions will span deeper into areas such as the family and even organizations such as houses of worship.

Major Issues That Need Attention

Despite tremendous interest in and empirical examination of interpersonal forgiveness over the past 2 decades, some important work remains. The central issue at hand is the need for further research to clarify and articulate a concise definition of forgiveness. In other words, we must ask, "What does forgiveness mean? (Exline, Worthington, Hill, & McCullough, 2003). It has long been acknowledged that there is some controversy with regard to the definition of forgiveness differences (Enright, Eastin, et al., 1992). However, it is no longer sufficient for social scientists and practitioners to simply acknowledge these differences. The development of diagnostic scales—such as the Forgiveness Attitudes Questionnaire (FAQ) by Kanz (2000)—and recent meta-analyses—such as those conducted by Baskin and Enright (2004) and Wade and Worthington (2005)—provide essential insight into the common components and effective conditions of interpersonal forgiveness. We must therefore incorporate these new findings into our operational definitions and processes of forgiveness. Furthermore, as the field of forgiveness research continues to inform and shape the implementation of forgiveness interventions, there is a concurrent need for valid and reliable measurement of the construct.

Research Box 21.1

INTERVENTION STUDIES ON FORGIVENESS: A META-ANALYSIS

Baskin, T. W., & Enright, R. D. (2004). Intervention studies on forgiveness: A meta-analysis. *Journal of Counseling and Development,* 82, 79–90.

Objective: To examine the type and effectiveness of empirical forgiveness interventions within a counseling context.

Method: The authors examined nine published empirical studies that implemented a forgiveness intervention within a counseling context. The studies were categorized based on the type of counseling model employed: decision model, process model within a group setting, and process model with individual treatment. In addition to the counseling model, the authors examined the sample population, forgiveness measure, and secondary psychological variable of interest. Effect sizes were calculated for the forgiveness and secondary psychological variables and compared among the three counseling models.

Results: Analysis of the data revealed a mean effect size for decision models of d = -0.04, a mean effect size for process models in a group setting of d = 0.82*, and a mean effect size for process models with individual treatment of d = 1.66*. Furthermore, the analysis of the secondary psychological variables revealed a similar patter: decision d = 0.16, process-group d = 0.59*, and process individual d = 1.42* (*p < .05).

Conclusion: The meta-analysis revealed that both process-based models of forgiveness intervention produced statistically significant effect sizes for forgiveness and the secondary psychological variables of interest. The process model within an individual setting was the most effective. Conversely, the decision-based models failed to yield statistically significant effect sizes.

Questions: What are the implications of these results for practitioners and researchers? How might these results shape future research in the field? Do these findings impact how we might best measure forgiveness? If construct-assessment match is an important measurement consideration, what characteristics might we expect to find in effective forgiveness assessment measures?

Conclusion

What surprises us, as we reflect back on the knowledge base in the psychology of forgiveness, is this: The field has developed quite quickly. In about 2 decades, the psychology of forgiveness has been shown to be quite effective for a wide variety of people suffering deep hurts. The effect sizes of the interventions are moderate to strong, a testimony to the robust nature of forgiveness within the helping professions. Although forgiveness would seem to be a rather amorphous concept, its assessment can be done with high reliability and good scientific validity.

We look forward to the creative contributions of others over the coming decades. We anticipate that even though the essence of forgiveness, in all likelihood, will be shown to be similar across cultures, the nuances of different cultural norms and religious practices will become clearer to those studying forgiveness and trying to help others forgive.

References

Al-Mabuk, R., Enright, R. D., & Cardis, P. (1995). Forgiveness education with parentally love-deprived college students. *Journal of Moral Education, 24,* 427–444.

Baskin, T. W., & Enright, R. D. (2004). Intervention studies on forgiveness: A meta-analysis. *Journal of Counseling and Development, 82,* 79–90.

Beck, A. T., & Steer, R. A. (1987). *Beck depression inventory.* San Antonio, TX: Psychological Corporation.

Bole, W., Christiansen, D., & Henemeyer, R. T. (2004). *Forgiveness in international politics.* Washington, DC: U.S. Conference of Catholic Bishops.

Bruyere, S. M., Van Looy, S. A., & Peterson, D. B. (2005). The International Classification of Functioning, Disability and Health: Contemporary literature overview. *Rehabilitation Psychology, 50*(2), 113–121.

Coopersmith, S. (1981). *Self-esteem inventories.* Palo Alto, CA: Consulting Psychologists Press.

Coyle, C. T., & Enright, R. D. (1997). Forgiveness intervention with post-abortion men. *Journal of Consulting and Clinical Psychology, 65*(6), 1042–1046.

DiBlasio, F. (1998). The use of a decision-based forgiveness intervention within intergenerational family therapy. *Journal of Family Therapy, 20,* 77–94.

DiBlasio, F. (2000). Decision-based forgiveness treatment in cases of marital infidelity. *Psychotherapy, 37*(2), 149–158.

Enright, R. D. (2000). Forgiveness within and among communities and nations. *The World of Forgiveness, 3*(3), 6–29.

Enright, R. D. (2001). *Forgiveness is a choice.* Washington, DC: APA Books.

Enright, R. D., Eastin, D. L., Golden, S., Sarinopoulos, I., & Freedman, S. R. (1992). Interpersonal forgiveness within the helping professions: An attempt to resolve differences of opinion. *Counseling and Values, 36*(2), 84–103.

Enright, R. D., & Fitzgibbons, R. P. (2000). *Helping clients forgive: An empirical guide for resolving anger and restoring hope.* Washington, DC: American Psychological Association.

Enright, R. D., Gassin, E. A., & Knutson, J. A. (2003). Waging peace through forgiveness education in Belfast, Northern Ireland: A review and proposal for mental health improvement of children. *Journal of Research in Education, 13,* 1–11.

Enright, R. D., Gassin, E. A., & Wu, C. (1992). Forgiveness: A developmental view. *Journal of Moral Education, 21,* 99–114.

Enright, R.D., Knutson Enright, J. A., Holter, A., Baskin, T., & Knutson, C. (2006). *A psychologist/teacher consultation model for anger reduction: Forgiveness interventions in Belfast, Northern Ireland.* Manuscript submitted for publication review.

Enright, R. D., & The Human Development Study Group. (1991). The moral development of forgiveness. In W. Kurtines & J. Gewirtz (Eds.), *Handbook of moral behavior and development* (Vol. 1, pp. 123–152). Hillsdale, NJ: Lawrence Erlbaum Associates.

Enright, R. D., & Rique, J. (1999). *The Enright forgiveness inventory.* Menlo Park, CA: Mind Garden, Inc.

Enright, R. D., Santos, M.J.O., & Al-Mabuk, R. H. (1989). The adolescent as forgiver. *Journal of Adolescence, 12,* 95–110.

Exline, J. J., Worthington, E. L., Jr., Hill, P., & McCullough, M. E. (2003). Forgiveness and justice: A research agenda for social and personality psychology. *Personality and Social Psychology Review, 7*(4), 337–348.

Freedman, S. R., & Enright, R. D. (1996). Forgiveness as an intervention goal with incest survivors. *Journal of Consulting and Clinical Psychology, 64*(5), 983–992.

Gambaro, M. E. (2002). *School-based forgiveness education in the management of trait anger in early adolescents.* Unpublished doctoral dissertation, University of Wisconsin–Madison.

Gassin, E. A. (1995). *Social cognition and forgiveness in adolescent romance: An intervention study.* Unpublished Doctoral Dissertation, University of Wisconsin–Madison.

Gassin, E. A., Enright, R. D., & Knutson J. A. (2005). Bringing peace to the central-city: Forgiveness education in Milwaukee. *Theory Into Practice, 44*(4), 319–328.

Hall, G. (1891). The moral and religious training of children and adolescents. *Pedagogical Seminary, 1,* 196–210.

Hebl, J. H., & Enright, R. D. (1993). Forgiveness as a psychotherapeutic goal with elderly females. *Psychotherapy, 30,* 658–667.

Huang, S. T., & Enright, R. D. (2000). Forgiveness and anger-related emotions in Taiwan: Implications for therapy. *Psychotherapy, 37,* 71–79.

Kanz, J. E. (2000). How do people conceptualize and use forgiveness? The Forgiveness Attitudes Questionnaire. *Counseling and Values, 44*(3), 174–188.

Killen, M., & Smetana, J. (Eds.). (2006). *Handbook of moral development.* Mahwah, NJ: Lawrence Erlbaum Associates.

Konstam, V., Chernoff, M., & Deveney, S. (2001). Toward forgiveness: The role of shame, guilt, anger, and empathy. *Counseling and Values, 46*(1), 26–39.

Lawler, K. A., Younger, J. W., Piferi, R. L., Billington, E., Jobe, R., Edmondson, K., et al. (2003). A change of heart: Cardiovascular correlates of forgiveness in response to interpersonal conflict. *Journal of Behavioral Medicine, 26,* 373–393.

Lin, W. F., Mack, D., Enright, R. D., Krahn, D., & Baskin, T. (2004). Effects of forgiveness therapy on anger, mood, and vulnerability to substance use among inpatient substance-dependent clients. *Journal of Consulting and Clinical Psychology, 72*(6),1114–1121.

Lipsley, M. W. (1990). *Design sensitivity: Statistical power for experimental research.* Newbury Park, CA: Sage.

Maltby, J., Day, L., & Barber, L. (2005). Forgiveness and happiness, the differing contexts of forgiveness using the distinction between hedonic and eudaimonic happiness. *Journal of Happiness Studies, 6*(1), 1–13.

McCullough, M. E., Pargament, K. I., & Thoresen, C. E. (2000). *Forgiveness: Theory, research, and practice.* New York: Guilford Press.

McCullough, M. E., & Worthington, E. L., Jr. (1995). Promoting forgiveness: The comparison of two brief psychoeducational interventions with a waiting-list control. *Counseling and Values, 40,* 55–68.

McCullough, M. E., Worthington, E. L., Jr., & Rachal, K. C. (1997). Interpersonal forgiving in close relationships. *Journal of Personality and Social Psychology, 73,* 321–336.

McLernon, F., Cairns, E., Hewstone, M., & Smith, R. (2004). The development of intergroup forgiveness in Northern Ireland. *Journal of Social Issues, 60*(3), 587–601.

Murphy, J. G. (2005). Forgiveness, self-respect, and the value of resentment. In E. L. Worthington, (Ed.), *Handbook of forgiveness* (Vol. 1, pp. 33–40). New York: Rutledge.

Nietzsche, F. W. (1887). *The genealogy of morals* (P. Watson, Trans.). London: S.P.C.K.

Reed, G. L., & Enright, R. D. (2006). The effects of forgiveness therapy on depression, anxiety, and posttraumatic stress for women after spousal emotional abuse. *Journal of Consulting and Clinical Psychology, 74*(5), 920–929.

Reed, G. M., Lux, J. B., Bufka, L. F., Trask, C., Peterson, D. B., Stark, S., et al. (2005). Operationalizing the International Classification of Functioning, Disability and Health in clinical settings. *Rehabilitation Psychology, 50*(2), 122–131.

Rye, M. S., Loiacono, D. M., Folck, C. D., Olszewski, B. T., Heim, T. A., & Madia, B. P. (2001). Evaluation of the psychometric properties of two forgiveness scales. *Current Psychology: Developmental, Learning, Personality, Social, 20*(3), 260–277.

Rye, M. S., Pargament, K. I., Pan, W., Yingling, D. W., Shogren, K. A., & Ito, M. (2005). Can group intervention facilitate forgiveness of an ex-spouse? A randomized clinical trial. *Journal of Consulting and Clinical Psychology, 73,* 880–892.

Sarinopoulos, I. (2000). *Forgiveness and physical health.* Unpublished Doctoral Dissertation, University of Wisconsin—Madison.

Seligman, M.E., & Csikszentmihalyi, M. (2000). Positive Psychology: An introduction. *American Psychologist, 55*(1), 5–14.

Smedes, L. (1984). *Forgive and forget.* New York: Harper & Row.

Spielberger, C. D., Gorsuch, R. L., Lushene, R., Vagg, P. R., & Jacobs, G. A. (1983). *State-trait anxiety inventory* (Form Y): *Self evaluation questionnaire.* Palo Alto, CA: Consulting Psychologists Press.

Subkoviak, M. J., Enright, R. D., Wu, C., Gassin, E., Freedman, S., Olson, L., et al. (1992, April). *Measuring interpersonal forgiveness.* Paper presented at the annual meeting of the American Educational Research Association, San Francisco.

Subkoviak, M. J., Enright, R. D., Wu, C., Gassin, E., Freedman, S., Olson, L., et al. (1995). Measuring interpersonal forgiveness in late adolescent and middle adulthood. *Journal of Adolescence, 18,* 641–655.

Sullivan, D., & Tifft, L. (Eds.). (2006). *Handbook of restorative justice: A global perspective.* London: Taylor and Francis.

Wade, N. G., & Worthington, E. L., Jr. (2005). In search of a common core: A content analysis of interventions to promote forgiveness. *Psychotherapy: Theory, Research, Practice, Training, 42*(2), 160–177.

World Health Organization. (2006). *About the International Classification of Functioning, Disability and Health (ICF).* Retrieved October 3, 2006, from: http://www.who.int/icidh

Worthington, E. L., Jr., & DiBlasio, F. (1990). Promoting mutual forgiveness within the fractured relationship. *Psychotherapy, 27,* 219–223.

Worthington, E. L, & Scherer, M. (2004). Forgiveness is an emotion-focused coping strategy that can reduce health risks and promote health resilience: Theory, review, and hypotheses. *Psychology and Health, 19*(3), 385–405.

Michael Ungar
Jessica R. Toste
Nancy L. Heath

Self-Efficacy and Resilience Measures

22

Overview

This chapter explores issues related to the assessment of resilience and self-efficacy in youth. First, we review current definitions of resilience and self-efficacy and relate these to the International Classification of Functioning, Disability, and Health (ICF; World Health Organization [WHO], 2001). The history of the assessment of resilience is explored with reference to critical aspects, such as risk and protective factors, culture, and context. The second half of the chapter focuses on specific guidelines for conducting an assessment of resilience, including quantitative and qualitative approaches. Finally, critical considerations in the assessment of resilience are discussed.

Learning Objectives

By the end of the chapter, the reader should be able to:

1. Obtain information pertaining to current definitions of, and concepts related to, resilience and self-efficacy;
2. Apply a framework for understanding resilience;
3. Describe the development of practice in the assessment of resilience across different cultures and contexts;
4. Demonstrate a complex culturally sensitive understanding of the interactions between risk and protective factors within a resilience framework;
5. Relate the client's resilience profile to the four essential ecological levels of resources; and
6. Conduct both quantitative and qualitative assessments of resilience.

Introduction

Rehabilitation is intended to discover and build upon the capacities of those who are in some way debilitated. Though much of the focus can be on remediation of dysfunction, an equally important aspect of this work should be to examine dimensions of healthy functioning that are in evidence despite disorder and infirmity. This shift in focus to health brings with it many useful opportunities for intervention. WHO and its international partners (Health and Welfare Canada, 1988) have argued that a distinction needs to be made between dimensions of health and the degree of incapacity caused by illness. They are not polar opposites of the same continuum but two interdependent factors that affect a person's overall well-being. One may experience many aspects of healthy functioning, such as self-efficacy, despite serious disorder related to disease or disability. In much the same way, a focus on resilience and related positive dimensions of healthy development focuses our attention as professionals on the capacity of individuals that is either potentiated or already in evidence in their lives. A shift in focus from alleviating disorder to building strengths is a much needed part of intervention.

Importance of Self-Efficacy and Resilience to Rehabilitation and Health

Definitions and Theories of Self-Efficacy and Resilience

Self-efficacy can be defined as "beliefs in one's capabilities to organize and execute the courses of action required to produce given attainments" (Bandura, 1997, p. 3). Beliefs of personal efficacy, therefore, are not dependent on an individual's own abilities but instead on what he/she believes may be accomplished with his/her personal skill set. Thus, self-efficacy has been thought to be a better predictor of success than skills, knowledge, or even past accomplishments (Multon, Brown, & Lent, 1991; Schunk, 1991). A sense of self-efficacy influences an individual's course of action, effort dedicated to certain endeavors, persistence in the face of obstacles, and coping in the face of adversity.

Most commonly, *resilience* refers to a dynamic, developmental process involving positive adjustment in the face of significant adversity (Luthar, Cicchetti, & Becker, 2000). Two conditions are central to this definition: (1) exposure to considerable threat or adversity and (2) the achievement of positive adaptation in spite of major assaults on one's development (Garmezy, 1990; Luthar & Zigler, 1991). While this theoretical definition is widely accepted among researchers studying resilience, there are numerous examples of alternative conceptualizations in the literature. Specifically, Masten, Best, and Garmezy (1991) differentiate among three groups of resilient individuals: those who demonstrate successful outcomes despite exposure to high-risk circumstances, sustained competence under continued stress, and positive recovery from trauma. Alternatively, Rutter (1987) construes resilience in a more general sense, as the positive end of a continuum of individual differences in responses to stress. It is important to note that despite these slight differences, the notion that an individual demonstrates positive adjustment despite enduring extremely challenging circumstances remains central to these conceptualizations. Thus, it makes sense to view resilience as intricately linked to the qualities of individuals' physical (housing, safety, transportation, etc.) and social (social supports, recreational opportunities, employment, etc.) ecologies. Resilience is as much a condition of the environment as it is an individual characteristic or aspect of developmental processes. As Ungar (2008) argues, a definition of resilience has three dimensions: first, resilience is the capacity of individuals to navigate their way to resources that sustain well-being; second, resilience is the capacity of individuals' physical and social ecologies to provide these resources; and third, resilience is the capacity of individuals, their families, and communities to negotiate culturally meaningful ways for resources to be shared. This definition emphasizes the self-efficacy of individuals as they exercise personal agency in their navigations toward the acquisition of health-related resources. These resources, in turn, must be both available and accessible in ways that are relevant to the individual within his or her culture and context.

Researchers have employed criteria for identification of "resilient," "invulnerable," or "successful" individuals within their own empirical explorations of resilience (Luthar & Zigler, 1991). However, in general, an individual's ability to use internal and external resources to achieve stage-salient developmental expectations is a common theme that unites varying definitions (Cicchetti & Schneider-Rosen, 1986; Luthar et al., 2000; Masten & Coatsworth, 1998; Sroufe & Rutter, 1984; Waters & Sroufe, 1983). Historically, researchers have relied on the absence of psychopathology or maladaptive behavior as an indication of resilience in an individual exposed to extreme stress (Luthar & Zigler, 1991). However, increasingly researchers are looking at defining resilience in terms of competence demonstrated in multiple dimensions of life, which for adults may include level of education, job satisfaction, and attainment of a leadership role (Gerber, Ginsberg, & Reiff, 1992).

Applicable ICF Aspects

As the application of the resilience paradigm requires there to be exposure to significant risk (it is not a proxy for all health-related phenomena), the presence of a disability that impairs functioning, especially when such impairment affects multiple domains of a person's life, is arguably a risk to an individual's well-being that may be associated with resilience. Individuals recovering from a major injury or disease or suffering from chronic illness are, in effect, those who endure acute and chronic stress related to environmental factors that create abnormal demands on their adaptability (Prilleltensky & Prilleltensky, 2005). The concept of resilience shifts our focus from the disorder and dysfunction causing the stress to both the capacity of individuals to thrive under adversity (of which disability can play a significant role) and the assets found in the individual's multilevel physical and social ecologies that facilitate growth and buffer the impact of exposure to risk. As such, a resilience perspective complements other forms of assessment necessary to understand both the pathological and salutogenic (health) related aspects of people's lives lived with a disability.

Understanding the patterns of intrinsic and facilitative coping that large numbers of individuals demonstrate under stress provides a reflexive engagement with the indices of health. Learning from those who demonstrate resilience, and documenting the relationship between personal and environmental strengths and health outcomes, can inform interventions with those who remain vulnerable. Investigations of resilience provide possible targets for interventions among those lacking the strengths and assets required to overcome their disability and other concurrent barriers to positive development. In this regard, this chapter examines dimensions of functioning relevant to the ICF, emphasizing the interface of contextual factors and personal strengths relevant to the plasticity of individuals who are confronted with the need to adapt. Resilience status, or health level, is likely a better predictor of future ability than a more restricted understanding that dysfunction and disability demonstrate. Within a resilience paradigm, it is reasoned that the more we understand what people are still able to do and the strengths they show, the more likely we will be to help them build further their capacity to cope (Peterson, 2005).

History of Research and Practice in the Assessment of Self-Efficacy and Resilience

The dominant approach to the study of resilience in North America has been to search for *protective factors,* or personal and community "developmental assets" (Lerner & Benson, 2003), that enable resilient individuals to achieve positive outcomes in the face of adversity. Self-efficacy can be interpreted not as an area of assessment on its own but as one facet in our multidimensional understanding of resilience. As an individual resource, one's self-efficacy increases resilient functioning. Individuals with a strong sense of self-efficacy will approach challenges with the intention and anticipation of mastery, intensifying their efforts and persistence accordingly. These individuals rapidly recover their lowered sense of efficacy after enduring failure or difficulty and attribute failure to insufficient effort or deficient knowledge. Within the context of rehabilitation and health settings, the failure or difficulty may be understood as physical loss or trauma or illness. According to Bandura (1997), the most influential source of efficacy information is *mastery experiences*. These experiences are prior performances that may be interpreted positively or negatively. Individuals interpret the results of prior performances and develop beliefs about their personal capabilities from the subsequent self-appraisal. Whereas successful performances strengthen personal efficacy beliefs, failed performances undermine one's sense of efficacy. Successful performances then contribute to the anticipation of future success. Information from mastery experiences provides the individual with a reliable foundation from which one can assess self-efficacy and predict the successful performance of future tasks. Furthermore, self-efficacy may cross domains. Thus, an individual who has a personal history of encountering challenges and succeeding will face a health challenge with a better attitude. It is for these reasons that an individual's sense of self-efficacy can be considered a protective factor leading to resilience when faced with adversity.

Garmezy, Masten, and Tellegen (1984) define protective factors as "dispositional attributes, environmental conditions, biological predispositions, and positive events that can act to contain the expression of deviance or pathology" (p. 109). In direct contrast, *risk factors* may be understood as the attributes, environmental conditions, biological predispositions, and negative events that may predispose an individual to a negative outcome (Fraser, 1997). Historically, research on resilience has been oriented toward understanding how the individuals' adjustment was compromised in several salient areas of functioning relative to peers (Kaplan, 1999) and the explanation for growth atypical of what was expected. Increasingly, however, researchers are shifting the focus of their studies to examinations of strengths in order to understand the constellation of factors that contribute to thriving regardless of the risks to which one is exposed. In relation to the assessment and remediation of a disability, a balance in focus that can account for both the barriers to growth and the capacities of individuals and their physical and social ecologies that contribute to development seems more synergistic with the needs of professionals and those they serve.

The *risk and resilience paradigm* is an example of one such model that has been applied to many vulnerable populations. It provides a useful framework for understanding the complex factors that increase, or decrease, an individual's susceptibility to poor outcomes (Cosden, 2001; Fraser, 1997). Given an individual who is particularly vulnerable to developing future difficulties, the presence of risk factors would increase the likelihood of the individual developing problems, while protective factors would decrease this probability. It is the complex and dynamic interaction between these risk and protective factors that ultimately determines the quality of one's adjustment. Research has revealed broad categories of risk and protective factors whose effects are ubiquitous in diverse populations, however, the importance of one's unique environmental context must not be underestimated. The assessment of risk and protective factors is contingent on understanding the larger ecological and social context around children and families (Boyden & Mann, 2005; Keogh & Weisner, 1993; Trickett & Birman, 2000). While this body of research has influenced both policy and interventions, it has also presumed that there is a universal set of developmental assets relevant to all individuals, irrespective of the outcomes they and their communities' value, the adversity they face, or the context in which they live (Ungar, 2005).

Broadly speaking, resilience researchers have sought to understand how the potential negative impact of risk factors, such as poverty, divorce, exposure to violence, immigration, or disability, can be mediated by protective factors,

Research Box 22.1

Luthar, S. S. (1991). Vulnerability and resilience: A study of high-risk adolescents. *Child Development, 62,* 600–616.

Objectives: This study sought to examine whether factors deemed "protective" for children would also act as protective factors, serving to improve functioning, for high-risk adolescents. Specifically, the study examined factors that served to maintain positive functioning for adolescents in the face of stress and risk factors.

Method: The sample consisted of 144 adolescents (62 male, 82 female) attending ninth grade at an inner-city public school. The participants ages ranged from 14 to 17.2 years (M = 15.3 years, SD = .78). Information was collected on negative and positive life events, social competence as rated by teachers and peers, social skills, school grades, depression, and anxiety.

Results: Aspects of personality, such as internal locus of control and social protectiveness, were found to be protective factors against stress. Ego development was found to be compensatory against stress (helps to improve competence levels, which are lowered by increased stress). Intelligence and positive life events were found to be vulnerability factors (high levels indicate that the individual is more susceptible to increased stress).

Conclusion: The diverse findings of this study suggested that perhaps protective and vulnerability factors were not continuous and that they may differ across settings and populations. Furthermore, it was suggested that resilience may not be a factor that is consistent over time and that it may develop or change based on the circumstances within which the individual is living.

Questions: Discuss Luthar's findings in relation to the influence of culture on resilience. Is it possible to identify "resilient" characteristics that will be consistent across all cultures and contexts? Consider a client or personal acquaintance who you would consider resilient in their current functioning. Would this person be considered resilient if they had grown up with different experiences, experienced trauma, or lived in a different environment?

including personality, family, peer, community, and cultural factors. More than 30 years ago, researchers such as Werner and Smith (1992), Rutter, Maughan, Mortimore, and Ouston (1979), and Garmezy (1976) began to structure quasi-experimental and longitudinal studies in mostly Western contexts. Through the study of children who were exposed to chronic and acute risk (e.g., extreme poverty, war, the mental illness of a parent, etc.), findings uniformly revealed that a significant proportion of the children showed positive cognitive, behavioral, and physical health outcomes. These children are often referred to as resilient, or as having "beaten the odds." Their resilience in the face of adversity was traced to a variety of protective factors.

These efforts have been followed more recently by studies that have examined which protective factors are most likely to mitigate the impact of risk on children in both clinical and nonclinical populations. For example, the Search Institute in the United States has studied the relationship between 40 developmental assets and outcomes in 99,462 children (Benson, 2003). The higher the number of assets available to a child, the more likely the child will abstain from drugs and remain in school. Consistent with this literature, other studies have documented a wide range of factors that correlate with healthy functioning in high-risk children, youth, and families (Anthony & Cohler, 1987; Combrinck-Graham, 1995; Gilgun, 1999; Glantz & Sloboda, 1999; Greene, 2003; McCubbin et al., 1998; Richman & Fraser, 2001). A study by Resiliency Canada (Hammond, 2004) of over 25,000 Canadian children has demonstrated that resilience can be enhanced when children's capacities and health resources are better understood. These include resources at all four ecological levels, such as individual resources (e.g., self-efficacy), relational resources (e.g., parental monitoring), community resources (e.g., meaningful involvement by youth), and cultural resources (e.g., values and beliefs).

In summary, research in the area of resilience suggests that self-efficacy may be best understood as one of the personal characteristics that both fosters resilience and is a proxy indicator that equates well with resilience as an outcome. Resilience is positive development in the face of significant adversity and frequently a result of a complex interplay between risk factors and protective factors, as well as the environments (including service environments provided by professionals) in which these factors are manifested. Recently, many researchers have documented known risk and protective factors that need to be assessed. These factors fall into four major domains: individual, relational, community, and cultural. A resilience focus shifts the role of assessors from identifiers of barriers to growth, incapacity, and ecological impediments to the assets available in all domains of an individual's life. Practitioners in the field of rehabilitation and health need to develop an understanding of this framework in order to conduct an appropriate evaluation of clients' resilience profile and to see how present risks are being coped with and future outcomes potentiated. This shift in focus may greatly enhance interventions. After all, the study of resilience offers a reflexive engagement with those who already are successful despite their disability. Understanding their success can contribute to a deeper understanding of what interventions are most efficacious and, therefore, might prudently be generalized across an entire population. Those who demonstrate resilience are, arguably, the experts on overcoming barriers.

The upcoming section reviews both quantitative and qualitative methods for evaluating resilience in individual, relational, community, and cultural domains.

Assessing Resilience

The significant amount of research in the area of resilience demonstrates different pathways to the examination of resilience. There are two critical considerations when selecting assessment instruments. First, one must determine the lens through which they are examining resilience. Do we wish to examine an individual's outcomes after the fact? Do we wish to examine protective factors and personal assets that will assist an individual in maintaining positive adjustment even in the face of adversity? Or do we wish to do both, assessing the current status of the individual and then determining the likelihood that they will have the resources to recover from the present challenge? The assessment instruments and approaches discussed in this section can be applied in either of these contexts, but it is essential that these questions are addressed prior to the assessment in order to ensure congruence between the pattern of assessment and the application of results.

The second consideration is the importance of utilizing multidimensional assessment measures in exploring an individual's resilience profile. It has been established through research that many individuals demonstrate competence in some domains but have difficulties in others. For example, a client who is struggling with a newly diagnosed chronic illness may have strong individual resources (e.g., strong self-efficacy) but very limited community resources (e.g., be isolated with limited services available). In light of these findings, the methods discussed here include instruments designed to assess both functioning and assets across domains. Specifically, to tap individual resources, we assess self-efficacy, social competence, emotional well-being, and behavioral adjustment. To assess relational resources, we include measures of social functioning, relationships (parent, sibling, peer, romantic partner), and relational aspects of life satisfaction. Community resources are tapped through the measure of life stressors, economic situation, school, living environment, and community connectedness. Cultural resources are evaluated through the measurement of values and beliefs within the individual's given context.

Researchers have identified four primary factors implicated in the development of resilience: individual resources, relational resources, community resources, and cultural resources (Masten & Garmezy, 1985; Ungar, 2006; Werner & Smith, 1992). For example, the following interpersonal characteristics are consistently found to exert protective effects: active coping strategies (Dumont & Provost, 1999; Herman-Stahl & Peterson, 1996); positive self-esteem and self-concept (Dumont & Provost, 1999; Neighbors, Forehand, & McVicar, 1993; Werner, 1993); internal locus of control (Grossman et al., 1992; Luthar, 1991; Werner, 1993); self-awareness (Beardslee, 1989; Smokowski, Reynolds, & Bezruczko, 2000); possessing a sense of purpose and hope for the future (Masten et al., 1988; Werner, 1993); and intelligence (Garmezy et al., 1984; Luthar, 1991; Masten et al., 1988). In addition to relational resources, such as positive peer relationships (Beardslee, 1989; Herman-Stahl & Peterson, 1996; Werner, 1993) and family relationships (Howard & Johnson, 2000; Werner, 1993), aspects of the broader community may also serve as protective factors. This includes availability of services and involvement in community-based programs (Howard & Johnson, 2000) as well as a sense of security and support (Werner, 1993). A final important consideration is the individual's cultural resources, including religious beliefs, values, and customs or traditions (Crawford, Wright, & Masten, 2005; Lerner, Alberts, Anderson, & Dowling, 2005). See Table 22.1 for a summary of the resources that need to be evaluated when assessing a client's resilience profile.

Due to the multidimensional nature of resilience, the assessment approaches and instruments detailed in this section frequently cross the four

22.1 Examples of Resources to Consider in Resilience Profile

Individual	Relational	Community	Cultural
• Adaptive coping skills • Positive self-esteem • Sense of self-efficacy • Internal locus of control • Self-awareness • Personal insight • Sense of purpose • Hope for future • Intelligence	• Peer relationships • Family relationships • Romantic relationships	• Availability of services • Involvement • Sense of security • Support network	• Religious beliefs • Values • Cultural beliefs

resource domains. Clinicians should maintain a conceptual framework of their client's profile and select specific instruments, as needed, following initial evaluation by informal interview.

Quantitative Assessment of Resilience

Using a quantitative approach provides an opportunity for a multidimensional assessment of an individual's resilient functioning based on normative data and expectations. This approach allows for an efficient assessment of the factors associated with an individual's functioning as compared with other individuals who are assumed to be comparably vulnerable. These measures are, however, not exclusive to populations with disabilities but instead were designed for populations of individuals facing constellations of risks of which disabilities may or may not play a part.

Given the sheer number of possible measures that can assess the multidimensionality of resilience, we have chosen to concentrate on one developmental phase: adolescence. Our choice is arbitrary, as there are many tools available to investigate the same themes investigated by these measures of positive development in adults and younger children.

Resiliency Scales for Adolescents—A Profile of Personal Strengths

The Resiliency Scales for Adolescents (RSA; Prince-Embury, 2006) provides a profile of personal strengths as well as vulnerabilities. There are three standalone global scales containing 19 to 24 items each, including the sense of mastery scale (optimism, self-efficacy, adaptivity), the sense of relatedness scale (trust, support, comfort, tolerance), and the emotional reactivity scale (sensitivity, recovery, impairment). The RSA is appropriate for youth aged 15 to 18 years and yields *T*-scores for global scales.

Individual Protective Factors Index

The Individual Protective Factors Index (IPFI; Springer & Philips, 1997) is a six-page self-report questionnaire designed to assess adolescent resiliency in three major domains: social bonding, personal competence, and social competence. Development of IPFI had a validation sample of 2,416 youths from 15 sites across the United States, and the inventory was found to have adequate reliability and validity.

Life Stressors and Social Resources Inventory

The Life Stressors and Social Resources Inventory (LISRES; Moos & Moos, 1994) provides an integrated picture of an individual's current life context. Different versions of the inventory are tailored to different age groups. The LISRES-Youth inventory assesses stable life stressors and social resources among youth aged 12 to 18 years; the 8 domains of the LISRES (and the LISRES-Youth) tap physical health status, home and money, relationships with parents, relationships with siblings, relationships with extended family, school, relationships with friends, and relationship with a boyfriend/girlfriend. The LISRES-Y has 16 scales; 9 measure life stressors and 7 measure social resources. To assess stressors, there is an index for each of the 8 domains and an index for negative life events over the past year. For social resources, there is an index for 6 of the 8 domains and an index of positive life events over the past year. The LISRES-Y was normed on 400 youth (179 boys and 221 girls). Internal consistency reliabilities range from 0.66 to 0.92 for Stressor scales and from 0.78 to 0.93 for Social Resources scales (Moos & Moos, 1994).

Search Institute Profile of Student Life Attitudes and Behaviors Assessment

The Profile of Student Life Attitudes and Behaviors Assessment (PSL-AB; Leffert et al., 1998) is a 156-item survey instrument that measures 8 principal asset domains: support, empowerment, boundaries and expectations, constructive use of time, commitment to learning, positive values, social competencies, and positive identity. It also measures 8 thriving indicators: succeeds in school, helps others, values diversity, maintains good health, exhibits leadership, resists danger, delays gratification, and overcomes adversity. The PSL-AB also measures 5 developmental deficits: being alone at home more then 2 hours per day, TV overexposure, physical abuse, victim of violence, and attendance at drinking parties. There is as well a measure of 24 risk-taking behaviors covering alcohol and drug use, sexual activity, and antisocial behavior. Reliability coefficients are above .60 for 19 asset scales, 4 are between .50 and .59, and 4 are less than .50. Search Institute explains that the low reliability of the 4 items is due to those items measuring individual assets across multiple contexts. An example of this is 3 of the questions that make up the asset of youth programs. The respondent is asked to report on the number of hours he or she spends on different types of youth program activities in both school and community contexts. For these items to be reliable as a scale, it would be necessary that young people who do one type of activity spend equal time doing other activities (Leffert et al. 1998).

Multidimensional Students Life Satisfaction Scale

The Multidimensional Students Life Satisfaction Scale (MSLSS; Huebner, 1994) is a 40-item self-report scale that examines general life satisfaction while retaining ratings of domain-specific satisfaction in the areas of school, family, friends, self, and living environment. Participants are asked to rate the extent of their satisfaction across the five domains of the MSLSS using a six-point Likert scale. The MSLSS has yielded acceptable psychometric properties across grades 3 to 8 (Bender, 1997) and high overall consistency across samples of students in grades 9 to 12 (Gilman, Huebner, & Laughlin, 2000). The internal consistency estimate of the total score was 0.91. The coefficient alpha for each MSLSS scale ranged from 0.86 to 0.79 (Gilman et al., 2000).

Adolescent Coping Orientation for Problem Experiences

The Adolescent Coping Orientation for Problem Experiences (A-COPE; Patterson & McCubbin, 1987) is a 54-item self-report questionnaire for individuals between the ages of 11 and 18 years. The A-COPE is designed to identify behaviors that adolescents find helpful in managing problems and taps 12 factors, including personal and social adjustment, responsibility, and independence. Three samples of adolescents were involved in the construction and validity testing of the A-COPE, and it was found to have good alpha reliability (.50 to .76).

Self-Efficacy Questionnaire for Children

The Self-Efficacy Questionnaire for Children (SEQ-C; Muris, 2001) is a 24-item scale designed to assess 3 domains of self-efficacy, and it has been normed with adolescents between the ages of 14 to 17 years. The SEQ-C is designed to assess social self-efficacy (perceived capability for positive relationships and independence), academic self-efficacy (perceived capability to manage one's own learning, master academic subjects, and fulfill expectations), and emotional self-efficacy (perceived capability to cope with negative emotions and life stressors). This scale has good internal consistently with the Cronbach's alpha for total score at .88 and the subscale scores ranging from .85 to .88.

Self-Perception Profile for Children

The Self-Perception Profile for Children (SPPC; Harter, 1985) is a 36-item measure of self-concept that is used to tap into the domain-specific judgments of children about their competence and global perceptions of self-esteem or self-worth. This measure focuses on 5 domains: scholastic competence (perception of academic skills), social acceptance (degree of peer acceptance and popularity), athletic competence (ability in sports and outdoor play), physical appearance (acceptance level of personal appearance), and behavioral conduct (perception of behavior and ability to perform right behavior). There is also a Global Dimension of Self-Worth that examines the child's overall judgment of whether the child likes him/herself. This scale was constructed on the assumption that an instrument providing separate measures of one's competence in different domains, as well as an independent assessment of one's global self-worth, would provide a more differentiated picture than those instruments providing only a single self-concept score. The SPPC also contains a parallel rating scale, where the parents and/or teacher provide a rating of the child's actual behavior to provide an independent judgment of the child's perceptions. In studies of reliability and validity of the SPPC, researchers have concluded that it demonstrates extremely good psychometric properties (Byrne & Schneider, 1988; Marsh & Gouvernet, 1989). Subscale reliability results range from .71 to .86 (Harter, 1985).

Self-Perception Profile for Adolescents

The Self-Perception Profile for Adolescents (SPPA; Harter, 1988) is a 45-item scale designed to measure adolescents' (9th through 12th grades) perceptions of their competence in, and the importance to them, of 8 domains: scholastic competence, social acceptance, athletic competence, physical appearance, job competence, romantic appeal, behavioral conduct, and close friendship. Similar to the SPPC, the SPPA provides a scale of global self-worth, which constitutes a global judgment of one's worth as a person, rather than domain-specific competency or adequacy. This instrument is used widely and has been found to have sound psychometric properties. The internal consistency ranges from 0.74 to 0.92 (Harter, 1988).

Behavior Assessment System for Children

The Behavior Assessment System for Children (BASC; Reynolds & Kamphaus, 1992) is used to tap overall well-being and adjustment among youth. The BASC is a coordinated system of instruments that evaluates the behaviors, thoughts, and emotions of children and adolescents. The Self-Report of Personality (SRP; Child and Adolescent forms) measures children's thoughts and feelings about themselves and their environments through a series of 170 true or false questions. The adolescent form is appropriate for use with youth between the ages of 12 and 18 and contains the following composite scales: clinical maladjustment (with subscales in the areas of anxiety, atypicality, locus of control, social stress, somatization), school maladjustment (attitude to school, attitude to teachers, sensation seeking), depression, sense of inadequacy, personal adjustment (relations with parents, interpersonal relations, self-esteem, self-reliance), and emotional symptoms index. The SRP *T*-scores and percentiles based either on a national norm group, by gender in the norm group, or in comparison to a group of seriously emotionally disturbed children. Internal consistency for the SRP is acceptable with alpha coefficients ranging from the mid .80s to .90s for adolescents (Reynolds & Kamphaus, 1992).

Child and Youth Resilience Measure

The Child and Youth Resilience Measure (CYRM; Ungar et al., 2008) is a 28-item measure developed by Ungar and his colleagues, an international team from 14 communities in 11 countries. Using a mixed methods iterative process of design, the CYRM taps aspects of resilience related to individual, relational, community, and cultural factors. Findings from an initial sample of 1,451 youth ranging in age from 12–23 suggest that scoring the CYRM be based on either total scores for subscales determined on a culture-by-culture basis or by tallying the overall score of the instrument, thereby treating resilience resources as a more coherent cross-culturally valid construct. Both strategies allow youth to demonstrate the value of aspects of resilience that are most predictive of positive development without necessarily biasing results to reflect only Western conceptions of health outcomes. Results have demonstrated the CYRM's capacity to measure resilience across cultures and contexts with sensitivity to differences.

Qualitative and Mixed Methods Approaches

Haase (2004), in her work investigating the resilience of adolescents who experience cancer, argues for a triangulation of methods, with multiphase research allowing for the identification of unique variables related to survival experiences. Haase's *Adolescent Resilience Model* is based on the resilience literature, a composite index of several normed measures of resilience, and interviews with youth themselves from which thematic analysis leads to additional questions. Such integration is crucial, we feel, to a contextually and culturally relevant investigation of resilience. Clinical interviews, especially, should address variability in the experiences of individuals in relation to the strength variables under study. Because resilience is such a complex construct, the interface between the person and his or her physical and social ecologies will always necessitate some degree of qualitative inquiry. Though it is beyond the scope of this chapter to orient the reader to phenomenological approaches to research and assessment, there are similarities between the work of qualitative researchers and a clinical interview. In both cases, the clinician is open to, and inquires after, localized (emic) understandings of people's experiences. Quality in qualitative inquiry adheres to principles of rigor roughly equivalent to those of validity and reliability in quantitative paradigms. We caution against making generalizations based on anecdotal qualitative evidence that is not analyzed fully using the principles associated with the methodological paradigm. These include contrasting truth claims from different individuals, bracketing the experiences of the investigators so as to acknowledge potential bias in interpretation, ensuring a length of engagement sufficient to respond to the questions asked, and other similar aspects of qualitative research that ensure trustworthy accounts of patients (Lincoln & Guba, 1985).

Critical Research Issues in Assessment of Self-Efficacy and Resilience

Conceptual Issues

Research in the area of resilience clearly suggests two major issues for consideration before undertaking an assessment in this area. First, the clinician must have a good theoretical understanding of the construct of resilience. Second, the clinician must also be aware of the multidimensionality and cultural specificity of resilience. The construct of resilience can be hugely problematic if not well-conceptualized by the clinician. He/She must clearly understand that resilience can be either an outcome measure (how is the patient now, following this health challenge?), an attempt to predict future recovery (how likely is it that this patient will respond well in the future to the health challenges he/she is facing?), or a combination of the two (how is he/she doing presently, and given his/her risk/protective factors or resilience profile, how is he/she likely to do in the future?).

In addition, research has demonstrated that a true assessment of resilience must be culturally sensitive and multidimensional. To limit an assessment of resilience to a single area of functioning is unacceptable. Too often, basic behavioral adjustment or adaptive behavior (e.g., client is functioning day-to-day) is the only measurement of resilience. Assessment across areas of individual, relational, community, and cultural domains is essential. This assessment may take many forms, including standardized measurement, qualitative measurement, informal interviews, or a combination of the three.

Self-Report Assessments

Self-report is arguably the most significant method of tapping an individual's perception of resilient functioning. The question is raised about how accurate these self-report measures truly are. In the area of resilience, it is more the individual's perceptions of their situation that predict future performance than their actual situation (Spekman, Herman, & Vogel, 1993). Therefore, in this area self-reports are essential, and when in conflict with others' reports, self-reports should take precedence. However, ideally, multiple informants (e.g., parents, teachers, significant others, self) should be used to obtain a convergent understanding of the client's current situation.

Cultural and Professional Issues That Impact the Counseling Aspects/Procedures

Influence of Culture on Resilience

The understanding of self-efficacy and resilience may differ between cultures and contexts. How do we come to decide what to measure and how much weight to give to specific aspects of healthy functioning? The question raises the issue of equivalence in measures across cultures, with contextually specific factors and constructions of meaning likely to shape response patterns. Even the very notion of what we accept as good science may be challenged by other ways of knowing prominent in aboriginal and non-Western contexts (see Smith, 1999). Of course, to date, many studies of resilience-related phenomena have attempted to account for cultural differences, at least in samples coming from Western democracies. An uneven set of results from Masten (2001), Luthar et al. (2000), Werner and Smith (1992), Rutter (1987), Egeland, Carlson, and Sroufe (1993), Brodsky (1996), Sampson and Laub (1997), Walsh (1998), and McCubbin et al. (1998) have shown that community and cultural factors confound patterns associated with healthy development. As helpful as these efforts have been, they do overlook increasingly the needs of diverse populations and the potentially flawed nature of measures that are exported to international contexts. They also ignore epistemological issues related to Western science and the possibility that bias embedded in the

Discussion Box 22.1

HOW WELL DO WE KNOW OURSELVES?

Some researchers argue that self-report of current functioning by children and adolescents may not be the most reliable information source. In contrast, other researchers argue that in assessing internal states (e.g., mood, self-esteem, perceived social support) the individual's perspective is the most relevant to their functioning and future progress. Many researchers and practitioners advocate a multi-informant approach, where the individual's perspective is evaluated as well as other significant figures in his/her life (e.g., parents, peers, and teachers). Discuss which perspective you would feel most pertinent in conducting an assessment of an individual's resilient functioning. Explore the issue of how you, as a clinician, would proceed in the event of contradictory reports. Whose report is most valid?

measures may homogenize populations who are either immigrants or living in international settings, imposing on them a set of criteria for successful development that may or may not be relevant. Thus, as Chan, Carlson, Trickett, and Earls (2003) caution, there is a heightened need for greater accountability to diverse geographic, ethnic, and racial communities if assessment of resilience is to be judged as valid. What's more, there may be latent strengths among specific populations that are overlooked by measures designed from only one cultural perspective. For example, Man-Kwong (2004) argues that to understand healthy adaptation among Hong Kong Chinese, one must account for the role shame plays in positive development: "Working in a Chinese culture means we need to have an increased cultural sensitivity to this experience of shame. I am sure shame exists in many cultures but it takes a particular form here" (p. 17).

It is with this caveat that we cautiously employ the measures discussed in this chapter. A qualitative process that encourages specific populations to comment on the meaning of the measure to them is one way to control bias. Reciprocity in analysis is another. Creating feedback loops in which individuals share their comments on the assessor's findings may help to ensure that interpretations of strengths (and weaknesses) are more reflective of culturally embedded norms. Trickett and Birman (2000) note: "If outcomes and wellness are to be understood as individual efforts to cope and adapt to the demands of the surrounding culture, community, and institutions, then the definition of what is positive will be different across situations, and even among individuals in similar circumstances" (p. 381). This contextually sensitive approach is not just good science, it is also ethically sound.

Multidisciplinary or Interdisciplinary Approaches

The very nature of resilience being a multidimensional ecologically layered construct makes it amenable to intervention at many different levels and,

Discussion Box 22.2

ARE RESILIENCE AND SELF-EFFICACY THE SAME IN EVERY CULTURE?

Some researchers argue that there are core aspects of resilience that cross all cultures and that these are what we should be measuring, whereas other researchers feel that culture and context are essential to the understanding of resilience and thus the assessment of resilience. Research is telling us both points of view have merit. There are likely some experiences we all share in common, such as a need to feel some say over our lives. Other aspects, such as what a disability means and how much it influences our self-esteem, are likely much more dependent on cultural values and norms. Think about your culture and context and what "health" means to you and those around you. What does healthy functioning look like? Now imagine someone from a country where life is very different from your own. Even better, interview a classmate or colleague who is a recent immigrant, or someone who has lived abroad. What is normative and expected functioning in that culture or context? How are people with disabilities viewed? What are the benchmarks of success? How accessible are the resources required to be successful to those whose functioning is impaired? What would the goals be for rehabilitation in that other place?

therefore, requires the effort of a group of professionals (and lay providers as well). As we have defined resilience as dependent on both individual factors and the physical and social ecologies in which individuals realize well-being, there are a range of interventions that bolster resilience. It is for this reason that we see the need for professionals from the medical as well as social side of individual's lives collaborating. While the nurse, the physiotherapist, the doctor, and the pharmacist may all play a significant role in alleviating symptoms, promoting health (as distinct from suppressing illness) will require the added contribution of the occupational therapist, the social worker, the homemaker, the financial aid worker, the employment counselor, the educator, and even the architect and engineer if we expand our thinking to encompass issues of accessibility. Resilience cannot result from individualized interventions alone; self-efficacy and other positive aspects of development require forums in which one can realize one's strengths.

It is for this reason that we see resilience as part of a plan to bring social justice to people living with disabilities. In their examination of resilience and its relationship to social justice, with a special emphasis on the impact of both concepts on the lives of people with disabilities, Prilleltensky and Prilleltensky (2005) write: "Resilience stems, in part, from the capacity and opportunity to understand the role of adversity in one's life and the role of individuals and groups to challenge systems of inequality and discrimination. Coping without challenging these systems may result in accepting the unacceptable" (pp. 92–93).

Specifically, they explain, "disability is not a personal tragedy that requires medical solutions but, rather, a social issue requiring social intervention" (p. 93). Thus, from an ecological perspective of resilience, there is the need to require professionals to address individual barriers to functioning and societal barriers concurrently. After all, a disability is more or less limiting to the extent that society facilitates inclusion or exclusion of the person with an impairment. The degree to which professionals work together, and work with communities, will determine whether resilience will be realized or thwarted. In rehabilitation and health, a critical aspect of resilience assessment, therefore, must be to understand the multifaceted nature of resilience—not examining an individual after the fact, but all aspects of an individual's life and working to support or foster areas of weakness in the resilience profile (weighing personal factors with available resources and advocating social justice to remediate gaps in service).

Summary

Resilient individuals are able to achieve positive outcomes in the face of adversity. Indeed, health-related phenomena and disabilities that impair functioning may be considered a potentially negative circumstance that threatens adaptive functioning and positive outcomes. Self-efficacy and resilience are critical considerations in understanding the adjustment of adolescents and their ability to maintain a positive mental state in the face of significant stress. While still an emerging field of research, there are many benefits to balancing a view of disorder and dysfunction with the detailed examination of the capacity individuals hold, even as they require rehabilitation services. A focus on resilience and self-efficacy that includes sensitivity to culturally and contextually embedded definitions of health is likely to change our perception of those with whom we work. If our intent is to avoid totalizing people's lives in relation solely to their disability, then our assessment of people's strengths despite adversity offers us a more holistic way to understand lives as they are lived. This more balanced approach to assessment offers the opportunity to see patients as people with the complexity of both strengths and weaknesses evident in their adaptations to their social and physical ecologies.

References

Anthony, E. J., & Cohler, B. J. (Eds.). (1987). *The invulnerable child.* New York: Guilford.

Bandura, A. (1997). *Self-efficacy: The exercise of control.* New York: Time Books.

Beardslee, W. R. (1989). The role of self-understanding in resilient individuals: The development of a perspective. *American Journal of Orthopsychiatry, 59,* 266–278.

Bender, T. A. (1997). Assessment of subjective well-being in children and adolescents. In G. Phye (Ed.), *Handbook of classroom assessment: Learning, achievement, and adjustment* (pp.199–225). San Diego, CA: Academic Press.

Benson, P. L. (2003). Developmental assets and asset-building community: Conceptual and empirical foundations. In R. Lerner & P. L. Benson (Eds.), *Developmental assets and asset-building communities: Implications for research, policy, and practice* (pp. 19–46). New York: Kluwer Academic/Plenum Publishers.

Boyden, J., & Mann, G. (2005). Children's risk, resilience, and coping in extreme situations. In M. Ungar (Ed.), *A handbook for working with children and youth: Pathways to resilience across cultures and contexts* (pp. 3–26). Thousand Oaks, CA: Sage.

Brodsky, A. E. (1996). Resilient single mothers in risky neighborhoods: Negative psychological sense of community. *Journal of Community Psychology, 24*(4), 347–363.

Byrne, B. M., & Schneider, B. H. (1988). Perceived Competence Scale for Children: Testing factorial validity and invariance across age and ability. *Applied Measurement in Education, 1,* 171–187.

Chan, B., Carlson, M., Trickett, B., & Earls, F. (2003). Youth participation: A critical element of research on child well-being. In R. M. Lerner & P. L. Benson (Eds.), *Developmental assets and asset-building communities: Implications for research, policy and Practice* (pp. 65–69). New York: Kluwer.

Cicchetti, D., & Schneider-Rosen, K. (1986). An organizational approach to childhood depression. In M. Rutter, C. Izard, & P. Read (Eds.), *Depression in young people, clinical and developmental perspectives* (pp. 71–134). New York: Guilford.

Combrinck-Graham, L. (Ed.). (1995). *Children in families at risk.* New York: Guilford.

Cosden, M. (2001). Risk and resilience for substance abuse among adolescents and adults with LD. *Journal of Learning Disabilities, 34,* 352–358.

Crawford, E., Wright, M. O., & Masten, A. (2005). Resilience and spirituality in youth. In E. C. Roehlkepartain, P. E. King, L. Wagener, & P. L. Benson (Eds.), *The handbook of spiritual development in childhood and adolescence* (pp. 355–370). Thousand Oaks, CA: Sage.

Dumont, M., & Provost, M. A. (1999). Resilience in adolescents: Protective role of social support, coping strategies, self-esteem, and social activities on the experience of stress and depression. *Journal of Youth and Adolescence, 28,* 343–363.

Egeland, B., Carlson, E., & Sroufe, L. A. (1993) Resilience as process. *Development and Psychopathology, 5,* 517–528.

Fraser, M. (Ed.). (1997). *Risk and resilience in childhood: An ecological perspective.* Washington, DC: NASW Press.

Garmezy, N. (1976). *Vulnerable and invulnerable children: Theory, research, and intervention.* Journal Supplement Abstract Service, APA.

Garmezy, N. (1990). A closing note: Reflections on the future. In J. Rolf, A. Masten, D. Cicchetti, K. Nuechterlein & S. Weintraub (Eds.), *Risk and protective factors in the development of psychopathology* (pp. 527–534). New York: Cambridge University Press.

Garmezy, N., Masten, A. S., & Tellegen, A. (1984). The study of stress and competence in children: A building block for developmental psychopathology. *Child Development, 55,* 97–111.

Gerber, P. J., Ginsberg, R., & Reiff, H. B. (1992). Identifying alterable patterns in employment success for highly successful adults with learning disabilities. *Journal of Learning Disabilities, 25,* 475–487.

Gilgun, J. F. (1999). Mapping resilience as process among adults with childhood adversities. In H. I. McCubbin, E. A. Thompson, A. I. Thompson, & J. A. Futrell (Eds.), *The dynamics of resilient families* (pp. 41–70). Thousand Oaks, CA: Sage.

Gilman, R., Huebner, E. S., & Laughlin, J. E. (2000). A first study of the Multidimensional Students' Life Satisfaction Scale with adolescents. *Social Indicators Research, 52,* 135–160.

Glantz, M. D., & Sloboda, Z. (1999). Analysis and reconceptualization of resilience. In M. D. Glantz & J. L. Johnson (Eds.), *Resilience and development: Positive life adaptations* (pp. 109–128). New York: Kluwer Academic/Plenum.

Greene, R. R. (Ed.). (2003). *Resiliency: An integrated approach to practice, policy, and research.* Washington, DC: NASW Press.

Grossman, F. K., Beinashowitz, J., Anderson, L., Sakuri, M., Finnin, L., & Flaherty, M. (1992). Risk and resilience in young adolescents. *Journal of Youth and Adolescence, 21,* 529–550.

Haase, J. E. (2004). The adolescent resilience model as a guide to interventions. *Journal of Pediatric Oncology Nursing, 21*(5), 289–299.

Hammond, W. (2004, August). *Resiliency Canada: Results.* Paper presentation at the 5th Annual Child Welfare Symposium, Ottawa, Ontario.

Harter, S. (1985). *Manual for the Self-Perception Profile for Children.* Denver: University of Denver.

Harter, S. (1988). *Manual for the Self-Perception Profile for Adolescents.* Denver: University of Denver.

Health and Welfare Canada. (1988). *Mental health for Canadians: Striking a balance.* Ottawa: Supply and Services Canada.

Herman-Stahl, M., & Petersen, A. C. (1996). The protective role of coping and social resources for depressive symptoms among young adolescents. *Journal of Youth and Adolescence, 25,* 733–753.

Howard, S., & Johnson, B. (2000). What makes the difference? Children and teachers talk about resilient outcomes for children "at risk." *Educational Studies, 26,* 321–337.

Huebner, E. S. (1994). Preliminary development and validation of a multidimensional life satisfaction scale for children. *Psychological Assessment, 6,* 149–158.

Kaplan, H. B. (1999). Toward an understanding of resilience: A critical review of definitions and models. In M. D. Glantz & J. L. Johnson (Eds.), *Resilience and development: Positive life adaptations* (pp. 17–84). New York: Kluwer/Plenum.

Keogh, B. K., & Weisner, T. (1993). An ecocultural perspective on risk and protective factors in children's development: Implications for learning disabilities. *Learning Disabilities Research & Practice, 8*(1), 3–10.

Leffert, N., Benson, P. L., Scales, P. C., Sharma, A. R., Drake, D. R., & Blyth, D. A. (1998). Developmental assets: Measurement and prediction of risk behaviors among adolescents. *Applied Developmental Science, 2*(4), 209–230.

Lerner, R. M., Alberts, A. E., Anderson, P. M., & Dowling, E. M. (2005). On making humans human: spirituality and the promotion of positive youth development. In E. C. Roehlkepartain, P. E. King, L. Wagener, & P. L. Benson (Eds.), *The handbook of spiritual development in childhood and adolescence* (pp. 60–72). Thousand Oaks, CA: Sage.

Lerner, R. M., & Benson, P. L. (Eds.). (2003). *Developmental assets and asset-building communities: Implications for research, policy, and practice.* New York: Kluwer Academic/Plenum Publishers.

Lincoln, Y. S., & Guba, E. G. (1985). *Naturalistic inquiry.* Newbury Park, CA: Sage.

Luthar, S. S. (1991). Vulnerability and resilience: A study of high-risk adolescents. *Child Development, 62,* 600–616.

Luthar, S. S., Cicchetti, D., & Becker, B. (2000). The construct of resilience: A critical evaluation and guidelines for future work. *Child Development, 71*(3), 543–562.

Luthar, S. S., & Zigler, E. (1991). Vulnerability and competence: A review of research on resilience in childhood. *American Journal of Orthopsychiatry, 61,* 6–22.

Man-Kwong, H. (2004). Overcoming craving: The use of narrative practices in breaking drug habits. *The International Journal of Narrative Therapy and Community Work, 1,* 17–24.

Marsh, H. W., & Gouvernet, P. J. (1989). Multidimensional self-concepts and perceptions of control: Construct validity of responses by children. *Journal of Educational Psychology, 81,* 57–69.

Masten, A. S. (2001). Ordinary magic: Resilience processes in development. *American Psychologist, 56*(3), 227–238.

Masten, A. S., Best, K. M., & Garmezy, N. (1991). Resilience and development: Contributions from the study of children who overcame adversity. *Development and Psychopathology, 2,* 425–444.

Masten, A. S., & Coatsworth, J. D. (1998). The development of competence in favourable and unfavourable environments: Lessons from research on successful children. *American Psychologist, 53,* 205–220.

Masten, A.S., & Garmezy, N. (1985). Risk, vulnerability, and protective factors in developmental psychopathology. In B. B. Lahey & A. E. Kazdin (Eds.), *Advances in Clinical Child Psychology* (Vol. 8, pp. 1–52). New York: Plenum.

Masten, A. S., Garmezy, N., Tellegen, A., Pellegrini, D. S., Larkin, K., & Larsen, A. (1988). Competence and stress in school children: The moderating effects of individual and family qualities. *Journal of Child Psychology and Psychiatry, 29,* 745–764.

McCubbin, H. I., Fleming, W. M., Thompson, A. I., Neitman, P., Elver, K. M., & Savas, S. A. (1998). Resiliency and coping in "at risk" African-American youth and their families. In H. I. McCubbin, E. A. Thompson, A. I. Thompson, & J. A. Futrell (Eds.), *Resiliency in African-American families* (pp. 287–328). Thousand Oaks, CA: Sage.

Moos, R. H., & Moos, B. S. (1994). *Manual for the Life Stressors and Social Resources Inventory—Youth Form.* Odessa, FL: Psychological Assessment Resources, Inc.

Multon, K. D., Brown, S. D., & Lent, R. W. (1991). Relation of self-efficacy beliefs to academic outcomes: A meta-analytic investigation. *Journal of Counseling Psychology, 38,* 30–38.

Muris, P. (2001). A brief questionnaire for measuring self-efficacy in youths. *Journal of Psychopathology and Behavioral Assessment, 33*(2), 145–149.

Neighbors, B., Forehand, R., & McVicar, D. (1993). Resilient adolescents and interparental conflict. *American Journal of Orthopsychiatry, 63,* 462–471.

Patterson, J. M., & McCubbin, H. I. (1987). Adolescent coping style and behaviors: Conceptualization and measurement. *Journal of Adolescence, 10,* 163–186.

Peterson, D. B. (2005). International Classification of Functioning, Disability and Health: An introduction for rehabilitation psychologists. *Rehabilitation Psychology, 50,* 105–112.

Prilleltensky, I., & Prilleltensky, O. (2005). Beyond resilience: Blending wellness and liberation in the helping professions. In M. Ungar (Ed.), *Handbook for working with children and youth: Pathways to resilience across cultures and contexts* (pp. 89–104). Thousand Oaks, CA: Sage.

Prince-Embury, S. (2006). *Resiliency Scales for Adolescents: A profile of personal strengths—Manual.* San Antonio, TX: Psychological Corporation.

Reynolds, C. R., & Kamphaus, R. W. (1992). *Manual for the Behavior Assessment System for Children.* Circle Pines, MN: American Guidance Service.

Richman, J. M., & Fraser, M. W. (Eds.). (2001). *The context of youth violence: Resilience, risk and protection.* Westport, CT: Praeger.

Rutter, M. (1987). Psychosocial resilience and protective mechanisms. *American Journal of Orthopsychiatry, 57,* 316–331.

Rutter, M., Maughan, B., Mortimore, P., & Ouston, J. (1979). *Fifteen thousand hours: Secondary schools and their effects on children.* Cambridge, MA: Harvard University Press.

Sampson, R. J., & Laub, J. H. (1997). A life-course theory of cumulative disadvantage and stability of delinquency. In T. P. Thornberry (Ed.), *Developmental theories of crime and delinquency* (pp. 133–161). New Brunswick, NJ: Transaction.

Schunk, D. H. (1991). Self-efficacy and academic motivation. *Educational Psychologist, 26,* 207–231.

Smith, L. T. (1999). *Decolonizing methodologies: Research and indigenous peoples.* New York: Zed.

Smokowski, P. R., Reynolds, A. J., & Bezruczko, N. (2000). Resilience and protective factors in adolescence: An autobiographical perspective from disadvantaged youth. *Journal of School Psychology, 37,* 425–448.

Spekman, N. J., Herman, K. L., & Vogel, S. A. (1993). Risk and resilience in individuals with learning disabilities: A challenge to the field. *Learning Disabilities Research & Practice, 8,* 59–65.

Springer, F., & Phillips, J. L. (1997). *Individual Protective Factors Index (IPFI): A measure of adolescent resiliency.* Folsom, CA: EMT Associates.

Sroufe, L. A., & Rutter, M. (1984). The domain of developmental psychopathology. *Child Development, 55,* 17–29.

Trickett, E. J., & Birman, D. (2000). Interventions with diverse children and adolescents: Contextualizing a wellness orientation. In D. Cicchetti, J. Rappaport, I. Sandler, & R. P. Weissberg (Eds.), *The promotion of wellness in children and adolescents* (pp. 371–394). Washington, DC: CWLA Press.

Ungar, M. (2005). Introduction: Resilience across cultures and contexts. In M. Ungar (Ed.), *Handbook for working with children and youth: Pathways to resilience across cultures and contexts* (pp. xv–xxxix). Thousand Oaks, CA: Sage.

Ungar, M. (2006). *Strengths-based counseling with youth at-risk.* Thousand Oaks, CA: Corwin Press.

Ungar, M. (2008). Resilience across cultures. *British Journal of Social Work, 38*(2), 218–235.

Ungar, M., Liebenberg, L., Boothroyd, R., Kwong, W. M., Lee, T. Y., Leblanc, J., et al. (2008). The study of youth resilience across cultures: Lessons from a pilot study of measurement development. *Research in Human Development, 5*(3), 166–180.

Walsh, F. (1998). *Strengthening family resilience.* New York: Guilford Press.

Waters, E., & Sroufe, L. A. (1983). Social competence as a developmental construct. *Developmental Review, 3,* 79–97.

Werner, E. (1993). Risk and resilience in individuals with learning disabilities: Lessons learned from the Kauai Longitudinal Study. *Learning Disabilities Research & Practice, 8,* 28–34.

Werner, E., & Smith, R. (Eds.). (1992). *Overcoming the odds: High risk children from birth to adulthood.* Ithaca, NY: Cornell University Press.

World Health Organization. (2001). *ICF: International Classification of Functioning, Disability*

23 Assessment in Rehabilitation and Health: Spirituality and Religiosity

David R. Brown
Mark S. Parrish
Elise P. Johnson

Overview

This chapter explores issues related to the assessment of spirituality and religiosity in the rehabilitation profession. Of primary concern is to discuss possible definitions of spirituality and religiosity. The history of the assessment of spirituality and religiosity is explored with special attention placed on the purpose of spiritual assessment in the diagnostic and therapeutic process, including benefits and limitations, cultural contexts, and the multidimensional characteristics of spirituality and religiosity. The remainder of the chapter focuses on quantitative and qualitative assessment approaches in spirituality and religiosity. The final parts of this chapter discuss critical considerations in the assessment of spirituality and religiosity in the rehabilitation profession.

Learning Objectives

By the end of the chapter, the reader should be able to:

1. Explain the importance of spirituality and religiosity in the health care field and in the rehabilitative and recovery process;
2. Critically consider the cultural context in the integration of spirituality into rehabilitation;
3. Compare qualitative and quantitative methods of assessing spirituality and religiosity;
4. Discuss specific issues related to the development and administration of spirituality and religiosity assessment instruments;
5. Evaluate the multifaceted dimension of the constructs of spirituality and religiosity and the subsequent lack of universality; and
6. List and describe religious and spiritual competencies to work with clients of diverse backgrounds.

Introduction

Within the past 2 decades, increasing attention has been placed on the role of spirituality and religiosity in mental health (Cashwell & Young, 2004; Kelly, 1994; Miller & Thoresen, 2003; Pate & High, 1995) and rehabilitation therapy (Boswell, Knight, Hamer, & McChesney, 2001; Faull et al., 2004; Fitchett, Rybarczyk, DeMarco, & Nicholas, 1999); this is reported specifically by Kelly (1994), who states that such integration began gaining popularity in the early 1980s. Although interest in spirituality and religiosity declined throughout most of the 20th century (Speck, 2005), resurgence in popularity has been noted through numerous research studies geared toward observing the positive influence of spirituality and religiosity in mental health and rehabilitation (Eliason, Hanley, & Leventis, 2001; Faull et al., 2004; Fitchett et al., 1999; Kelly, 1992, 1994; Miller & Thoresen; Seybold & Hill, 2001; Young, Cashwell, Wiggins-Frame, & Belaire, 2002). In fact, Young, Wiggins-Frame, and Cashwell (2007) recently published research reporting that interest in integrating spirituality in the helping professions is still increasing. This perspective is supported by Revheim and Greenberg (2007) who state that spiritual experiences result in decreased recovery time and reduced frequency of hospitalization. These positive experiences provide a convincing testimony to the efficacy of integrating spirituality and religiosity into the rehabilitation and recovery therapeutic process.

Importance of Spirituality and Religiosity to Rehabilitation and Health

Spirituality and religiosity are reportedly important aspects in the lifestyles of most Americans, according to Gallup polling (as cited in Kelly, 1994; Pate & High, 1995) and U.S. census data (U.S. Census Bureau, 2001, 2006). Much effort has been focused on integrating spirituality into various aspects of the helping professions. Defined as a multicultural issue by the Council on Rehabilitation Education (CORE; 2004), American Counseling Association (ACA; 2005), and the Council for the Accreditation of Counseling and Related Educational Programs (CACREP, 2001), spirituality and religiosity are articulated in rehabilitation counseling training programs. For example, spirituality and religiosity appear in graduate-level counseling courses (Curtis & Glass, 2002; Fukuyama & Sevig, 1997; Ingersoll, 1997; Souza, 2002), holistic wellness models (Adams, Bezner, Drabbs, Zambarano, & Steinhardt, 2000; Sweeney & Witmer, 1991), the therapeutic and recovery process (Faull et al., 2004; Fitchett et al., 1999; Revheim & Greenberg, 2007), and assessment instruments (Hall & Edwards, 2002; Hill & Hood, 1999; Moberg, 1984; Slater, Hall, & Edwards, 2001; Stanard, Sandhu, & Painter, 2000).

Definitions and Theories of Spirituality and Religiosity

Speck (2005) and Ardell (1999) suggest that the primarily limitation to integrating spirituality and religiosity into training programs is the impasse in providing an acceptable definition for these terms. Definitions of spirituality range from ecstatic, transcendental experiences to existential searches for purpose and meaning. Speck illustrates this definitional dilemma when stating that "to harmonize these definitions would be a herculean [sic] task because they point to competing worldviews that are not always fully articulated in the literature, helping to explain why the definitions rely on abstractions" (p. 4). Although many definitions have been proposed, for the purposes of this chapter, *spirituality* will be defined according to that suggested by Burke et al. (1999): an appreciation of human life and existence, as well as a sense of connectedness to a higher power and openness to the infinite beyond human existence and experience. This definition also suggests a relationship with *religion,* which represents an organized and/or structured approach to spirituality. Although many similarities exist, enough differences can be identified to create a different understanding. Therefore, *religion* will also be defined according to the definition provided by Burke et al.: "an institutionalized set of beliefs and practices by which groups and individuals relate to the ultimate" (p. 252). *Religiosity,* as Burke et al. suggest, may represent to some as a set of dogmatic beliefs that must be implicitly followed. Although many individuals consider spirituality and religion to be inseparable, the purpose of this chapter is not to differentiate between personal beliefs and practices. This chapter is primarily concerned with the integration of spiritual and/or religious assessment into the rehabilitation process and describing the benefits of assessing the spiritual and religious needs of clients.

Applicable International Classification Functioning and Health Aspects

Addressing spiritual needs in rehabilitation and health can bridge the gap between multidimensional approaches to assessment by promoting a holistic model of intervention and wellness. Including the assessment of spiritual needs ensures a multicultural system where diversity is valued and differences are

Discussion Box 23.1

WHY SPIRITUALITY AND RELIGIOSITY?

Despite the lack of consensus in defining spirituality and religiosity, and the variety of ways in which one may experience them, most researchers agree that spirituality is a vital component of well-being. The term *spirituality* comes from the Latin word *spiritus,* which means "breath of life," which some researchers suggest indicates a connection with life and being, something larger and more significant than the individual. Spirituality and *spiritual formation* occurs through personal experiences and practices, which can profoundly affect an individual's well-being. Consider and discuss how spirituality and religiosity can positively and negatively affect an individual's well-being. Explore how you, as a clinician, would integrate spirituality and religiosity into your practice. What is the best way to proceed?

embraced in the assessment process (ACA, 2005) and rehabilitative services (Smith, 2006). Health care professionals are able to target specific needs and help determine areas of improvement not typically addressed through traditional health care delivery models (Gleason, 1999). This may offer clients new insight about making meaning of their lives. Talking with clients about spiritual issues may also help them assess their current level of mind-body-spirit wellness, which can promote increased self-understanding (Adams et al., 2000). Despite the difficulty in assessing personal factors, such as spirituality and religiosity, research indicates the effectiveness of supplementing therapeutic interventions with spiritual and/or religious themes.

Assessing spirituality and addressing spiritual needs has proven beneficial with multiple populations, such as: gerontology patients (Blazer, 2006; Lewis, 2001; Phillips, 2003), addictions patients (MacKinnon, 2004; Olive, 2004), persons with anxiety and other mood disorders (Boscaglia, Clarke, Jobling, & Quinn, 2005; Davis, Kerr, & Kurpius, 2003), victims of traumatic events such as societal and domestic violence (Briggs, Apple, & Aydlett, 2004; Connor, Davidson, & Lee, 2003), college students (Bowen-Reid & Smalls, 2004; Hindeman, 2002), patients with terminal illnesses (Dunbar, Mueller, Medina, & Wolf, 1998; Johnson, 2003), and women (Gatz & Fisk, 2003). In general, assessing spiritual concerns within any health care setting provides a framework from which professionals can effectively and holistically approach the treatment process.

History of Research and Practice in the Assessment of Spirituality and Religiosity

Spirituality and religiosity were first discussed in professional literature through the works of Parsons and Galton (McCormick, 2004), and since that time, the presence of spirituality and religiosity in the helping professions has become increasingly popular and accepted in a variety of aspects of the counseling and rehabilitation professions. Miller and Thoresen (2003), Kelly (1992, 1994), and the U.S. Census Bureau (2001, 2006) all provide convincing statistics that indicate the importance of spirituality and religiosity to the American population. Indeed, Miller and Thoresen indicate that "Many Americans have stated that their faith is a central guiding force in their lives" (p. 24). Additionally, research indicates a more effective and beneficial therapeutic process if professionals integrate spiritual and religious beliefs into the health care process (Adams et al., 2000; Cook, 2004; Fallot, 2007; Miller & Thoresen; Seybold & Hill, 2001; Skevington, Sartorius, & Amir, 2004).

Additional requirements include ethical obligations for therapists to seek greater competency in integrating spirituality and religiosity into the recovery and rehabilitation process (ACA, 2005; CORE, 2004). Current research indicates two important lessons for helping professionals: (1) the increasing number of research studies indicates that spirituality is a very important aspect of many people's lives, and (2) an increasing amount of literature addresses the assessment of spirituality and religiosity in rehabilitation and health care (Fallot, 2007; Kelly, 1992, 1994; Miller & Thoresen, 2003; Young et al., 2007). These methods of assessing spirituality and religiosity are discussed throughout this chapter.

Spirituality and Religiosity in Assessment

Because the rehabilitation field is primarily concerned with helping others recover and/or regain ability, the assessment of spirituality and religiosity can be a particularly useful tool in increasing wellness (Stanard et al., 2000). To be useful constructs in the recovery and rehabilitation process, accurate means must be developed to adequately and correctly assess spirituality and religiosity. Through their review of all published assessments of spirituality and religiosity, Hill and Hood (1999) defined and described various related constructs. They placed 125 assessment instruments in 17 categories. These categories both define various spiritual constructs and assist professionals in selecting the proper assessment instrument. The 17 categories are: (1) religious beliefs and practices, (2) religious attitudes, (3) religious orientation, (4) religious development, (5) religious commitment and involvement, (6) religious experience, (7) religious/moral values or personal characteristics, (8) multidimensional religiousness, (9) religious coping and problem solving, (10) spirituality and mysticism, (11) God concept, (12) religious fundamentalism, (13) death/afterlife, (14) divine intervention/religious attribution, (15) forgiveness, (16) institutional religion, and (17) related constructs. These 17 categories characterize the multidimensional characteristics of spirituality and indicate the numerous ways spirituality may be integrated into the rehabilitation therapeutic process.

Current Assessment Methods in Spirituality and Religiosity

The categories created by Hill and Hood (1999) to classify assessments of spirituality and religiosity not only describe the constructs of spirituality and religiosity, they also illustrate the wide variety of approaches to experience spirituality. The categories range from beliefs and practices to related constructs, object relations (Hall & Edwards, 2002), implicit and explicit attitudes (Bassett et al., 2005), and subjective measures of well-being (Daaleman & Frey, 2004; Slater et al., 2001). Despite Hill and Hood's efforts, much still depends upon the individual understanding of these concepts. Speck (2005) states that definitional dilemmas and social factors have continually plagued the use of spiritual constructs in the recovery process.

The assessment of spirituality and religiosity in the rehabilitation profession centers primarily on the evaluation of levels of spirituality and spiritual well-being, spiritual experiences, coping skills, life satisfaction, and quality of life—spiritual and religious experiences that may aid in the recovery process. Well-developed and researched wellness models also provide useful interventions in rehabilitation and recovery (Adams et al., 2000; Myers, Sweeney, & Witmer, 2000; Sweeney & Witmer, 1991; Witmer & Sweeney, 1992). It is through these constructs that rehabilitation, recovery, and other health care professionals may quantitatively and qualitatively measure a sense of well-being. Each construct characterizes a different aspect of spirituality and religiosity and how it may increase one's ability to recover from illness or debilitation. Each construct also provides a diagnostic and therapeutic base for helping professionals.

Despite the perceived difficulties, assessing and evaluating the role of spirituality and religiosity (if any) with clients is important. The information gained from an assessment of spirituality and religiosity may provide pertinent information related to existential concerns, coping skills, sense of meaning or purpose, sense of hope for the future, and/or a relationship with a higher power or higher being. Stanard et al. (2000) supports the provision of a therapeutic rationale for assessing spirituality:

> *Richards and Bergin (1997) cited five major reasons for including spiritual assessment in therapeutic protocols. These reasons are obtaining a better understanding of the client's worldview, determining if a religious orientation is healthy or unhealthy, finding out if a client's community is a source of help, ascertaining which spiritual interventions are helpful, and determining how a client's problems are related to spiritual issues. (p. 205)*

Similar information is gathered by therapists for diagnostic purposes, such as ensuring the client has developed an adequate support network (or encouraging the client to do so), working with the client to determine a plan of action to address his or her concerns, working to fully understand the client's concerns, and addressing any hidden or underlying concerns that the client may not fully articulate. This information is gathered with a primary concern of helping those with some type of disorder or infirmity to increase their level of functioning, life satisfaction, and/or sense of meaning and purpose.

Evaluation of Spirituality and Spiritual Well-Being

With the assessment of spirituality, well-being is an important aspect of the assessment process. As Stanard et al. (2000) suggest, rehabilitation professionals must evaluate all available tools and interventions that may be useful in the recovery and therapeutic process. Depending upon the nature of the client's needs, spiritual experiences may be useful in the recovery process. Miller and Thoresen (2003) reported numerous research studies that indicate the beneficence of integrating spirituality into the recovery and therapeutic process.

Seybold and Hill (2001) also suggest that spirituality may be a helpful component to the therapeutic process. They state that spirituality and religiosity should be fully integrated and not considered a separate activity. Indeed, an increasing amount of research indicates that involvement in spiritual and religious activities shows promising results to the health care fields, as evidenced through work commissioned by the Fetzer Institute and the National Institute on Aging (NIA). Ten dimensions of religion and spirituality were identified as prominent areas in recent research: religious-spiritual history, preference-affiliation, social participation, private practices, coping styles, beliefs and values, commitment, experiences, sense of support, and motivation for regulating and reconciling relationships (Fetzer Institute/NIA, 1999, cited in Seybold & Hill). In this example, Seybold and Hill defined spiritual and religious constructs and categories similar to those defined by Hill and Hood (1999). The Fetzer Institute/NIA report also indicates that in an effort to provide better health care to clients, the helping professions must seek all available resources. Thus, both awareness and understanding of spiritual and religious issues with clients must be included in the client assessment process.

Both wellness and spirituality are highly subjective and personal; therefore, it is difficult to devise a single measure that can be generalized across numerous populations. However, Hill and Hood (1999) indicate that although several assessments have been developed to assess spirituality and overall spiritual well-being, each scale measures aspects of spirituality from different perspectives. Rehabilitation professionals may determine which assessment instrument will best meet the client's needs.

Spiritual Assessment Inventory

Partially based on an object relations maturity perspective (Hall, Brokaw, Edwards, & Pike, 2000), the Spiritual Assessment Inventory (SAI; Hall & Edwards, 1996, 2002) was developed to measure spiritual development or spiritual maturity from two perspectives: object relations and contemplative spirituality (Tisdale, 1999). The SAI was designed to be used in both a research and a clinical practice environment (Stanard et al., 2000). Because it is grounded in a spiritual, theological, and a psychological foundation, it may be used to "measure both the spiritual and psychological aspects of spiritual maturity defined in the context of one's experienced relationship with God" (Hall & Edwards, 1996, p. 244). Consisting of 43 total items presented on a 5-point Likert-type scale, the assessment is intended "to be a tool that would assist in identifying individuals' strengths and weaknesses, thus providing direction for pastoral counseling or psychotherapy" (p. 353).

Spiritual Well-Being Scale

The Spiritual Well-Being Scale (SWBS; Ellison, 1983; Paloutzian & Ellison, 1982, 1991) was developed in an effort to provide "a general measure of the subjective quality of life" (Boivin, Kirby, Underwood, & Silva, 1999, p. 382). The SWBS is reportedly one of the most widely used assessments of spirituality and religiosity in clinical research (Paloutzian & Ellison, 1991), and it was designed to be holistic in nature, not to focus on a specific religious organization or community. The SWBS combines both psychology and spirituality to measure an individual's global perception of spiritual well-being on two subscales: existential well-being (EWB) and religious well-being (RWB). The SWBS consists of 20 items where higher scores represent higher levels of well-being. This assessment instrument appears to be a good choice for rehabilitation and recovery professionals to assess related variables, such as psychological, religious, health, and inter/intrapersonal relations (Ellison & Smith, 1991, cited in Boivin et al.).

Spiritual Themes and Religious Responses Test

The Spiritual Themes and Religious Responses Test (STARR; Saur & Saur, 1993a, 1993b) is a projective assessment designed to provide information regarding individual religious experiences. The assessment consists of 11 black and white photographs of people, which is designed to elicit themes of prayer, "solitude, grief, joy, awe, celebration of life, family relatedness, and death" (Brokaw, 1999, p. 372). This assessment was modeled after the Thematic Apperception Test (TAT), and it is also assumed that individuals will project their own perceptions and experiences. It should be noted, however, that this assessment should only be administered and interpreted by professionals trained in the use of projective testing.

Spiritual Well-Being Questionnaire

The Spiritual Well-Being Questionnaire (SWB; Moberg, 1984) was developed as a multidimensional measure of spiritual growth and maturity. This instrument is considered a comprehensive assessment because it includes items and sections of "social attitudes, self-perceptions, theological orientation, religious beliefs, opinions, experiences, preferences, affirmations, and various charitable endeavors" (Boivin, 1999, p. 375).

Evaluation of Spiritual Experiences

The evaluation of spiritual experiences can also reveal important and necessary information for the rehabilitation professional. Just as evaluating the level and significance of spirituality and religiosity in an individual is important in the diagnostic process, helping professionals should also seek to identify the client's most significant spiritual experiences. Knowledge of these experiences will help the rehabilitation profession determine to what extent they may integrate spirituality into the therapeutic process. Moberg (2002) states that the best way to measure spirituality is through qualitative methods—if assessed in this manner, individuals are able to describe and explain their experiences in their own words. The qualitative and mixed-methods approach will evaluate spirituality from an individual perspective.

Index of Core Spiritual Experiences

The Index of Core Spiritual Experiences (INSPIRIT; Kass, Friedman, Leserman, Zuttermeister, & Benson, 1991) was designed to identify the intensity and concreteness of experiences related to the existence of God or a higher power. By measuring a variety of elements related to spirituality by addressing a distinct spiritual event that occurred in the individual's life, the INSPIRIT appraises this event to determine if it resulted in a conviction of God's existence, and it assesses their relationship with God. Consisting of seven items, higher numerical values on the INSPIRIT indicate a more distinct spiritual experiences. Data indicates the INSPIRIT may be helpful in the following areas: (1) positive psychological attitudes, (2) reduction of medical symptoms, (3) improved quality of life less burdened by illness, (4) less depression, (5) greater life satisfaction, (6) lower blood pressure, (7) lower mortality rates from coronary artery disease and cardiac surgery, (8) improved obstetric outcomes, and (9) the utilization of fewer health services in general (Hinebaugh-Igoe, 1999; Kass et al., 1991).

The Mysticism Scale: Research Form D

The Mysticism Scale: Research Form D (M Scale; Hood, 1975) was designed to assess intense experiences (sense of unity and/or "nothingness") that may or may not be characterized as religious experiences (Burris, 1999). The M Scale consists of 32 items that measure mystical experiences based on 8 criteria, where higher scores indicate more intense experiences. Additionally, it has been suggested that the M Scale is "nonsectarian, nonsexist in wording and content, and can therefore be administered without modification across a broad range of samples" (Burris, p. 364).

Evaluation of Spiritual Coping Skills

When dealing with a loss or disability, an individual may use a variety of coping strategies. Schaefer and Gorsuch (1991) suggest that coping skills illustrate psychological adjustment to negative life events. Additionally, according to Tyler (1978, 1979, cited in Hathaway & Pargament, 1990), research indicated that "effective coping involves three dimensions: a favorable self-attitude, a positive self-world attitude, and a realistic, active coping style" (p. 426). These tenets are supported by research compiled by Pargament et al. (1988), which identified three styles of religious problem solving: collaborative, self-directing, and deferring. These styles depict the manner in which individuals may cope with negative life events.

Religious Problem-Solving Scale

The Religious Problem-Solving Scale (RPS; Pargament et al., 1988) was originally published to evaluate religious coping and problem-solving styles. The primary reason for the development of this assessment was to ascertain the relationship between religious problem-solving style and mental health (Thurston, 1999). The RPS is designed to evaluate the manner in which individuals attempt to use the sacred to solve problems and make decisions (Pargament & Mahoney, 2005). The RPS has 36 items, and higher scores indicate a greater endorsement level of a religious coping style. This data collected by Pargament et al. is supported by research conducted by Fox, Blanton, and Morris (1998), Hathaway and Pargament (1990), and Schaefer and Gorsuch (1991) on religious coping and problem solving.

Religious Coping Activities Scale

The Religious Coping Activities Scale (RCAS; Pargament et al., 1990) was developed on the heels of the RPS in an effort to measure to what extent individuals use religiosity to cope with negative life events with a "more sophisticated index of religiously based coping responses" (Watson, 1999, p. 344). Measuring 6 types of religious coping (spiritually-based coping, good deeds, discontent, interpersonal religious support, plead, and religious avoidance) and consisting of 31 items (higher scores indicate a greater endorsement of a coping activity), the RCAS was designed from previous research in coping activities, client writings, and interviews with clergy and religious individuals.

The Royal Free Interview for Religious and Spiritual Beliefs

Designed to discern how spiritual, religious, and/or philosophical beliefs can influence the outcomes of illness, the Royal Free Interview (RFI) for Religious and Spiritual Beliefs was developed using a population of inpatients suffering from acute physical illness (King, Speck, & Thomas, 1995). Considered a qualitative measure, the RFI consists of three sections of interviews. Additionally, the RFI was designed so that interview questions may "branch" depending upon the answers given by the subject. It should be noted that although no special training is required to administer the assessment, the administrator is responsible for determining if the individual's response was "a religious understanding, a spiritual understanding without religious observance, or a philosophical understanding without any religious or spiritual understanding" (Seybold, 1999, p. 351).

Summary

Although many more spirituality and religiosity assessment instruments have been developed than have been discussed here, the assessments described appear to be highly valid and reliable. Although some limitations do exist for each assessment (these are discussed later in this chapter), the theoretical and research bases for the assessments have consistently been proven sound. Hill and Hood's (1999) reviews allow rehabilitation professionals to easily peruse and select assessment instruments to supplement current diagnostic and therapeutic materials, integrate assessment of the sacred into the rehabilitation and recovery process, increase research, and potentially resolve the limitations of these assessments so they may become useful to a greater array of helping professionals.

Research Critical to Issues in the Assessment of Spirituality and Religiosity

The Institute of Medicine has defined *spiritual needs* as "the needs and expectations that humans have to find meaning, purpose and value in their life" (Murray et al., 2004, p. 40, cited in Taylor, 2006). This definition suggests that all people have basic belief systems that provide meaning and purpose to life, regardless of their religiosity. With the increased interest of the assessment and use of spirituality and religiosity measures in contemporary mental and rehabilitative health care, much research has been facilitated in assessing and potentially utilizing these components in the delivery of health care services. This section considers those issues that are critical to the development, validation, and utilization of spirituality and religiosity measures by mental health practitioners. This includes considerations such as: (1) the importance of assessing spirituality and religiosity, (2) the multidimensional nature of spirituality and religiosity, (3) the social context of spirituality and religiosity, (4) the potential health implications, and (5) the benefits and limitations of assessing spirituality and religiosity.

One of the consistent themes found in the research points to the multifaceted dimension of spirituality and religiosity and, therefore, the profession's inability to strictly define the constructs of either (Seybold & Hill, 2001). Seybold and Hill note that the development of definitive constructs is blocked by the lack of a specific set of beliefs and/or behaviors that are inherent to any particular spiritual or religious concept. Thus, the development of spirituality and religiosity measures are inhibited by this same roadblock. An example of the diversity of this issue of defining spirituality and religiosity is demonstrated in the 10 dimensions developed by the Fetzer Institute and the NIA, where they attempted to conceptualize the constructs of spirituality and religiosity within an individual. These issues have been the focus of recent research and appear to have the potential to enhance the delivery of health care services (Fetzer Institute/NIA, 1999).

From another perspective, Miller and Thoresen (2003) describe spirituality and religiousness as *latent constructs* that conceptually underlie all entities and can be inferred from observable dimensions of the individual. In a broader sense, spirituality or religiousness is a characteristic of all individuals, regardless of their affiliation (or lack thereof) with any formal religion. Latent constructs are generally complex and multidimensional, lacking a single measure or dimension that captures their essential meaning. Thus, from a scientific perspective, spirituality and religiousness as a broad set of component dimensions must be considered in developing an operational definition that may be distinguishable yet with overlapping constructs (Miller & Thoresen). Additionally, several factors have been correlated to spirituality and religiosity, including altruistic behavior (Schwartz, Meisenhelder, Ma, & Reed, 2003, cited in Miller, 2004) and the prediction of psychosocial functioning in the areas of stress and coping, as well as other domains of life, for a diverse set of populations (Connor, Davidson, & Lee, 2003; Tanyi & Werner, 2003; Wink & Dillon, 2003, cited in Miller, 2004).

Research Box 23.1

ADDRESSING SPIRITUALITY AND RELIGIOSITY IN REHABILITATION COUNSELOR EDUCATION

Green, R. L., Benshoff, J. J., & Harris-Forbes, J. A. (2001). Spirituality in rehabilitation counselor education: A pilot survey. *Journal of Rehabilitation, 67,* 55–60.

Objectives: This study was to identify if spirituality is integrated into rehabilitation counseling training programs. Specifically, the authors sought to determine the preparedness of faculty to teach this topic, if spirituality was considered an important aspect of rehabilitation, and familiarity with CACREP standards.

Method: This study consisted of a survey sent to 76 program directors with 28 responding, for a 37% response rate. Data was collected on seven yes/no questions and an eighth question for write-in responses.

Results: The results indicated that although a majority of respondents (64%) considered spirituality an important aspect of rehabilitation counseling, only a small percentage (7%) offered such training as a specific course, although a larger number (39%) indicated it was offered in several courses within their training program. Additionally, a majority of respondents (61%) were not familiar with the CACREP standards regarding spirituality.

Conclusion: The authors discovered the rehabilitation programs offering drug and alcohol abuse training were more likely to offer coursework on spirituality. Additionally, the results indicated that although many considered spirituality an important factor in rehabilitation counseling, few training programs offered such training. The authors suggested that until such training is offered, rehabilitation counseling students must seek alternative sources of training in spirituality.

Questions:

Discuss the results from Green et al. (2001) in regards to the current consideration of spirituality and religiosity in your rehabilitation counselor training program; are their results accurate? What alternatives might be available if spirituality training is not provided at your institution? Describe and provide examples of how a rehabilitation counseling training program might integrate spirituality and religiosity into the curricula.

Multidimensional Nature

The inherent theme in research related to spirituality and religiosity consists of attempts to universalize those issues that individuals define as their spiritual and/or religious values. Moberg (2002) discusses numerous attempts to design sociopsychometric scales that have the intent to measure these constructs appropriately for all people, due to the inherent common humanity believed to be consistent through diverse populations, with only minor allowances considered for social, cultural, and linguistic differences. However, in his research he found evidence that existential issues, such as personal fulfillment, holistic wellness, life satisfaction, spiritual well-being, and analogous concepts, occur in a wide variety of sociocultural frames of reference and cannot be generalized.

Hill and Hood (1999) offer a vivid example of the breadth of the multidimensional nature of attempting to develop assessment tools related to spirituality and religiosity in their publication of over 125 measures. A review of these instruments clearly demonstrates that the breadth of the measurement issue is not only related to the diversity of the constructs of spirituality and religiosity but also to the breadth of the researchers' approaches to developing measures to assess them. In addition to the Fetzer Institute and NIA's dimensions, Hill and Hood's research shows additional dimensions, including scales for religion and spirituality beliefs and practices, attitudes, religious orientation and development, commitment and involvement, religious coping, mysticism, and views of death and afterlife (Kass et al., 1991; Pargament, 1997; Seybold & Hill, 2001). Still other research looks at components of spirituality, such as unifying interconnectedness, purpose and meaning in life, innerness or inner resources, and transcendence, which seems to broaden the components beyond the level of some religious beliefs (Hodges, 2002; Howden, 1992). Other scholars have identified five features related to the diversity of spirituality and religiosity, including: (1) connectedness to the sacred, (2) importance and embeddedness of spiritual or religious traditions in people's lives, (3) the ways in which individuals create and revise those components through the life experience, (4) whether their beliefs and practices are emotional or intellectual in nature, and (5) the constructs of their conceptions and practices related to their spirituality and/or religiosity (Moberg, 2002).

A review of the research demonstrates that the assessment of an individual's spirituality and/or religiosity should not be oversimplified due to the multidimensional nature of one's worldview on religiosity, faith development, faith maturity, and spiritual health or wellness (Hill & Hood, 1999). Moberg (2002) offers specific considerations in the development and utilization of such assessments (see Chapter 23 appendix, A). The author further identifies common guidelines for those considering research on spirituality due to the complications of definitions, normative values, methodologies, and other issues associated with spirituality. The implications of these issues are directly related to the development and utilization of evaluative assessments and research (see Chapter 23 appendix, B).

Spirituality and Religiosity: A Social Context

Numerous research scholars have identified the social contextual nature of spirituality and religion as they have reviewed and critiqued a number of assessment measures (Glock & Stark, 1966; Hill & Kilian, 2003; Hill et al., 2000; Hilty & Morgan, 1985; Krause, 1999; Lenski, 1961; Moberg, 1984; Pargament, 1997). It is important to consider the inherent sociocultural nature of one's support system in assessing the context of the accepted spiritual and religious belief system. Vogt, Mullooly, Ernst, Pope, and Hollis (1992) found that individuals report receiving substantial physical and mental benefits when they are well-connected within their spiritual and religious communities and thus are impacted by that social belief system. Additionally, Pargament et al. (1988) identified three religious coping styles to assist in working through negative life events, and Kass et al. (1991) has identified a strong correlation between spiritual experiences (both individually and communally) and positive health outcomes. These results suggest that spirituality and religiosity exists in a variety of contexts and must be assessed in the client's chosen perspective.

Benefits of Spirituality and Religiosity

There is a substantial body of evidence that spirituality and religiosity often impact psychological, social, and physical adjustment of people to crises through the development of coping and problem-solving mechanisms that provide individuals the ability to cope with stressful situations in life (Fox et al., 1998; Hathaway & Pargament, 1990; Hill & Kilian, 2003; Pargament et al., 1988). Other studies have shown positive outcomes related to the perceived outcomes of prayer, religious and spiritual social support, relationship with a higher power, participation in spiritual and religious ceremonies, and the development of meaning in one's life that comes from spirituality and religion (Larson et al., 1992; Kass et al., 1991). Watters's (1992) review of the literature indicates a general positive effect of religion and spirituality on mental health outcomes in the studies reviewed (Boscaglia et al., 2005; Kass et al.; Seybold & Hill, 2001).

Boscaglia et al. (2005) discuss the impact of spirituality on cancer patients and how their beliefs and attitudes provided a basis for meaning and purpose in their lives through a sense of connectedness, including between self and others, with the natural environment, with a higher power, and with other supernatural forces. They additionally found that spirituality was positively correlated with improvements of psychosocial adjustment, quality of life, death distress, and anxiety adjustment among those with life-threatening illnesses.

Limitations of Spirituality and Religiosity

According to Stanard et al. (2000), many of the spiritual assessments being widely used today are based "on a Judeo-Christian perspective or a belief in God or a Higher Power as the basis of measurement" (p. 209). In Koenig's 1995 review of religion and spirituality studies (Moberg, 2002), only 5 of the 282 studies reviewed dealt with religious or spiritual contexts other than Judeo-Christian. This strong bias toward a single belief system in the development of assessments ignores a vast portion of our global and continental population (Moberg, 2002). Therefore, the results are not fully representative of the general population and may not accurately address a client's spiritual issues or needs at all.

Health care professionals must also consider the information being sought; Moberg (2002) suggests that a qualitative instrument may provide more descriptive

Research Box 23.2

CAN SPIRITUALITY AND RELIGIOSITY IMPROVE QUALITY OF LIFE?

Kim, J., Heinemann, A. W., Bode, R. K., Sliwa, J., & King, R. B. (2000). Spirituality, quality of life, and functional recovery after medical rehabilitation. *Rehabilitation Psychology, 45,* 365–385.

Objectives: The purpose of this research was to measure how spiritual well-being, emotional well-being, life satisfaction, and functional status changed during and after the rehabilitation process. As a longitudinal study, the authors also considered the relationship among these variables.

Method: This study consisted of 155 adult rehabilitation inpatients (45% male, 55% female). The participants completed four assessments (the Spiritual Well-Being Scale, the Life Satisfaction Questionnaire, the Short-Form Health Questionnaire, and the Functional Independence Measure) on three different occasions: upon entering the hospital, at discharge, and 3 months after discharge.

Results: The authors discovered that the respondents' emotional well-being increased throughout the rehabilitation process, although they found that the respondents' life satisfaction and spiritual well-being did not change. Additionally, the authors reported that some variables moderately increased over time.

Conclusion: According to the results reported by the authors, although some respondents indicated increased gains in emotional well-being, those who reported less gains during rehabilitation were also less likely to report emotional well-being. The evidence provided by the authors appears to endorse the efficacy of factors of spirituality in the rehabilitation process. Furthermore, the results also indicate that those who experience the greatest level of gains in functionality also reported the highest levels of spiritual and emotional well-being and life satisfaction.

Questions:
Discuss the results reported by Heinemann et al. (2000). What did the authors report as the most significant factor in experiencing spiritual well-being? Discuss and explain what you would consider a limitation in this study. How would you correct this limitation? Explain your answer.

and useful information about the larger concept of spirituality than a quantitative measure. Another study reveals that of the 125 instruments reviewed, Hill and Kilian (2003) found little validation of instruments using clinical populations. Additionally, many of the published spiritual assessments have small

Discussion Box 23.2

CAN THE ASSESSMENT OF SPIRITUALITY AND RELIGIOSITY BE GENERALIZED?

A look into current literature regarding spirituality and religiosity reveals a definitional dilemma. Additionally, researchers have found that the multidimensional facets of spirituality occur differently through diverse cultural perspectives. However, researchers were also able to define five common elements regarding spirituality and religiosity in diverse cultural contexts: (1) a connection to the sacred, (2) the embeddedness of spiritual and religious traditions, (3) how spiritual and religious traditions are created and revised, (4) if spiritual beliefs and practices are emotional or intellectual, and (5) the characteristics of practices and spiritual and religious beliefs. To what extent do you believe these five elements factor into the assessment of spirituality and religiosity in diverse cultures? Can these elements be generalized to all cultural settings? How might the rehabilitation profession best assess and utilize spirituality and religiosity with multicultural clients?

norming samples, are not well-constructed, and cannot be deemed either reliable or valid. Therefore, knowledge and sound professional judgment is imperative when selecting and using spirituality assessments.

In considering the potential utilization of spirituality and religiosity measures in the delivery of mental and physical health services, practitioners must also consider how to measure the outcomes of those health-related issues that are being treated. Although, many health-related outcomes may have specific determinants (e.g., loss of mobility, substance abuse, and/or debilitating illnesses), many of these health outcomes are subjectively measured as well (e.g., depression, anxiety, and/or wellness). Seybold and Hill (2001) identify the ambiguous nature of some findings that they assert to the inconsistencies in defining or measuring religion and spirituality and are thus conflicted when research attempts to link those outcomes to the mental and physical health issues being treated.

Cultural, Legislative, and Professional Issues Impacting Specific Counseling Aspects or Procedures

According to Watts (2001), the scope of the integration of spirituality and religiosity in the delivery of mental health services has hit an all-time high, with approximately 95% of the American public identifying a belief in God or some higher power. This figure is further supported by Gallup and Lindsay (1999, as cited in Miller & Thoresen, 2003), who cite the same numerical statistics. Because the American public consists of numerous ethnically and culturally diverse groups with their own spiritual and religious worldviews, it is incumbent upon the helping profession to adequately accommodate these unique perspectives in the consideration of spirituality and religiosity assessment. Many of these unique populations cannot be understood without understanding the history and nature of their spiritual beliefs.

As previously discussed, Richards and Bergin (2000) describe several imperatives related to the need for rehabilitation and health care professionals to develop religious and spiritual competencies in anticipation of dealing with clients of diverse backgrounds. In some situations, Moberg (2002) points out that the norms are so diverse that the spiritual health indicators of one tradition are negative symptoms in another. Such incongruence with the clinician's traditional worldview may have a significant impact on the therapeutic process without the development of spiritual and religious competencies that are consistent with those of the client.

Spirituality and religiosity in the helping professions has been largely defined and defended under the umbrella of multiculturalism and diversity (ACA, 2005; CACREP, 2001; CORE, 2004). Because current CACREP and CORE training standards define spirituality as a multicultural issue, it is a required aspect of training and development. Also, considering it a multicultural issue, Hodge (2005) asserts that spirituality is defined within a cultural context, where individual perceptions of spirituality and religiosity become a worldview. Unfortunately, singular worldviews cannot be generalized to the larger population. Despite these complications, the helping professions perceive spirituality and religiosity as an important aspect of the therapeutic process. As such, the Association of Counselor Education and Supervision (ACES) and the Association for Spiritual, Ethical, and Religious Values in Counseling (ASERVIC) also recognize spirituality as a multicultural issue. The 1999 collaboration between ACES and ASERVIC resulted in the establishment of nine spirituality competencies (see Chapter 23 appendix, C). The ASERVIC spiritual competencies do not attempt to define spirituality and religiosity. Instead, the competencies attempt to evaluate the individual worldview, understanding spirituality to encompass both individual and communal experiences. Thus, the competencies approach spirituality from a multicultural perspective, looking to understand the person as a unique individual rather than how they fit into a cultural norm.

CORE (2004), CACREP (2001), and ACA (2005), as well as other sanctioning, accrediting, and professional bodies for the helping professions, offers competency mandates (as illustrated previously) for their programs and professional members to facilitate culturally sensitive and effective training, treatment implementation, and supervision. A consistent theme of these directives deals with the ethical and legal treatment of religious and spiritual values in those individuals being served (CACREP). These standards highlight the responsibilities of helping professionals to facilitate diversity consideration in the processes of treatment planning and implementation to clients and communities of diverse origins and beliefs, including spirituality and religiosity. Thus, it appears that several organizations in the helping professions are collaboratively discussing directives to ensure that the spiritual needs of clients are being considered in the therapeutic process.

The presidents of nine national associations of mental health professionals, representing over 600,000 professionals across the United States, met on

February 20, 1997, to consider the entitlement of clients' rights who present for mental health services. This group developed and implemented the Principles for the Provision of Mental Health and Substance Abuse Treatment Services: A Bill of Rights (American Psychological Association [APA], 2007). This document represents the helping professions' assurance of the availability of quality mental health and substance abuse treatment to all who seek such services. This Mental Health Bill of Rights has resulted in laws that require clinicians to educate their clients as to their rights to receive mental health services and the equitable expectations they may have as recipients of these services (Cantor, 1998). Integrated into this bill of rights is the directive for clinicians to provide quality mental health services to all individuals without regard to race, color, religion, national origin, gender, age, sexual orientation, or disability (APA). Thus, not only has the mental health profession mandated consideration of an individual's spirituality and religiosity within numerous ethical codes of professional organizations, but the profession has carried that mandate into a legislatively grounded consumer bill of rights for mental health clients.

Multidisciplinary or Interdisciplinary Approaches

Spirituality assessment is not unique to the mental health profession. In fact, assessing spiritual needs is common in other health care settings and has been shown to benefit patients in numerous ways. Assessing spirituality and addressing related concerns have become integral components across disciplines, including counseling and mental health (Hall, Dixon, & Mauzey, 2004), nursing (McSherry & Ross, 2002), and psychiatric rehabilitation (Blanch, 2007; Fallot, 2007; Russinova & Blanch, 2007). Research has pointed to the importance of implementing a more holistic approach to mental and physical health assessment and treatment (Adams, et al., 2000). This research has generated increased expectations for providing culturally competent care while attending to clients' desires to find meaning and purpose in their circumstances and lives.

Assessing spirituality can promote health and wellness while providing patients with a framework for making important health care decisions (Adams et al., 2000; Ehman, Ott, & Short, 1999; Sweeney & Witmer, 1991; Witmer & Sweeney, 1992). Research studies suggest that addressing spiritual concerns promotes more positive health care experiences and enhances the therapeutic relationship between the patient and the health care professional (Joint Commissions on Accreditation of Health care Organizations, 2005). Studies have also shown decreased levels of depression for many patients while helping them effectively cope with difficult illnesses (Westgate, 1996). Simply acknowledging the spiritual wishes and needs of patients has resulted in improved outcomes for some patients, and many are able to find meaning in their specific situations as well as in life overall (Blanch, 2007).

The American Association of Colleges of Nursing advises that nurse education programs should ensure nurses' competence in comprehending "the meaning of human spirituality in order to recognize the relationships of beliefs to culture, behavior, health and healing" (1986, p. 5, cited in McSherry & Ross, 2002, p. 481). The ACA *Code of Ethics* (2005) has also provided ethical guidelines for the integration of spirituality into the counseling process in areas such as informed consent (Section A.2.a.), developmental and cultural sensitivity (Section A.2.c.), personal values (Section A.4.b.), advocacy (Section A.6.a.), quality of life (Section A.9.a.), counselor competence (Section A.9.b.), multicultural and/or diversity considerations (Section B.1.a.), counselor credentials (Section C.4.b.), nondiscrimination (Section C.5.), and evaluation, assessment, and interpretation (Section E.). Many ACA divisions define similar areas of spirituality awareness and competence, thus requiring members to attend to spiritual issues in the diagnostic and therapeutic processes.

An essential element shared by disciplines is the provision of quality care, where counselors, nurses, and other health care specialists are encouraged to foster an environment where spiritual beliefs, values, and customs are respected (ACA, 2005; McSherry & Ross, 2002). Research studies continue to grow in number, and they support the belief that addressing the spiritual dimension is critical in preventative and rehabilitative treatment (Johnson, 2003; MacKinnon, 2004). A proliferation of quantitative assessment measures has surfaced alongside the increased attention given to assessing spirituality (Hill & Hood, 1999; Hill & Kilian, 2003). However, other disciplines look to more qualitative methods for facilitating a client's search for meaning through the use of "creative arts, writing, guided imagery, music, reflective readings, and rituals" (Johnson, 2003, p. 235). Regardless of the method, assessment tools should be adaptable to the context of care, nonintrusive, nonthreatening, and free of judgment (McSherry & Ross).

Major Issues That Need Attention in Spirituality and Religiosity Assessment

Despite the increased attention and effort being placed on assessing clients' beliefs and needs related to spirituality and religiosity, several issues remain. Numerous articles state that the lack of consensus on a definition for spirituality and its various constructs is a problem (Burke et al., 1999; Slater et al., 2001; Speck, 2005). Spirituality and religiosity both involve a sense of purpose or meaning and draw upon relational variables; although these commonalities are intrinsic to most helping models, many professionals offering rehabilitative services lack adequate training in assessing clients with spiritual and/or religious concerns. Specific training for assessing spirituality and addressing related issues is essential if rehabilitation professionals are to work effectively with individuals from a variety of cultural backgrounds (Fallot, 2007).

As stated earlier, assessments based solely on one spiritual and/or religious perspective are likely to produce culturally biased results (Moberg, 2002; Stanard et al., 2000). Many instruments measure spiritual constructs that are viewed as specific pieces to a more complex spiritual whole. Knowledge of the intended use of the assessment and determining the specific construct to be measured relative to the client's needs are essential. Some published spirituality assessments, as reported by Hill and Hood (1999), do not report norming or validity data; others are acknowledged and strictly defined as research instruments and should not be used without careful consideration. Therefore, health care professionals must be trained in the selection and administration of assessment instruments in order to ensure valid and meaningful results. Understanding the limitations of any spirituality assessment, whether used for research or treatment purposes, is imperative.

Summary

Because of the popularity of spiritual and religious issues in the American population (Daaleman & Frey, 2004; Kelly, 1992, 1994; Miller & Thoresen, 2003; Seybold & Hill, 2001; Skevington et al., 2004; U.S. Census Bureau, 2001, 2006; Young et al., 2002; Young et al., 2007), more emphasis is placed upon integrating the sacred into the diagnostic and therapeutic process. Spirituality and religiosity will continue to be the focus of academic inquiry and scientific research as health professionals investigate more effective methods of health care delivery. It is apparent from the current and past research literature that patients look beyond the health care provider to facilitate wellness, especially as they search for meaning and purpose in life. The challenge to the health care profession is to develop effective methodologies for the assessment and utilization of the spiritual and religious tools that patients bring into the treatment process. This practice is endorsed by Richards and Bergin (1997; as cited by Stanard et al., 2000), who encourage professionals to regularly and consistently include an assessment of spirituality and religiosity in the diagnostic process, as these beliefs and experiences may significantly impact the client's worldview.

As discussed in this chapter, numerous issues impact how spiritual and religious beliefs, attitudes, and practices manifest in our patients; their sociocultural and family systems often complicate the assessment process. This complexity especially complicates the development, administration, and analysis of assessment instruments. Thus, the need for further investigation, research, and reflection upon how best to utilize the client's spiritual and religious strengths (or their absence) is essential to the effectiveness of promoting wellness with our patients. Furthermore, with the growing consideration of diversity and cross-cultural treatment methodologies, the inclusion of spiritual and religious components becomes essential in order to accommodate our patients' traditional worldviews related to healing and wellness. This approach is not only a humanistic one from the perspective of treating the patient within his or her own context, but it is rapidly becoming the standard approach to treatment as evidenced by numerous professional codes of ethics, training standards, and legislative initiatives (ACA, 2005; CACREP, 2001; CORE, 2004).

Acknowledgments

Assistance provided by Rebecca Stanard, PhD (University of West Georgia), and Jamie Carney, PhD (Auburn University).

Chapter 23 Appendix

A. Research and Assessment Issues in Spirituality and Religiosity

1. Investigating the spiritual side of human nature is extremely complex and multidimensional.

2. No single research tool will adequately accommodate the multidimensional complexity of spirituality and religiosity.
3. The indicators utilized to assess and measure spirituality and religiosity are merely observations of the spiritual manifestations, not the phenomenon itself. (e.g., behavior, beliefs, attitudes, feelings, interpersonal relationships of social participation, social welfare concerns, love, and stewardship responsibilities to God, self, humanity, and the environment.)
4. Any measure is an imperfect reflection of the true phenomenon.
5. The intensity of one's spirituality and religiosity is difficult to express in temporal secular concepts.
6. The illusion of feelings exists both in the physical and spiritual realm, and self-ratings of spirituality can be deceptive.
7. Universality of measures and evaluations is not conducive to such a multidimensional multicultural application of a construct.
8. Universal measures of spirituality may oppress minorities and negate ethnic, academic, religious, sociopolitical, or scientific minority characteristics that are uniquely interpreted as essential to the spiritual nature of those unique groups.
9. The utilization of universalistic instruments to evaluate spirituality results in the loss of distinctive features of specific groups resulting in the use of the most generic common denominators consistent within the groups.
10. The issue of validity remains the most significant concern in assessment and research on spirituality in which the implicit and explicit values upon which operational definitions, methodologies, and evaluations rest are of primary consideration.

From Moberg, D. O. (2002). Assessing and measuring spirituality: Confronting dilemmas of universal and particular evaluative criteria. *Journal of Adult Development, Special issue: Spirituality and adult development, 9,* 47–60.

B. Guidelines for Research on Spirituality and Religiosity

1. Any spirituality scale reflects only limited aspects of a highly complex, multidimensional construct in which numerous factors impact the outcomes.
2. A specific approach, unique to the religious and ideological group being assessed, will provide more valid results for comparative analyses.
3. Application of each group's own criteria of what constitutes spiritual wellness will provide more valid results than the application of researcher-centered criteria (Headland, Pike, & Harris, 1990, cited in Moberg, 2002).
4. The use of comparative and cross-disciplinary studies of spirituality will avoid the result of universal or generic spirituality assessment outcomes.
5. Develop typologies of spirituality and its components while avoiding the reinforcement of stereotypes, which may confuse the multidimensional nature of the topic.
6. The use of precise operational definitions and careful linguistic/philosophical analyses are essential to avoid misunderstandings across diverse populations and their interpretations of the concepts being described and their meanings.

7. The development of valid and reliable assessments and measures of spirituality must be conscientiously targeted so that both particularistic and universal goals are considered.
8. The use of both quantitative and qualitative methods from a variety of professions and disciplines to learn from different perspectives.

From Moberg, D. O. (2002). Assessing and measuring spirituality: Confronting dilemmas of universal and particular evaluative criteria. *Journal of Adult Development, Special issue: Spirituality and adult development, 9,* 47–60.

C. ASERVIC Spirituality Competencies

1. Explain the relationship between religion and spirituality, including similarities and differences.
2. Describe religious and spiritual beliefs and practices in a cultural context.
3. Engage in self-exploration of his/her religious and spiritual beliefs in order to increase sensitivity, understanding, and acceptance of his/her belief system.
4. Describe one's religious and/or spiritual belief system, and explain various models of religious/spiritual development across the lifespan.
5. Demonstrate sensitivity to and acceptance of a variety of religious and/or spiritual expression in the client's communication.
6. Identify the limits of one's understanding of a client's spiritual expression, and demonstrate appropriate referral skills and general possible referral sources.
7. Assess the relevance of the spiritual domains in the client's therapeutic issues.
8. Be sensitive to and respectful of the spiritual themes in the counseling process as benefits each client's expressed preference.
9. Use the client's spiritual beliefs in pursuit of the client's therapeutic goals as befits the client's expressed preference.

From Miller, G. (1999). The development of the spiritual focus in counseling and counselor education. *Journal of Counseling & Development, 77,* 498–501.

References

Adams, T. B., Bezner, J. R., Drabbs, M. E., Zambarano, R. J., & Steinhardt, M. A. (2000). Conceptualization and measurement of the spiritual and psychological dimensions of wellness in a college population. *College Health, 48,* 165–173.

American Counseling Association. (2005). *Code of ethics.* Alexandria, VA: Author.

American Psychological Association. (2007). *Mental Health Bill of Rights: Principles for the provision of mental health and substance abuse treatment services.* Retrieved May 26, 2007, from: http://www.apa.org/topics/rights/#nondiscrimination

Ardell, D. (1999). Spirituality. *Ardell Wellness Report, 51,* 3.

Bassett, R. L., Thrower, J., Barclay, J., Powers, C., Smith, A., Tindall, M., et al. (2005). One effort to measure implicit attitudes toward spirituality and religion. *Journal of Psychology and Christianity, 24,* 210–218.

Blanch, A. (2007). Integrating religion and spirituality in mental health: The promise and the challenge. *Psychiatric Rehabilitation Journal, 30,* 251–260.

Blazer, D. G. (2006). Spirituality, depression, and the elderly. *Southern Medical Journal, 99,* 1178–1179.

Boivin, M. J. (1999). Review of the Spiritual Well-Being Questionnaire. In P. C. Hill & R. W. Hood, Jr. (Eds.), *Measures of religiosity* (pp. 375–381). Birmingham, AL: Religious Education Press.

Boivin, M. J., Kirby, A. L., Underwood, L. K., & Silva, H. (1999). Review of the Spiritual Well-Being Scale. In P. C. Hill & R. W. Hood, Jr. (Eds.), *Measures of religiosity* (pp. 382–385). Birmingham, AL: Religious Education Press.

Boscaglia, N., Clarke, D. M., Jobling, T. W., & Quinn, M. A. (2005). The contribution of spirituality and spiritual coping to anxiety and depression in women with a recent diagnosis of gynecological cancer. *International Journal of Gynecological Cancer, 15,* 755–761.

Boswell, B. B., Knight, S., Hamer, M., & McChesney, J. (2001). Disability and spirituality: A reciprocal relationship with implications for the rehabilitation process. *Journal of Rehabilitation, 67,* 20–25.

Bowen-Reid, T. L., & Smalls, C. (2004). Stress, spirituality and health promoting behaviors among African American college students. *The Western Journal of Black Studies, 28,* 283–291.

Briggs, M. K., Apple, K. J., & Aydlett, A. E. (2004). Spirituality and the events of September 11: A preliminary study. *Counseling and Values, 48,* 174–182.

Brokaw, B. F. (1999). Review of the Spiritual Themes and Religious Responses Test. In P. C. Hill & R. W. Hood, Jr. (Eds.), *Measures of religiosity* (pp. 371–374). Birmingham, AL: Religious Education Press.

Burke, M. T., Hackney, H., Hudson, P., Miranti, J., Watts, G. A., & Epp, L. (1999). Spirituality, religion, and CACREP curriculum standards. *Journal of Counseling & Development, 77,* 251–257.

Burris, C. T. (1999). Review of The Mysticism Scale: Research Form D. In P. C. Hill & R. W. Hood, Jr. (Eds.), *Measures of religiosity* (pp. 363–367). Birmingham, AL: Religious Education Press.

Cantor, D. W. (1998). Achieving a mental health bill of rights. *Professional Psychology: Research & Practice, 29,* 315–316.

Cashwell, C. S., & Young, J. S. (2004). Spirituality in counselor training: A content analysis of syllabi from introductory spirituality courses. *Counseling & Values, 48,* 96–109.

Connor, K. M., Davidson, J. R. T., & Lee, L. (2003). Spirituality, resilience, and anger in survivors of violent trauma: A community survey. *Journal of Traumatic Stress, 16,* 487–494.

Cook, C. C. H. (2004). Addiction and spirituality. *Addiction, 99,* 539–551.

Council for the Accreditation of Counseling and Related Educational Programs. (2001). *2001 Standards.* Retrieved June 1, 2006, from: http://www.cacrep.org/2001Standards.html

Council on Rehabilitation Education. (2004). *Standards.* Retrieved February 1, 2007, from: http://www.core-rehab.org/manual/c-accman0207.pdf

Curtis, R. C., & Glass, J. S. (2002). Spirituality and counseling class: A teaching model. *Counseling & Values, 47,* 3–12.

Daaleman, T. P., & Frey, B. B. (2004). The Spirituality Index of Well-Being: A new instrument for health-related quality-of-life research. *Annals of Family Medicine, 2,* 499–503.

Davis, T. L., Kerr, B. A., & Kurpius, S.E.R. (2003). Meaning, purpose, and religiosity in at-risk youth: The relationship between anxiety and spirituality. *Journal of Psychology and Theology, 31,* 356–365.

Dunbar, H. T., Mueller, C. W., Medina, C., & Wolf, T. (1998). Psychological and spiritual growth in women living with HIV. *Social Work, 43,* 144–154.

Ehman, J. W., Ott, B. B., & Short, T. H. (1999). Do patients want physicians to inquire about their spiritual or religious beliefs if they become gravely ill? *Archive of Internal Medicine, 159,* 1803–1806.

Eliason, G. T., Hanley, C., & Leventis, M. (2001). The role of spirituality in counseling: Four theoretical orientations. *Pastoral Psychology, 50,* 77–91.

Ellison, C. W. (1983). Spiritual well-being: Conceptualization and measurement. *Journal of Psychology and Theology, 11,* 330–340.

Fallot, R. D. (2007). Spirituality and religion in recovery: Some current issues. *Psychiatric Rehabilitation Journal, 30,* 261–270.

Faull, K., Hills, M. D., Cochrane, C., Gray, J., Hunt, M., McKenzie, C. et al. (2004). Investigation of health perspectives of those with physical disabilities: The role of spirituality as a determinant of health. *Disability and Rehabilitation, 26,* 129–144.

Fetzer Institute/National Institute on Aging. (1999). *Multidimensional measurement of religiousness/spirituality for use in health research: A report of the Fetzer Institute/National Institute on Aging working group.* Kalamazoo, MI: John E. Fetzer Institute.

Fitchett, G., Rybarczyk, B. D., DeMarco, G. A., & Nicholas, J. J. (1999). The role of religion in medical rehabilitation outcomes: A longitudinal study. *Rehabilitation Psychology, 44,* 333–253.

Fox, C. A., Blanton, P. W., & Morris, M. L. (1998). Religious problem-solving styles: Three styles revisited. *Journal for the Scientific Study of Religion, 37,* 673–677.

Fukuyama, M. A., & Sevig, T. D. (1997). Spiritual issues in counseling: A new course. *Counselor Education & Supervision, 36,* 233–244.

Gatz, M., & Fisk, A. (2003). Aging women and depression. *Professional Psychology: Research and Practice, 34,* 3–9.

Gleason, J. J. (1999). The four worlds of spiritual assessment and care. *Journal of Religion and Health, 38,* 305–317.

Glock, C., & Stark, R. (1966). *Christian beliefs and anti-Semitism.* New York: Harper & Row.

Green, R. L., Benshoff, J. J., & Harris-Forbes, J. A. (2001). Spirituality in rehabilitation counselor education: A pilot survey. Journal *of Rehabilitation, 67,* 55–60.

Hall, R. W., Dixon, W. A., & Mauzey, E. D. (2004). Spirituality and religion: Implications for counselors. *Journal of Counseling & Development, 82,* 504–507.

Hall, T. W., Brokaw, B. F., Edwards, K. J., & Pike, P. L. (2000). An empirical exploration of psychoanalysis and religion: Spiritual maturity and object relations development. *Journal for the Scientific Study of Religion, 37,* 303–313.

Hall, T. W., & Edwards, K. J. (1996). The initial development and factor analysis of the Spiritual Assessment Inventory. *Journal of Psychology and Theology, 24,* 233–246.

Hall, T. W., & Edwards, K. J. (2002). The Spiritual Assessment Inventory: A theistic model and measure for assessing spiritual development. *Journal for the Scientific Study of Religion, 41,* 341–357.

Hathaway, W. L., & Pargament, K. I. (1990). Intrinsic religiousness, religious coping, and psychosocial competence: A covariance structure analysis. *Journal for the Scientific Study of Religion, 29,* 423–441.

Hill, P. C., & Hood, R. W., Jr. (Eds.). (1999). *Measures of religiosity.* Birmingham, AL: Religious Education Press.

Hill, P. C., & Kilian, M. K. (2003). Assessing clinically significant religious impairment in clients: applications from measures in the psychology of religion and spirituality. *Religion & Culture, 6,* 149–160.

Hill, P. C., Pargament, K. I., Hood, R. W., Jr., Mccullough, M. E., Sawyers, J. P., & Larson, D. B. (2000). Conceptualizing religion and spirituality: Points of commonality, points of departure. *Journal for the Theory of Social Behavior, 30,* 51–77.

Hilty, D. M., & Morgan, R. L. (1985). Construct validation for the Religious Involvement Inventory: Replication. *Journal for the Scientific Study of Religion. 24,* 75–86.

Hindeman, D. M. (2002). From splintered lives to whole persons: Facilitating spiritual development in college students. *Religious Education, 97,* 165–182.

Hinebaugh-Igoe, L. (1999). Review of the Index of Core Spiritual Experiences. In P. C. Hill & R. W. Hood, Jr. (Eds.), *Measures of religiosity* (pp. 360–363). Birmingham, AL: Religious Education Press.

Hodge, D. R. (2005). Developing a spiritual assessment toolbox: A discussion of the strengths and limitations of five different assessment methods. *Health & Social Work, 30,* 314–323.

Hodges, S. (2002). Mental health, depression, and dimensions of spirituality and religion. *Journal of Adult Development, 9,* 109–115.

Hood, R. W., Jr. (1975). The construction and preliminary validation of a measure of reported mystical experience. *Journal for the Scientific Study of Religion, 14,* 29–41.

Howden, J. (1992). *Development and psychometric characteristics of the Spirituality Assessment Scale.* Unpublished doctoral dissertation. Denton, TX: Texas Women's University.

Ingersoll, R. E. (1997). Teaching a course on counseling and spirituality. *Counselor Education & Supervision, 36,* 224–232.

Johnson, L. S. (2003). Facilitating spiritual meaning-making for the individual with a diagnosis of a terminal illness. *Counseling and Values, 47,* 230–240.

Joint Commissions on Accreditation of Healthcare Organizations. (2005). Evaluating your spiritual assessment process. *Joint Commission, The Source, 3,* 6–7. Retrieved March 10, 2007, from: http://www.pastoralreport.com/archives/spiritual.pdf

Kass, J. D., Friedman, R., Leserman, J., Zuttermeister, P. C., & Benson, H. (1991). Health outcomes and a new Index of Spiritual Experience. *Journal for the Scientific Study of Religion, 30,* 203–211.
Kelly, E. W., Jr. (1992). *Religious and spiritual issues in university-based counselor education programs: A national survey of current status and practice. Final report of a research project* (EDRS No. 350496). Alexandria, VA: American Association for Counseling and Human Development Foundation.
Kelly, E. W., Jr. (1994). The role of religion and spirituality in counselor education: A national survey. *Counselor Education & Supervision, 33,* 227–237.
Kim, J., Heinemann, A. W., Bode, R. K., Sliwa, J., & King, R. B. (2000). Spirituality, quality of life, and functional recovery after medical rehabilitation. *Rehabilitation Psychology, 45,* 365–385.
King, M., Speck, P., & Thomas, A. (1995). The Royal Free Interview for Religious and Spiritual Beliefs: Development and standardization. *Psychological Medicine, 25,* 1125–1134.
Koenig, H. G. (1995). *Research on religion and aging: An annotated bibliography.* Westport, CT: Greenwood Press.
Krause, N. (1999). Religious support. In John E. Fetzer Institute, *Multidimensional measurement of religiousness / spirituality for use in health research: A report of the Fetzer Institute / National Institute on Aging Working Group* (pp. 57–64). Kalamazoo, MI: Author.
Larson, D. B., Sherrill, K. A., Lyons, J. S., Craigie, F. C., Thielman, S. B., Greenwood, M. A., et al. (1992). Associations between dimensions of religious commitment and mental health reported in the *American Journal of Psychiatry* and *Archives of General Psychiatry:* 1978–1989. *American Journal of Psychiatry, 149,* 557–559.
Lenski, G. (1961). *The religious factor.* Garden City, NY: Doubleday & Co.
Lewis, M. M. (2001). Spirituality, counseling, and elderly: An introduction to the spiritual life review. *Journal of Adult Development, 8,* 231–240.
MacKinnon, S. V. (2004). Spirituality: Its role in substance abuse, treatment and recovery. *DATA: The Brown University Digest of Addiction Theory & Application, 23,* 8.
McCormick, D. J. (2004). Galton on spirituality, religion, and health [Letter to the editor]. *American Psychologist, 59,* 52.
McSherry, W., & Ross, L. (2002). Dilemmas of spiritual assessment: Considerations for nursing practice. *Journal of Advanced Nursing, 38,* 479–488.
Miller, E. D. (2004). The development and validation of a new measure of spirituality. *North American Journal of Psychology, 6,* 423–430.
Miller, G. (1999). The development of the spiritual focus in counseling and counselor education. *Journal of Counseling & Development, 77,* 498–501.
Miller, W. R., & Thoresen, C. E. (2003). Spirituality, religion, and health: An emerging research field. *American Psychologist, 58,* 24–35.
Moberg, D. O. (1984). Subjective measures of spiritual well-being. *Reviews of Religious Research, 25,* 351–364.
Moberg, D. O. (2002). Assessing and measuring spirituality: Confronting dilemmas of universal and particular evaluative criteria. *Journal of Adult Development, Special issue: Spirituality and adult development, 9,* 47–60.
Myers, J. E., Sweeney, T. J., & Witmer, J. M. (2000). The wheel of wellness, counseling for wellness: A holistic model for treatment planning. *Journal of Counseling & Development, 78,* 251–266.
Olive, K. E. (2004). Religion and spirituality: Important psychosocial variables frequently ignored in clinical research. *Southern Medical Journal, 97,* 1152–1153.
Paloutzian, R. F., & Ellison, C. W. (1982). Loneliness, spiritual well-being, and quality of life. In L. A. Peplau & D. Perlman (Eds.), *Loneliness: A sourcebook of current theory, research, and therapy* (pp. 224–237). New York: Wiley Interscience.
Paloutzian, R. F., & Ellison, C. W. (1991). *Manual for the Spiritual Well-Being Scale.* Nyack, NY: Life Advance, Inc.
Pargament, K. I. (1997). *The psychology of religion and coping.* New York: Guilford Press.
Pargament, K. I., Ensing, D. S., Falgout, K., Olsen, H., Reilly, B., Van Haitsma, K., et al. (1990). God help me; (I): Religious coping efforts as predictors of the outcomes to significant negative life events. *American Journal of Community Psychology, 18,* 793–824.
Pargament, K. I., Kennell, J., Hathaway, W., Grevengoed, N., Newman, J., & Jones, W. (1988). Religion and problem-solving process: Three styles of coping. *Journal for the Scientific Study of Religion, 27,* 90–104.

Pargament, K. I., & Mahoney, A. (2005). Sacred matters: Sanctification as a vital topic for the psychology of religion. *The International Journal for the Psychology of Religion, 15,* 179–198.

Pate, R. H., Jr., & High, H. J. (1995). The importance of client religious beliefs and practices in the education of counselors in CACREP-accredited programs. *Counseling & Values, 40,* 2–5.

Phillips, I. (2003). Infusing spirituality into geriatric health care. *Topics in Geriatric Rehabilitation, 19,* 249–256.

Revheim, N., & Greenberg, W. M. (2007). Spirituality matters: Creating a time and place for hope. *Psychiatric Rehabilitation Journal, 30,* 307–310.

Richards, P. S., & Bergin, A. E. (Eds.). (2000). *Handbook of psychotherapy and religious diversity.* Washington, DC: American Psychological Association.

Russinova, Z., & Blanch, A. (2007). Supported spirituality: A new frontier in the recovery-oriented mental health system. *Psychiatric Rehabilitation Journal, 30,* 247–249.

Saur, M. S., & Saur, W. G. (1993a). *Spiritual Themes and Religious Responses Test (STARR): Preliminary manual.* Chapel Hill, NC: Author.

Saur, M. S., & Saur, W. G. (1993b). Transitional phenomena as evidenced in prayer. *Journal of Religion and Health, 32,* 55–65.

Schaefer, C. A., & Gorsuch, R. L. (1991). Psychological adjustment and religiousness: the multivariate Belief-Motivation Theory of Religiousness. *Journal for the Scientific Study of Religion, 30,* 448–461.

Seybold, K. S. (1999). Review of The Royal Free Interview for Religious and Spiritual Beliefs. In P. C. Hill & R. W. Hood, Jr. (Eds.), *Measures of religiosity* (pp. 351–357). Birmingham, AL: Religious Education Press.

Seybold, K. S., & Hill, P. C. (2001). The role of religion and spirituality in mental and physical health. *Current Directions in Psychological Science, 10,* 21–24.

Skevington, S. M., Sartorius, M., & Amir, M. (2004). Developing methods for assessing quality of life in different cultural settings: The history of the WHOQOL instruments. *Social Psychiatry & Psychiatric Epidemiology, 39,* 1–8.

Slater, W., Hall, T. W., & Edwards, K. J. (2001). Measuring religion and spirituality: Where are we and where are we going? *Journal of Psychology and Theology, 29,* 4–21.

Smith, D. (2006). Rehabilitation counselor willingness to integrate spirituality into client counseling sessions. *Journal of Rehabilitation, 72*(3), 4–11.

Souza, K. Z. (2002). Spirituality in counseling: what do counseling students think about it? *Counseling & Values, 46,* 213–217.

Speck, B. W. (2005). What is spirituality? *New Directions for Teaching and Learning, 104,* 3–13.

Stanard, R. P., Sandhu, D. S., & Painter, L. C. (2000). Assessment of spirituality in counseling. *Journal of Counseling & Development, 78,* 204–210.

Sweeney, T. J., & Witmer, J. M. (1991). Beyond social interest: Striving toward optimum health and wellness. *Individual Psychology, 47,* 527–540.

Tanyi, R. A., & Werner, J. S. (2003). Adjustment, spirituality, and health in women on hemodialysis. *Clinical Nursing Research, 12,* 229–245.

Taylor, E. J. (2006). Prevalence and associated factors of spiritual needs among patients with cancer and family caregivers. *Oncology Nursing Forum, 33,* 729–735.

Thurston, N. S. (1999). Review of the Religious Problem-Solving Scale. In P. C. Hill & R. W. Hood, Jr. (Eds.), *Measures of religiosity* (pp. 347–350). Birmingham, AL: Religious Education Press.

Tisdale, T. C. (1999). Review of the Spiritual Assessment Inventory. In P. C. Hill & R. W. Hood, Jr. (Eds.), *Measures of religiosity* (pp. 368–371). Birmingham, AL: Religious Education Press.

U.S. Census Bureau. (2001). *Monthly estimates of the United States population: April 1, 1980 to July 1, 1999, with short-term projections to November 1, 2000.* Washington, DC: Author.

U.S. Census Bureau. (2006). *Statistical abstract of the population.* Washington, DC: Author.

Vogt, T., Mullooly, J., Ernst, D., Pope, C., & Hollis, J. (1992). Social networks as predictors of ischemic heart disease, cancer, stroke and hypertension: Incidence, survival and mortality. *Journal of Clinical Epidemiology, 45,* 659–666.

Watson, P. J. (1999). Review of the Religious Coping Activities Scale. In P. C. Hill & R. W. Hood, Jr. (Eds.), *Measures of religiosity* (pp. 344–347). Birmingham, AL: Religious Education Press.

Watters, W. (1992). *Deadly doctrine: Health, illness, and Christian God-talk.* Amherst, NY: Prometheus Books.

Watts, R. E. (2001). Addressing spiritual issues in secular counseling and psychotherapy: Response to Helminiak's (2001) views. *Counseling and Values, 45,* 207–217.

Westgate, C. E. (1996). Spiritual wellness and depression. *Journal of Counseling & Development, 75,* 26–35.

Witmer, J. M., & Sweeney, T. J. (1992). A holistic model for wellness and prevention over the life span. *Journal of Counseling & Development, 71,* 140–148.

Young, J. S., Cashwell, C. S., Wiggins-Frame, M., & Belaire, C. (2002). Spiritual and religious competencies: A national survey of CACREP-accredited programs. *Counseling & Values, 47,* 22–33.

Young, J. S., Wiggins-Frame, M., & Cashwell, C. S. (2007). Spirituality and counselor competence: A national survey of American Counseling Association members. *Journal of Counseling & Development, 85,* 47–52.

Lawrence R. Burns
Amy N. Evans

24 Measures of Perfectionism

Without halting, without rest,
Lifting better up to Best;

—Ralph Waldo Emerson

Overview

This chapter presents a brief review of conceptual and assessment issues related to perfectionism. Examining five different assessment measures reveals theoretical similarities and meaningful conceptual divergences. A paucity of research specific to the area of perfectionism and rehabilitation is noted. The chapter concludes with a review of some recent work examining various correlates of perfectionism and the multidisciplinary or interdisciplinary overlap with health and health-related domains.

Learning Objectives

By the end of the chapter, the reader should be able to:

1. Describe current research and practices on measures of perfectionism;
2. Distinguish between the various models of perfectionism;
3. Show how the various measures of perfectionism are related to their conceptual models;
4. Explain the place of role attributions in treatment;
5. Examine the utility of personality correlates in rehabilitation and assessment; and
6. Evaluate the value of perfectionism in goal attainment, general health, and rehabilitation.

Introduction

Contrasting winter's raising with the anticipation of spring's, Emerson's harbinger poem, *May-Day,* reflects striving, acceptance, and recovery. And not unlike the word *raise,* perfectionism has become a modern day contronym—a word with two opposite meanings. Initially construed as pathological (Burns, 1980; Horney, 1950; Pacht, 1984), ample recent research has found that, for some, perfectionism is concomitant with a healthy outlook on life (Stoeber & Otto, 2006; Stoeber, Harris, & Moon, 2007; Stumpf & Parker, 2000; Terry-Short, Owens, Slade, & Dewey, 1995). The World Health Organization's (WHO) recently revised International Classification of Functioning, Disability and Health (ICF; WHO, 2001) prompts a similar shift in perspectives of disability by promoting a more inclusive focus on one's functioning and health (Stucki, Ewert, & Cieza, 2003).

This chapter has one central goal—introducing the reader to the idea that perfectionism can be either dysfunctional or beneficial in conjunction with rehabilitation and health. To accomplish this, we first present a brief overview of perfectionism and rehabilitation; then we review significant historical perspectives and recent advances in definitions of perfectionism; third, we provide a limited review of the many available assessment instruments and some of the associated treatment paradigms; fourth, we discuss some of the current findings in the field and how broad multidisciplinary considerations may inform future research.

Importance of Perfectionism to Rehabilitation and Health

Optimally, rehabilitation incorporates an effective multi- and interdisciplinary management of a person's functioning and health. A central goal is to minimize symptoms and disability and maximize independent functioning (Deaton, 1998; Stucki et al., 2003). "The [ICF's] current framework of disability ... attempts to achieve a synthesis ... of different perspectives of health from a biological, individual, and social perspective" (Stucki et al., 2003, p. 630). Similarly, Cohen and Rodriguez (1995) present an expanded psychological model that includes cognitive and behavioral pathways (along with biological and social) as explanations for the development and maintenance of co-occurring psychological and physical disorders. Client outcomes in rehabilitation inevitably reflect the interplay between rehabilitation service capacity and client participation: Counseling outcomes improve as client participation increases (Mpofu & Bishop, 2006; Mpofu, Beck, & Weinrach, 2004).

In the last 3 decades, a fundamental shift away from the symptom-based psychiatric/medical-model-as-psychopathology has occurred. Nowhere is this change more evident than in the recent WHO ICF adoption of the biopsychosocial model. This approach mirrors an international trend yielding a steadily increasing body of research emphasizing a phenomenological shift and a corresponding focus on some of the basic mental operations underlying various forms of emotional disturbance (Brown & Beck, 2002; Burns, Selke, Stein, & Poston, 2002; Üstün, Chatterji, Bickenbach, Kostanjsek, & Schneider, 2003). Notably, rehabilitation research now incorporates different cognitive, behavioral, and affective correlates (Gatchel, Peng, Peters, Fuchs, & Turk, 2007; Kiviniemi, Voss-Humke, & Seifert, 2007; Suzuki, Krahn, McCarthy, & Adams, 2007). The same is true of work involving perfectionism (Andersson, Airikka, Buhrman, & Kaldo, 2005; Bergman, Nyland, & Burns, 2007; Bieling, Israeli, & Antony, 2004). Both rehabilitation and perfectionism research have independently examined important, and often similar, indices of functioning in adults, but little effort has been made to integrate these two productive areas of investigation (Bruyère, Van Looy, & Peterson, 2005; Ueda & Okawa, 2003).

Established relationships linking perfectionism with functional limitations and/or processes of rehabilitation are limited, yet there is ample reason to bridge them. The diathesis-stress model provides one well-established model linking the tasks in a rehabilitation setting with the utility of perfectionism. When activated by stressful situations, psychological vulnerabilities can moderate one's coping style. Certain dimensions of perfectionism are moderated by different coping styles and can result in healthy coping, whereas other dimensions result in unhealthy coping (Blankstein, Lumley, & Crawford, 2007; O'Connor & O'Connor, 2003).

Consider perfectionism and rehabilitation and recent work involving research on hope. According to Snyder, Lehman, Kluck, and Monsson (2006), hope is an important goal-directed cognitive motivational process associated with adaptive coping mechanisms. People with higher levels of hope are better at setting and obtaining goals, and they appear to be better at creating clearer, more sustainable goals, which results in a greater sense of agency. Some sustainable goal orientations are beneficial, others detrimental (Payne, Youngcourt, & Beaubien, 2007). Positive perfectionism is clearly related to successful goal-directed cognitions and behaviors or positive outcome cognitions; negative perfectionism is not (Burns, Dittman, Nguyen, & Mitchelson, 2000; Burns & Fedewa, 2005; Chang, 2006).

Meaningful links between perfectionism and physical health include affect (Molnar, Reker, Culp, Sadava, & DeCourville, 2006), negative social interactions and avoidant coping (Dunkley, Sanislow, Grilo, & McGlashan, 2006), tinnitus distress (Andersson et al., 2005), anorexia nervosa (Cockell et al., (2002), and recurrent pain (Hadjistavropoulos, Dash, Hadjistavropoulos, & Sullivan, 2007).

A growing body of research pertaining to people with physical disabilities and their health includes affect (Cohen & Rodriquez, 1995); body esteem (Taleporos & McCabe, 2005); activity limitations (Schröder et al., 2007); health-related quality of life (Geyh, Cieza, Kollerits, Grimby, & Stucki, 2007); self-efficacy and interpersonal support (Suzuki et al., 2007); coping, social problem solving, and perceived communications skills (Blais & Boisvert, 2007); health perceptions (Jang, Bergman, Schofeld, & Molinari, 2007); romantic attachment (Hwang, Johnston, & Smith, 2007); and psychological adjustment (Noronha & Faust, 2007). We believe that future empirical work examining meaningful connections between perfectionism, particularly healthy perfectionism, and rehabilitation is called for based on the numerous conceptual links we've identified.

History of Research and Practice in the Assessment of Perfectionism

Current research on perfectionism is focused on two broad, interrelated empirical questions: Is a one-dimensional or multidimensional construct more representative of perfectionism, and is there sufficient evidence of two different types of perfectionism—healthy/unhealthy? As Flett and Hewitt (2002) note, perfectionists strive for flawlessness, and those with extremes of this quality attempt to achieve perfection in all the things they do. Hollender (1978, p. 384) defined perfectionism as "the practice of demanding of oneself or others a higher quality of performance than is required by the situation."

Initial conceptualizations were predicated on one-dimensional models of perfectionism as a personality trait, and assessment instruments provided a single-scale score. Burns (1980) developed his scale based on items from the Dysfunctional Attitude Scale (Weissman & Beck, 1978). In the early 1990s, two independent research groups developed different multidimensional measures of perfectionism (Frost, Marten, Lahart, & Rosenblate, 1990; Hewitt & Flett, 1991b). This work prompted studies examining the factor structure of various measures of perfectionism (Flett & Hewitt, 2002). The majority of research post-1990 reflects a multidimensional approach to assessment, but some recent clinical work has challenged this assertion with the return to a one-dimensional model (Dominic, Brown, Fairburn, & Shafran, 2007; Rhéaume, Ladouceur, & Freeston, 2000; Riley, Michelle, Zafra, Fairburn, & Shafran, 2007; Riley & Shafran, 2005; Shafran, Cooper, & Fairburn, 2002).

Hamachek (1978) proposed two types of perfectionism—normal and neurotic. Almost 30 years later, Stoeber and Otto's (2006) comprehensive review of 35 studies presented compelling support for Hamachek's basic two-factor model. Variously labeled as normal and neurotic, adaptive and maladaptive, positive and negative, or healthy and unhealthy, two factors have been consistently obtained in factor-analytic studies. Flett and Hewitt (2002) raise two assessment-related concerns about these findings: No definition of perfectionism has been agreed upon, and they emphasize the importance of ascertaining the distinction between *perfectionistic standards* and the attainment of these standards. As Hewitt and Flett specifically note, "[definitions] of perfectionism, however, should be restricted to perfectionistic strivings and that individual

Discussion Box 24.1

ARE YOU A HEALTHY PERFECTIONIST?

Are you a healthy perfectionist? Some researchers contend that being a perfectionist is inherently fraught with problems: from addiction and eating disorders to hopelessness and suicide. Others feel that holding high personal standards and being highly motivated to succeed can be beneficial. Dr. Hamachek, in 1978, made an important clinical observation about perfectionists that holds true to this day—the ability to accept a less-than-perfect outcome, combined with an ability to feel a genuine sense of pride and accomplishment when one achieved a goal, are indicative of healthy perfectionism. Dr. Hamachek also offered some clinical advice about dealing with troubling perfectionistic tendencies by identifying areas in one's life where perhaps one is not self-critical. By identifying less demanding areas of one's life and generalizing the lack of distress to areas that are troubling, a person may be able to decrease or even relinquish their distress. Alternately, if you are comfortable notching it down if the situation demands it of you, or if you're able to feel a genuine thrill of success and accomplishment for a job well done, then perhaps you're a positive perfectionist.

Questions:
Reflect on some recent examples of your responses to success or failure situations, and discuss how your reactions might indicate what type of perfectionist you might be. Do you feel that Hamachek's advice is relevant to your situation?

differences in perceived discrepancies should be seen as part of a related but distinct construct that emphasizes self-evaluation" (p. 15).

Stoeber and Otto (2006) propose an elegant model that successfully integrates dimensional and categorical components. They identify two distinct dimensions: perfectionistic concerns and perfectionistic striving. Accordingly, categorically healthy perfectionists are defined as reporting low levels of perfectionistic concerns and high levels of perfectionistic striving, whereas negative perfectionists are the reverse. As the Figure 24.1 illustrates, perfectionism has come full circle and now reflects two sides of the same coin—in some cases detrimental, in others, beneficial.

Assessment of Perfectionism

Data from personality tests are most applicable to the ICF domains of Participation, Environmental Factors, and Personal Factors (Joyce & Rossen, 2008). The primary role of personality assessment in rehabilitation is to determine, if possible, premorbid and transient or other changes in one's traits as may affect adaptation during the rehabilitation process. Typically, personality characteristics

24.1

Common conceptual framework combining both dimensional and group-based conceptions of the two basic forms of perfectionism. Two basic dimensions of perfectionism are distinguished (perfectionistic strivings, perfectionistic concerns) and can be used to differentiate between groups of perfectionists (healthy perfectionists, unhealthy perfectionists, nonperfectionists).

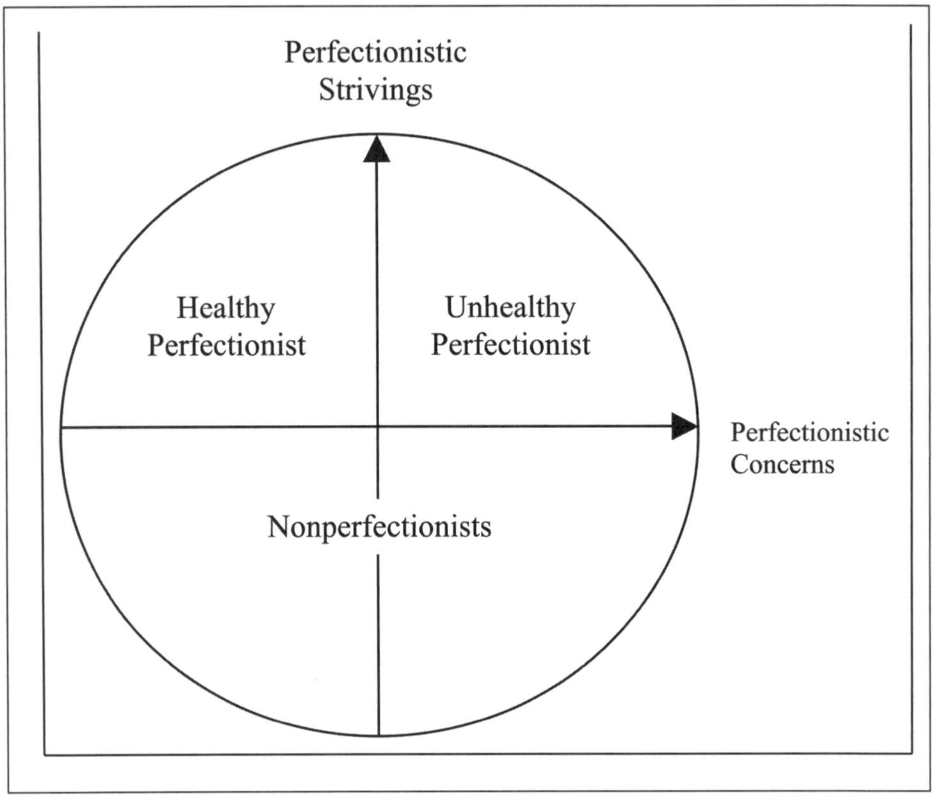

are considered relatively stable over time and exist within the person rather than the situation (Butcher, 1995). However, circumstances encountered by rehabilitative clients may result in brief or temporary changes in personality characteristics (e.g., elevated anxiety). These changes may be due to environmental stressors or cognitive impairments (Joyce & Rossen, 2008). More transient changes can indicate states of functioning rather than traits. To determine appropriate short-term and long-term rehabilitation interventions, therapists should consider whether observed behaviors reflect contextual states or stable traits of personality (Joyce & Rossen, 2008).

As mentioned, the detrimental effects of perfectionism have been a primary research focus of the past few decades. More recently, however, researchers have begun in earnest to explore the positive, or healthy, aspects associated with this personality trait. The variety of available models and measures require a clinician to determine which approach best suits his/her therapeutic objective. It is important to recognize that the study of perfectionism relies heavily on self-report questionnaires as its primary tool for generating quantifiable results.

In order to narrow the scope of choices, this section, of necessity, presents only five practical, self-report instruments that may be used for assessing perfectionism. Each reflects different perspectives of perfectionism. The focus and format of each measure is briefly introduced; including its theoretical origins. A discussion of the reliability and validity of each measurement follows. The perfectionism measures are presented in chronological order, beginning with one of the early clinically-based multidimensional measures and concluding with one of the most current and clinically promising assessment measures.

The assessment of perfectionism relies heavily on self-report questionnaires as its primary tool for generating quantifiable results. Several models and measures of perfectionism are available. A clinician should consider which approach best suits his/her therapeutic objective.

Self-Report Assessment Instruments

Dysfunctional Attitude Scale

The Dysfunctional Attitude Scale (DAS; Weissman & Beck, 1978; Weissman, 1979) assesses depressive symptoms associated with perfectionism. Predictive of depression years later, perfectionism may be a useful way to anticipate vulnerability to depression. Conversely, perfectionism has proven to be detrimental in the treatment of depression. Being cognizant of the client's degree and *type* of perfectionism can be helpful and may allow clinicians to focus initially on the treatment of depression.

Originally the DAS consisted of 100 items, but it has since been condensed into 2 parallel 40-item measures labeled as Form A and Form B. DAS Form A (DAS-A) is a two-factor, self report scale that measures *perfectionism* and the *need for social approval*. DAS items were generated using suggestions from practicing clinical psychologists to reflect patterns of maladaptive thinking and depressive ideation in particular. Participants are asked to rate how well they relate to each item on a 7-point Likert-type scale from *strongly disagree* to *strongly agree*. Examples of the items include: "If I fail at my work, then I am a failure as a person" (perfectionism), and "What other people think about me is very important" (need for social approval).

Extensive studies confirm the reliability and validity of DAS. Some provide evidence for the internal validity of DAS and its predictive validity in appropriately distinguishing perfectionism and vulnerability to depression (Dunkley et al., 2006; Floyd, Scogin, & Chaplin, 2004; Imber et al., 1990). The DAS has helped clinicians tap into symptoms of perfectionism that ultimately reflect maladaptive qualities, such as "high levels of daily stress (e.g., negative social interactions), avoidant coping, and negative perceptions of social support" (Dunkley et al., 2006, p. 113).

Sometimes the treatment of perfectionism prefaces treatment of other psychiatric disorders. Glover, Brown, Fairburn, and Shafran (2007) developed a cognitive-behavioral therapy focused on treating perfectionism in eating disorder clients. Three months after treatment, approximately 70% of participants showed signs of improvement for perfectionism. Dunkley et al. (2006) offered a more specific form of treatment, postulating that by "decreasing [perfectionists'] avoidant coping and negative social interactions, and increasing their perceptions of social support availability" (p. 113), vulnerability to later depressive symptoms may be greatly reduced.

Briefly, for those interested in work pertaining to children, D'Alessandro and Burton (2006) extended Beck's cognitive diathesis-stress theory in assessing vulnerability for depression in children. Using a sample of school-aged children between 8–14 years of age, D'Alessandro and Burton, present a shortened version of the Dysfunctional Attitudes Scale specifically for use with children (DAS-C). They conclude that assessing dysfunctional cognitions in children as young as 11 years may be of clinical interest worthy of further research.

Multidimensional Perfectionism Scale

The Multidimensional Perfectionism Scale (MPS; Hewitt & Flett, 1991b) consists of three dimensions of perfectionism: (1) self-oriented perfectionism (demanding perfection of oneself), (2) other-oriented perfectionism (demanding perfection of others), and (3) socially prescribed perfectionism (perception of others demanding perfection of oneself).

Based on considerable clinical experience, Hewitt and Flett theorized that interpersonal relationships contributed substantially to the regulation of personal standards and expectations, prompting the development of the MPS. The MPS began as a compilation of 122 potential items but was reduced to a 45-item self report measure. Participants are asked to rate how well they relate to each item on a 7-point Likert-style scale, ranging from (1) *strongly agree* to (7) *strongly disagree*. This assessment focuses on self-oriented perfectionism, other-oriented perfectionism, and socially prescribed perfectionism. Items on the MPS reflect the direction and origin of perfectionistic behavior. Examples include: "I must always be successful at school or work" (self-oriented perfectionism), "The people around me expect me to succeed at everything I do" (socially prescribed perfectionism), and "I do not have very high standards for those around me" (other-oriented perfectionism).

The MPS has been widely used and accepted. Numerous studies have replicated its dimensions across differing populations, and its convergent and discriminant validity has been well-documented (Hewitt & Flett, 1993). When used with clinical samples, the MPS retained its reliability and validity. Studies observing test–retest reliability in a clinical setting revealed slightly lower scores for psychiatric clients compared to those of the community, excluding socially prescribed perfectionism (Flett & Hewitt, 2002). This finding is consistent with previous studies that have found socially prescribed perfectionism to be positively correlated with maladaptive psychological symptoms. More specifically, socially prescribed perfectionism has been found to be associated with feelings of "hopelessness, helplessness, and loss of control that can lead to depression and suicide" (Blankstein & Winkworth, 2004, p. 273).

Flett, Besser, and Davis (2003) also found that all three perfectionism dimensions correlated negatively with unconditional self-acceptance. Those low in unconditional self-acceptance have higher levels of self-oriented, other-oriented, and socially prescribed perfectionism. Predictably, people reporting difficulty with self-acceptance typically endorse lower levels of self-esteem, higher levels of depression and anxiety, and a diminished sense of happiness and life satisfaction (Chamberlain & Haaga, 2001).

The discussion of self-acceptance is important for therapeutic reasons. It is the self-oriented perfectionism dimension that contains some adaptive qualities. This is the case because self-oriented perfectionism is characterized by two factors: *personal* perfectionistic strivings (rather than being predicated on the demands of others) and *acceptance* of nonperfection. Utilizing these criteria, different categories of self-oriented perfectionism can be generated. Positive perfectionism reflects the category of perfectionists who (a) strive for perfection and (b) are able to accept nonperfection. Negative perfectionism, on the other hand, reflects the category of perfectionists who (a) strive for perfection and (b) are unable to accept nonperfection. Lundh also identifies a third nonperfectionist category of people. By recognizing which category reflects a client's predominant cognitive style, or range of behaviors, a therapist is better equipped to assist in the treatment process (Lundh, 2004).

Other-oriented perfectionism works in a parallel way. Despite a paucity of experimental evidence, other-acceptance is thought to be associated with other-oriented perfectionism to the extent that acceptance or, inversely, one's degree of expectation (and lack of acceptance) is imposed on another person. For example, if person A provides unconditional acceptance to person B despite some failure on the part of person B, then person B may be more apt to develop a robust degree of self-acceptance. It is important to note that these theoretical assumptions should be explored further using experimental means (Lundh, 2004).

The differing MPS dimensions of perfectionism have been explored extensively. Recent studies have revealed a connection between perfectionism and attributional style. Attributions can reveal a perfectionist's tendency to blame certain factors for his/her failures; particularly important is the loci of the attribution—that is, either internal or external. Socially prescribed perfectionists tend to attribute negative events internally to a lack of personal control. These findings may also contain therapeutic implications. By recognizing a person's perception of causal factors as well as his/her type of perfectionism, a therapist is better prepared to address these attributions and associated cognitions. This approach may enable the client to better accept events with respect to their appropriate causal factors, thus stimulating feelings of control over the occurrence (Blankstein & Winkworth, 2004; Burns et al., 2000).

Almost Perfect Scale

The Almost Perfect Scale (APS; Slaney, Ashby, & Trippi, 1995) contains four dimensions of perfectionism that assess elevated personal standards and orderliness (Standards and Order), struggles in interpersonal relationships (Relationships), struggles with procrastination (Procrastination), and struggles with anxiety (Anxiety). The Standards and Order dimension is intended to assess adaptive perfectionistic behavior; the other three (Relationships, Procrastination, and Anxiety) are aimed at assessing maladaptive perfectionistic behavior (Slaney, Rice, & Ashby, 2002).

According to Slaney et al. (1995), the APS began as a collection of 62 items intended to measure the existence of the four dimensions of perfectionism and how it was condensed into a 32-item self-report measure. Participants are asked to rate how well they relate to each item on a 7-point Likert-type scale ranging from (1) *strongly agree* to (7) *strongly disagree*. Example items include: "I like to always be organized and disciplined" (Standards and Order), "I feel uncomfortable in intimate relationships" (Relationships), "I tend to put things off for as long as I can" (Procrastination), and "I often feel anxious when I strive to complete a task" (Anxiety; Slaney et al., 2002).

Studies examining the reliability and validity of the initial APS revealed various limitations, which prompted a revision of the APS. For example, several items within the Relationship dimension lacked significant face validity because several of the items failed to discriminate between perfectionism and nonperfectionism, as well as adaptive and maladaptive perfectionism (Johnson & Slaney, 1996). As a result, Slaney, Mobley, Trippi, Ashby, and Johnson (1996) developed a preliminary revised version of the APS, and a fully revised version appeared in 2001 (APS-R; Slaney, Rice, Mobley, Trippi, & Ashby, 2001).

The APS-R consists of three (not four) dimensions measuring the "perceived discrepancy between one's standards and one's actual performance" (p. 629); these include: High Standards, Order, and Discrepancy (Mobley, Slaney, & Rice, 2005). Examples of the 23-item measure include "I expect the best from myself" (High Standards), "I like to always be organized and disciplined" (Order), and "I rarely live up to my high standards" (Discrepancy).

While the dimensions High Standards and Order intend to measure the adaptive qualities of perfectionism, the Discrepancy dimension intends to measure the maladaptive qualities. Several studies have found that higher scores on the Discrepancy dimension reflect maladaptive perfectionism (Rice & Slaney, 2002).

Studies using the APS-R have demonstrated its reliability and validity. The internal consistency has been found to be relatively high, and when compared with other instruments for measuring perfectionism, the APS-R retained its concurrent validity (Slaney et al., 2001). Cultural validity has also been established in a series of interesting studies including participants of various cultures and ethnicities (Mobley et al., 2005; Wang, Slaney, & Rice, 2006).

Positive and Negative Perfectionism Scale

The Positive and Negative Perfectionism (PNP; Terry-Short et al., 1995) Scale contains two primary subscales drawn from: (1) positive perfectionism (behavior associated with positive reinforcement), (2) personal perfectionism (striving to meet personally set goals), (3) negative perfectionism (behavior associated with negative reinforcement), and (4) socially prescribed perfectionism (the perception of others setting goals for oneself). Terry-Short et al. generated the PNP as a function of Skinner's (1968) learning theory based on positive and negative reinforcement. Accordingly, the PNP assumes that perfectionistic behavior resulting from positive reinforcement is adaptive, and the avoidance of negative reinforcement is maladaptive. Hence, it assesses both the positive and negative aspects of perfectionism (Terry-Short et al., 1995).

Terry-Short et al.'s PNP scale is composed, in part, using items drawn from Hewitt and Flett's (1991a) MPS: self-oriented perfectionism and socially prescribed perfectionism. As a result, each dimension consists of 20 items—10 measuring positive perfectionism and 10 measuring negative perfectionism. When completing the 40-item assessment, participants are asked to rate how well they relate to each item on a 5-point Likert-type scale ranging from (1) *strongly disagree* to (5) *strongly agree*. Examples of the items include: "Producing a perfect performance is a reward in its own right" (self-oriented, positive perfectionism), and "I gain great approval from others by the quality of my accomplishments" (socially prescribed, positive perfectionism). These items further reflect the dual process model of perfectionism (Slade & Owens, 1998), which advances the premise that while the observable behavior of positive and negative perfectionists may seem indistinguishable, the latent motivations differ, as well as the emotional, psychological, and even physical consequences for the two types of perfectionists.

Despite its relatively recent development, several studies have provided support for the validity of the PNP. Work using the PNP supports the assumption that there exists two distinguishable types of perfectionism, both positive and negative, and that they differ in cognitive and behavioral processes (Bergman et al., 2007; Burns & Fedewa, 2005). Support for the dual process model has also been found with clinical and nonclinical participants (Terry-Short et al., 1995), as well as athletes and individuals suffering from an eating disorder (Slade & Owens, 1998).

The therapeutic implications of the dual process model of perfectionism center on cognitive-behavioral therapy. More explicitly, individuals driven by the avoidance of negative reinforcers can be exposed to the feared possibility of failure while being given positive feedback despite this perceived failure. Therapists should focus on the overall enhancement of self-esteem. As for those individuals driven by the hope for success, a decision about the necessity of treatment may be made depending on the overt behavior exhibited by the individual. Although positive perfectionism has primarily healthy motivations, this is not always the case. For example, individuals suffering from an eating disorder may be characterized by a desire for thinness. In cases such as these, a therapist should challenge the individual's ideal body size, while also exploring other means of reinforcement (Slade & Owens, 1998).

Performance Perfectionism Scale

The Performance Perfectionism Scale (PPS; Chang, 2006) is an assessment tool that offers a clinically useful, theoretically rigorous measure of positive and negative perfectionism, predicated on specific sets of outcome cognitions in response to imposed standards of performance. *Performance perfectionism* is defined as "high standards of performance involving positive and negative outcome cognitions" (Chang, 2006, p. 679). Similar to Terry-Short et al. (1995), Chang's model contrasts two orthogonal dimensions of perfectionism—the self versus others (as sources of high standards) and adaptive versus maladaptive outcome cognitions. This produces a total of four quadrants of performance perfectionism: positive self-oriented performance perfectionism (high performance standards placed on oneself concerning positive outcome cognitions), negative self-oriented performance perfectionism (high performance standards placed on oneself concerning negative outcome cognitions), positive socially prescribed performance perfectionism (high performance standards placed on oneself by others and concerning positive outcome cognitions), and negative socially prescribed performance perfectionism (high performance standards placed on oneself by others and concerning negative outcome cognitions).

Chang's PPS began as a pool of 143 items compiled by graduate students and faculty members experienced in the study of perfectionism. After extensive revision of the items, a series of studies were conducted by Chang in order to isolate the items that resulted in the most functional assessment of performance perfectionism. This produced a 32-item measure accounting for both positive and negative aspects of performance perfectionism predicated upon attendant outcome cognitions and behavior. When completing the PPS, participants are asked to rate how well they relate to each item on a 5-point Likert-style scale ranging from (1) *extremely untrue of me* to (5) *extremely true of me*. Examples of the items include: "It is because of my high standards that I have accomplished many great things" (positive self-oriented performance perfectionism), "When I try to meet my high standards, my work suffers" (negative self-oriented performance perfectionism), "My performance is always made better when others expect more from me" (positive socially prescribed performance perfectionism), and "My work suffers when others push me to meet their high standards" (negative socially prescribed performance perfectionism).

Initial studies have been quite promising and offer support concerning convergent and discriminant validity of the PPS. Although results were obtained from college students at a large midwestern university, preliminary findings suggest a high degree of consistency among the items, good test–retest reliability, meaningful association with differing personality traits and psychological functioning, and the capacity to predict academic performance. Replication and further examination of the PPS is necessary. Chang (2006) has identified several important cross-cultural considerations, particularly insights regarding treatment issues and perfectionism.

Comment

Although several treatment implications for perfectionism were suggested throughout this section, there are no established treatments as of yet (Glover et al., 2007). Our conclusions and suggestions are strictly preliminary and are in need of future research. Perfectionism, in specific, and personality, in general, as they pertain to health and rehabilitation, reflect a youthful and vibrant area of theoretical and clinical work of interest to a wide audience, including aspiring and experienced clinicians (Joyce & Rossen, 2008).

Critical Research Issues in the Assessment of Perfectionism

Several treatment suggestions have been presented in this chapter, but further research must be conducted to investigate their utility. Self-report assessments of perfectionism are diagnostically effective, but to better assist clinicians in treating clients with perfectionism, generalized treatment standards may be beneficial. This section presents several critical issues concerning the assessment and treatment of perfectionism.

There are various issues regarding the assessment of perfectionism. The first major issue is the lack of unity in the terminology. Although most researchers are in agreement that perfectionism has both positive or healthy and negative or unhealthy characteristics, there are several differing labels, including: positive striving and maladaptive evaluation concerns (Frost, Heimberg, Holt, Mattia, & Neubauer, 1993), active and passive perfectionism (Adkins & Parker, 1996), positive and negative perfectionism (Terry-Short et al., 1995), adaptive and maladaptive perfectionism (Rice, Ashby, & Slaney, 1998), functional and dysfunctional perfectionism (Rhéaume et al., 2000), healthy and unhealthy perfectionism (Stumpf & Parker, 2000), personal standards and evaluative concerns perfectionism (Blankstein & Dunkley, 2002), conscientious and self-evaluative perfectionism (Hill et al., 2004), and healthy and unhealthy, or perfectionistic striving and perfectionistic concerns (Stoeber & Otto, 2006).

A second major concern in the assessment of perfectionism is the discrepancy in conceptualizations that address the two aspects. Along with the different labels, researchers have also identified different dimensions, or subcategories, of perfectionism (Stoeber & Otto, 2006). For example, although Frost et al. (1990) and Hewitt and Flett (1991b) each developed a multidimensional perfectionism scale, Frost et al. (1990) identified the following dimensions for their measure: concern over mistakes, doubts about actions, personal standards, parental expectations, parental criticism, and organization. Hewitt and Flett (1991b) identified the following three dimensions for their measure: self-oriented, other-oriented, and socially prescribed perfectionism. These two scales have been used extensively despite the fact that perfection as assessed by each measure is conceptually quite different. This is just one example of the lack of consensus in the field at the present time.

Thirdly, as mentioned earlier, research has usually been based on one of two approaches when studying perfectionism. Generally the case has been that either a dimensional approach or a categorical, group-based approach is used. The dimensional approach assesses individuals on a continuum, with a person possibly endorsing none to significant amounts of some specific aspect of perfectionism—such as self-oriented or socially prescribed perfectionism. Alternately, the categorical approach simply tries to differentiate between groups, for instance, dichotomously identifying people as being perfectionistic or not. Stoeber and Otto (2006) bridge these two theoretical approaches by utilizing both theoretical approaches. Their model juxtaposes one's degree of "perfectionistic strivings" with one's degree of "perfectionistic concerns." Using these as orthogonal dimensions, Stoeber and Otto are then able to identify three subsequent categories: high striving and low concerns, or "healthy perfectionism"; high striving and high concerns, or "unhealthy perfectionism"; and those low on both, or "nonperfectionists." While unanimity is not always indicative of theoretical cohesion, currently the study of perfectionism is clearly preparadigmatic. It is also the case that low levels of perfectionistic concerns, in tandem with high perfectionistic strivings, (i.e., healthy perfectionism), have not been found to be exclusively correlated with positive characteristics.

Nonetheless, this dimensional pattern remains definitive of positive perfectionism (Stoeber & Otto, 2006).

A final significant drawback regarding the assessment of perfectionism is observed in the simple fact that the field is based almost exclusively on self-report measures. This poses a possible limitation. It is plausible that people may not be fully aware of the intensity of their perfectionistic tendencies, or they may downplay or deny them. One promising alternative method of assessment may be the use of an interview-based measure of perfectionism. Thus far, its use has been sparse, but the Interview for Perfectionistic Behavior (IPB) may serve in this capacity. The IPB is loosely structured, and measures the degree to which participants relate to items that describe cognitions, such as a need to be perfect, a fear of mistakes, satisfaction with performance, and so forth. This interview assessment is highly reflective of Hewitt and Flett's (1991b) multidimensional model and their MPS (Hewitt, Flett, Flynn, & Neilsen, 1995). Preliminary results suggest high reliability and validity (Cockell et al., 2002). Cockell et al.'s findings highlight a few benefits of using interview assessments, the most significant being that they may identify heightened perfectionism more accurately than self-report measures. At the same time, impression management is one potential drawback using an interview-based assessment measure. Importantly, the IPB may allow for the option of verbally assessing one's degree of perfectionism, especially in situations involving injury or other functional limitation to the extent that only verbal, as opposed to written assessment, is viable.

Originally, perfectionism was characterized as a strictly maladaptive quality. Progress in the field has indicated that specific types of perfectionist cognitions can facilitate beneficial outcomes, as well. Despite this, the question remains concerning which multidimensional approach is most indicative of perfectionism. The future of perfectionism research lies in the hope for convergent terminology, dimensions, and assessment measures, which may lead to a more systemized understanding of the construct. Meeting these objectives may also yield person-specific cognitive-behavioral treatment protocols.

Cultural, Legislative, or Professional Issues That Impact the Specific Counseling Aspects or Procedures

Mpofu (2002) outlines a thoughtful series of potential benefits associated with the inclusion of culture as a focus of psychological inquiry. Such work meaningfully informs rehabilitation practice, education, and research. Surprisingly, even when assessment focuses on a single construct and various international parties agree on similar terminology, Oakland, Mpofu, Grégoire, and Faulkner (2007) indicate that many cultural difficulties may still arise. Many of these cross-cultural issues are also acknowledged as assessment concerns affecting research and clinical practice within the United States (see also Mpofu et al., 2004), particularly as relates to people with disabilities and minority status (Mpofu & Conyers, 2004, see also Wyatt & Gilbert, 1998). Chang and Banks (2007) conclude that more research is clearly needed "before we can draw definitive implications for cultivating agentic and pathways thinking across and within different racial/ethnic groups" (p. 101).

Generally speaking, negative perfectionism is a detrimental personality trait for people of other cultures, and conversely, positive or adaptive perfectionism is of benefit. Sumi and Kanda (2002) found neurotic perfectionism to be a significant predictor of depression and psychosomatic symptoms in Japanese male college students. According to Castro and Rice (2003), perfectionism explained significant variance in depressive symptoms and cumulative grade point averages for Asian and African Americans. Chang (1998) found that Asian Americans were generally more perfectionistic than Caucasian Americans. While empirical work is limited, the past decade has certainly seen an increase in the focus on culturally-based psychological research. Recent findings related to negative perfectionism offer some useful clinical insights and provide clear and specific suggestions for future research.

Gilman, Ashby, Sverko, Florell, and Varjas (2005), in a sample of Croatian youth, found that similar to American youth, adaptive perfectionists reported higher levels of satisfaction across many life domains. Both de Jonge and Waller (2003) and Mobley et al. (2005) report positive findings related to the cultural validity of multidimensional measures of perfectionism in samples of African American students (see also, Watkins, Akande, & Mpofu, 1996).

Discussion Box 24.2

WHAT IS PERFECTIONISM ANYWAY?

What is perfectionism anyway? Some authors have questioned whether living in a Western culture is synonymous with perfectionistic expectations. Such expectations, overt or tacit, are ubiquitous in the media—these range from advertisers telling us what we're supposed to eat, or how we're supposed to look, to what supposedly constitutes a "perfect" lifestyle or relationship. While we may scoff and claim that we're not influenced by (these) unrealistic media depictions, when was the last time you deliberately bought an apple with a bruise in it? When was the last time you thought to thank your automobile mechanic for a less-than-perfect repair to your car? Extending this logic, some of our mainstream social expectations imply that *people* with disabilities are themselves flawed rather than placing the notion of failure on the environment. In fact, some have suggested that being a person with a disability makes people feel like anything they do must be twice as good as what anyone else might do.

Questions:
Do you feel our culture encourages making snap character judgments of people based on physical characteristics? Why or why not? Can you think of examples that affirm or dispute this characterization of Western culture?

These findings are encouraging and consistent with Mpofu's (2002) observations that such work adds to the richness and global relevance of psychology.

Multidisciplinary or Interdisciplinary Approaches

A major limitation regarding perfectionism has to do with the current lack of research related to persons with disabilities. As mentioned previously, there have been various studies examining perfectionism and correlates with psychological health issues such as optimism and pessimism, positive and negative affect, high and low self-esteem, and the likelihood of developing psychological disorders, such as depression, anxiety, or eating disorders. Very few studies have examined perfectionism, coping behavior, and treatment outcomes for persons with functional diversity. One promising area of study for future research may involve the study of perfectionism and attributions. While positive perfectionism may serve as a buffer, adding resiliency to individuals confronted with the need for rehabilitation, this section concentrates exclusively on attributions of distress and blame. It offers guidance to those interested in investigating the overall effects of perfectionism on injury and rehabilitation.

Negative perfectionism has been found to not only instigate the development of depression but also to hinder the course of treatment (Dunkley et al., 2006). Persons dealing with functional diversity are more susceptible to psychological disorders such as depression and/or anxiety. Individuals may experience these disorders for various reasons, including pain, physical limitations, lifestyle changes, or stigma due to injury, disease, or impairment. Understanding a particular client's attribution, or attributions, in specific can be an important consideration in facilitating treatment and personal well-being in the client. For example, if a client claims to be depressed or anxious due to pain, plausibly, treatment would include consideration of pain-relieving medications; however, the role of personal factors, for example, perfectionism, can be considerable. Conversely, if a client claims that limitations to physical activity are at the core of his/her depressed or anxious feelings, a likely treatment choice might start with consideration of negative outcome cognitions, including perfectionism, along with a focus on teaching the client to complete tasks in a new way (Schröder et al., 2007).

Also worth taking into consideration is a client's attribution of blame. According to DeGood and Kiernan (1996), "perception, or attribution, of blame is an important element in the pain behavior of some clients and may contribute to a poor response to treatment" (p. 159). Following their study on clients with chronic pain, they found that when compared to clients who reported no source of blame, those who believed that the pain was the result of someone else's mistake reported significantly greater distress, significantly lower anticipated gain from treatment, and significantly greater negative outcomes from treatments in the past. They inferred that when a client focuses on attributing blame, he/she is less likely to develop the emotional and cognitive skills necessary when coping with chronic pain (DeGood & Kiernan, 1996). This discussion of internal and external causes resembles that of Hewitt and Flett's self-oriented and socially prescribed perfectionism in the sense that, depending on a person's source of perfectionistic strivings, treatment of psychological distress may be

Research Box 24.1

PATIENT ATTRIBUTIONS: THE ROLE OF BLAME ATTRIBUTIONS AND SUBJECTIVE WELL-BEING

Hart, T., Hanks, R., Bogner, J. A., Millis, S., & Esselman, P. E. (2007). Blame attribution in intentional and unintentional traumatic brain injury: Longitudinal changes and impact on subjective well-being. *Rehabilitation Psychology, 52,* 152–161.

Objectives: This study was designed to examine longitudinal changes in the attributions of blame (to self or other) in both intentional (violence-related) and unintentional (accidental) traumatic brain injury (TBI) and how these attributions related to subjective well-being at 1-year postinjury.

Method: This longitudinal study used a prospective, observational design, including 124 men admitted to the in-client rehabilitation units of four collaborating TBI Model System (TBIMS) centers. The sample included 99 men with unintentional TBI and 25 men with intentional TBI who sustained moderate to severe injury. Measures of blame attribution, general health, neurobehavioral functioning, depression, satisfaction with life, and community participation were included.

Results: At both time points, participants with intentional TBI blamed others more, while those with unintentional TBI blamed themselves more. Other-blame at 1 year predicted depression but not life satisfaction. Increasing concern over cause/blame from acute rehabilitation to follow-up was associated with high levels of emotional distress.

Conclusion: Blame attribution issues may be markers of TBI-related emotional distress regardless of injury etiology, particularly when others are blamed for the injury and/or concerns over cause of injury do not resolve over time.

Questions:
Discuss different causes of injury and your observations of (possible) differences in how people cope based on the cause of the injury. Do you think people are typically more inclined to view injury as a fault of others' behavior (e.g., reckless driving) versus accidental injury (e.g., kicked by a horse) or accidental self-harm (e.g., diving into a shallow river or quarry)? Why might the origin of the injury play a role in recovery? In certain cases, is it possible that the injury itself is obscured by diminished capacity or levels of self-awareness? What aspects of a person's premorbid personality might serve a beneficial function postinjury?

Discussion Box 24.3

CAN PREMORBID PERSONALITY TRAITS INFLUENCE RECOVERY AND ADJUSTMENT?

Due to technological advances in body armor and the speedy transfer of injured personnel to hospital care, recent reports suggest that almost half the surviving casualties in the Iraq war suffer from various degrees of traumatic brain injury (TBI). Given the relative youth of this cohort and innovative medical treatments both in the field and in the hospital in comparison to previous wars, more and more of our surviving soldiers will be placed in-home or in community care of some sort.

Questions:
From what you've heard or read about the predominant types of injury, do you feel perfectionism, from caregivers or from those recovering from these types of injuries, will play a role in recovery and rehabilitation? Given the initial significant life-saving success, do you feel rehabilitative efforts will mirror these improvements? Are there other premorbid personality traits you feel will be equally or more important than perfectionism?

more, or less, responsive to treatment. The same could be true for individuals with an acute injury or chronic impairment.

As noted, personality traits, including negative perfectionism, can affect the treatment process and outcome of depression (Blatt, Quinlan, Pilkonis, & Shea, 1995). These findings give rise to questions concerning personality traits, specifically perfectionism, and its affects on the coping behavior and treatment of physical disability. Physical disability can increase the likelihood of developing a psychological disorder such as depression and/or anxiety. Negative perfectionism, too, increases the likelihood of experiencing depression and/or anxiety. Predictably, the comorbidity of these two would most likely result in a prolonged course of rehabilitation.

According to Bandura (1997), control cognitions affect both effort and achievement (Schröder et al., 2007). This finding suggests that if a client does not feel in control of his/her injury or treatment outcome, he/she may put forth less effort and, therefore, achieve fewer rehabilitation goals. For example, unexpected limitations in activity may lower a person's efficacy, generating feelings of inadequacy in coping with or overcoming his/her condition (Schröder et al., 2007). For this reason, it is important that clients be offered both cognitive and emotional treatment in order to enhance their physical rehabilitation.

Although this section has focused largely on the detrimental effects of perfectionism on the outcome of rehabilitation, it should be noted that there are positive aspects as well. In fact, a significant correlation between positive perfectionism and coping behaviors has been found. This effect may be related to the task-oriented characteristic of self-oriented perfectionism, which was correlated with conscientiousness and efficacy. "By taking steps to engage their problems actively and to distract themselves in emotionally healthy ways, positive perfectionists, appear to be more tolerant and effective, instead of ruminating about their problems or misfortunes" (Burns & Fedewa, 2005, p. 110).

Summary

As noted vis-à-vis this chapter and others in this section of the text, assessment is, in large part, determined by etiological premises and treatment objectives. Underlying assumptions of a given theoretical model will inevitably guide its assessment design and format. Albrecht and Devlieger (1999) emphasize the importance of "establishing and maintaining a harmonious set of relationships within the person's social context and external environment," especially to the extent that one's quality of life is, "dependent upon finding a balance between body, mind, and spirit" (p. 977). At the present time, there is no single "correct" way to assess perfectionism. Taylor, Thordarson, and Söchting (2002) conclude, "A useful method is one that provides a systematic way of developing a model of the causes and cures of the client's problems" (p. 210). More research is needed to build upon the present findings so that we may better and more fully appreciate the many causes, correlates, and consequences linking the ICF Personal Factors to rehabilitation and indices of health within our diverse and changing society.

We offer one final caveat concerning the role of feedback in the assessment process. This important aspect of assessment is often overlooked. A central question to be asked is: How can one share the results of any particular assessment beneficially? Smith, Wiggins, and Gorske (2007) indicate that "[psychologists] who spend more time conducting feedback sessions were more likely to indicate positive effects, particularly as with regard to facilitating a collaborative working dialogue" (p. 316). And, as Stocker (2001) notes, "I want for my students, as I want for myself, engagement with theory that is liberating, not dissociated with life" (p. 169). Understanding that perfectionism can be either dysfunctional or beneficial is helpful in construing personal striving, acceptance, and recovery. It also provides a useful context for students, practitioners, and persons in the process of rehabilitation, namely, that of lifting better up to best.

Acknowledgment

The authors would like to thank Jacobus Donders, PhD, Psychology Department Mary Free Bed Hospital, and Barbara J. Palombi, PhD, ABPP, Director, Counseling and Career Center, Grand Valley State University for generously providing the excellent case studies presented in this chapter. We would also like to thank Lee Doyle and Dr. Mary Bower-Russa for their insightful comments and constructive criticisms of an earlier draft of this chapter.

References

Adkins, K. K., & Parker, W. D. (1996). Perfectionism and suicidal preoccupation. *Journal of Personality, 64*, 529–543.

Albrecht, G. L., & Devlieger, P. J. (1999). The disability paradox: high quality of life against all odds. *Social Science & Medicine, 48,* 977–988.

Andersson, G., Airikka, M., Buhrman, M., & Kaldo, V. (2005). Dimensions of perfectionism and tinnitus distress. *Psychology, Health, & Medicine, 10,* 78–87.

Bandura, A. (1997). *Self-efficacy: The exercise of control.* New York: W.H. Freeman/Times Books/ Henry Holt & Co.

Bergman, A. J., Nyland, J. E., & Burns, L. R. (2007). Correlates with perfectionism and the utility of a dual process model. *Personality and Individual Differences, 43,* 389–399.

Bieling, P. J., Israeli, A. L., & Antony, M. M. (2004). Is perfectionism good, bad, or both? Examining models of the perfectionism construct. *Personality and Individual Differences, 36,* 1373–1385.

Blais, M. C., & Boisvert, J. (2007). Psychological adjustment and marital satisfaction following head injury. Which critical personal characteristics should both partners develop? *Brain Injury, 21,* 357–372.

Blankstein, K. R., & Dunkley, D. M. (2002). Evaluative concerns, self-critical, and personal standards perfectionism: A structural equation modeling strategy. In G. L. Flett & P. L. Hewitt (Eds.), *Perfectionism, theory, research, and treatment* (pp. 285–315). Washington, DC: American Psychological Association.

Blankstein, K. R., Lumley, C. H., & Crawford, A. (2007). Perfectionism, hopelessness, and suicide ideation: Revisions to diathesis-stress and specific vulnerability models. *Journal of Rational-Emotive & Cognitive-Behavior Therapy, 25,* 279–319.

Blankstein, K. R., & Winkworth, G. R. (2004). Dimensions of perfectionism and levels of attributions for grades: relations with dysphoria and academic performance. *Journal of Rational-Emotive & Cognitive-Behavioral Therapy, 22,* 271–299.

Blatt, S. J., Quinlan, D. M., Pilkonis, P. A., & Shea, M. T. (1995). Impact of perfectionism and need for approval on the brief treatment of depression: The National Institute of Mental Health Treatment of Depression collaborative Research Program revisited. *Journal of Consulting and Clinical Psychology, 63,* 125–132.

Brown, G. P., & Beck, A. T. (2002). Dysfunctional attitudes, perfectionism, and models of vulnerability to depression. In G. L. Flett & P. L. Hewitt (Eds.), *Perfectionism, theory, research, and treatment* (pp. 231–251). Washington, DC: American Psychological Association.

Bruyère, S. M., Van Looy, S. A., & Peterson, D. B. (2005). The International Classification of Functioning, Disability, and Health: Contemporary literature overview. *Rehabilitation Psychology, 50,* 113–121.

Burns, D. (1980, November). The perfectionist's script for self-defeat. *Psychology Today,* 34–51.

Burns, L. R., Dittman, K., Nguyen, N., & Mitchelson, J. K. (2000). Academic procrastination, perfectionism, and control: Associations with vigilant and avoidant coping. In J. R. Ferrari & T. A. Pychyl (Eds.), Procrastination: Current issues and new directions (Special Issue). *Journal of Social Behavior and Personality, 15,* 35–46.

Burns, L. R., & Fedewa, B. A. (2005). Cognitive styles: Links with perfectionistic thinking. *Personality and Individual Differences, 38,* 103–113.

Burns, L. R., Selke, K., Stein, R. J., & Poston, W.S.C. (2002). Taking the body into account. In N. D. Sundberg, A. A. Winebarger, & J. R. Taplin (Eds.), *Clinical psychology: Evolving theory, practice, and research* (pp. 330–365). Upper Saddle River, NJ: Prentice Hall.

Butcher, J. N. (1995). *Clinical personality assessment: Practical approaches.* New York: Oxford.

Castro, J. R., & Rice, K. G. (2003). Perfectionism and ethnicity: Implications for depressive symptoms and self-reported academic achievement. *Cultural Diversity and Ethnic Minority Psychology, 9,* 64–78.

Chamberlain, J. D., & Haaga, D.A.F. (2001). Unconditional self-acceptance and psychological health. *Journal of Rational-Emotive & Cognitive-Behavioral Therapy, 19,* 163–176.

Chang, E. C. (1998). Cultural differences, perfectionism, and suicidal risk in a college population: Does social problem solving still matter? *Cognitive Therapy and Research, 22,* 237–254.

Chang, E. C. (2006). Conceptualization and measurement of adaptive and maladaptive aspects of performance perfectionism: Relations to personality, psychological functioning, and academic achievement. *Cognitive Therapy and Research, 30,* 677–697.

Chang, E. C., & Banks, K. H. (2007). The color and texture of hope: Some preliminary findings and implications for Hope Theory and counseling among diverse racial/ethnic groups. *Cultural Diversity and Ethnic Minority Psychology, 13,* 94–103.

Cockell, S. J., Hewitt, P. L., Seal, B., Sherry, S., Goldner, E. M., Flett, G. L., et al. (2002). Trait and self-presentational dimensions of perfectionism among women with anorexia nervosa. *Cognitive Therapy and Research, 26,* 745–758.

Cohen, S., & Rodriguez, M. S. (1995). Pathways linking affective disturbances and physical disorders. *Health Psychology, 14,* 374–380.

D'Alessandro, D. U., & Burton, K. D. (2006). Development and validation of the Dysfunctional Attitudes Scale for children: Tests of Beck's cognitive diathesis-stress theory of depression, of its causal mediation component, and of developmental effects. *Cognitive Therapy and Research, 30,* 335–353.

Deaton, A. V. (1998). Treating conversion disorders: Is a pediatric rehabilitation hospital the place? *Rehabilitation Psychology, 43,* 56–62.

DeGood, D. E., & Kiernan, B., (1996). Perceptions of fault in clients with chronic pain. *Pain, 64,* 153–159.

de Jonge, L. van Hanswick, & Waller, G. (2003). Perfectionism levels in African-American and Caucasian adolescents. *Personality and Individual Differences, 34,* 1447–1451.

Dominic, G. S., Brown, G. P., Fairburn, C. G., & Shafran, R. (2007). A preliminary evaluation of cognitive-behaviour therapy for clinical perfectionism: A case series. *British Journal of Clinical Psychology, 46*(1), 85–94.Dunkley, D. M., Sanislow, C. A., Grilo, C. M., & McGlashan, T. H. (2006). Perfectionism and depressive symptoms 3 years later: Negative social interactions, avoidant coping, and perceived social support as mediators. *Comprehensive Psychiatry, 47,* 106–115.Emerson, W. E. (Ed.) (1918). *The collected works of Ralph Waldo Emerson.* Boston: Houghton, Mifflin Company.

Flett, G. L., & Hewitt, P. L. (2002). Perfectionism and Maladjustment: An overview of theoretical, definitional, and treatment issues. In G. L. Flett & P. L. Hewitt (Eds.), *Perfectionism, theory, research, and treatment* (pp. 5–31). Washington, DC: American Psychological Association.

Flett, G. L., Besser, A., & Davis, R. A. (2003). Dimensions of perfectionism, unconditional self-acceptance, and depression. *Journal of Rational-Emotive & Cognitive-Behavior Therapy, 21,* 119–138.

Floyd, M., Scogin, F., & Chaplin, W. F. (2004). The Dysfunctional Attitudes Scale: Factor structure, reliability, and validity with older adults. *Aging & Mental Health, 8,* 153–160.

Frost, R. O., Heimberg, R. G., Holt, C. S., Mattia, J. I., & Neubauer, A. L. (1993). A comparison of two measures of perfectionism. *Personality and Individual Differences, 14,* 119–126.

Frost, R. O., Marten, P., Lahart, C. M., & Rosenblate, R. (1990). The dimensions of perfectionism. *Cognitive Therapy and Research, 14,* 449–468.

Gatchel, R. J., Peng, Y. B., Peters, M. L., Fuchs, P. N., & Turk, D. C. (2007). The biopsychosocial approach to chronic pain: Scientific advances and future directions. *Psychological Bulletin, 133,* 581–624.

Geyh, S., Cieza, A., Kollerits, B., Grimby, G., & Stucki, G. (2007). Content comparison of health-related quality of life measures used in stroke based on the International Classification of Functioning, Disability and Health (ICF): A systematic review. *Quality of Life Research, 16,* 833–851.

Gilman, R., Ashby, J. S., Sverko, D., Florell, D., & Varjas, K. (2005). The relationship between perfectionism and multidimensional life satisfaction among Croatian and American youth. *Personality and Individual Differences, 39,* 155–166.

Glover, D. S., Brown, G. P., Fairburn, C. G., & Shafran, R. (2007). A preliminary evaluation of cognitive-behavioral therapy for clinical perfectionism: A case series. *British Journal of Clinical Psychology, 46,* 85–94.

Hadjistavropoulos, H., Dash, H., Hadjistavropoulos, T., & Sullivan, T. (2007). Recurrent pain among university students: Contributions of self-efficacy and perfectionism to the pain experience. *Personality and Individual Differences, 42,* 1081–1091.

Hamachek, D. E. (1978). Psychodynamics of normal and neurotic perfectionism. *Psychology, 15,* 27–33.

Hart, T., Hanks, R., Bogner, J. A., Millis, S., & Esselman, P. E. (2007). Blame attribution in intentional and unintentional traumatic brain injury: Longitudinal changes and impact on subjective well-being. *Rehabilitation Psychology, 52,* 152–161.

Hewitt, P. L., & Flett, G. L. (1991a). Dimensions of perfectionism in unipolar depression. *Journal of Abnormal Psychology, 100,* 98–101.

Hewitt, P. L., & Flett, G. L. (1991b). Perfectionism in the self and social contexts: conception, assessment, and association with psychopathology. *Journal of Personality and Social Psychology, 60,* 456–470.

Hewitt, P. L., & Flett, G. L. (1993). Dimensions of perfectionism, daily stress, and depression: A test of the specific vulnerability issue. *Journal of Abnormal Psychology, 102,* 58–65.

Hewitt, P. L., Flett, G. L., Flynn, C., & Nielsen, A. (1995). Development and validation of an interview measure of perfectionistic behaviour. *Canadian Psychology, 36,* 223.

Hill, R. W., Huelsman, T. J., Furr, R. M., Kibler, J., Vicente, B. B., & Kennedy, C. (2004). A new measure of perfectionism: The Perfectionism Inventory. *Journal of Personality Assessment, 82,* 80–91.

Hollender, M. H. (1978). Perfectionism, a neglected personality trait. *Journal of Clinical Psychiatry, 39,* 384.

Horney, K. (1950). *Neurosis and human growth.* New York: Norton.

Hwang, K., Johnston, M., & Smith, J. K. (2007). Romantic attachment in individuals with physical disabilities. *Rehabilitation Psychology, 52,* 184–195.

Imber, S. D., Pilkonis, P. A., Sotsky, S. M., Elkin, I., Watkins, J. T., Collins, J. F., et al. (1990). Mode-specific effects among three treatments for depression. *Journal of Consulting and Clinical Psychology, 58*(3), 352–359.

Jang, Y., Bergman, E., Schonfeld, L., & Molinari, V. (2007). The mediating role of health perceptions in the relation between physical and mental health. *Journal of Aging and Health, 19,* 439–452.

Johnson, D. G., & Slaney, R. B. (1996). Perfectionism: Scale development and a study of perfectionistic clients in counseling. *Journal of College Student Development, 37,* 29–41.

Joyce, D., & Rossen, E. (2010). Personality. In E. Mpofu & T. Oakland (Eds.), *Assessment in rehabilitation and health* (pp. 295–309.: Upper Saddle, NJ: Pearson.

Kiviniemi, M. T., Voss-Humke, A. M., & Siefert, A. L. (2007). How do I feel about the behavior? The interplay of affective associations with behaviors and cognitive beliefs as influences on physical activity behavior. *Health Psychology, 26,* 152–158.

Lundh, L. G. (2004). Perfectionism and acceptance. *Journal of Rational-Emotive & Cognitive-Behavioral Therapy, 22,* 255–269.

Mobley, M., Slaney, R. B., & Rice, K. G. (2005). Cultural validity of the almost perfect scale—revised for African American college students. *Journal of Counseling Psychology, 52,* 629–639.

Molnar, D. S., Reker, D. L., Culp, N. A., Sadava, S. W., & DeCourville, N. H. (2006). A mediated model of perfectionism and physical health. *Journal of Research in Personality, 40,* 482–500.

Mpofu, E. (2002). Psychology in sub-Saharan Africa: Challenges, prospects and promises. *International Journal of Psychology, 37,* 179–186.

Mpofu, E., Beck, R., & Weinrach, S. G. (2004). Multicultural rehabilitation counseling: Challenges and strategies. In F. Chan, N. L. Berven, & K. R. Thomas (Eds.), *Counseling theories and techniques for rehabilitation health professionals* (pp. 386–402). New York: Springer.

Mpofu, E., & Bishop, M. (2006). Value change and adjustment to disability: Implications for rehabilitation education, practice, and research. *Rehabilitation Education, 20,* 147–161.

Mpofu, E., & Conyers, L. M. (2004). A Representational Theory perspective of minority status and people with disabilities: Implications for rehabilitation education and practice. *Rehabilitation Counseling Bulletin, 47,* 142–151.

Noronha, D. O., & Faust, J. (2007). Identifying the variables impacting post-burn psychological adjustment: A meta-analysis. *Journal of Pediatric Psychology, 32,* 380–391.

Oakland, T., Mpofu, E., Grégoire, J., & Faulkner, M. (2007). An exploration of learning disabilities in four countries: Implications for test development and use in developing countries. *International Journal of Testing, 7,* 53–70.

O'Connor, R. C., & O'Connor, D. B. (2003). Predicting hopelessness and psychological distress: The role of perfectionism and coping. *Journal of Counseling Psychology, 50,* 362–372.

Pacht, A. R. (1984). Reflections on perfectionism. *American Psychologist, 39,* 386–390.

Payne, S. C., Youngcourt, S. S., & Beaubien, J. M. (2007). A meta-analytic examination of the goal orientation nomological net. *Journal of Applied Psychology, 92,* 128–150.

Rhéaume, J., Ladouceur, R., & Freeston, M. H. (2000). The prediction of obsessive-compulsive tendencies: Does perfectionism play a significant role? *Personality and Individual Differences, 28,* 583–592.

Rice, K. G., Ashby, J. S., & Slaney, R. B. (1998). Self-esteem as a mediator between perfectionism and depression: A structural equations analysis. *Journal of Counseling Psychology, 45,* 304–314.

Rice, K. G., & Slaney, R. B. (2002). Clusters of perfectionists: Two studies of emotional adjustment and academic achievement. *Measurement and Evaluation, 35,* 35–48.

Riley, C., Michelle, L., Zafra, C., Fairburn, C. G., & Shafran, R. (2007). A randomized controlled trial of cognitive-behaviour therapy for clinical perfectionism: A preliminary study. *Behaviour Research and Therapy, 45,* 2221–2231.

Riley, C., & Shafran, R. (2005). Clinical Perfectionism: A preliminary qualitative analysis. *Behavioural and Cognitive Psychotherapy, 33,* 369–374.

Schröder, C., Johnston, M., Morrison, V., Teunissen, L., Notermans, N., & van Meeteren, N. (2007). Health condition, impairment, activity limitations: Relationships with emotions and control cognitions in people with disabling conditions. *Rehabilitation Psychology, 52,* 280–289.

Shafran, R., Cooper, Z., & Fairburn, C. G. (2002). Clinical perfectionism: A cognitive-behavioural analysis. *Behaviour Research and Therapy, 40,* 773–791.

Skinner, B. F. (1968). *Contingencies of reinforcement: A theoretical analysis.* New York: Appleton Century Crofts.

Slade, P. D., & Owens, R. G. (1998). A dual process model of perfectionism based on reinforcement theory. *Behavior Modification, 22,* 372–390.

Slaney, R. B., Ashby, J. S., & Trippi, J. (1995). Perfectionism: Its measurement and career relevance. *Journal of Career Assessment, 3,* 279–297.

Slaney, R. B., Mobley, M., Trippi, J., Ashby, J., & Johnson, D. G. (1996). *Almost Perfect Scale—Revised.* Unpublished manuscript, Pennsylvania State University at University Park.

Slaney, R. B., Rice, K. G., & Ashby, J. S. (2002). A programmatic approach to measuring perfectionism: The almost perfect scales. In G. L. Flett & P. L. Hewitt (Eds.), *Perfectionism, theory, research, and treatment* (pp. 231–251). Washington, DC: American Psychological Association.

Slaney, R. B., Rice, K. G., Mobley, M., Trippi, J., & Ashby, J. (2001). The Almost Perfect Scale—Revised. *Measurement and Evaluation in Counseling and Development, 34,* 130–145.

Smith, S. R., Wiggins, C. M., & Gorske, T. T. (2007). A survey of psychological assessment feedback practices. *Assessment, 14,* 310–319.

Snyder, C. R., Lehman, K. A., Kluck, B., & Monsson, Y. (2006). Hope for rehabilitation and vice versa. *Rehabilitation Psychology, 51,* 89–112.

Stocker, S. (2001). Disability and Identity: Overcoming perfectionism. *Frontiers, 22,* 154–173.

Stoeber, J., Harris, R. A., & Moon, P. S. (2007). Perfectionism and the experience of pride, shame, and guilt: Comparing healthy, unhealthy, and non-perfectionists. *Personality and Individual Differences, 43,* 131–141.

Stoeber, J., & Otto, K. (2006). Positive conceptions of perfectionism: approaches, evidence, challenges. *Personality and Social Psychology Review, 10,* 295–319.

Stucki, G., Ewert, T., & Cieza, A. (2003). Value and application of the ICF in rehabilitation medicine. *Disability and Rehabilitation, 25,* 628–634.

Stumpf, H., & Parker, W. D. (2000). A hierarchical structural analysis of perfectionism and its relation to other personality characteristics. *Personality and Individual Differences, 28,* 837–852.

Sumi, K., & Kanda, K. (2002). Relationship between neurotic perfectionism, depression, anxiety, and psychosomatic symptoms: a prospective study among Japanese men. *Personality and Individual Differences, 32,* 817–826.

Suzuki, R., Krahn, G. L., McCarthy, M. J., & Adams, E. J. (2007). Understanding health outcomes: Physical secondary conditions in people with spinal cord injury. *Rehabilitation Psychology, 52,* 338–350.

Taleporos, G., & McCabe, M. P. (2005). The relationship between the severity and duration of physical disability and body esteem. *Psychology and Health, 20,* 637-650.

Taylor, S., Thordarson, D. S., & Söchting, I. (2002). Obsessive-compulsive disorder. In M. M. Antony & D. H. Barlow (Eds.), *Handbook of assessment and treatment planning for psychological disorders* (pp. 182–214). New York: The Guilford Press.

Terry-Short, L. A., Owens, R. G., Slade, P. D., & Dewey, M. E. (1995). Positive and negative perfectionism. *Personality and Individual Differences, 18,* 663–668.

Ueda, S., & Okawa, Y. (2003). The subjective dimension of functioning and disability: What is it and what is it for? *Disability and rehabilitation, 25,* 596–601.Wang, K. T., Slaney, R. B., &

Rice, K. G. (2006). Perfectionism in Chinese university students from Taiwan: A study of psychological well-being and achievement motivation. *Personality and Individual Difference, 42,* 1279–1290.

Watkins, D., Akande, A., & Mpofu, E. (1996). Assessing self-esteem: An African perspective. *Personality and Individual Differences, 20,* 163–169.

Weissman, A. N. (1979). The Dysfunctional Attitude Scale: A validation study. *Dissertation Abstracts International, 40,* 1389B–1390B. (UMI No. 79-19, 533).

Weissman, A. N., & Beck, A. T. (1978, November). *Development and validation of the Dysfunctional Attitude Scale: A preliminary investigation.* Paper presented at the meeting of the Association for the Advancement of Behavior therapy, Chicago.

World Health Organization. (2001). *International Classification of Functioning, Disability, and Health.* Geneva: Author.

Wyatt, R., & Gilbert, P. (1998). Dimensions of perfectionism: A study exploring their relationship with perceived social rank and status. *Personality and Individual Differences, 24,* 71–79.

Part 4

Measures of Participation

Carl V. Granger
Michael Gilewski
Marsha Carlin

25 Measures of Functional Performance

Overview

Since the development of medical rehabilitation functional assessment tools that meet the scientific requirements of validity, reliability, responsiveness to change, feasibility for use, and meaningfulness for clinicians, the medical rehabilitation field has been documenting change in functional status and measuring outcomes. Different types of scales measure functional performance: *quality of life* scales are the most general; *instrumental activities of daily living* scales measure the ability to accomplish activities to maintain the living environment; and *activities of daily living* scales, which are the most specific, are used most extensively in medical rehabilitation (Granger, Black, & Braun, 2006). The ideal is a continuum of care, whereby scales track patients from inpatient to outpatient, adult day services, and home care. This ideal is being implemented, as patients are tracked through the various clinical settings.

Learning Objectives

By the end of the chapter, the reader should be able to:

1. Name and describe the key qualities of the most widely used functional assessment instruments;
2. Explain the concepts of outcomes management and quality improvement;
3. Understand how a continuum of care is used to track patients over time and care settings;
4. Identify the changes in functional deficits in a patient by reviewing a case example patient record that a clinician would use; and
5. Relate the clinical application of the most frequently used instruments and systems to the World Health Organization's International Classification of Functioning, Disability, and Health.

Introduction

An individual's *quality of daily living* is a direct result of balancing functional abilities with functional limitations (Granger et al., 2006). In medical rehabilitation, the term *quality of daily living* is preferred to the more general term *quality of life*. Quality of daily living is specific and relates closely to the term *activities of daily living*. Functional assessment in medical rehabilitation is the measurement of an individual's abilities and limitations in performing these activities of daily living in numerous physical, emotional, and cognitive domains. In the last 20 to 30 years, medical rehabilitation functional measurement tools have been developed that meet the strict scientific requirements of validity, reliability, responsiveness to change, feasibility for use, and meaningfulness for clinicians (Granger et al., 2006). Functional status data now joins medical status data, creating a complete profile of a medical rehabilitation patient's strengths and deficits as related to his or her disability. Measuring functional status provides documentation of functional change, guides treatment, and estimates the types and amounts of care that must be provided by familial or hired caregivers, supportive devices, and environmental alterations. Because medical rehabilitation's mission is caring for those with chronic and debilitating illnesses and disabilities and helping them achieve the highest possible level of functional independence, measurement of function in activities of daily living takes on the utmost importance. The first author of this chapter, Carl V. Granger, MD, offers this watchword: As we function, so shall we live.

The Basis for Functional Assessment

The basis for functional assessment is in the disablement model created by the World Health Organization (WHO) in 1980 and updated in 2001, (World Health

Organization, 1980, 2001) now named the International Classification of Functioning, Disability, and Health (ICF). Key roles for human survival are stated: orientation, physical independence, mobility, occupation, social integration, and economic self-sufficiency. Functional skills help achieve these goals. The ability to participate in vocational and other roles and interact socially influences a rehabilitation patient's satisfaction with life.

It has been a challenging process applying measurement principles to function. Physical performance is readily measured as muscle strength, velocity of contraction, timed ambulation, endurance, or oxygen uptake; whereas level of competence in activities of daily living is an abstract concept. As well, measuring pain, social interactions, and role participation has been an arduous task (Granger et al., 2006). A new measurement approach and standardized system were needed, and ultimately were implemented, to describe and quantify functional ability in persons with disabilities.

Research and Practice

Functional assessment documents type and severity of disabilities and functionality, usually at the beginning and end of treatment but also during treatment and at follow-up points, to measure functional change—positive or negative—and treatment outcomes. Assessment is used to set and reset therapeutic goals, monitor the clinical course of disease, predict outcomes, connect patients to appropriate care, and place patients in appropriate settings at appropriate times. Anticipating the course or progression of a chronic illness is useful to prescribing treatment, triaging patients to appropriate treatment settings, and measuring outcomes. Predictive information is available through analysis of large functional assessment databases, described later in this chapter.

Medical rehabilitation functional assessment in its early years was based on less-than-scientifically developed scales, which were used with undefined descriptive terms, such as *mild, moderate,* and *severe.* This changed when the American Congress of Rehabilitation Medicine formed the interdisciplinary Task Force on Measurement and Evaluation, which included representatives of the disciplines of physiatry, physical therapy, occupational therapy, rehabilitation nursing, psychology, and rehabilitation counseling. The task force in 1992 published *Measurement Standards for Interdisciplinary Medical Rehabilitation* (Johnston, Keith, & Hinderer, 1992), guidelines for the creation and use of assessment tools for measurement for the disciplines allied with medical rehabilitation. According to these standards, one of the most important requirements in development of a functional measurement tool is scientific validity, meaning the tool is appropriate to its specific and intended use. Researchers developing functional assessment tools have relied on content validity, predictive validity, concurrent validity, and construct validity (Granger et al., 2006). *Content validity* indicates items are appropriate to a domain. For example, an item measuring indoor mobility should be included in an instrument measuring independence in activities of daily living. *Concurrent validity* is the degree to which the scores on an instrument relate to scores on another established instrument used at the same time. *Construct validity* is the degree to which an instrument measures what it is intended to measure. *Predictive validity* is the extent to which an instrument can predict an event or outcome of interest. The standards also call for reliability characteristics in scales (Johnston et al., 1992). Testing results must be in agreement despite changes in raters, time, or subjects. The standards also address measures applied at group levels, rather than at the level of individual patients. Individual outcomes typically are aggregated into averages, but care must be taken when comparing individuals to group averages. Outcomes are shaped not only by effectiveness of treatment but also by type and severity of a patient's disability. Patient grouping by disability type and severity, as measured by functional assessment, is discussed further in the section on legislative issues.

There are numerous scales, listed here from general to specific, that measure performance in medical rehabilitation patients: quality of life scales, instrumental activities of daily living scales, and activities of daily living scales. Quality of life scales are the most general, look at a wide range of capabilities, and are not criterion-referenced. Examples are the MOS 36-Item Short Form Survey (Ware & Sherbourne, 1992), the Sickness Impact Profile (Carter, Bobbitt, Bergner, & Gilson, 1976), and the LIFEware℠ System (Baker, Granger, & Fiedler, 1997; Baker, Granger, & Ottenbacher, 1996; Granger, Ottenbacher, Baker, & Sehgal, 1995). Instrumental activities of daily living scales measure the ability to accomplish activities to maintain the living environment, such as shopping, preparing meals, and managing money. Examples are the Functional Health Status (Rosow & Breslau, 1966), the Older Americans Resources and Services Multidimensional Functional Assessment Questionnaire (Duke University Center for the Study of Aging and Human Development, 1978), and the Philadelphia Geriatric Instrumental Activities of Daily Living (Lawton, 1971). Activities of daily living scales are the most extensively used scales in medical rehabilitation and usually are administered by clinician observers. These scales measure capabilities in those basic skills necessary to caring for oneself, such as eating, bathing, grooming, dressing, transfers, continence, and locomotion. Examples of activities of daily living scales that have met validity and reliability standards are: Barthel Index (Mahoney & Barthel, 1965), Index of Independence in Activities of Daily Living (Katz, Ford, Moskowitz, Jackson & Jaffe, 1963), Kenny Self-Care Evaluation (Schoening & Iversen, 1968), FIM™ instrument (Uniform Data System for Medical Rehabilitation [UDSMR], 1997), WeeFIM® instrument (UDSMR, 1998/2002, 2005b), Level of Rehabilitation Scale (LORS) and LORS American Data System (LADS; Carey & Posavac, 1978), and the Patient Evaluation and Conference System (PECS; Marianjoy Rehabilitation Hospital and Clinics).[1]

Outcomes Management and Quality Improvement

Documentation of outcomes in medical rehabilitation and achieving quality care through outcomes management are required by several organizations: the Commission on Accreditation of Rehabilitation Facilities (CARF, 2004), the Joint Commission (formerly named the Joint Commission on Accreditation of Healthcare Organizations) (JCAHO, 1992), state health departments, and other health agencies.

1. FIM, AlphaFIM, WeeFIM, and LIFEware are trademarks of the Uniform Data System for Medical Rehabilitation, a division of UB Foundation Activities, Inc.

Outcomes management has been described as a way to measure effectiveness and efficiency of medical rehabilitation programs (CARF, 2004). Structure, process, and outcomes all can be considered (Granger et al., 2006). Structural data may provide information about certification of professional health care providers. Process data may describe treatment, in terms of numbers and types. Outcomes evaluation gives information about the level of functional independence patients achieve and the level of patient satisfaction. An outcomes management system in a rehabilitation facility (hospital unit or freestanding hospital) may contain a mission statement, a program structure, program goals, program objectives, methods of applying measures, and utilization of outcome data. Effectiveness is the extent to which outcomes are achieved. Efficiency is the amount of resources used to reach program goals. For a stroke program, for example, objectives might include optimization of self-care skills, sphincter management, transfer abilities, locomotion, communication and social-cognition skills, and the patient's return to the community. Functional assessment tells whether these goals have been achieved. Facilities also gather data on patient age and sex distribution, length of stay, program interruptions, and payment sources. These data assist quality improvement and third-party payers. The ultimate goal for a facility is quality improvement, sometimes achieved by making changes to rehabilitation treatment programs (Granger et al., 2006).

Most Frequently Used Instruments/Systems

At about the same time as the American Congress of Rehabilitation Medicine had its interdisciplinary Task Force on Measurement and Evaluation developing guidelines for assessment tools, first author Carl V. Granger, MD, with a grant from the U.S. Department of Education's National Institute on Disability and Rehabilitation Research, served as project director of a national task force to develop a uniform data set for medical rehabilitation that could document the outcomes and costs of inpatient medical rehabilitation. The work culminated in the late 1980s in the development of a data set that included the FIM instrument (UDSMR, 1997), which became the most frequently used adult inpatient rehabilitation instrument. (The section on legislation describes the use of the instrument by the U.S. government.) The FIM instrument consists of 18 items that assess performance of activities of daily living skills: 13 motor items and 5 cognition items. Rehabilitation inpatients are rated by clinicians observing patients' abilities to complete the 18 functional items using a scale from 1 to 7, with 1 representing total assistance needed, 7 representing complete independence, and the numbers in-between representing well-defined levels of dependence and independence in completing the activities. The item ratings then are summed, with total-FIM instrument ratings ranging from 18 (lowest function) to 126 (highest function). The motor items are: Eating, Grooming, Bathing, Dressing-upper body, Dressing-lower body, Toileting, Bladder management, Bowel management, Transfers-bed/chair/wheelchair, Transfers-toilet, Transfers-tub/shower, Locomotion-walk/wheelchair, and Locomotion-stairs. The cognition items are: Comprehension, Expression, Social interaction, Problem solving, and Memory. The FIM instrument is administered by trained and tested clinicians in approximately 15 to 30 minutes at inpatient admission, discharge, and follow-up. The data set also includes demographic and diagnostic information. Subscribing inpatient rehabilitation facilities (IRFs) send data to the UDSMR in Amherst, New York, and receive back reports on the outcomes of their facility's medical rehabilitation services, which are compared to other U.S. IRFs. UDSMR has a Program Evaluation Model for its IRF subscribers that ranks each facility's performance relative to nearly 70% of the IRFs in the United States, which was designed to help IRFs quickly identify strengths and opportunities for improvement and to raise performance of all subscribing facilities. U.S. IRFs must send admission data to the federal government for Medicare Part A payment. (Medicare is described in the section on U.S. legislation.)

Another important feature of the FIM instrument is that it has been shown to have the capability of estimating *burden of care,* defined as hours/minutes of assistance needed per day from another person for personal care. Studies were conducted in homes with persons who had stroke, spinal cord injury, multiple sclerosis, and head injury (Granger, Cotter, Hamilton, & Fiedler, 1993; Granger, Cotter, Hamilton, Fiedler, & Hens, 1990; Granger, Divan, & Fiedler, 1995; Heinemann et al., 1997). Remembering that total-FIM instrument ratings range from 18 (lowest function) to 126 (highest function), here are examples of the relationships between ratings and burden of care. A total-FIM instrument rating of 60 indicates functional deficits too severe for care at home because 4 or more hours of personal care from another person could be required. Patients, on average, enter inpatient rehabilitation with a rating of 60. At a rating of 70, they could require 3 hours of care, which also would not be manageable in most homes. At a rating of 80, 2 hours are required; at 90, 1 hour; at 100, a quarter hour to a half hour; and at 110, a quarter of an hour to none. At ratings of 80 and higher, most patients are manageable at home. On average, patients are discharged from inpatient rehabilitation at a rating of 80 to 90. Quantifying need for personal assistance helps triage patients from the acute-care hospital to appropriate rehabilitation venues and serves to establish the amount of care needed once the patient reaches home and the financial costs if help is hired. Most often, home care must be provided by family members. Care can be needed for weeks, months, or years, and care need levels can fluctuate over time.

To foster a continuum of care from the acute-care hospital to the various rehabilitation settings, the AlphaFIM® instrument was developed (UDSMR, 2005a). It is a 6-item version of the 18-item FIM instrument. The AlphaFIM instrument has the same 7-level rating system with 1 representing total assistance needed and 7 representing complete independence, with well-defined levels of dependence and independence in-between. The item ratings are totaled and range from 6 (lowest function) to 42 (highest function). The AlphaFIM instrument has 4 motor items (Eating, Grooming, Bowel management, and Transfers-toilet); and 2 cognition items (Expression and Memory). The AlphaFIM instrument was constructed using Rasch (1993) analysis, which converted the 18-item FIM instrument raw scores into equal-interval, unidimensional motor and cognition measures with hierarchical rating structures. These structures showed which items are easier and which are more difficult for the acute-care hospital patient. The easier items were deemed most appropriate to be included in the AlphaFIM instrument.

Research Box 25.1

THE FIM™ INSTRUMENT AND PHARMACEUTICAL TESTING

Granger, C. V., Wende, K., & Brownscheidle, C. M. (2003). Use of the FIM™ instrument in a trial of intramuscular interferon β-1a for disease progression in relapsing-remitting multiple sclerosis. *American Journal of Physical Medicine & Rehabilitation, 82*(6), 427–436.

This is a description of research on use of the FIM instrument to measure function of subjects in a trial of an interferon β-1a pharmaceutical for multiple sclerosis.

Objective: To investigate the effect of interferon β-1a on disability in patients with relapsing-remitting multiple sclerosis, using the FIM instrument to assess levels of decline in total, motor, and cognitive function.

Methods: Of the 301 patients enrolled in the trial, 274 subjects with relapsing-remitting multiple sclerosis with baseline FIM instrument and Kurtzke Expanded Disability Status Scale scores were studied, and patients were measured every 6 months. Mildly disabled patients were chosen, with a Kurtzke Expanded Disability Status Scale score of 1.0–3.5. Subjects received either interferon β-1a or placebo. Analysis was by Kaplan-Meier methodology. The Mann-Whitney test (log rank) compared mean change and Spearman's rank-correlation test determined correlation.

Results: There was a significant difference in treatment groups, with a FIM instrument rating decline of ≥4 points, with placebo subjects showing greater loss of function than subjects receiving interferon β-1a. There was no statistically significant difference in total, cognition, or motor activities, with a decline of ≤3 points.

Conclusion: Disability, as measured by the FIM instrument, was slowed by treatment with interferon β-1a, compared with placebo. The treatment effect determined using the FIM instrument, with its motor and cognition components, shows response to therapy for mild to moderate multiple sclerosis.

Question:

1. The use of pharmaceuticals by multiple sclerosis patients can help minimize disabling events, but multiple sclerosis remains a chronic condition. For multiple sclerosis patients taking pharmaceuticals, what might functional assessment show?

The 18-item FIM instrument also has been shown to be an effective tool in measuring function for patients in pharmaceutical studies. One example is use of the FIM instrument in a clinical trial of an interferon pharmaceutical for patients with multiple sclerosis (Granger, Wende, & Brownscheidle, 2003).

For children, the FIM instrument was adapted as the WeeFIM instrument, which is used in inpatient and outpatient pediatric settings for children generally 6 months through 7 years of age (UDSMR, 1998/2002, 2005b). The WeeFIM instrument motor items are: Eating, Grooming, Bathing, Dressing-upper body, Dressing-lower body, Toileting, Bladder management, Bowel management, Transfers-bed/chair/wheelchair, Transfers-toilet, Transfers-tub/shower, Locomotion-walk/wheelchair/crawl, and Locomotion-stairs. The WeeFIM instrument cognition items are: Comprehension, Expression, Social interaction, Problem solving, and Memory. There is also a WeeFIM II® System: 0–3 Module (UDSMR, 2005b), with three domains: motor, cognitive, and behavioral. The instrument's 0–3 Module was developed to improve sensitivity of the assessment for children up to and including the age of 3 years, and its items are considered the precursors to: self-feeding, hand use, tool use, mobility (prone antigravity control, getting to an upright position, and locomotion), cognition (attention to task, joint attention, problem solving, memory, comprehension, and expression), and burden of care, in terms of sleeping, bathing, dressing, calming, and separation anxiety.

Functional assessment instruments typically use ordinal scales to rate a patient's performance, that is, the numbers increase with increasing function, or responses are rank-ordered from least to greatest. For example, in the FIM instrument (UDSMR, 1997), a rating of 1 represents lowest function, and 7 represents highest function. For purposes of analysis of the ratings obtained on these scales, nonparametric statistical techniques must be used to observe latent traits, such as functional activities. Ordinal data are interpreted differently than interval or ratio data. For example, a rating of 4 does not represent twice the functionality of a rating of 2, and the difference between ratings of 1 and 2 is not the same as the difference between ratings of 3 and 4. Rasch analysis is a technique used to transform ordinal scores into equal-interval measures of latent traits (Linacre & Wright, 2000). This method looks at all the items in a scale in relationship to each other and computes the probability of an individual being able to perform a task based on having performed other tasks in the scale. In Rasch analysis, the instrument items are arranged along a hierarchy from easiest to most difficult. This property is called *unidimensionality*. The subjects also are arranged along the same hierarchy, according to their abilities to perform the tasks on the scale. This property, called *conjoint additivity*, yields an objective measure of ability for each subject and an objective measure of difficulty for each item. At that point where the subject's ability equals the item's difficulty, the probability of the subject's success on that item is.50. Items below that point should be within the subject's ability, and items above that point may be too difficult (Linacre & Wright, 2000). There has been established a hierarchy of difficulty in completing tasks of the FIM instrument. For example, on average, the item called Stairs (a task of locomotion, defined as ascending or descending 12–14 stairs) is the most difficult task, and the item called Eating is the easiest task, as explained by research on structure and stability of the FIM instrument (Linacre, Heinemann, Wright, Granger, & Hamilton, 1994). Again, this is the average, as a patient with upper-limb impairment likely would have more difficulty eating than using stairs. Clinicians must be aware of the hierarchy of easy-to-difficult items, but never make assumptions about a patient's performance of difficult tasks based on the patient's performance of easier tasks.

For adult outpatients, the LIFEware System (Baker et al., 1997; Baker et al., 1996; Granger, Ottenbacher et al., 1995) assesses functional status, through self-reporting, of persons with musculoskeletal, neurological, cardiac, and other conditions. Responses are from the outpatient's point of view about his or her own functional abilities. The LIFEware System is a series of measures of physical functioning, pain experience, emotional/mood state, cognitive status, social interaction, selected role participation, and satisfaction with the treatment process. Most often, the LIFEware System assesses these three domains: physical functioning (Body Movement and Control [BMC] measure of 10 items), affective sense of well-being or mood state (PLACID measure of seven items), and experience with pain (PAINFREE measure of six items and the LIFEware® Visual Analog Scale; Baker et al., 1997; Baker et al., 1996; Granger, Ottenbacher et al., 1995). Subscribing facilities can customize their forms for each outpatient by selecting from more than 130 measures and scales. For example, the adult day services version gathers information on memory, medication, and nutrition; and the cardiac version asks questions about breathing, chest pain/discomfort, and fatigue. The LIFEware System approaches pain measurement in three ways. The Painfree measure asks about type of pain, using these adjectives: "throbbing," "sharp," "aching," "tender," "splitting," "tiring-exhausting," "fearful," "punishing-cruel," "cramping," and "hot-burning." The Painscale and a LIFEware Visual Analog Scale (LVAS) measure intensity of pain, and sometimes both are used with a patient in order to confirm pain levels. The Painscale asks about the extent of pain in the last 3 days, including the day of assessment. Its descriptors include "none," "mild," "discomforting," "distressing," "horrible," and "excruciating." The LVAS is a Likert scale asking that pain be rated from 0 to 10, from "no pain" to the "worst imaginable pain." An outpatient can complete a form in 10 to 15 minutes. All LIFEware System measures and scales are transferred to a 0 to 100 rating, with 100 representing the best rating, meaning no physical limitations, no emotional distress, and no pain (Baker et al., 1997; Baker et al., 1996; Granger, Ottenbacher et al., 1995). For most LIFEware measures, a response level of 70 on items appears to be the most probable threshold of clinical significance, or the academic equivalent of a passing grade, whereas a response level below 70 usually indicates remediation is needed. However, each item and each measure has a prespecified threshold of clinical significance (designated as an expected value), based on Rasch modeling with thousands of cases. LIFEware measures are derived using the Rasch measurement model. Raw scores on the self-report questionnaire are transformed into unidimensional, equal-interval measures through Rasch analysis (Linacre & Wright, 2000). Subscribing outpatient facilities send data to, and receive outcomes reports from, the UDSMR.

The FIM instrument is not restricted to use for inpatients only, and sometimes is appropriate for use with outpatients with more severe disablement. The FIM instrument (UDSMR, 1997) and the LIFEware System (Baker et al., 1997; Baker et al., 1996; Granger, Ottenbacher et al., 1995) sometimes are combined, using a common rating scale of 0 to 100, to follow inpatient to outpatient progress, or follow a patient through lengthy outpatient care. This is described in the section on the continuum of care.

The earlier discussion of standards (Johnston et al., 1992) that address measures applied at group levels supports the collection of combined facility data by the UDSMR for the purpose of analysis of many factors related to outcomes. Since 1987, the UDSMR has been the largest U.S. repository for performance measurement systems data from medical rehabilitation facilities. From its subscribing facilities, it has collected over 15 million assessments (pre-admission, interim, and follow-up) completed for adults and children. The UDSMR is a not-for-profit data management service that also provides such ancillary services as training to use its instruments and related data analysis and reporting systems. The number of subscribing facilities for all products increased from 57 in 1988 to 1,550 in 2009. The UDSMR instruments and systems are used in the United States, Canada, Italy, Finland, Sweden, South Africa, Australia, Hong Kong, Singapore, Saudi Arabia, Chile, Israel, Belgium, Iceland, Mexico, and Spain.

U.S. Legislative Issues

It has been estimated that about 70% of inpatient medical rehabilitation is utilized in the United States by Medicare beneficiaries. Medicare is the government-funded health, hospital, and drug insurance program for Americans 65 and older, Americans under 65 with certain disabilities, and all Americans with end-stage renal disease. U.S. medical rehabilitation facilities traditionally had been reimbursed for Medicare patients under a cost-based system, meaning they were paid for actual care costs. However, in recent years, U.S. Congressional mandates changed this payment system. Beginning in 2002, the U.S. Centers for Medicare & Medicaid Services (CMS), which oversees Medicare, substituted a prospective payment system, which is a method of reimbursement based on a predetermined, fixed amount, derived from a classification system (U.S. Department of Health and Human Services, Centers for Medicare & Medicaid Services, n.d.). CMS also added the requirement that IRFs use an Inpatient Rehabilitation Facility-Patient Assessment Instrument (IRF-PAI) to collect data in order to receive reimbursement (HHS/CMS Web site). The FIM instrument, slightly modified, is central to the IRF-PAI, which collects data for submission to the CMS for reimbursement for Medicare Part A inpatient rehabilitation services. Payment now is based on type and level of severity of the patient's disability at admission, derived from a functional assessment. The grouping of patients by type and severity of disability is based on the FIM-FRG (function-related group) system developed for the FIM instrument (Stineman et al., 1994). Grouping was changed in recent years to the CMG (case-mix group) system based on work by the RAND Corporation (U.S. Department of Health and Human Services, Centers for Medicare & Medicaid Services, 2002). The coding conventions, available in detail from the CMS, must be thoroughly understood by medical rehabilitation team members to ensure that documentation is accurate.

A more recent U.S. Congressional mandate, the U.S. Deficit Reduction Act of 2005, directed CMS to conduct a research project to compare all the post-acute rehabilitation settings to find the most cost-effective settings for individual patients. This could lead to a new post-acute payment system for Medicare recipients for all the types of facilities providing medical rehabilitation after acute hospital care. CMS is to report to the U.S. Congress in 2011 on this payment reform demonstration.

Clinical Application of Measures of Functional Performance

The Continuum of Care

Health care can be delivered in many settings and over long periods of time, and this especially is true for medical rehabilitation. Patients experiencing such problems as, for example, stroke, spinal cord injury, or brain injury may be stabilized in acute-care hospitals, but they usually are left with functional deficits. The goal of medical rehabilitation is to help the patient maintain or, if possible, restore function. Patients likely are moved into one or more types of facilities, but not in any established order after the acute hospital stay: freestanding rehabilitation hospitals or in-hospital rehabilitation units, subacute facilities, skilled nursing facilities, or outpatient facilities. Patients may also receive home care or adult day services. Some patients remain in the same post-acute rehabilitation setting for a long time. One goal of UDSMR is to follow patients' function over time and through various venues of care, and this continuum of care is being implemented (Granger, 1999). A continuum of care helps to measure and manage outcomes and predict which types of patients benefit most in which settings at which times during their illness and the duration of services and costs. Managed care capitation is forcing health care institutions to achieve cost-effective outcomes. Therefore, maintaining beginning-to-end care information on patients becomes useful.

The UDSMR continuum of care follows inpatient-to-outpatient medical rehabilitation using its FIM instrument and LIFEware System. For this purpose, assessments for both instruments are on a common scale of 0 to 100, with 100 reflecting best function. One picture is created of a patient's functional history. In the patient's longitudinal record, the values called *absolute values* are totals for all items in each measure, shown as *above expected* (in green) or *below expected* (in red), based on thousands of cases in the database. (This color-coded differentiation is not shown in this publication but appears on the actual record used by clinicians.) Only those individual items from a measure that are below expected appear on the record. These are the functional items that pose problems for the patient and therefore warrant clinical attention. (Items at or above expected do not appear on the record.) Minus signs indicate the number of points the item rating values are below the expected item value. Clinicians can refer to the patients' medical records to identify the causes of change in functional status.

Case Example: Stroke, Inpatient and Outpatient

This case example longitudinal record (Table 25.1) shows the functional status of a 60-year-old stroke patient, a woman, with 7 assessments over 18 months

Research Box 25.2

USE OF THE ALPHAFIM® INSTRUMENT TO PROJECT PATIENT FUNCTION

Stillman, G., Granger, C., & Niewczyk, P. (2009). Projecting function of stroke patients in rehabilitation using the AlphaFIM® instrument in acute care. *Physical Medicine & Rehabilitation, 1*(3), 234–239.

Being able to predict, while a patient is in an acute-care hospital, how long that patient later stays in an inpatient rehabilitation facility and whether that patient can return to community living after rehabilitation could be important for projecting the resources needed to properly care for that patient. This research on two assessment instruments has shown that some valuable prediction is possible.

Objective: To test if the AlphaFIM instrument (a 6-item version of the 18-item FIM instrument) administered in the acute-care hospital would: approximate the FIM instrument ratings at admission to and discharge from an inpatient rehabilitation facility, show inpatient rehabilitation length of stay, and predict likelihood of patients being discharged from inpatient rehabilitation to the community.

Methods: A prospective cohort study of 144 stroke patients in an acute-care stroke unit who were transferred to an inpatient rehabilitation facility.

Results: The AlphaFIM instrument showed predictive capabilities with regard to inpatient rehabilitation admission and discharge ratings and length of stay but was a weak predictor of return to the community.

Conclusion: The AlphaFIM instrument, easily administered in the acute-care hospital, can be helpful in predicting patient rehabilitation needs.

Question:
This research showed that functional assessment can be used to predict stroke patients' needs in terms of levels of rehabilitation care. If this was tested and shown to work for other diagnoses, how could all this research be valuable to the rehabilitation industry?

while receiving inpatient and outpatient rehabilitation treatment that included psychological counseling. The first two assessments use only FIM instrument ratings, indicating she was in an inpatient rehabilitation unit or rehabilitation hospital. The next three assessments utilize FIM instrument and LIFEware System ratings, indicating she moved to outpatient care but had more serious functional problems. The last two assessments show that only LIFEware System ratings were used, indicating continued care on an outpatient basis. In the patient's longitudinal record, specific functional deficits appear: These are individual items with minus signs next to their values that are problematic

25.1 Longitudinal Record, Case Example

LIFEWARE® LONGITUDINAL RECORD OF FUNCTIONAL STATUS FOR CASE EXAMPLE
CONDITION: NEUROLOGICAL PROBLEM: STROKE

Patient code: xxxxxxxxx	Gender: Female	Birth: xx/xx/xx	Case open: 2003
Subscriber: xxxxx	Marital: N/A	Onset: N/A	Case close: N/A
Employment: N/A	Living with: N/A	Clinicians: xxx	Age: 60 years

NOTE – Absolute Range is 0 to 100

DATE	FIMALL	PAINSCALE	PLACID	LBM	COMMUNITY/ SATISFACTION
08/18/03	65 Absolute –2 Grooming	Incomplete	Incomplete	Incomplete	Incomplete
08/25/03	70 Absolute None below expected	Incomplete	Incomplete	Incomplete	Incomplete
09/02/03	82 Absolute None below expected	100 Absolute None below expected	71 Absolute –61 Panic –12 Irritated –10 Uptight	84 Absolute –20 Walking –3 Lifting	Participation 30% Social Primary Role 20% Work
05/10/04	97 Absolute None below expected	75 Absolute None below expected	87 Absolute –15 Morbid	75 Absolute –20 Walking –11 Right lower limb	Participation 50% Social Primary Role 70% Work Treatment 100% Overall 100% Planning 100% Waiting 100% Decisions 100% Achievement
08/19/04	97 Absolute None below expected	45 Absolute –30 Painscale	66 Absolute –30 Uptight –21 Panic –15 Blame –15 Morbid –12 Irritated	54 Absolute –40 Walking –35 Getting up –28 Standing –11 Left lower limb –3 Lifting	Participation 30% Social Primary Role 70% Work

(continued)

25.1 Longitudinal Record, Case Example — *Continued*

DATE	FIMALL	PAINSCALE	PLACID	LBM	COMMUNITY/ SATISFACTION
10/12/04	Incomplete	75 Absolute None below expected	76 Absolute –21 Panic –15 Blame –10 Uptight	Incomplete –3 Lifting	Participation 40% Social Primary Role 80% Work Treatment 100% Overall 100% Planning 100% Waiting 100% Decisions 100% Achievement
02/15/05	Incomplete	75 Absolute None below expected	89 Absolute –10 Uptight	47 Absolute –68 Getting up –35 Stairs –28 Standing –25 Kneeling –23 Lifting	Participation 70% Social Primary Role 100% Work

 Source: Uniform Data System for Medical Rehabilitation

and need to be addressed by clinicians. (Again, items that are not problematic do not appear on the longitudinal record.) Absolute values (totals for all items in each measure) as above/below expected would be color-coded green/red on the patients' longitudinal records that are provided to subscribing facilities. (This color-coding is not shown here.) Over the first year, the FIMALL measure (18 motor and cognition FIM instrument items) indicates improvement, as shown by the increasing value of the absolute ratings, and then the appearance of a note that no items were below expected. The Grooming item initially appears as a minor problem, two points below expected. PAINSCALE (pain) appears as a problem about halfway through treatment; then is resolved. Under the PLACID measure, these item problems appear: Panic, Irritated, Uptight, Morbid thoughts, and Blaming oneself. The LBM (Lower Body Movement) measure items increase as problems about halfway through treatment: Walking, Lifting, Right lower limb, Getting up, Standing, Left lower limb, Stairs, and Kneeling. The increases in LBM problems and pain are associated with a diagnosis of multilevel low back facet arthropathy and degenerative disc disease with spinal stenosis and foramen outlet stenosis, causing back pain and decline in lower body function. Clinicians must refer to the patient's medical record to learn the causes of functional changes. Community and Satisfaction role participation ratings improve over time: to 70% social and 100% work. Satisfaction with treatment is 100%.

Mapping ICF Categories With the FIM Instrument and the Lifeware System

UDSMR's instruments and systems are used worldwide, as is the ICF (WHO, 2001). The ICF classification offers numerous categories divided over three components: Body Functions and Body Structures, Participation and Activities, and Environmental Factors. The ICF allows for the documentation of degrees of disability and has performance and capacity qualifiers, but it is generally not considered a functional measurement instrument or system. It can be used concurrently with traditional measurement systems in clinical practice to follow an individual's function and guide an individual's treatment, but used alone it may present practicability issues, perhaps due in part to its comparative length and complexity. A recently completed review of the literature on the ICF since the WHO endorsement concluded that clinical application of the ICF is limited at this time, possibly because it was so recently introduced (Bruyère, VanLooy, & Peterson, 2005). The article said several authors have stated that the ICF is promising in rehabilitation research, while others have expressed reservations and concerns. Other authors "hold that routine collection of functional status information across settings in the health care delivery system can facilitate more effective evaluation of outcomes, comparison of the effectiveness and cost effectiveness of treatment modalities, and prediction and management of costs" (Bruyère et al., 2005, p. 114). The UDSMR functional measurement instruments and systems are complementary to the ICF and go further than the ICF: They are the most widely used in medical rehabilitation clinical settings to document functional status over time and to measure medical rehabilitation outcomes. The UDSMR instruments and systems are used to make decisions about treatment types and duration, measure treatment outcomes, estimate the burden of care that must be provided by others, and provide documentation for payment for care. According to an informal matching project completed by UDSMR, for all 18 FIM instrument items there are corresponding ICF classifications; and for the LIFEware System's approximately 250 items, ICF classifications match about 85% of them. The LIFEware System has items for which there are no corresponding ICF classifications, for example, temporomandibular joint problems and satisfaction with treatment. This UDSMR matching preceded important ICF validation research published in 2006 (Grill, Stucki, Scheuringer, & Melvin, 2006), which concluded that ICF lines up with the concepts of the most frequently used measures, including the FIM instrument. (This research did not include the LIFEware System or the WeeFIM instrument.)

The ICF classifications corresponding to the continuum of care items from the combined FIM instrument and LIFEware System, for the case example (Table 25.1) longitudinal record, is shown in Table 25.2. This table shows those items with below-expected values that appear on the longitudinal record for clinician attention.

25.2 Comparison With ICF Classifications, Case Example

FIM™ Item/Description	ICF	ICF Description
Grooming: Includes oral care, hair grooming, washing the hands and face, and either shaving the face or applying make-up	Caring for teeth (d5201)	Looking after dental hygiene, such as by brushing teeth, flossing, and taking care of a dental prosthesis or othosis
	Caring for hair (d5202)	Looking after the hair on the head and face, such as by combing, styling, shaving, or trimming
	Washing body parts (d5100)	Applying water, soap, and other substances to body parts, such as hands, face, feet, hair, or nails, in order to clean them
	Drying oneself (d5102)	Using a towel or other means for drying some part or parts of one's body, or the whole body, such as after washing
	Caring for skin (d5200)	Looking after the texture and hydration of one's skin, such as by removing calluses or corns and using moisturizing lotions or cosmetics
LIFEware® Item	**ICF**	**ICF Description**
Painscale	Sensation of pain (b280)	Sensation of unpleasant feeling indicating potential or actual damage to some body structure
Blaming yourself/guilt	Optimism (b1265)	Mental functions that produce a personal disposition that is cheerful, buoyant and hopeful, as contrasted to being downhearted, gloomy, and despairing
	Confidence (b1266)	Mental functions that produce a personal disposition that is self-assured, bold and assertive, as contrasted to being timid, insecure, and self-effacing
	Other specified (b1268)	Temperament and personality functions, other specified
Morbid/gloomy thoughts Pessimistic about future	Optimism (b1265)	Mental functions that produce a personal disposition that is cheerful, buoyant, and hopeful, as contrasted to being downhearted, gloomy, and despairing
Uptight/tense/stressed	Handling stress (d2401)	Carrying out simple or complex and coordinated actions to cope with pressure, emergencies, or stress associated with task performance
Panic attacks	Emotional functions—Regulation of emotion (b1521)	Mental functions that control the experience and display of affect
	Emotional functions—Range of emotion (b1522)	Mental functions that produce the spectrum of experience of arousal of affect or feelings, such as love, hate, anxiousness, sorrow, joy, fear, and anger

25.2 Comparison With ICF Classifications, Case Example — *Continued*

LIFEware® Item	ICF	ICF Description
Easily irritated/annoyed	Psychic stability (b1263)	Mental functions that produce a personal disposition that is even-tempered, calm, and composed as contrasted to being irritable, worried, erratic, and moody
Lift	Lifting (d4300)	Raising up an object in order to move it from a lower to a higher level, such as when lifting a glass from the table
Walk	Walking (d450)	Moving along a surface on foot, step-by-step, so that one foot is always on the ground, such as when strolling, sauntering, walking forwards, backwards, or sideways
Getting up from a low seat like a sofa	Standing (d4104)	Getting into or out of a standing position or changing body position from standing to any other position, such as lying down or sitting down
Climbing a flight of stairs	Climbing (d4551)	Moving the whole body upwards or downwards, over surfaces or objects, such as climbing steps, rocks, ladders or stairs, curbs, or other objects
Standing a long time, like for 30 minutes	Maintaining a standing position (d4154)	Staying in a standing position for some time as required, such as when standing in a queue
Kneeling or bending down to the floor	Kneeling (d4102)	Getting into and out of a position where the body is supported by the knees with legs bent, such as during prayers, or changing body position from kneeling to any other position, such as standing up
	Bending (d4105)	Tilting the back downwards or to the side, at the torso, such as in bowing or reaching down for an object
Limitation of right lower limb	Mobility of several joints (b7101)	Functions of the range and ease of movement of more than one joint
	Structure of lower leg (s7501, s7502)	—
Limitation of left lower limb	Mobility of several joints (b7101)	Functions of the range and ease of movement of more than one joint
	Structure of lower leg (s7501, s7502)	—

(continued)

25.2 Comparison With ICF Classifications, Case Example — *Continued*

LIFEware® Item	ICF	ICF Description
Satisfaction with treatment	No corresponding code	No corresponding code
Primary role: Work	Remunerative employment (d850)	Engaging in all aspects of work, as an occupation, trade, profession, or other form of employment, for payment, as an employee, full or part time, or self-employed, such as seeking employment and getting a job, doing the required tasks of the job, attending work on time as required, supervising other workers or being supervised, and performing required tasks alone or in groups
Social participation	Socializing (d9205)	Engaging in any form of play, recreational, or leisure activity, such as informal or organized play and sports; programs of physical fitness, relaxation, amusement, or diversion; going to art galleries, museums, cinemas, or theatres; engaging in crafts or hobbies; reading for enjoyment; playing musical instruments; sightseeing, tourism, and traveling for pleasure

The Future of Measures of Functional Performance

At one time, function had been considered impossible to measure. So instead, clinicians measured those objective signs considered reproducible and less likely to be affected by variables, such as patient motivation. However, now it is clear that measuring how people function in their daily lives not only is possible, but it can lie closer to actual human experience than other tests. It has been determined that functional measurement instruments made of a minimum set of items describe important aspects of patient experience, predict burden of care, and measure effectiveness and efficiency of the rehabilitation process.

Functional assessment will continue to be important for describing outcomes of patient care, particularly for persons with varying degrees of disablement secondary to chronic health conditions, and especially as the U.S. population ages and utilizes a larger share of health services. Attention will be given to the structures of measures with respect to how well item ratings relate to each other in a predictable unidimensional hierarchy and the extent to which a patient's strengths and weaknesses can be readily identified. Then, interventions may be targeted. This will lead to more cost-effective care. In health and rehabilitation care delivery systems of the future, there will need to be a balance among: costs of delivering services; quality, evident in benefit conferred; and value, including satisfaction. Functional performance measures will need to be an integral part of health and rehabilitation care delivery systems.

Discussion Box 25.1

AGING AND ASSESSMENT

Health care planning for an aging world population must take place now. Global demographic and socioeconomic trends offer a view of a future of care that might be available only to those who can afford to pay for it. In poor countries, aging is but one cause of disablement. Equally threatening is impairment resulting from disease pandemics, wars, terrorism, and natural disasters. Disability prevention programs, such as those promoted by the World Health Organization, may help identify and treat problems early, to prevent some disabling conditions. In the United States, demand will escalate for medical rehabilitation for the elderly as the population ages (especially the proportionately large numbers of post–World War II baby boomers) and life expectancy increases due to medical advances. U.S. estimates show that by the year 2030, there will be 71 million older persons (≥65 years), or twice as many as there were in year 2000 (U.S. Department of Health and Human Services, Centers for Disease Control and Prevention, n.d.). Without early large-scale systematic planning, problems will emerge for health care facilities, clinicians, patients, and families. Also, the U.S. budget could be strained, as publicly funded Medicare resources are needed for increasing numbers of elderly patients with multiple, complex, and chronic disabling health conditions. Primarily, these elderly consumers will need rehabilitation services associated with stroke, orthopedic problems, cardiac disorders, and deconditioning. They will require care in inpatient medical rehabilitation facilities, skilled nursing facilities, and long-term care hospitals, as well as outpatient care and home care. The challenges will be to keep demand from outpacing resources and to deliver quality care. There is a role for assessment in this future of rehabilitation care. The FIM™ instrument can estimate burden of care, which is the amount of assistance, in hours/minutes, needed from another individual for personal care. Quantifying need for personal assistance helps triage patients from the acute-care hospital to appropriate rehabilitation settings and serves to establish the amount of care needed once the patient reaches home. This is important to families who must provide care themselves, or hire assistance. (Heinemann et al., 1997; Granger et al., 1990; Granger et al., 1993; Granger, Divan et al., 1995). Assessment instruments also could be used to document and analyze the functional status of large numbers of aging patients in different settings over time, to determine trends and help guide health care policy.

Question:

1. Using functional assessment instruments to monitor the functional status of large numbers of patients in rehabilitation care settings over time would provide researchers with data, as they examine lengths of stay, admission and discharge functional status, and costs of care. In what ways could this information be applied to health care planning for the future?

Summary

Since the development of medical rehabilitation functional assessment tools that meet the scientific requirements of validity, reliability, responsiveness to change, feasibility for use, and meaningfulness for clinicians, the medical rehabilitation field has been documenting change in functional status and measuring outcomes (Granger et al., 2006). This has enhanced treatment for persons with chronic and debilitating illnesses and helped them achieve the highest possible level of functional independence.

It was a challenging process creating functional assessment instruments that describe motor and cognitive domains, in terms of level of competence in activities of daily living, and pain, as self-reported by patients. A new measurement approach and standardized systems were needed for many years and, ultimately, were implemented. In the United States, outcomes management and quality improvement are required by various accrediting agencies, state health departments, and other health agencies (Granger et al., 2006).

There are different types of scales that measure functional performance (Granger et al., 2006). Quality of life scales are the most general, looking at a wide range of capabilities. Instrumental activities of daily living scales measure the ability to accomplish activities to maintain the living environment, such as shopping, preparing meals, and managing money. Activities of daily living scales are the most specific and are the most extensively used in medical rehabilitation. These scales measure capabilities in those basic skills necessary to care for oneself, including eating, bathing, grooming, dressing, transfers, continence, and locomotion. The ideal is a continuum of care, with scales that are compatible, tracking patients from inpatient to outpatient care, adult day services, and home care.

UDSMR's instruments and systems are used in many countries, as is the ICF (WHO, 2001). The ICF is a taxonomy that allows for the documentation of degrees of disability and has performance and capacity qualifiers, but it is generally not considered a traditional functional measurement instrument/system. The UDSMR instruments and systems are complementary to the ICF and go further than the ICF and complement it through the use of metrics: They are being used in medical rehabilitation clinical settings to document functional status over time, through various care venues, and to measure rehabilitation outcomes.

In research and in practice, it has been shown that assessment is used successfully to set and reset therapeutic goals, monitor the clinical course of disease, predict outcomes, and to connect the patient to the appropriate care settings at the appropriate times.

References

Baker, J. G., Granger, C. V., & Fiedler, R. C. (1997). A brief outpatient functional assessment measure: Validity using Rasch measures. *American Journal of Physical Medicine & Rehabilitation, 76*(1), 8–13.

Baker, J. G., Granger, C. V., & Ottenbacher, K. J. (1996). Validity of a brief outpatient functional outcome assessment measure. *American Journal of Physical Medicine & Rehabilitation, 75*(5), 356–363.

Bruyère, S., Van Looy, S., & Peterson D. (2005). The International Classification of Functioning, Disability and Health (ICF): Contemporary literature overview. *Rehabilitation Psychology, 50*(2), 113–121.

Carey, R. G., & Posavac, E. J. (1978). Program evaluation of a physical medicine and rehabilitation unit: A new approach. *Archives of Physical Medicine and Rehabilitation, 59*(7), 330–337.

Carter, W. B., Bobbitt, R. A., Bergner, M., & Gilson, B. S. (1976). Validation of an interval scaling: The Sickness Impact Profile. *Health Services Research, 11*(4), 516–528.

Commission on Accreditation of Rehabilitation Facilities. (2004). *Standards manual.* Tucson, AZ: CARF.

Duke University Center for the Study of Aging and Human Development. (1978). *Multidimensional functional assessment: The OARS methodology.* Durham, NC: Duke University.

Granger, C. V. (1999). Continuum of care: Measuring medical rehabilitation outcomes. *Popular Measurement: Journal of the Institute for Objective Measurement, 2*(1), 60–62.

Granger, C. V., Black, T., & Braun S. L. (2006). Quality and outcome measures for medical rehabilitation. In R. L. Braddom (Ed.), *Physical medicine & rehabilitation* (3rd ed., pp. 151–164). Elsevier.

Granger, C. V., Cotter, A. C., Hamilton, B. B., & Fiedler, R. C. (1993). Functional assessment scales: A study of persons after stroke. *Archives of Physical Medicine and Rehabilitation, 74*(2), 133–138.

Granger, C. V., Cotter, A. C., Hamilton, B. B., Fiedler, R. C., & Hens, M. M. (1990). Functional assessment scales: A study of persons with multiple sclerosis. *Archives of Physical Medicine and Rehabilitation, 71*(11), 870–875.

Granger, C. V., Divan, N., & Fiedler, R. C. (1995). Functional assessment scales: A study of persons after traumatic brain injury. *American Journal of Physical Medicine & Rehabilitation, 74*(2), 107–113.

Granger, C. V., Ottenbacher, K. J., Baker, J. G., & Sehgal, A. (1995). Reliability of a brief outpatient functional outcome assessment measure. *American Journal of Physical Medicine & Rehabilitation, 74*(6), 469–475.

Granger, C. V., Wende, K., & Brownscheidle, C. M. (2003). Use of the FIM™ instrument in a trial of intramuscular interferon β-1a for disease progression in relapsing-remitting multiple sclerosis. *American Journal of Physical Medicine & Rehabilitation, 82*(6), 427–436.

Grill, E., Stucki, G., Scheuringer, M., & Melvin, J. (2006). Validation of International Classification of Functioning, Disability, and Health (ICF) core sets for early postacute rehabilitation facilities. *American Journal of Physical Medicine & Rehabilitation, 85*(8), 640–649.

Heinemann, A. W., Kirk, P., Hastie, B. A., Semik, P., Hamilton, B. B., Linacre, J. M., et al. (1997). Relationships between disability measures and nursing effort during medical rehabilitation for patients with traumatic brain and spinal cord injury. *Archives of Physical Medicine and Rehabilitation, 78*(2), 143–149.

Johnston, M. V., Keith, R. A., & Hinderer S. (1992). Measurement standards for interdisciplinary medical rehabilitation. *Archives of Physical Medicine and Rehabilitation, 73*(Suppl), S3–S23.

Joint Commission on Accreditation of Healthcare Organizations. (1992). *1993 accreditation manual for hospitals.* Oakbrook Terrace, IL: Author.

Katz, S., Ford, A. B., Moskowitz, R. W., Jackson, B. A., & Jaffe, M. W. (1963). Studies of illness in the aged: The index of ADL: a standardized measure of biological and psychological functioning. *Journal of the American Medical Association, 185,* 914–919.

Lawton, M. P. (1971). The functional assessment of elderly people. *Journal of the American Geriatric Society, 19*(6), 465–481.

Linacre, J. M., Heinemann, A. W., Wright, B. D., Granger, C. V., & Hamilton, B. B. (1994). The structure and stability of the Functional Independence Measure. *Archives of Physical Medicine and Rehabilitation, 5*(2), 127–132.

Linacre, J. M., & Wright, B. D. (2000). *A user's guide to Winsteps.* Chicago: MESA Press.

Mahoney, F. I., & Barthel, D. W. (1965). Functional evaluation: The Barthel Index. *Maryland State Medical Journal, 14,* 61–65.

Marianjoy Rehabilitation Hospital and Clinics. *Patient Evaluation and Conference System (PECS).* Wheaton, IL: Author.

Rasch, G. (1993). *Probabilistic models for some intelligence and attainment tests.* Chicago: Mesa Press.

Rosow, I., & Breslau, N. (1966). A Guttman health scale for the aged. *Journal of Gerontology, 21*(4), 556–559.

Schoening, H. A., & Iversen, I. A. (1968). Numerical scoring of self-care status: A study of the Kenny Self-Care Evaluation. *Archives of Physical Medicine and Rehabilitation, 49*(4), 221–229.

Stillman, G., Granger, C., & Niewczyk, P. (2009). Projecting function of stroke patients in rehabilitation using the AlphaFIM® instrument in acute care. *Physical Medicine & Rehabilitation, 1*(3), 234–239.

Stineman, M. G., Escarce, J. J., Goin, J. E., Hamilton, B. B., Granger, C. V., & Williams, S. V. (1994). A case mix classification system for medical rehabilitation. *Medical Care, 32*(4), 366–379.

Uniform Data System for Medical Rehabilitation. (1997). *Guide for the Uniform Data Set for Medical Rehabilitation (Including the FIM™ Instrument), Version 5.1.* Buffalo, NY: Author.

Uniform Data System for Medical Rehabilitation. (1998/2002). *WeeFIM System℠ Clinical Guide, Version 5.01.* Buffalo, NY: Author.

Uniform Data System for Medical Rehabilitation. (2005a). *The AlphaFIM® Instrument Guide, Version 2.1.* Buffalo, NY: Author.

Uniform Data System for Medical Rehabilitation. (2005b). *WeeFIM II™ Clinical Guide, Version 6.0.* Buffalo, NY: Author.

U.S. Department of Health and Human Services, Centers for Disease Control and Prevention. (n.d.) *Public Health and Aging: Trends in Aging—United States and Worldwide.* Retrieved January 14, 2009, from: http://www.cdc.gov/mmwr/preview/mmwrhtml/mm5206a2.htm

U.S. Department of Health and Human Services, Centers for Medicare & Medicaid Services. (2002). *Inpatient Rehabilitation Facility-Patient Assessment Instrument (IRF-PAI).* (OMB-0938–0842). Baltimore, MD: Author.

U.S. Department of Health and Human Services, Centers for Medicare & Medicaid Services. (n.d.). Retrieved March 10, 2008, from: http://www.cms.hhs.gov/ProspMedicareFeeSvc PmtGen/

Ware, J. E., & Sherbourne, C. D. (1992).The MOS 36-Item Short-Form Health Survey (SF-36). I. Conceptual framework and item selection. *Medical Care, 30*(6), 473–483.

World Health Organization. (1980). *International Classification of Impairments, Disabilities and Handicaps.* Geneva: Author.

World Health Organization. (2001). *International Classification of Functioning, Disability and Health.* Geneva: Author.

Mary G. Brownsberger
Mary Hibbard

26 Assessment of Community Integration

Overview

When a person enters rehabilitation, the typical image is that of physical, and perhaps psychological, restoration. But if restoration of social functioning, that is, reintegration within one's community, is not considered, the rehabilitation mission of facilitating full recovery or adjustment is incomplete.

The goals of this chapter are to become familiar with the concepts underlying community integration (CI) and to understand how measurement of CI is important not only to the consumer of rehabilitation services but to rehabilitation professionals who provide services to these consumers. The most common measures of CI, including inherent strengths and limitations, are outlined, and current research efforts to enhance the sensitivity of these measures are discussed. The influence of current CI research on rehabilitation practice and implications for sociopolitical policy are also discussed.

Learning Objectives

By the end of the chapter, the reader should be able to:

1. Identify the most commonly utilized CI assessment tools;
2. Discuss the development of CI measures and their current definition;
3. Assess the strengths and limitations of CI measurement tools; and
4. Discuss relevant rehabilitation practice and sociopolitical issues related to issues of CI measurement.

Introduction

CI is a multidimensional construct, and a solid consensus as to its precise definition is lacking. Stakeholders (i.e., rehabilitation professionals, policy makers, funding agencies, and consumers of rehabilitation services) agree that CI involves participation in one's community of choice. Most professionals consider CI to include participation in both home activities (housekeeping, personal finance management, etc.) and community activities (working or going to school, attending religious or social functions, having friends or close relationships outside the home, etc.) and that measurement of CI must include some indicator of levels of participation within each domain. When assessing CI, measurement of potential barriers to CI must also be addressed. These barriers include environmental factors outside a person's control, such as lack of physical access or negative societal attitudes, and unique personal barriers, such as physical, cognitive, or emotional challenges, that can impact CI. A final consideration of CI is the concept of individualized choice. What a person values and how one chooses to participate in his/her community can vary greatly yet still be considered within the bounds of "normal." The importance of individual preference, priorities, and values has not been well-addressed within either the conceptual definition of CI or its measurement. This is a significant shortfall given that the primary goal of rehabilitation professionals is to design and measure rehabilitation outcomes that are guided by individualized priorities and values, rather than purely assessing a fixed array of rehabilitation service delivery systems. Rehabilitation, particularly when considering how to best facilitate an individual's ability to participate in the community, is not "one size fits all." As this chapter highlights, the greatest challenge is the need to expand and reshape the established CI definition and measurement in a way that is specific yet allows for individualized preferences.

Early Developmental History of CI

The concept of CI is not a new idea. Wright (1959), in her discussion of the early development of rehabilitation as a specialized entity, described the concept of *convalescence,* which has evolved over time from "a period of waiting for time and nature to complete healing" to encouraging the person to become "involved in purposeful activity" as quickly as physically possible (p. 12). Wright emphasized that a person cannot successfully be reintegrated into her or his community without the social setting being altered in a way that facilitates participation. Thus, two key components of CI, that is, reintegration into community and facilitation of participation in community, were linked early in the history of rehabilitation.

Following the civil rights movement of the 1960s, the disability rights movement (also known as the independent living movement—IL) gained momentum. By the 1970s, the field of rehabilitation was in a prime position to impact social policy for those with disabilities. The values of empowerment and normalization of individuals with disabilities, long endorsed by rehabilitation professionals (e.g., Wright, 1959), were sanctioned by federal mandate with the Rehabilitation Act of 1973 and further expanded within the Americans with Disabilities Act (ADA) in 1990 (Larson & Sachs, 2000). The ADA is viewed as the culmination of a long effort to achieve equal rights for individuals with disabilities and prohibits discrimination based on a person's level of ability in employment, public services and accommodations, and telecommunications. It has been called the "Emancipation Proclamation for the Disability Community" (Equal Employment Opportunity Commission, 2002).

Current Definitions of CI

Three organizations share a common mission in enhancing rehabilitation outcomes to maximize CI for consumers: the World Health Organization (WHO), the National Institute on Disability and Rehabilitation Research (NIDRR), and the Commission for Accreditation of Rehabilitation Facilities (CARF). While each organization has its own functions, they are inextricably linked in their influence on how rehabilitation outcomes, including CI, are defined and on how services designed to achieve those outcomes are provided and evaluated.

Applicable ICF—WHO Constructs

WHO views disability from a biopsychosocial perspective. CI is defined using a system that addresses how impairments, abilities, and environmental factors influence an individual's ability to function in the community. WHO developed the International Classification of Functioning, Disability and Health (ICF), formerly codified as the International Classification of Impairment, Disability and Health (ICIDH; WHO, 2001). In addition to classifications of physical function, the ICF includes indicators of individual activity and participation levels and of environmental factors that can impact a person's ability to be active and/or participate in the community (WHO, 2001).

In the ICF, the term *participation* is synonymous with CI and is defined as "involvement in a life situation" (WHO, 2002). Participation involves examining how health conditions, physical function and structure, personal and environmental contextual factors, and levels of activity interact to influence an individual's level of participation. Specific domains considered as core components of CI, or participation, include: learning and applying knowledge; general tasks and demands; communication; mobility; self-care; domestic life; interpersonal interactions and relationships; major life areas; and community, social, and civic life.

NIDRR

Under the auspices of the U.S. Department of Education, NIDRR is the lead agency providing federal funding for rehabilitation outcome research. NIDRR places a high priority on the funding of community integration research focused on improving independent living outcomes. In NIDRR's most recent long-range plan, CI is included as one of five priority funding domains (NIDRR, 2006). Utilizing concepts from the ICF, CI is viewed as including both participation and community living, with the term *participation* broadly defined to include all aspects of independent living and community integration. In NIDRR's view, CI "focus(es) on the extent to which people with disabilities are participating in the community in a manner that is meaningful to them" (NIDRR, 2006, p. 8,182). NIDRR's focus on CI outcomes serves to define both agency policy and funding decisions and ensures that future research and program development remain focused on ways to enhance CI among individuals with disabilities.

CARF

CARF is a nationally recognized accreditation agency whose purview is to accredit rehabilitation agencies and facilities that provide services in the areas of behavioral health, medical rehabilitation, and employment/community support. In its mission, CARF emphasizes the need for enhanced outcome measurement, particularly regarding how specific rehabilitation services enhance positive outcomes for their consumers (Wilkerson, Shen, & Duhaime, 1998). In CARF's view, CI outcomes are defined as "community inclusion and participation by persons served" (Wilkerson et al, 1998, p. 83). CARF highlights the need to develop quantifiable, scientifically sound CI measures that can be used to evaluate programs in a uniform manner, thus empowering consumers to make sound decisions regarding which rehabilitation services are best for them. CARF's role in enhancing CI lies in its capacity to accredit organizations working with individuals with disabilities that are able to demonstrate enhanced CI outcomes for its consumers.

In summary, while all three agencies approach CI in a slightly different fashion due to different missions and focus, all embrace WHO's ICF definition of "involvement in a life situation." In this chapter, the terms *CI* and *participation* are used interchangeably.

CI Assessment Methodology

Throughout the 1980s and 1990s, rehabilitation researchers developed a wide variety of CI measures, with most tools used to assess CI for groups of consumers with specific disabilities or medical conditions. Examples of these CI tools are listed here:

- Frenchay Activities Index (Wade, Leigh-Smith, & Hewer, 1985)—measures the frequency of participation in social activities among stroke survivors.
- Reintegration to Normal Living Index (Wood-Dauphinee, Opzoomer, Williams, Marchand, & Spitzer, 1988)—an 11-item instrument that assesses a person's level of participation and satisfaction. Those who participated in the initial testing of this instrument included individuals who were primarily cancer and heart attack survivors.
- Edinburgh Rehabilitation Status Scale (ERSS; Affleck, Aitkin, Hunter, McGuire, & Roy, 1988)—measures independence, activity level, social integration, and effect of symptoms on lifestyle among individuals who received rehabilitation following amputation, stroke, musculoskeletal surgery, or other neurological conditions.
- Personal Independence Profile (PIP; Nosek, Fuhrer, & Howland, 1992)—includes measures of the environmental and psychological aspects of independence.
- London Handicap Scale (Harwood, Gompertz, & Ebrahim, 1994)—measures the level of handicap, as defined by WHO (for more details, see description of CHART below), among stroke survivors.
- Living Life After Traumatic Brain Injury (LLATBI; Gordon, Brown, & Hibbard, 1998)—developed to capture the "insider perspective" of disability after brain injury (BI) while focusing on social roles and extent of community integration after BI.
- LIFE-H (Fougeyrollas et al., 1998)—designed to assess independent functioning, social roles, and level of handicap among individuals with spinal cord injury.
- Community Outcome Scale (Stilwell, Stilwell, Hawley, & Davies, 1998)—measures the impact of handicapping problems on achieving CI among individuals with brain injury.
- Brain Injury Community Rehabilitation Outcome Scales (BICRO-39; Powell, Beckers, & Greenwood, 1998)—assesses problems experienced by individuals with brain injury who live in the community;.
- Subjective Index of Physical and Social Outcome (SIPSO; Trigg, Wood, & Hewer, 1999)—measures social integration following stroke.
- Community Integration Measure (CIM; McColl, Davies, Carlson, Johnston, & Minnes, 2001)—designed to measure CI among individuals with brain injury.
- AIMS (Minnes et al., 2001)—a qualitative measure of CI based on acculturation theory that has been used with brain injury survivors.
- Sydney Psychosocial Reintegration Scale (SPRS; Kuipers, Kendall, Fleming, & Tate, 2004),—measures CI among brain injury survivors.

In a recent meta-analysis of CI outcomes, Brownsberger (2005) found that the aforementioned measures have been infrequently used by other researchers in the field.

Research Box 26.1.

Brownsberger, M. G. (2005). *Community integration outcomes in physical rehabilitation: An exploratory meta-analysis.*
Poster presented at the Midwinter Conference of Division 22 (Rehabilitation Psychology), Reno, NV.

Objective: To examine extant body of research to ascertain whether there is consistency in the definition, methodology rigor, and measurement of community integration (CI) outcomes that will allow a meaningful aggregation of findings.

Design: Sources included all published empirical studies related to CI among adults with sudden- or late-onset disabling conditions. Consistency of CI definitions, variables studied, and methodological characteristics were evaluated in terms of impact on overall effect size.

Results: Most studies used the WHO definition of CI or the CIQ or CHART as measures of CI. Included studies produced a moderate overall effect size. Residence status, physical health status, and functional status were statistically significant predictors of community integration outcome. Marital status, education level, and cognitive status demonstrated clinical significance.

Conclusions: Study quality and which variables have been studied must be considered when interpreting results. The type of statistic from which effect size could be derived, study design, and statistical power all had a substantial impact on findings, leading to a strong recommendation for improved methodology rigor in original research. Many variables that may be related to CI outcomes could not be fully explored due to small volume of studies.

Questions to consider:
How would you utilize the findings of this study to improve the study of community integration outcomes? In what way might these issues influence how you decide to assess community integration?

Three CI tools have been more widely used. Two of these tools were initially designed to assess CI in individuals with brain injury: the Community Integration Questionnaire (CIQ; Willer, Rosenthal, Kreutzer, Gordon, & Rempel, 1993) and the Mayo-Portland Adaptability Inventory (MPAI; Malec, Smigielski, DePompolo, & Thompson, 1993). The Craig Handicap Assessment and Reporting Technique (CHART; Whiteneck, Charlifue, Gerhart, Overholser, & Richardson, 1992) was developed to assess CI in individuals with spinal cord injury. The reader is directed to the following Web site for additional information regarding these and other measures used in rehabilitation: http://www.tbims.org/combi. Each of these measures, as well as a much newer measure

26.1 Psychometrics of Common CI Assessments

Assessment	CIQ	CHART	MPAI—Participation Subscale
Unit of measure	Tasks/activities	Tasks/activities	Problems experienced
Metric	Frequency	Frequency	Level of independence
Test-retest reliability	Acceptable (.83–.97)	Acceptable (.80–.93)	n/a
Inter-rater reliability	Acceptable (.42–.94)	Acceptable (.28–.84)	Acceptable (.74–.89)
Internal consistency	Acceptable (coefficient alpha > .80)	n/a	Acceptable (coefficient alpha = .85)
Validity	Good correlation with CHART	Good comparison with professional eval of subjects	Good correlation with Disability Rating Scale, Rancho, Neuropsych measures
Subscale/ Item categories			
Physical/ Cognitive		X	X
Home integration/ Domestic life	X		X
Mobility/ Transportation		X	X
Social integration	X	X	X
Employment/Economic self-sufficiency	X	X	X
Interpersonal relationships			X

Note: For additional psychometric information, please visit http://www.tbims.org/combi.
Although the above measures include items in similar categories, and they are similarly named, they do not necessarily measure the same constructs.

that has recently been incorporated into the Uniform Data System for Medical Rehabilitation (UDSMR), is described in greater detail in the following paragraphs. Also, please see Table 26.1, which summarizes the similarities and differences in the measures.

Community Integration Questionnaire

The CIQ (Willer et al., 1993) was developed to measure CI among individuals who have survived brain injury. This measure was designed to accommodate both the cognitive and physical impairments of this disability group. The CIQ is one of the most frequently used measures of CI for individuals with BI. It was designed as a brief 15-item questionnaire that could produce a meaningful self-report of CI within three main areas of functioning: home, social, and productive activities. The CIQ is currently incorporated into a long-term outcome database for survivors of traumatic brain injury (TBI) who received services from one of NIDRR Model Systems of Care for individuals with TBI.

The CIQ consists of three subscales: the *home integration subscale,* which includes such activities as grocery shopping, meal preparation and housework; the *social integration subscale,* which includes activities such as visiting with friends, going shopping, and engaging in leisure activities; and the *productivity subscale,* which contains activities focused on employment, volunteer activities, and continuing education. Some activities are scored on a six-point scale, while others are scored on a three-point scale. Overall level of CI is computed based on a summation of the three subscales with possible values ranging from 0 to 29; higher scores indicate a higher level of CI.

The primary benefit of the CIQ is the measure's brevity. It asks a limited number of unambiguous questions designed to accommodate those with cognitive impairments and/or those who fatigue easily (both common challenges following brain injury). The CIQ has demonstrated acceptable test–retest reliability (Willer et al, 1993). It has demonstrated concurrent validity with other CI measures (most notably CHART, described later) and is able to differentiate levels of CI between those with brain injury and controls (Willer, Ottenbacher, & Coad, 1994). Because the CIQ is an integral component of the outcome data collected across all TBI Model Systems and is utilized across a wide variety of other rehabilitation settings, it has provided researchers and service providers in the area of BI a common tool with which to assess CI. However, findings of a recent study have challenged the sensitivity of CIQ. More specifically, when self and proxy (either significant others or professionals who are well-acquainted) report on the CIQs were compared, discrepancies have been apparent with higher values (i.e., greater report of CI) reported by the brain injury survivor (Dijkers, 2000). Findings such as these have highlighted the need for revisions of even well-used CI measurement tools in the field.

The Mayo-Portland Adaptability Inventory

The MPAI (Malec et al., 1993) was designed to assess functioning in the areas of emotional behavior, functional abilities, and physical impairments among individuals with traumatic or acquired brain injury. The MPAI was derived from Lezak's Portland Adaptability Inventory (Malec et al, 1993). It has undergone several modifications over the years and now includes a subscale that addresses participation. The current version, MPAI-4, contains 35 items that result in three indices: *Ability* (physical and cognitive functioning, such as mobility, vision, memory, attention), *Adjustment* (emotional functioning, such as anxiety, depression, pain, fatigue, self-awareness), and *Participation* (social functioning, such as initiation, social contact, leisure activities, self-care). The instrument is designed to be completed by either individuals with brain injury and/or their proxies. The Participation index, consisting of eight items, can be used either as a part of the entire instrument or separately. Each item is scored on a

Likert-type scale from zero, indicating no problems in that area, to four, indicating severe problems. The instrument has demonstrated good psychometric properties (Malec, 2005).

An advantage of the MPAI-4 is its comprehensiveness; it includes a broad range of CI challenges that a brain injury survivor may encounter, lending itself well to use in a variety of clinical and research settings. Unfortunately, the MPAI's comprehensiveness has also made it difficult to contrast MPAI findings with findings from other CI measures (see Table 26.1).

The Craig Handicap Assessment and Reporting Technique

The CHART was first utilized with individuals with spinal cord injury (SCI; Whiteneck et al., 1992) and is a frequently used CI measurement tool in the study of individuals following SCI. The CHART is incorporated into a long-term outcome database for SCI survivors as part of NIDRR-funded Model System Programs for individuals with SCI. As with the CIQ, this measure has undergone extensive reliability and validity testing, and psychometric characteristics have been published (see Table 26.1). It was designed to measure WHO's concept of handicap, using the ICIDH model, which preceded the ICF. The ICIDH model describes the level of handicap, or inability to function independently, in six key areas: orientation to surroundings, physical existence, mobility, occupation, social integration, and economic self-sufficiency. The CHART was initially developed to quantify functioning in 5 of the 6 ICIDH-described areas and contained 27 items; it was recently modified to include the 6th ICIDH domain, orientation, and now contains 32 items (Mellick, 2000). The maximum score on each subscale (physical and cognitive independence, mobility, occupation, social integration, and economic self-sufficiency) is 100 points, with a total of 500 points possible. Higher scores indicate higher levels of functioning. A briefer version, CHART-SF, was developed in 2000. It has 19 items that yield the same subscales as the original CHART.

The CHART has demonstrated good reliability and validity, with good participant-proxy agreement (Whiteneck et al, 1992). It has become the "gold standard" for measurement of CI among individuals with SCI. Its items, while similar to the CIQ, contain additional items targeted to assess the level of assistance needed with mobility, a relevant issue for many individuals with SCI (e.g., ability to enter and exit home without assistance).

PAR-PRO

A more recent CI tool, called the PAR-PRO (Ostir et al., 2006), was developed to closely parallel the ICF. This 20-item measure demonstrates good psychometric properties and is intended to be utilized in conjunction with existing measures of physical and cognitive functioning, such as the Functional Independence Measure (FIM), an outcome tool widely used in inpatient rehabilitation settings to assess functional improvement overtime. The PAR-PRO is designed to capture levels of participation for the year prior to hospitalization, at hospital discharge, and at 30-day follow-up. The instrument includes a patient evaluation of rehabilitation services provided. The PAR-PRO has been incorporated into the UDSMR.

Factors Impacting CI: A Summary of the Research

Using the numerous CI measurement tools described in the previous section, researchers have attempted to examine variables impacting CI outcomes. Most research has been directed at examination of personal factors (e.g., physical, cognitive, emotional, behavioral), environmental factors, and rehabilitation effectiveness as influencing CI outcomes.

Personal factors impacting CI outcomes include a range of concepts such as pre- or post-injury personality characteristics, a self-identity that includes one's disability status, pre- or post-injury cognitive or psychological deficits, and pre- or post-injury social skills. Many authors have discussed the impact of sudden-onset disability on an individual's activities, social participation, and resumption of social roles (e.g., residence status, marital status, employment, education level) and recommend areas for further research and intervention (e.g., Bell & Pepping, 2001; Burton, Leahy, & Volpe, 2003; Colantonio et al., 2004).

Environmental factors impacting CI outcomes focus on the attitudes and accessibility of the community vis-à-vis individuals with disabilities. These also include the availability of services and social supports and systems that allow individuals with disabilities to make independent choices regarding the utilization of services. Several authors discuss the importance of community acceptance of individuals with disabilities. For example, Pomeroy (1983) proposes that recreation can be an avenue toward CI. While people with disabilities are acquiring new physical skills, there is also the potential for increased interaction with nondisabled individuals, which then increases the potential for acceptance of another's disability on the part of the nondisabled person.

Rehabilitation effectiveness factors impacting CI outcomes focus primarily on the availability of services along a continuum of care (from in-patient acute care through community-reentry) and through involvement of independent living centers. Research regarding the effectiveness of specific rehabilitation interventions in CI outcomes is extremely limited. Two studies in which specific rehabilitation interventions have been shown to be effective in increasing CI include a study of service dog ownership (Allen & Blascovich, 1996) and a study of athletic participation (Slater & Meade, 2004). Allen and Blascovich used the CIQ to measure changes in CI after wheelchair users had received service dogs, finding a significant increase in CI following the intervention. Using the CHART as an outcome measure, Slater and Meade found that CI increased when individuals with disabilities participated in athletics.

The limited number of studies suggests critical areas in which to focus future research and enhance the sensitivity of current CI measures.

Challenges to Current CI Assessment Measures

Researchers have begun to challenge the adequacy of current CI assessment measurement tools. The first challenge has been the lack of a universal standard for measuring CI. For example, measurement of physical function is easily suited to "objective standards," that is, there are broadly used and well-accepted

Research Box 26.2

A RANDOMIZED, CONTROLLED STUDY OF CI OUTCOMES

Allen, K., & Blaskovich, J. (1996). The value of service dogs for people with severe ambulatory disabilities. *Journal of the American Medical Association, 275*(13), 1001–1006.

The following represents one of the few randomized, controlled studies (RCT) of CI outcomes of a specific intervention. In a recent meta-analysis of CI research (see Research Box 26.1), it was excluded from the quantitative meta-analysis because its effect size was so large that, in comparison with other included studies, it was an outlier. It is this type of rigorous research, however, to which future efforts should aspire.

Objective: To assess the value of service dogs for people with ambulatory disabilities.

Design: Randomized, controlled clinical trial.

Setting: Environment of study participants.

Participants: Forty-eight individuals with ambulatory mobility impairments were recruited, matched on age, sex, marital status, race, and disability diagnosis and severity, and randomized into experimental and wait-list control groups.

Intervention: Experimental group members received trained service dogs 1 month after study began. Wait-list group members received dogs in month 13.

Main Outcome Measures: Self-reported psychological well-being (Affect Balance Scale), internal locus of control (Spheres of Control Scale), self-esteem (Rosenberg Self-esteem Scale), community integration (Community Integration Questionnaire), school attendance, part-time work status, marital status, living arrangements, and number of biweekly paid and unpaid assistance hours. Assessment data were collected every 6 months throughout the course of the study.

Results: All participants showed significant positive changes in self-esteem, internal locus of control, psychological well-being, and community integration, as well as increases in employment or school activities and reduced personal assistance requirements. Community integration levels, as measured by the CIQ (score range of 0-30), increased for both groups from an average of just over 2 to over 25 after 1 year of dog ownership.

Conclusions: Trained service dogs can be highly beneficial and potentially cost-effective components of independent living for people with physical disabilities.

> **Questions to consider:**
> In looking at the relationship of service dog ownership and community integration, it appears that there is indeed a strong effect. However, consider the limitations of how community integration is assessed, as described in this chapter. How might that influence interpretation of study results, or influence future assessment or interventions?

standards related to better vs. poorer CI (e.g., walking is a higher level of physical function than use of a wheelchair), while in measurement of CI, no such "objective" standards exist. A second challenge has been the varied scope of activities assessed across measurement tools. For example, while most CI measures are similar at the broadest level (i.e., all purport to measure CI as generally defined by the ICF or its predecessor ICIDH), each CI measure focuses on slightly different domains of functioning. A third challenge has been the varied ways in which a given CI activity is measured across CI measures (e.g., frequency of activity per week vs. time spent in a specific activity each day vs. extent of assistance needed to perform the activity), making comparison across outcome findings difficult, if not impossible (Dijkers, Whiteneck, & El-Jaroudi, 2000).

Perhaps the greatest challenge to established CI measures is one concerning validity because established CI measures fail to include subjective indicators of which activities are most important or valued to an individual (e.g., Brown et al., 2004). In current CI measurement, CI outcomes are objective and defined by the researcher; subjective views of the person about the inherent value of a given activity are neither obtained nor considered in determining adequacy of CI. For example, in traditional CI outcome measurement, competitive employment is viewed as more desirable than part-time work, volunteering, or not working. Yet, one person may view being competitively employed full time as a high value, while another person may not consider full-time work as a desirable or valued CI outcome. Therefore, using traditional measurement, a person may be perceived as less "community integrated" merely because one is engaged in activities at a level consistent with one's personal value system.

In a multicultural society such as the United States, there is no single set of "desirable" roles to which individuals aspire. Thus, a clear idea of what is undesirable is also difficult to define. After years of methodological disregard by the scientific community, the early concept of the "insider perspective" espoused by social and early rehabilitation psychologists (e.g., Wright, 1959) has re-emerged as a missing element of CI measurement.

Expansion of CI Outcome Measurement

While it is critical to measure how an individual is functioning in society and establish rehabilitation goals accordingly (Whiteneck et al., 1992), it is equally

Case Study 26.1

The following was presented as an illustrative case study for a program designed to increase community integration and social interaction skills through the collaboration of a rehabilitation program and a community college. Individuals with brain injury enrolled in an adult education class designed to improve social functioning. Instructors were therapeutic recreation specialists with experience in brain injury rehabilitation, and class size was limited to eight students to facilitate effectiveness. Meeting weekly, each class followed a structured routine that included social skill development and practice, planning and organizational skill development, and community participation activities. It was hypothesized that skill development would generalize to other settings, thus increasing participants' community integration.

Greg is a 30-year-old white male who sustained TBI at the age of 15 years. He was involved in inpatient rehabilitation, outpatient programs, and several employment assistance programs. He had attempted to work; however, he was unable to keep a job for any length of time. Typically, he could perform the tasks required for the job but had difficulty using good judgment when making social decisions, such as when to take a break, talking excessively, flirting with females, and so forth. When he began the class at the community college, he had not worked in several years. His activity level was very low. The majority of his time was spent reading or watching television. He did occasionally assist with tasks around the house. Greg attended the Compensatory Education class for a little over 1 year. During his involvement in the class, Greg was able to make progress in improving the intelligibility of his speech, controlling his disinhibition, and increasing his awareness of others and their needs. In addition, he improved his dependability with attendance as well as using his appointment book so he could assume responsibility for his plans and actions. When Greg first began attending the class, he often would miss class and not call in. He frequently made inappropriate comments to females on campus. He was very self-centered and frequently did not acknowledge others in the class with a greeting when joining the class or leaving. He made steady gains in all of these areas, resulting in his readiness and decision to graduate from his class.

Greg did not want to just stop attending the class when he graduated. He needed to progress to another form of activity. He did not feel he was ready to make the time commitment for paid employment, so Greg decided to explore the possibility of volunteer work. The consideration of volunteer work demonstrated a big change in Greg's previously rigid values. When Greg became involved in the class, he stated that it was better not to work at all than to do volunteer work. Greg identified several factors he felt would be important for him to enjoy a volunteer position. Some of those included a job routine, a variety of job tasks, outside work, and involvement with people. Greg accepted a volunteer position at a local rose garden park. His job tasks included upkeep of the grounds, raking grass, spreading pine needles, and trimming the roses. Greg received job coaching for his volunteer job by one of the therapeutic recreation specialists through their involvement at the rehabilitation center.

Job coaching assisted Greg with developing strategies to recall his job tasks and their procedures. Job coaching also provided Greg with the training to determine when to request assistance from his supervisor and when he could initiate his job tasks on his own. Greg has frequent contact with other employees and his supervisor and limited contact with the public. To date, he has demonstrated good conversation skills, an awareness of when to work and when to take a break, respect for his supervisor and thus appropriate interaction with her, and a sense of dependability. Currently, the management at the rose garden is considering including some of Greg's work time in the budget and paying him for some of the time that he spends working there. Greg has gradually increased his hours working from one 2-hour day to two 4-hour days. Greg reports that the volunteer job has given structure and meaning to his life. He feels his quality of life has improved because of his involvement. (Guerrier & Bostick, 2001, p. 37)

important to prioritize those activities in a way that is meaningful to a given individual. To address this challenge, researchers are in the process of developing and/or modifying existing CI measures to include the "insider's perspective" (e.g., Brown et al., 2004; Cicerone, Mott, Azulay, & Friel, 2004; Johnston, Goverover, & Dijkers, in press) and are redefining the concepts underlying CI (Whiteneck, Heinemann, Corrigan, Bogner, & Brooks, 2007). This shift in focus has resulted in an expansion of CI methodology to include both objective assessment of CI, that is, how an individual is participating in her or his community, and subjective assessment of CI, that is, the specific values and priorities of an individual when formulating their own rehabilitation outcomes.

Expanding CI to Include the "Insider Perspective"

Recent research efforts are being directed at expanding CI measures to include both objective and subjective indicators of participation. In the field of TBI, the Participation Objective, Participation Subjective (POPS; Brown et al., 2004) was designed to assess both objective and subjective components of given CI activities. In the POPS, subjective assessment includes both ratings of the importance of a given CI activity to the person and level of satisfaction with the current level of participation in the specific activity. Thus, the POPS was the first CI metric to incorporate the "insider perspective" and to utilize weighted scoring of CI based on an individual's preferences and priorities, as well as satisfaction with current participation in a given activity. The POPS consists of 26 activities; scores are weighted based on individual responses to calculate a mean level of subjective participation. The POPS is available for use by clinicians and researchers via the Web site, http://www.tbims.org/combi.

Several other authors in the area of TBI have pursued similar avenues. Cicerone and colleagues (2004) developed the Quality of Community Integration Questionnaire (QCIQ), in which parallel questions regarding satisfaction with activity levels and cognitive functioning were added to each of the items within the CIQ. Johnston et al. (in press) included questions regarding satisfaction and value levels for each item of the CIQ. Jette, Keysor, Coster, Penshen, and Haley (2005) developed the Participation Measure for Post-Acute Care (PM-PAC), which is designed to measure participation outcomes of rehabilitation services provided to individuals with a variety of disabilities and medical conditions in outpatient or home-care settings.

These most recent research efforts point to the importance of using objective and subjective measures of CI (Brown et al., 2004, Cicerone et al., 2004; Johnston et al., in press; Keysor, Jette, Coster, Prvu-Bettger, & Haley, 2006) and highlight the value of an individual's perception of environmental or social barriers, as well as the value of a particular activity to the individual. Clearly, "next generation" CI measures will include evaluation of the importance of a given community activity by the individual.

Discussion Box 26.1

THE CURRENT CHALLENGE: TO DEFINE CI WITH ENOUGH SPECIFICITY THAT IT IS MEASURABLE AND ALSO ALLOWS FOR THE INCLUSION OF AN INDIVIDUAL'S VALUES AND PRIORITIES

Most measures of CI assess objective levels of activity in various settings. While this is the most easily quantified way of assessing CI, there is growing agreement that this approach is less than adequate because it lacks inclusion of an individual's values and priorities within measurement. Each individual has unique ideas regarding what constitutes CI and what level of participation is optimal. Preferences are influenced by culture and language of origin and the norms of one's chosen community as well as by personality and physical, cognitive, and emotional challenges.

Thus, the challenge to the field is to develop a CI measure that is reliable and valid across cultures and takes into account individual values and preferences (subjective) that may impact levels of activity (objective) in various settings. Furthermore, assessment must consider what barriers to participation the individual perceives, such as whether physical access is available, or whether society values participation of individuals with disabilities, when assessing an individual's level of CI.
Core Issue Questions: Is CI a "society" or an "individual" problem?
Is a universal definition and/or measure of CI possible?

Redefining the Concept of CI

Other researchers are re-examining the concepts underlying CI by using the voice of the consumer and state-of-the-art test theory to guide instrument development (A. Heinemann, personal communication, February 16, 2007). Whiteneck and colleagues (2007) are developing a more comprehensive CI tool called the Community Participation Index (CPI). They have utilized focus groups and Kelly's Role Construct Repertory test with all stakeholders who have a vested interest in rehabilitation outcomes (i.e., consumers of rehabilitation services, caregivers, rehabilitation professionals, insurers, and policy makers) to "identify components of participation as a basis for item development" (p.1). Items have been piloted in interviews with individuals with disabilities and former consumers of rehabilitation services. Qualitative analysis revealed a cluster of values that define the concept of participation: active and meaningful engagement, personal choice and control, society access and opportunity, inclusion, and membership. Pilot testing revealed a spectrum of participation ranging from low, indicated by involuntary isolation and not leaving one's house often, to high, indicated by time spent in civic and cultural activities, employment, school attendance, and holding leadership roles. The CPI is now a 41-item instrument being implemented in a state-wide, population-based telephone survey of the general population (Whiteneck et al., 2007). Future plans include enlargement of the item pool and utilization of computer adaptive testing to further tailor assessment administration to each individual. A tailored assessment approach will facilitate a greater ability to develop rehabilitation goals that target the challenges most important to each consumer of rehabilitation services.

Challenges to Inclusion of the Insider's Perspective Within CI Measurement

There are also critics of the need for inclusion of subjective criteria in CI measures. Some researchers argue that CI constructs become too loosely defined and are thus meaningless except to the specific individual. From these critics' viewpoints, subjective instruments are neither reliable nor valid. Similarly, weighting of subjective responses to objective CI items based upon an individual's preference is considered not to be reliable or valid by traditional test theorists (e.g., Nunnally & Bernstein, 1994; Wainer, 1976). These concerns have been countered by other theorists. For example, Dijkers, Diamond, and Marion (2003) suggest that while psychometric theory may be more appropriate in certain settings, clinicians of various disciplines often use subjective and weighted measures. Furthermore, a subjective approach may have more validity when a construct is as complex as CI.

Collaborative Efforts to Design More Universal CI Measurement Tools

While existing instruments each have positive attributes, all have limitations, and none are recognized as the universal tool for measuring CI. The CIQ and CHART, currently the most frequently used measures, and the tools included in the Model Systems of Care databases for brain injury and spinal cord injury, respectively, also have shortcomings, as noted in the prior discussion. Recent efforts at embedding subjective components into existing measures have been fruitful, but further work is needed.

Two collaborative research efforts are underway to develop instruments that combine the best items from existing instruments, while including both objective and subjective measures. In a current collaborative study (NIDRR Grant No. H133B040033), investigators from eight TBI Model Systems of Care for individuals with TBI are combining items from the CIQ, CHART, MPAI, and POPS to derive and test a new measure called the Participation Assessment with Recombined Tool, or the PART. The PART consists of an objective component (PART) as well as its subjective counterpart, the PART-OS (PART Objective and Subjective). Currently, the PART (objective component) consists of 78 questions; 70 are completed by the person with brain injury and 8 by the interviewer, with input from other individuals who are well-acquainted with the brain injury survivor. It is anticipated that the final instrument will be reduced to 10 to 15 of the most sensitive items. The PART-OS (subjective component) is currently in development, with input obtained from individuals with brain injury regarding phrasing of key questions. Qualitative data will be utilized to develop a standardized questionnaire to complement the objective ratings of the PART, which will then be piloted in participating model systems (M. Hibbard, personal communication, March 14, 2007).

A similar effort is underway among SCI Model Systems of Care. In this project, investigators are utilizing items from the PART-OS, CPI, PM-PAC, CIM, and PAR-PRO, with the goal to create a stream-lined and effective measure of participation that is stakeholder-focused (i.e., consumers, professionals, policy makers), emphasizes the "insider perspective," focuses on positive aspects of disability, and utilizes contemporary measurement approaches (Whiteneck et al., 2007).

Legislative and Advocacy Issues

Addressing Funding Disparities

While CI research has been conducted in relation to many disability groups, including stroke, burn, cancer, and cardiac disease, the preponderance of research and thus instrument development has been focused on two major groups: those individuals with spinal cord injury and those with traumatic brain injury. This disparity in CI research emphasis appears to reflect the differential funding streams available to support disability research; that is, NIDRR funding has been directed at specific groups (SCI and TBI). While NIDRR funds research in other disability areas, for example, burns, pediatric TBI, aging, stroke, and so forth, these programs are more limited in that only one or two sites will be funded for a given disability focus. As a result, there has been less opportunity to reach the same level of maturity in measure development as the other NIDRR-funded programs. Despite limited federal financial support for CI research, individuals with other disabilities face similar CI challenges that remain largely unaddressed. There is a clear need for rehabilitation professionals to increase advocacy efforts for improved public policy and funding related to CI outcomes across the wider spectrum of disability so that individuals, regardless of specific disability, are better served.

Striving for Cultural Inclusion

As our world becomes increasingly integrated, policies that protect human rights are becoming more common across cultures. However, acknowledging rights for individuals with disabilities and establishing public policies that facilitate improved physical and attitudinal access are far from the norm, even in some Western cultures. When our focus is on long-term outcomes, such as CI, we cannot consider only a specific individual's ability to function. We must also consider the culture and the environment in which individuals exist.

While the ICF is a great boon to this effort, it is only a starting point. WHO recommendations do not hold the weight of law or public policy in any country, and in some countries, these guidelines are not even considered. The next step requires advocacy and activism to implement policies that facilitate greater access and participation for all individuals across cultures and countries. While the disability rights movement in the United States has played a significant role in the passage of critical legislation such as the ADA, similar efforts in other countries have not yet had similar impact. Furthermore, the field of rehabilitation is in its infancy in many countries and must be supported by rehabilitation professionals in order to achieve successful CI outcomes for all with disabilities.

Expanded Support for Long-Term CI Outcome Research

While the need to measure the impact of interventions at each stage of rehabilitation, including long-term follow-up, may seem obvious, it is a difficult standard to achieve. The NIDRR-funded Model Systems of Care for individuals with SCI and TBI provide longitudinal follow-up assessments at 1 year, 5 years, and 10 years post-injury, serving as a model for longitudinal follow-up for individuals with other types of disabilities. Long-term follow up, even in NIDRR model system programs, is a significant challenge with many people lost to follow-up over time. The ability to follow individuals with other disabilities is equally valued but lacking adequate financial or institutional support. Thus, attempts to identify which rehabilitation interventions are most likely to result in positive long-term outcomes remains the challenge of future researchers. The key to successful implementation of longitudinal outcome research is a steady and expanded funding stream.

Research Challenges

Enhanced Research Methodology

To better understand CI outcomes, the field needs to strive for a universally accepted definition and single measure of CI outcome. This will allow for more comprehensive and rigorous CI outcome methodology and permit comparison across disability groups. A recent meta-analysis of CI outcomes research (Brownsberger, 2005; see Research Box 26.1) concluded that research quality was a critical factor in being able to synthesize results across studies. Of particular issue is the need to focus on statistical power and effect size in determining the clinical significance of results (rather than statistical significance, e.g., McAweeney, Forschheimer, & Tate, 1997). Studies should maximize power through the use of comparison or control groups and adequate sample sizes (e.g., McAweeney & Klockars, 1998). Research should also be replicated in order to validate results and establish solid foundations on which to build the knowledge base (e.g., Ottenbacher, 1995). At the same time, investigators must conduct research that includes the subjective "insider perspective" (e.g., Brown et al., 2004) to ensure that study is focused on those aspects of CI that are most important to the people we serve.

It is through study of our current practices and their impact on long-term outcomes that we can hope to achieve better CI outcomes in the future. The ultimate goal is to develop rehabilitation methods that are generally successful and that can be customized to meet the specific needs of each individual.

Moderating Variables

While much research of factors that impact CI has been completed, many possible factors have not yet been studied adequately. These include variables such as cultural and racial differences, socioeconomic status, familial support, comorbid psychological disorders including substance abuse, and personality constructs such as self-efficacy.

Summary

CI is a multidimensional construct. Most authors consider it to comprise the following: living situation, social relationships, social roles, economic status, daily activities, and interaction with mainstream society. Also inherent in the concept of CI are the equally important but more difficult to quantify concepts of rights, power, and freedom of action. The ICF definition of participation is synonymous with CI. One's level of participation, or CI, is determined by the interaction of health condition, physical function and structure, personal and environmental contextual factors, and opportunities to participate. Researchers have identified many factors that impact CI outcomes and recognize that positive outcomes require the interaction of personal, social, and environmental characteristics. Understanding each individual's unique characteristics allows us to flexibly modify empirically validated interventions to be as effective as possible.

While specific definitions and terms may change, the underlying concept of CI has not shifted dramatically over time. Restoring the capacity to participate in meaningful and valued activities in the community is arguably the ultimate goal of rehabilitation. In addition to WHO's development of the ICF, two agencies have supported the need for ongoing evaluation of CI outcomes: NIDRR, in its funding of CI research program efforts, and CARF, in its accrediting rehabilitation organizations emphasizing CI as a key outcome of rehabilitation efforts.

The most frequently used measures of CI are the CIQ and the MPAI, primarily for individuals with TBI, and the CHART, primarily for individuals with SCI. These measures assess objective levels of activity in home, social, and work settings. Current measure development efforts are now focused on the inclusion of subjective components of CI, that is, the individual's values and priorities as related to specific CI activities, with revisions of these CI tools to include the "insider's perspective" now underway.

Future research needs to focus on the creation of a single CI outcome tool, expanding assessment to include the broadest range of disability types and addressing potential moderators, such as cultural, race, and socioeconomic differences, within newly developed CI measurement. Finally, the rehabilitation system must achieve a seamless continuum of care that facilitates the best long-term outcomes for individuals we serve.

References

Affleck, J. W., Aitkin, R.C.B., Hunter, J.A.A., McGuire, R. J., & Roy, C. W. (1988, January 30). Rehabilitation status: A measure of medicosocial dysfunction. *Lancet, 1*(8579), 230–233.

Allen, K., & Blascovich, J. (1996). The value of service dogs for people with severe ambulatory disabilities. *Journal of the American Medical Association, 275,* 1001–1006.

Bell, K. R., & Pepping, M. (2001). Women and traumatic brain injury. *Physical Medicine and Rehabilitation Clinics of North America, 12,* 169–182.

Brown, M., Dijkers, M. P., Gordon, W. A., Ashman, T., Charatz, H., & Cheng, Z. (2004). Participation objective, participation subjective: A measure of participation combining outsider and insider perspectives. *Journal of Head Trauma Rehabilitation, 19,* 459–481.

Brownsberger, M. G. (2005). *Community Integration Outcomes in Physical Rehabilitation: An Exploratory Meta-Analysis.* Poster presented at the Midwinter Conference of Division 22 (Rehabilitation Psychology), Reno, NV.

Burton, L. A., Leahy, D. M., & Volpe, B. (2003). Traumatic brain injury brief outcome interview. *Applied Neuropsychology, 10,* 145–152.

Cicerone, K. D., Mott, T., Azulay, J., & Friel, J. C. (2004). Community integration and satisfaction with functioning after intensive cognitive rehabilitation for traumatic brain injury. *Archives of Physical Medicine and Rehabilitation, 85*(6), 943–950.

Colantonio, A., Ratcliff, G., Chase, S., Kelsey, S., Escobar, M., & Vernich, L. (2004). Long-term outcomes after moderate to severe traumatic brain injury. *Disability and Rehabilitation, 26,* 253–261.

Dijkers, M. (2000). The Community Integration Questionnaire. *The Center for Outcome Measurement in Brain Injury.* Retrieved January 11, 2007, from: http://www.tbims.org/combi/ciq

Dijkers, M.P.J., Diamond, J. J., & Marion, R. (2003). Methodologist's corner: Psychometrics and clinimetrics in assessing environments: A comment suggested by MacKenzie et al., 2002. *Journal of Allied Health, 32*(1), 38–45.

Dijkers, M. P., Whiteneck, G., & El-Jaroudi, R. (2000). Measures of social outcomes in disability research. *Archives of Physical Medicine and Rehabilitation, 81*(12 Suppl. 2), S63–S80.

Equal Employment Opportunity Commission. (2002). *The Americans with Disabilities Act (ADA): 1990–2002.* Washington, DC: Author. Retrieved January 20, 2007, from: http://www.eeoc.gov/ada

Fougeyrollas, P., Noreau, L., Bergeron, H., Cloutier, R., Dion, S. A., & St-Michel, G. (1998). Social consequences of long-term impairments and disabilities: Conceptual approach and assessment of handicap. *International Journal of Rehabilitation Research, 21,* 127–141.

Gordon, W. A., Brown, M., & Hibbard, M. (1998). *Living life after TBI.* New York: RTC on Community Integration of Individuals with TBI, Mount Sinai School of Medicine.

Guerrier, T., & Bostick, A. (2001). Community integration through collaboration between a community college and a rehabilitation program. *Cognitive Technology, 6*(1), 33–37.

Harwood, R. H., Gompertz, P., & Ebrahim, S. (1994). Handicap one year after a stroke: Validity of a new scale. *Journal of Neurology, Neurosurgery, and Psychiatry, 57,* 825–829.

Jette, A., Keysor, J., Coster, W., Penshen, N., & Haley, S. (2005). Beyond function: Predicting participation outcomes in a rehabilitation cohort. *Archives of Physical Medicine and Rehabilitation, 86,* 2087—2094.

Johnston, M. V., Goverover, Y., & Dijkers, M. P. (in press). Community activities and individuals' satisfaction with them: Quality of life in the first year after traumatic brain injury. *Archives of Physical Medicine and Rehabilitation.*

Keysor, J. J., Jette, A. M., Coster, W., Prvu-Bettger, J., & Haley, S. M. (2006). Association of environmental factors with levels of home and community participation in an adult rehabilitation cohort. *Archives of Physical Medicine and Rehabilitation, 87,* 1566–1582.

Kuipers, P., Kendall, M., Fleming, J. M., & Tate, R. (2004). Comparison of the Sydney Psychosocial Reintegration Scale (SPRS) with the Community Integration Questionnaire (CIQ): Psychometric properties. *Brain Injury, 18,* 161–177.

Larson, P. C., & Sachs, P. R. (2000). A history of Division 22 (Rehabilitation Psychology). *Unification through division: Histories of the divisions of the American Psychological Association.* Washington, DC: American Psychological Association.

Malec, J. (2005). The Mayo-Portland Adaptability Inventory. *The Center for Outcome Measurement in Brain Injury.* Retrieved January 11, 2007, from: http://www.tbims.org/combi/mpai

Malec, J. F., Smigielski, J. S., DePompolo, R. W., & Thompson, J. M. (1993). Outcome evaluation and prediction in a comprehensive-integrated post-acute outpatient brain injury rehabilitation programme. *Brain Injury, 7,* 15–29.

McAweeney, M. J., Forschheimer, M., & Tate, D. G. (1997). Improving outcome research in rehabilitation psychology: Some methodological recommendations. *Rehabilitation Psychology, 42,* 125–135.

McAweeney, M. J., & Klockars, A. J. (1998). Maximizing power in skewed distributions: Analysis and assignment. *Psychological Methods, 3,* 117–122.

McColl, M. A., Davies, D., Carlson, P., Johnston, J., & Minnes, P. (2001). The Community Integration Measure: Development and preliminary validation. *Archives of Physical Medicine and Rehabilitation, 82,* 429–434.

Mellick, D. (2000). The Craig Handicap Assessment and Reporting Technique. *The Center for Outcome Measurement in Brain Injury.* Retrieved January 11, 2007, from: http://www.tbims.org/combi/chart

Minnes, P., Buell, K., Nolte, M. L., McColl, M. A., Carlson, P., & Johnston, J. (2001). Defining community integration of persons with brain injuries as acculturation: A Canadian. *NeuroRehabilitation, 16,* 3–10.

National Institute on Disability and Rehabilitation Research. (2006). Department of Education: National Institute on Disability and Rehabilitation Research—Notice of final long range plan for fiscal years 2005—2009. *Federal Register, 71*(31), 8166–8200. Retrieved February 14, 2007, from: http://www.ed.gov/legislation/FedRegister/other/2006-1/021506d.pdf

Nosek, M., Fuhrer, M. J., & Howland, C. (1992). Independence among people with disabilities: II: Personal independence profile. *Rehabilitation Counseling Bulletin, 36,* 21–36.

Nunnally, J. C., & Bernstein, I. H. (1994). *Psychometric theory* (3rd ed.). New York: McGraw Hill.

Ostir, G. V., Granger, C. V., Black, T., Roberts, P., Burgos, L., Martinkewiz, P., et al. (2006). Preliminary results for the PAR-PRO: A measure of home and community participation. *Archives of Physical Medicine and Rehabilitation, 87,* 1043—1051.

Ottenbacher, K. J. (1995). Why rehabilitation research does not work (as well as we think it should). *Archives of Physical Medicine and Rehabilitation, 76,* 123–129.

Pomeroy, J. (1983). Community recreation for persons with disabilities. *Annual Review of Rehabilitation, 3,* 268–291.

Powell, J. H., Beckers, K., & Greenwood, R. J. (1998). Measuring progress and outcome in community rehabilitation after brain injury with a new assessment instrument—the BICRO-39 Scales. *Archives of Physical Medicine and Rehabilitation, 79,* 1213–1223.

Slater, D., & Meade, M. A. (2004). Participation in recreation and sports for persons with spinal cord injury: Review and recommendations. *NeuroRehabilitation, 19,* 121–129.

Stilwell, P., Stilwell, J., Hawley, C., & Davies, C. (1998). Measuring outcome in community based rehabilitation services for people who have suffered traumatic brain injury: The Community Outcome Scale. *Clinical Rehabilitation, 12,* 521–531.

Trigg, R., Wood, V. A., & Hewer, R. L. (1999). Social reintegration after stroke: The first stages in the development of the Subjective Index of Physical and Social Outcome (SIPSO). *Clinical Rehabilitation, 13,* 341–353.

Wade, D. T., Leigh-Smith, J., & Hewer, R. L. (1985). Social activities after stroke: Measurement and natural history using the Frenchay activities index. *International Journal of Rehabilitation Medicine, 7,* 176–181.

Wainer, H. (1976). Estimating coefficients in linear models: It don't make no nevermind. *Psychological Bulletin, 83*(2), 213–217.

Whiteneck, G. G., Charlifue, S. W., Gerhart, K. A., Overholser, J. D., & Richardson, G. N. (1992). Quantifying handicap: A new measure of long-term rehabilitation outcomes. *Archives of Physical Medicine and Rehabilitation, 73,* 519–526.

Whiteneck, G. G., Heinemann, A., Corrigan, J., Bogner, J., & Brooks, C. A. (2007, February). *The Community Participation Index: A measure based on constituency input and evaluated in rehabilitation client and general population surveys.* Paper presented at Symposium on Post-Acute Rehabilitation, State of the Science, Arlington VA.

Wilkerson, D., Shen, D., & Duhaime, M. (1998). *Performance indicators for rehabilitation programs* (version 1.1). Tucson, AZ: CARF. Retrieved February 15, 2007, from: http://www.carf.org

Willer, B., Ottenbacher, K. J., & Coad, M. L. (1994). The Community Integration Questionnaire: A comparative examination. *American Journal of Physical Medicine and Rehabilitation, 73,* 103–111.

Willer, B., Rosenthal, M., Kreutzer, J. S., Gordon, W. A., & Rempel, R. (1993). Assessment of community integration following rehabilitation for traumatic brain injury. *Journal of Head Trauma Rehabilitation, 8*(2), 75–87.

Wood-Dauphinee, S. L., Opzoomer, M. A., Williams, J. I., Marchand, B., & Spitzer, W. O. (1988). Assessment of global function: The reintegration to normal living index. *Archives of Physical Medicine and Rehabilitation, 69,* 583–590.

World Health Organization. (2001). *ICF Introduction. Geneva: World Health Organization.* Retrieved April 3, 2004, from: http://www.who.int

World Health Organization. (2002). *Towards a Common Language for Functioning, Disability and Health: ICF. Geneva: World Health Organization.* Retrieved September 10, 2006, from: http://www3.who.int/icf/beginners/bg.pdf

Wright, B. A. (1959). *Psychology and rehabilitation.* Washington, DC: American Psychological Association.

Michael J. Prince
Elias Mpofu
Trevor Hawkins
Patrick Devlieger

27 Social Safety Net Assessments

Overview

This chapter examines a major problem that confronts all modern states, namely, providing some form of social protection against the loss of income due to serious illness, injury, or disablement. Social safety net (SSN) policies, procedures used for eligibility assessment, accessibility, and efficiency of services are the focus of this chapter. What are social safety nets (SSNs)? What are the most common types of SSNs? How is the International Classification of Functioning, Disability and Health (ICF; World Health Organization, 2001) framework helpful to understanding the role of SSN in health and well-being? What assessment practices are relevant to SSN policy evaluations? We consider these and other significant issues on SSN as health and well-being support systems. We also consider examples of SSN type evaluations with people with chronic illness and disability and ways in which the quality of these evaluations can be enhanced.

Learning Objectives

By the end of the chapter, the reader should be able to:

1. Define SSN as a public policy concept;
2. Locate the place of SSNs within the ICF structure on chronic illness and disability;
3. Identify the five main categories of SSNs in public policy practice programming;
4. Describe different criteria used for assessing SSN eligibility and access with chronic illness or disability; and
5. Discuss key considerations for rehabilitation professionals in assessment for SSN eligibility, access, and provider system efficiency.

Introduction

State and federal governments have complex and varied bundles of social programs that serve people with chronic illness and disability. Social safety nets help the disadvantaged of a society to access basic social services, prevent social exclusion, and use coping strategies to manage adverse shocks from events, circumstances, or developments. Disadvantaged groups are distinct from others in the society from characteristics or circumstances considered unfair and significant in relation to mainstream population or their political recognition as a stigmatized minority (Mpofu & Conyers, 2004; Mpofu, Crystal, & Feist-Price, 2000).

At the policy proposal stage, SSN programs generate expectations by groups for certain resources, rights, or duties, prompting organizations to mobilize to advance their interests. At the design stage, safety net programs can shape the obstacles and the openings for access to vital financial assistance and essential goods and services to enable people with various disadvantages to participate more equally in society. The design of SSN programs directly influences the construction of personal identities and formation of the social status of groups. At the delivery stage of provision, safety net programs have consequences for the practice of inclusion and the meaning of citizenship for those most vulnerable in political society. How social programs actually perform, or are thought to operate, also has implications for future demands for reforms to enhance their access and relevance to consumer constituencies (Barnes, 2002).

Social Safety Nets: Definition and Analytical Framework

SSN programs in their diversity contain collective provisions for addressing some assortment of economic risks, social problems, special needs, and life transitions of individuals and groups. These provisions can be in the form of direct income payments, tax relief and assistance, various health and social services, and laws and regulations. Although there are overlaps across the categories, in practice each has a definite policy orientation, tending to emphasize a particular set of functions and a focus on specific issues and client groups (Armitage, 2003; Dinitto, 1999; Karger & Stoesz, 2006).

A wider conception of SSN equates them with income security as in public transfer of monies, through direct spending and through tax measures, to a range of groups for a range of needs. These groups and needs span the entire life course of people and a series of transitions and social risks: children and youth, families of various forms, needy students, the unemployed, those with chronic illness or disability, the injured from work, the loss of the main earner from premature death, the poor and homeless, veterans, indigenous peoples (e.g., Native Americans in the United States or, in Canada, Aboriginal peoples), recent immigrants, other minority groups (e.g., African Americans, Hispanic Americans, or Asian Americans), and retired persons and the elderly. A still wider concept of SSN includes the provision of several human services, namely, education, public health and medical care, social housing, employment policies, and an array of personal and community social services. This chapter concentrates on SSNs typically provided by programs for people with chronic illness or disability.

SSNs and Vulnerabilities

SSNs help cushion beneficiaries from social risks for which they are inadequately prepared and that would threaten their livelihood or survival. They are intended to provide an accessible and reliable portfolio of assets to offset or ameliorate the impact of adverse social events, such as the experience of significant illness, disability, or other social disadvantage. SSNs make it possible to bridge socioeconomic vulnerabilities from both acute (transient/adventitious) and chronic (cyclical) social shocks by enabling in beneficiaries coping behaviors to contain the negative effects of the social shocks, such as the experience of disability and poverty.

Disability and Poverty

Disability may lead to poverty from lower access to work opportunities because of social discrimination by "gate-keepers" to employment networks, social participation, and other resources for well-being (Mitra, 2005). Disability could also add significantly to the personal cost of work and social participation because of the expenses related to medical care, assistive technology, adaptations to home and work stations, transportation, and personal care. In addition, courtesy poverty, the loss of household resources because of the direct or indirect costs of a family member's disability, is likely to occur in households with a person with disabilities. For example, family members may forego earnings in order to spend time to care for the family member with a disability. Women with disabilities are more vulnerable to poverty because of their historical disadvantage as a socially oppressed minority; rural residents and the semiliterate or illiterate are also more vulnerable because they may not have ready access to the social services that may help them mitigate the effects of living with a disability. Of course, poverty itself can lead to disability as a result of malnutrition and

Research Box 27.1

CAREGIVING, WORK–FAMILY CONFLICT, AND WELL-BEING

Marks, N. F. (1998). Does it hurt to care? Caregiving, work–family conflict, and midlife well-being. *Journal of Marriage and the Family, 60,* 951–966.

Objectives: To examine the effects of caregiving for disabled children, spouses, parents, and other kin and nonkin on multiple positive and negative dimensions of psychological well-being and development.

Methods: Quantitative analysis of data from a population sample of employed, middle-aged men and women in a Wisconsin Longitudinal Study 1992–1993 (n = 5,782).

Results: Contemporary social organization leads to conflicting demands across the role identities of employee and caregiver, and this conflict is an important factor in accounting for the negative effects of caregiving on well-being.

Conclusions: Does it hurt to care? Not always and not necessarily the same for all groups. Negative effects for caregiving are most likely for women caring for disabled children. If differences in work and family conflict between caregivers and noncaregivers are eliminated, the caregiving role would more often have positive effects on well-being.

Questions:
1. What are some beneficial effects of caregiving for the caregiver as well as for the care recipient?
2. Based on your experience, what other people may be affected by these work–family conflicts?
3. When making decisions about rehabilitation, how could you use these results to inform your thinking and recommendations?

poorer health care (Elwan, 1999; Mitra, 2005). SSNs are important to facilitating the participation of people with disabilities in activities of their communities in comparable ways to typically developing peers, thereby reducing poverty in that population. SSNs can also prevent disability from the consequences of disease, impairment, and social exclusion.

Types of SSN

Various classifications of SSN have been proposed (International Labor Office, 1982; World Bank, 1999). Five types of SSN widely used by social programs are: (a) social allowance, (b) social assistance, (c) economic inclusion, (d) health and

27.1 Types of SSN Policies

Type	Function	Target Groups	Labor Market Status	Program Examples
Social Assistance	Basic income and social protection	Indigenous peoples Persons with disabilities Single parents Low-income families Homeless	Unemployed Unemployable Working poor Marginal work force	Income support/ welfare Disability assistance Emergency shelter programs
Economic Inclusion	Broadening labor force participation	Indigenous peoples Persons with disabilities Youth Visible minorities Displaced older workers	Unemployed Marginal work force	Workfare Job creation schemes Literacy and language programs Training
Health and Social Security	Income replacement and stabilization Health support	Farmers in need Injured and disabled workers Unemployed workers Citizens in need of health care	Employed Many benefits based on regular and recent attachment to labor force	Crop insurance Workers' compensation Employment insurance Public health insurance
Human Capital Investment	Learning, skills, and infrastructure development	College and university students Researchers and scientists	Employed in good positions and or with good prospects	Student loans and grants Tax assistance Research funds

social security, and (e) human capital investment. These are briefly outlined in Table 27.1.

Social Allowance Programs

Social allowance programs are entitlement programs for people in designated categories (e.g., children, the elderly, and people with disabilities). They are not means tested. Examples of social allowance programs used in the international community include the orphan care, vulnerable groups, school feeding program, old age pension, and community home–based care.

Social Assistance Programs

Social assistance SSNs are programs of "last resort," means-tested or needs-tested, with a minimal level of support. Client groups for social assistance programs typically have no attachment to the labor force or have irregular or nonstandard work history. The narrowest conception of the social assistance nets equates them with public welfare or the basic income assistance provided to individuals and families when all other personal, private, and public resources have been exhausted. Examples of social assistance programs in the international community include the destitute persons' and needy student's allowance. In the North American welfare states of the United States and Canada, such social assistance is administered separately by each state or province. Eligibility involves a detailed investigation by public authorities into a person's or family's income and assets. The level of assistance is based on a minimum or subsistence concept of income support. The policy goals are typically to relieve misery, ease somewhat the burdens of poverty, and according to many commentators, to make low-wage work more attractive financially and more acceptable socially compared to welfare.

Access to social assistance is not a right of citizenship but is a result of satisfying an assessment. These financial assessments are often accompanied by a loss of privacy and assaults on dignity, and they are shrouded with public stigma and private shame. Traditionally, social assistance programs have included little, if any, vocational or social rehabilitation.

Economic Inclusion Programs

Economic inclusion programs aim to support the participation in the labor force of historically marginalized groups (e.g., people with disabilities, remote rural inhabitants, indigenous peoples, youth at risk, unemployed older workers, recent immigrants, and single parents with younger children). Examples of economic inclusion SSNs include literacy programs, apprenticeships, skill development and training initiatives, wage subsidies, job creation measures, and other employability techniques. The focus is on groups traditionally marginalized in the labor force: Policy goals seek to increase the workforce participation of these disadvantaged groups, thereby better integrating members of minority groups into society, promoting work ethic and personal responsibility, and decreasing welfare caseloads and payments. In this way, SSNs are seen as complementary to, and a positive instrument of, economic development.

Health and Social Security Programs

Health and social security programs include social insurance and general access benefits based on adequacy and income replacement. Instances of health and social security are disability pensions, employment insurance, hospital insurance, and medical care insurance, public pensions, veterans' benefits, and workers' compensation. The aim is to replace lost income in whole or in large part to ensure a large degree of income stability. A right to support is typically established through general taxes or specific premiums that clients have paid toward the program to insure themselves against these contingencies. Clients for the health and social security SSNs usually have or had a firm attachment to the labor force.

It is worth noting, too, that private disability and life insurance plans (including automobile insurance for road accidents and personal injuries) play a larger role in the SSN systems of Canada and the United States than in European countries. Such a divergence in SSNs is explained by differences in historical developments, private economic interests, public opinion values, and political cultures. Social assistance, economic inclusion, and health and social security programs are collectively referred to as social protection (SP).

Human Capital Development Programs

Human capital development SSNs target training in skills for industry and economic development or self-sustenance to increase resilience and reduce vulnerability. Illustrations of human capital investment SSNs are student grants and loans for post-secondary education, tax assistance with college and university for students and their families, and support for research councils and university research activities. The central policy goal is to foster a well-educated, skilled, and adaptable workforce. Investments are also targeted at economic and social infrastructure for science and technology. These SSNs are aimed at today's generation and the next generation of entrepreneurs, managers, scientists, researchers, and professors. It represents a project for upward mobility, further technological achievement, and personal success, thus adding to productivity and economic growth. Applied to vulnerable populations, human resource development SSN are poverty reduction strategies. The goal is to develop a capable, self-reliant citizenry able to contribute to the national economy. Poverty reduction goals of SSNs are likely to be met by involving people with disabilities in human resource development SSN and other SSN so they can access competitive employment.

Although SSN policies may be classified as social assistance, economic inclusion, health and social security, and human capital investment, in reality, there are overlaps and gaps among these subsystems of the welfare state. Nonetheless, this network of policies strongly suggests that the contribution of social programs to economic development is more substantial, potentially and in actual practice, than is often assumed or asserted by many policy analysts.

Applicable ICF Concepts

The ICF defines *disability* in terms of the individual, societal, and body-related aspects of impairments, activity limitations, and participation restrictions in the environment (see chapter 1). The model of health and well-being based on the ICF proposes dynamic, reciprocal relationships between the various health-related conditions within the context of environmental and personal factors. A specific impairment on its own does not portend a disability in the absence of the type of activities that the individual engages. In this regard, disability is conceptualized as a function of the dynamic interaction between health conditions in individuals and contextual factors. From an ICF perspective, SSN programs can be environmental supports for community participation with a chronic illness or disability. Disability is about activity and participation limitations from health conditions and, particularly, the environment in which people with disabilities live. Practical uses of the ICF are twofold: first, as a framework for understanding health and well-being in the context of social welfare programs; and, second, in monitoring progress toward the inclusion of persons with disabilities or impairments, whether that be in assistive technologies, caregiving, education,

Research Box 27.2

KEEPING THE UNEMPLOYED HEALTHY: THE EFFECT OF SOCIAL BENEFITS ON PEOPLE

Rodriguez, E. (2001). Keeping the unemployed healthy: The effect of means-tested and entitlement benefits in Britain, Germany, and the United States. *Am J Public Health, 91,* 1403–1411.

Objectives: To examine the role that means-tested and social insurance benefit programs could have in ameliorating the health impact of unemployment on people experiencing job loss and economic insecurity.

Methods: Quantitative analysis of panel data from three countries, Britain, Germany, and the United States, during the mid-1980s and early 1990s.

Results: Evidence found differences in perceived health status between groups of unemployed people characterized by the types of benefits they receive. When socioeconomic characteristics and previous health and employment status are controlled for, means-tested benefits do not seem sufficient to reduce the impact of unemployment on health.

Conclusions: Monitoring the possible effects of changes in public assistance benefits should be given priority in the research and political agenda.

Questions:
1. What are key differences between means-tested and social insurance benefit programs?
2. What are some implications of these results for public education or advocacy work by rehabilitation associations?
3. How might you use these findings to inform your own professional practice, be that in a clinical, service provision, or research setting?

employment, leisure, or general social participation. As a matter of fact, SSNs afford vulnerable populations the resources to engage in activities of daily living in the presence of social stressors (e.g., chronic illness or disability).

For the most part, SSN programs across welfare states predate the ICF, with assessment procedures that vary by program area and types of client groups. In no liberal democratic society is there a single coherent model of disability contained in all legislative, expenditure, taxation, and service measures.

Where the ICF might increasingly be used in an SSN is in identifying domains for health and well-being for needs assessment and planning and for impact or outcome evaluation, by providing standard frameworks for indicators for the health status of at-risk populations (Hurst, 2003; Üstün, Chatterji, Bickenbach, Kostanjsek, & Schneider 2003). Some policy analysis, however, goes beyond individualistic and medical views of disadvantage, highlighting structural causes and conditions located within societal culture, the labor market, or a country's political economy. In this regard, a number of disability scholars raise concerns over the ICF's approach to understanding health and well-being in people with disabilities (e.g., Anderberg, 2005; Barnes, 2002; Smart, 2005). Structural sources of disadvantage addressed in SSN policies include relatively high unemployment rates, different kinds of adverse prejudice or intolerance toward people with disabilities or ethnic groups, regional disparities in resources and wealth, gender-related disparities, and low-income and poverty (Moss & Teghtsoonian, 2008; Prince, 2009).

History of Research and Practice in SSN Assessments

The history on SSNs varies greatly across countries, depending upon the political philosophy and particular economic and social history of a country. Even within a single country, especially one with a federal system of governance such as Australia, Canada, Germany, and the United States, the practices in SSNs and associated policies differ. In this brief section, we present a conceptually inclusive but brief digest on the history of the development of SSNs, mindful that the account can be supplemented variously to speak more accurately to specific settings. We also deliberately focus on SSNs historic to people with chronic illness and disability.

Rehabilitation Foundations

Any description of what constitutes the history of SSNs must appreciate this multifaceted historical field of ideas, techniques, and working relationships. For instance, types of SSNs traditional to rehabilitation services include the provision of orthopedic prostheses, acoustic equipment, Braille equipment, special education programs, and sheltered workshops for persons with various physical and or mental disabilities. From working with veterans from World War I and World War II, state and federal rehabilitation programs provided SSNs aimed at minimizing or eliminating the disablement and restoring physical abilities of the individual through the use of an assortment of technologies by experts at institutional centers of care. Critiques of these SSNs pointed to the limited voice for people with disabilities and the ascendancy of professionals in this clinical and individualized relationship.

Since the 1970s, other types of SSNs have emerged, including community-based programs in which persons with disabilities have a direct role in the design and delivery of services (Jongbloed & Crichton, 1990). The premise here is that individuals with disabilities know a good deal about their own circumstances, vulnerabilities, strengths, aspirations, and what might be possible accommodations. Expectations shifted away from paternalistic SSN models of service provision to ones in which the consumer controlled or at least had a major voice in determining the operation of programs. In education settings, segregated classes gave way to inclusive education; real jobs with real pay have replaced sheltered workshops in some places; and self-advocacy groups and rights organizations have emerged over the past generation, with mandates of defending human rights and promoting equal opportunities for persons with disabilities and other health conditions (Rice & Prince, 2000).

Since the 1990s, programs and services were designed to help persons with disabilities obtain and maintain employment. People with disability had SSN to support their return to work—be it their former job as it was or reconfigured, a new job, or self-employment. The return-to-work SSNs were supported by the appearance on the market of new technologies and assistive devices and the changing attitudes of the employability of people with disabilities.

Workers' Compensation Programs

A fuller understanding of the history of practices in SSNs comes from looking more closely at income programs for disability, injury, and sickness. To do so, the following discussion examines briefly workers' compensation, veterans' pensions, public disability insurance plans, and sickness benefits.

Workers' compensations (WC) programs are among the oldest and most common social welfare programs and are primarily designed to pay financial support to a worker for loss of function or to his or her survivors for loss of life of the breadwinner. An important group not typically covered under WC programs are the self-employed, a growing segment of the labor market in many countries. WC programs are not neutral as to the etiology (cause or origins) of the disability, disease, or injury. A core element of the assessment process in WC programs is determining if the disability or injury (or death) is work-connected. If it is determined that the health condition is not directly attributable to the place of employment, then usually no income support or rehabilitation services are provided by the WC plan. When deemed eligible, WC programs do offer benefits for a partial disability that has occurred at work.

In some political federations, for example, Australia, Canada, and the United States, subnational governments (states, provinces, and territories) design and administer the WC programs. Consequently, in these countries there are numerous disparate programs for worker's compensation, each program different in terms of the proportion of the workforce covered and in the scope of diseases and injuries protected. Even work-related injuries and diseases are not necessarily recognized by WC programs. Illnesses typically excluded or sharply limited in coverage include musculoskeletal disorders as well as chronic fatigue syndrome, fibromyalgia, and repetitive strain injuries (Gunderson & Hyatt, 2000; Lippel, 2008). An important difference between WC programs on one hand, and most long-term public disability insurance programs and short-term sickness benefits on the other, is the strong emphasis WC plans place on vocational rehabilitation of injured and sick workers. No doubt, this rehabilitation focus reflects the coverage of temporary and partial disabilities and accident cases by WC plans (Puttee, 2002).

In a way similar to WC programs, veterans' pensions provide compensation for service-connected injuries, disabilities, and deaths, along with rehabilitation services of various kinds. Indeed, veterans' programs, many of which emerged shortly after the Great War of 1914–1918, include assessments of the loss of body function and structure for the determination of benefits and related health and social services. Veterans' pensions are recognition of personal sacrifices, performance of national duty, and compensation for lost opportunities and capacities.

Current Practices in SSN Assessments

Whatever the definition used, the systems of SSNs in place in modern societies are immensely complex and varied and highly significant for the health and well-being of vulnerable groups. SSN policies are designed, financed, and delivered by national governments, state or provincial governments, territorial governments, and local and urban governments. There are social security agreements that nation states sign with other countries along with being a signatory to a whole host of other international conventions, protocols, and accords. We consider SSN assessments typical to services transacted by people with chronic illness or disability.

Social Policies and Assessments

Diagnostic tools or assessment techniques in social safety net programs vary and are fragmented, due to the ad hoc and piecemeal development of social programs, over many decades, in modern societies. Consequently, programs can be confusing to clients, inefficient in delivery, unfair in their accessibility, and inequitable in their effects (Mpofu, Lopez, Tapologo, & Magweva, 2008).

In income security programs, common indicators for SSN eligibility include the following:

- Age (e.g., children under age 6 or persons aged 65 and over);
- Citizenship or residency (such as a set number of months or maybe years in a given jurisdiction to qualify for a given program);
- Family structure (e.g., single persons, number of children, or lone parent status);
- Prior contribution of premium payments, often through payroll deductions, for unemployment insurance and disability protection;
- Record of recent labor force attachment and availability for employment;
- Income and/or asset levels of individual or household and financial need for essential items of living;
- Military and war service (in some cases, eligibility is also determined by length and place of service, and by military rank);
- Occupation (in many workers' compensation schemes, some occupational groups are excluded from coverage);
- Enrollment in an educational institution (high school, college, technical institute, training program, or university);
- Employment status and history (self-employed and part-time are often not entitled to certain benefits or job protections);
- Incapacity to work and or return to work for pursuing gainful employment; and,
- Capacity to undertake activities of daily living (as measured by the severity of anatomical, physiological, or psychological impairments).

These indicators are used in various combinations depending on the type of SSN in question and the context or social policy system in which the SSNs are administered. The notion of due process or natural justice is another consideration that overlays the SSN assessment criteria. Among other principles, due process includes the idea of informed consent. In some fact situations, rulings by administrative tribunals and courts shape SSN assessment procedures and modify actual decisions in a fashion that asserts an entitlement or prevents the disentitlement or exclusion of a benefit to a certain group (Chambers, 1993).

Eligibility Criteria

Most SSN programs, if not all, contain two or more of these eligibility criteria. Income programs that offer basic social assistance (welfare), social insurance–based programs such as disability insurance, and workers' compensation typically include several conditions that must be met before a benefit or service is provided to an applicant (Karger & Stoesz, 2006). The final two of these criteria rely a good deal on medical, legal, and rehabilitation professionals in assessing the functional status of claimant people. We present brief case examples of SSN determination assessments in three Organization for Economic Cooperation and Development (OECD) countries, Australia, Canada, the United States, and in the European Union.

Australia SSN Eligibility With Disabilities

In Australia, support for persons with long-term and or significant illness, injury, or disability, whether the condition is permanent (Disability Support Pension) or temporary (Sickness Allowance), is administered by Centrelink (www.centrelink.gov.au). It is these two benefits (Disability Support Pension and Sickness Allowance) that form the major safety net support for injured or ill Australians. Those persons who have some capacity to work now or in the near future may be eligible for alternate payments in the form of Newstart Allowance, Youth Allowance, Parenting Payment, or Special Benefit.

As is the case in most developed countries, the determination of eligibility is based primarily on:

1. Medical evidence that the condition exists and is ongoing and is debilitating. This involves the condition attracting a rating of 20 points or above on standard impairment tables, which are used nationally. However, these ratings are not always determined by medical practitioners or those with medical training but are based on medical evidence provided by the individual.
2. Assessment of the continuing incapacity of the individual to participate in work (Job Capacity Assessment) for at least 15 hours per week within 2 years (the "work test") in order to independently generate an income, or to engage in formal or work-based vocational training or a program of support (e.g., counseling) in preparation for work. If the disability is severe and rated so by the medical practitioner, a Job Capacity Assessment will not be required because the severity of the disability is deemed to be manifest eligibility for ongoing income support.

Information about the Job Capacity Assessment can be accessed at http://www.humanservices.gov.au/jca/index.html

Issues of period of residency in Australia (10 years or more) and whether the illness or disability occurred while the individual was an Australian resident also impact upon granting of the benefit.

The amount of income an individual can receive in the form of a government-funded benefit also depends on income and assets tests. Persons who have received monies (a lump sum payment) or are continuing to receive ongoing monies in the form of weekly workers' compensation payments will only be eligible to receive a lesser amount of benefit despite the fact that they may have met the basic criteria for the granting of Disability Support Pension of Sickness Allowance outlined previously. This is because of the impact of the money on the person's income. Those individuals who received monies as part of a motor vehicle accident claim (not work-related) may also only be eligible for a reduced benefit because of the impact of that money on the income and assets status of the individual.

Once the benefit is granted, income is paid according to the determination made in relation to income and assets test guidelines and also whether the individual is single, married, or in a de facto relationship.

The benefit includes a weekly payment (paid every 2 weeks), and depending on circumstances, the individual may be eligible for rent assistance, a mobility allowance, a concession card for travel and pharmaceuticals, and telephone and utilities allowances.

Eligibility for continuation of benefits is assessed in irregular reviews called Service Update Contacts, which look at medical and nonmedical eligibility. These reviews may be carried out face-to-face and may require the individual to undertake a further Job Capacity Assessment.

Individuals have the right to appeal against decisions to not grant or not continue to pay a long-term disability or sickness benefit. While this appeal is taking place, the individual is placed on one of the other short-term work incapacity benefits outlined previously.

Canada

The Canada Pension Plan (CPP) disability program is the country's largest public disability insurance program.[1] Established in the mid-1960s, the primary policy goal is providing a degree of income protection or financial security that complements private insurance, personal savings, and employment benefit programs by replacing a portion of the earnings of contributors who cannot work because of a severe and prolonged mental or physical disability. This aim reflects the social insurance nature of the program's design. Other policy goals are: promoting a return to work by supporting at least some CPP disability beneficiaries to undertake gainful employment; ensuring program integrity and accountability so that benefits are paid correctly, appeals heard fairly and promptly, and fraud and errors are avoided; and, ensuring the financial sustainability and affordability of the CPP for present and future generations.

1. The province of Quebec has a separate, parallel program, the Quebec Pension Plan, with fairly comparable features in retirement pensions and disability and survivor benefits.

In recent years, more than $3 billion in benefit payments has gone to approximately 380,000 people. Behind this substantial expenditure, CPP disability has a national vocational rehabilitation program and other related return-to-work support services and incentives. There also is the decision-making process on applications and a three-stage appeal system for adjudicating benefit claims. Moreover, a series of information-sharing agreements exist with provincial governments and comparable agreements with provincial workers' compensation boards, along with reimbursement agreements with private sector insurers and international social security agreements with numerous countries.

In the case of CPP disability, applicants encounter knowledge systems and rules from administrative, medical, vocational rehabilitation, actuarial/financial, income security, and judicial discourses. These discursive practices regulate the experiences of individuals seeking to obtain benefits to which they believe they qualify and are entitled. The multiple diagnoses include self-assessments, medical examinations, legal deliberations, rehabilitation evaluations, and even actuarial considerations regarding the "financial health" of the program itself. This multiplicity of discourses and associated diagnoses are integral to the nature of contestation in claiming their benefits.

For many working Canadians with disabilities, the experience of seeking this social right of income support is one of rejection and denial of benefits. The "earned right" of CPP disability, even though based on contributions and work force participation, does not guarantee the automatic provision of benefits. While labor force attachment is a prerequisite for entitlement to the CPP disability, as a work-related insurance plan, it is not a sufficient condition for eligibility. Further conditions must be satisfied for a worker with a disability to actually qualify and obtain financial support from the program. In addition to having sufficient valid contributions to the CPP, these conditions are that the individual is assessed medically with having a severe mental or physical disability that is prolonged.

This is a crucial point: The CPP disability program insures against a specific category of disability—severe in condition and prolonged in duration, preventing a person from being able to pursue any gainful employment. A related point is that CPP does not provide partial benefits; a person either qualifies for the full benefit or gets nothing at all from the program. To determine if the person has a severe and prolonged disability, information is compiled from the applicant, their physician, and employer to produce a profile of the applicant and to determine medical eligibility for the income benefit. Labor market considerations, too, enter into decisions, informed by the relative strength of the economy and the extent of employment opportunities in a local area that may match the skills or background of an applicant.

The interplay of these eligibility requirements as presented, interpreted, and, at times, negotiated and challenged, affects a person's ability to receive benefits. Assessing benefits is certainly not free of numerous kinds of interventions into the personal lives of individuals. Medical judgments and administrative decisions on eligibility are shaped not just by professional knowledge and expertise but also by economic factors, political calculations, service traditions, and bureaucratic constraints. With detailed investigations, reviews, and various encounters with complex organizations, for many people this social insurance program can feel a lot like a social assistance program.

U.S. Social Security Administration (SSA) Determination

There are many SSN programs and determination procedures in the United States (SSA, 2006; see also Cox & Goldberg, in press). We consider only the SSN by the SSA, which is the major public SSN administration program in the United States. The Social Security Disability Insurance (SSDI) and Supplemental Security Income (SSI) programs are two of the main SSN for people with disabilities in the United States. To qualify for the SSDI and SSI, a five-step disability test is used: initial work test, severity of disabling condition, medical listings test, previous work test, and comprehensive work test. Eligibility can be denied at any of the five stages depending on the stage specific result. For the *initial work test evaluation,* an applicant for SSN with a disability must be earning below a minimum amount of $810 per month (and this is higher if with blindness). If this condition is met, the person moves to the test of the *severity of the disabling condition.* Medical evidence is submitted at this stage. To qualify, the person must have a disability severe enough to present him or her from engaging in gainful employment or basic work activities. For the *medical listings test,* the Disability Determination Service (DDS) expert checks whether a client's identified disability is on the list of eligible conditions, in which case the client automatically qualifies for SSDI and/or SSI. If the client's identified condition is not listed, the SSA determines whether the client's disability is as severe as that of a listed condition. If the condition does not lead to automatic eligibility based on the medical listing test, the previous work test is engaged. The *previous work test* is an evaluation of whether the person can perform the type of work he or she did before. In the event that the person can perform previous work, the determination is stopped at this point and eligibility denied. If the previous work test suggests that the person could not perform the work he or she did before, the case is moved to the comprehensive work test. The *comprehensive work test* is for determining if the individual could perform any work that exists in the national economy, regardless of the availability of any such work position in the local job market. To make that determination, factors such as age, qualifications, and experience of the applicant are considered. If the result of the comprehensive work test suggests that the applicant could perform a job available in the national economy, then the application for SSN is denied. A claimant can appeal a denied disability benefit application to a SSA law judge retaining only the evidence already submitted. The claim is accepted if the person passes the comprehensive work test.

Unlike many OECD countries, SSN eligibility with a disability in the United States requires total disability. Determinations in other OECD countries, with the exception of Canada and the United Kingdom, are far less stringent. About 50% disability is sufficient for SSN eligibility in a majority of OECD countries (Andrews, 1998).

Belgium and the European Union

In European countries, and specifically in Belgium, disability policy may be the responsibility of different government administrations, depending on the particular matter. In Belgium, the responsibility may belong to the Flemish community, the Walloon region, the French community commission of the Brussels region, and the German-language community. Employment of disabled people, education and training, housing, and allowance of technical aids belong to the responsibility of these four entities.

The SSN in terms of monetary allowances for disabled people belongs to the responsibility of the Belgian Federal Government. To clarify the system, Belgium follows the rules set out by the Directorate General for Persons with Disabilities, who maintains the system (see FOD, 2007). Apart from examining requests for allowances, the Directorate-General for Persons with Disabilities also coordinates the medical examinations in the context of fiscal and social advantages (telephone, transport, utilities, and parking) that are allocated to persons with disabilities, and in the context of increased child allowances that are awarded to children who have a chronic illness or disability.

Types of Allowances

There are two specific allowances for disabled people in Belgium: an allowance that replaces income and an allowance to facilitate integration. Both allowances intend to replace or compensate for the inability of the person with a disability to obtain a sufficient income, or for the person who has to carry additional charges caused by the disability. The replacement income allocation is awarded to persons who cannot gain more than one-third of the income of an able-bodied person in a profession in the general employment market. The integration allocation is awarded to a person with a disability who has a lack or a decreased ability of providing for oneself without assistance from others and the associated costs to fit into societal life. The two allowances can be awarded separately or jointly to accommodate for someone whose income may not be affected but nevertheless experiences great problems in providing for oneself and vice versa.

Eligibility

The eligibility criteria for these allocations are dependent on age, nationality, residence, income, exemptions on income, and disability. A person with a disability is eligible from the age of 21, and the request must be made before the age of 65. People who have been awarded allocations before the age of 65 continue to receive these after the 65th birthday. Persons with disabilities who are or were married and who have the charge of children are considered to be equal to a person of 21 years old. Also, a person whose disability started after the age of receiving child allowances and before the age of 21 is eligible.

Nationality

In terms of nationality, a person who is Belgian, a national of the European Union (EU), a refugee, or stateless, is eligible, also, a person who is a national of Algeria, Iceland, Lichtenstein, Morocco, Norway, Tunesia, or Switzerland and who is subject to the social security of a country of the EU or of his own country (as an employee or self-employed). A person of another nationality is eligible provided that he is the spouse, the legal partner, or a family member (child, parent, or parent-in-law) of an eligible person. For example, a woman from

Surinam who is married to a Belgian meets the nationality criterion and can request an allocation for persons with disabilities. A person is considered as a charge when that person lives under the same roof and for whom there is a charge of the obligatory insurance for health and unemployment. The person who has been awarded an increased child allowance up to the age of 21 years is equally eligible.

Residence

In terms of residence, the person to whom the allocation is awarded must live in Belgium at the time of the request and for the period during which the allocation is granted. Exemptions are made for up to 90 days per calendar year, stays abroad for medical or employment reasons, accompaniments to relatives that are obligatory, stays of more than 90 days because of exceptional reasons, and provided permission from the Minister. Persons with a disability who leave the country are obliged to inform the service for allocations at least 1 month in advance, with a mention of the duration and the reason.

Thresholds

The income replacing allocation and the integration allocation can only be allocated when the amounts of income do not exceed certain thresholds. The part of the income that exceeds these thresholds is deducted from the base amounts of the allocations. The income is calculated on the basis of the taxable income of the person with a disability and the income of the person with whom the person with a disability lives together in the same household. These amounts are indicated on the taxation form, delivered by the administration for direct taxes of the Federal Government Service for Finances. For persons who do not have a taxation form, the service for allocation will calculate the real income of the person with a disability and the persons with whom a household exists.

Exemptions

The calculation of the replacing income takes also into account certain exemptions. Certain parts of the income of the person with whom the person with the disability forms a household are exempted and certain parts of the professional income of the person with the disability and as well as a portion of other income sources are exempted. In 2006, an income from 6,119.88 euro onwards was not being exempted. Also, for the calculation of the integration allocation, certain parts of the income are exempted.

In order to be able to be awarded an income-replacing allocation, it needs to be determined that a person, because of his physical or mental situation, cannot gain more than a third of an able-bodied person on the general employment market. A lack or decrease of providing for oneself needs to be determined, taking into account the possibility of mobility, the possibility of preparing or feeding oneself, the possibility of providing for one's personal hygiene and dressing oneself, the possibility of maintaining one's living space and doing household work, the possibility of living without supervision and of being aware of danger, and the possibility of communication and social interaction.

Medical Evidence

A physician examines each of the functions and provides a response, namely, no problems (0 points), limited problems (1 point), extended problems (2 points), or impossible without help from others (3 points). The amount of points is added and leads a person with a disability to be categorized in one of the following categories: category 1 (7 or 8 points), category 2 (9 to 11 points), category 3 (12 to 14 points), category 4 (15 or 16 points) and category 5 (17 or 18 points). Less than 7 points does not allow a person the right to an integration allocation.

The medical examination is executed by a physician of the Medical Service of the Federal Government Service for Social Security or by an appointed physician. In certain circumstances, it is also possible to have the medical examination at the home of the person with the disability. In certain cases, there is no need for a medical exam, for example when there are detailed and recent reports already available.

Allocations

The amount of the allocations is connected to the index of consumption prices. The income replacing allocation is 5.261,63 EUR per year, allocated to persons who belong to a household category A. It is increased with 50% for persons belonging to household category B (7.892,45 EUR) and with 100% for persons belonging to household category C (10.523,26 EUR). The household is defined as two people who are not relatives that live together in a single major residence. A person with a disability belongs to category C if he has a household or has one or more children in charge. A person with a disability belongs to category B if he is a person who lives by himself or who does not belong to category C and resides in an institution day and night during a period of 3 months. A person belongs to category A if that person does not belong to category B nor C.

The amount of the integration allocation varies according to the degree to which one can provide for oneself and according to the category of disability in which the person with the disability belongs. The person with a disability who lives in an institution that is wholly or partly covered by the state, or by social security, receives an integration allocation that is diminished by one-third. People who are imprisoned or interned in an institution for social protection receive no such allocations.

To file a request for an allocation, a person with a disability can be represented by a person to whom he gives the authority. This person must be of age and carrier of an authorization. The request for an allocation must be filed with the mayor of commune where the person is enrolled in the population register or foreigner register.

SSN Access Evaluations

SSNs, if they are accessed by intended beneficiaries in a timely manner, generally meet the purpose for which they are intended. Both inclusive and targeted SSN are used in the international community. Inclusive SSN tend to be open to a variety of vulnerable groups and, for that reason, have broader eligibility criteria. Targeted SSN are exclusive to specified groups with vulnerability.

Within an inclusive SSN program delivery system, clients typically self-target for the services for which they believe they are eligible. Self-targeting involves initiating and following through with access to the appropriate SSN programs. In some inclusive SSN programs, people with disabilities are helped in targeting the specific SSN that typically are accessed by people with disabilities. SSN access evaluations are important to the practical implementation. A number of SSN access instruments have been proposed in the literature. The more comprehensive assessments cover key outcome indicators, such as accessibility, coverage, targeting, and actual benefit to people with disabilities. The toolkit by Mitra (2005; see Table 27.2) is particularly useful for assessing the extent to which people with disabilities are able to access inclusive SSNs and also for evaluating the impact of the SSN on poverty alleviation and reduction in that population relative to typically developing others.

In most jurisdictions, an inadequate supply of appropriate supports for people with disabilities or chronic illness to access SSN puts them at risk for poor SSN access, aggravating existing vulnerabilities if not contributing to additional risks (Mpofu et al., 2008). Given program budget limits and specific program

27.2 Design for the Assessment of SSN Accessibility, Design and Impact

Dimension	Relevant Analytical Instruments
1. Program Implementation	
1.1. Physical Accessibility	
• What is the accessibility of the built environment, including SSN facilities and transport system?	Direct observation and review of program manuals of operation or guidelines.
• Can social workers and rehabilitation personnel conduct home visits to persons with disabilities?	Administrative data on beneficiaries, if available.
• Can a family representative apply, enroll, and receive benefits on behalf of a person with a disability?	Analysis of legislative framework.
• Are there any geographical asymmetries in program coverage (by region, urban vs. rural)?	
1.2. Communication and Social Accessibility	
• Is program information available in different formats (e.g., Braille)?	Review of existing information materials; semistructured interviews and focus group discussions with current and potential beneficiaries with disabilities and with program staff.
• How does the program deal with illiteracy among potential and actual beneficiaries?	
• Is program information delivered through different channels besides the government policy documents (media, community outreach)?	
• Do attitudes of SSN staff prevent or discourage access to benefits for persons with disabilities?	
• Do some of the SSN staff have disabilities?	

(*continued*)

27.2 Design for the Assessment of SSN Accessibility, Design and Impact — *Continued*

Dimension	Relevant Analytical Instruments
2. Program Design	
• Is the cost to apply or collect benefits high for persons with disabilities? • Are some of the eligibility conditions difficult to meet for persons with disabilities?	Semistructured interviews and focus group discussions with current and potential beneficiaries with disabilities and program staff. Incidence analysis.
3. Program Evaluation	
3.1. Program Coverage • What is the proportion of eligibles with disabilities that participate in the program?	Household data collection and analysis Social sector studies.
• What are the profiles of participants with disabilities compared to nonparticipant eligibles with disabilities (e.g., demographic characteristics, type of disability)?	Comparison of group at risk (people with disabilities) and coverage of individual SSN. Incidence analysis (to determine the share of SSN program benefits that reach people with disabilities across vulnerability quartiles).
3.2. Program Impact on poverty • What poverty alleviation and reduction impact does the program have on persons with disabilities?	Household data collection and analysis Poverty study (e.g., UNDP). World Bank Living Standard Measurement Survey (LSMS). Newspaper stories. Qualitative Poverty Study.
3.3. Program's Impact on Inequality • How does this poverty alleviation and reduction impact compare to the one that is found for typically developing others?	Household data collection and analysis. Human Development Reports. World Development Reports. Qualitative inequality study.

criteria, for some people in need, the role of SSN programs assessments seems to be more to screen rather than to serve. At times, the real effect of these constraints on applicants and on professionals means assessment procedures are used to prove the disablement in order to qualify for a program, rather than to assess the overall functionality of the individual, which may cast them in a light of not being sick or impaired enough to receive the income benefit or clinical service.

27.3 SSN Institution, Organization, and Environment Capacity Analysis Toolkit

Component	Assessment Foci	Relevant Analytical Tools	Summary and Implications
1. Country Environment	1.1. What is the level of poverty in the country?	Document review: country studies, Web page, sector studies, interviews with country leaders and specialists. Information on GDP	What are the levels of poverty within people with disabilities? What implications does this have about SSN needs? How does the country compare with others with similar resources? What can the country realistically achieve?
	1.2. What is the political environment?	Indices of good governance	
	1.3. How developed is the infrastructure?	Document review: country studies, Web page, sector studies, interviews with country leaders and specialists.	
	1.4. How does the country's SSN program compare with others in the region?	Benchmark study	
2. Main Actors in SSN	2.1. Is there a national SSN policy and legal framework? 2.2. Who does what in the field of SSN (public, NGO, private providers) 2.3. How do SSN interventions relate to each other? 2.4. How do people with disabilities perceive SSN?	Document review: social policy, constitution, country studies. Sector studies, interviews with program staff, NGO umbrella representative, etc.	What are the gaps, strengths, and limitations in SSN actors? What aspects require change? What can be realistically changed?
3. Institution and Organization Capacity of Policy Development and Planning	3.1. Which organizational unit(s) is/are in charge of SSN policy development and planning as well as accountable for implementation? 3.2. What is the unit's organizational structure (what are their mandates and tasks)? 3.3. Is there a functional Management Information System (MIS) for SSN? 3.7. Is there a functional interministerial/intersectorial coordinating body?	Document review: previous SSN studies, legal provisions, organigrams, policy circulars, etc.; Focus group discussion with program staff; participatory observation in a coordination meeting	What are the gaps, strengths, and limitations? What aspects require change? What can be realistically changed?
4. Administrative Structure	4.1. Are resources for SNN interventions adequate at the local level?	1. Interview chief admin officers at the local levels 2. Interview ministries in charge of SSN and also expert NGO	What are the gaps, strengths, and limitations? What aspects require

(continued)

27.3 SSN Institution, Organization, and Environment Capacity Analysis Toolkit — *Continued*

Component	Assessment Foci	Relevant Analytical Tools	Summary and Implications
	4.2. What is the local admin capacity level? 4.3. Are there mechanisms that facilitate the inclusion of consumer views.		change? What can be realistically changed? What should the structure be like ideally?
5. Service Delivery	5.1. How are SSN delivered?		What are the gaps, strengths, and limitations? What aspects require change? What can be realistically changed? What should the structure be like ideally?
6. Organizational and Institutional Capacity Agencies Implementing SSN	6.1. What is the SSN provider's organizational capacity? 6.2. What is the capacity of eligibility evaluations? 6.3. What bottom-up accountability systems are in operation? How do service providers interact with other SSN actors?		What are the gaps, strengths, and limitations? What aspects require change? What can be realistically changed? What should the structure be like ideally?
7. Community Characteristics and Community Capacity	7.1. How is the community organized? 7.2. What kind of self-help culture prevails? 7.3. What is the institutional and organizational capacity of the community committees?		
8. The NGO Sector and Interorganizational Relations	8.1. What is the nature of national NGO sector? How do the public, private, and voluntary sectors interact with each other?		What are the gaps, strengths, and limitations? What aspects require change? What can be realistically changed? What interorganizational interaction be like ideally?

Institutional and Organization Efficiency Evaluations

SSN outcomes are mediated by institutional and organizational design and environmental factors so that loosely coordinated delivery programs tend to be less efficient and are duplicative in roles and functions. They also raise the cost of access for the person with a disability as a result of the fragmentation of SSN service provider functions (e.g., from higher time and travel investment between providers; Mathauer, 2004). Actual benefit to clients also is significantly reduced, due to losses in efficiency, duplication of roles and functions, and contradictory program delivery manuals. For example, SSN programs in most developing countries are provided by several government agencies with overlapping functions, and coordination issues in their delivery have an impact on effectiveness and efficiency. An institutional and organizational analysis toolkit is helpful for assessing the extent to which institutional and organization design factors influence SSN accessibility, coverage, targeting, and actual benefit to people with disabilities (see Table 27.3). The toolkit is particularly helpful for determining gaps, strengths, and weaknesses in SSN as a basis for the design of solutions and implementation plans to remedy inefficiencies in institutional, organizational, and environmental conditions. Based on an institutional and organizational analysis, it is possible to identify and exploit synergies among SSN delivery systems, eliminate program management overlaps, reduce coverage gaps, and take stock of responsibilities for program implementation, monitoring, evaluation, and coordination. From this analysis, it is possible to identify strengths that should be maintained or resources needed to develop more efficient ways for SSN to serve people with disabilities.

Life-Span–Life-Space Issues Evaluations

SSN needs with disabilities are influenced by the specific type of disability and also by evolving life-span and developmental needs. For example, people over the age of 60 are at an elevated risk for disability compared to those in early to middle adulthood. Necessarily, they have age-related developmental health and functioning needs for which particular SSN would be appropriate. A Social Risk Management (SRM) framework has been proposed to assess the differential impact of demographics on SSN access and use in populations (Holzmann & Steen, 2000). The SRM framework allows for the systematic study of the distribution of SSN types across ages within populations and also by main risks. Between groups, comparisons of accessibility of specific SSN are also possible. Data from these analyses are helpful for accurate understanding of the SSN situation within special categories of consumers and also for solution design and implementation.

Major Issues Requiring Attention in SSN Assessment

These relate to the interpretive nature of eligibility criteria, how disability is defined, and historical influences of SSN social policies. We briefly consider each in turn.

The Interpretive Nature of Eligibility Criteria

SSN eligibility outcomes could be different for people with similar medical statuses. Given the inevitable interpretive nature of eligibility criteria, SSN program officials derive a degree of discretion in assessing clients and determining eligibility for benefits, goods, and services. This discretion is further enhanced if the official occupies a particular professional role with its attendant expert knowledge, delegated authority, specialized vocabulary, and social standing. It is no real surprise, in this context, that SSN clients with chronic illness or disease feel professionals dominate the human services and that their own voices are weakly heard (Mpofu et al., 2008).

Medical, behavioral, and psychological assessments are prominent in certain social program areas such as short-term sickness benefits, long-term disability benefits, and compensation for workplace-related injuries and impairments (Andrews, 1998; Mitra, 2005). Assessment issues in social programs include whether the diagnosis is done by a single practitioner or a multidisciplinary team and, if the latter, which kinds of disciplinary knowledge (and criteria and types of evidence) are used and how they interrelate with one another. Another challenge for practitioners concerns multiple or overlapping

Discussion Box 27.1

WHAT ARE THE ROLES OF THE REHABILITATION PROFESSIONAL?

Rehabilitation professionals are often involved in eligibility assessments as either expert witnesses or primary determination of eligibility. In work-related injury or compensation SSN claims, a client may be in conflict with an insurer, a private company, and/or governmental agency that deals with accidents, injuries, illness, or long-term disability over satisfying eligibility criteria or justifying the continuation of a service or income benefit. In these circumstances, which can become quite adversarial and upsetting to the client, the rehabilitation professional may be called upon to advocate on behalf of the client to defend their interests. The rehabilitation specialist may be placed in a situation of acting as an adjudicator for the insurer to determine the authenticity of the client's claim or to discern a client's apparent lack of progress in recovery.

Questions:

1. How may SSN evaluations be designed to avoid potential conflicts of interest as noted in this case? Discuss with reference to practices in your own setting. Is there an inherent tension between person-centered rehabilitation and evidence-based practice?
2. If you were faced this set of expectations in your work, how would you try to manage the situation?

eligibility for individual clients, which raises questions about rationalization of SSN resources.

Definition of Disabilities

How disability is defined determines the eligibility for SSN. In navigating through myriad SSN programs, clients and even professionals are often baffled to discover that programs within a government (never mind across governments) use different definitions of disability in the determination of eligibility for benefits and services (Andrews, 1998; Moss & Teghtsoonian, 2008). Along these lines, disability is assessed separately and differently for social security disability insurance, workers' compensation, income assistance, veterans' programs, and disability-related tax measures. Under one program, then, an applicant might be assessed as permanently or severely impaired and, thus, eligible for certain benefits, yet, they may not qualify for another disability program by the same organization. The outcome can produce anger, confusion, and uncertainty as well as possible negative health effects.

A basic reason for this complex state of affairs is that disability programs and social policy more generally comprise a multilayered historical field of choices and activities. This is why today social policy is many things at the same time for different people and even for the same people with similar issues or needs.

Impairment-oriented definitions prevalent in developing countries may underreport the prevalence of disability and inadvertently exclude people with disabilities from SSN services they deserve. Definitions of disability based on activity and participation limitations tend to be more inclusive and are likely to result in a higher census of eligibles for SSN (Mitra, 2005). Thus, a key issue for people with disabilities seeking SSN is whether a program's assessment is diagnostically driven or functionally oriented.

Historical Influences

Social safety nets contain a diverse pattern of policy choices, made over many decades, concerning who to help, how, and why. They also contain a distinctive discourse on how to talk about disadvantage and disadvantaged groups. These ideas and programs reflect the diversities of the human condition as well as the differences in the cultural, economic, geographical, historical, and political contexts in which we live and work. In this sense, we can still speak of a Canadian approach to social policy or an American, Japanese, or Ugandan approach. Social safety net policies address the insecurities of industrialism—a concern of social programs for the past 150 years or more–and also the risks of everyday life and the opportunities and challenges presented by the new economy. Experiences across many countries indicate, however, that SSN policies are not, by themselves, enough to deal with issues of economic growth and social justice. A broader infrastructure of social programs and public services is essential: These include the justice system and rule of law, a broad system of progressive taxation on income, public spaces for parks, and other community amenities for sports, the arts, leisure, and recreation.

In modern times, social policies serve multiple functions, for multiple groups, and governed in multiple ways. Economic change by itself cannot solve the problems of poverty, discrimination, homelessness, or youth unemployment. Public social programs are required to address the human costs of economic change, to foster opportunities in the economy, and to promote fairness and social justice. Social development and economic development must be considered together; there are policy issues of priorities and balance in the allocation of limited public and private resources. Both are necessary parts of a policy aimed at broadening opportunities and removing barriers for disadvantaged groups in society.

Issues for Research and Other Forms of Scholarship in SSN Assessments

Assessment procedures sensitive to targeted SSN (those specific to identified vulnerable groups) and inclusive SSN (those for the general population) need to be developed. In addition, SSN policy implementation instruments to expose proactively likely systemic inefficiencies or service gaps (e.g., Mathauer, 2004) need further study. For example, the right mix of public to private SSN programs and the instruments for determining the best packaging and the best fit to particular welfare contexts is unknown. Evidence is also needed on the disability determination process that would yield the same objective outcomes within welfare contexts. The ICF could serve as a framework for planning disability determinations and evaluation outcomes.

Targeted or Inclusive SSN

Evidence is needed to assess the conditions under which SSN targeted to people with disabilities should (1) be preferred over inclusive SSN or (2) used together with inclusive SSN. Mitra (2005) developed a flowchart to guide SSN program policy implementation with and without targeting. A brief screening instrument for decisions regarding whether claimants with vulnerability could be better served by targeted SSN and/or inclusive SSN would enhance both quality and efficiency in SSN policy implementation. Many countries have adopted assessment waiver procedures for SSN for participants with visible or documented disabilities. The extent to which assessment for inclusive SSN services serve people with chronic illness efficiently as compared to assessments for targeted services is to be determined.

SSN Assessment Inequities

Government or public disability insurance programs typically provide income maintenance payments for workers who have made regular financial contributions to such programs (and to the survivors of these contributors) and who have become seriously disabled. While these disability insurance programs vary in details among industrial states (OECD, 2003), generally they do not address the etiology of a disability or impairment but rather focus on the degree of disability. Many public disability insurance plans offer coverage only or primarily to those workers medically assessed to have a severe and prolonged impairment that, in turn, prevents them from pursuing their own job, a comparable one, or perhaps any gainful occupation.

In addition to disability insurance programs for long-term needs, many countries have short-term sickness benefits (Kangas, 2004). Often, these sickness benefit programs are administered separately from the disability insurance programs in order to deal with the contingencies of short-term and temporary illnesses that result in a person leaving the labor force for just a few weeks or a few months (OECD, 2003). Assessment procedures are not as involved or elaborate as with disability insurance plans because the clients are expected to receive benefits for a relatively short period of time and then return to work.

As noted previously, for some SSN programs, income social protection is for work-related injuries and diseases, while for others, a direct attachment to the workplace is not a requirement for coverage. We also see that some programs offer protection for disabilities that are partial and total as well as permanent and temporary in nature; other programs offer protection for just temporary ailments; and, still other programs target only total disablement over the longer term. Furthermore, in programs for WC and veterans, rehabilitation serves a major part, while for long-term disability insurance and short-term sickness benefits, rehabilitation serves a minor part in program delivery. What these programs all share, however, is the safety net policy goal of compensating labor force participants for lost income due to sickness, injury, disease or disability.

This uneven array of income programs comprise a complex and fragmented system of support to individuals and families (European Commission, 2003; Ison, 1994). This fragmented system raises serious issues of horizontal equity—that is, of treating people in comparable circumstances in comparable ways. At present, in most social safety net systems worldwide, how people are treated in terms of income protection depends on how and where their injury, disease, or disablement came about. As a result, horizontal inequities prevail. In the words of one social policy analyst: "people with disabilities in similar situations can be treated very differently depending on which programs they qualify for, which in turn reflects how their disability arose and in which province [or state] they live" (Puttee, 2002, p. 97). Research is needed on best practices in SSN eligibility assessment that accurately accept qualified claimants.

Stigma Issues

In market societies, recipients of needs-based programs (such as people with chronic illness or disability) frequently have a negative status as dependent and wealth takers rather than as independent contributors to the wealth of nations. The actual, perceived, or preferred fit between welfare transfers and market values continually plays out in numerous debates, one of which concerns the necessity, morality, or efficacy of mandatory work requirements for able-bodied recipients of public assistance, the so-called workfare issue. These debates are important and can have decisive effects on the design and assessment of SSN programs and on the quality of life of many individuals and families living in vulnerable circumstances (Karger, Midgley, & Brown, 2002).

Research Box 27.3

KEEPING THE UNEMPLOYED HEALTHY: THE EFFECT OF SOCIAL BENEFITS ON PEOPLE

Marlow, S. (2006). A safety net or ties that bind? Women, welfare and self-employment. *International Journal of Sociology and Social Policy, 26*(9/10), 397–410.

Objectives: To examine the challenges facing benefit-dependent lone mothers who seek to engage with self-employment.

Methods: Qualitative case study, based on semistructured interviews, of three women in Britain considering the transition from welfare benefit dependency to self-employment.

Results: The current welfare system discourages lone mothers from entering formal self-employment due to the system's close surveillance, lack of trust, limited freedom to make choices, and the absence of appropriate supports for making the transition.

Conclusions: Questions are raised regarding the efficacy of current welfare to work policies that, in this case, appear to encourage informal working but impede enterprising behavior into waged work.

Questions:
The results of this study suggest that welfare-to-work programs have unintended adverse consequences for women on welfare.

1. How is the relationship between welfare and work addressed in rehabilitation assessment procedures?
2. Why is shame and stigma often connected with receiving welfare benefits?
3. What other research and information would you require in order to understand more completely this phenomenon?

Summary and Conclusion

Social programs can and do serve as facilitators or as barriers to the activities and participation of people with chronic health conditions and functional impairments. Social safety net programs are important in the community participation of people with chronic illness or disability and, indeed, for their health and well-being. The ways in which SSN assessments are carried out at the individual and institution level influence the ease with which people with chronic illness or disability access SSN services. The manner and efficiency with which SSN eligibility and service delivery qualities are assessed can enable or discourage the involvement of consumers in the design and delivery of health, education, rehabilitation, and community services. Increasingly, there is a growing awareness of the need for client-friendly SSN assessment procedures, including the greater involvement of caregivers or family members in the determination evaluation processes.

In this chapter, we noted the fact that disabilities are assessed differently for SSN such as disability insurance, workers' compensation, basic income assistance, veterans' programs, and sickness benefits. In most social safety net systems worldwide, how people are treated in terms of income protection depends on how and where their injury, disease, or disablement came about, raising serious issues of equity and effectiveness.

Clients may also present with multiple disabilities, and discretionary decisions may be required in weighting eligibility qualifications.

References

Anderberg, P. (2005). Making both ends meet. *Disability Studies Quarterly, 25*(3), 1–9.

Andrews, E. S. (1998). *Disability insurance: Programs and practices.* Washington, DC: World Bank.

Armitage, A. (2003). *Social welfare in Canada* (4h ed.). Toronto: Oxford University Press.

Barnes, C. (2002). Introduction: Disability, policy and politics. *Policy & Politics, 30,* 311–318.

Chambers, D. E. (1993). *Social policy and social programs: A method for the practical public policy analyst* (2nd ed.). New York: Macmillan.

Cox, D. R., & Goldberg, A. L. (in press). Assessing disability: Social Security Disability evaluations. In E. Mpofu & T. Oakland (Eds.), *Assessment in rehabilitation and health.* Boston, MA: Pearon/Merrill.

Dinitto, D. M. (1999). *Social welfare: Politics and public policy* (5th ed.). Old Tappan, NJ: Allyn & Bacon.

Elwan, A. (1999). *Poverty and disability: A survey of the literature. Social Protection Discussion Paper Series, No. 9932.* Washington, DC: The World Bank.

European Commission. (2003). *Social protection of people with disabilities. Mutual Information System on Social Protection (MISSOC)—Info 01/2003.* Retrieved January 7, 2009, from: http://www.europa.eu

FOD. (2007). Inkomensvervangende Tegemoetkoming en Integratietegemoetkoming [Income replacing and integration allocations]. Retrieved January 7, 2009, from: http://www.handicap.fgov.be

Gunderson, M., & Hyatt, D. (Eds.). (2000). *Workers' compensation: Foundations for reform.* Toronto: University of Toronto Press.

Holzmann, R., & Steen, J. (2000). *Social risk management: A new conceptual framework and beyond.* Washington, DC: World Bank.

Hurst, R. (2003). The international disability rights movement and the ICF. *Disability and Rehabilitation, 25*(11–12), 572–576.

International Labor Office. (1984). *Introduction to social security.* Geneva: Author.

Ison, T. (1994). *Compensation systems for injury and disease: The policy choices.* Toronto: Butterworths.

Jongbloed, L., & Crichton, A. (1990). A new definition of disability: Implications for rehabilitation practice and social policy. *Canadian Journal of Occupational Therapy, 57*(1), 32–38.

Kangas, O. (2004). Institutional development of sickness cash-benefit programmes in 18 OECD Countries. *Social Policy & Administration, 38*(2), 190–203.

Karger, H. J., Midgley, J., & Brown, C. B. (Eds.). (2002). *Controversial issues in social policy* (2nd ed.). Old Tappan, NJ: Allyn & Bacon.

Karger, H. J., & Stoesz, D. (2006). *American social welfare policy: A pluralist approach* (5th ed.). Old Tappan, NJ: Allyn & Bacon.

Lippel, K. (2008). Workers' compensation and controversial illnesses. In P. Moss & K. Teghtsoonian (Eds.), *Contesting illness: Processes and practices* (pp. 47–68). Buffalo: University of Toronto Press.

Marks, N. F. (1998). Does it hurt to care? Caregiving, work–family conflict, and midlife well-being. *Journal of Marriage and the Family, 60,* 951–966.

Marlow, S. (2006). A safety net or ties that bind? Women, welfare and self-employment. *International Journal of Sociology and Social* Policy, *26*(9/10), 397–410.

Mathauer, I. (2004). *Institutional analysis toolkit for safety net interventions. Social Protection Discussion Paper Series.* Washington, DC: The World Bank.

Mitra, S. (2005). *Disability and social safety nets in developing countries. Social Protection Discussion Paper Series, No. 0509.* Washington, DC: The World Bank.

Moss, P., & Teghtsoonian, K. (Eds.). (2008). *Contesting illness: Processes and practices.* Buffalo: University of Toronto Press.

Mpofu, E., & Conyers, L. M. (2004). A representational theory perspective of minority status and people with disabilities: Implications for rehabilitation education and practice. *Rehabilitation Counselling Bulletin, 47,* 142–151.

Mpofu, E., Crystal, R., & Feist-Price, S. (2000). Tokenism among rehabilitation clients: Implications for rehabilitation education. *Rehabilitation Education, 14,* 243–256.

Mpofu, E., Lopez, L. L., Tapologo, M., & Magweva, I. (2008). *Comprehensive study of social safety nets for people with disabilities in Botswana.* Gaborone, Botswana: Ministry of Health.

Organization for Economic Cooperation and Development. (2003). *Transforming disability into ability: Policies to promote work and income security for disabled people.* Paris: Author.

Prince, M. J. (2009) *Absent citizens: Disability politics and policy in Canada.* Toronto: University of Toronto Press.

Puttee, A. (2002). Reforming the disability insurance system: A Collaborative approach. In A. Puttee (Ed.), *Federalism, democracy and disability policy in Canada* (pp. 79–120). Montreal: McGill-Queen's University Press.

Rice, J. J., & Prince, M. J. (2000). *Changing politics of Canadian social policy.* Toronto: University of Toronto Press.

Rodriguez, E. (2001). Keeping the unemployed healthy: The effect of means-tested and entitlement benefits in Britain, Germany, and the United States. *Am J Public Health, 91,* 1403–1411.

Smart, J. (2005). The promise of the International Classification of Functioning, Disability and Health (ICF). *Rehabilitation Education, 19*(2&3), 191–199.

Social Security Administration. (2006). *Disability evaluation under Social Security—January 2006.* Retrieved from http://www.ssa.gov/disability/professionals/bluebook/

Üstün, T. B., Chatterji, S., Bickenbach, J., Kostanjsek, N., & Schneider, M. (2003). The International Classification of Functioning, Disability and Health: A new tool for understanding disability and health. *Disability and Rehabilitation, 25*(11–12), 565–571.

World Bank. (1999). *Social risk management: Intellectual underpinnings of the social protection strategy.* Washington, DC: Author.

World Health Organization. (2001). *The International Classification of Functioning, Disability and Health.* Geneva: Author.

Sexual Functioning Assessments

28

Jill Harris

Overview

Sexual functioning is a complex construct that includes biopsychosocial factors affecting the sexual response cycle. While sexual functioning problems are not uncommon in the general population, prevalence of sexual difficulties may be even higher among people with physical disabilities or chronic health issues. The increased prevalence may be due in part to physical features of the disability/illness, medication effects, and/or psychosocial aspects such as societal barriers, emotional concerns, and body image issues. Assessment techniques include interviews, self-report diaries or questionnaires, physiological measures, and physical examination. Assessment strategies should take into consideration the sensitivity associated with sexual functioning, cultural influences, and the extent that the measurement tool is applicable to the population. Future work on assessment of sexual functioning in rehabilitation and health is likely to focus on attention to cognitive and behavioral flexibility in addressing sexual functioning as well as developing measures that are brief, have been standardized with special populations, and better lend themselves to intervention.

Learning Objectives

By the end of the chapter, the reader should be able to:

1. Identify aspects of sexual function for which assessment would be important;
2. List reasons why people with disabilities or health concerns may be at greater risk for sexual functioning difficulties;
3. Discuss the pros and cons of interview, self-reported questionnaire, and physiological techniques in the assessment of sexual health;
4. Examine the appropriateness of procedures for conducting a successful interview to assess sexual functioning; and
5. Identify and describe three barriers to effective assessment and treatment of sexual difficulties of people with disabilities or chronic medical illness.

Introduction

Sexual functioning is complex. It encompasses physical, emotional, behavioral, and social areas and is influenced by a myriad of factors including, but not limited to, health, culture, and attitude. For people with disabilities, assessment of sexual functioning is often overlooked, but it is as essential to understanding the whole person as it is for people without disabilities.

This chapter highlights issues related to definitions of sexual functioning; history of research on sexual functioning; approaches to assessment; cultural, legislative, and professional issues; multidisciplinary approaches to assessment and treatment of sexual functioning; and major issues for future research and practice related to sexual functioning for people with disabilities or chronic health conditions.

Importance of Sexual Functioning to Rehabilitation and Health

Sexual functioning is a complex construct that is associated with personal well-being, quality of life, and relationship stability among the general population, as well as those with disabilities or illnesses. For those with acute medical issues, the attention of both the patient and health care staff typically is focused on managing the health crisis. As the acute crisis abates and medical issues become more chronic, energy often turns to how to incorporate the health condition into all aspects of functioning for the patient, as well as his/her significant others. While satisfaction with sexual function may not be critical for sustaining life, sexual functioning is associated with personal happiness. As many chronic medical illnesses or disabilities affect sexual functioning, it is important to address this issue within rehabilitation and health care settings. In order to do so, terms must be adequately defined and reliable and valid assessment instruments must be developed. Valid assessment is essential to accurately determine the need for treatment and the effectiveness of interventions (Heiman, 2002).

Definitions and Theories of Sexual Functioning

One can narrowly define sexual functioning in terms of the sexual response cycle. According to the works of Masters and Johnson (1966), the sexual response cycle consists of the phases of sexual desire, excitement, orgasm, and resolution. The *desire phase* refers to fantasies about sexual activity and interest in having sexual activity. The *excitement phase* refers to a subjective sense of pleasure plus physiological, genital changes. In males, the major changes are penile tumescence and erection. In females, the major physiological changes involve vaginal lubrication and expansion and swelling of the external genitalia. The *orgasm phase* consists of peaking of sexual pleasure, release of sexual tension, and rhythmic contraction of the perineal muscles and reproductive organs. For males, there is a sense of inevitable ejaculation, followed by ejaculation of semen. The *resolution phase* refers to *a* sense of relaxation and well-being. Males are physiologically unable to experience erection or orgasm for a variable period of time during this phase, whereas females may be able to respond to sexual stimulation without delay (Masters & Johnson, 1966).

This definition may be overly simplistic, however, as it may fail to fully account for the biopsychosocial influences on sexual response. Further, what is considered "normal" in regard to sexual functioning may vary depending on factors such as gender, age, personal attributes, and societal, religious, and cultural values (National Cancer Institute, n.d., 1). Thus, determination of sexual functioning will be influenced by how it is defined as well as what is measured. For example, a person may experience sexual functioning difficulties due to biological factors related to health status, social factors related to attitudinal barriers, psychological factors such as perception of inadequacy/adequacy or anxiety about sexual performance, and/or interpersonal factors such as quality of the relationship with a partner (Matthew et al., 2005). Other factors, such as the importance one attaches to the role of sexual functioning within self esteem and within a relationship, will affect one's sense of sexual satisfaction. Thus, if the definition of sexual functioning does not account for the factors pertinent to the individual, then inaccurate conclusions may be reached.

If sexual functioning refers to satisfactory sexual response, then what is sexual *dysfunction?* The *Diagnostic and Statistical Manual of Mental Disorders* (4th ed., text revision; *DSM-IV-TR*) provides one commonly used system for categorizing sexual dysfunction. Sexual dysfunctions are characterized by disturbance in sexual desire and physiological changes involved in the sexual response cycle that cause marked distress and interpersonal difficulty (American Psychiatric Association, 2002). Disorders are further categorized by onset (lifelong versus acquired), context (generalized versus situational), and presumed etiology (due to psychological factors versus due to combined factors).

The sexual dysfunctions listed in *DSM-IV-TR* are:

- Sexual Desire Dysfunctions (Hypoactive Sexual Desire Disorder; Sexual Aversion Disorder)
- Sexual Arousal Disorders (Female Sexual Arousal Disorder; Male Erectile Disorder)
- Orgasmic Disorders (Female Orgasmic Disorder; Male Orgasmic Disorder, Premature Ejaculation)
- Sexual Pain Disorders (Dyspareunia; Vaginismus)
- Sexual Dysfunction due to a General Medical Condition
- Substance-induced Sexual Dysfunction
- Sexual Dysfunction not Otherwise Specified

Masters and Johnson's (1966) portrayal of the linear nature of the sexual response cycle and the *DSM* categorization of sexual dysfunctions have been challenged in regard to applicability to women. Sexual response in females may be affected by sexual priorities and experiences such that desire does not necessarily lead to excitement and orgasm, for example (Basson, 2002). An international consensus panel of experts recommended that additional subcategories be created under Female Sexual Arousal Disorder: Physical/Genital Sexual Arousal Disorder; Psychological Sexual Arousal Disorder; and Combined Physical and Psychological Sexual Arousal Disorder (Basson et al., 2004). The additional subcategories are felt to better reflect the differences between subjective and physiological aspects of sexual response in women.

Lack of consensus regarding definition may influence prevalence estimates of sexual dysfunction. Indeed, there is wide variation with estimates of sexual problems in the general population ranging from 10%–52% of men and 25%–63% of women (Heiman, 2002). The wide range is likely due to differences among definitions of sexual problems, assessment techniques, and comfort level of respondents. The prevalence of sexual problems among people with physical disabilities or chronic medical illness is often estimated to be as high, or higher (Rosen et al., 2004), than that of the general population. For example, 40%–100% of people with cancer (Derogatis & Kourlesis, 1981) and 30%–60% of patients with epilepsy (Fishman, Ettinger, & Callanan, 2006) have been estimated to experience sexual problems. Prevalence of sexual difficulties among people with traumatic brain injury is also felt to be higher than in the general population (Hibbard, Gordon, Flanagan, Haddad, & Labinsky, 2000).

There are a number of reasons why people with disabilities or health conditions may have difficulties involving sexual functioning. Effects may be due to physical effects of the actual illness/injury such as nerve damage from spinal cord injury or diabetes, pain from illnesses such as cancer, or reduced blood flow from illnesses such as cardiac conditions. Treatments for medical conditions can also negatively impact sexual functioning. Many medications are known to have sexual side effects. Chemotherapy, for example, may disrupt hormones, decrease energy, cause weight gain or weight loss, or cause diarrhea, all of which may affect body image and desire. Surgery may negatively impact sexual functioning due to loss of tissue, nerve damage, or reduction in mobility, for example. Radiation may cause vascular compromise and build-up of scar tissue and/or nerve damage, which may lead to pain, infertility, erectile dysfunction, or vaginal dryness, among other effects (Lamb, 1996).

Sipski and Alexander (1997) provide a helpful method of examining the effects of illness on sexual functioning. First, consider the overall effect of the disability or illness. Next, consider the secondary complications from the illness, such as spasticity or contractures from cerebral palsy or other brain injury, that may impact sexual activity. Consider whether the illness is progressive or static because psychological and physical adjustment to change may place additional strain on the individual. Consider iatrogenic effects of treatment, such as side-effects of medication, surgery, and radiation. Consider if the illness is congenital or acquired, age at onset, stress associated with the illness, and potential barriers to finding a partner. Applying this model to a woman diagnosed with multiple sclerosis (MS) as an example, the illness, itself, may cause neurological changes that may affect sexual functioning directly. These changes may include, for example, decreased libido or numbness of genital sensation. Secondary complications of MS, such as weakness or incoordination, may affect sexual function by limiting sexual positions and decreasing satisfaction. As MS can have progressive as well as static periods, patients may find that interest in and expectations for sexual activity may be affected. Fluctuations in the disease process may also cause mood changes, which may impact sexual interest and satisfaction. Medication may affect libido. Stress of living with MS may lead to worries about attracting or maintaining a sexual relationship, worries about satisfying a partner and one's own sexual satisfaction, and concerns about body image and attractiveness, as well as many other issues that may impact sexual functioning. Thus, assessment and treatment of sexual functioning within rehabilitation and health care settings need to recognize the complexity of all these factors.

Applicable Aspects of the ICF

Sexual function is listed as a Body Function (b640–b6409) within the International Classification of Functioning, Disability, and Health (ICF) system. In regards to Activity and Participation, it falls within the realm of Interpersonal Interactions and Relationships. Relevant Environmental Factors that influence sexual functioning include Support and Relationships and Attitudes (personal and societal). Capacity for sexual functioning may be quite different from performance due to personal and societal barriers. An individual with a disability or health condition may or may not require assistance, such as use of an assistive device (e.g., to achieve and maintain an erection) or personal assistant (e.g., to assist with positioning), to perform sexually.

History of Research and Practice in the Assessment of Sexual Functioning

Published case studies of sexual dysfunction and the "psychology of sex" have dated back to the 1880s (Krafft-Ebing, reprinted 1998). Krafft-Ebing considered any sexual activity not for the purpose of procreation to be a "perversion." He felt that homosexuality was part of nature and should be studied rather than condemned. In the 1930s through 1950s, large-scale population surveys became a popular way to study sexual behavior. Kinsey and colleagues conducted personal interviews with approximately 12,000 males and females (Kinsey, Pomeroy, & Martin, 1948; Kinsey, Pomeroy, Martin, & Gebhard, 1953). His studies were viewed as highly controversial and were subject to public opposition, including opposition from law enforcement.

In the 1950s, William Masters and Virginia Johnson veered away from Kinsey's approach by conducting lab studies to examine the physiological basis of human sexual response (Masters & Johnson, 1966, 1970). Their treatment included both cognitive and behavioral methods. Some critics at the time viewed them as biased in their population samples and methods and considered their work to be an unacceptable departure from traditional medicine (Gerdes, 1997).

Helen Kaplan Singer was another pioneer in the study of sexual functioning. She integrated psychodynamic, behavioral, medical, and relational models in discussing assessment and treatment of sexual dysfunction (Kaplan, 1974). She was among the first to consider performance anxiety as an area worthy of intervention. She also described an approach to assessment that is now referred to as the Kaplan model (discussed later).

Since the 1980s, sexual functioning research has increasingly focused on medication and its role in treating males with erectile dysfunction. More recent focus has expanded to address premature or rapid ejaculation as well as reduced sexual desire in females. Research with females tends to focus more on self-report rather than physiological measures due to the greater variability and less visibility of female sexual response in comparison to males.

The increased availability of pharmaceutical treatment of sexual dysfunction has led to further discussion of appropriate "endpoints" for measuring treatment outcomes and resulted in the development of an increasing number of sexual functioning assessment measures in the past 15 years. The *Journal of Sexual Medicine* published a series of articles in 2004, describing consensus recommendations related to sexual medicine. The recommendations were the result of meetings with over 200 international multidisciplinary experts conducted over 2 years (e.g., Hatzichristou et al., 2004; Heiman et al., 2004; Hirsch et al., 2004). These articles were intended to help clarify definitions and practices and thus advance the field of sexual functioning research. Despite these advances, clinical practice involving sexual assessment and treatment for people with disabilities may still be woefully inadequate. For example, McAlonan, (1996) found that a majority of clients with spinal cord injury reported dissatisfaction with the quantity and quality of sexuality-related services they received. Services were felt to inadequately address client needs, readiness, or preference for type of information and format for service delivery.

Current Assessment Methods in Sexual Functioning

Overall approaches to assessment of sexual function include the following models: Kaplan (1983), PLISSIT (Annon, 1976), and ALLOW (Hatzichristou et al., 2004). The Kaplan model focuses on the chief complaint, sexual status, psychiatric status, family and psychosocial history, relationship assessment, summary, and recommendations. Kaplan notes the need to take the initiative when discussing sexuality with clients, as well as the need to be approachable. At the same time, the Kaplan model recognizes the limitations of the clinic setting and the importance of referring the client to an expert when necessary (Kaplan, 1983). Applying the Kaplan model, the primary physician may introduce the topic of sexual health as part of a well-patient visit. Maintaining a calm and accepting manner would help demonstrate that the physician is approachable about sexual functioning. Interviewing may reveal that the male patient has been experiencing some anxiety regarding job stability. The resulting stress may be impacting his relationship with his partner with subsequent episodes of erectile dysfunction. If the physician is uncertain how to address these issues, he/she might then refer that patient to a mental health therapist, urologist, or other sexual health specialist.

The PLISSIT model is a framework for assessment and treatment that is often used in rehabilitation settings. PLISSIT stands for *P*ermission to discuss sexuality, provision of *L*imited *I*nformation regarding sexuality, *S*pecific *S*uggestions regarding the person's sexual issues, and *I*ntensive *T*herapy with an expert when needed (Annon, 1976). Using the same example of the male patient described in the Kaplan model, a health care professional using the PLISSIT model likely would also initiate discussion of sexual health and demonstrate approachability. Unlike Kaplan, PLISSIT draws the distinction between providing general information (e.g., regarding effect of stress and anxiety on erections) versus suggestions more specific to the patient (e.g., exploring the reaction of the partner to the patient's job instability). Like Kaplan, referrals to specialists would be made if the health care professional did not feel qualified to address the issue further.

The ALLOW model acronym stands for *A*sk the patient about sexual function and activity, *L*egitimize the client's problems by acknowledging that sexual function is clinically relevant, *L*imitations (limited knowledge or comfort of client or clinician), *O*pen up the discussion including consideration of referral to specialist/expert, and *W*ork together to develop a treatment plan (Hatzichristou et al., 2004). The main difference between the ALLOW model and the Kaplan and PLISSIT models is the greater emphasis on the collaborative relationship between the patient and the health care professional. Applying the ALLOW model, the clinician likely would explore the comfort level of the male patient described previously in discussing his sexual issue. The clinician would also acknowledge his/her own comfort level with the discussion (at least to himself/herself). Finally, even if referral was made to a specialist, the clinician would participate in the development of the treatment plan (e.g., by assisting in location of a specialist, monitoring medication that may be needed as an adjunct to therapy, etc.). All these approaches have the common features of encouraging the clinician to take initiative when discussing sexuality and to know when to refer to an expert.

Regardless of the overall approach, the tools used to assess sexual functioning include interview, self-report measures including questionnaires and diaries, physiological measures, and/or physical examination. All assessment tools should be administered with sensitivity and regard to the unique cultural, ethnic, and personal background of the client. Regardless of the type of assessment tool used, consideration of the particular domain of interest for a particular client is essential.

Interviews

Interviews typically include detailed medical, psychosocial, and sexual history. The medical history should include consideration of lifestyle factors. Lifestyle factors, such as substance abuse and/or smoking, for example, may negatively impact libido, quality of erections, or ability to achieve orgasm. Because psychosocial difficulties in the absence of any health issues may also lead to sexual problems, it is important that the interview assess any possible comorbidities in this area, such as the presence of an anxiety or depressive disorder, which may lead to performance anxiety, reduced sexual interest, or negatively impact quality of relationships. The sexual history section of the interview may include questions regarding sexual response, sexual functioning prior to the disability or illness, relationship status, and sexual perceptions. Because flexibility may be a crucial risk factor in sexual adjustment, especially for people with chronic health conditions, it is an important area to assess (Barsky, Friedman, & Rosen, 2006).

One way to structure the interview is to start with general, less sensitive questions about the patient's overall history, then proceed to more specific, sensitive history of sexual functioning difficulties, duration of the problem, change in sexual functioning over time, behavioral contingencies related to sexual functioning, and the effects of the difficulties on other aspects of the client's life (Pollets, Ducharme, & Pauporte, 1999). Because discussions about sexuality are often sensitive for the patient as well as the clinician, it is important to establish rapport, comfort, and a sense of acceptance. In order to do this, the following tips for conducting a sexual history interview may be helpful (from Fishman et al., 2006; Gregoire, 1999; Lefebvre, 1997):

- Initiate discussion by starting with questions that might be less sensitive in nature. For female clients, start by asking about reproductive history and contraceptive use history, then proceed to discussing sexual activity. For male clients, consider starting with questions regarding urinary issues.
- To help promote a sense of acceptance, introduce sexual questions with a normalizing statement such as, "Sexual health is important to overall health so I always ask about it. . ." Or, "many people with [name of illness/disability] often have concerns about. . ."
- To aid conversational flow and reduce embarrassment, use transitional statements between sensitive subject areas.
- Avoid unrealistic optimism, such as reassuring the patient that he/she will find a partner. This may reduce clinician credibility and lead to false expectations from the client.
- To improve comfort level and respect autonomy, allow patient to feel in control of the interview by noting that he/she can choose not to discuss a topic if preferred.
- Keep questions open-ended so patient does not feel interrogated or rushed.

- Avoid assumptions about sexual orientation so the patient does not feel judged or embarrassed.
- Watch physical reactions during interview, such as increased activity level, rapid speech, or blushing, for cues when to slow questions down.
- Avoid judgmental reactions or comments in order to reduce barriers between the patient and interviewer.
- To reduce patient discomfort or sense of distancing, avoid jargon.
- To help ensure rapport and good communication, check for own and client understanding.
- Destigmatize and normalize by noting that other clients may have similar concerns and that such concerns would be expected given the nature of the illness and/or the experiences of the client.
- Assess flexibility by asking questions such as "Do you think there are ways to have a good sex life without sexual intercourse?"
- To assess how central sexual functioning is to client self-esteem, ask questions such as "How important is sexual activity to how you view yourself?" Responses related to flexibility and centrality help lay the groundwork for design of cognitive-behavioral interventions. (Barsky et al., 2006)

The pros of the interview technique for assessing sexual functioning include the ability to assess how the client relates to the interviewer. This may give clues to interpersonal style impacting relationships, which are not as easily assessed using self-report or other measures. Further, the interview allows the possibility of assessing the client alone or with his/her partner in order to gather important information regarding the viewpoint of the partner and the quality of the relationship, an often key component to sexual functioning (Pollets et al., 1999). Interviews also allow for elaboration on questions as necessary, clarification of questions, and probing when responses are unclear or contradictory.

Self-Report Questionnaires

Advantages of self-report questionnaires (SRQs) include their potential utility to track sexual functioning over time and response to treatment using a standard metric (Rosen, 2006). SRQs may be less biased than interviews and less costly in terms of professional time and effort (Pollets et al., 1999). SRQs also help the clinician maintain documentation in a systematic manner. SRQs can be useful in directing the discussion between the clinician and client and may be less embarrassing to the client than direct interview questions. They also may lend themselves to computerized formats, which can be more efficient and cost-effective for both client and clinician and may allow completion at home or in the office waiting area, rather than during an appointment (Rosen, 2006). Further, SRQs may allow the client to organize thoughts in a reflective manner (Pollets et al., 1999). Additionally, SRQs place a lower burden on the client in comparison to physiological measures (Heiman et al., 2004).

Disadvantages of the SRQ, however, include its subjectivity. For example, the client may endorse a particular response on the SRQ but not feel that the behavior is a particular problem. Thus, the clinician may want to supplement

Discussion Box 28.1

SENSITIVITY OF TOPIC AND EFFECT ON ACCURACY OF RESPONSE

Sexual functioning is typically perceived to be a sensitive, potentially threatening topic. Research on assessment of threatening topics notes that accuracy of responses may be influenced by the mode of questions and responses, context of questions, and structure or wording of the questions (Schaeffer, 1999).

Discuss how various question formats related to sexual functioning may influence accuracy of responses. How might the way the patient processes the question influence the accuracy of the response?

the SRQ items by asking about the particular bother of a symptom or behavior to the client. Additionally, SRQs typically do not take into account the sexual knowledge of the client as a potential barrier to sexual function. SRQs can limit the responses that a client can give. The format of the SRQ may need to be modified to allow for accessibility to clients whose disability or reading level may inhibit ability to respond (Lefebvre, 1997). Further, questions regarding frequency of sexual activity may be affected by lack of opportunity for people with disabilities, rather than lack of interest or ability.

Criteria for selecting a particular questionnaire include brevity of the measure, specificity to sexual functioning versus using a more generic instrument (such as a quality of life measure), inclusion of questions specific to the gender of interest, applicability regardless of sexual orientation or availability of a partner, questions perceived as nonintrusive, sensitive enough to assess changes over time/response to treatment, ability to separate effects of illness from medication effects, adequate reliability and validity, cross-cultural applicability and translation into other languages, and whether it has been used with the population of interest (Fishman et al., 2006). The degree to which the tool can discriminate between those with adequate sexual functioning from those with dysfunction is important if the tool is to be used to establish a sexual-related diagnosis.

The specific SRQs reviewed in the following paragraphs were chosen based on the frequency with which they were cited in published studies, relative brevity, and, in most cases, adequate specification of psychometric properties. Tools that have sensitivity to discriminate between those with and without sexual dysfunction have utility in establishing diagnosis. Tools that are sensitive in detecting changes resulting from treatment have utility as outcome measures. Selection of a particular tool should also consider whether published norms are available for the population and age group of interest. Listed tools are described as having "adequate" reliability if mean internal consistency (e.g., Cronbach's alpha) was over 0.70 for reported subscales or test–retest reliability coefficient was over 0.50. Validity is described as "adequate" if attempts were made to compare the measure to accepted measures of the same construct (concurrent validity) or measures of a construct felt to be unrelated (divergent validity). Chapter 28 appendix, A (see the end of this chapter), lists some commonly used SRQs that are applicable to either gender. It is not meant to include all available measures. Measures specific to a particular disability or illness (e.g., multiple sclerosis measure described in Szasz, Paty, Lawton-Speert, & Eisen, 1984) were not reviewed due to their lack of generalizability to other populations.

Most of the measures listed in section A of the appendix report adequate internal consistency, test–retest reliability, and construct and/or divergent validity. Some of the measures do not report psychometric qualities and should thus only be used with caution. The Derogatis Interview for Sexual Functioning (DISF/DISF-SR; Derogatis, 1997) and the Golombok-Rust Inventory of Sexual Satisfaction (GRISS; 1986) have been translated into several languages. The Changes in Sexual Functioning Questionnaire (CSFQ; Clayton, Owens, & McGarvey, 1995) and the Inventory of Sexual Experiences and Response in Disability (IEReSDI; Rodarte & Munoz, 2004) are available in Spanish and have been shown to have good validity in Spanish. The CSFQ is also available in a computerized format. Several measures, including the DISF and the GRISS, have shown utility in discriminating people with sexual dysfunction from a control population. The Arizona Sexual Experience Scale (ASEX; McGahuey, Gelenberg, Lankes, Moreno, & Delgado, 2000), CSFQ, and GRISS have been noted to demonstrate utility in measuring response to treatment (Clayton, 2001). Those SRQs that include items related to frequency of specific sexual activity, such as the Modified Rush Sexual Inventory (MRSI; Rao, Zajecka, & Skubiak, 2005) and the DISF-SR, may be viewed by clients as intrusive. The MRSI is unique in that it includes medical history, free response, and visual analogue sections. Those measures that were specifically designed for use with a disability population include the Physical Disability Sexual and Body Esteem Scale (PDSBE; Taleporas & McCabe, 2001), the Sexual Health Needs Survey (SHNS; Fisher et al.,2002), and the IEReSDI. The IEReSDI also was validated on a wider age range (i.e., 14 years old and up) than most measures. Some of the measures designed for the general population have also been used for people with disabilities (e.g., DISF and spinal cord injuries, CSFQ and patients with cancer).

Chapter 28 appendix, B, lists SRQs for men. Many of the measures designed for use with men focus exclusively on erectile function (Rosen, 2006). The Male Sexual Health Questionnaire (MSHQ; Rosen, 2006) is more comprehensive than most SRQs because it assesses domains related to ejaculatory dysfunction and sexual satisfaction, as well as to erectile function. Validation studies using the MSHQ have been with males ages 45 and older, thus, utility with younger men is unclear at this point. The International Index of Erectile Functioning (IIEF; Rosen et al., 1997) has been internationally validated and has been used as the major endpoint in many studies related to effectiveness of treatment for erectile dysfunction. The IIEF, however, does not assess ejaculation or partner variables and is not applicable to homosexual men (Rosen, 2006). While the Brief Male Sexual Function Inventory (BMSFI; O'Leary et al., 1995) is multidimensional, it has shown only a modest level of sensitivity to change, which may limit its utility to measure response to treatment (Rosen, 2006). The Florida Sexual History Questionnaire (FSHQ; Geisser et al., 1991) is one of the few measures that were validated against a physiological measure (e.g., nocturnal tumescence). While the FSHQ has been used with male diabetics, data is lacking regarding use of most of these measures with men who have disabilities or chronic medical illness.

Chapter 28 appendix, C, lists SRQs for women. The SRQs listed in Appendix C report adequate internal consistency and test–retest reliability, with the exception of moderate internal consistency for the domains of Arousal and Receptivity on the Brief Index of Sexual Function for Women (BISF-W; Taylor, Rosen, & Leiblum, 1994). As with the SRQs designed for either gender or for males only, selection of a specific SRQ for females should be based on how well the domains match the clinical questions. Many of the SRQs that were developed for women were developed specifically to assess transition to menopause. Some examine global sexual functioning in women, such as the BISF-W, while others are more specific in focus, such as the Sexual Interest and Desire Inventory-Female (SIDI-F; Clayton et al., 2006). Some have utility in diagnosing specific aspects of sexual dysfunction, such as hypoactive sexual desire (SIDI-F) or sexual arousal disorder, as in the Female Sexual Function Index (FSFI; Rosen et al., 2000), while the BISF-W reliably discriminates between women with and without nonspecific sexual disorders (Meston & Derogatis, 2002). The BISF-W has shown sensitivity to change as a result of treatment (i.e., therapy or medication). Data are lacking regarding the extensive use of any of the female-specific listed measures with women who have a disability or illness. Gender-specific SRQs are available, however, that are specific to a particular illness group, such as the Sexual Functioning after Gynecological Illness Scale (Bransfield, Horiot, & Nabid, 1984).

Self-Report Diaries

Diaries for assessing sexual functioning typically refer to sexual event logs. The information recorded may be nominal in nature, such as whether an event was attempted (e.g., intercourse attempted: yes/no; erection upon awakening: yes/no), or may be used to record subjective impressions (self-report of level of desire, arousal, or satisfaction). Diaries have been criticized, however, as placing a degree of burden on the client that may result in lack of compliance or inaccurately reported entries (Althof et al., 2005). Using hand-held devices or telephone call-in methodologies may improve compliance, although inaccuracies may remain. These authors argue that self-report questionnaires are likely to be more valuable as primary endpoints for outcome measurement, although diaries may have value as *secondary* endpoints (Althof et al., 2005).

Physiological Measures

Physiological measures are sometimes used as adjuncts to other assessment activities, such as the physical examination, self-report measures, and/or interviews. While physiological measures may be viewed as more scientific than other assessment tools, disadvantages include expense, intrusiveness, and time burden (Rosen, 2006). Further, physiological measures should not be the sole endpoint measure for assessing response to intervention. For example, a study of use of sexual assistance aids following prostate surgery found that psychological factors such as anxiety about using the device, quality of the nonsexual

Research Box 28.1

RELIABILITY AND VALIDITY OF SELF-REPORT

Daker-White, G. (2002). Reliability and validity of self-report outcome measures in sexual (dys)function: A systematic review. *Archives of Sexual Behavior, 31,* 197–209.

Objective: Review of psychometric qualities of published self-report outcome measures in sexual (dys)function.

Method: Searched *Embase* database for works published from 1980–1999 that reported on psychometric qualities of sexual function questionnaires.

Results: Of 23 reviewed studies, only 14 reported adequate reliability and validity.

Conclusion: Most measures are designed for people in current, heterosexual relationships and were validated with mostly White, middle-class North Americans. Selection of a SRQ should consider the relevant domain measured as well as whether the measure was validated with the particular population of interest.

Questions:
Is an instrument with adequate psychometric qualities relevant for a population of people with disabilities or illnesses if it has only been validated with a general population? What differences might be expected in domains or item selection for measures used with populations of people with disabilities or illnesses?

relationship with the partner, and expectation were better predictors of use of the aid than the actual physiological response produced by the assistance device (Matthew et al., 2005).

Examples of physiological measures for males include measurement of nocturnal penile tumescence (i.e., Rigiscan, a computerized electronic instrument), volumetric devices, strain gauges, thermistor devices, vascular assessment, penile ultrasound and blood pressure, penile nerve conduction, penile biothesiometry assessment of penile sensory pathway, and use of mini vibrators to assess penile sensitivity. Examples of female physiological measures for females include vaginal maturation index to measure estrogenization, vaginal photoplethymography to assess changes in blood flow to the vagina, Doppler ultrasonography to measure clitoral blood flow, and measures of heat dissipation in genitalia (Gerdes, 1997). Hormonal assays may be used with either gender.

A thorough physical examination is an important element in determining possible factors affecting sexual function, especially to help differentiate organic from psychogenic factors. The physical examination screens for medical risk or comorbidities with attention to the cardiovascular, neurological, and genital system. The physical exam also is essential in identifying possible sources of pain that may impact sexual activity. Key elements of the exam include (from Hatzichristou et al., 2004; Sipski, 1997):

- Complete genital exam
- Secondary sexual characteristics
- Body hair and fat distribution
- Blood pressure, heart rate, peripheral pulses, and edema
- Vibratory sensation
- Lower extremity strength and coordination
- Salivary production and swallowing
- Limitations in movement due to reduced range of movement or pain
- Scarring, areas of tenderness, hypersensitivity, or reduced sensation

Lab tests may include basic fasting glucose, cholesterol, lipids, and hormonal profiles. Thyroid function tests are also sometimes done (Hatzichristou et al., 2004).

Research Critical to Assessment of Sexual Functioning

One concern related to assessment in a rehabilitation population includes accessibility of the assessment tool. People with limited vision, cognitive, fine-motor, or reading level may require adaptations in any assessment tool in order for results to be valid. Because people with disabilities may be at higher risk for sexual abuse (Sobsey & Doe, 1991; Young, Nosek, Howland, Champong, & Rintala, 1997), it is especially important that the assessment format allow them to clearly communicate issues related to sexual behavior. Increased risk for sexual abuse may be due to perception of vulnerability, social isolation that may contribute to confusion regarding acceptable behavior, and confusion regarding body boundaries resulting from dependence on others for assistance with activities of daily living. A client with a communication disability may have difficulty notifying others if abuse has occurred. The credibility of clients with cognitive disabilities, for example, may be questioned when they report sexual abuse.

Bell and Cameron (2003) presented a case study that addressed these concerns. A young woman with cognitive and communicative impairments presented as a possible victim of sexual abuse. The psychology and speech/language therapists teamed to create an augmentative device using picture symbols, which enabled the patient to indicate her level of sexual knowledge and attitudes. This is an encouraging study because it suggests adaptations that may reduce barriers and bias when assessing and treating sexual function with particular populations of people with disabilities.

The Patient Reported Outcome Measurement Information System (PROMIS) model (Reeve, 2006), sponsored by the National Institutes of Health, is an area of research that is likely to advance assessment of sexual functioning as well as other aspects of quality of life. The PROMIS model incorporates a review of items from existing SRQs for a particular domain. The items are clustered into topic bins and then winnowed to eliminate redundancy or poorly worded questions. Final items are selected based on ability to discriminate and assist with determining diagnosis. The PROMIS model encourages the use of computer-assisted technology that is designed to encourage assessment that is efficient, valid, and reliable. Because computerized assessment tools may yield more accurate data when assessing sensitive topics (Schaeffer, 1999), this model may be especially relevant for the assessment of sexual functioning. To date, the PROMIS model for sexual functioning assessment has only focused on clients with cancer (D. Jeffrey, personal communication, November 8, 2006).

Cultural, Legislative, and Professional Issues

In cultures and religions where sexuality may be rarely discussed or where sex roles may be highly restrictive, it is likely that assessment and treatment related to sexual functioning may also be very limited. The comfort of the client in discussing sexual function may vary widely depending on how openly sex is discussed within the culture. The client may consider sexuality to be a private topic, a source of embarrassment and stigma, or unrelated to medical issues and, thus, be reluctant to initiate a discussion with professionals or others. Indeed, Solursh and colleagues (2003) found that 14% of patients initiate discussion of sexual concerns, but 55% disclose a sexual concern if the health care staff directly question the patient. Thus, it is critical to train staff how to initiate as well as how to respond to sexual functioning issues.

Cultural and societal barriers may occur regarding whether people with disabilities are viewed as sexual beings. People with disabilities or medical illnesses may be infantilized or sexually marginalized by assuming that they either have no sexual interest or that sexual activity is unrealistic (Sipski & Alexander, 1997).

Legislative issues include impact of insurance coverage for sexual assessment or treatment. Within the medical fields, such discussions are typically included within routine medical evaluation and treatment charges. In the mental health field, use of Health and Behavior CPT codes may be relevant when sexual issues are likely to be the result of a diagnosed medical disorder and, thus, potentially covered by medical insurance. If the sexual problem occurred

Discussion Box 28.2

SOCIETAL BARRIERS TO SEXUAL OPPORTUNITY

Experts note that people with disabilities may be able to demonstrate adequate capacity for sexual function but may have limited opportunities to participate in sexual activity. Discuss how societal barriers may limit sexual opportunities for people with disabilities or chronic health concerns.

prior to the disability or illness, it may meet the definition for one of the sexual dysfunctions listed in *DSM-IV-TR* and, thus, may be covered by mental health insurance.

Professional issues related to sexual functioning assessment include the lack of education that health care professionals have on this topic. Although the National Institutes of Health Consensus Conference of 1993 recognized that graduate school curricula for all health care workers should include courses on human sexuality, how to take a detailed sexual history, diagnosis and management of sexual dysfunction, and interdisciplinary approach to diagnosis and treatment, Solursh and colleagues found that 61% of North American medical schools devote less than 10 hours of curriculum to teaching about sexuality (Solursh et al., 2003). Personal discomfort with the topic, fear of offending the patient, and cultural/religious/moral concerns regarding discussing sexuality may negatively impact effective staff–patient communication related to sexuality. Research detailing sexuality education practices in the training programs of nonphysicians is even more limited.

Multidisciplinary or Interdisciplinary Approaches

Perhaps the most important determinant of who should carry out the assessment is the comfort level of the particular staff member. Comfort, approachability, and specific knowledge are needed. This may involve *any* member of the health care team. For some people with disabilities or health conditions, their primary care physician or nurse practitioner may have most frequent contact and, thus, may be the person with whom the patient is most comfortable. For other patients, their medical specialist or rehabilitation therapist may be the point person. Every member of the health care team could be involved in this area because teachable moments occur within the course of evaluation and treatment in a wide variety of disciplines. Physicians and nurses may best be able to address physical concerns or concerns related to medical treatment. The physical therapist working on mobility and endurance can address questions regarding sexual activity, positioning, and community access. Occupational therapists working on activities of daily living may address questions related to privacy, toileting, and sexual self-care. Speech therapists may address concerns regarding effect of social communication difficulties or control of secretions, for example, on social relationships. Psychotherapists certainly may address issues related to relationships, body image, sexuality, and self-esteem along with many other aspects of sexual functioning. Psychotherapists may also be well-suited for encouraging a cognitive-behavioral approach to treatment, an intervention that is likely to be more effective than medication approaches for most people with chronic health conditions (Barsky et al., 2006). Recreation therapists may be able to assist with social reintegration issues.

Booth and colleagues describe methods for determining training needs, approaches to training, and effectiveness of training health care staff in sexuality rehabilitation (Booth, Kendall, Fronek, Miller, & Geraghty, 2003; Fronek, Booth, Kendall, Miller, & Geraghty, 2005). While their approach was used with staff involved in spinal cord injury rehabilitation, it is applicable to a variety of settings and populations.

Discussion Box 28.3

ADOLESCENTS WITH DISABILITIES

While adolescents with disabilities or chronic medical illnesses are often as sexually active as teens in the general population, their sexual knowledge, sexual safety, and satisfaction may be lower. What may be some factors to account for this discrepancy? In what ways might the age at onset of the disability/illness be expected to impact sexual functioning?

Preventive Health Intervention

When sexual functioning assessment occurs is important. Anticipatory guidance related to sexual functioning is needed from the point of diagnosis and at every phase of treatment in order to help patients and their families know what to expect. Because anticipatory guidance helps to normalize and destigmatize possible sexual functioning issues, it also aids communication between the health care staff and patient/family as well as between the patient and his/her partner(s).

Disability Management

For some disabilities, readiness to discuss sexual functioning may be a factor. Fisher and colleagues (2002) conducted a longitudinal study of adults with spinal cord injuries. They suggest that the optimal time to address sexual health may be approximately 6 months after discharge from inpatient rehabilitation. Prior to that time, many patients report that their energies are focused on achieving medical stability and learning other aspects of self-care. Nevertheless, clients note that it is important to "put a bug in the patient's ear" during inpatient rehabilitation that sexual functioning may be affected and that information is available (Fisher et al., 2002).

Health Policy

Readiness of the health care institution to provide sexual assessment and treatment is typically a critical factor. Tepper (1997) provides excellent guidelines to assess institutional readiness. For example, the facility should have institutional support to address this topic, a policy related to comprehensive sexual health care, staff training, and sexuality resources. He feels that patients need to be told early in rehabilitation that sexuality is a part of their rehabilitation process and that resources are available, both on request and offered periodically. General questions regarding sexuality should be included at intake and documented within the history and physical. Each team member needs to be able to recognize teachable moments. Opportunities for peer discussions and outpatient follow-up also need to occur. Lamb's (1996) description of nursing care approaches within cancer treatment provides one excellent example of how to incorporate sexual functioning assessment and treatment into the health care plan for people with disabilities or health issues.

International Practices

An international, multidisciplinary consortium of experts in sexual health has published consensus recommendations regarding diagnostic and treatment practices in the area of sexual dysfunction (Hatzichristou et al., 2004; Heiman et al., 2004; Hirsch et al., 2004). Their goal was to attempt to standardize care and encourage best practices. It is not clear how much variability in actual practice or research focus now exists cross-culturally. While most measures have been developed in the United States and then translated into other languages, it is important that the translated versions also be validated for use in non–English-speaking populations. Rellini and colleagues, for example, found that domain factors differed from the original, English version of the McCoy Female Sexuality Questionnaire when it was administered in Italian to Italian women (Rellini et al., 2005).

Major Issues That Need Attention in Sexual Functioning Assessment

Given the significant impact of disability and illness on sexual functioning, there appears to be a need to normalize assessment and treatment of sexual problems and improve access at all phases of treatment: within acute care, rehabilitation, and chronic care. Much of the work related to sexual functioning among people with disabilities or illness focuses on impairments caused by traumatic or acquired injury (e.g., spinal cord injury, traumatic brain injury, stroke) or illness diagnosed in adulthood (e.g., adult cancer, heart disease, multiple sclerosis). Incorporating quality and individualized sexuality assessment, education, and other treatment for people with congenital or developmental disabilities also needs to occur in order to promote healthy body image, self-esteem, and sexual health in those populations. Attention to the sexual health needs of children with acquired injury or chronic conditions also is lacking. These children typically do not receive specialized sexuality education either in their school or health care settings. Absence of specialized information may lead to increased sense of social isolation or creation of misinformation that may jeopardize safe sexual practices.

While much of the focus of intervention for sexual dysfunction has been on pharmaceutical approaches, these are unlikely to have widespread or long-term effectiveness for most people with chronic health conditions (Barsky et al., 2006). Barsky and colleagues argue that a more effective treatment approach is to encourage cognitive and behavioral flexibility in order to maximize coping. Improved flexibility includes widening one's definition of sexual activity beyond sexual intercourse and decreasing the centrality of sexual functioning to one's self-esteem. This may involve increasing emphasis on other forms of intimacy within a relationship or attention to nonsexual relationships and other role functions.

Controversies exist regarding access to sexual activities for people with disabilities, especially those in institutional settings. For example, privacy may be limited, and sexual contact between clients or involving visitors may be restricted. Restrictions may be due to various concerns, including safety and health issues, but they also may be due to attitudinal barriers. Other controversies regarding access include whether sexual surrogates should be provided or whether caregivers should assist clients who have limited movement to masturbate for sexual release.

Increased attention to ethnicity in studies of sexual function is needed. While ethnic differences have been noted in reports of sexual satisfaction, for example (Rellini et al., 2005), only 7.3% of articles in *Archives of Sexual Behavior* and *Journal of Sexual Research* between 1971–1995 considered ethnicity as a relevant variable (Wiederman, Maynard, & Fretz, 1996).

Future work is needed to address these issues involving education, provision of care, and ethical guidelines. Development of more efficient, less intrusive, and more accurate methods of assessment that include assessment of possible barriers, such as access to an available partner, lack of sexual knowledge, negative body image, and increasing cognitive and behavioral flexibility, is needed in order to advance the assessment and treatment of sexual dysfunction.

Summary

Attention to sexual functioning has evolved since the early work of Masters and Johnson (1966), which focused on the linear nature of a sexual response cycle. Current models of sexual functioning now acknowledge the biopsychosocial factors that impact functioning. Sexual problems are common in the general population, with those having physical disability or chronic medical illness likely to be further impacted due to the negative effects of the actual injury/illness, as well as treatment effects and societal barriers.

Methods for assessment of sexual functioning include interview, self-report questionnaires (SRQs) and diaries, physiological measures, and physical examination, all of which have pros and cons. Most research involving effectiveness of sexual functioning treatment use SRQs as a primary endpoint outcome measure. Future assessment tools may emphasize computer-assisted technology to improve efficiency, accuracy, and comprehensiveness of assessment.

Training of health care professionals to address knowledge, skills, comfort, and attitudes regarding sexual functioning is crucial. Institutional readiness to provide sexual assessment and treatment and timing of the service in relation to the onset of the injury/illness is important. While maintaining sensitivity to cultural, ethnic, and religious attitudes, it is essential to recognize that people with disabilities or illnesses are sexual beings who are entitled to equal access to a healthy and satisfying sexual life if they so choose. The onus is on health care professionals to initiate discussions regarding sexual health and to be approachable and knowledgeable on this topic in order to promote quality of life.

Chapter 28 Appendix

A. Self-Reported Questionnaires of Sexual Function for Either Gender

Measure	#Items	Reliability	Validity	Domains	Comments
Arizona Sexual Experience Scale (ASEX; McGahuey, Gelenberg, Lankes, Moreno, & Delgado, 2000)	5	adequate i.c/t.r	adequate c.v/d.v	sex drive, arousal, vaginal lubrication/penile erection, ability to reach orgasm, satisfaction w/orgasm	measures reduced or enhanced function; not restricted to sexual orientation; less intrusive
Brief Sexual Symptom Checklist (BSSC; Hatzichristou et al. 2005)	4	?		satisfaction w/sexual funct; duration & type of problem; willingness to discuss w/staff	not restricted to sexual orientation; does not consider lack of access to partner
Changes in Sexual Functioning Questionnaire (CSFQ/CSFQ-14; Clayton, Owens, & McGarvey, 1995; Keller, McGarvey, & Clayton, 2006)	14–36	adequate for females i.c./t.r.	adequate c.v.	desire and interest, arousal, release & physiological competence, interpersonal	has been used with cancer & depressed clients to assess sexual changes due to meds versus illness; available in many languages & computerized format
Derogatis Interview for Sexual Functioning (DISF/DISF-SR; Derogatis, 1997)	25	adequate i.c/t.r/i.r.	adequate c.v./d.v	cognition, arousal, behavior, orgasm, drive/relationship	combination interview & SRQ; translated into many languages; used w/SCI pop.
Golombok-Rust Inventory of Sexual Satisfaction (GRISS; Rust & Golombok, 1986)	28	adequate i.c/t.r.	adequate c.v/ d.v	frequency of sexual contact, noncommunication	translated into Dutch; used to assess response to treatment in couples

Inventory of Sexual Experiences & Response in Disability (IEReSDI; Rodarte & Munoz, 2004)	39	adequate i.c.=.89-.94	n.r.	satisfaction, response (desire arousal, orgasm), factors that interfere w/sexuality	used with variety of disabilities, ages 14-up; study done in Mexico; includes wider variety of activities than most SRQs
Modified Rush Sexual Inventory (MRSI; Rao, Zajecka, & Skubiak, 2005)	24–31	adequate i.c.	adequate c.v.	desire, satisfaction, pain, functioning, behavior, sensitivity	shortened version of Rush Sexual Inventory, used w/ depressive pop., includes medical hx, free response & visual analogue sections
Physical Disability Sexual & Body Esteem Scale (PDSBE; Taleporos & McCabe, 2001)	10	adequate i.c/t.r	adequate d.v/c.c	sexual esteem, attractiveness to others, body esteem	not restricted to sexual orientation, has been used with disabled
Sexual Desire Inventory (SDI; Spector, Carey, & Steinberg, 1996)	14	adequate i.c	adequate c.v.	dyadic desire, solitary desire	not designed to assess change in response to treatment
Sexual Evaluation Scale (SES; Othmer & Othmer, 1987)	16	adequate t.r.	adequate d.v.	sexual interest, arousal, performance	does not address satisfaction or sexual drive
Sexual Health Needs Survey (SHNS; Fisher et al., 2002)	?	?	?	sexual activity, concerns, interest, partner factors, educational needs, sexual adjustment	has been used with SCI; has inpatient & outpatient versions

Reliability: n.r. = not reported; i.c. = internal consistency; t.r. = test–retest reliability; i.r. = interrater reliability
Validity: n.r. = not reported; c.c. = construct validity; d.v. = divergent validity

B. Self-Reported Questionnaires of Sexual Function for Males

Measure	#Items	Reliability	Validity	Domains	Comments
Brief Male Sexual Function Inventory (BMSFI; O'Leary-et al., 1995)	11	adequate i.c/t.r	adequate c.v.	sex drive, erectile function, ejaculation, bother, overall satisfaction w/sex life	modest sensitivity as outcome measure; ejaculation eval limited to amt only
Florida Sexual History Questionnire (FSHQ; Geisser et al., 1991)	20	adequate i.c.	adequate c.v.	interest & desire, sexual development, current behavior, satisfaction	focuses on vaginal intercourse only; inclusion of sexual dev domain is helpful; has been used with diabetics
International Index of Erectile Functioning (IIEF; Rosen et al., 1997)	15	adequate i.c./t.r	adequate c.v.	erectile function, orgasm, sexual desire; intercourse satisfaction; overall satisfaction	focuses on vaginal intercourse only; does not assess partner relationship; translated into many languages
Male Sexual Health Questionnaire (MSHQ; Rosen, 2006)	25	adequate i.c/t.r.	adequate d.v/c.v.	erection, desire, ejaculation, satisfaction	used for men with ejaculatory dysfunction but not necessarily disabled groups

Reliability: i.c. = internal consistency; t.r. = test–retest reliability
Validity: d.v. = divergent or discriminant validity; c.v. = construct or concurrent validity

C. Self-Reported Questionnaires of Sexual Function for Females

Measure	#Items	Reliability	Validity	Domains	Comments
Brief Index of Sexual Function for Women (BISF-W; Taylor, Rosen, & Leiblum, 1994)	22	moderate i.c./t.r.	adequate c.v./d.v.	thoughts/desire, arousal, frequency of sexual activity, receptivity, pleasure/orgasm, relationship satisfaction, problems affecting sexuality	sensitive to treatment effects; data not reported for disability groups
Female Sexual Function Index (FSFI; Rosen et al., 2000)	19	adequate i.c./t.r.	adequate c.v./d.v.	desire, arousal, lubrica tion, orgasm, pain, satisfaction	focuses on arousal disorder; data not reported for disability groups
McCoy Female Sexuality Questionnaire (MFSQ; McCoy, 2000)	19	adequate i.c/t.r.	adequate c.v./d.v.	interest, satisfaction with frequency of sex, vaginal lubrication, sex partner, orgasm	focuses on menopausal transition, translated into many languages
Shortened Personal Experiences Questionnaire (SPEQ; Dennerstein, Anderson-Hunt, Dudley, 2002)	9	adequate t.r.	adequate c.v.	responsiveness, frequency of activities, libido, feelings in partner, pain, partner's problems	developed as shorter version of MFSQ. Focuses on meno-pausal transition; data reported for disability groups
Sexual Interest and Desire Inventory-Female (SIDI-F; Clayton et al., 2006)	13	adequate i.c.	adequate d.v/c.v	desire, co-morbid sexual dysfunction, sexual behavior, sexual relationship	focuses on assessment of hypoactive sexual desire, data not reported with disability population but includes unscored items related to health

Reliability: i.c. = internal consistency; t.r. = test–retest reliability
Validity: d.v. = divergent ordiscriminant validity; c.v. = construct or concurrent validity

References

Althof, S., Rosen, R., Derogatis, L., Corty, E., Quirk, F., & Symonds, T. (2005). Outcome measurement in female sexual dysfunction clinical trials. *Journal of Sexual & Marital Therapy, 31,* 153–166.

American Psychiatric Association. (2002). *Diagnostic and statistical manual of mental disorders* (4th ed., text revision). Washington, DC: Author.

Annon, J. (1976). The PLISSIT model: A proposed conceptual scheme for the behavioral treatment of sexual problems. *Journal of Sexual Educational Therapy, 2,* 1–15.

Barsky, J., Friedman, M., & Rosen, R. (2006). Sexual dysfunction and chronic illness: The role of flexibility in coping. *Journal of Sex & Marital Therapy, 32,* 235–253.

Basson, R. (2002). Sexual health of women with disabilities. *Canadian Medical Association Journal, 159,* 359–362.

Basson, R., Leiblum, S., Brotto, L., Derogatis, L., Fourcroy, J., Fugl-Meyer, K., et al. (2004). Definitions of women's sexual dysfunction reconsidered: Advocating expansion and revision. *Journal of Psychosomatic Obstetrics and Gynecology, 24,* 221–229.

Bell, D., & Cameron, L. (2003). The assessment of the sexual knowledge of a person with a severe learning disability and a severe communication disorder. *British Journal of Learning Disabilities, 31,* 123–129.

Booth, S., Kendall, M., Fronek, P., Miller, D., & Geraghty, T. (2003). Training the interdisciplinary team in sexuality rehabilitation following spinal cord injury: A needs assessment. *Sexuality and Disability, 21,* 249–261.

Bransfield, D., Horiot, J., & Nabid, A. (1984). The development of a scale for the assessment of sexual functioning after treatment for gynecological malignancy. *Journal of Psychosocial Oncology, 2,* 3–19.

Clayton, A. (2001). Recognition and assessment of sexual dysfunction associated with depression. *Journal of Clinical Psychiatry, 62*(Suppl 3), 5–9.

Clayton, A., Owens, J., & McGarvey, E. (1995). Assessment of paroxetine-induced sexual dysfunction using the Changes in Sexual Functioning Questionnaire. *Psychopharmacology Bulletin, 31,* 397–413.

Clayton, A., Segraves, R., Leiblum, S., Basson, R., Pyke, R., Cotton, D., et al. (2006). Reliability and validity of the Sexual Interest and Desire Inventory-Female (SIDI-F), a scale designed to measure severity of female hypoactive sexual desire disorder. *Journal of Sex and Marital Therapy, 32,* 115–135.

Daker-White, G. (2002). Reliability and validity of self-report outcome measures in sexual (dys) function: A systematic review. *Archives of Sexual Behavior, 31,* 197–209.

Dennerstein, L., Anderson-Hunt, M., & Dudley, E. (2002). Evaluation of a short scale to assess female sexuality. *Journal of Sex and Marital Therapy, 28,* 389–397.

Derogatis, D. (1997). The Derogatis Interview for Sexual Functioning (DISF/DISF-SR): An introductory report. *Journal of Sex and Marital Therapy, 23,* 291–304.

Derogatis, L., & Kourlesis, S. (1981). An approach to evaluation of sexual problems in the cancer patient. *Canadian-American Cancer Journal for Clinicians, 31,* 46–50.

Fisher, T., Laud, P., Byfield, M., Brown, T., Hayat, M., & Fiedler, I. (2002). Sexual health after spinal cord injury: A longitudinal study. *Archives of Physical Medicine and Rehabilitation, 83,* 1043–1051.

Fishman, O., Ettinger, A., & Callanan, M. (2006). Sexual dysfunction in patients with epilepsy: Communication strategies and assessment tools. *CNS Spectrums, 11*(Suppl 9), 38–45.

Fronek, P., Booth, S., Kendall, M., Miller, D., & Geraghty, T. (2005). The effectiveness of a sexuality training program for the interdisciplinary spinal cord injury rehabilitation team. *Sexuality and Disability, 23,* 51–63.

Geisser, M., Jefferson, T., Spevak, M., Boaz, T., Thomas, R., & Murray, F. (1991). Reliability and validity of the Florida Sexual History Questionnaire. *Journal of Clinical Psychology, 47,* 519–528.

Gerdes, C. (1997). Psychophysiological and laboratory testing. In M. L. Sipski & C. J. Alexander (Eds.), *Sexual function in people with disabilities and chronic illness* (pp. 47–74). Gaithersburg, MD: Aspen Publishers.

Gregoire, A. (1999). ABCs of sexual health: Assessing and managing male sexual problems. *British Medical Journal, 318,* 315–317.

Hatzichristou, D., Moysidis, K., Aposolidis, A., Bekos, A., Tzortzis, V., & Hatzimouratis, K. (2005). Sildenafil failures may be due to inadequate patient instructions and follow up: A study on 100 non-responders. *European Urology, 47,* 518–522.

Hatzichristou, D., Rosen, R., Broderick, G., Clayton, A., Cuzin, B., Derogatis, L., et al. (2004). Clinical evaluation and management strategy for sexual dysfunction in men and women. *Journal of Sexual Medicine, 1,* 49–57.

Heiman, J. (2002). Sexual dysfunction: Overview of prevalence, etiological factors, and treatments. *The Journal of Sex Research, 39,* 73–78.

Heiman, J., Guess, M., Connell, K., Melman, A., Hyde, J., Segraves, T., et al. (2004). Standards for clinical trials in sexual dysfunctions of women: Research designs and outcomes assessment. *Journal of Sexual Medicine, 1,* 92–97.

Hibbard, M., Gordon, W., Flanagan, S., Haddad, L., & Labinsky, E. (2000). Sexual dysfunction after traumatic brain injury. *NeuroRehabilitation, 15,* 107–120.

Hirsch, M., Donatucci, C., Glina, S., Montague, D., Montorsi, F., & Wyllie, M. (2004). Standards for clinical trials in male sexual dysfunction: Erectile dysfunction and rapid ejaculation. *The Journal of Sexual Medicine, 1,* 87–91.

Kaplan, H. (1974). *Disorders of sexual desire.* New York: Brunner/Mazel.

Kaplan, H. (1983). *The evaluation of sexual disorders: Psychological and medical aspects.* New York: Brunner/Mazel.

Keller, A., McGarvey, E., & Clayton, A. (2006). Reliability and construct validity of the Changes in Sexual Functioning Questionnaire Short Form (CSFQ-14). *Journal of Sex & Marital Therapy, 32,* 43–52.

Kinsey, A., Pomeroy, W., & Martin, C. (1948). *Sexual behavior in the human male.* Philadelphia: W.B. Saunders.

Kinsey, A., Pomeroy, C., Martin, C., & Gebhard, P. (1953). *Sexual behavior in the human female.* Philadelphia: W.B. Saunders.

Krafft-Ebing, R. (1998). *Psychopathia sexualis* (reprint). New York: Arcade Publishing.

Lamb, M. (1996). Sexuality and sexual functioning. In R. McCorckle, M. Grant, M. Frank-Stromberg, & S. Baird (Eds), *Cancer nursing: A comprehensive textbook* (2nd ed., pp. 1105–1127). Philadelphia: W.B. Saunders Company.

Lefebvre, K. (1997). Performing a sexual evaluation on the person with disability or illness. In M. L. Sipski & C. J. Alexander (Eds.), *Sexual function in people with disabilities and chronic illness* (pp. 19–45). Gaithersburg, MD: Aspen Publications

Masters, W., & Johnson, V. (1966). *Human sexual response.* Boston: Little, Brown.

Masters, W., & Johnson, V. (1970). *Human sexual inadequacy.* Boston: Little, Brown.

Matthew, A., Goldman, A., Trachtenberg, J., Robinson, J., Horsburgh, S., Currie, K., et al. (2005). Sexual dysfunction after radical prostatectomy: Prevalence, treatments, restricted use of treatments and distress. *The Journal of Urology, 174,* 2105–2110.

McAlonan, S. (1996). Improving sexual rehabilitation services: The patient's perspective. *American Journal of Occupational Therapy, 50,* 826–834.

McCoy, N. (2000). The McCoy Female Sexuality Questionnaire. *Quality of Life Research, 9,* 739–745.

McGahuey, C., Gelenberg, A., Lankes, C., Moreno, F., & Delgado, P. (2000). The Arizona Sexual Experience Scale (ASEX): Reliability and validity. *Journal of Sexual & Marital Therapy, 26,* 25–40.

Meston, C., & Derogatis, L. (2002). Validated instruments for assessing female sexual function. *Journal of Sexual & Marital Therapy, 28*(Suppl 1), 155–164.

National Cancer Institute. (n.d.). *The prevalence and types of sexual dysfunction in people with cancer.* Retrieved November 16, 2007, from: http://www.nci.nih.gov/cancertopics/pdq/supportivecare/sexuality/HealthProfessional

National Institutes of Health Consensus Conference on Impotence. (1993). *Journal of the American Medical Association, 270,* 83–90.

O'Leary, M., Fowler, F., Lenderking, W., Barber, B., Sagniero, P., Guess, H., et al. (1995). A brief male sexual function inventory for urology. *Urology, 46,* 697–706.

Othmer, E., & Othmer, S. (1987). Evaluation of sexual dysfunction. *Journal of Clinical Psychiatry, 48,* 191–193.

Pollets, D., Ducharme, S., & Pauporte, J. (1999). Psychological considerations in the assessment of erectile dysfunction. *Sexuality & Disability, 17,* 129–145.

Rao, D., Zajecka, J., & Skubiak, T. (2005). The modified Rush Sexual Inventory: Preliminary psychometric findings. *Psychiatry Research, 137,* 175–181.

Reeve, B. (2006). Special issues for building computerized adaptive tests for measuring patient-reported outcomes: The NIH's investment in new technology. *Medical Care, 44*(Suppl 3), 5198–5204.

Rellini, A., Nappi, R., Vaccaro, P., Ferdeghini, F., Abbiati, I., & Meston, C. (2005). Validity of the McCoy Female Sexuality Questionnaire in an Italian sample. *Archives of Sexual Behavior, 34,* 641–647.

Rodarte, I., & Munoz, M. (2004). Inventory of sexual experiences and response in disability (IEReSDI): Construction and validation of the scale of the sexual response in people. *Sexuality and Disability, 22,* 181–195.

Rosen, R. (2006). Assessment of sexual dysfunction in patients with benign prostatic hyperplasia. *British Journal of Urology International, 97*(Suppl 2), 29–33.

Rosen, R., Brown, C., Heiman, J., Leiblum, S., Meston, C., Shabsigh, R., et al. (2000). The Female Sexual Function Index (FSFI): A multidimensional self-report instrument for the assessment of female sexual function. *Journal of Sex and Marital Therapy, 26,* 191–208.

Rosen, R., Fisher, W., Eardley, I., Niederberger, C., Nadel, A., & Saud, M. (2004). The multinational Men's Attitudes to Life Events and Sexual functioning (MALES) study: I. Prevalence of erectile dysfunction and related health concerns in the general Population. *Current Medical Research and Opinion, 20,* 607–617.

Rosen, R., Riley, A., Wagner, G., Osterloh, I., Kirkpatrick, J., & Mishra, A. (1997). The International Index of Erectile Function (IIEF): A multidimensional scale for assessment of erectile dysfunction. *Urology, 49,* 823–830.

Rust, J., & Golombok, S. (1986). *The Golombok-Rust Inventory of Sexual Satisfaction.* Odessa, FL: Psychological Assessment Resources.

Schaeffer, N. (1999). Asking questions about threatening topics: A selective overview. In A. Stone et al. (Eds.), *The science of self-report: Implications for research and practice* (pp. 105–122). Mahwah, NJ: Lawrence Erlbaum Associates.

Sipski. M. (1997). Performing the medical sexual history and physical. In M. Sipski & C. Alexander (Eds.), *Sexual function in people with disability and chronic illness* (pp. 13–17). Gaithersburg, MD: Aspen Publications.

Sipski, M., & Alexander, C. (1997). Impact of disability or chronic illness on sexual function. In M. Sipski & C. Alexander (Eds.), *Sexual function in people with disability and chronic illness* (pp. 3–12). Gaithersburg, MD: Aspen Publications.

Sobsey, D., & Doe, T. (1991). Patterns of sexual abuse and assault. *Sexuality and Disability, 9,* 243–260.

Solursh, D., Ernst, J., Lewis, R., Prisant, M., Mills, T., Solursh, L., et al. (2003). The human sexuality education of physicians in North American medical schools. *International Journal of Impotence Research, 15*(Suppl 5), S41–S45.

Spector, I., Carey, M., & Steinberg, L. (1996). The Sexual Desire Inventory: Development, factor structure, and evidence of reliability. *Journal of Sexual & Marital Therapy, 22,* 175–190.

Szasz, G., Paty, D., Lawton-Speert, S., & Eisen, K. (1984). A sexual functioning scale in multiple sclerosis. *Acta Neurology Scandinavia, 101,* 37–43.

Taleporos, G., & McCabe, M. (2001). Physical disability and sexual esteem. *Sexuality and Disability, 19*(2), 131–148.

Taylor, J., Rosen, R., & Leiblum, S. (1994). Self report assessment of female sexual function: Psychometric evaluation of the Brief Index of Sexual Functioning for Women. *Archives of Sexual Behavior, 23,* 225–232.

Tepper, M. (1997). Editorial: Guidelines to address the fluid issue of readiness. *Sexuality & Disability, 15,* 129–130.

Wiederman, M., Maynard, C., & Fretz, A. (1996). Ethnicity in 25 years of published sexuality research: 1971–1995. *Journal of Sex Research, 33,* 339–342.

Young, M., Nosek, M., Howland, C., Champong, G., & Rintala, D. (1997). Prevalence and abuse of women with physical disabilities. *Archives of Physical Medicine and Rehabilitation, 78*(Suppl 5), S34–S38.

Assessing Recreation and Leisure Participation

Norma J. Stumbo
Marcia J. Carter

29

Overview

The following chapter considers the significance of recreation and leisure during rehabilitation, introducing a model to frame the discussion of recreation and therapeutic recreation assessment in the International Classification of Functioning, Disability, and Health (ICF) schema. The chapter first considers the significance of recreation and leisure in quality of life and therapeutic recreation's contribution to the rehabilitation process. The Information Seeking and Health Spectrum Model provides the theoretical foundation for considering the relationship of the therapeutic recreation process (assessment, planning, implementation, and evaluation) to the rehabilitation experience and the application of the ICF. Concluding sections of the chapter overview assessment in therapeutic recreation, assessment tools available to gather information from clients during various stages or levels of the rehabilitation process, and implications of the ICF for therapeutic recreation assessment. A closing section outlines research and practice issues presented by introducing the ICF and a quality of life approach to professionals in recreation and therapeutic recreation.

Learning Objectives

By the end of the chapter, the reader should be able to:

1. Comprehend information on definitions of leisure, leisure education, therapeutic recreation, and assessment;
2. Describe the benefits of leisure in life and the rehabilitation process;
3. Discuss the inherent features of the Information Seeking and Health Spectrum Model;
4. Outline a classification of client assessments in therapeutic recreation; and
5. Critically examine the relationships of therapeutic recreation assessment and the Information Seeking and Health Spectrum Model to the ICF schema.

Introduction

Leisure is both an every day occurrence and an enigma. Leisure is common in our lives and yet elusive to many. Leisure is vital to our well-being but can also be misspent and misused. Leisure can be a prerequisite for, as well as the end result of, health and well-being. A number of leisure researchers have noted it is likely that reciprocal relations of causality exist, in that those who feel healthier and happier will be more likely to engage in leisure activities and feel positively toward leisure, and those who engage in and have positive attitudes toward leisure are likely to feel happier and healthier (Cassidy, 1996; Iso-Ahola, 1997) and report higher life satisfaction (Drummond, Parker, Gladman, & Logan, 2001; Edginton, Jordan, DeGraaf, & Edginton, 2002; Parker, Gladman, & Drummond, 1997). "Leisure participation can affect and be affected by life satisfaction or well-being variables. Leisure, in fact, can be an important component contributing to the daily well-being of an individual" (Edginton et al., 2002, p. 8).

No one would argue that leisure and recreation are vitally important to a person's health and wellness as well as to the health and wellness of entire societies. The debate begins when one tries to extricate the relationships and design rehabilitation programs and measure leisure's degree of impact on health and wellness. According to Jackson (2005, p. 1),

> *Leisure is integral to the social, cultural, and economic development of developing and developed societies alike. However, there are many beliefs, interpretations, and perspectives about how and to what extent leisure contributes to the quality of life in general, and in particular health outcomes and other benefits at the individual and societal level.*

This brings to mind several questions: What exactly is leisure? What is leisure's relationship to health and wellness and especially to the rehabilitation process of individuals with illnesses, disabilities, and/or special needs? How should leisure be measured with respect to its contribution to rehabilitation, health, and wellness? What is leisure's relationship to a person's activity level and participation within society? Does leisure "fit" under the umbrella term *health-related quality of life* (HRQoL)?

This chapter first explores the relationship between leisure and recreation participation and a person's quality of life (QoL), health, and well-being. It then addresses the profession of therapeutic recreation and its contribution to the rehabilitation and health processes of individuals with illnesses, disabilities, and/or special needs. Leisure education is used to impart information that aids clients in rehabilitation as they assume responsibility for a leisure lifestyle. The chapter introduces a model, the Information Seeking and Health Spectrum Model, that provides a framework to consider the role of leisure education and the relationship of the therapeutic recreation process of assessment, planning, implementation, and evaluation (or APIE) to the ICF. The assessment process used within therapeutic recreation as well as a convenience classification of several common instruments is then discussed. The chapter then provides a discussion about how therapeutic recreation, a profession that focuses on the leisure, health, and well-being of individuals, benefits from holistic perspectives, such as that of the ICF, that encompass the interactions between the individual, his or her limitations, and the environment in which he or she lives. The chapter concludes with an exploration of the needed research in the area of leisure, health, and quality of life.

Leisure and Recreation: A Key to Quality of Life

Leisure and recreation, like health, wellness, and quality of life, are fluid concepts and are dependent on a number of lifestyle and functioning factors. Leisure has typically been approached from one of three perspectives: (a) as a measure of time (i.e., leisure time as opposed to work time), (b) as a container of activity (i.e., sky diving is a leisure activity, filing income taxes is not), and (c) in terms of meaning (defined by the feelings of perceived freedom, intrinsic motivation, perceived competence, and positive affect; Caldwell, 2005; Cassidy, 1996; Iso-Ahola, 1997; Iwasaki & Mannell, 2000; Jackson, 2005; Mannell, 2006; Mannell & Kleiber, 1997; Wankel, 1994). Many authors have linked leisure and recreation participation with health and quality of life. Exhibit 29.1 displays some of these works.

In addition, several benefits of leisure and recreation participation have been noted (Cohen-Gewerc & Stebbins, 2007; Coyle, Kinney, Riley, & Shank, 1991; Stumbo & Peterson, 2009). These benefits, although largely overlapping and interrelated, can be separated into the following major categories of human functioning: (a) physical, (b) emotional and psychological, and (c) social health. The following lists help illustrate these benefits valued by health, human service, and rehabilitation service providers.

Exhibit 29.1

VIEWS OF THE RELATIONSHIPS BETWEEN LEISURE AND HEALTH

Both leisure and health vary on a continuum. Some leisure experiences are better than others. Similarly, even in the absence of illness, some people are healthier than others. (Iso-Ahola, 1997, p. 131)

To a large degree, to experience leisure with the characteristics of perceived freedom, competence, self-determination, satisfaction, and perceived quality of life is to experience a subjective state of health. In this sense, the development of a broad repertoire of leisure skills to facilitate rich, meaningful experiences provides the foundation for extending such holistic quality experiences to all of life. Personal initiative, choice, meaningful involvement, and enjoyable, supportive social networks—key aspects for leisure—also have important implications for well-being. In the more extreme subjective view, distinctions between leisure and health disappear. (Wankel, 1994, p. 28)

Leisure can influence health in two principal ways. First, in and of itself, leisure is conducive to health. The mere existence of leisure in a person's everyday life has consequences for health. The fact that an individual acknowledges, values, and engages in leisure for its own sake, for its inherent characteristics, is one way in which leisure contributes to health. Another way is where leisure is used as a tool to achieve certain health outcomes. An example of this is a person who takes time to exercise regularly; leisure provides time for him or her to exercise. (Iso-Ahola, 1997, p. 132)

Individual health and well-being are important aspects of quality of life…and leisure behavior can contribute to health and well-being. (Mannell, 2006, p. 65)

Leisure may be restorative and beneficial and move one toward health (p. 8)…Leisure can contribute to physical, social, emotional, and cognitive health through prevention, coping (adjustment, remediation, diversion) and transcendence [rising above adverse conditions]. (Caldwell, 2005, p. 15)

Physical Health and Leisure

- Reduction of numerous health problems such as high blood pressure, heart disease, and premature morbidity
- Improved physical health indicators, such as bone density, heart rate, and joint mobility
- Potential counteragent to lifestyle choices, such as smoking and obesity

- Reduction of secondary conditions, such as depression, decubiti, and urinary tract infections
- Higher levels of reported self-efficacy, social support, perceived freedom, and intrinsic motivation
- Improved general health as a factor in perceived quality of life and life satisfaction

Emotional and Psychological Health and Leisure

Kleiber, Hutchinson, and Williams (2002) and Hutchinson and Kleiber (2005) noted that leisure involvement improved coping with and adjustment to negative life events. They suggested that leisure plays four important roles in transcending negative life events:

- Leisure activities, often offering immediate distraction and "distance," may buffer the impact of negative life events.
- Leisure activities, providing temporary relief and escape, buffer the impact of negative life events by generating optimism and hope about the future.
- Leisure activities buffer the impact of negative life events by aiding the reconstruction of a life story that is continuous with the past, providing "normalcy" in times of disruption.
- Leisure activities may be used in the wake of negative life events as vehicles of personal transformation to attain new goals and head in new directions.

In terms of emotional and psychological health and leisure, a number of research studies have found evidence of the following psychological benefits of leisure participation:

- Improved self-exploration, self-identification, and self-actualization
- Improved opportunities for planning, making choices, and taking responsibility
- Improved opportunities for expression of freedom, control, and intrinsic motivation
- Improved ability to prevent, manage, and cope with stress
- Improved ability to adjust to and be less distressed by negative life events
- Decreased symptoms of anxiety and depression
- Improved quality of life, life satisfaction, and psychological well-being

Social Health and Leisure

- Development, practice, and application of social interaction skills
- Development, maintenance, and use of social support networks
- Improved ability to handle stress due to higher perceived levels of physical and mental health
- Creation and nurturing of relationships with significant others

- Improved interaction with and acceptance by individuals without disabilities
- Improved familial relationships

Leisure and Life Satisfaction

Caldwell (2005) noted a number of ways in which leisure involvement can "protect" against the "risk" factors often brought about by disability, illness, and/or special needs. Among those typical leisure-related protective factors are:

- Personal meaning derived from intrinsic leisure involvement
- Social support, friendships, and social acceptance in leisure
- Competence and self-efficacy derived from leisure participation
- The sense of challenge and absorption brought about in leisure
- The sense of self-determination, autonomy, and control during leisure
- Relaxation, disengagement from stress, and distraction from negative life events through leisure involvement
- The sense of continuity in life that leisure provides after experiencing disability

It is easy to see the relationship of leisure participation and involvement with a person's quality of life through these examples. Mannell (2006) provided a list of nine principles related to leisure, health, and well-being that have been reasonably well-established in the leisure research literature. These include:

- Leisure positively influences physical, psychological, and spiritual health and well-being through opportunities for making meaningful choices and reaping the benefits provided by specific activities.
- Leisure is not automatically good for health and well-being. Leisure choices and activities can have neutral and negative effects and can displace positive behaviors that contribute to health and well-being.
- The benefits from physically active leisure are scientifically well-documented, and the evidence for psychological and social health and well-being are emerging.
- Some evidence exists that leisure involvements contribute to individual health and well-being by structuring free time and replacing idleness with constructive behavioral alternatives.
- Research suggests that fun and pleasurable activities not only enhance the quality of the present moment but also accumulate in long-term psychological well-being.
- Leisure contributes to identity formation and affirmation, and the evidence suggests that under some circumstances it may contribute to personal psychological growth.
- Sufficient evidence is emerging that leisure can promote coping and personal growth in response to daily stress and significant negative life events that include disability and illness.
- Leisure engagement contributes to health and well-being by positively influencing other domains of life, such as work, family, and interpersonal

Discussion Box 29.1

LEISURE AND HEALTH

How does leisure contribute to health? Several ideas are presented in Exhibit 29.1. Consider each and discuss the benefit categories of physical, emotional/psychological, and social health. What role does leisure assume in each category? What is leisure's relationship to health, well-being, and life satisfaction?

relationships. Alternatively, leisure can also detract from these same domains.

- Health, well-being, and leisure research has been reported largely by Western researchers, and only recently has international research and cross-cultural research been undertaken. Eventually this total body of research will enlighten leisure practice.

Leisure, Health, and Therapeutic Recreation

It is clear that leisure plays important roles in a person's physical, psychological, and social well-being and contributes to his/her life satisfaction. Therapeutic recreation, as the discipline that focuses on the leisure abilities of individuals with disabilities, illnesses, and/or special needs, therefore, has much to contribute to the health and well-being of these individuals. Therapeutic recreation is based on several assumptions.

The first assumption is that every human being needs, wants, and deserves leisure. Leisure presents opportunities to try new behaviors, experience mastery, learn new skills, meet new people, deepen existing relationships, and develop a clearer sense of self. Leisure provides the context in which people can learn, interact, express individualism, and self-actualize (Kelly, 1996). Leisure tends to have less serious boundaries and consequences than do other activities, such as work. The benefits of leisure are numerous, diverse, and defined by the individual, his or her life experiences, and, to a large degree, his or her culture.

The second assumption is that many, if not most, individuals experience barriers to full and satisfying leisure. For example, some individuals may view leisure as wasteful; some may not know how to access information about leisure opportunities; some may lack skills in meeting new people or establishing meaningful relationships; some may have safety and welfare concerns that prevent them from entering leisure facilities; and some may feel they have inadequate discretionary money to spend on leisure. Although many adults overcome these barriers or learn to compensate for their consequences, many are constrained from full and satisfying leisure experiences, and therefore, do not benefit fully from satisfying and healthful participation. Whereas some individuals may seek help and guidance in negotiating these constraints, many individuals do not, and thus reduce their chances for fulfilling leisure and the resulting benefits of leisure participation.

It then follows that many individuals with disabilities and/or illnesses may experience more frequent, severe, or lasting barriers than their counterparts without disabilities, simply due to the presence of their disability and/or illness, their reactions or perceptions about their disability and/or illness, or the environment in which they live and work. For example, some individuals may experience difficulty with the lack of physical accessibility in recreation or tourist facilities; some may be addicted to substances that challenge their sober participation; some may have reduced physical endurance, coordination, or strength; some may have few skills due to lack of exposure to typical recreation and leisure opportunities; some may have difficulty making friends due to social isolation or societal attitudes; and some may be unaware of leisure opportunities that are available to someone with their disabling condition. For some individuals, these barriers and constraints are quite limiting and ultimately affect their leisure lifestyle, quality of life, health, and overall happiness or satisfaction.

Because they are likely to experience greater difficulty in full and satisfying leisure participation, many individuals with disabilities and/or illnesses need the additional help of a therapeutic recreation specialist to eliminate, reduce, overcome, or compensate for their leisure barriers. A therapeutic recreation specialist helps reduce clients' barriers to leisure involvement through the provision of functional intervention, leisure education, and recreation participation services. The reduction of these barriers or constraints allows the individual to participate more fully in leisure experiences of his or her choice. The ultimate outcome of therapeutic recreation services is the improved ability of the individual to make and act on choices for leisure participation that are meaningful, rewarding, and successful. That is, the ultimate outcome of therapeutic recreation services is the improved ability of the individual to engage in a successful, meaningful, and culturally appropriate leisure lifestyle that, in turn, leads to improved health, quality of life, and well-being. When the individual can successfully engage in leisure of his or her own choice, the individual has the chance to receive the psychological, physical, and social benefits as well as the more global benefits of improved health, wellness, and quality of life (Stumbo & Peterson, 2009).

Leisure Education

The unique role of therapeutic recreation specialists (TRSs) is to assist individuals with illnesses and disabilities to engage in a leisure lifestyle that is satisfying and leads to enhanced quality of life experiences through improvements in functioning and behaviors. Leisure professionals use three categories of service (functional intervention, leisure education, and recreation participation) to create options that foster health and quality of life regardless of one's status in the health spectrum. Leisure education is a prominent and widely used process through which individuals develop an understanding of leisure, the significance of self in leisure, and the facilitation of a leisure lifestyle that is compatible with their needs, values, and goals (Mundy, 1998). This developmental process is unique to each person as the interrelationships and values among the self and leisure are explored and skills acquired and nurtured in order to achieve optimal health. Clients in the rehabilitation process experience a disproportionate amount of leisure and may also need to learn or relearn knowledge and skills to incorporate the effects of the disability into their desired lifestyle (Stumbo & Peterson, 2009).

A number of educational models have outlined the information in content areas critical to a healthy leisure lifestyle (Dattilo, 1999; Mundy, 1998; Stumbo & Peterson, 2009). The commonly apparent threads are leisure awareness, knowledge of leisure resources, leisure participation skills, decision-making skills, and social skills (Shank & Coyle, 2002). Leisure awareness helps individuals explore the benefits of leisure as well as their attitudes and barriers to leisure. Knowledge of leisure resources considers options and use of leisure in the client's community, for example, and is represented in the ICF by d910 Community Life. Leisure participation skills relate directly to the ICF schema in two ways: First, the ICF uses qualifiers, performance and capacity, to describe discrepancies between the client's ability to participate in a life situation (performance) and completion of the experience in a standardized testing environment (capacity). Therapists aid clients in reducing the differences between performance and capacity during participation in leisure experiences. Second, this leisure education content area includes recreation and leisure experiences found in d920 of the ICF. Finally decision making and social skills are crucial to the client's ability to select and engage in recreation and leisure that are compatible with their needs and facilitate adequate levels of group engagement. In the ICF schema, several categories relate to this leisure education content area, including communication; interpersonal interactions and relationships; and community, social, and civic life. Through assessment, barriers and limitations to full participation in community and social life are identified. Leisure education interventions are selected to reduce these barriers and minimize difficulties in performance.

Information Seeking and Health Spectrum Model

Stumbo and Caldwell (2002) proposed a model to indicate the level of information that is appropriate to an individual, depending on his or her stage in the rehabilitation and recovery process. As individuals progress through various stages of the health spectrum, the perception of challenge may present varying demands on the individual's ability to cope, adapt, and respond. Cognitive learning theory would suggest that the individual's ability to intake new information depends on their previous cognitive framework, as well as the novelty and degree of arousal present. Figure 29.1 provides a proposed relationship between interest in leisure and energy to expend toward knowledge acquisition and participation (adapted from Sullivan, as cited in Babcock & Miller, 1994).

Leisure Education in Acute Stage

Clients' leisure education needs vary during the recovery and rehabilitation process. When a client is in an acute stage, whether this means a drug or

29.1

Information seeking and health spectrum model.

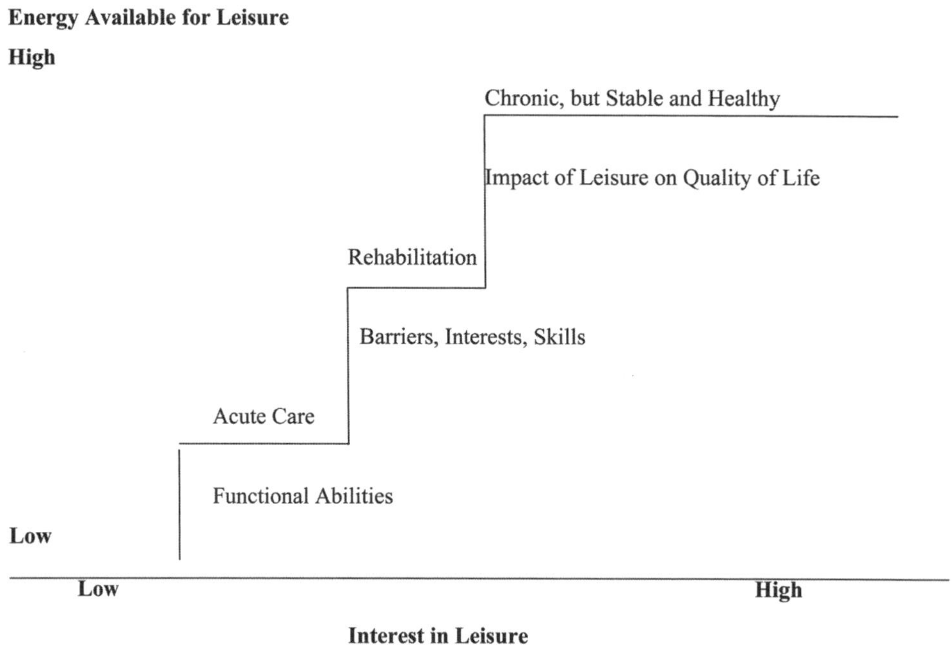

From Leisure education and learning theory, by N. J. Stumbo & L. L. Caldwell, 2002, *ADOZ: Boletin del Centro de Docmentacion en Ocio, 23* (Spanish version pp. 29–35; English version, pp. 35–40). Adapted with permission.

substance detoxification ward, an intensive medical care unit, or an intake section of the penitentiary, the energy and attention devoted to leisure needs may be minimal. The individual's attention and focus is narrowed on physical and psychic survival, and minimal energy remains for the appreciation and application of leisure. Learning at this stage is very limited, focused, and concrete.

Leisure Education in Rehabilitation

In the recovery or rehabilitation stage, individuals become more concerned about what they can do to "survive" and promote their own longevity and health. Their goal, if rehabilitation efforts are successful, is to optimize their own individual health and return to their original life to the greatest degree possible. They seek specific information to return as quickly as possible to a normally functioning (familiar) state. In this stage, individuals may be more interested in learning leisure activities as a "means" to achieve rehabilitation goals rather than as an "end" of the leisure experience.

Leisure Education With Chronic but Healthy and Stable Conditions

For those who will live with the condition for a long time, such as those who have incurred a stroke, an amputation, or who are incarcerated for a long term, information that will help them make adaptations to their total lifestyle, including leisure, is sought. What are the new rules for participation? Is physical access required? Do old skills need to be modified in order to participate once again? In what types of leisure situations is a former inmate accepted? What kinds of experiences and opportunities are available for a recovering alcoholic? In this stage, the individual seeks information about the changes to his or her individual lifestyle that are necessary to regain a degree of homeostasis. It involves overlaying new information and ways of doing things on the cognitive frameworks previously held by the individual.

The learning needs of individuals seeking health information with the ultimate goal of increased wellness are multifaceted. Leisure education services for this category of individuals should explore the broad range of leisure experiences and opportunities available to promote wellness. It may include factual information, such as nutrition and heart rate calculations, as well as attitudes toward incorporating leisure into daily patterns. A broad spectrum of information is needed in order to develop and maintain a satisfying and independent leisure lifestyle.

At each stage in the continuum, individuals have different needs from leisure education service providers. Professionals who desire to be prepared for all levels of service must be familiar with cognitive learning theory, leisure education models and content, and stages in the total health spectrum. Each stage prompts a different amount and kind of information to be shared with the individual. Types of leisure education information used by TRSs are influenced by the levels of client health and desired outcomes of rehabilitation. Our success in providing leisure education services depends on our own readiness to respond to these diverse needs.

Client Assessment

Assessment is an important process that aids in establishing client needs, which, in turn, allows the professional to target the right services to meet those client's needs, thus moving the client toward improved outcomes. Stumbo and Peterson (2009, p. 251) provided the following definition:

> *Client assessment is the systematic process of gathering and analyzing selected information about an individual client and using the results for placement into a program(s) that is designed to reduce or eliminate the individual's problems or deficits with his or her leisure, and that enhances the individual's ability to independently function in leisure pursuits. This definition has several key concepts. Assessment involves:*

- Gathering selected pieces of data
- About an individual, involving a

- Systematic process of collecting, analyzing, and reporting that
- Results in the ability to make decisions for placement into therapeutic recreation programs that
- Have been designed to reduce or eliminate problems so that the
- Individual can independently function in his or her leisure.

This list implies that the specialist needs to make numerous decisions during the assessment, planning, and implementation process. For example, the specialist needs to decide *what information* is important for program placement; what *data collection technique(s)* (e.g., observations, interviews, etc.) is best to gather the information; how the *data will be interpreted* for decisions about program placement; and how the assessment and program placement *relate to the individual's future lifestyle.* Assessment decisions are foundational to and closely parallel programming decisions. Assessment is the initial step in a systematic process of assessment, planning, implementation, and evaluation (or APIE) that identifies client needs and preferences. With this information, the specialist designs goals to address desired changes in functioning and behaviors in order to improve health and well-being. From the goals, interventions are selected and implemented to facilitate client engagements that result in growth and lifestyle enhancements. Evaluation determines if the implemented programs enabled achievement of goals written to address client needs. The APIE process is the framework for systematic decision making that places clients in interventions to optimize their health.

Purposes of Client Assessment

Client assessment tools may serve a variety of functions, beyond indicating program placement, monitoring progress, and evaluating involvement (Stumbo, 2002). For example, the information gathered from client assessments is used for the following reasons and purposes:

- Individual client information
    - Initial baseline assessment (treatment planning/program placement)
    - Monitoring progress (formative information)
    - Summarizing progress (summative information)
- Research on program efficacy and effectiveness
- Communication within and among disciplines
- Administrative requirements

The first purpose is to identify the problem(s) of the client so that appropriate interventions can be designed, monitored, and evaluated. Client assessment is clearly important to determining clients' needs for placement into therapeutic recreation intervention programs. Without appropriate client assessment, clients are likely to be placed into programs that are not designed to meet their needs and, therefore, cannot produce the outcomes intended from participation (Palmer & McMahon, 1997; Stumbo, 2002). On the other hand, quality assessment processes can lead to appropriate placement into programs that are designed to address the clients' needs and move them toward valued outcomes. Quality assessment procedures are necessary for changing client behavior in desired and predictable ways.

Within the first purpose of identifying client problems and needs, additional uses of assessment are appropriate. As noted by Gronlund (1993), Hoy and Gregg (1994), Salvia and Ysseldyke (1998), and Ward and Murray-Ward (1999), assessment information can be used for (a) placement decisions, (b) formative (on-going progress) decisions, and (c) summative (end-of-services) decisions. Client assessment provides baseline information about the attitudes, knowledge, skills, and abilities that clients possess prior to receiving intervention. That baseline information is important for: (a) establishing what programs should be selected for clients; (b) monitoring and reporting on clients' status (progression or regression) as they participate in the program; and (c) comparing clients' attitudes, knowledge, skills, and abilities as they exit the intervention program. All three purposes, placement, monitoring, and evaluation, are dependent on collecting the right baseline information accurately.

For placement decisions, assessment needs to be fine-tuned enough to distinguish client problems and needs and match those problems and needs with the appropriate intervention programs. In this case, the assessment procedure must detail the problems and needs of the client so that the most efficient yet effective intervention can be provided. In speaking about psychology, Palmer and McMahon (1997) explained:

> *Diagnosis involves matching signs and symptoms of [the] client with a known cluster of symptoms (a syndrome)...The purpose of making a diagnosis is to allow the counselor to intervene in the most effective way possible... [However] change is only possible within the limitations set by the system or systems of which the person is a part and with the resources at the person's disposal. (pp. 7–8)*

Obviously, assessment decisions closely parallel the program planning, implementation, and evaluation processes. During the course of the intervention and at the end of services, the specialist can use a well-designed assessment that produces valid and reliable results for measuring the client's progress during and after the end of the client's participation in the program. While shortened lengths of stay and the sheer volume of clients affect how well this can be accomplished, the fact remains that a measurement process that produces valid and reliable results can be used at different intervals to measure a person's movement toward and at a final outcome.

The second major reason for assessment is for research purposes to ascertain the most effective interventions possible for future clients. Baseline assessment data can be used for quality improvement and research purposes (Palmer & McMahon, 1997; Sneegas, 1989; Stumbo & Peterson, 2009). Beyond the implications for programming, baseline assessment data can be used to monitor the overall efficacy or effectiveness of the therapeutic recreation intervention program for a client, a particular group of clients, or all clients entering and exiting the program. This data can assist with performance improvement efforts as well as result in research to determine for whom which programs are most effective. Starting with an effective assessment is one of the easiest ways to determine client outcomes that result from program participation.

The third major reason is for "knowledge, communication, and memory" (Palmer & McMahon, 1997, p. 11) so that people within the discipline may be able to communicate with each other as well as with other professionals. Professionals within a discipline need a common language in order to communicate and, therefore, need a common knowledge base and common definitions of professional terms. In therapeutic recreation, such terms as *leisure barriers, leisure education, leisure awareness, perceived freedom, client assessment, leisure lifestyle,* and even *therapeutic recreation* need to have common meanings for professional understanding to occur. These definitions and understandings sometimes may be specialized to the discipline and sometimes must be in alignment with those used by other disciplines (Palmer & McMahon, 1997).

A fourth major purpose is related to administrative requirements from external and professional bodies, as well as local agency mandates. Three organizations have significant influence on the therapeutic recreation profession at the national level: (a) the Joint Commission on Accreditation of Healthcare Organizations (JCAHO), (b) the Rehabilitation Accreditation Commission (CARF), and (c) the Centers for Medicare and Medicaid Services (CMS; formerly the Health Care Financing Administration [HCFA]). These three organizations affect all health care professions because they set standards for health care quality that, in turn, affects reimbursement for services. All three of these organizations monitor specific requirements for client assessment that affects therapeutic recreation services in the United States.

What Should Leisure and Recreation Assessments Measure?

The question of "What should leisure and recreation assessments measure?" has both a simple and yet dauntingly complex set of answers. On one hand, there seems to be some agreement about the content side of that question. For example, here are some comments from experts in the field:

- "The current, future, and oftentimes past leisure behavior of the client are important areas of focus for the therapeutic recreation specialist. Relevant information to be gathered may include leisure interests, use of leisure time, ability to participate in individual or group activities, ability to experience fun and enjoyment, leisure skills, leisure attitudes and awareness, and knowledge of leisure resources as well as any physical, cognitive, or social limitations affecting leisure lifestyle" (Sneegas, 1989, pp. 223–224).
- "Others describe leisure assessment as a process of systematic inquiry about client attitudes, needs, interests, values, behaviors, and patterns where some type or degree of intervention is desired" (Howe, 1989, p. 209).
- "Assessment should aid us to determine client strengths, interests, and expectations and to identify the nature and extent of problems or concerns.

Determining client strengths and interests will allow us to construct a strengths list on which to base interventions during the planning phase. Identifying client expectations helps us to determine treatment or rehabilitation goals" (Austin, 2004, p. 188).

- "A sound assessment identifies the client's health status, needs, and strengths" (Austin, 2001, p. 47).
- Therapeutic recreation specialists "assess physical, cognitive, social, emotional, and behavioral functioning, as it relates to leisure behavior, leisure knowledge and skills, and functional independence in life activities" (Kinney & Witman, 1997, p. 9).

Some of the generic commonalties among these insights include (a) functional abilities, (b) clients' strengths and limitations, and (c) leisure patterns, attitudes, knowledge, skills, and abilities. Although several taxonomies have been suggested to classify client assessments within therapeutic recreation (cf. Burlingame & Blaschko, 2002; Howe, 1984; Stumbo, 1991, 1992, 2002; Stumbo & Thompson, 1986), the following will be used for this chapter:

- Functional Abilities;
- Leisure Attitudes, Barriers, Skills, and Interests; and
- Leisure Constructs (e.g., motivation, satisfaction).

The reader will note that these three areas roughly equate to the levels within Figure 29.1. Functional abilities are the prime concern for individuals in acute care; attitudes, barriers, interests, and skills—new and premorbid—are of interest during the rehabilitation phase, and leisure constructs, such as leisure motivation, leisure satisfaction, and quality of life, are instrumental in minimizing the influence of disability and enhancing one's health throughout the life course.

Sneegas (1989) and Sylvester, Voelkl, and Ellis (2001) noted that measuring complex phenomena, such as human behavior and attitudes, is difficult at best. How do we adequately measure such complex phenomena as "leisure behavior" or "leisure attitudes" or "health and well-being?" Such measurements often require more than just a simple checklist of "activity interests" or "activity participation." Addressing the measurement of leisure behavior, Sneegas indicated:

> *Identifying and measuring participation in various activities is alone not a valid and sufficient measure of the full spectrum of leisure behavior. In order to obtain more meaningful information, the antecedents and consequences of activity involvement—that is, the preexisting need and subsequent effects of leisure involvement ... as well as the subjective experiences of the individuals—need to be examined.... There is currently a lack of appropriate measurement tools, or instrumentation, which reflect the complexity of leisure behavior. Whereas time diaries and activity checklists provide a measure of time use and activity involvement, they do not generally provide any information detailing the whys and wherefores of the behavior, information on the subjective experience of the individual's involvement. (p. 225)*

This quote provides a small indication of some of the difficulties encountered in selecting and developing tools and procedures for assessing and measuring the complexities of the leisure experience, such as barriers, attitudes, interests, skills, motivations, and outcomes.

At the micro-level, the content of the program remains important in deciding what the assessment should measure. The intent and content of the program and the purpose and function of the assessment both have a large impact on determining what content needs to be included in the assessment instrument. While these decisions are not impossible to make, many find it difficult because a great deal of knowledge and expertise, as well as professional judgment, must accompany these decisions. It is not that the answers are vague and unobtainable, it is that they are often unique to the therapeutic recreation department and program. No single assessment will fit all therapeutic recreation programs, largely because few therapeutic recreation programs across the country (globe) are similar nor are individuals' leisure patterns and interests easily categorized.

Examples of Assessment Tools Aligned With the Information Seeking and Health Spectrum Model

The levels of the Information Seeking and Health Spectrum Model can be used to roughly translate the categories of client assessments: (a) functional ability; (b) recreation skills/participation patterns, including attitudes, barriers, skills, and interests; and (c) leisure constructs involved with life satisfaction and quality of life. A sampling of commercially available tools illustrates the nature of assessment tools, although admittedly limited, found in settings reflective of the intent of programming intervention in each tier of the model. Assessments listed are representative of those with established psychometric qualities. The assessments listed are presented to share examples of tools available to assess constructs within each level of the model.

Functional Abilities: Acute Care

This level of intervention addresses the areas commonly acknowledged as prerequisites to successful involvement in daily life and leisure. Assessments may focus on one area, such as physical or cognitive functioning, or address all areas perceived as important to negotiating and managing life and leisure activities.

1. **Comprehensive Evaluation in Recreation Therapy—Psychiatric/Behavioral** (CERT-Psych). Parker, R. A., Ellison, C. H., Kirby, T. F., & Short, M. J. (1975). The comprehensive evaluation in recreation therapy scale: A tool for patient evaluation. *Therapeutic Recreation Journal, 9*(4), 143–152. This assessment measures a person's ability to successfully integrate into society using his/her social skills.
2. **Comprehensive Evaluation in Recreation Therapy—Physical Disabilities** (CERT-P/D). Parker, R. A., & Downie, G. (1981). Recreation therapy: A model for consideration. *Therapeutic Recreation Journal, 15*(3), 22–26. This assessment measures baseline skills in eight areas: gross motor, fine motor, locomotion, motor skills, sensory, cognition, communication, and behavior.

3. **Leisure Competence Measure** (LCM). Kloseck, M., Crilly, R. G., Ellis, G. D., & Lammers, E. (1996). Leisure competence measure: Development and reliability testing of a scale to measure functional outcomes in therapeutic recreation. *Therapeutic Recreation Journal, 30*(1), 13–26. The purpose of this tool is to categorize and summarize information related to a client's ability to participate independently in the community; the tool is designed to be consistent with the Functional Independence Measure (FIM), and the philosophy and tenets of the ICF.

Leisure Attitudes, Barriers, Skills, and Interests: Rehabilitation

This assessment area considers factors that either inhibit or support the development of a leisure lifestyle. Assessment ascertains motivators and obstacles to participation.

1. **Leisure Diagnostic Battery** (LDB). Ellis, G. D., & Witt, P. A. (1986). The Leisure Diagnostic Battery: Past, present, future. *Therapeutic Recreation Journal, 20*(4), 31–47. This tool consists of a number of scales to use with individuals with and without disabilities to assess leisure functioning (how a person feels about their leisure experiences and the kinds of outcomes that result from these experiences) and the areas where improvement might be necessary.
2. **State Technical Institute Leisure Assessment Process** (STILAP). Navar, N. (1980). A rationale for leisure skill assessment with handicapped adults. *Therapeutic Recreation Journal, 14*(4), 21–28. This tool assesses then categorizes leisure skill participation patterns to help clients achieve a balanced leisure lifestyle.

Impact of Leisure on Quality of Life: Chronic but Stable and Healthy

This level of intervention and assessment is associated with the World Health Organization's (WHO's) definition of QoL: the person's perception of their position in life within the cultural context and value system as it relates to their goals and expectations. Assessments often consider subjective elements about life and leisure.

1. **Leisure Motivation Scale** (LMS). Beard, J. G., & Ragheb, M. G. (1983). Measuring leisure motivation. *Journal of Leisure Research, 12*(1), 20–33. This scale measures client's motivation to engage in leisure activities; four subscales assess intellectual, social, competency-mastery, and stimulus-avoidance motivators to establish what components need to be present to motivate client participation.
2. **Leisure Attitude Scale/Measurement** (LAS). Ragheb, M. G., & Beard, J. G. (1982). Measuring leisure attitude. *Journal of Leisure Research, 14*(2), 155–167. This scale assesses the three components of attitudes—cognitive, affective, and behavioral; each scale may be administered separately or all

Discussion Box 29.2

LEISURE AND THE ICF

How do client assessments in therapeutic recreation address the ICF schema descriptors for capacity and performance? The ICF assessment process addresses holistic health in the broadest sense by considering contextual variables such as family support, attitudes of friends, and lifestyle or social and environmental barriers influencing clients living with chronic conditions. What primary function is served by therapeutic recreation assessments as client capacity and performance are investigated?

together and identifies factors that may be preventing active participation in leisure.

3. **Leisure Boredom Scale** (LBS). Iso-Ahola, S. E., & Weissinger, E. (1990). Perceptions of boredom in leisure: Conceptualization, reliability and validity of the leisure boredom scale. *Journal of Leisure Research, 22*(1), 1–17. This tool measures perceptions of leisure (too much time available and too little to do) as boredom; clients are not likely to be intrinsically motivated if they lack awareness, attitudes, and skills to facilitate leisure participation and perceive constraints negatively impacting quality of life.

Relationship of Assessments and the ICF

The conceptual framework of the ICF presents several opportunities for the TRS to reexamine and reposition assessments in rehabilitation management. First, as depicted in the Information Seeking and Health Spectrum Model, the opportunity is presented to expand our way of thinking about the scope and practice of assessment in the rehabilitation process (Bruyère, VanLooy, & Peterson, 2005). As a result, the ICF offers a conceptual framework to guide TRSs in organizing already existing assessments in accordance with related ICF codes used in rehabilitation practice (Reed et al., 2005). Second, while TR assessments have measured the direct relationship between the ability to perform an activity and the context in which it is being executed (Porter & Van Puymbroeck, 2007), the ICF identities two relevant domains, Activities and Participation and Environmental Factors (WHO, 2001), for which HRQoL assessments may be developed through multidisciplinary practice. The level of detail to apply assessments in our field to the ICF does not yet exist; once developed and applied, the conceptual framework of the ICF supports the relevance of TR assessments to documentation and communication of rehabilitation results with peer professionals and clients and caregivers involved in the selection of interventions (Reed et al.). The key to rehabilitation management is understanding the relationship between disability and health and the psychosocial and environmental factors that exacerbate or minimize them (Stucki, Ewert, & Cieza, 2003). Consequently, a third opportunity is presented to the TRS by the nature of the ICF coding schema that uses qualifiers, performance and capacity, to describe the client's ability to complete an action. In this context, the TRS selects interventions to minimize the differences clients experience between capacity and performance (Peterson, 2005). Inclusion of subjective influences in the ICF framework, therefore, presents the opportunity for TRS to select interventions that define outcome measures pertinent to the rehabilitation process (Mermis, 2005), within the context of holistic health. Consequently, it is anticipated that the ICF will create the "opportunity for greater awareness of TR services" in the future (Howard, Browning, & Lee, 2007, p. 77).

Howard et al. (2007) recommended that, in the absence of specific TR assessments designed and based on the ICF, a starting point is "crosswalking" our assessments with the ICF. This approach would result in the identification of items from different assessments that are compatible with specific ICF codes (Perenboom & Chorus, 2003). To illustrate, items from the Leisure Diagnostic Battery (LDB) relate to the ICF code, chapter 9—Community, Social, and Civic Life, d920 recreation and leisure; or items from the Comprehensive Evaluation in Recreational Therapy-Physical Disabilities (CERT-PD) relate to the ICF code, chapter 4—Mobility, d410 changing and maintaining basic body position and d450 walking and moving. The compatibility between corresponding TR assessment instrument items and the ICF codes would have to be determined (Stucki et al., 2003). In other words, the TR assessment item score, for example, would have to be mapped to the performance and capacity qualifiers in the ICF to explain the magnitude of the activity limitation or participation restriction or the extent to which the environmental factor is a barrier or facilitator (Stucki et al.) in the rehabilitation process. The consequences of undertaking this compatibility check might be the operationalization of the ICF concepts, especially Activities and Participation and Environmental Factors, to health care settings that use standardized TR assessments.

The second opportunity presented by the ICF is the design and application of new assessment tools to support a multidisciplinary rehabilitation process. Through leisure education paradigms (Stumbo, 2002; Stumbo & Peterson, 2009), TRSs have tools that assess leisure motivation, satisfaction, and barriers (Porter & Van Puymbroeck, 2007). Further TRSs assess and address clients' needs within the context of activities occurring in the natural environment (Stumbo). Thus, with respect to the ICF model, our expertise is encompassed by the terms *activity* (execution of a task or action), *participation* (involvement in a life situation), and *environmental factors* ("the physical, social and attitudinal environment in which people live and conduct their lives"; WHO, 2001, p. 10). TRSs, therefore, have the opportunity to develop relevant assessments that measure potential to perform and be successful in the context of holistic health. Specifically, the profession is in a position to design tools that assess performance and capacity qualifiers and environmental barriers and facilitators (WHO, 2002). One recently developed tool, the Leisure Competence Measure (LCM; Kloseck et al., 1996; Kloseck, Crilly, & Hutchinson-Troyer, 2001), captures environmental factors relative to independent participation in community leisure activities and is intended to be used with the Functional Independent Measure (FIM), a tool used widely in rehabilitation practice. The design of new assessment tools that document the influence of environmental factors on a person's ability to perform an activity, therefore, appears to be within the professional scope of practice.

The third opportunity created by the ICF relates to the identification of outcome measures pertinent to the rehabilitation process. The ICF schema

Research Box 29.1

INCORPORATING THE ICF IN LEISURE ASSESSMENT

Tasiemski, T., Gardner, B. P., & Taylor, N. (2005). The association of sports and physical recreation with life satisfaction in a community sample of people with spinal cord injuries. *NeuroRehabilitation, 20*(4), 253–265.

Objectives: This study intended to assess satisfaction with life domains (life as a whole, ability to manage self-care, leisure situation, vocational situation, financial situation, sexual life, partnership relations, family life, and contacts with friends and acquaintances) and the role of sports and physical recreation with life satisfaction in SCI.

Method: The sample consisted of 985 individuals from three spinal injury centers, with SCI at C5 or below, wheelchair dependent, between 18 and 50 chronological age, injured at least 1 year prior to the study. The measures used included the Sports Participation Questionnaire, the Life Satisfaction Questionnaire, and the Hospital Anxiety and Depression Scale.

Results: Hours of participation in sports decreased after injury with those who participate in sports or physical recreation experiencing higher life satisfaction than those not participating in physical activities. 40% of the respondents were satisfied with their leisure, 67% with family life, and 56% with contacts and friends. Mood, marital status, loss of independence, and sports participation are predictors of life satisfaction.

Conclusion: Nearly half, 47%, of the study respondents were involved in physical recreation after injury, and their life satisfaction was significantly higher than those not active in sports. Efforts to increase awareness among the SCI population about the psychological and physical health benefits of sport should be undertaken.

Questions:
Which areas of the ICF might be included in an assessment tool that would attempt to determine the factors that contribute to increased sports participation among clients with SCI? What aspects of leisure education are crucial to clients with SCI gaining an awareness of the significance of sports participation to QoL and their life satisfaction? How could these be measured? Which benefits introduced in the chapter might be investigated as potential client outcomes with SCI participating in physical activity? How might a study be designed to determine specific health benefits?

uses the qualifiers *performance* and *capacity* to describe the client's difficulty to participate in a life situation (performance) and ability to complete an action in a standardized testing environment (capacity; Porter & Van Puymbroeck, 2007). TRSs select interventions that reduce, eliminate, or minimize the differences between the client's capacities and performances. Further, TRSs plan for a continuum of growth and well-being as clients transition from one level of assistance to another or from one experience to another (Carter, Van Andel, & Robb, 2003). TRSs expertise emanates from the activity and task analyses used to select and sequence interventions. Through these processes, TRSs design relevant and meaningful activities "considered essential for the well-being of any human being" (Weigl et al., 2004, p. 16).

Client assessments affirm the degree to which interventions reduce or eliminate deficits that create differences between capacity and performance. The assessment of contextual variables, such as family support or attitudes of friends and lifestyle or fitness, recognizes the broadest influences on the rehabilitation process and its outcomes (Mermis, 2005). The assessment, planning, implementation, and evaluation (APIE) process used in therapeutic recreation services targets benefits valued by rehabilitation team members and that are "frequently reported in the literature with other health conditions under the umbrella term Health-Related Quality of Life" (Cieza et al., 2004, p. 67). Consequently, the ICF presents the opportunity to identify outcome measures pertinent to the rehabilitation process while crafting assessments that measure intervention benefits significant to holistic health.

Assessment Imposing the ICF Model on the Information Seeking and Health Spectrum Model

The ICF framework presents the opportunity to design universally applicable assessment tools for activity levels and levels of participation in basic functioning areas, for the whole person, and for the social engagements of the person (WHO, 2002). TRSs design and use assessment tools that measure functional improvement as well as improvements that facilitate access to social engagements. The design of these tools takes into consideration activity limitations and performance restrictions or the differences between the ability to complete the activity in a standardized setting and the ability to perform the activity within the context of day-to-day life. If the ICF model were to be superimposed on the Information Seeking and Health Spectrum Model, professionals might consider three levels of assessment that explore activity limitations and participation restrictions relevant to environments in acute care, rehabilitation, and as persons live with chronic impairments. With each of these levels of disability and health, TRSs consider the information clients need relative to leisure and quality of life. To illustrate, in the acute stage, while the client's attention to leisure needs is minimal, the TRS might assess functional abilities and report premorbid factors and potential for rehabilitation; likewise, during the rehabilitation stage, the TRSs might focus assessment on specific activity limitations and participation restrictions experienced during selected treatment interventions, such as aquatic or animal-assisted therapies

As the client transitions to living with a chronic condition, the TRS addresses the differences between capacity and performance qualifiers for specific experiences (e.g., wheelchair mobility during recreational games vs. competitive sports), while reducing barriers and facilitating participation in the client's social environment. The results of assessments identify how TRSs may build the social environment to be more accessible and enable transition to the next level of health and well-being.

Vignette

This vignette illustrates the use of one of the sampled assessments with a client who is experiencing the rehabilitation process, commencing with acute care, transitioning to the rehabilitation phase, and eventually living with the chronic disability. The case illustrates the application of the Information Seeking and the Health Spectrum Model to the concepts of capacity and performance as defined by the ICF schema.

TRSs using the CERT-P/D with clients having strokes, for example, during acute care, under standardized inpatient conditions, would assess "transfer ability" and note "complete difficulty" (4) as the extent of activity limitation or capacity because the client has no ability to assist in a transfer more than 95% of the time, which disrupts the client's ability to engage in hobbies (d9204) and socialize (d9205; WHO, 2002). The same assessment may be repeated following transition to a rehabilitation unit and result in a code of "moderate difficulty" (2) because the extent of activity limitation or capacity occurs about 50% of the time as the client attempts to transfer with assistance during recreation therapy when engaging in group leisure experiences (WHO, 2002). With this reassessment information, the TRS documents progress in capacity or reduced difficulty by two levels under standardized conditions; in this case, during inpatient interventions. This decrease in difficulty recognizes that assistance is necessary to execute the task under standardized conditions.

During rehabilitation while on a community outing, the TRS might discover that assistance is required to transfer to seating in a restaurant and theater, for example. As a consequence, in real-life situations, according to the ICF coding schema, participation restriction(s) would be coded at "complete difficulty" (4) resulting in a difference of two levels between execution of the task under standardized conditions (inpatient intervention) and life situations (outpatient intervention). In this example, the environment has become a barrier. The ICF coding schema presents the opportunity to code environmental factors that impinge upon the rehabilitation process. The environmental factor (design, construction and building products; e150) became a barrier during the community outing. As a consequence, on a scale of 0–4, the TRS would use the code 3 to indicate that a severe barrier resulted from construction and, as a consequence, weighed negatively on the client's performance, causing a difference of two levels between capacity and ability to complete the task in a real-life situation (WHO, 2002). For this illustration, when the client and TRS consider living with a chronic condition, level three of the Information Seeking and the Health Spectrum Model, the TRS is challenged to determine what interventions will decrease the level of impairment or discrepancy between capacity (standardized conditions) and performance (life situations). Thus, the TRS needs to determine what social and environmental factors require adaptations in order to minimize challenges experienced as the client lives with the chronic condition: As the client considers engaging in desired hobbies and social engagements, the TRS provides the information necessary for reducing the variance between capacity and performance. When assessments are designed to measure transition challenges and identify the cause for discrepancy between capacity and performance, TRSs justify intervention selections, create the means to document progress, and validate their role in the rehabilitation process. Additionally, data are provided to explain levels of functioning and the leisure needs of persons with various levels of disability.

Research and Practice Issues on Recreation and Leisure Assessment in Rehabilitation and Quality of Life

Many issues and much work remain to improve the quality and functionality of recreation and therapeutic recreation assessments to ensure that the therapeutic recreation profession remains in alignment with world health trends (such as the ICF) and that consumers of recreation and leisure services remain well-served. As suggested by other authors in this volume, the ICF presents a welcomed opportunity to rethink former classifications and ideas about health, functioning, and disability. This, in turn, requires much work reconceptualizing notions of quality health care service delivery and evaluation.

Three particular areas of research and focused energy will be needed in the immediate future for recreation and leisure assessments. First, current instruments need to be mapped to the ICF in ways that align with other health professions and provide optimal assessment information to colleagues and clients. Some efforts in this direction have been seen, although much work remains. The second line of research and effort will be to develop and test recreation and leisure assessments that specifically address indicators, performance, and capacity as outlined in the ICF itself. For reasons outlined earlier in this chapter about the complex nature of leisure behavior, we suspect this assessment development and testing process may be slow in being realized. The third area of needed research is that which focuses on service outcomes that reflect the intent of the ICF and provide sufficient evidence from which professionals can design, implement, and evaluate the best services for client involvement.

Summary

Leisure and recreation experiences produce numerous physical, social, emotional, and cognitive benefits and are essential to health and well-being. The relationships between leisure and recreation participation and a person's QoL, health, and well-being are complex and multifaceted. Therapeutic recreation is the profession that focuses on leisure and recreation experiences of individuals with illnesses, disabilities, and/or special needs. Leisure education is used to impart information that aids clients in rehabilitation as they assume responsibility for a meaningful, healthful, and satisfying leisure lifestyle. The Information Seeking and Health Spectrum Model provides a schematic to address the role of leisure education and the relationship of the therapeutic recreation process of assessment, planning, implementation, and evaluation (or APIE) to the ICF. This model was also used to highlight a few of the assessment tools available within therapeutic recreation. The chapter then provides a discussion about the alignment of therapeutic recreation practices and the ICF and ends with an exploration of the needed research.

References

Austin, D. R. (2001). The therapeutic recreation process. In D. R. Austin & M. E. Crawford (Eds.), *Therapeutic recreation and introduction* (3rd ed., pp. 45–56). Boston: Allyn and Bacon.

Austin, D. R. (2004). *Therapeutic recreation processes and techniques* (5th ed.). Champaign, IL: Sagamore.

Babcock, D. E., & Miller, M. A. (1994). *Client education: Theory and practice.* St. Louis: Mosby.

Beard, J. G., & Ragheb, M. G. (1983). Measuring leisure motivation. *Journal of Leisure Research, 12*(1), 20–33.

Bruyère, S. M., VanLooy, S. A., & Peterson D. B. (2005). The International Classification of Functioning, Disability and Health: Contemporary literature overview. *Rehabilitation Psychology, 50*(2), 113–121.

Burlingame, J., & Blaschko, T. M. (2002). *Assessment tools for recreational therapy and related fields* (3rd ed.). Ravensdale, WA: Idyll Arbor.

Caldwell, L. L. (2005). Leisure and health: Why is leisure therapeutic? *British Journal of Guidance & Counselling, 33*(1), 7–26.

Carter, M. J., Van Andel, G. E., & Robb, G. M. (2003). *Therapeutic recreation a practical approach* (3rd ed.). Prospect Heights, IL: Waveland Press.

Cassidy, T. (1996). All work and no play: A focus on leisure time as a means for promoting health. *Counseling Psychology Quarterly, 9*(1), 77–90.

Cieza, A., Stucki, G., Weigl, M., Kullmann, L., Stoll, T., Kamen, L., et al. (2004). ICF core sets for chronic widespread pain. *Journal of Rehabilitation Medicine Supplement, 44,* 63–68.

Cohen-Gewerc, E., & Stebbins, R. A. (2007). *The pivotal role of leisure education: Finding personal fulfillment in this century.* State College, PA: Venture.

Coyle, C., Kinney, W., Riley, B., & Shank, J. (Eds.). (1991). *Benefits of therapeutic recreation: A consensus view.* Ravensdale, WA: Idyll Arbor.

Dattilo, J. (1999). *Leisure education program planning: A systematic approach* (2nd ed.). State College, PA: Venture.

Drummond, A.E.R, Parker, C. J., Gladman, J.R.F., & Logan, P. A. (2001). Development and validation of the Nottingham Leisure Questionnaire (NLQ). *Clinical Rehabilitation, 15,* 647–656.

Edginton, C. R., Jordan, D. J., DeGraaf, D. G., & Edginton, S. R. (2002). *Leisure and life satisfaction: Foundational perspectives* (3rd ed.). Boston: McGraw-Hill.

Ellis, G. D., & Witt, P. A. (1986). The Leisure Diagnostic Battery: Past, present, future. *Therapeutic Recreation Journal, 20*(4), 31–47.

Gronlund, N. E. (1993). *How to make achievement tests and assessments* (5th ed.). Boston: Allyn and Bacon.

Howard, D., Browning, C., & Lee Y. (2007). The International Classification of Functioning, Disability, and Health: Therapeutic recreation code sets and salient diagnostic core sets. *Therapeutic Recreation Journal, 41*(1), 61–81.

Howe, C. Z. (1984). Leisure assessment instrumentation in therapeutic recreation. *Therapeutic Recreation Journal, 18*(2), 14–24.

Howe, C. Z. (1989). Assessment instruments in therapeutic recreation: To what extent do they work? In D. Compton (Ed.), *Issues in therapeutic recreation: A profession in transition* (pp. 205–221). Champaign, IL: Sagamore Publishing.

Hoy, C., & Gregg, N. (1994). *Assessment: The special educator's role.* Pacific Grove, CA: Brooks/Cole.

Hutchinson, S., & Kleiber, D. (2005). Leisure, constraints, and negative life events: Paradox and possibilities. In E. L. Jackson (Ed.), *Constraints to leisure* (pp. 137–152). State College, PA: Venture.

Iso-Ahola, S. E. (1997). A psychological analysis of leisure and health. In J. T. Haworth (Ed.), *Work, leisure and well-being* (pp. 131–144). New York: Routledge.

Iso-Ahola, S. E., & Weissinger, E. (1990). Perceptions of boredom in leisure: Conceptualization, reliability and validity of the leisure boredom scale. *Journal of Leisure Research, 22*(1), 1–17.

Iwasaki, Y., & Mannell, R. C. (2000). Hierarchical dimensions of leisure stress coping. *Leisure Sciences, 22,* 163–181.

Jackson, E. L. (Ed.). (2005). *Constraints to leisure.* State College, PA: Venture.

Kelly, J. R. (1996). *Leisure* (3rd ed.). Needham Heights, MA: Allyn and Bacon.

Kinney, T., & Witman, J. (1997). *Guidelines for competency assessment and curriculum planning in therapeutic recreation: A tool for self-evaluation.* Alexandria, VA: American Therapeutic Recreation Association.

Kleiber, D. A., Hutchinson, S. L., & Williams, R. (2002). Leisure as a resource in transcending negative life events: Self-protection, self-restoration, and personal transformation. *Leisure Sciences, 24,* 219–235.

Kloseck, M., Crilly, R. G., Ellis, G. D., & Lammers, E. (1996). Leisure competence measure: Development and reliability testing of a scale to measure functional outcomes in therapeutic recreation. *Therapeutic Recreation Journal, 30*(1), 13–26.

Kloseck, M., Crilly, R. G., & Hutchinson-Troyer, L. (2001). Measuring therapeutic recreation: Further testing of the Leisure Competence Measure. *Therapeutic Recreation Journal, 35*(1), 31–42.

Mannell, R. (2006). Health, well-being, and leisure. In E. L. Jackson (Ed.), *Leisure and the quality of life: Impacts on social, economic, and cultural development* (pp. 65–74). Hangzhou, China: Zhejiang University Press.

Mannell, R. C., & Kleiber, D. A. (1997). *A social psychology of leisure.* State College, PA: Venture.

Mermis, B. J. (2005). Developing a taxonomy for rehabilitation outcome measurement. *Rehabilitation Psychology, 50*(1), 15–23.

Mundy, J. (1998). *Leisure education theory and practice* (2nd ed.). Champaign, IL: Sagamore.

Navar, N. (1980). A rationale for leisure skill assessment with handicapped adults. *Therapeutic Recreation Journal, 14*(4), 21–28.

Palmer, S., & McMahon, G. (1997). *Client assessment.* Thousand Oaks, CA: Sage.

Parker, C. J., Gladman, J.R.F., & Drummond, A.E.R. (1997). The role of leisure in stroke rehabilitation. *Disability Rehabilitation, 19,* 1–5.

Parker, R. A., & Downie, G. (1981). Recreation therapy: A model for consideration. *Therapeutic Recreation Journal, 15*(3), 22–26.

Parker, R. A. Ellison, C. H., Kirby, T. F., & Short, M. J. (1975). The comprehensive evaluation in recreation therapy scale: A tool for patient evaluation. *Therapeutic Recreation Journal, 9*(4), 143–152.

Perenboom, R.J.M., & Chorus, A.M.J. (2003). Measuring participation according to the International Classification of Functioning, Disability and Health (ICF). *Disability and Rehabilitation, 25*(11–12), 577–587.

Peterson, D. B. (2005). International Classification of Functioning, Disability and Health: An introduction for rehabilitation psychologists. *Rehabilitation Psychology, 50*(2), 105–112.

Porter, H. R., & Van Puymbroeck, M. (2007). Utilization of the International Classification of Functioning, Disability, and Health within therapeutic recreation practice. *Therapeutic Recreation Journal, 41*(1), 47–60.

Ragheb, M. G., & Beard, J. G. (1982). Measuring leisure attitude. *Journal of Leisure Research, 14*(2), 155–167.

Reed, G. M., Lux, J. B., Bufka, L. F., Peterson, D. B., Threats, T. T., Trask, C., et al. (2005). Operationalizing the International Classification of Functioning, Disability and Health in clinical settings. *Rehabilitation Psychology, 50*(2), 122–131.

Salvia, J., & Ysseldyke, J. E. (1998). *Assessment* (7th ed.). Boston: Houghton-Mifflin.

Shank, J., & Coyle, C. (2002). *Therapeutic recreation in health promotion and rehabilitation.* State College, PA: Venture.

Sneegas, J. J. (1989). Can we really measure leisure behavior of special populations and individuals with disabilities? In D. Compton (Ed.), *Issues in therapeutic recreation: A profession in transition* (pp. 223–236). Champaign, IL: Sagamore.

Stucki, G., Ewert, T., & Cieza, A. (2003). Value and application of the ICF in rehabilitation medicine. *Disability and Rehabilitation, 25*(11–12), 628–634.

Stumbo, N. J. (1991). Selected assessment resources: A review of instruments and references. *Annual in Therapeutic Recreation, 2,* 8–24.

Stumbo, N. J. (1992). Re-thinking activity interest inventories. *Illinois Parks and Recreation, 23*(2), 17–21.

Stumbo, N. J. (2002). *Client assessment in therapeutic recreation services.* State College, PA: Venture.

Stumbo, N. J., & Caldwell, L. L. (2002). Leisure education and learning theory. *ADOZ: Boletin del Centro de Docmentacion en Ocio, 23* (Spanish version pp. 29–35; English version, pp. 35–40).

Stumbo, N. J. & Peterson, C. A. (2009). *Therapeutic recreation program design: Principles and procedures* (5th ed.). San Francisco, CA: Pearson Benjamin Cummings.

Stumbo, N. J., & Thompson, S. R. (1986). *Leisure education: A manual of activities and resources.* State College, PA: Venture.

Sylvester, C., Voelkl, J. E., & Ellis, G. D. (2001). *Therapeutic recreation programming: Theory and practice.* State College, PA: Venture.

Tasiemski, T., Gardner, B. P., & Taylor, N. (2005). The association of sports and physical recreation with life satisfaction in a community sample of people with spinal cord injuries. *NeuroRehabilitation, 20*(4), 253–265.

Wankel, L. M. (1994). Health and leisure: Inextricably linked. *Journal of Physical Education, Recreation and Dance, 65*(4), 28–33.

Ward, A. W., & Murray-Ward, M. (1999). *Assessment in the classroom.* Belmont, CA: Wadsworth.

Weigl, M., Cieza, A., Anderson, C., Kollerits, B., Amann, E., & Stucki, G. (2004). Identification of relevant ICF categories in patients with chronic health conditions: A Delphi exercise. *Journal of Rehabilitation Medicine Supplement, 44,* 12–21.

World Health Organization. (2001). International classification of functioning, disability, and health. Retrieved January 1, 2003 from: http://www3.who.int/icf/icftemplate.cfm?myurl=omepage.html&mytitle=ome%20Page

World Health Organization. (2002). *Towards a common language for Functioning, Disability and Health ICF.* Geneva: Author.

Jolie Haun

30 Health Literacy Assessment

Overview

This chapter addresses the assessment of health literacy within the context of the health care setting and rehabilitation. Literacy is identified as a primary indicator of one's health status. However, nearly half of the American population lacks adequate health literacy skills to effectively use health information and navigate the health care process. The Institute of Medicine (IOM) estimates approximately 90 million people lack literacy skills needed to function in the health environment. This health issue affects millions of people and costs billions of dollars in health care resources annually. Each year, inadequate health

Acknowledgment: The author wishes to thank Lorraine S. Wallace, PhD, for her careful review and constructive feedback regarding this chapter during its development.

literacy results in a diversity of adverse health-related outcomes approximating $58–$73 billion in unnecessary health care costs. Understanding the scope of health literacy, what it means to be functionally health literate, and how to assess and respond to individuals' health literacy needs is essential to advancing health and wellness. This chapter provides an introduction to the construct of health literacy and a review of key factors associated with health literacy assessment within the context of the World Health Organization's (WHO) International Classification of Functioning, Disability, and Health (ICF). Further, this chapter reviews current research and identifies validated formal and informal assessment methods. Critical issues in the field of health literacy assessment are briefly discussed. Resources also are identified for responding appropriately to individuals' health literacy needs.

Learning Objectives

By the end of the chapter, the reader will be able to

1. Discuss current definitions of health literacy;
2. Describe health literacy within the context of WHO's ICF;
3. Review current research in health literacy assessment and identify formal and informal methods for assessing health literacy needs in clinical practice;
4. Discuss critical issues in health literacy assessment; and
5. Identify resources for responding to health literacy needs in clinical practice.

The Importance of Health Literacy in Rehabilitation and Health

Although adequate health literacy is critical for functioning efficiently throughout the health care process, at least 46% of the adult population, approximately 90 million people, lack a sufficient foundation of basic skills to function successfully; including reading basic materials, comprehension, and providing and seeking information (National Institute for Literacy, n.d.). More conservative, yet consistent, estimates suggest 40% to 48% of adult Americans struggle with functional literacy tasks (Andrus & Roth, 2002; Kirsch, Jungeblut, Jenkins, & Kolstad, 1993). Further, Kutner, Greenberg, and Baer (2005) suggest more than one-third of English-speaking patients and more than one-half of primarily Spanish-speaking patients have low health literacy.

Partnership for Clear Health Communication (n.d.) suggests that people with low health literacy are often less likely to comply with prescribed treatment and self-care regimens, they often fail to seek preventive care, and they are at higher (more than double) risk for hospitalization. In addition, they often remain in the hospital nearly 2 days longer than adults with higher health literacy, and they often require additional care that results in annual health care costs that are four times higher than for those with higher literacy skills.

The impact of health literacy affects the health process in many ways. Pawlak (2005) suggests, "Low literacy, an aging population, prevalence in chronic conditions, and a complicated health care system influence and magnify health disparities in the United States" (p. 174). Inadequate health literacy is associated with less health-related knowledge, decreased comprehension of medical information, poorer health status, poor compliance rates, infrequent and delayed use of preventative services, increased hospitalization, increased use of emergency services, increased health care costs, and inadequate management of chronic illness (Andrus & Roth, 2002; Dewalt, Berkman, Sheridan, Lohr, & Pignone, 2004; Pawlak, 2005).

In addition, the average individual reads at the eighth- to ninth-grade level; however, most health-related materials are written at a higher reading level (Partnership for Clear Health Communication, n.d.). Limited general literacy skills (eighth- to ninth-grade level) combined with complex health content written at advanced reading levels result in inadequate use and comprehension of health information. Due to the compounded nature of this problem, nearly half of the population is unprepared to effectively access, navigate and engage in the health care process and, therefore, put themselves at risk of inadequate care, negative outcomes, and unnecessary costs.

Most experts will admit concerns about the nation's health care system being overburdened and nearing collapse. Low health literacy skills for millions of Americans is a contributing factor, with inadequate health literacy translating into tens of billions of dollars a year in U.S. health system costs (Partnership for Clear Health Communication, n.d.). The Center on an Aging Society at Georgetown University (1999) estimates that low health literacy costs the nation at least $73 billion annually. The incurring costs of medical errors, unnecessary hospitalization, extended hospital stays, medical nonadherence, and delayed onset of health care all contribute to the exorbitant cost incurred annually by Americans. Identifying and responding to patients' health literacy needs can significantly contribute to improving the quality of the health care process and outcomes while simultaneously conserving limited resources. Continued efforts in responding to health literacy needs are critical in addressing the nation's health care priorities.

Professional Definitions of Health Literacy

Defining health literacy provides a descriptive context for understanding what skills are required to function effectively throughout the health care process. *Health literacy* is identified as a complex construct with many contributing variables, such as: reading, seeking, exchanging, understanding, and using health information. *Healthy People 2010* defines health literacy as, "The degree to which individuals have the capacity to obtain, process, and understand basic health information and services needed to make appropriate health decisions" (U.S. Department of Health and Human Services, 2000, pp. 11–20). Additionally, the National Health Education Standards define health literacy as, "the capacity of individuals to obtain, interpret, and understand basic health information and services and the competence to use such information and services in ways which enhance health" (Joint Committee on National Health Education Standards, 1995, p. 5). Thus, health literacy is not only the ability to read and comprehend health materials, but also requires the application of listening, analyzing, and decision-making skills in a diversity of health situations (Consumer Health Advisory Committee, 2000).

The Council of Scientific Affairs of the American Medical Association (1999) refers to functional health literacy as, "the ability to read and comprehend prescription bottles, appointment slips, and the other essential health-related materials required to successfully function as a patient" (p. 552). This definition implies not only a basis of knowledge, but also the ability to apply knowledge and *function* as an active participant in one's own health care. In addition to basic reading, writing, and communication skills, functional health literacy includes the capability to understand instructions on prescription drug bottles and medical education materials, comprehend doctor's instructions, find information, and analyze health information (Committee on Health Literacy, 2004). Other functional health literacy skills include actively participating in health encounters; understanding and giving consent; advocating rights; and the general ability to access, negotiate, and navigate within complex health care systems (Committee on Health Literacy, 2004). Not only are there many skills required to proficiently participate in one's health care, but health literacy capabilities vary by context and setting and are not contingent on years of education or general reading capability. An individual who is literate, in general, may have inadequate functional health literacy capabilities in the health care environment (Consumer Health Advisory Committee, 2000).

As individuals navigate through the health care process, they use forms of communication, such as writing, reading, analysis, and comprehension, to effectively interact with health care providers and participate in decision making. Health literacy skills are critical in equipping individuals with what they need to interact with health care providers and understand health information, function with competency within the health care system, and make health care and self-care decisions to effectively mange their health condition. If individuals have difficulty with any of these skills, they are at increased risk of experiencing poor health-related outcomes (Partnership for Clear Health Communication, n.d.). Because patients rely on these basic forms of communication and comprehension to progress through the health care system, an adequate level of health literacy is critical for experiencing an optimal health care process.

Further, Baker (2006) suggests several factors contribute to the measurement of one's health literacy level, including reading fluency, prior knowledge, complexity of health information, oral complexity, culture, social norms, and barriers. Pawlak (2005) proposes the following determinants of health literacy: age, genetics (cognition and ability), language, race and ethnicity (culture), education (reading level and technologic competence), employment, socioeconomic status, and environment (access to care and technology). Because there are many contributing variables to being functionally health literate anyone is likely to need assistance with the various capabilities required, regardless of demographics or socioeconomic status (U.S. Department of Health and Human Services, 2000).

Overall, authoritative sources suggest preventing adverse outcomes related to low health literacy skills can potentially prevent unnecessary health care costs. Currently, ideal practice standards include increasing provider awareness and screening patients for inadequate health literacy skills to allow timely assistance. Appropriate timely interventions and support can promote a high quality health care experience and optimal outcomes for patients in diverse health care settings.

Historical Development of Health Literacy Assessment

Health literacy was conceptualized in 1974 in the context of health education (Simonds, 1974). Over the years, the concept has grown into a field of study with an increasing amount of national attention. Development of health literacy assessment progressed in the early nineties with the development of the Rapid Estimate of Adult Literacy in Medicine (REALM; Davis et al., 1993) and the Test of Functional Health Literacy in Adults (TOFHLA; Parker, Baker, Williams, & Nurss, 1995), which, to date, are still the most commonly used assessments of health literacy.

Health literacy was identified as a national priority in 2000 in the *Healthy People 2010* report, which identified health literacy as a significant factor in increasing health and the quality of health and reducing disparities for the nation's citizens. Further reports, in 2004, by the IOM and the Agency for Healthcare Research and Quality, put the topic of health literacy in the spotlight of national health care. The impact of these reports was illustrated by the release of the 2005 National Assessment of Adult Literacy (NAAL) data, suggesting a significant portion of the nation's population lacked adequate literacy skills (Kutner et al., 2005). Safeer and Keenan (2005) summarize the current status of health literacy in the medical environment and their recommendations to rectify identified problems as follows:

> *Though most adults read at an eighth-grade level, and twenty percent of the population reads at or below a fifth-grade level, most healthcare materials are written at a 10th-grade level. Older patients are particularly affected because their reading and comprehension abilities are influenced by their cognition and their vision and hearing status. Inadequate health literacy can result in difficulty accessing healthcare, following instructions from a physician, and taking medication properly. Patients with inadequate health literacy are more likely to be hospitalized than patients with adequate skills. Patients understand medical information better when spoken to slowly, simple words are used, and a restricted amount of information is presented. For optimal comprehension and compliance, patient education material should be written at a sixth-grade or lower reading level, preferably including pictures and illustrations. All patients prefer reading medical information written in clear and concise language. Physicians should be alert to this problem because most patients are unwilling to admit that they have literacy problems. (p. 463)*

Though the history of health literacy is brief, it is clear that health literacy will remain a central factor in increasing the quality of health care and outcomes for individuals to promote the nation's health priorities. Central to this lofty goal is developing and documenting effective and efficient health literacy screening assessments that can be used to quickly and accurately assess patients' health literacy needs.

30.1

Health literacy within the context of WHO's ICF Model.

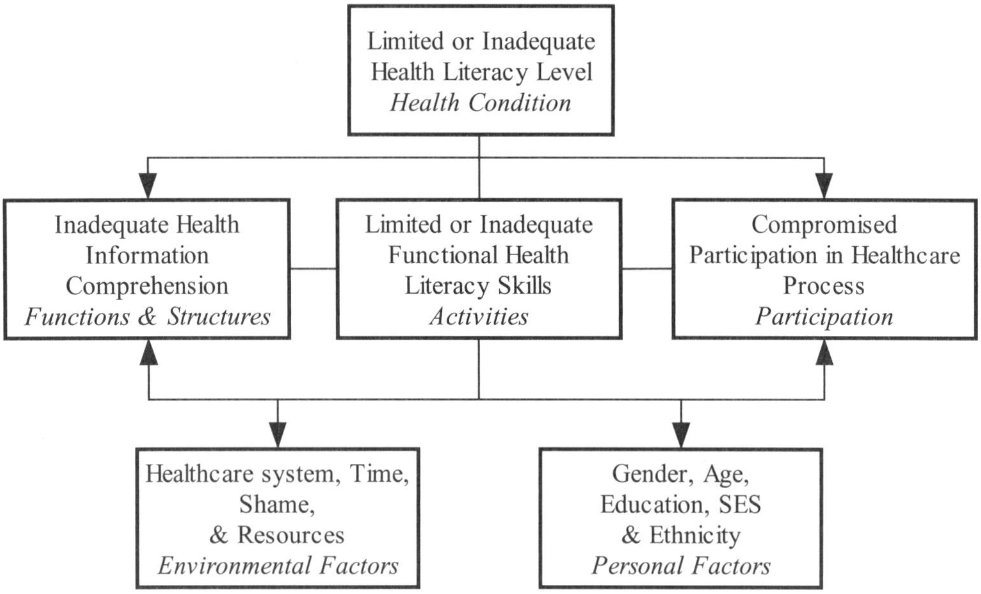

Health Literacy Within the ICF

As with most other important health care topics, health literacy assessment in rehabilitation and health is better understood within the context of WHO's ICF model (see Figure 30.1). This section addresses the core issues in health literacy screening within WHO's ICF model.

Functioning and Disability

Body Functions and Structures

Unlike many other disabilities and health conditions, health literacy does not directly affect the human body. However, limited or inadequate health literacy can be understood as a limited cognitive function, thus affecting the psychological structure of the individual. This cognitive limitation can adversely affect an individual and their health care process and outcomes in many ways. These adverse outcomes are further discussed in the following section.

Activities and Participation

Though adequate health literacy is critical for functioning efficiently throughout the health care process, approximately 90 million people lack a sufficient foundation of basic skills to function successfully, including reading basic materials, comprehension, and providing and seeking information (National Institute for Literacy, n.d.). More conservative, yet consistent, estimates suggest 40%–48% of adult Americans struggle with functional literacy tasks (Andrus & Roth, 2002; Kirsch et al., 1993). Of adults in the United States, 14% have a below basic level of prose literacy; 12% have below basic document literacy; and 22% have below basic quantitative literacy (Kutner et al., 2005). In adults 64 years of age or older, 23% have below basic prose literacy; 27% have below basic document literacy; and 34% have below basic quantitative literacy (Kutner et al.). If an individual does not demonstrate adequate general literacy, it can be inferred that complex health information will also present issues with comprehension. Thus, inadequate literacy skills are an indicator of an individual's health literacy skills. According to the *National Assessment of Adult Literacy,* among adults in the United States, 14% have a below basic level of prose literacy, 12% have below basic document literacy, and 22% have below basic quantitative literacy (Kutner et al., 2005). In adults 64 years of age or older, 23% have below basic prose literacy, 27% have below basic document literacy, and 34% have below basic quantitative literacy (Kutner et al., 2005). Estimates suggest 40%–48% of adult Americans struggle with functional literacy tasks (Andrus & Roth, 2002; Kirsch et al., 1993). Specific to the measure of health literacy, the *Institute of Medicine* suggests 90 million people lack a sufficient foundation of basic health literacy skills to function successfully, including reading basic materials, comprehension, and providing and seeking information. With a conservative estimate of 1 in 3 individuals lacking necessary skills to properly use health information, it is apparent that a significant portion of the American population is unable to access, navigate, and properly use health services within the healthcare system, compromising their healthcare process and health related outcomes.

Contextual Factors

Environmental Factors

There are several environmental factors that can adversely affect individuals with limited or inadequate health literacy. Most health care systems in our nation are not adequately supplied with resources to properly implement a health literacy initiative that is supported by screening and response resources. However, beyond this general limitation, two primary environmental factors that adversely affect individuals with limited or inadequate health literacy are *time* and *shame.*

Shame

Practitioners and educators should first realize that individuals with inadequate health literacy often do not realize or acknowledge their lack of health literacy (Parker, Davis, & Williams, 1999). Due to the stigma associated with the inability to read, people with inadequate literacy skills often feel ashamed when they have trouble reading. Thus, individuals will often hide their inability to read and comprehend information (Baker et al., 1996; Parikh, Parker, Nurss, Baker, & Williams, 1996). Often individuals with low literacy do not bring anyone to help them, and they do not ask for assistance (Parikh et al., 1996). This can make identifying individuals with inadequate literacy difficult. Further, recent

Research Box 30.1

Parikh, N. S., Parker, R. M., Nurss, J. R., Baker, D. W., & Williams, M. V. (1996). Shame and health literacy: The unspoken connection. *Patient Education Counseling, 27*(1), 33–39.

Objective: To understand the connection between limited health literacy and shame in the health care setting.

Methods: Demographic survey, the Test of Functional Health Literacy in Adults, and interview questions about difficulty reading and shame were collected from 202 predominantly African American participants in a large public hospital in Atlanta, Georgia.

Results: Of those interviewed, 42.6% had limited or inadequate health literacy skills. Of those with limited and inadequate health literacy, 67.4% admitted they have trouble reading and understanding health materials, and 40% admitted experiencing shame. Sixty-seven percent of patients with low literacy did not tell their spouse, 53.4% did not tell their children, and 19% reported never telling anyone about their difficulty with reading.

Conclusion: Patients who have difficulty reading experience shame and hide their inability to read. It is important to understand how shame influences the way patients interact with health care providers. Further research is needed to understand how providers can best deal with shame in the health care setting when responding to patients health literacy needs.

Questions:
How can researchers and clinicians collaborate to create shame-free environments that support patients health literacy needs?

Often information that is obvious to the provider may be new and confusing to a patient, regardless of their education or background. What strategies can providers use to avoid condescending behavior, promote patient understanding, and provide a safe supportive environment that invites patients to openly acknowledge their literacy needs?

findings suggest there is potential for harm resultant from shame and alienation, subsequent to clinical screening. Creating a supportive, nonstigmatizing environment for low literacy patients can promote proactive behaviors rather than perpetuate feelings of shame (Parker, 2000). Clinicians and researchers can collaborate in efforts to prevent shame and alienation associated with limited literacy skills and to promote implementation of innovative strategies to empower and support patients who have difficulty with health information. Providing a shame-free empowering environment will reinforce patients' ability to effectively communicate and navigate through the health care system.

Time

Although health literacy screening is a logical solution to identifying patients with health literacy needs, time constraints are a significant barrier to getting health professionals to assess their patients' health literacy levels. On average, a general practitioner conducts 120,000 to 160,000 patient interviews in a 40-year career (Center for the Advancement of Health, 2003). The average length of a patient–physician interaction is 20.4 minutes, up from 16.3 minutes in 1989 (Mechanic, McAlpine, & Rosenthal, 2001). Researchers note that although this amount of time is adequate, patients are often unable to disclose all their concerns, ask important questions, and engage in meaningful dialogue because they are constantly interrupted in an already limited time period (Thompson, 1998). Patients trying to behave and act as a "good patient" are silent in order to not take up the valuable time of a rushed provider. Even if medical encounters allow enough time for discussion, individuals who are not equipped with functional health literacy skills may be unlikely to assert themselves in discussions with their doctor. Finally, if clinicians do screen their patients, they are then responsible for intervening when necessary, which may require additional time. Unfortunately, many clinicians are not adequately prepared with skills and resources to effectively intervene with patients' health literacy needs.

Personal Factors

Because there are many contributing variables to being functionally health literate, anyone is likely to need assistance with the various capabilities required, regardless of demographical status (U.S. Department of Health and Human Services, 2000). However, certain populations, such as the elderly, minorities, immigrants, and individuals with low socioeconomic status, are disproportionately affected by the negative outcomes of low and marginal health literacy skills (Kirsch et al., 1993). For example, Sudore and colleagues (2006) analyzed the relationship between health literacy, demographics, and access to health care. Their findings suggest, "After adjusting for socio-demographics, associations remained between limited health literacy and being male, being black, and having low income and education, diabetes mellitus, depressive symptoms, and fair/poor self-rated health ($P < .02$)" (p. 770).

Further, after adjusting for sociodemographics, health status, and comorbidities, older people with a sixth-grade reading level or lower were twice as likely to have any of the three indicators of poor health care access (odds ratio = 1.96, 95% confidence interval = 1.34–2.88) (Sudore et al., 2006). Limited health literacy was prevalent and was associated with low socioeconomic status, comorbidities, and poor access to health care, suggesting, "It may be an independent risk factor for health disparities in older people" (Sudore et al., p. 770). The majority of adults 60 years old and older have inadequate or marginal literacy skills, half of welfare recipients read below the fifth-grade level, and 40%–50% of minorities have reading problems (Kirsch et al., 1993). Low levels of health literacy can affect the health care process in many ways, and cumulating risk factors can have a negative additive effect.

Cultural barriers significantly moderate the likelihood of patient involvement (Thompson, 1998). Ethnicity and cultural background can influence patient–provider communication and patients' level of functional health literacy in at least three ways: (1) they may have different languages or dialects, (2) preferred styles of communication may differ, and (3) people from different cultures have different explanatory models for health and illness (Cooper & Roter, 2003; Cooper-Patrick et al., 1999).

Other factors that might adversely impact a patient's active participation in his/her health care include entry into the health care encounter while ill with considerable emotional strain, being disrobed during the interaction led by a provider who typically limits patient responses. Cumulative effects of these complex personal variables compound an already complex interaction.

Health Literacy Assessment Methods

There are several measures designed to evaluate an individual's literacy level. Andrus and Roth (2002) and Pawlak (2005) have identified the most popular assessments, as illustrated in Table 30.1. Specific to health literacy, several assessments have been developed for clinical assessment of patients' health literacy skills. The Rapid Estimate of Adult Literacy in Medicine (REALM) and the Test of Functional Health Literacy in Adults (TOFHLA) are the most commonly used measures of health literacy; however, even with extensive research, "neither test is a comprehensive assessment of an individual's capacities. Rather, the tests measure selected domains that are thought to be markers for an individual's overall capacity ... [and are] clearly inadequate" (Baker, 2006, p. 880).

As educators and practitioners prepare to assist individuals with low health literacy, it is important to have an understanding of the general levels of literacy. Sometimes general reading assessments are based on criteria for four to five levels (on a scale from 0 to 500), which can provide an indication of level of health literacy abilities (see Table 30.2). Individuals scoring at level one have the ability to perform simple tasks, and those who score at levels four and five are able to perform long complex tasks requiring higher cognitive levels of analysis (National Institute for Literacy, n.d.). Commonly, both general and health literacy assessments focus on a three-point scale with the first level being subaverage, mid-level being marginal, and the higher level being a gradation of proficiency. More commonly, general literacy levels are indicated by academic grade levels or equivalencies, with the numerical value correlating with the individual's grade level. For example, if a fifth grader reads and applies skills on grade level, then the individual's score is a "5"; if below grade level, then a "3" or "4" depending on their skills and abilities (Committee on Health Literacy, 2004).

The following sections discuss three of the most commonly used assessments of Health Literacy: the TOFHLA, the REALM, and the Newest Vital Sign (NVS). Health literacy screening items, which have been clinically tested in multiple settings, are reviewed. Informal assessment methods are also reviewed.

Test of Functional Health Literacy in Adults

The Test of Functional Health Literacy in Adults (TOFHLA; Parker et al., 1995; Nurss, Parker, Williams, & Baker, 2001), which is commonly used as an indicator for level of health literacy skills, divides scores into three criterion levels: (1) inadequate (0–16), (2) marginal (17–22), and (3) adequate (23–36; see Table 30.2). Individuals' scoring at level one on the TOFHLA do not possess the necessary

30.1 Common General Literacy and Health Literacy Screening Assessments

Variable	WRAT-R	REALM	MART	SORT-R	PIAT-R	IDL	NVS-S	BRIEF	TOFHLA
Description	Word Recognition Test	Medical Word Recognition Test (multiple versions)	Medical Word Recognition Test	Word Recognition Test	Reading Recognition & Comprehension Test	Reading Comprehension Test	Food Label Comprehension	Self-Report	Reading Comprehension & Numerical Ability Test
Age	5–74 years	Adults Only	High school	4 years and older	All ages	All ages	Adults Only	Adults Only	Adults Only
Time to Administer (minutes)	3–5	2–7	3–5	5–10	60	20–30	3	1–2	22 (7 for short-form version)
Scoring	Raw score of 1–57, converted to grade equivalent	Approximate grade level: 3rd and below; 4th–6th, 7th–8th, or 9th and above	Raw score converted to grade equivalent	Results converted to age and grade equivalent	Comprehension subtest score determines grade level	0–8, 0 = failure at first grade level, 8 = 8th grade level or above	Raw score 0–6: 0–1 = high likelihood of limited literacy; 2–3 = possibly limited literacy; 4–6 = almost always adequate literacy	Raw score 4–20: 4–12 = inadequate literacy; 13–16 = marginal literacy; 17–20 = adequate literacy	Comprehension and numeracy test: inadequate, marginal, or functional health literacy
Advantages	Quick	Quick, uses medical terminology	Quick, nonthreatening	Quick	Assesses Comprehension	Available in Spanish	Quick and available in Spanish	Quick and easy to administer	Available in Spanish
Limitations	Difficult	Assigns only grade range equivalent	Limited clinical validation	Small print; many items; intimidating	Long	Long	Doesn't address all aspects of health literacy; limited clinical validation	Limited clinical validation	Long, but short version is also available STOFHLA
Correlation with other Tests (r value)	PIAT-R 0.62-0.91	WRAT 0.88, SORT-R 0.96, PIAT-R 0.97, TOFHLA 0.84	WRAT 0.98	PIAT-R 0.83-0.90	Not Available	0.65–0.70 with other English assessments	TOFHLA .49	REALM .40, STOFHLA 42	WRAT 0.74, REALM 0.84

WRAT-R = Wide Range Achievement Test-Revised; REALM = Rapid Estimate of Adult Literacy in Medicine; MART = Medical Terminology Achievement Reading Test; SORT-R = Slosson Oral Reading Test-Revised; PIAT-R = Peabody Individual Achievement Test-Revised; IDL = Instrument for the Diagnosis of Reading; NVS = Newest Vital Sign Short Form; BRIEF = BRIEF Health Literacy Screening Tool; TOFHLA = Test of Functional Health Literacy in Adults.

From "Health Literacy: A Review," by M. R. Andrus and M. T. Roth, 2002, *Pharmacotherapy, 22,* 284–285. Adapted with permission. Published in "Economic Considerations of Health Literacy," by R. Pawlak, 2005, *Nursing Economics, 23,* 173–180.

30.2 Scale for Levels of TOFHLA/S-TOFHLA and General Literacy Skills

TOFHLA Level	TOFHLA Score	General Literacy Score	Skills and Abilities
Inadequate	0–16	0–225	Able to perform uncomplicated tasks involving brief and uncomplicated texts and documents.
Marginal	17–22	226–275	Able to locate information in text, make low level inferences using printed materials, and integrate easily identifiable pieces of information.
		275–325	Able to integrate information from relatively long or dense texts or documents, determine appropriate arithmetic operations based on information contained in the directive, and identify quantities needed to perform operation.
Adequate	23–36	326–375 376–500	Adults at these levels demonstrate proficiencies associated with long and complex documents and text passages; able to determine and interpret qualitative and quantitative data needed to perform an operation.

skills to function efficiently when executing health literacy–related tasks. Individuals scoring at level 2 have marginal skills that allow for achieving simple tasks, but not complex tasks; whereas those scoring at level three have the skills necessary to accomplish health literacy–related tasks proficiently.

The S-TOFHLA is a shortened version of the original TOFHLA (Parker et al., 1995; Nurss et al., 2001). S-TOFHLA is made up of 2 prose passages with 36 fill-in-the-blank response items worth 1 point each. The possible score range is 0–36. The maximum time for administration is 7 minutes. S-TOFHLA scores divide health literacy skills into three criterion levels: (1) inadequate (0–16), (2) marginal (17–22), and (3) adequate (23–36). In a group of 211 patients, Cronbach's alpha for the S-TOFHLA was 0.97. Spearman's correlation between the S-TOFHLA and the REALM was 0.80 (Baker, Williams, Parker, Gazmararian, & Nurss, 1999).

Rapid Estimate of Adult Literacy in Medicine

The Rapid Estimate of Adult Literacy in Medicine (REALM; Davis et al., 1993) has three levels, which correspond to the general reading grade levels with scores ranging from 0 to 66 (see Table 30.3). These levels allow for an interchangeable scaling system for evaluating general and health literacy. The REALM assesses health literacy through the use of 3 columns of 22 words each. The words in each column are listed in ascending order of difficulty. The REALM produces

30.3 Levels for Grade Equivalent Scale of the Rapid Estimate of Adult Literacy in Medicine (REALM)

REALM Level	REALM Score	Grade Level	Skills and Abilities
Limited	0–44	0–6	Not able to read most low literacy health materials; will need repeated oral instructions; materials should be composed of illustrations or video tapes. Will need low literacy materials; may not be able to read a prescription label.
Marginal	45–60	7–8	Will struggle with most patient education materials.
Adequate	61–66	9 and above	Will be able to read and comprehend most patient education materials.

a summed score based on the number of correctly pronounced words in each column. REALM scores range from 0 to 66 and are divided into three criterion levels, namely, limited (0–44), marginal (45–60), and adequate (61–66). Davis and colleagues (1993) tested the REALM with three other standardized reading tests—the reading recognition section of the Peabody Individual Achievement Test-Revised (PIAT-R), the Wide Range Achievement Test-Revised (WRAT-R), and the Slosson Oral Reading Test-Revised (SORT-R)—to establish instrument validity with a sample of 203 patients. The REALM correlated well with the three other tests. Correlation coefficients were 0.97 (PIAT-R), 0.88 (WRAT-R), and 0.96 (SORT-R), ($p < .0001$). To determine test—retest reliability, 100 inmates at a state prison were given the REALM twice, 1 week apart. Test–retest reliability was 0.99 ($p < .001$). Intrasubject reliability for REALM has been reported as 0.97 (Davis et al., 1993).

More recently, Bass, Wilson, and Griffith (2003) tested an 8-item revised version of the REALM, the REALM-R. The REALM-R was administered to 157 patients. The REALM-R was correlated with Wide Range Achievement Test-Revised (WRAT-R;.64) and demonstrated a Cronbach's alpha of 0.91. The REALM-R identified a substantial number of people who scored poorly on the WRAT-R.

The Newest Vital Sign

The Newest Vital Sign (NVS) is a recently published health literacy assessment and simulates a functional health literacy using a nutrition label task (note: nutrition labels and prescription labels are most commonly identified as misunderstood health information). The NVS is a bilingual (English and Spanish) screening tool that can be administered in 3 minutes. It is based on the comprehension and use of nutrition label information from an ice cream container. Patients are given the label and then asked six questions about the information on the label. Based on the number of correct responses, the health care provider can assess the patient's health literacy level. The raw score range is 0–6: 0–1 = high likelihood of limited literacy, 2–3 = possibly limited literacy, 4–6 = almost always indicates adequate literacy. The NVS-S moderately correlated with the TOFHLA ($r = 0.49$, $p < .001$). The NVS-S also gleaned an area under the ROC curve for predicting TOFHLA-S scores was 0.72 (95% CI, 0.62–0.76; $p < .001$); for the NVS-S, 0.69 (95% CI, 0.62–0.76; $p < .001$). Scoring less than 2 on the NVS-S showed 77% sensitivity and 57% specificity for predicting limited health literacy; whereas scoring less than 4 gleaned 100% sensitivity and 19% specificity (Weiss et al., 2005). Subsequent research by Osborn et al. (2007) suggested that when the NVS was tested against the S-TOFHLA, the area under the ROC curve was 0.71–0.73; however, NVS scores were not associated with health outcomes.

Health Literacy Screening Items

Chew, Bradley, and Boyko (2004) examined 16 screening questions to determine which best identified individuals with marginal or inadequate health literacy skills. Three of the screening questions were effective in detecting inadequate health literacy: "How often do you have someone help you read hospital materials?" "How confident are you filling out medical forms by yourself?" and "How often do you have problems learning about your medical condition because of difficulty understanding written information?" The area under the receiver operating characteristic curve (AUROC) was 0.87, 0.80, and 0.76. Wallace, Rogers, Roskos, Holiday, and Weiss (2006) continued Chew and colleagues' (2004) work and tested the three individual items with 305 participants. They computed the AUROC for each item, using REALM scores as a reference standard. In Wallace and colleagues' sample, 54 (17.7%) had limited and 52 (17.0%) had marginal health literacy skills. One screening question, "How confident are you filling out medical forms by yourself?" was accurate in detecting limited (AUROC of 0.82; 95% confidence interval [CI] = 0.77 to 0.86) and limited/marginal (AUROC of 0.79; 95% CI = 0.74 to 0.83) health literacy skills; the item had a significantly greater AUROC than the other questions ($P < .01$). (Note: Wallace conducted further research with these items in a surgery setting. For details see the section "Health Literacy Assessment for Specific Populations, Diseases, and Healthcare Settings—Surgery.")

Based on these findings, Haun and colleagues (in press) conducted a study, using the three items with the addition of a fourth item, "How often do you have a problem understanding what is told to you about your medical condition?" in an attempt to increase the construct validity of the tool by addressing the comprehension of oral health information. The addition of this item completed the development of the 4-item BRIEF health literacy screening tool to be validated against the previously published REALM and S-TOFHLA.

The study tested four items using the S-TOFHLA and REALM: (1) How often do you have someone help you read hospital materials? (2) How confident are you filling out medical forms by yourself? (3) How often do you have a problem learning about your medical condition because of difficulty understanding written information? and (4) How often do you have a problem understanding what is told to you about your medical condition? Response options were offered in a five-point Likert scale for each of the items. Items 1, 3, and

4 (1 = always to 5 = never); and item 2 (1 = not at all to 5 = extremely). This study gleaned a positive significant correlation between the BRIEF, REALM, & S-TOFHLA; r (378) =.40, p <.01 for the BRIEF and REALM; r (378) =.42, p <.01 for the BRIEF and S-TOFHLA; and r (378) =.61, p <.01 for the REALM and S-TOFHLA (Haun et al., in press). A Principal Component Analysis findings suggest the BRIEF health literacy screening tool measures one distinct construct—"health literacy" (eigenvalue = 2.388) accounting for 60% of score variance. The BRIEF gleaned an area under the ROC curve, .79 (95% CI =.70–.87), versus inadequate and marginal, .69 (95% CI =.64–.75), with the REALM. With the S-TOFHLA, findings indicate the BRIEF items identify individuals with inadequate health literacy skills, .76 (95% CI =.69–.83), with slightly more accuracy than individuals with inadequate or marginal health literacy skills, .74 (95% CI =.67–.80). All of the items had an AUROC greater than 0.5 at 95% CI (Haun et al., in press). The BRIEF had a higher AUROC than any of the single items, indicating the BRIEF is a better screening tool than the single items. An Analysis of Variance (ANOVA) was conducted to determine if the group differences for the score intervals were significant; findings indicate the three proposed BRIEF levels were significantly different from one another on the REALM (F = 28.63, p <.000) and S-TOFHLA (F = 35.32, p <.000). Based on previous research (Chew et al., 2004; Haun et al., in press; Wallace et al., 2006) and statistical findings, three levels are recommended for interpreting BRIEF score intervals: 4–12 = inadequate, 13–16 = marginal, and 17–20 = adequate. Implementing these items in the clinical setting takes between 1 and 2 minutes.

Research concerning these screening items indicates clinicians can use at least one screening item, related to an individual's confidence level when filling out medical form, to assess patients' health literacy level, if necessary. However, with the addition of three brief items, the BRIEF screening tool addresses diverse functional health literacy skills, including reading comprehension, auditory health information, and the ability to learn about one's medical condition. This information can be most informative when determining how to best respond to patients' health literacy needs.

Informal Assessment of Health Literacy

Informal assessments can also be made to identify individuals who might need formal assessment and assistance with health information. For example, a practitioner can ask patients about their education level. Though some individuals with limited education can learn to effectively comprehend and use health information, individuals with an eighth-grade education or less are likely to have inadequate health literacy (Parker, 2000). Individuals with a ninth-grade education or higher are harder to identify for health literacy problems and usually require formal assessment (Parker, 2000). Providers can use the following check list of patient behaviors as informal indicators of limited health literacy:

- Providing inaccurate or incomplete histories
- Difficulty navigating the health care system
- Asking staff for help
- Bringing along someone who can read
- Inability to keep appointments

- Making excuses ("I forgot my glasses")
- Noncompliance with medication
- Poor adherence to recommended interventions
- Postponing decision making ("I'll read through this when I get home")
- Not seeking preventive care
- Incorrectly filling out forms
- Watching others (mimicking behavior)
- Answering all items in an identical fashion
- Concrete thinking; literal interpretation of words and visuals
- Missing principal features and/or getting lost in details
- Inability to interpret perceptual information
- Avoidance of printed materials
- Often looking around with poor eye contact when receiving information

Though these indicators can assist providers in identifying individuals who need assistance with health information, research indicates that providers accurately identify individuals with low literacy only 40% of the time. This percentage warrants efforts in research and practice to develop valid formal screening assessments and interventions for patients with limited or inadequate health literacy skills.

Health Literacy Assessment for Specific Populations, Diseases, and Health Care Settings

As development of health literacy assessment has progressed, researchers and clinicians have recognized the need to create instruments for specific populations. This allows researchers to develop instrumentation that aligns assessment with content specific to particular populations and diseases. This section identifies some current research efforts in developing health literacy assessments to meet the needs of specific populations and diseases.

Genetics

Health information, such as genetic information, presents challenges to all patients. Erby, Roter, Larson, and Cho (2008) developed the Rapid Estimate of Adult Literacy in Genetics (REAL-G), which provides a screening tool that can be used to quickly identify patients with low literacy skills in the clinical genetics context. This tool is similar to the REALM, using word recognition, in English, with varying degrees of difficulty.

Dentistry

Richman et al. (2007) developed and tested another tool similar to the REALM, the Rapid Estimate of Adult Literacy in Dentistry (REALD-99), for measuring dental health literacy. The REALD-99 scores had a possible range of 0 (low literacy) to 99 (high literacy); REALM scores ranged from 0 to 66. With a sample of 102, the REALD-99 was positively correlated with REALM (PCC = 0.80);

REALD-99 had good reliability (Cronbach's alpha = 0.86). Lee, Rozier, Lee, Bender, and Ruiz (2007) also developed a shorter version, the Rapid Estimate of Adult Literacy in Dentistry (REALD-30), which consisted of 30 common dental words with a range of difficulty. REALD-30 scores were also significantly correlated with REALM scores.

Diabetes

The Literacy Assessment for Diabetes (LAD) instrument is a word recognition test composed of three-word lists in ascending difficulty, similar to the REALM. Nath, Sylvester, Yasek, and Gunel (2001) developed this literacy test to measures patients' ability to pronounce terms that they would encounter while receiving care for diabetes. Using the Wide Range Achievement Test (WRAT3) and the REALM, they tested the LAD with 203 participants. LAD measured word recognition ability similar to the REALM and WRAT3. The raw score of the LAD is scaled to a reading grade level.

Surgery

Using items previously tested, Wallace and colleagues (2007) tested three items in a surgery clinic: "How often do you have someone (like a family member, friend, or hospital worker) help you read hospital materials?" (AUROC of 0.83; 95% confidence interval [CI] = 0.73, 0.92); "How often do you have problems learning about your medical condition because of difficulty understanding written information?" (AUROC of 0.77; 95% CI = 0.67, 0.86); and "How confident are you filling out medical forms by yourself?" (AUROC of 0.76; 95% CI = 0.66, 0.86). Findings indicated each were effective in detecting those with limited/marginal skills in a surgery-based setting. Most recently, using the S-TOFHLA and REALM, Chew and colleagues (2008) evaluated three questions to detect inadequate and marginal health literacy. Based on a large sample of 1,796, "How confident are you filling out medical forms by yourself?" had the largest AUROC of 0.74 (95% CI: 0.69–0.79) and 0.84 (95% CI: 0.79–0.89).

Youth Populations

Sanders. Zacur, Haecker, and Klass (2004) tested seven screening questions to determine which is most useful for identifying parents with adequate health literacy. Two factors were independently associated with adequate health literacy: more than 10 adults' books or more than 10 children's books in the home, with a positive predictive value of 91%. Findings suggest having more than 10 children's books in the home is a useful, independent indicator of adequate parent health literacy. Clinicians can ask parents about the number of adults' and/or children's books in the home to identify parents with adequate health literacy.

Davis and colleagues (2006) tested the Rapid Estimate of Adolescent Literacy in Medicine (REALM-Teen), a word-recognition test similar to the REALM, with 1,533 adolescents aged 10 to 19 years. Davis et al. (2006) tested the REALM-Teen using the Wide Range Achievement Test–Revised (WRAT-3) and Slosson Oral Reading Test–Revised (SORT-R). The REALM-Teen was determined to be strongly correlated with both the WRAT-R and SORT-R; five reading level categories were identified: 3rd grade and below, 4th to 5th grade, 6th to 7th grade, 8th to 9th grade, and 10th grade and above. The REALM-Teen takes only 3 minutes to administer.

As clinicians, researchers, and administrators continue to recognize the importance of assessing health literacy within the health care and rehabilitation setting, population and disease specific assessments will continue to be developed, tested, and published. Clinicians and researchers can benefit from staying current with published health literacy research—as population and disease specific assessments are increasing in availability for both research and clinical practice.

Critical Issues in Health Literacy Assessment

While several health literacy screening assessments have been developed, many require specialized materials, time, and scoring interpretation. The greatest weakness of current health literacy assessments is their partial measurement of the larger holistic concept of functional health literacy. Baker (2006) concludes, despite extensive validation research, the REALM and the TOFHLA are "clearly inadequate" (p. 880). Although these two tools are the most commonly used measures of health literacy, Baker proposes neither adequately test "individual's capacities. Rather, the tests measure selected domains that are thought to be markers for an individual's overall capacity" (p. 880). Baker asserts that the inconsistencies between Chew and Wallace's work indicate a need for further research. Further, he and others suggest that additional research is needed to assess health literacy. Parker and Kindig (2006) state that, "More research is needed ... a continued need to advance measuring individual skills. Efforts to advance population-level measurement and indicators are also greatly needed" (pp. 891–892).

Some researchers suggest health literacy screening programs for limited literacy have not been effective and have potential for harm resultant from shame and alienation (Paasche-Orlow & Wolf, 2008). However, they do suggest health literacy assessment instruments warrant further investigation and may have a place in practice when they can be followed up by effective interventions. Some clinicians suggest modifying practice and health information materials to anticipate health literacy needs. Some suggestions for helping patients exchange, understand, and use health information are discussed in the following section.

What to Do: Responding to Health Literacy Needs

Providers and health administrators can implement immediate strategies to assist patients with limited health literacy skills. For example, facilities can provide patients with surrogate readers or advocates to assist them when getting information from practitioners, thereby promoting a support system for successful health care outcomes (Potter & Martin, 2003). Patients identified as having low levels of health literacy should be provided with support, verbal explanations, written materials with only the necessary information presented in

Discussion Box 30.1

Paasche-Orlow, M. K., & Wolf, M. S. (2008). Evidence does not support clinical screening of literacy. *Journal of General Internal Medicine, 23*(1),100–102.

A recent article published by the *Journal of General Internal Medicine* by Paasche-Orlow and Wolf (2008) suggests "Evidence does not support clinical screening of literacy." As the title indicates, these experts in health literacy suggest that although limited health literacy is a risk factor for adverse health outcomes, no screening program for limited literacy has been shown to be effective. Further, they state there is potential for harm resultant from shame and alienation, subsequent to clinical screening. The authors recommend screening for literacy at this time should not be implemented. However, they also suggest there are tools that do warrant further investigation and may be warranted for use in the future when adequate interventions for limited health literacy emerge.

With current efforts in various health organizations supporting health literacy screening, how will the concerns of these authors potentially influence further implementation of screening programs?

If organizations do cease to screen patients for limited health literacy, how will they properly respond to the health literacy needs of their patient populations?

As the authors of this article suggest, appropriate effective interventions must be available to respond to screening outcomes. Discuss and identify current resources and strategies available to practitioners to respond to the needs of individuals with limited health literacy. Are these resources adequate, and do current health care settings support implementation of your identified resources?

How can clinicians and researchers work together to overcome the identified barriers to health literacy screening and promote the development of effective and supportive responses to patients' health literacy needs?

simple terms and pictures, and alternative resources such as videotapes (Parker, 2000; Potter & Martin, 2003).

Providers can use the following check list of strategies to respond to the needs of all patients, particularly those with limited health literacy skills:

- Create a safe supportive environment.
- Be respectful, caring, and sensitive.
- Empower patients to participate.
- Slow down, and take time to assess skills.
- Speak slowly.
- Use clear and concise language and simple words.
- Limit information.

- Print instructions—No scribbling.
- Health/Education materials should be written at a fifth- to sixth-grade or lower reading level.
- Show or draw pictures and illustrations.
- Repeat instructions.
- Use a "teach back" or "show me" method.
- Color code medications.
- Provide a daily pill box to organize medications.
- Leave the room. Give the patient time to think. Come back for questions.
- Get family members/advocates involved.

Implementing these practices will decrease the stigma associated with needing assistance and emphasize the importance of understanding health materials in a shame-free environment. Health care facilities can prepare practitioners to be sensitive to low literacy individuals to promote a shame-free environment (Parikh et al., 1996). Efforts to empower patients with functional health literacy skills, and instill them with the self-efficacy to use them, will promote optimal health care outcomes and an economical and ethical practice. Additionally, when facilities formally implement a health literacy screening process, policy can be implemented to allow clinicians to post patient health literacy scores in patients' medical records to alert the health care team of the patients' health literacy needs. These organizational efforts can not only support individual patient needs, but also support clinicians in responding to patient needs.

Summary

Adverse health outcomes associated with low health literacy affect one in three Americans, approximately 90 million people. Low literacy consumes health care resources equivalent to billions of dollars annually. Authoritative resources suggest health care providers need to identify and respond to patients' literacy skills to prevent personal and system loss. National organizations of health suggest clinicians can screen patients' to alert health care team members of patients' individual health literacy needs. Upon screening, clinicians can refer patients to an official evaluation and/or patient education intervention and tailor their clinical practice to meet the individual needs of patients. However, some health literacy research experts indicate a need for further research to validate the efficacy of such measures. Many variables are associated with inadequate health literacy, yet, the exact relationships between patient variables and health literacy outcomes are unclear. Current research has produced a variety of tools that measure health literacy using methods pronunciation, reading comprehension, and self reports. One limitation of assessments, currently, is these tools measure varying aspects of the construct *health literacy*. Evidence-based research efforts continue to develop culturally sensitive reliable and valid screening tools that address the complexity of functional health literacy to inform research and practice. Maybe, more important than screening patients for health literacy needs is anticipating and responding to individuals who have limited or inadequate health literacy. Providers can equip themselves with innovative strategies to promote effective communication with their patient population, particularly those individuals with limited or inadequate health literacy skills. Statistics suggest health literacy is a national issue that adversely affects 90 million people, however proper assessment and effective supportive interventions can promote an optimal health care process one person at a time.

References

American Medical Association. (1999). *Health Literacy: Report of the Council on Scientific Affairs.* Ad Hoc Committee on Health Literacy for the Council on Scientific Affairs, AMA. *JAMA, 281*(6), 552–557.

Andrus, M. R., & Roth, M. T. (2002). Health literacy: A review. *Pharmacotherapy, 22*(3), 282–302.

Baker, D. W. (2006). The meaning and the measure of health literacy. *Journal of General Internal Medicine, 21*(8), 878–883.

Baker, D. W., Parker, R. M., Williams, M. V., Pitkin, K., Parikh, N. S., Coates, W., et al. (1996). The health care experience of patients with low literacy. *Archives of Family Medicine, 5*(6), 329–334.

Baker, D. W., Williams, M. V., Parker, R. M., Gazmararian, J. A., & Nurss, J. (1999). Development of a brief test to measure functional health literacy. *Patient Education and Counseling, 38*(1), 33–42.

Bass, P. F., Wilson, J. F., & Griffith, C. H. (2003). A shortened instrument for literacy screening. *J Gen Intern Med, 18,* 1036–1038.

Chew, L. D., Bradley, K. A., & Boyko, E. J. (2004). Brief questions to identify patients with inadequate health literacy. *Family Medicine, 36*(8), 588–594.

Chew, L. D., Griffin, J. M., Partin, M. R., Noorbaloochi, S., Grill, J. P., Snyder, A., et al. (2008). Validation of screening questions for limited health literacy in a large VA outpatient population. *Journal of General Internal Medicine, 23*(5), 561–566.

Center for the Advancement of Health. (2003). Talking the talk: Improving patient-provider communication. *Facts of Life: Issue Briefings for Health Reporters, 8*(3). Retrieved January 21, 2007, from: http://www.cfah.org/factsoflife/vol8no3.cfm

Center on an Aging Society at Georgetown University. (1999). *Low health literacy skills increase annual health care expenditures by $73 Billion.* Retrieved May 14, 2004, from: http://ihcrp.georgetown.edu/agingsociety/pubhtml/healthlit.html

Committee on Health Literacy. (2004). *Health Literacy: Prescription to End Confusion.* Washington, DC: Institute of Medicine, The National Academies Press.

Consumer Health Advisory Committee. (2000). *Consumer health manual. National Network of Libraries of Medicine: South Central Region.* Retrieved February 19, 2007, from: http://nnlm.gov/outreach/consumer/

Cooper, L. A., & Roter, D. L. (2003). Patient-provider communication: The effect of race and ethnicity on process and outcomes of healthcare. In Brian D. Smedley, Adrienne Y. Stith, & Alan R. Nelson (Eds.) *Unequal treatment: Confronting racial and ethnic disparities in health care* (pp. 552–593). Washington, DC: The National Academies Press.

Cooper-Patrick, L., Gallo, J. J., Vu, H. T., Powe, N. R., Nelson, C., & Ford, D. E. (1999). Race, gender, and partnership in the patient-provider relationship. *Journal of the American Medical Association, 282,* 583–589.

Davis, T. C., Long, S. W., Jackson, R. H., Mayeaux, E. J., George, R. B., Murphy, P. W., et al. (1993). Rapid estimate of adult literacy in medicine: a shortened screening instrument. *Family Medicine, 25*(6), 391–395.

Davis, T. C., Wolf, M. S., Arnold, C. L., Byrd, R. S., Long, S. W. Springer, T., et al. (2006). Development and validation of the rapid estimate of adolescent literacy in medicine (REAL-Teen): A tool to screen adolescents for below-grade reading in health care settings. *Pediatrics, 118,* e1707–1714.

Dewalt, D. A., Berkman, N. D., Sheridan, S., Lohr, K. N., & Pignone, M. P. (2004). Literacy and health outcomes: A systematic review of the literature. *Journal of General Internal Medicine, 19,* 1128–1139.

Erby, L. H., Roter, D., Larson, S., & Cho, J. (2008). The rapid estimate of adult literacy in genetics (REAL-G): A means to assess literacy deficits in the context of genetics. *American Journal of Medical Genetics, 146A,* 174–181.

Haun, J., Noland-Dodd, V. J., Varnes, J. W., Graham-Pole, J., Rienzo, B. A., & Donaldson, P. (in press). Testing a health literacy screening tool: Implications for utilization of a BRIEF health literacy indicator. *Federal Practitioner.*

Institute of Medicine, Health Literacy. (2004). *A prescription to end confusion.* Washington, DC: National Academies Press.

Joint Committee on National Health Education Standards. (1995). *National health education standards.* Reston, VA: The American School Health Association, The Association for the Advancement of Health Education.

Kirsch, I., Jungeblut, A., Jenkins, L., & Kolstad, A. (1993). *Adult literacy in America: A first look at the findings of the National Adult Literacy Survey (NALS).* Washington, DC: National Center for Education Statistics, U.S. Department of Education.

Kutner, M., Greenberg, E., & Baer, J. (2005). *National Assessment of Adult Literacy (NAAL). A first look at the literacy of America's adults in the 21st century.* Retrieved October 22, 2006, from: http://nces.ed.gov/naal

Lee, J. Y., Rozier, R. G., Lee, S. Y., Bender, D., & Ruiz, R. E. (2007). Development of a word recognition instrument to test health literacy in dentistry: The REALD-30. *Journal of Public Health Dentistry, 67,* 94–98.

Mechanic, D., McAlpine, D., & Rosenthal, M. (2001). Are patient-physician visits getting shorter? *New England Journal of Medicine, 344,* 198–204.

Nath, C. R., Sylvester, S. T., Yasek, V., & Gunel, E. (2001). Development and validation of a literacy assessment tool for persons with diabetes. *The Diabetes Educator, 27,* 857–864.

National Institute for Literacy. (n.d.). *Frequently asked questions.* Retrieved June 19, 2004, from: http://www.nifl.gov/nifl/faqs.html#literacy%20rates

Nurss, J. R., Parker, R., Williams, M., & Baker, D. (2001). *Test of functional health literacy in adults.* Snow Camp, NC: Peppercorn Books & Press.

Osborn, C. Y., Weiss, B. D., Davis, T. C., Skripkauskas, S., Rodrigue, C., Bass III, P. F., et al. (2007). Measuring adult literacy in healthcare: Performance of the Newest Vital Sign. *American Journal of Health Behavior, 31*(Suppl 3), S36–S46.

Paasche-Orlow, M. K., & Wolf, M. S. (2008) Evidence does not support clinical screening of literacy. *Journal of General Internal Medicine, 23*(1), 100–102.

Parikh, N. S., Parker, R. M., Nurss, J. R., Baker, D. W., & Williams, M. V. (1996). Shame and health literacy: The unspoken connection. *Patient Education Counseling, 27*(1), 33–39.

Parker, R. (2000). Health literacy: A challenge for American patients and their health care providers. *Health Promotion International, 15*(4), 277–283.

Parker, R. M., Baker, D. W., Williams, M. V., & Nurss, J. R. (1995). The test of functional health literacy in adults: A new instrument for measuring patients' literacy skills. *Journal of General Internal Medicine, 10*(10), 537–541.

Parker, R. M., Davis, T. C., & Williams, M. V. (1999). Patients with limited health literacy. In W. B. Bateman, E. J. Kramer, & K. S. Glassman (Eds.), *Patient and family education in managed care and beyond* (pp. 63–71). New York: Springer.

Parker, R. M., & Kindig, D. A. (2006). Beyond the Institute of Medicine health literacy report: Are the recommendations being taken seriously? *Journal of General Internal Medicine, 21*(8), 891–892.

Partnership for Clear Health Communication. (n.d.). *Ask Me 3. What is Health literacy?* Retrieved August 15, 2005, from: http://www.askme3.org

Pawlak, R. (2005). Economic considerations of health literacy. *Nursing Economics, 23*(4), 173–180.

Potter, L., & Martin, C. (2003). *Strategies to assist low-literate health care consumers.* Center for Health Care Strategies, Inc. Retrieved June 1, 2004, from: http://www.chcs.org/publications3960/publications_show.htm?doc_id=213131

Richman, J. A., Lee, J. Y., Rozier, R. G., Gong, D. A., Pahel, B. T., & Vann, W. F. (2007). Evaluation of a word recognition instrument to test health literacy in dentistry: The REALD-99. *Journal of Public Health Dentistry, 67,* 99–104.

Safeer, R. S., & Keenan, J. (2005). Health literacy: The gap between physicians and patients. *American Family Physician, 72*(3), 463–468.

Sanders, L. M., Zacur, G., Haecker, T., & Klass, P. (2004). Number of children's books in the home: an indicator of parent health literacy. *Ambulatory Pediatrics, 4*(5), 424–428.

Simonds, S. (1974). Health education as social policy. In *Health Education Monograph 2* (pp. 1–25). Baltimore: Johns Hopkins University.

Sudore, R. L., Mehta, K. M., Simonsick, E. M., Harris, T. B., Newman, A. B., Satterfield, S., et al. (2006). Limited literacy in older people and disparities in health and healthcare access. *Journal of the American Geriatrics Society, 54*(5), 770–776.

Thompson, T. L. (1998). The patient/professional relationship. In L. D. Jackson & B. K. Duffy (Eds.), *Health communication research: A guide to development and directions* (pp. 37–55). Westport, CT: Greenwood Press.

U.S. Department of Health and Human Services. (2000). *Healthy People 2010. Understanding and improving health and objectives for improving health* (2nd ed., 2 vols.). Washington, DC: U.S. Government Printing Office.

Wallace, L. S., Cassada, D. C., Rogers, E. S., Freeman, M. B., Grandas, O. H., Stevens, S. L., et al. (2007). Can screening items identify surgery patients at risk of limited health literacy? *Journal of Surgical Research, 140,* 208–213.

Wallace, L. S., Rogers, E. S., Roskos, S. E., Holiday, D. B., & Weiss, B. D. (2006). BRIEF REPORT: Screening items to identify patients with limited health literacy skills. *Journal of General Internal Medicine, 21*(8), 874–877.

Weiss, B. D., Mays, M. Z., Martz, W., Castro, K. M., DeWalt, D. A., Pignone, M. P., et al. (2005). Quick assessment of literacy in primary care: The Newest Vital Sign. *Annals of Family Medicine, 3,* 514–522.

Part 5

Looking Ahead

Trends in Rehabilitation and Health Assessments

Elias Mpofu
Thomas Oakland

31

Overview

Assessment practices in rehabilitation and health are continually evolving, and measures that map the International Classification of Functioning, Disability, and Health (ICF) domains are likely to be preferred over time for their value in linking assessments to quality of life outcomes. Social factors that influence behavioral health outcomes will increasingly receive attention, as will their interface with measures of physical function in everyday settings. Prospectively, consumers will have a greater say in the assessments in which they participate and the implications for their health and well-being. Use of objective measures of health outcomes could result in fewer, and more efficient, measures for treatment intervention in rehabilitation and health settings.

Learning Objectives

By the end of the chapter, the reader should be able to:

1. Identify and briefly describe social factors important to rehabilitation and health assessment.
2. Discuss the significance of social factors in rehabilitation and health assessment.
3. Characterize how partnerships between consumers and service providers influence the types, quality, and focus of rehabilitation assessments.
4. Identify two types of objective measures described in this chapter and how their wider use would add to the quality of rehabilitation and health assessments.

Introduction

We conclude this book as we began it, with a note of optimism about the future of rehabilitation as a science and practice as well as the important contributions the use of tests and other assessment methods make to them. The ICF (World Health Organization [WHO], 2001) provides a useful road map for the design of instruments and other assessment methods to address domains of participation consequential to the full community inclusion of people with disabilities. This model shifts the focus from cause to impact, places all health conditions on an equal footing, and allows them to be compared using a common metric—the ruler of health and disability. These changes have several implications for the development of assessments for use in rehabilitation and health. We consider several themes that we believe are important to the continued growth and use of assessment expertise in rehabilitation and health.

Social Factors Are Important Indicators of Health and Well-Being

The current WHO (2001) model of disablement recognizes that disability involves both medical and social factors. The ICF model helps bring to light the complex interaction between physical, psychological, social, personal, and environmental qualities. The model refocuses our attention from diagnosing behaviors to describing them in ways that show the impact of these interactions on practical and important daily events in the lives of our clients. The ICF takes into account the social aspects of disability and does not see disability only as a medical or biological dysfunction. By including contextual (e.g., environmental) factors in understanding participation with chronic illness and disability, the ICF enables one to record the impact of the environment on the person's functioning. There has been comparatively more progress in the development of measures of physical function than of social and community functioning (Mpofu, Oakland, Herbert, & O'Donnel, 2010). However, an impressive number of measures of social and community functioning has been developed over the past 2 decades. That trend is likely to continue as consumers and health care service providers partner to develop instruments useful for supporting quality of life interventions with chronic illness or disability.

Partnerships for Health Continue to Grow

We are challenged to acquire a greater understanding of the interaction between a person's physical, psychological, social, personal, and environmental qualities as well as their combined impact on efforts to develop and maintain desired activities and participation. We also are challenged to link assessment information with empirically supported interventions. A better understanding of the complexities that arise from their interactions and counter-influencing systems is likely to be achieved through consumer and designer partnerships that lead to the development of new consumer-oriented assessments for use in health and rehabilitation, including those that focus on preferences, needs, and values.

The potential for researchers and health care service providers to be guided by a shared conceptual framework for understanding the disablement process and the impact of disability on quality of life should add to the flow of information between researchers and practitioners who may feel less estranged from each other due to this shared understanding. Health care service providers may become increasingly open to adopting newer and more efficient behavioral measures of health care that they perceive to address areas of activity and participation displayed by those with chronic conditions or a disability. Researchers in assessment also are more likely to develop behavioral instruments that have direct relevance to bedside practice or are useful for supporting decisions on community living.

Health and well-being transcend discipline-specific concepts and technologies. Compared to discipline-focused assessment, interdisciplinary health care assessment design merges key concepts and procedures in understanding disablement and participation, resulting in a more holistic approach to assessments for health and well-being. Thus, information technology engineers collaborate with rehabilitation professionals to design measures that address problems of daily living. The development of instruments with universal design features and the use of virtual tools to assess everyday functioning with chronic illness or disability exemplify interdisciplinary thinking. Interdisciplinary work leading to the design of rehabilitation and health assessments is likely to become mainstream as health service providers, the assessment industry, and consumers explore options to maximize the use of well tested assessment protocols whose access to a wider population of users may have been limited due to their technical–administrative inaccessibility. Interdisciplinary work brings various advantages. For example, those engaged in this work educate others and become educated by others by sharing important principles and practices common to their work. Everyone fully engaged in this work experiences professional growth. Learning never stops.

Interdisciplinary delivery of services requires people to interact in ways that allow professionals to deliver the best their professions allow and in a personally cordial and respectful manner. Although tried and tested discipline specific assessments are likely to be used for their value in assessing aspects of activity and participation with chronic illness and disability, the more successful assessment instruments of the future will be designed by teams of professionals to reflect the interdisciplinary nature of their practices and to address the impact of disability at several layers of complexity. Achieving greater success in applying interdisciplinary knowledge by working with others in ways that educate and motivate them to lead healthy lifestyles remains an exciting challenge.

Diversity in the primary consumers of assessment services also will encourage partnerships in the design of effective rehabilitation and health interventions. For example, those engaged in providing rehabilitation and health services are working with more premature infants, many of whom later exhibit chronic needs best met through coordinated rehabilitation services. We remain challenged by our aging population, whom exhibit deteriorating neuroanatomical and muscular, physical, cognitive, and social qualities. Methods used to prevent and treat acute and often chronic needs displayed by members of our armed forces, including high rates of post traumatic stress disorders and traumatic brain injury, deserve a high priority. Many persons engaged in rehabilitation and health research and service wonder if empirically based treatments and sufficiently prepared professional personnel will be available to address client's needs. This information can be used to help ensure personnel who constitute work teams display respect for one's self and others as well as possess needed knowledge and skills.

We are challenged to develop measures that help us understand biopsychosocial interactions in the disabling process and adjustment to disability. However, we cannot rely on tests alone to achieve this understanding. Tests typically are developed to assess more discrete behaviors, not the confluence of many qualities. Thus, we first must engage in research and other forms of scholarship that help us better understand the impact of the interaction between an individual's biopsychosocial qualities and their environmental qualities on their development, recovery, and continued display of desired behaviors. Research in the behavioral sciences has not taken this broad view and instead focuses on smaller issues. Thus, research has overlooked the complex array of conditions and qualities that impact personal activities and participation. Subsequent revisions of this book hopefully will provide information on advances in this important topic.

Professional judgments that rest on solid data constitute a cornerstone of professional service. Thus, those engaged in rehabilitation services can make great strides in implementing the ICF model by using all assessment methods, not only tests, that provide reliable and valid information. Experienced professionals are able to combine the science and art associated with their practices, expressed through seasoned professional judgments, as to the impact of the interactions between a client's biopsychosocial and environmental qualities on his or her development, recovery, and continued display of desired behaviors. The status of test development and use never will negate a need to use sound professional judgment.

More Complex Measurement Designs Are Applied

Complex measurement designs are likely to be applied with greater prominence, leading to the construction of instruments to support clinical decisions at the individual person level and the use of efficient measures, or those that reduce the burden of health care, to both consumers and providers of health services. The use of measures constructed using item response theory (IRT) promises to yield robust measures that map the continuum of health and well-being in ways not possible previously. IRT-derived measures have the added advantage of allowing for shorter measures that reduce the burden of assessment, while providing data at the test item level needed to inform intervention designs (see chapter 5). The increasing use of geospatial systems and mapping to understand the epidemiology of health (Janelle, 2009) increasingly will lead to a better understanding of health systems and their interplay with health and well-being at the individual person level. Interest will also develop in the use of mixed-method approaches, and narrative inquiry to better understand constructions of health and well-being by individuals and communities also can be expected. Narrative inquiry data captures the authentic meanings people with chronic illness and disability impute that influence their sense of health and wellness (Albright, Duggan, & Epstein, 2008). These personal meanings are critical to the recovery process and living with a disability (Mpofu & Oakland, 2006). Econometric measurement heuristics also will be applied to link consumer responses to health service qualities to the cost of health care (see also chapter 8) and to health management capitation plans structured to reflect such understanding. Finally, more assessments will be developed to identify behavioral markers of underlying biophysical functioning (see chapter 9), resulting in immense benefits through screening for preventive, targeted health, and well-being interventions; reduced costs for heath care by using reliable noninvasive methods; and better understanding the interplay between biobehavioral health systems.

In-Situ Reporting of Health and Well-Being Data Methods

An important concern with post-dictive self-report data is that its reliability may be reduced by memory decay and other information retrieval challenges. Diary methods appear to be better able to address limitations with retrospective recall. With diary methods, patients record their health and well-being related experiences as these occur and may use a personal assistant data tool (PDA, such as a Palm pilot). The collection of self-report data on health status experience can also include biophysical information (e.g., galvanic skin response, ambulatory heart rate) so that physical reactions are captured together with any behavioral–emotional data and in the setting in which these reactions co-occur (Bogler, Davis, & Rafaeli, 2003; Seekins, Ipsen, & Arnold, 2007; see also chapter 6). Diary methods allow for more valid explanations of varied health and well-being responses in the absence of intervention, which information is helpful to designing tailored interventions suited to individuals in their particular circumstances. We project wider use of these in-vivo type data collection approaches, particularly for the additional benefit they give in allowing a window to view health and well-being functioning in the context of a person's routine or everyday activities.

Conclusion

Chapters in this book were selected, in part, to promote an understanding of the ICF model and assessment methods that complement it. The model's full implementation may take decades and is likely to undergo changes. Its deployment is likely to lead to new assessment procedures, especially those that address the domains of activity and participation.

Professionals rely heavily on knowledge from their discipline and others to inform their assessment and intervention practices. The editors of this book trust the contents of the prior 29 chapters in *Rehabilitation and Health Assessment: Applying ICF Guidelines* inform those entering the rehabilitation professions and refresh the knowledge of the more senior professionals. The 4 chapters in Part 1 provide a foundation for the ICF and other forms of rehabilitation services. The 11 chapters in Part 2 reflect the rich array of tests and other assessment methods useful to rehabilitation science and service.

The topics discussed in Part 3 (e.g., values, subjective well-being, pain, forgiveness, self-efficacy and resilience, spirituality and religiosity, and perfectionism) were selected because they constitute personal qualities that have been found to impact rehabilitation outcomes. Thus, our knowledge of them informs our services and other professional decision-making processes. The topics discussed in Part 4 (i.e., functional performance, community integration, society safety, sexual functioning, and assessing recreation) were selected because they help inform us of qualities that may impact a person's ability to participate in meaningful ways at home, in the neighborhood, and in the community. Thus, although we may lack tests that assess all desired qualities, we have considerable solid information on which to draw when making sound professional judgments.

Self-Check Questions

1. Identify and briefly describe social factors important to rehabilitation and health assessment.
2. What is the significance of social factors in rehabilitation and health assessment?
3. How may partnerships between consumers and service providers influence the types, quality, and focus of rehabilitation assessments?
4. Identify two types of objective measures described in this chapter. How would their wider use add to the quality of rehabilitation and health assessments?
5. How would the greater use of assessments of function in everyday settings likely influence the types of questions asked in rehabilitation and health assessments and also the interventions based on those assessments?

Field-Based Learning Tasks

1. Interview a behavioral health professional with a rehabilitation or health facility in your community and determine the types of social factors he or she typically takes into account in his or her client evaluations and why. Briefly outline what other social factors he or she should be addressing. Give reasons for your selection.
2. Interview a rehabilitation and health professional to learn of any initiatives that he or she is considering to enhance the types of assessments that he or she typically carries out. Consider such initiatives in relation to how they characterize current trends in rehabilitation and health assessments.

References

Albright, K. J., Duggan, C. H., & Epstein, M. J. (2008). Analyzing trauma narratives: Introducing the narrative from index to matrix. *Rehabilitation Psychology, 53,* 400–411.

Bogler, N., Davis, A., Rafaeli, E. (2003). Diary methods: Capturing life as it is lived. *Annual Review of Psychology, 54,* 579–616.

Janelle, D. (2009). *Spatio-temporal approaches in the social and behavioral sciences as illustrated in the spacetime ecologies of cities.* Brisbane: Australian Research Council.

Mpofu, E., & Oakland, T. (2006). Assessment of value change in adults with acquired disabilities. In M. Hersen (Ed.), *Clinician's handbook of adult behavioral assessment* (pp. 601–630). New York: Elsevier Press.

Mpofu, E., Oakland, T., Herbert, T., & O'Donnel, P. (2010). Testing and assessment: History context, and prevailing issues. In E. Mpofu & T. Oakland (Eds.), *Assessment in rehabilitation and health* (pp. 3–21). Upper Saddle, NJ: Merrill.

Seekins, T., Ipsen, C., & Arnold, N. L. (2007). Using ecological momentary assessment to measure participation: A preliminary study. *Rehabilitation Psychology, 52,* 319–330.

World Health Organization. (2001). *ICF: International Classification of Functioning, Disability and Health.* Geneva: Author.

Index